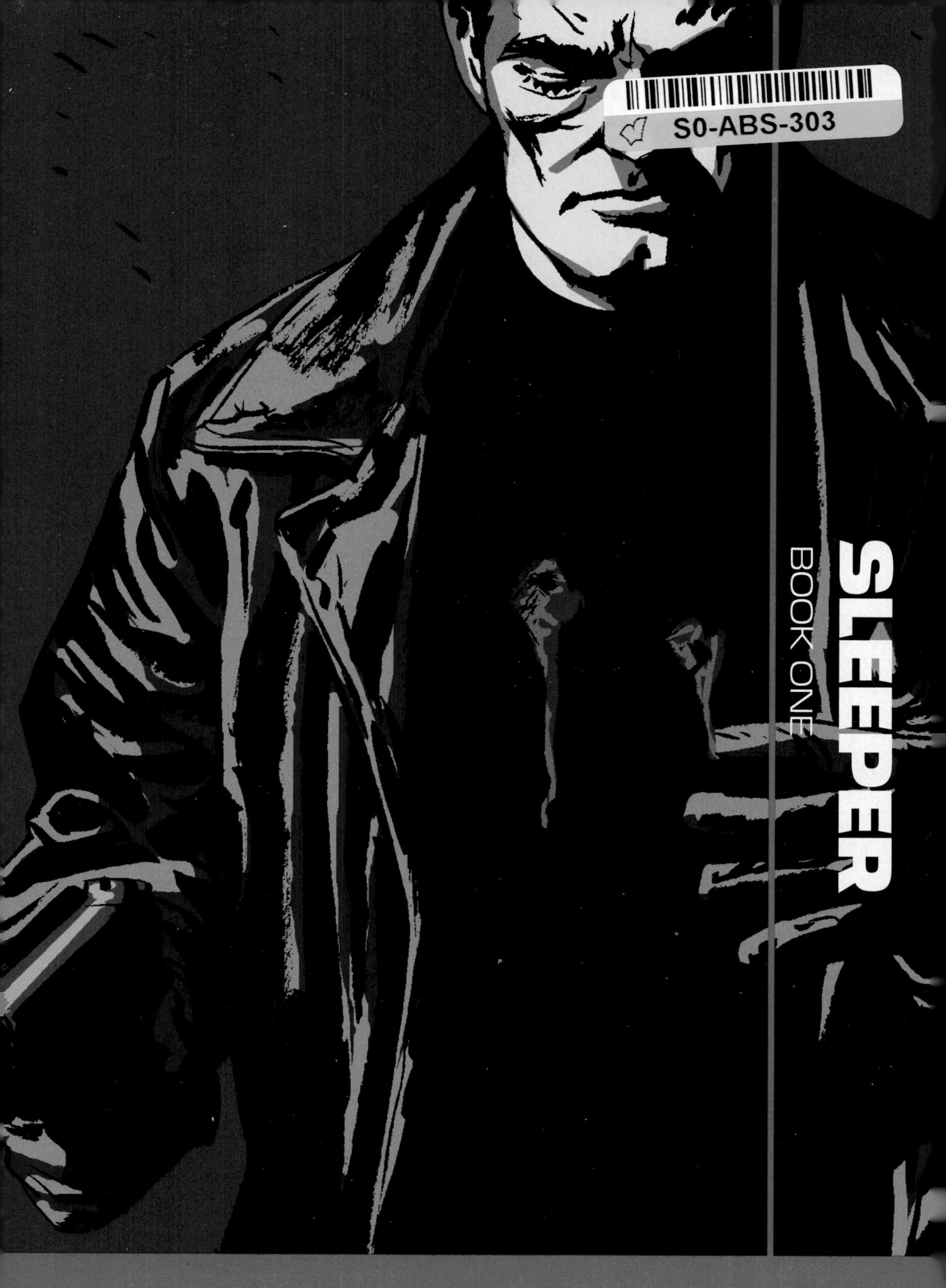
SLEEPER
BOOK ONE

WILDSTORM CLASSIC

ED BRUBAKER
writer

SEAN PHILLIPS
COLIN WILSON
artists

TONY AVIÑA
JANET GALE
RANDY MAYOR
colorists

JIMMY BETANCOURT \ ROB LEIGH
KENNY LOPEZ \ BILL OAKLEY
RICHARD STARKINGS
letterers

SEAN PHILLIPS
collection cover artist

SLEEPER created by **ED BRUBAKER** and **SEAN PHILLIPS**

SLEEPER
BOOK ONE

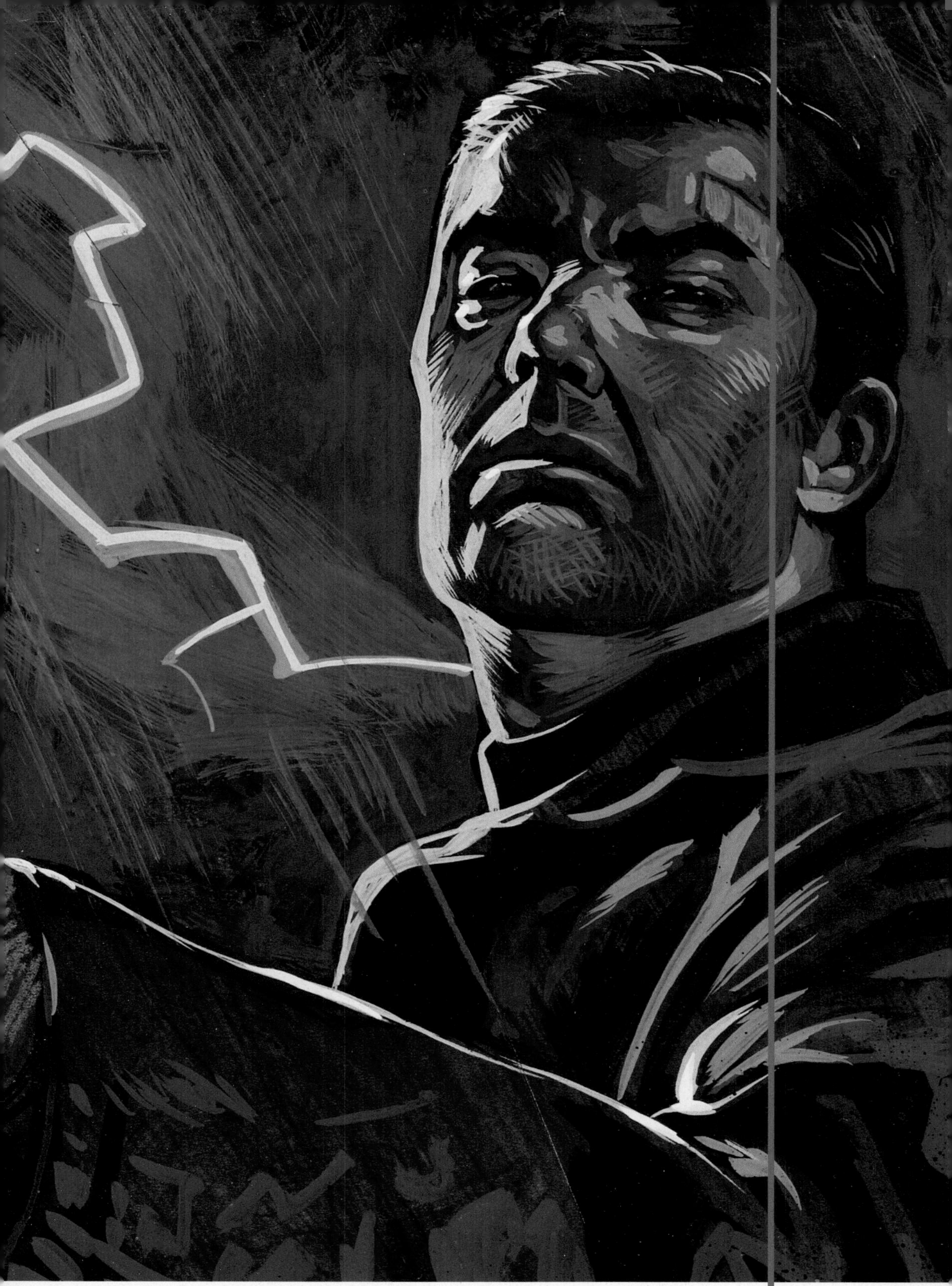

SCOTT DUNBIER EDITOR – ORIGINAL SERIES
KRISTY QUINN ASSISTANT EDITOR – ORIGINAL SERIES
JEB WOODARD GROUP EDITOR – COLLECTED EDITIONS
STEVE COOK DESIGN DIRECTOR – BOOKS
MONIQUE NARBONETA PUBLICATION DESIGN

BOB HARRAS SENIOR VP – EDITOR-IN-CHIEF, DC COMICS
PAT McCALLUM EXECUTIVE EDITOR, DC COMICS

DIANE NELSON PRESIDENT
DAN DiDIO PUBLISHER
JIM LEE PUBLISHER
GEOFF JOHNS PRESIDENT & CHIEF CREATIVE OFFICER
AMIT DESAI EXECUTIVE VP – BUSINESS & MARKETING STRATEGY,
          DIRECT TO CONSUMER & GLOBAL FRANCHISE MANAGEMENT
SAM ADES SENIOR VP & GENERAL MANAGER, DIGITAL SERVICES
BOBBIE CHASE VP & EXECUTIVE EDITOR, YOUNG READER & TALENT DEVELOPMENT
MARK CHIARELLO SENIOR VP – ART, DESIGN & COLLECTED EDITIONS
JOHN CUNNINGHAM SENIOR VP – SALES & TRADE MARKETING
ANNE DePIES SENIOR VP – BUSINESS STRATEGY, FINANCE & ADMINISTRATION
DON FALLETTI VP – MANUFACTURING OPERATIONS
LAWRENCE GANEM VP – EDITORIAL ADMINISTRATION & TALENT RELATIONS
ALISON GILL SENIOR VP – MANUFACTURING & OPERATIONS
HANK KANALZ SENIOR VP – EDITORIAL STRATEGY & ADMINISTRATION
JAY KOGAN VP – LEGAL AFFAIRS
JACK MAHAN VP – BUSINESS AFFAIRS
NICK J. NAPOLITANO VP – MANUFACTURING ADMINISTRATION
EDDIE SCANNELL VP – CONSUMER MARKETING
COURTNEY SIMMONS SENIOR VP – PUBLICITY & COMMUNICATIONS
JIM (SKI) SOKOLOWSKI VP – COMIC BOOK SPECIALTY SALES & TRADE MARKETING
NANCY SPEARS VP – MASS, BOOK, DIGITAL SALES & TRADE MARKETING
MICHELE R. WELLS VP – CONTENT STRATEGY

SLEEPER BOOK ONE

Published by DC Comics. Compilation and all new material Copyright © 2018 DC Comics. All Rights Reserved.
Originally published in single magazine form in POINT BLANK 1-5, SLEEPER 1-12. Copyright © 2002, 2003 DC
Comics. All Rights Reserved. All characters, their distinctive likenesses and related elements featured in this
publication are trademarks of DC Comics. The stories, characters and incidents featured in this publication are
entirely fictional. DC Comics does not read or accept unsolicited submissions of ideas, stories or artwork.

DC Comics, 2900 West Alameda Ave., Burbank, CA 91505
Printed by LSC Communications, Kendallville, IN. USA. 3/23/18. First Printing.
ISBN: 978-1-4012-7844-1

Library of Congress Cataloging-in-Publication Data is available.

PEFC Certified

Printed on paper from
sustainably managed
forests, controlled
sources

PEFC™
PEFC/29-31-337   www.pefc.org

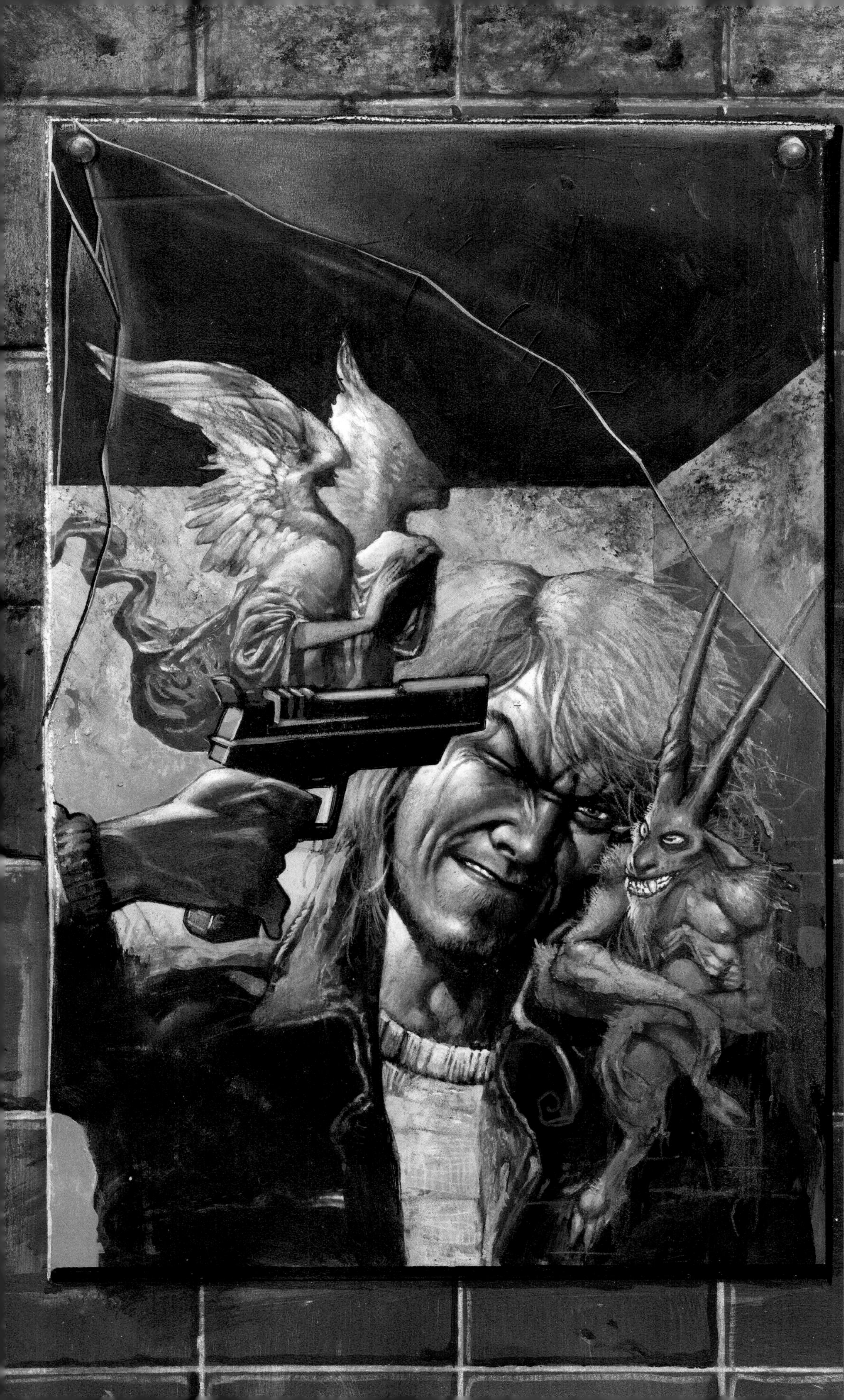

Cover by SIMON BISLEY

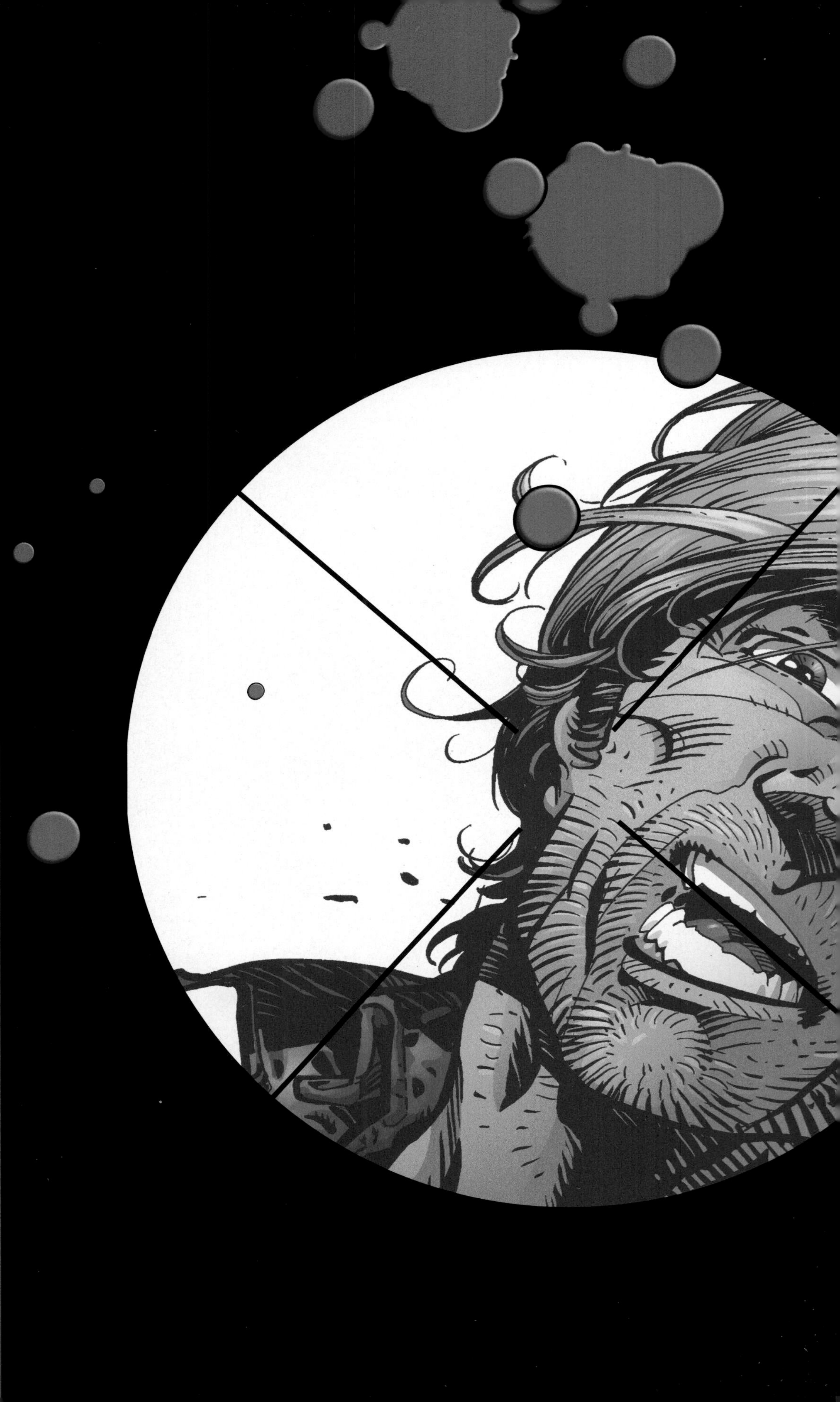

POINT BLANK #1 Variant Cover by COLIN WILSON

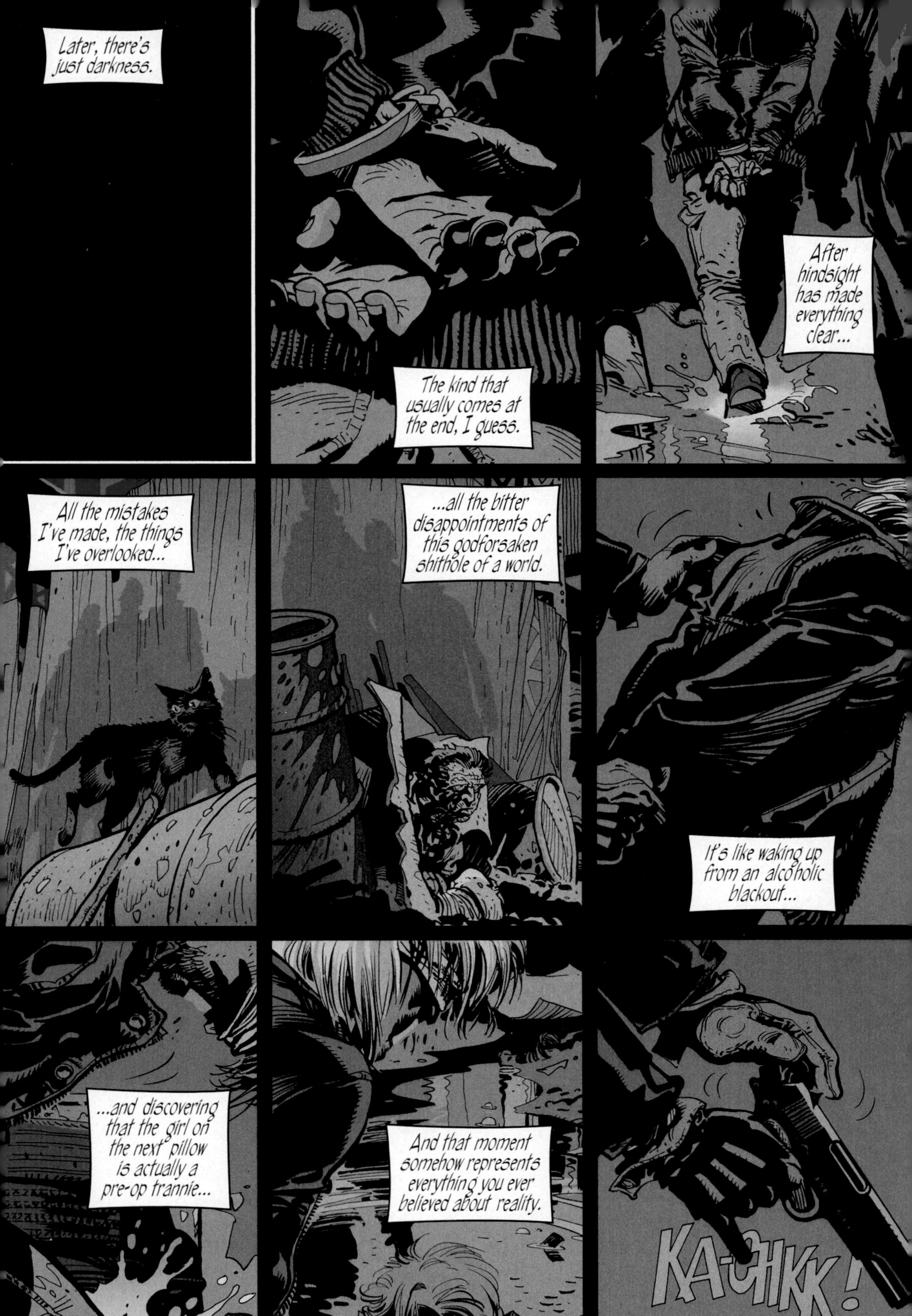
Later, there's just darkness.
The kind that usually comes at the end, I guess.
After hindsight has made everything clear...
All the mistakes I've made, the things I've overlooked...
...all the bitter disappointments of this godforsaken shithole of a world.
It's like waking up from an alcoholic blackout...
...and discovering that the girl on the next pillow is actually a pre-op trannie...
And that moment somehow represents everything you ever believed about reality.
KA-CHKK!
But, of course, by then it's too late...

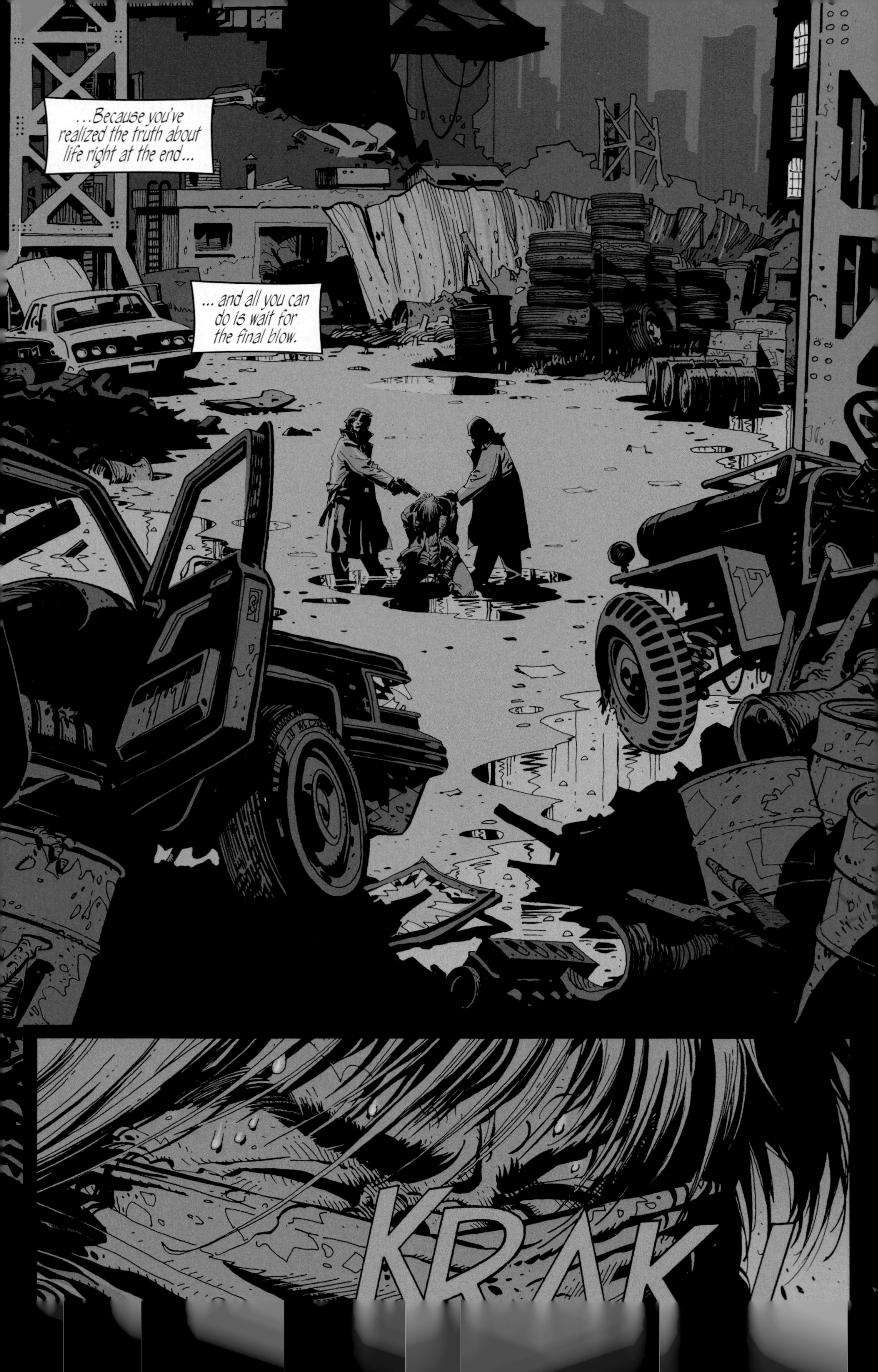
...Because you've realized the truth about life right at the end...
...and all you can do is wait for the final blow.
KRAK

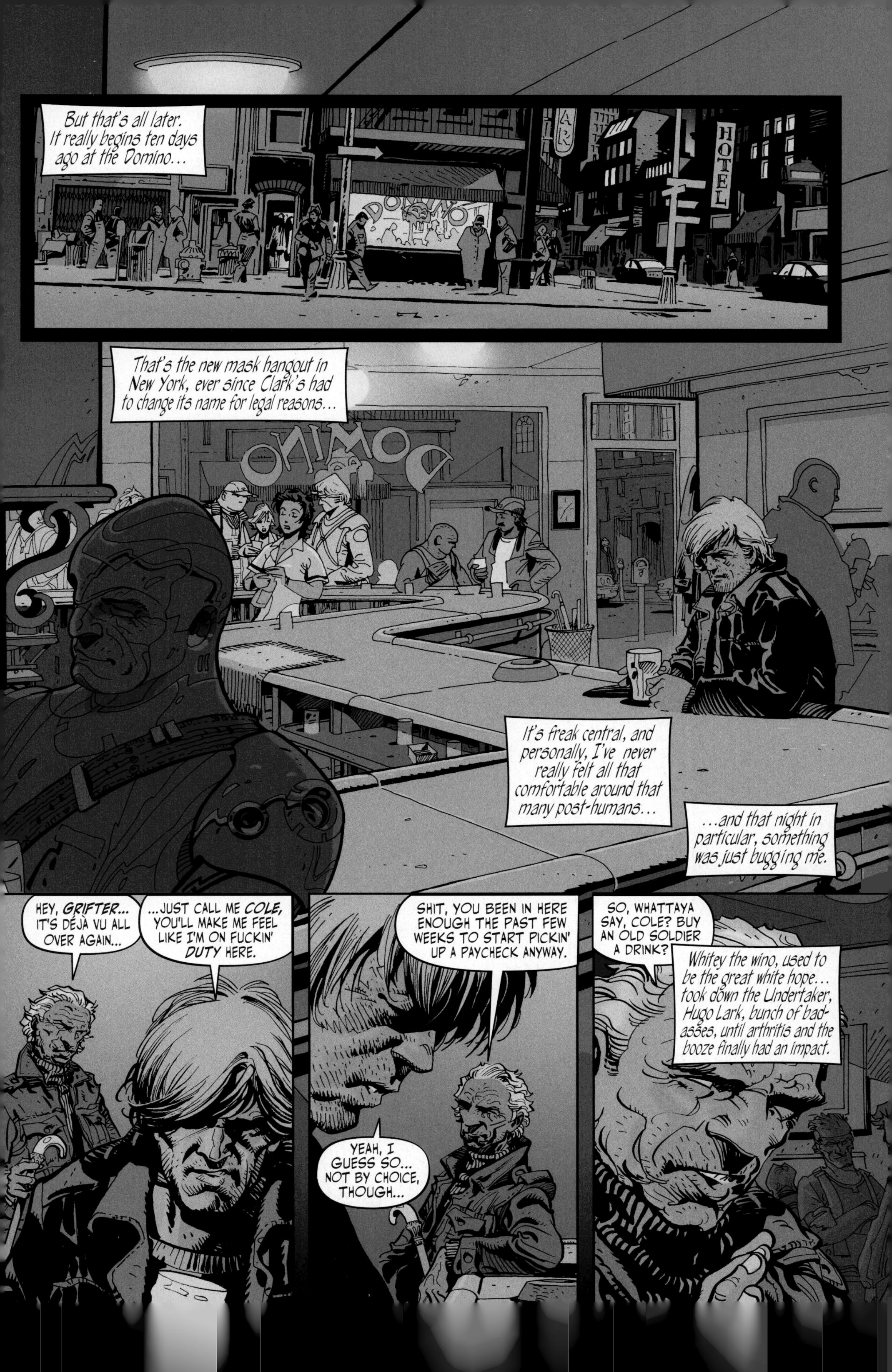
But that's all later. It really begins ten days ago at the Domino...
HOTEL
That's the new mask hangout in New York, ever since Clark's had to change its name for legal reasons...
DOMINO
It's freak central, and personally, I've never really felt all that comfortable around that many post-humans...
...and that night in particular, something was just bugging me.
HEY, GRIFTER... IT'S DÉJÀ VU ALL OVER AGAIN...
...JUST CALL ME COLE, YOU'LL MAKE ME FEEL LIKE I'M ON FUCKIN' DUTY HERE.
SHIT, YOU BEEN IN HERE ENOUGH THE PAST FEW WEEKS TO START PICKIN' UP A PAYCHECK ANYWAY.
YEAH, I GUESS SO... NOT BY CHOICE, THOUGH...
SO, WHATTAYA SAY, COLE? BUY AN OLD SOLDIER A DRINK?
Whitey the wino, used to be the great white hope... took down the Undertaker, Hugo Lark, bunch of bad-asses, until arthritis and the booze finally had an impact.

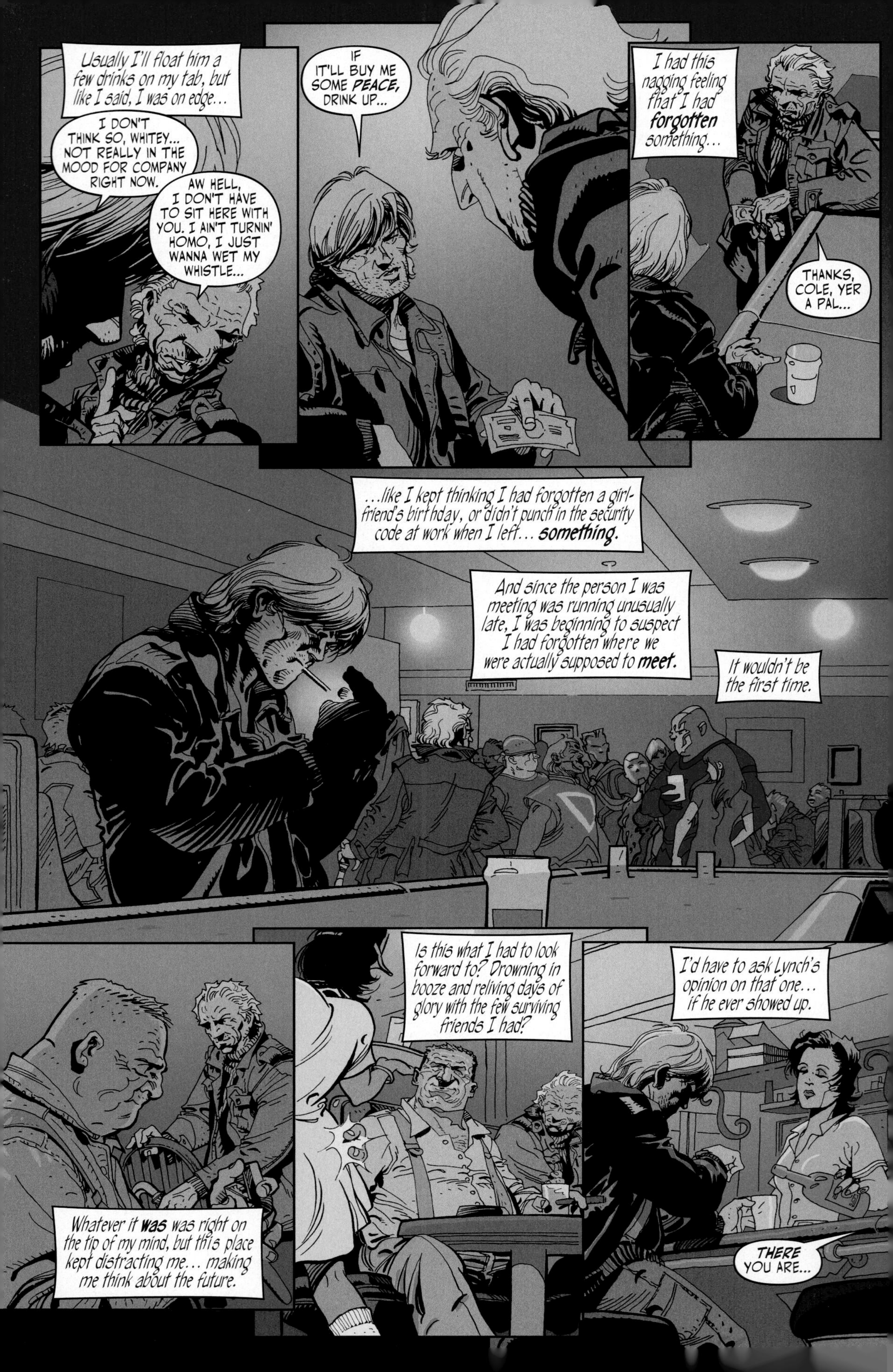

Usually I'll float him a few drinks on my tab, but like I said, I was on edge...
I DON'T THINK SO, WHITEY... NOT REALLY IN THE MOOD FOR COMPANY RIGHT NOW.
AW HELL, I DON'T HAVE TO SIT HERE WITH YOU. I AIN'T TURNIN' HOMO, I JUST WANNA WET MY WHISTLE...
IF IT'LL BUY ME SOME PEACE, DRINK UP...
I had this nagging feeling that I had forgotten something...
THANKS, COLE, YER A PAL...
...like I kept thinking I had forgotten a girl-friend's birthday, or didn't punch in the security code at work when I left... something.
And since the person I was meeting was running unusually late, I was beginning to suspect I had forgotten where we were actually supposed to meet.
It wouldn't be the first time.
Whatever it was was right on the tip of my mind, but this place kept distracting me... making me think about the future.
Is this what I had to look forward to? Drowning in booze and reliving days of glory with the few surviving friends I had?
I'd have to ask Lynch's opinion on that one... if he ever showed up.
THERE YOU ARE...

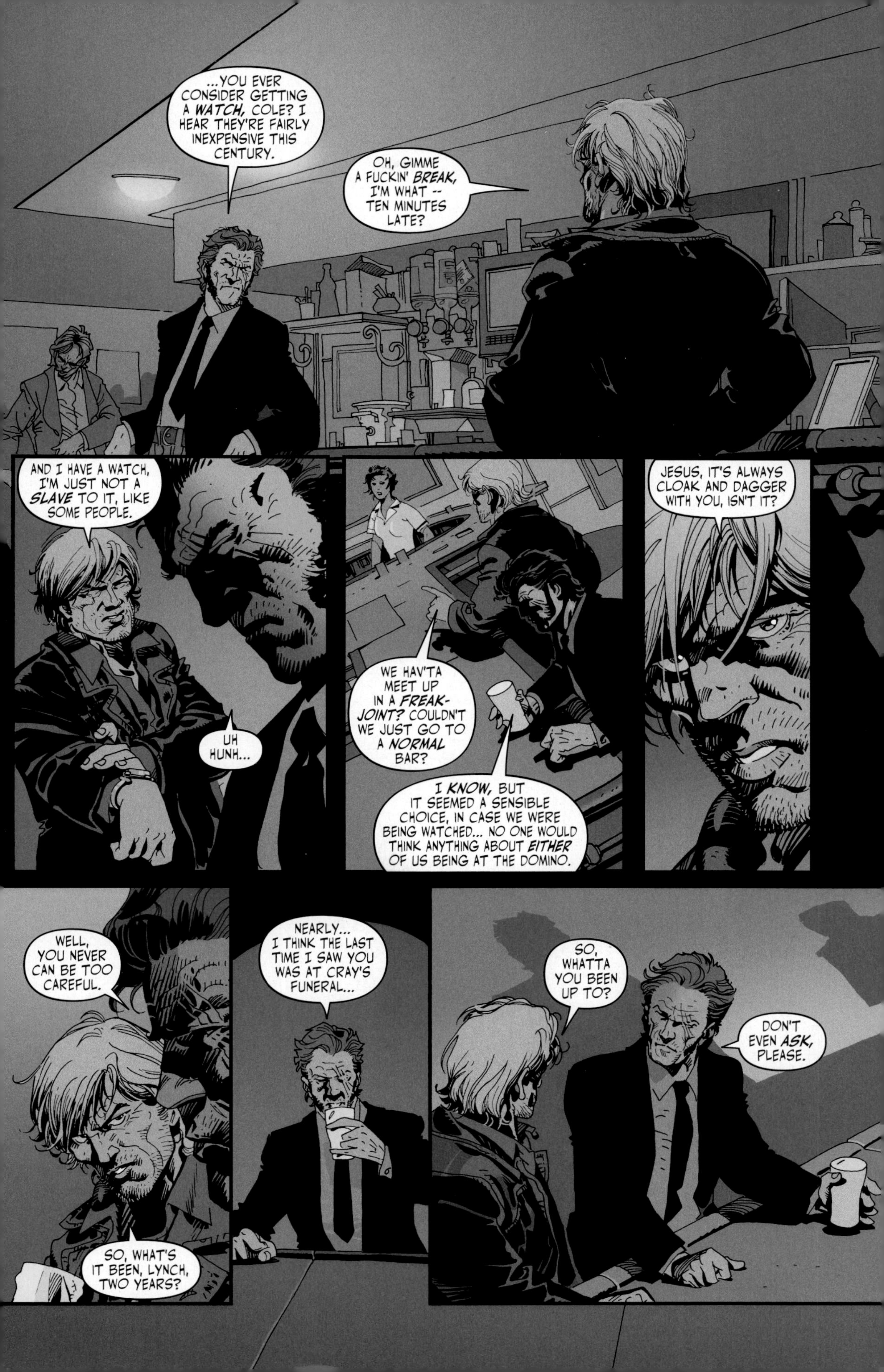
...YOU EVER CONSIDER GETTING A WATCH, COLE? I HEAR THEY'RE FAIRLY INEXPENSIVE THIS CENTURY.
OH, GIMME A FUCKIN' BREAK, I'M WHAT -- TEN MINUTES LATE?
AND I HAVE A WATCH, I'M JUST NOT A SLAVE TO IT, LIKE SOME PEOPLE.
UH HUNH...
WE HAV'TA MEET UP IN A FREAK-JOINT? COULDN'T WE JUST GO TO A NORMAL BAR?
I KNOW, BUT IT SEEMED A SENSIBLE CHOICE, IN CASE WE WERE BEING WATCHED... NO ONE WOULD THINK ANYTHING ABOUT EITHER OF US BEING AT THE DOMINO.
JESUS, IT'S ALWAYS CLOAK AND DAGGER WITH YOU, ISN'T IT?
WELL, YOU NEVER CAN BE TOO CAREFUL.
SO, WHAT'S IT BEEN, LYNCH, TWO YEARS?
NEARLY... I THINK THE LAST TIME I SAW YOU WAS AT CRAY'S FUNERAL...
SO, WHATTA YOU BEEN UP TO?
DON'T EVEN ASK, PLEASE.

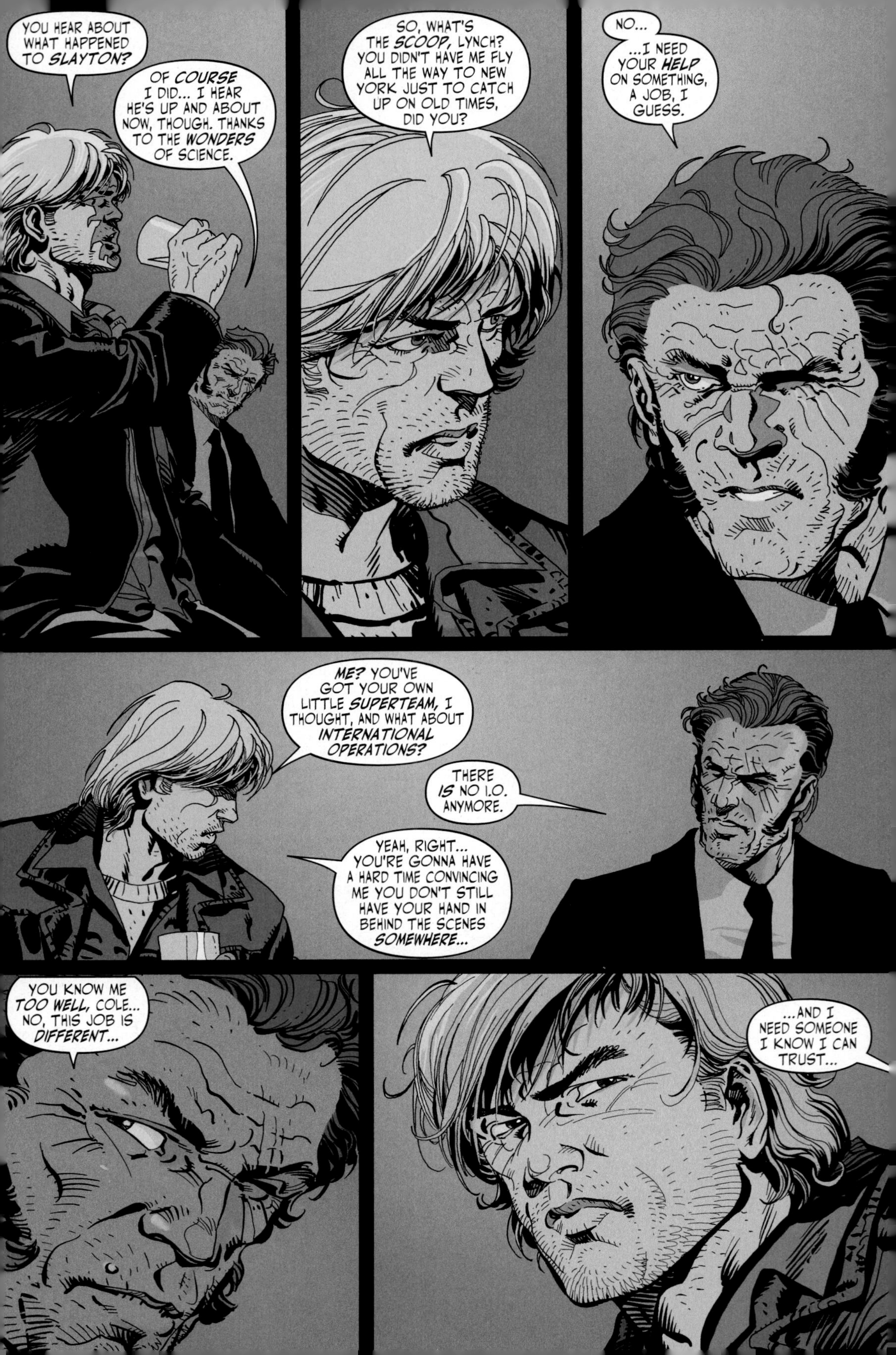
YOU HEAR ABOUT WHAT HAPPENED TO SLAYTON?
OF COURSE I DID... I HEAR HE'S UP AND ABOUT NOW, THOUGH. THANKS TO THE WONDERS OF SCIENCE.
SO, WHAT'S THE SCOOP, LYNCH? YOU DIDN'T HAVE ME FLY ALL THE WAY TO NEW YORK JUST TO CATCH UP ON OLD TIMES, DID YOU?
NO...
...I NEED YOUR HELP ON SOMETHING, A JOB, I GUESS.
ME? YOU'VE GOT YOUR OWN LITTLE SUPERTEAM, I THOUGHT, AND WHAT ABOUT INTERNATIONAL OPERATIONS?
THERE IS NO I.O. ANYMORE.
YEAH, RIGHT... YOU'RE GONNA HAVE A HARD TIME CONVINCING ME YOU DON'T STILL HAVE YOUR HAND IN BEHIND THE SCENES SOMEWHERE...
YOU KNOW ME TOO WELL, COLE... NO, THIS JOB IS DIFFERENT...
...AND I NEED SOMEONE I KNOW I CAN TRUST...

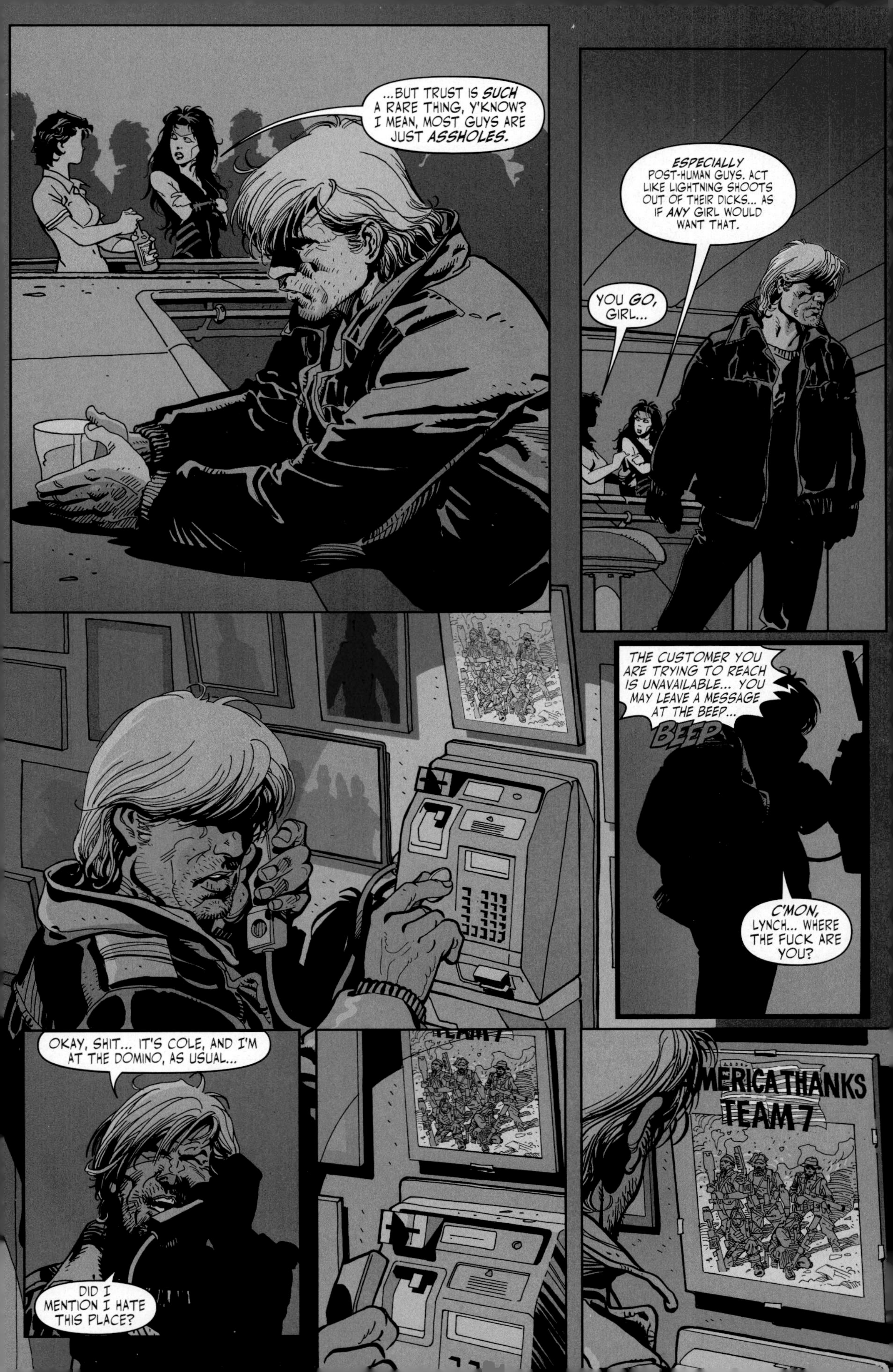
...BUT TRUST IS SUCH A RARE THING, Y'KNOW? I MEAN, MOST GUYS ARE JUST ASSHOLES.
ESPECIALLY POST-HUMAN GUYS. ACT LIKE LIGHTNING SHOOTS OUT OF THEIR DICKS... AS IF ANY GIRL WOULD WANT THAT.
YOU GO, GIRL...
THE CUSTOMER YOU ARE TRYING TO REACH IS UNAVAILABLE... YOU MAY LEAVE A MESSAGE AT THE BEEP...
BEEP
C'MON, LYNCH... WHERE THE FUCK ARE YOU?
OKAY, SHIT... IT'S COLE, AND I'M AT THE DOMINO, AS USUAL...
DID I MENTION I HATE THIS PLACE?
AMERICA THANKS TEAM 7

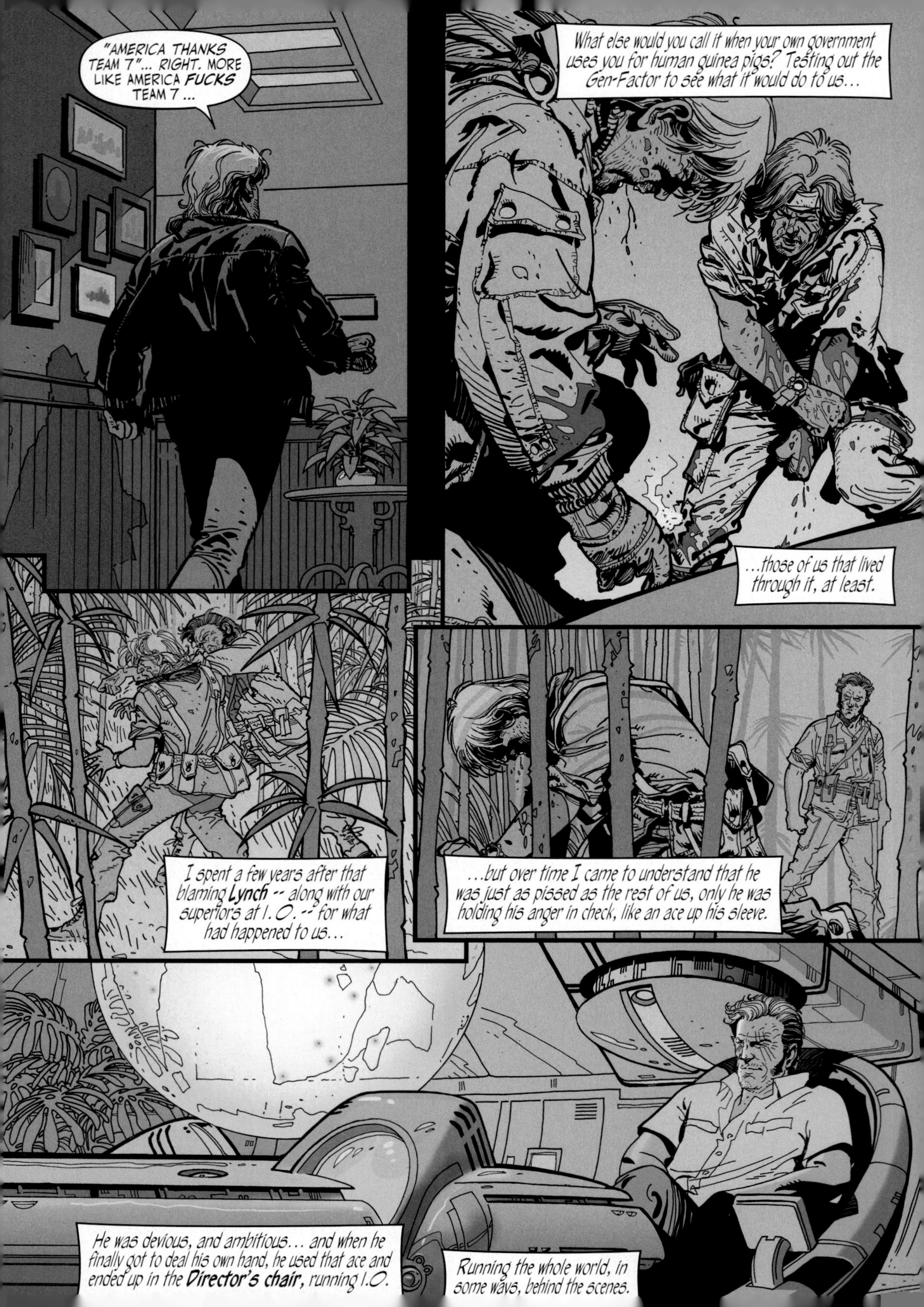
"AMERICA THANKS TEAM 7"... RIGHT. MORE LIKE AMERICA FUCKS TEAM 7 ...
What else would you call it when your own government uses you for human guinea pigs? Testing out the Gen-Factor to see what it would do to us...
...those of us that lived through it, at least.
I spent a few years after that blaming Lynch -- along with our superiors at I.O. -- for what had happened to us...
...but over time I came to understand that he was just as pissed as the rest of us, only he was holding his anger in check, like an ace up his sleeve.
He was devious, and ambitious... and when he finally got to deal his own hand, he used that ace and ended up in the Director's chair, running I.O.
Running the whole world, in some ways, behind the scenes.

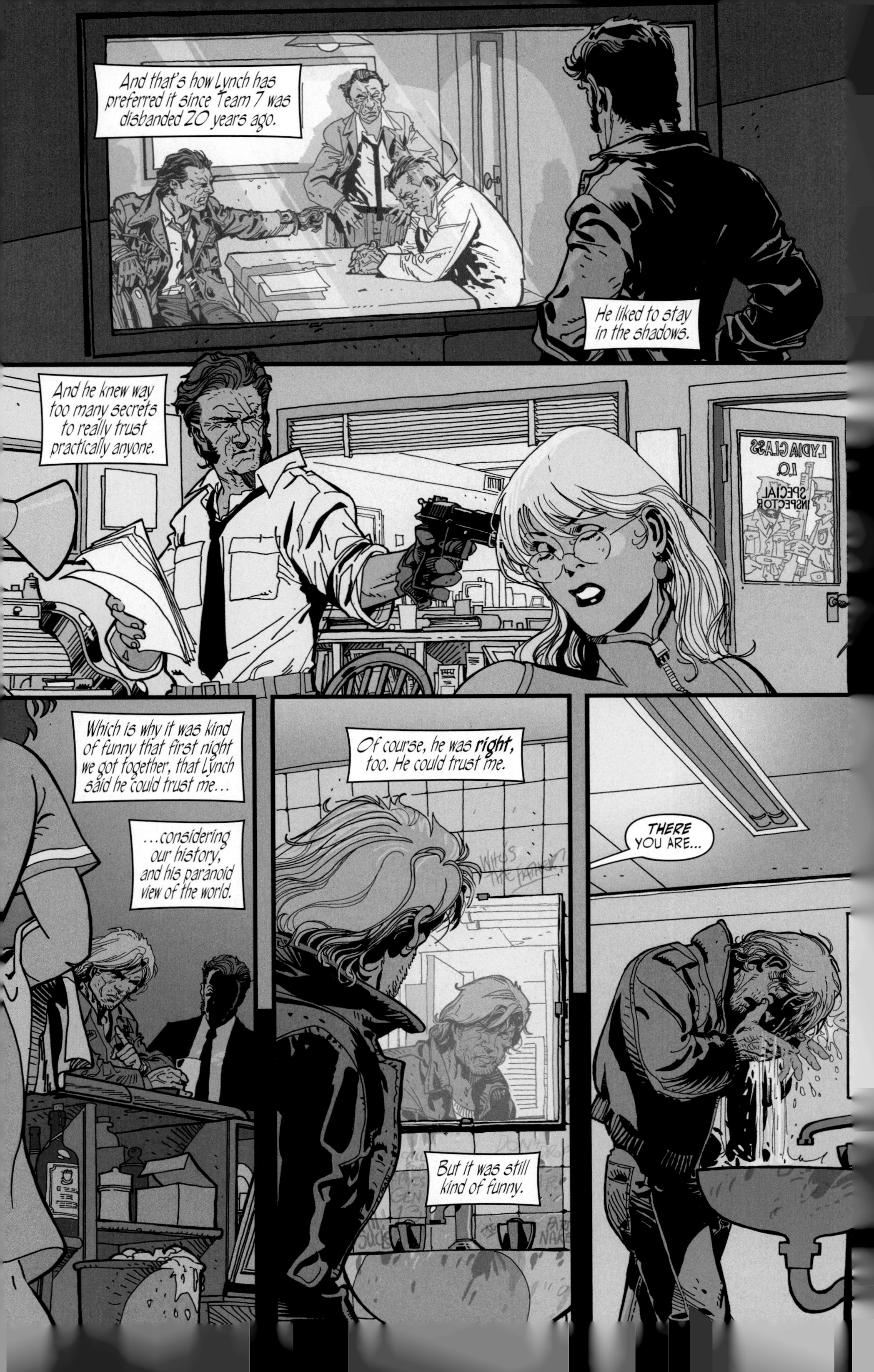
And that's how Lynch has preferred it since Team 7 was disbanded 20 years ago.
He liked to stay in the shadows.
And he knew way too many secrets to really trust practically anyone.
LYDIA GLASS
I.O.
SPECIAL INSPECTOR
Which is why it was kind of funny that first night we got together, that Lynch said he could trust me...
...considering our history, and his paranoid view of the world.
Of course, he was **right**, too. He could trust me.
But it was still kind of funny.
THERE YOU ARE...

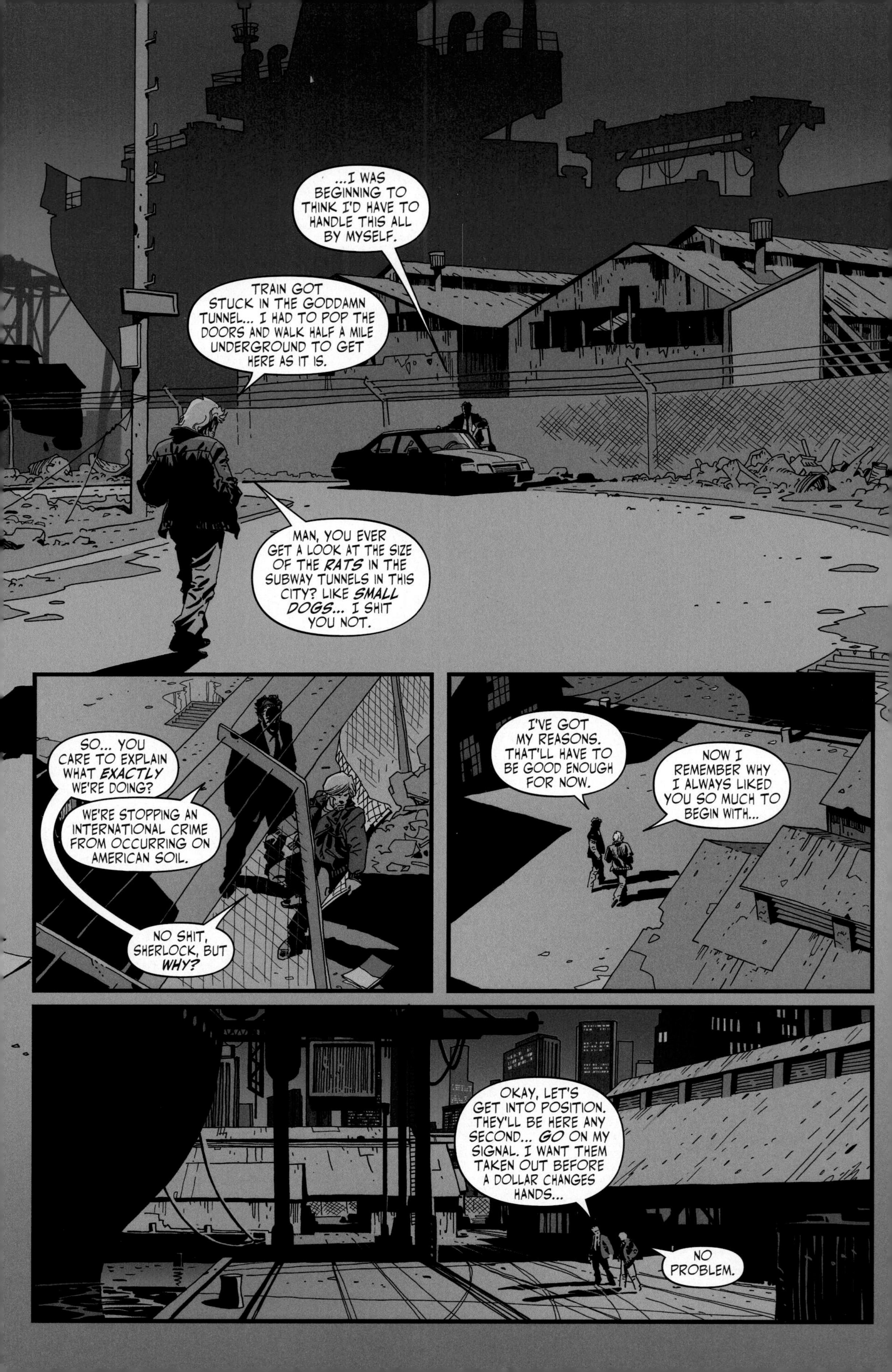
...I WAS BEGINNING TO THINK I'D HAVE TO HANDLE THIS ALL BY MYSELF.
TRAIN GOT STUCK IN THE GODDAMN TUNNEL... I HAD TO POP THE DOORS AND WALK HALF A MILE UNDERGROUND TO GET HERE AS IT IS.
MAN, YOU EVER GET A LOOK AT THE SIZE OF THE RATS IN THE SUBWAY TUNNELS IN THIS CITY? LIKE SMALL DOGS... I SHIT YOU NOT.
SO... YOU CARE TO EXPLAIN WHAT EXACTLY WE'RE DOING?
WE'RE STOPPING AN INTERNATIONAL CRIME FROM OCCURRING ON AMERICAN SOIL.
NO SHIT, SHERLOCK, BUT WHY?
I'VE GOT MY REASONS. THAT'LL HAVE TO BE GOOD ENOUGH FOR NOW.
NOW I REMEMBER WHY I ALWAYS LIKED YOU SO MUCH TO BEGIN WITH...
OKAY, LET'S GET INTO POSITION. THEY'LL BE HERE ANY SECOND... GO ON MY SIGNAL. I WANT THEM TAKEN OUT BEFORE A DOLLAR CHANGES HANDS...
NO PROBLEM.

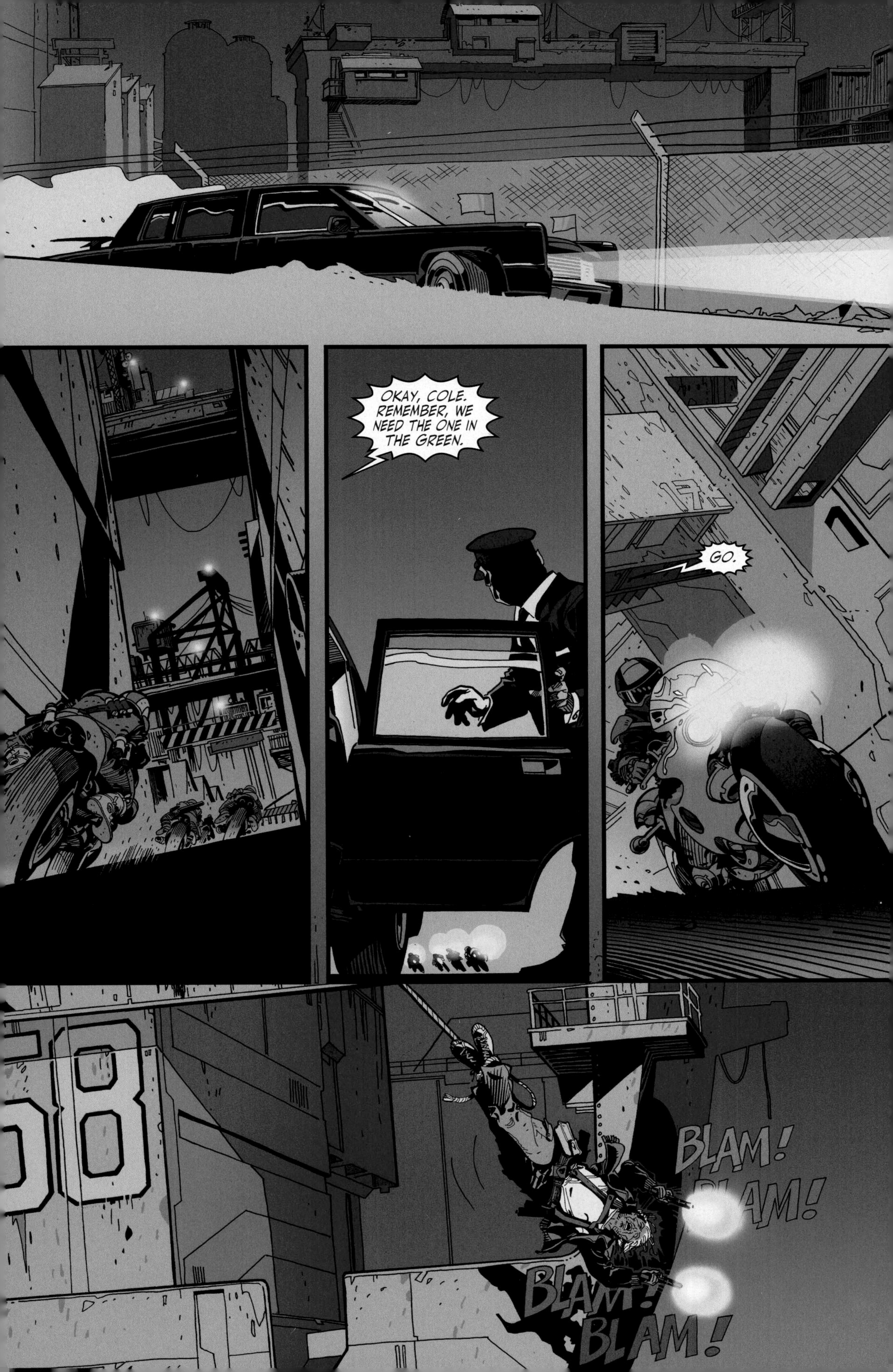
OKAY, COLE. REMEMBER, WE NEED THE ONE IN THE GREEN.
GO.
BLAM! BLAM!
BLAM! BLAM!

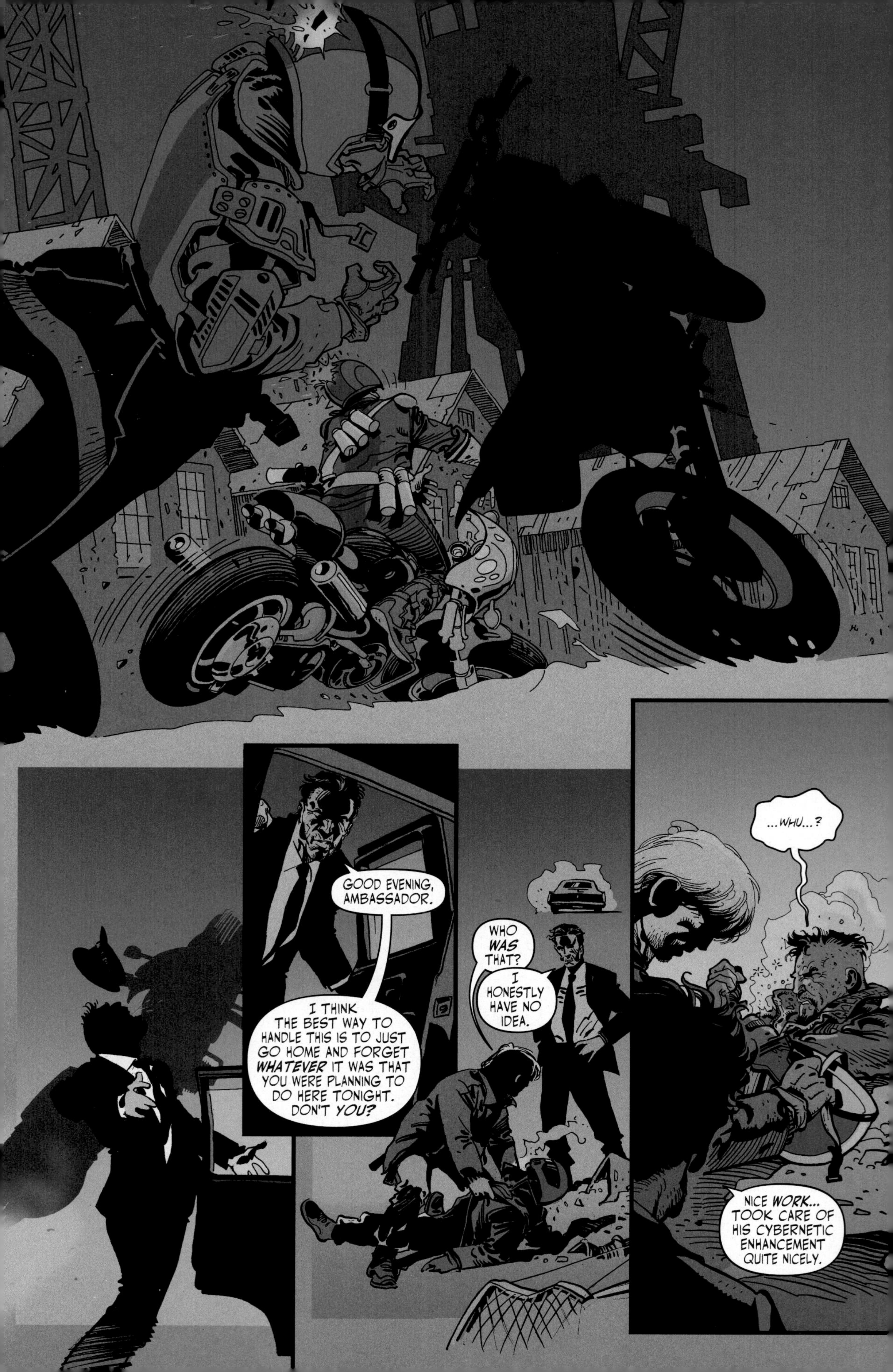
GOOD EVENING, AMBASSADOR.
I THINK THE BEST WAY TO HANDLE THIS IS TO JUST GO HOME AND FORGET WHATEVER IT WAS THAT YOU WERE PLANNING TO DO HERE TONIGHT. DON'T YOU?
WHO WAS THAT?
I HONESTLY HAVE NO IDEA.
...WHU...?
NICE WORK... TOOK CARE OF HIS CYBERNETIC ENHANCEMENT QUITE NICELY.

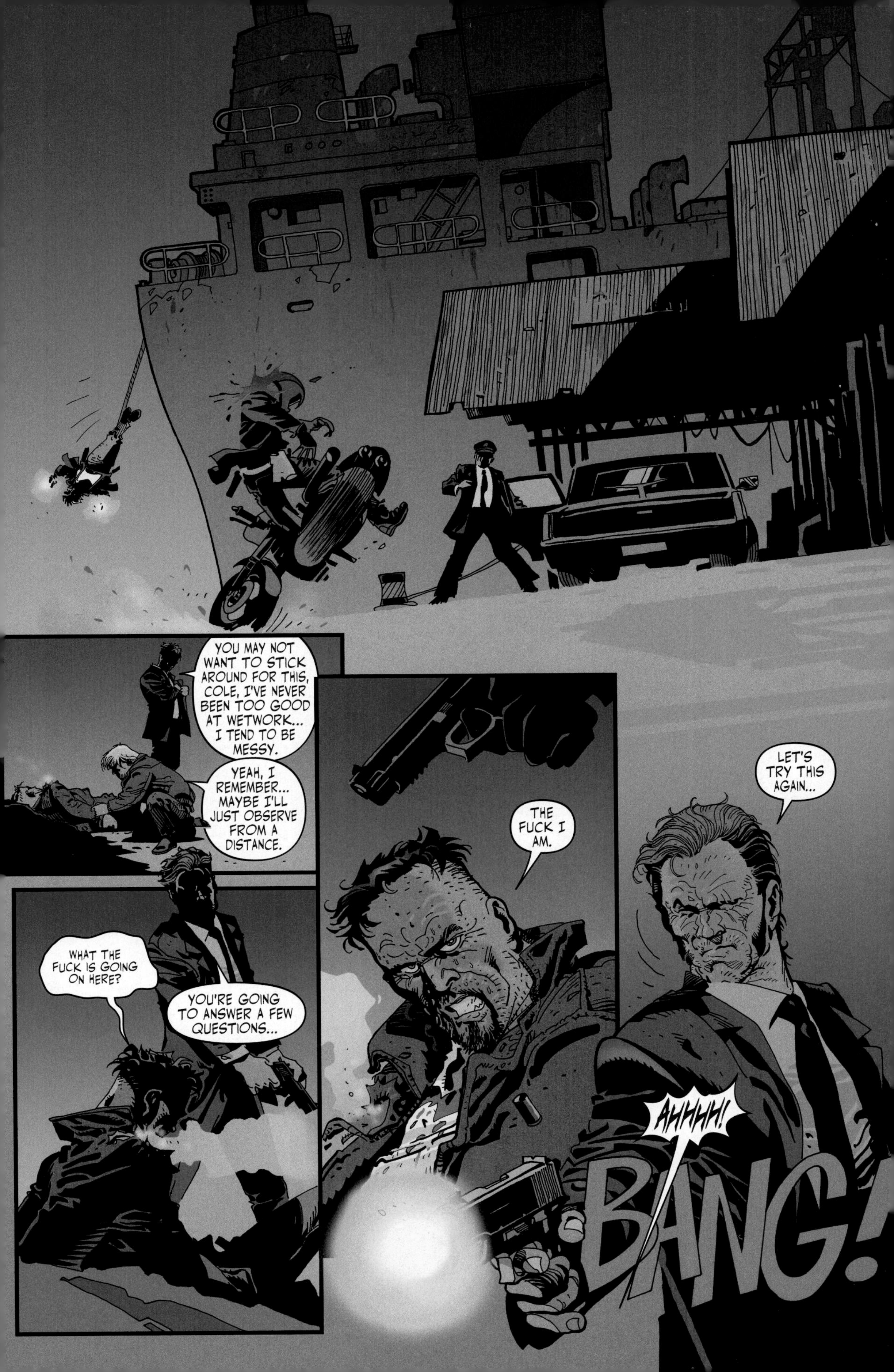
YOU MAY NOT WANT TO STICK AROUND FOR THIS, COLE, I'VE NEVER BEEN TOO GOOD AT WETWORK... I TEND TO BE MESSY.
YEAH, I REMEMBER... MAYBE I'LL JUST OBSERVE FROM A DISTANCE.
WHAT THE FUCK IS GOING ON HERE?
YOU'RE GOING TO ANSWER A FEW QUESTIONS...
THE FUCK I AM.
LET'S TRY THIS AGAIN...
AHHHH!
BANG!

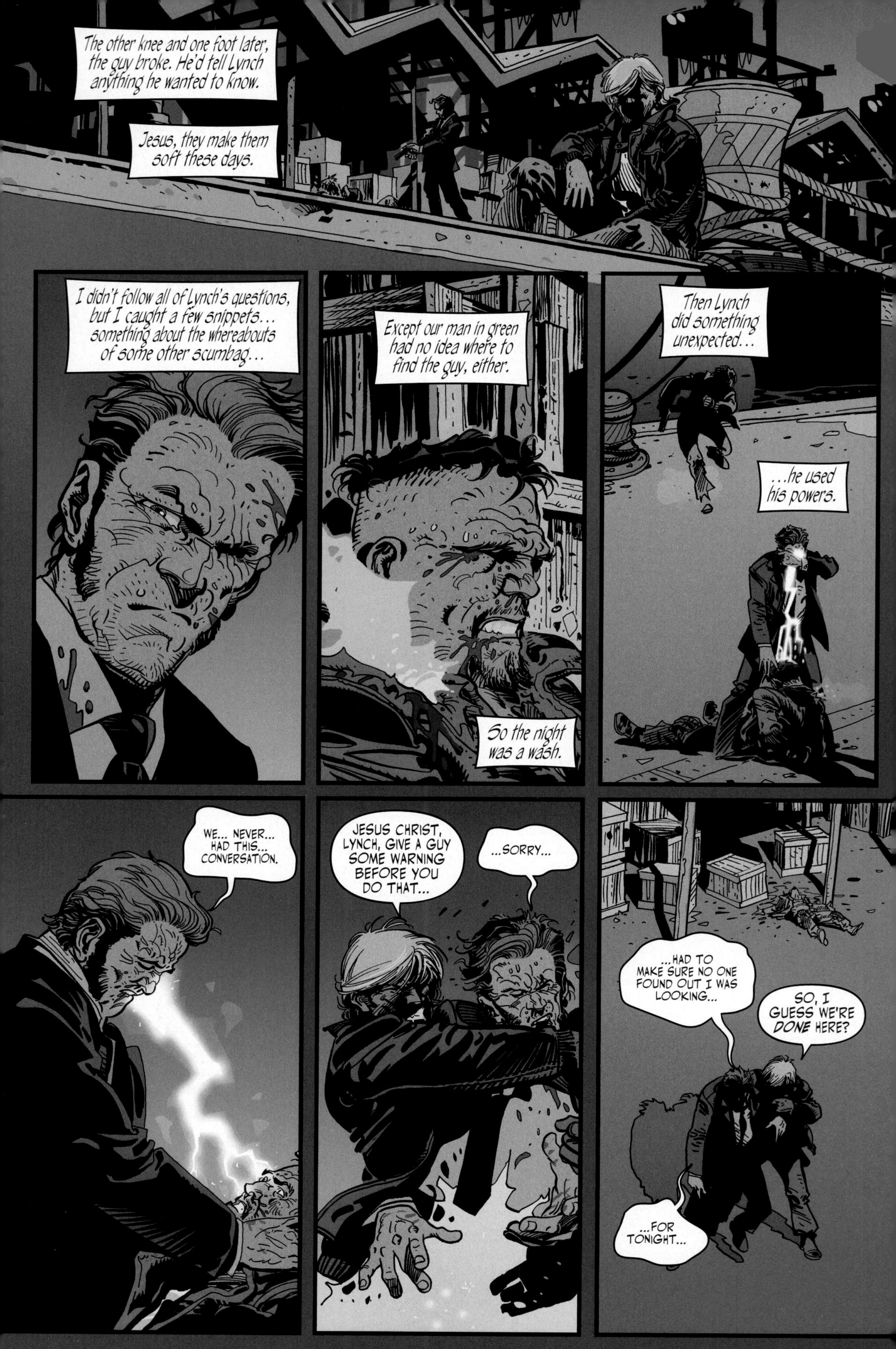
The other knee and one foot later, the guy broke. He'd tell Lynch anything he wanted to know.
Jesus, they make them soft these days.
I didn't follow all of Lynch's questions, but I caught a few snippets... something about the whereabouts of some other scumbag...
Except our man in green had no idea where to find the guy, either.
So the night was a wash.
Then Lynch did something unexpected...
...he used his powers.
WE... NEVER... HAD THIS... CONVERSATION.
JESUS CHRIST, LYNCH, GIVE A GUY SOME WARNING BEFORE YOU DO THAT...
...SORRY...
...HAD TO MAKE SURE NO ONE FOUND OUT I WAS LOOKING...
SO, I GUESS WE'RE *DONE* HERE?
...FOR TONIGHT...

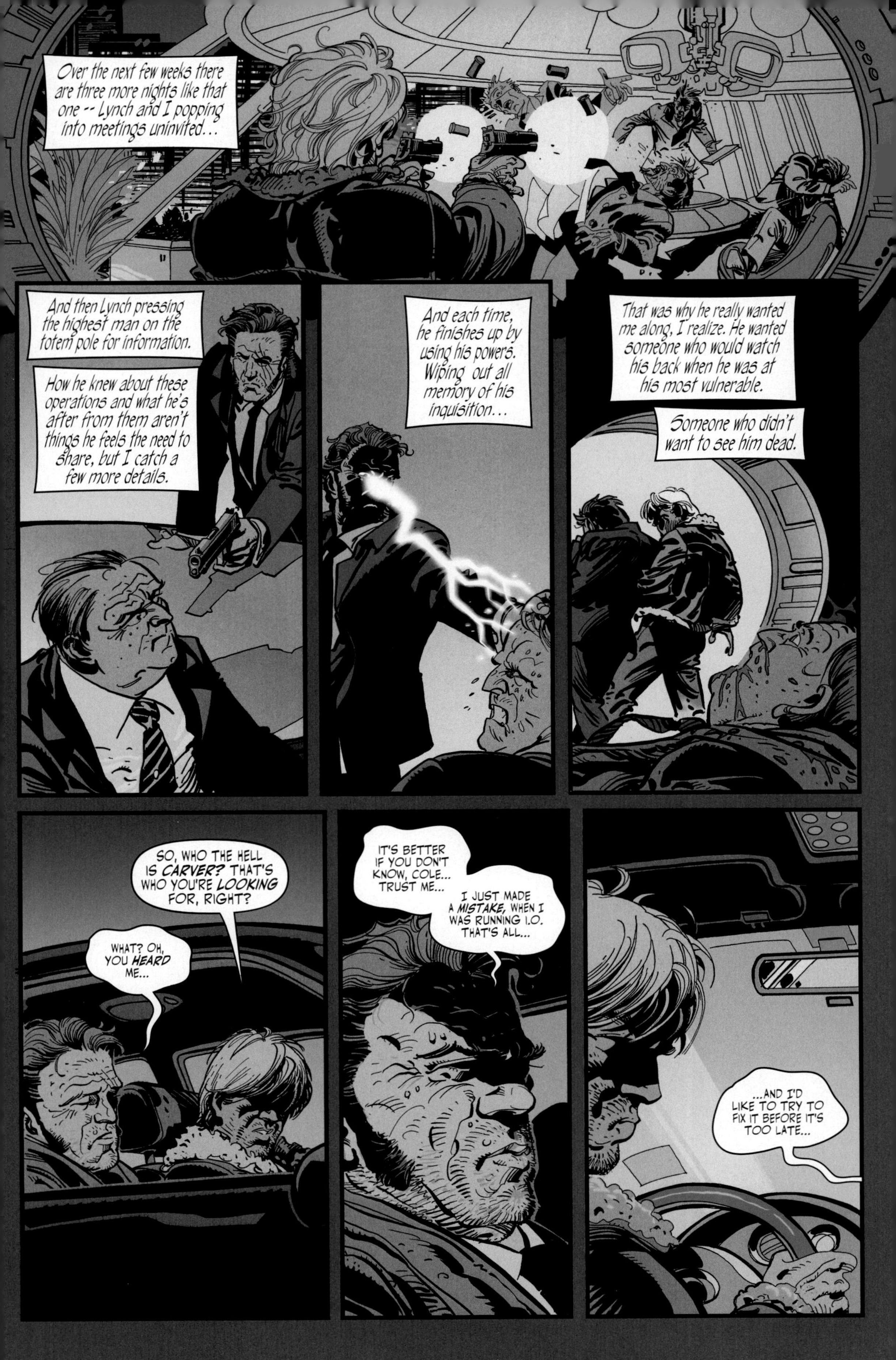

Over the next few weeks there are three more nights like that one -- Lynch and I popping into meetings uninvited...
And then Lynch pressing the highest man on the totem pole for information.
How he knew about these operations and what he's after from them aren't things he feels the need to share, but I catch a few more details.
And each time, he finishes up by using his powers. Wiping out all memory of his inquisition...
That was why he really wanted me along, I realize. He wanted someone who would watch his back when he was at his most vulnerable.
Someone who didn't want to see him dead.
SO, WHO THE HELL IS CARVER? THAT'S WHO YOU'RE LOOKING FOR, RIGHT?
WHAT? OH, YOU HEARD ME...
IT'S BETTER IF YOU DON'T KNOW, COLE... TRUST ME...
I JUST MADE A MISTAKE, WHEN I WAS RUNNING I.O. THAT'S ALL...
...AND I'D LIKE TO TRY TO FIX IT BEFORE IT'S TOO LATE...

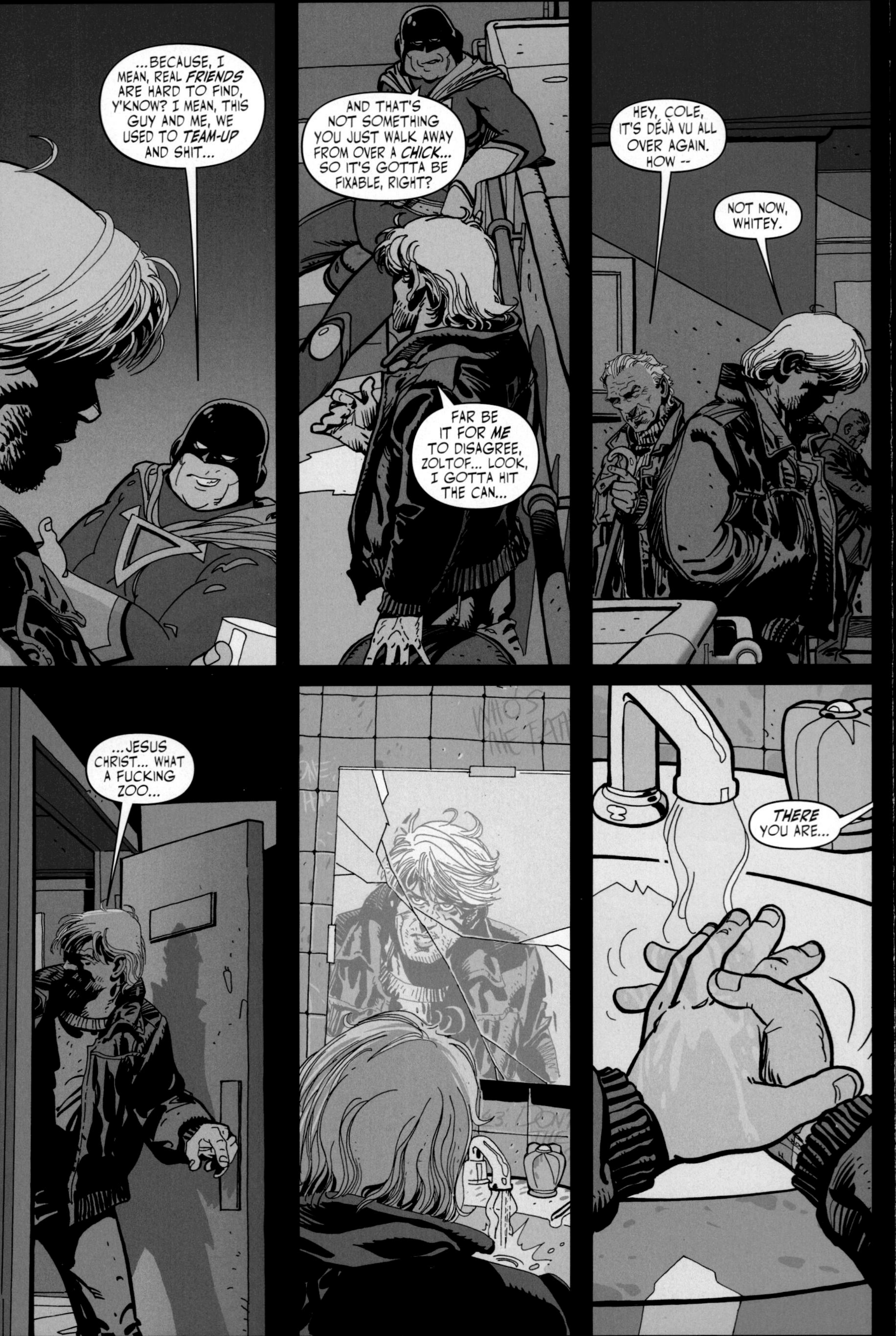
...BECAUSE, I MEAN, REAL *FRIENDS* ARE HARD TO FIND, Y'KNOW? I MEAN, THIS GUY AND ME, WE USED TO *TEAM-UP* AND SHIT...
AND THAT'S NOT SOMETHING YOU JUST WALK AWAY FROM OVER A *CHICK*... SO IT'S GOTTA BE FIXABLE, RIGHT?
FAR BE IT FOR *ME* TO DISAGREE, ZOLTOF... LOOK, I GOTTA HIT THE CAN...
HEY, COLE, IT'S DÉJÀ VU ALL OVER AGAIN. HOW --
NOT NOW, WHITEY.
...JESUS CHRIST... WHAT A FUCKING ZOO...
THERE YOU ARE...

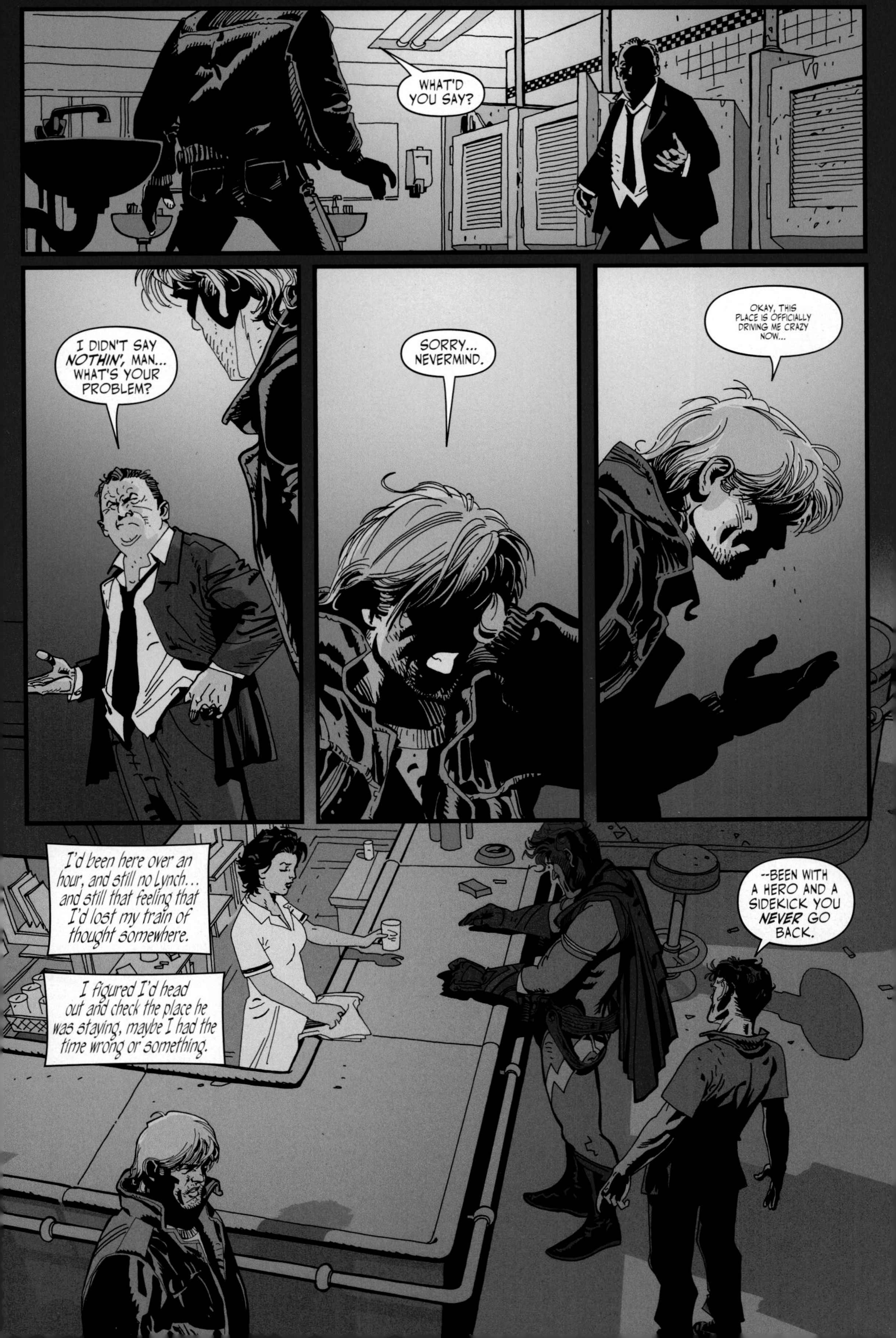
WHAT'D YOU SAY?
I DIDN'T SAY NOTHIN', MAN... WHAT'S YOUR PROBLEM?
SORRY... NEVERMIND.
OKAY, THIS PLACE IS OFFICIALLY DRIVING ME CRAZY NOW...
I'd been here over an hour, and still no Lynch... and still that feeling that I'd lost my train of thought somewhere.
I figured I'd head out and check the place he was staying, maybe I had the time wrong or something.
--BEEN WITH A HERO AND A SIDEKICK YOU NEVER GO BACK.

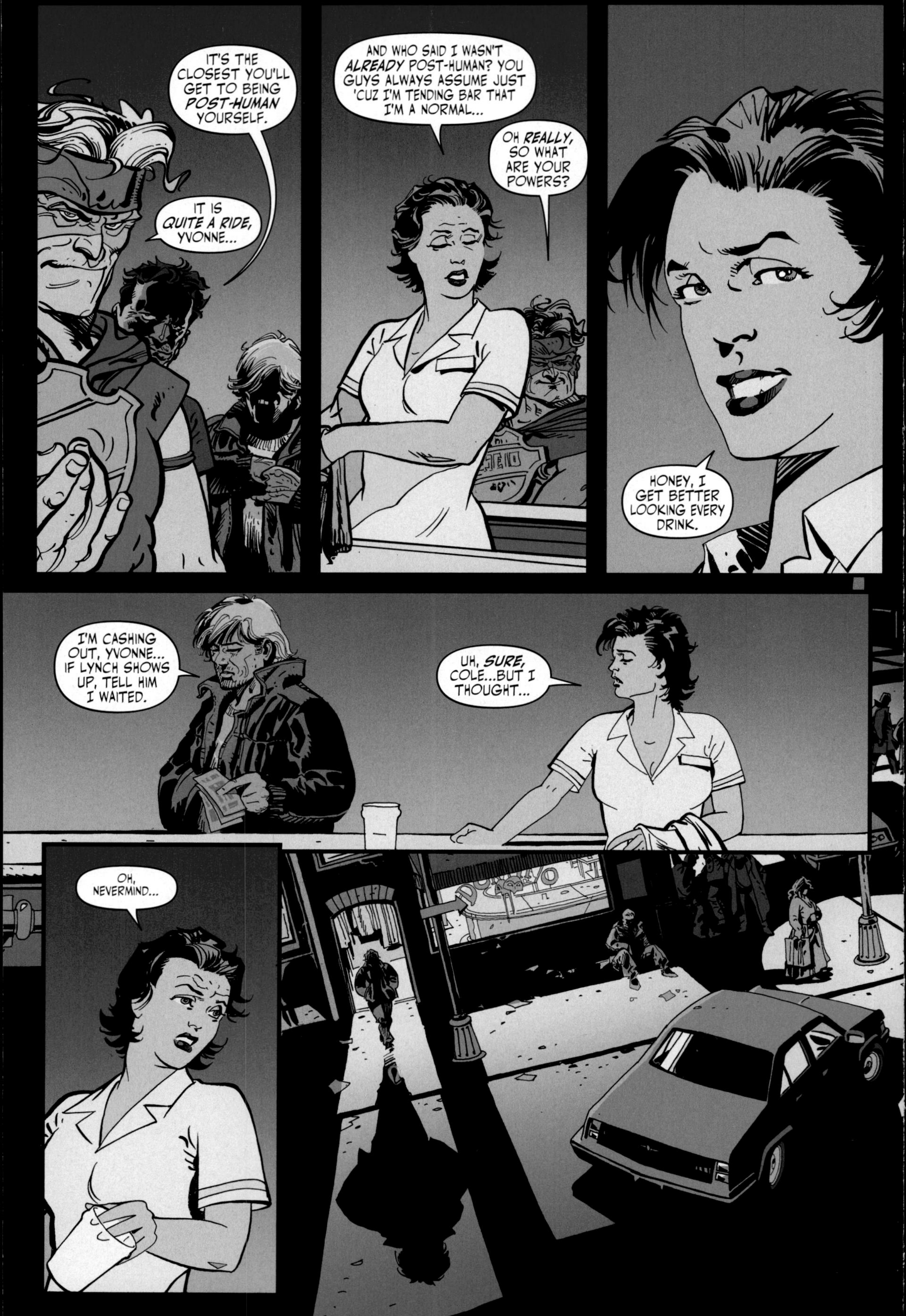
IT'S THE CLOSEST YOU'LL GET TO BEING *POST-HUMAN* YOURSELF.
IT IS *QUITE A RIDE,* YVONNE...
AND WHO SAID I WASN'T *ALREADY* POST-HUMAN? YOU GUYS ALWAYS ASSUME JUST 'CUZ I'M TENDING BAR THAT I'M A NORMAL...
OH *REALLY,* SO WHAT ARE YOUR POWERS?
HONEY, I GET BETTER LOOKING EVERY DRINK.
I'M CASHING OUT, YVONNE... IF LYNCH SHOWS UP, TELL HIM I WAITED.
UH, *SURE,* COLE...BUT I THOUGHT...
OH, NEVERMIND...

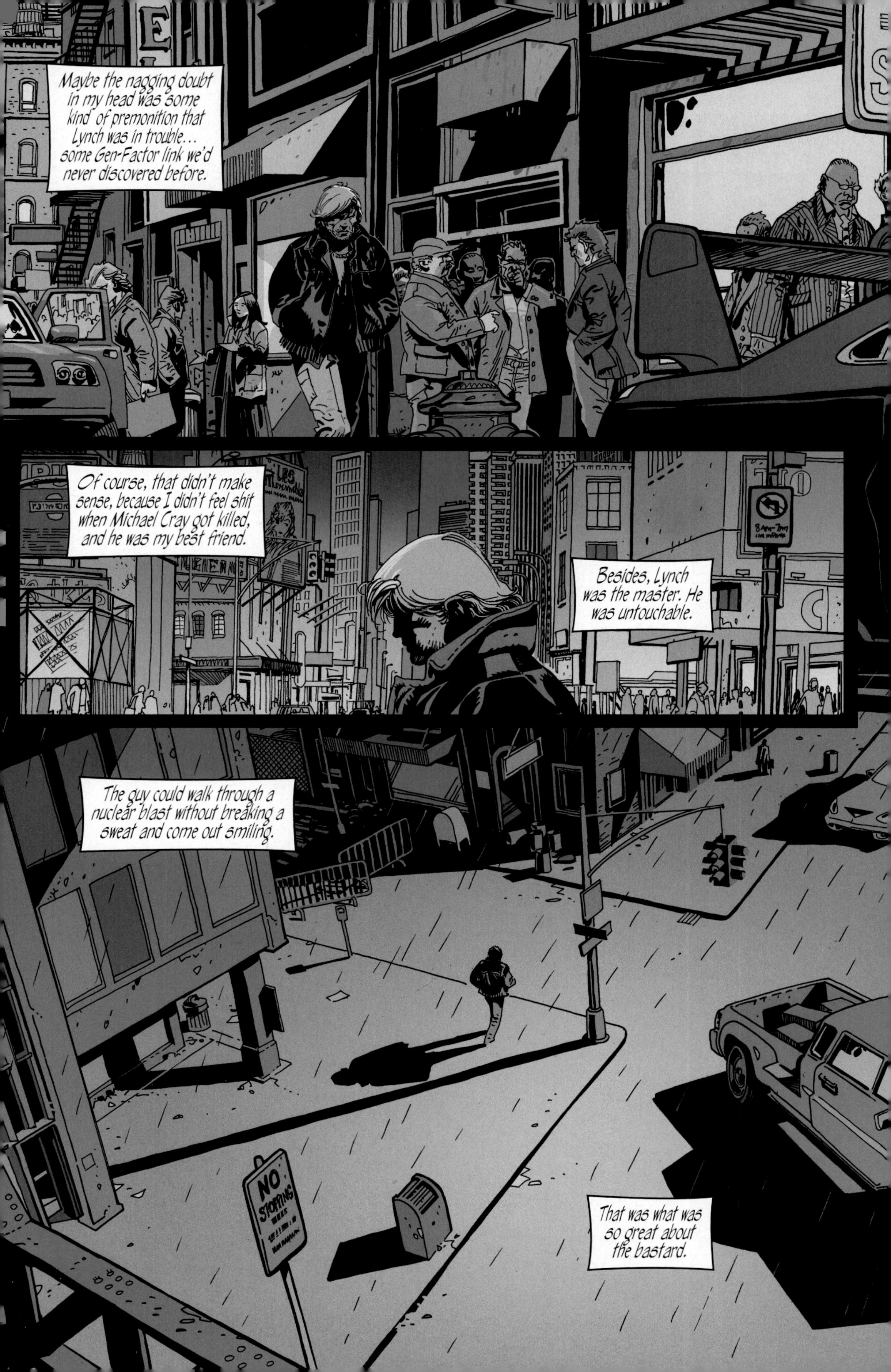
Maybe the nagging doubt in my head was some kind of premonition that Lynch was in trouble... some Gen-Factor link we'd never discovered before.
Of course, that didn't make sense, because I didn't feel shit when Michael Cray got killed, and he was my best friend.
Besides, Lynch was the master. He was untouchable.
The guy could walk through a nuclear blast without breaking a sweat and come out smiling.
NO STOPPING
That was what was so great about the bastard.

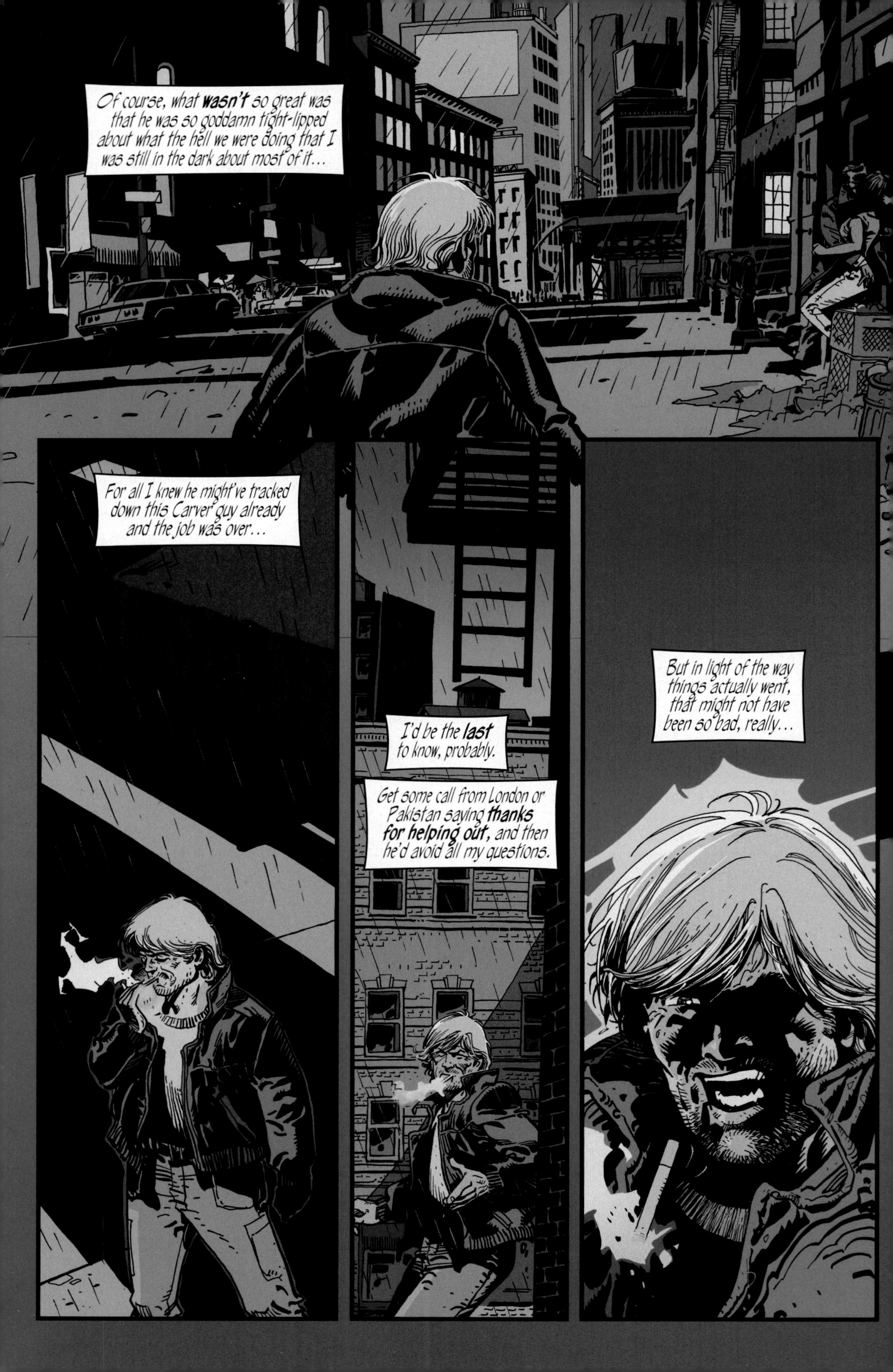
Of course, what **wasn't** so great was that he was so goddamn tight-lipped about what the hell we were doing that I was still in the dark about most of it...
For all I knew he might've tracked down this Carver guy already and the job was over...
I'd be the **last** to know, probably.
Get some call from London or Pakistan saying **thanks for helping out**, and then he'd avoid all my questions.
But in light of the way things actually went, that might not have been so bad, really...

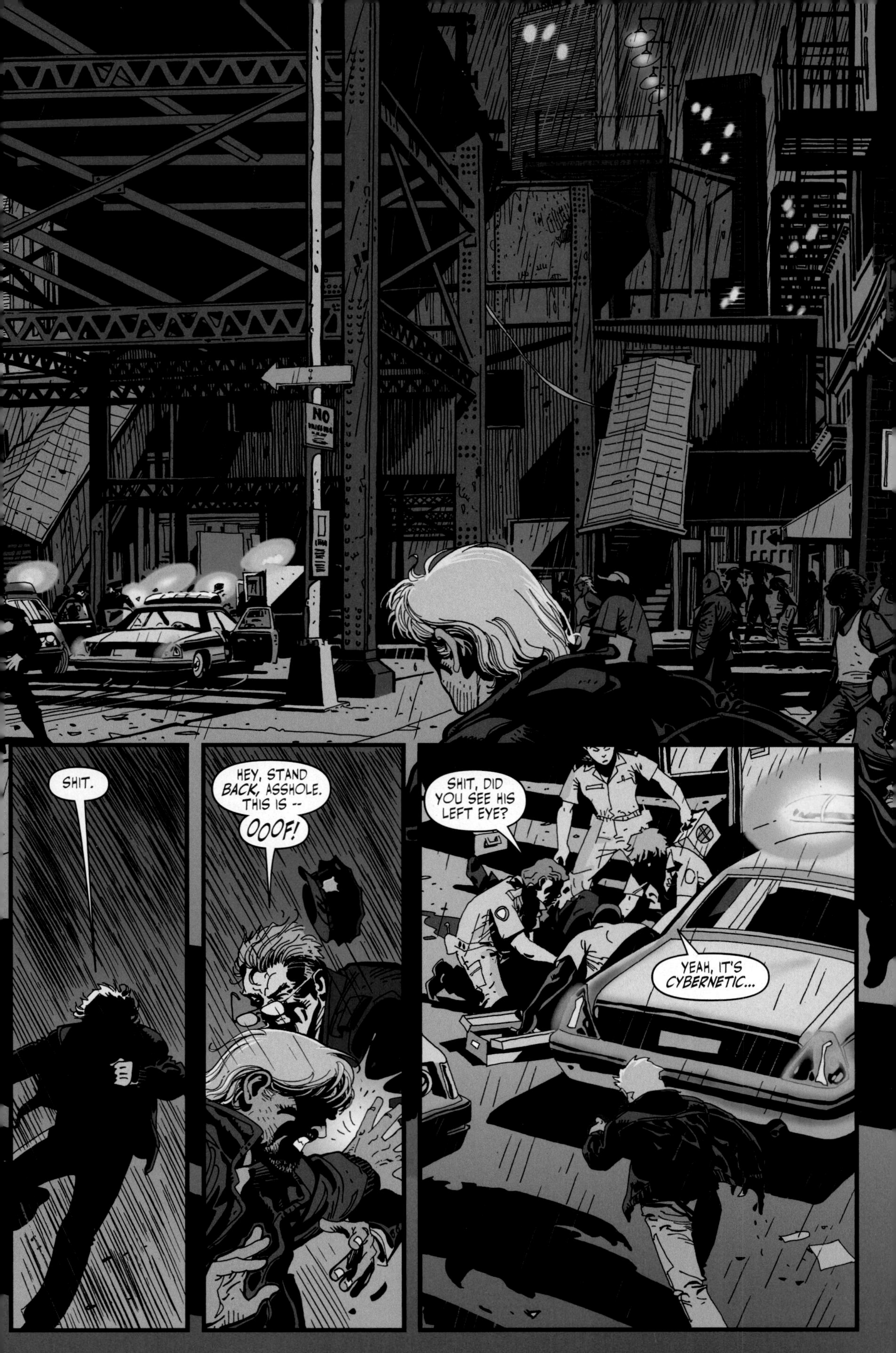
NO
SHIT.
HEY, STAND BACK, ASSHOLE. THIS IS --
OOOF!
SHIT, DID YOU SEE HIS LEFT EYE?
YEAH, IT'S CYBERNETIC...

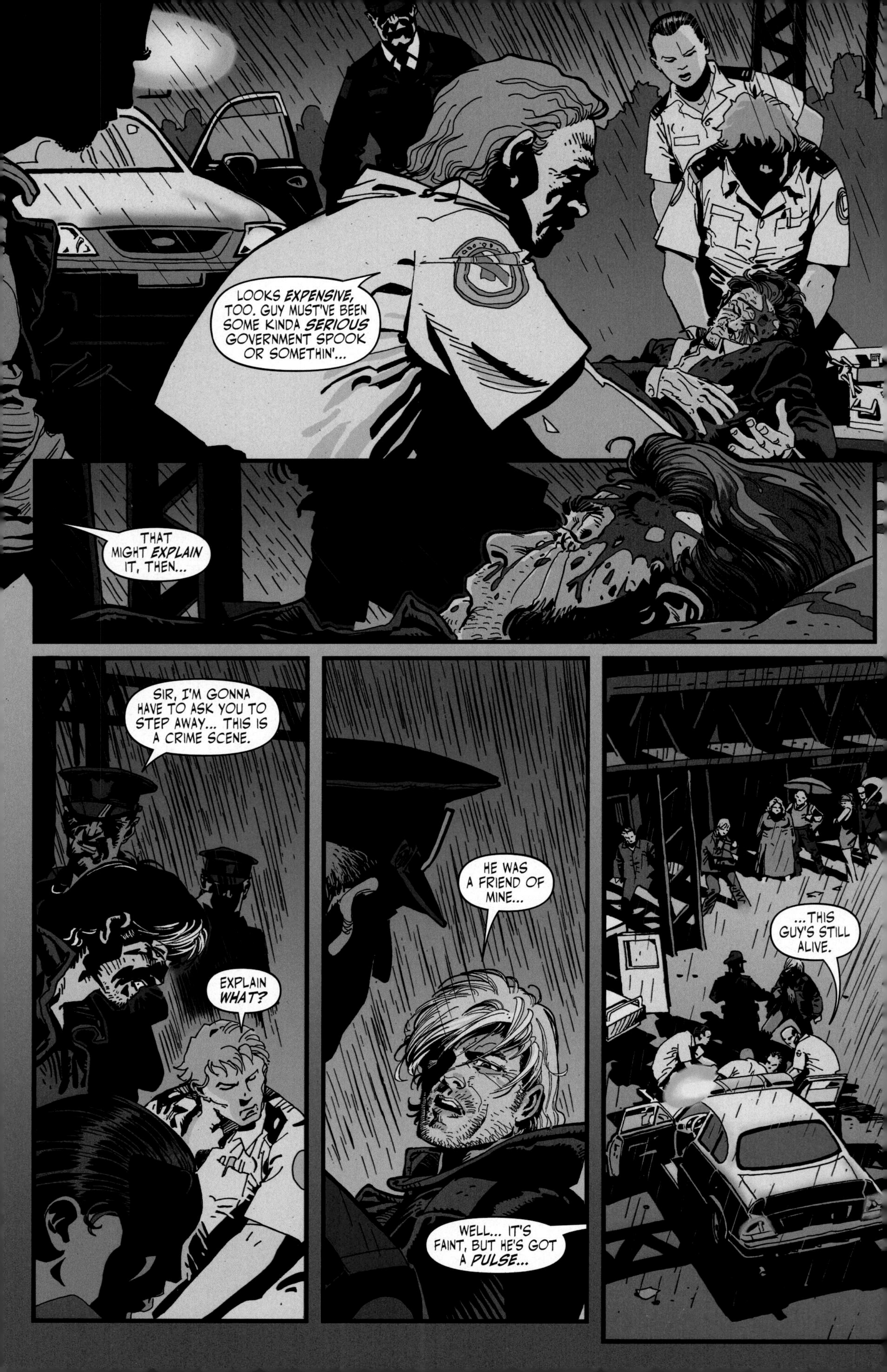
LOOKS EXPENSIVE, TOO. GUY MUST'VE BEEN SOME KINDA SERIOUS GOVERNMENT SPOOK OR SOMETHIN'...
THAT MIGHT EXPLAIN IT, THEN...
SIR, I'M GONNA HAVE TO ASK YOU TO STEP AWAY... THIS IS A CRIME SCENE.
EXPLAIN WHAT?
HE WAS A FRIEND OF MINE...
WELL... IT'S FAINT, BUT HE'S GOT A PULSE...
...THIS GUY'S STILL ALIVE.

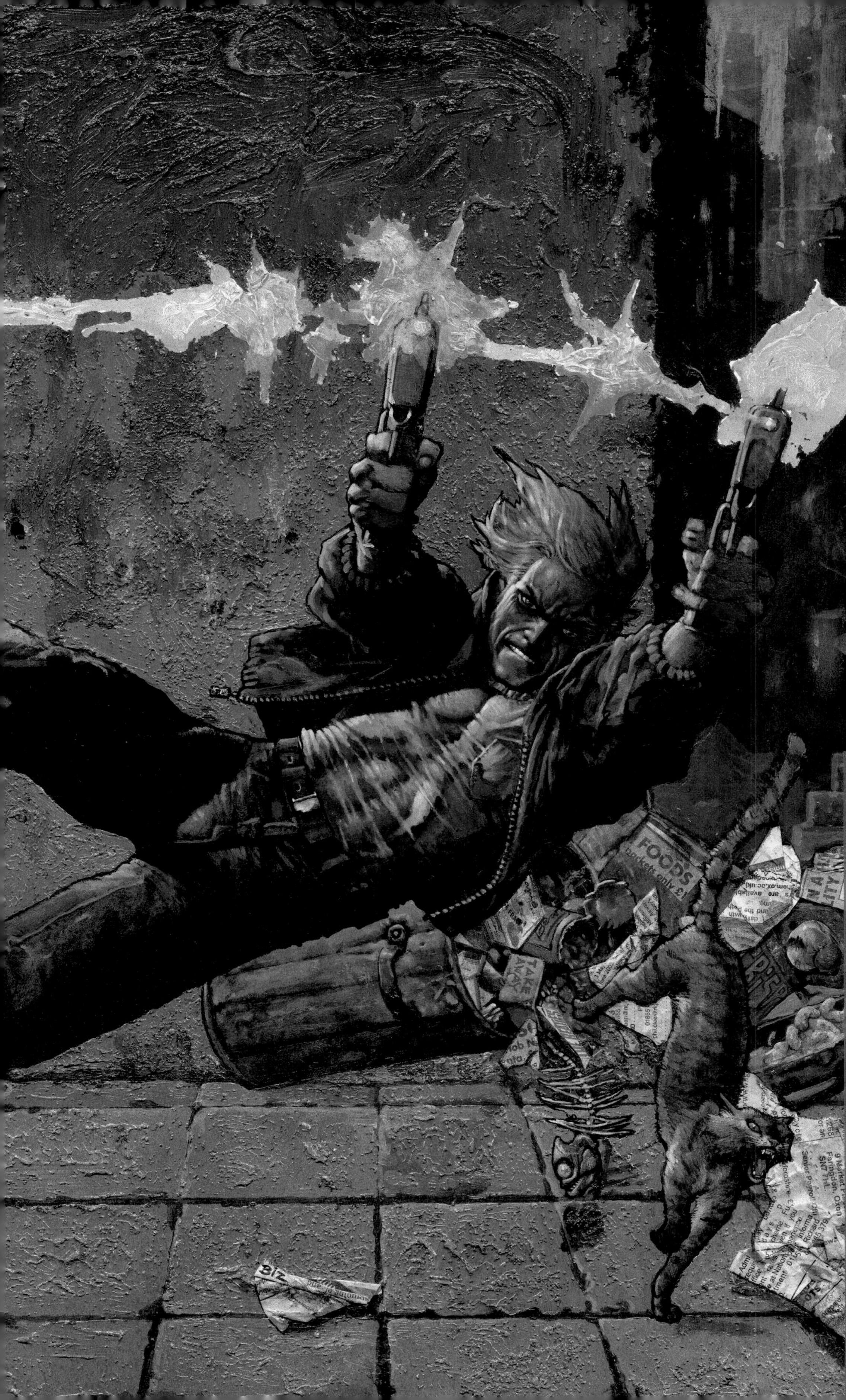
FOODS

Cover by SIMON BISLEY

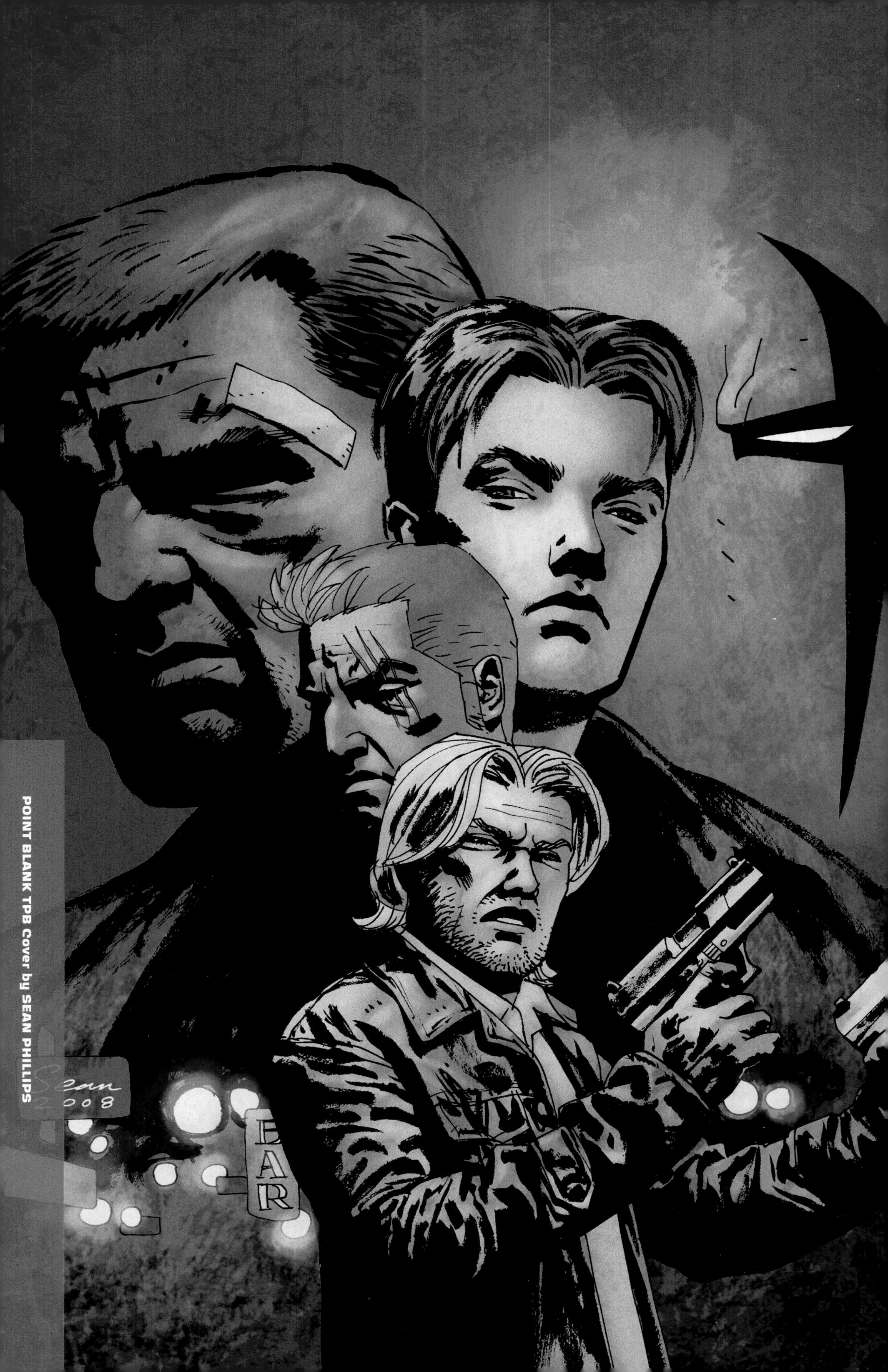
Sean
2008
BAR

POINT BLANK TPB Cover by SEAN PHILLIPS

When we were kids, my brother Max was always trying to come up with **get-rich-quick** schemes...

...he figured since our last name was *Cash*, we should be loaded.

But I remember Max's last great idea... something he came up with the night our mother died...

Of course, he didn't realize that we **would be** loaded someday... loaded with ammunition and death...

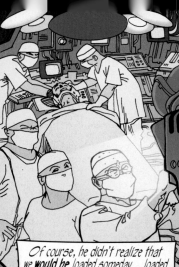

We'd been at the hospital for days... Max was too young to really understand what was happening, and Dad seemed a million miles away.

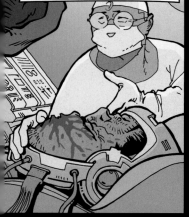

When the doctor finally came out and told us she was gone, we followed Dad as he wandered aimlessly down the halls of the building, trying to find the exit...

And the only thing that he said was "God, I need a drink..."

Then Max had his brilliant idea. There should be **bars** in hospitals.

Bars were so much more fun than churches, anyway, and think of the **money** you could make...

He said all the sad people would have places to go, then, besides the chapels, where we had seen so many of them praying...

The stupid kid couldn't shut up about it, he was so excited... and so oblivious to Dad's pain.

Dad beat the shit out of him in the parking lot...

...and Max never talked about get-rich-quick schemes again.

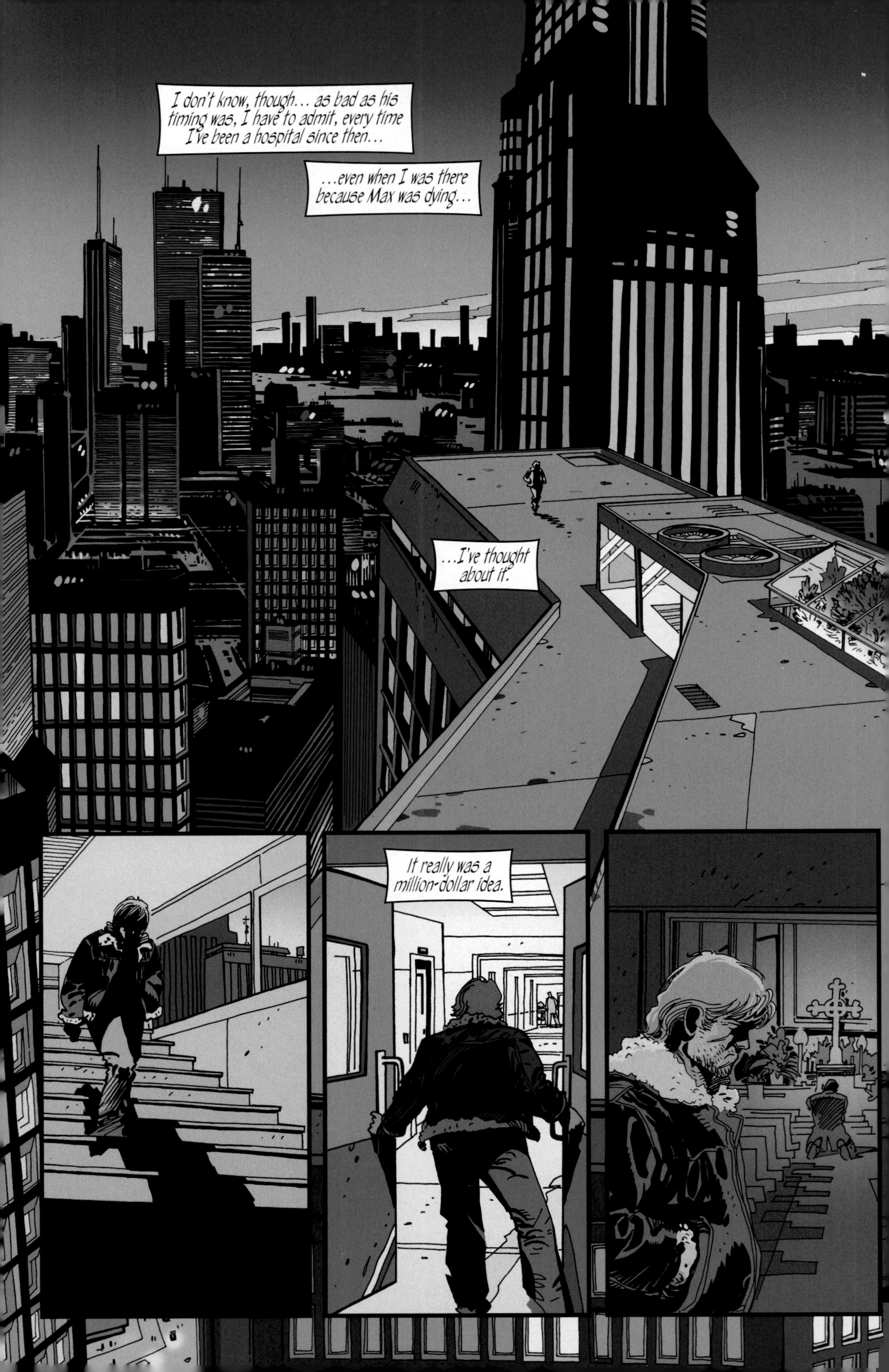
I don't know, though... as bad as his timing was, I have to admit, every time I've been a hospital since then...
...even when I was there because Max was dying...
...I've thought about it.
It really was a million-dollar idea.

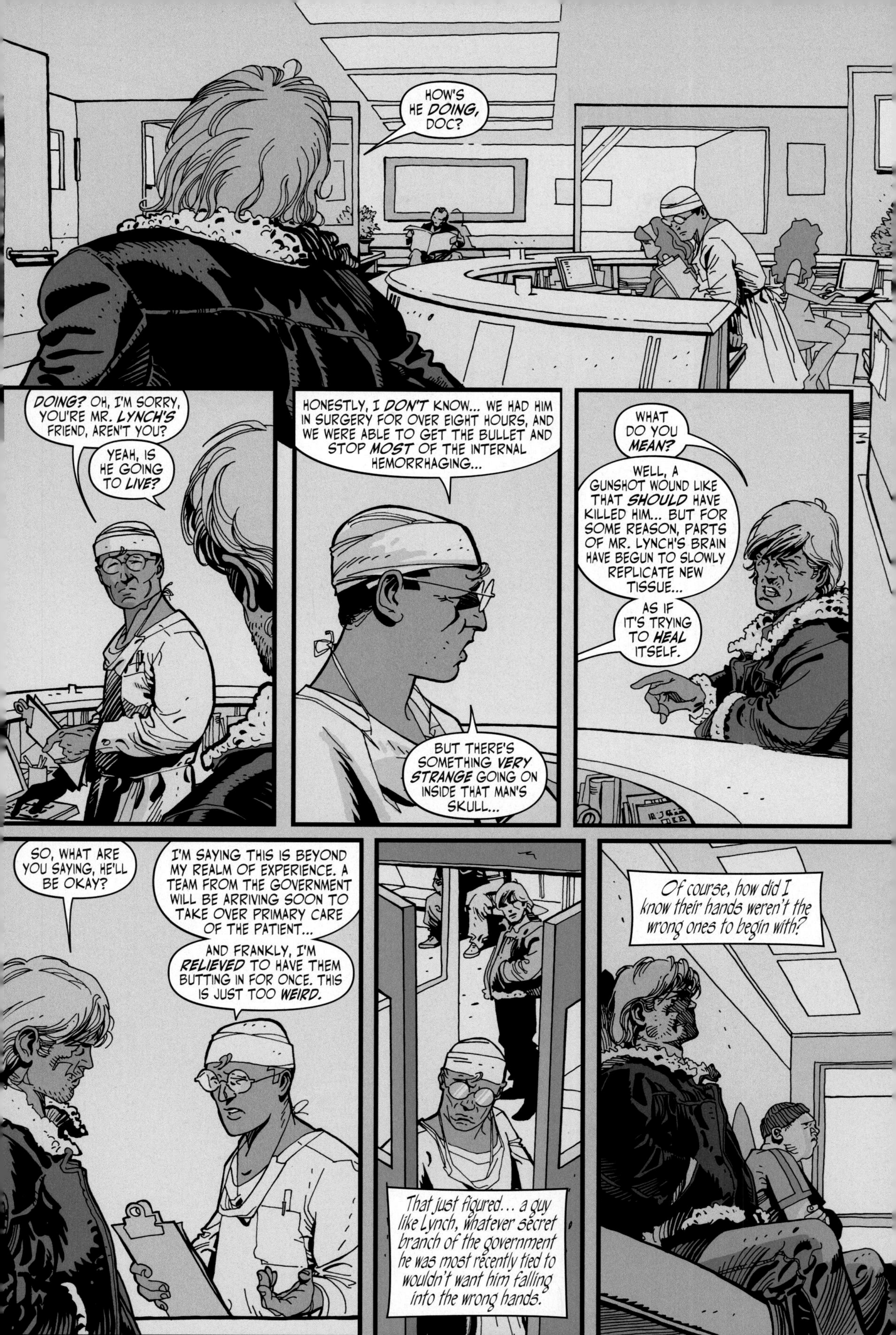
HOW'S HE DOING, DOC?
DOING? OH, I'M SORRY, YOU'RE MR. LYNCH'S FRIEND, AREN'T YOU?
YEAH, IS HE GOING TO LIVE?
HONESTLY, I DON'T KNOW... WE HAD HIM IN SURGERY FOR OVER EIGHT HOURS, AND WE WERE ABLE TO GET THE BULLET AND STOP MOST OF THE INTERNAL HEMORRHAGING...
BUT THERE'S SOMETHING VERY STRANGE GOING ON INSIDE THAT MAN'S SKULL...
WHAT DO YOU MEAN?
WELL, A GUNSHOT WOUND LIKE THAT SHOULD HAVE KILLED HIM... BUT FOR SOME REASON, PARTS OF MR. LYNCH'S BRAIN HAVE BEGUN TO SLOWLY REPLICATE NEW TISSUE...
AS IF IT'S TRYING TO HEAL ITSELF.
SO, WHAT ARE YOU SAYING, HE'LL BE OKAY?
I'M SAYING THIS IS BEYOND MY REALM OF EXPERIENCE. A TEAM FROM THE GOVERNMENT WILL BE ARRIVING SOON TO TAKE OVER PRIMARY CARE OF THE PATIENT...
AND FRANKLY, I'M RELIEVED TO HAVE THEM BUTTING IN FOR ONCE. THIS IS JUST TOO WEIRD.
That just figured... a guy like Lynch, whatever secret branch of the government he was most recently tied to wouldn't want him falling into the wrong hands.
Of course, how did I know their hands weren't the wrong ones to begin with?

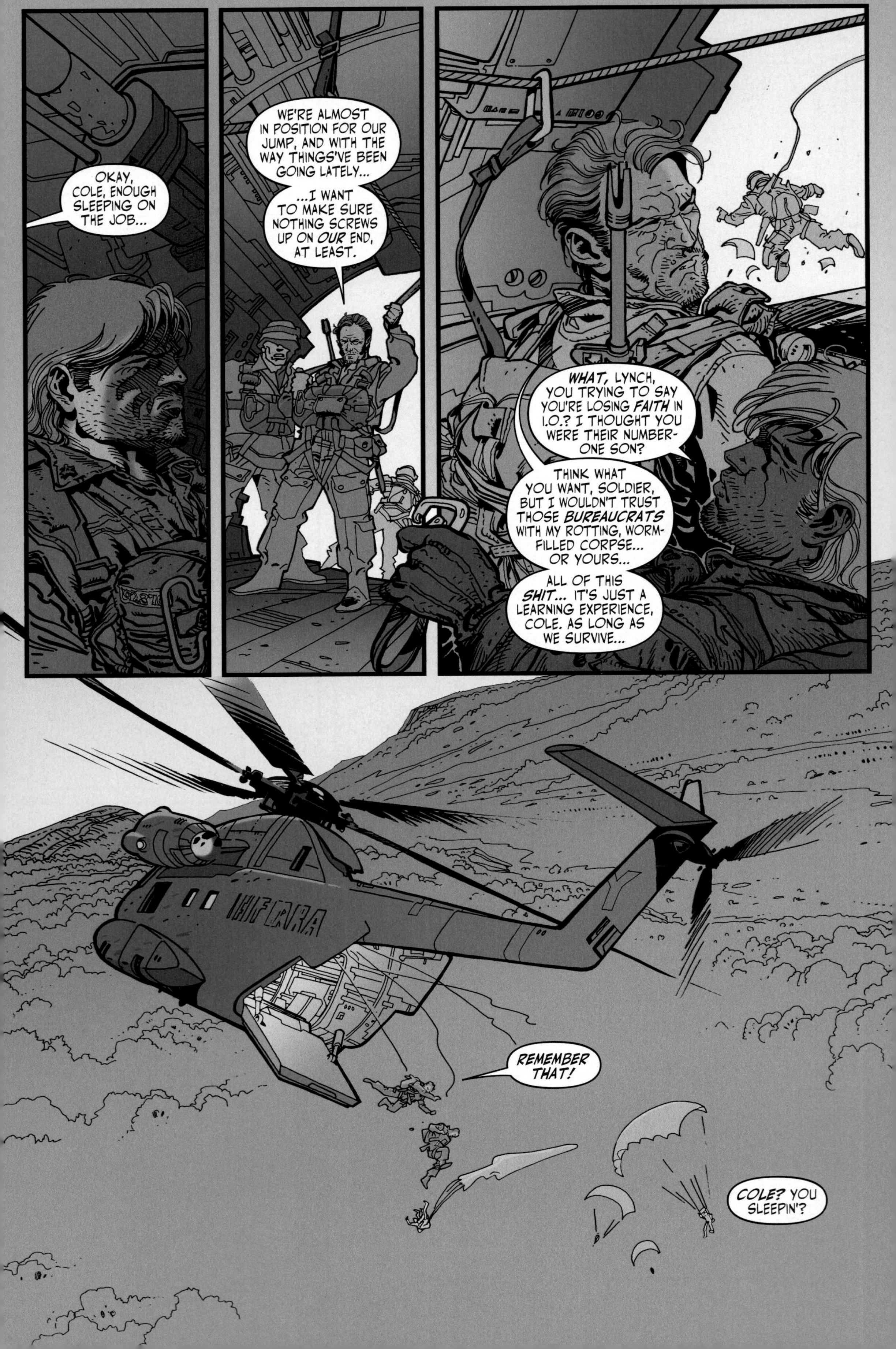
OKAY, COLE, ENOUGH SLEEPING ON THE JOB...
WE'RE ALMOST IN POSITION FOR OUR JUMP, AND WITH THE WAY THINGS'VE BEEN GOING LATELY...
...I WANT TO MAKE SURE NOTHING SCREWS UP ON OUR END, AT LEAST.
WHAT, LYNCH, YOU TRYING TO SAY YOU'RE LOSING FAITH IN I.O.? I THOUGHT YOU WERE THEIR NUMBER-ONE SON?
THINK WHAT YOU WANT, SOLDIER, BUT I WOULDN'T TRUST THOSE BUREAUCRATS WITH MY ROTTING, WORM-FILLED CORPSE... OR YOURS...
ALL OF THIS SHIT... IT'S JUST A LEARNING EXPERIENCE, COLE. AS LONG AS WE SURVIVE...
REMEMBER THAT!
COLE? YOU SLEEPIN'?

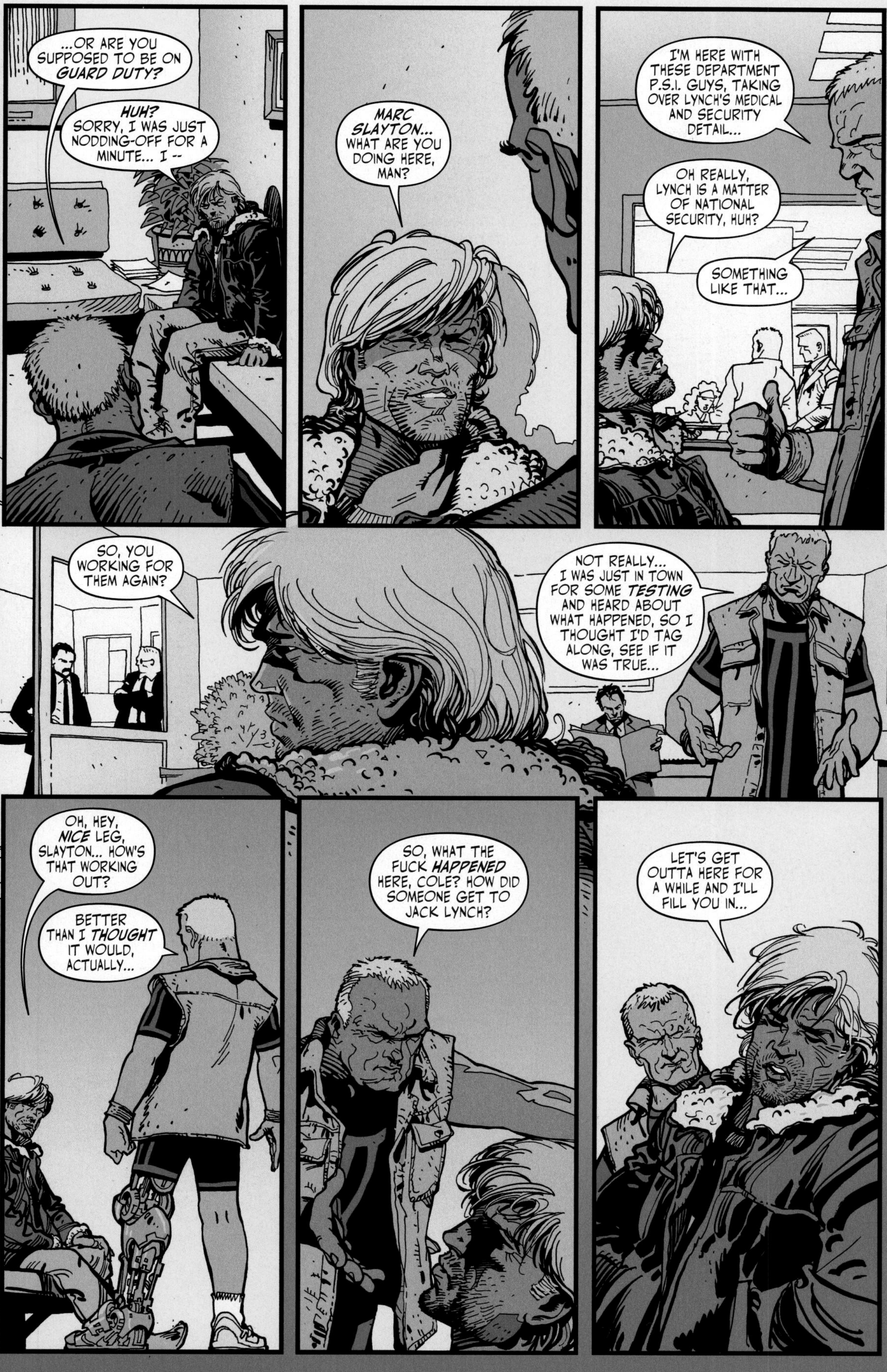
...OR ARE YOU SUPPOSED TO BE ON GUARD DUTY?
HUH? SORRY, I WAS JUST NODDING-OFF FOR A MINUTE... I --
MARC SLAYTON... WHAT ARE YOU DOING HERE, MAN?
I'M HERE WITH THESE DEPARTMENT P.S.I. GUYS, TAKING OVER LYNCH'S MEDICAL AND SECURITY DETAIL...
OH REALLY, LYNCH IS A MATTER OF NATIONAL SECURITY, HUH?
SOMETHING LIKE THAT...
SO, YOU WORKING FOR THEM AGAIN?
NOT REALLY... I WAS JUST IN TOWN FOR SOME TESTING AND HEARD ABOUT WHAT HAPPENED, SO I THOUGHT I'D TAG ALONG, SEE IF IT WAS TRUE...
OH, HEY, NICE LEG, SLAYTON... HOW'S THAT WORKING OUT?
BETTER THAN I THOUGHT IT WOULD, ACTUALLY...
SO, WHAT THE FUCK HAPPENED HERE, COLE? HOW DID SOMEONE GET TO JACK LYNCH?
LET'S GET OUTTA HERE FOR A WHILE AND I'LL FILL YOU IN...

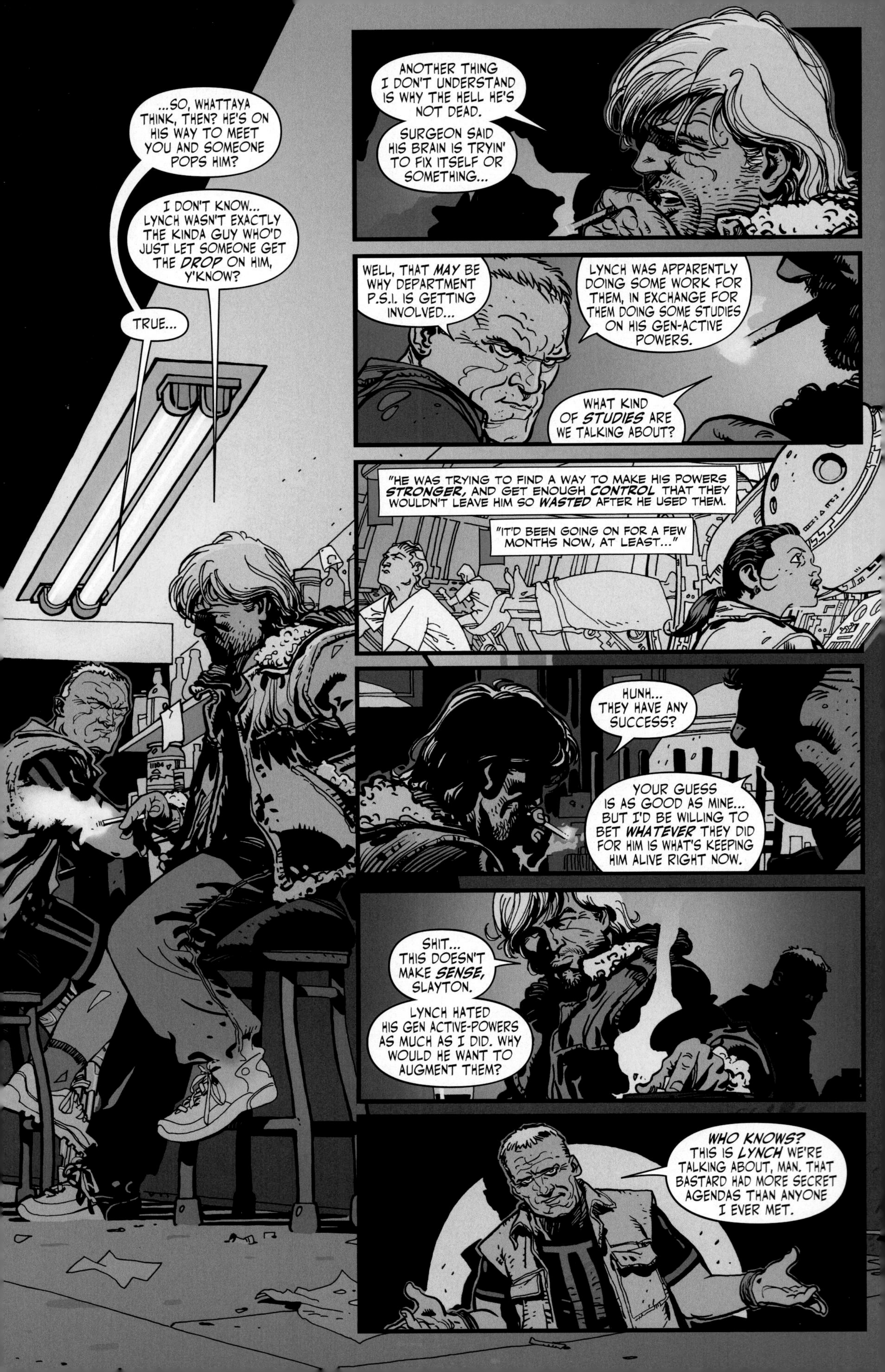
...SO, WHATTAYA THINK, THEN? HE'S ON HIS WAY TO MEET YOU AND SOMEONE POPS HIM?
I DON'T KNOW... LYNCH WASN'T EXACTLY THE KINDA GUY WHO'D JUST LET SOMEONE GET THE DROP ON HIM, Y'KNOW?
TRUE...
ANOTHER THING I DON'T UNDERSTAND IS WHY THE HELL HE'S NOT DEAD.
SURGEON SAID HIS BRAIN IS TRYIN' TO FIX ITSELF OR SOMETHING...
WELL, THAT MAY BE WHY DEPARTMENT P.S.I. IS GETTING INVOLVED...
LYNCH WAS APPARENTLY DOING SOME WORK FOR THEM, IN EXCHANGE FOR THEM DOING SOME STUDIES ON HIS GEN-ACTIVE POWERS.
WHAT KIND OF STUDIES ARE WE TALKING ABOUT?
"HE WAS TRYING TO FIND A WAY TO MAKE HIS POWERS STRONGER, AND GET ENOUGH CONTROL THAT THEY WOULDN'T LEAVE HIM SO WASTED AFTER HE USED THEM.
"IT'D BEEN GOING ON FOR A FEW MONTHS NOW, AT LEAST..."
HUNH... THEY HAVE ANY SUCCESS?
YOUR GUESS IS AS GOOD AS MINE... BUT I'D BE WILLING TO BET WHATEVER THEY DID FOR HIM IS WHAT'S KEEPING HIM ALIVE RIGHT NOW.
SHIT... THIS DOESN'T MAKE SENSE, SLAYTON.
LYNCH HATED HIS GEN ACTIVE-POWERS AS MUCH AS I DID. WHY WOULD HE WANT TO AUGMENT THEM?
WHO KNOWS? THIS IS LYNCH WE'RE TALKING ABOUT, MAN. THAT BASTARD HAD MORE SECRET AGENDAS THAN ANYONE I EVER MET.

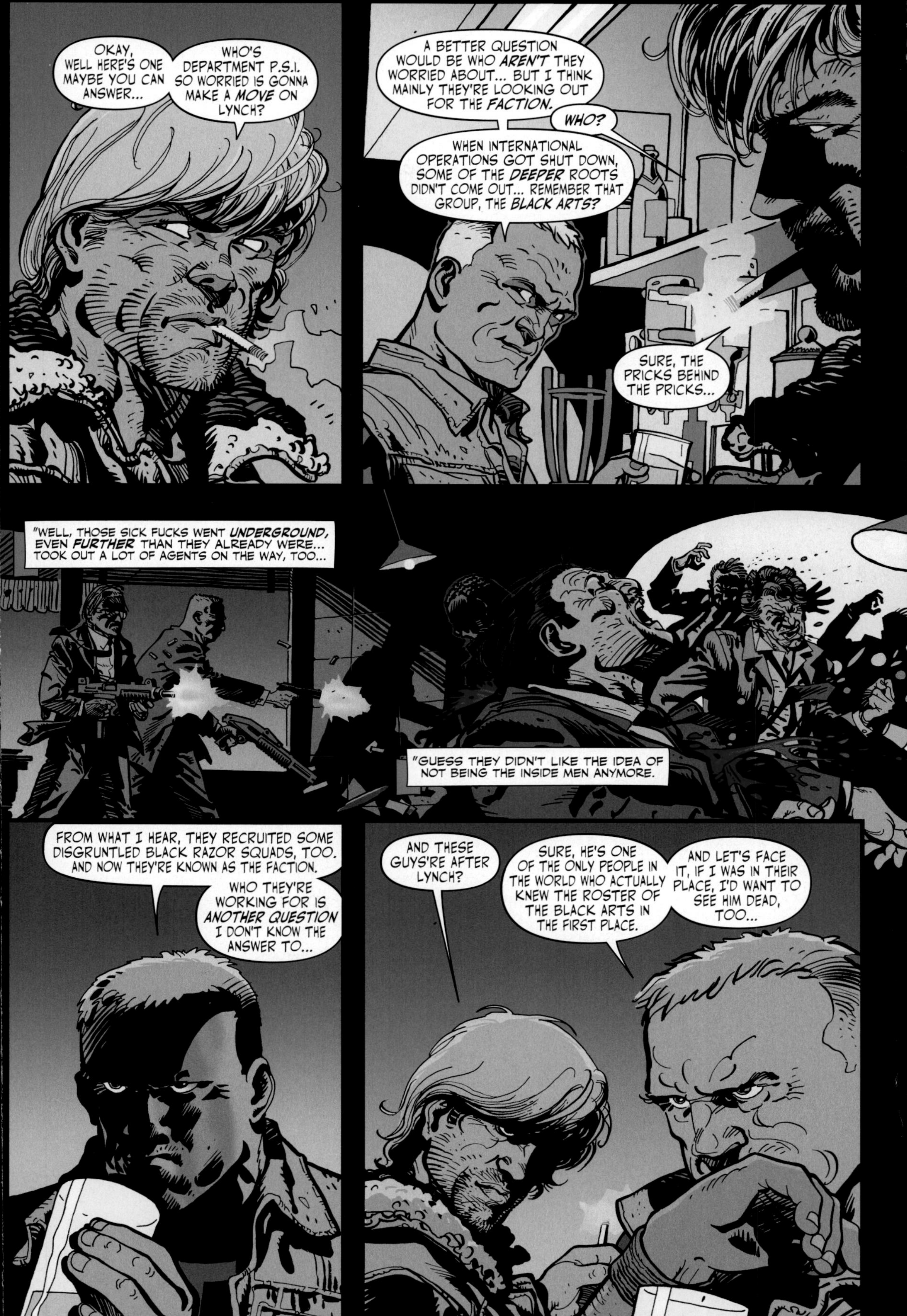
OKAY, WELL HERE'S ONE MAYBE YOU CAN ANSWER...
WHO'S DEPARTMENT P.S.I. SO WORRIED IS GONNA MAKE A *MOVE* ON LYNCH?
A BETTER QUESTION WOULD BE WHO *AREN'T* THEY WORRIED ABOUT... BUT I THINK MAINLY THEY'RE LOOKING OUT FOR THE *FACTION.*
WHO?
WHEN INTERNATIONAL OPERATIONS GOT SHUT DOWN, SOME OF THE *DEEPER* ROOTS DIDN'T COME OUT... REMEMBER THAT GROUP, THE *BLACK ARTS?*
SURE, THE PRICKS BEHIND THE PRICKS...
"WELL, THOSE SICK FUCKS WENT *UNDERGROUND,* EVEN *FURTHER* THAN THEY ALREADY WERE... TOOK OUT A LOT OF AGENTS ON THE WAY, TOO...
"GUESS THEY DIDN'T LIKE THE IDEA OF NOT BEING THE INSIDE MEN ANYMORE.
FROM WHAT I HEAR, THEY RECRUITED SOME DISGRUNTLED BLACK RAZOR SQUADS, TOO. AND NOW THEY'RE KNOWN AS THE FACTION.
WHO THEY'RE WORKING FOR IS *ANOTHER QUESTION* I DON'T KNOW THE ANSWER TO...
AND THESE GUYS'RE AFTER LYNCH?
SURE, HE'S ONE OF THE ONLY PEOPLE IN THE WORLD WHO ACTUALLY KNEW THE ROSTER OF THE BLACK ARTS IN THE FIRST PLACE.
AND LET'S FACE IT, IF I WAS IN THEIR PLACE, I'D WANT TO SEE HIM DEAD, TOO...

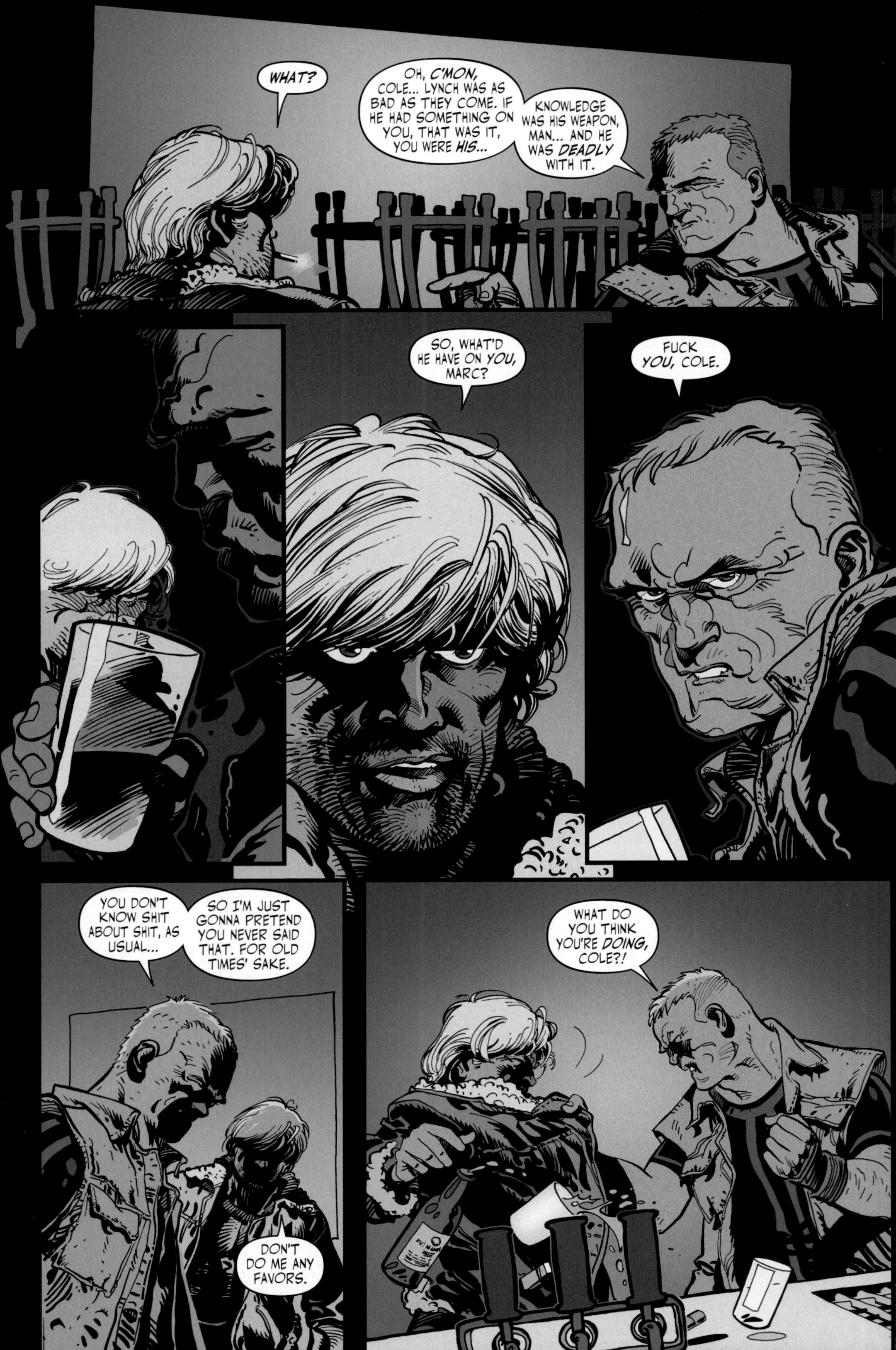
WHAT?
OH, C'MON, COLE... LYNCH WAS AS BAD AS THEY COME. IF HE HAD SOMETHING ON YOU, THAT WAS IT, YOU WERE HIS...
KNOWLEDGE WAS HIS WEAPON, MAN... AND HE WAS DEADLY WITH IT.
SO, WHAT'D HE HAVE ON YOU, MARC?
FUCK YOU, COLE.
YOU DON'T KNOW SHIT ABOUT SHIT, AS USUAL...
SO I'M JUST GONNA PRETEND YOU NEVER SAID THAT. FOR OLD TIMES' SAKE.
DON'T DO ME ANY FAVORS.
WHAT DO YOU THINK YOU'RE DOING, COLE?!

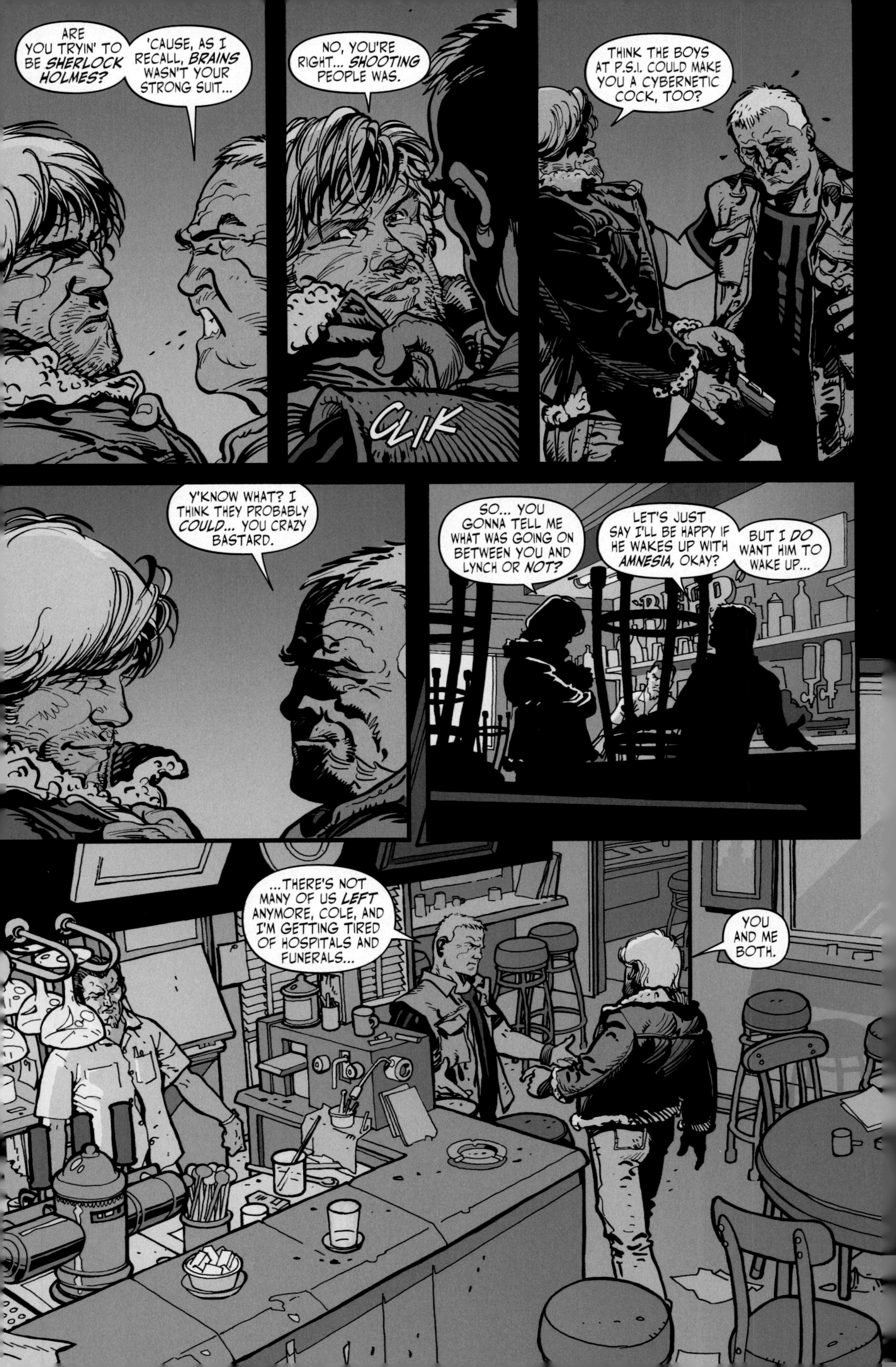
ARE YOU TRYIN' TO BE SHERLOCK HOLMES?
'CAUSE, AS I RECALL, BRAINS WASN'T YOUR STRONG SUIT...
NO, YOU'RE RIGHT... SHOOTING PEOPLE WAS.
CLIK
THINK THE BOYS AT P.S.I. COULD MAKE YOU A CYBERNETIC COCK, TOO?
Y'KNOW WHAT? I THINK THEY PROBABLY COULD... YOU CRAZY BASTARD.
SO... YOU GONNA TELL ME WHAT WAS GOING ON BETWEEN YOU AND LYNCH OR NOT?
LET'S JUST SAY I'LL BE HAPPY IF HE WAKES UP WITH AMNESIA, OKAY?
BUT I DO WANT HIM TO WAKE UP...
...THERE'S NOT MANY OF US LEFT ANYMORE, COLE, AND I'M GETTING TIRED OF HOSPITALS AND FUNERALS...
YOU AND ME BOTH.

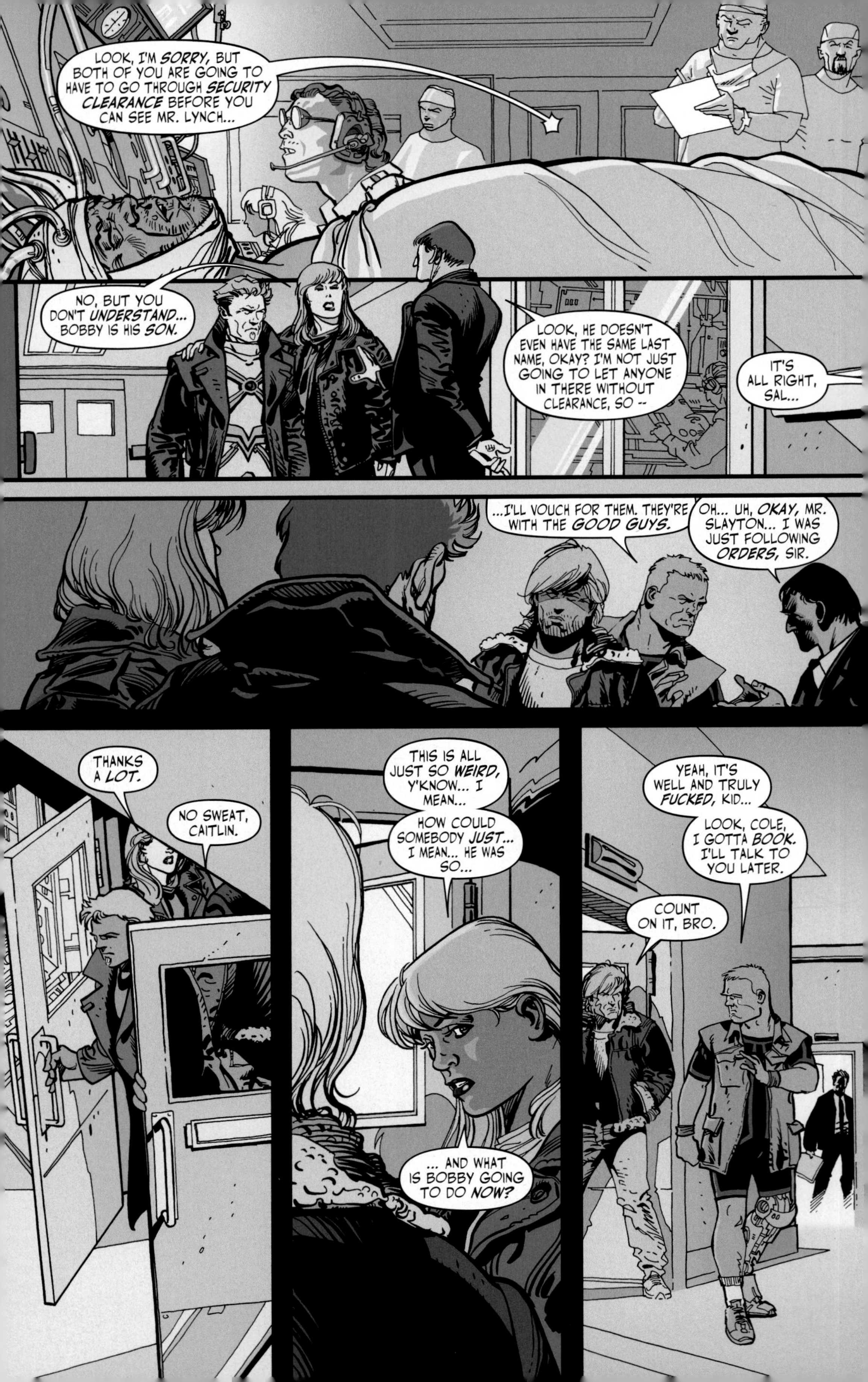
LOOK, I'M SORRY, BUT BOTH OF YOU ARE GOING TO HAVE TO GO THROUGH SECURITY CLEARANCE BEFORE YOU CAN SEE MR. LYNCH...
NO, BUT YOU DON'T UNDERSTAND... BOBBY IS HIS SON.
LOOK, HE DOESN'T EVEN HAVE THE SAME LAST NAME, OKAY? I'M NOT JUST GOING TO LET ANYONE IN THERE WITHOUT CLEARANCE, SO --
IT'S ALL RIGHT, SAL...
...I'LL VOUCH FOR THEM. THEY'RE WITH THE GOOD GUYS.
OH... UH, OKAY, MR. SLAYTON... I WAS JUST FOLLOWING ORDERS, SIR.
THANKS A LOT.
NO SWEAT, CAITLIN.
THIS IS ALL JUST SO WEIRD, Y'KNOW... I MEAN...
HOW COULD SOMEBODY JUST... I MEAN... HE WAS SO...
... AND WHAT IS BOBBY GOING TO DO NOW?
YEAH, IT'S WELL AND TRULY FUCKED, KID...
LOOK, COLE, I GOTTA BOOK. I'LL TALK TO YOU LATER.
COUNT ON IT, BRO.

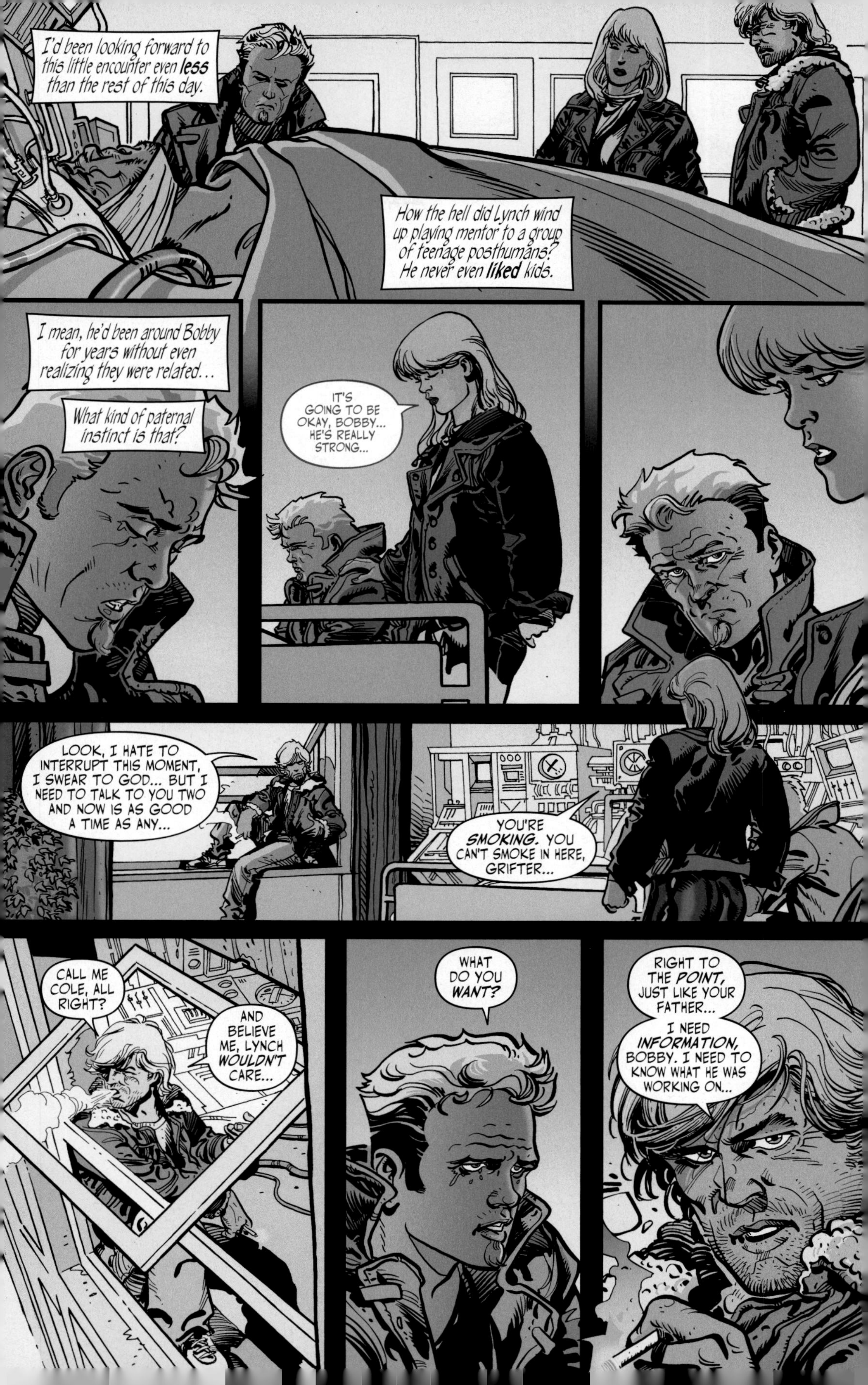
I'd been looking forward to this little encounter even **less** than the rest of this day.
How the hell did Lynch wind up playing mentor to a group of teenage posthumans? He never even **liked** kids.
I mean, he'd been around Bobby for years without even realizing they were related...
What kind of paternal instinct is that?
IT'S GOING TO BE OKAY, BOBBY... HE'S REALLY STRONG...
LOOK, I HATE TO INTERRUPT THIS MOMENT, I SWEAR TO GOD... BUT I NEED TO TALK TO YOU TWO AND NOW IS AS GOOD A TIME AS ANY...
YOU'RE *SMOKING.* YOU CAN'T SMOKE IN HERE, GRIFTER...
CALL ME COLE, ALL RIGHT?
AND BELIEVE ME, LYNCH *WOULDN'T* CARE...
WHAT DO YOU *WANT?*
RIGHT TO THE *POINT,* JUST LIKE YOUR FATHER...
I NEED *INFORMATION,* BOBBY. I NEED TO KNOW WHAT HE WAS WORKING ON...

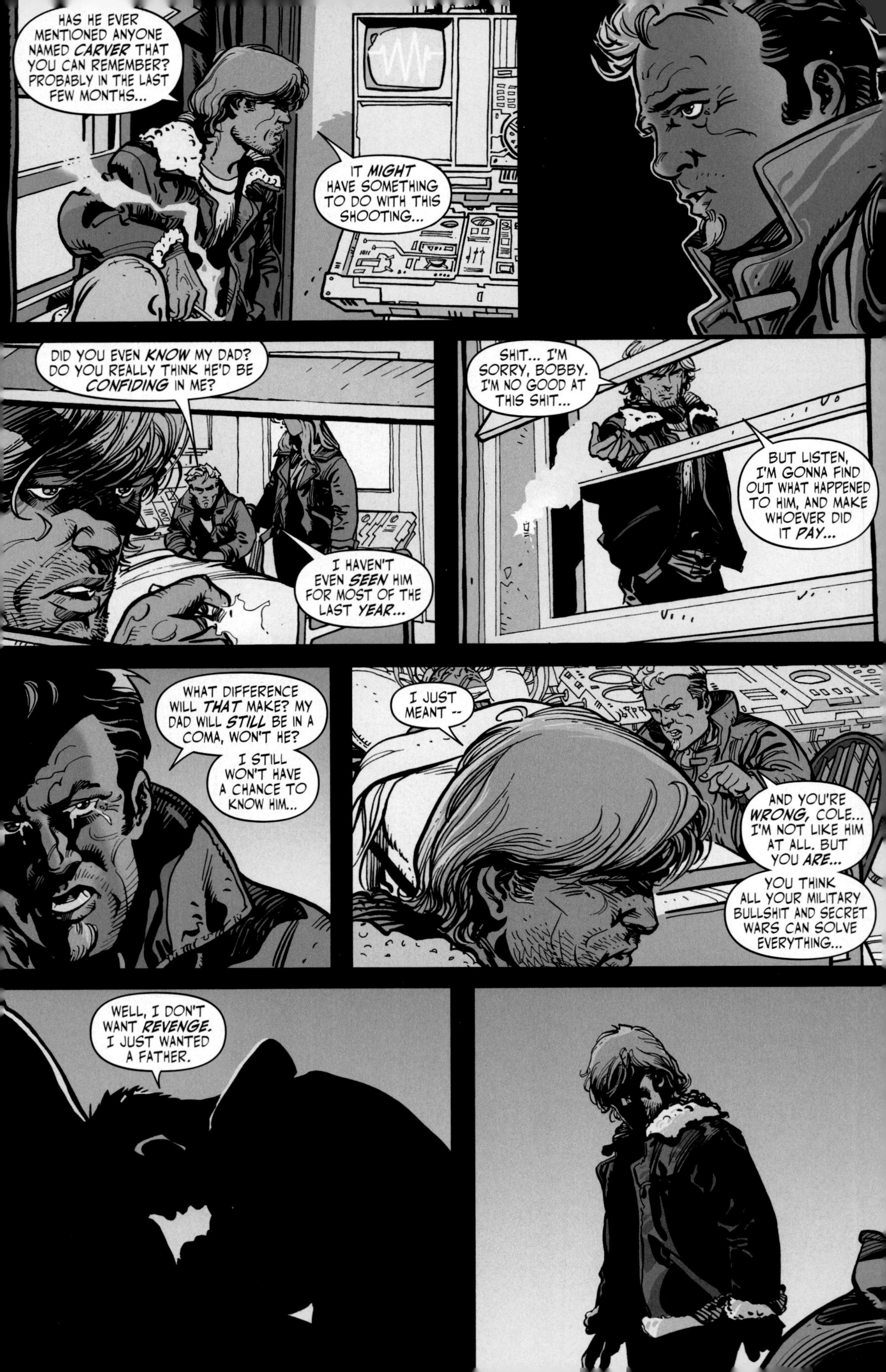
HAS HE EVER MENTIONED ANYONE NAMED CARVER THAT YOU CAN REMEMBER? PROBABLY IN THE LAST FEW MONTHS...
IT MIGHT HAVE SOMETHING TO DO WITH THIS SHOOTING...
DID YOU EVEN KNOW MY DAD? DO YOU REALLY THINK HE'D BE CONFIDING IN ME?
I HAVEN'T EVEN SEEN HIM FOR MOST OF THE LAST YEAR...
SHIT... I'M SORRY, BOBBY. I'M NO GOOD AT THIS SHIT...
BUT LISTEN, I'M GONNA FIND OUT WHAT HAPPENED TO HIM, AND MAKE WHOEVER DID IT PAY...
WHAT DIFFERENCE WILL THAT MAKE? MY DAD WILL STILL BE IN A COMA, WON'T HE?
I STILL WON'T HAVE A CHANCE TO KNOW HIM...
I JUST MEANT --
AND YOU'RE WRONG, COLE... I'M NOT LIKE HIM AT ALL. BUT YOU ARE...
YOU THINK ALL YOUR MILITARY BULLSHIT AND SECRET WARS CAN SOLVE EVERYTHING...
WELL, I DON'T WANT REVENGE. I JUST WANTED A FATHER.

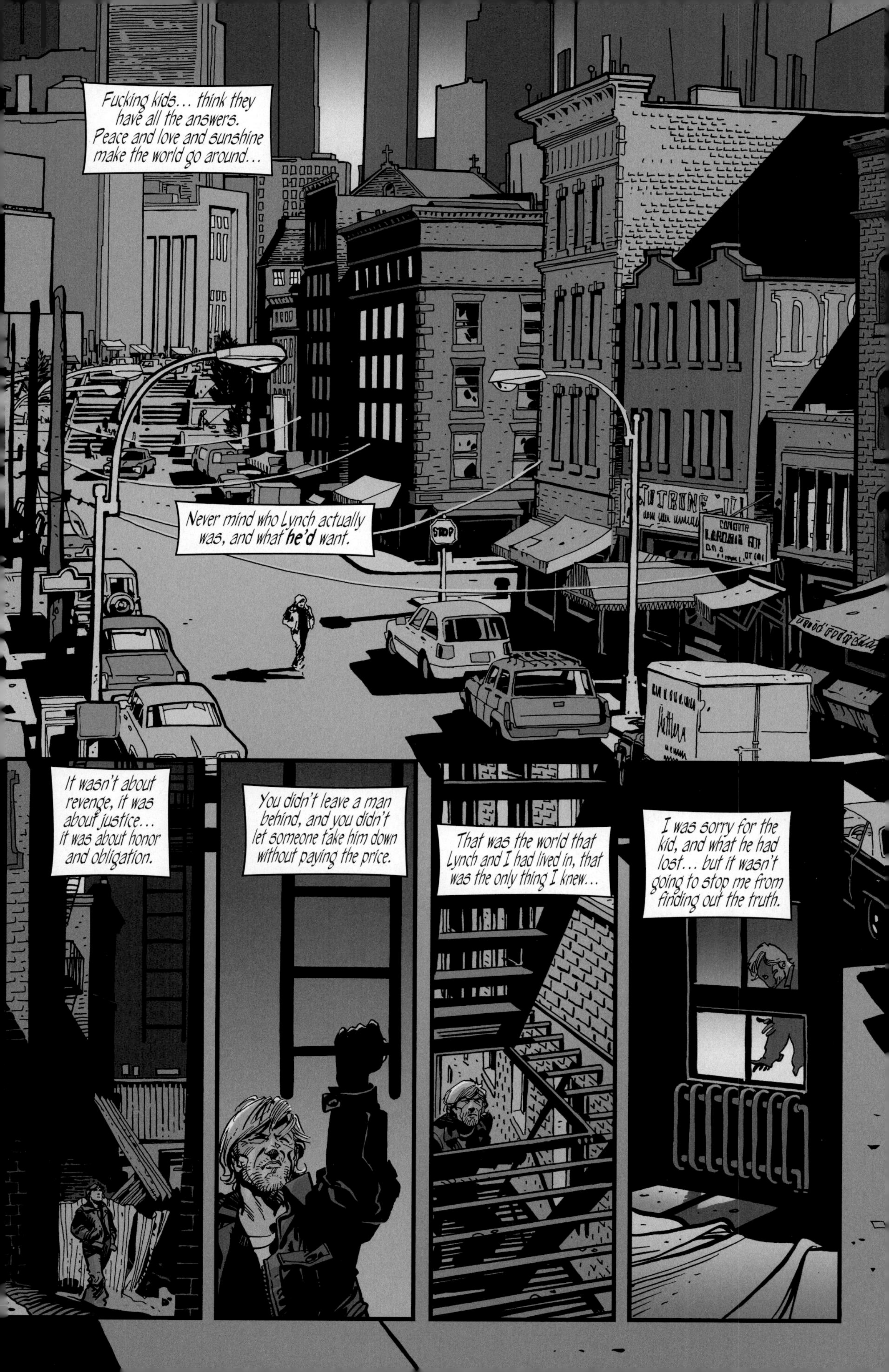
Fucking kids… think they have all the answers. Peace and love and sunshine make the world go around…
Never mind who Lynch actually was, and what **he'd** want.
STOP
It wasn't about revenge, it was about justice… it was about honor and obligation.
You didn't leave a man behind, and you didn't let someone take him down without paying the price.
That was the world that Lynch and I had lived in, that was the only thing I knew…
I was sorry for the kid, and what he had lost… but it wasn't going to stop me from finding out the truth.

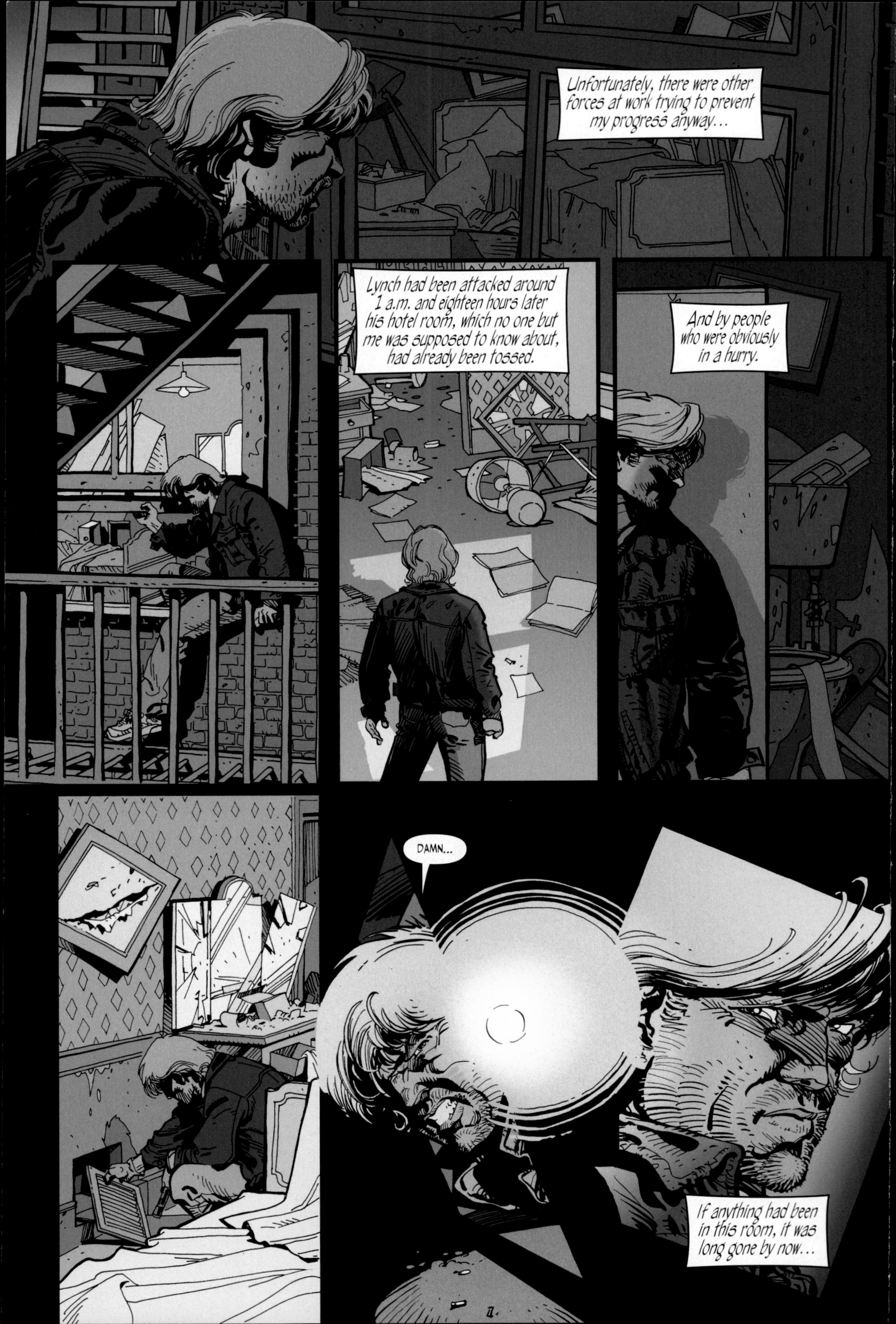
Unfortunately, there were other forces at work trying to prevent my progress anyway...
Lynch had been attacked around 1 a.m. and eighteen hours later his hotel room, which no one but me was supposed to know about, had already been tossed.
And by people who were obviously in a hurry.
DAMN...
If anything had been in this room, it was long gone by now...

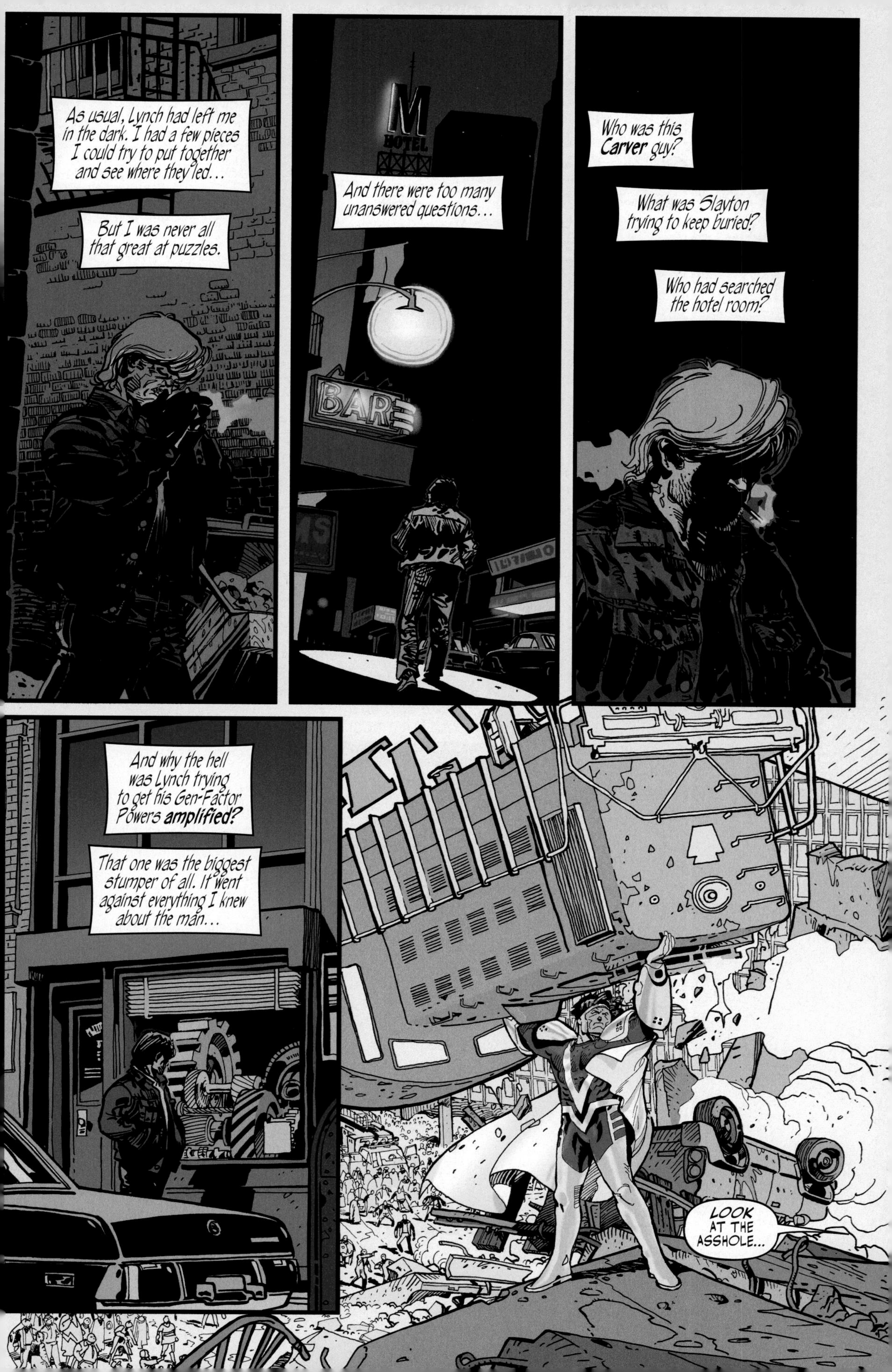
As usual, Lynch had left me in the dark. I had a few pieces I could try to put together and see where they led...
But I was never all that great at puzzles.
M
HOTEL
And there were too many unanswered questions...
BAR
Who was this **Carver** guy?
What was Slayton trying to keep buried?
Who had searched the hotel room?
And why the hell was Lynch trying to get his Gen-Factor Powers **amplified?**
That one was the biggest stumper of all. It went against everything I knew about the man...
LOOK AT THE ASSHOLE...

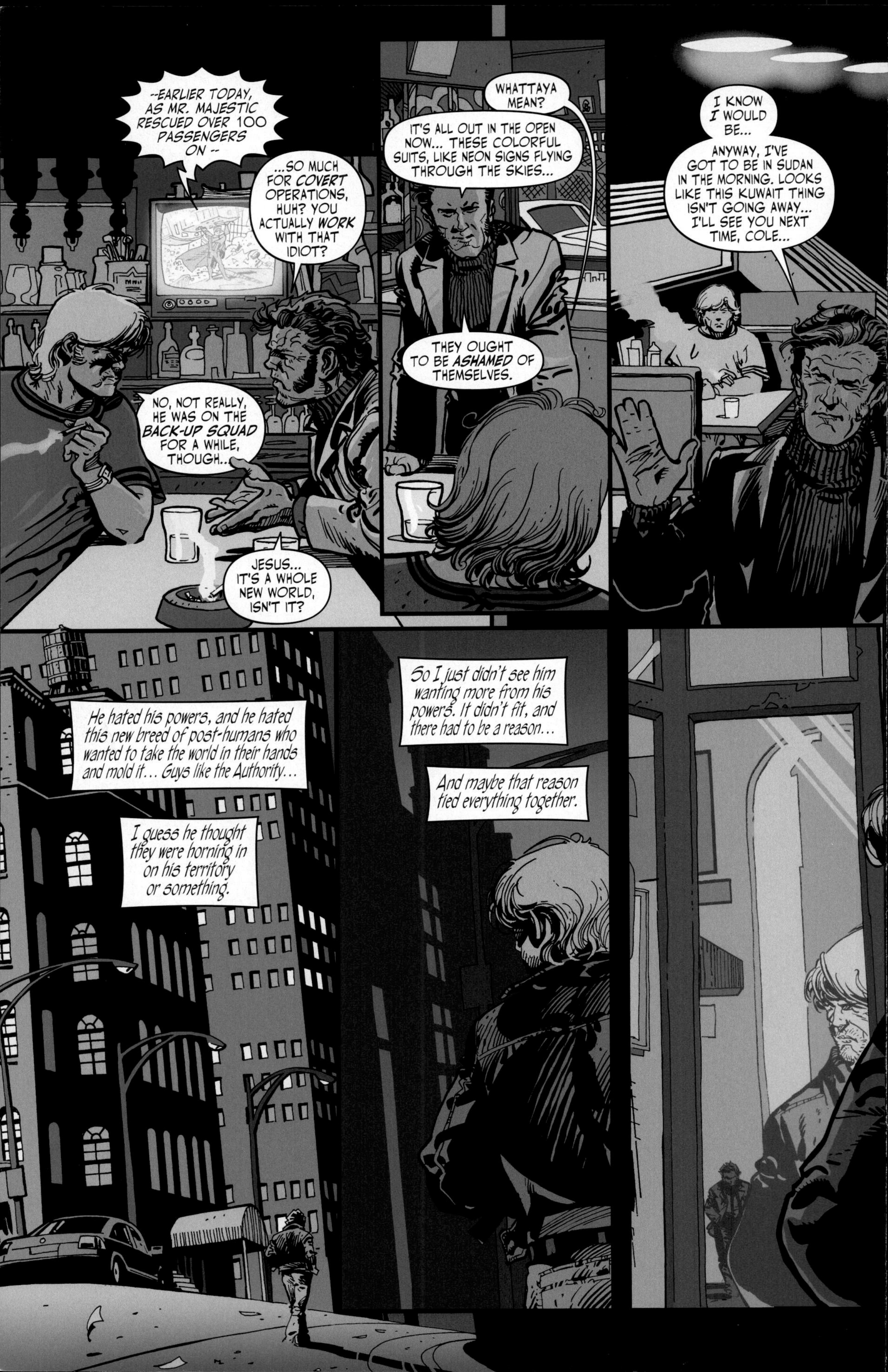

--EARLIER TODAY, AS MR. MAJESTIC RESCUED OVER 100 PASSENGERS ON --
...SO MUCH FOR COVERT OPERATIONS, HUH? YOU ACTUALLY WORK WITH THAT IDIOT?
NO, NOT REALLY, HE WAS ON THE BACK-UP SQUAD FOR A WHILE, THOUGH...
JESUS... IT'S A WHOLE NEW WORLD, ISN'T IT?
WHATTAYA MEAN?
IT'S ALL OUT IN THE OPEN NOW... THESE COLORFUL SUITS, LIKE NEON SIGNS FLYING THROUGH THE SKIES...
THEY OUGHT TO BE ASHAMED OF THEMSELVES.
I KNOW I WOULD BE...
ANYWAY, I'VE GOT TO BE IN SUDAN IN THE MORNING. LOOKS LIKE THIS KUWAIT THING ISN'T GOING AWAY... I'LL SEE YOU NEXT TIME, COLE...
He hated his powers, and he hated this new breed of post-humans who wanted to take the world in their hands and mold it... Guys like the Authority...
I guess he thought they were horning in on his territory or something.
So I just didn't see him wanting more from his powers. It didn't fit, and there had to be a reason...
And maybe that reason tied everything together.

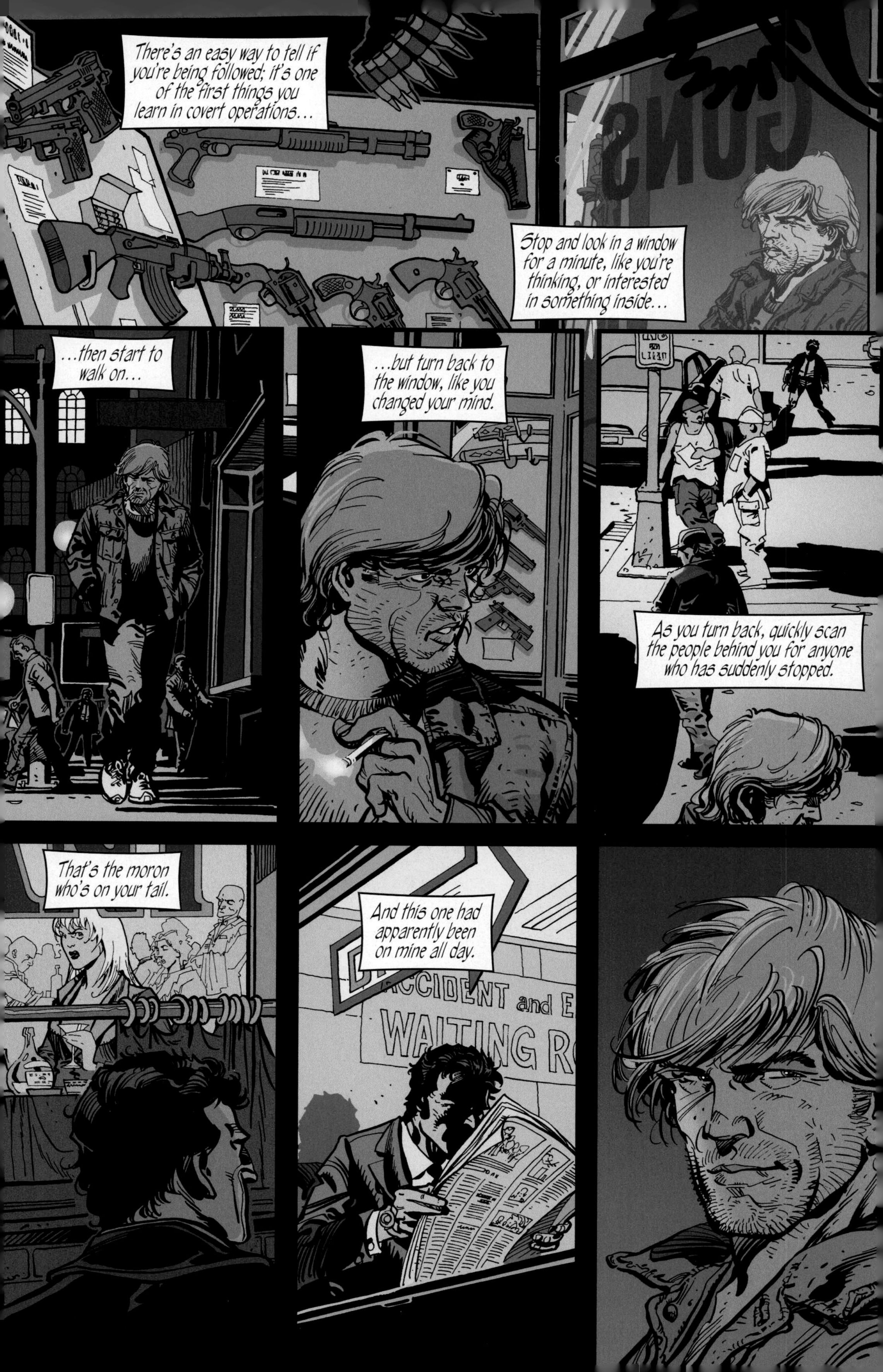

There's an easy way to tell if you're being followed; it's one of the first things you learn in covert operations...
GUNS
Stop and look in a window for a minute, like you're thinking, or interested in something inside...
...then start to walk on...
...but turn back to the window, like you changed your mind.
As you turn back, quickly scan the people behind you for anyone who has suddenly stopped.
That's the moron who's on your tail.
And this one had apparently been on mine all day.
ACCIDENT and E
WAITING R

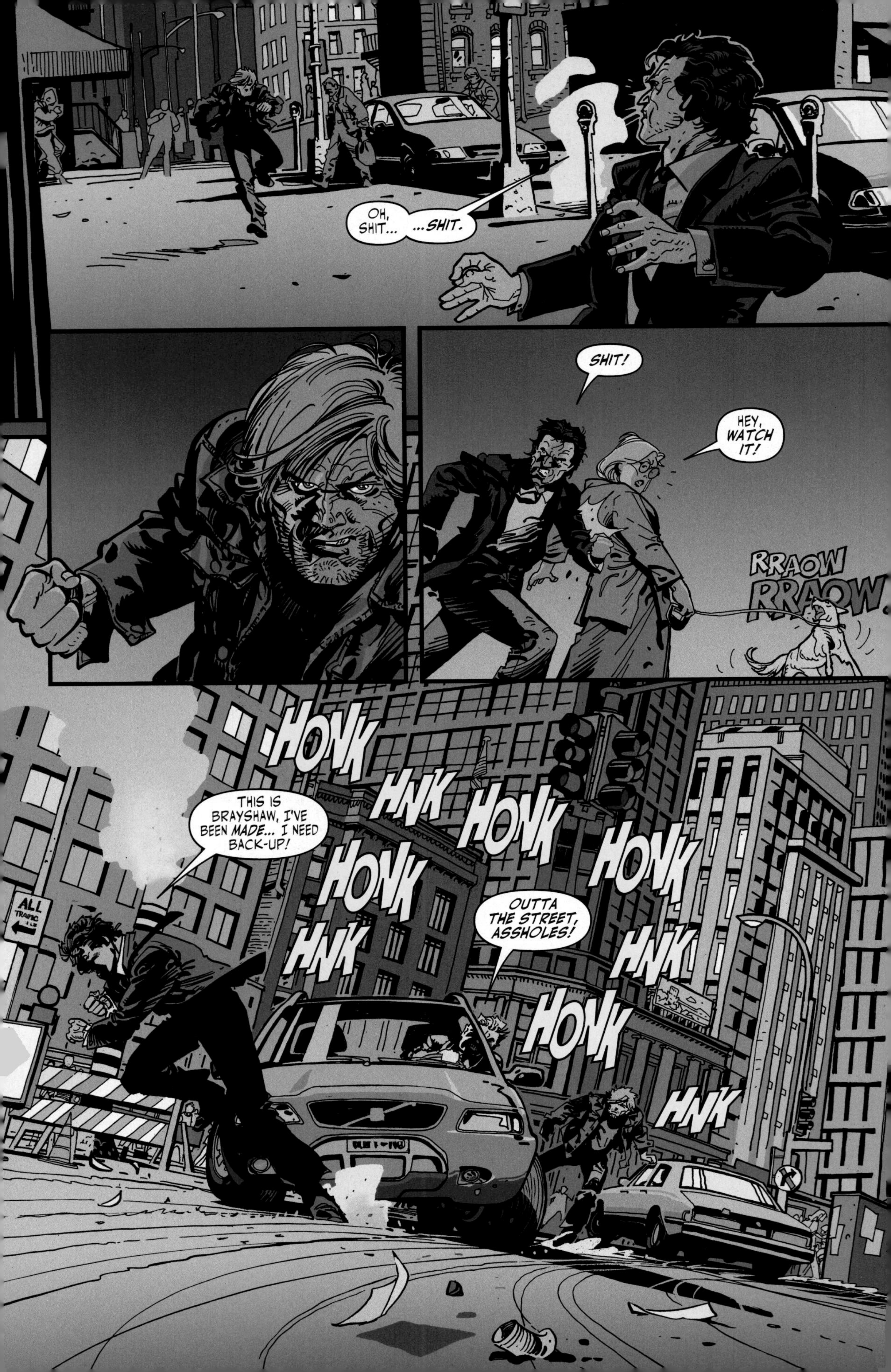
OH, SHIT...
...SHIT.
SHIT!
HEY, WATCH IT!
RRAOW RRAOW
THIS IS BRAYSHAW, I'VE BEEN MADE... I NEED BACK-UP!
HONK HNK HONK HONK HONK HNK
OUTTA THE STREET, ASSHOLES!
HNK HONK HNK
ALL TRAFFIC

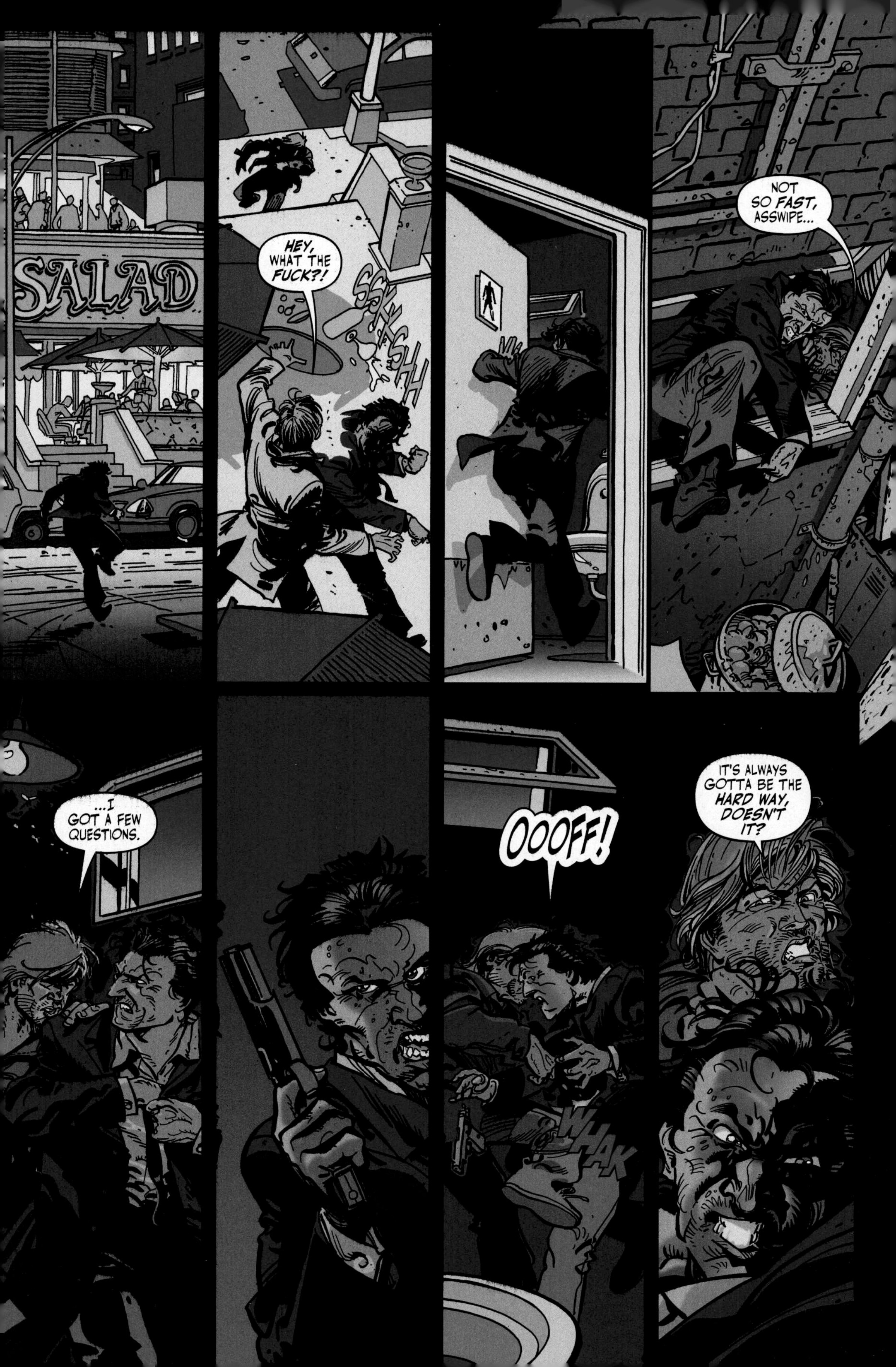
SALAD
HEY, WHAT THE FUCK?!
SSKSHH
NOT SO FAST, ASSWIPE...
...I GOT A FEW QUESTIONS.
OOOFF!
WHAK
IT'S ALWAYS GOTTA BE THE HARD WAY, DOESN'T IT?

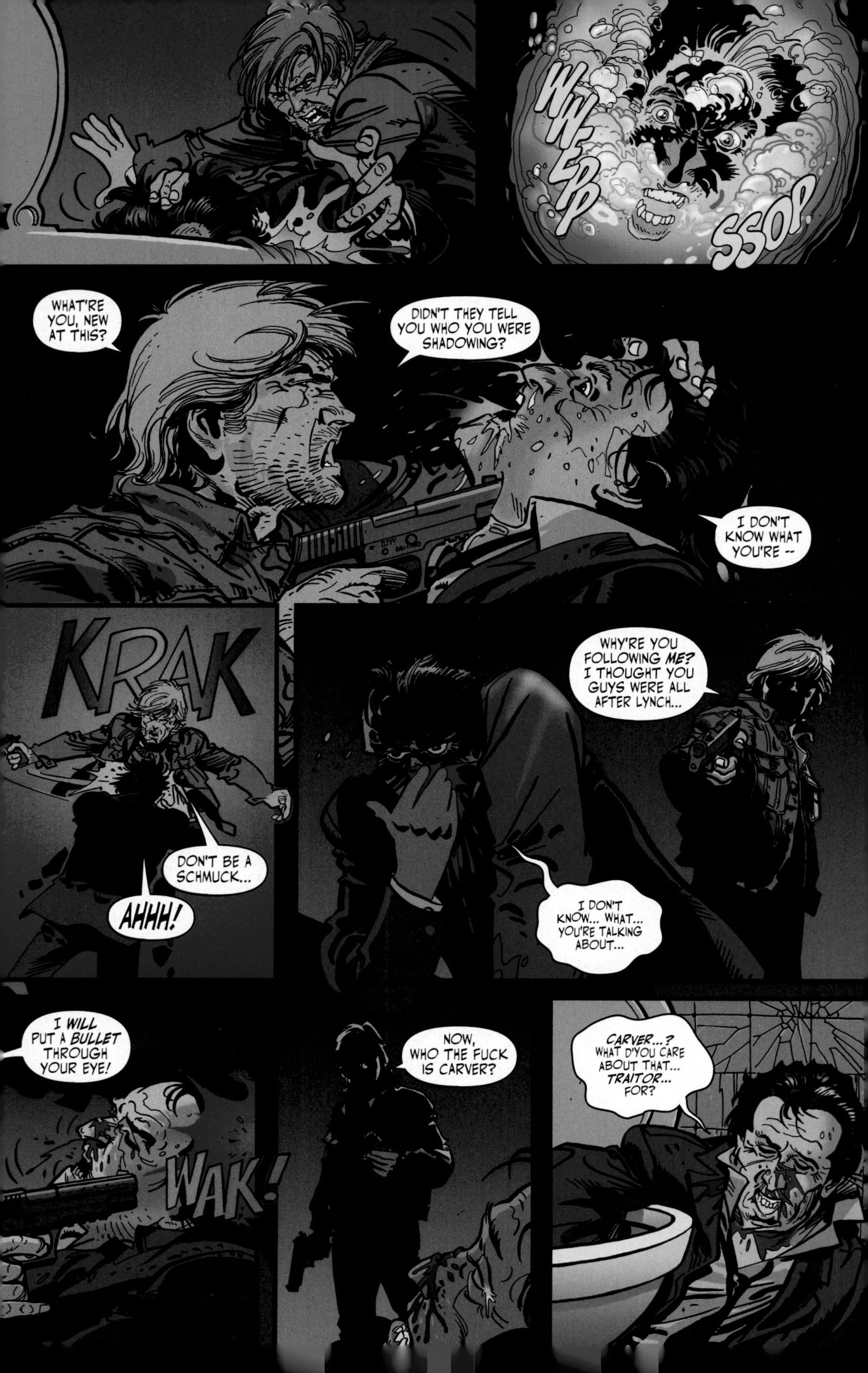
WWEEP
SSOP
WHAT'RE YOU, NEW AT THIS?
DIDN'T THEY TELL YOU WHO YOU WERE SHADOWING?
I DON'T KNOW WHAT YOU'RE --
KRAK
DON'T BE A SCHMUCK...
AHHH!
WHY'RE YOU FOLLOWING ME? I THOUGHT YOU GUYS WERE ALL AFTER LYNCH...
I DON'T KNOW... WHAT... YOU'RE TALKING ABOUT...
I WILL PUT A BULLET THROUGH YOUR EYE!
WAK!
NOW, WHO THE FUCK IS CARVER?
CARVER...? WHAT D'YOU CARE ABOUT THAT... TRAITOR... FOR?

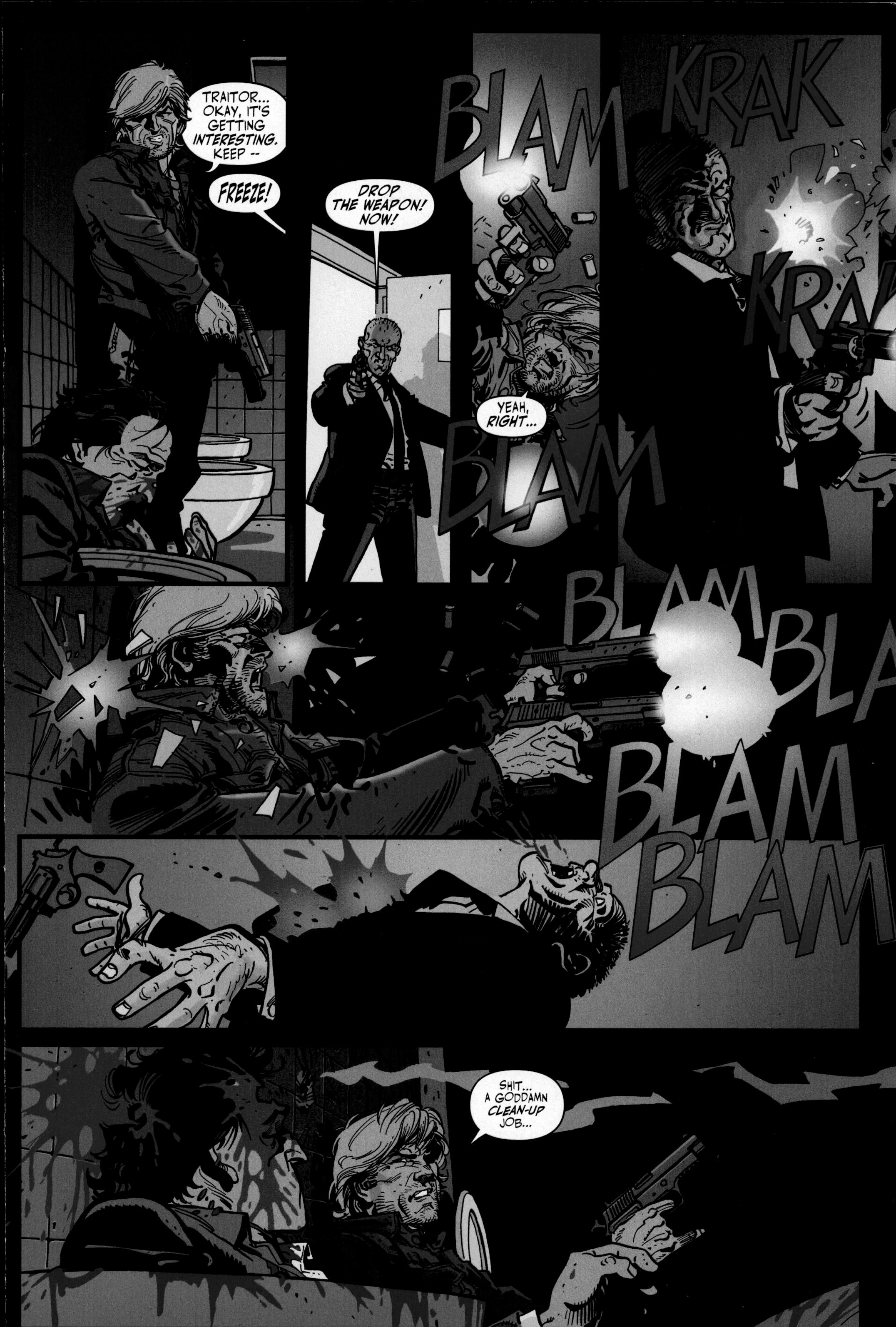

TRAITOR... OKAY, IT'S GETTING INTERESTING. KEEP --
FREEZE!
DROP THE WEAPON! NOW!
BLAM
YEAH, RIGHT...
BLAM
KRAK
KRAK
BLAM
BLAM
BLAM
BLAM
SHIT... A GODDAMN CLEAN-UP JOB...

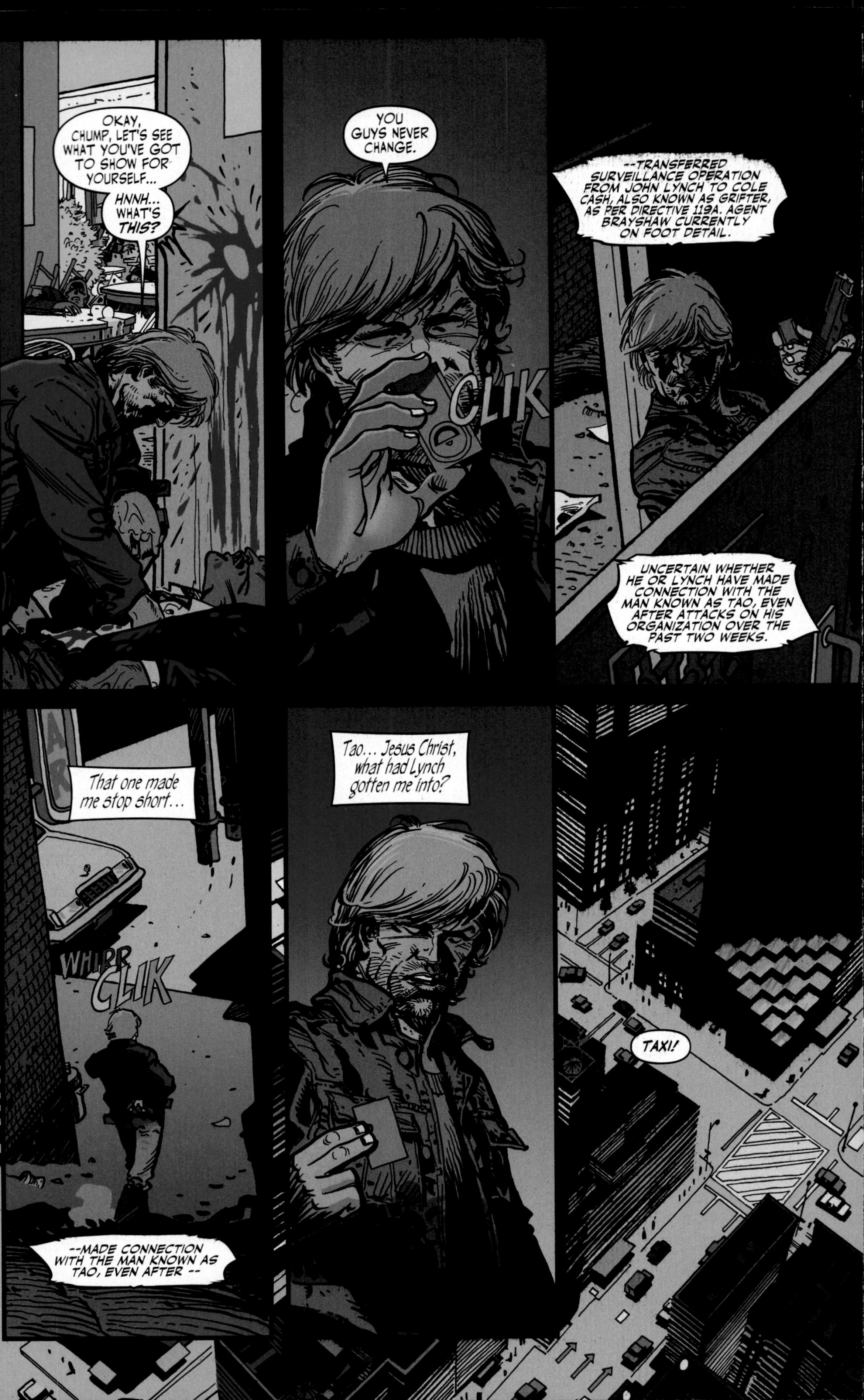
OKAY, CHUMP, LET'S SEE WHAT YOU'VE GOT TO SHOW FOR YOURSELF...
HNNH... WHAT'S THIS?
YOU GUYS NEVER CHANGE.
CLIK
--TRANSFERRED SURVEILLANCE OPERATION FROM JOHN LYNCH TO COLE CASH, ALSO KNOWN AS GRIFTER, AS PER DIRECTIVE 119A. AGENT BRAYSHAW CURRENTLY ON FOOT DETAIL.
UNCERTAIN WHETHER HE OR LYNCH HAVE MADE CONNECTION WITH THE MAN KNOWN AS TAO, EVEN AFTER ATTACKS ON HIS ORGANIZATION OVER THE PAST TWO WEEKS.
That one made me stop short...
WHIRR
CLIK
--MADE CONNECTION WITH THE MAN KNOWN AS TAO, EVEN AFTER --
Tao... Jesus Christ, what had Lynch gotten me into?
TAXI!

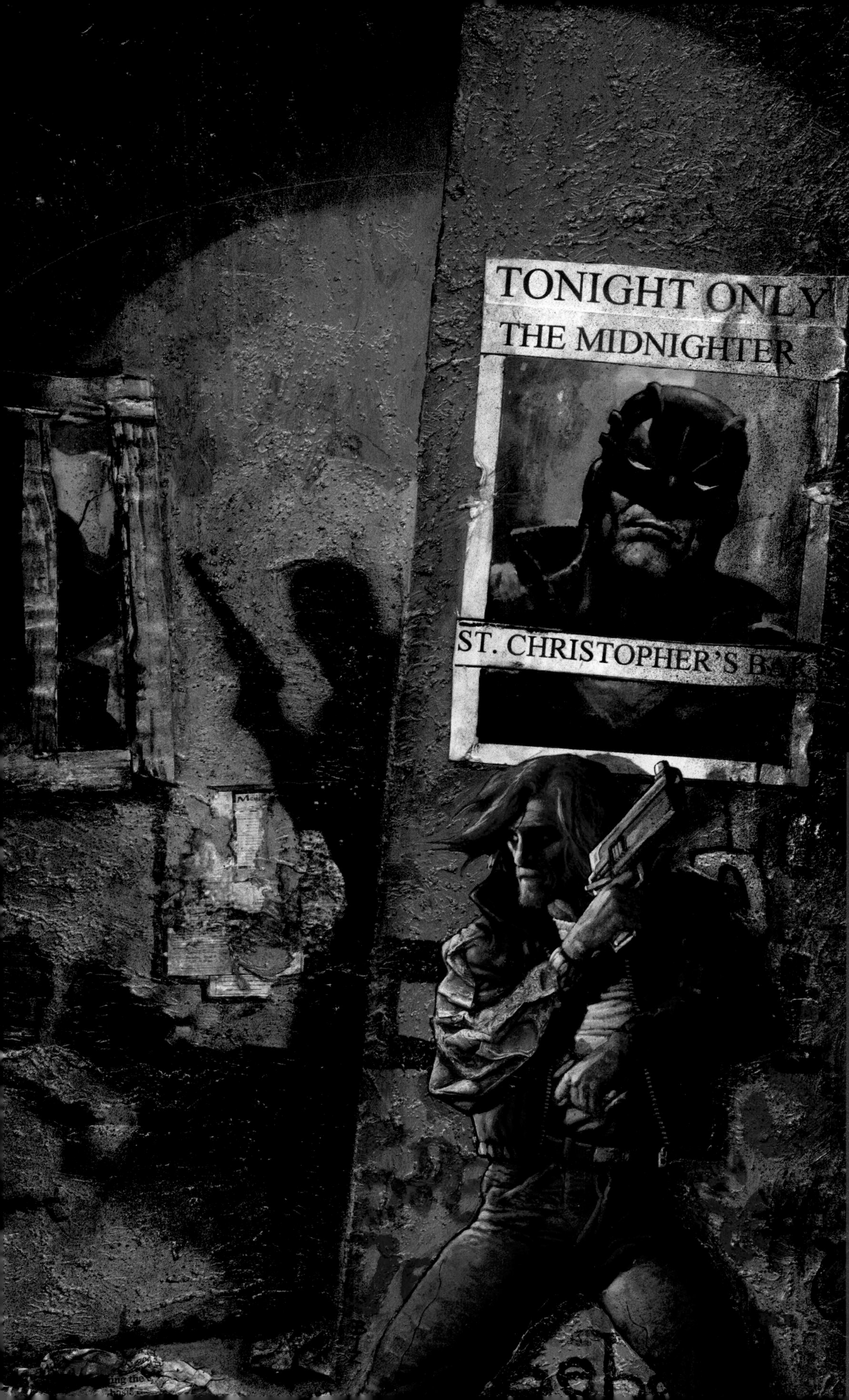
TONIGHT ONLY
THE MIDNIGHTER
ST. CHRISTOPHER'S

Cover by SIMON BISLEY

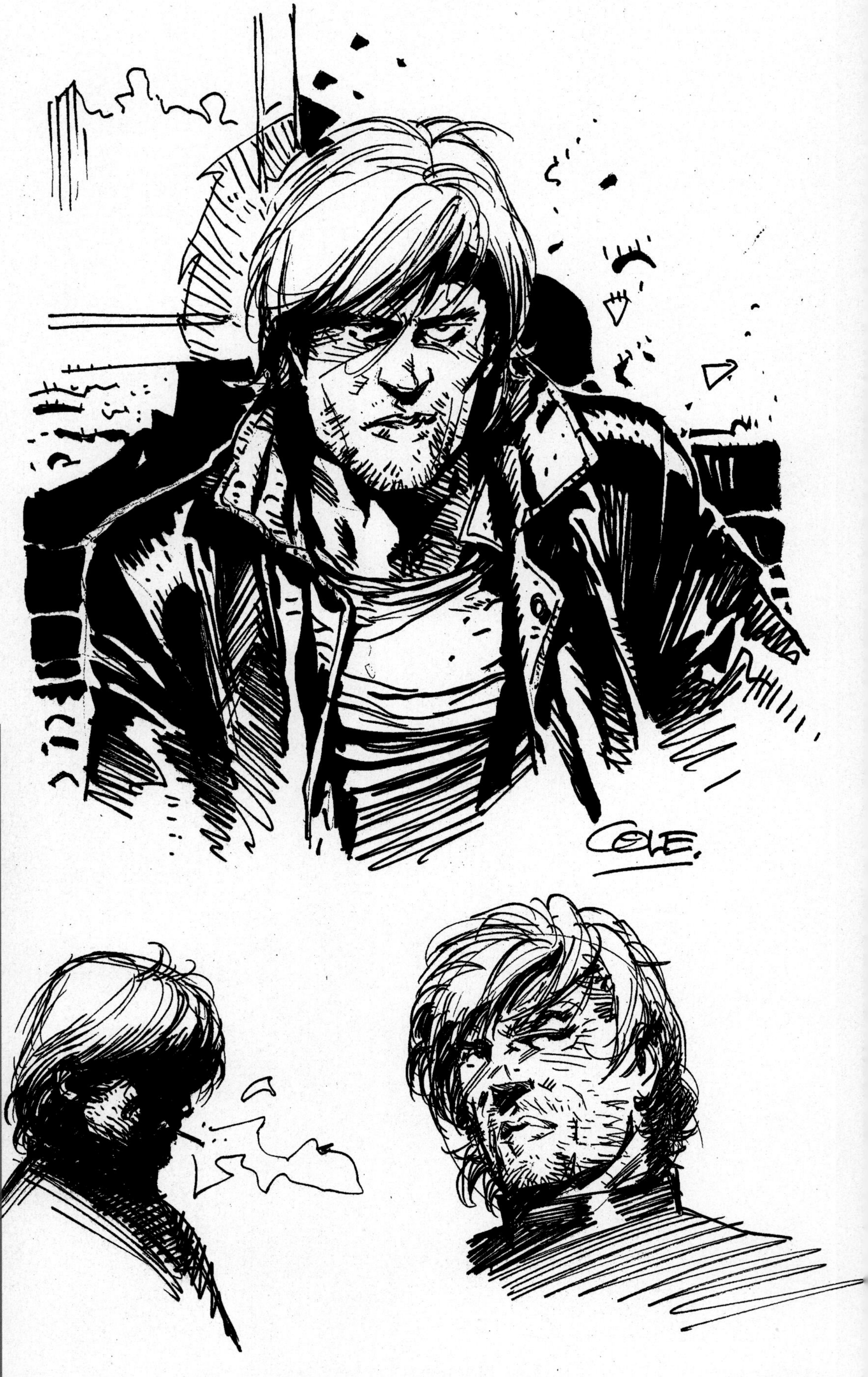
COLE.

GRIFTER Sketches by COLIN WILSON

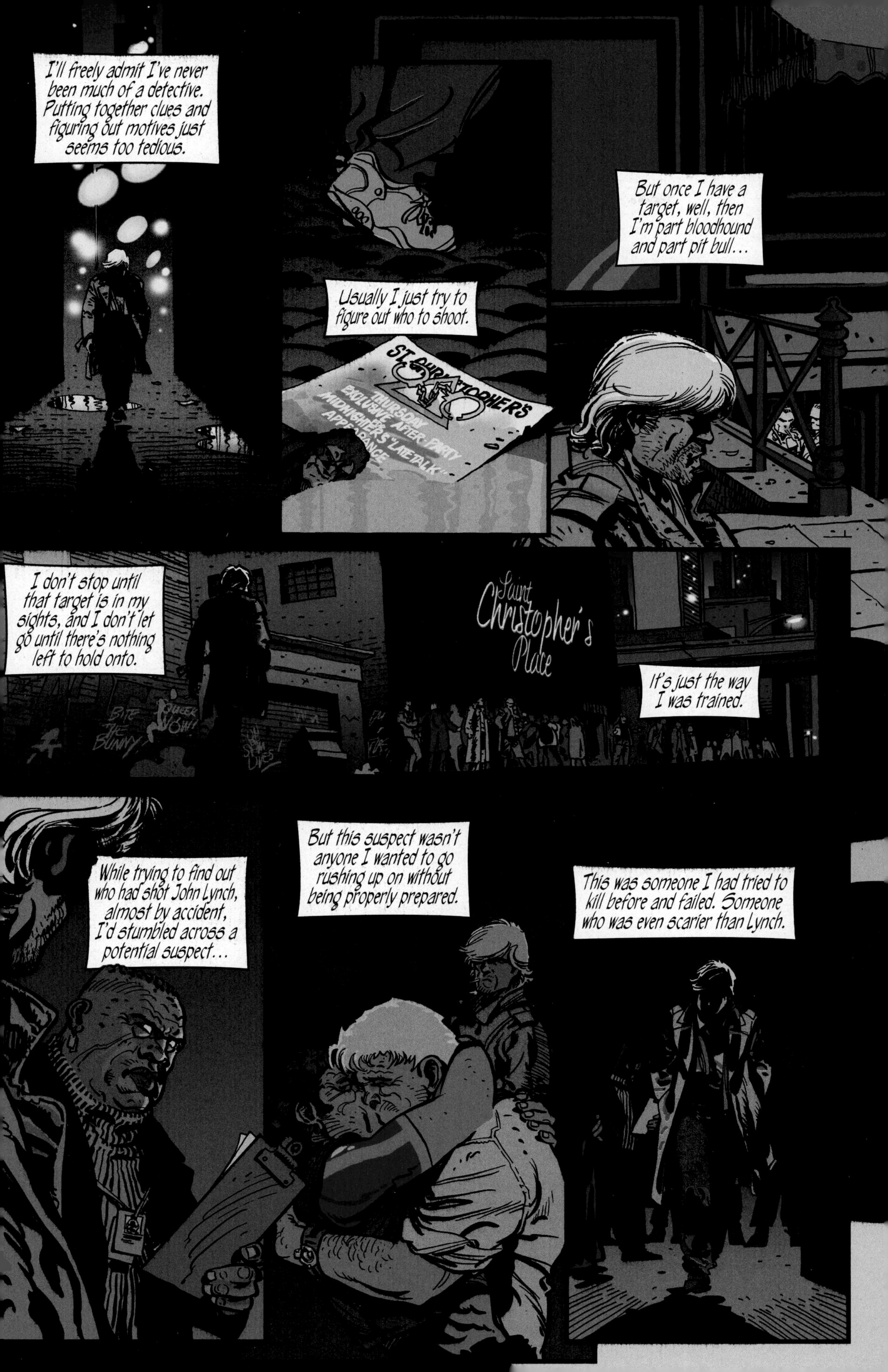
I'll freely admit I've never been much of a detective. Putting together clues and figuring out motives just seems too tedious.
Usually I just try to figure out who to shoot.
THURSDAY
EXCLUSIVE AFTER-PARTY
But once I have a target, well, then I'm part bloodhound and part pit bull...
I don't stop until that target is in my sights, and I don't let go until there's nothing left to hold onto.
BITE THE BUNNY
QUEER NOW!
Saint Christopher's Place
It's just the way I was trained.
While trying to find out who had shot John Lynch, almost by accident, I'd stumbled across a potential suspect...
But this suspect wasn't anyone I wanted to go rushing up on without being properly prepared.
This was someone I had tried to kill before and failed. Someone who was even scarier than Lynch.

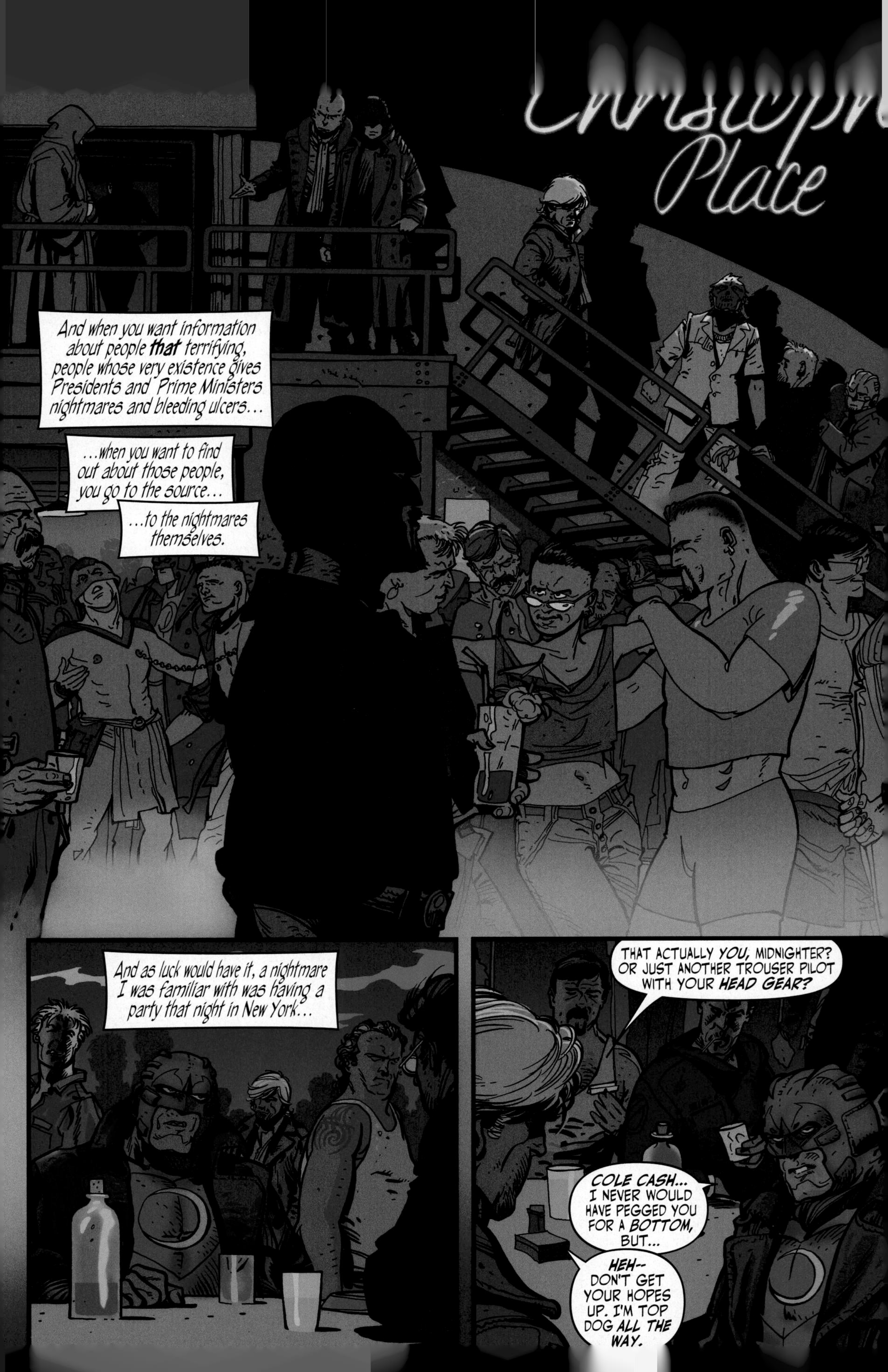
Christopher Place
And when you want information about people *that* terrifying, people whose very existence gives Presidents and Prime Ministers nightmares and bleeding ulcers...
...when you want to find out about those people, you go to the source...
...to the nightmares themselves.
And as luck would have it, a nightmare I was familiar with was having a party that night in New York...
THAT ACTUALLY *YOU*, MIDNIGHTER? OR JUST ANOTHER TROUSER PILOT WITH YOUR *HEAD GEAR?*
COLE CASH... I NEVER WOULD HAVE PEGGED YOU FOR A *BOTTOM*, BUT...
HEH-- DON'T GET YOUR HOPES UP. I'M TOP DOG *ALL THE WAY.*

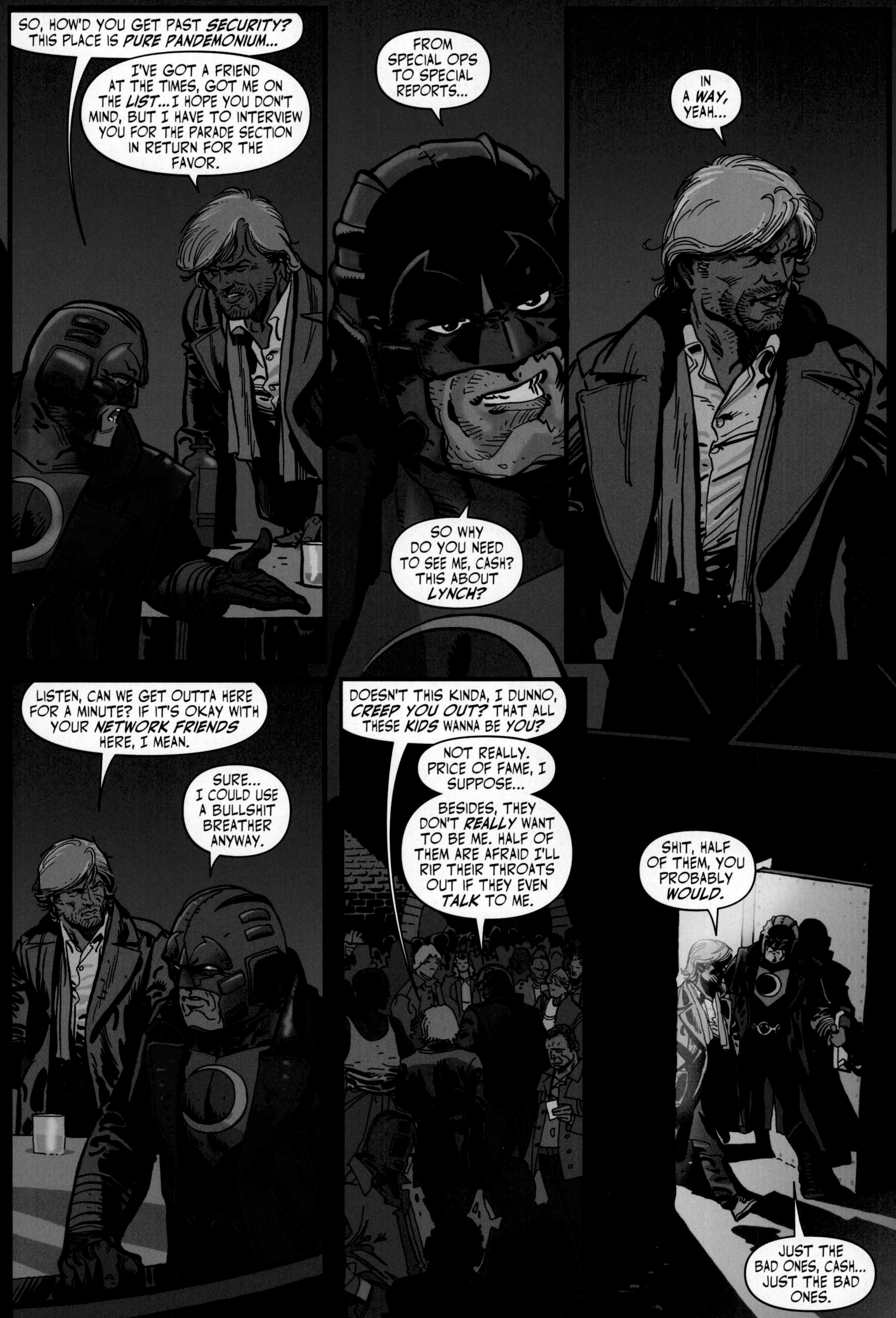
SO, HOW'D YOU GET PAST SECURITY? THIS PLACE IS PURE PANDEMONIUM...
I'VE GOT A FRIEND AT THE TIMES, GOT ME ON THE LIST... I HOPE YOU DON'T MIND, BUT I HAVE TO INTERVIEW YOU FOR THE PARADE SECTION IN RETURN FOR THE FAVOR.
FROM SPECIAL OPS TO SPECIAL REPORTS...
SO WHY DO YOU NEED TO SEE ME, CASH? THIS ABOUT LYNCH?
IN A WAY, YEAH...
LISTEN, CAN WE GET OUTTA HERE FOR A MINUTE? IF IT'S OKAY WITH YOUR NETWORK FRIENDS HERE, I MEAN.
SURE... I COULD USE A BULLSHIT BREATHER ANYWAY.
DOESN'T THIS KINDA, I DUNNO, CREEP YOU OUT? THAT ALL THESE KIDS WANNA BE YOU?
NOT REALLY. PRICE OF FAME, I SUPPOSE...
BESIDES, THEY DON'T REALLY WANT TO BE ME. HALF OF THEM ARE AFRAID I'LL RIP THEIR THROATS OUT IF THEY EVEN TALK TO ME.
SHIT, HALF OF THEM, YOU PROBABLY WOULD.
JUST THE BAD ONES, CASH... JUST THE BAD ONES.

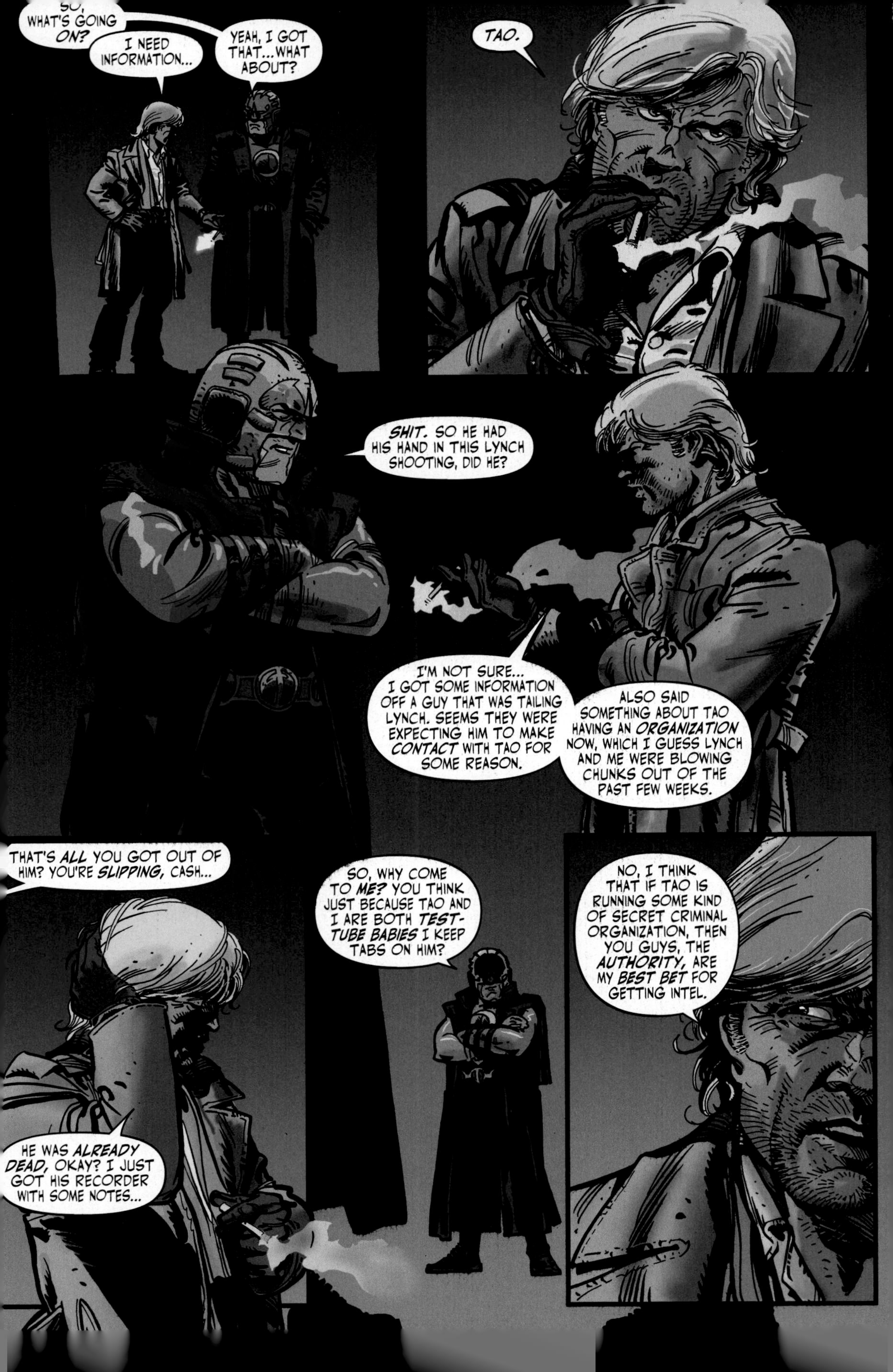
SO, WHAT'S GOING ON?
I NEED INFORMATION...
YEAH, I GOT THAT...WHAT ABOUT?
TAO.
SHIT. SO HE HAD HIS HAND IN THIS LYNCH SHOOTING, DID HE?
I'M NOT SURE... I GOT SOME INFORMATION OFF A GUY THAT WAS TAILING LYNCH. SEEMS THEY WERE EXPECTING HIM TO MAKE CONTACT WITH TAO FOR SOME REASON.
ALSO SAID SOMETHING ABOUT TAO HAVING AN ORGANIZATION NOW, WHICH I GUESS LYNCH AND ME WERE BLOWING CHUNKS OUT OF THE PAST FEW WEEKS.
THAT'S ALL YOU GOT OUT OF HIM? YOU'RE SLIPPING, CASH...
HE WAS ALREADY DEAD, OKAY? I JUST GOT HIS RECORDER WITH SOME NOTES...
SO, WHY COME TO ME? YOU THINK JUST BECAUSE TAO AND I ARE BOTH TEST-TUBE BABIES I KEEP TABS ON HIM?
NO, I THINK THAT IF TAO IS RUNNING SOME KIND OF SECRET CRIMINAL ORGANIZATION, THEN YOU GUYS, THE AUTHORITY, ARE MY BEST BET FOR GETTING INTEL.

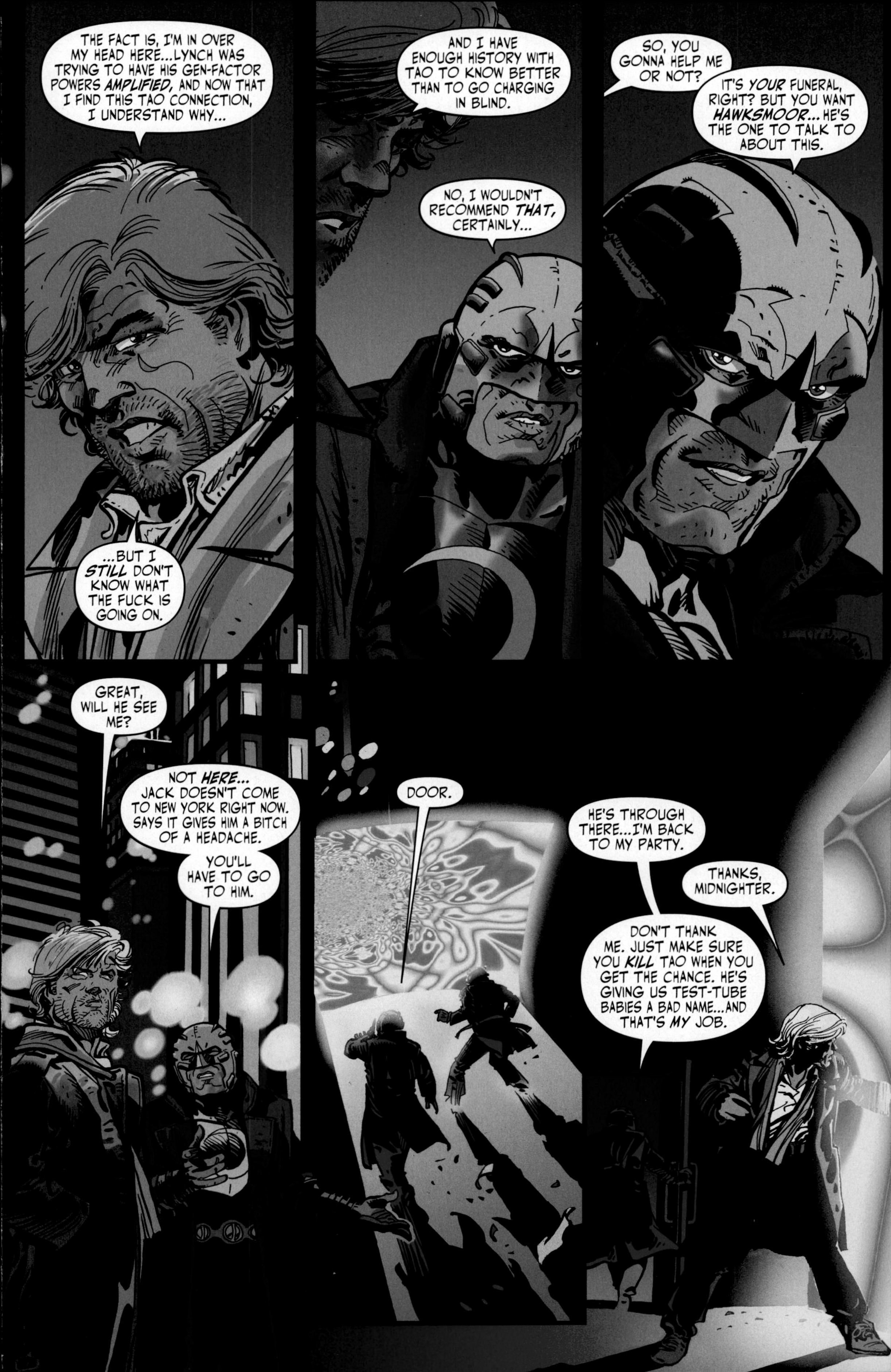
THE FACT IS, I'M IN OVER MY HEAD HERE...LYNCH WAS TRYING TO HAVE HIS GEN-FACTOR POWERS AMPLIFIED, AND NOW THAT I FIND THIS TAO CONNECTION, I UNDERSTAND WHY...
...BUT I STILL DON'T KNOW WHAT THE FUCK IS GOING ON.
AND I HAVE ENOUGH HISTORY WITH TAO TO KNOW BETTER THAN TO GO CHARGING IN BLIND.
NO, I WOULDN'T RECOMMEND THAT, CERTAINLY...
SO, YOU GONNA HELP ME OR NOT?
IT'S YOUR FUNERAL, RIGHT? BUT YOU WANT HAWKSMOOR... HE'S THE ONE TO TALK TO ABOUT THIS.
GREAT, WILL HE SEE ME?
NOT HERE... JACK DOESN'T COME TO NEW YORK RIGHT NOW. SAYS IT GIVES HIM A BITCH OF A HEADACHE.
YOU'LL HAVE TO GO TO HIM.
DOOR.
HE'S THROUGH THERE...I'M BACK TO MY PARTY.
THANKS, MIDNIGHTER.
DON'T THANK ME. JUST MAKE SURE YOU KILL TAO WHEN YOU GET THE CHANCE. HE'S GIVING US TEST-TUBE BABIES A BAD NAME...AND THAT'S MY JOB.

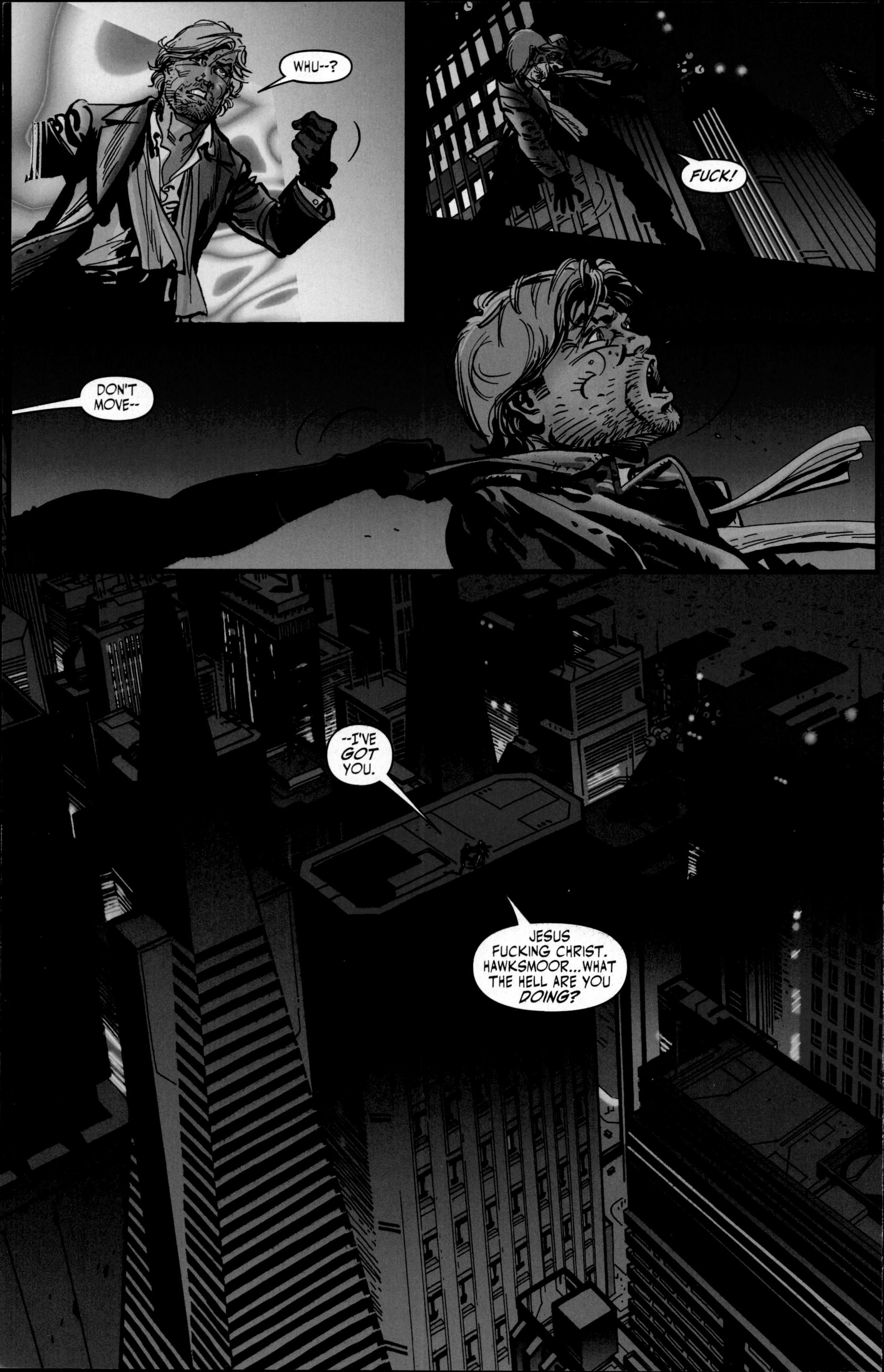
WHU--?
FUCK!
DON'T MOVE--
--I'VE GOT YOU.
JESUS FUCKING CHRIST. HAWKSMOOR...WHAT THE HELL ARE YOU DOING?

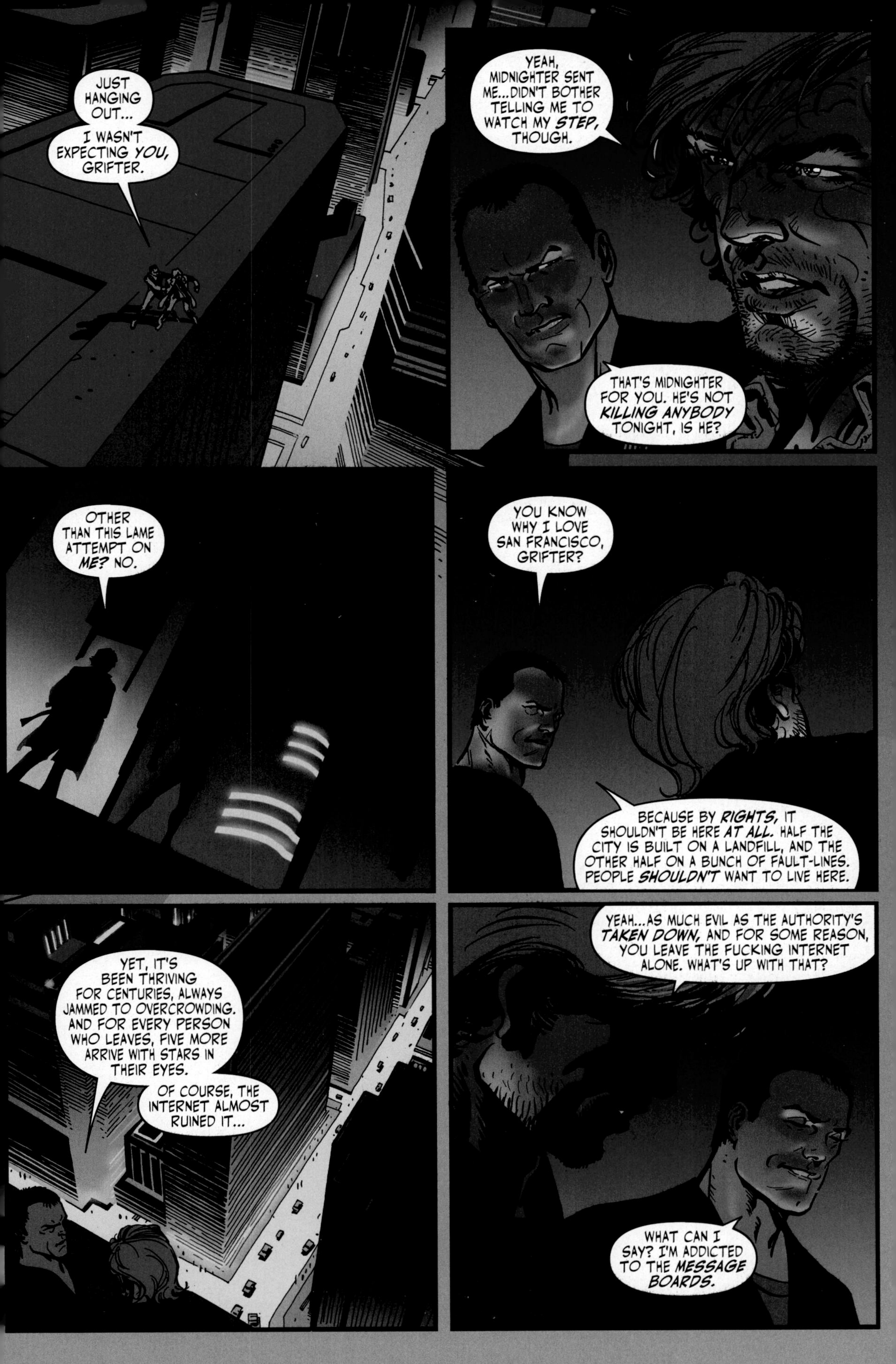
JUST HANGING OUT...
I WASN'T EXPECTING YOU, GRIFTER.
YEAH, MIDNIGHTER SENT ME...DIDN'T BOTHER TELLING ME TO WATCH MY STEP, THOUGH.
THAT'S MIDNIGHTER FOR YOU. HE'S NOT KILLING ANYBODY TONIGHT, IS HE?
OTHER THAN THIS LAME ATTEMPT ON ME? NO.
YOU KNOW WHY I LOVE SAN FRANCISCO, GRIFTER?
BECAUSE BY RIGHTS, IT SHOULDN'T BE HERE AT ALL. HALF THE CITY IS BUILT ON A LANDFILL, AND THE OTHER HALF ON A BUNCH OF FAULT-LINES. PEOPLE SHOULDN'T WANT TO LIVE HERE.
YET, IT'S BEEN THRIVING FOR CENTURIES, ALWAYS JAMMED TO OVERCROWDING. AND FOR EVERY PERSON WHO LEAVES, FIVE MORE ARRIVE WITH STARS IN THEIR EYES.
OF COURSE, THE INTERNET ALMOST RUINED IT...
YEAH...AS MUCH EVIL AS THE AUTHORITY'S TAKEN DOWN, AND FOR SOME REASON, YOU LEAVE THE FUCKING INTERNET ALONE. WHAT'S UP WITH THAT?
WHAT CAN I SAY? I'M ADDICTED TO THE MESSAGE BOARDS.

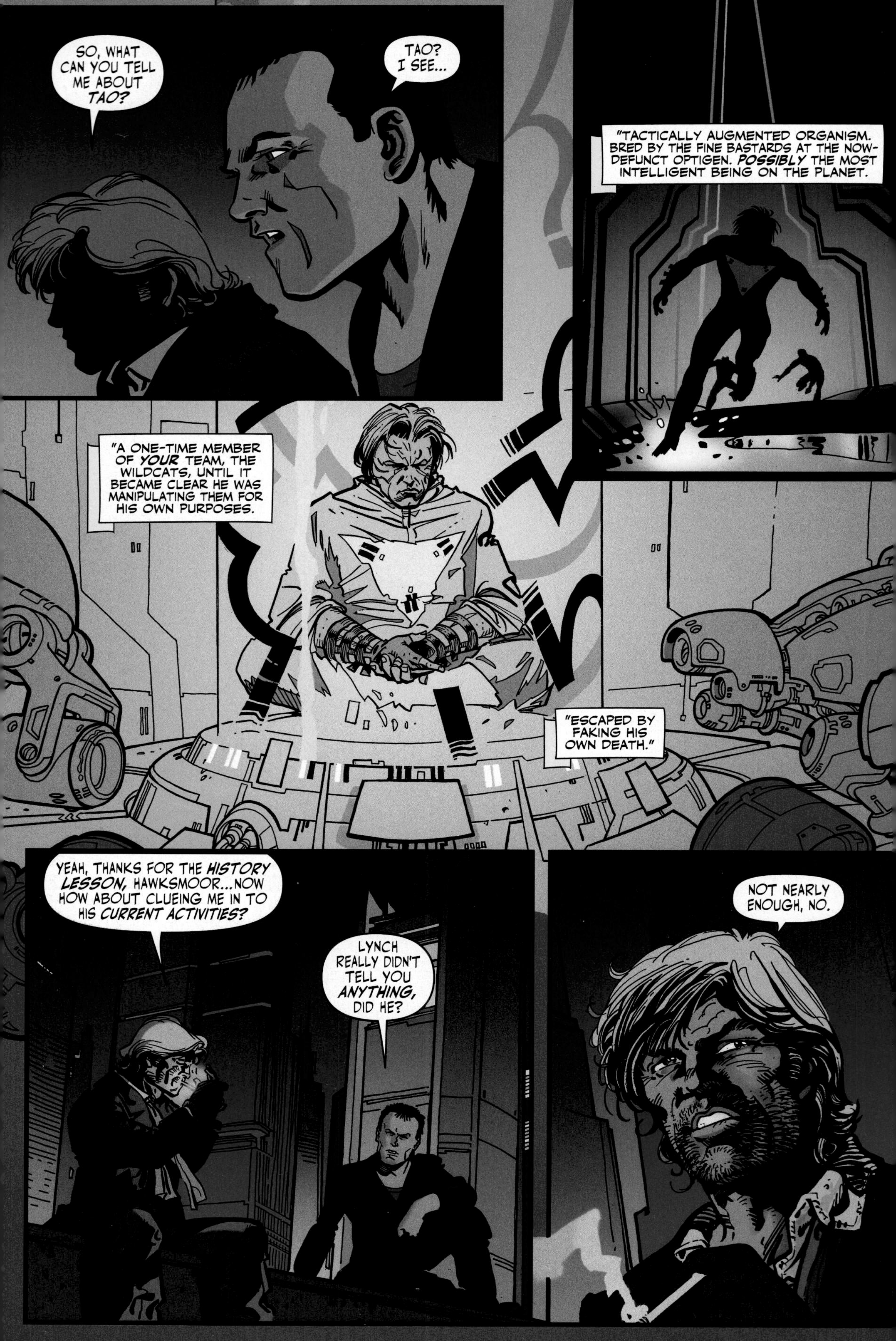
SO, WHAT CAN YOU TELL ME ABOUT TAO?
TAO? I SEE...
"TACTICALLY AUGMENTED ORGANISM. BRED BY THE FINE BASTARDS AT THE NOW-DEFUNCT OPTIGEN. POSSIBLY THE MOST INTELLIGENT BEING ON THE PLANET.
"A ONE-TIME MEMBER OF YOUR TEAM, THE WILDCATS, UNTIL IT BECAME CLEAR HE WAS MANIPULATING THEM FOR HIS OWN PURPOSES.
"ESCAPED BY FAKING HIS OWN DEATH."
YEAH, THANKS FOR THE HISTORY LESSON, HAWKSMOOR...NOW HOW ABOUT CLUEING ME IN TO HIS CURRENT ACTIVITIES?
LYNCH REALLY DIDN'T TELL YOU ANYTHING, DID HE?
NOT NEARLY ENOUGH, NO.

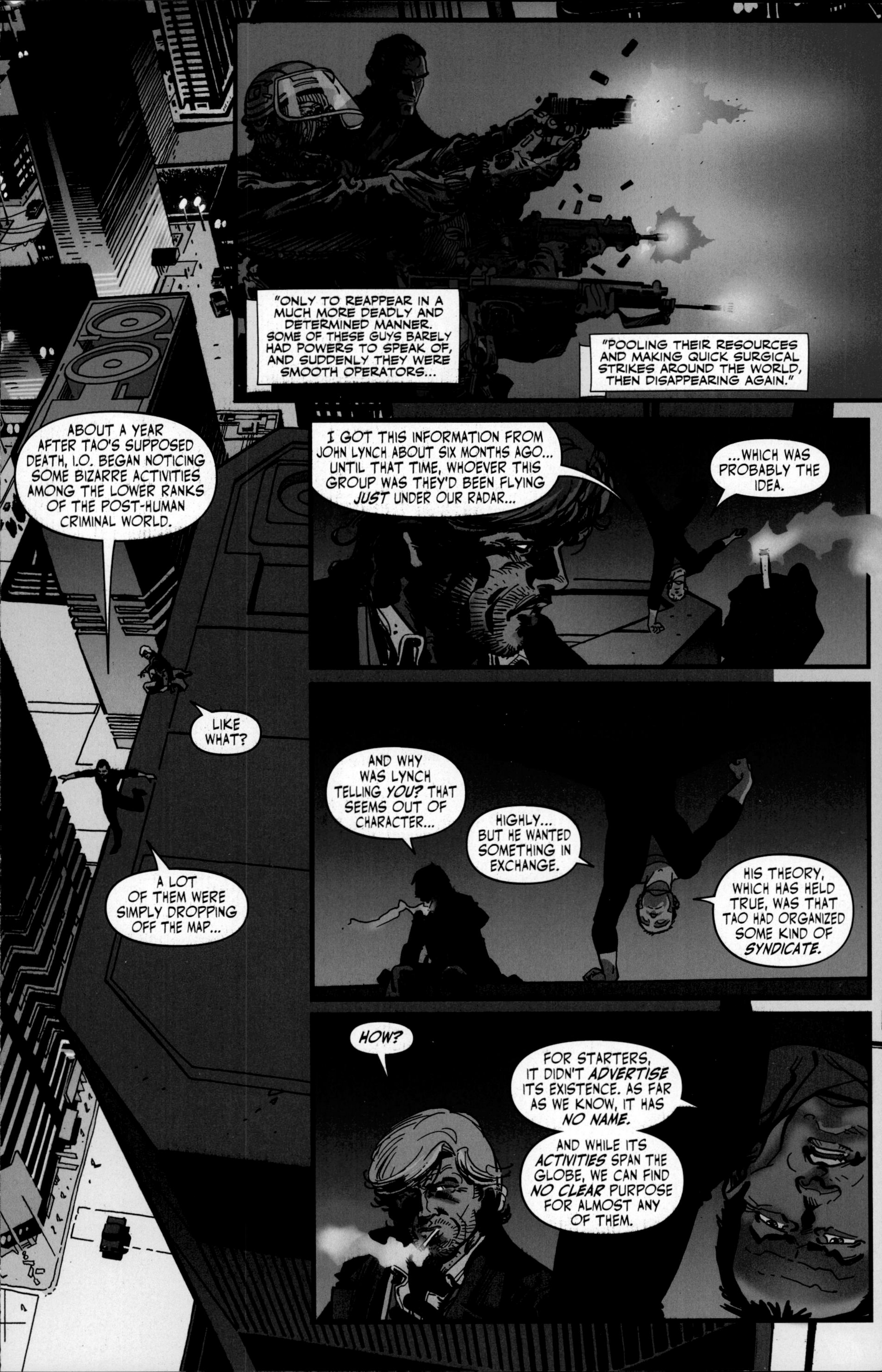
"ONLY TO REAPPEAR IN A MUCH MORE DEADLY AND DETERMINED MANNER. SOME OF THESE GUYS BARELY HAD POWERS TO SPEAK OF, AND SUDDENLY THEY WERE SMOOTH OPERATORS...
"POOLING THEIR RESOURCES AND MAKING QUICK SURGICAL STRIKES AROUND THE WORLD, THEN DISAPPEARING AGAIN."
ABOUT A YEAR AFTER TAO'S SUPPOSED DEATH, I.O. BEGAN NOTICING SOME BIZARRE ACTIVITIES AMONG THE LOWER RANKS OF THE POST-HUMAN CRIMINAL WORLD.
LIKE WHAT?
A LOT OF THEM WERE SIMPLY DROPPING OFF THE MAP...
I GOT THIS INFORMATION FROM JOHN LYNCH ABOUT SIX MONTHS AGO... UNTIL THAT TIME, WHOEVER THIS GROUP WAS THEY'D BEEN FLYING JUST UNDER OUR RADAR...
...WHICH WAS PROBABLY THE IDEA.
AND WHY WAS LYNCH TELLING YOU? THAT SEEMS OUT OF CHARACTER...
HIGHLY... BUT HE WANTED SOMETHING IN EXCHANGE.
HIS THEORY, WHICH HAS HELD TRUE, WAS THAT TAO HAD ORGANIZED SOME KIND OF SYNDICATE.
HOW?
FOR STARTERS, IT DIDN'T ADVERTISE ITS EXISTENCE. AS FAR AS WE KNOW, IT HAS NO NAME.
AND WHILE ITS ACTIVITIES SPAN THE GLOBE, WE CAN FIND NO CLEAR PURPOSE FOR ALMOST ANY OF THEM.

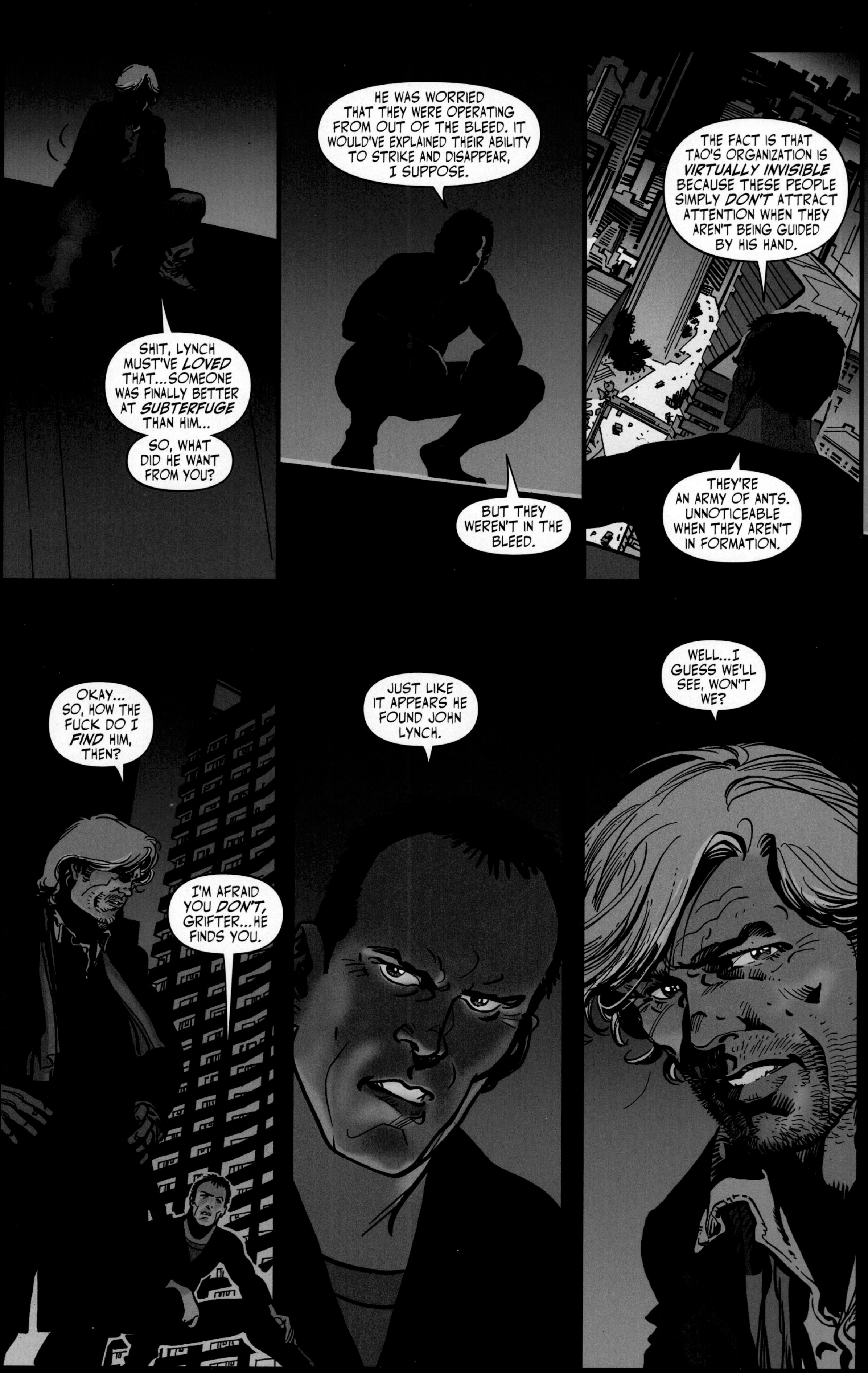
SHIT, LYNCH MUST'VE *LOVED* THAT...SOMEONE WAS FINALLY BETTER AT *SUBTERFUGE* THAN HIM...
SO, WHAT DID HE WANT FROM YOU?
HE WAS WORRIED THAT THEY WERE OPERATING FROM OUT OF THE BLEED. IT WOULD'VE EXPLAINED THEIR ABILITY TO STRIKE AND DISAPPEAR, I SUPPOSE.
BUT THEY WEREN'T IN THE BLEED.
THE FACT IS THAT TAO'S ORGANIZATION IS *VIRTUALLY INVISIBLE* BECAUSE THESE PEOPLE SIMPLY *DON'T* ATTRACT ATTENTION WHEN THEY AREN'T BEING GUIDED BY HIS HAND.
THEY'RE AN ARMY OF ANTS. UNNOTICEABLE WHEN THEY AREN'T IN FORMATION.
OKAY... SO, HOW THE FUCK DO I *FIND* HIM, THEN?
I'M AFRAID YOU *DON'T,* GRIFTER...HE FINDS YOU.
JUST LIKE IT APPEARS HE FOUND JOHN LYNCH.
WELL...I GUESS WE'LL SEE, WON'T WE?

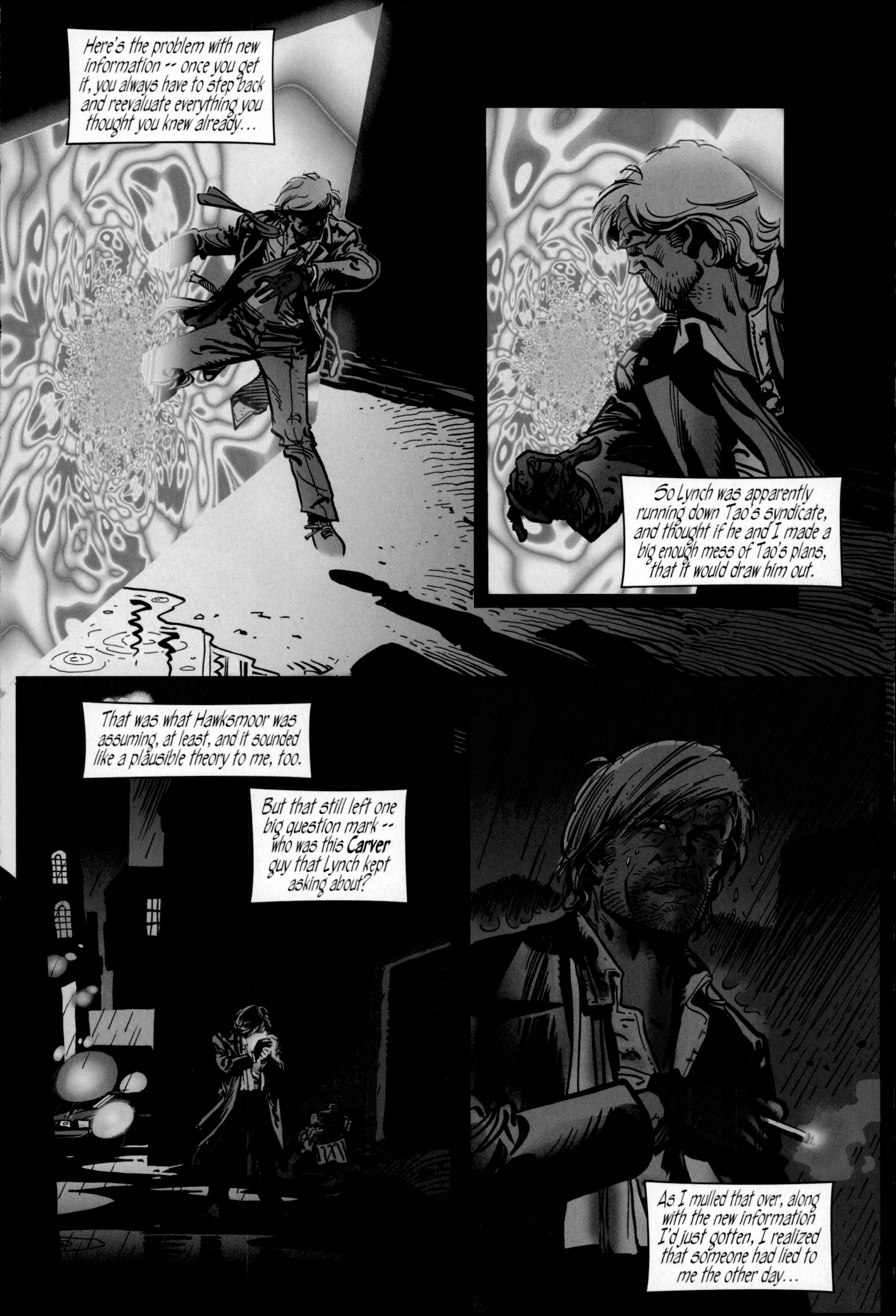
Here's the problem with new information -- once you get it, you always have to step back and reevaluate everything you thought you knew already...
So Lynch was apparently running down Tao's syndicate, and thought if he and I made a big enough mess of Tao's plans, that it would draw him out.
That was what Hawksmoor was assuming, at least, and it sounded like a plausible theory to me, too.
But that still left one big question mark -- who was this Carver guy that Lynch kept asking about?
As I mulled that over, along with the new information I'd just gotten, I realized that someone had lied to me the other day...

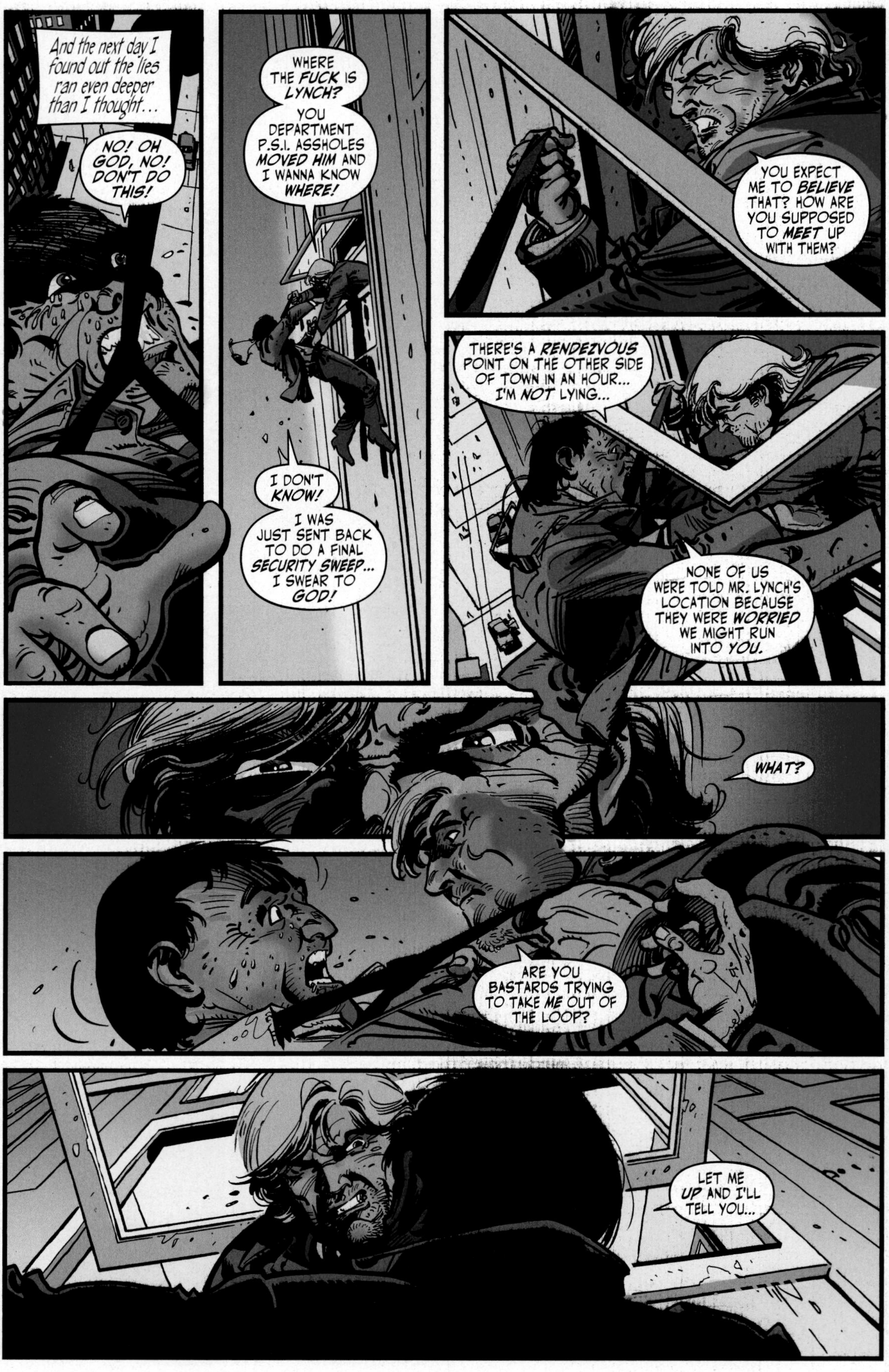
And the next day I found out the lies ran even deeper than I thought...
NO! OH GOD, NO! DON'T DO THIS!
WHERE THE FUCK IS LYNCH?
YOU DEPARTMENT P.S.I. ASSHOLES MOVED HIM AND I WANNA KNOW WHERE!
I DON'T KNOW!
I WAS JUST SENT BACK TO DO A FINAL SECURITY SWEEP... I SWEAR TO GOD!
YOU EXPECT ME TO BELIEVE THAT? HOW ARE YOU SUPPOSED TO MEET UP WITH THEM?
THERE'S A RENDEZVOUS POINT ON THE OTHER SIDE OF TOWN IN AN HOUR... I'M NOT LYING...
NONE OF US WERE TOLD MR. LYNCH'S LOCATION BECAUSE THEY WERE WORRIED WE MIGHT RUN INTO YOU.
WHAT?
ARE YOU BASTARDS TRYING TO TAKE ME OUT OF THE LOOP?
LET ME UP AND I'LL TELL YOU...

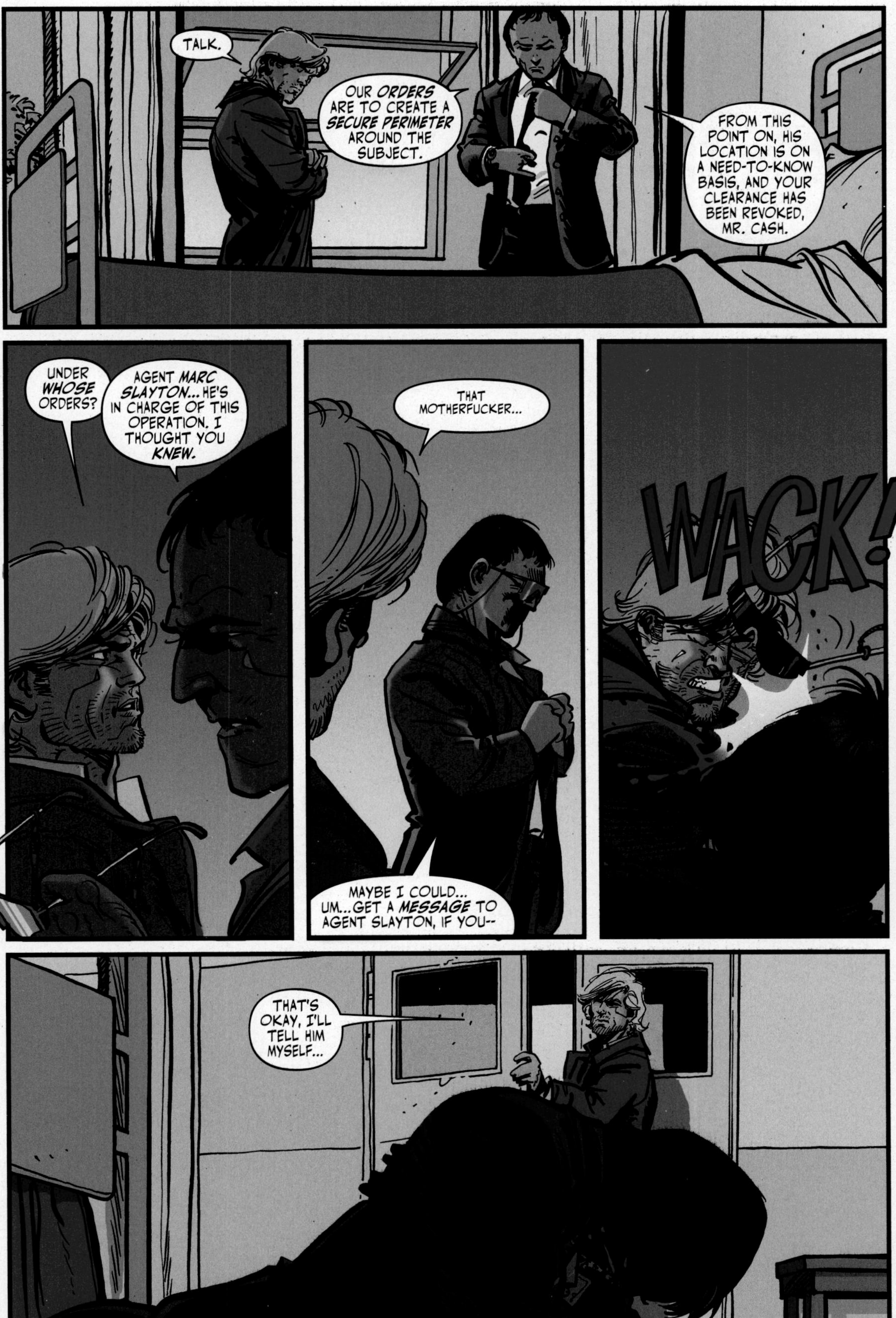
TALK.
OUR ORDERS ARE TO CREATE A SECURE PERIMETER AROUND THE SUBJECT.
FROM THIS POINT ON, HIS LOCATION IS ON A NEED-TO-KNOW BASIS, AND YOUR CLEARANCE HAS BEEN REVOKED, MR. CASH.
UNDER WHOSE ORDERS?
AGENT MARC SLAYTON... HE'S IN CHARGE OF THIS OPERATION. I THOUGHT YOU KNEW.
THAT MOTHERFUCKER...
MAYBE I COULD... UM...GET A MESSAGE TO AGENT SLAYTON, IF YOU--
WACK!
THAT'S OKAY, I'LL TELL HIM MYSELF...

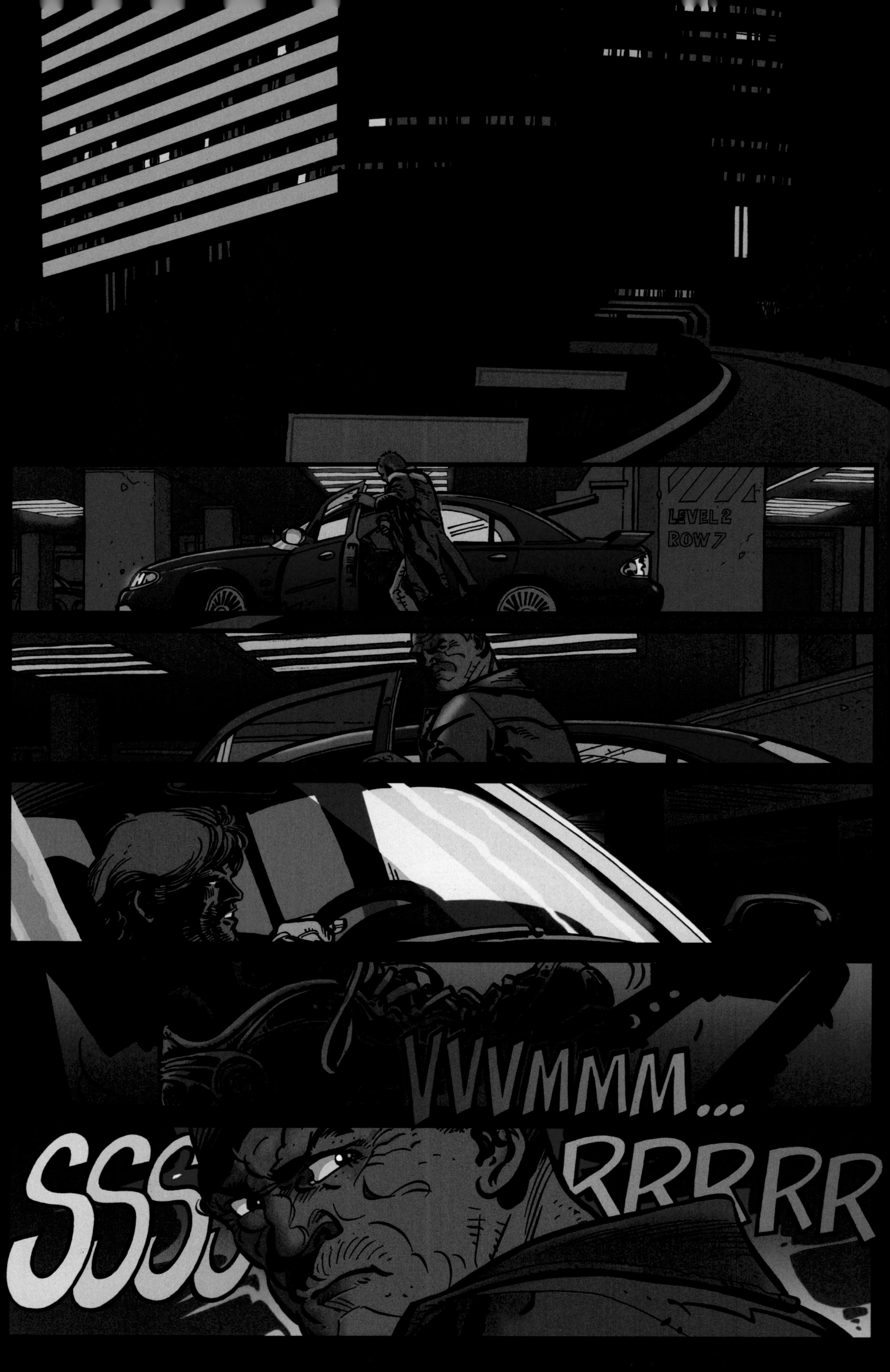
LEVEL 2
ROW 7
VVVMMM...
SSS
RRRRR

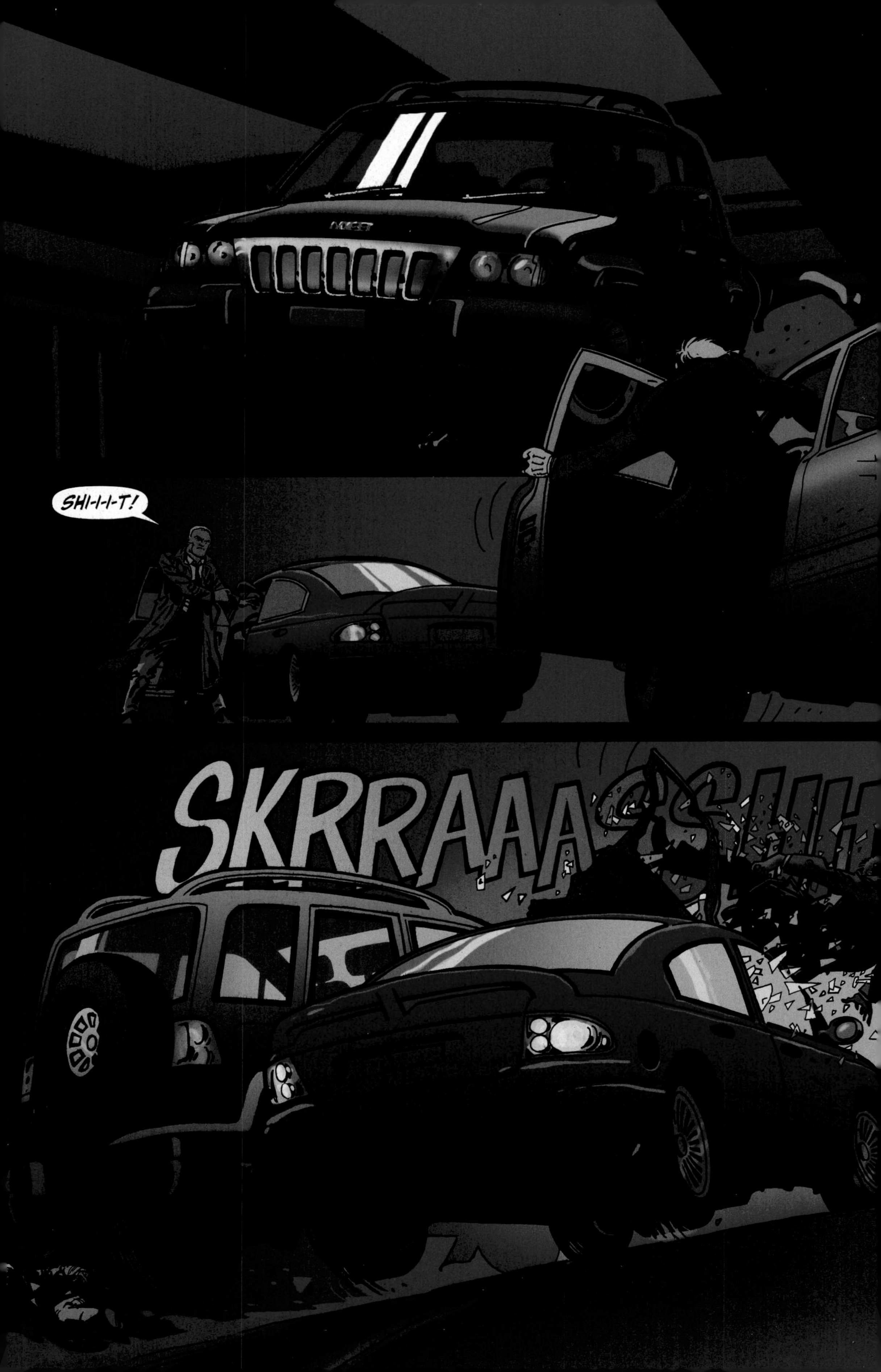
SHI-I-I-T!
SKRRAAASSHH

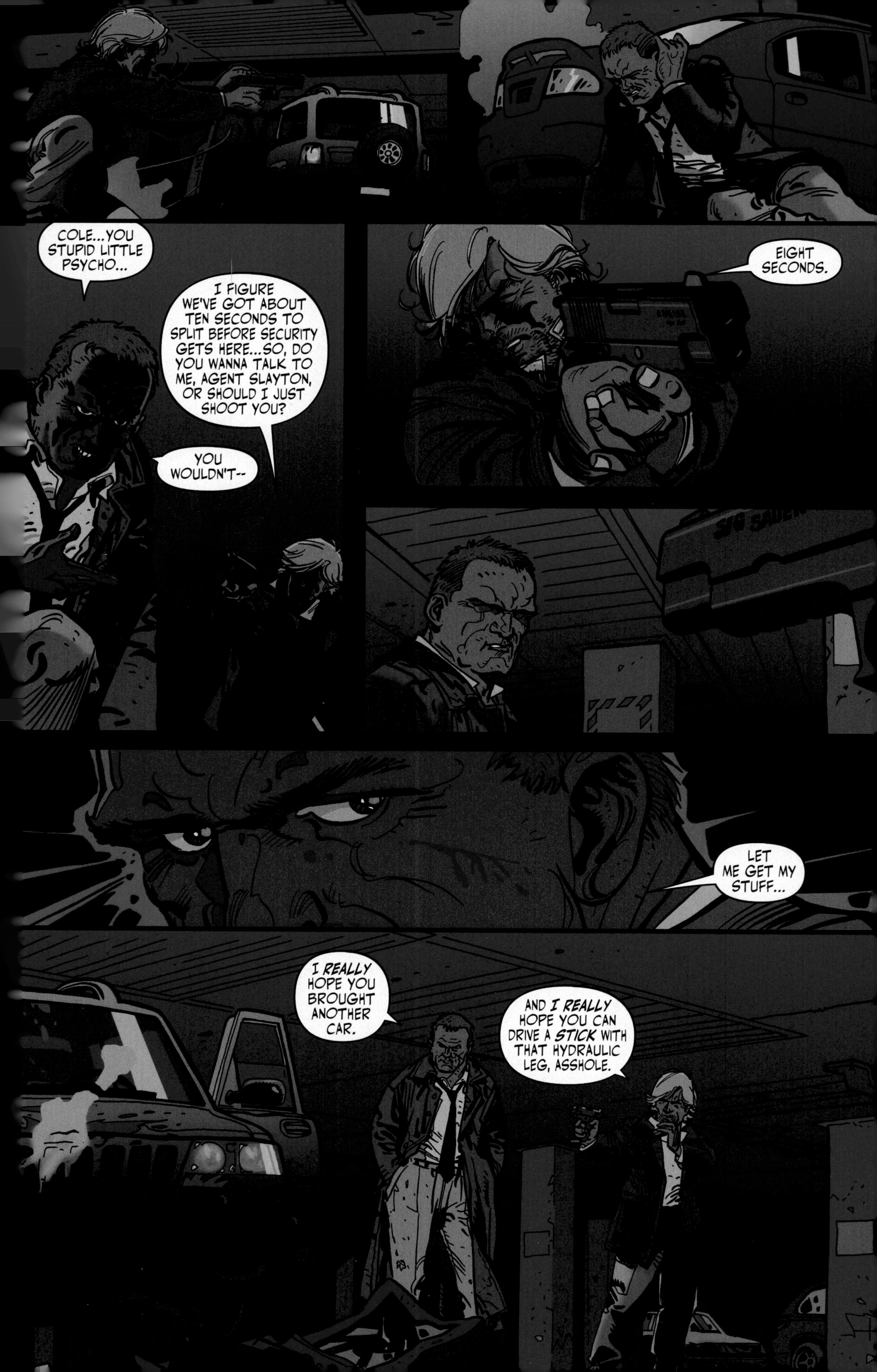

COLE...YOU STUPID LITTLE PSYCHO...
I FIGURE WE'VE GOT ABOUT TEN SECONDS TO SPLIT BEFORE SECURITY GETS HERE...SO, DO YOU WANNA TALK TO ME, AGENT SLAYTON, OR SHOULD I JUST SHOOT YOU?
YOU WOULDN'T--
EIGHT SECONDS.
LET ME GET MY STUFF...
I *REALLY* HOPE YOU BROUGHT ANOTHER CAR.
AND *I REALLY* HOPE YOU CAN DRIVE A *STICK* WITH THAT HYDRAULIC LEG, ASSHOLE.

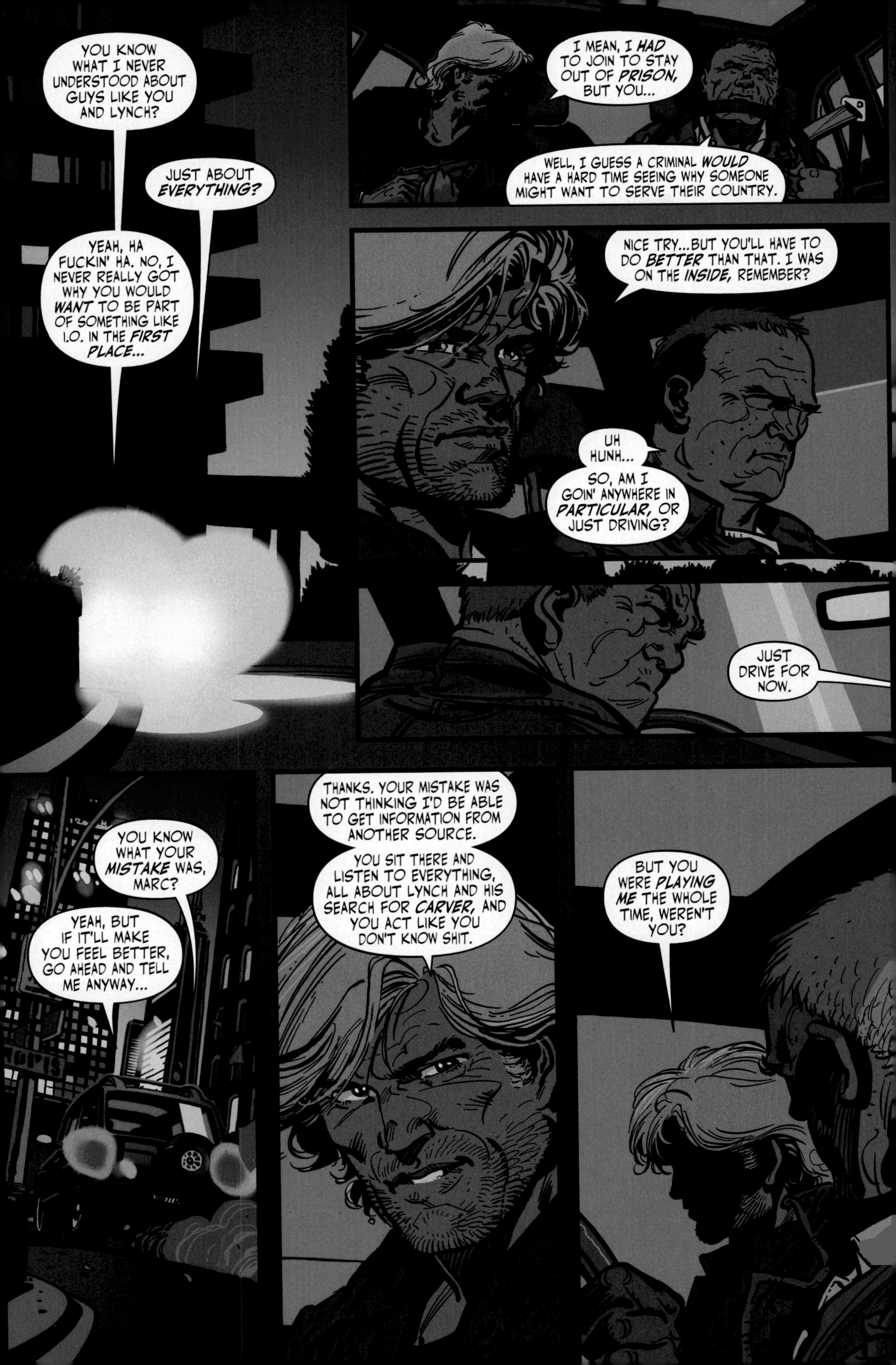
YOU KNOW WHAT I NEVER UNDERSTOOD ABOUT GUYS LIKE YOU AND LYNCH?
JUST ABOUT EVERYTHING?
YEAH, HA FUCKIN' HA. NO, I NEVER REALLY GOT WHY YOU WOULD WANT TO BE PART OF SOMETHING LIKE I.O. IN THE FIRST PLACE...
I MEAN, I HAD TO JOIN TO STAY OUT OF PRISON, BUT YOU...
WELL, I GUESS A CRIMINAL WOULD HAVE A HARD TIME SEEING WHY SOMEONE MIGHT WANT TO SERVE THEIR COUNTRY.
NICE TRY...BUT YOU'LL HAVE TO DO BETTER THAN THAT. I WAS ON THE INSIDE, REMEMBER?
UH HUNH...
SO, AM I GOIN' ANYWHERE IN PARTICULAR, OR JUST DRIVING?
JUST DRIVE FOR NOW.
YOU KNOW WHAT YOUR MISTAKE WAS, MARC?
YEAH, BUT IF IT'LL MAKE YOU FEEL BETTER, GO AHEAD AND TELL ME ANYWAY...
THANKS. YOUR MISTAKE WAS NOT THINKING I'D BE ABLE TO GET INFORMATION FROM ANOTHER SOURCE.
YOU SIT THERE AND LISTEN TO EVERYTHING, ALL ABOUT LYNCH AND HIS SEARCH FOR CARVER, AND YOU ACT LIKE YOU DON'T KNOW SHIT.
BUT YOU WERE PLAYING ME THE WHOLE TIME, WEREN'T YOU?

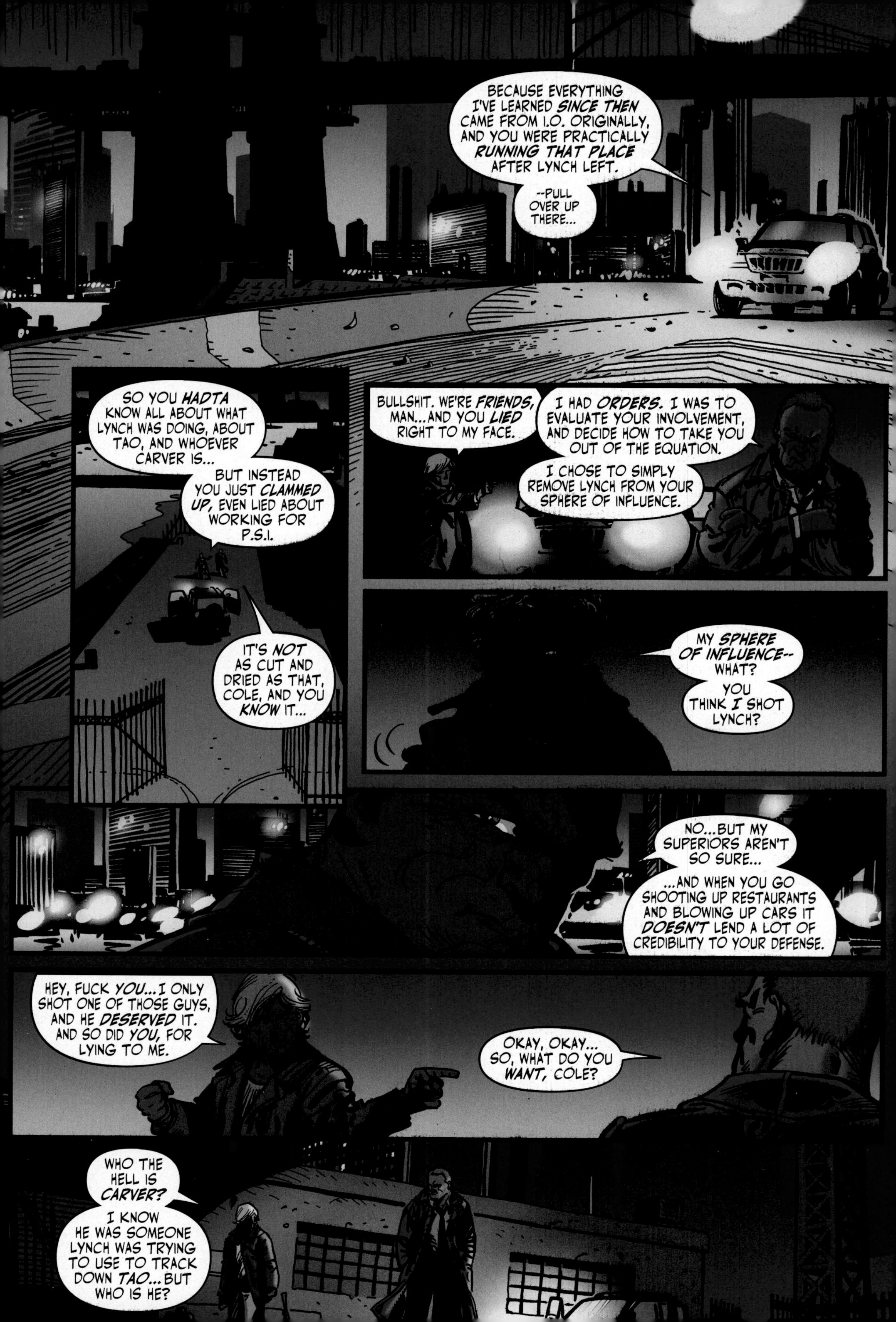
BECAUSE EVERYTHING I'VE LEARNED SINCE THEN CAME FROM I.O. ORIGINALLY, AND YOU WERE PRACTICALLY RUNNING THAT PLACE AFTER LYNCH LEFT.
--PULL OVER UP THERE...
SO YOU HADTA KNOW ALL ABOUT WHAT LYNCH WAS DOING, ABOUT TAO, AND WHOEVER CARVER IS...
BUT INSTEAD YOU JUST CLAMMED UP, EVEN LIED ABOUT WORKING FOR P.S.I.
IT'S NOT AS CUT AND DRIED AS THAT, COLE, AND YOU KNOW IT...
BULLSHIT. WE'RE FRIENDS, MAN...AND YOU LIED RIGHT TO MY FACE.
I HAD ORDERS. I WAS TO EVALUATE YOUR INVOLVEMENT, AND DECIDE HOW TO TAKE YOU OUT OF THE EQUATION.
I CHOSE TO SIMPLY REMOVE LYNCH FROM YOUR SPHERE OF INFLUENCE.
MY SPHERE OF INFLUENCE-- WHAT?
YOU THINK I SHOT LYNCH?
NO...BUT MY SUPERIORS AREN'T SO SURE...
...AND WHEN YOU GO SHOOTING UP RESTAURANTS AND BLOWING UP CARS IT DOESN'T LEND A LOT OF CREDIBILITY TO YOUR DEFENSE.
HEY, FUCK YOU...I ONLY SHOT ONE OF THOSE GUYS, AND HE DESERVED IT. AND SO DID YOU, FOR LYING TO ME.
OKAY, OKAY... SO, WHAT DO YOU WANT, COLE?
WHO THE HELL IS CARVER?
I KNOW HE WAS SOMEONE LYNCH WAS TRYING TO USE TO TRACK DOWN TAO... BUT WHO IS HE?

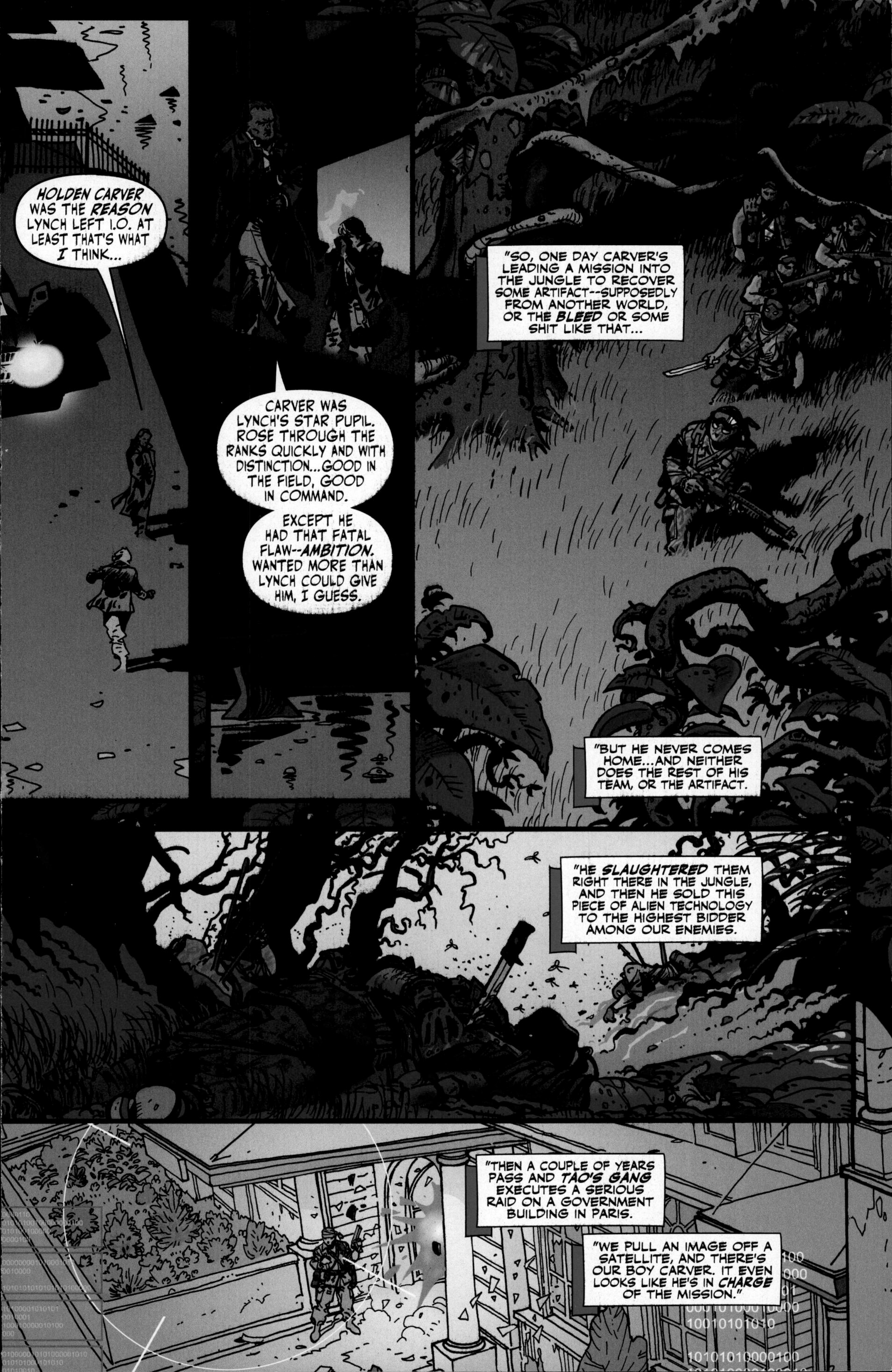
HOLDEN CARVER WAS THE REASON LYNCH LEFT I.O. AT LEAST THAT'S WHAT I THINK...
CARVER WAS LYNCH'S STAR PUPIL. ROSE THROUGH THE RANKS QUICKLY AND WITH DISTINCTION...GOOD IN THE FIELD, GOOD IN COMMAND.
EXCEPT HE HAD THAT FATAL FLAW--AMBITION. WANTED MORE THAN LYNCH COULD GIVE HIM, I GUESS.
"SO, ONE DAY CARVER'S LEADING A MISSION INTO THE JUNGLE TO RECOVER SOME ARTIFACT--SUPPOSEDLY FROM ANOTHER WORLD, OR THE BLEED OR SOME SHIT LIKE THAT...
"BUT HE NEVER COMES HOME...AND NEITHER DOES THE REST OF HIS TEAM, OR THE ARTIFACT.
"HE SLAUGHTERED THEM RIGHT THERE IN THE JUNGLE, AND THEN HE SOLD THIS PIECE OF ALIEN TECHNOLOGY TO THE HIGHEST BIDDER AMONG OUR ENEMIES.
"THEN A COUPLE OF YEARS PASS AND TAO'S GANG EXECUTES A SERIOUS RAID ON A GOVERNMENT BUILDING IN PARIS.
"WE PULL AN IMAGE OFF A SATELLITE, AND THERE'S OUR BOY CARVER. IT EVEN LOOKS LIKE HE'S IN CHARGE OF THE MISSION."

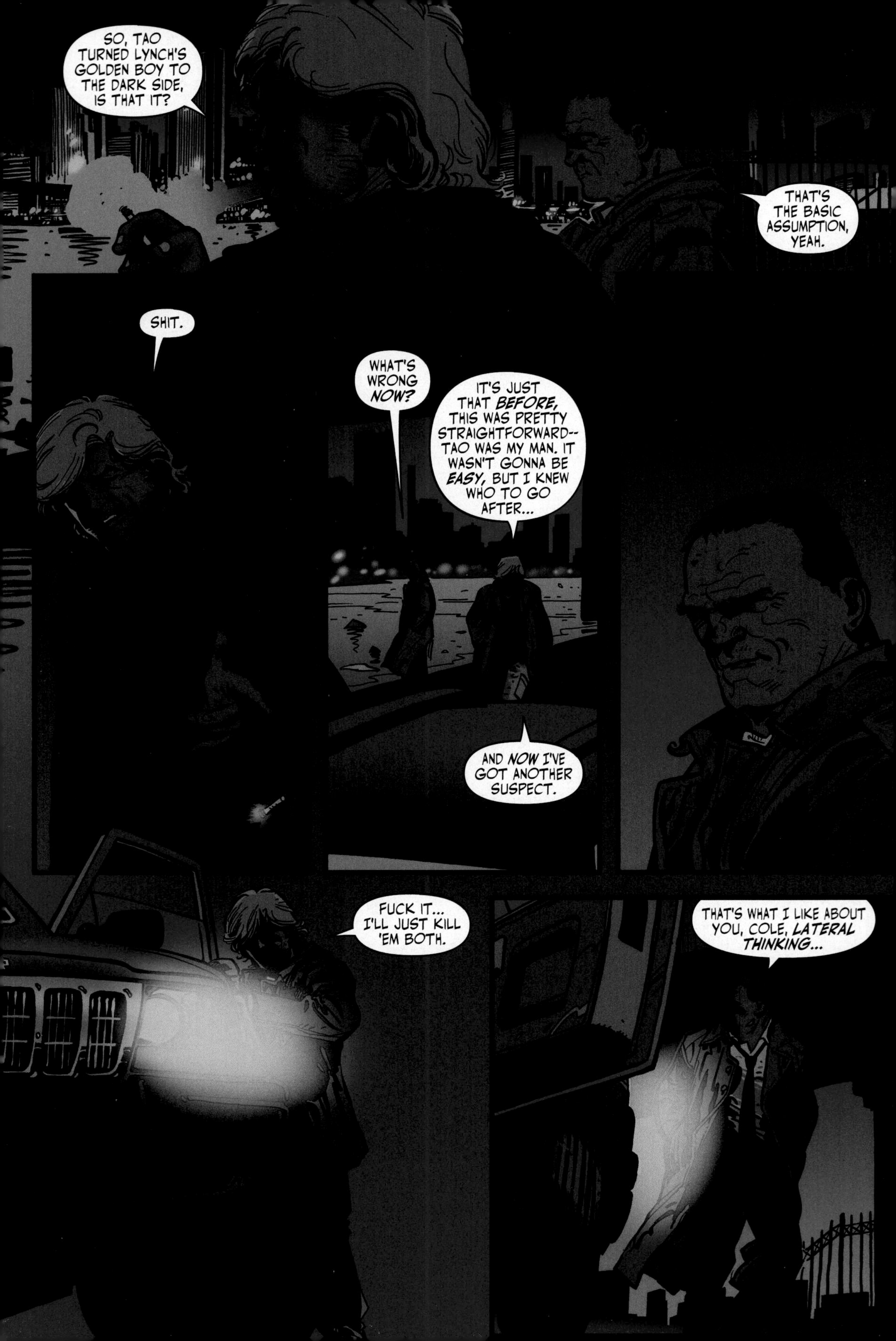
SO, TAO TURNED LYNCH'S GOLDEN BOY TO THE DARK SIDE, IS THAT IT?
THAT'S THE BASIC ASSUMPTION, YEAH.
SHIT.
WHAT'S WRONG NOW?
IT'S JUST THAT BEFORE, THIS WAS PRETTY STRAIGHTFORWARD-- TAO WAS MY MAN. IT WASN'T GONNA BE EASY, BUT I KNEW WHO TO GO AFTER...
AND NOW I'VE GOT ANOTHER SUSPECT.
FUCK IT... I'LL JUST KILL 'EM BOTH.
THAT'S WHAT I LIKE ABOUT YOU, COLE, LATERAL THINKING...

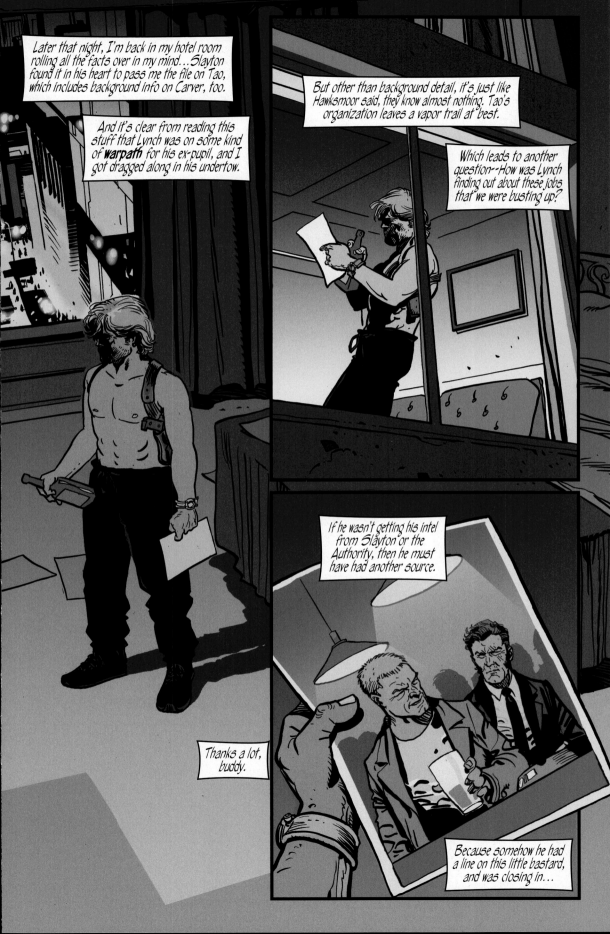

Later that night, I'm back in my hotel room rolling all the facts over in my mind...Slayton found it in his heart to pass me the file on Tao, which includes background info on Carver, too.

And it's clear from reading this stuff that Lynch was on some kind of **warpath** for his ex-pupil, and I got dragged along in his undertow.

But other than background detail, it's just like Hawksmoor said, they know almost nothing. Tao's organization leaves a vapor trail at best.

Which leads to another question--How was Lynch finding out about these jobs that we were busting up?

If he wasn't getting his intel from Slayton or the Authority, then he must have had another source.

Thanks a lot, buddy.

Because somehow he had a line on this little bastard, and was closing in...

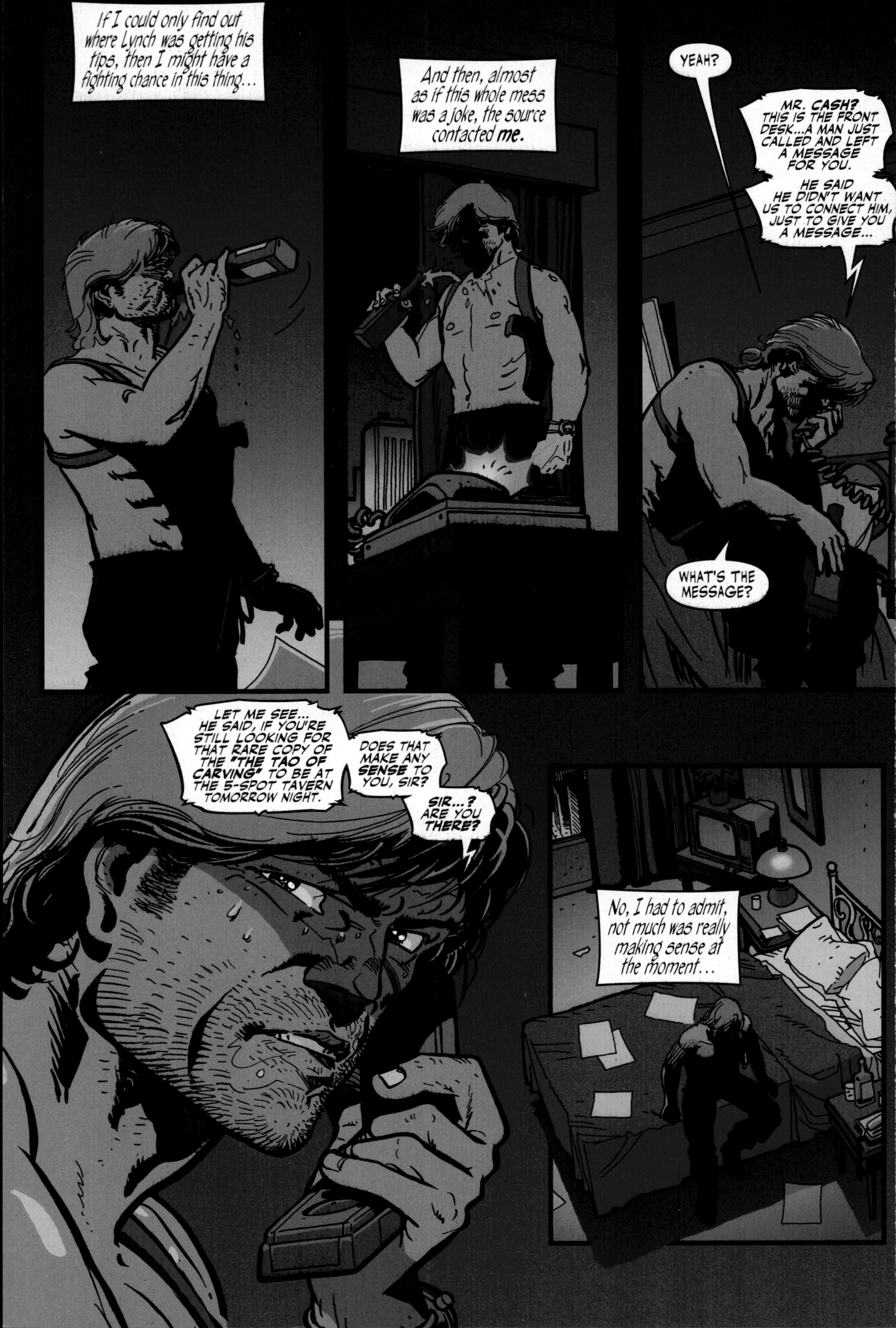
If I could only find out where Lynch was getting his tips, then I might have a fighting chance in this thing...
And then, almost as if this whole mess was a joke, the source contacted **me.**
YEAH?
MR. **CASH?** THIS IS THE FRONT DESK...A MAN JUST CALLED AND LEFT A MESSAGE FOR YOU.
HE SAID HE DIDN'T WANT US TO CONNECT HIM, JUST TO GIVE YOU A MESSAGE...
WHAT'S THE MESSAGE?
LET ME SEE... HE SAID, IF YOU'RE STILL LOOKING FOR THAT **RARE** COPY OF THE **"THE TAO OF CARVING"** TO BE AT THE 5-SPOT TAVERN TOMORROW NIGHT.
DOES THAT MAKE ANY **SENSE** TO YOU, SIR?
SIR...? ARE YOU THERE?
No, I had to admit, not much was really making sense at the moment...

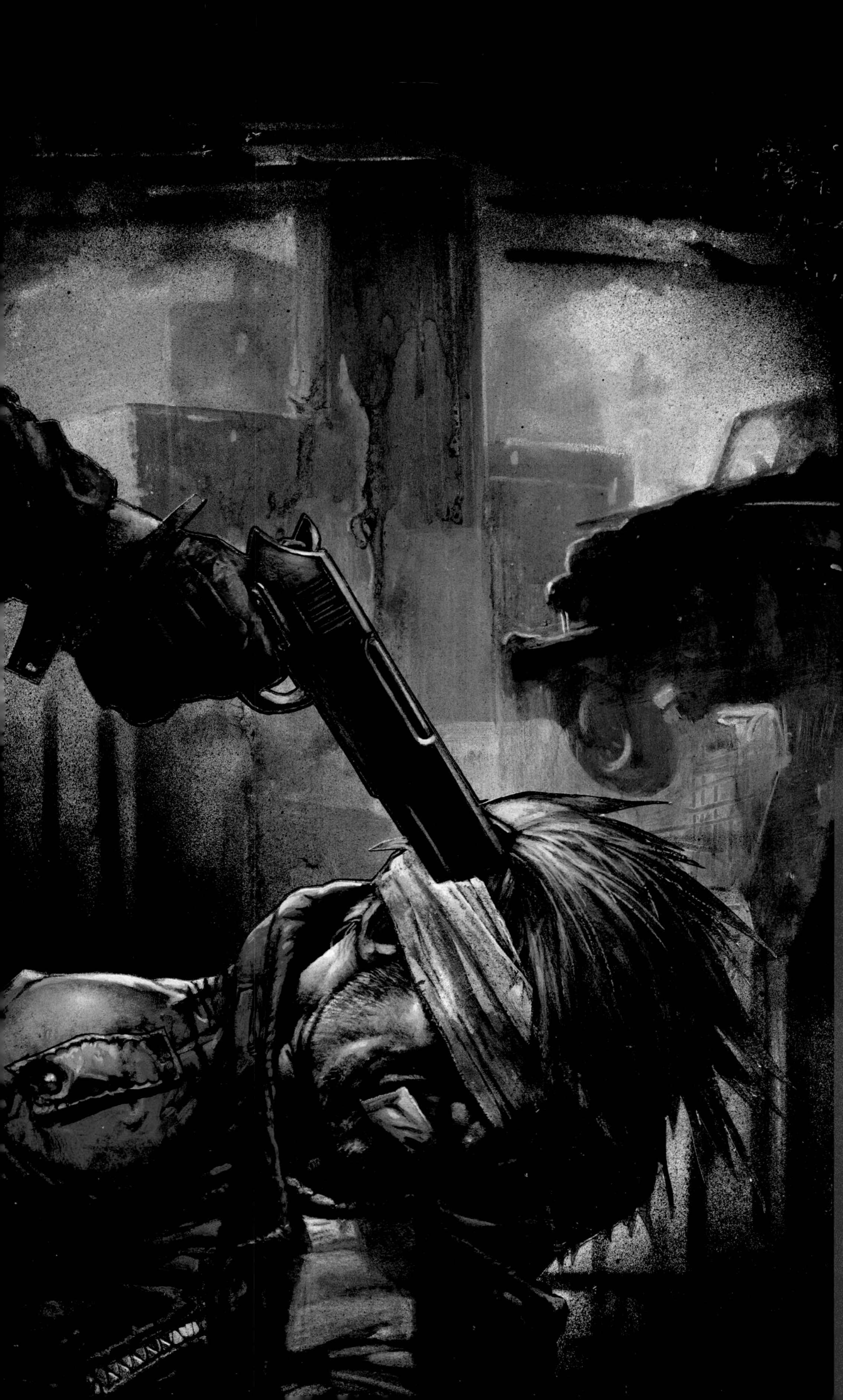

Cover by SIMON BISLEY

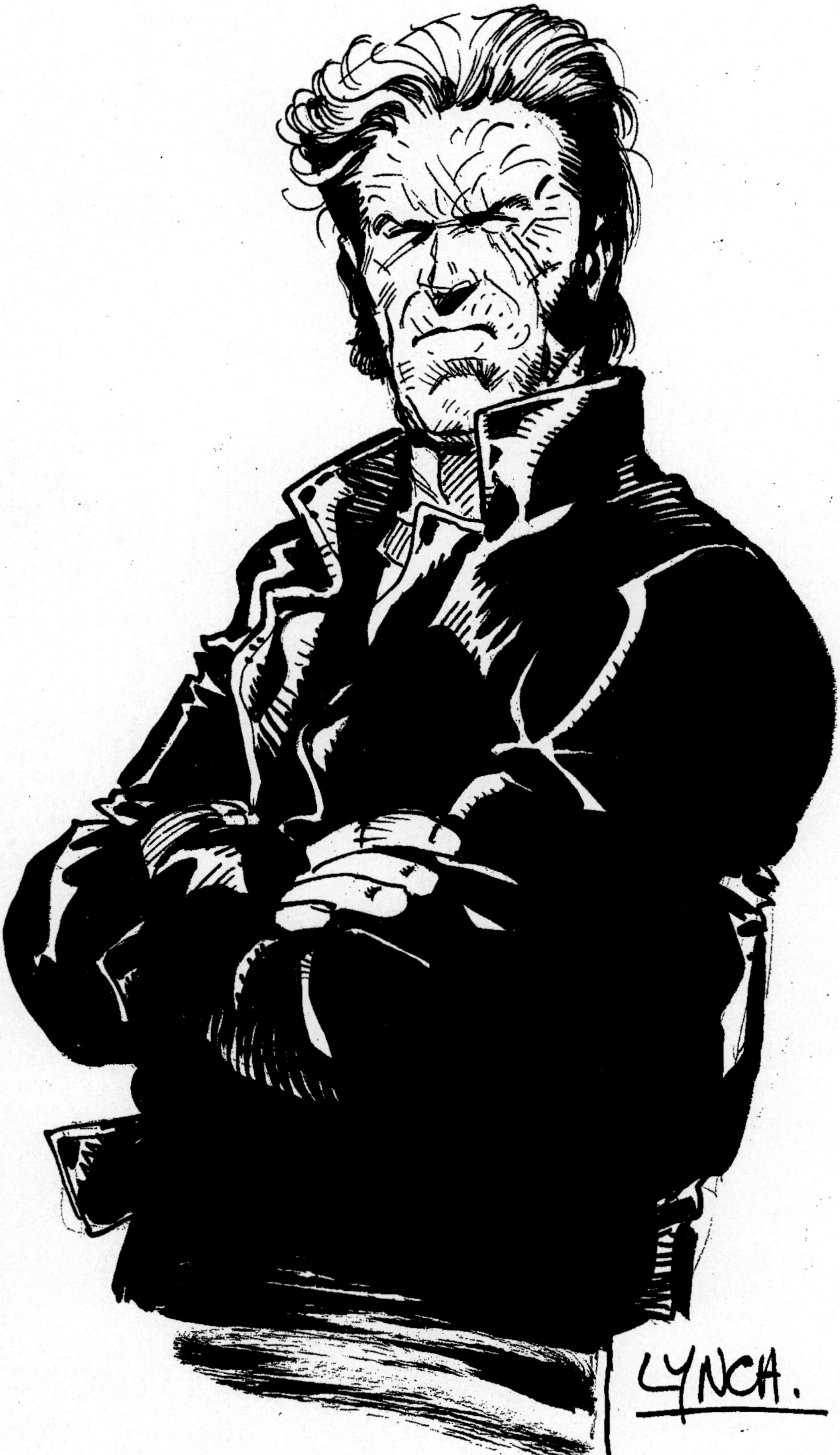
LYNCH.

LYNCH sketch by COLIN WILSON

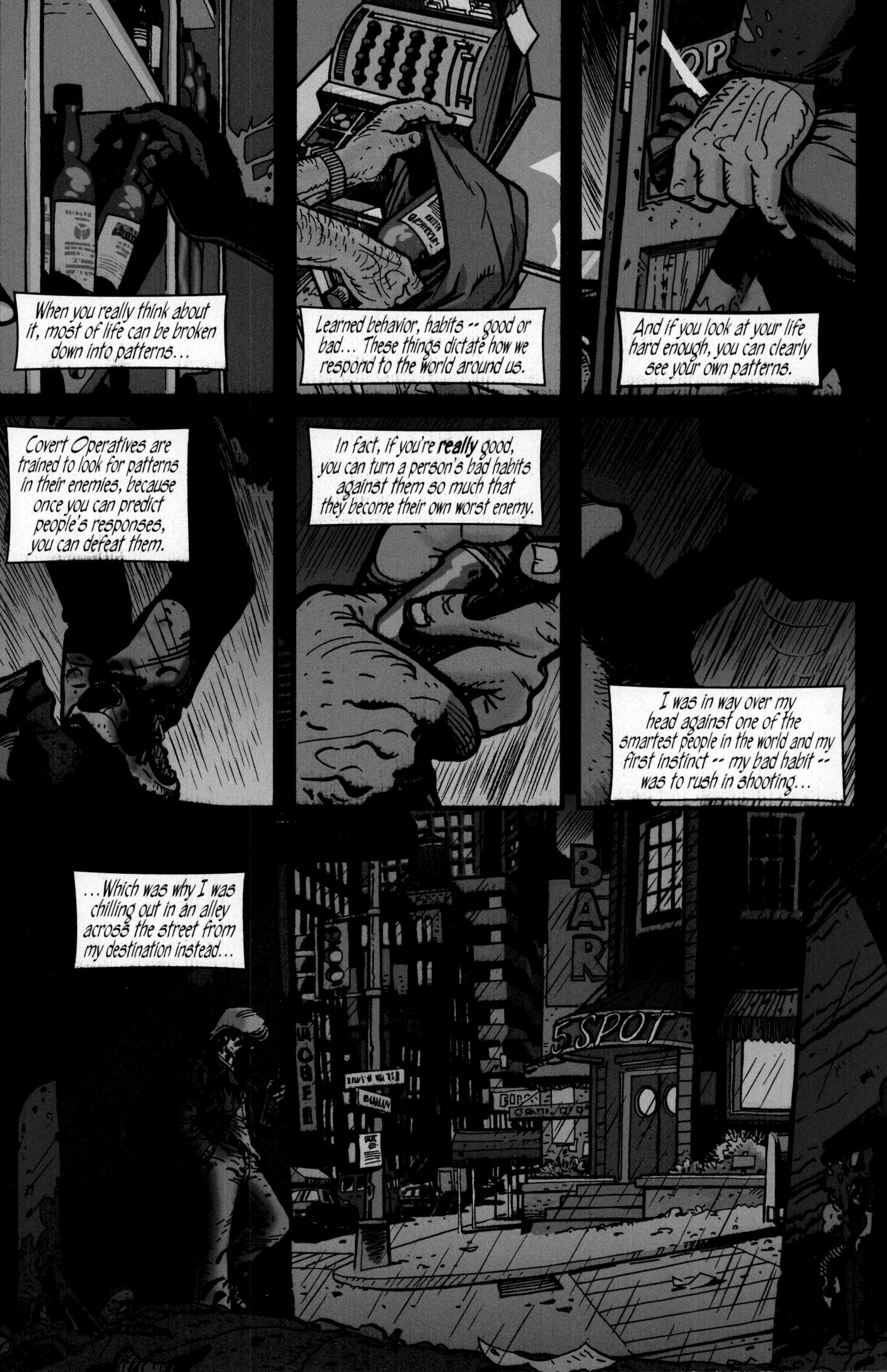
When you really think about it, most of life can be broken down into patterns...
Learned behavior, habits -- good or bad... These things dictate how we respond to the world around us.
And if you look at your life hard enough, you can clearly see your own patterns.
Covert Operatives are trained to look for patterns in their enemies, because once you can predict people's responses, you can defeat them.
In fact, if you're **really** good, you can turn a person's bad habits against them so much that they become their own worst enemy.
I was in way over my head against one of the smartest people in the world and my first instinct -- my bad habit -- was to rush in shooting...
...Which was why I was chilling out in an alley across the street from my destination instead...
BAR
5 SPOT

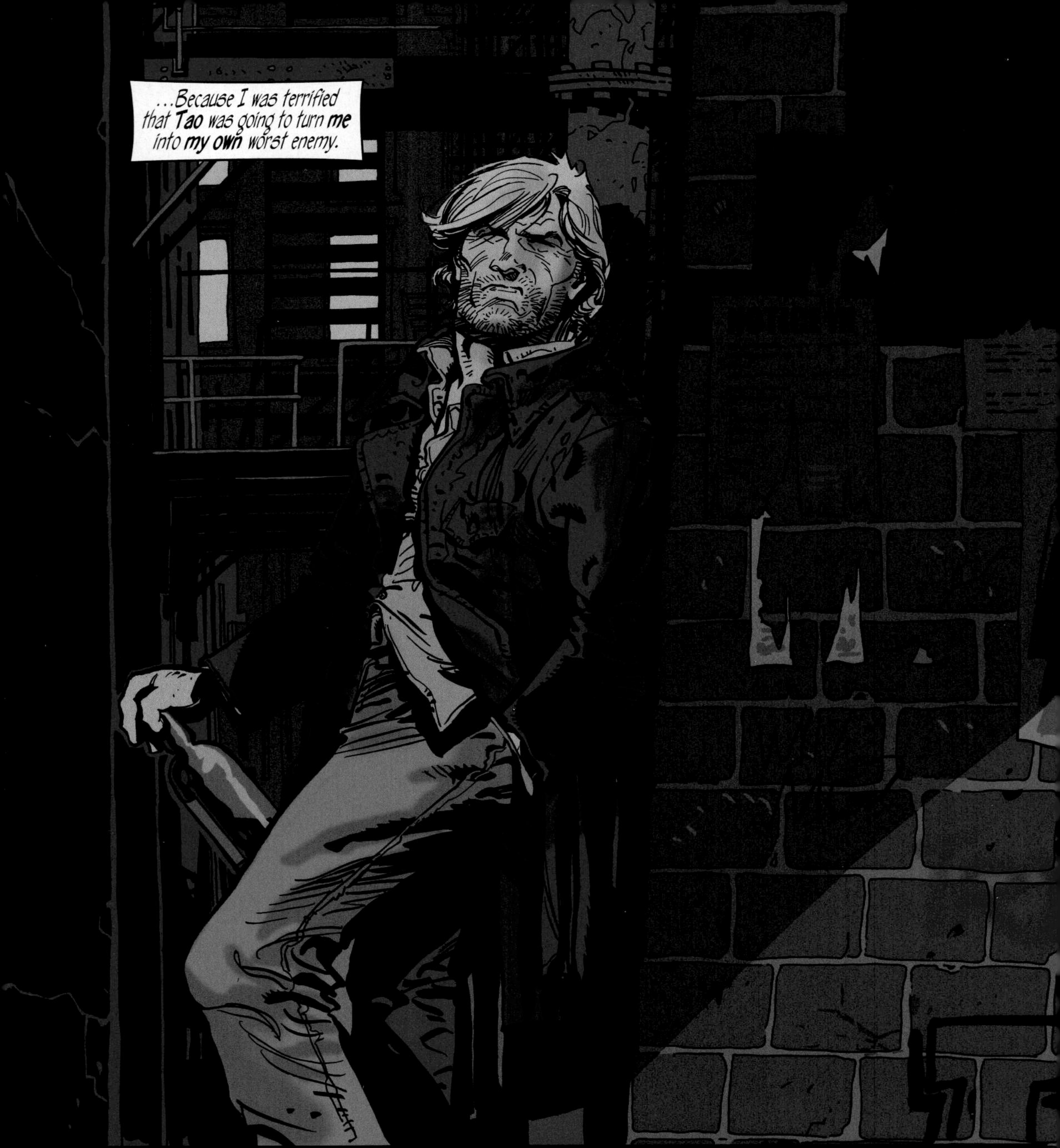
...Because I was terrified that **Tao** was going to turn **me** into **my own** worst enemy.
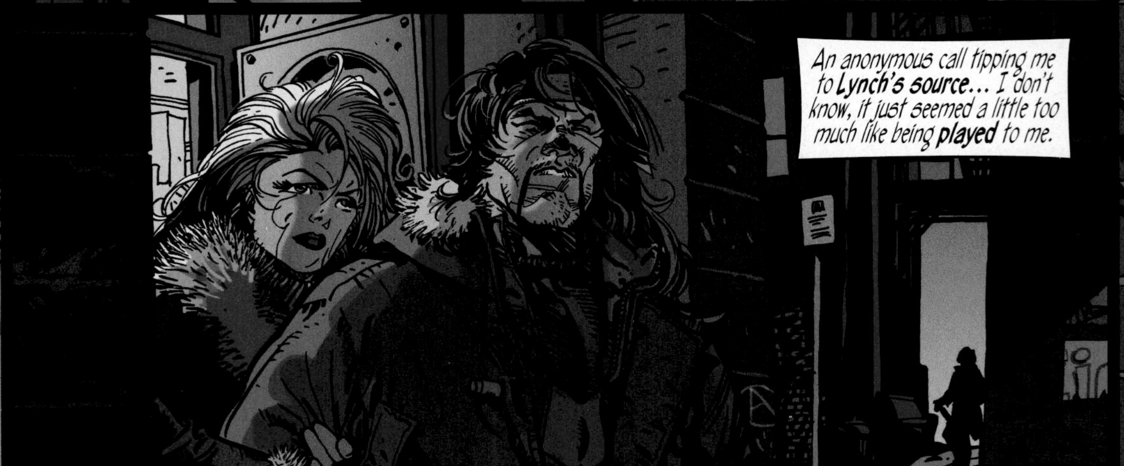
An anonymous call tipping me to **Lynch's source**... I don't know, it just seemed a little too much like being **played** to me.

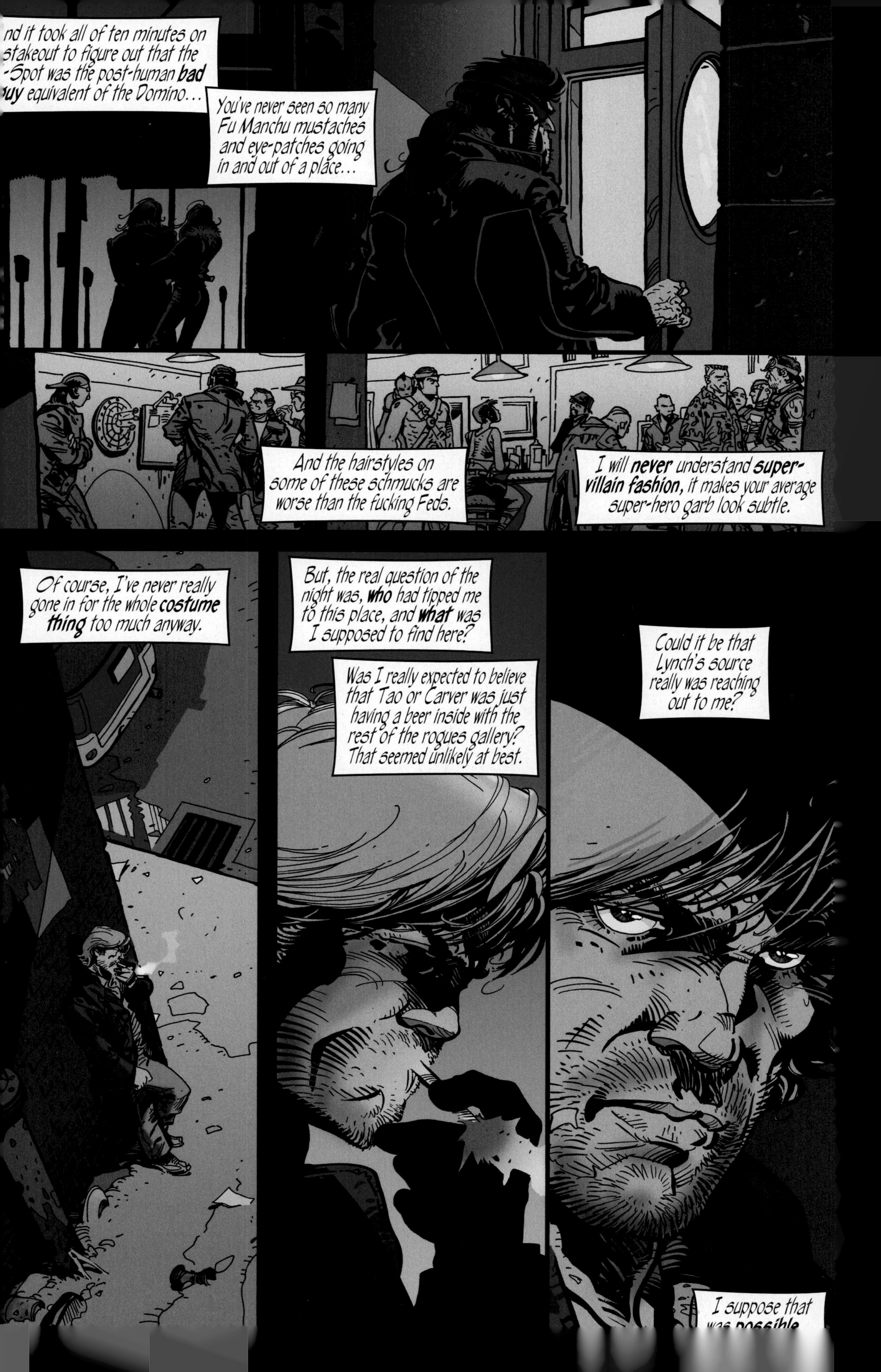
nd it took all of ten minutes on stakeout to figure out that the -Spot was the post-human bad uy equivalent of the Domino...
You've never seen so many Fu Manchu mustaches and eye-patches going in and out of a place...
And the hairstyles on some of these schmucks are worse than the fucking Feds.
I will never understand super-villain fashion, it makes your average super-hero garb look subtle.
Of course, I've never really gone in for the whole costume thing too much anyway.
But, the real question of the night was, who had tipped me to this place, and what was I supposed to find here?
Was I really expected to believe that Tao or Carver was just having a beer inside with the rest of the rogues gallery? That seemed unlikely at best.
Could it be that Lynch's source really was reaching out to me?
I suppose that

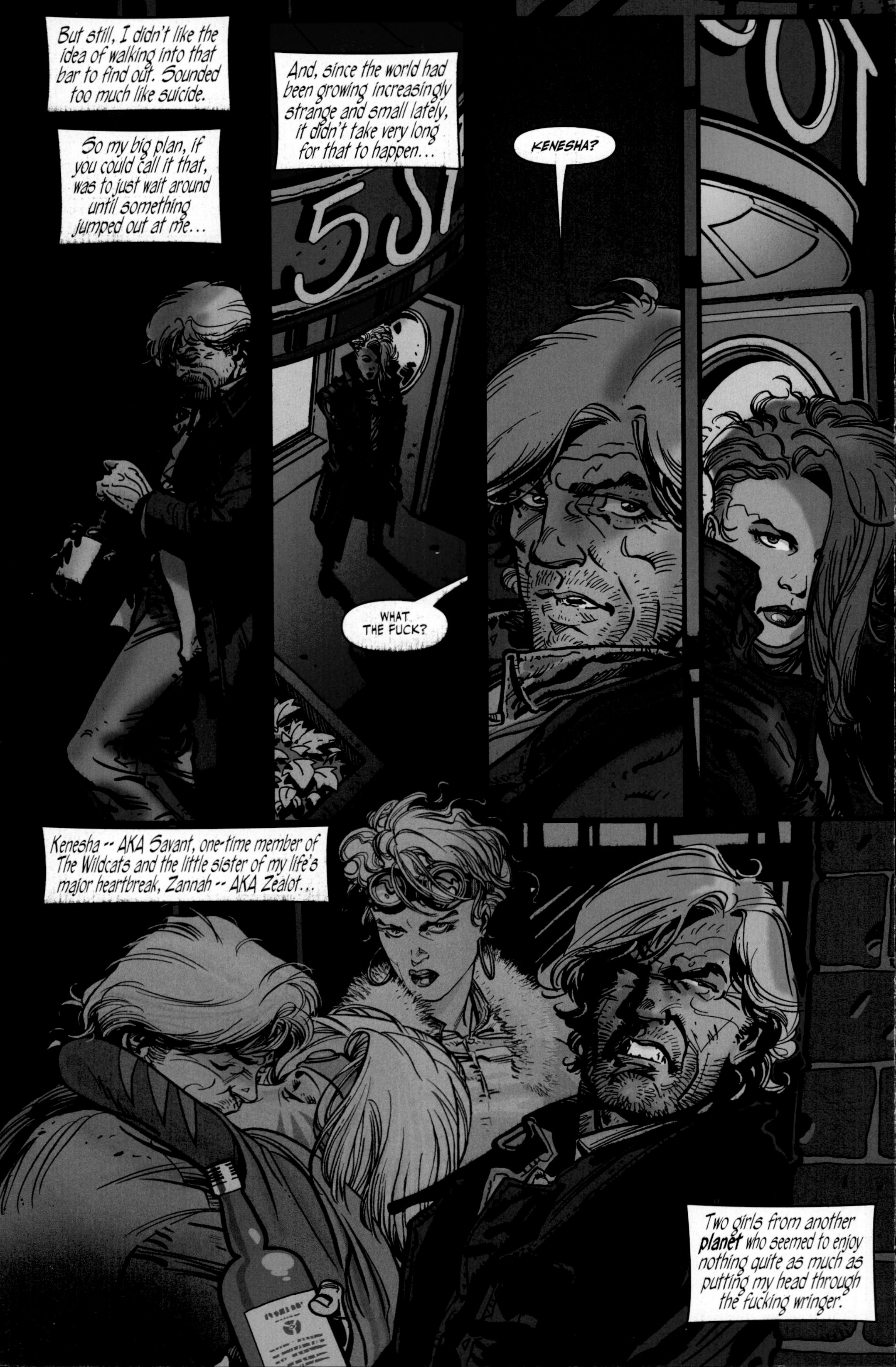
But still, I didn't like the idea of walking into that bar to find out. Sounded too much like suicide.
So my big plan, if you could call it that, was to just wait around until something jumped out at me...
And, since the world had been growing increasingly strange and small lately, it didn't take very long for that to happen...
WHAT THE FUCK?
KENESHA?
Kenesha -- AKA Savant, one-time member of The Wildcats and the little sister of my life's major heartbreak, Zannah -- AKA Zealot...
Two girls from another planet who seemed to enjoy nothing quite as much as putting my head through the fucking wringer.

Could **she** be Lynch's source?

When we all thought Tao was a **good guy**, Kenesha and he were **quite** the hot little item. Maybe she still had a line on him somehow...

She always was a **font** of information. According to Zealot, Kenesha had the entire history of mankind at her disposal in some secret hideout somewhere...

No wonder she and Tao hit it off -- he's a freak and she's an alien anthropologist.

The next guy out the door was another surprise...

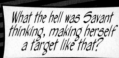

Nicky Zapp -- a minor league post-human thug with electrical powers...

And the way he was sneaking down the block, it looked like he was hoping that taking out an ex-Wildcat might move him up to the **big leagues**.

What the hell was Savant thinking, making herself a target like that?

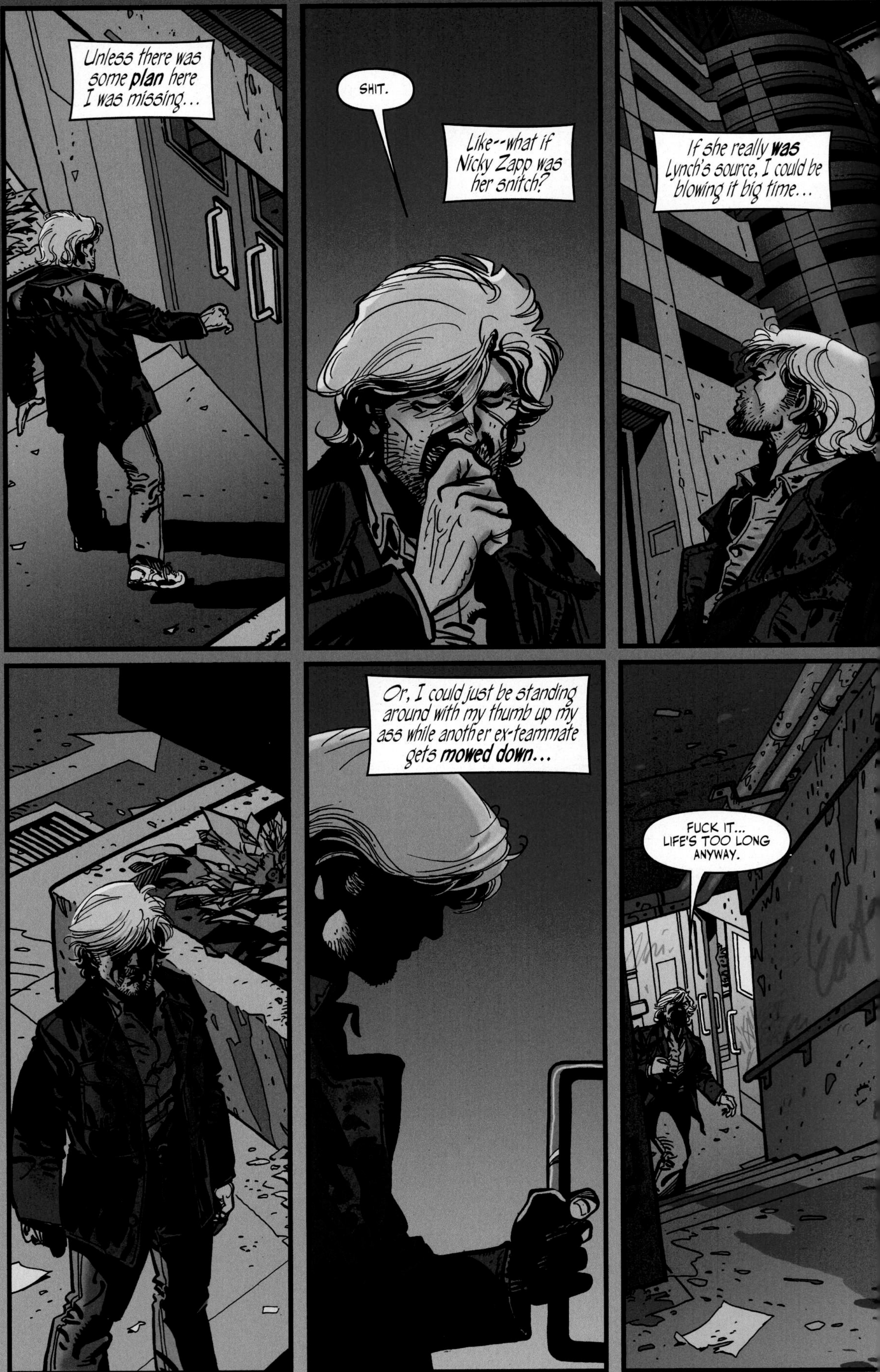

Unless there was some **plan** here I was missing...
SHIT.
Like--what if Nicky Zapp was her snitch?
If she really **was** Lynch's source, I could be blowing it big time...
Or, I could just be standing around with my thumb up my ass while another ex-teammate gets **mowed down**...
FUCK IT... LIFE'S TOO LONG ANYWAY.

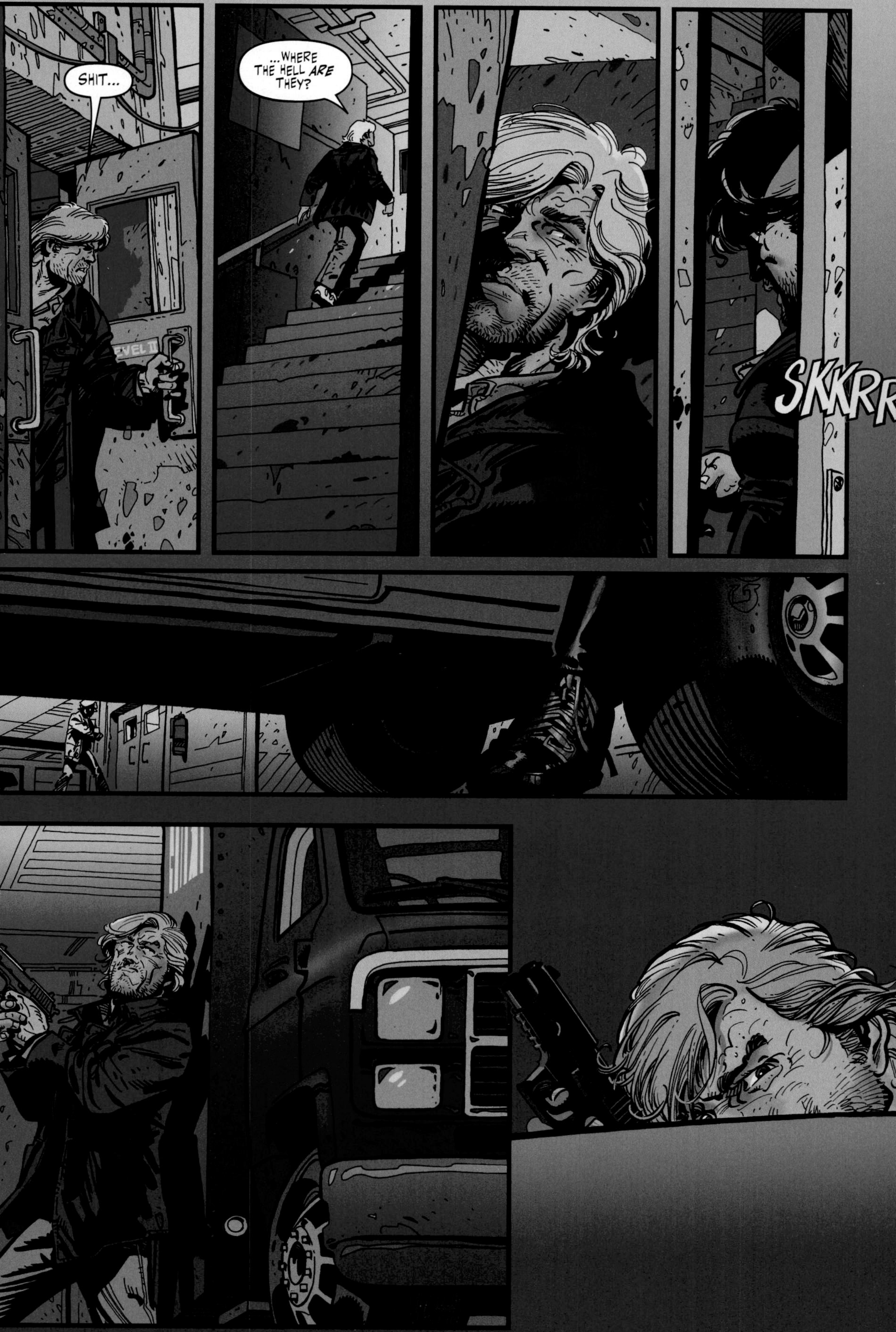
SHIT...
...WHERE THE HELL *ARE* THEY?
SKKRR

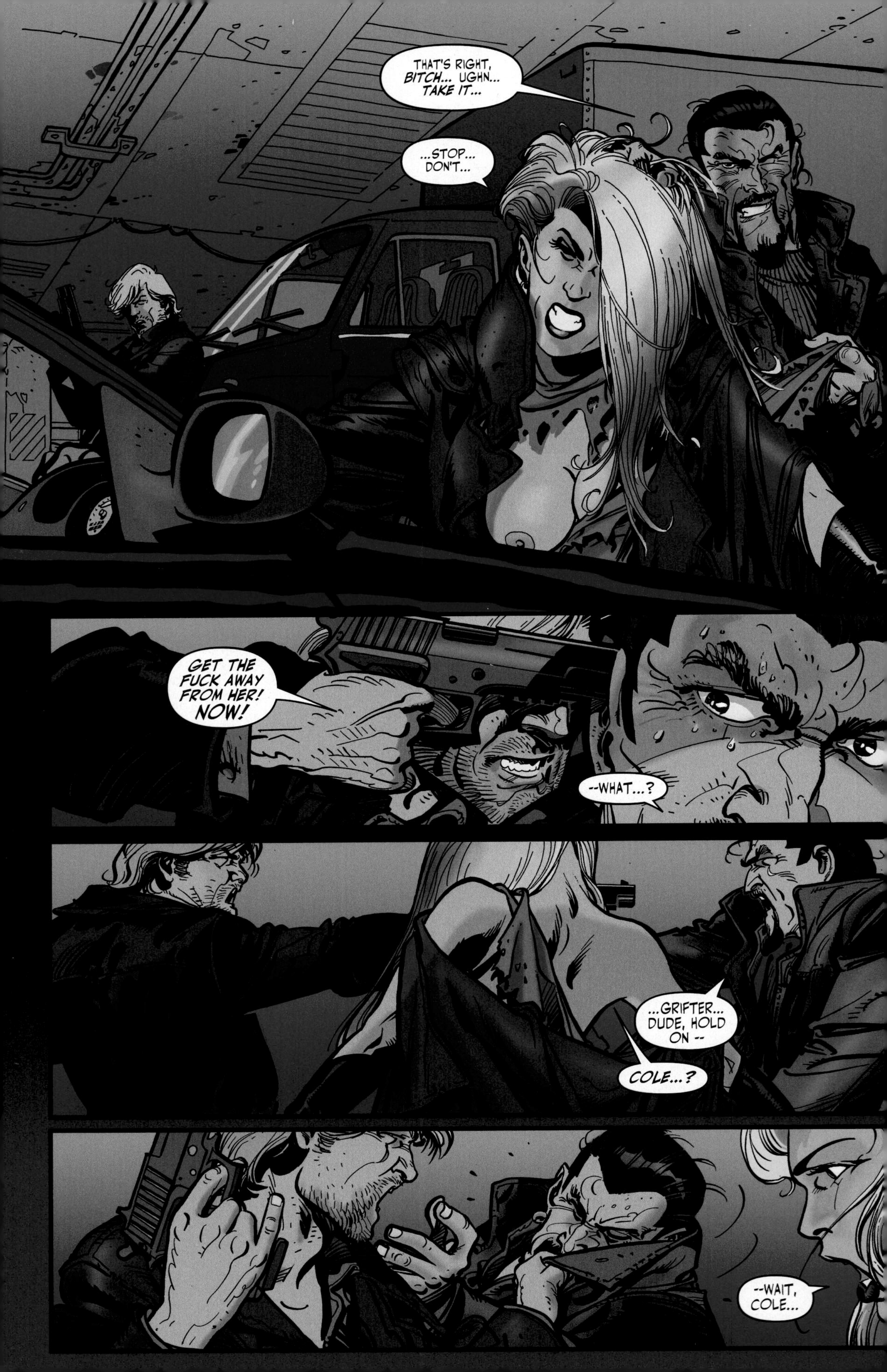
THAT'S RIGHT, BITCH... UGHN... TAKE IT...
...STOP... DON'T...
GET THE FUCK AWAY FROM HER! NOW!
--WHAT...?
...GRIFTER... DUDE, HOLD ON --
COLE...?
--WAIT, COLE...

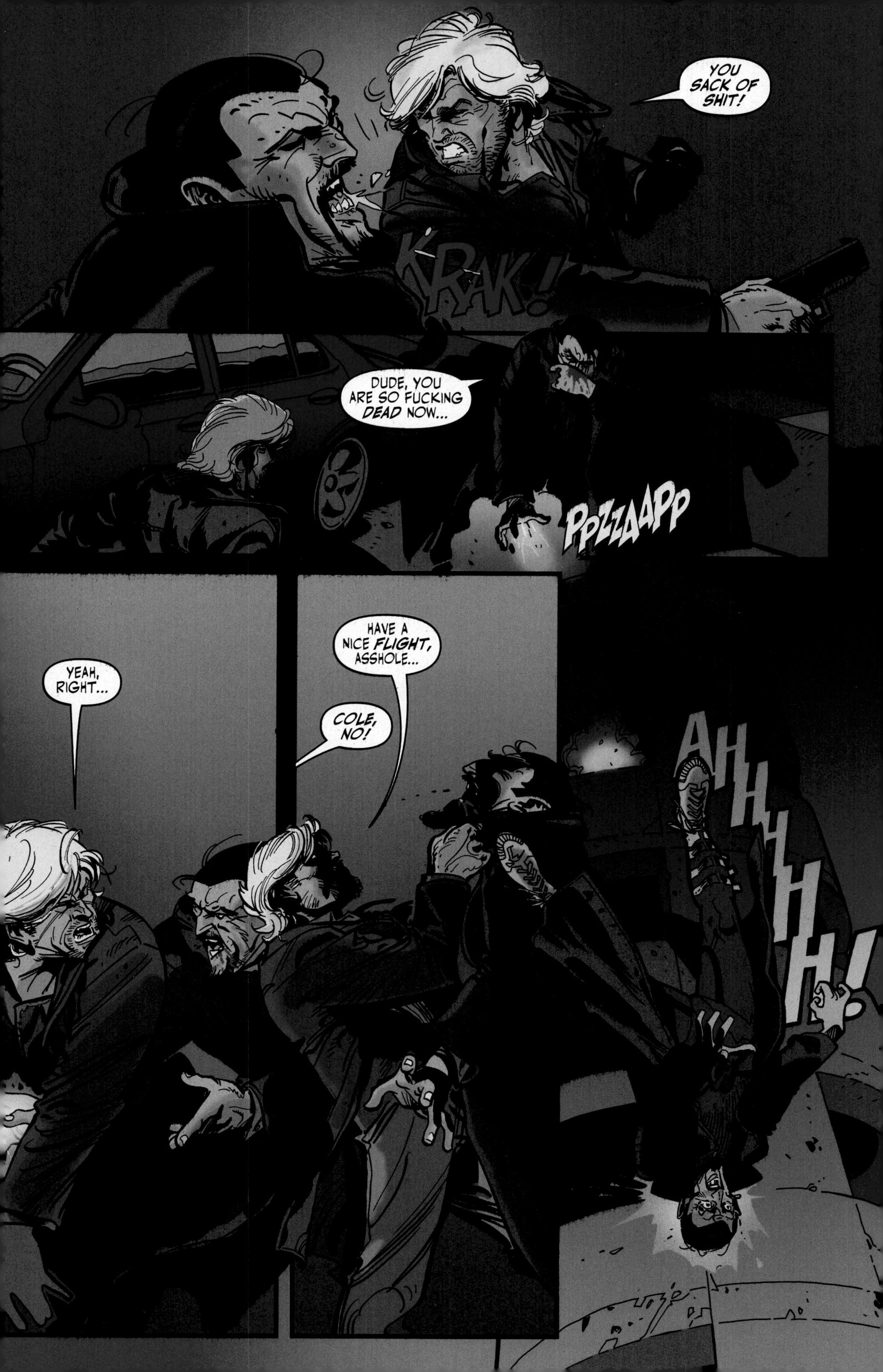

YOU SACK OF SHIT!
KRAK!
DUDE, YOU ARE SO FUCKING DEAD NOW...
PPZZAAPP
YEAH, RIGHT...
HAVE A NICE FLIGHT, ASSHOLE...
COLE, NO!
AHHHHH!

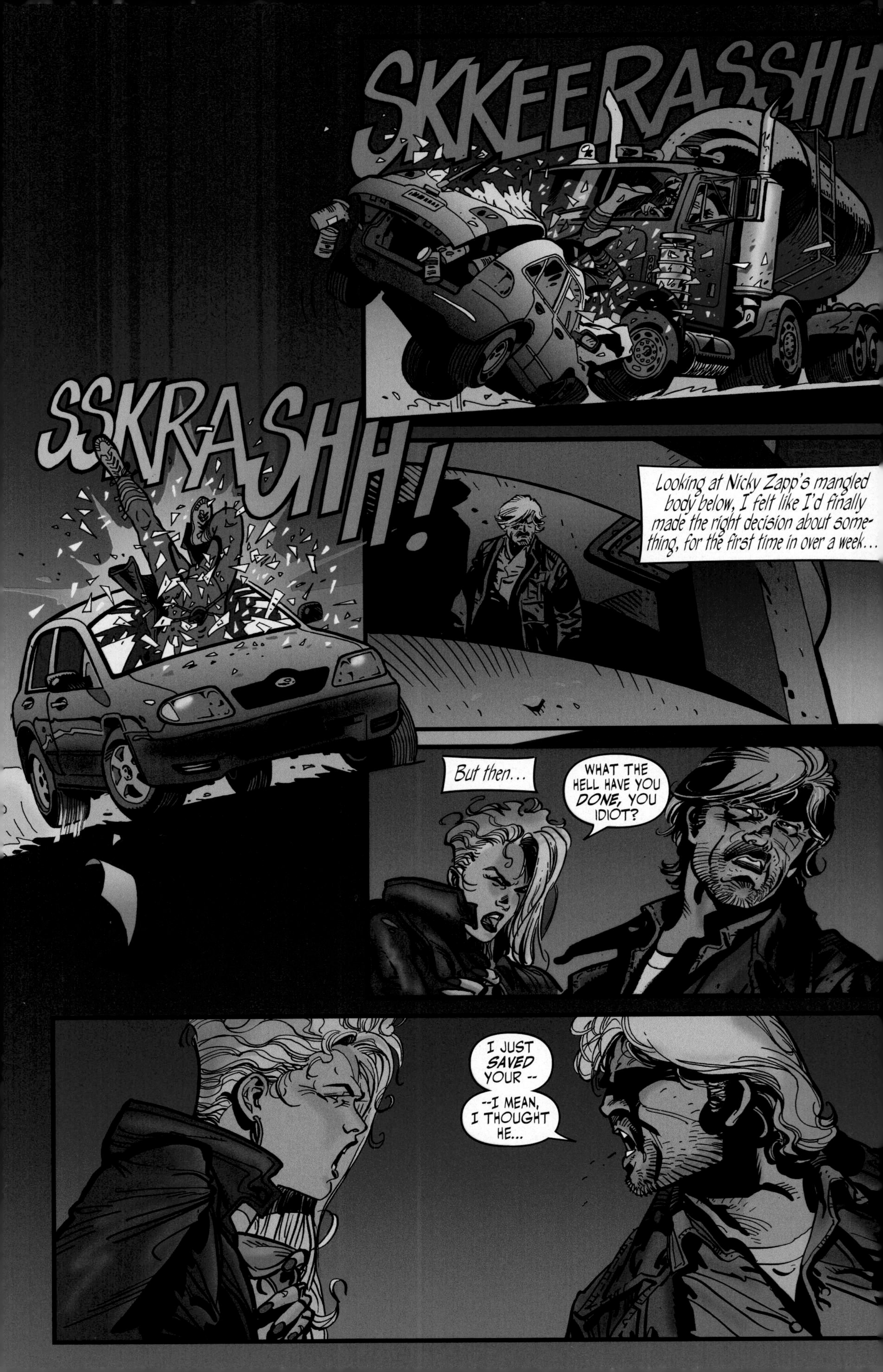

SKKEERASSHH
SSKRASHH!
Looking at Nicky Zapp's mangled body below, I felt like I'd finally made the right decision about something, for the first time in over a week…
But then…
WHAT THE HELL HAVE YOU DONE, YOU IDIOT?
I JUST SAVED YOUR --
--I MEAN, I THOUGHT HE...

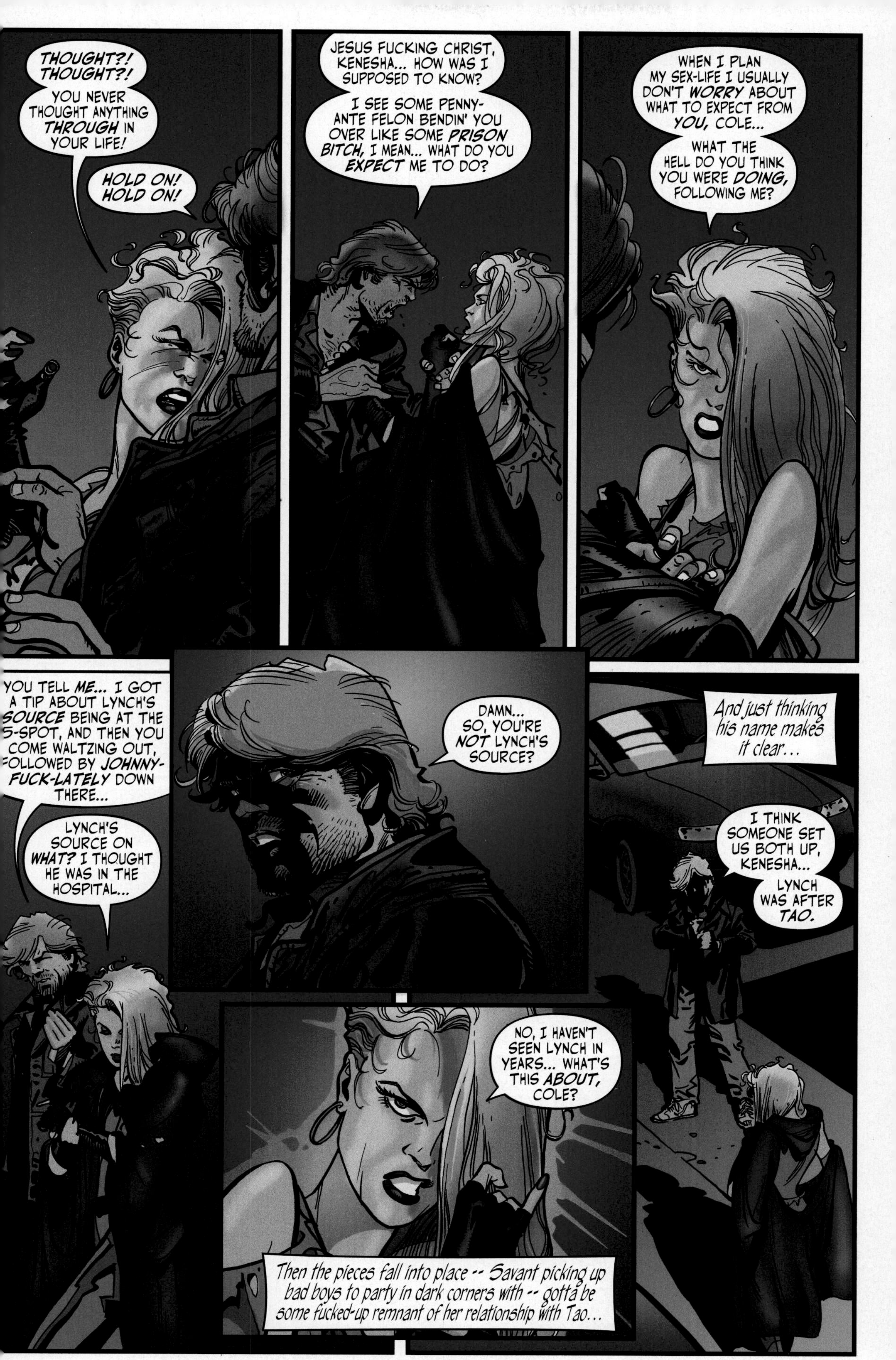
THOUGHT?! THOUGHT?!
YOU NEVER THOUGHT ANYTHING THROUGH IN YOUR LIFE!
HOLD ON! HOLD ON!
JESUS FUCKING CHRIST, KENESHA... HOW WAS I SUPPOSED TO KNOW?
I SEE SOME PENNY-ANTE FELON BENDIN' YOU OVER LIKE SOME PRISON BITCH, I MEAN... WHAT DO YOU EXPECT ME TO DO?
WHEN I PLAN MY SEX-LIFE I USUALLY DON'T WORRY ABOUT WHAT TO EXPECT FROM YOU, COLE...
WHAT THE HELL DO YOU THINK YOU WERE DOING, FOLLOWING ME?
YOU TELL ME... I GOT A TIP ABOUT LYNCH'S SOURCE BEING AT THE 5-SPOT, AND THEN YOU COME WALTZING OUT, FOLLOWED BY JOHNNY-FUCK-LATELY DOWN THERE...
LYNCH'S SOURCE ON WHAT? I THOUGHT HE WAS IN THE HOSPITAL...
DAMN... SO, YOU'RE NOT LYNCH'S SOURCE?
NO, I HAVEN'T SEEN LYNCH IN YEARS... WHAT'S THIS ABOUT, COLE?
And just thinking his name makes it clear...
I THINK SOMEONE SET US BOTH UP, KENESHA...
LYNCH WAS AFTER TAO.
Then the pieces fall into place -- Savant picking up bad boys to party in dark corners with -- gotta be some fucked-up remnant of her relationship with Tao...

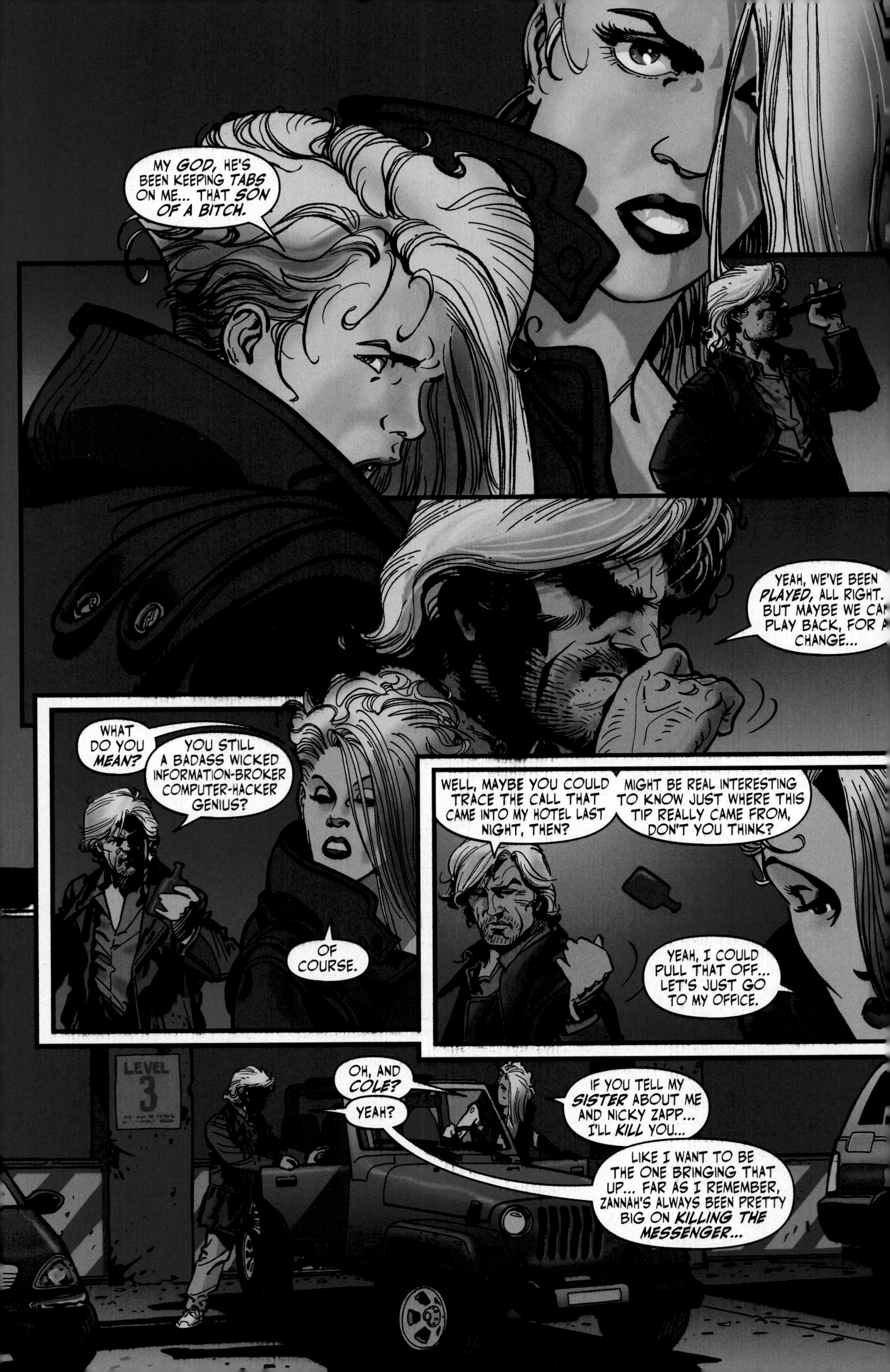
MY GOD, HE'S BEEN KEEPING TABS ON ME... THAT SON OF A BITCH.
YEAH, WE'VE BEEN PLAYED, ALL RIGHT. BUT MAYBE WE CAN PLAY BACK, FOR A CHANGE...
WHAT DO YOU MEAN?
YOU STILL A BADASS WICKED INFORMATION-BROKER COMPUTER-HACKER GENIUS?
OF COURSE.
WELL, MAYBE YOU COULD TRACE THE CALL THAT CAME INTO MY HOTEL LAST NIGHT, THEN?
MIGHT BE REAL INTERESTING TO KNOW JUST WHERE THIS TIP REALLY CAME FROM, DON'T YOU THINK?
YEAH, I COULD PULL THAT OFF... LET'S JUST GO TO MY OFFICE.
LEVEL 3
OH, AND COLE?
YEAH?
IF YOU TELL MY SISTER ABOUT ME AND NICKY ZAPP... I'LL KILL YOU...
LIKE I WANT TO BE THE ONE BRINGING THAT UP... FAR AS I REMEMBER, ZANNAH'S ALWAYS BEEN PRETTY BIG ON KILLING THE MESSENGER...

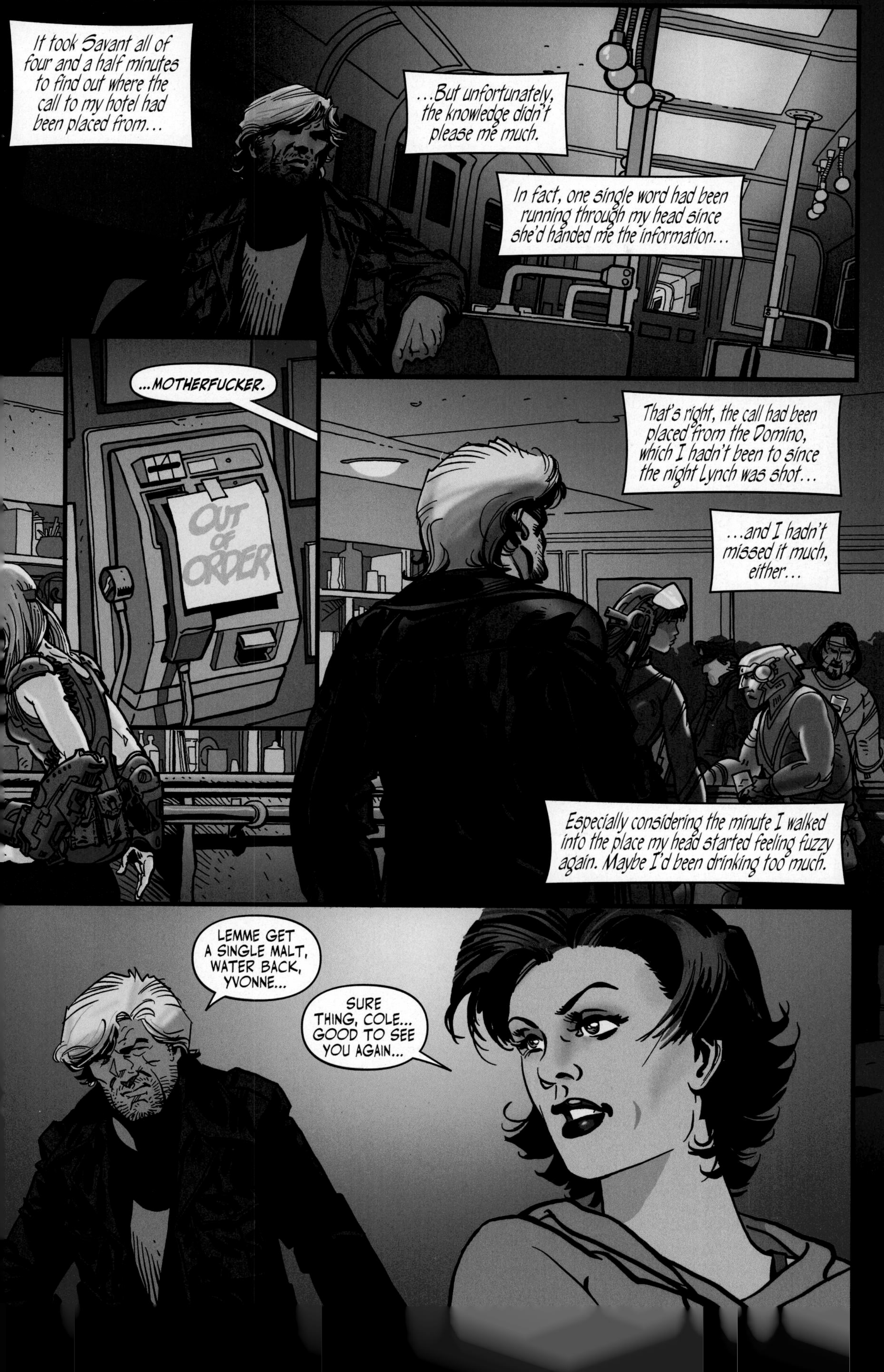

It took Savant all of four and a half minutes to find out where the call to my hotel had been placed from...
...But unfortunately, the knowledge didn't please me much.
In fact, one single word had been running through my head since she'd handed me the information...
...MOTHERFUCKER.
OUT OF ORDER
That's right, the call had been placed from the Domino, which I hadn't been to since the night Lynch was shot...
...and I hadn't missed it much, either...
Especially considering the minute I walked into the place my head started feeling fuzzy again. Maybe I'd been drinking too much.
LEMME GET A SINGLE MALT, WATER BACK, YVONNE...
SURE THING, COLE... GOOD TO SEE YOU AGAIN...

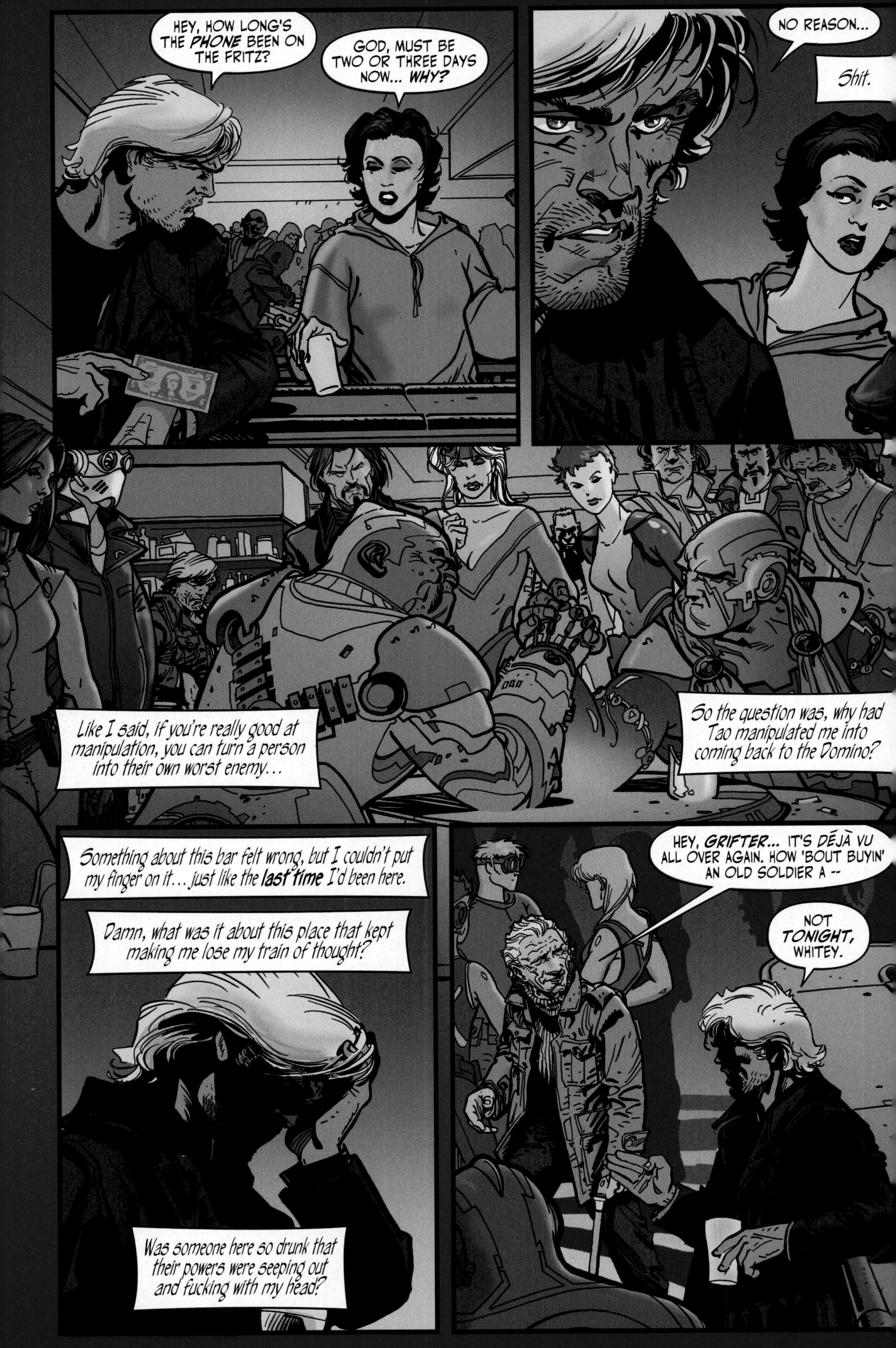
HEY, HOW LONG'S THE *PHONE* BEEN ON THE FRITZ?
GOD, MUST BE TWO OR THREE DAYS NOW... *WHY?*
NO REASON...
Shit.
Like I said, if you're really good at manipulation, you can turn a person into their own worst enemy...
So the question was, why had Tao manipulated me into coming back to the Domino?
*Something about this bar felt wrong, but I couldn't put my finger on it... just like the **last time** I'd been here.*
Damn, what was it about this place that kept making me lose my train of thought?
Was someone here so drunk that their powers were seeping out and fucking with my head?
HEY, *GRIFTER*... IT'S *DÉJÀ* VU ALL OVER AGAIN. HOW 'BOUT BUYIN' AN OLD SOLDIER A --
NOT *TONIGHT,* WHITEY.

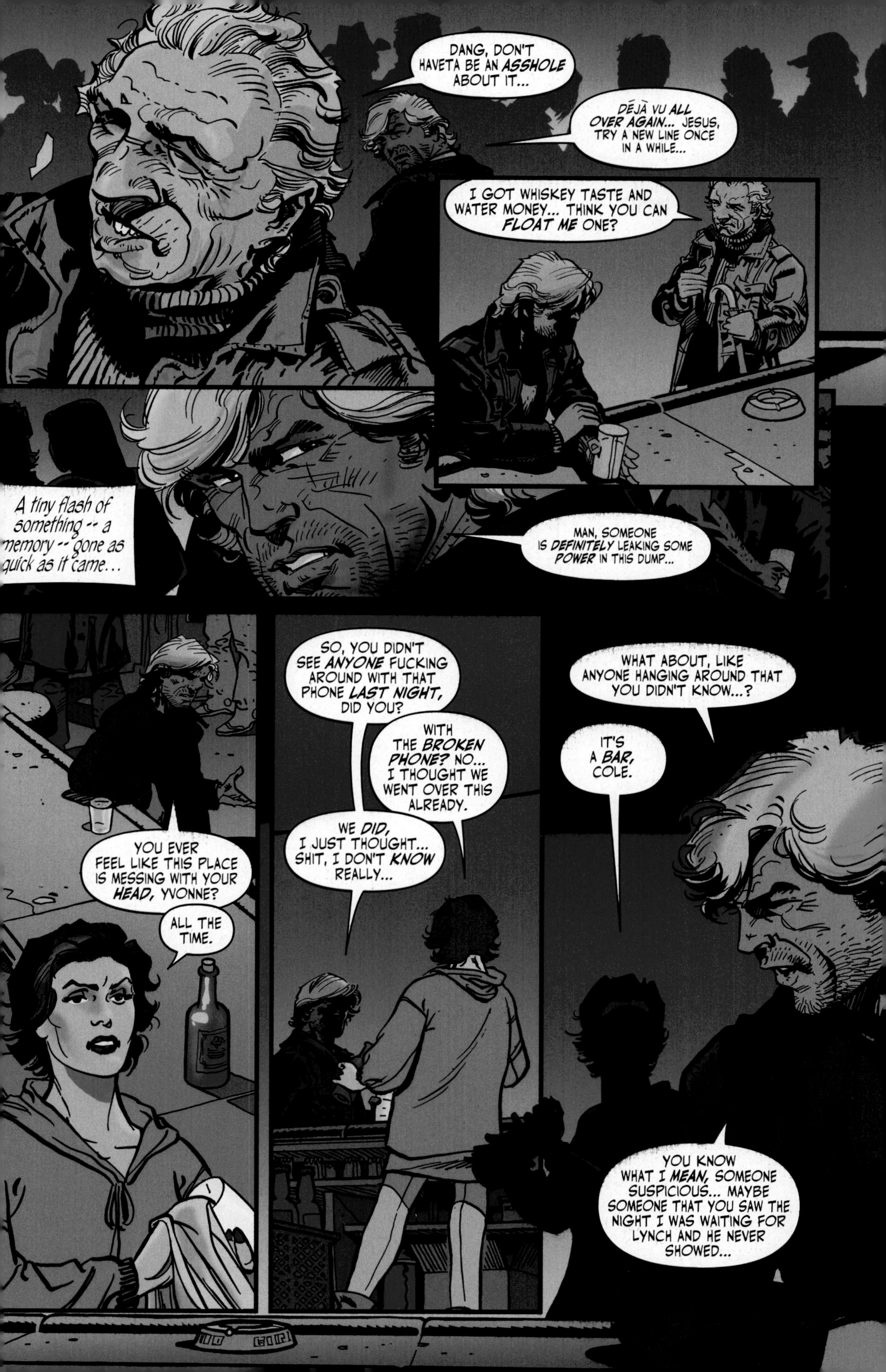

DANG, DON'T HAVETA BE AN ASSHOLE ABOUT IT...
DÉJÀ VU ALL OVER AGAIN... JESUS, TRY A NEW LINE ONCE IN A WHILE...
I GOT WHISKEY TASTE AND WATER MONEY... THINK YOU CAN FLOAT ME ONE?
A tiny flash of something -- a memory -- gone as quick as it came...
MAN, SOMEONE IS DEFINITELY LEAKING SOME POWER IN THIS DUMP...
YOU EVER FEEL LIKE THIS PLACE IS MESSING WITH YOUR HEAD, YVONNE?
ALL THE TIME.
SO, YOU DIDN'T SEE ANYONE FUCKING AROUND WITH THAT PHONE LAST NIGHT, DID YOU?
WITH THE BROKEN PHONE? NO... I THOUGHT WE WENT OVER THIS ALREADY.
WE DID, I JUST THOUGHT... SHIT, I DON'T KNOW REALLY...
WHAT ABOUT, LIKE ANYONE HANGING AROUND THAT YOU DIDN'T KNOW...?
IT'S A BAR, COLE.
YOU KNOW WHAT I MEAN, SOMEONE SUSPICIOUS... MAYBE SOMEONE THAT YOU SAW THE NIGHT I WAS WAITING FOR LYNCH AND HE NEVER SHOWED...

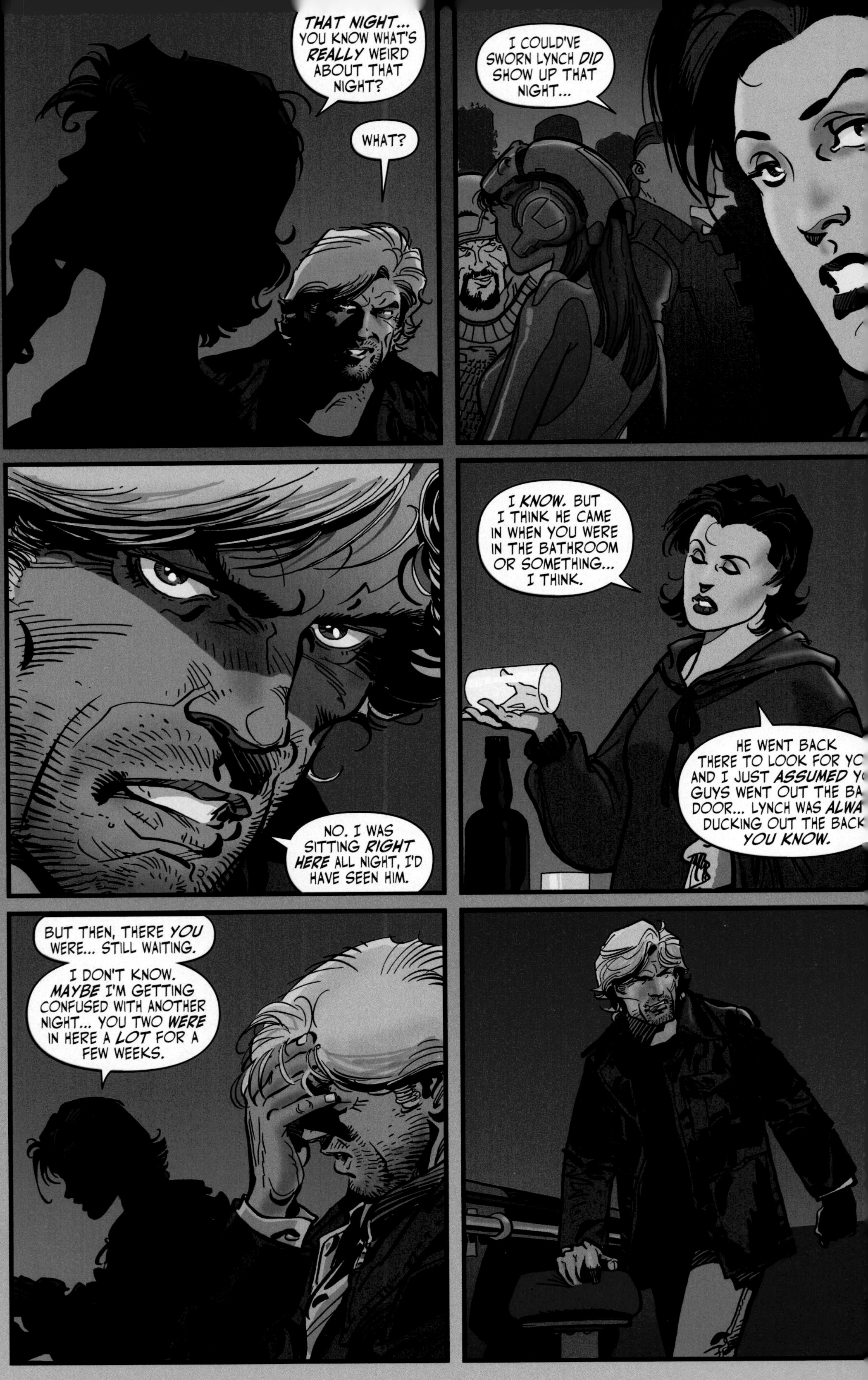
THAT NIGHT... YOU KNOW WHAT'S REALLY WEIRD ABOUT THAT NIGHT?
WHAT?
I COULD'VE SWORN LYNCH DID SHOW UP THAT NIGHT...
NO. I WAS SITTING RIGHT HERE ALL NIGHT, I'D HAVE SEEN HIM.
I KNOW. BUT I THINK HE CAME IN WHEN YOU WERE IN THE BATHROOM OR SOMETHING... I THINK.
HE WENT BACK THERE TO LOOK FOR YO AND I JUST ASSUMED YO GUYS WENT OUT THE BA DOOR... LYNCH WAS ALWA DUCKING OUT THE BACK YOU KNOW.
BUT THEN, THERE YOU WERE... STILL WAITING.
I DON'T KNOW. MAYBE I'M GETTING CONFUSED WITH ANOTHER NIGHT... YOU TWO WERE IN HERE A LOT FOR A FEW WEEKS.

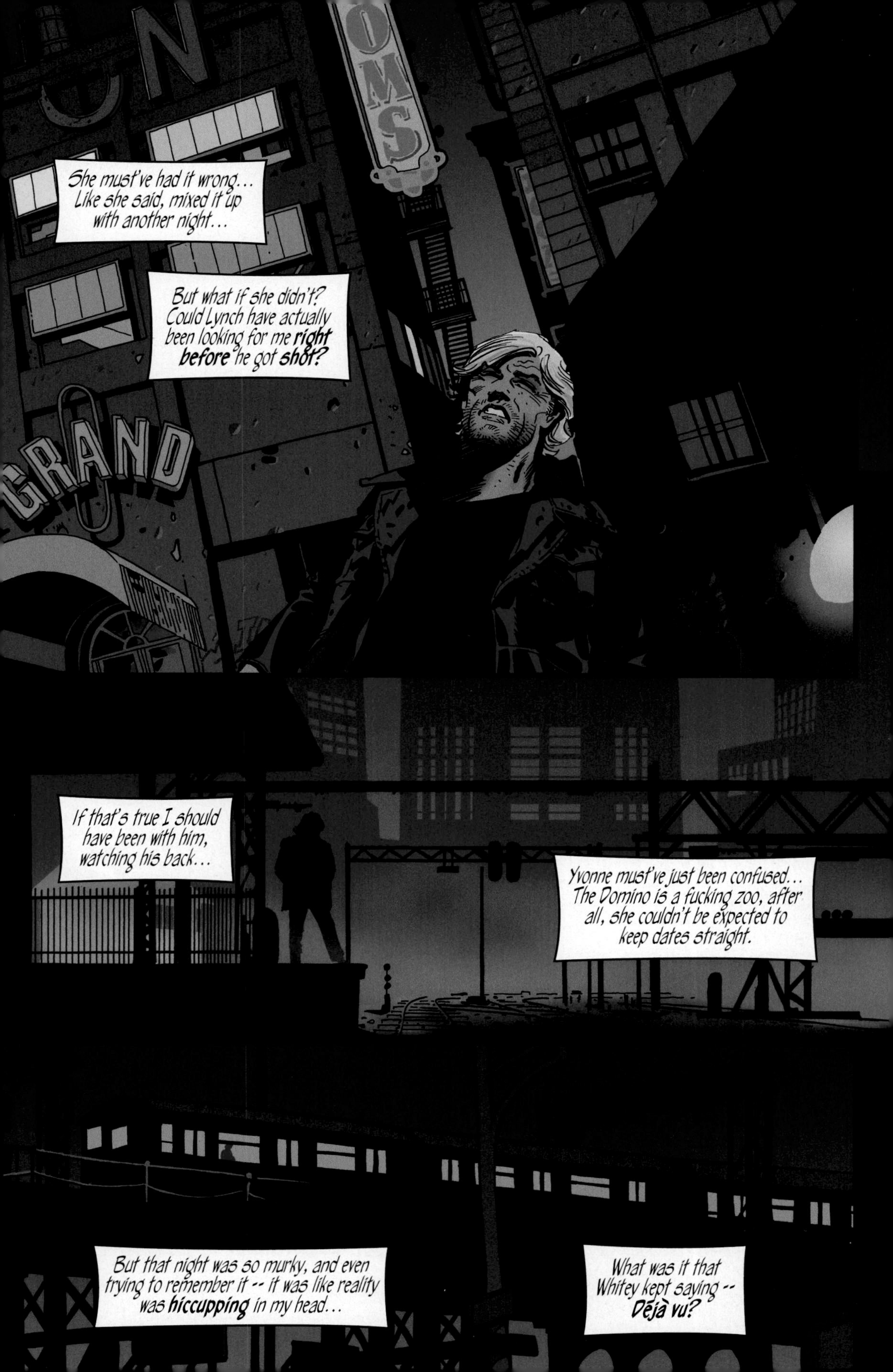
She must've had it wrong... Like she said, mixed it up with another night...
But what if she didn't? Could Lynch have actually been looking for me **right before** he got **shot?**
GRAND
If that's true I should have been with him, watching his back...
Yvonne must've just been confused... The Domino is a fucking zoo, after all, she couldn't be expected to keep dates straight.
But that night was so murky, and even trying to remember it -- it was like reality was **hiccupping** in my head...
What was it that Whitey kept saying -- **Déjà vu?**

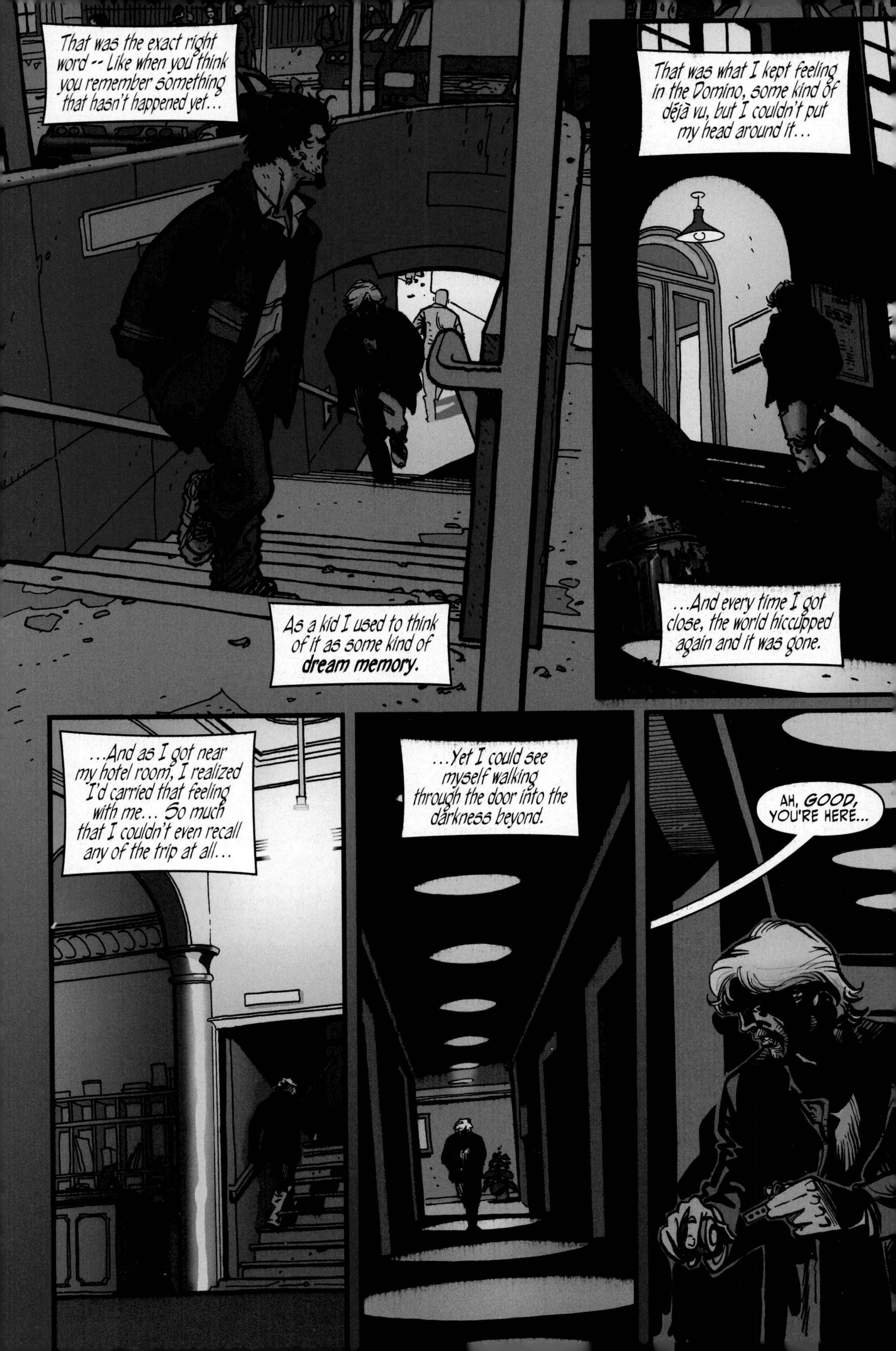
That was the exact right word -- Like when you think you remember something that hasn't happened yet...
As a kid I used to think of it as some kind of **dream memory.**
That was what I kept feeling in the Domino, some kind of déjà vu, but I couldn't put my head around it...
...And every time I got close, the world hiccupped again and it was gone.
...And as I got near my hotel room, I realized I'd carried that feeling with me... So much that I couldn't even recall any of the trip at all...
...Yet I could see myself walking through the door into the darkness beyond.
AH, *GOOD,* YOU'RE HERE...

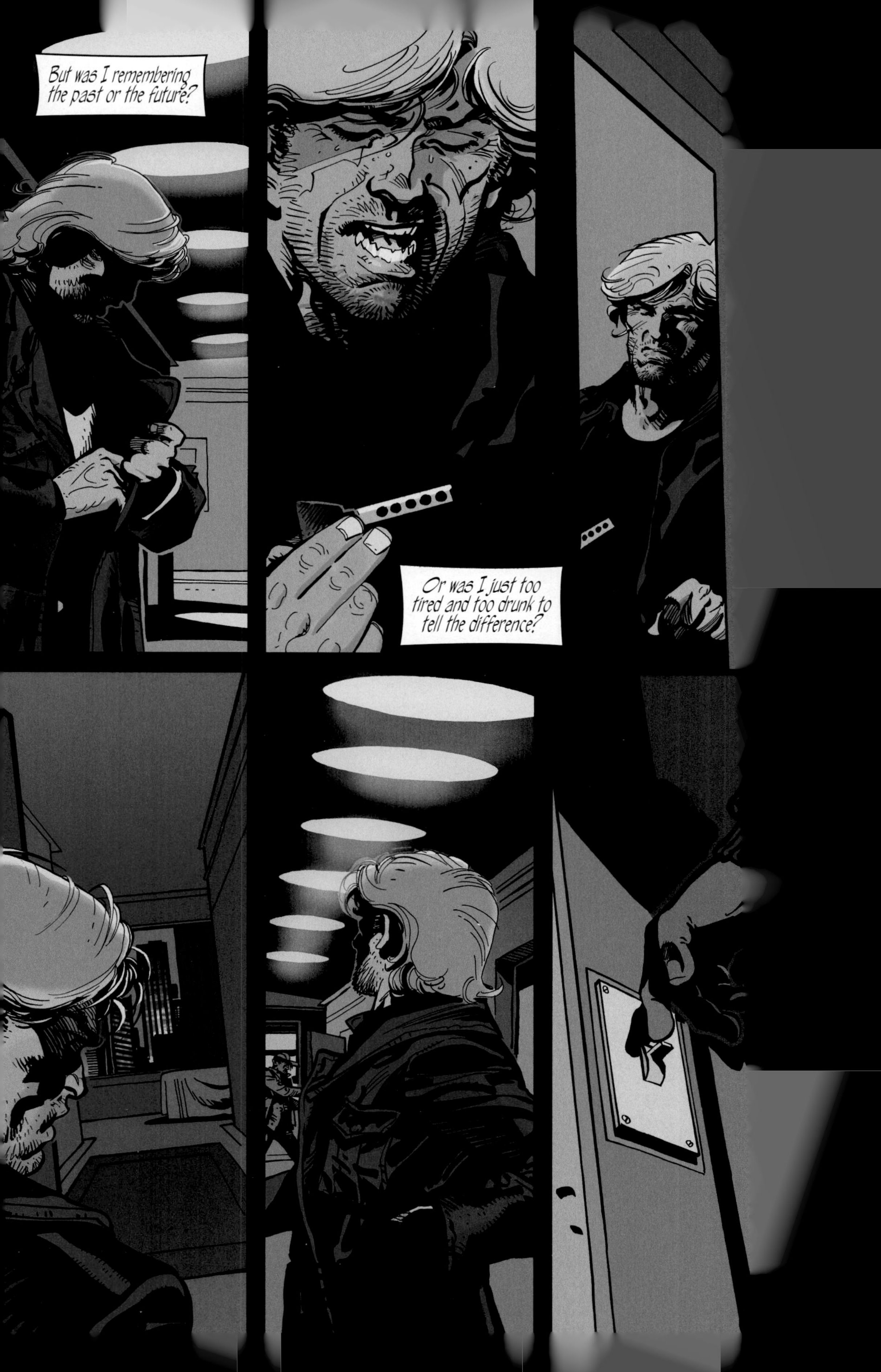
But was I remembering the past or the future?
Or was I just too tired and too drunk to tell the difference?

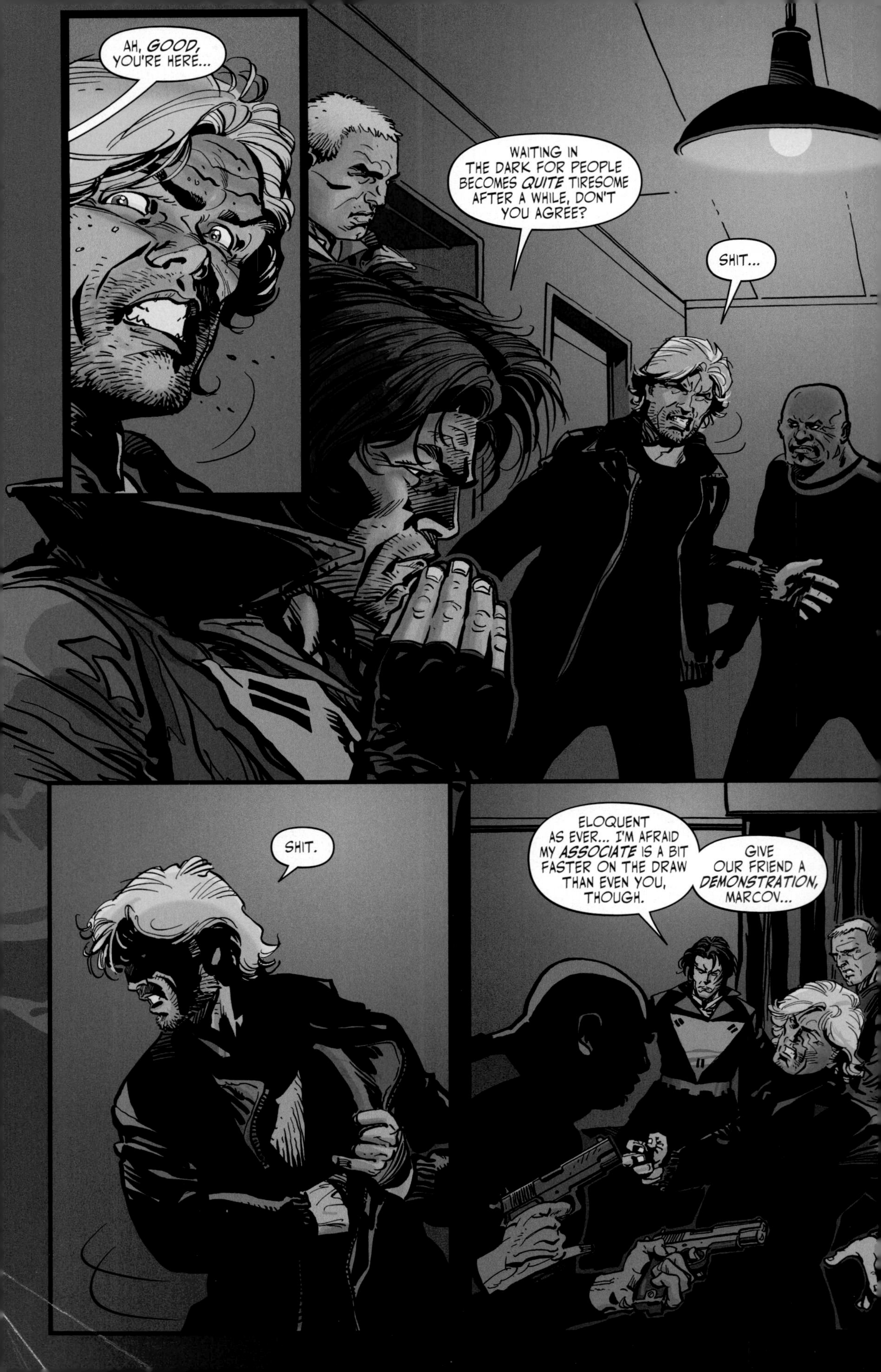
AH, *GOOD*, YOU'RE HERE...
WAITING IN THE DARK FOR PEOPLE BECOMES *QUITE* TIRESOME AFTER A WHILE, DON'T YOU AGREE?
SHIT...
SHIT.
ELOQUENT AS EVER... I'M AFRAID MY *ASSOCIATE* IS A BIT FASTER ON THE DRAW THAN EVEN YOU, THOUGH.
GIVE OUR FRIEND A *DEMONSTRATION*, MARCOV...

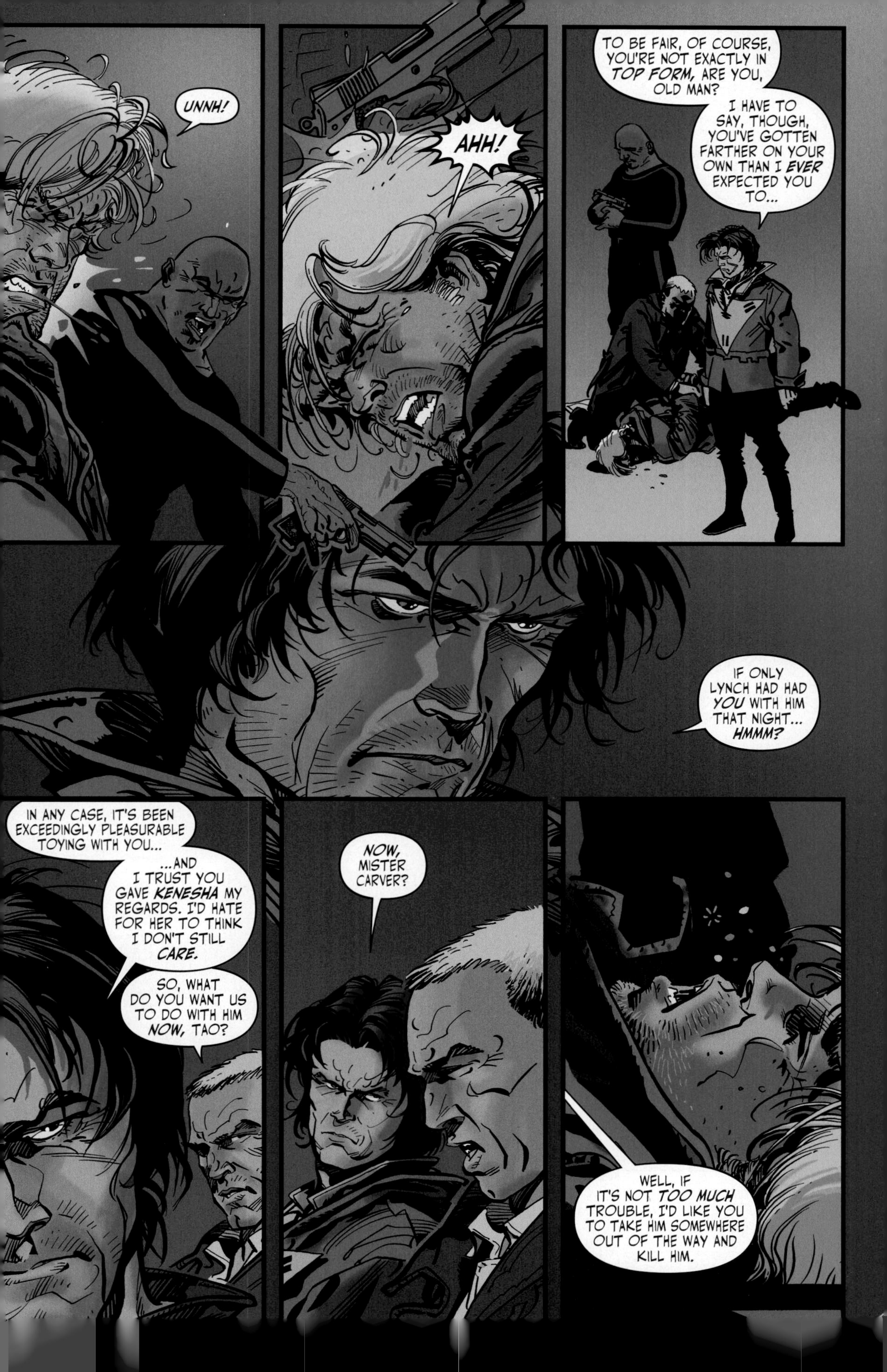
UNNH!
AHH!
TO BE FAIR, OF COURSE, YOU'RE NOT EXACTLY IN *TOP FORM,* ARE YOU, OLD MAN?
I HAVE TO SAY, THOUGH, YOU'VE GOTTEN FARTHER ON YOUR OWN THAN I *EVER* EXPECTED YOU TO...
IF ONLY LYNCH HAD HAD *YOU* WITH HIM THAT NIGHT... *HMMM?*
IN ANY CASE, IT'S BEEN EXCEEDINGLY PLEASURABLE TOYING WITH YOU...
...AND I TRUST YOU GAVE *KENESHA* MY REGARDS. I'D HATE FOR HER TO THINK I DON'T STILL *CARE.*
SO, WHAT DO YOU WANT US TO DO WITH HIM *NOW,* TAO?
NOW, MISTER CARVER?
WELL, IF IT'S NOT *TOO MUCH* TROUBLE, I'D LIKE YOU TO TAKE HIM SOMEWHERE OUT OF THE WAY AND KILL HIM.

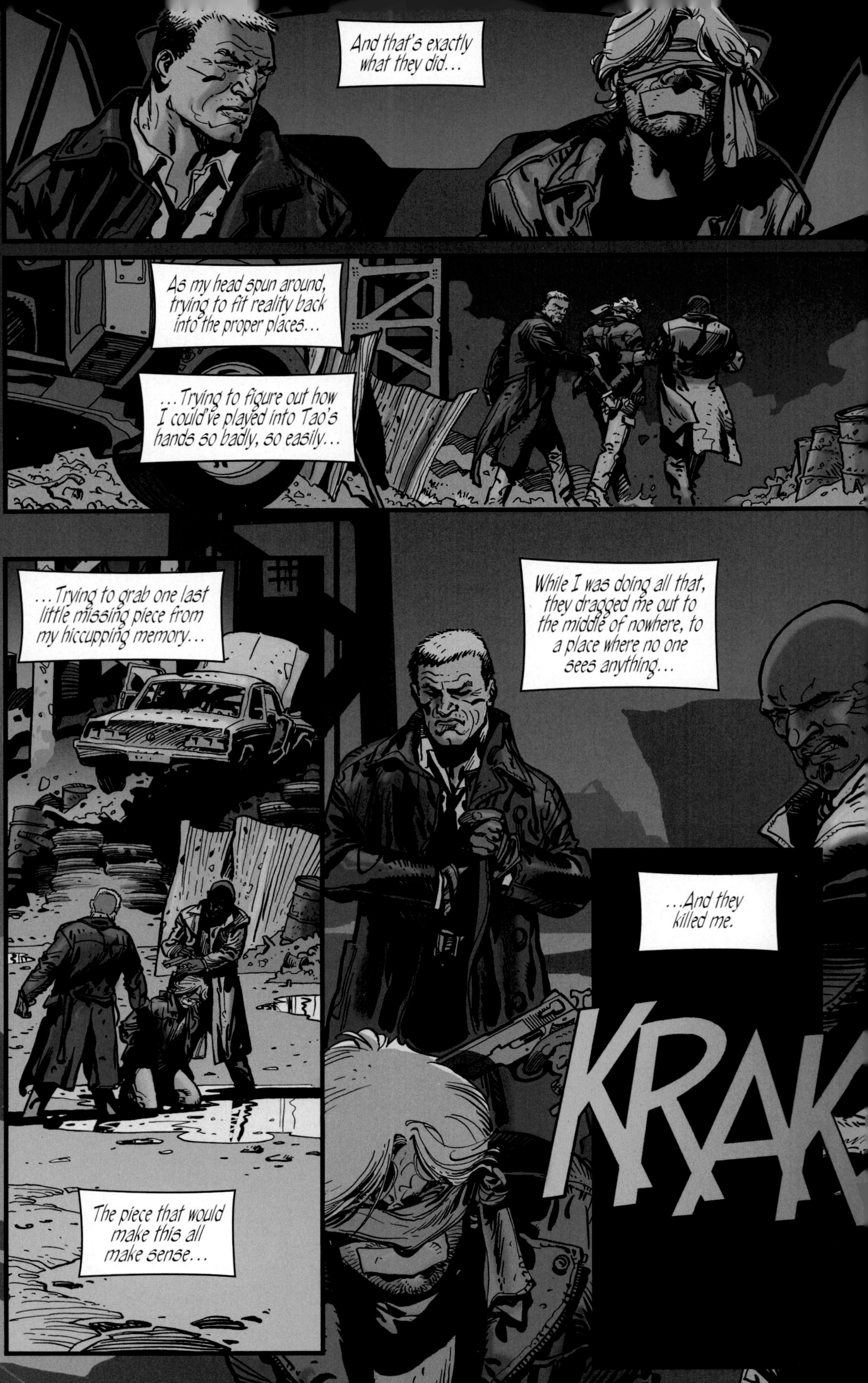
And that's exactly what they did...
As my head spun around, trying to fit reality back into the proper places...
...Trying to figure out how I could've played into Tao's hands so badly, so easily...
...Trying to grab one last little missing piece from my hiccupping memory...
The piece that would make this all make sense...
While I was doing all that, they dragged me out to the middle of nowhere, to a place where no one sees anything...
...And they killed me.
KRAK

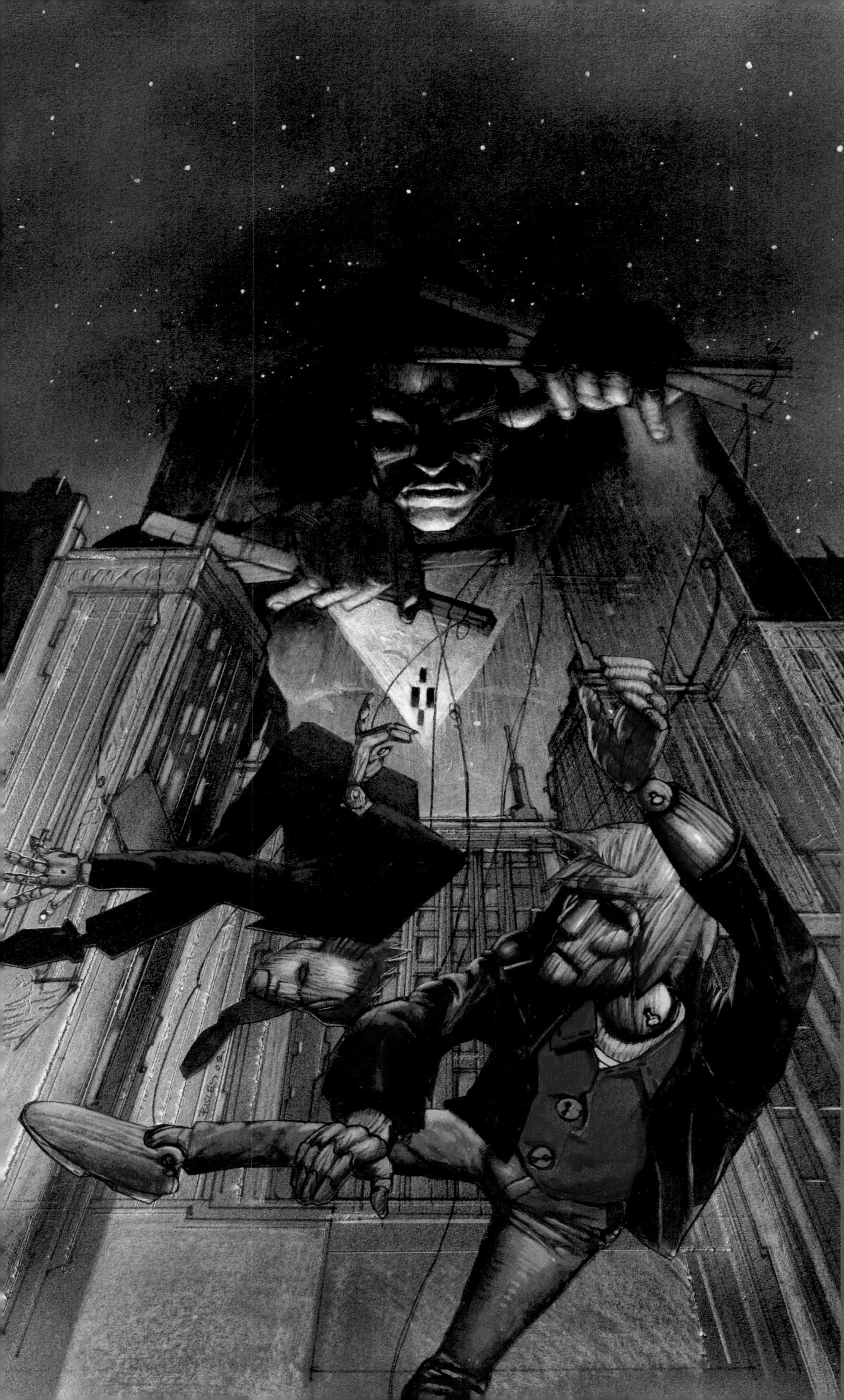

Cover by SIMON BISLEY

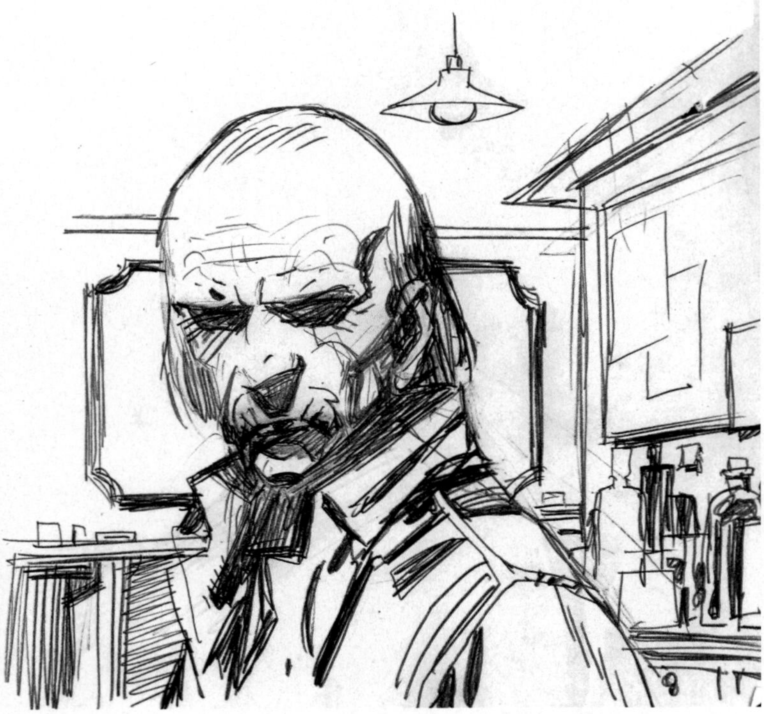

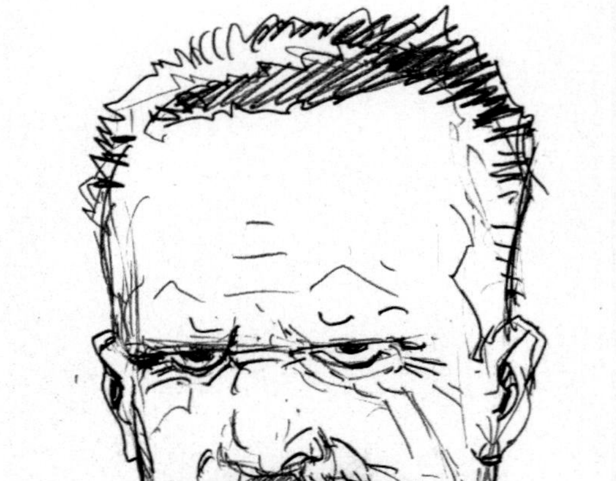

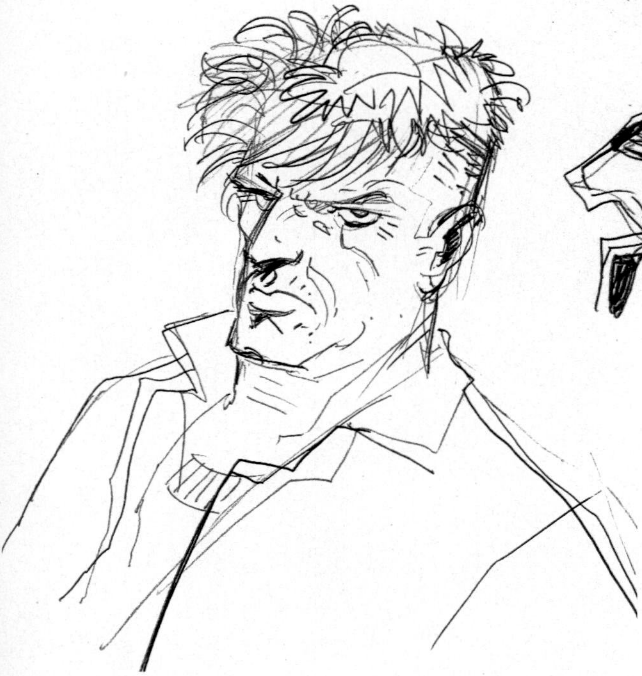

WHITEY sketches by COLIN WILSON

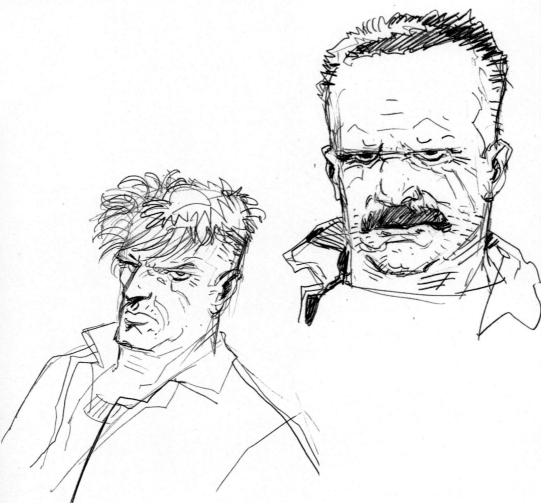

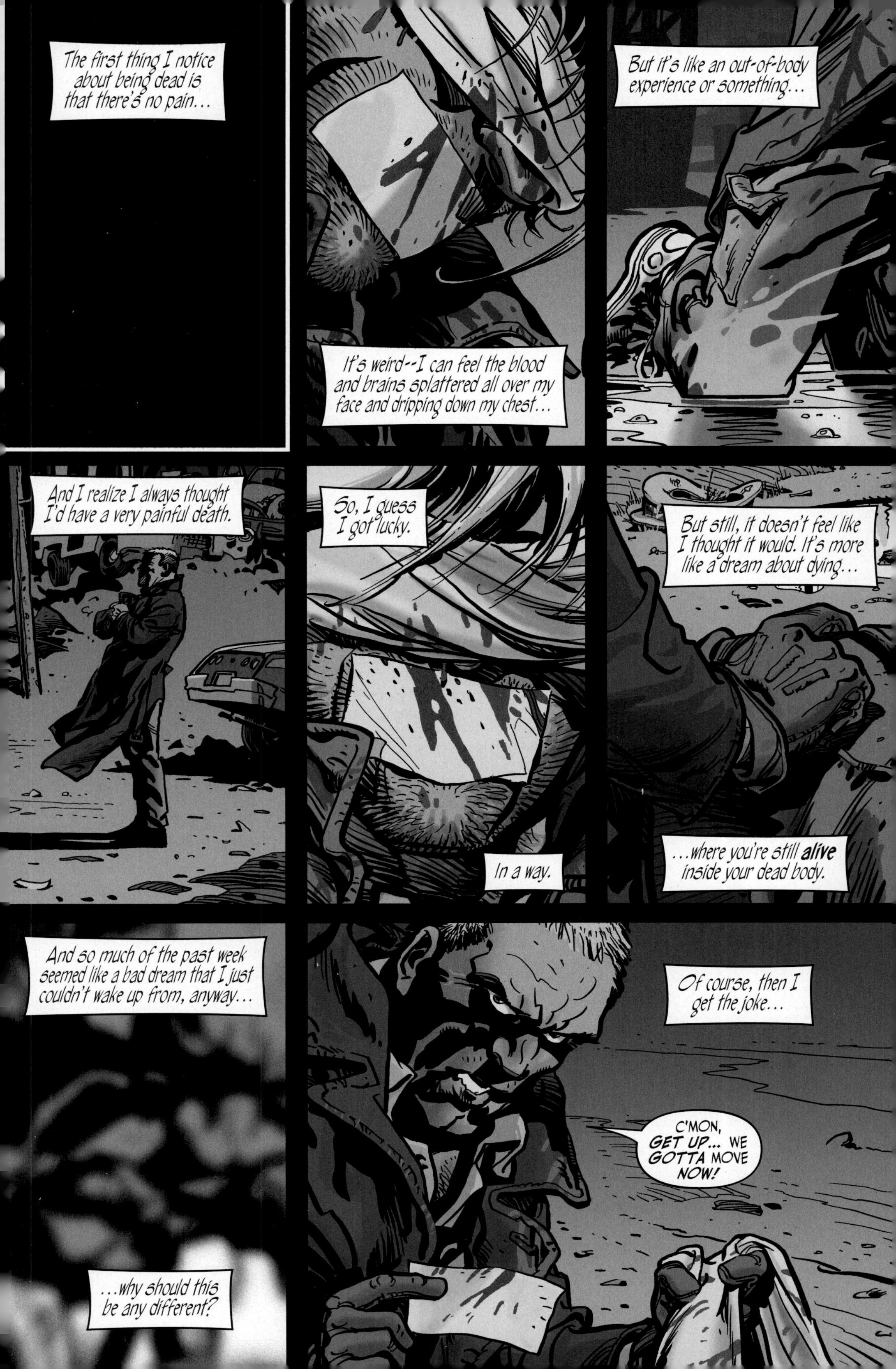
The first thing I notice about being dead is that there's no pain...
It's weird--I can feel the blood and brains splattered all over my face and dripping down my chest...
But it's like an out-of-body experience or something...
And I realize I always thought I'd have a very painful death.
So, I guess I got lucky.
In a way.
But still, it doesn't feel like I thought it would. It's more like a dream about dying...
...where you're still **alive** inside your dead body.
And so much of the past week seemed like a bad dream that I just couldn't wake up from, anyway...
...why should this be any different?
Of course, then I get the joke...
C'MON, **GET UP...** WE **GOTTA** MOVE **NOW!**

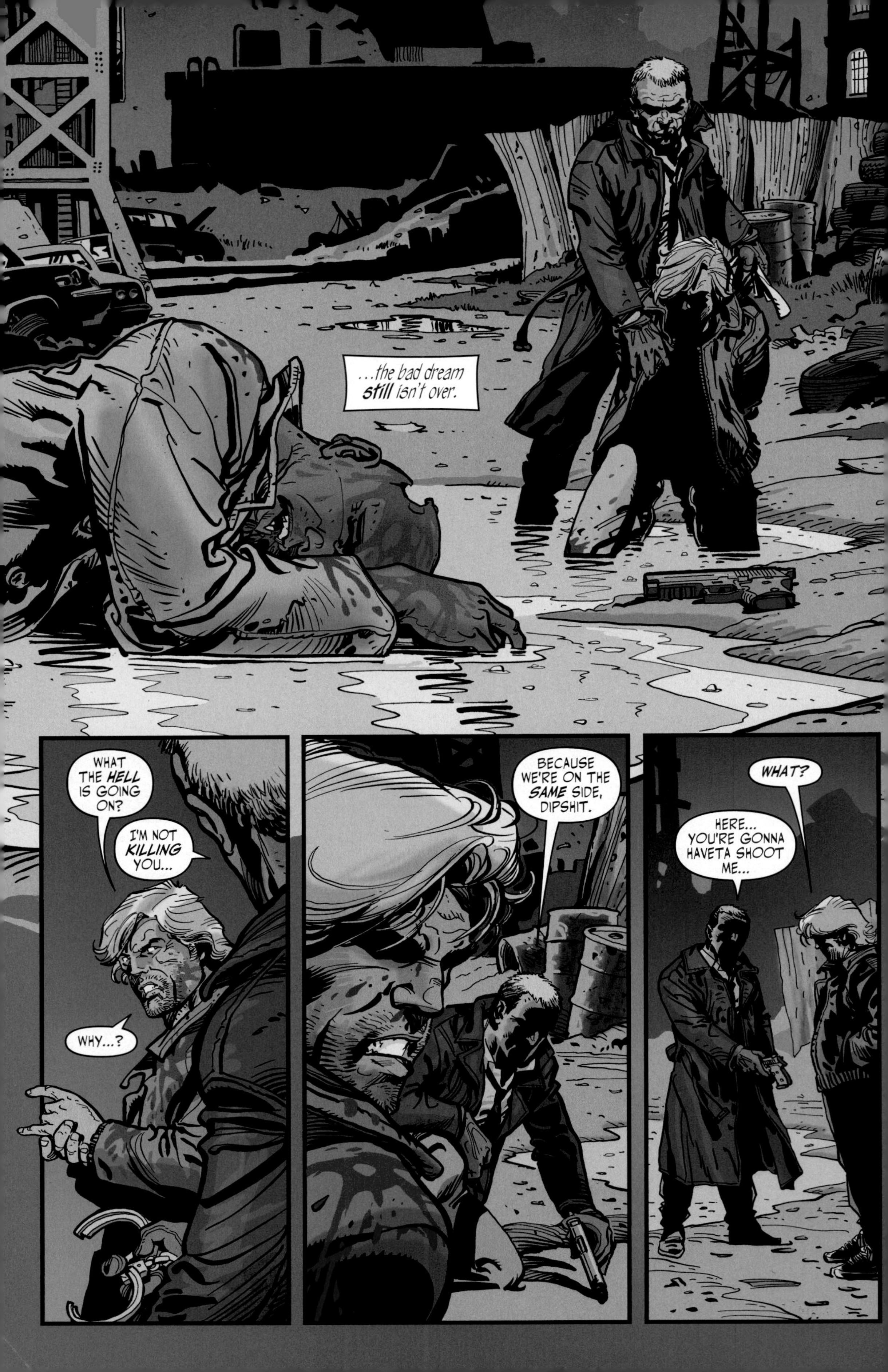
...the bad dream **still** isn't over.
WHAT THE **HELL** IS GOING ON?
I'M NOT **KILLING** YOU...
WHY...?
BECAUSE WE'RE ON THE **SAME** SIDE, DIPSHIT.
WHAT?
HERE... YOU'RE GONNA HAVETA SHOOT ME...

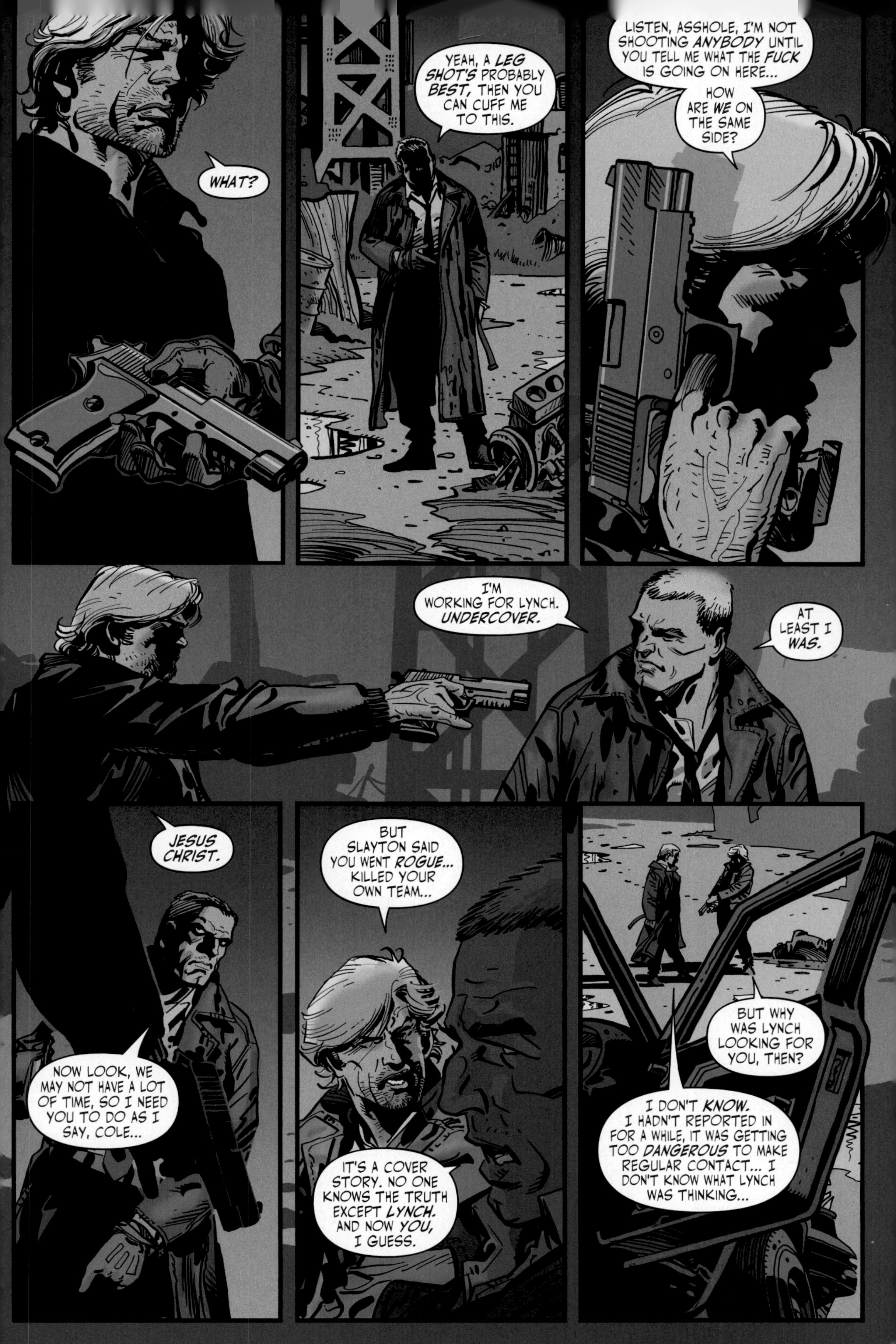
WHAT?
YEAH, A LEG SHOT'S PROBABLY BEST, THEN YOU CAN CUFF ME TO THIS.
LISTEN, ASSHOLE, I'M NOT SHOOTING ANYBODY UNTIL YOU TELL ME WHAT THE FUCK IS GOING ON HERE...
HOW ARE WE ON THE SAME SIDE?
I'M WORKING FOR LYNCH. UNDERCOVER.
AT LEAST I WAS.
JESUS CHRIST.
NOW LOOK, WE MAY NOT HAVE A LOT OF TIME, SO I NEED YOU TO DO AS I SAY, COLE...
BUT SLAYTON SAID YOU WENT ROGUE... KILLED YOUR OWN TEAM...
IT'S A COVER STORY. NO ONE KNOWS THE TRUTH EXCEPT LYNCH. AND NOW YOU, I GUESS.
BUT WHY WAS LYNCH LOOKING FOR YOU, THEN?
I DON'T KNOW. I HADN'T REPORTED IN FOR A WHILE, IT WAS GETTING TOO DANGEROUS TO MAKE REGULAR CONTACT... I DON'T KNOW WHAT LYNCH WAS THINKING...

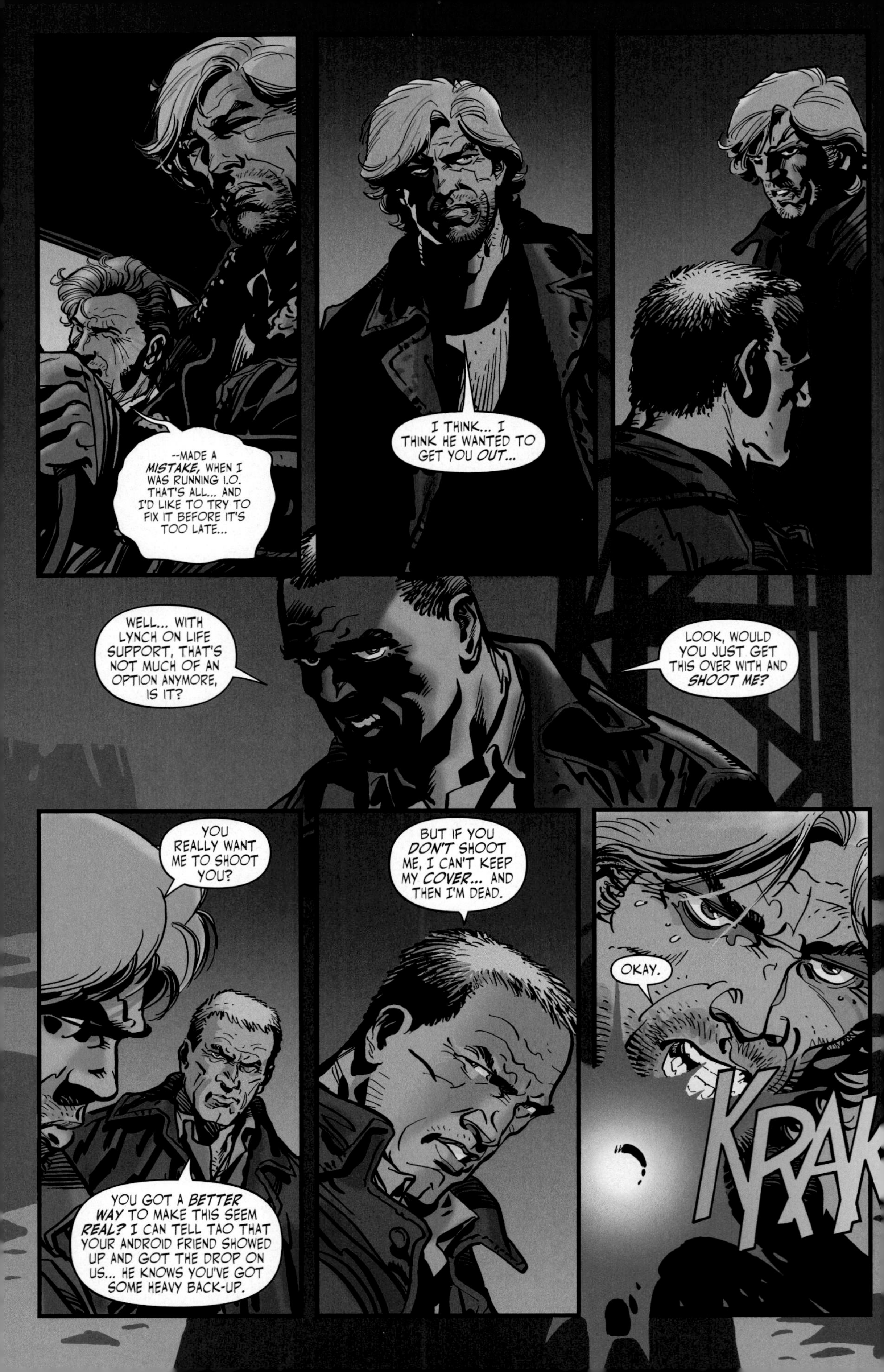
--MADE A MISTAKE, WHEN I WAS RUNNING I.O. THAT'S ALL... AND I'D LIKE TO TRY TO FIX IT BEFORE IT'S TOO LATE...
I THINK... I THINK HE WANTED TO GET YOU OUT...
WELL... WITH LYNCH ON LIFE SUPPORT, THAT'S NOT MUCH OF AN OPTION ANYMORE, IS IT?
LOOK, WOULD YOU JUST GET THIS OVER WITH AND SHOOT ME?
YOU REALLY WANT ME TO SHOOT YOU?
YOU GOT A BETTER WAY TO MAKE THIS SEEM REAL? I CAN TELL TAO THAT YOUR ANDROID FRIEND SHOWED UP AND GOT THE DROP ON US... HE KNOWS YOU'VE GOT SOME HEAVY BACK-UP.
BUT IF YOU DON'T SHOOT ME, I CAN'T KEEP MY COVER... AND THEN I'M DEAD.
OKAY.
KRAK

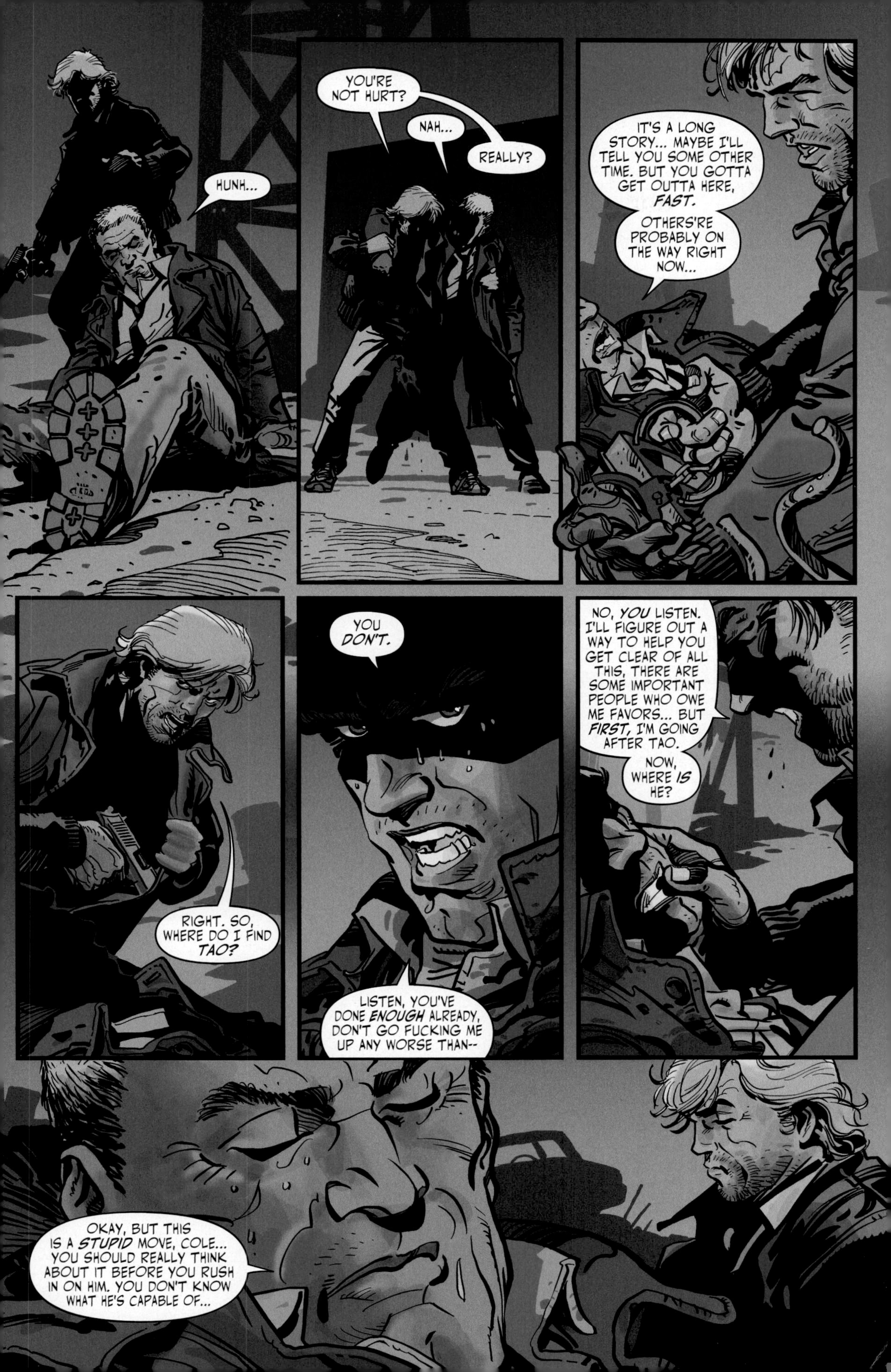
HUNH...
YOU'RE NOT HURT?
NAH...
REALLY?
IT'S A LONG STORY... MAYBE I'LL TELL YOU SOME OTHER TIME. BUT YOU GOTTA GET OUTTA HERE, FAST.
OTHERS'RE PROBABLY ON THE WAY RIGHT NOW...
RIGHT. SO, WHERE DO I FIND TAO?
YOU DON'T.
LISTEN, YOU'VE DONE ENOUGH ALREADY, DON'T GO FUCKING ME UP ANY WORSE THAN--
NO, YOU LISTEN. I'LL FIGURE OUT A WAY TO HELP YOU GET CLEAR OF ALL THIS, THERE ARE SOME IMPORTANT PEOPLE WHO OWE ME FAVORS... BUT FIRST, I'M GOING AFTER TAO.
NOW, WHERE IS HE?
OKAY, BUT THIS IS A STUPID MOVE, COLE... YOU SHOULD REALLY THINK ABOUT IT BEFORE YOU RUSH IN ON HIM. YOU DON'T KNOW WHAT HE'S CAPABLE OF...

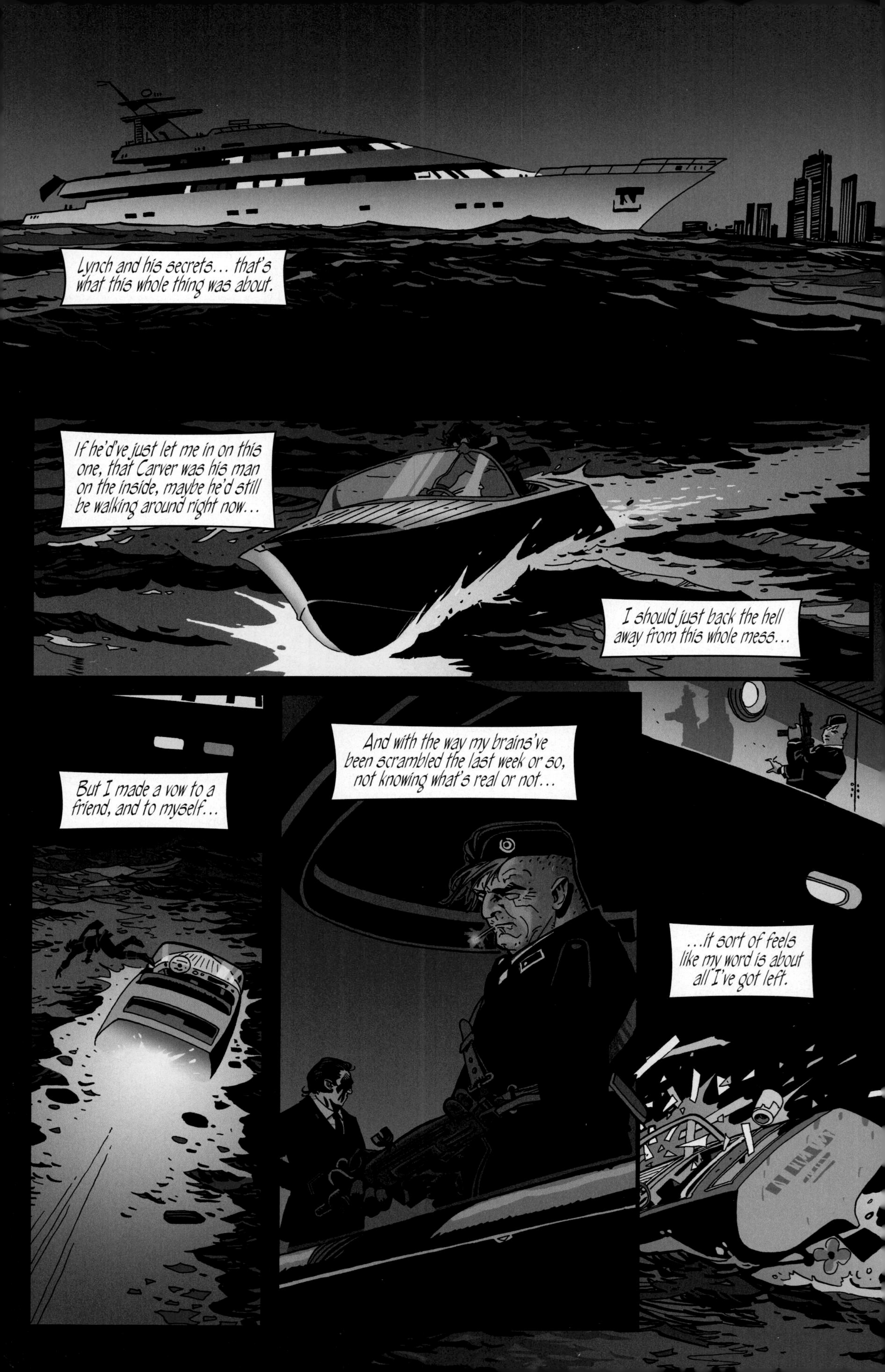
Lynch and his secrets… that's what this whole thing was about.
If he'd've just let me in on this one, that Carver was his man on the inside, maybe he'd still be walking around right now…
I should just back the hell away from this whole mess…
But I made a vow to a friend, and to myself…
And with the way my brains've been scrambled the last week or so, not knowing what's real or not…
…it sort of feels like my word is about all I've got left.

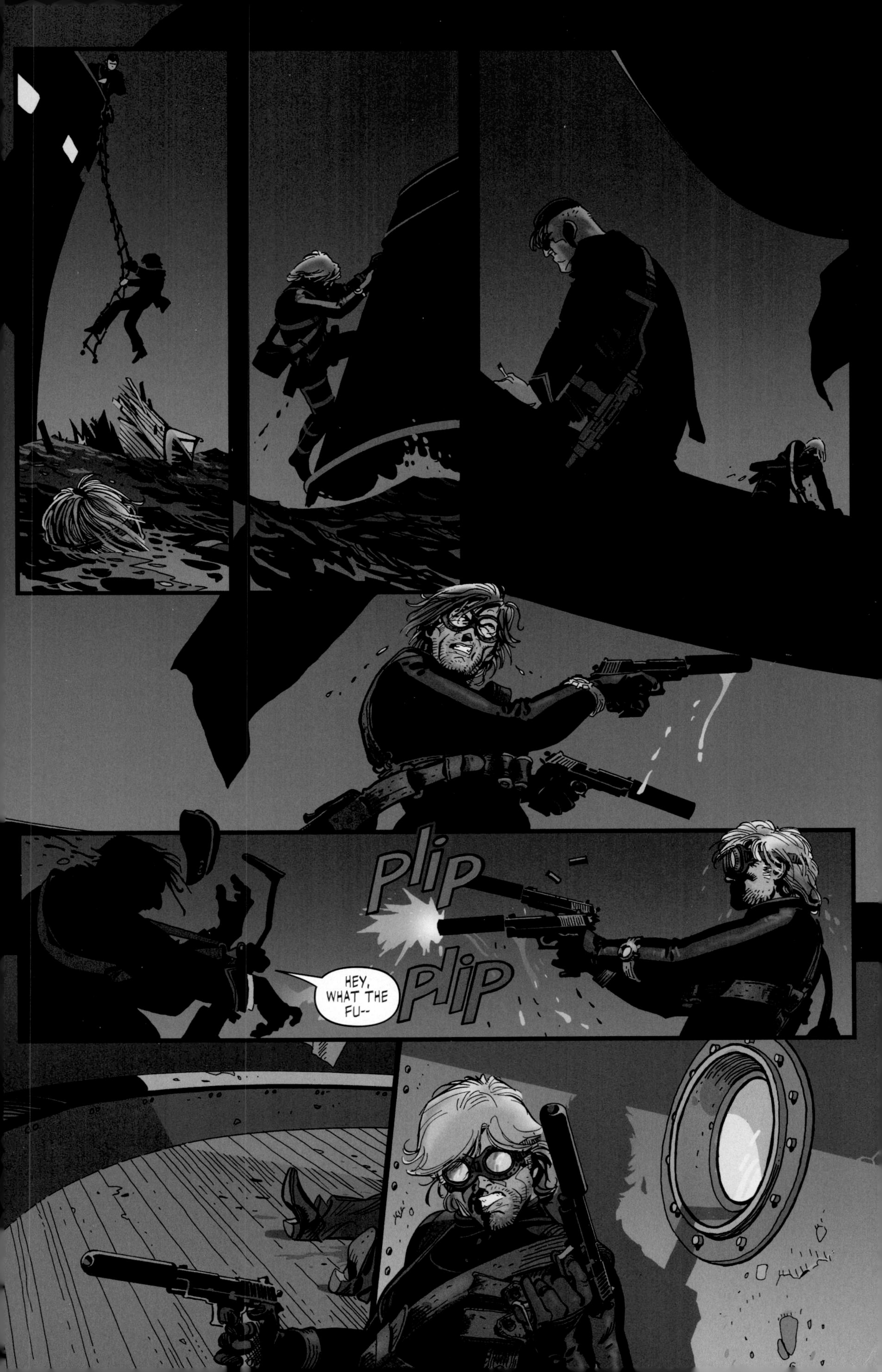
plip
HEY, WHAT THE FU--
plip

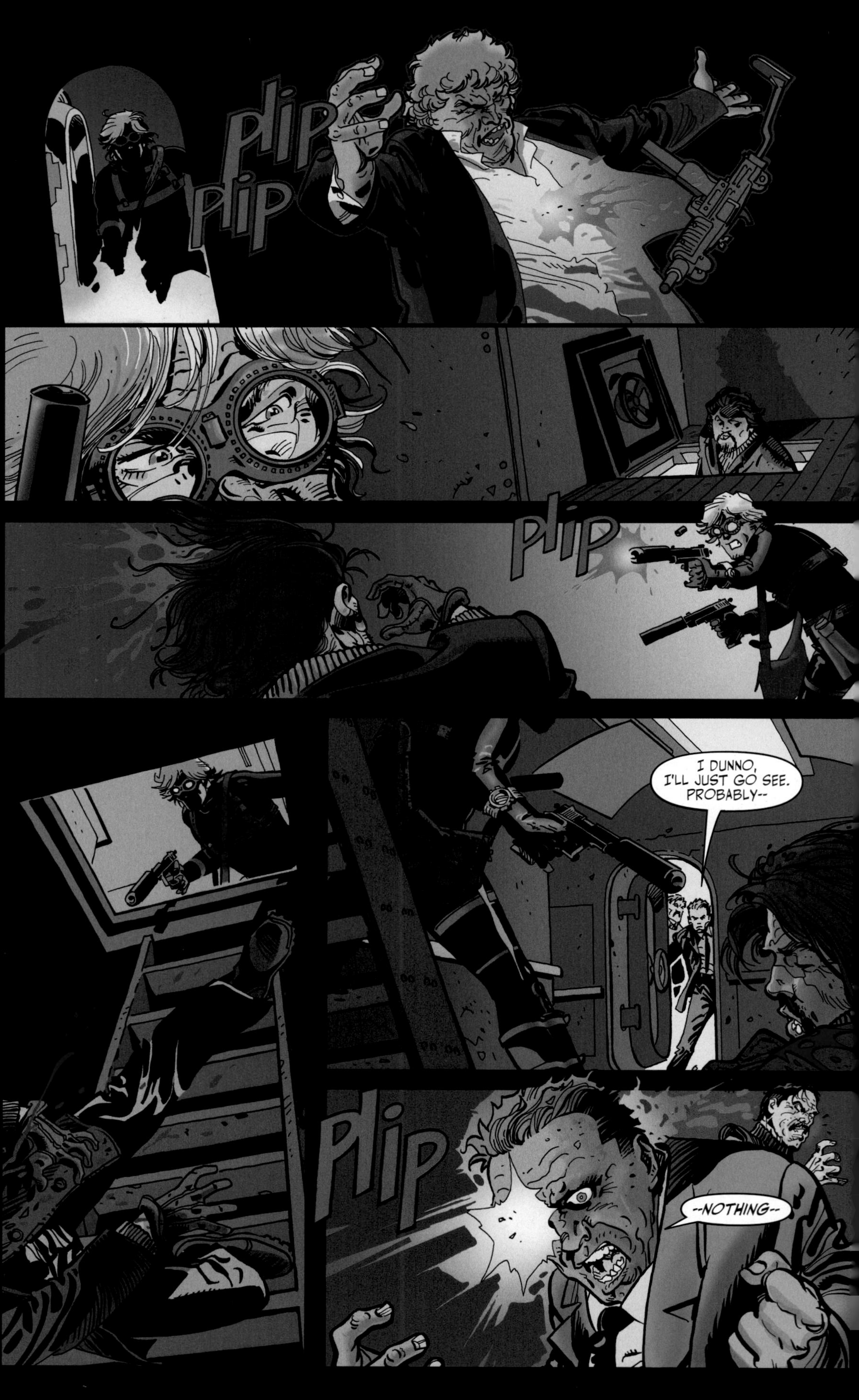

PLIP
PLIP
PLIP
I DUNNO, I'LL JUST GO SEE. PROBABLY--
PLIP
--NOTHING--

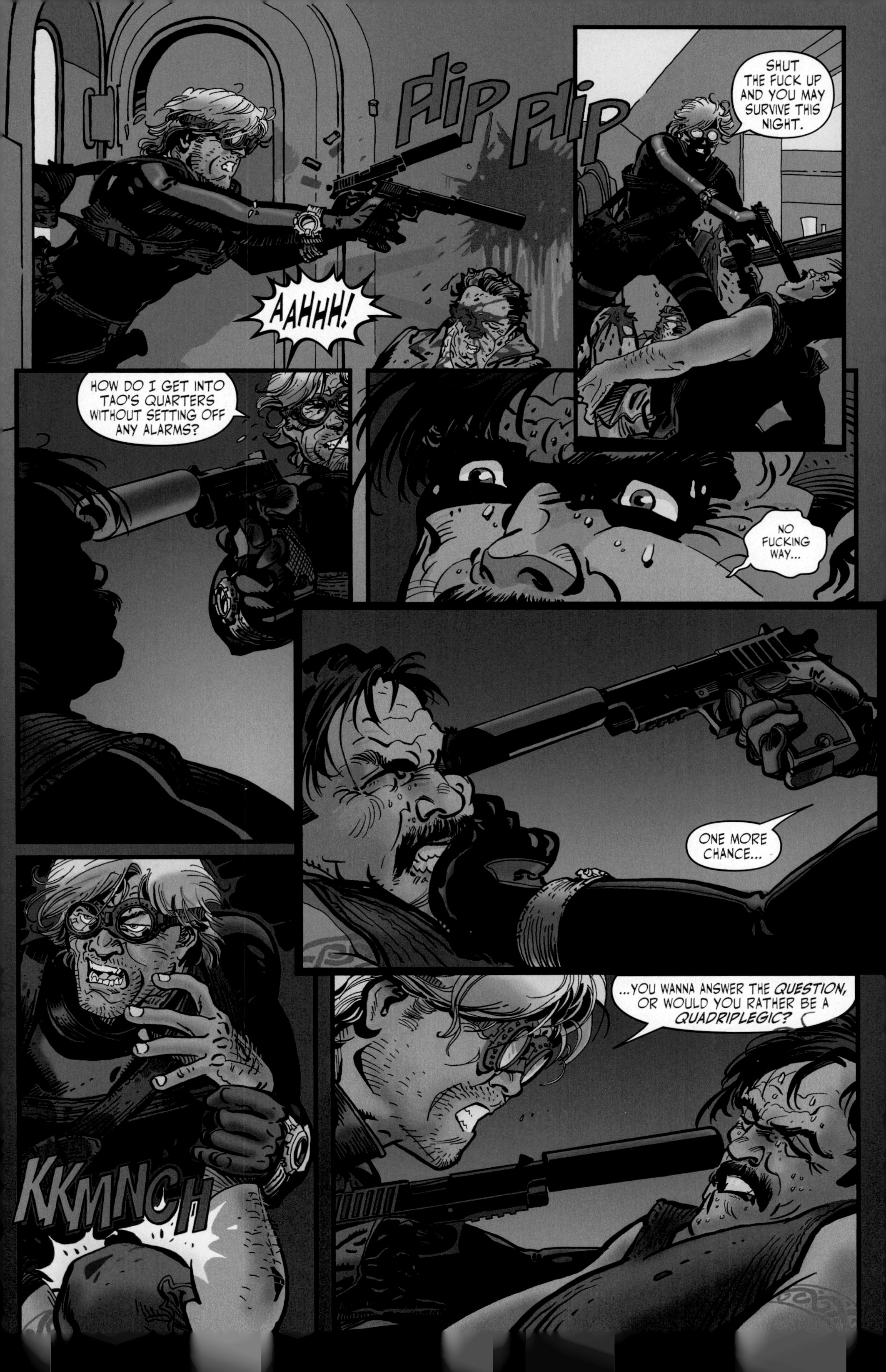
PLIP PLIP
AAHHH!
SHUT THE FUCK UP AND YOU MAY SURVIVE THIS NIGHT.
HOW DO I GET INTO TAO'S QUARTERS WITHOUT SETTING OFF ANY ALARMS?
NO FUCKING WAY...
ONE MORE CHANCE...
KKMNCH
...YOU WANNA ANSWER THE *QUESTION*, OR WOULD YOU RATHER BE A *QUADRIPLEGIC*?

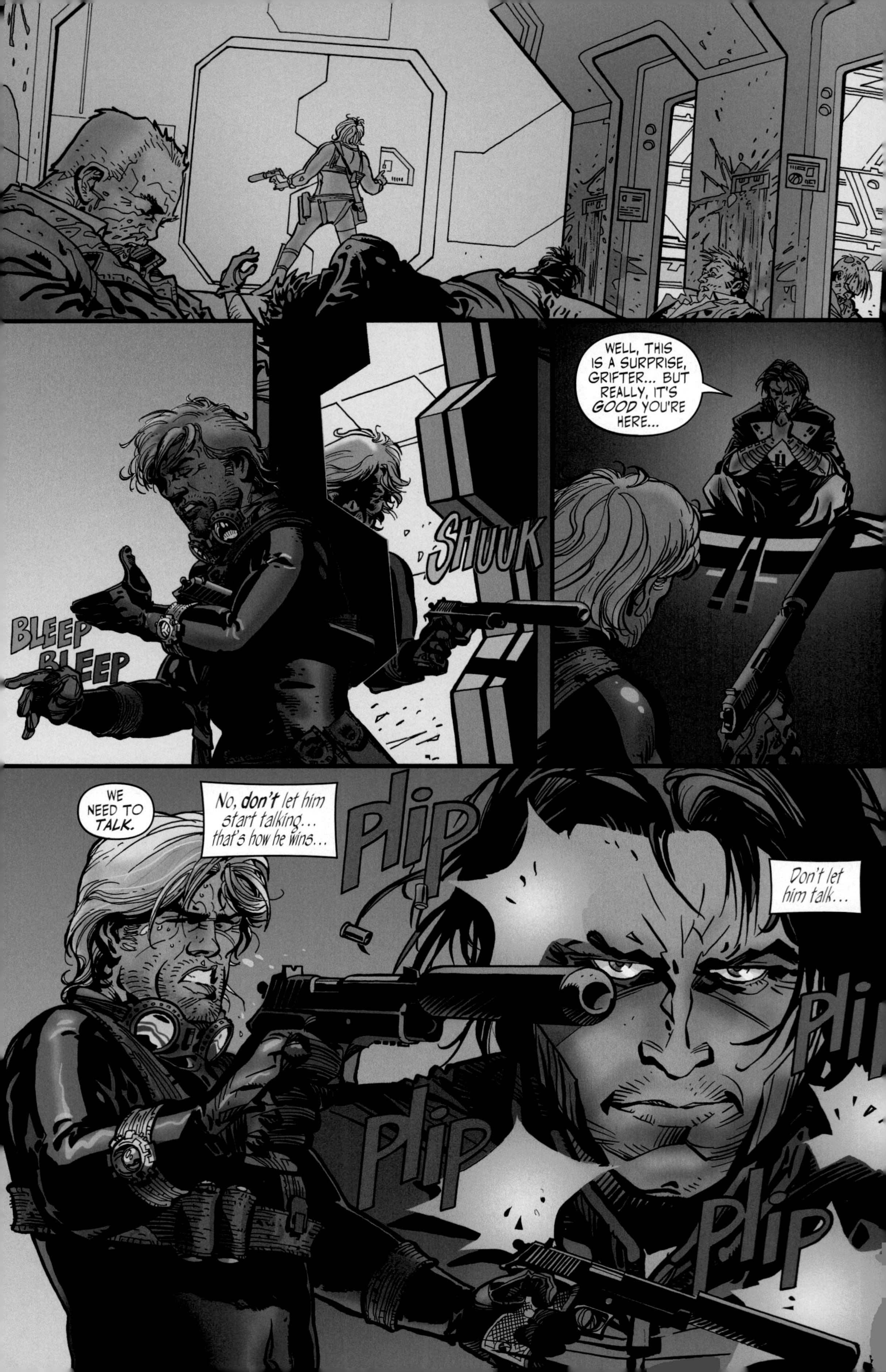
BLEEP
BLEEP
SHUUK
WELL, THIS IS A SURPRISE, GRIFTER... BUT REALLY, IT'S *GOOD* YOU'RE HERE...
WE NEED TO **TALK.**
No, **don't** let him start talking... that's how he wins...
plip
Don't let him talk...
plip
plip
plip

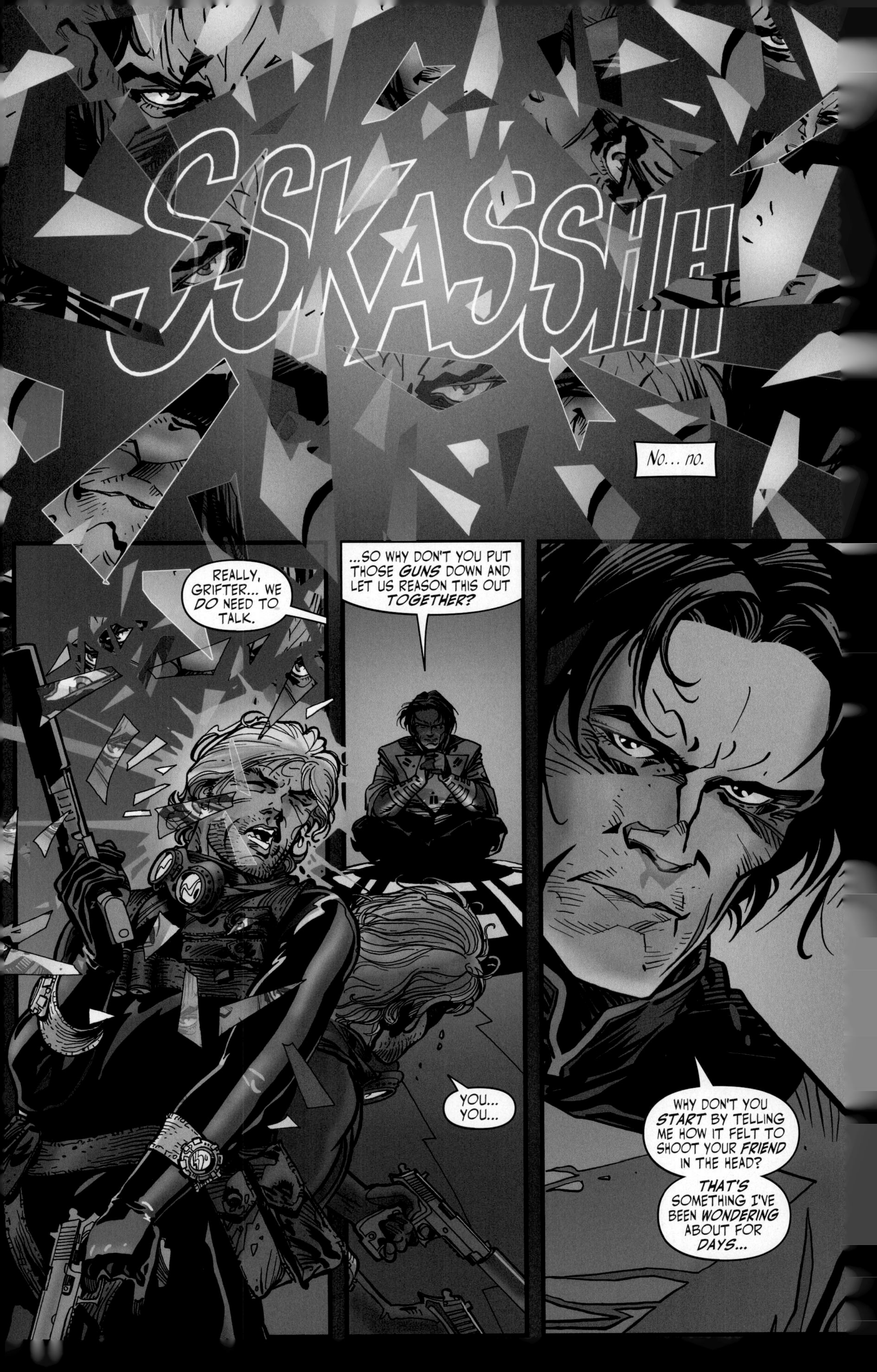
SSKASSHH
No... no.
REALLY, GRIFTER... WE DO NEED TO TALK.
...SO WHY DON'T YOU PUT THOSE GUNS DOWN AND LET US REASON THIS OUT TOGETHER?
YOU... YOU...
WHY DON'T YOU START BY TELLING ME HOW IT FELT TO SHOOT YOUR FRIEND IN THE HEAD?
THAT'S SOMETHING I'VE BEEN WONDERING ABOUT FOR DAYS...

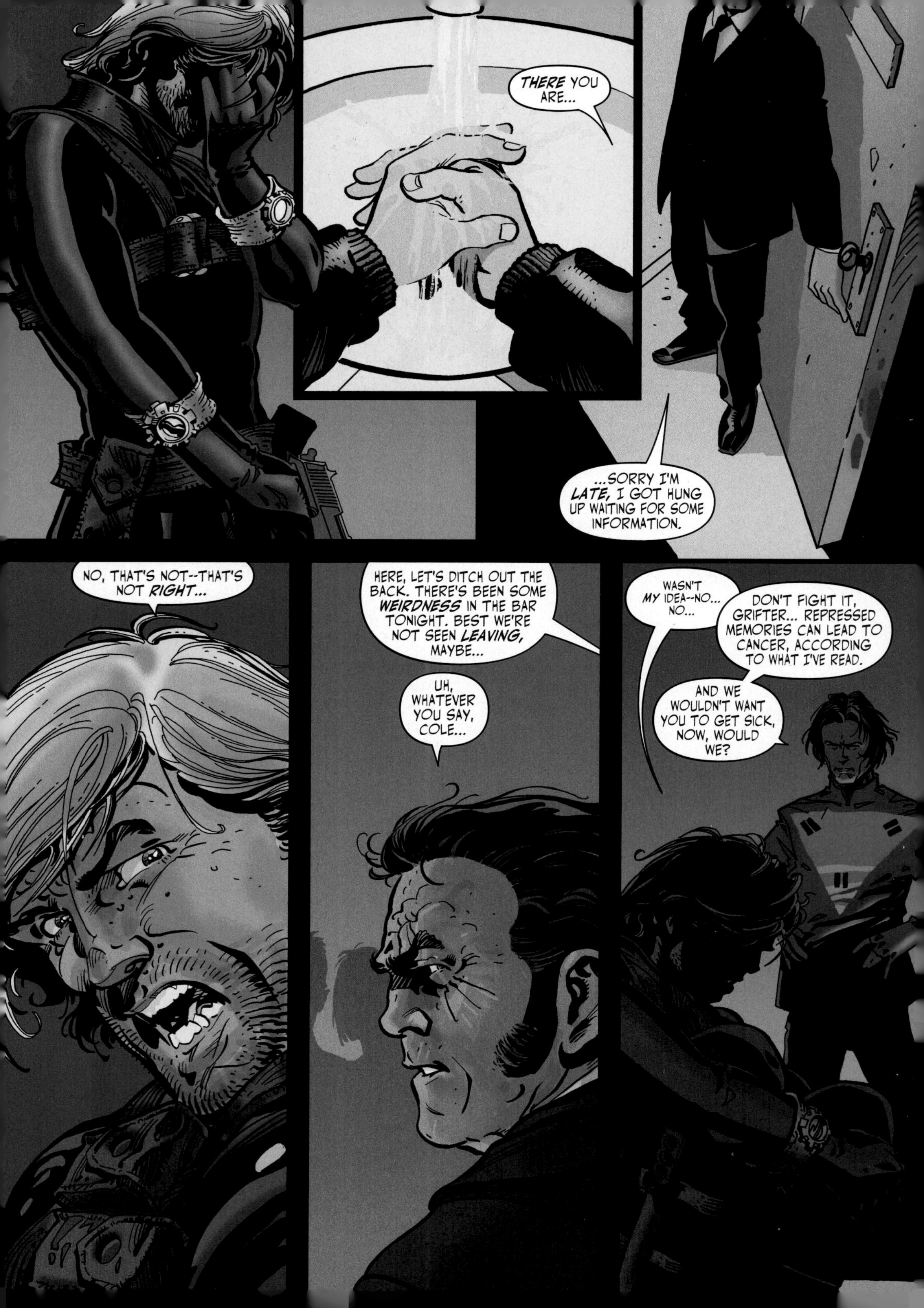
THERE YOU ARE...
...SORRY I'M LATE, I GOT HUNG UP WAITING FOR SOME INFORMATION.
NO, THAT'S NOT--THAT'S NOT RIGHT...
HERE, LET'S DITCH OUT THE BACK. THERE'S BEEN SOME WEIRDNESS IN THE BAR TONIGHT. BEST WE'RE NOT SEEN LEAVING, MAYBE...
UH, WHATEVER YOU SAY, COLE...
WASN'T MY IDEA--NO... NO...
DON'T FIGHT IT, GRIFTER... REPRESSED MEMORIES CAN LEAD TO CANCER, ACCORDING TO WHAT I'VE READ.
AND WE WOULDN'T WANT YOU TO GET SICK, NOW, WOULD WE?

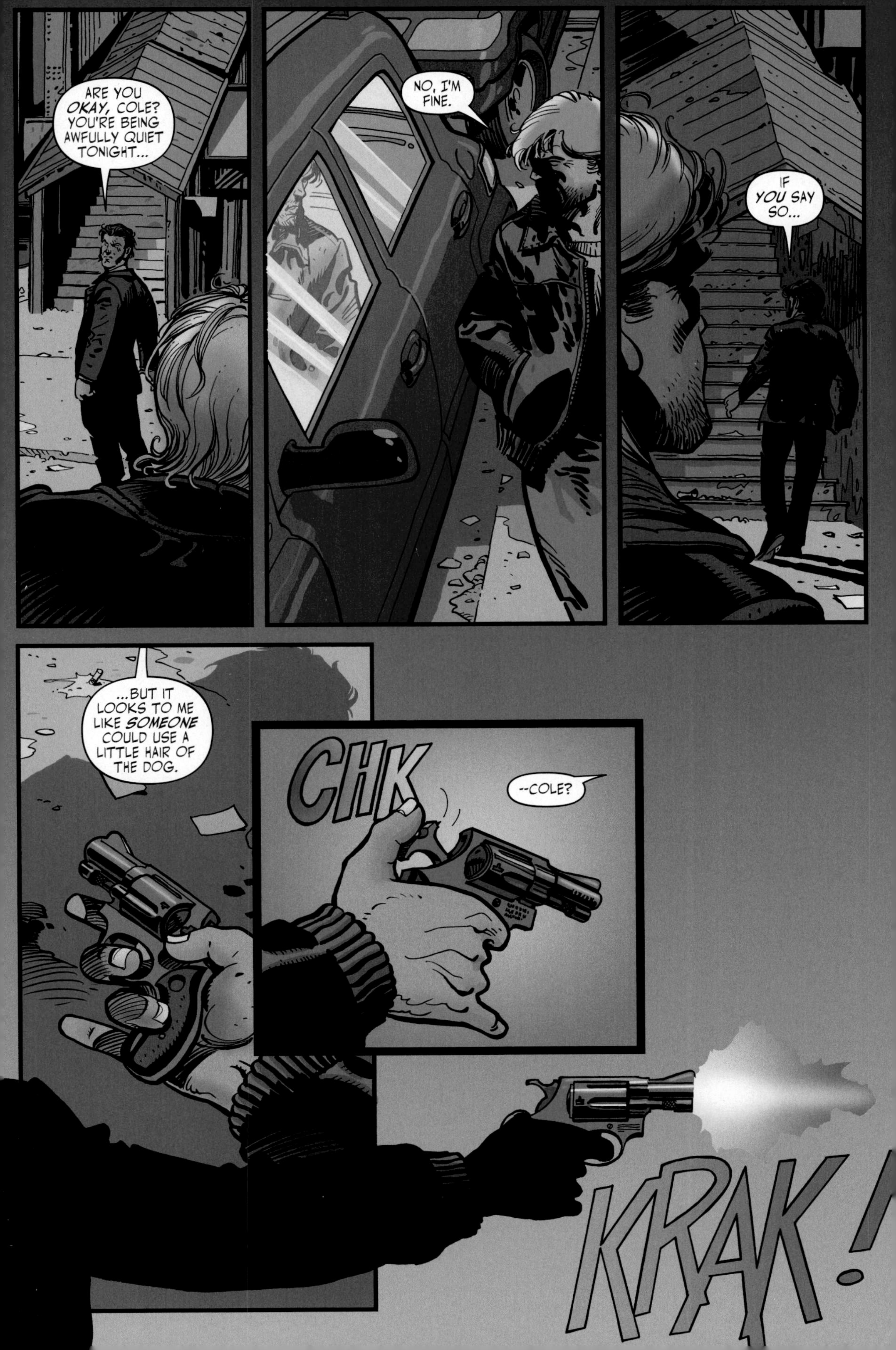
ARE YOU OKAY, COLE? YOU'RE BEING AWFULLY QUIET TONIGHT...
NO, I'M FINE.
IF YOU SAY SO...
...BUT IT LOOKS TO ME LIKE SOMEONE COULD USE A LITTLE HAIR OF THE DOG.
CHK
--COLE?
KRAK!

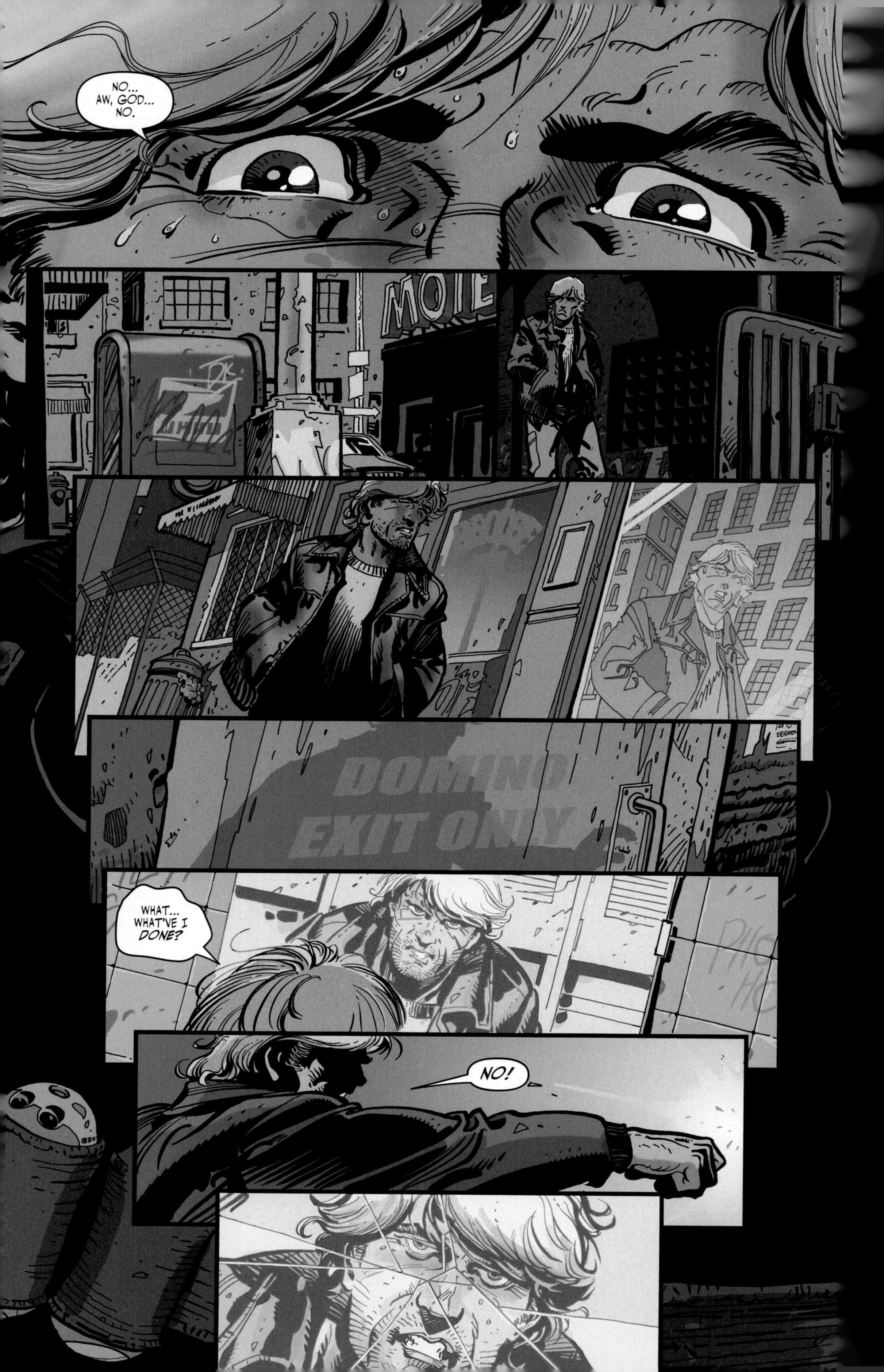
NO... AW, GOD... NO.
MOTE
DOMINO
EXIT ONLY
WHAT... WHAT'VE I *DONE?*
NO!

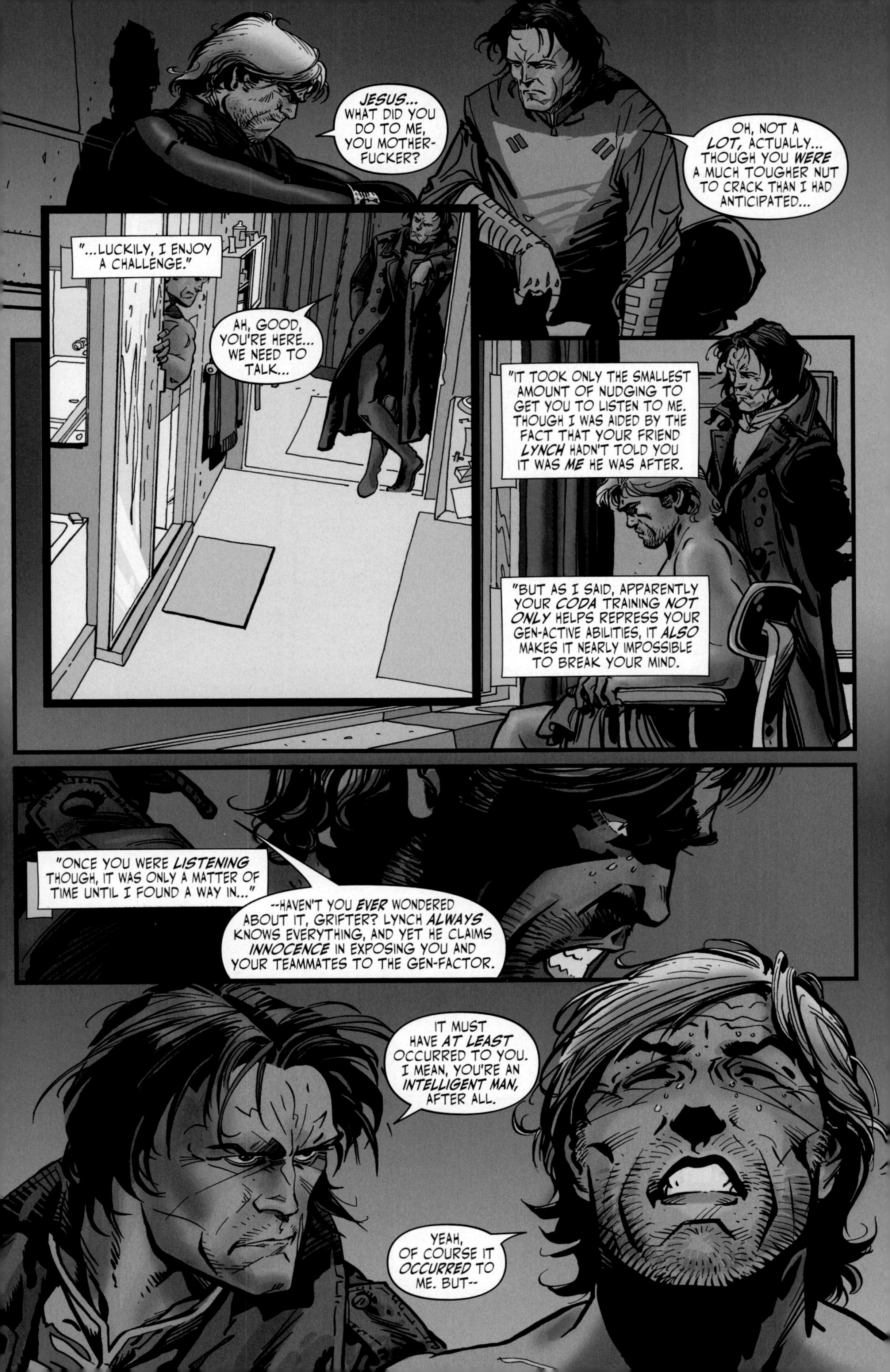
JESUS... WHAT DID YOU DO TO ME, YOU MOTHER-FUCKER?
OH, NOT A LOT, ACTUALLY... THOUGH YOU WERE A MUCH TOUGHER NUT TO CRACK THAN I HAD ANTICIPATED...
"...LUCKILY, I ENJOY A CHALLENGE."
AH, GOOD, YOU'RE HERE... WE NEED TO TALK...
"IT TOOK ONLY THE SMALLEST AMOUNT OF NUDGING TO GET YOU TO LISTEN TO ME. THOUGH I WAS AIDED BY THE FACT THAT YOUR FRIEND LYNCH HADN'T TOLD YOU IT WAS ME HE WAS AFTER.
"BUT AS I SAID, APPARENTLY YOUR CODA TRAINING NOT ONLY HELPS REPRESS YOUR GEN-ACTIVE ABILITIES, IT ALSO MAKES IT NEARLY IMPOSSIBLE TO BREAK YOUR MIND.
"ONCE YOU WERE LISTENING THOUGH, IT WAS ONLY A MATTER OF TIME UNTIL I FOUND A WAY IN..."
--HAVEN'T YOU EVER WONDERED ABOUT IT, GRIFTER? LYNCH ALWAYS KNOWS EVERYTHING, AND YET HE CLAIMS INNOCENCE IN EXPOSING YOU AND YOUR TEAMMATES TO THE GEN-FACTOR.
IT MUST HAVE AT LEAST OCCURRED TO YOU. I MEAN, YOU'RE AN INTELLIGENT MAN, AFTER ALL.
YEAH, OF COURSE IT OCCURRED TO ME. BUT--

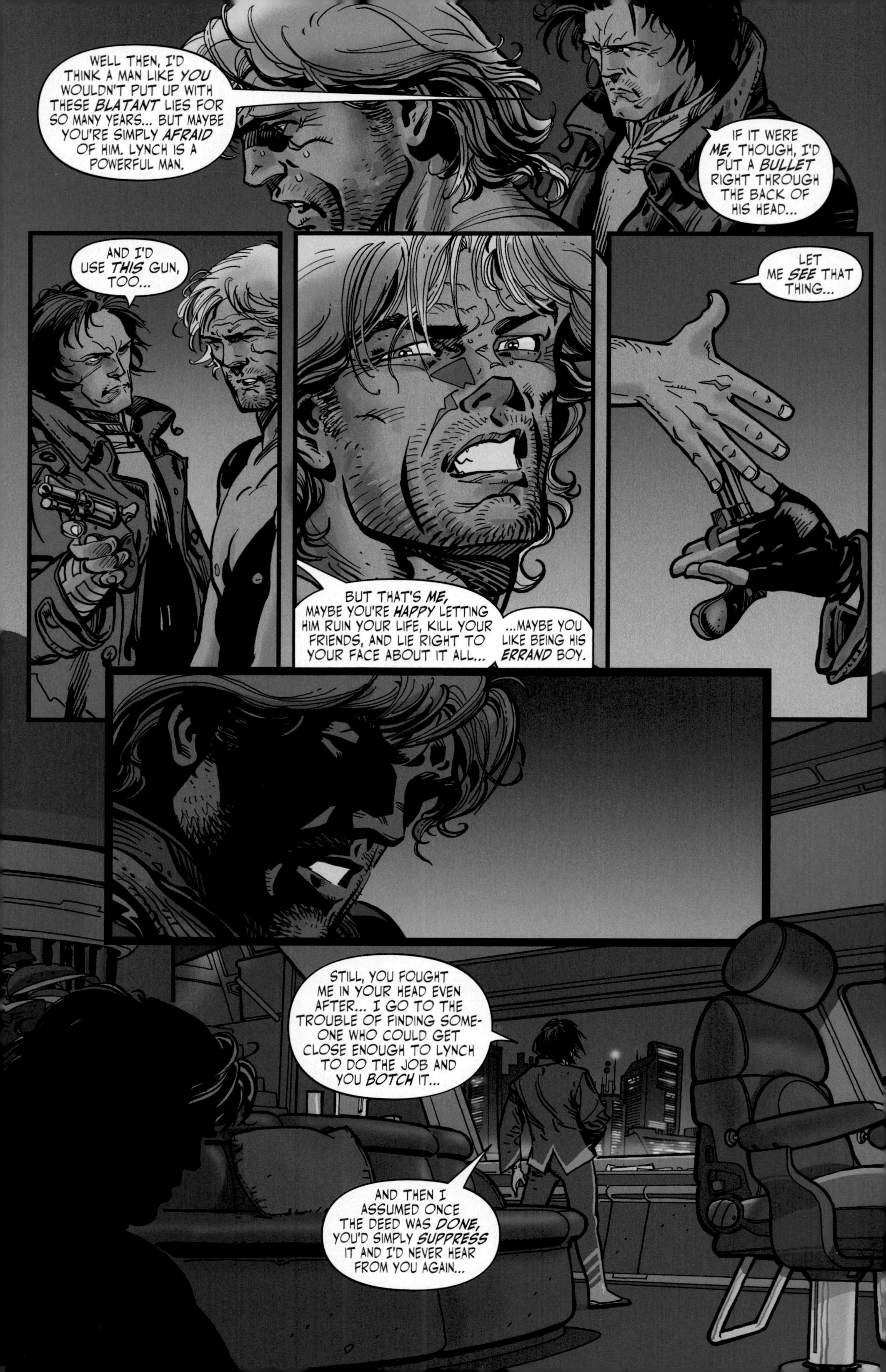
WELL THEN, I'D THINK A MAN LIKE YOU WOULDN'T PUT UP WITH THESE BLATANT LIES FOR SO MANY YEARS... BUT MAYBE YOU'RE SIMPLY AFRAID OF HIM. LYNCH IS A POWERFUL MAN.
IF IT WERE ME, THOUGH, I'D PUT A BULLET RIGHT THROUGH THE BACK OF HIS HEAD...
AND I'D USE THIS GUN, TOO...
BUT THAT'S ME, MAYBE YOU'RE HAPPY LETTING HIM RUIN YOUR LIFE, KILL YOUR FRIENDS, AND LIE RIGHT TO YOUR FACE ABOUT IT ALL...
...MAYBE YOU LIKE BEING HIS ERRAND BOY.
LET ME SEE THAT THING...
STILL, YOU FOUGHT ME IN YOUR HEAD EVEN AFTER... I GO TO THE TROUBLE OF FINDING SOME-ONE WHO COULD GET CLOSE ENOUGH TO LYNCH TO DO THE JOB AND YOU BOTCH IT...
AND THEN I ASSUMED ONCE THE DEED WAS DONE, YOU'D SIMPLY SUPPRESS IT AND I'D NEVER HEAR FROM YOU AGAIN...

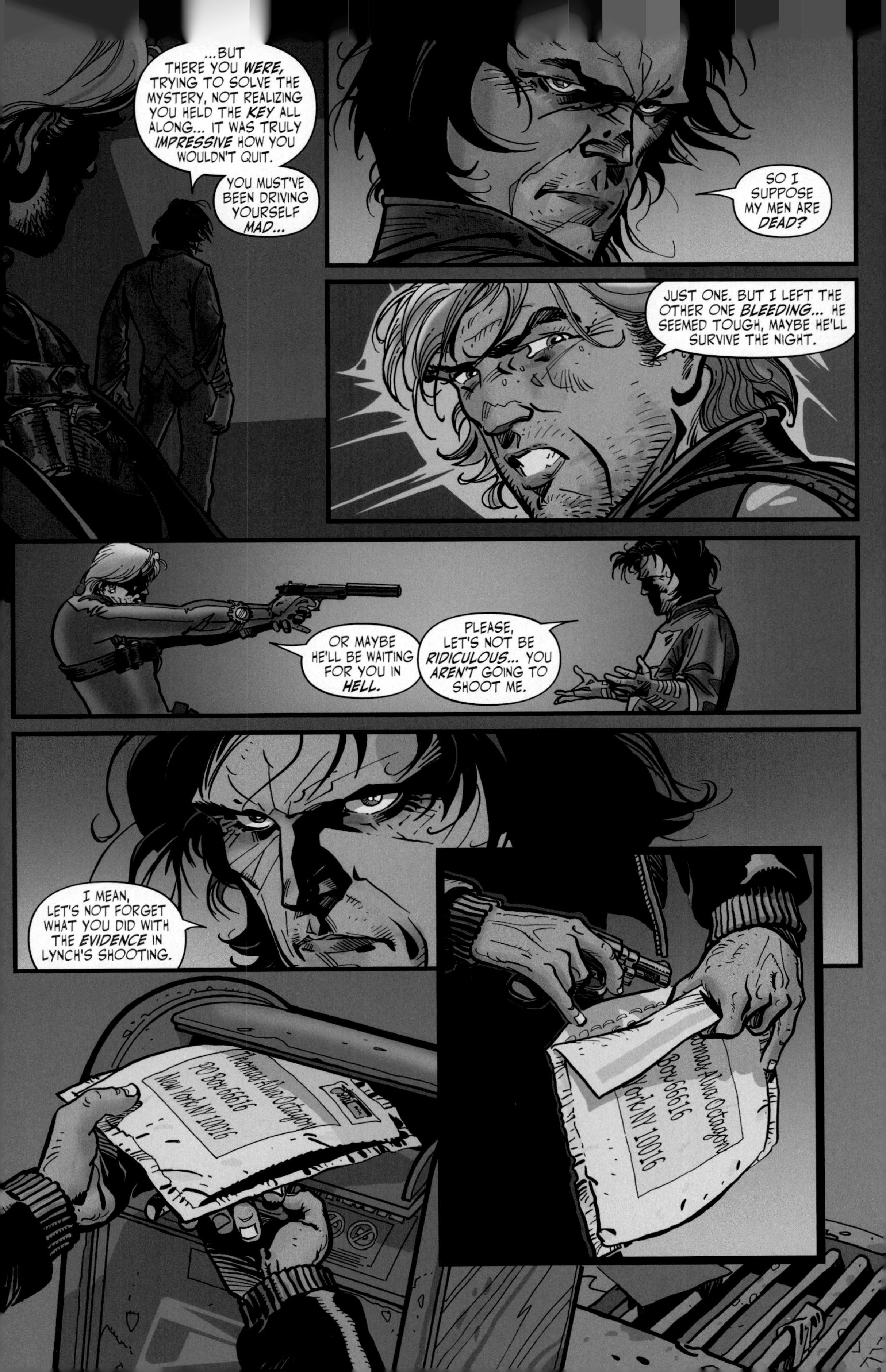
...BUT THERE YOU WERE, TRYING TO SOLVE THE MYSTERY, NOT REALIZING YOU HELD THE KEY ALL ALONG... IT WAS TRULY IMPRESSIVE HOW YOU WOULDN'T QUIT.
YOU MUST'VE BEEN DRIVING YOURSELF MAD...
SO I SUPPOSE MY MEN ARE DEAD?
JUST ONE. BUT I LEFT THE OTHER ONE BLEEDING... HE SEEMED TOUGH, MAYBE HE'LL SURVIVE THE NIGHT.
OR MAYBE HE'LL BE WAITING FOR YOU IN HELL.
PLEASE, LET'S NOT BE RIDICULOUS... YOU AREN'T GOING TO SHOOT ME.
I MEAN, LET'S NOT FORGET WHAT YOU DID WITH THE EVIDENCE IN LYNCH'S SHOOTING.
Thomas Alva Octagon
PO Box 66616
New York NY 10016

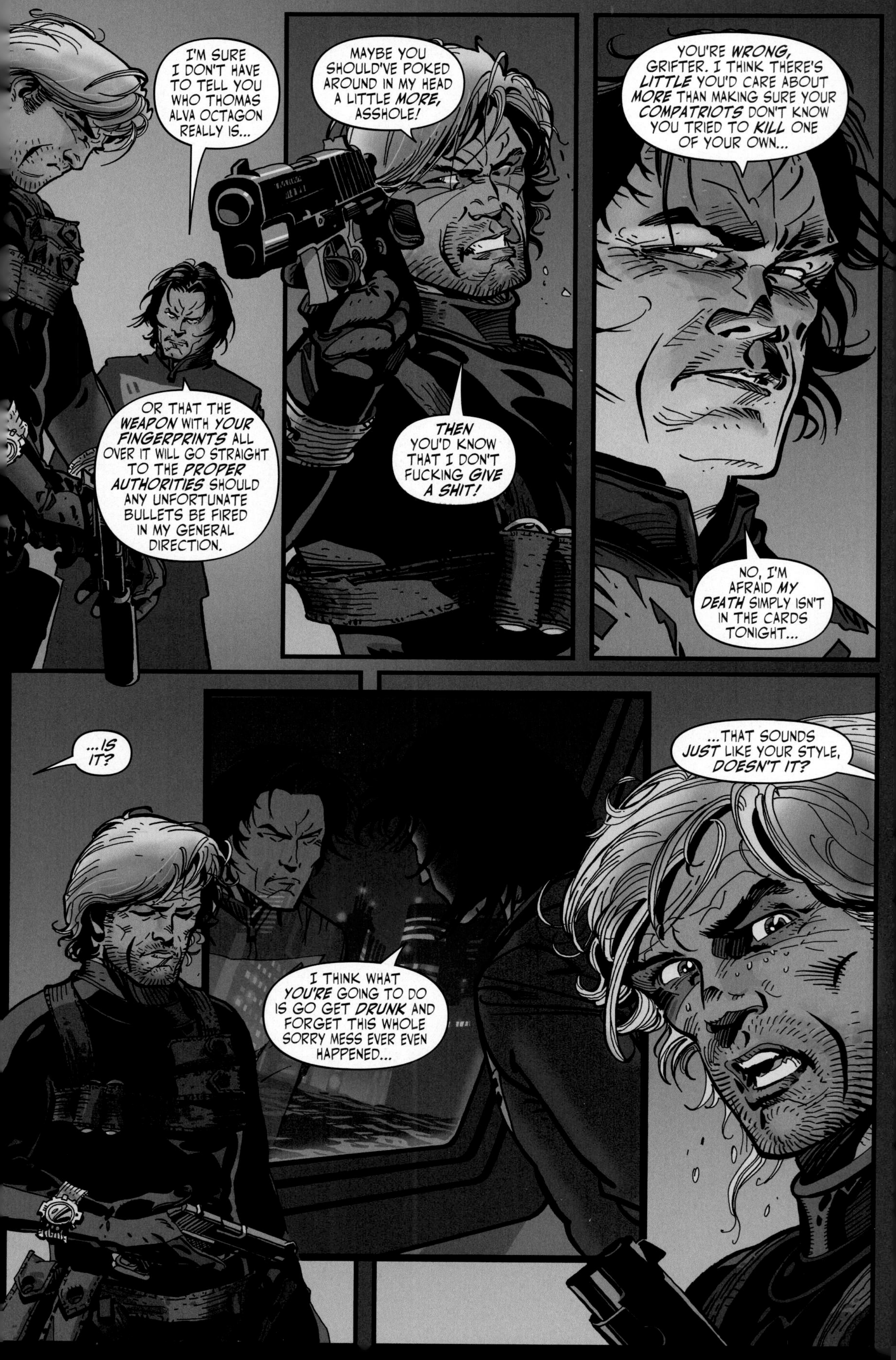
I'M SURE I DON'T HAVE TO TELL YOU WHO THOMAS ALVA OCTAGON REALLY IS...
OR THAT THE WEAPON WITH YOUR FINGERPRINTS ALL OVER IT WILL GO STRAIGHT TO THE PROPER AUTHORITIES SHOULD ANY UNFORTUNATE BULLETS BE FIRED IN MY GENERAL DIRECTION.
MAYBE YOU SHOULD'VE POKED AROUND IN MY HEAD A LITTLE MORE, ASSHOLE!
THEN YOU'D KNOW THAT I DON'T FUCKING GIVE A SHIT!
YOU'RE WRONG, GRIFTER. I THINK THERE'S LITTLE YOU'D CARE ABOUT MORE THAN MAKING SURE YOUR COMPATRIOTS DON'T KNOW YOU TRIED TO KILL ONE OF YOUR OWN...
NO, I'M AFRAID MY DEATH SIMPLY ISN'T IN THE CARDS TONIGHT...
...IS IT?
I THINK WHAT YOU'RE GOING TO DO IS GO GET DRUNK AND FORGET THIS WHOLE SORRY MESS EVER EVEN HAPPENED...
...THAT SOUNDS JUST LIKE YOUR STYLE, DOESN'T IT?

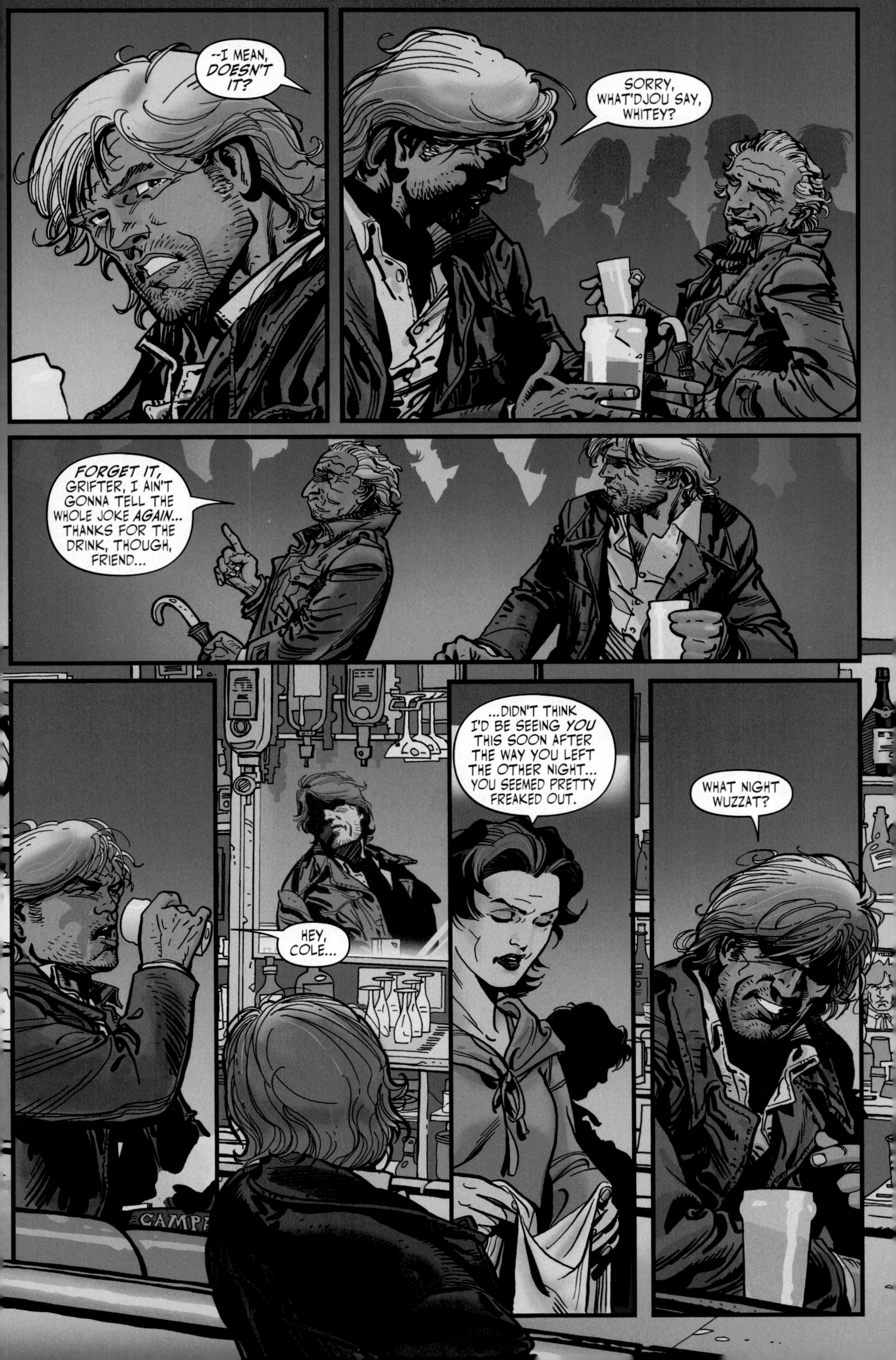
--I MEAN, DOESN'T IT?
SORRY, WHAT'DJOU SAY, WHITEY?
FORGET IT, GRIFTER, I AIN'T GONNA TELL THE WHOLE JOKE AGAIN... THANKS FOR THE DRINK, THOUGH, FRIEND...
HEY, COLE...
...DIDN'T THINK I'D BE SEEING YOU THIS SOON AFTER THE WAY YOU LEFT THE OTHER NIGHT... YOU SEEMED PRETTY FREAKED OUT.
WHAT NIGHT WUZZAT?
CAMPA

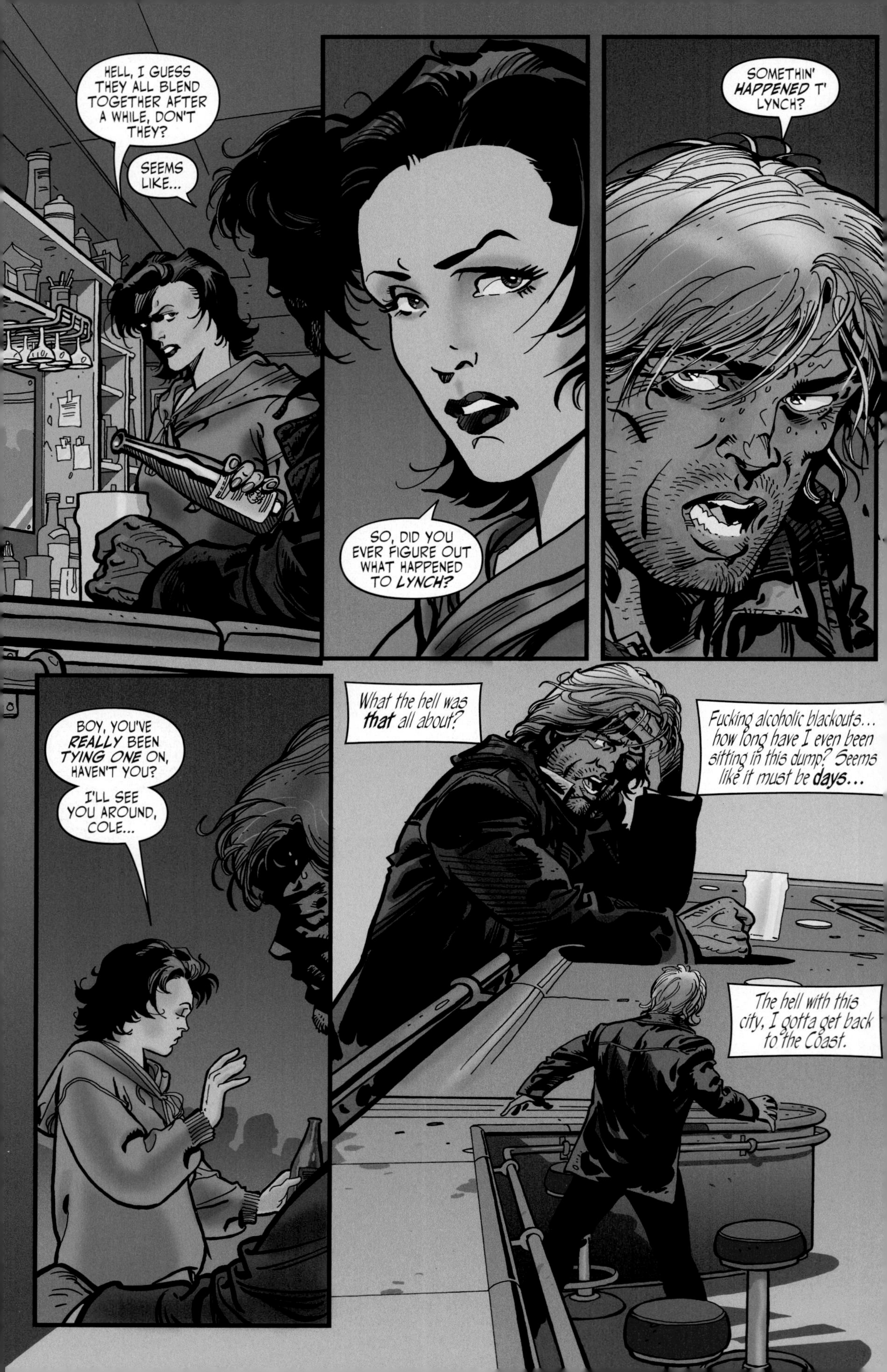
HELL, I GUESS THEY ALL BLEND TOGETHER AFTER A WHILE, DON'T THEY?
SEEMS LIKE...
SO, DID YOU EVER FIGURE OUT WHAT HAPPENED TO *LYNCH?*
SOMETHIN' *HAPPENED* T' LYNCH?
BOY, YOU'VE *REALLY* BEEN *TYING ONE ON,* HAVEN'T YOU?
I'LL SEE YOU AROUND, COLE...
What the hell was **that** all about?
Fucking alcoholic blackouts... how long have I even been sitting in this dump? Seems like it must be **days...**
The hell with this city, I gotta get back to the Coast.

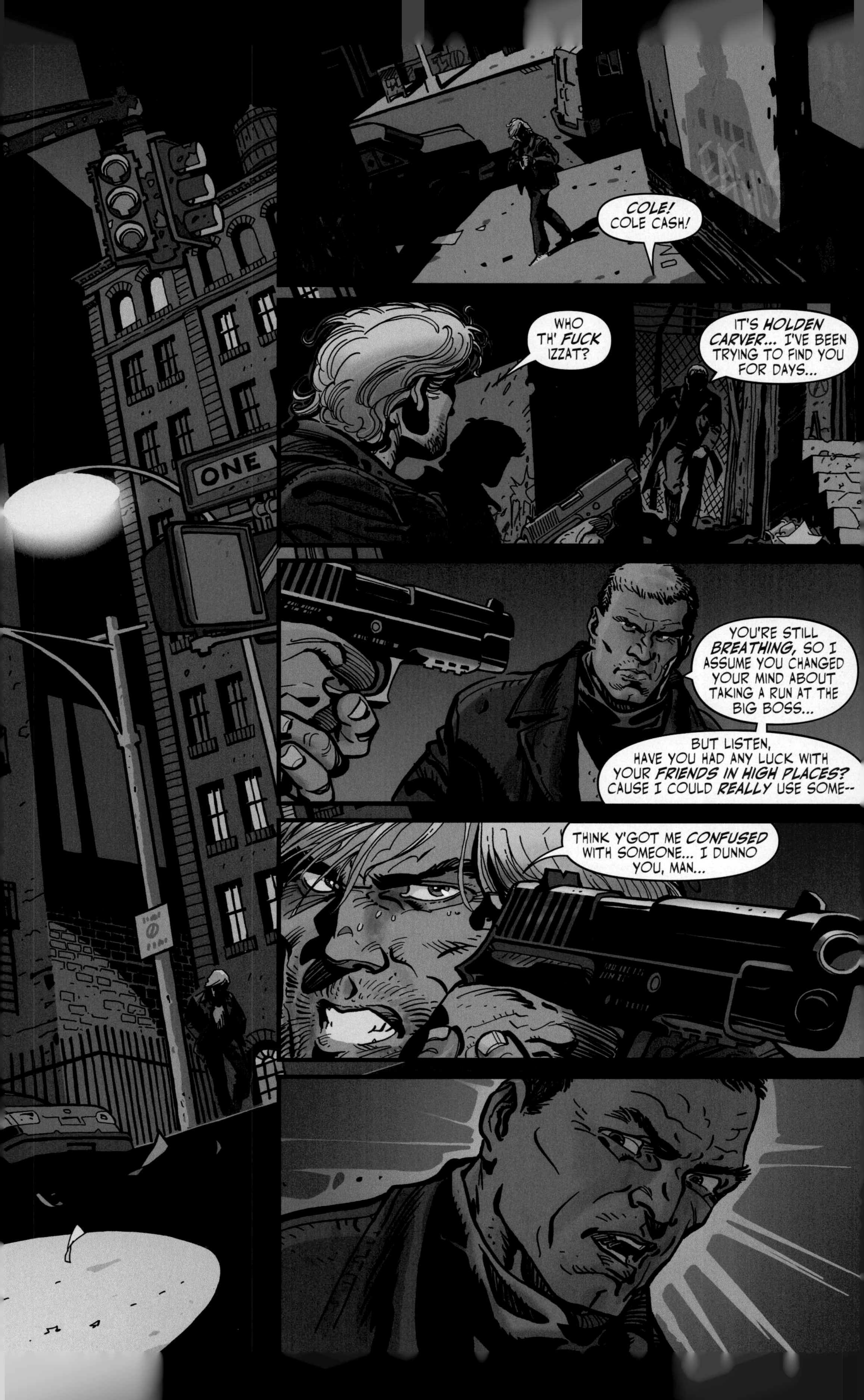
COLE! COLE CASH!
WHO TH' FUCK IZZAT?
IT'S HOLDEN CARVER... I'VE BEEN TRYING TO FIND YOU FOR DAYS...
ONE W
YOU'RE STILL BREATHING, SO I ASSUME YOU CHANGED YOUR MIND ABOUT TAKING A RUN AT THE BIG BOSS...
BUT LISTEN, HAVE YOU HAD ANY LUCK WITH YOUR FRIENDS IN HIGH PLACES? CAUSE I COULD REALLY USE SOME--
THINK Y'GOT ME CONFUSED WITH SOMEONE... I DUNNO YOU, MAN...

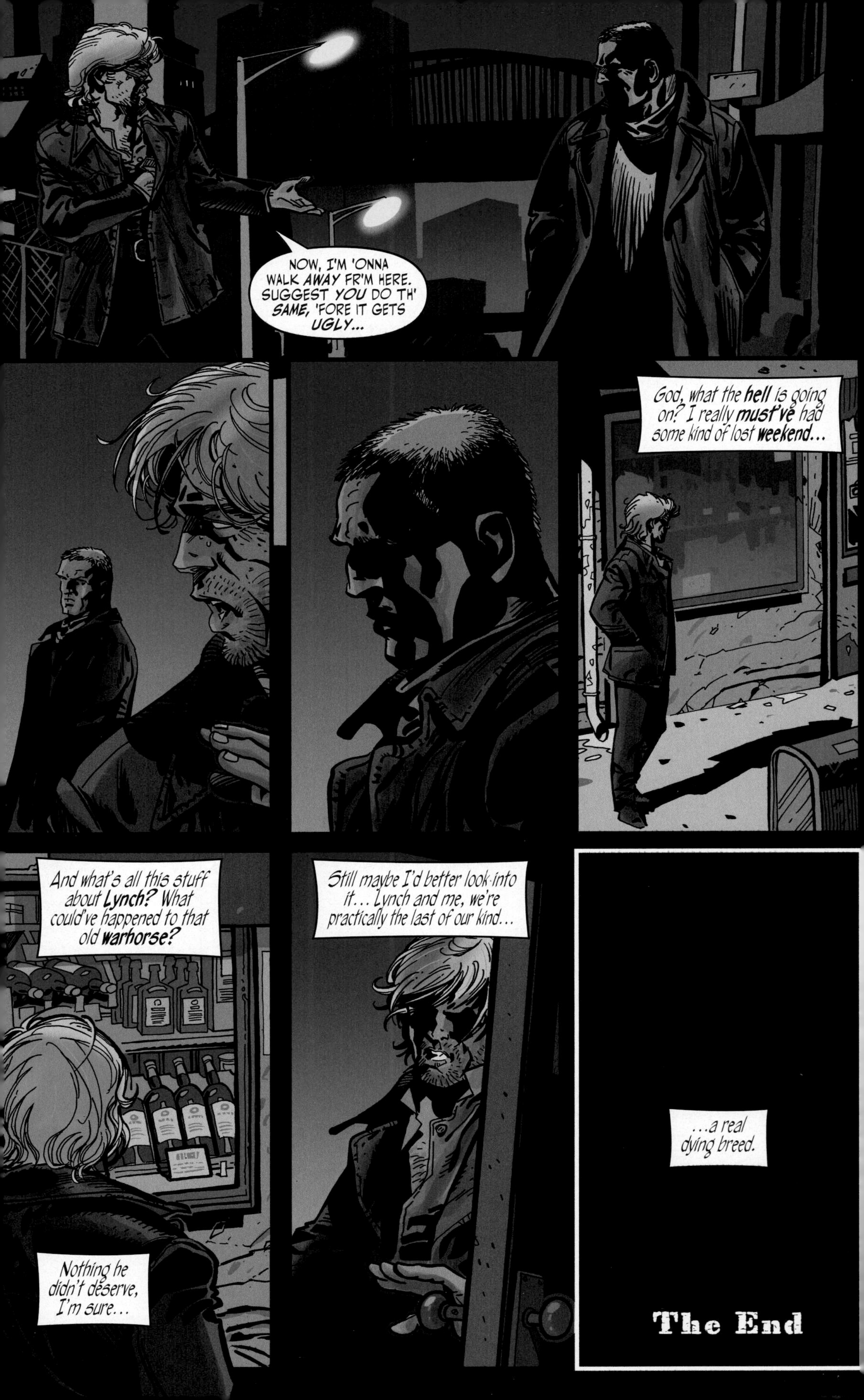

NOW, I'M 'ONNA WALK AWAY FR'M HERE. SUGGEST YOU DO TH' SAME, 'FORE IT GETS UGLY...
God, what the hell is going on? I really must've had some kind of lost weekend...
And what's all this stuff about Lynch? What could've happened to that old warhorse?
Nothing he didn't deserve, I'm sure...
Still maybe I'd better look into it... Lynch and me, we're practically the last of our kind...
...a real dying breed.
The End

AFTERWORD

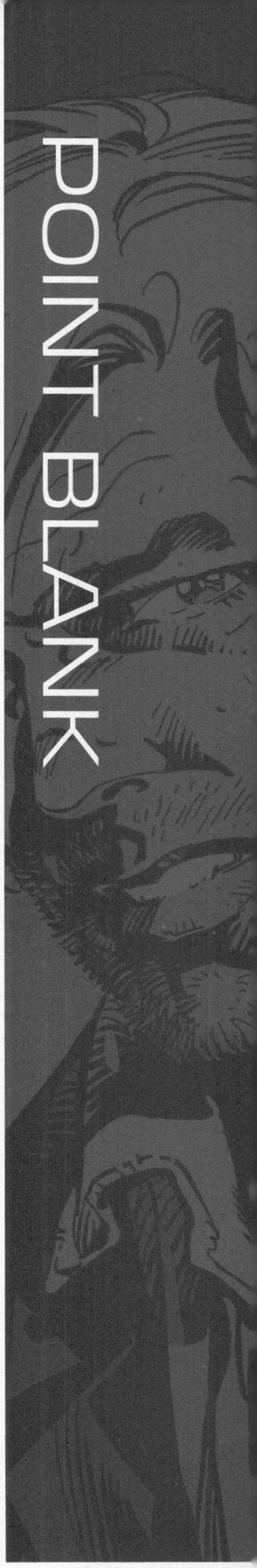
POINT BLANK

A violent little Möbius strip is what POINT BLANK was always intended to be. And I don't mean Moebius the cartoonist, but the thing he named himself after—a story that has no ending, that loops endlessly back onto itself. I always liked stories like that, when they were done well, and that's why the end of our story has Cole wondering if he should look into what happened to Lynch. Who knows how many times he'll go through the exact same experience? How many times will TAO mindfuck him? It could go on forever. Writers are at their best when they're being mean to their characters, I find.

There are a few things of note about the experience of creating this project. It went through many evolutions, for one thing, and it started with a phone call from Scott Dunbier one day asking me if I had any interest in writing a murder mystery that took place in the WildStorm Universe. I did, of course, because given my druthers, I'd almost always rather write a murder mystery. Of course, Lynch doesn't actually die, though. That was Jim Lee's idea. After thinking about it for a while, he just couldn't let us kill the old bastard, and thank god he didn't, because he's gone on to become one of my favorite characters to write, even though he's been in a coma for over a year now.

Another thing of note is the villain of our piece, TAO. Scott wanted me to use TAO, created by Alan Moore during his run on WildC.A.T.s, because Scott thought he was a great character that had never been utilized to his full potential after Alan left that book. I am a huge Alan Moore fan, and the opportunity to write characters he created was a thrill.

And inspired by the inclusion of TAO, and once the book became Mature Readers, things really opened up for me. I found myself asking what Mature Readers superhero comics should be. As you can see, I decided they should be really complicated. They should demand the reader's attention more than the average comic. They should assume intelligence on the part of the Mature Reader. Of course, assuming intelligence is not usually that commercial of a formula, though, is it? Still, I wanted a book that had the flavor of things like WATCHMEN or *The Limey*. I wanted scenes that cut quickly into other scenes, where the reader had to look back. I wanted a puzzle whose pieces had to be forced together.

Some readers got it immediately, and some did not. I think it benefits from being under one cover, though—I think the story works better, and it was really meant to be read in one sitting, so while you may have had to flip back, you didn't have to dig through last month's pile of comics and reread the past issue to make sense of it all. Also, I was trying to write an espionage story, where characters appeared and disappeared and all you needed to know about them was what was given to you on the page. It's obvious that Slayton and Cole have a history, and that Savant and Cole have more history, but we don't need to know what it is, more than what we see. The problem is that comics readers have a bizarre desire to know everything about any character if they've ever appeared elsewhere. And since part of this story was a tour of the WildStorm Universe, some readers felt compelled to know more than they needed to. But I'm telling you right now: everything you need to know is right here in this book.

When we were talking about it later, Scott pointed out that if WATCHMEN had actually featured the Charlton Comics characters instead of Alan Moore's and Dave Gibbons' new creations, a lot of readers would have complained that they couldn't understand the story because they didn't know enough about Charlton continuity. I think he might be right.

In any case, I had a lot of fun with this book. Cole Cash is a great noir character, and I was glad to have the chance to add to his guilty conscience, even if it's just on a subconscious level so far. And I had a great time working with Colin Wilson, who is a legend in the UK and Europe, but just getting known over here in the U.S. I learned early on that Colin, much like his friend Dave Gibbons, would draw anything you wrote in the panel description. That poor bastard. I ran him ragged after that.

And of course, after all the changes the project went through, from being a murder story, to an almost murder story, from a general audience book to a Mature Readers book, one day Scott called me up and asked if I had any ideas for an ongoing book to sort of spin out of POINT BLANK. I had none, but then thinking about Lynch in a coma, I suddenly came up with one, and the project changed one last time. Now Lynch's nebulous missions with Cole had more purpose. He had a deep-cover operative out there in the cold, and he was trying to bring him in.

So, what happens to a deep-cover operative when the only person who knows he's not a bad guy is in a coma? That's what SLEEPER with artist Sean Phillips is about, another gritty noir spy story with super-powered overtones, except this time we focus on the villain's side of the story.

ED BRUBAKER
2003

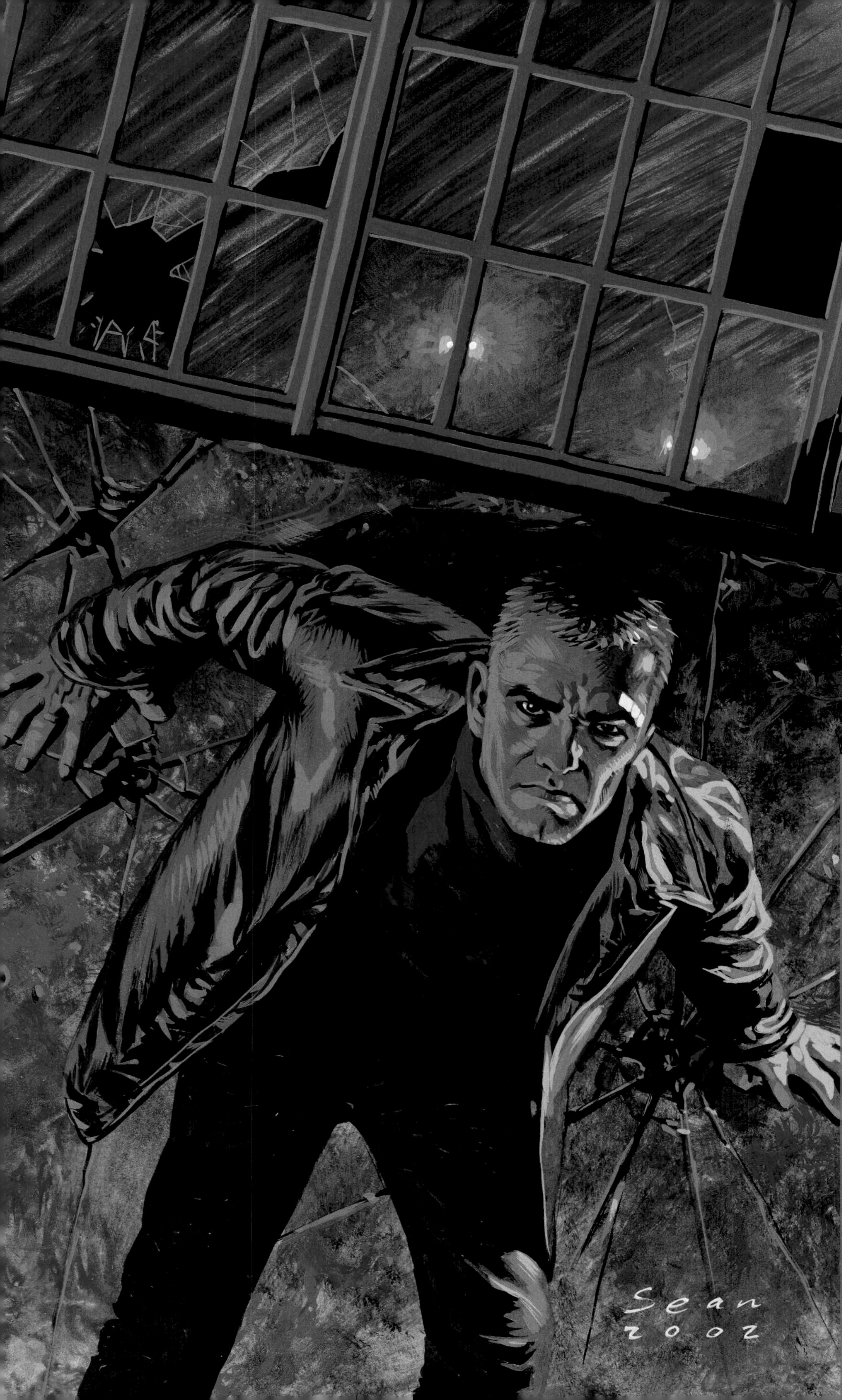
Sean
2002

Cover by SEAN PHILLIPS

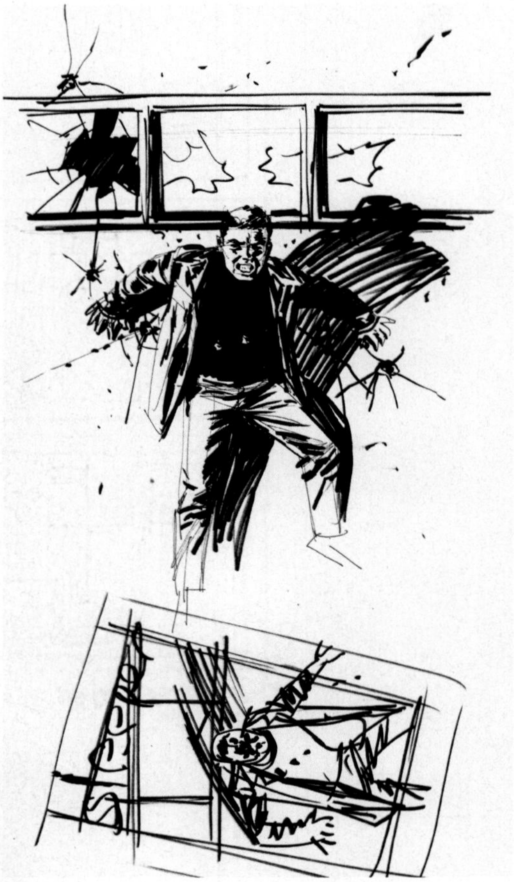

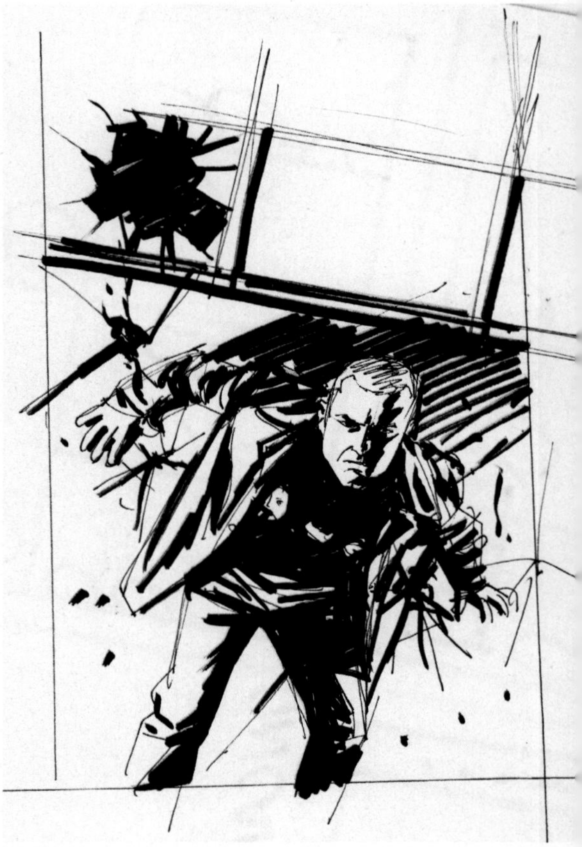

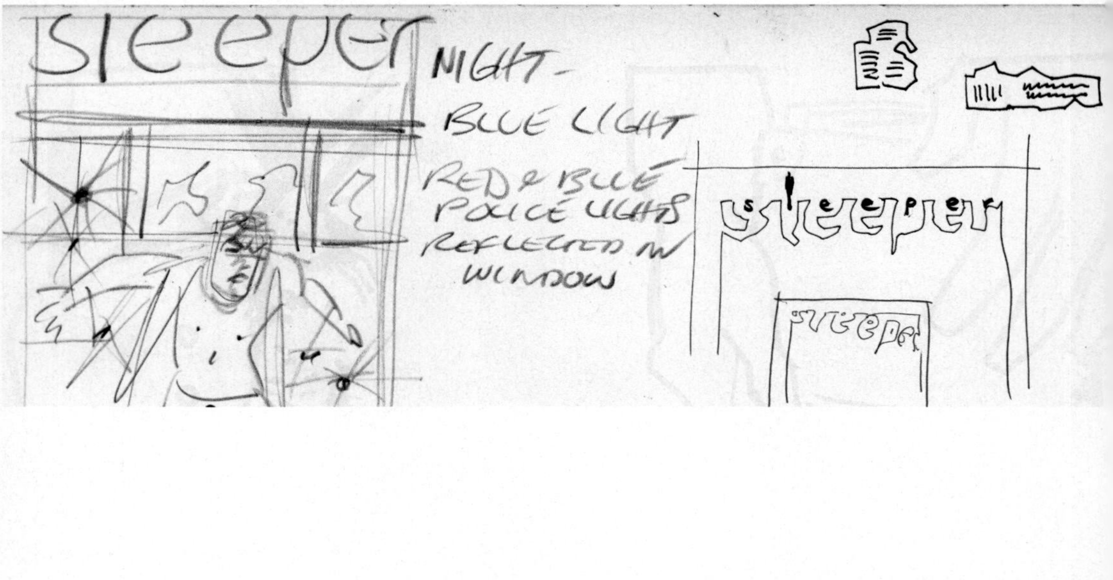
sleeper
NIGHT -
BLUE LIGHT
RED & BLUE POLICE LIGHTS REFLECTED IN WINDOW
sleeper
sleeper

SLEEPER #1 Cover Sketches by SEAN PHILLIPS

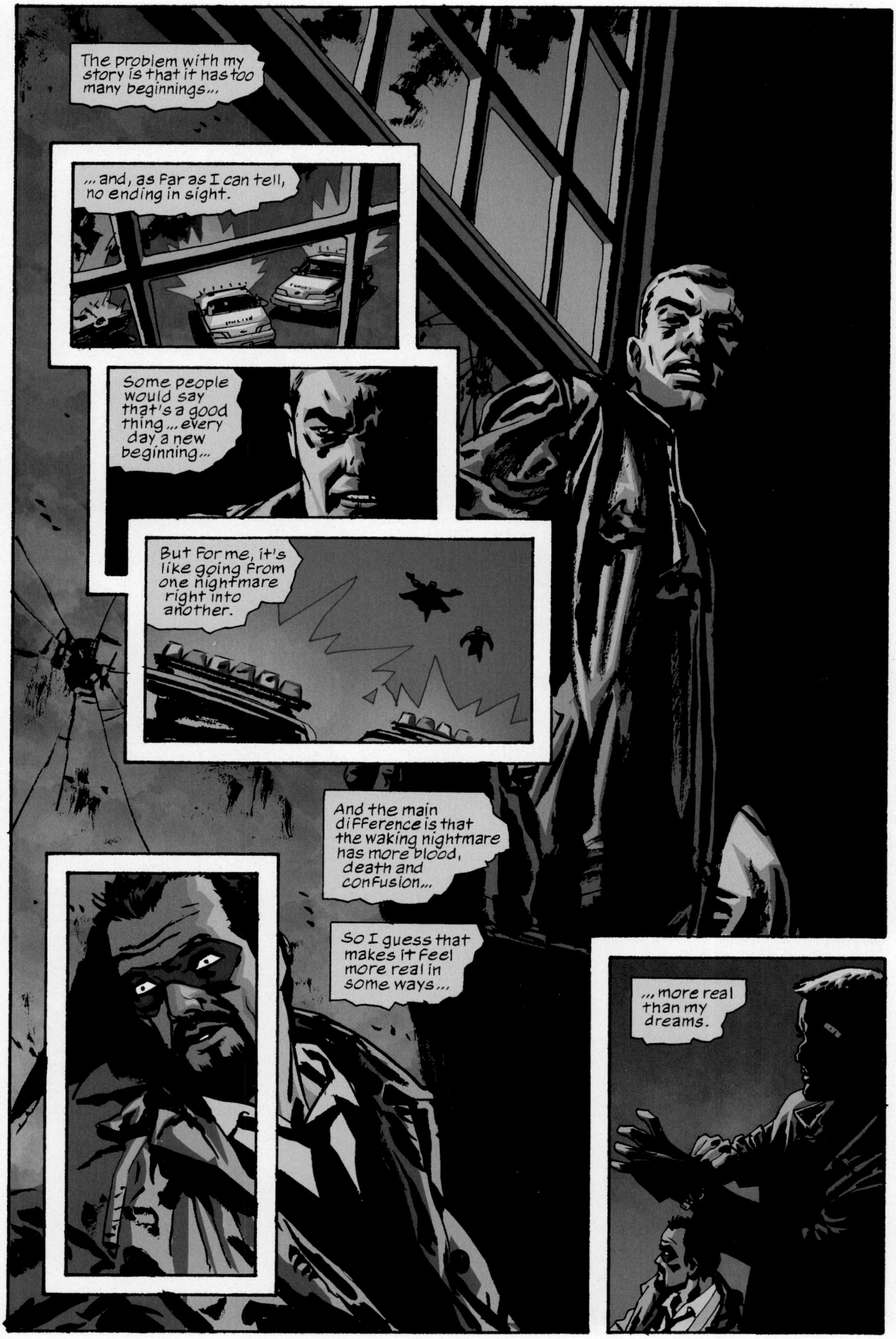

The problem with my story is that it has too many beginnings...
...and, as far as I can tell, no ending in sight.
Some people would say that's a good thing... every day a new beginning...
But for me, it's like going from one nightmare right into another.
And the main difference is that the waking nightmare has more blood, death and confusion...
So I guess that makes it feel more real in some ways...
...more real than my dreams.

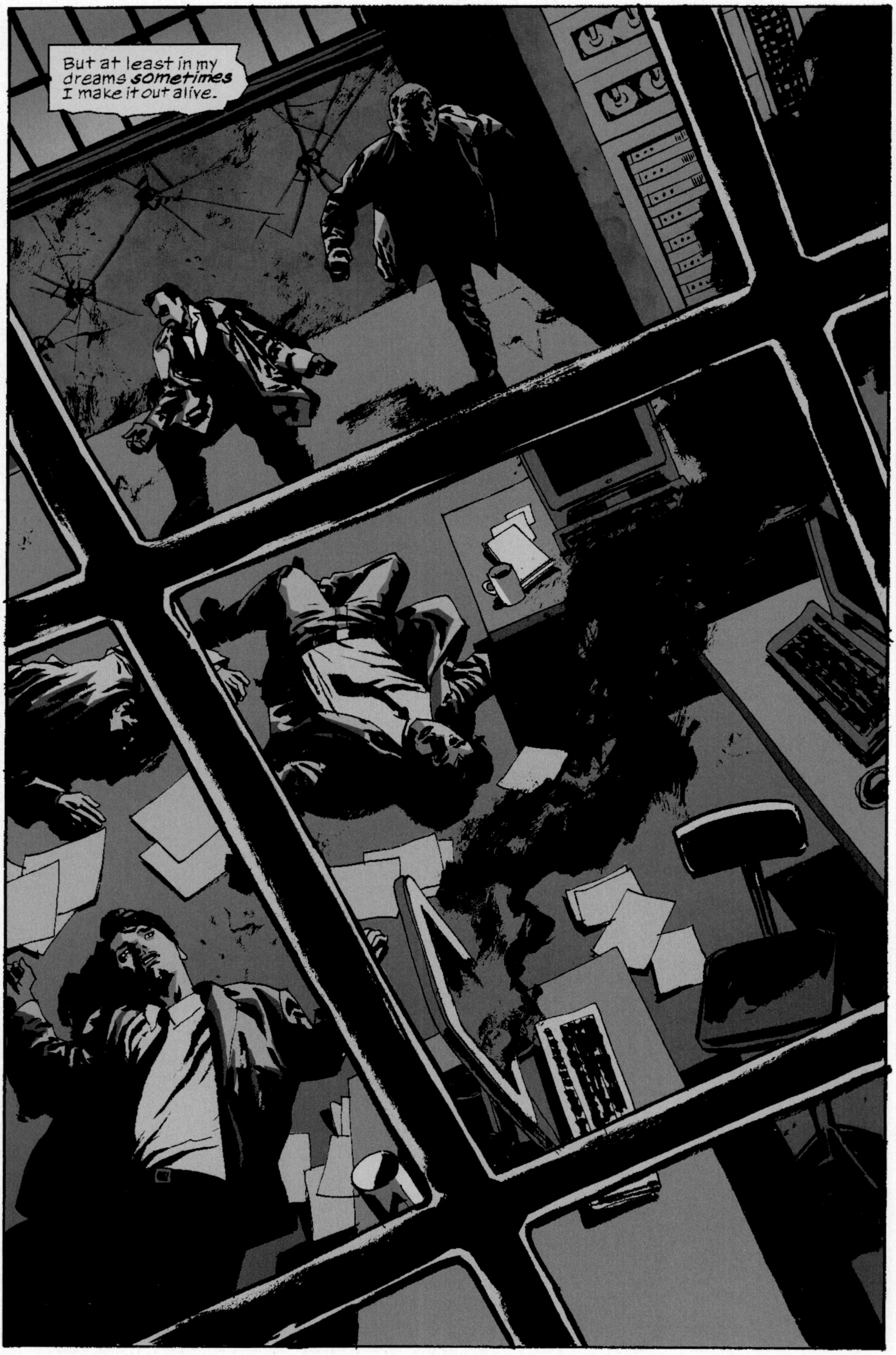
But at least in my dreams sometimes I make it out alive.

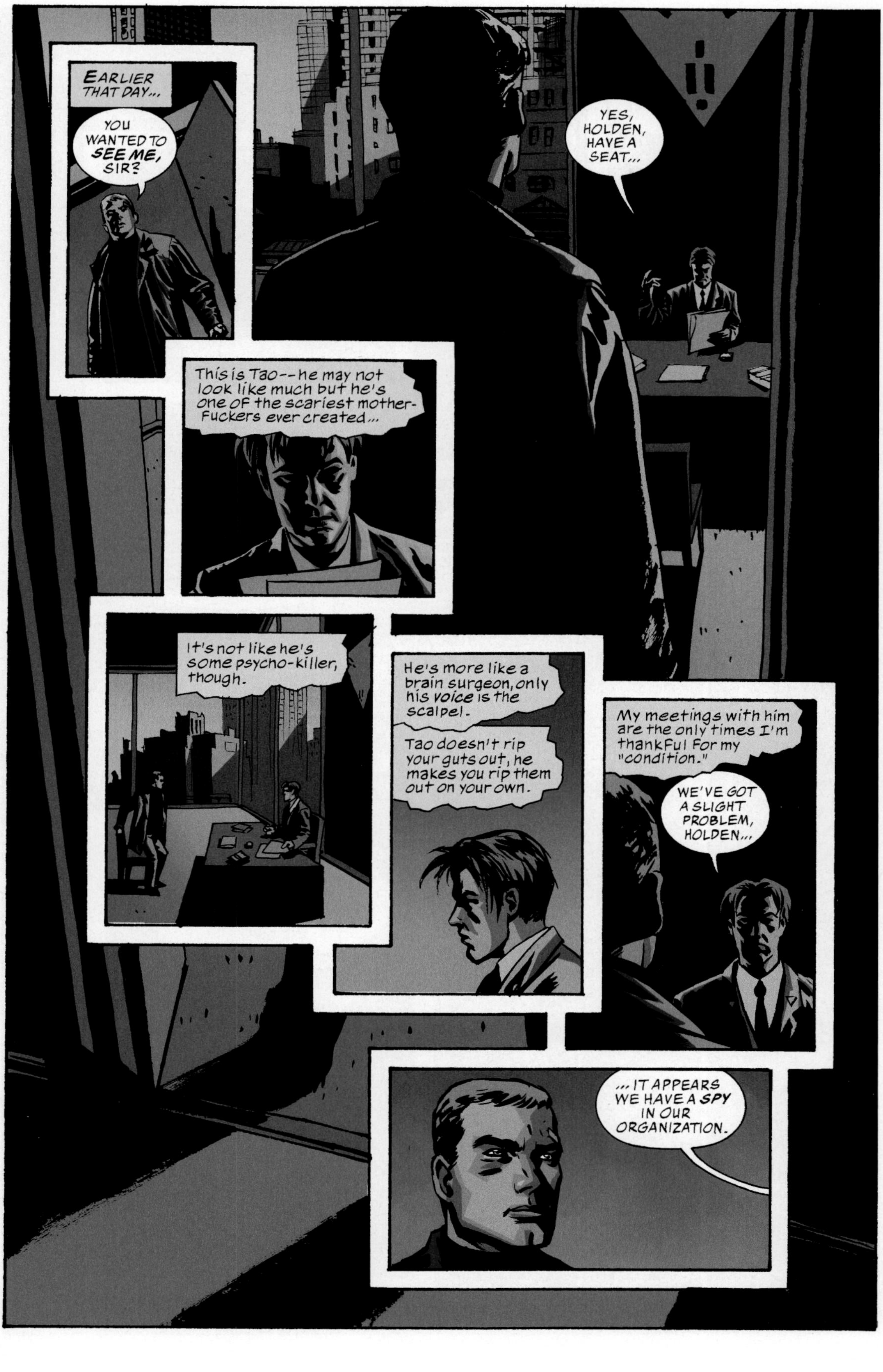
EARLIER THAT DAY...
YOU WANTED TO SEE ME, SIR?
YES, HOLDEN, HAVE A SEAT...
This is Tao--he may not look like much but he's one of the scariest mother-fuckers ever created...
It's not like he's some psycho-killer, though.
He's more like a brain surgeon, only his voice is the scalpel.
Tao doesn't rip your guts out, he makes you rip them out on your own.
My meetings with him are the only times I'm thankful for my "condition."
WE'VE GOT A SLIGHT PROBLEM, HOLDEN...
...IT APPEARS WE HAVE A SPY IN OUR ORGANIZATION.

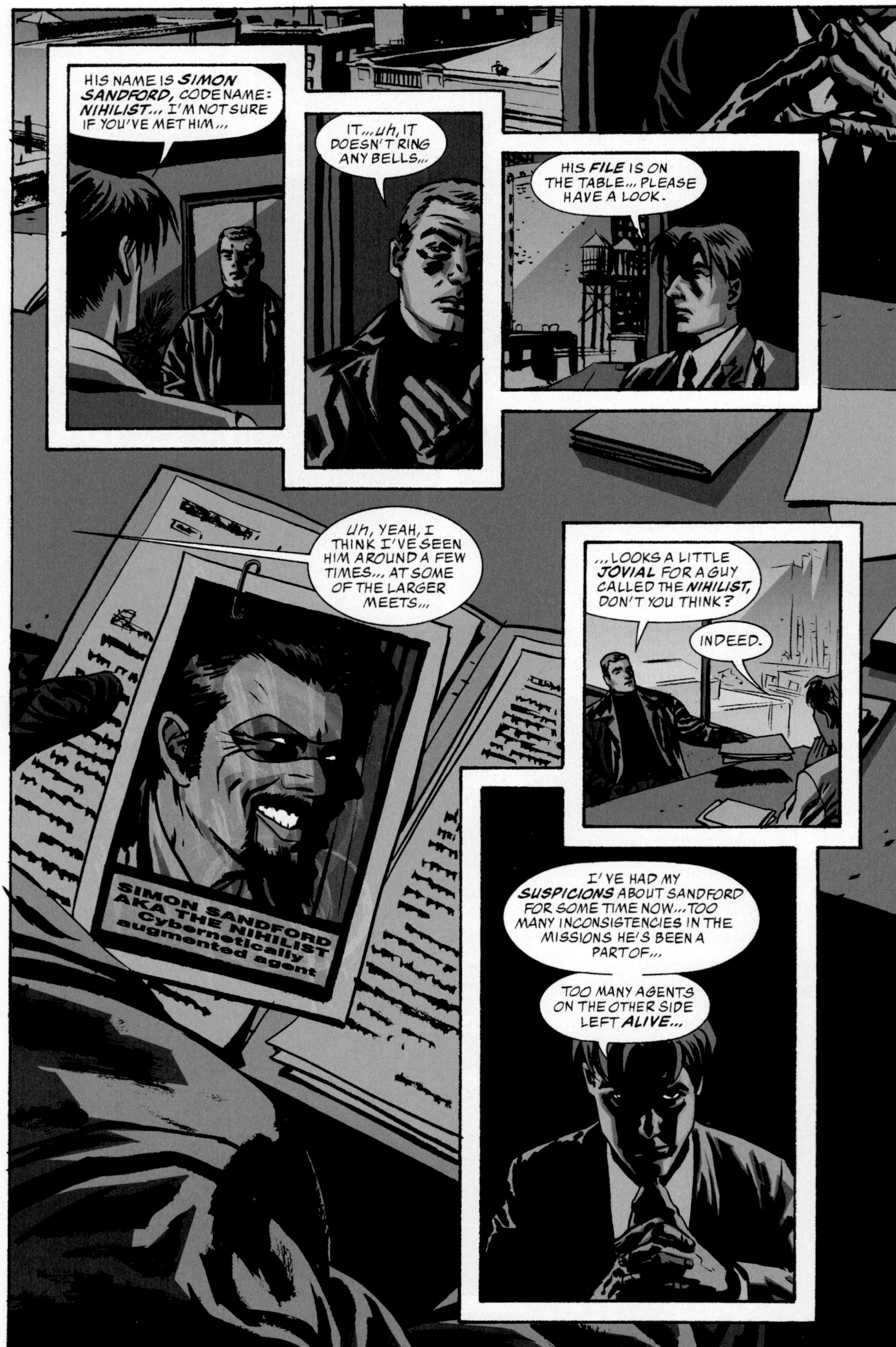
HIS NAME IS SIMON SANDFORD, CODENAME: NIHILIST... I'M NOT SURE IF YOU'VE MET HIM...
IT... uh, IT DOESN'T RING ANY BELLS...
HIS FILE IS ON THE TABLE... PLEASE HAVE A LOOK.
uh, YEAH, I THINK I'VE SEEN HIM AROUND A FEW TIMES... AT SOME OF THE LARGER MEETS...
SIMON SANDFORD AKA THE NIHILIST Cybernetically augmented agent
...LOOKS A LITTLE JOVIAL FOR A GUY CALLED THE NIHILIST, DON'T YOU THINK?
INDEED.
I'VE HAD MY SUSPICIONS ABOUT SANDFORD FOR SOME TIME NOW... TOO MANY INCONSISTENCIES IN THE MISSIONS HE'S BEEN A PART OF...
TOO MANY AGENTS ON THE OTHER SIDE LEFT ALIVE...

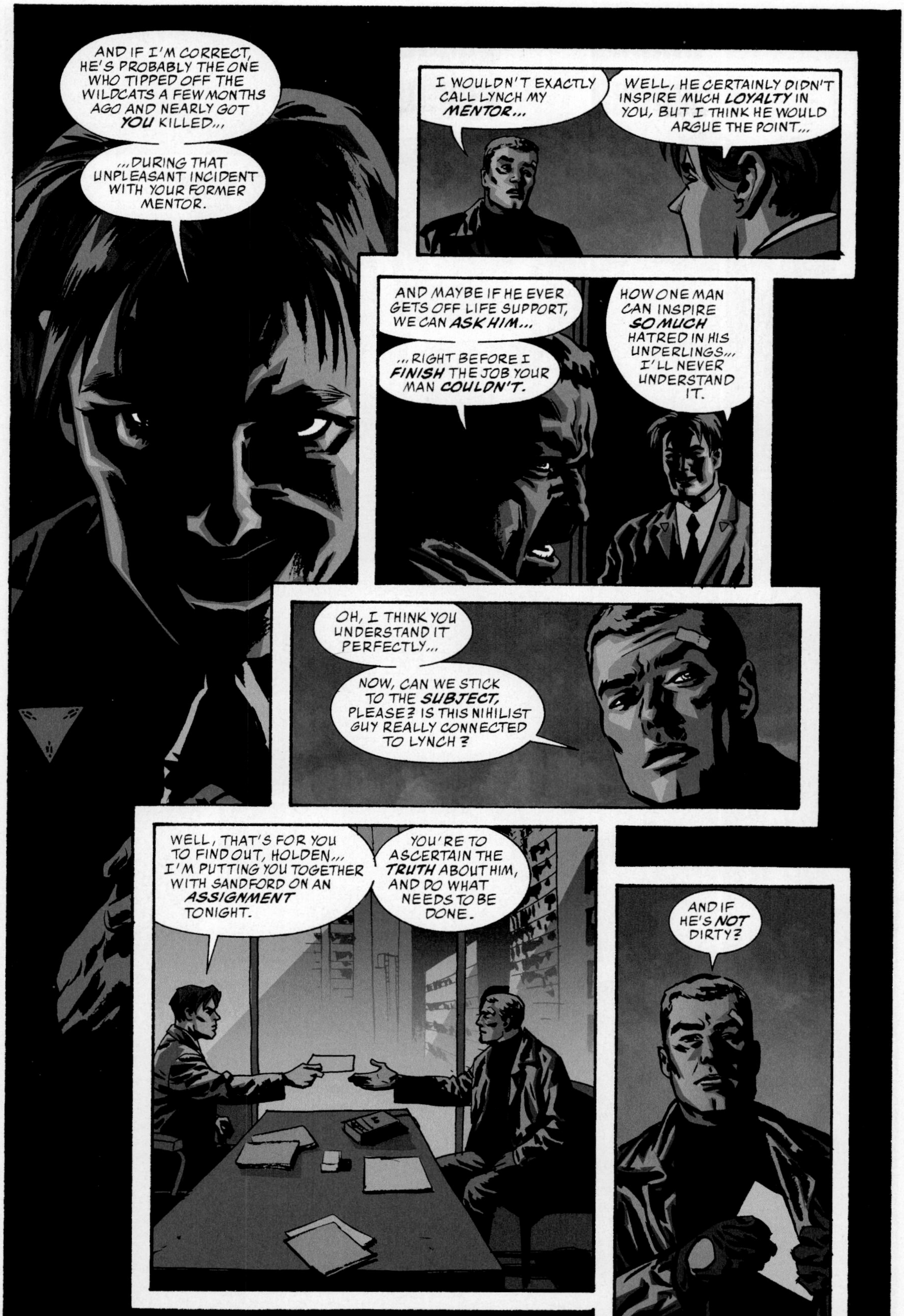
AND IF I'M CORRECT, HE'S PROBABLY THE ONE WHO TIPPED OFF THE WILDCATS A FEW MONTHS AGO AND NEARLY GOT YOU KILLED...
...DURING THAT UNPLEASANT INCIDENT WITH YOUR FORMER MENTOR.
I WOULDN'T EXACTLY CALL LYNCH MY MENTOR...
WELL, HE CERTAINLY DIDN'T INSPIRE MUCH LOYALTY IN YOU, BUT I THINK HE WOULD ARGUE THE POINT...
AND MAYBE IF HE EVER GETS OFF LIFE SUPPORT, WE CAN ASK HIM...
...RIGHT BEFORE I FINISH THE JOB YOUR MAN COULDN'T.
HOW ONE MAN CAN INSPIRE SO MUCH HATRED IN HIS UNDERLINGS... I'LL NEVER UNDERSTAND IT.
OH, I THINK YOU UNDERSTAND IT PERFECTLY...
NOW, CAN WE STICK TO THE SUBJECT, PLEASE? IS THIS NIHILIST GUY REALLY CONNECTED TO LYNCH?
WELL, THAT'S FOR YOU TO FIND OUT, HOLDEN... I'M PUTTING YOU TOGETHER WITH SANDFORD ON AN ASSIGNMENT TONIGHT.
YOU'RE TO ASCERTAIN THE TRUTH ABOUT HIM, AND DO WHAT NEEDS TO BE DONE.
AND IF HE'S NOT DIRTY?

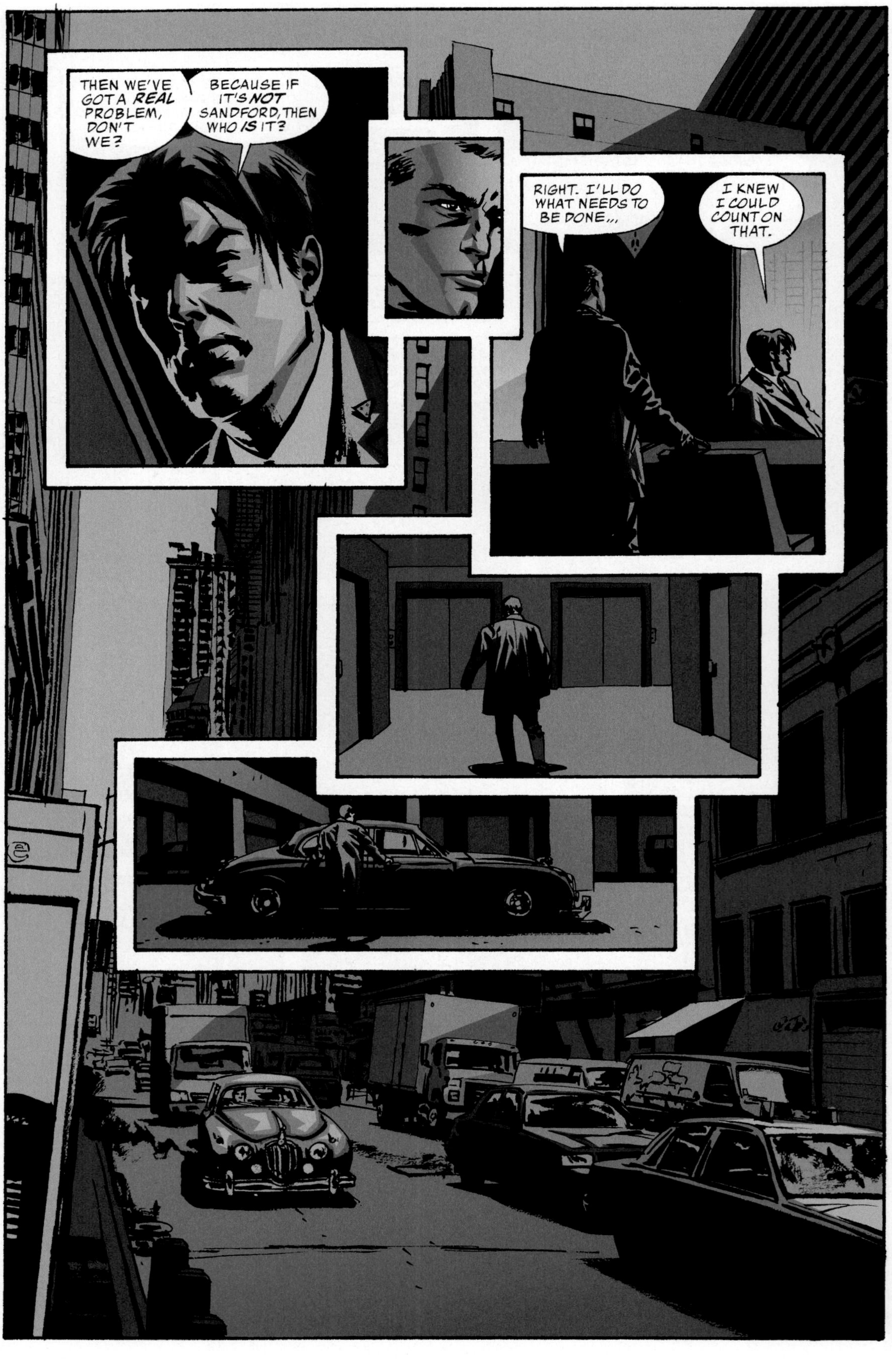
THEN WE'VE GOT A REAL PROBLEM, DON'T WE?
BECAUSE IF IT'S NOT SANDFORD, THEN WHO IS IT?
RIGHT. I'LL DO WHAT NEEDS TO BE DONE...
I KNEW I COULD COUNT ON THAT.

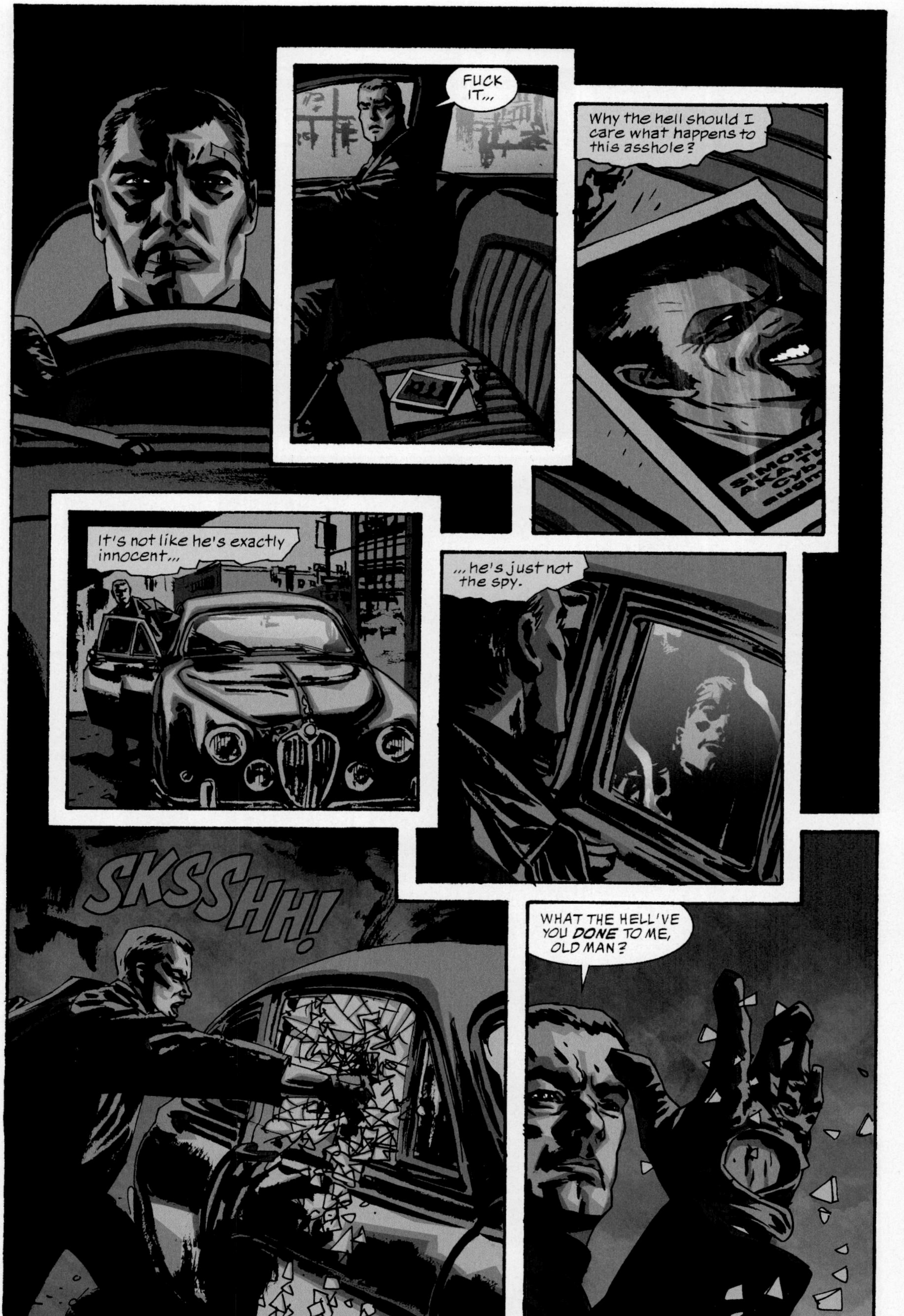
FUCK IT...
Why the hell should I care what happens to this asshole?
It's not like he's exactly innocent...
...he's just not the spy.
SKSSHH!
WHAT THE HELL'VE YOU DONE TO ME, OLD MAN?

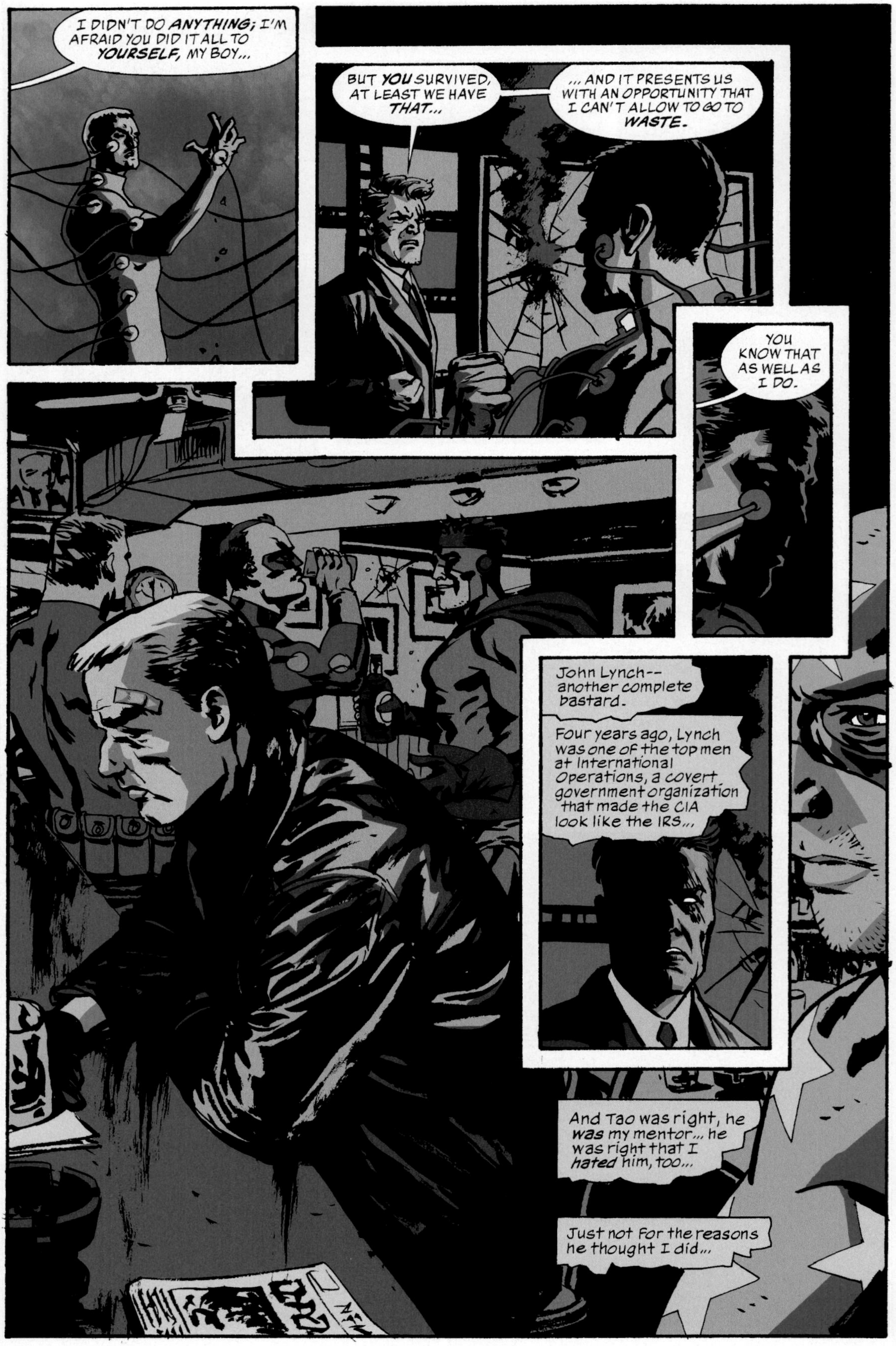
I DIDN'T DO ANYTHING; I'M AFRAID YOU DID IT ALL TO YOURSELF, MY BOY...
BUT YOU SURVIVED, AT LEAST WE HAVE THAT...
...AND IT PRESENTS US WITH AN OPPORTUNITY THAT I CAN'T ALLOW TO GO TO WASTE.
YOU KNOW THAT AS WELL AS I DO.
John Lynch-- another complete bastard.
Four years ago, Lynch was one of the top men at International Operations, a covert government organization that made the CIA look like the IRS...
And Tao was right, he was my mentor... he was right that I hated him, too...
Just not for the reasons he thought I did...

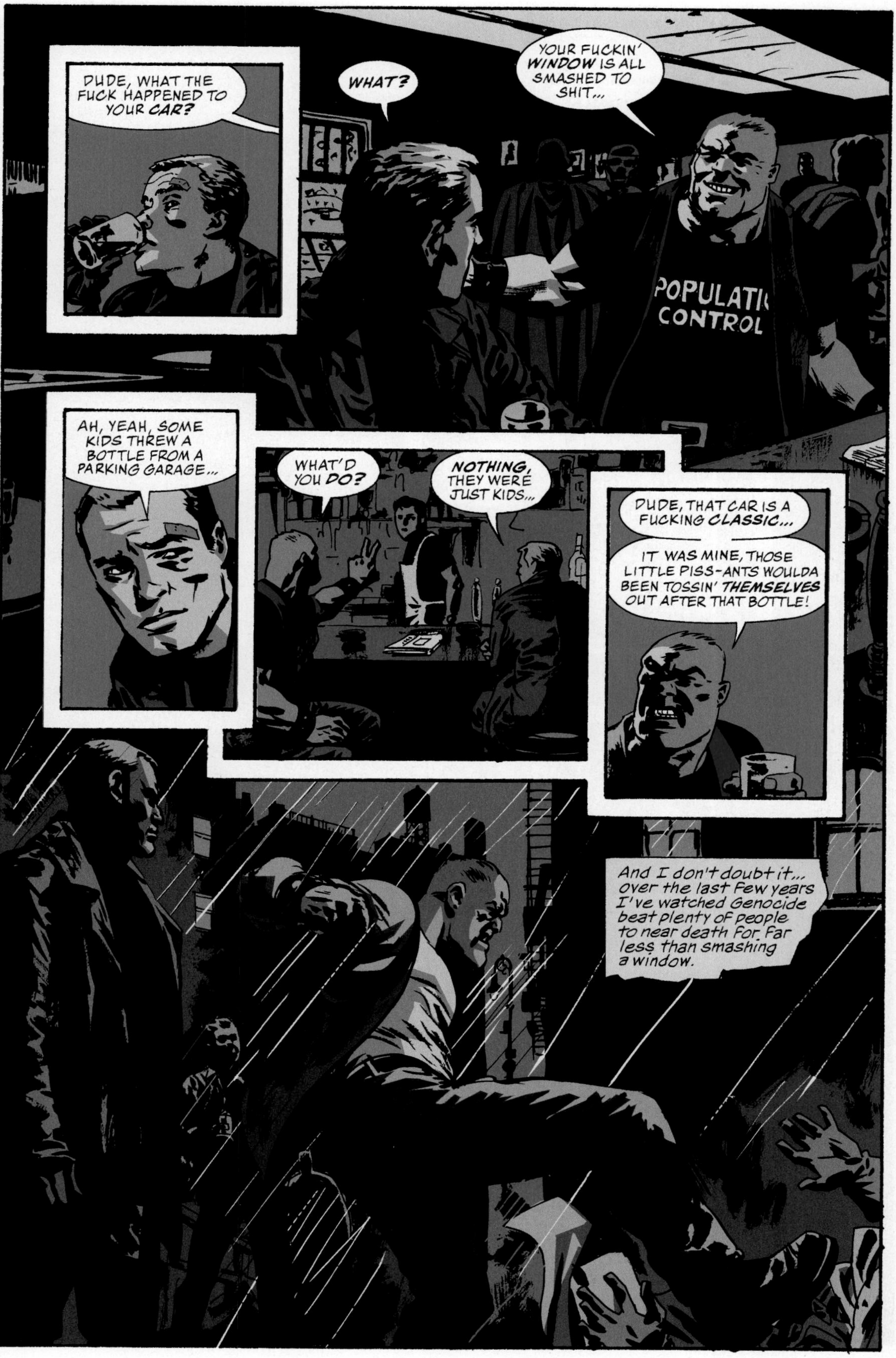
DUDE, WHAT THE FUCK HAPPENED TO YOUR CAR?
WHAT?
YOUR FUCKIN' WINDOW IS ALL SMASHED TO SHIT...
POPULATIO CONTROL
AH, YEAH, SOME KIDS THREW A BOTTLE FROM A PARKING GARAGE...
WHAT'D YOU DO?
NOTHING, THEY WERE JUST KIDS...
DUDE, THAT CAR IS A FUCKING CLASSIC...
IT WAS MINE, THOSE LITTLE PISS-ANTS WOULDA BEEN TOSSIN' THEMSELVES OUT AFTER THAT BOTTLE!
And I don't doubt it... over the last few years I've watched Genocide beat plenty of people to near death for far less than smashing a window.

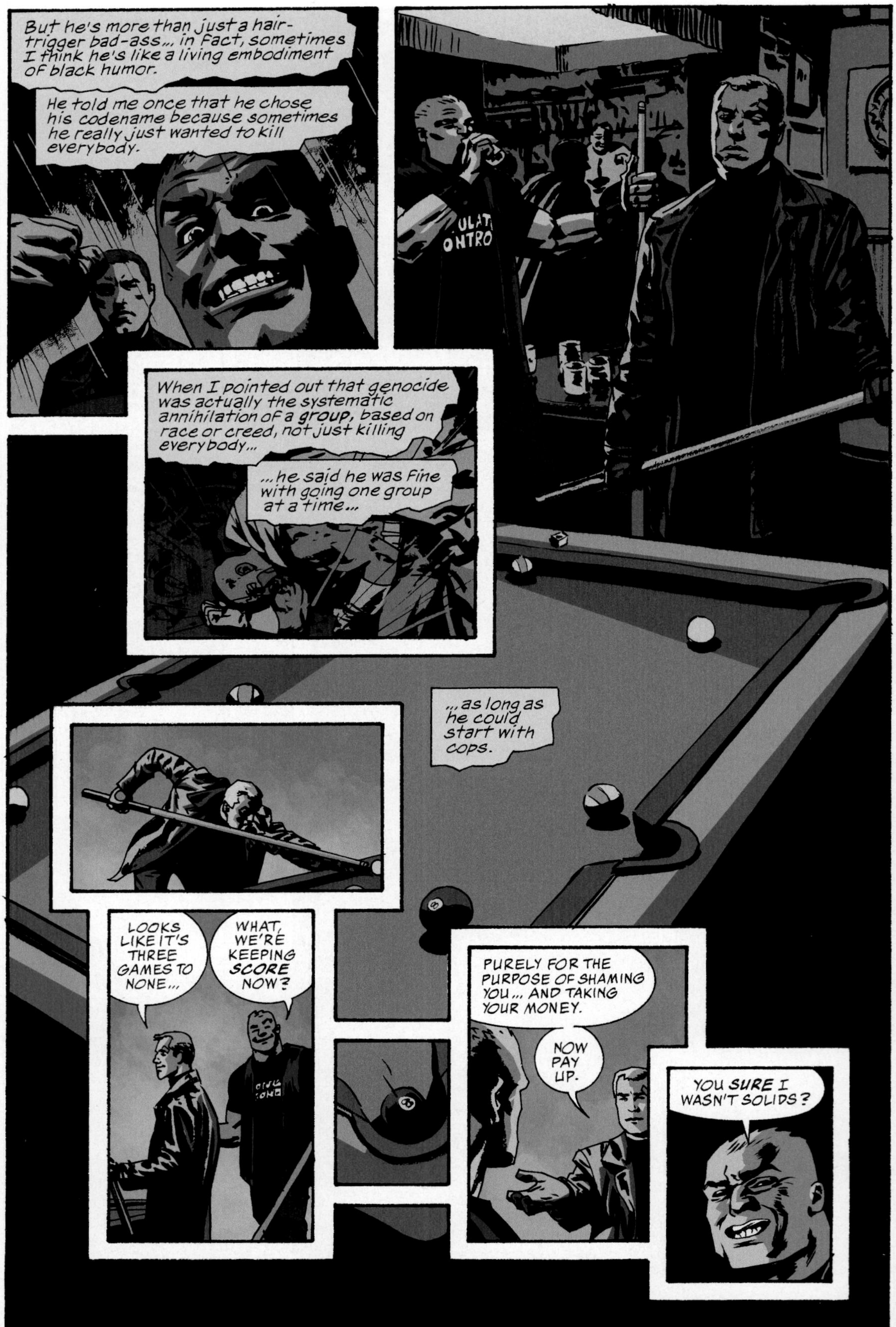
But he's more than just a hair-trigger bad-ass... in fact, sometimes I think he's like a living embodiment of black humor.
He told me once that he chose his codename because sometimes he really just wanted to kill everybody.
When I pointed out that genocide was actually the systematic annihilation of a group, based on race or creed, not just killing everybody...
...he said he was fine with going one group at a time...
...as long as he could start with cops.
LOOKS LIKE IT'S THREE GAMES TO NONE...
WHAT, WE'RE KEEPING SCORE NOW?
PURELY FOR THE PURPOSE OF SHAMING YOU... AND TAKING YOUR MONEY.
NOW PAY UP.
YOU SURE I WASN'T SOLIDS?

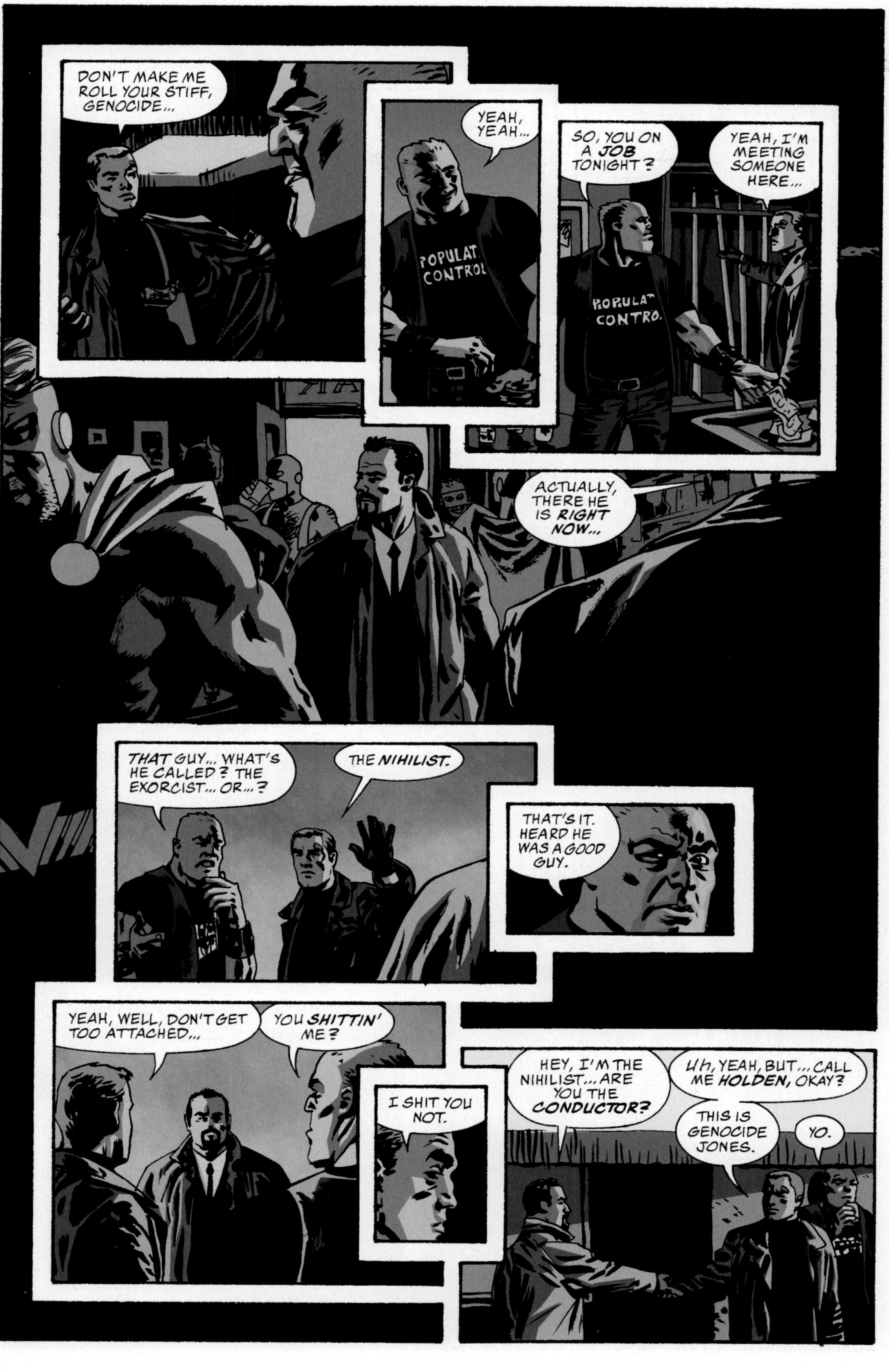
DON'T MAKE ME ROLL YOUR STIFF, GENOCIDE...
YEAH, YEAH...
POPULAT. CONTROL
SO, YOU ON A JOB TONIGHT?
YEAH, I'M MEETING SOMEONE HERE...
ACTUALLY, THERE HE IS RIGHT NOW...
THAT GUY... WHAT'S HE CALLED? THE EXORCIST... OR...?
THE NIHILIST.
THAT'S IT. HEARD HE WAS A GOOD GUY.
YEAH, WELL, DON'T GET TOO ATTACHED...
YOU SHITTIN' ME?
I SHIT YOU NOT.
HEY, I'M THE NIHILIST... ARE YOU THE CONDUCTOR?
Uh, YEAH, BUT... CALL ME HOLDEN, OKAY?
THIS IS GENOCIDE JONES.
YO.

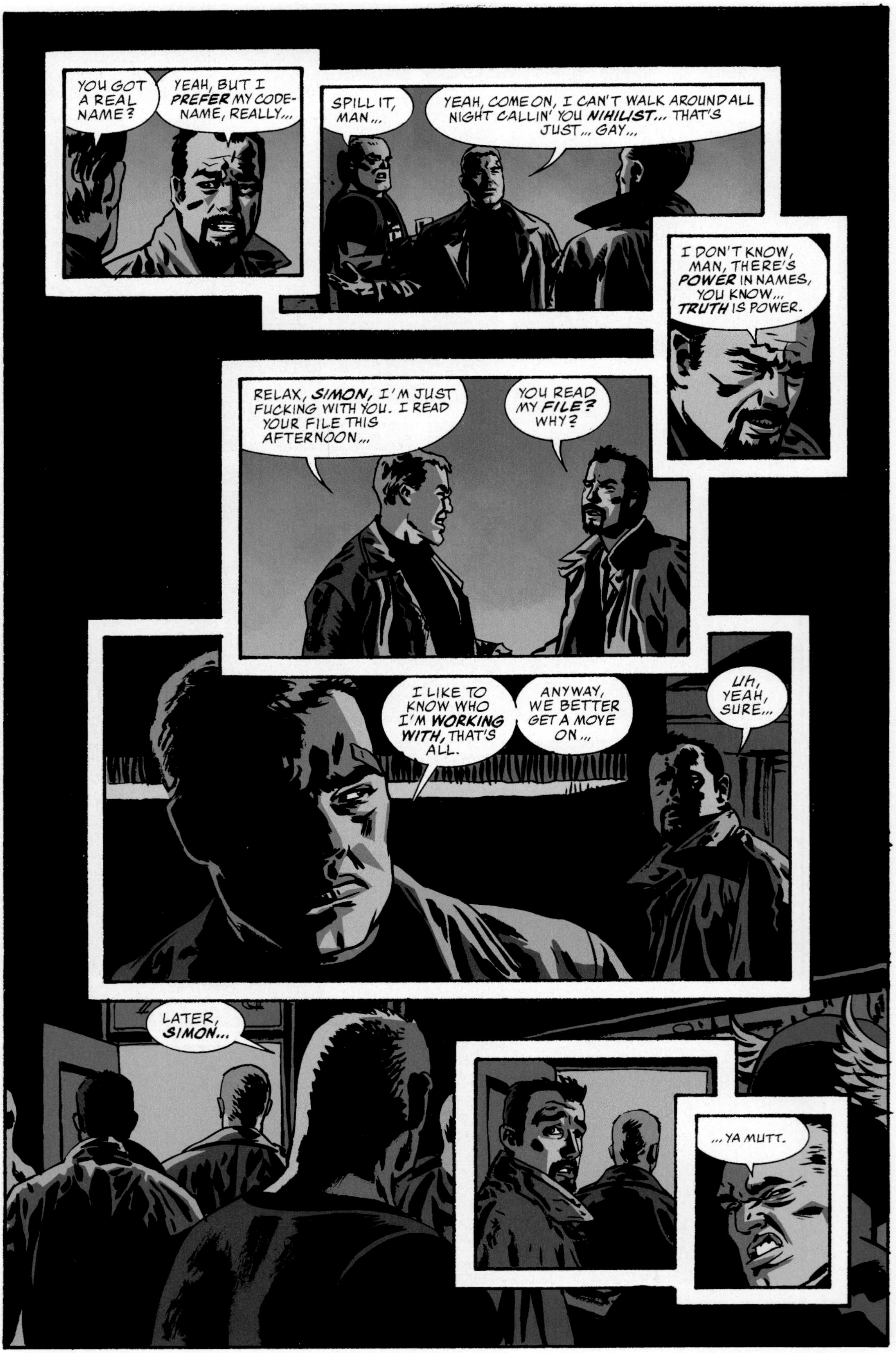
YOU GOT A REAL NAME?
YEAH, BUT I PREFER MY CODE-NAME, REALLY...
SPILL IT, MAN...
YEAH, COME ON, I CAN'T WALK AROUND ALL NIGHT CALLIN' YOU NIHILIST... THAT'S JUST... GAY...
I DON'T KNOW, MAN, THERE'S POWER IN NAMES, YOU KNOW... TRUTH IS POWER.
RELAX, SIMON, I'M JUST FUCKING WITH YOU. I READ YOUR FILE THIS AFTERNOON...
YOU READ MY FILE? WHY?
I LIKE TO KNOW WHO I'M WORKING WITH, THAT'S ALL.
ANYWAY, WE BETTER GET A MOVE ON...
UH, YEAH, SURE...
LATER, SIMON...
...YA MUTT.

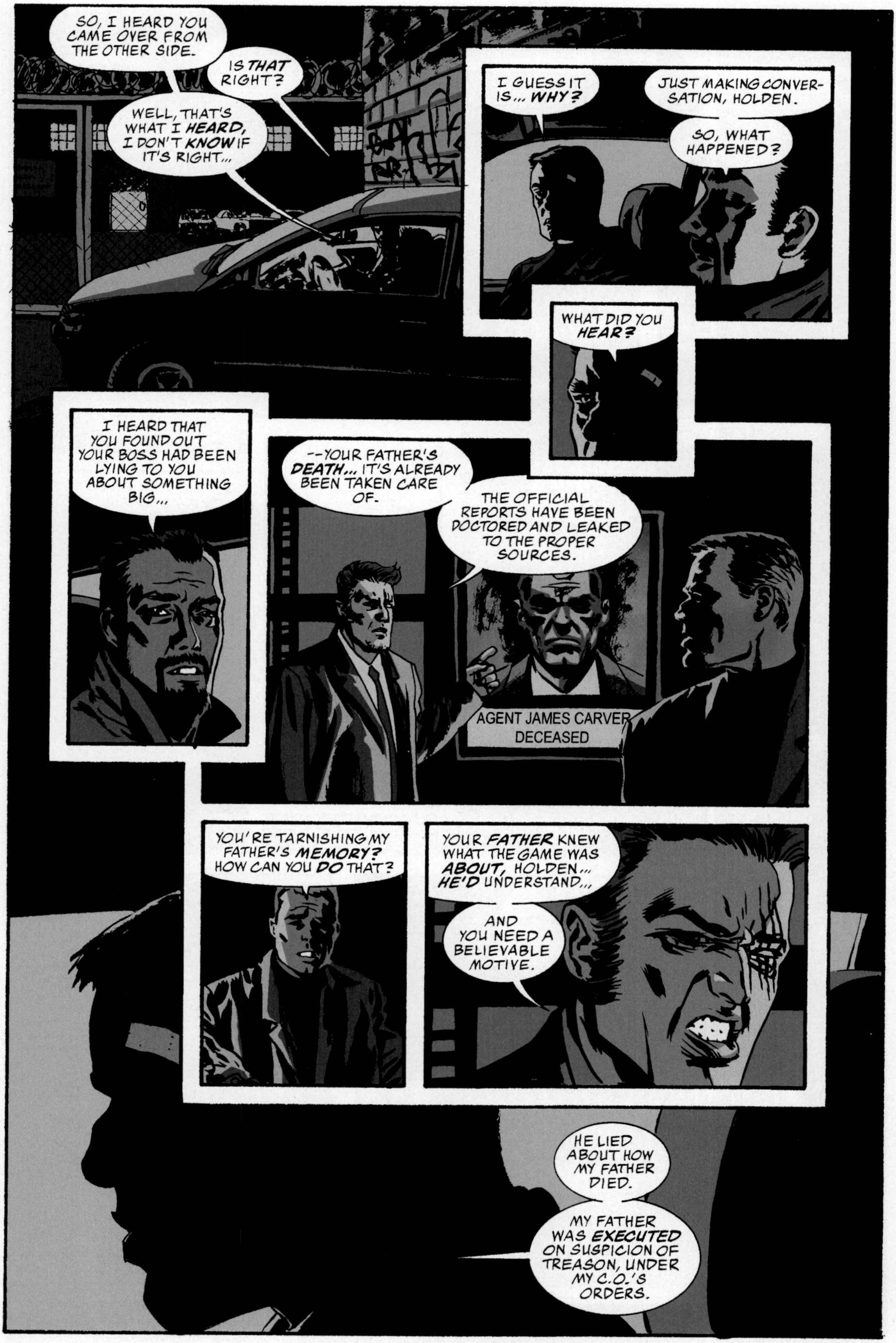

SO, I HEARD YOU CAME OVER FROM THE OTHER SIDE.
IS THAT RIGHT?
WELL, THAT'S WHAT I HEARD, I DON'T KNOW IF IT'S RIGHT...
I GUESS IT IS... WHY?
JUST MAKING CONVER-SATION, HOLDEN.
SO, WHAT HAPPENED?
WHAT DID YOU HEAR?
I HEARD THAT YOU FOUND OUT YOUR BOSS HAD BEEN LYING TO YOU ABOUT SOMETHING BIG...
--YOUR FATHER'S DEATH... IT'S ALREADY BEEN TAKEN CARE OF.
THE OFFICIAL REPORTS HAVE BEEN DOCTORED AND LEAKED TO THE PROPER SOURCES.
AGENT JAMES CARVER
DECEASED
YOU'RE TARNISHING MY FATHER'S MEMORY? HOW CAN YOU DO THAT?
YOUR FATHER KNEW WHAT THE GAME WAS ABOUT, HOLDEN... HE'D UNDERSTAND...
AND YOU NEED A BELIEVABLE MOTIVE.
HE LIED ABOUT HOW MY FATHER DIED.
MY FATHER WAS EXECUTED ON SUSPICION OF TREASON, UNDER MY C.O.'S ORDERS.

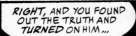 RIGHT, AND YOU FOUND OUT THE TRUTH AND *TURNED* ON HIM...

WENT ON SOME CRAZY *BLACK OPS* MISSION AFTER SOME *ALIEN* ARTIFACT--

WASN'T *ALIEN*... IT WAS SOMETHING FROM THE BLEED.

WHAT'S THE FUCKING *BLEED?*

I'M NOT EXACTLY SURE. SOME KIND OF DIMENSION BETWEEN REALITIES...

REALLY? TRIP OUT.

YEAH, I COULD NEVER ENTIRELY GET *MY* HEAD AROUND IT, EITHER.

SO THEN I HEARD YOU *KILLED* ALL YOUR MEN AND TOOK THIS *ARTIFACT* FOR YOURSELF...

--AND ACCORDING TO WHAT I.O. HAVE BEEN ABLE TO TRACK, IT *APPEARS* YOU WERE PAID A *PRETTY PENNY* FOR IT BY A MIDDLE EASTERN EMIRATE...

THIS WAY, I DON'T HAVE TO WORRY ABOUT *YOU* APPROACHING TAO... ONCE WE GET YOU OUT OF HERE, HIS *PEOPLE* WILL APPROACH YOU.

BECAUSE YOU'RE ALREADY *ONE OF THEM.*

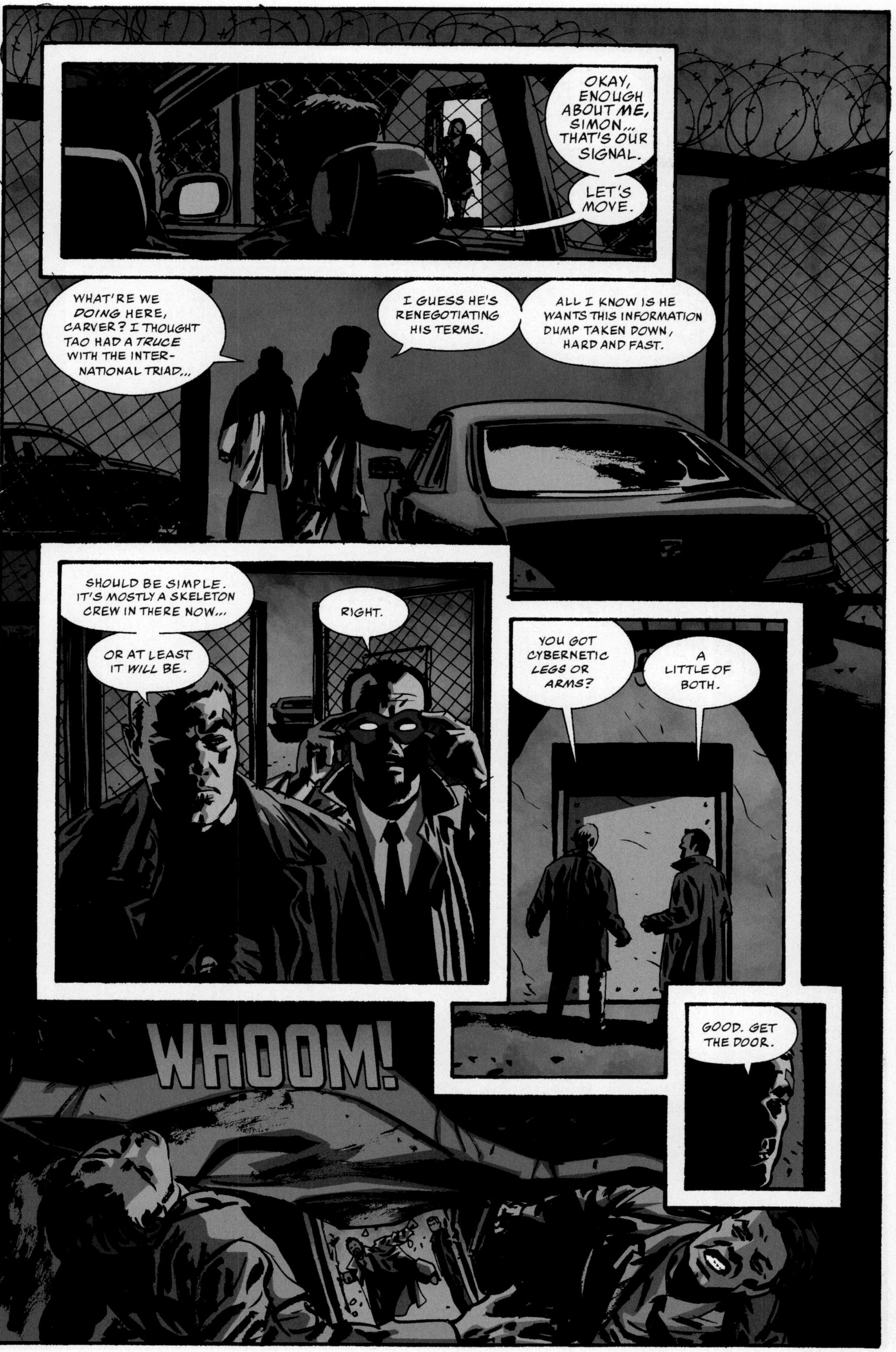
OKAY, ENOUGH ABOUT *ME*, SIMON... THAT'S OUR SIGNAL.
LET'S MOVE.
WHAT'RE WE *DOING* HERE, CARVER? I THOUGHT TAO HAD A *TRUCE* WITH THE INTER-NATIONAL TRIAD...
I GUESS HE'S RENEGOTIATING HIS TERMS.
ALL I KNOW IS HE WANTS THIS INFORMATION DUMP TAKEN DOWN, HARD AND FAST.
SHOULD BE SIMPLE. IT'S MOSTLY A SKELETON CREW IN THERE NOW...
OR AT LEAST IT *WILL* BE.
RIGHT.
YOU GOT CYBERNETIC *LEGS* OR *ARMS*?
A LITTLE OF BOTH.
GOOD. GET THE DOOR.
WHOOM!

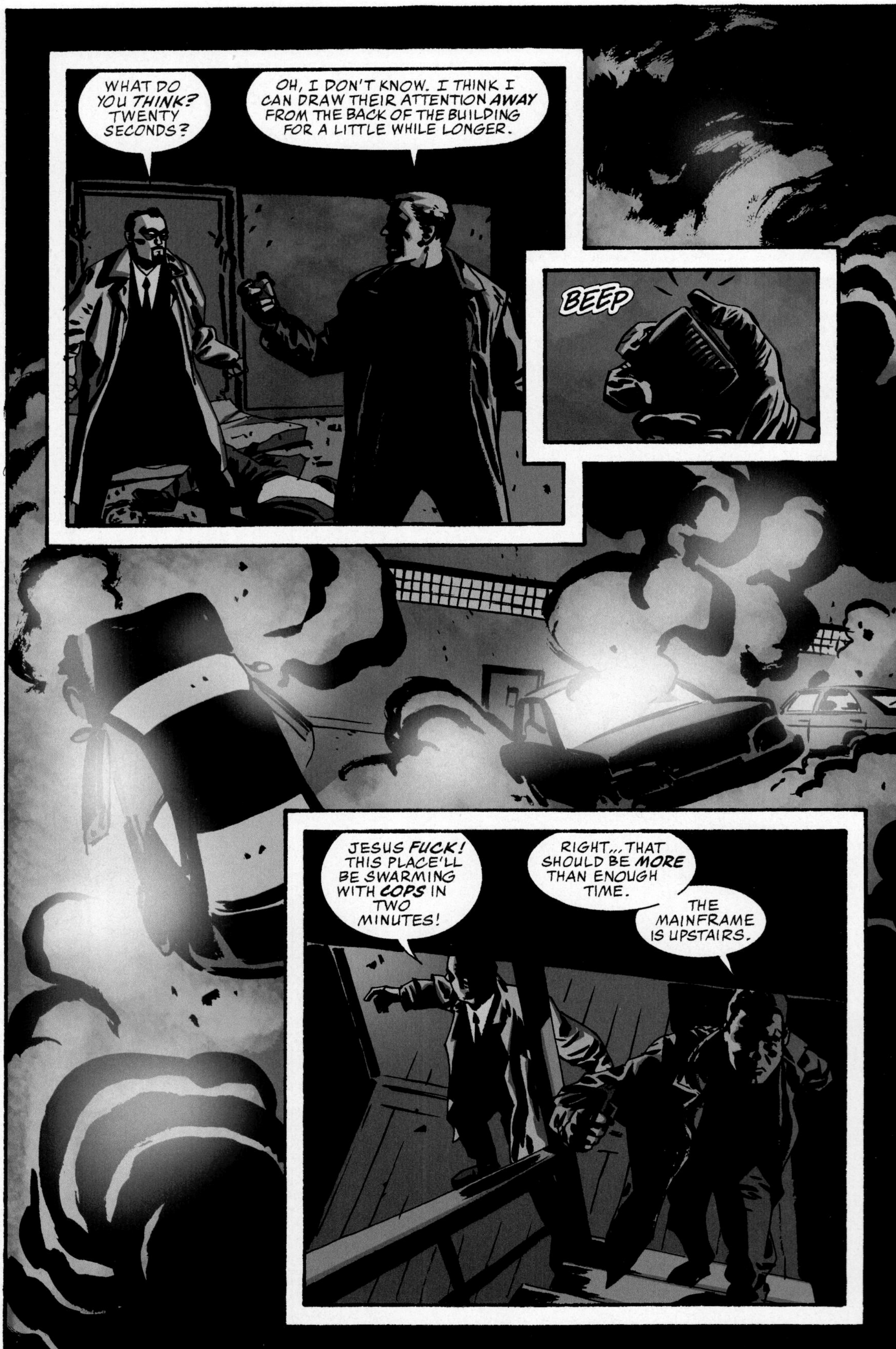
WHAT DO YOU THINK? TWENTY SECONDS?
OH, I DON'T KNOW. I THINK I CAN DRAW THEIR ATTENTION AWAY FROM THE BACK OF THE BUILDING FOR A LITTLE WHILE LONGER.
BEEP
JESUS FUCK! THIS PLACE'LL BE SWARMING WITH COPS IN TWO MINUTES!
RIGHT... THAT SHOULD BE MORE THAN ENOUGH TIME.
THE MAINFRAME IS UPSTAIRS.

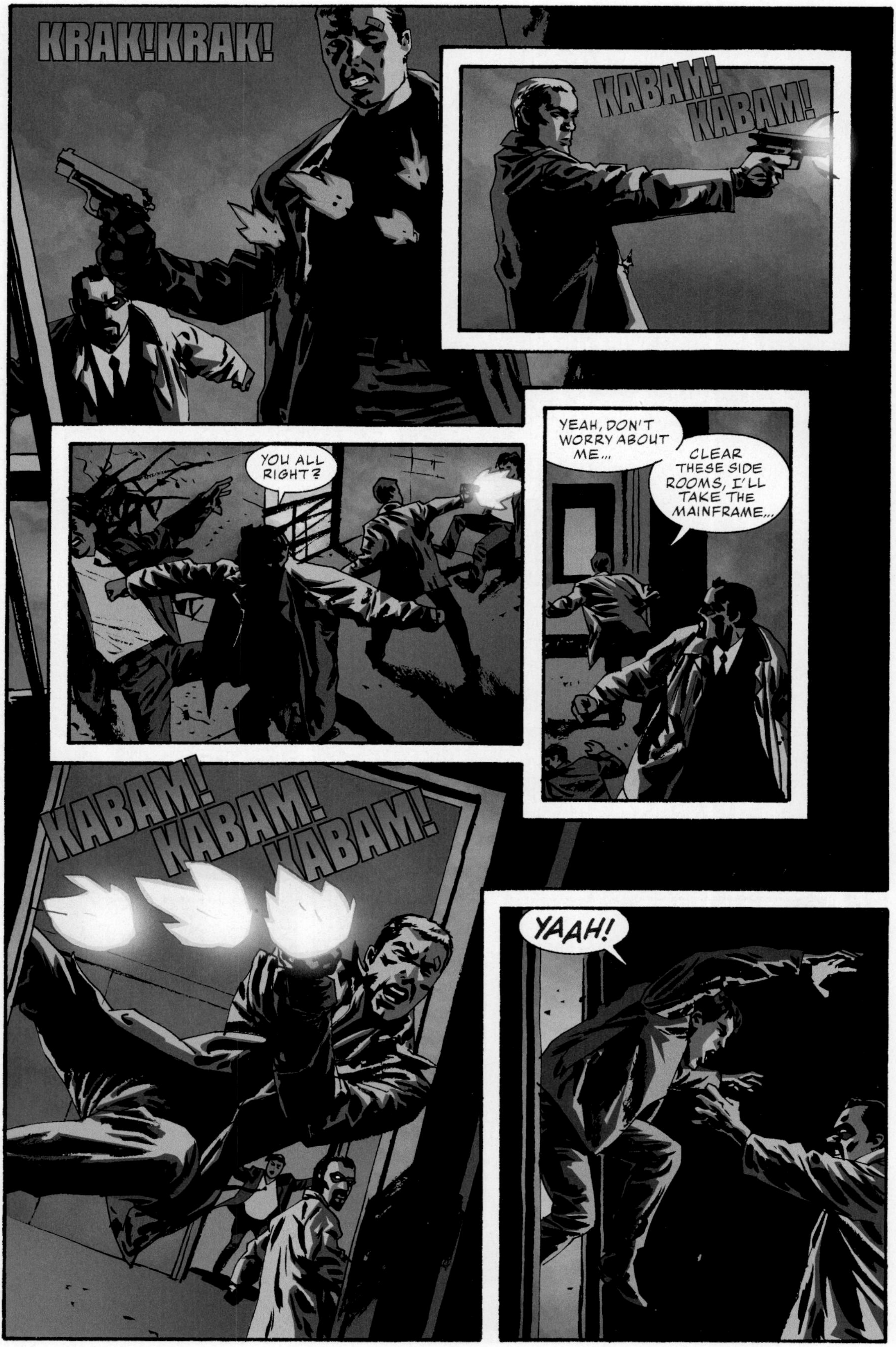
KRAK!KRAK!
KABAM! KABAM!
YOU ALL RIGHT?
YEAH, DON'T WORRY ABOUT ME...
CLEAR THESE SIDE ROOMS, I'LL TAKE THE MAINFRAME...
KABAM! KABAM! KABAM!
YAAH!

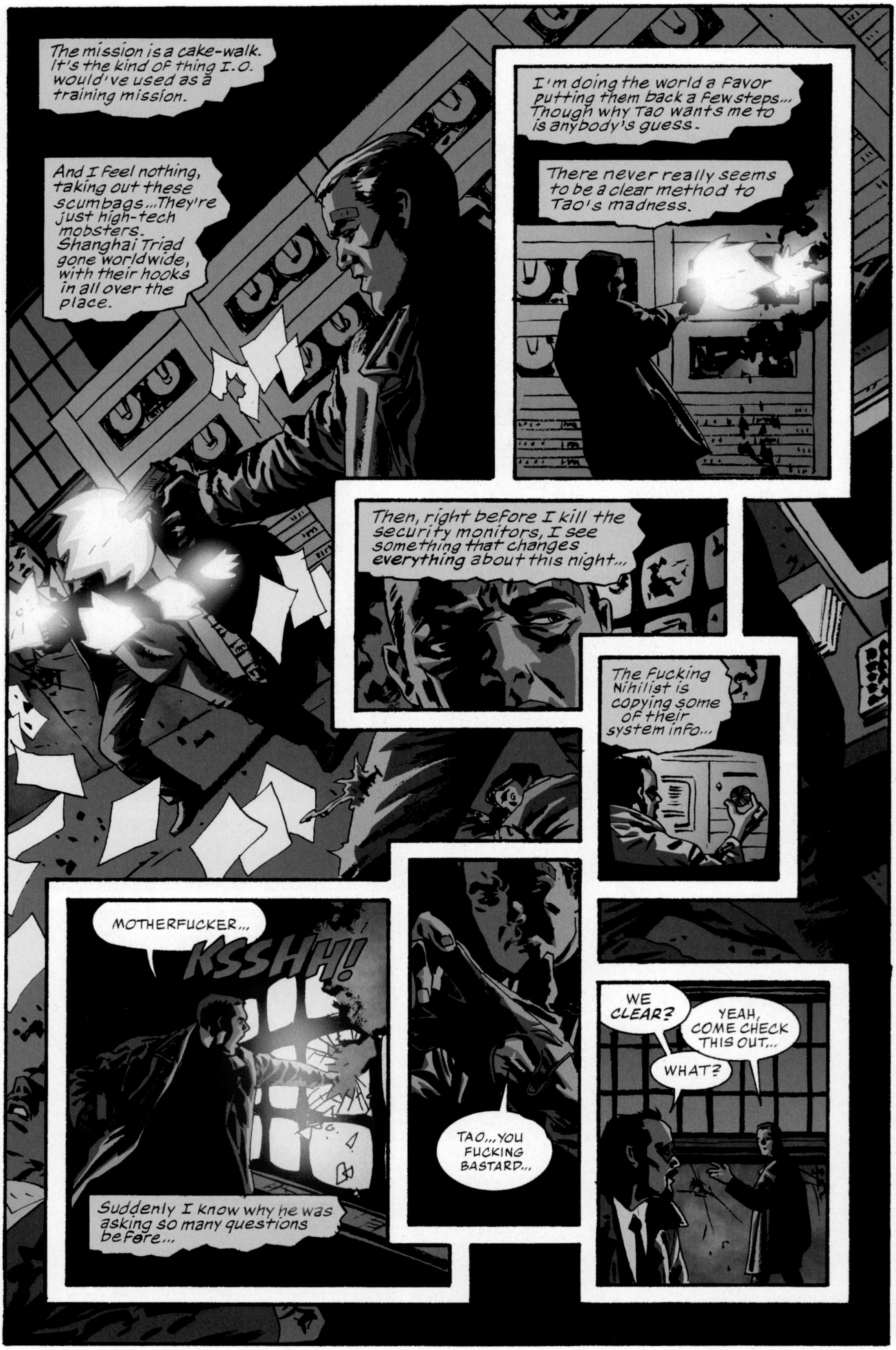

The mission is a cake-walk. It's the kind of thing I.O. would've used as a training mission.
And I feel nothing, taking out these scumbags...They're just high-tech mobsters. Shanghai Triad gone worldwide, with their hooks in all over the place.
I'm doing the world a favor putting them back a few steps... Though why Tao wants me to is anybody's guess.
There never really seems to be a clear method to Tao's madness.
Then, right before I kill the security monitors, I see something that changes **everything** about this night...
The fucking Nihilist is copying some of their system info...
MOTHERFUCKER...
KSSHH!
Suddenly I know why he was asking so many questions before...
TAO...YOU FUCKING BASTARD...
WE CLEAR?
YEAH, COME CHECK THIS OUT...
WHAT?

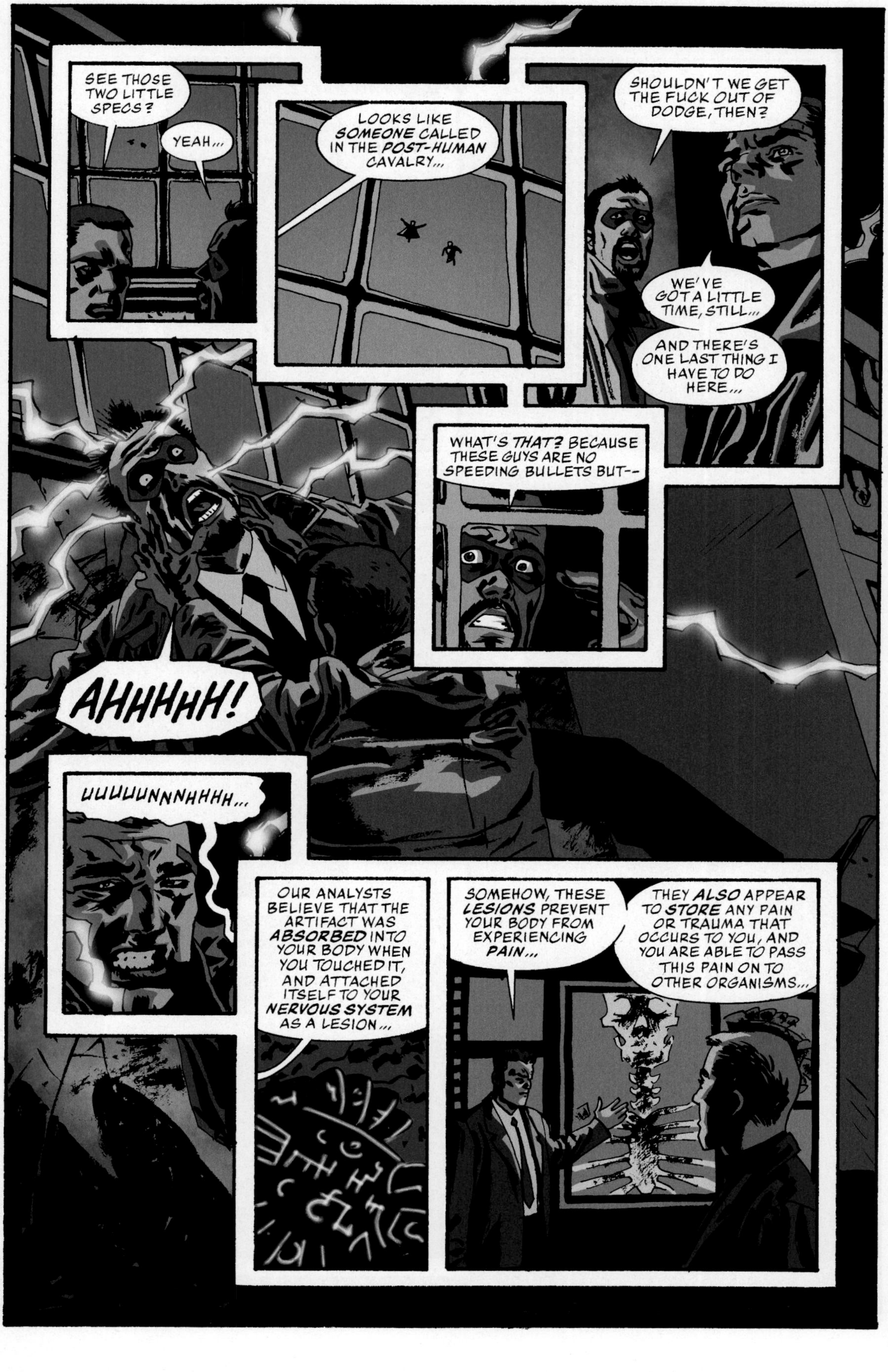
SEE THOSE TWO LITTLE SPECS?
YEAH...
LOOKS LIKE SOMEONE CALLED IN THE POST-HUMAN CAVALRY...
SHOULDN'T WE GET THE FUCK OUT OF DODGE, THEN?
WE'VE GOT A LITTLE TIME, STILL...
AND THERE'S ONE LAST THING I HAVE TO DO HERE...
WHAT'S THAT? BECAUSE THESE GUYS ARE NO SPEEDING BULLETS BUT--
AHHHHH!
UUUUUNNHHHH...
OUR ANALYSTS BELIEVE THAT THE ARTIFACT WAS ABSORBED INTO YOUR BODY WHEN YOU TOUCHED IT, AND ATTACHED ITSELF TO YOUR NERVOUS SYSTEM AS A LESION...
SOMEHOW, THESE LESIONS PREVENT YOUR BODY FROM EXPERIENCING PAIN...
THEY ALSO APPEAR TO STORE ANY PAIN OR TRAUMA THAT OCCURS TO YOU, AND YOU ARE ABLE TO PASS THIS PAIN ON TO OTHER ORGANISMS...

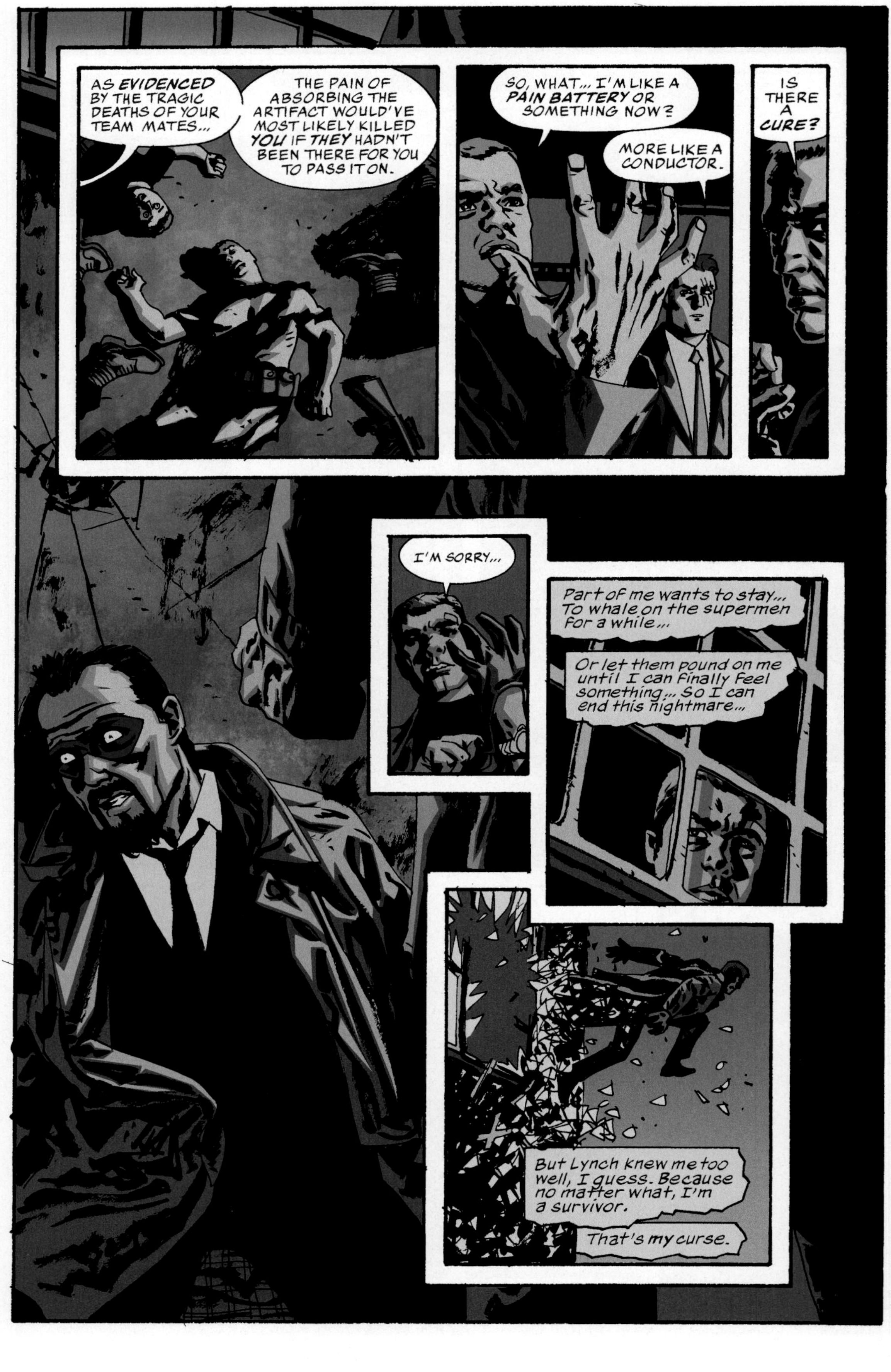

AS EVIDENCED BY THE TRAGIC DEATHS OF YOUR TEAM MATES...
THE PAIN OF ABSORBING THE ARTIFACT WOULD'VE MOST LIKELY KILLED YOU IF THEY HADN'T BEEN THERE FOR YOU TO PASS IT ON.
SO, WHAT... I'M LIKE A PAIN BATTERY OR SOMETHING NOW?
MORE LIKE A CONDUCTOR.
IS THERE A CURE?
I'M SORRY...
Part of me wants to stay... To whale on the supermen for a while...
Or let them pound on me until I can finally feel something... So I can end this nightmare...
But Lynch knew me too well, I guess. Because no matter what, I'm a survivor.
That's my curse.

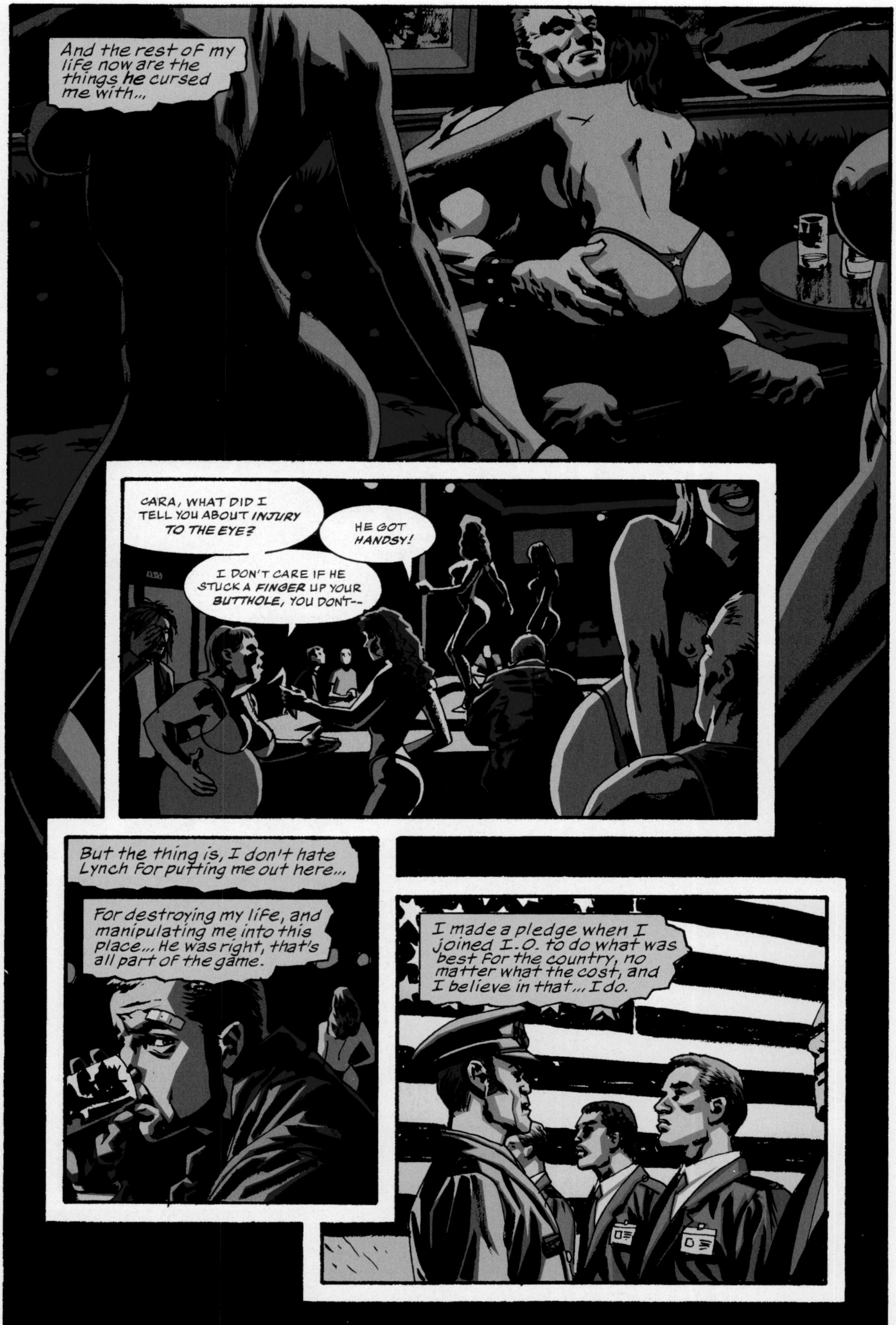
And the rest of my life now are the things he cursed me with...
CARA, WHAT DID I TELL YOU ABOUT INJURY TO THE EYE?
HE GOT HANDSY!
I DON'T CARE IF HE STUCK A FINGER UP YOUR BUTTHOLE, YOU DON'T--
But the thing is, I don't hate Lynch for putting me out here...
For destroying my life, and manipulating me into this place... He was right, that's all part of the game.
I made a pledge when I joined I.O. to do what was best for the country, no matter what the cost, and I believe in that... I do.

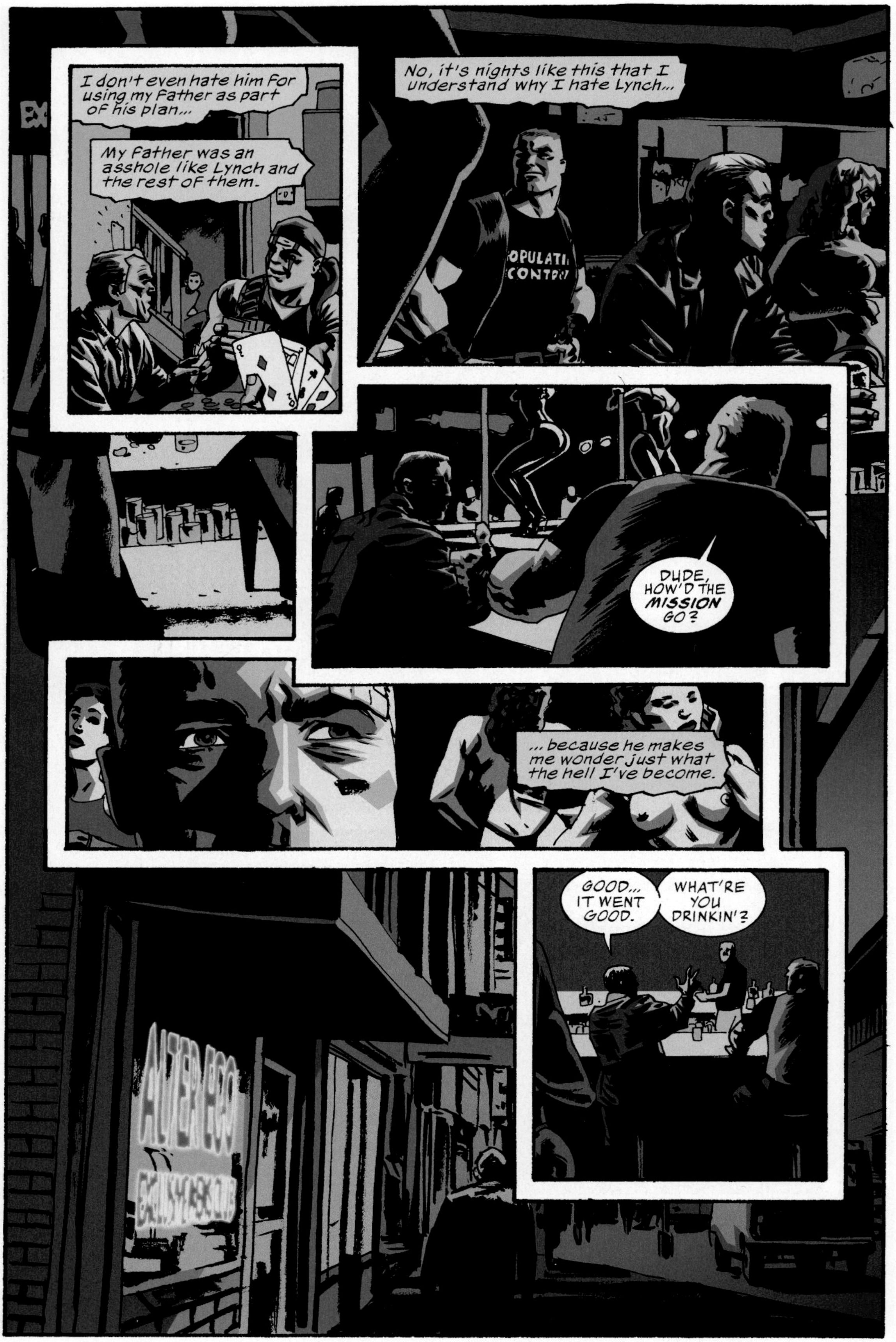
I don't even hate him for using my father as part of his plan...
My father was an asshole like Lynch and the rest of them.
No, it's nights like this that I understand why I hate Lynch...
DUDE, HOW'D THE MISSION GO?
...because he makes me wonder just what the hell I've become.
GOOD... IT WENT GOOD.
WHAT'RE YOU DRINKIN'?
ALTER EGO

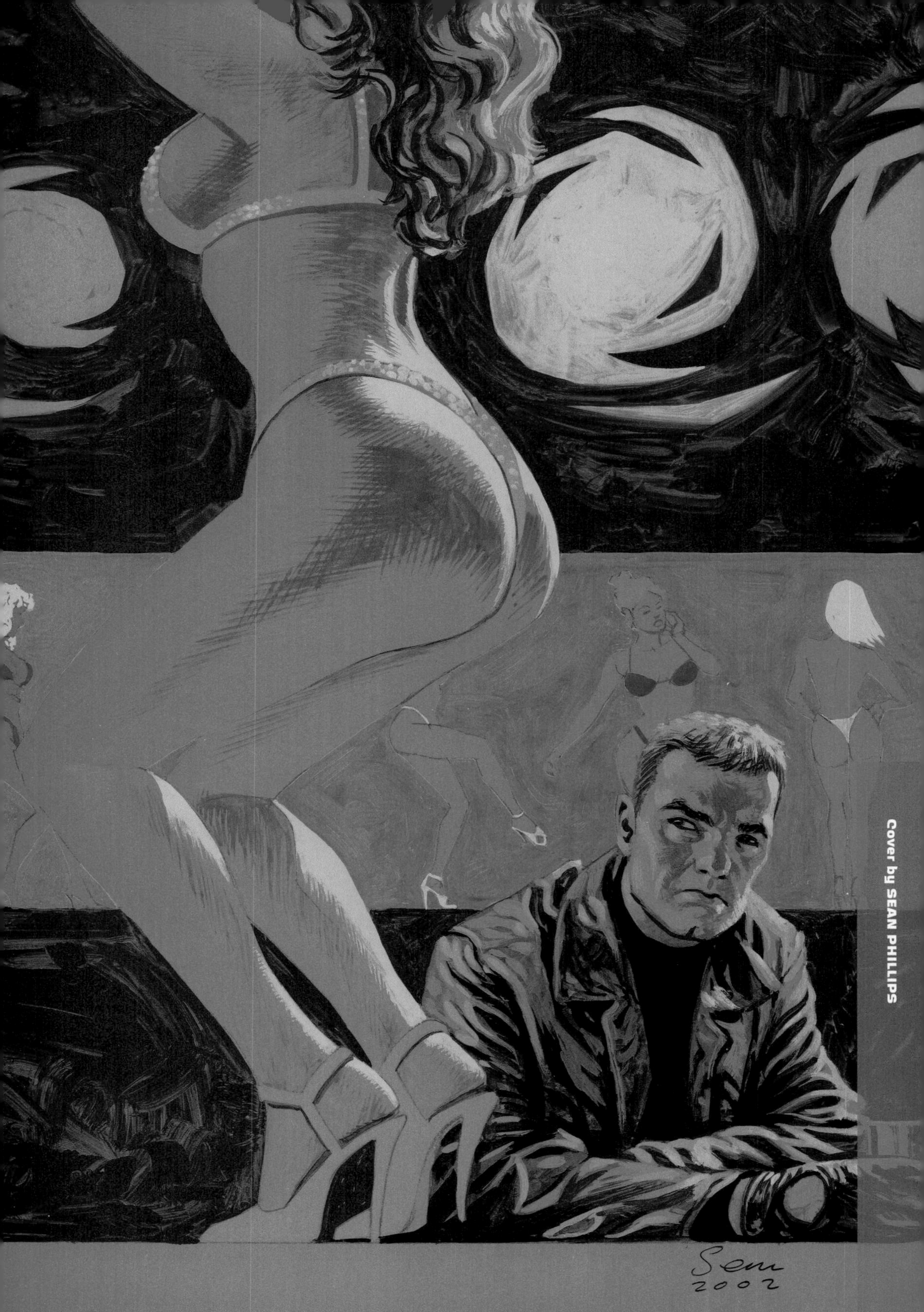
Sean
2002

Cover by SEAN PHILLIPS

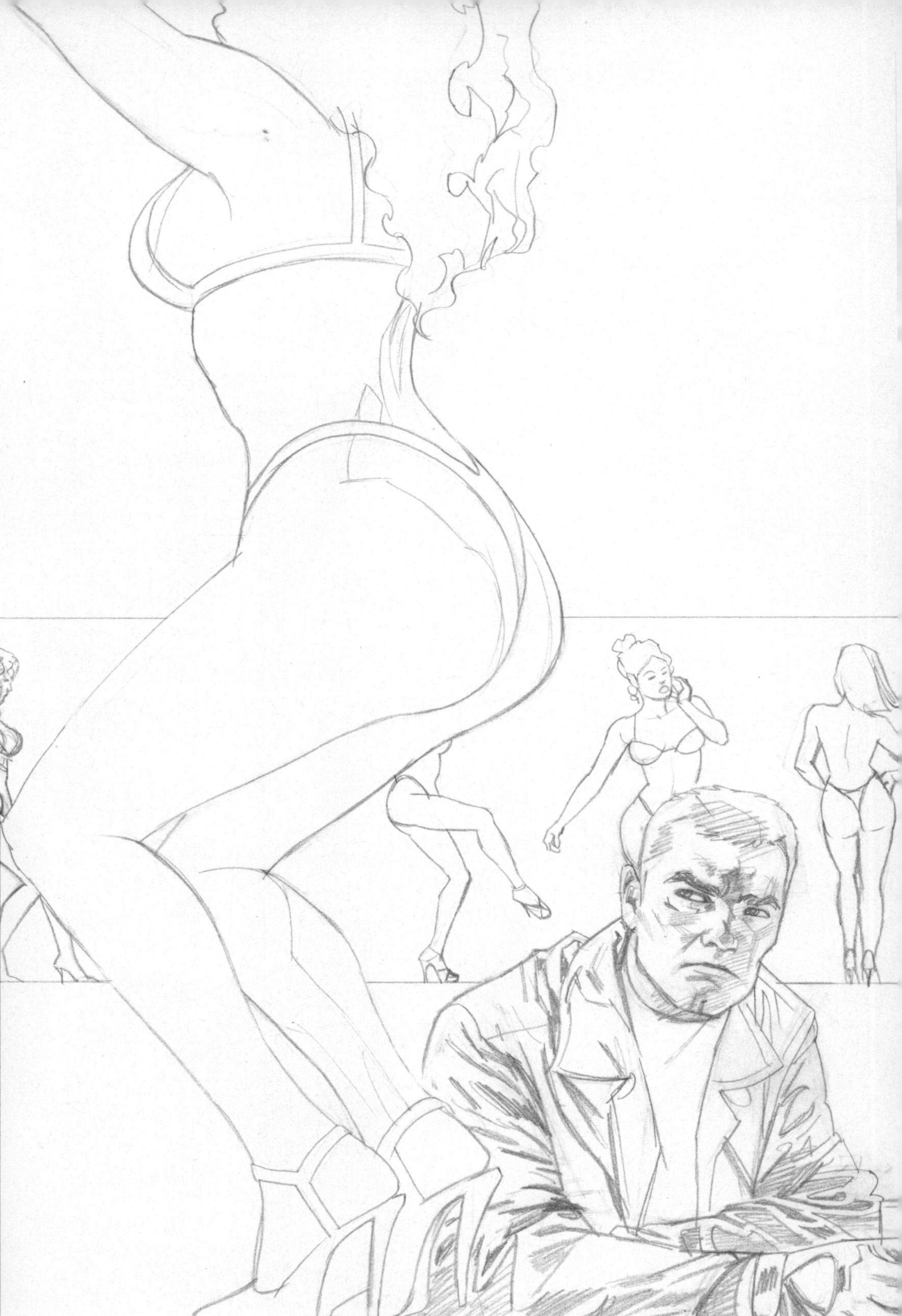

SLEEPER #2 Cover Pencils by SEAN PHILLIPS

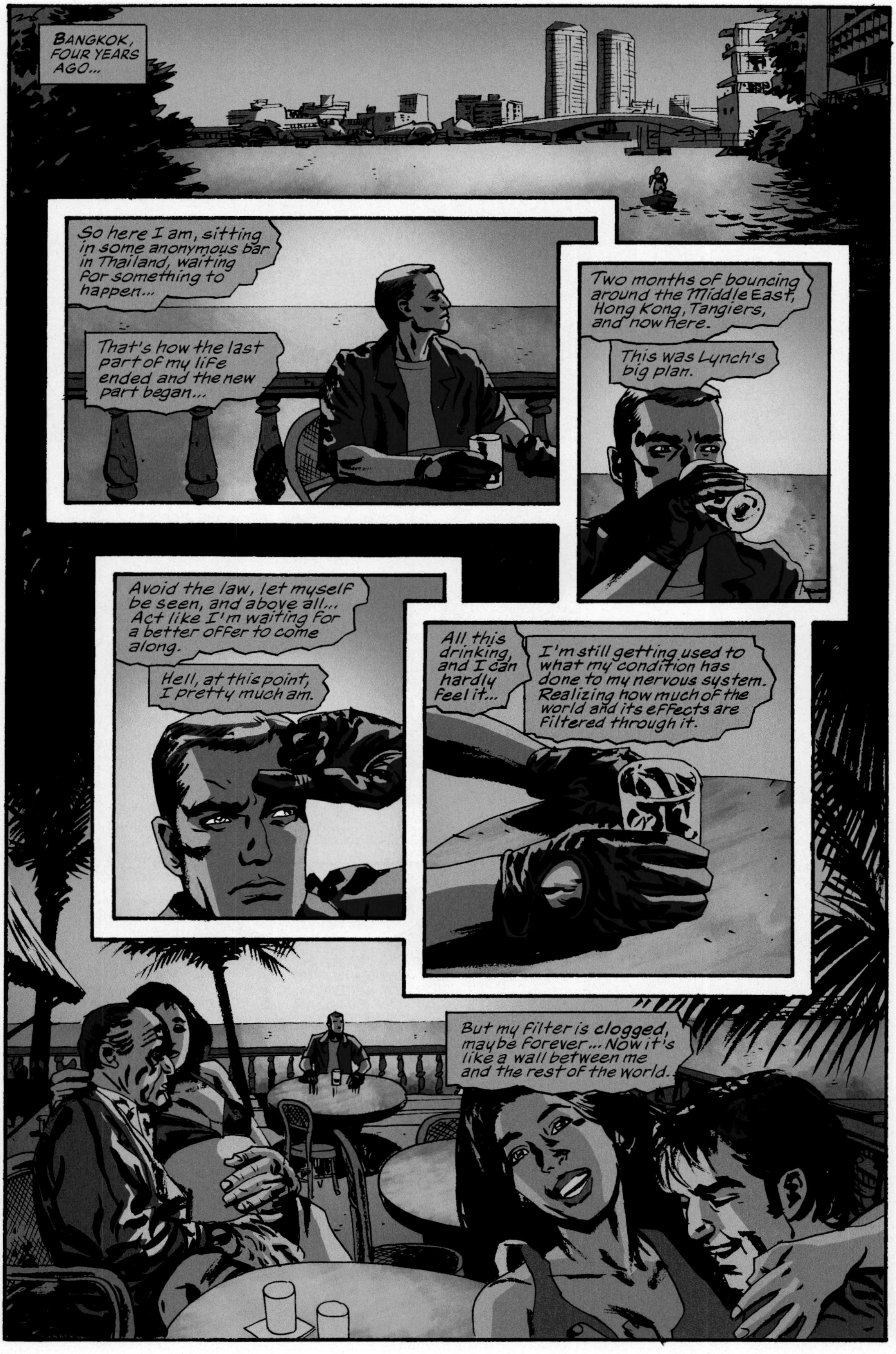
BANGKOK, FOUR YEARS AGO...
So here I am, sitting in some anonymous bar in Thailand, waiting for something to happen...
That's how the last part of my life ended and the new part began...
Two months of bouncing around the Middle East, Hong Kong, Tangiers, and now here.
This was Lynch's big plan.
Avoid the law, let myself be seen, and above all... Act like I'm waiting for a better offer to come along.
Hell, at this point, I pretty much am.
All this drinking, and I can hardly feel it...
I'm still getting used to what my condition has done to my nervous system. Realizing how much of the world and its effects are filtered through it.
But my filter is clogged, maybe forever... Now it's like a wall between me and the rest of the world.

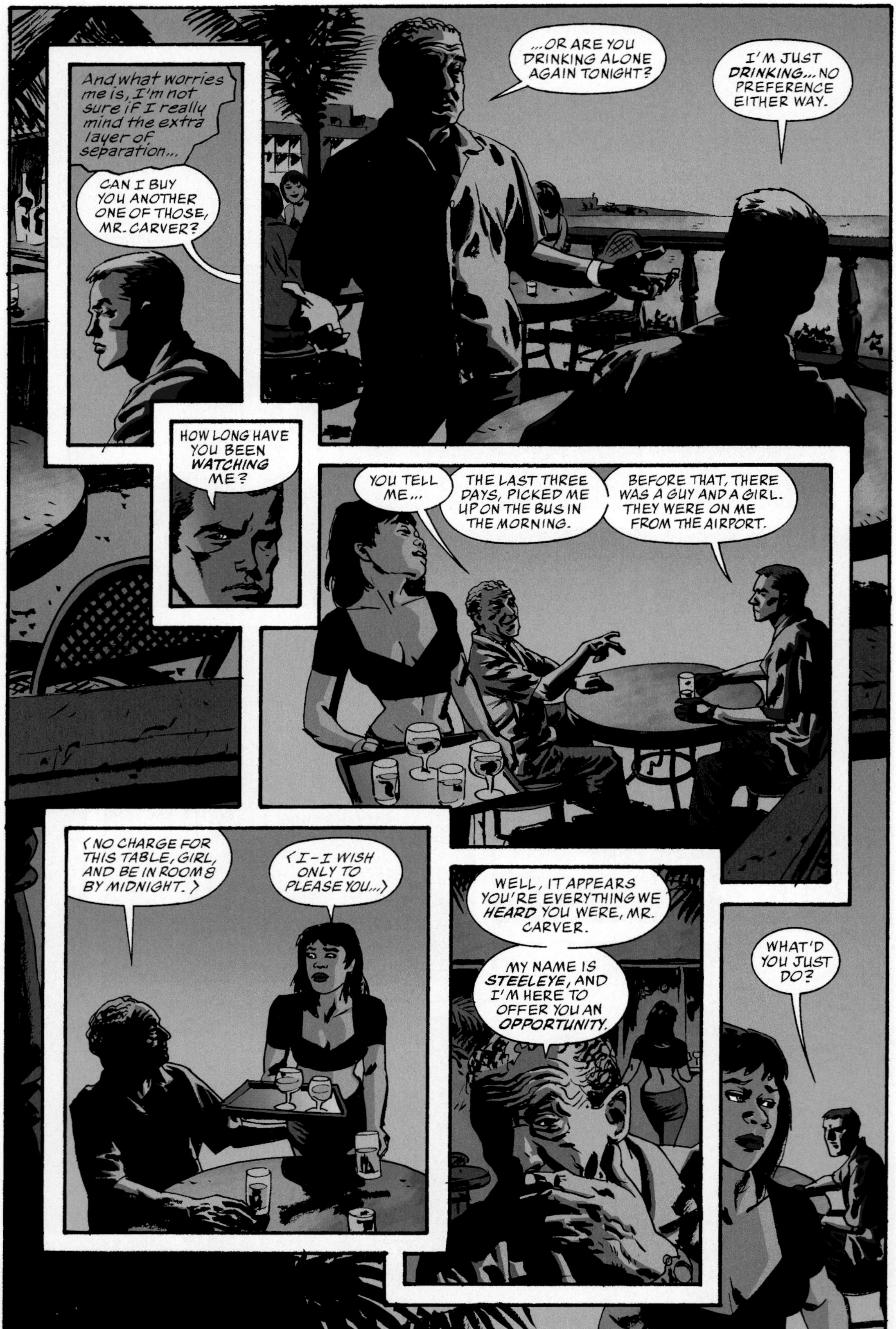
And what worries me is, I'm not sure if I really mind the extra layer of separation...
CAN I BUY YOU ANOTHER ONE OF THOSE, MR. CARVER?
...OR ARE YOU DRINKING ALONE AGAIN TONIGHT?
I'M JUST DRINKING... NO PREFERENCE EITHER WAY.
HOW LONG HAVE YOU BEEN WATCHING ME?
YOU TELL ME...
THE LAST THREE DAYS, PICKED ME UP ON THE BUS IN THE MORNING.
BEFORE THAT, THERE WAS A GUY AND A GIRL. THEY WERE ON ME FROM THE AIRPORT.
<NO CHARGE FOR THIS TABLE, GIRL, AND BE IN ROOM 8 BY MIDNIGHT.>
<I-I WISH ONLY TO PLEASE YOU...>
WELL, IT APPEARS YOU'RE EVERYTHING WE HEARD YOU WERE, MR. CARVER.
MY NAME IS STEELEYE, AND I'M HERE TO OFFER YOU AN OPPORTUNITY.
WHAT'D YOU JUST DO?

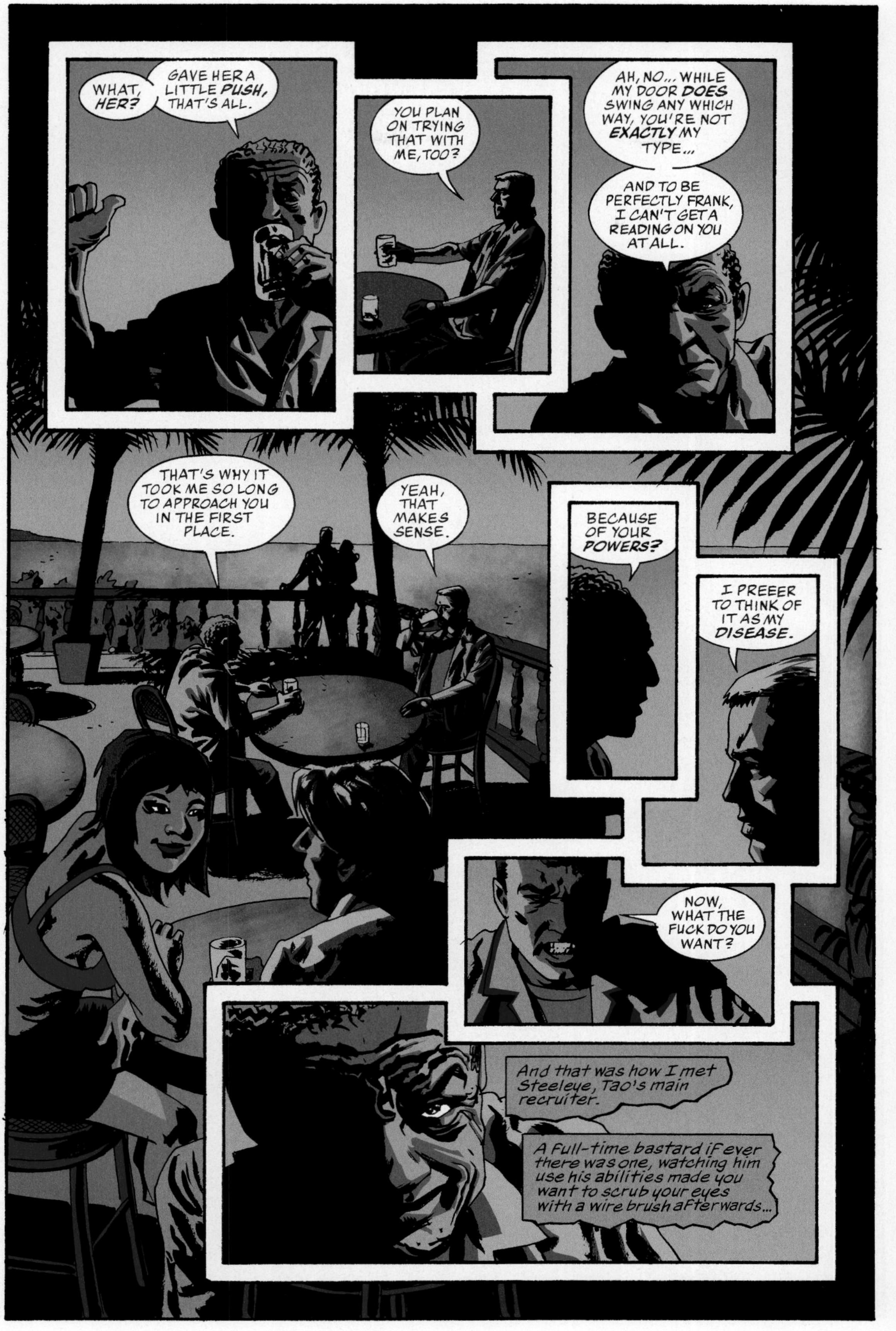

WHAT, HER?
GAVE HER A LITTLE PUSH, THAT'S ALL.
YOU PLAN ON TRYING THAT WITH ME, TOO?
AH, NO... WHILE MY DOOR DOES SWING ANY WHICH WAY, YOU'RE NOT EXACTLY MY TYPE...
AND TO BE PERFECTLY FRANK, I CAN'T GET A READING ON YOU AT ALL.
THAT'S WHY IT TOOK ME SO LONG TO APPROACH YOU IN THE FIRST PLACE.
YEAH, THAT MAKES SENSE.
BECAUSE OF YOUR POWERS?
I PREEER TO THINK OF IT AS MY DISEASE.
NOW, WHAT THE FUCK DO YOU WANT?
And that was how I met Steeleye, Tao's main recruiter.
A full-time bastard if ever there was one, watching him use his abilities made you want to scrub your eyes with a wire brush afterwards...

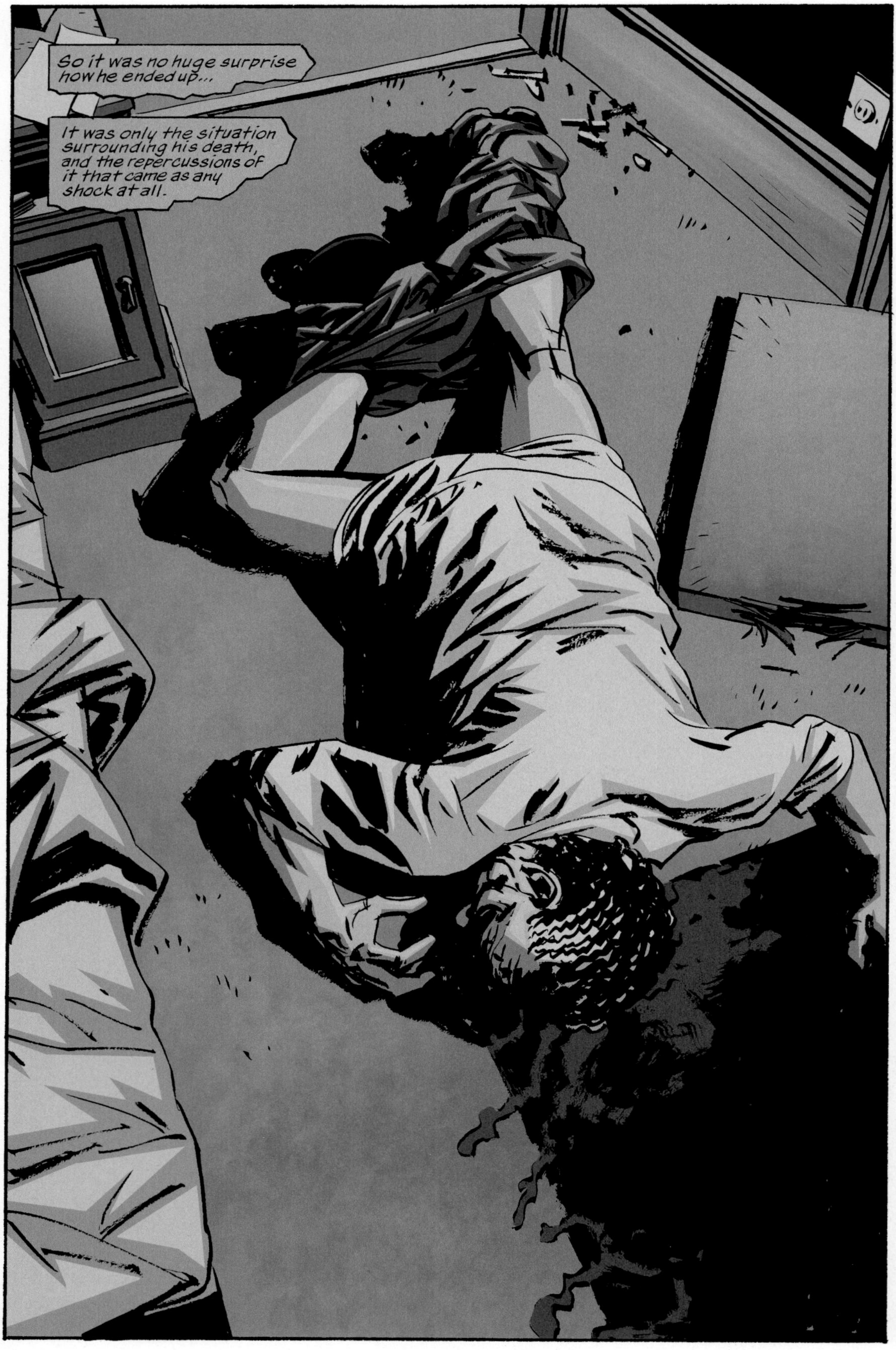
So it was no huge surprise how he ended up...
It was only the situation surrounding his death, and the repercussions of it that came as any shock at all.

NEW YORK, LAST WEEKEND...

While the good guys have their secret headquarters in space and on the moon, those of us on the other side of the fence have an assortment of hangouts...

...and an assortment of hanger-ons.

Wannabes and groupies. Kids who wish they were bad, and young girls who just need to be close to bad for a few hours at a time.

In the old days, major villains like Doctor Mind, Hugo Lark, the Undertaker...They wouldn't have been caught dead around here. Those guys had class...

...But the super-powered badasses of our modern era spend a considerable part of their lives in underground dumps like this...

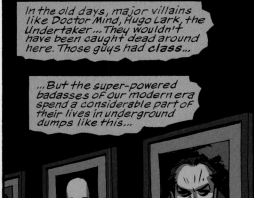

...Because who the fuck doesn't want to be treated like a rock star?

It's the curse of the 21st century.

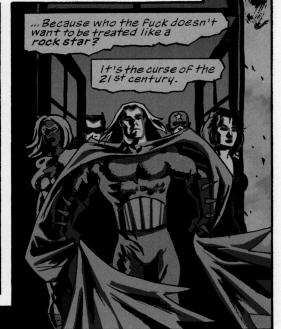

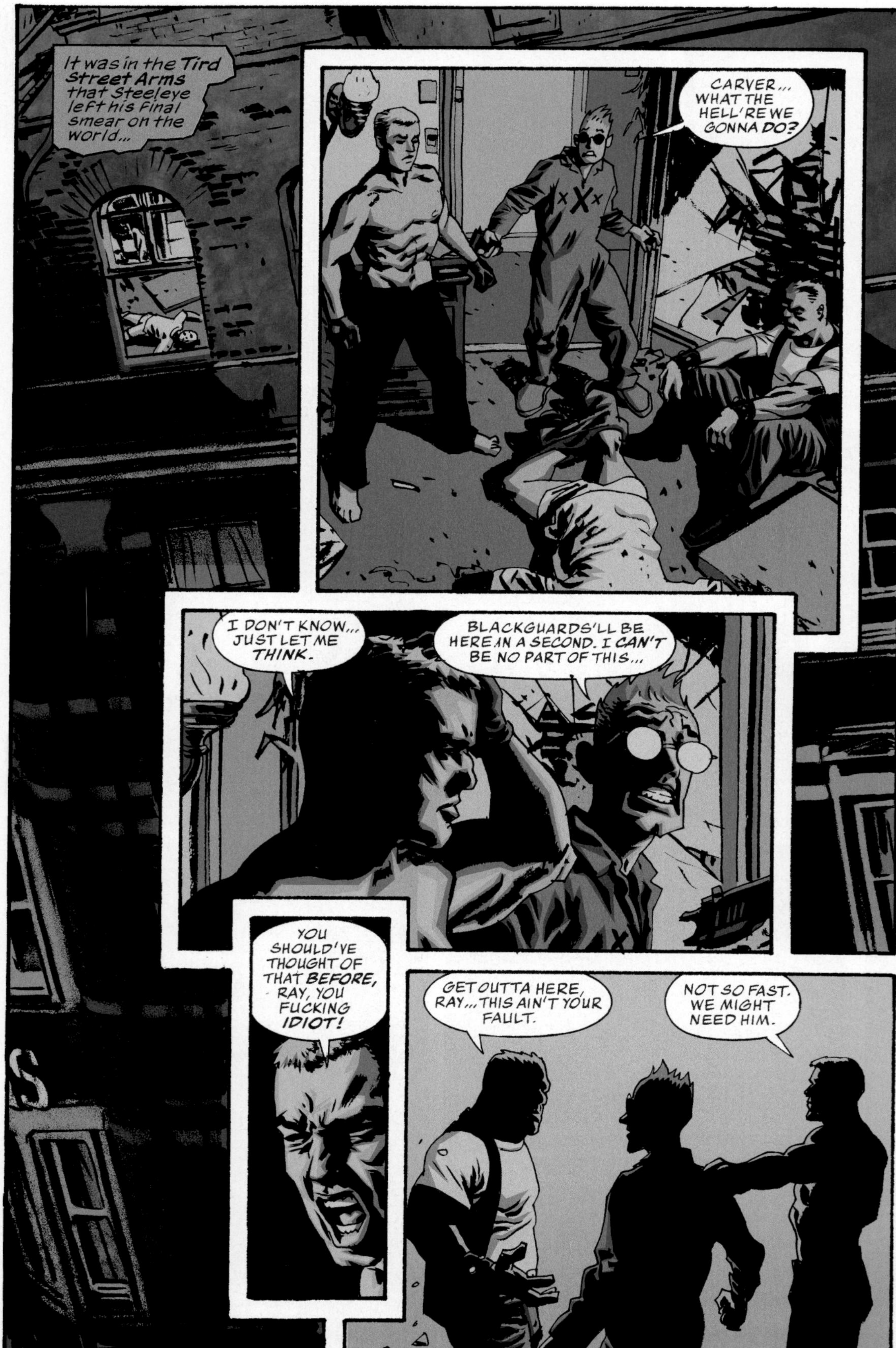
It was in the Tird Street Arms that Steeleye left his final smear on the world...
CARVER... WHAT THE HELL'RE WE GONNA DO?
I DON'T KNOW... JUST LET ME THINK.
BLACKGUARDS'LL BE HERE IN A SECOND. I CAN'T BE NO PART OF THIS...
YOU SHOULD'VE THOUGHT OF THAT BEFORE, RAY, YOU FUCKING IDIOT!
GET OUTTA HERE, RAY... THIS AIN'T YOUR FAULT.
NOT SO FAST. WE MIGHT NEED HIM.

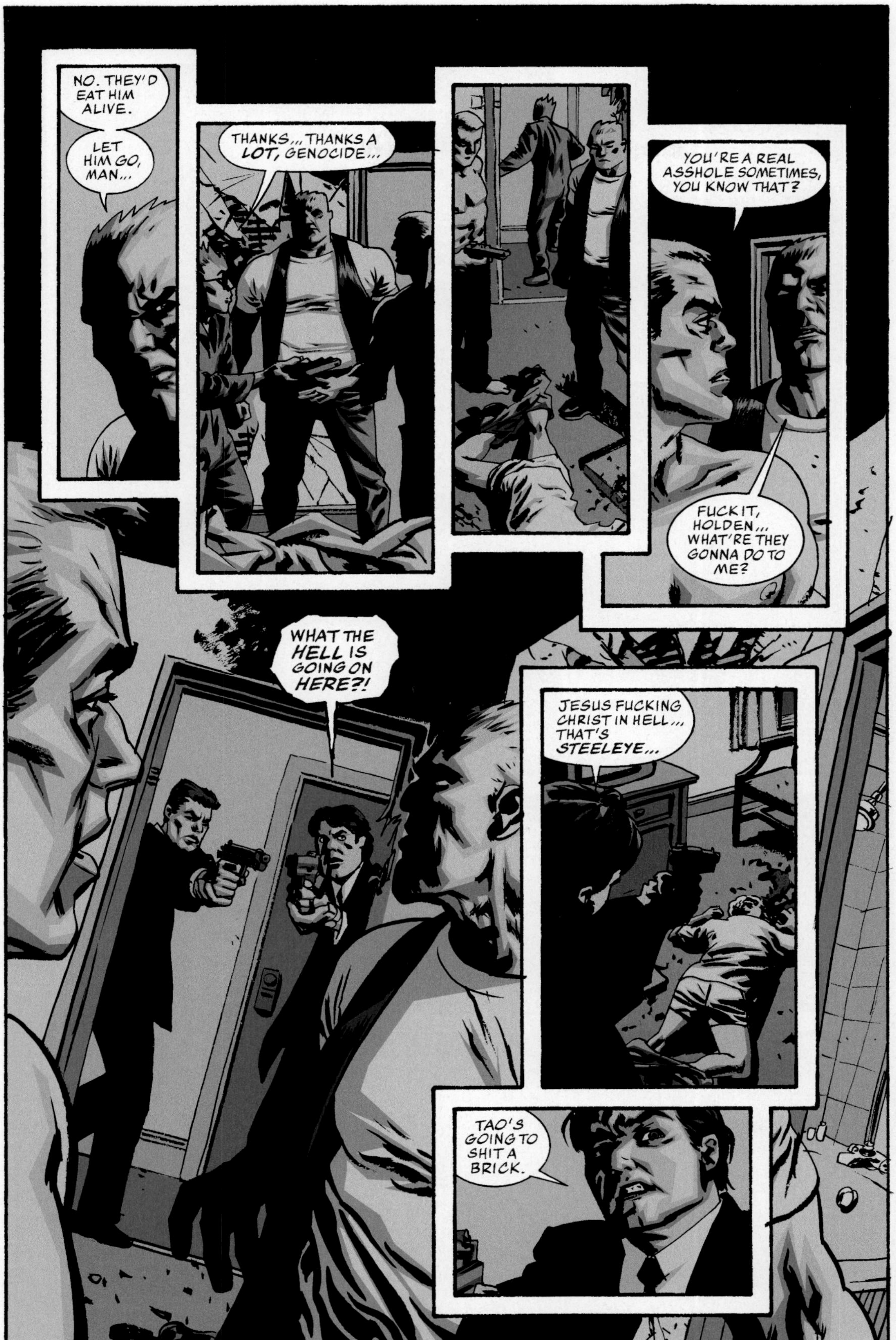
NO. THEY'D EAT HIM ALIVE.
LET HIM GO, MAN...
THANKS... THANKS A LOT, GENOCIDE...
YOU'RE A REAL ASSHOLE SOMETIMES, YOU KNOW THAT?
FUCK IT, HOLDEN... WHAT'RE THEY GONNA DO TO ME?
WHAT THE HELL IS GOING ON HERE?!
JESUS FUCKING CHRIST IN HELL... THAT'S STEELEYE...
TAO'S GOING TO SHIT A BRICK.

Of course, that's not a very accurate description. Tao doesn't shit bricks. He doesn't even get mad.

He just deals with problems in a meticulous and methodical way.

It's the lack of emotion involved that makes it scary.

LET ME START BY SAYING HOW *OBJECTION-ABLE* IT IS TO BE HERE UNDER SUCH *CIRCUM-STANCES...*

... STEELEYE WAS A *VALUED* MEMBER OF OUR ORGANIZATION. MORE THAN THAT, HE WAS A *PRODIGAL.*

SO, I WANT TO KNOW *EXACTLY* WHAT HAPPENED.

AND *THEN* WE'LL SORT OUT WHAT TO DO WITH THE BOTH OF YOU.

Under normal circumstances, if either Genocide or I had killed another operative, it wouldn't be such a big deal.

Nobody would be thrilled, necessarily, but there wouldn't be an inquiry. Hell, half the time someone ended up dead, you could almost assume Tao *wanted* it that way.

But Steeleye's death was different because we had broken chain of command.

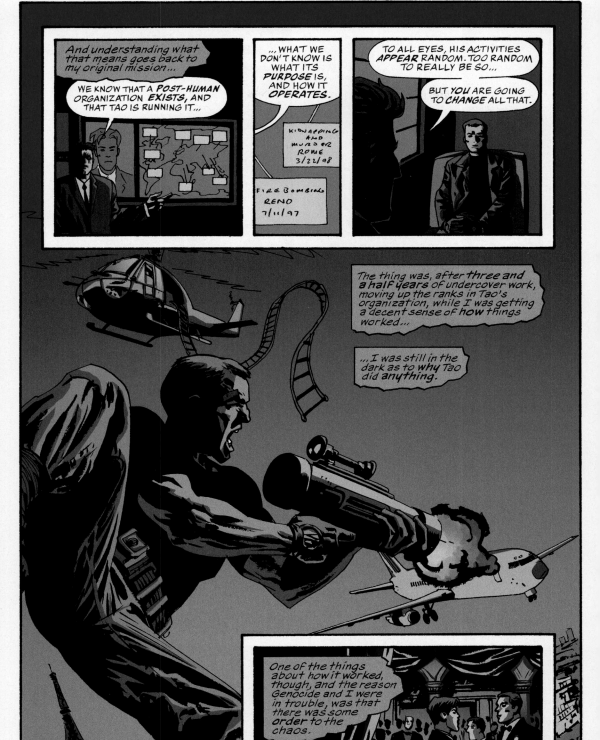

And understanding what that means goes back to my original mission...

WE KNOW THAT A *POST-HUMAN* ORGANIZATION *EXISTS*, AND THAT TAO IS RUNNING IT...,

...WHAT WE DON'T KNOW IS WHAT ITS *PURPOSE* IS, AND HOW IT *OPERATES*.

KIDNAPPING AND MURDER ROWE 3/22/98

FIRE BOMBING RENO 7/11/97

TO ALL EYES, HIS ACTIVITIES *APPEAR* RANDOM. TOO RANDOM TO REALLY BE SO...

BUT *YOU* ARE GOING TO *CHANGE* ALL THAT.

The thing was, after *three and a half years* of undercover work, moving up the ranks in Tao's organization, while I was getting a decent sense of *HOW* things worked...

...I was still in the dark as to *WHY* Tao did anything.

One of the things about how it worked, though, and the reason Genocide and I were in trouble, was that there was some *order* to the chaos.

There was a *hierarchy*.

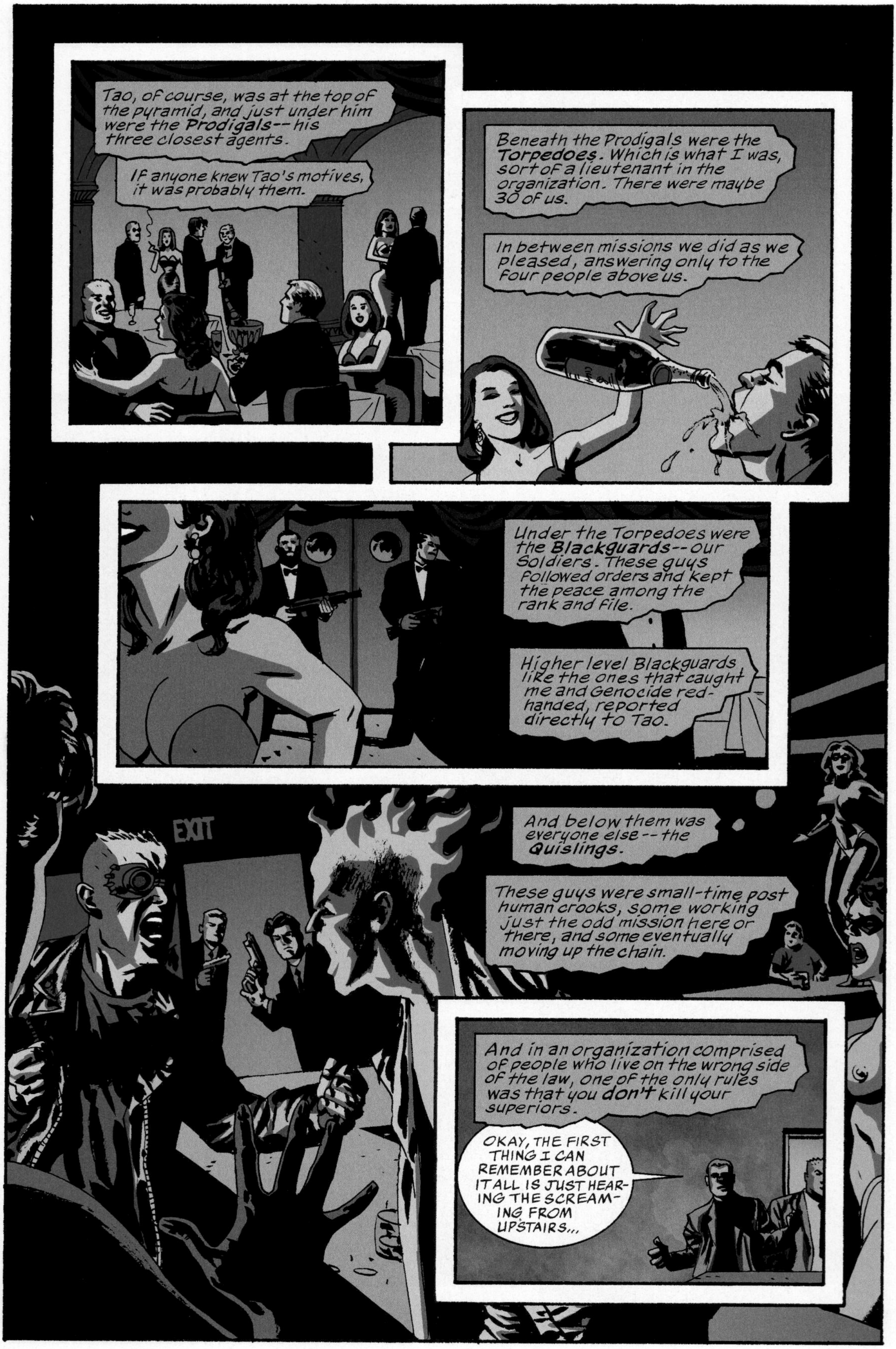
Tao, of course, was at the top of the pyramid, and just under him were the **Prodigals**-- his three closest agents.
If anyone knew Tao's motives, it was probably them.
Beneath the Prodigals were the **Torpedoes**. Which is what I was, sort of a lieutenant in the organization. There were maybe 30 of us.
In between missions we did as we pleased, answering only to the four people above us.
Under the Torpedoes were the **Blackguards**--our Soldiers. These guys followed orders and kept the peace among the rank and file.
Higher level Blackguards like the ones that caught me and Genocide red-handed, reported directly to Tao.
EXIT
And below them was everyone else -- the **Quislings**.
These guys were small-time post human crooks, some working just the odd mission here or there, and some eventually moving up the chain.
And in an organization comprised of people who live on the wrong side of the law, one of the only rules was that you **don't** kill your superiors.
OKAY, THE FIRST THING I CAN REMEMBER ABOUT IT ALL IS JUST HEARING THE SCREAMING FROM UPSTAIRS...

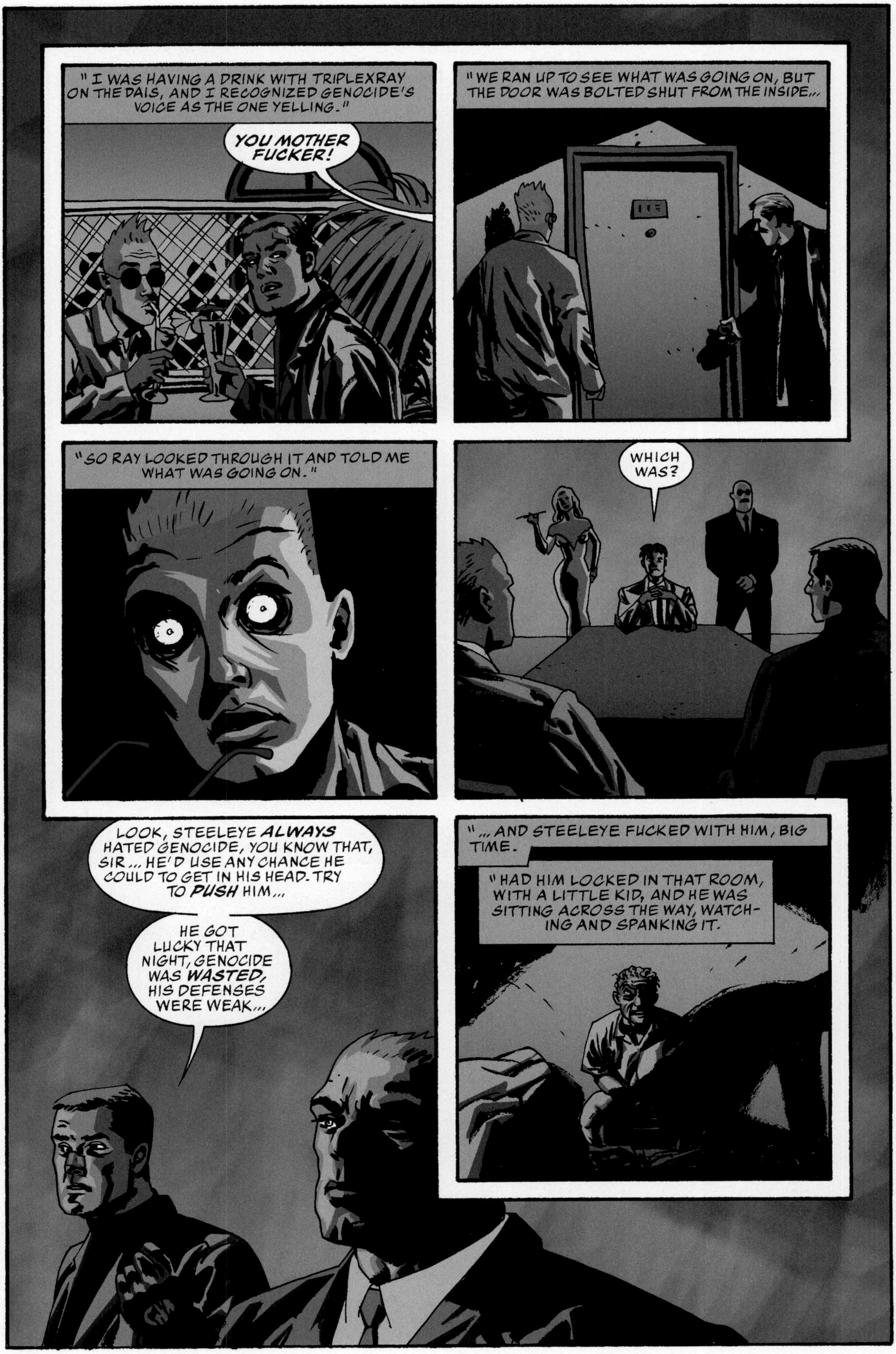
"I WAS HAVING A DRINK WITH TRIPLEXRAY ON THE DAIS, AND I RECOGNIZED GENOCIDE'S VOICE AS THE ONE YELLING."
YOU MOTHER FUCKER!
"WE RAN UP TO SEE WHAT WAS GOING ON, BUT THE DOOR WAS BOLTED SHUT FROM THE INSIDE...
"SO RAY LOOKED THROUGH IT AND TOLD ME WHAT WAS GOING ON."
WHICH WAS?
LOOK, STEELEYE ALWAYS HATED GENOCIDE, YOU KNOW THAT, SIR... HE'D USE ANY CHANCE HE COULD TO GET IN HIS HEAD. TRY TO PUSH HIM...
HE GOT LUCKY THAT NIGHT, GENOCIDE WAS WASTED, HIS DEFENSES WERE WEAK...
"...AND STEELEYE FUCKED WITH HIM, BIG TIME.
"HAD HIM LOCKED IN THAT ROOM, WITH A LITTLE KID, AND HE WAS SITTING ACROSS THE WAY, WATCHING AND SPANKING IT.

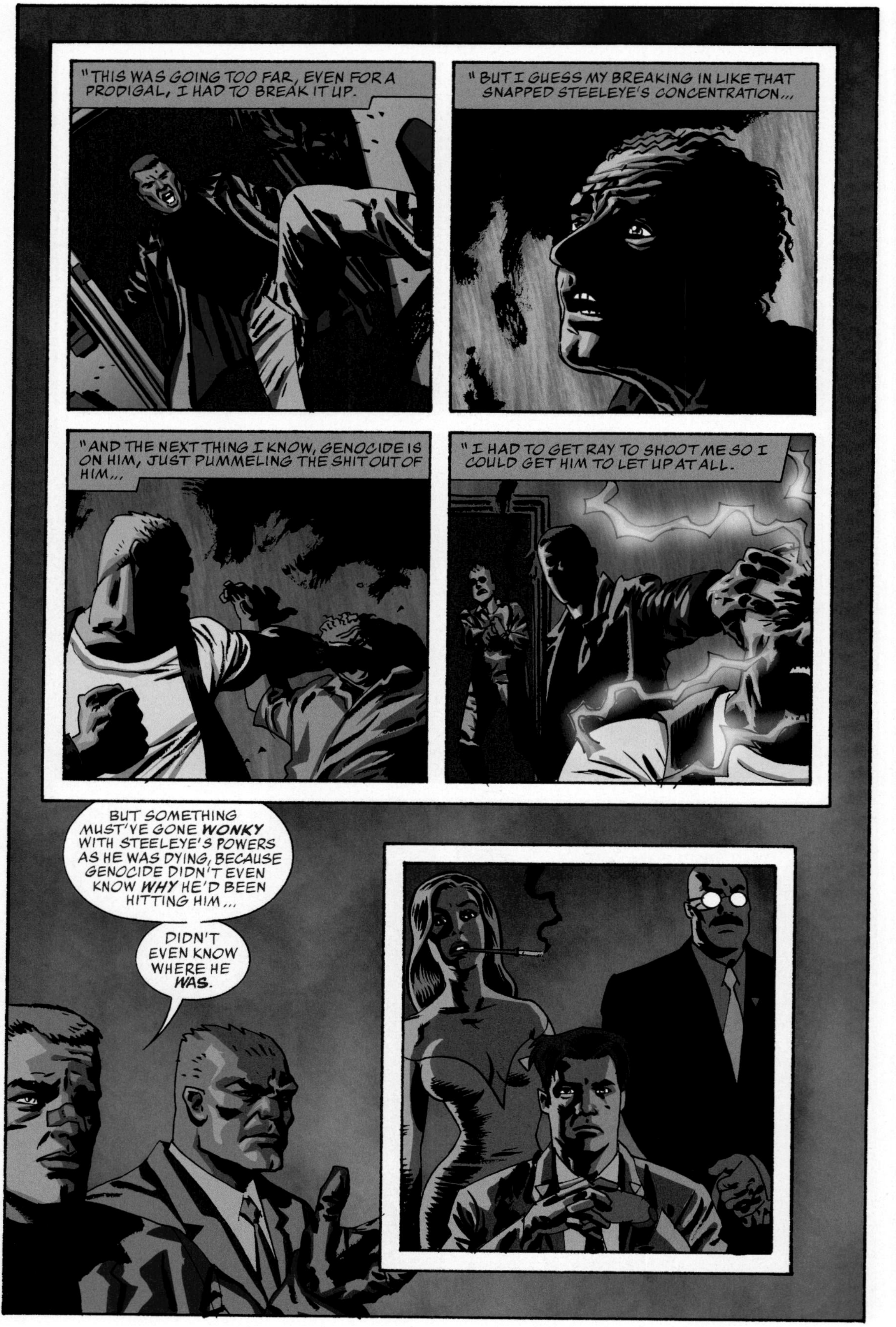
"THIS WAS GOING TOO FAR, EVEN FOR A PRODIGAL, I HAD TO BREAK IT UP.
"BUT I GUESS MY BREAKING IN LIKE THAT SNAPPED STEELEYE'S CONCENTRATION...
"AND THE NEXT THING I KNOW, GENOCIDE IS ON HIM, JUST PUMMELING THE SHIT OUT OF HIM...
"I HAD TO GET RAY TO SHOOT ME SO I COULD GET HIM TO LET UP AT ALL.
BUT SOMETHING MUST'VE GONE WONKY WITH STEELEYE'S POWERS AS HE WAS DYING, BECAUSE GENOCIDE DIDN'T EVEN KNOW WHY HE'D BEEN HITTING HIM...
DIDN'T EVEN KNOW WHERE HE WAS.

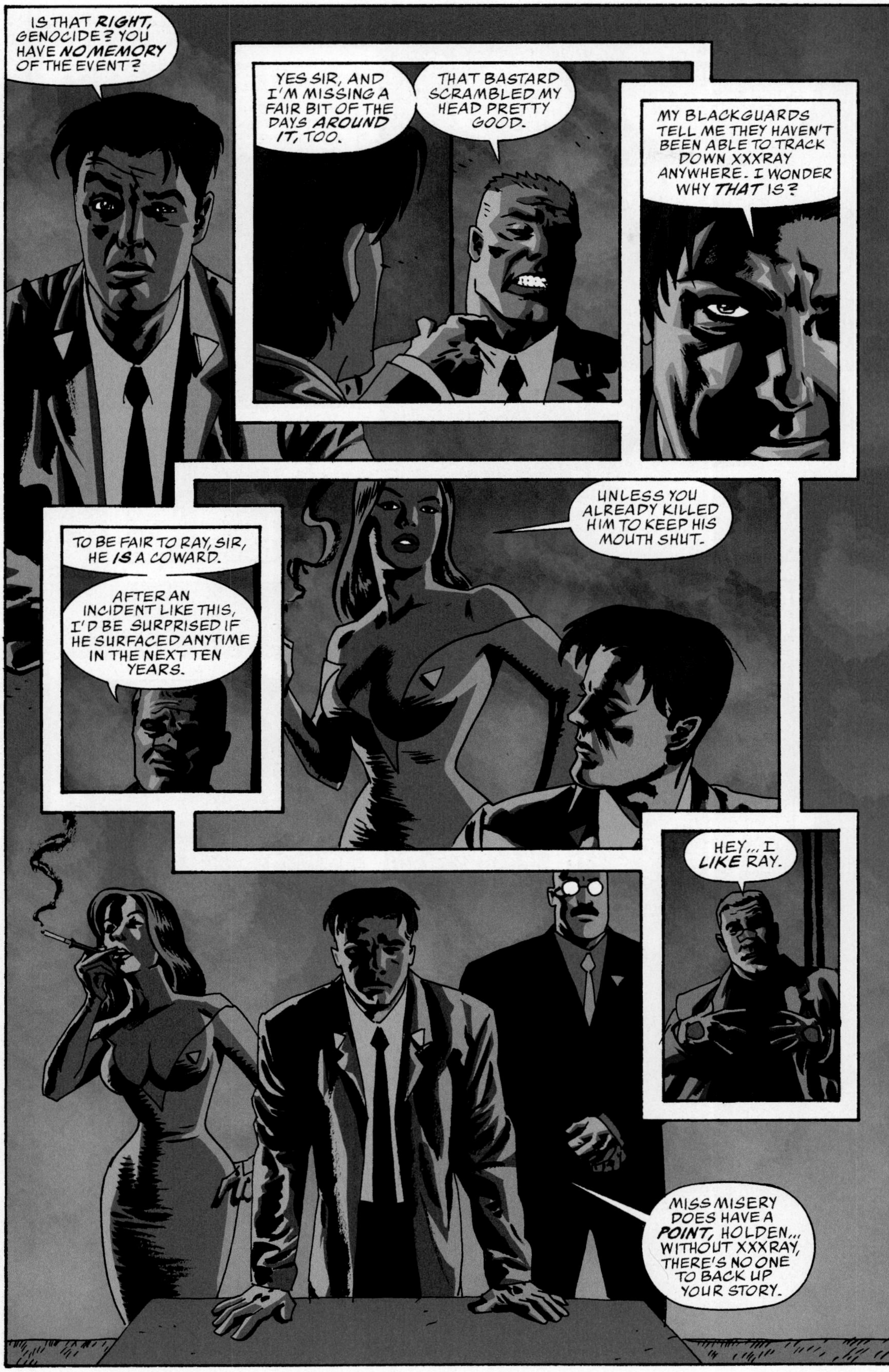
IS THAT RIGHT, GENOCIDE? YOU HAVE NO MEMORY OF THE EVENT?
YES SIR, AND I'M MISSING A FAIR BIT OF THE DAYS AROUND IT, TOO.
THAT BASTARD SCRAMBLED MY HEAD PRETTY GOOD.
MY BLACKGUARDS TELL ME THEY HAVEN'T BEEN ABLE TO TRACK DOWN XXXRAY ANYWHERE. I WONDER WHY THAT IS?
UNLESS YOU ALREADY KILLED HIM TO KEEP HIS MOUTH SHUT.
TO BE FAIR TO RAY, SIR, HE IS A COWARD.
AFTER AN INCIDENT LIKE THIS, I'D BE SURPRISED IF HE SURFACED ANYTIME IN THE NEXT TEN YEARS.
HEY... I LIKE RAY.
MISS MISERY DOES HAVE A POINT, HOLDEN... WITHOUT XXXRAY, THERE'S NO ONE TO BACK UP YOUR STORY.

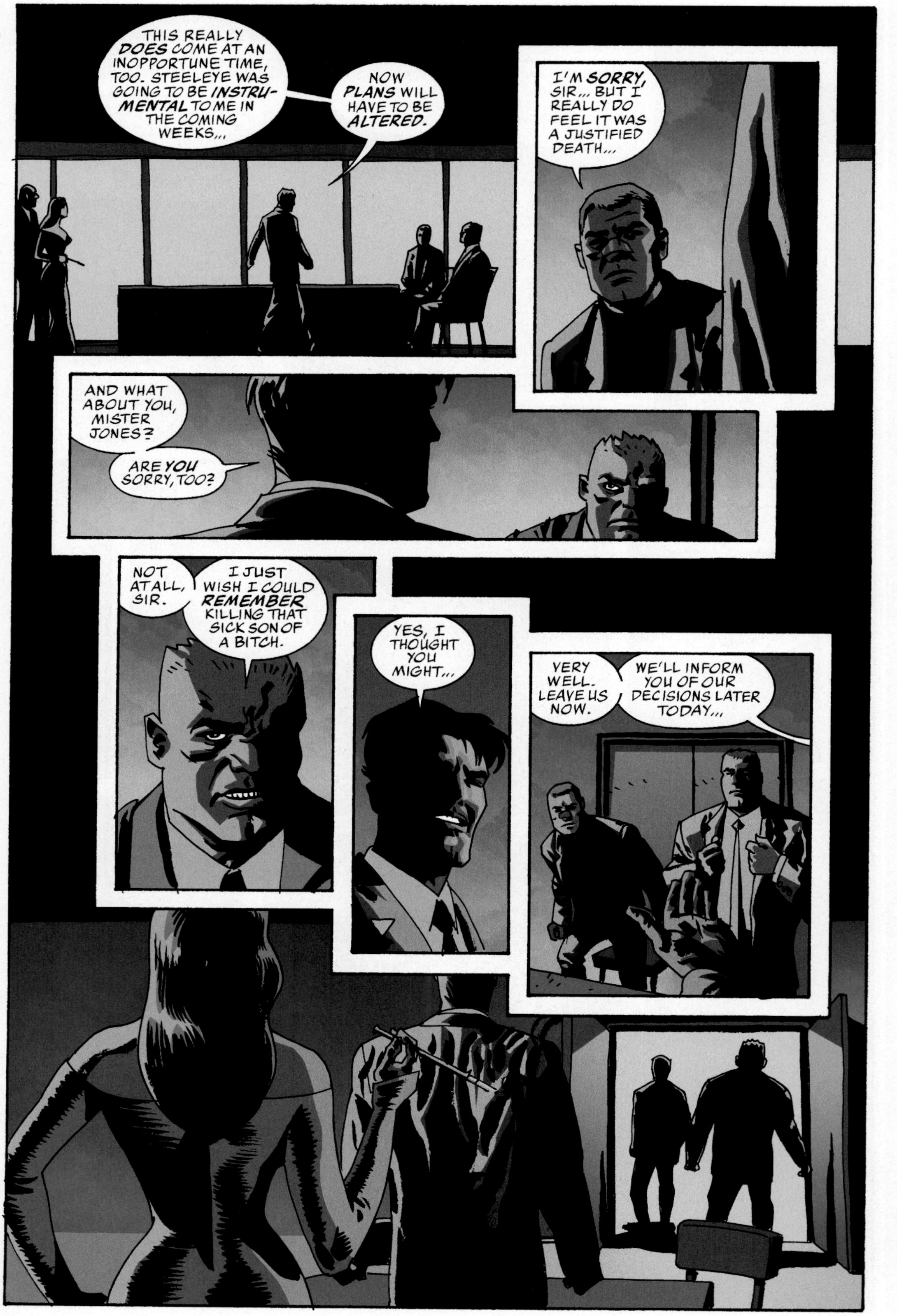
THIS REALLY DOES COME AT AN INOPPORTUNE TIME, TOO. STEELEYE WAS GOING TO BE INSTRUMENTAL TO ME IN THE COMING WEEKS...
NOW PLANS WILL HAVE TO BE ALTERED.
I'M SORRY, SIR... BUT I REALLY DO FEEL IT WAS A JUSTIFIED DEATH...
AND WHAT ABOUT YOU, MISTER JONES?
ARE YOU SORRY, TOO?
NOT AT ALL, SIR.
I JUST WISH I COULD REMEMBER KILLING THAT SICK SON OF A BITCH.
YES, I THOUGHT YOU MIGHT...
VERY WELL. LEAVE US NOW.
WE'LL INFORM YOU OF OUR DECISIONS LATER TODAY...

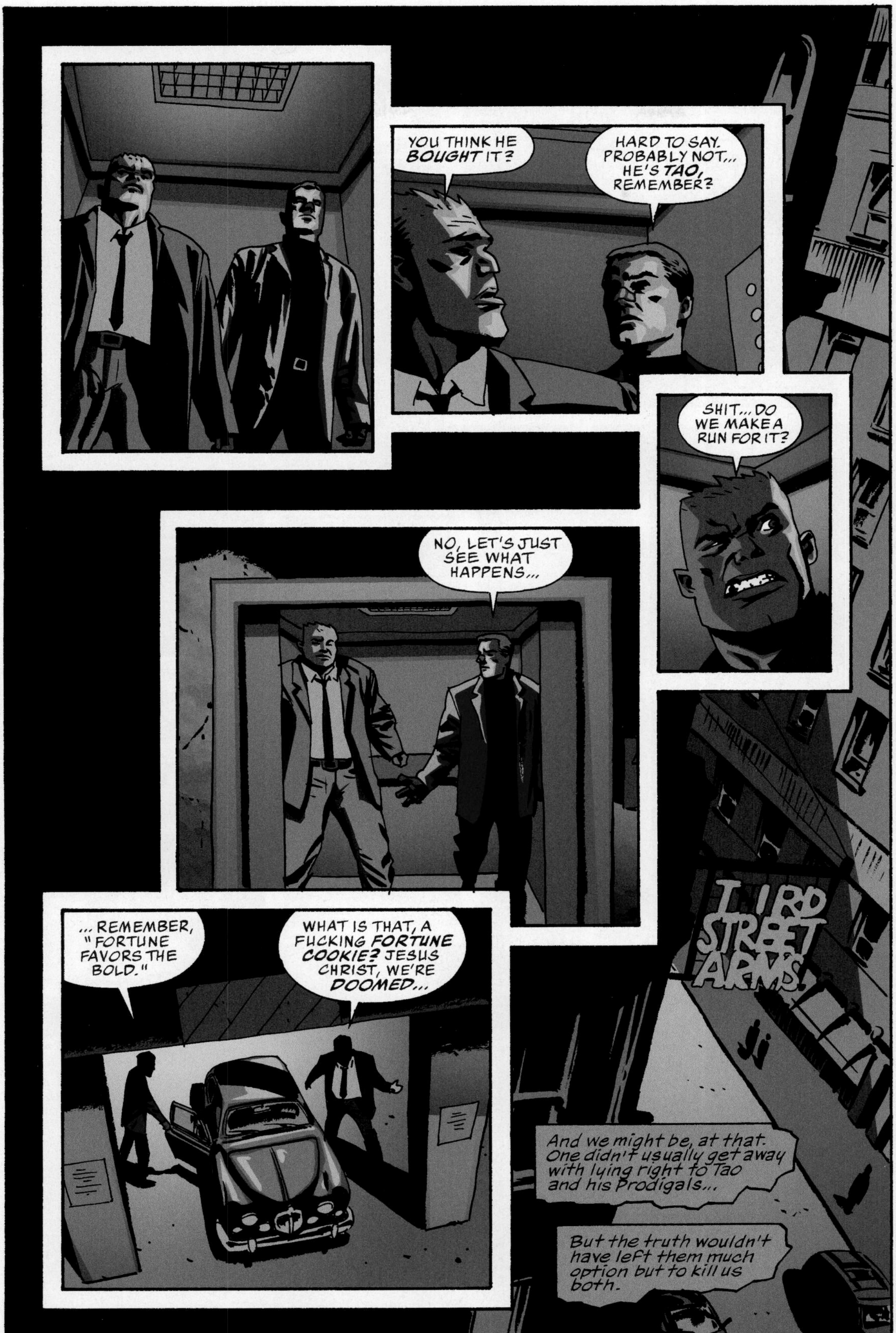
YOU THINK HE BOUGHT IT?
HARD TO SAY. PROBABLY NOT... HE'S TAO, REMEMBER?
SHIT... DO WE MAKE A RUN FOR IT?
NO, LET'S JUST SEE WHAT HAPPENS...
...REMEMBER, "FORTUNE FAVORS THE BOLD."
WHAT IS THAT, A FUCKING FORTUNE COOKIE? JESUS CHRIST, WE'RE DOOMED...
And we might be, at that. One didn't usually get away with lying right to Tao and his Prodigals...
But the truth wouldn't have left them much option but to kill us both.

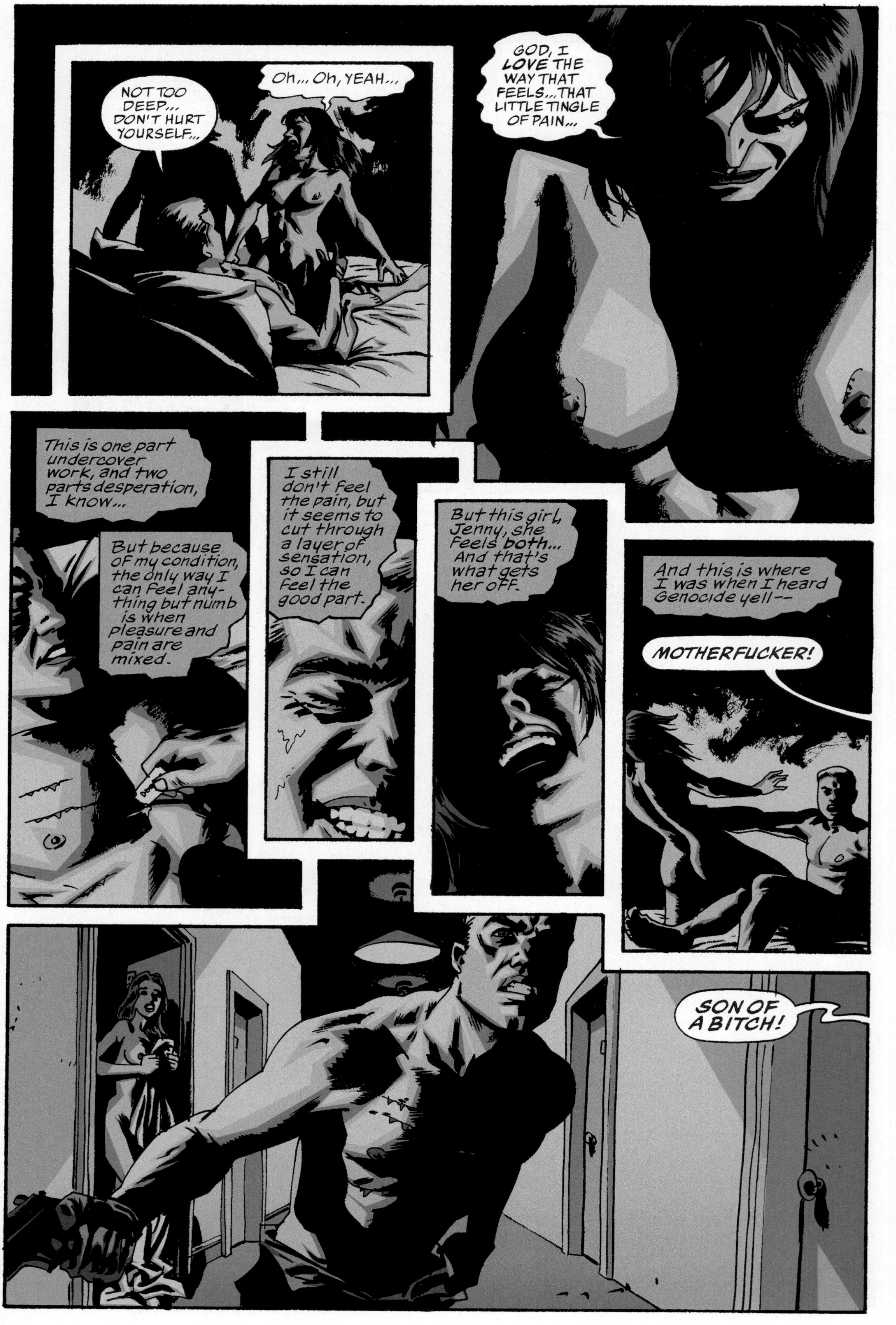

NOT TOO DEEP... DON'T HURT YOURSELF...
Oh... Oh, YEAH...
GOD, I LOVE THE WAY THAT FEELS... THAT LITTLE TINGLE OF PAIN...
This is one part undercover work, and two parts desperation, I know...
But because of my condition, the only way I can feel anything but numb is when pleasure and pain are mixed.
I still don't feel the pain, but it seems to cut through a layer of sensation, so I can feel the good part.
But this girl, Jenny, she feels both... And that's what gets her off.
And this is where I was when I heard Genocide yell--
MOTHERFUCKER!
SON OF A BITCH!

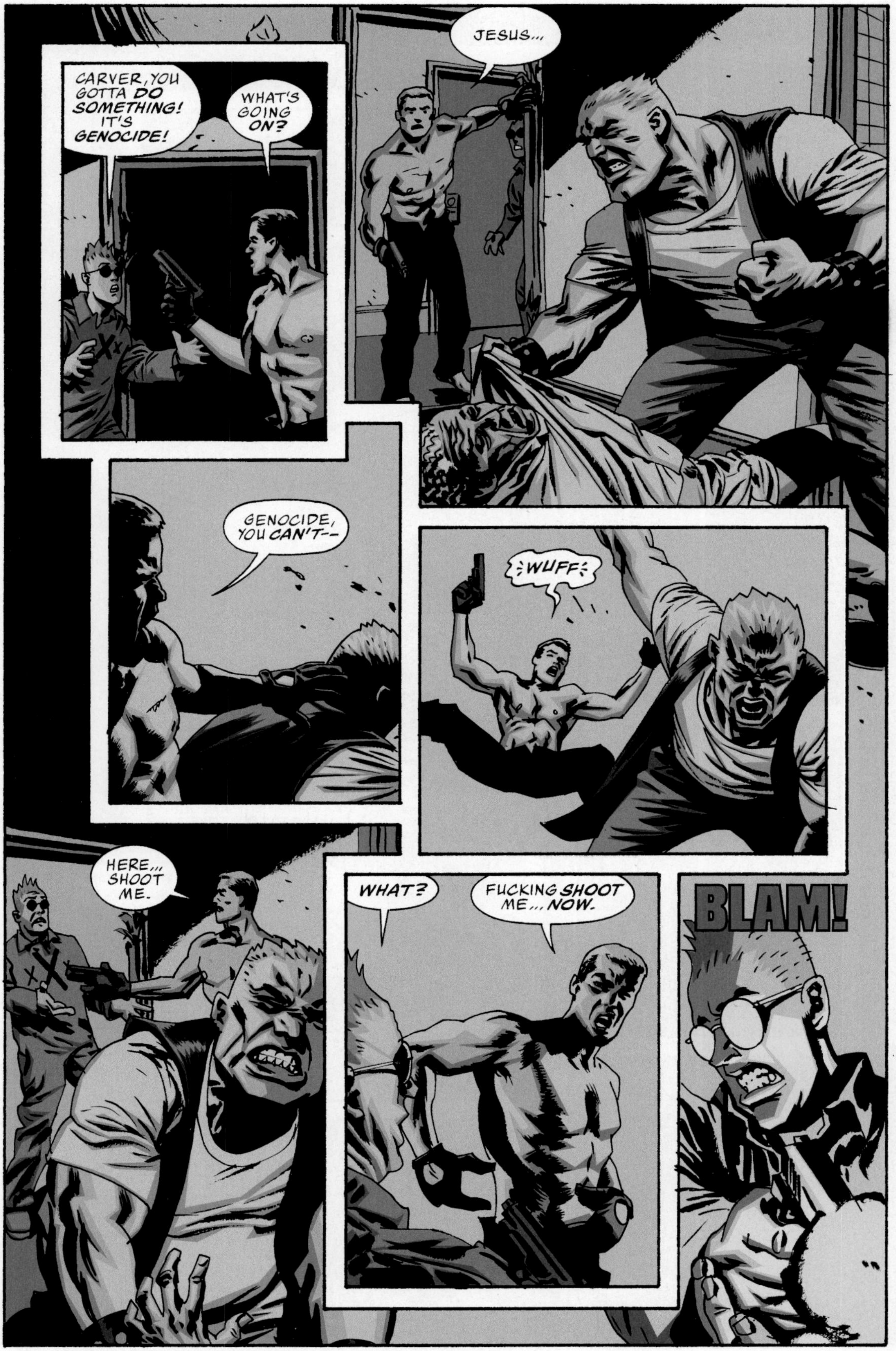

CARVER, YOU GOTTA DO SOMETHING! IT'S GENOCIDE!
WHAT'S GOING ON?
JESUS...
GENOCIDE, YOU CAN'T--
WUFF
HERE... SHOOT ME.
WHAT?
FUCKING SHOOT ME... NOW.
BLAM!

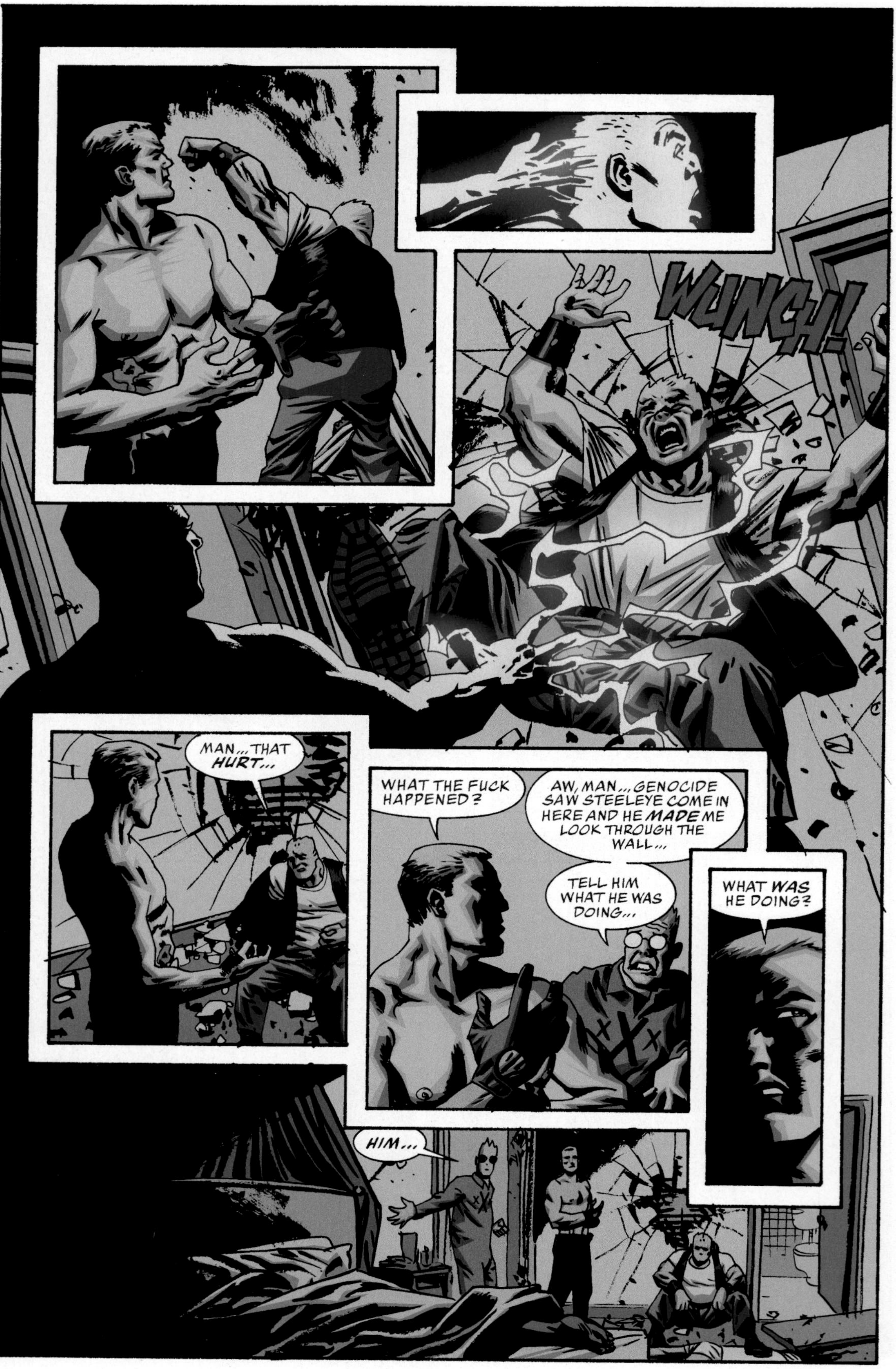
WUNCH!
MAN... THAT HURT...
WHAT THE FUCK HAPPENED?
AW, MAN... GENOCIDE SAW STEELEYE COME IN HERE AND HE MADE ME LOOK THROUGH THE WALL...
TELL HIM WHAT HE WAS DOING...
WHAT WAS HE DOING?
HIM...

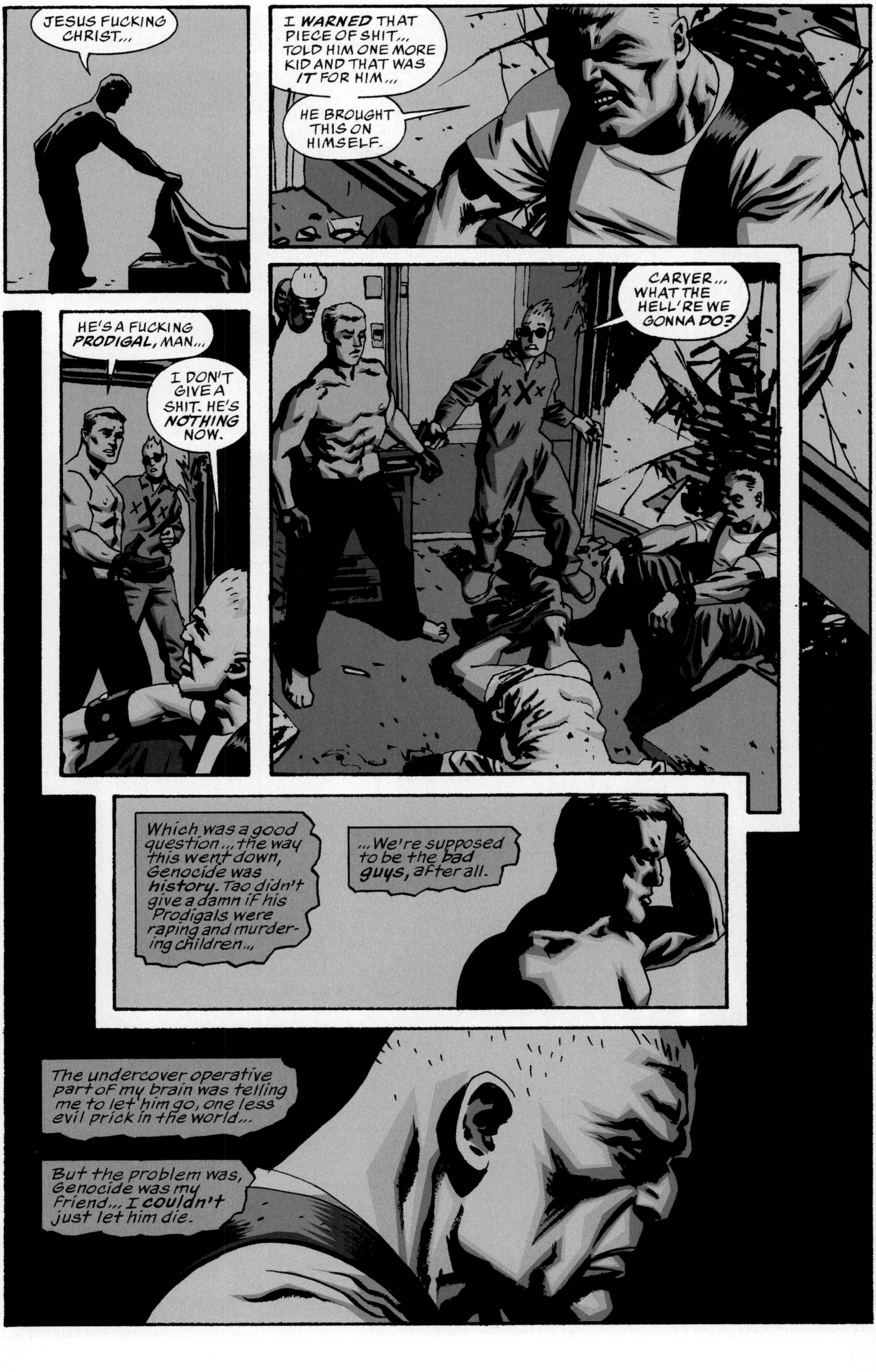

JESUS FUCKING CHRIST...
I WARNED THAT PIECE OF SHIT... TOLD HIM ONE MORE KID AND THAT WAS IT FOR HIM...
HE BROUGHT THIS ON HIMSELF.
HE'S A FUCKING PRODIGAL, MAN...
I DON'T GIVE A SHIT. HE'S NOTHING NOW.
CARVER... WHAT THE HELL'RE WE GONNA DO?
Which was a good question... the way this went down, Genocide was history. Tao didn't give a damn if his Prodigals were raping and murdering children...
...We're supposed to be the bad guys, after all.
The undercover operative part of my brain was telling me to let him go, one less evil prick in the world...
But the problem was, Genocide was my friend... I couldn't just let him die.

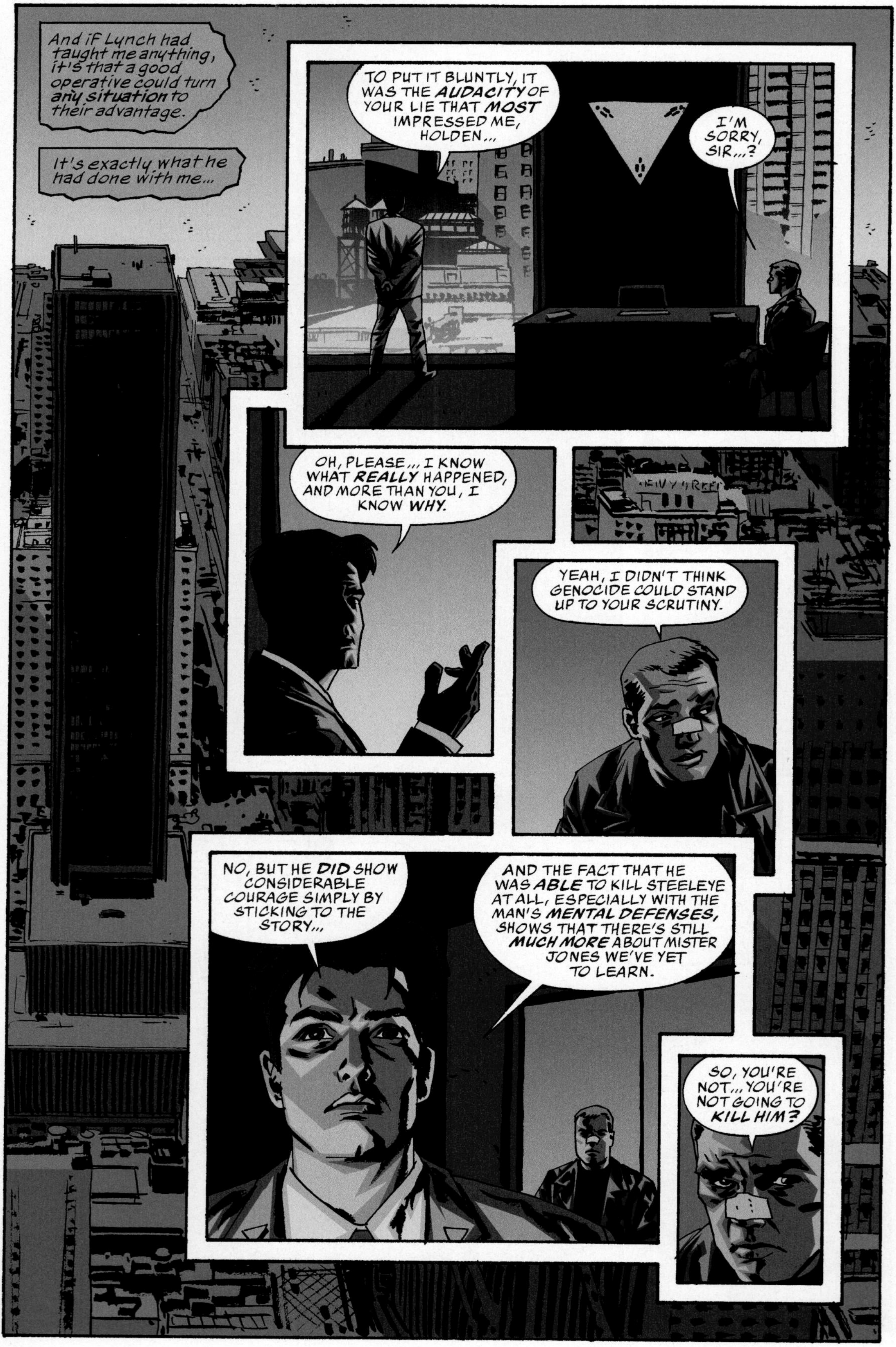
And if Lynch had taught me anything, it's that a good operative could turn any situation to their advantage.
It's exactly what he had done with me...
TO PUT IT BLUNTLY, IT WAS THE AUDACITY OF YOUR LIE THAT MOST IMPRESSED ME, HOLDEN...
I'M SORRY, SIR...?
OH, PLEASE... I KNOW WHAT REALLY HAPPENED, AND MORE THAN YOU, I KNOW WHY.
YEAH, I DIDN'T THINK GENOCIDE COULD STAND UP TO YOUR SCRUTINY.
NO, BUT HE DID SHOW CONSIDERABLE COURAGE SIMPLY BY STICKING TO THE STORY...
AND THE FACT THAT HE WAS ABLE TO KILL STEELEYE AT ALL, ESPECIALLY WITH THE MAN'S MENTAL DEFENSES, SHOWS THAT THERE'S STILL MUCH MORE ABOUT MISTER JONES WE'VE YET TO LEARN.
SO, YOU'RE NOT... YOU'RE NOT GOING TO KILL HIM?

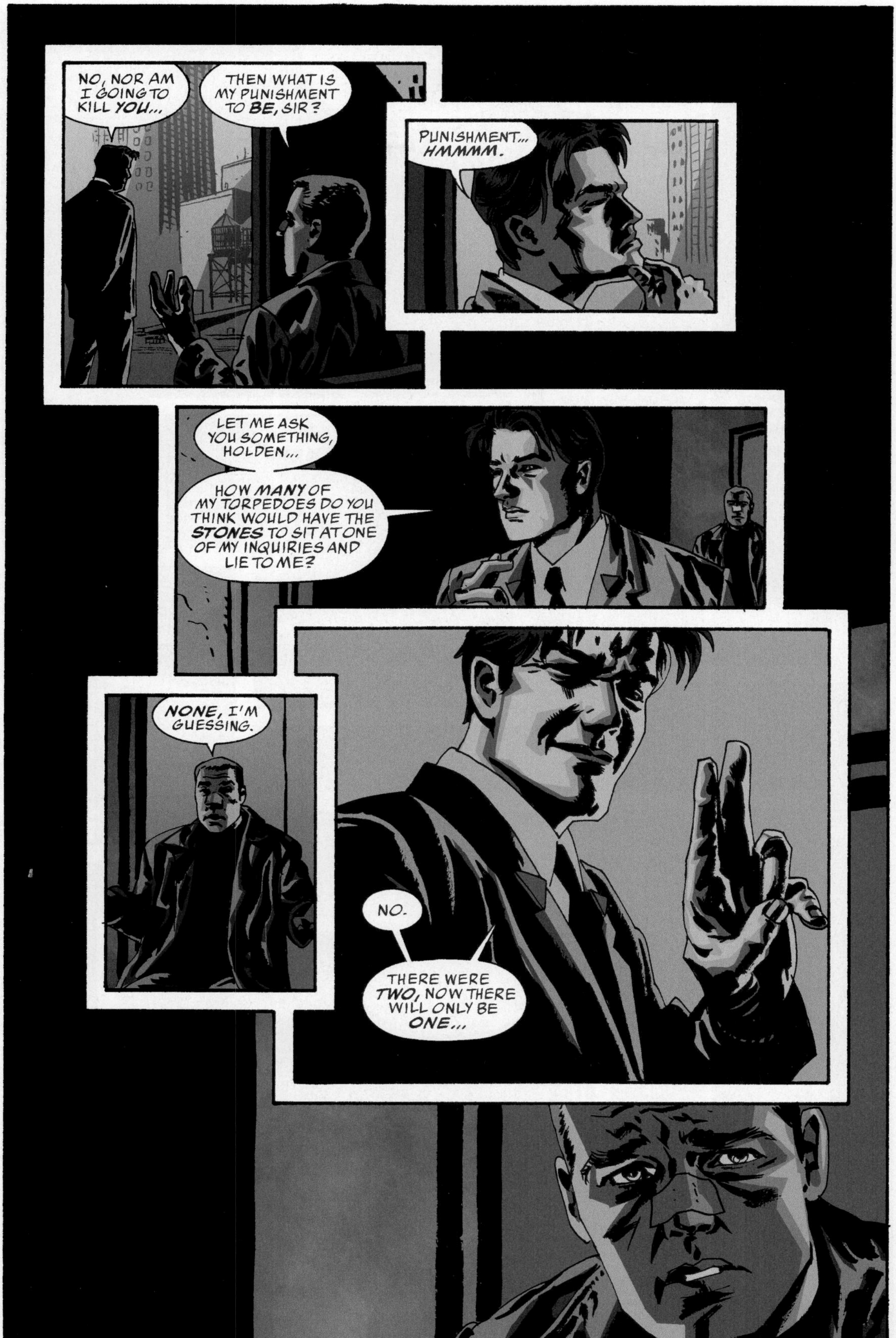
NO, NOR AM I GOING TO KILL YOU...
THEN WHAT IS MY PUNISHMENT TO BE, SIR?
PUNISHMENT... HMMMM.
LET ME ASK YOU SOMETHING, HOLDEN...
HOW MANY OF MY TORPEDOES DO YOU THINK WOULD HAVE THE STONES TO SIT AT ONE OF MY INQUIRIES AND LIE TO ME?
NONE, I'M GUESSING.
NO.
THERE WERE TWO, NOW THERE WILL ONLY BE ONE...

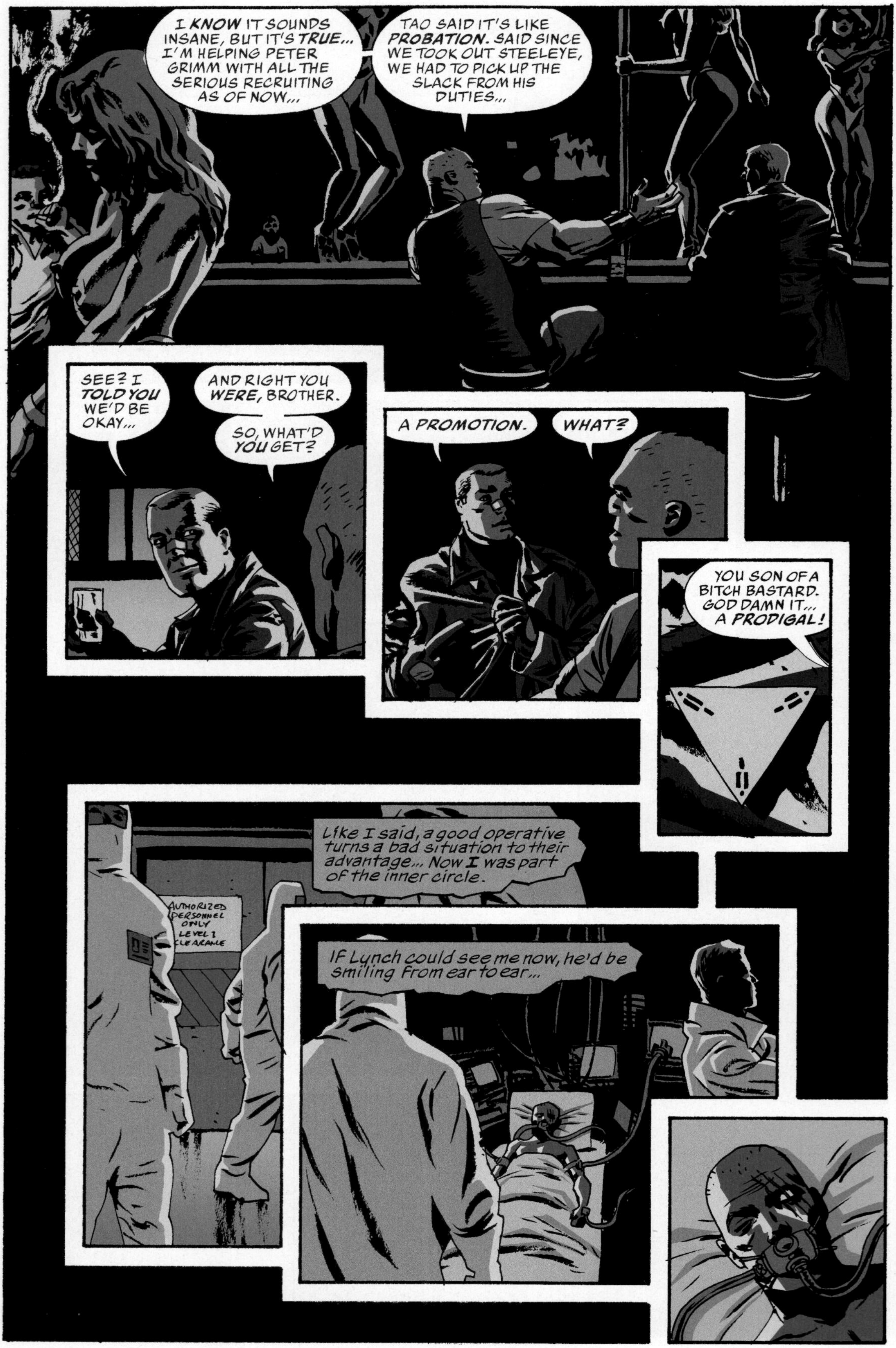
I KNOW IT SOUNDS INSANE, BUT IT'S TRUE... I'M HELPING PETER GRIMM WITH ALL THE SERIOUS RECRUITING AS OF NOW...
TAO SAID IT'S LIKE PROBATION. SAID SINCE WE TOOK OUT STEELEYE, WE HAD TO PICK UP THE SLACK FROM HIS DUTIES...
SEE? I TOLD YOU WE'D BE OKAY...
AND RIGHT YOU WERE, BROTHER.
SO, WHAT'D YOU GET?
A PROMOTION.
WHAT?
YOU SON OF A BITCH BASTARD. GOD DAMN IT... A PRODIGAL!
Like I said, a good operative turns a bad situation to their advantage... Now I was part of the inner circle.
AUTHORIZED PERSONNEL ONLY LEVEL 1 CLEARANCE
If Lynch could see me now, he'd be smiling from ear to ear...

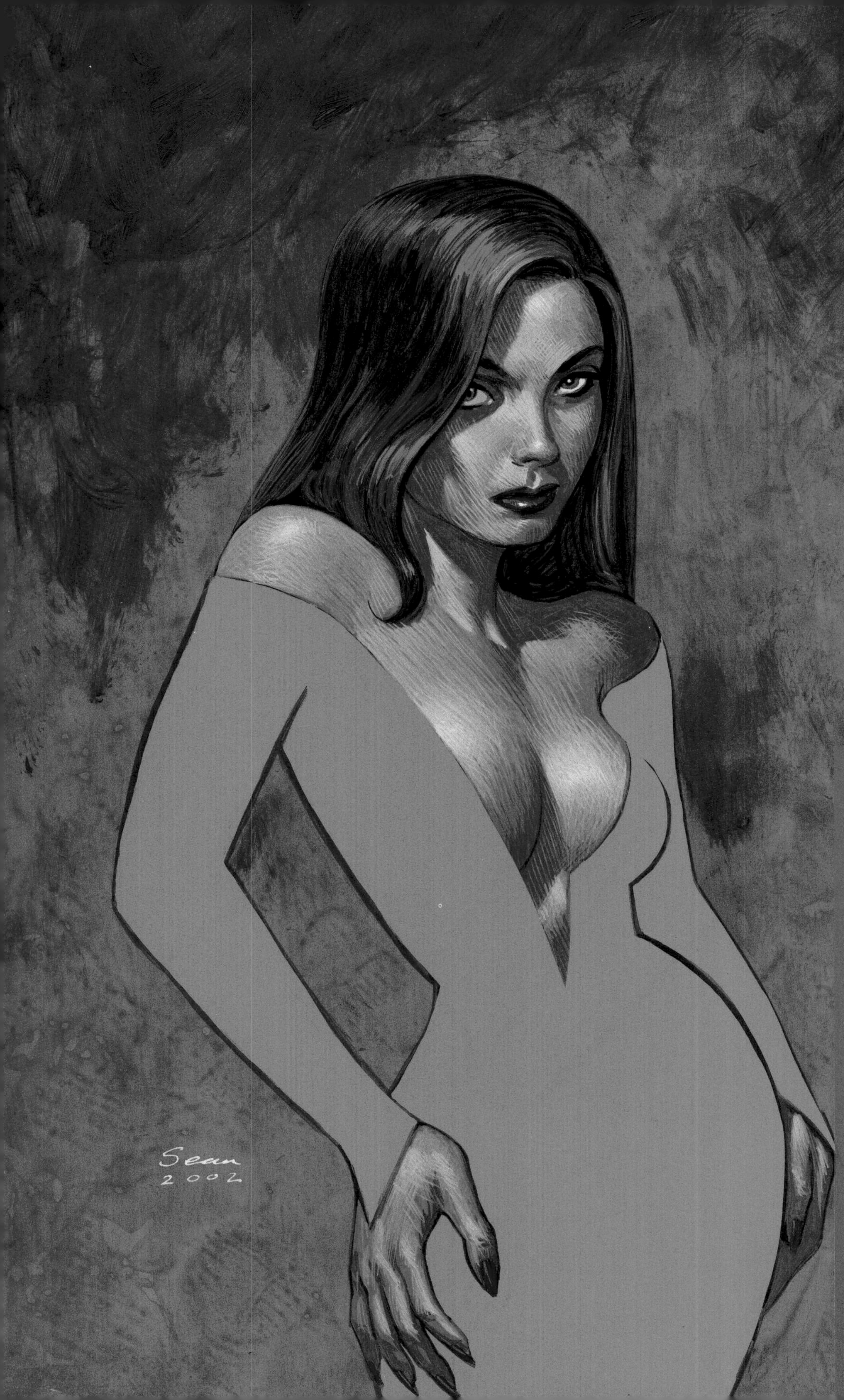
Sean
2002

Cover by SEAN PHILLIPS

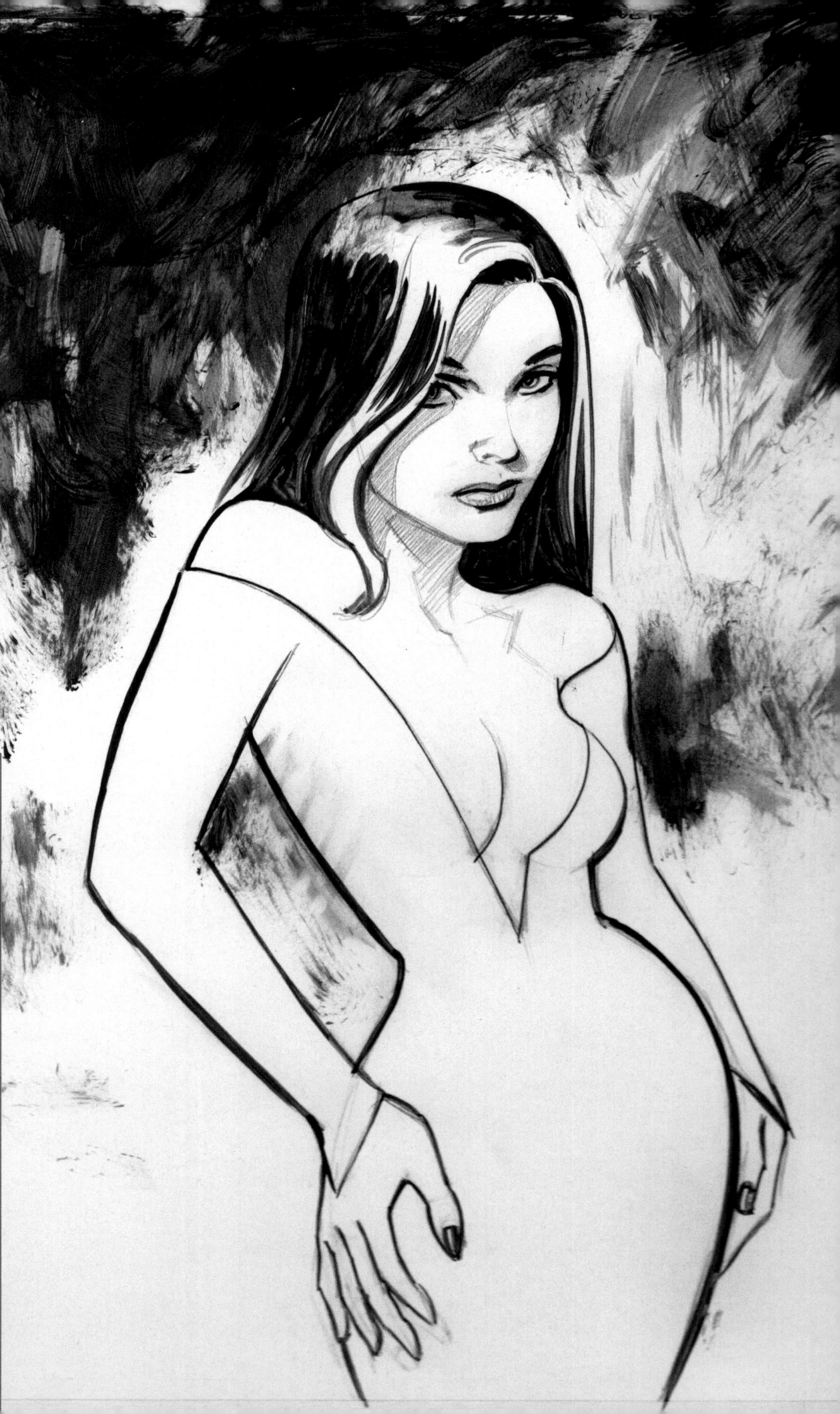

SLEEPER #3 Cover Inks by SEAN PHILLIPS

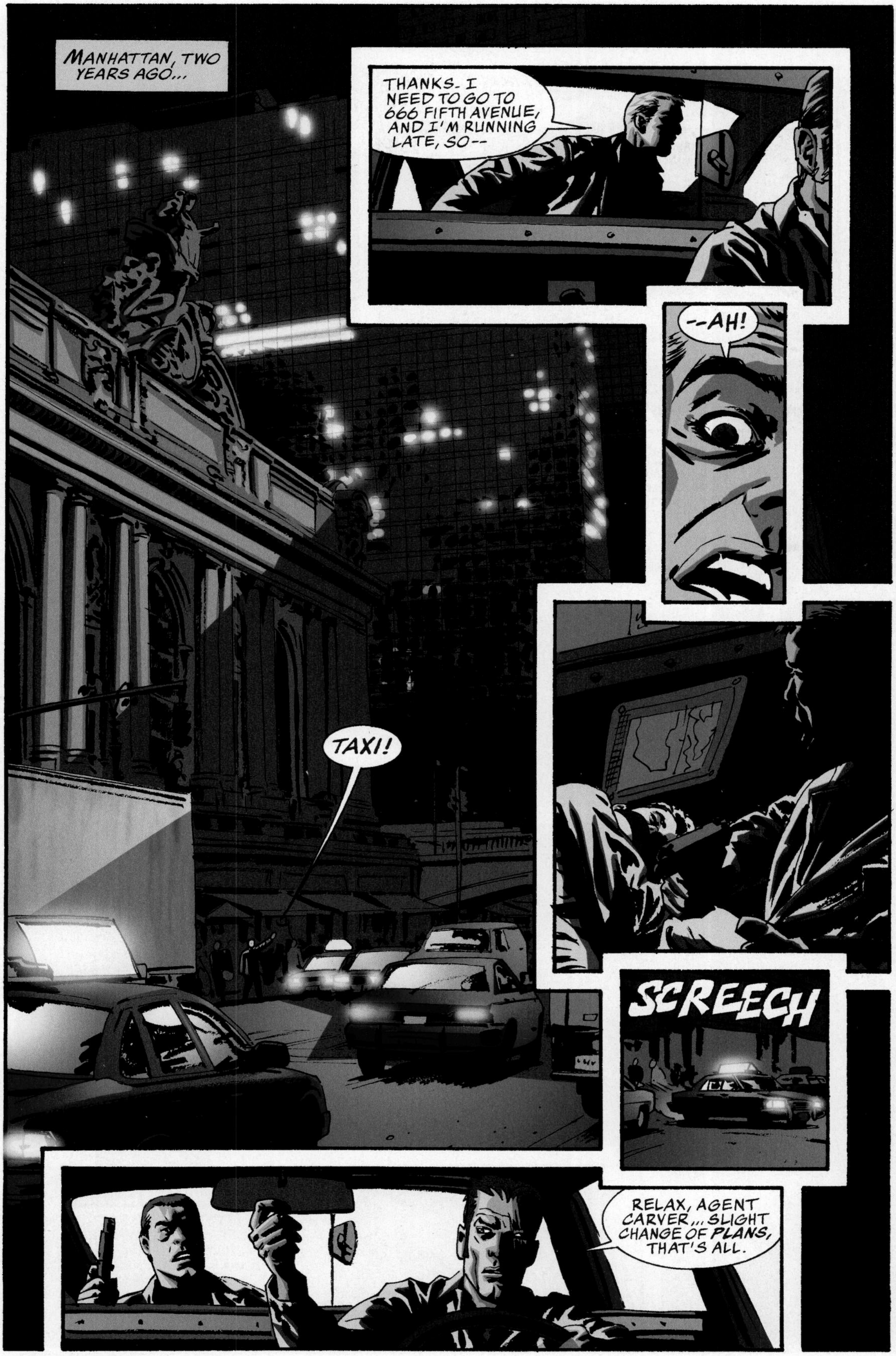
MANHATTAN, TWO YEARS AGO...
THANKS. I NEED TO GO TO 666 FIFTH AVENUE, AND I'M RUNNING LATE, SO--
--AH!
TAXI!
SCREECH
RELAX, AGENT CARVER... SLIGHT CHANGE OF PLANS, THAT'S ALL.

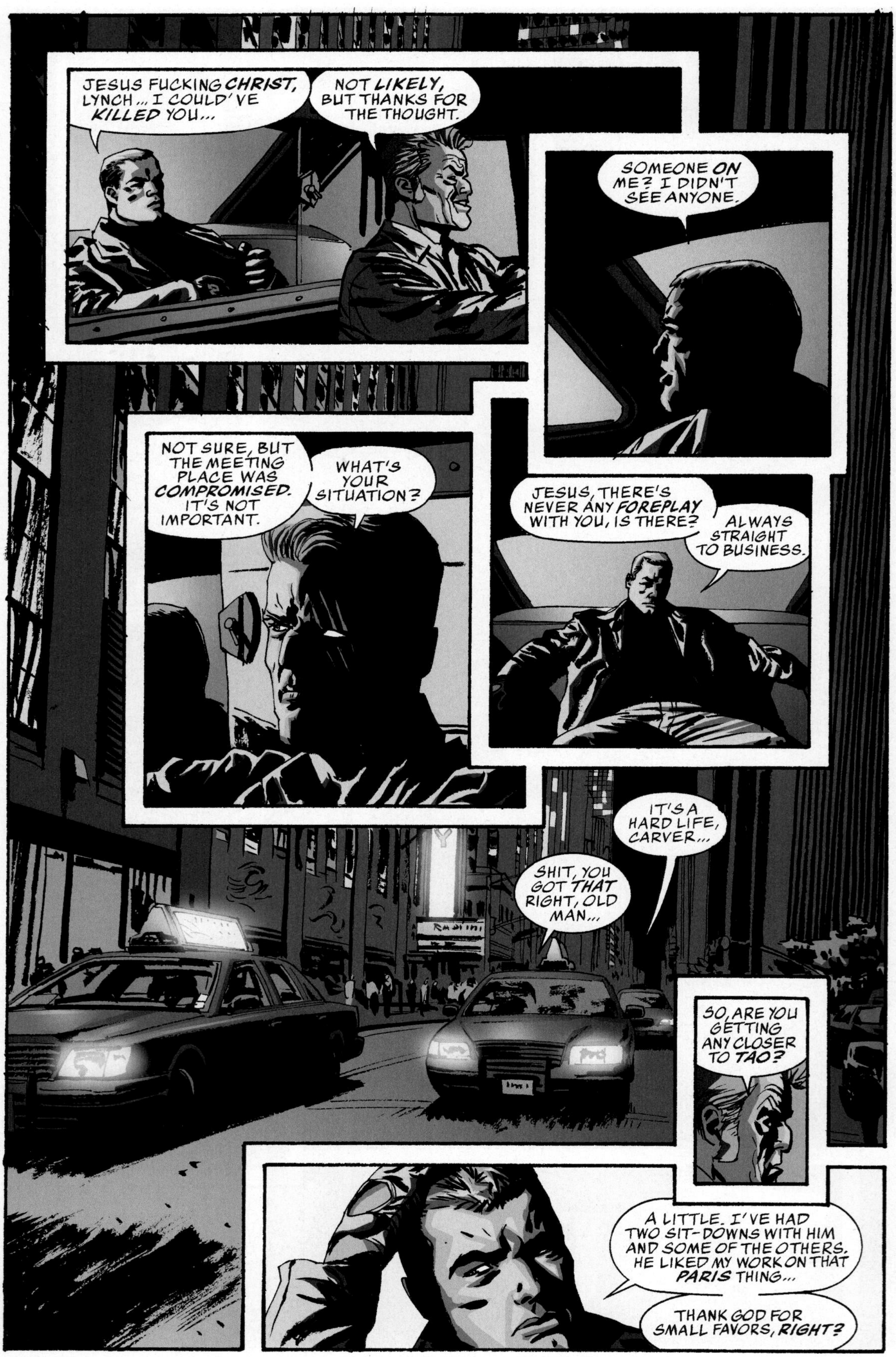

JESUS FUCKING CHRIST, LYNCH... I COULD'VE KILLED YOU...
NOT LIKELY, BUT THANKS FOR THE THOUGHT.
SOMEONE ON ME? I DIDN'T SEE ANYONE.
NOT SURE, BUT THE MEETING PLACE WAS COMPROMISED. IT'S NOT IMPORTANT.
WHAT'S YOUR SITUATION?
JESUS, THERE'S NEVER ANY FOREPLAY WITH YOU, IS THERE?
ALWAYS STRAIGHT TO BUSINESS.
IT'S A HARD LIFE, CARVER...
SHIT, YOU GOT THAT RIGHT, OLD MAN...
SO, ARE YOU GETTING ANY CLOSER TO TAO?
A LITTLE. I'VE HAD TWO SIT-DOWNS WITH HIM AND SOME OF THE OTHERS. HE LIKED MY WORK ON THAT PARIS THING...
THANK GOD FOR SMALL FAVORS, RIGHT?

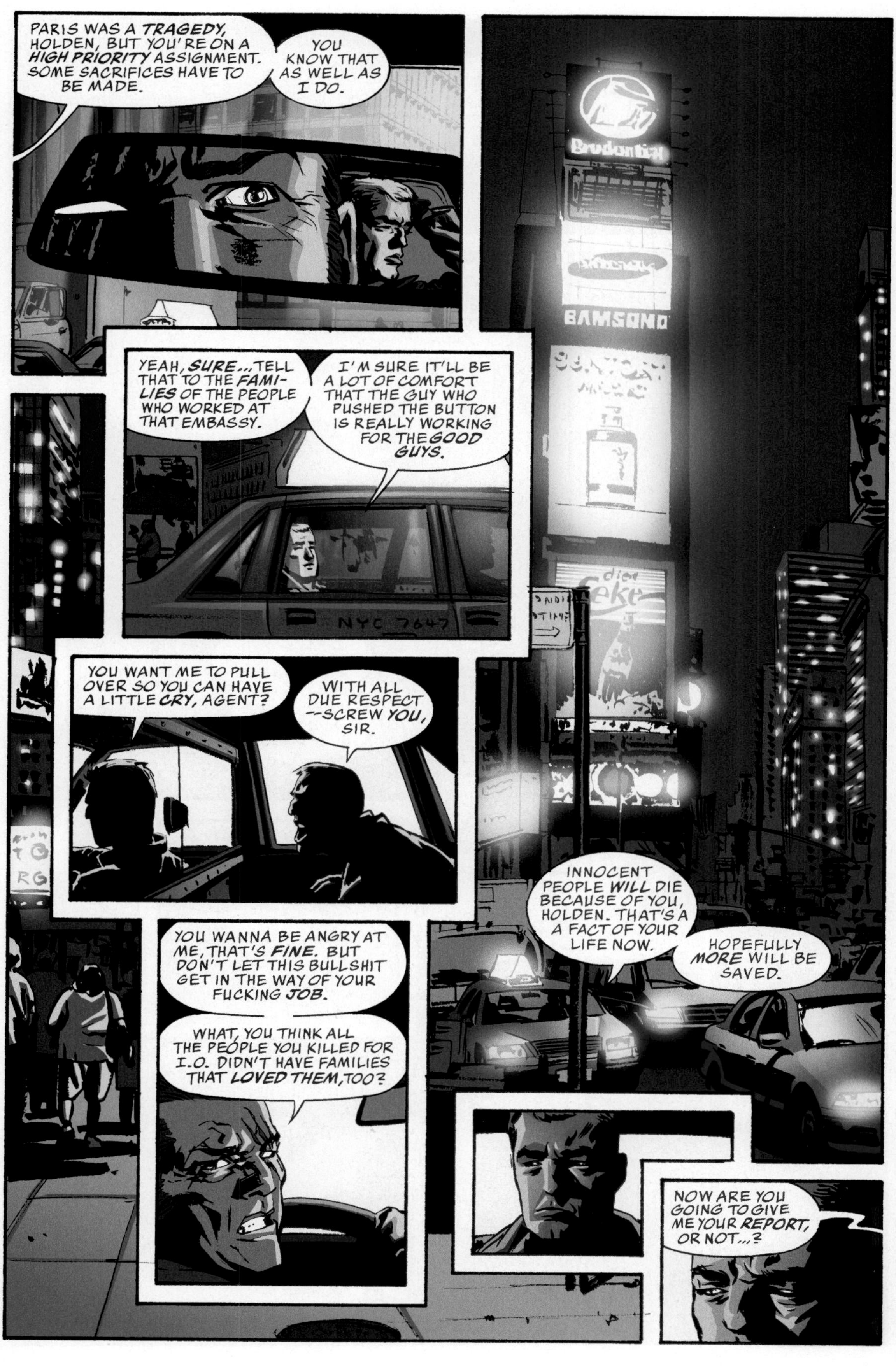
PARIS WAS A TRAGEDY, HOLDEN, BUT YOU'RE ON A HIGH PRIORITY ASSIGNMENT. SOME SACRIFICES HAVE TO BE MADE.
YOU KNOW THAT AS WELL AS I DO.
YEAH, SURE... TELL THAT TO THE FAMI-LIES OF THE PEOPLE WHO WORKED AT THAT EMBASSY.
I'M SURE IT'LL BE A LOT OF COMFORT THAT THE GUY WHO PUSHED THE BUTTON IS REALLY WORKING FOR THE GOOD GUYS.
NYC 7647
YOU WANT ME TO PULL OVER SO YOU CAN HAVE A LITTLE CRY, AGENT?
WITH ALL DUE RESPECT --SCREW YOU, SIR.
YOU WANNA BE ANGRY AT ME, THAT'S FINE. BUT DON'T LET THIS BULLSHIT GET IN THE WAY OF YOUR FUCKING JOB.
WHAT, YOU THINK ALL THE PEOPLE YOU KILLED FOR I.O. DIDN'T HAVE FAMILIES THAT LOVED THEM, TOO?
INNOCENT PEOPLE WILL DIE BECAUSE OF YOU, HOLDEN. THAT'S A A FACT OF YOUR LIFE NOW.
HOPEFULLY MORE WILL BE SAVED.
NOW ARE YOU GOING TO GIVE ME YOUR REPORT, OR NOT...?

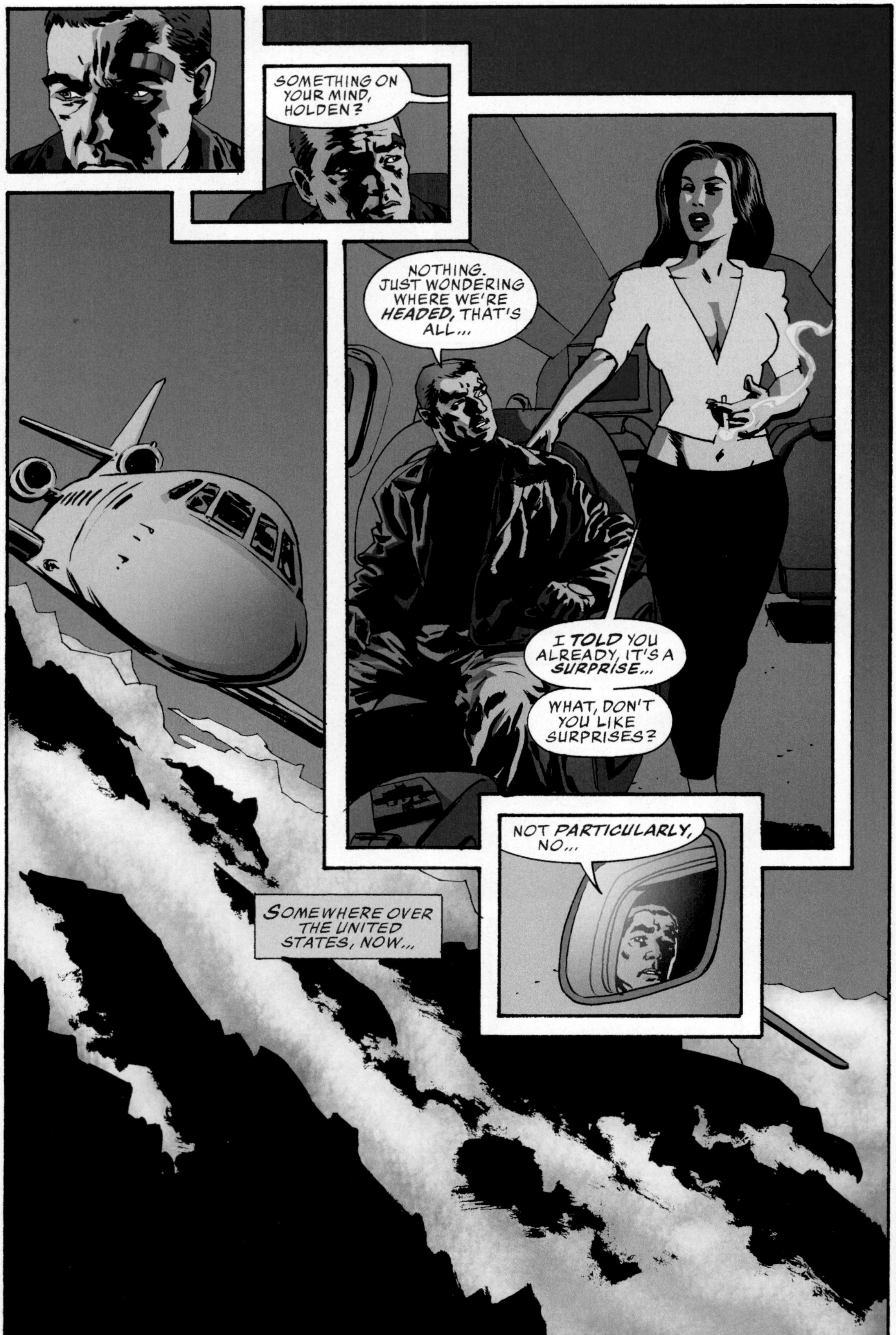
SOMETHING ON YOUR MIND, HOLDEN?
NOTHING. JUST WONDERING WHERE WE'RE HEADED, THAT'S ALL...
I TOLD YOU ALREADY, IT'S A SURPRISE...
WHAT, DON'T YOU LIKE SURPRISES?
SOMEWHERE OVER THE UNITED STATES, NOW...
NOT PARTICULARLY, NO...

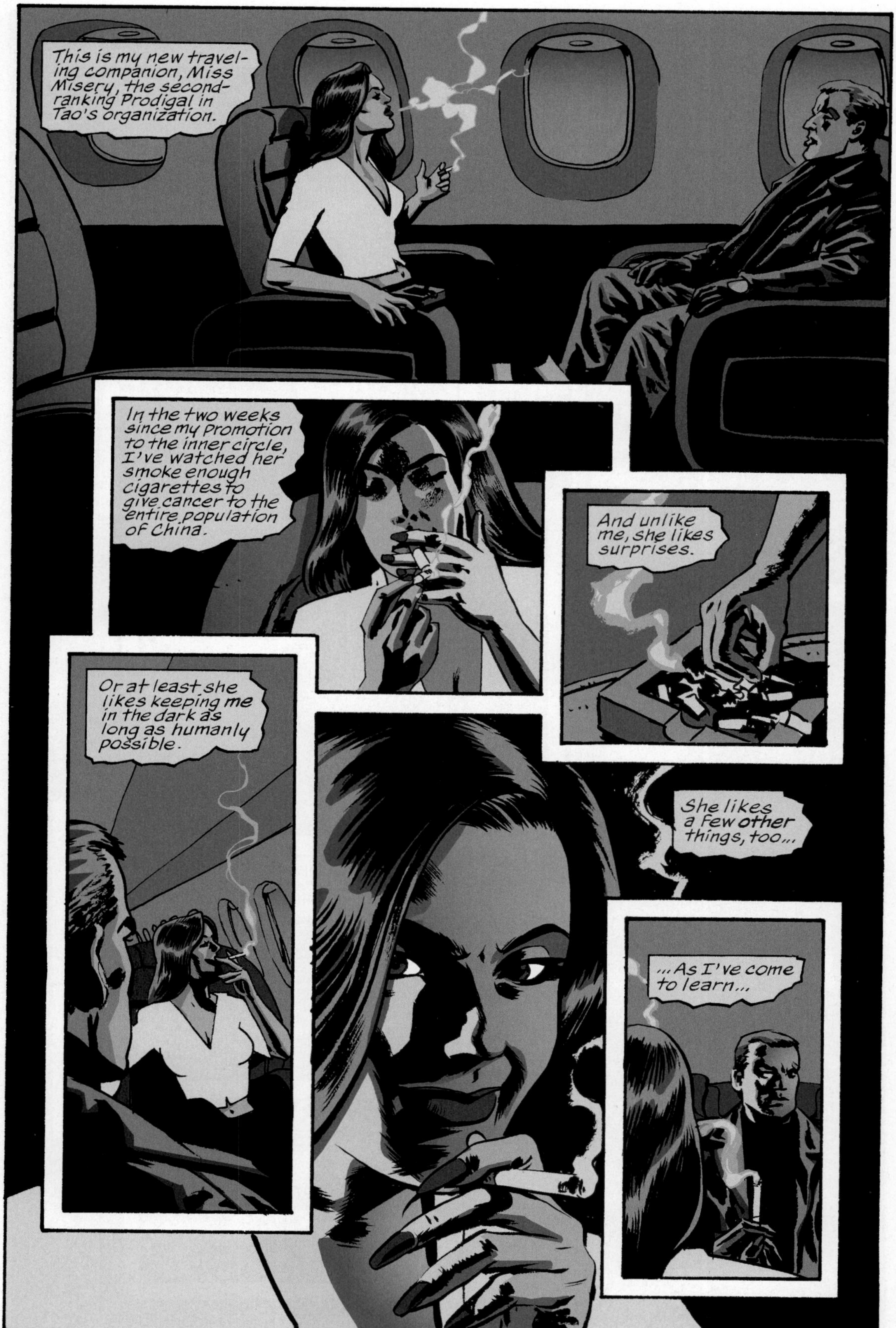
This is my new traveling companion, Miss Misery, the second-ranking Prodigal in Tao's organization.
In the two weeks since my promotion to the inner circle, I've watched her smoke enough cigarettes to give cancer to the entire population of China.
And unlike me, she likes surprises.
Or at least she likes keeping me in the dark as long as humanly possible.
She likes a few other things, too...
...As I've come to learn...

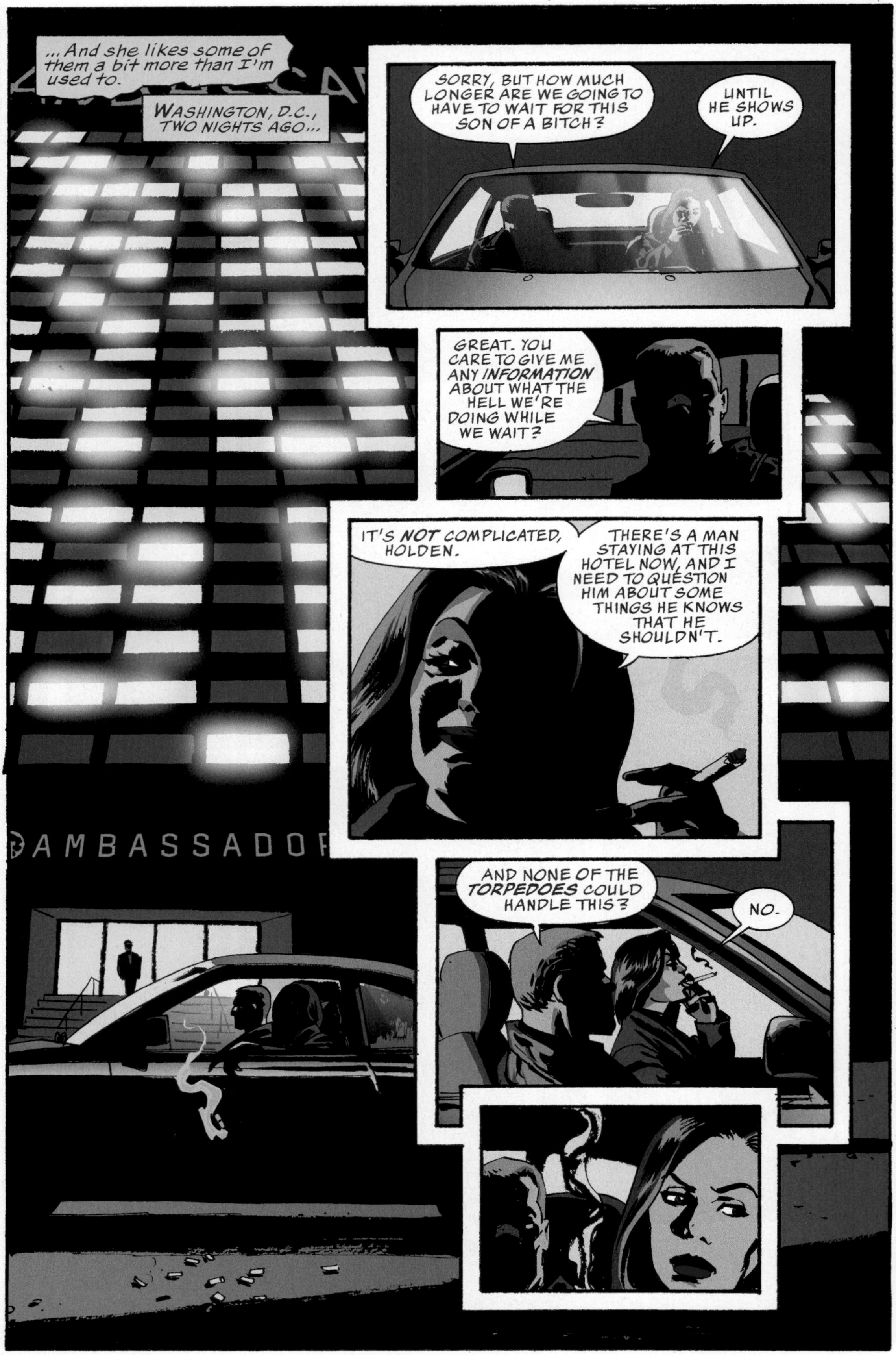

...And she likes some of them a bit more than I'm used to.
WASHINGTON, D.C., TWO NIGHTS AGO...
SORRY, BUT HOW MUCH LONGER ARE WE GOING TO HAVE TO WAIT FOR THIS SON OF A BITCH?
UNTIL HE SHOWS UP.
GREAT. YOU CARE TO GIVE ME ANY *INFORMATION* ABOUT WHAT THE HELL WE'RE DOING WHILE WE WAIT?
IT'S *NOT* COMPLICATED, HOLDEN.
THERE'S A MAN STAYING AT THIS HOTEL NOW, AND I NEED TO QUESTION HIM ABOUT SOME THINGS HE KNOWS THAT HE SHOULDN'T.
AMBASSADOR
AND NONE OF THE *TORPEDOES* COULD HANDLE THIS?
NO.

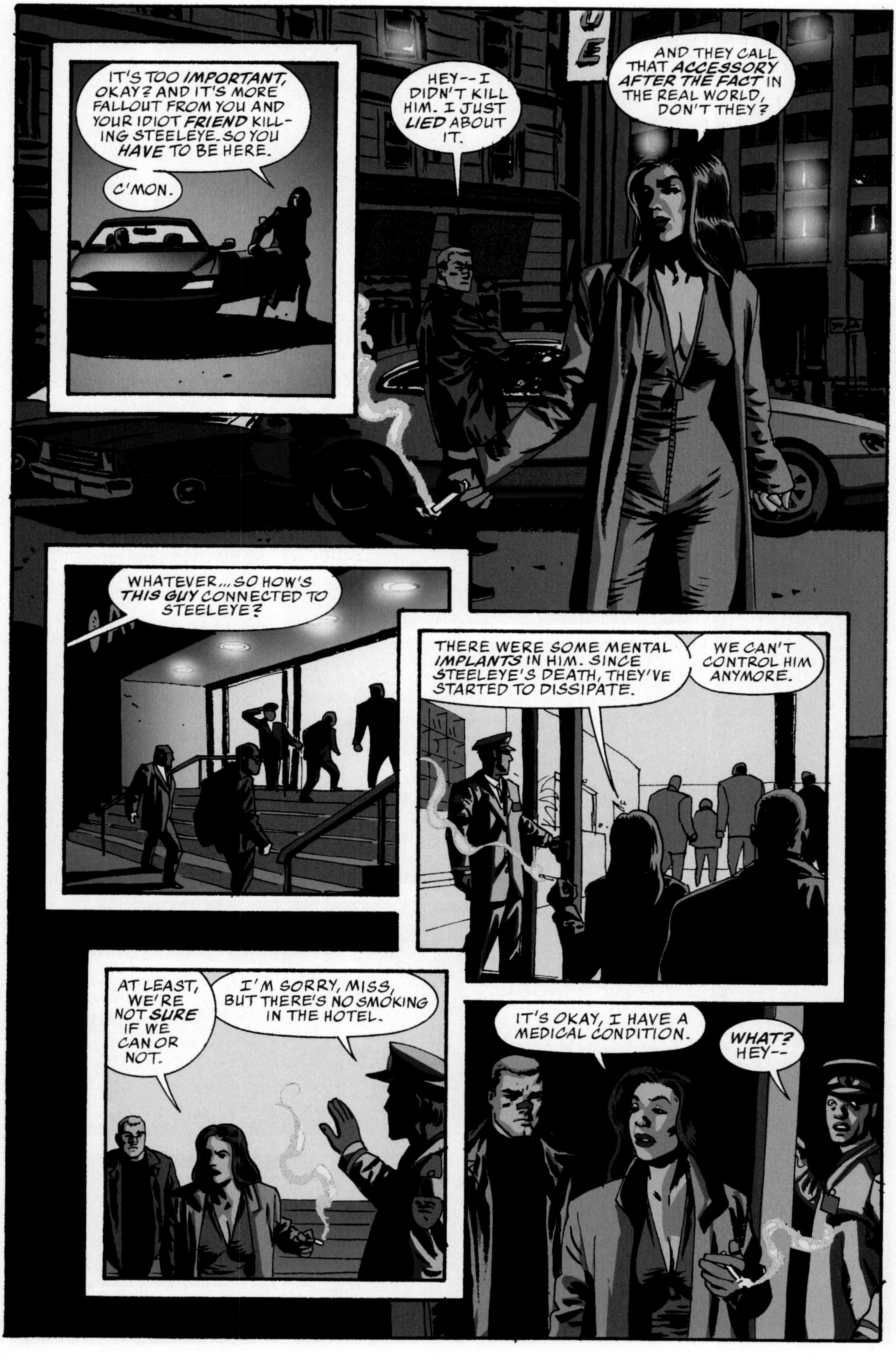
IT'S TOO IMPORTANT, OKAY? AND IT'S MORE FALLOUT FROM YOU AND YOUR IDIOT FRIEND KILLING STEELEYE. SO YOU HAVE TO BE HERE.
C'MON.
HEY-- I DIDN'T KILL HIM. I JUST LIED ABOUT IT.
AND THEY CALL THAT ACCESSORY AFTER THE FACT IN THE REAL WORLD, DON'T THEY?
WHATEVER... SO HOW'S THIS GUY CONNECTED TO STEELEYE?
THERE WERE SOME MENTAL IMPLANTS IN HIM. SINCE STEELEYE'S DEATH, THEY'VE STARTED TO DISSIPATE.
WE CAN'T CONTROL HIM ANYMORE.
AT LEAST, WE'RE NOT SURE IF WE CAN OR NOT.
I'M SORRY, MISS, BUT THERE'S NO SMOKING IN THE HOTEL.
IT'S OKAY, I HAVE A MEDICAL CONDITION.
WHAT? HEY--

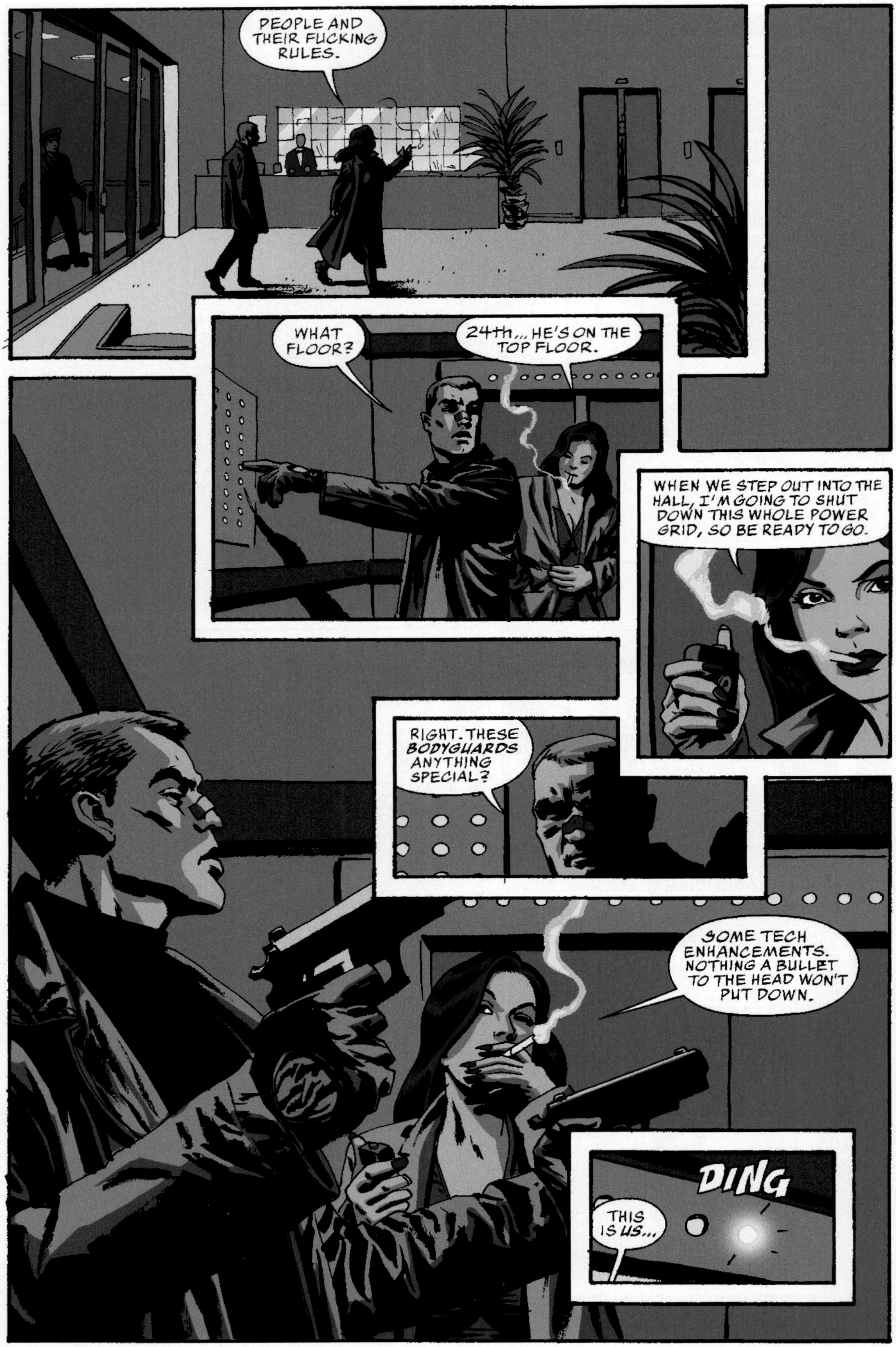
PEOPLE AND THEIR FUCKING RULES.
WHAT FLOOR?
24th... HE'S ON THE TOP FLOOR.
WHEN WE STEP OUT INTO THE HALL, I'M GOING TO SHUT DOWN THIS WHOLE POWER GRID, SO BE READY TO GO.
RIGHT. THESE BODYGUARDS ANYTHING SPECIAL?
SOME TECH ENHANCEMENTS. NOTHING A BULLET TO THE HEAD WON'T PUT DOWN.
DING
THIS IS US...

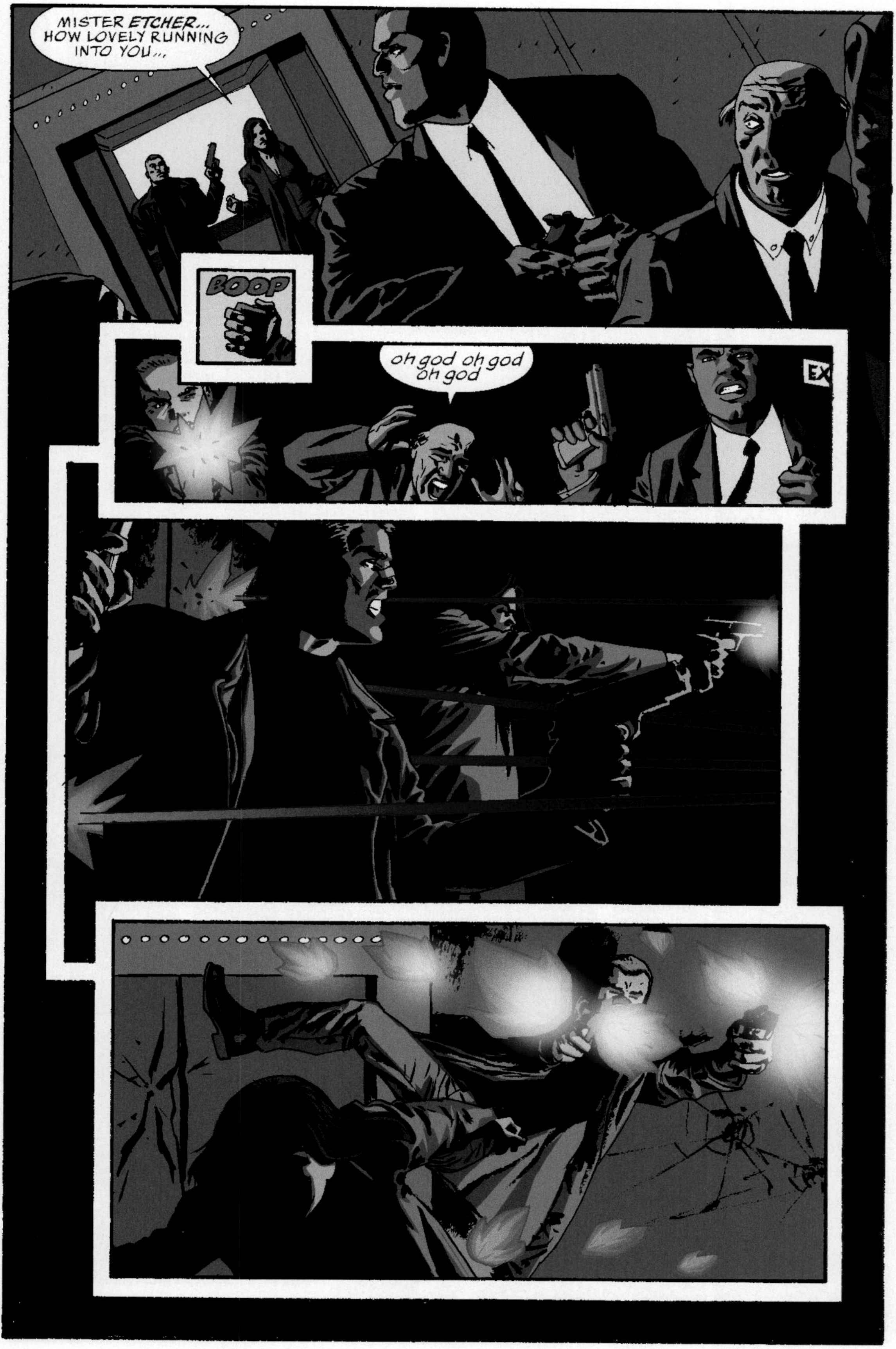
MISTER ETCHER...
HOW LOVELY RUNNING INTO YOU...
BOOP
oh god oh god oh god
EX

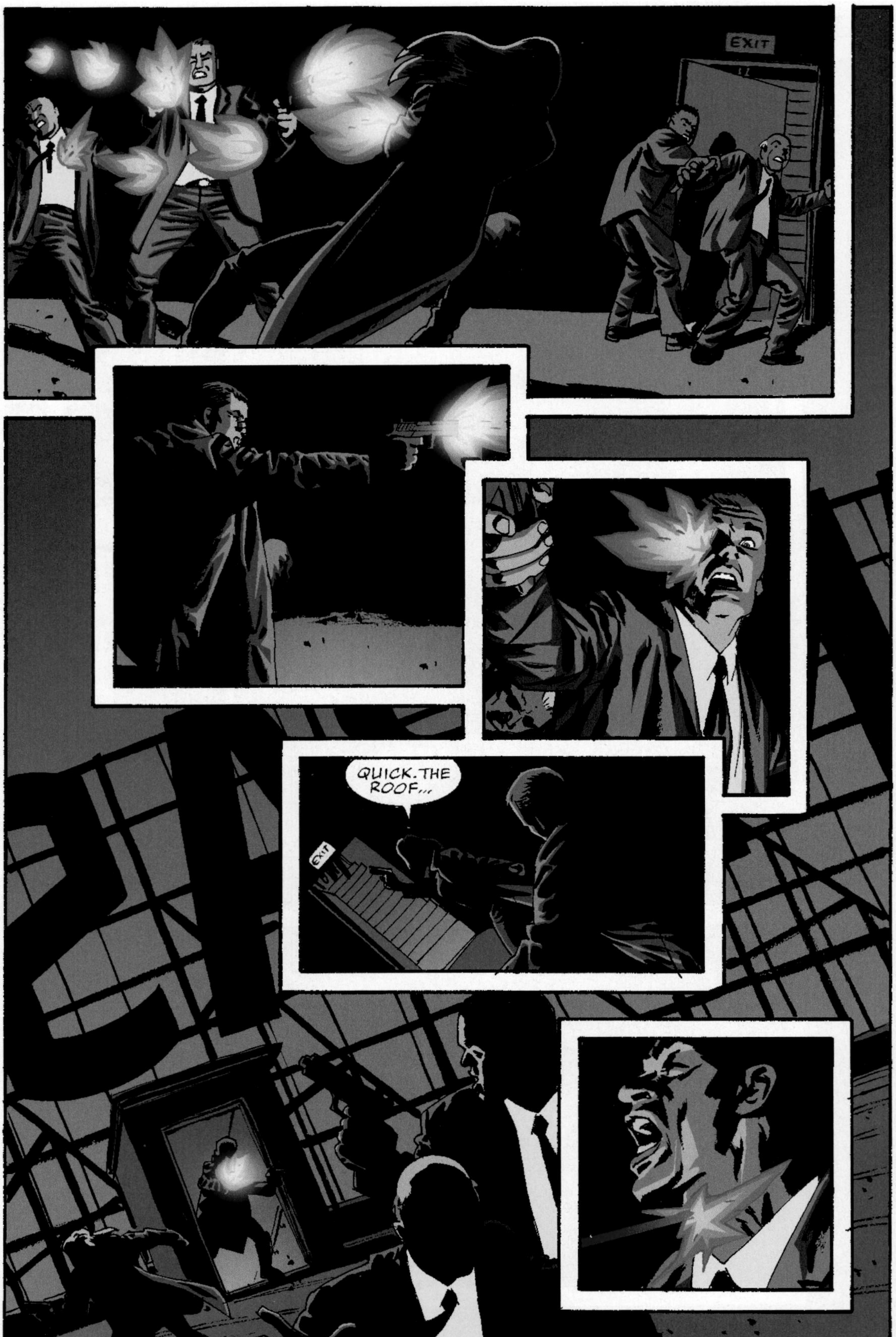
EXIT
QUICK. THE ROOF...
EXIT

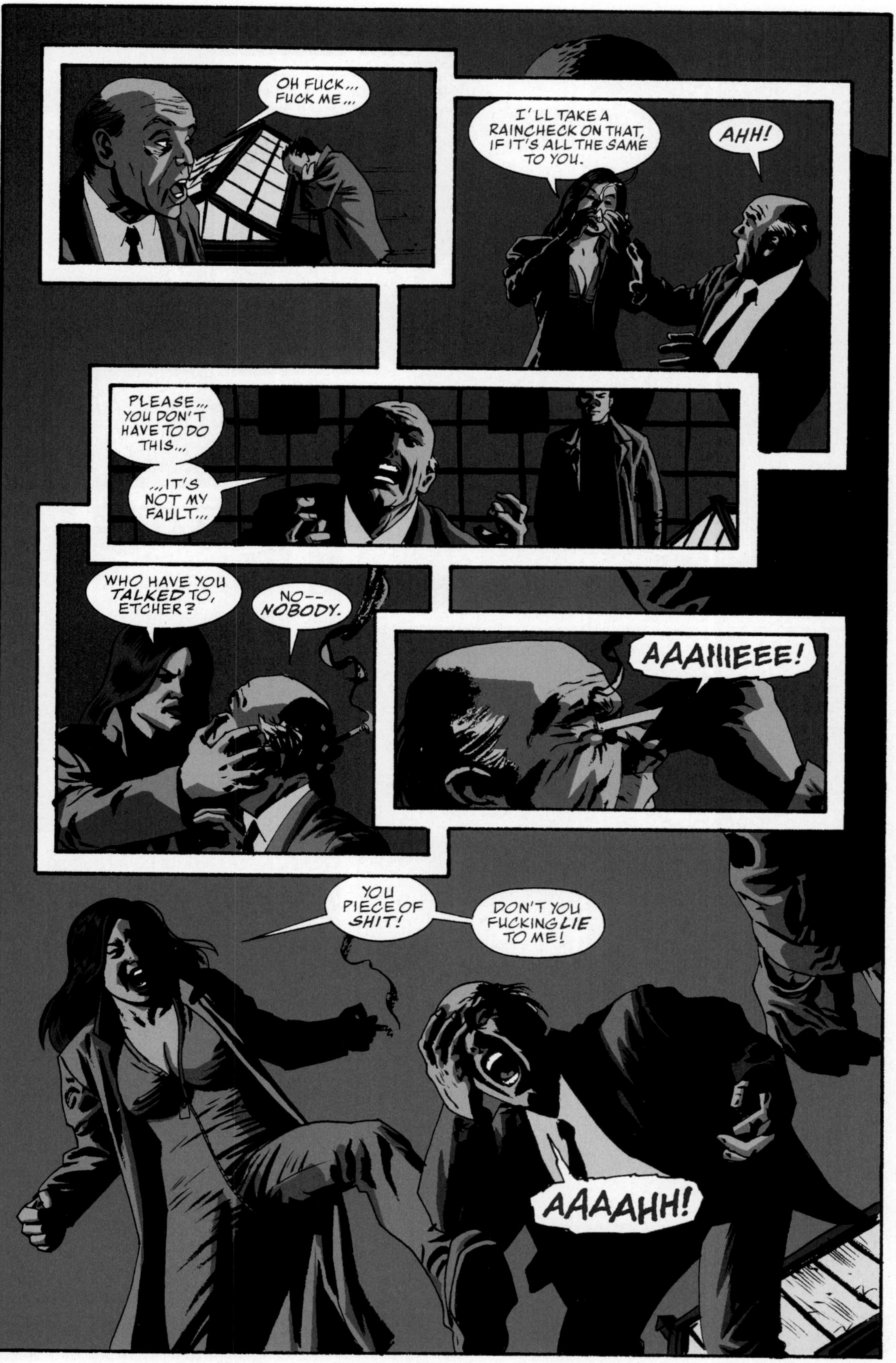
OH FUCK... FUCK ME...
I'LL TAKE A RAINCHECK ON THAT, IF IT'S ALL THE SAME TO YOU.
AHH!
PLEASE... YOU DON'T HAVE TO DO THIS...
...IT'S NOT MY FAULT...
WHO HAVE YOU TALKED TO, ETCHER?
NO-- NOBODY.
AAAIIIEEE!
YOU PIECE OF SHIT!
DON'T YOU FUCKING LIE TO ME!
AAAAHH!

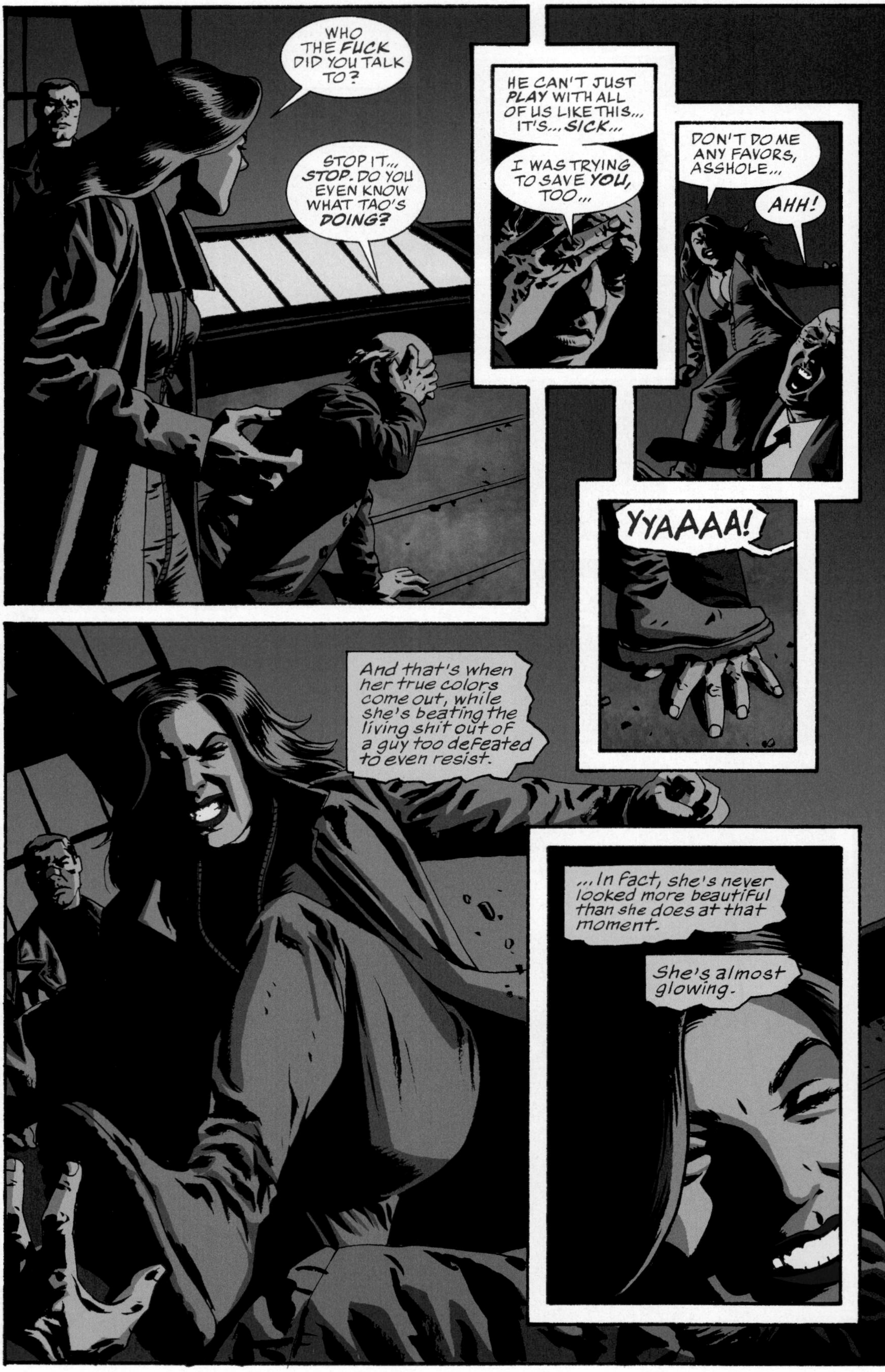
WHO THE FUCK DID YOU TALK TO?
STOP IT... STOP. DO YOU EVEN KNOW WHAT TAO'S DOING?
HE CAN'T JUST PLAY WITH ALL OF US LIKE THIS... IT'S... SICK...
I WAS TRYING TO SAVE YOU, TOO...
DON'T DO ME ANY FAVORS, ASSHOLE...
AHH!
YYAAAA!
And that's when her true colors come out, while she's beating the living shit out of a guy too defeated to even resist.
...In fact, she's never looked more beautiful than she does at that moment.
She's almost glowing.

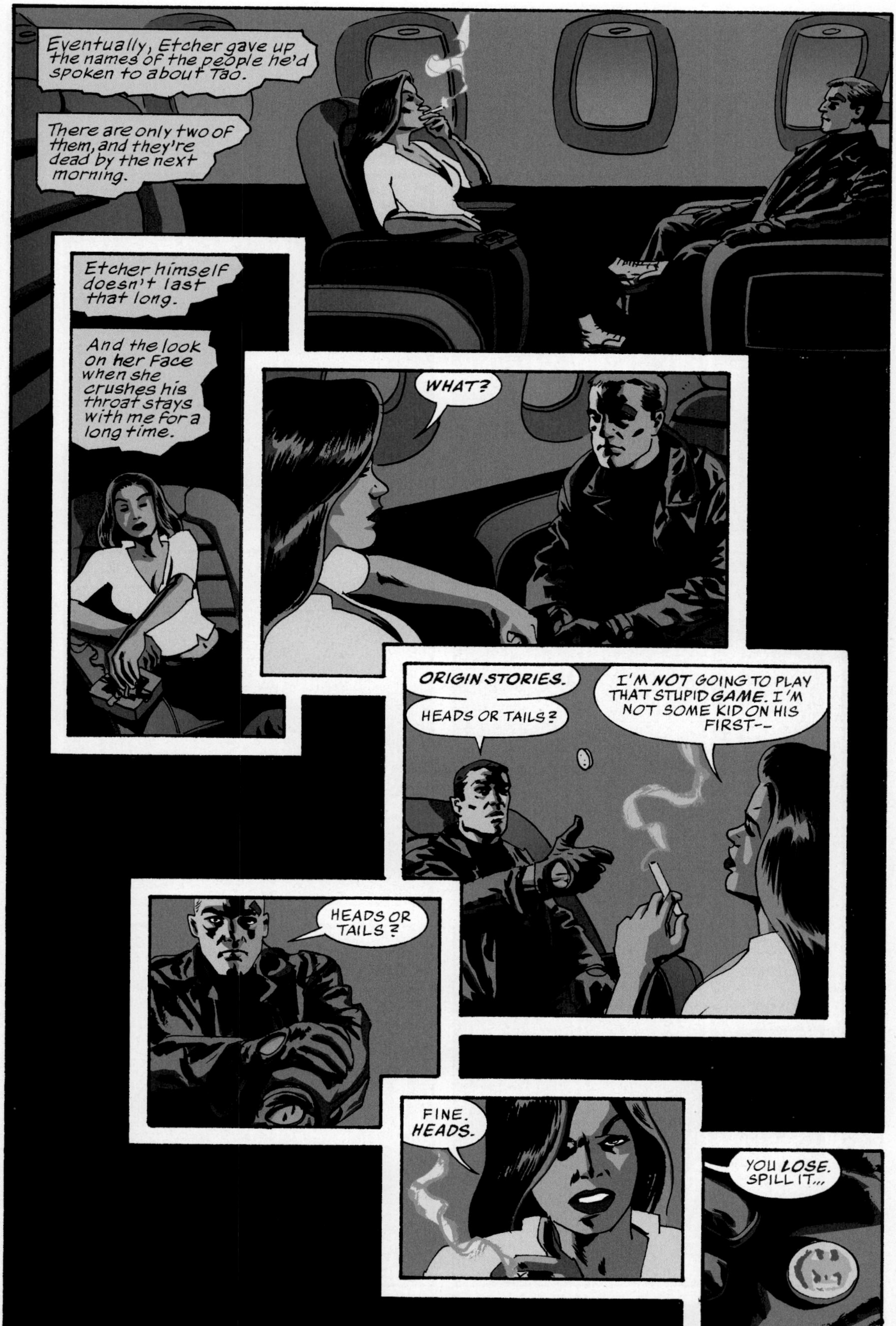
Eventually, Etcher gave up the names of the people he'd spoken to about Tao.
There are only two of them, and they're dead by the next morning.
Etcher himself doesn't last that long.
And the look on her face when she crushes his throat stays with me for a long time.
WHAT?
ORIGIN STORIES.
HEADS OR TAILS?
I'M NOT GOING TO PLAY THAT STUPID GAME. I'M NOT SOME KID ON HIS FIRST--
HEADS OR TAILS?
FINE. HEADS.
YOU LOSE. SPILL IT...

ALL RIGHT, GOD.... LET ME SEE IF I CAN EVEN *REMEMBER* HOW TO DO THIS...

"ONCE UPON A TIME THERE WAS A NICE YOUNG GIRL NAMED GRETCHEN MACDONALD. SHE WAS THE KIND OF GIRL EVERY PARENT WANTS THEIR CHILD TO BE...

"... CLASS VALEDICTORIAN, BELIEVED IN GOD, DIDN'T DRINK, SMOKE, FUCK, OR DO DRUGS.

" SHE WAS AS BORING AND HAPPY AS ANY WHITE GIRL IN AMERICA COULD EVER HOPE TO BE. HAD BIG PLANS FOR THE FUTURE... CAREER, KIDS, THE WHOLE APPLE PIE DREAM.

" EXCEPT SOMETHING WENT WRONG FOR POOR GRETCHEN. SHE STARTED TO GET SICK. *REALLY* SICK...

" AND NO ONE COULD FIGURE OUT EXACTY WHAT WAS WRONG WITH HER.... SOME DOCTORS THOUGHT IT WAS MENTAL, SOME SAID ENVIRONMENTAL...

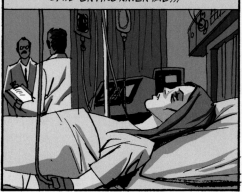

" IT DIDN'T SEEM *FAIR*, REALLY, SINCE HER WHOLE LIFE SHE'D ALWAYS DONE ALL THE RIGHT THINGS...

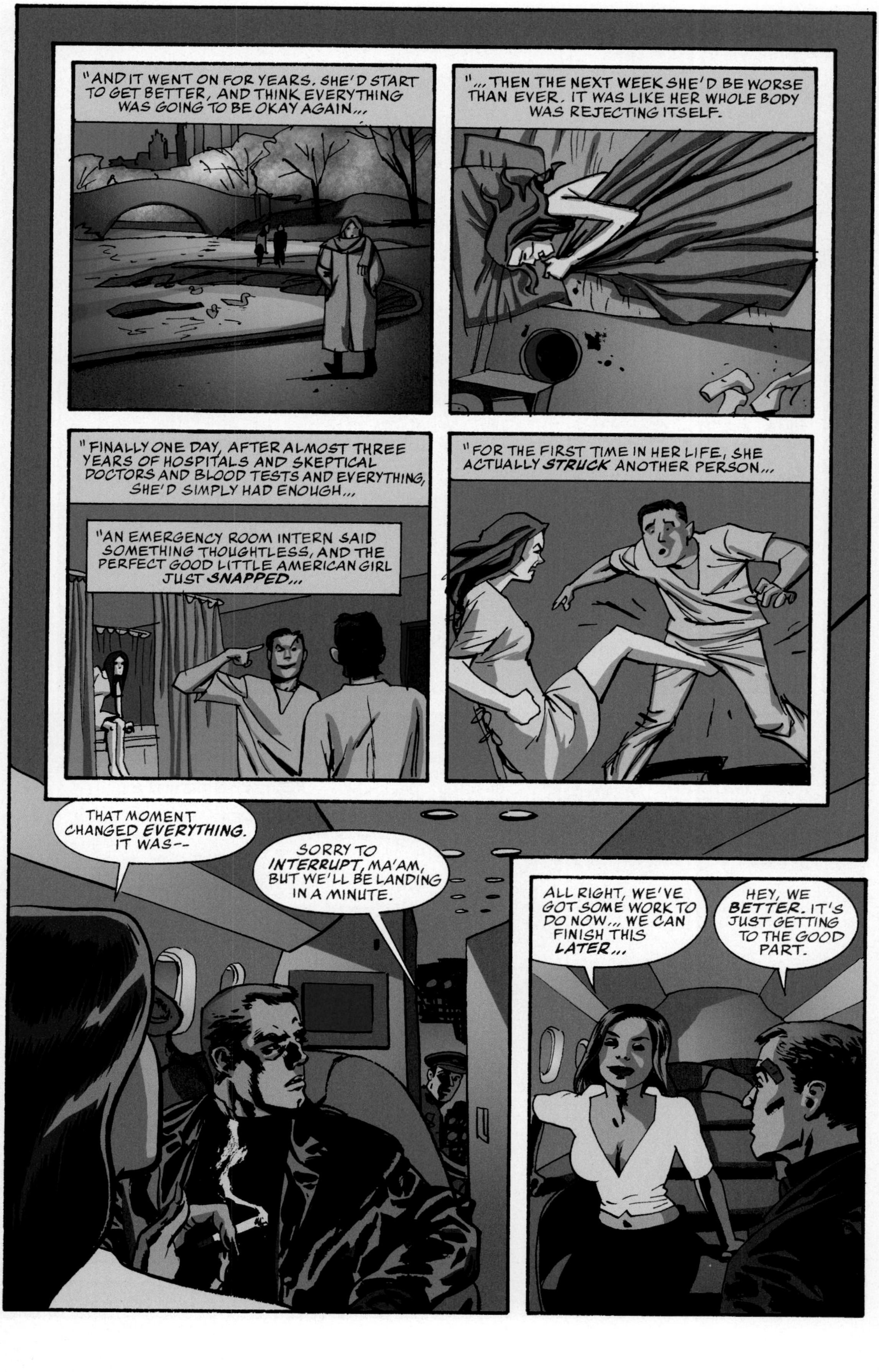
"AND IT WENT ON FOR YEARS. SHE'D START TO GET BETTER, AND THINK EVERYTHING WAS GOING TO BE OKAY AGAIN...
"...THEN THE NEXT WEEK SHE'D BE WORSE THAN EVER. IT WAS LIKE HER WHOLE BODY WAS REJECTING ITSELF.
"FINALLY ONE DAY, AFTER ALMOST THREE YEARS OF HOSPITALS AND SKEPTICAL DOCTORS AND BLOOD TESTS AND EVERYTHING, SHE'D SIMPLY HAD ENOUGH...
"AN EMERGENCY ROOM INTERN SAID SOMETHING THOUGHTLESS, AND THE PERFECT GOOD LITTLE AMERICAN GIRL JUST SNAPPED...
"FOR THE FIRST TIME IN HER LIFE, SHE ACTUALLY STRUCK ANOTHER PERSON...
THAT MOMENT CHANGED EVERYTHING. IT WAS--
SORRY TO INTERRUPT, MA'AM, BUT WE'LL BE LANDING IN A MINUTE.
ALL RIGHT, WE'VE GOT SOME WORK TO DO NOW... WE CAN FINISH THIS LATER...
HEY, WE BETTER. IT'S JUST GETTING TO THE GOOD PART.

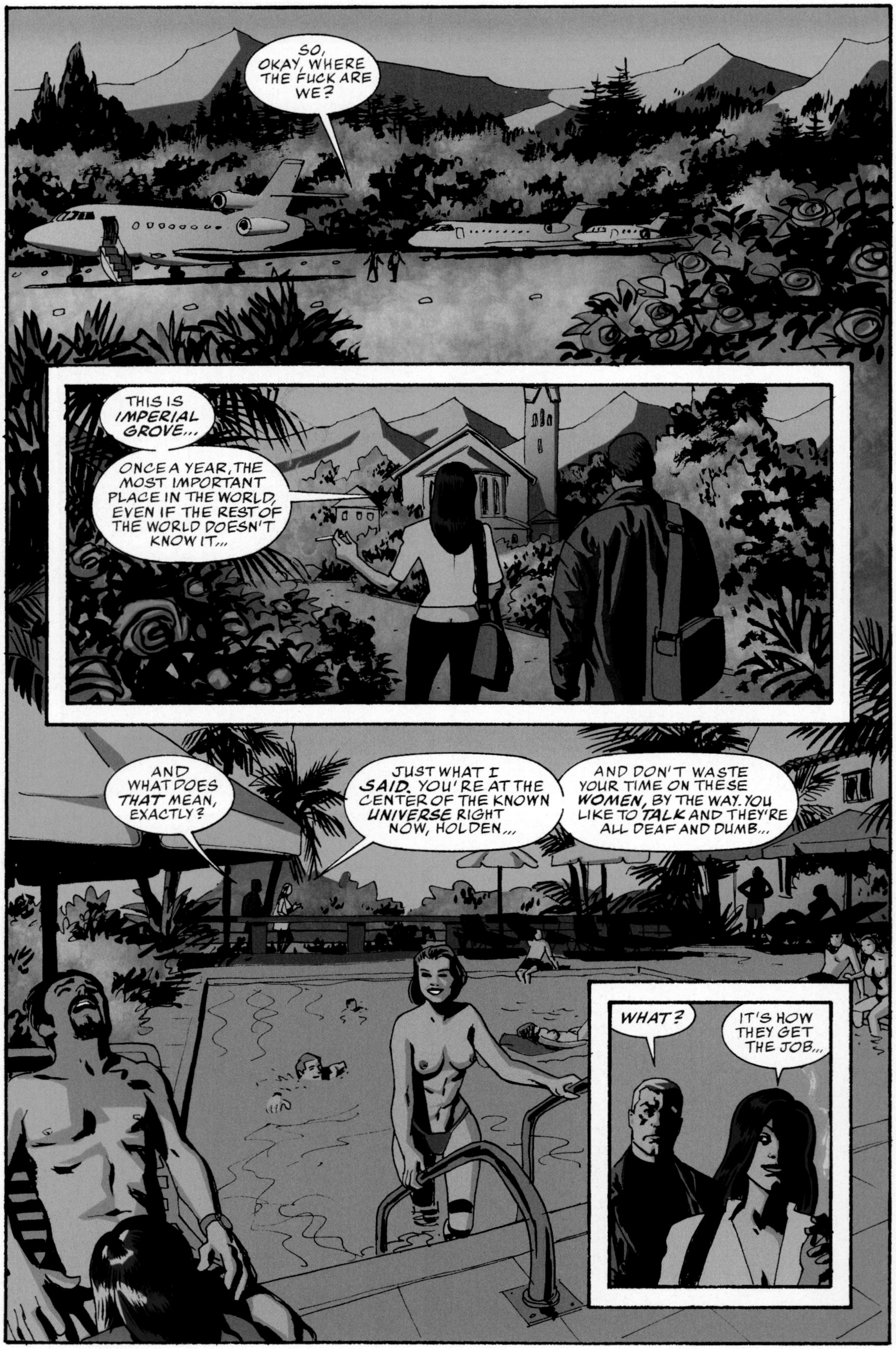
SO, OKAY, WHERE THE FUCK ARE WE?
THIS IS IMPERIAL GROVE...
ONCE A YEAR, THE MOST IMPORTANT PLACE IN THE WORLD, EVEN IF THE REST OF THE WORLD DOESN'T KNOW IT...
AND WHAT DOES THAT MEAN, EXACTLY?
JUST WHAT I SAID. YOU'RE AT THE CENTER OF THE KNOWN UNIVERSE RIGHT NOW, HOLDEN...
AND DON'T WASTE YOUR TIME ON THESE WOMEN, BY THE WAY. YOU LIKE TO TALK AND THEY'RE ALL DEAF AND DUMB...
WHAT?
IT'S HOW THEY GET THE JOB...

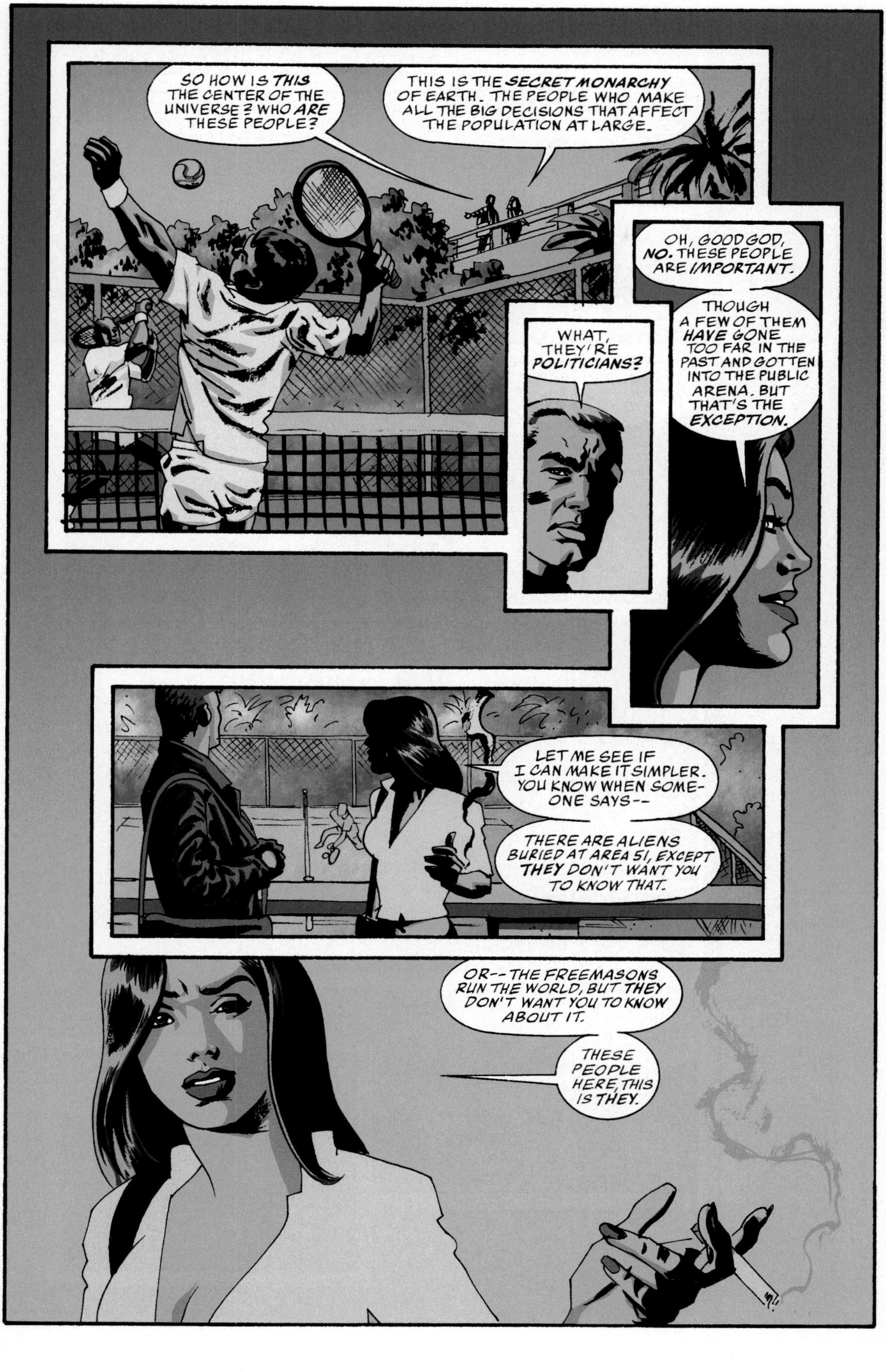
SO HOW IS THIS THE CENTER OF THE UNIVERSE? WHO ARE THESE PEOPLE?
THIS IS THE SECRET MONARCHY OF EARTH. THE PEOPLE WHO MAKE ALL THE BIG DECISIONS THAT AFFECT THE POPULATION AT LARGE.
WHAT, THEY'RE POLITICIANS?
OH, GOOD GOD, NO. THESE PEOPLE ARE IMPORTANT.
THOUGH A FEW OF THEM HAVE GONE TOO FAR IN THE PAST AND GOTTEN INTO THE PUBLIC ARENA. BUT THAT'S THE EXCEPTION.
LET ME SEE IF I CAN MAKE IT SIMPLER. YOU KNOW WHEN SOME-ONE SAYS--
THERE ARE ALIENS BURIED AT AREA 51, EXCEPT THEY DON'T WANT YOU TO KNOW THAT.
OR--THE FREEMASONS RUN THE WORLD, BUT THEY DON'T WANT YOU TO KNOW ABOUT IT.
THESE PEOPLE HERE, THIS IS THEY.

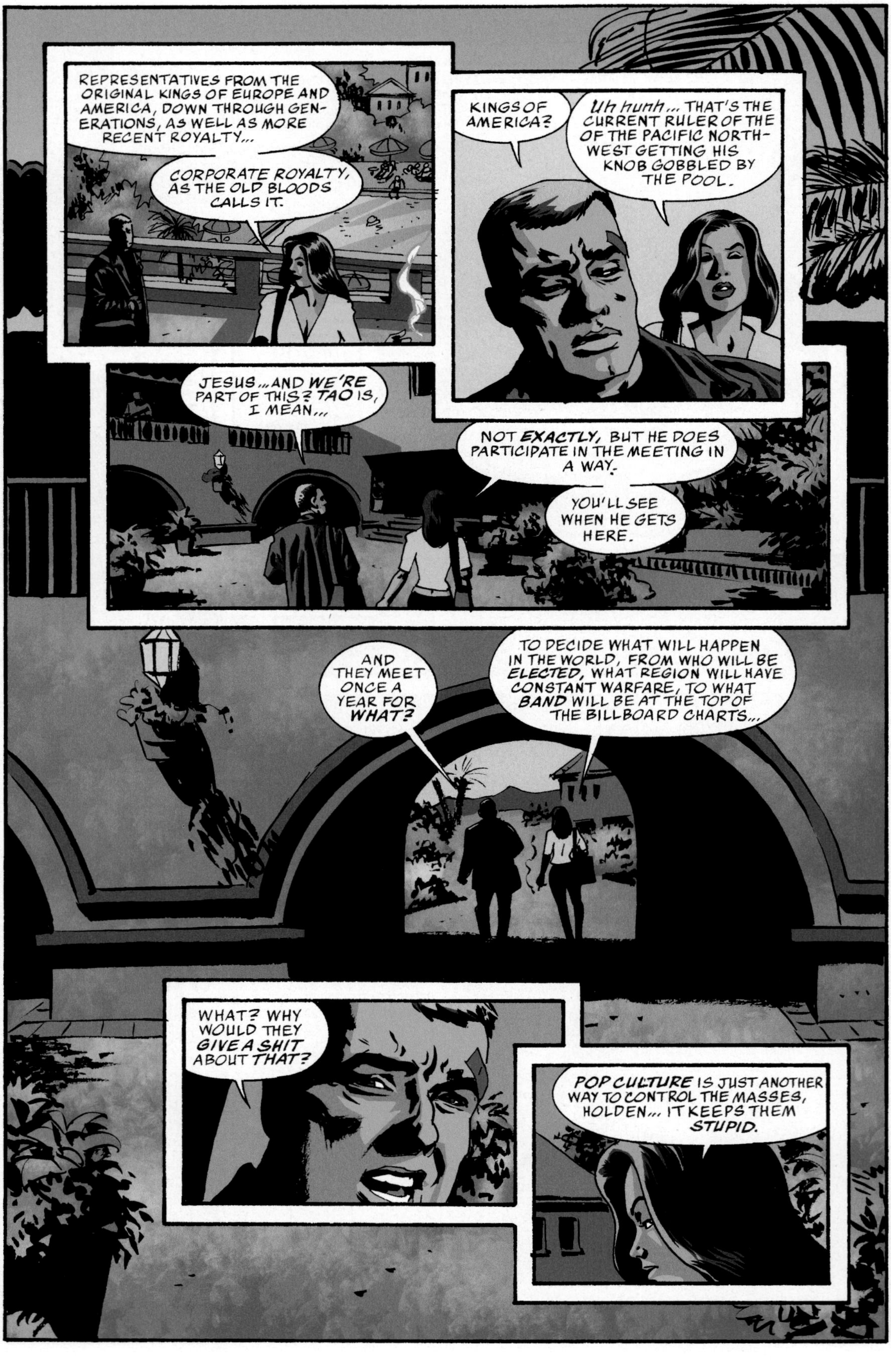

REPRESENTATIVES FROM THE ORIGINAL KINGS OF EUROPE AND AMERICA, DOWN THROUGH GENERATIONS, AS WELL AS MORE RECENT ROYALTY...
CORPORATE ROYALTY, AS THE OLD BLOODS CALLS IT.
KINGS OF AMERICA?
Uh hunh... THAT'S THE CURRENT RULER OF THE OF THE PACIFIC NORTH-WEST GETTING HIS KNOB GOBBLED BY THE POOL.
JESUS...AND WE'RE PART OF THIS? TAO IS, I MEAN...
NOT EXACTLY, BUT HE DOES PARTICIPATE IN THE MEETING IN A WAY.
YOU'LL SEE WHEN HE GETS HERE.
AND THEY MEET ONCE A YEAR FOR WHAT?
TO DECIDE WHAT WILL HAPPEN IN THE WORLD, FROM WHO WILL BE ELECTED, WHAT REGION WILL HAVE CONSTANT WARFARE, TO WHAT BAND WILL BE AT THE TOP OF THE BILLBOARD CHARTS...
WHAT? WHY WOULD THEY GIVE A SHIT ABOUT THAT?
POP CULTURE IS JUST ANOTHER WAY TO CONTROL THE MASSES, HOLDEN... IT KEEPS THEM STUPID.

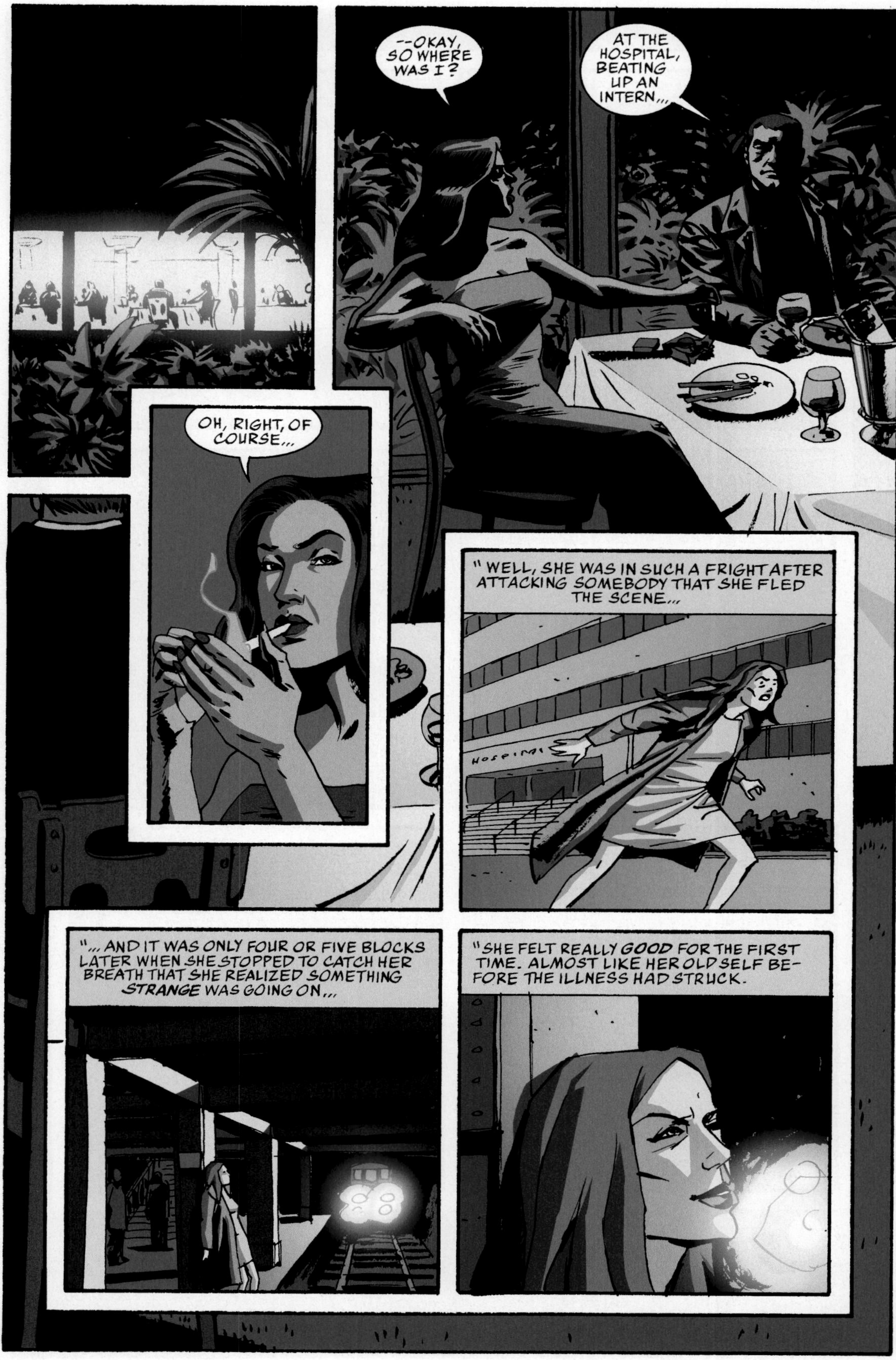
--OKAY, SO WHERE WAS I?
AT THE HOSPITAL, BEATING UP AN INTERN...
OH, RIGHT, OF COURSE...
"WELL, SHE WAS IN SUCH A FRIGHT AFTER ATTACKING SOMEBODY THAT SHE FLED THE SCENE...
"...AND IT WAS ONLY FOUR OR FIVE BLOCKS LATER WHEN SHE STOPPED TO CATCH HER BREATH THAT SHE REALIZED SOMETHING *STRANGE* WAS GOING ON...
"SHE FELT REALLY *GOOD* FOR THE FIRST TIME. ALMOST LIKE HER OLD SELF BEFORE THE ILLNESS HAD STRUCK.

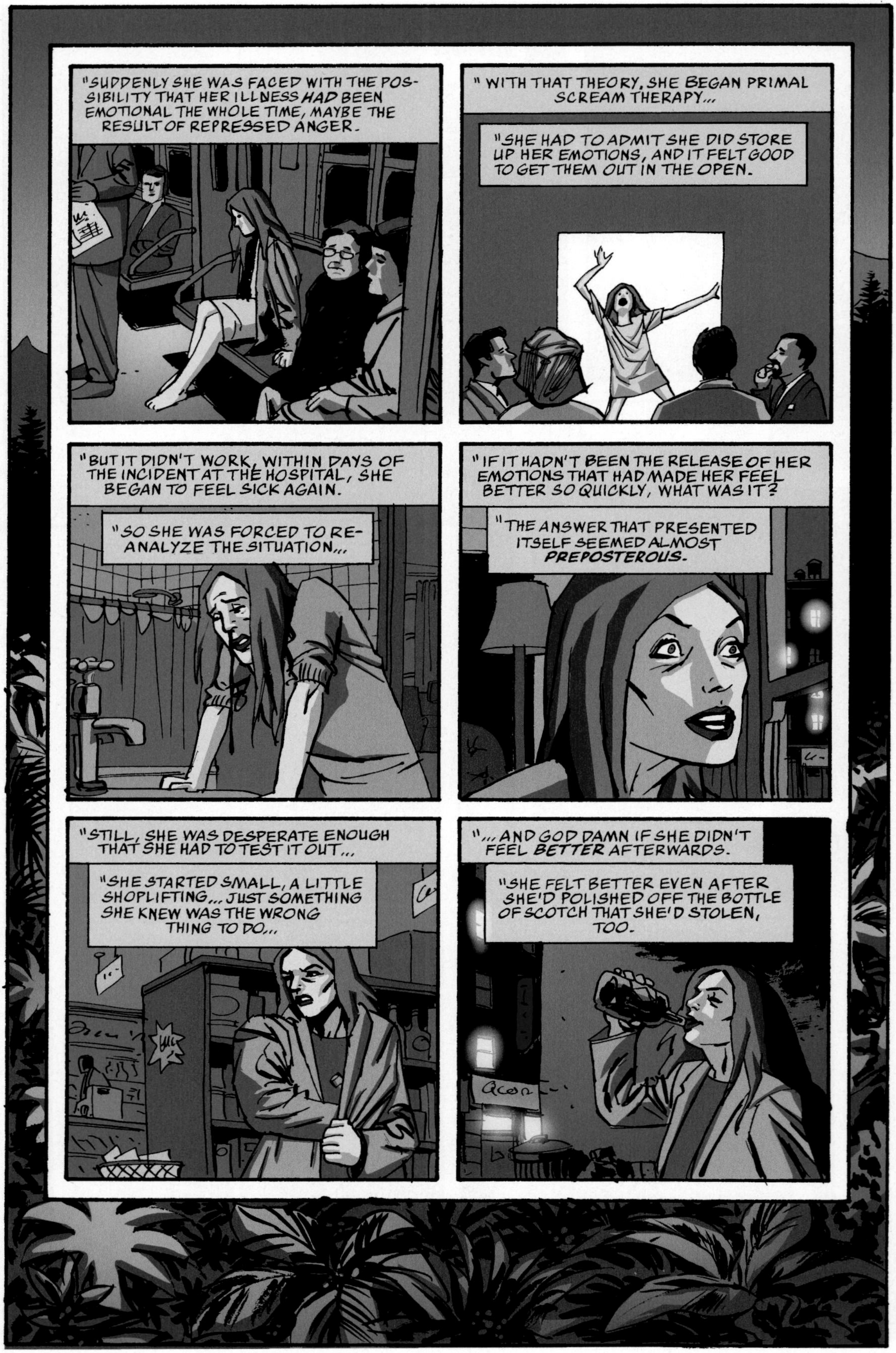
"SUDDENLY SHE WAS FACED WITH THE POSSIBILITY THAT HER ILLNESS HAD BEEN EMOTIONAL THE WHOLE TIME, MAYBE THE RESULT OF REPRESSED ANGER.
" WITH THAT THEORY, SHE BEGAN PRIMAL SCREAM THERAPY...
"SHE HAD TO ADMIT SHE DID STORE UP HER EMOTIONS, AND IT FELT GOOD TO GET THEM OUT IN THE OPEN.
"BUT IT DIDN'T WORK. WITHIN DAYS OF THE INCIDENT AT THE HOSPITAL, SHE BEGAN TO FEEL SICK AGAIN.
"SO SHE WAS FORCED TO RE-ANALYZE THE SITUATION...
"IF IT HADN'T BEEN THE RELEASE OF HER EMOTIONS THAT HAD MADE HER FEEL BETTER SO QUICKLY, WHAT WAS IT?
"THE ANSWER THAT PRESENTED ITSELF SEEMED ALMOST PREPOSTEROUS.
"STILL, SHE WAS DESPERATE ENOUGH THAT SHE HAD TO TEST IT OUT...
"SHE STARTED SMALL, A LITTLE SHOPLIFTING... JUST SOMETHING SHE KNEW WAS THE WRONG THING TO DO...
"...AND GOD DAMN IF SHE DIDN'T FEEL BETTER AFTERWARDS.
"SHE FELT BETTER EVEN AFTER SHE'D POLISHED OFF THE BOTTLE OF SCOTCH THAT SHE'D STOLEN, TOO.

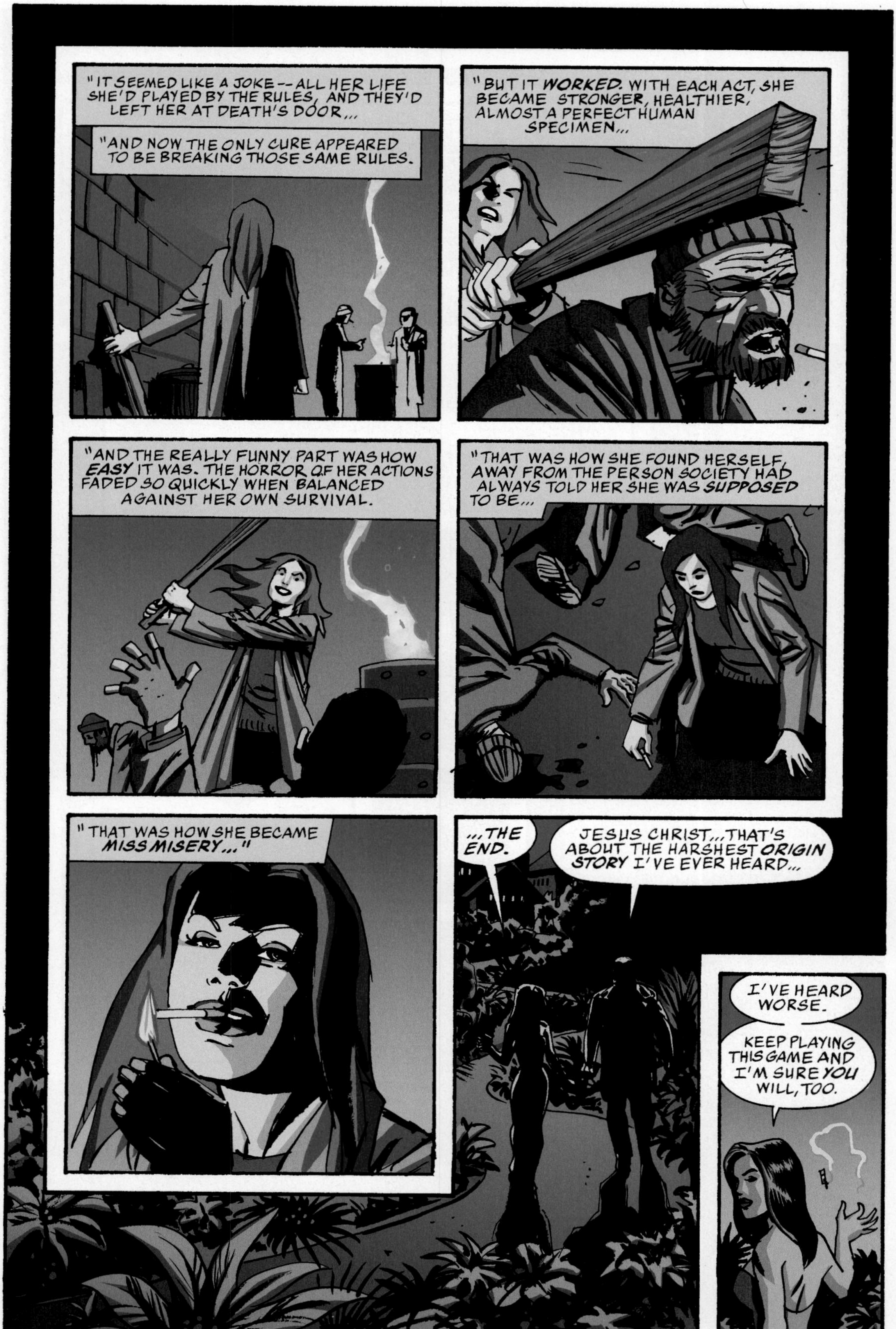
"IT SEEMED LIKE A JOKE -- ALL HER LIFE SHE'D PLAYED BY THE RULES, AND THEY'D LEFT HER AT DEATH'S DOOR...
"AND NOW THE ONLY CURE APPEARED TO BE BREAKING THOSE SAME RULES.
"BUT IT WORKED. WITH EACH ACT, SHE BECAME STRONGER, HEALTHIER, ALMOST A PERFECT HUMAN SPECIMEN...
"AND THE REALLY FUNNY PART WAS HOW EASY IT WAS. THE HORROR OF HER ACTIONS FADED SO QUICKLY WHEN BALANCED AGAINST HER OWN SURVIVAL.
"THAT WAS HOW SHE FOUND HERSELF, AWAY FROM THE PERSON SOCIETY HAD ALWAYS TOLD HER SHE WAS SUPPOSED TO BE...
"THAT WAS HOW SHE BECAME MISS MISERY..."
...THE END.
JESUS CHRIST... THAT'S ABOUT THE HARSHEST ORIGIN STORY I'VE EVER HEARD...
I'VE HEARD WORSE.
KEEP PLAYING THIS GAME AND I'M SURE YOU WILL, TOO.

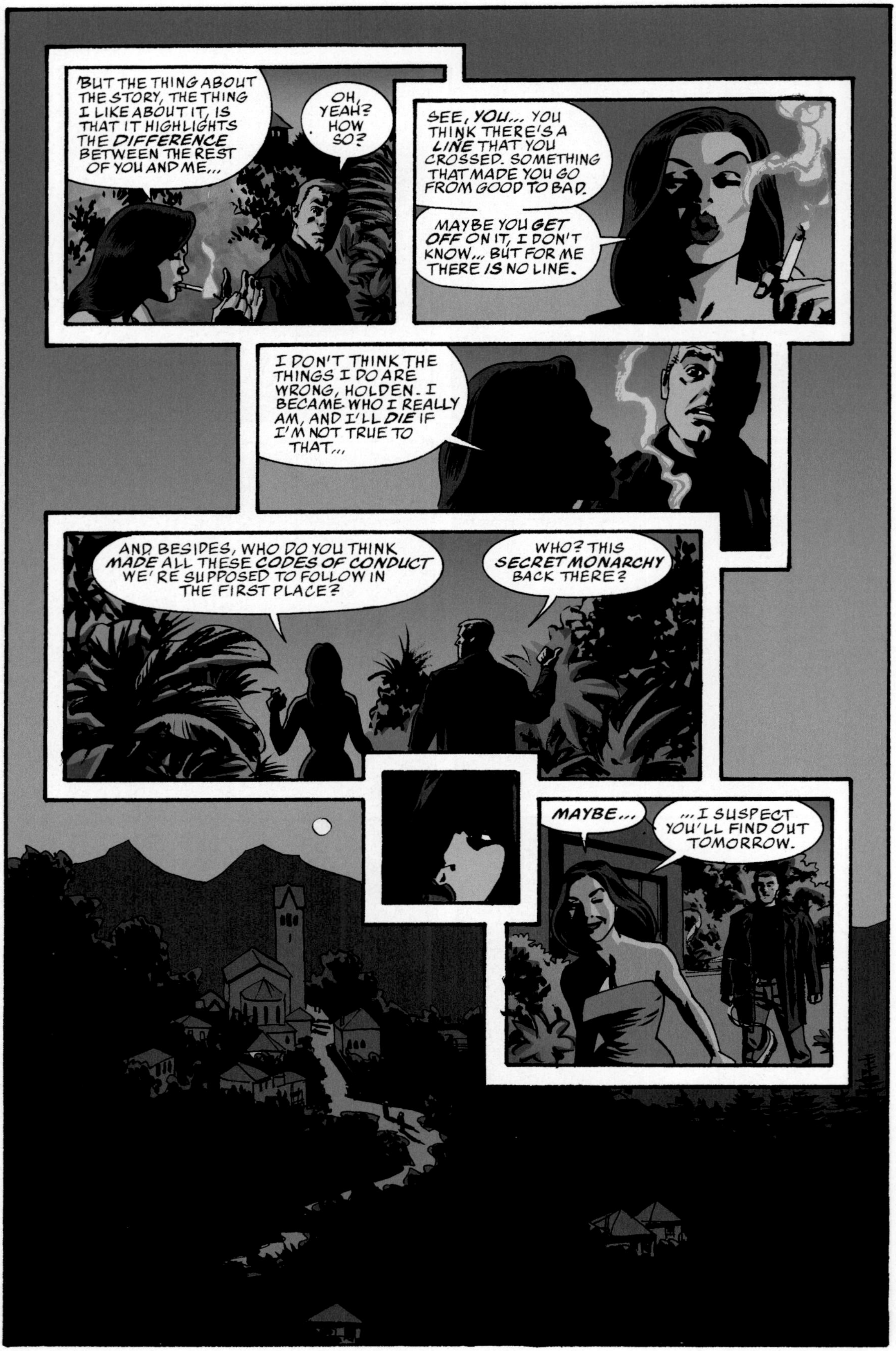
'BUT THE THING ABOUT THE STORY, THE THING I LIKE ABOUT IT, IS THAT IT HIGHLIGHTS THE DIFFERENCE BETWEEN THE REST OF YOU AND ME...
OH, YEAH? HOW SO?
SEE, YOU... YOU THINK THERE'S A LINE THAT YOU CROSSED. SOMETHING THAT MADE YOU GO FROM GOOD TO BAD.
MAYBE YOU GET OFF ON IT, I DON'T KNOW... BUT FOR ME THERE IS NO LINE.
I DON'T THINK THE THINGS I DO ARE WRONG, HOLDEN. I BECAME WHO I REALLY AM, AND I'LL DIE IF I'M NOT TRUE TO THAT...
AND BESIDES, WHO DO YOU THINK MADE ALL THESE CODES OF CONDUCT WE'RE SUPPOSED TO FOLLOW IN THE FIRST PLACE?
WHO? THIS SECRET MONARCHY BACK THERE?
MAYBE...
...I SUSPECT YOU'LL FIND OUT TOMORROW.

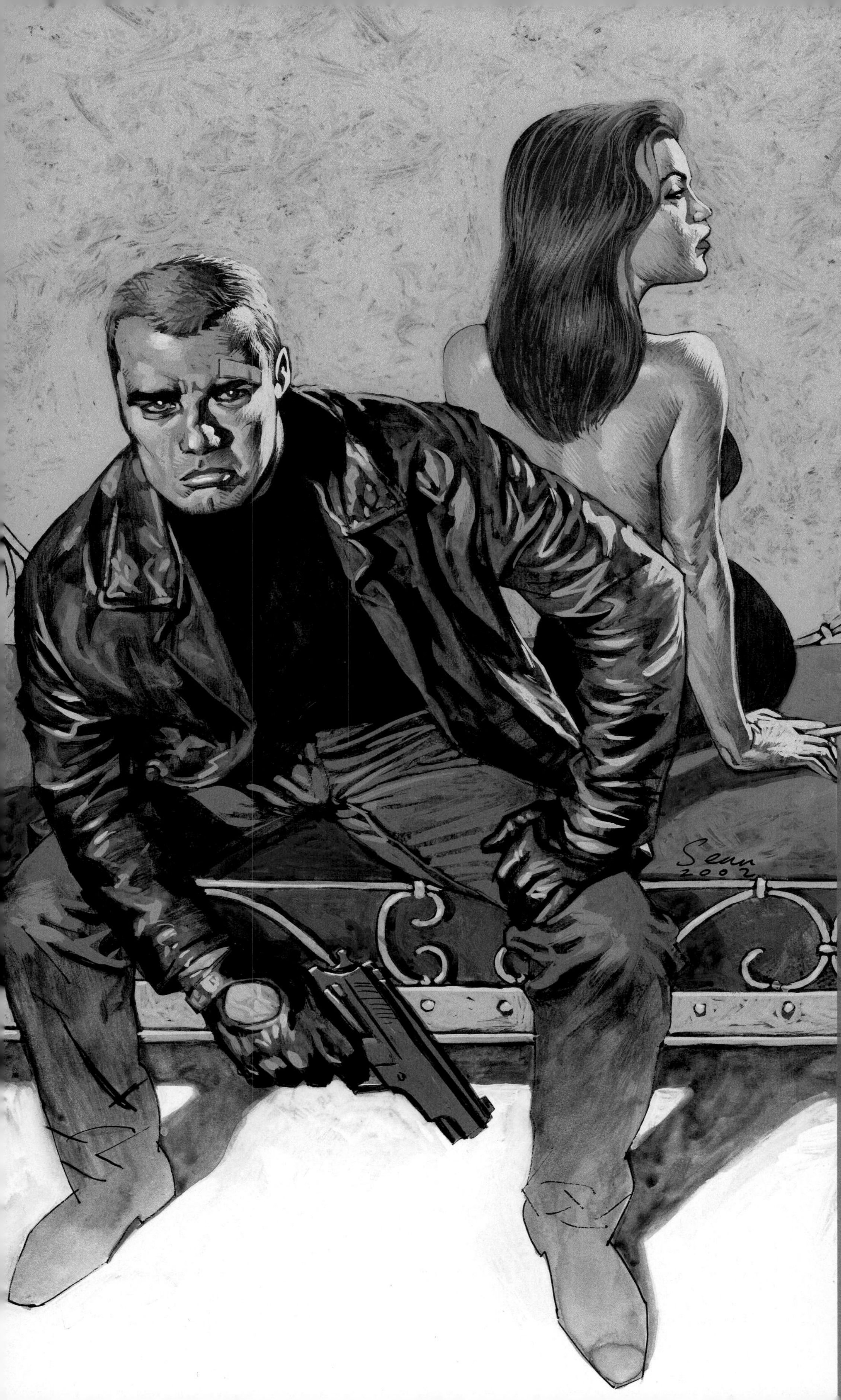
Sean 2002

Cover by SEAN PHILLIPS

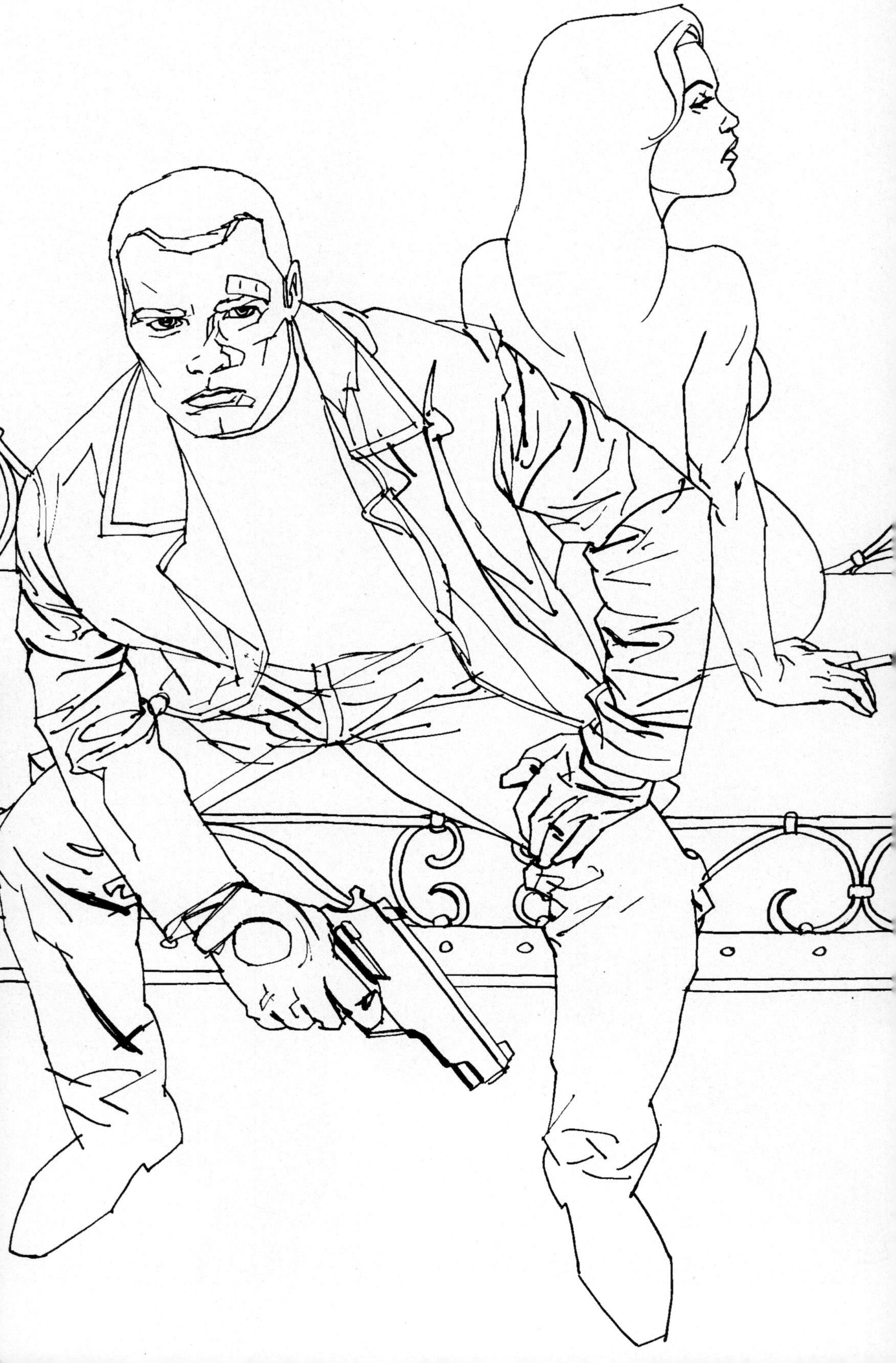

SLEEPER #4 Cover Inks by SEAN PHILLIPS

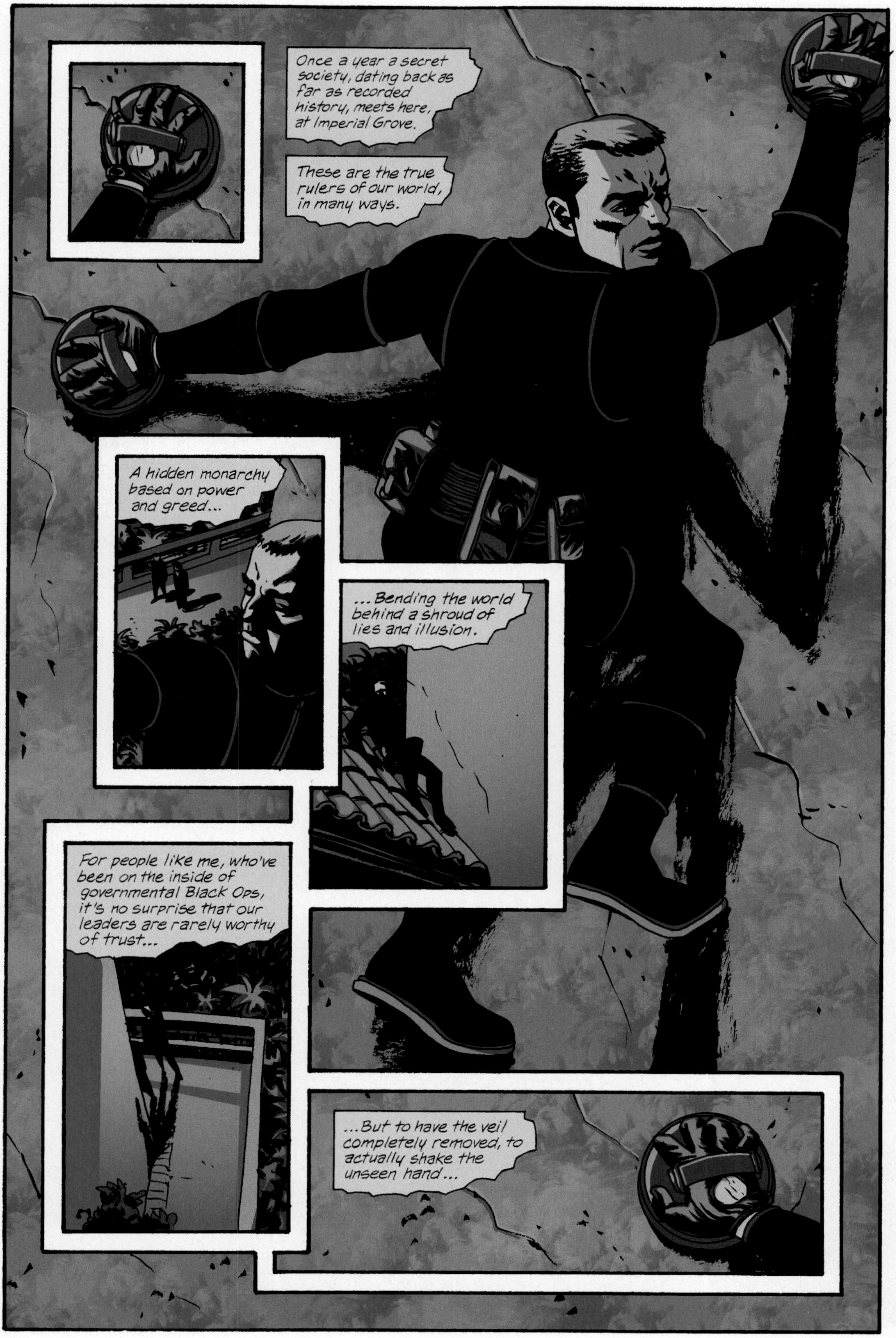
Once a year a secret society, dating back as far as recorded history, meets here, at Imperial Grove.
These are the true rulers of our world, in many ways.
A hidden monarchy based on power and greed...
...Bending the world behind a shroud of lies and illusion.
For people like me, who've been on the inside of governmental Black Ops, it's no surprise that our leaders are rarely worthy of trust...
...But to have the veil completely removed, to actually shake the unseen hand...

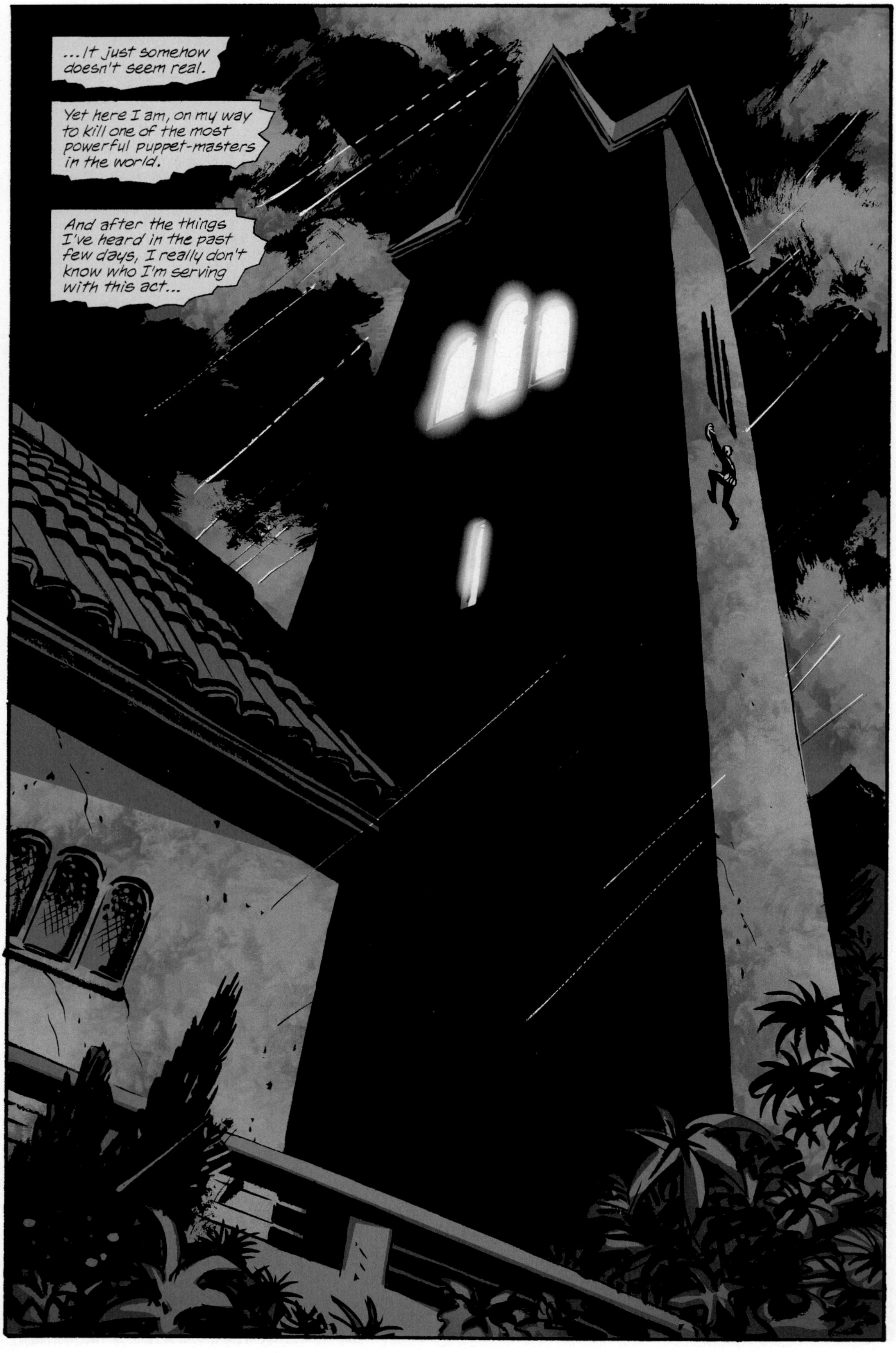
...It just somehow doesn't seem real.
Yet here I am, on my way to kill one of the most powerful puppet-masters in the world.
And after the things I've heard in the past few days, I really don't know who I'm serving with this act...

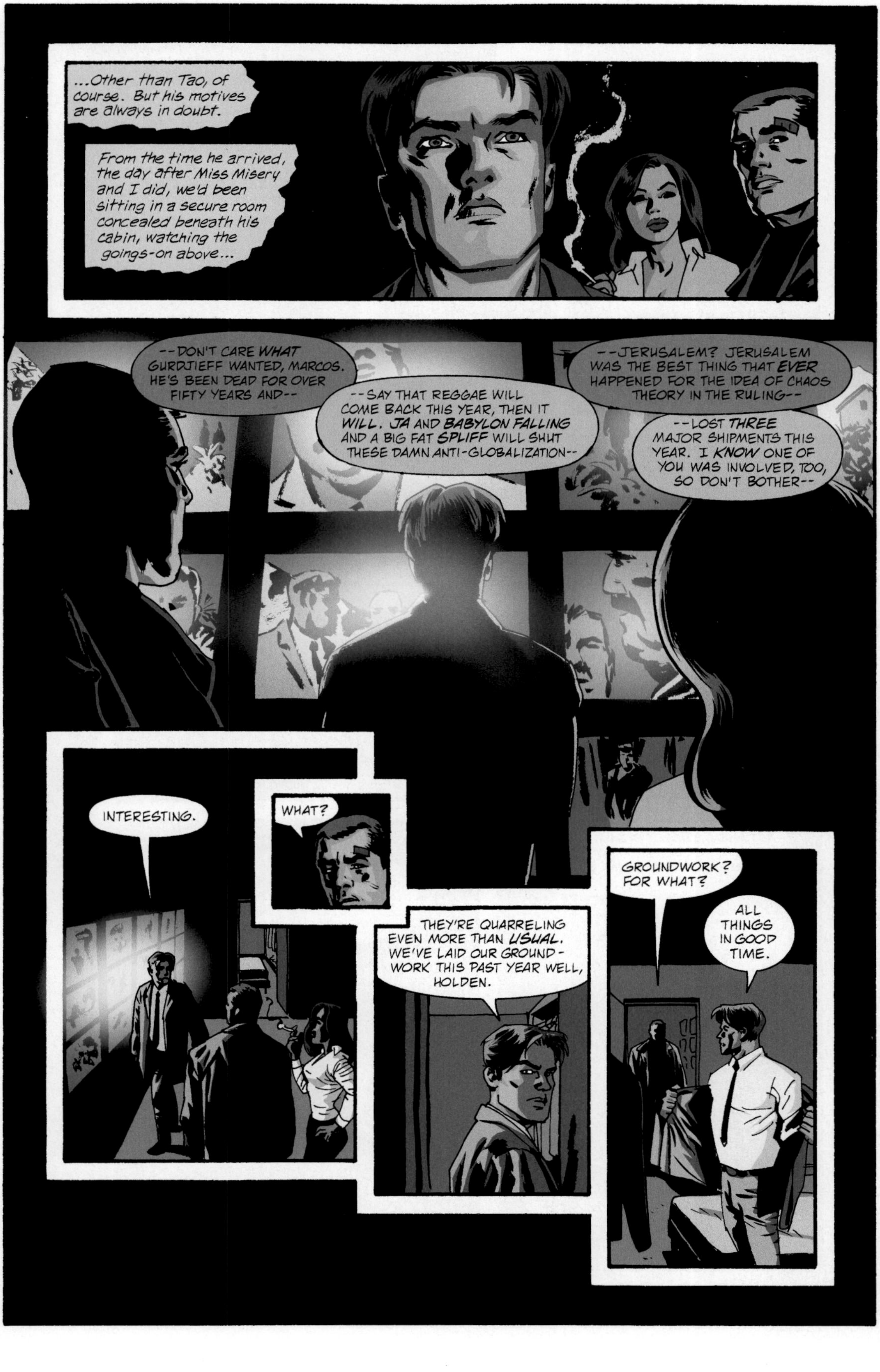
...Other than Tao, of course. But his motives are always in doubt.
From the time he arrived, the day after Miss Misery and I did, we'd been sitting in a secure room concealed beneath his cabin, watching the goings-on above...
--DON'T CARE WHAT GURDJIEFF WANTED, MARCOS. HE'S BEEN DEAD FOR OVER FIFTY YEARS AND--
--SAY THAT REGGAE WILL COME BACK THIS YEAR, THEN IT WILL. JA AND BABYLON FALLING AND A BIG FAT SPLIFF WILL SHUT THESE DAMN ANTI-GLOBALIZATION--
--JERUSALEM? JERUSALEM WAS THE BEST THING THAT EVER HAPPENED FOR THE IDEA OF CHAOS THEORY IN THE RULING--
--LOST THREE MAJOR SHIPMENTS THIS YEAR. I KNOW ONE OF YOU WAS INVOLVED, TOO, SO DON'T BOTHER--
INTERESTING.
WHAT?
THEY'RE QUARRELING EVEN MORE THAN USUAL. WE'VE LAID OUR GROUND-WORK THIS PAST YEAR WELL, HOLDEN.
GROUNDWORK? FOR WHAT?
ALL THINGS IN GOOD TIME.

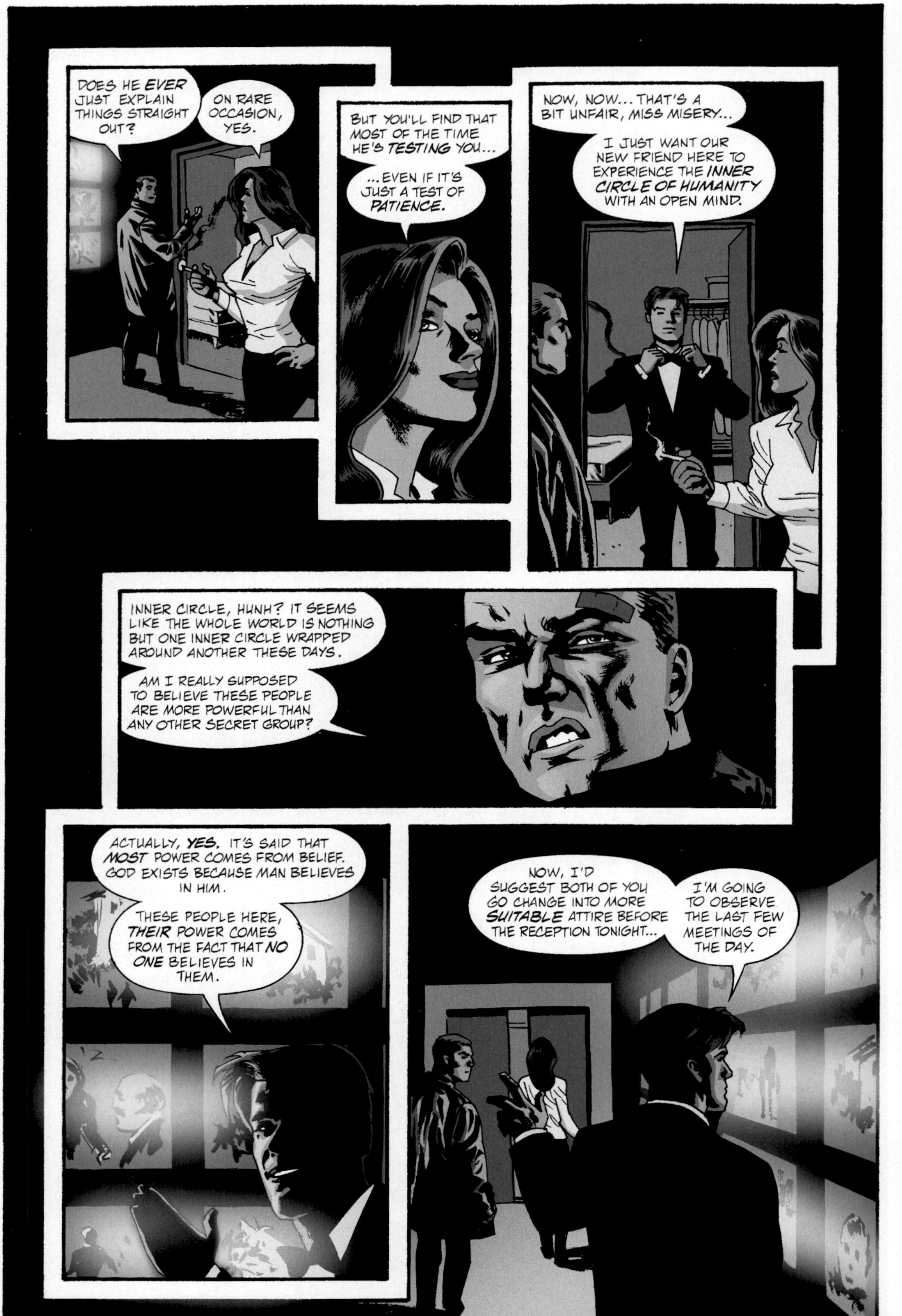
DOES HE EVER JUST EXPLAIN THINGS STRAIGHT OUT?
ON RARE OCCASION, YES.
BUT YOU'LL FIND THAT MOST OF THE TIME HE'S TESTING YOU...
...EVEN IF IT'S JUST A TEST OF PATIENCE.
NOW, NOW... THAT'S A BIT UNFAIR, MISS MISERY...
I JUST WANT OUR NEW FRIEND HERE TO EXPERIENCE THE INNER CIRCLE OF HUMANITY WITH AN OPEN MIND.
INNER CIRCLE, HUNH? IT SEEMS LIKE THE WHOLE WORLD IS NOTHING BUT ONE INNER CIRCLE WRAPPED AROUND ANOTHER THESE DAYS.
AM I REALLY SUPPOSED TO BELIEVE THESE PEOPLE ARE MORE POWERFUL THAN ANY OTHER SECRET GROUP?
ACTUALLY, YES. IT'S SAID THAT MOST POWER COMES FROM BELIEF. GOD EXISTS BECAUSE MAN BELIEVES IN HIM.
THESE PEOPLE HERE, THEIR POWER COMES FROM THE FACT THAT NO ONE BELIEVES IN THEM.
NOW, I'D SUGGEST BOTH OF YOU GO CHANGE INTO MORE SUITABLE ATTIRE BEFORE THE RECEPTION TONIGHT...
I'M GOING TO OBSERVE THE LAST FEW MEETINGS OF THE DAY.

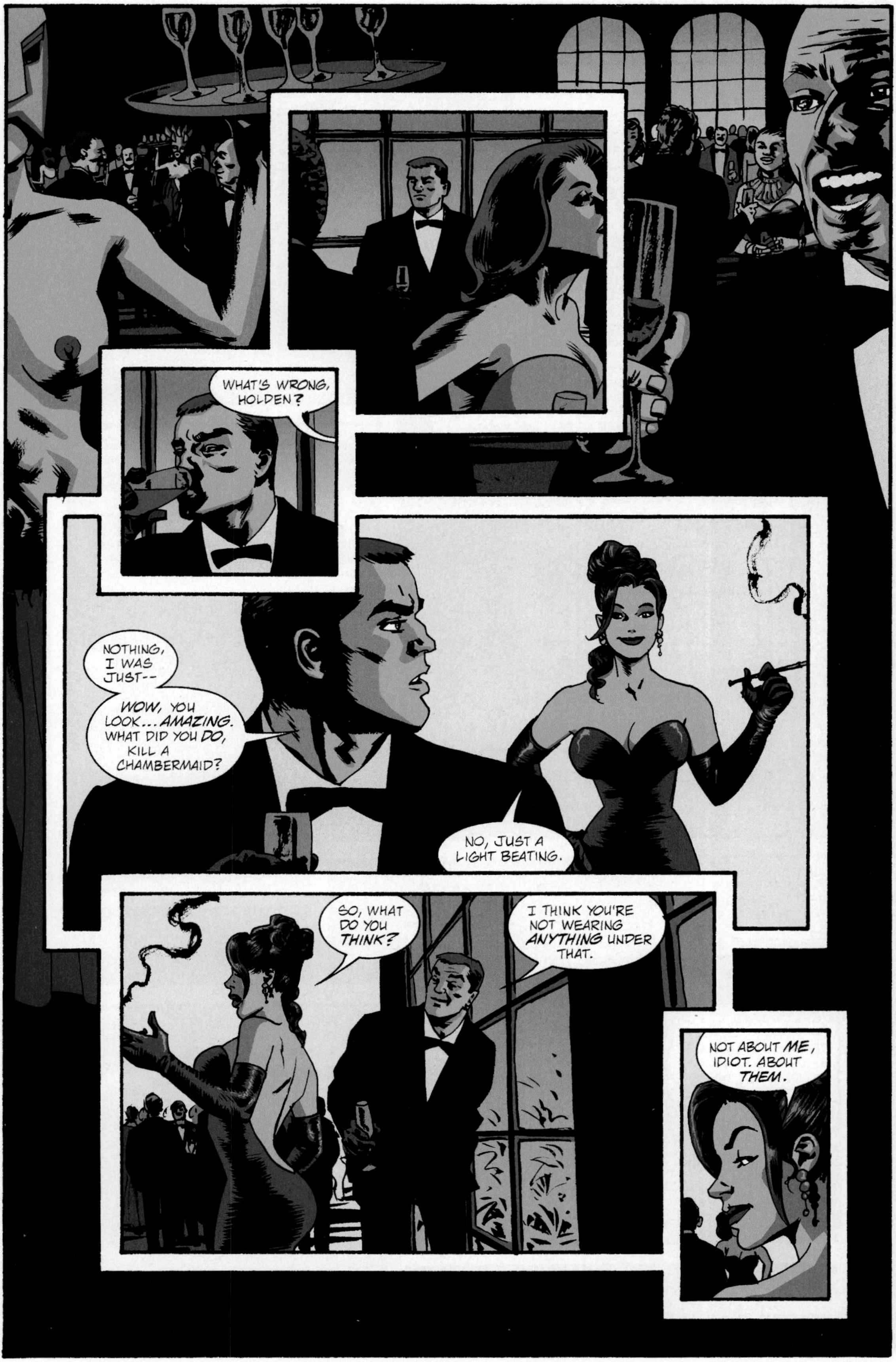
WHAT'S WRONG, HOLDEN?
NOTHING, I WAS JUST--
WOW, YOU LOOK... AMAZING. WHAT DID YOU DO, KILL A CHAMBERMAID?
NO, JUST A LIGHT BEATING.
SO, WHAT DO YOU THINK?
I THINK YOU'RE NOT WEARING ANYTHING UNDER THAT.
NOT ABOUT ME, IDIOT. ABOUT THEM.

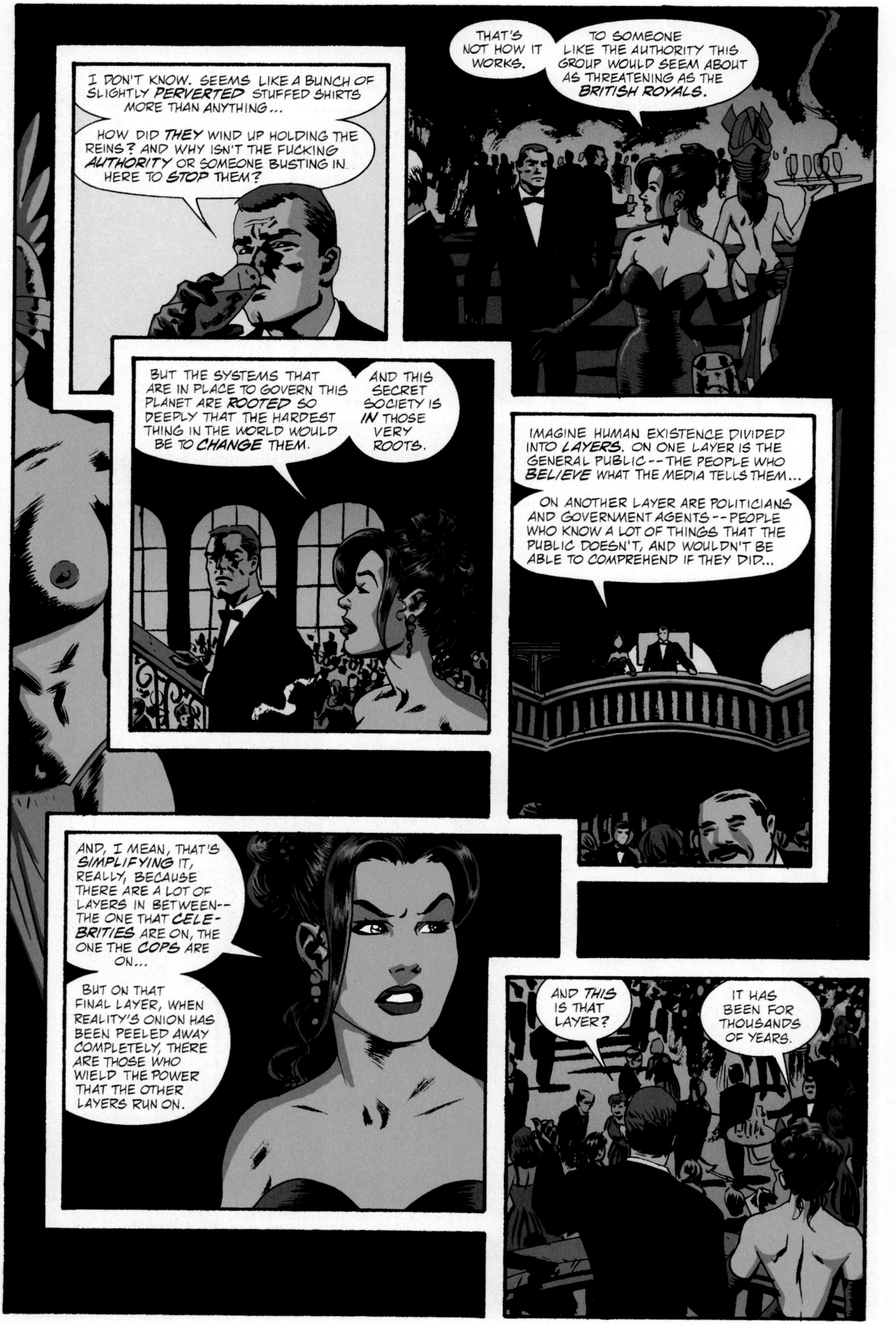
I DON'T KNOW. SEEMS LIKE A BUNCH OF SLIGHTLY PERVERTED STUFFED SHIRTS MORE THAN ANYTHING...
HOW DID THEY WIND UP HOLDING THE REINS? AND WHY ISN'T THE FUCKING AUTHORITY OR SOMEONE BUSTING IN HERE TO STOP THEM?
THAT'S NOT HOW IT WORKS.
TO SOMEONE LIKE THE AUTHORITY THIS GROUP WOULD SEEM ABOUT AS THREATENING AS THE BRITISH ROYALS.
BUT THE SYSTEMS THAT ARE IN PLACE TO GOVERN THIS PLANET ARE ROOTED SO DEEPLY THAT THE HARDEST THING IN THE WORLD WOULD BE TO CHANGE THEM.
AND THIS SECRET SOCIETY IS IN THOSE VERY ROOTS.
IMAGINE HUMAN EXISTENCE DIVIDED INTO LAYERS. ON ONE LAYER IS THE GENERAL PUBLIC--THE PEOPLE WHO BELIEVE WHAT THE MEDIA TELLS THEM...
ON ANOTHER LAYER ARE POLITICIANS AND GOVERNMENT AGENTS--PEOPLE WHO KNOW A LOT OF THINGS THAT THE PUBLIC DOESN'T, AND WOULDN'T BE ABLE TO COMPREHEND IF THEY DID...
AND, I MEAN, THAT'S SIMPLIFYING IT, REALLY, BECAUSE THERE ARE A LOT OF LAYERS IN BETWEEN--THE ONE THAT CELE-BRITIES ARE ON, THE ONE THE COPS ARE ON...
BUT ON THAT FINAL LAYER, WHEN REALITY'S ONION HAS BEEN PEELED AWAY COMPLETELY, THERE ARE THOSE WHO WIELD THE POWER THAT THE OTHER LAYERS RUN ON.
AND THIS IS THAT LAYER?
IT HAS BEEN FOR THOUSANDS OF YEARS.

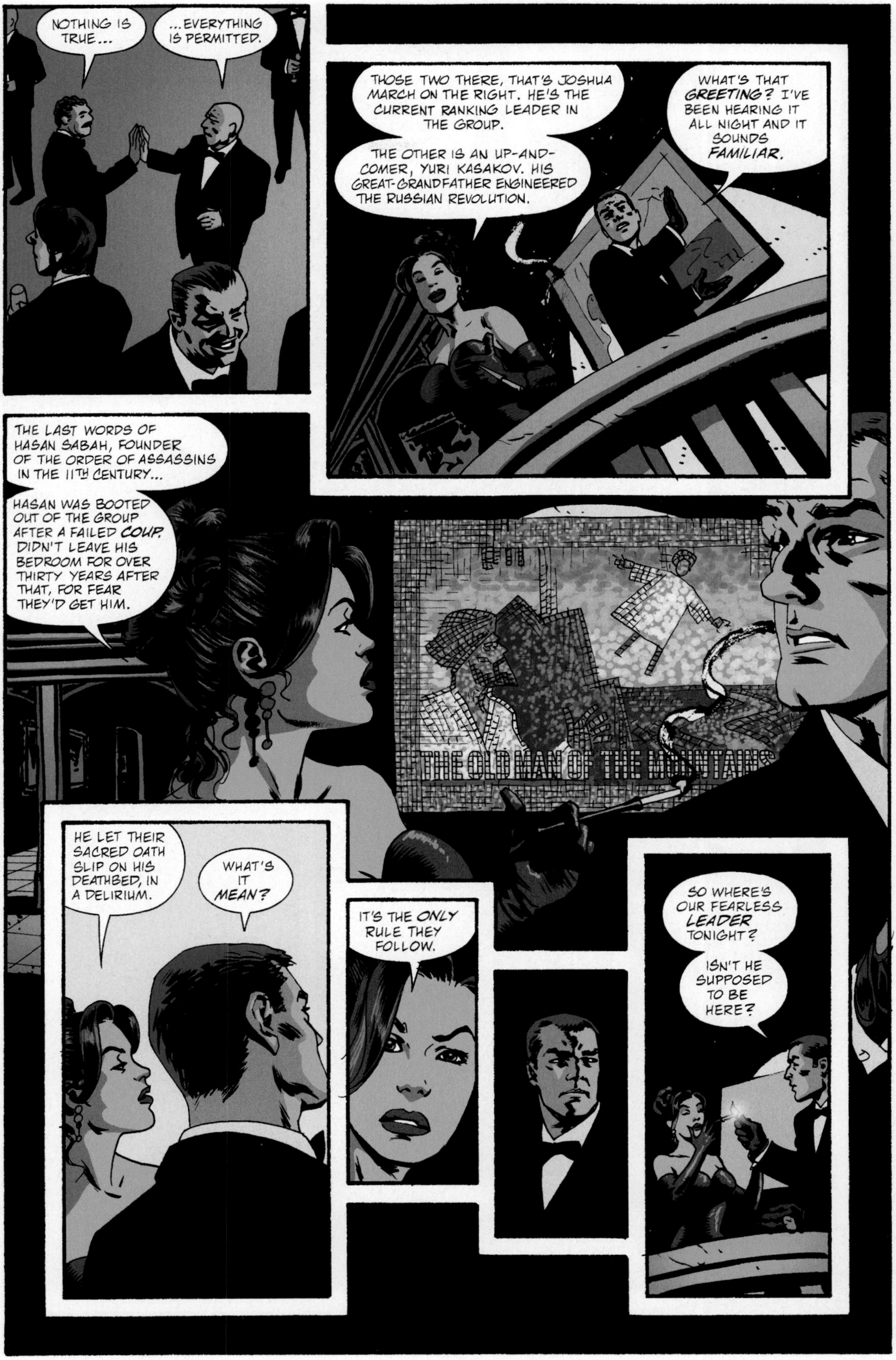
NOTHING IS TRUE...
...EVERYTHING IS PERMITTED.
THOSE TWO THERE, THAT'S JOSHUA MARCH ON THE RIGHT. HE'S THE CURRENT RANKING LEADER IN THE GROUP.
THE OTHER IS AN UP-AND-COMER, YURI KASAKOV. HIS GREAT-GRANDFATHER ENGINEERED THE RUSSIAN REVOLUTION.
WHAT'S THAT GREETING? I'VE BEEN HEARING IT ALL NIGHT AND IT SOUNDS FAMILIAR.
THE LAST WORDS OF HASAN SABAH, FOUNDER OF THE ORDER OF ASSASSINS IN THE 11TH CENTURY...
HASAN WAS BOOTED OUT OF THE GROUP AFTER A FAILED COUP. DIDN'T LEAVE HIS BEDROOM FOR OVER THIRTY YEARS AFTER THAT, FOR FEAR THEY'D GET HIM.
THE OLD MAN OF THE MOUNTAINS
HE LET THEIR SACRED OATH SLIP ON HIS DEATHBED, IN A DELIRIUM.
WHAT'S IT MEAN?
IT'S THE ONLY RULE THEY FOLLOW.
SO WHERE'S OUR FEARLESS LEADER TONIGHT?
ISN'T HE SUPPOSED TO BE HERE?

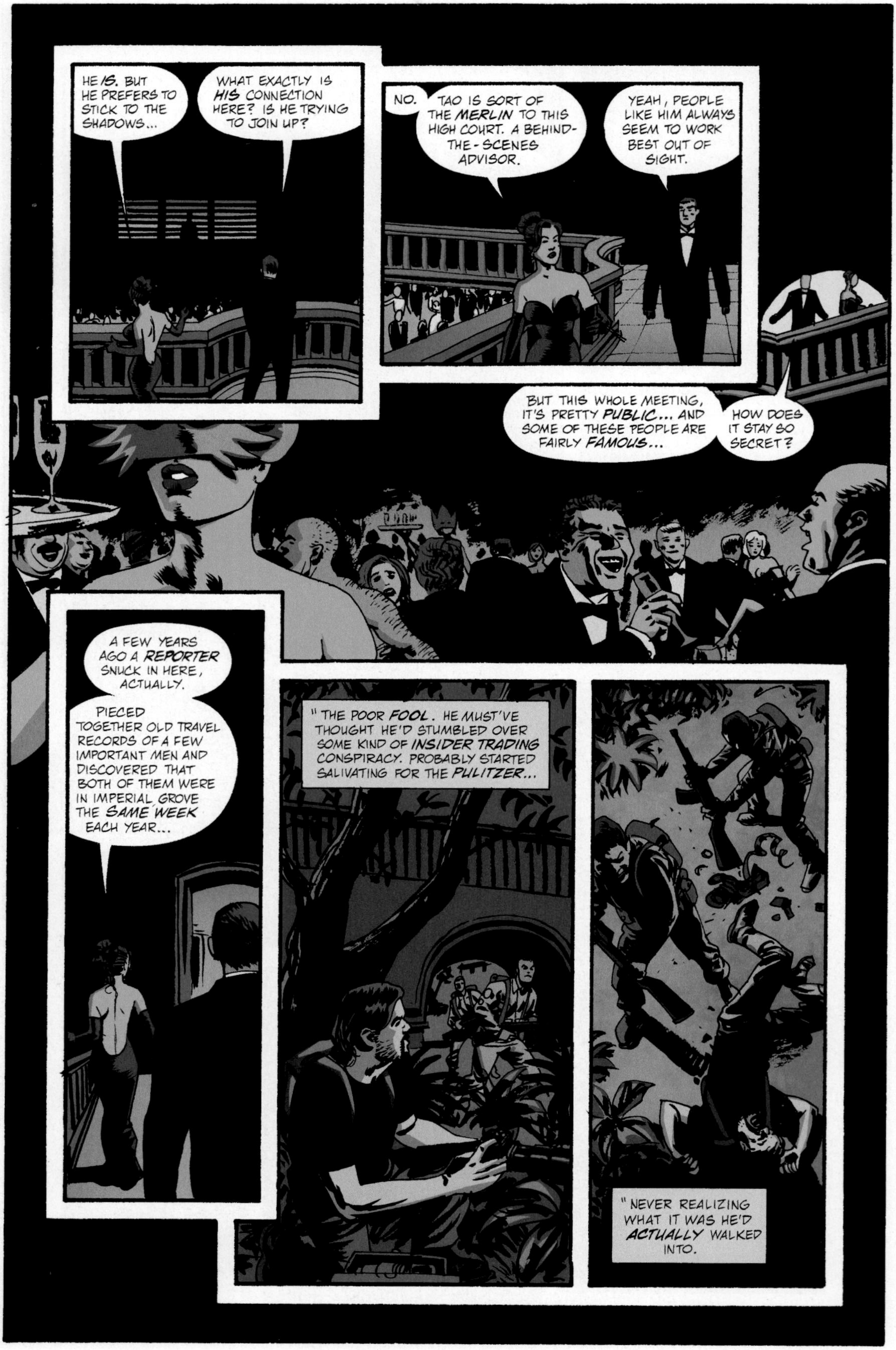
HE IS. BUT HE PREFERS TO STICK TO THE SHADOWS...
WHAT EXACTLY IS HIS CONNECTION HERE? IS HE TRYING TO JOIN UP?
NO.
TAO IS SORT OF THE MERLIN TO THIS HIGH COURT. A BEHIND-THE-SCENES ADVISOR.
YEAH, PEOPLE LIKE HIM ALWAYS SEEM TO WORK BEST OUT OF SIGHT.
BUT THIS WHOLE MEETING, IT'S PRETTY PUBLIC... AND SOME OF THESE PEOPLE ARE FAIRLY FAMOUS...
HOW DOES IT STAY SO SECRET?
A FEW YEARS AGO A REPORTER SNUCK IN HERE, ACTUALLY.
PIECED TOGETHER OLD TRAVEL RECORDS OF A FEW IMPORTANT MEN AND DISCOVERED THAT BOTH OF THEM WERE IN IMPERIAL GROVE THE SAME WEEK EACH YEAR...
"THE POOR FOOL. HE MUST'VE THOUGHT HE'D STUMBLED OVER SOME KIND OF INSIDER TRADING CONSPIRACY. PROBABLY STARTED SALIVATING FOR THE PULITZER...
"NEVER REALIZING WHAT IT WAS HE'D ACTUALLY WALKED INTO.

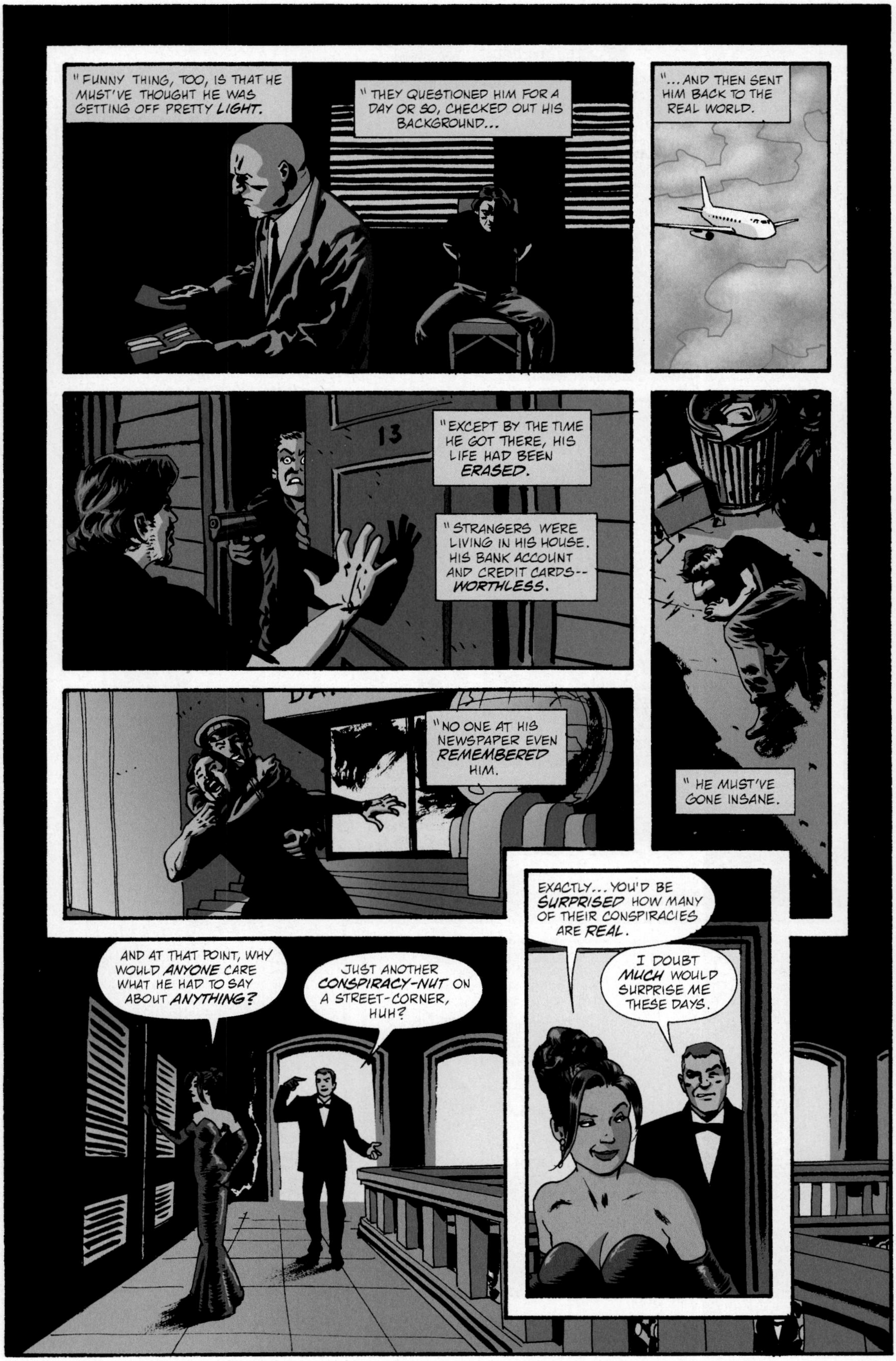
"FUNNY THING, TOO, IS THAT HE MUST'VE THOUGHT HE WAS GETTING OFF PRETTY LIGHT.
"THEY QUESTIONED HIM FOR A DAY OR SO, CHECKED OUT HIS BACKGROUND...
"...AND THEN SENT HIM BACK TO THE REAL WORLD.
13
"EXCEPT BY THE TIME HE GOT THERE, HIS LIFE HAD BEEN ERASED.
"STRANGERS WERE LIVING IN HIS HOUSE. HIS BANK ACCOUNT AND CREDIT CARDS--WORTHLESS.
"NO ONE AT HIS NEWSPAPER EVEN REMEMBERED HIM.
"HE MUST'VE GONE INSANE.
AND AT THAT POINT, WHY WOULD ANYONE CARE WHAT HE HAD TO SAY ABOUT ANYTHING?
JUST ANOTHER CONSPIRACY-NUT ON A STREET-CORNER, HUH?
EXACTLY... YOU'D BE SURPRISED HOW MANY OF THEIR CONSPIRACIES ARE REAL.
I DOUBT MUCH WOULD SURPRISE ME THESE DAYS.

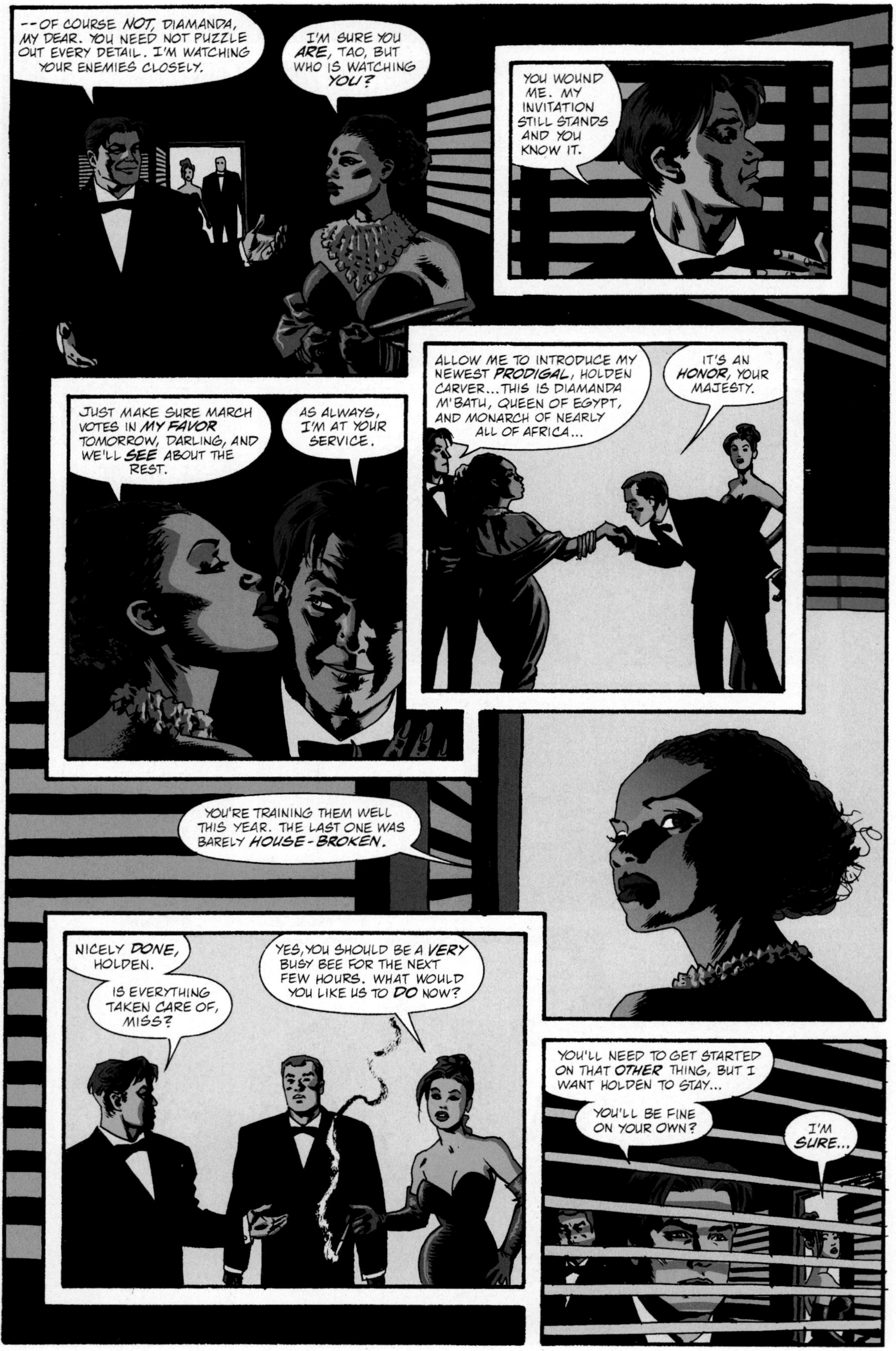
--OF COURSE NOT, DIAMANDA, MY DEAR. YOU NEED NOT PUZZLE OUT EVERY DETAIL. I'M WATCHING YOUR ENEMIES CLOSELY.
I'M SURE YOU ARE, TAO, BUT WHO IS WATCHING YOU?
YOU WOUND ME. MY INVITATION STILL STANDS AND YOU KNOW IT.
JUST MAKE SURE MARCH VOTES IN MY FAVOR TOMORROW, DARLING, AND WE'LL SEE ABOUT THE REST.
AS ALWAYS, I'M AT YOUR SERVICE.
ALLOW ME TO INTRODUCE MY NEWEST PRODIGAL, HOLDEN CARVER... THIS IS DIAMANDA M'BATU, QUEEN OF EGYPT, AND MONARCH OF NEARLY ALL OF AFRICA...
IT'S AN HONOR, YOUR MAJESTY.
YOU'RE TRAINING THEM WELL THIS YEAR. THE LAST ONE WAS BARELY HOUSE-BROKEN.
NICELY DONE, HOLDEN.
IS EVERYTHING TAKEN CARE OF, MISS?
YES, YOU SHOULD BE A VERY BUSY BEE FOR THE NEXT FEW HOURS. WHAT WOULD YOU LIKE US TO DO NOW?
YOU'LL NEED TO GET STARTED ON THAT OTHER THING, BUT I WANT HOLDEN TO STAY...
YOU'LL BE FINE ON YOUR OWN?
I'M SURE...

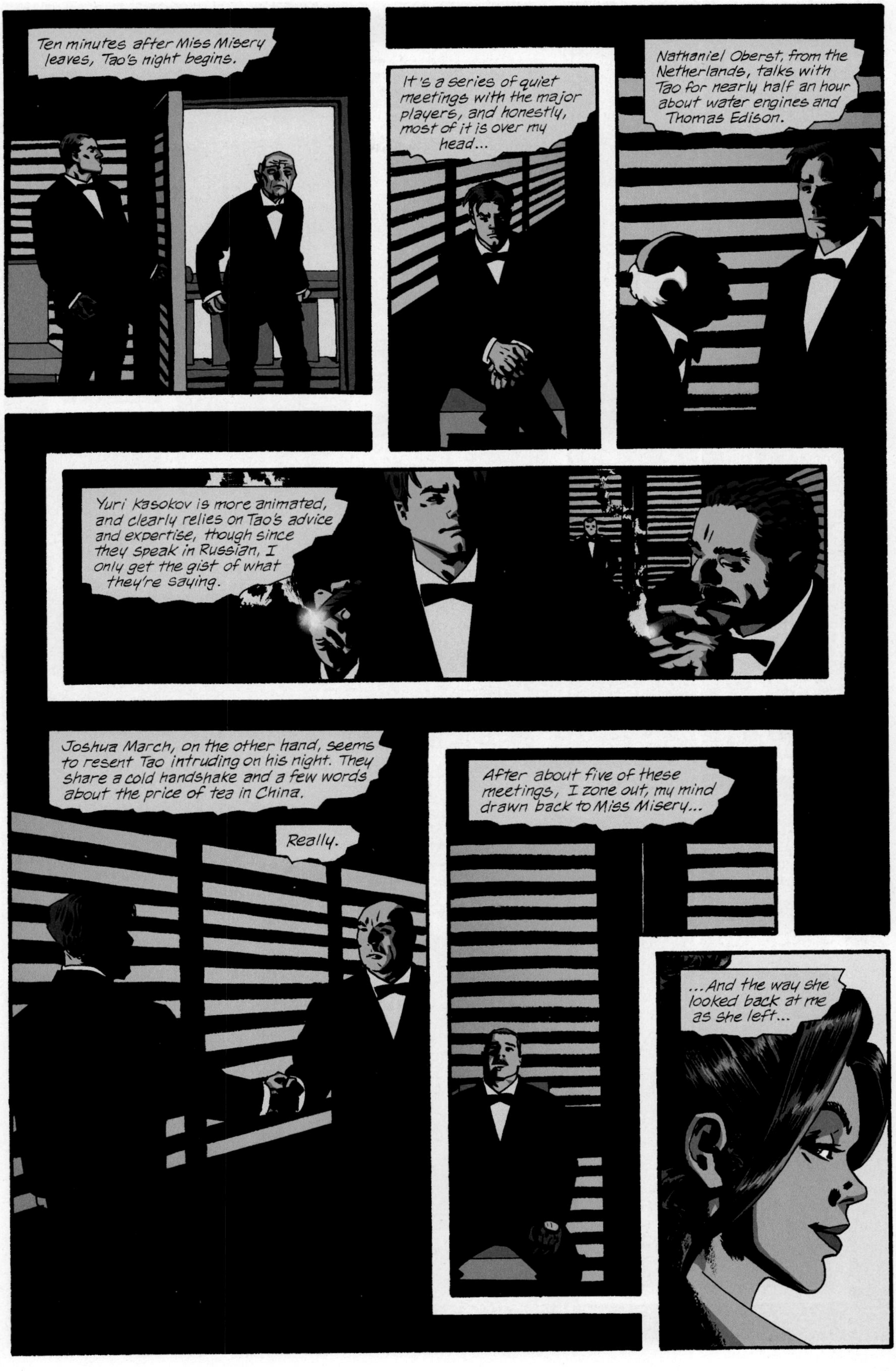

Ten minutes after Miss Misery leaves, Tao's night begins.
It's a series of quiet meetings with the major players, and honestly, most of it is over my head...
Nathaniel Oberst, from the Netherlands, talks with Tao for nearly half an hour about water engines and Thomas Edison.
Yuri Kasokov is more animated, and clearly relies on Tao's advice and expertise, though since they speak in Russian, I only get the gist of what they're saying.
Joshua March, on the other hand, seems to resent Tao intruding on his night. They share a cold handshake and a few words about the price of tea in China.
Really.
After about five of these meetings, I zone out, my mind drawn back to Miss Misery...
...And the way she looked back at me as she left...

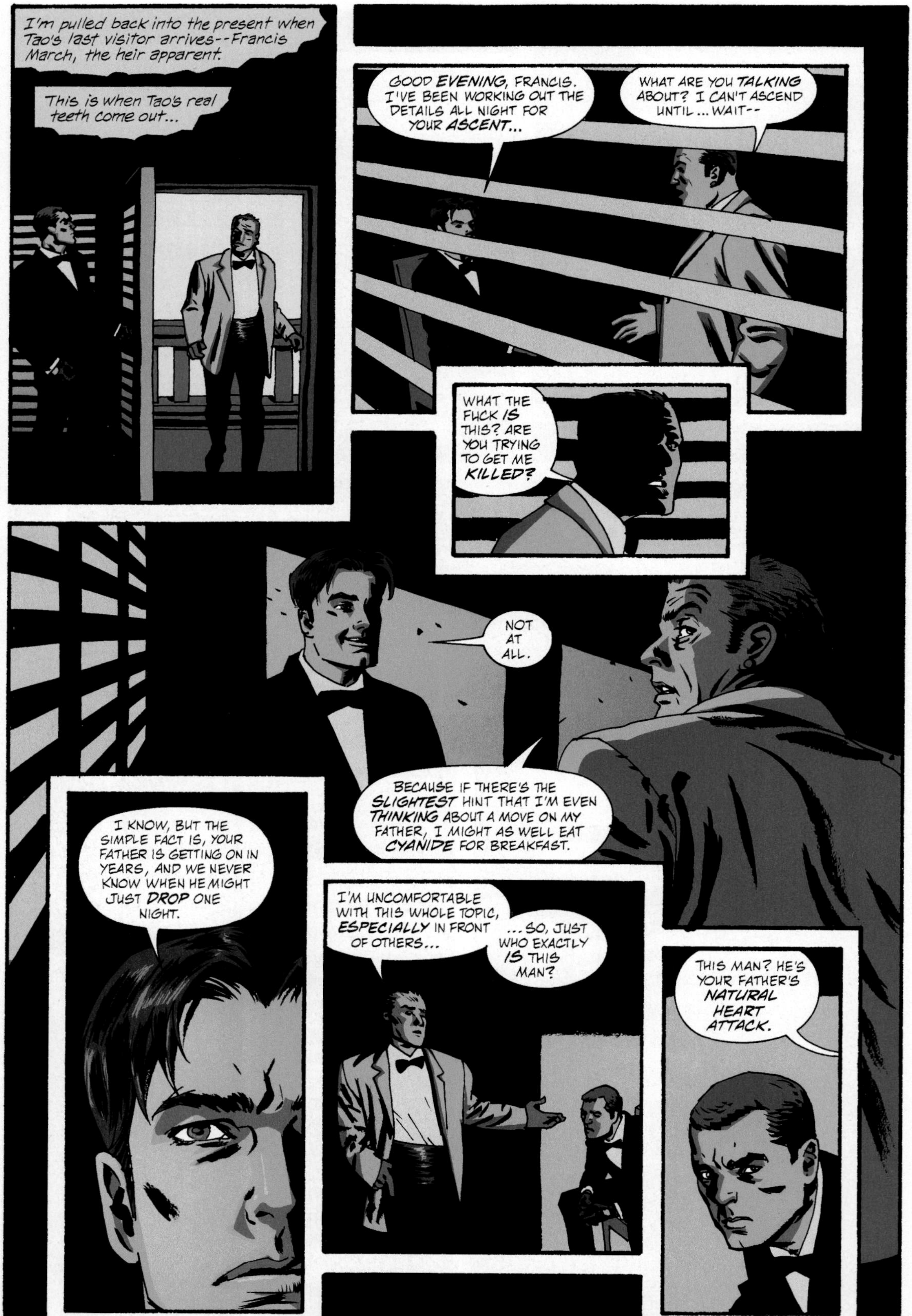
I'm pulled back into the present when Tao's last visitor arrives--Francis March, the heir apparent.
This is when Tao's real teeth come out...
GOOD EVENING, FRANCIS. I'VE BEEN WORKING OUT THE DETAILS ALL NIGHT FOR YOUR ASCENT...
WHAT ARE YOU TALKING ABOUT? I CAN'T ASCEND UNTIL ... WAIT--
WHAT THE FUCK IS THIS? ARE YOU TRYING TO GET ME KILLED?
NOT AT ALL.
BECAUSE IF THERE'S THE SLIGHTEST HINT THAT I'M EVEN THINKING ABOUT A MOVE ON MY FATHER, I MIGHT AS WELL EAT CYANIDE FOR BREAKFAST.
I KNOW, BUT THE SIMPLE FACT IS, YOUR FATHER IS GETTING ON IN YEARS, AND WE NEVER KNOW WHEN HE MIGHT JUST DROP ONE NIGHT.
I'M UNCOMFORTABLE WITH THIS WHOLE TOPIC, ESPECIALLY IN FRONT OF OTHERS...
...SO, JUST WHO EXACTLY IS THIS MAN?
THIS MAN? HE'S YOUR FATHER'S NATURAL HEART ATTACK.

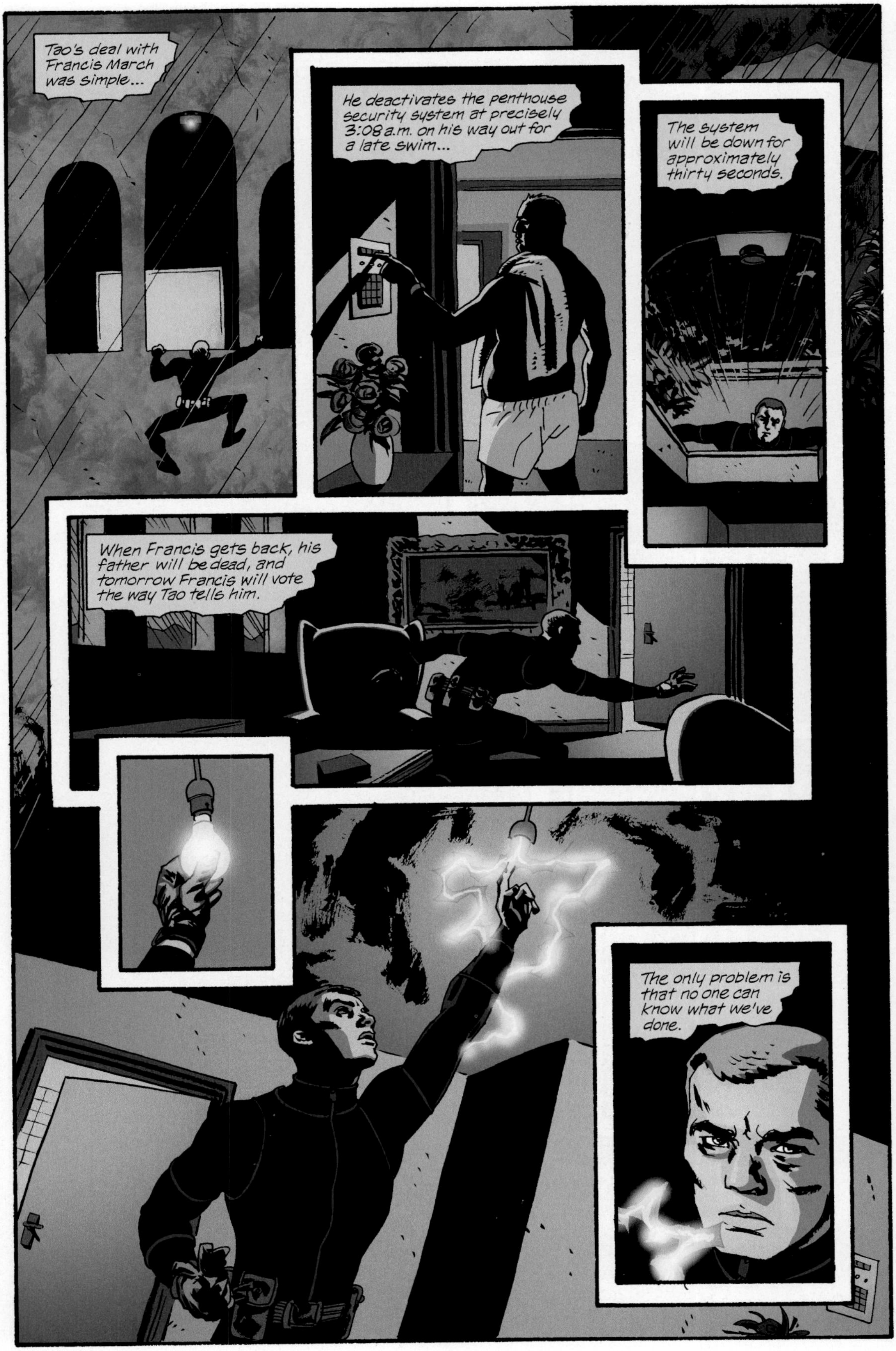
Tao's deal with Francis March was simple...
He deactivates the penthouse security system at precisely 3:08 a.m. on his way out for a late swim...
The system will be down for approximately thirty seconds.
When Francis gets back, his father will be dead, and tomorrow Francis will vote the way Tao tells him.
The only problem is that no one can know what we've done.

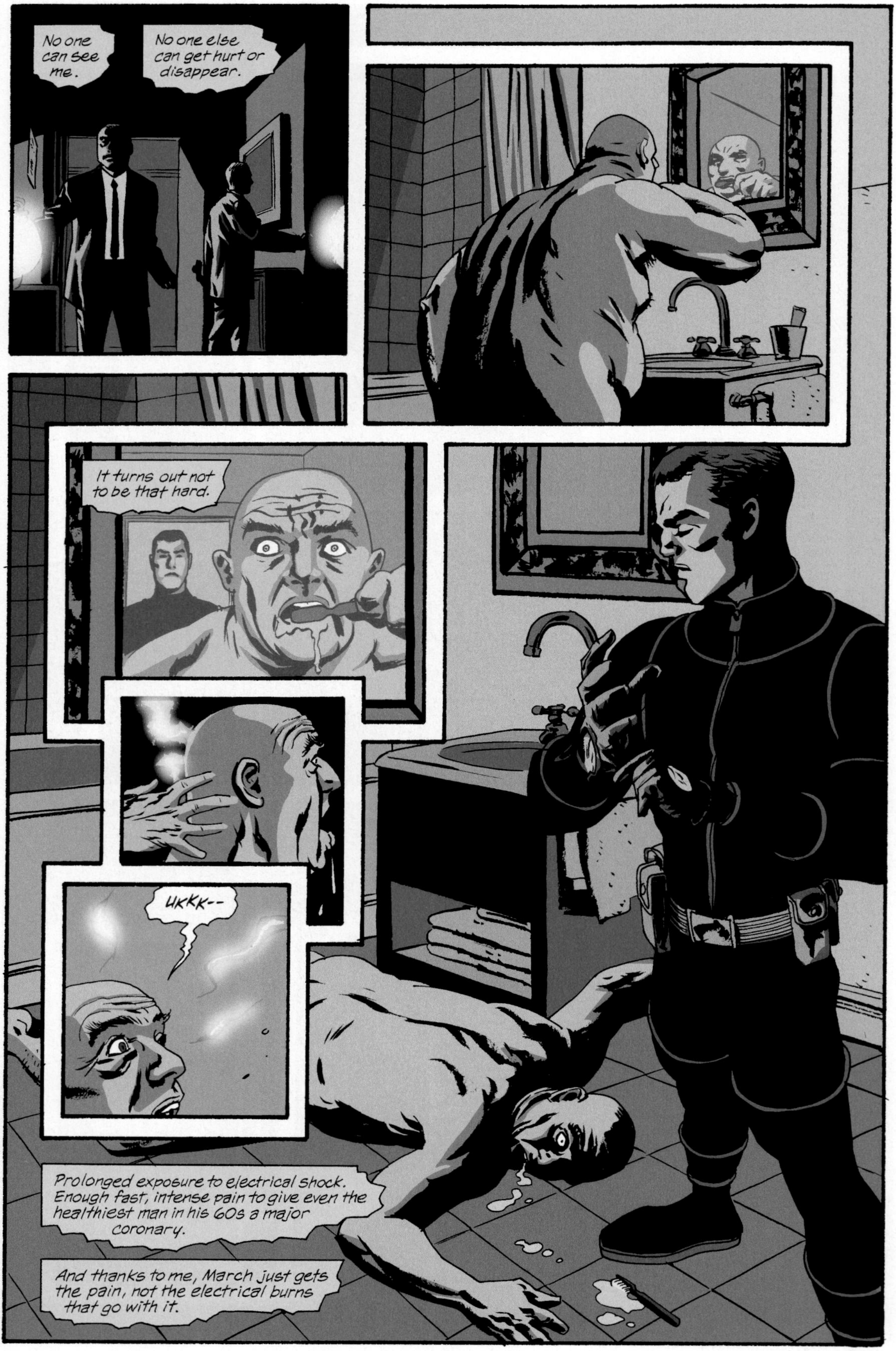
No one can see me.
No one else can get hurt or disappear.
It turns out not to be that hard.
UKKK--
Prolonged exposure to electrical shock. Enough fast, intense pain to give even the healthiest man in his 60s a major coronary.
And thanks to me, March just gets the pain, not the electrical burns that go with it.

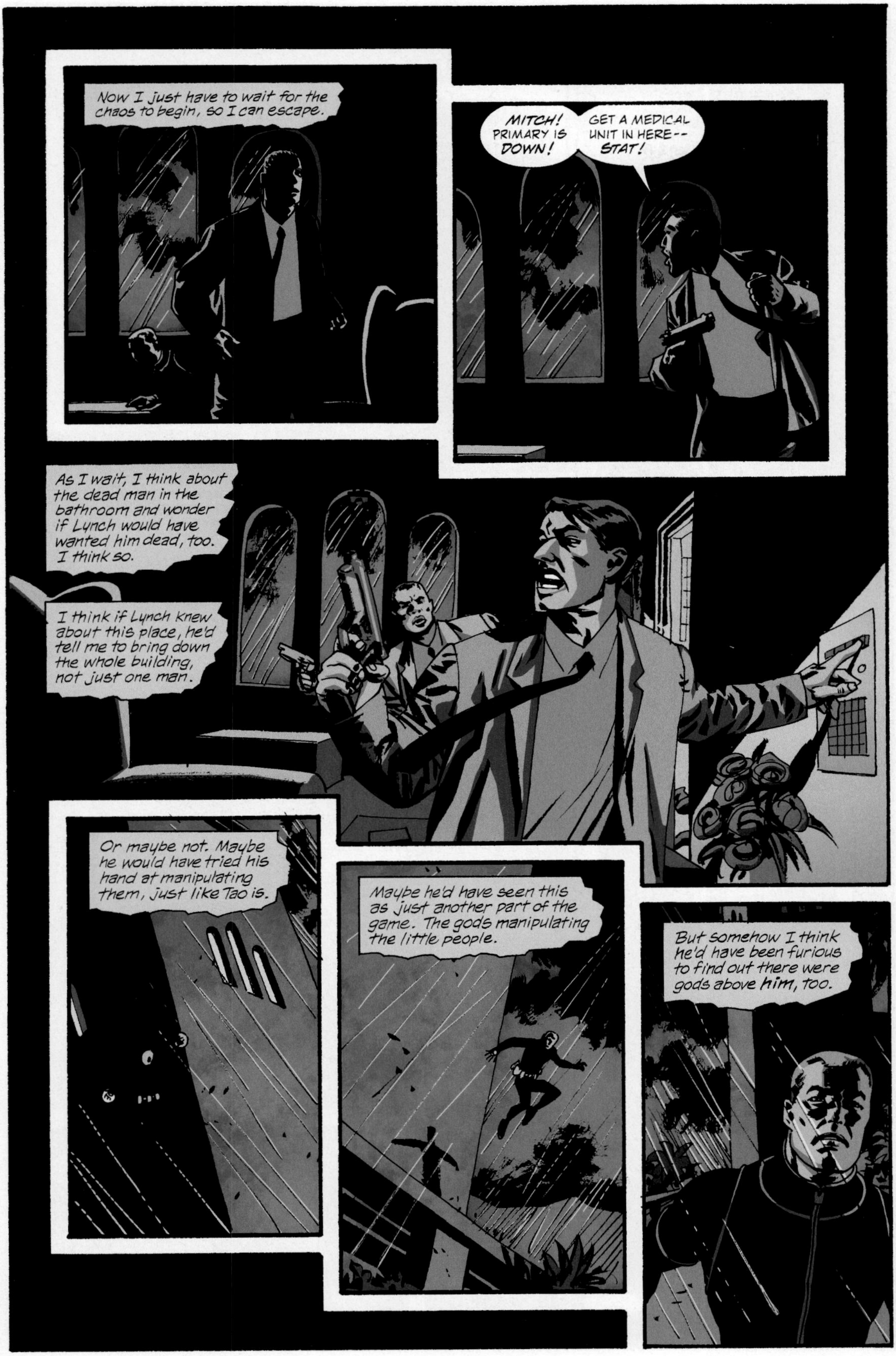
Now I just have to wait for the chaos to begin, so I can escape.
MITCH! PRIMARY IS DOWN!
GET A MEDICAL UNIT IN HERE-- STAT!
As I wait, I think about the dead man in the bathroom and wonder if Lynch would have wanted him dead, too. I think so.
I think if Lynch knew about this place, he'd tell me to bring down the whole building, not just one man.
Or maybe not. Maybe he would have tried his hand at manipulating them, just like Tao is.
Maybe he'd have seen this as just another part of the game. The gods manipulating the little people.
But somehow I think he'd have been furious to find out there were gods above him, too.

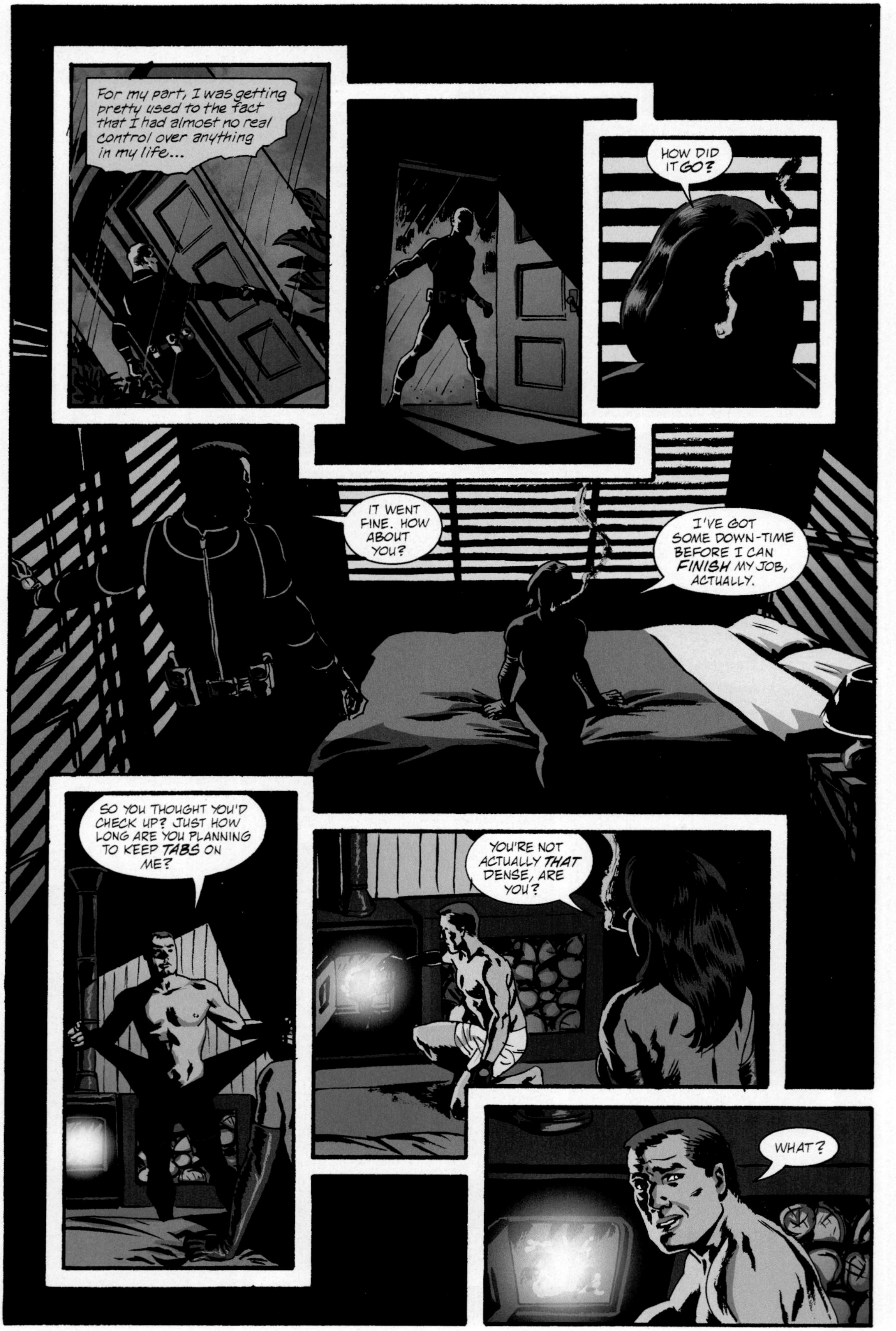
For my part, I was getting pretty used to the fact that I had almost no real control over anything in my life...
HOW DID IT GO?
IT WENT FINE. HOW ABOUT YOU?
I'VE GOT SOME DOWN-TIME BEFORE I CAN FINISH MY JOB, ACTUALLY.
SO YOU THOUGHT YOU'D CHECK UP? JUST HOW LONG ARE YOU PLANNING TO KEEP TABS ON ME?
YOU'RE NOT ACTUALLY THAT DENSE, ARE YOU?
WHAT?

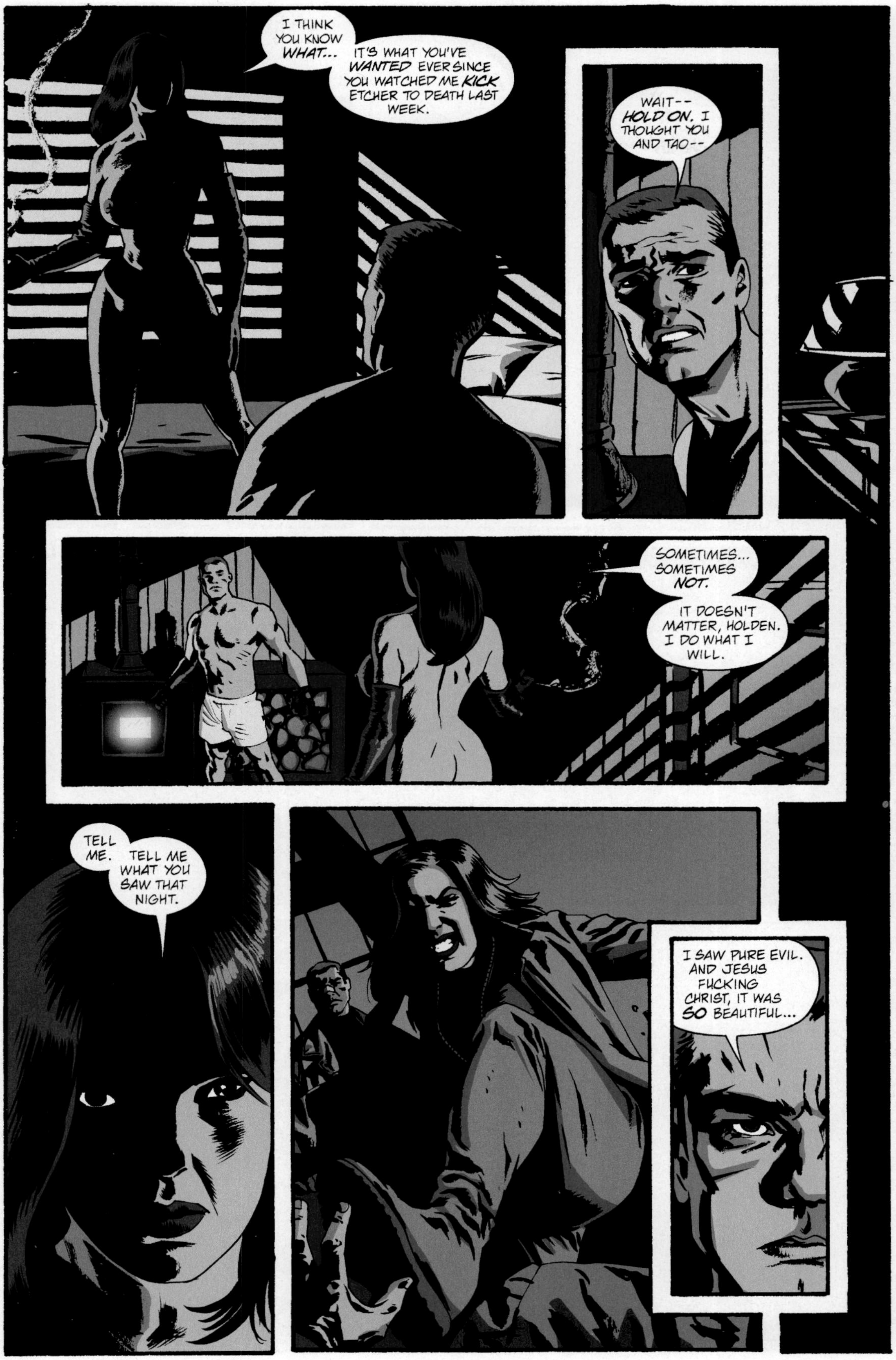

I THINK YOU KNOW WHAT...
IT'S WHAT YOU'VE WANTED EVER SINCE YOU WATCHED ME KICK ETCHER TO DEATH LAST WEEK.
WAIT-- HOLD ON. I THOUGHT YOU AND TAO--
SOMETIMES... SOMETIMES NOT.
IT DOESN'T MATTER, HOLDEN. I DO WHAT I WILL.
TELL ME.
TELL ME WHAT YOU SAW THAT NIGHT.
I SAW PURE EVIL. AND JESUS FUCKING CHRIST, IT WAS SO BEAUTIFUL...

DID IT MAKE YOUR COCK HARD?

WHY DON'T YOU TELL ME?

She gives me just enough pain so that I can feel how good she is. And each lash she tears across my back only makes her more perfect, more desirable.

With each fevered kiss, I taste my own blood in her mouth.

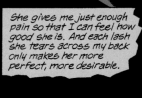

Afterwards, she nearly glows, and I remember how stunned I was by her that night on the roof. She was right, I *had* wanted her since then.

But why had she come to me?

Simple--Because Tao would *kill us* if he ever found out.

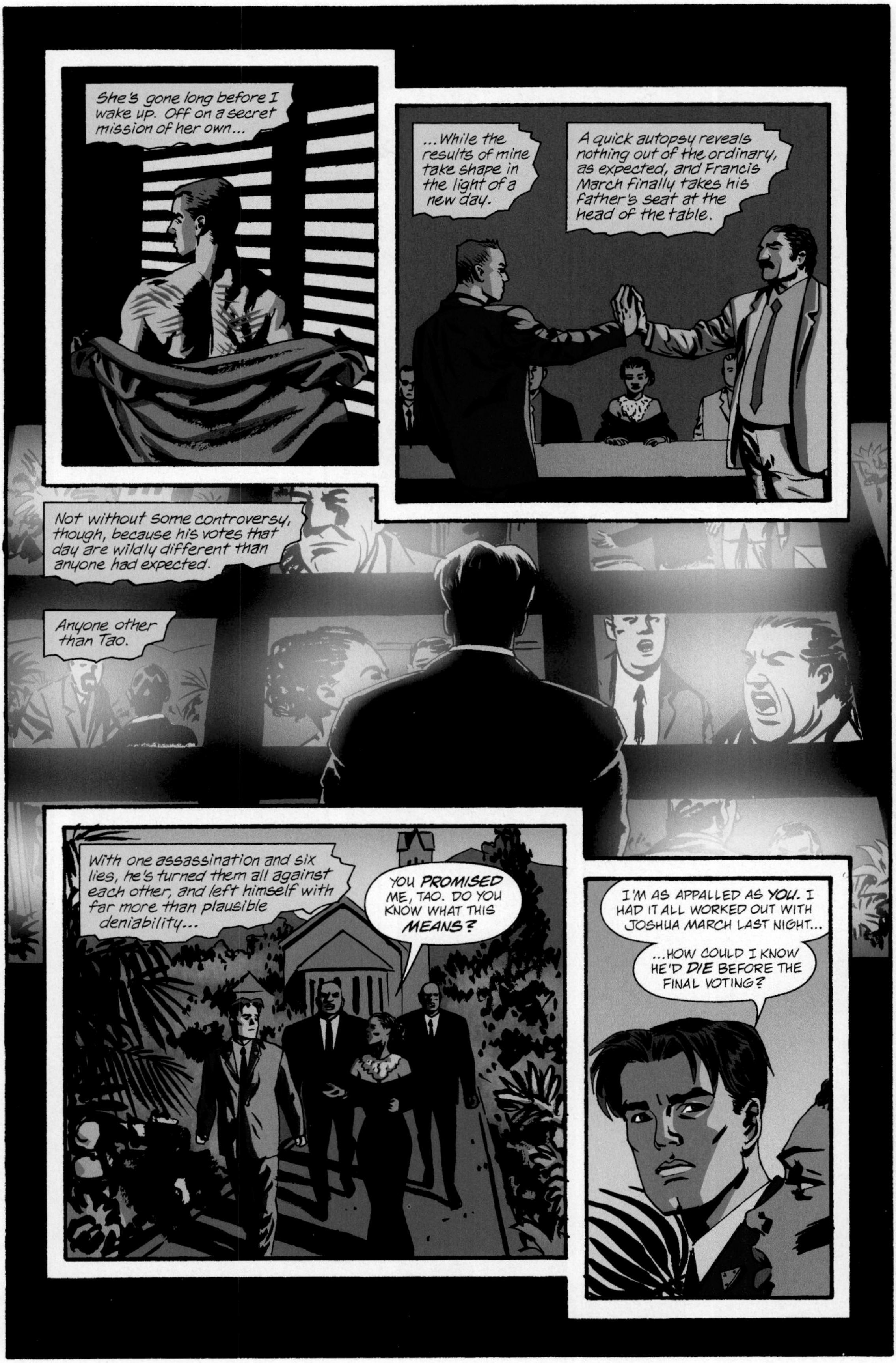
She's gone long before I wake up. Off on a secret mission of her own...
...While the results of mine take shape in the light of a new day.
A quick autopsy reveals nothing out of the ordinary, as expected, and Francis March finally takes his father's seat at the head of the table.
Not without some controversy, though, because his votes that day are wildly different than anyone had expected.
Anyone other than Tao.
With one assassination and six lies, he's turned them all against each other, and left himself with far more than plausible deniability...
YOU **PROMISED** ME, TAO. DO YOU KNOW WHAT THIS **MEANS?**
I'M AS APPALLED AS **YOU**. I HAD IT ALL WORKED OUT WITH JOSHUA MARCH LAST NIGHT...
...HOW COULD I KNOW HE'D **DIE** BEFORE THE FINAL VOTING?

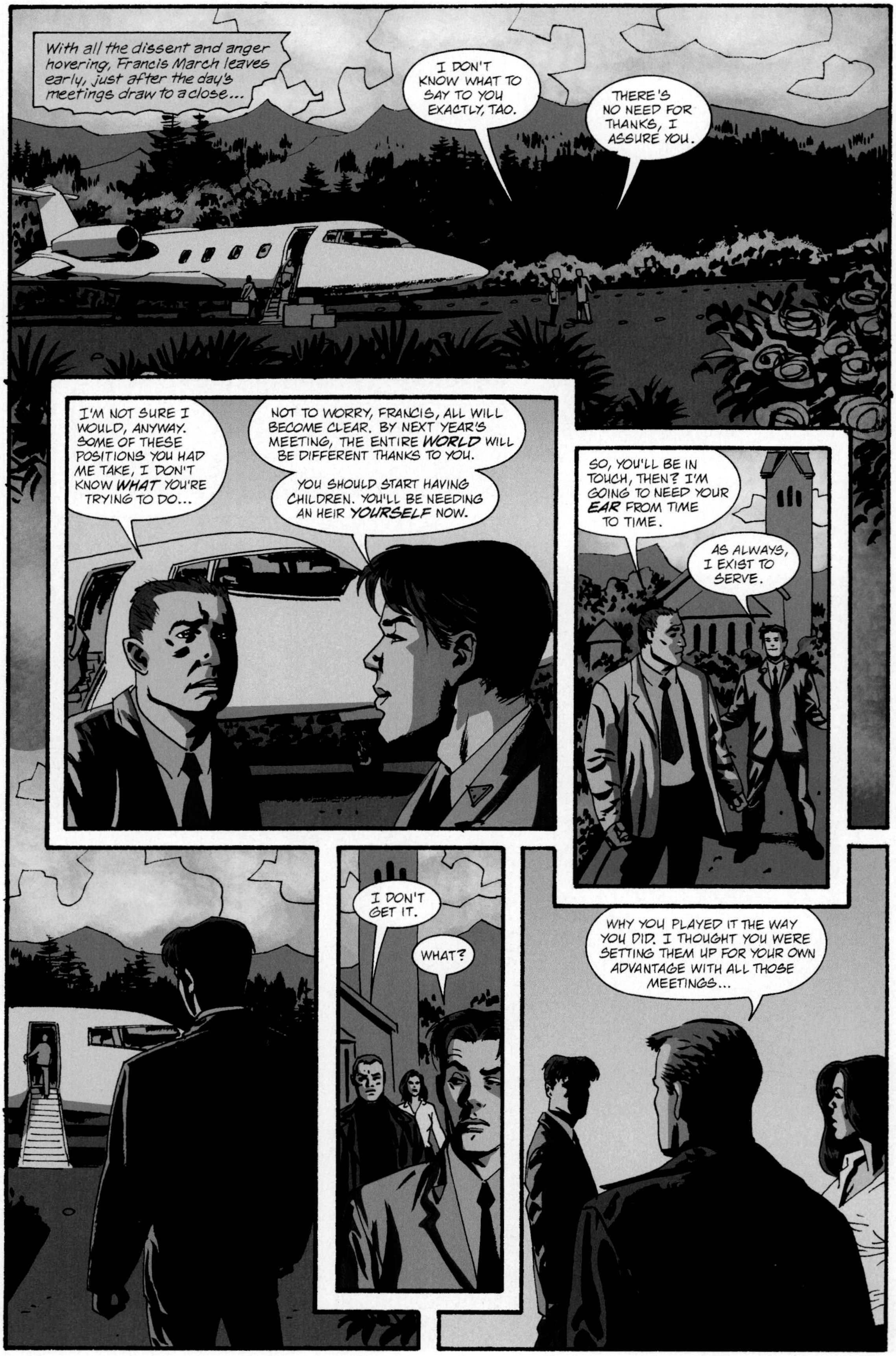
With all the dissent and anger hovering, Francis March leaves early, just after the day's meetings draw to a close...
I DON'T KNOW WHAT TO SAY TO YOU EXACTLY, TAO.
THERE'S NO NEED FOR THANKS, I ASSURE YOU.
I'M NOT SURE I WOULD, ANYWAY. SOME OF THESE POSITIONS YOU HAD ME TAKE, I DON'T KNOW WHAT YOU'RE TRYING TO DO...
NOT TO WORRY, FRANCIS, ALL WILL BECOME CLEAR. BY NEXT YEAR'S MEETING, THE ENTIRE WORLD WILL BE DIFFERENT THANKS TO YOU.
YOU SHOULD START HAVING CHILDREN. YOU'LL BE NEEDING AN HEIR YOURSELF NOW.
SO, YOU'LL BE IN TOUCH, THEN? I'M GOING TO NEED YOUR EAR FROM TIME TO TIME.
AS ALWAYS, I EXIST TO SERVE.
I DON'T GET IT.
WHAT?
WHY YOU PLAYED IT THE WAY YOU DID. I THOUGHT YOU WERE SETTING THEM UP FOR YOUR OWN ADVANTAGE WITH ALL THOSE MEETINGS...

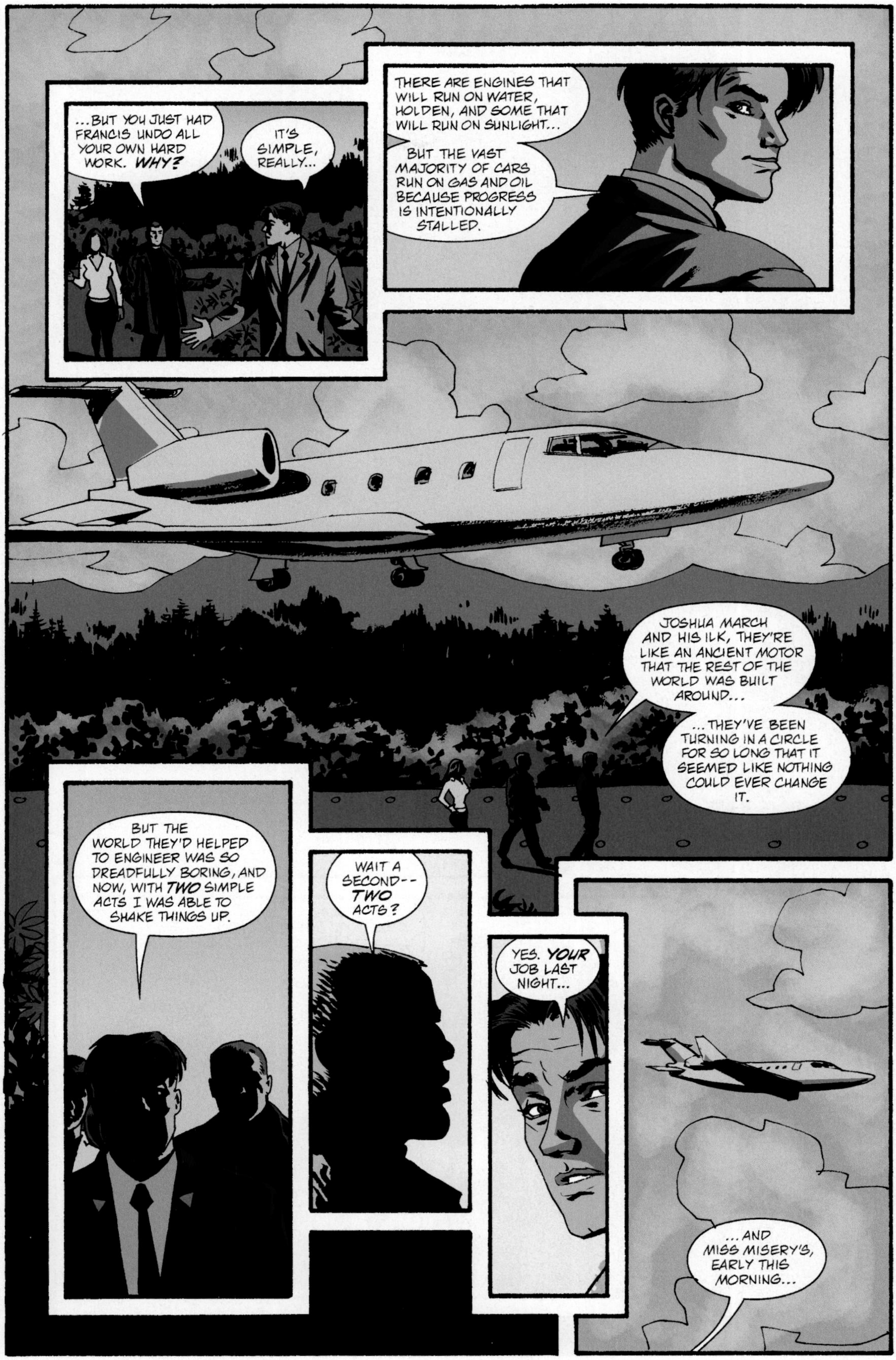
...BUT YOU JUST HAD FRANCIS UNDO ALL YOUR OWN HARD WORK. WHY?
IT'S SIMPLE, REALLY...
THERE ARE ENGINES THAT WILL RUN ON WATER, HOLDEN, AND SOME THAT WILL RUN ON SUNLIGHT...
BUT THE VAST MAJORITY OF CARS RUN ON GAS AND OIL BECAUSE PROGRESS IS INTENTIONALLY STALLED.
JOSHUA MARCH AND HIS ILK, THEY'RE LIKE AN ANCIENT MOTOR THAT THE REST OF THE WORLD WAS BUILT AROUND...
...THEY'VE BEEN TURNING IN A CIRCLE FOR SO LONG THAT IT SEEMED LIKE NOTHING COULD EVER CHANGE IT.
BUT THE WORLD THEY'D HELPED TO ENGINEER WAS SO DREADFULLY BORING, AND NOW, WITH TWO SIMPLE ACTS I WAS ABLE TO SHAKE THINGS UP.
WAIT A SECOND--TWO ACTS?
YES. YOUR JOB LAST NIGHT...
...AND MISS MISERY'S, EARLY THIS MORNING...

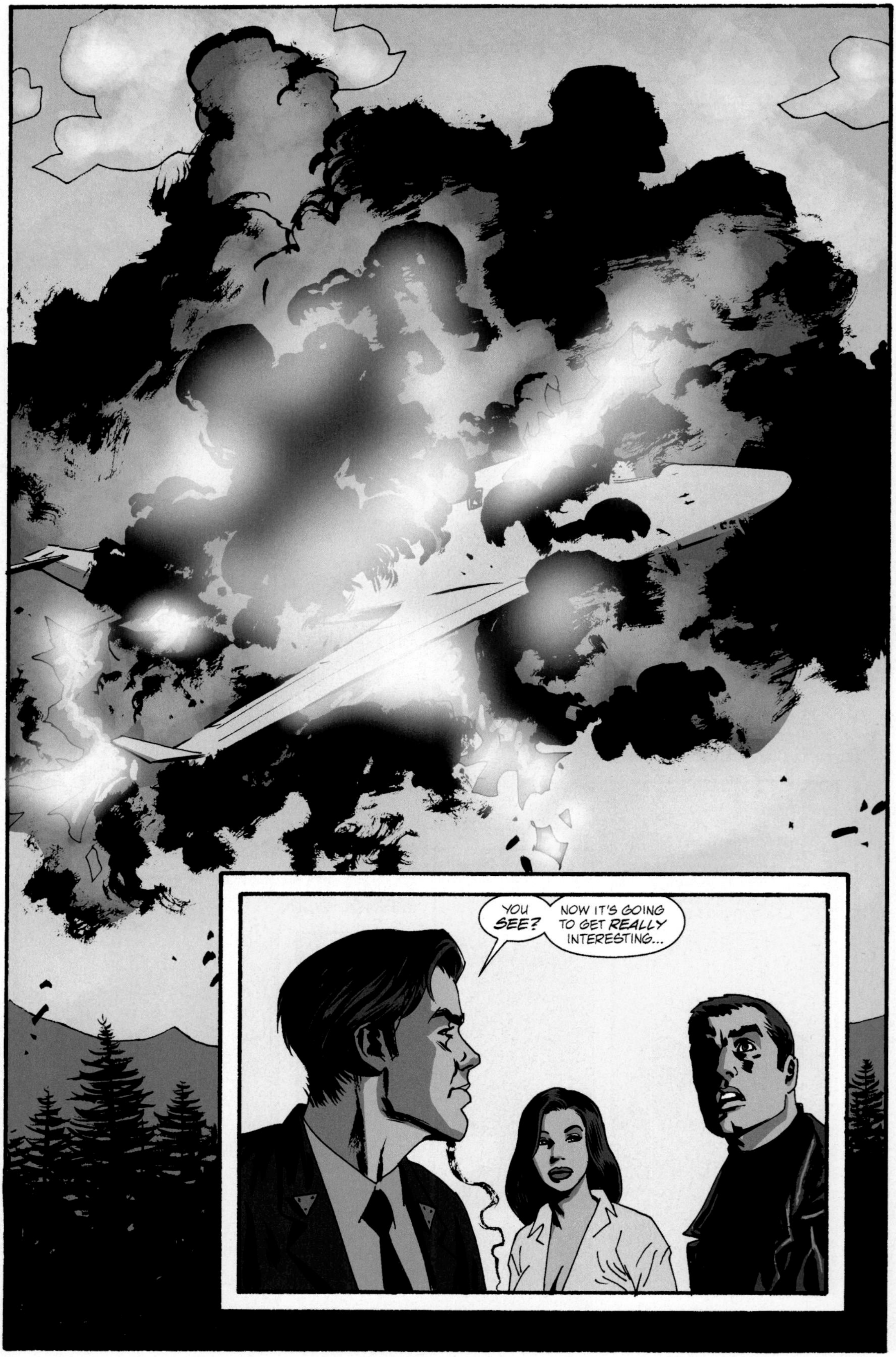
YOU SEE?
NOW IT'S GOING TO GET REALLY INTERESTING...

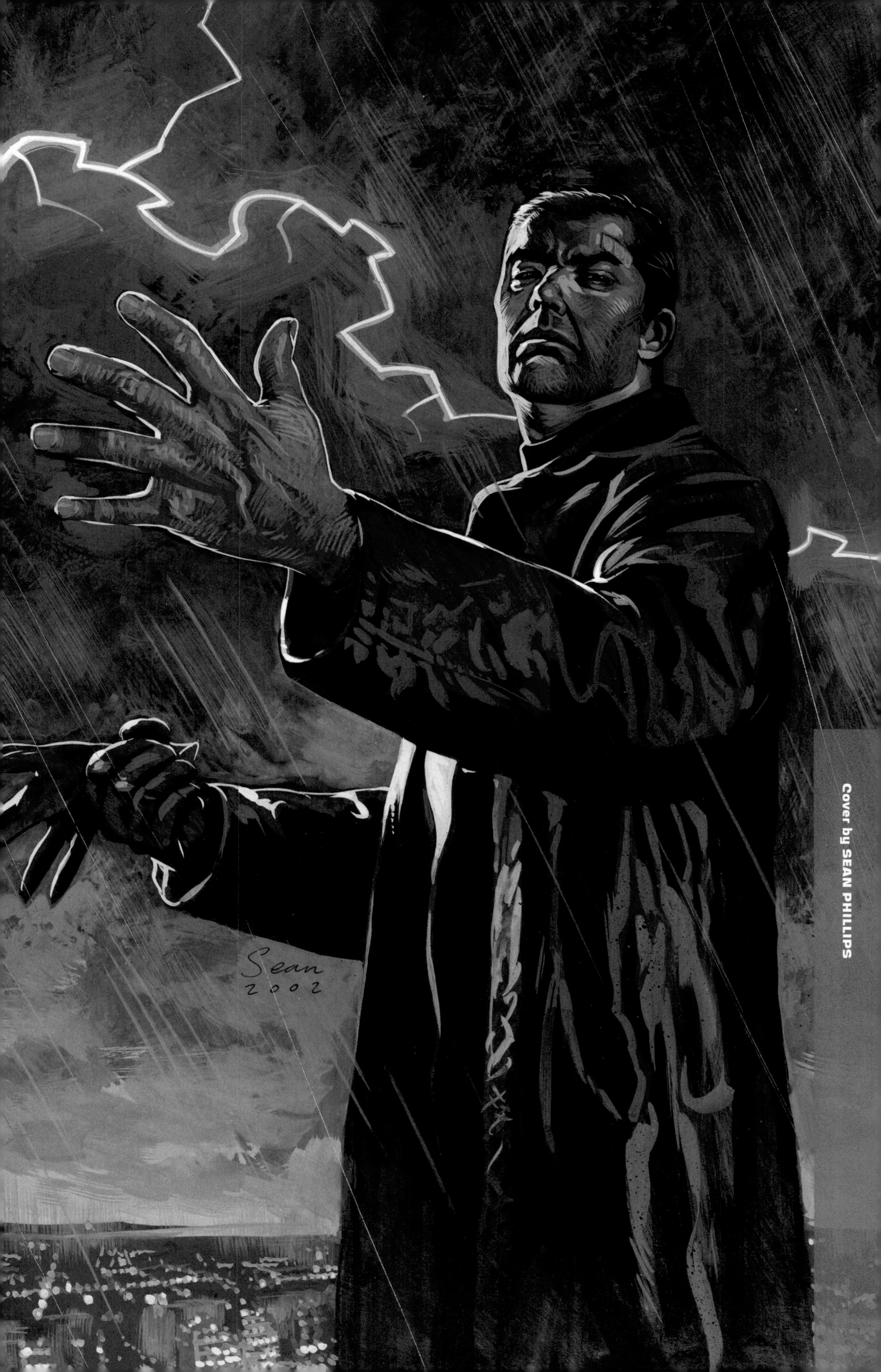
Sean
2002

Cover by SEAN PHILLIPS

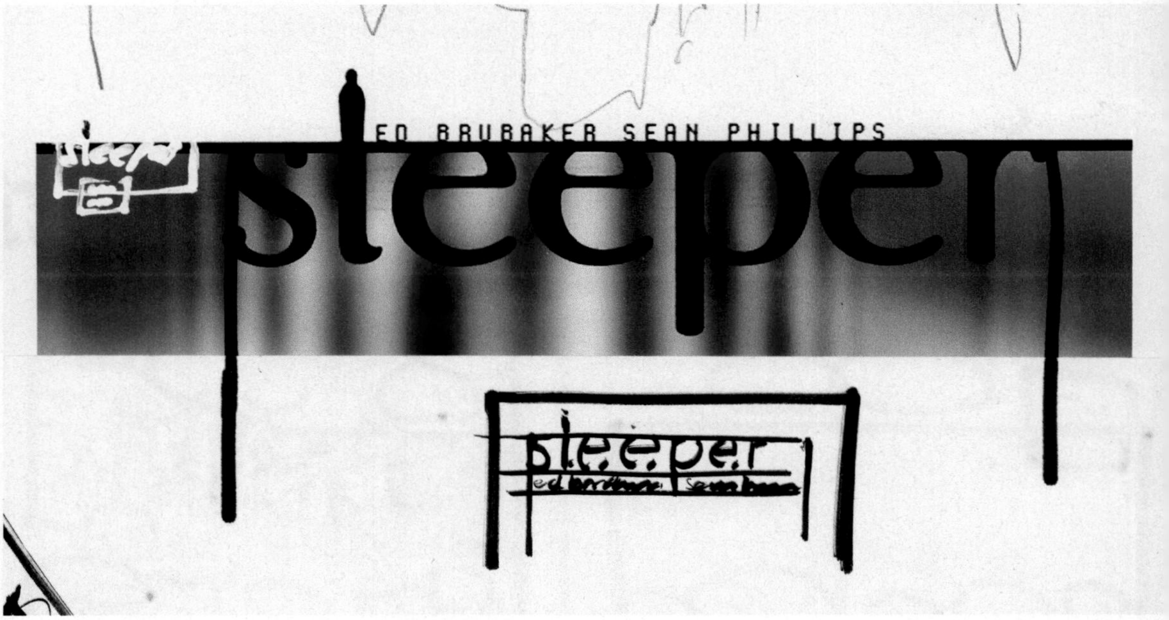
ED BRUBAKER SEAN PHILLIPS
sleeper
sleeper

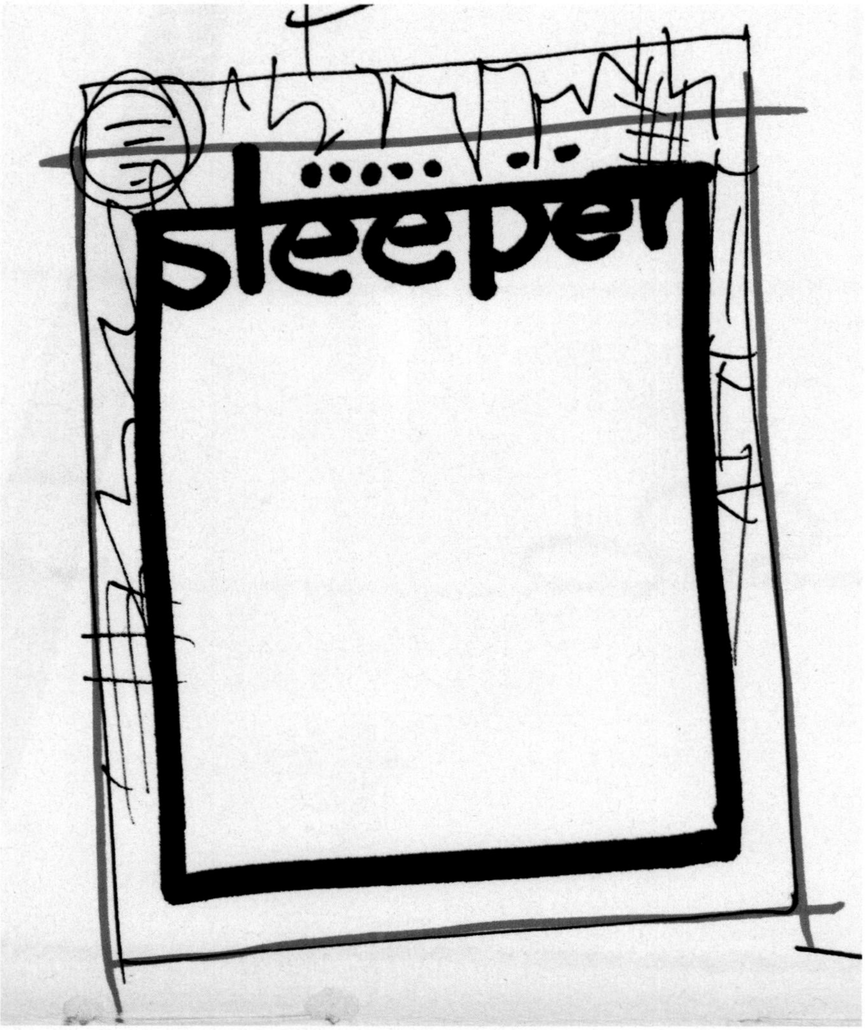
sleeper

SLEEPER Logo and Layout Sketches by SEAN PHILLIPS

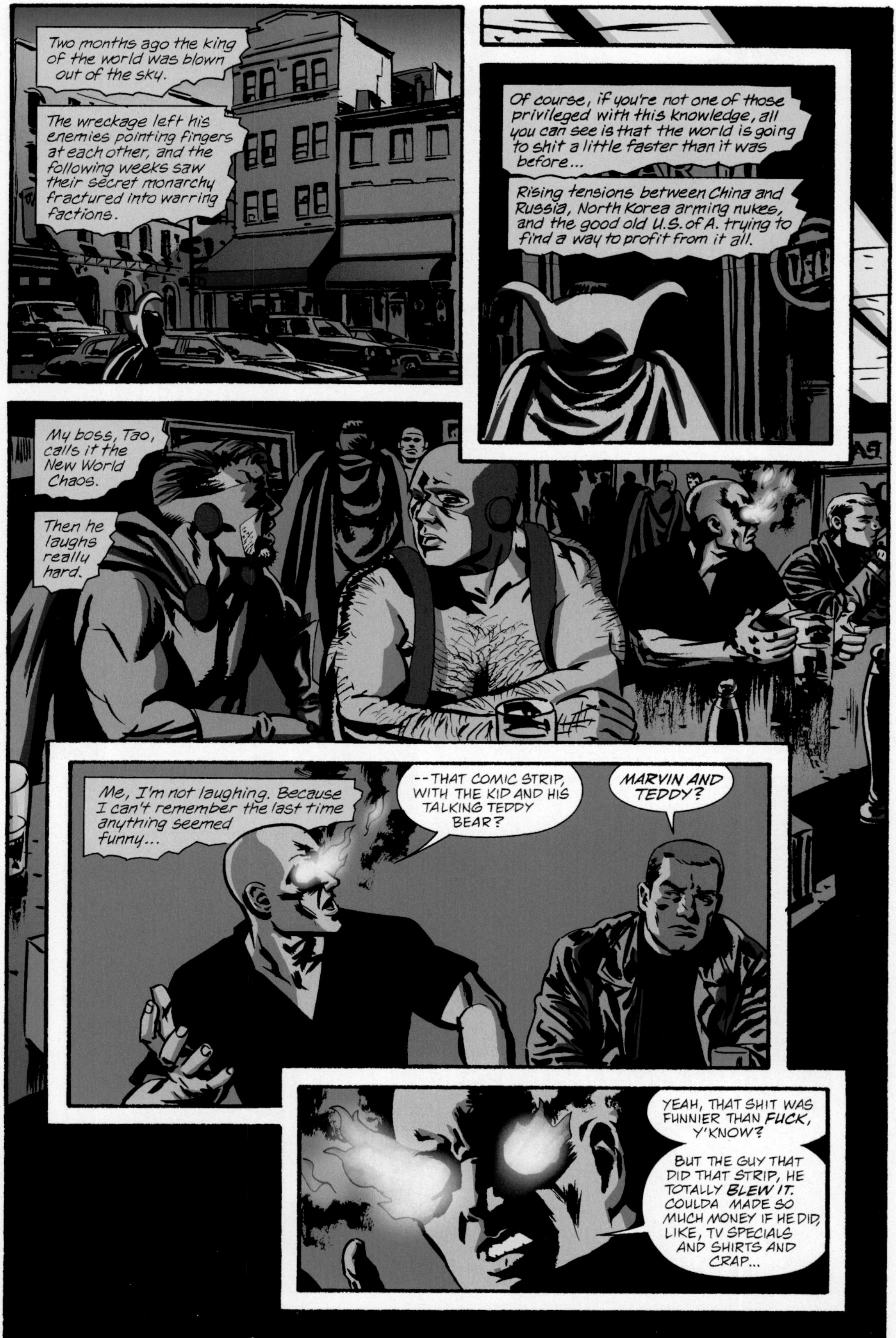
Two months ago the king of the world was blown out of the sky.
The wreckage left his enemies pointing fingers at each other, and the following weeks saw their secret monarchy fractured into warring factions.
Of course, if you're not one of those privileged with this knowledge, all you can see is that the world is going to shit a little faster than it was before...
Rising tensions between China and Russia, North Korea arming nukes, and the good old U.S. of A. trying to find a way to profit from it all.
My boss, Tao, calls it the New World Chaos.
Then he laughs really hard.
Me, I'm not laughing. Because I can't remember the last time anything seemed funny...
--THAT COMIC STRIP, WITH THE KID AND HIS TALKING TEDDY BEAR?
MARVIN AND TEDDY?
YEAH, THAT SHIT WAS FUNNIER THAN FUCK, Y'KNOW?
BUT THE GUY THAT DID THAT STRIP, HE TOTALLY BLEW IT. COULDA MADE SO MUCH MONEY IF HE DID, LIKE, TV SPECIALS AND SHIRTS AND CRAP...

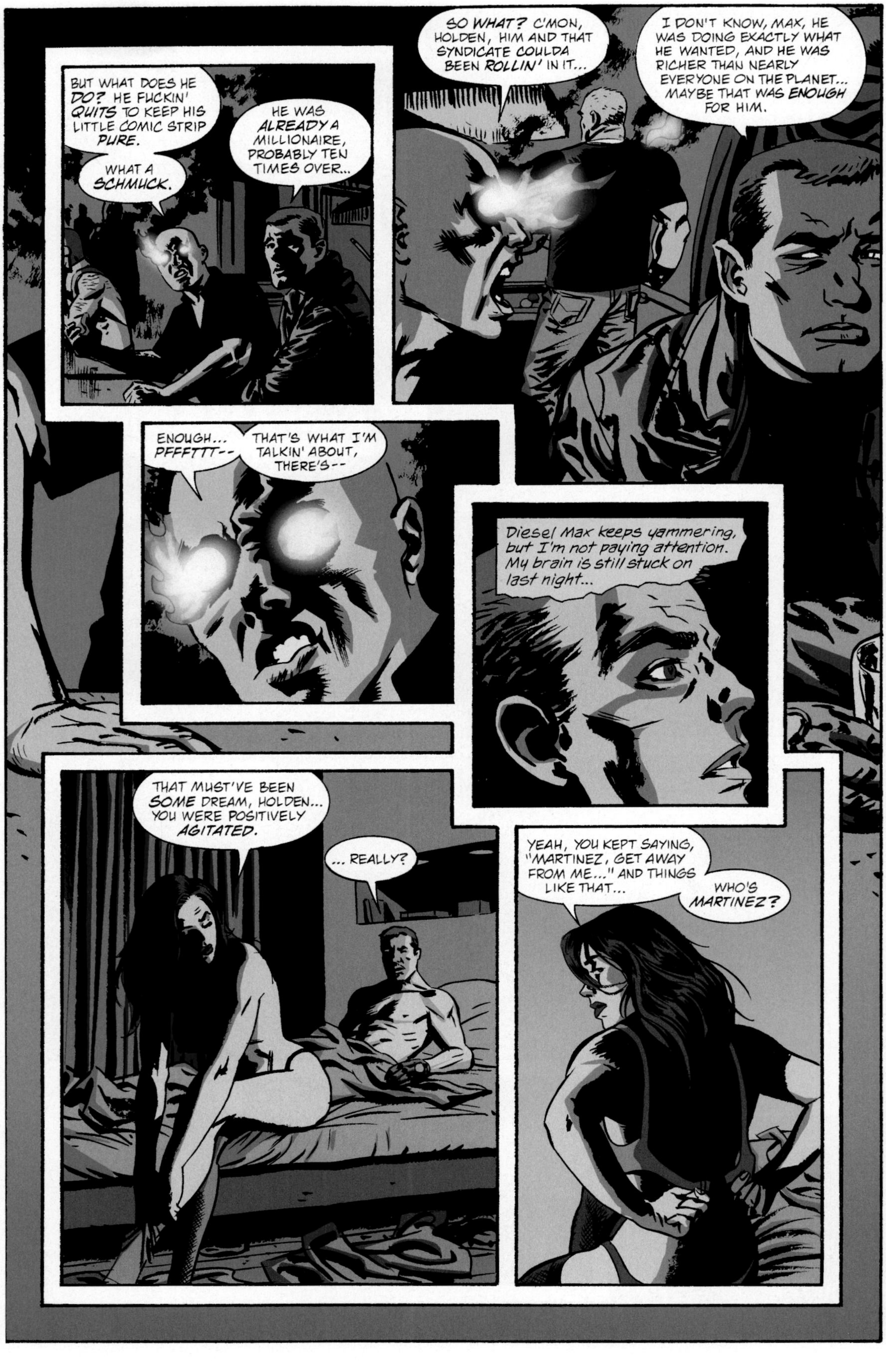
BUT WHAT DOES HE DO? HE FUCKIN' QUITS TO KEEP HIS LITTLE COMIC STRIP PURE.
WHAT A SCHMUCK.
HE WAS ALREADY A MILLIONAIRE, PROBABLY TEN TIMES OVER...
SO WHAT? C'MON, HOLDEN, HIM AND THAT SYNDICATE COULDA BEEN ROLLIN' IN IT...
I DON'T KNOW, MAX, HE WAS DOING EXACTLY WHAT HE WANTED, AND HE WAS RICHER THAN NEARLY EVERYONE ON THE PLANET... MAYBE THAT WAS ENOUGH FOR HIM.
ENOUGH... PFFFTTT--
THAT'S WHAT I'M TALKIN' ABOUT, THERE'S--
Diesel Max keeps yammering, but I'm not paying attention. My brain is still stuck on last night...
THAT MUST'VE BEEN SOME DREAM, HOLDEN... YOU WERE POSITIVELY AGITATED.
... REALLY?
YEAH, YOU KEPT SAYING, "MARTINEZ, GET AWAY FROM ME..." AND THINGS LIKE THAT...
WHO'S MARTINEZ?

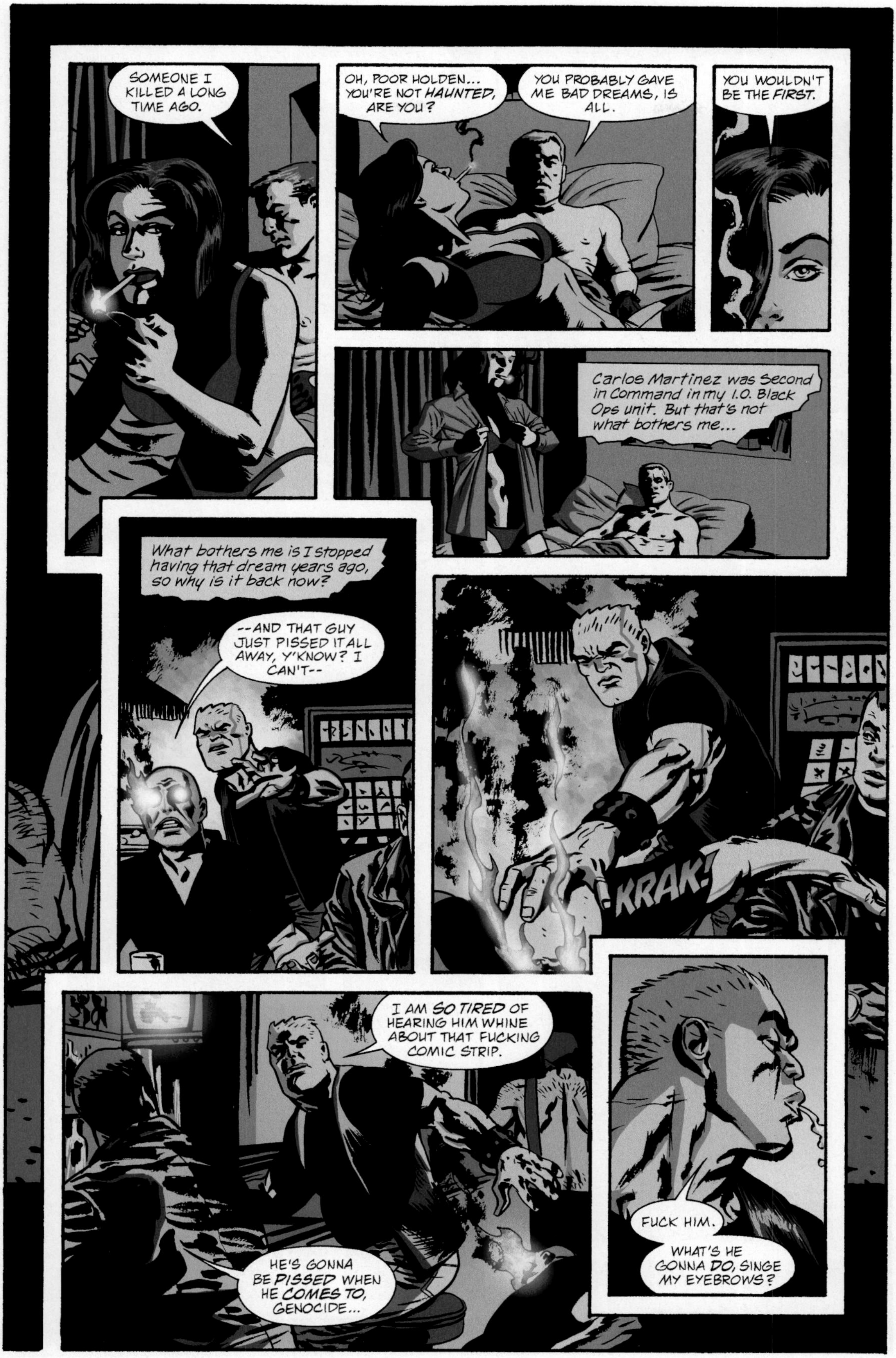
SOMEONE I KILLED A LONG TIME AGO.
OH, POOR HOLDEN... YOU'RE NOT HAUNTED, ARE YOU?
YOU PROBABLY GAVE ME BAD DREAMS, IS ALL.
YOU WOULDN'T BE THE FIRST.
Carlos Martinez was Second in Command in my I.O. Black Ops unit. But that's not what bothers me...
What bothers me is I stopped having that dream years ago, so why is it back now?
--AND THAT GUY JUST PISSED IT ALL AWAY, Y'KNOW? I CAN'T--
KRAK!
I AM SO TIRED OF HEARING HIM WHINE ABOUT THAT FUCKING COMIC STRIP.
HE'S GONNA BE PISSED WHEN HE COMES TO, GENOCIDE...
FUCK HIM.
WHAT'S HE GONNA DO, SINGE MY EYEBROWS?

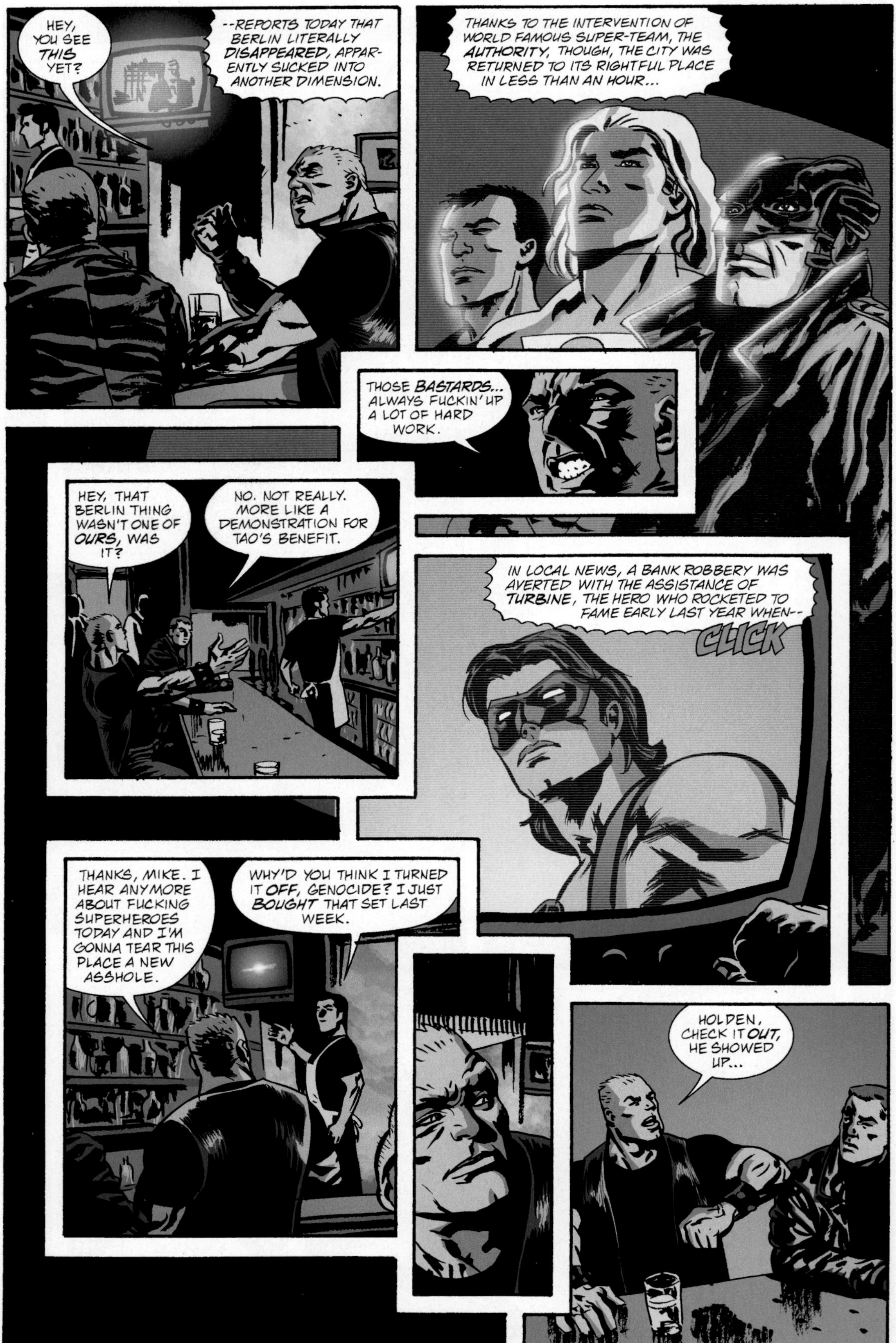
HEY, YOU SEE THIS YET?
--REPORTS TODAY THAT BERLIN LITERALLY DISAPPEARED, APPARENTLY SUCKED INTO ANOTHER DIMENSION.
THANKS TO THE INTERVENTION OF WORLD FAMOUS SUPER-TEAM, THE AUTHORITY, THOUGH, THE CITY WAS RETURNED TO ITS RIGHTFUL PLACE IN LESS THAN AN HOUR...
THOSE BASTARDS... ALWAYS FUCKIN' UP A LOT OF HARD WORK.
HEY, THAT BERLIN THING WASN'T ONE OF OURS, WAS IT?
NO. NOT REALLY. MORE LIKE A DEMONSTRATION FOR TAO'S BENEFIT.
IN LOCAL NEWS, A BANK ROBBERY WAS AVERTED WITH THE ASSISTANCE OF TURBINE, THE HERO WHO ROCKETED TO FAME EARLY LAST YEAR WHEN--
CLICK
THANKS, MIKE. I HEAR ANYMORE ABOUT FUCKING SUPERHEROES TODAY AND I'M GONNA TEAR THIS PLACE A NEW ASSHOLE.
WHY'D YOU THINK I TURNED IT OFF, GENOCIDE? I JUST BOUGHT THAT SET LAST WEEK.
HOLDEN, CHECK IT OUT, HE SHOWED UP...

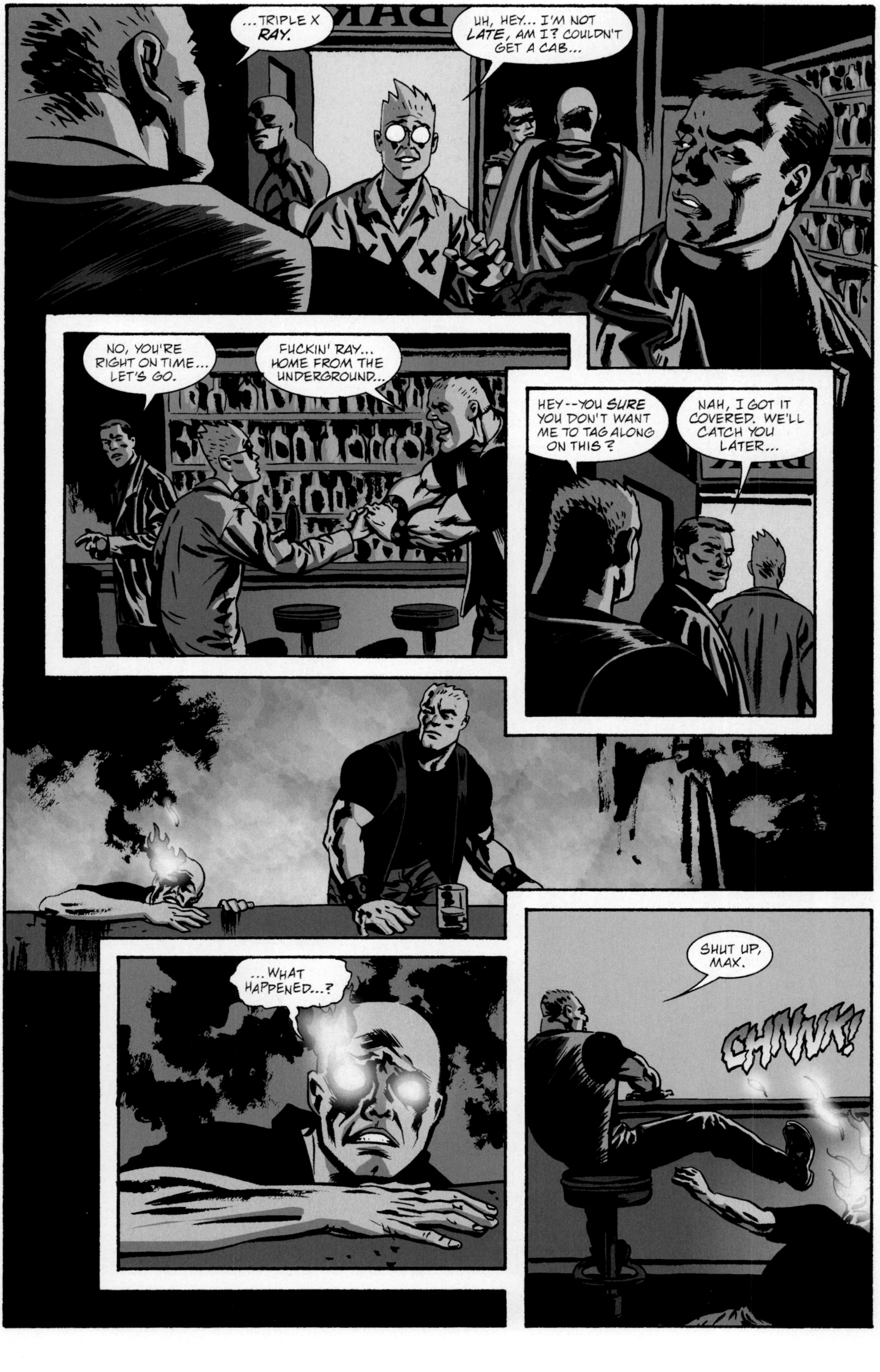
...TRIPLE X RAY.
UH, HEY... I'M NOT LATE, AM I? COULDN'T GET A CAB...
NO, YOU'RE RIGHT ON TIME... LET'S GO.
FUCKIN' RAY... HOME FROM THE UNDERGROUND...
HEY--YOU SURE YOU DON'T WANT ME TO TAG ALONG ON THIS?
NAH, I GOT IT COVERED. WE'LL CATCH YOU LATER...
...WHAT HAPPENED...?
SHUT UP, MAX.
CHNNK!

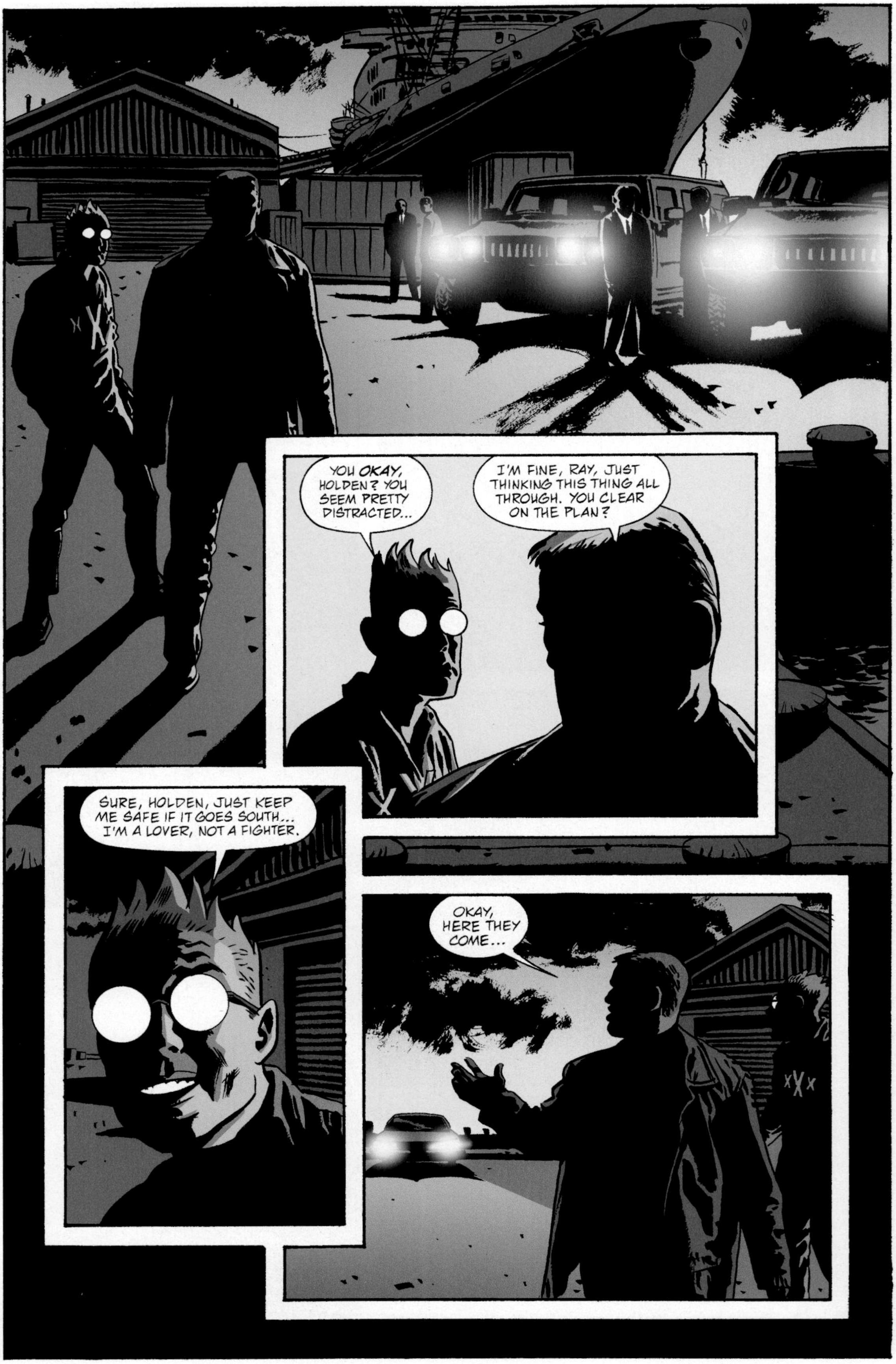
YOU OKAY, HOLDEN? YOU SEEM PRETTY DISTRACTED...
I'M FINE, RAY, JUST THINKING THIS THING ALL THROUGH. YOU CLEAR ON THE PLAN?
SURE, HOLDEN, JUST KEEP ME SAFE IF IT GOES SOUTH... I'M A LOVER, NOT A FIGHTER.
OKAY, HERE THEY COME...

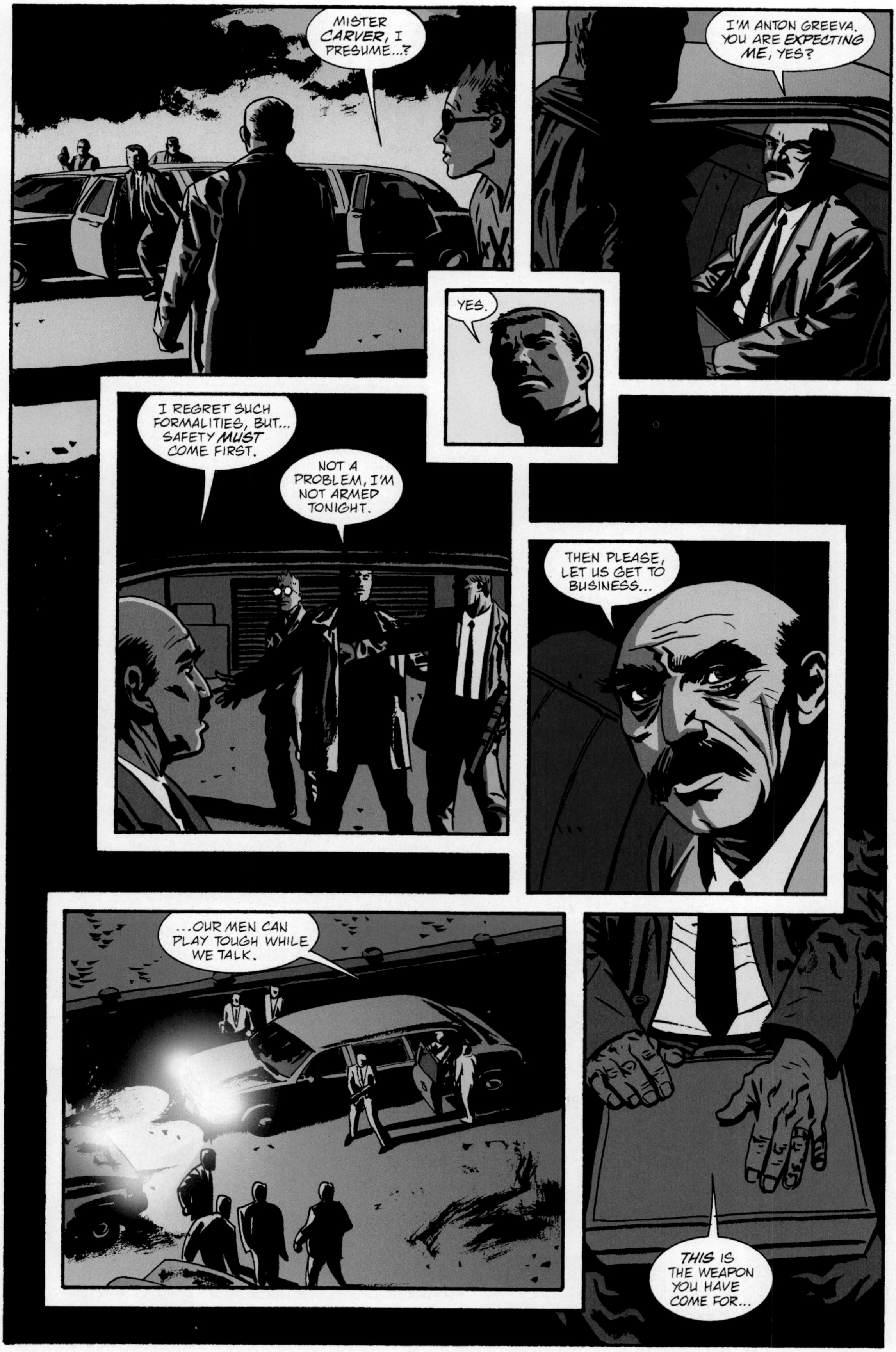

MISTER CARVER, I PRESUME...?
I'M ANTON GREEVA. YOU ARE EXPECTING ME, YES?
YES.
I REGRET SUCH FORMALITIES, BUT... SAFETY MUST COME FIRST.
NOT A PROBLEM, I'M NOT ARMED TONIGHT.
THEN PLEASE, LET US GET TO BUSINESS...
...OUR MEN CAN PLAY TOUGH WHILE WE TALK.
THIS IS THE WEAPON YOU HAVE COME FOR...

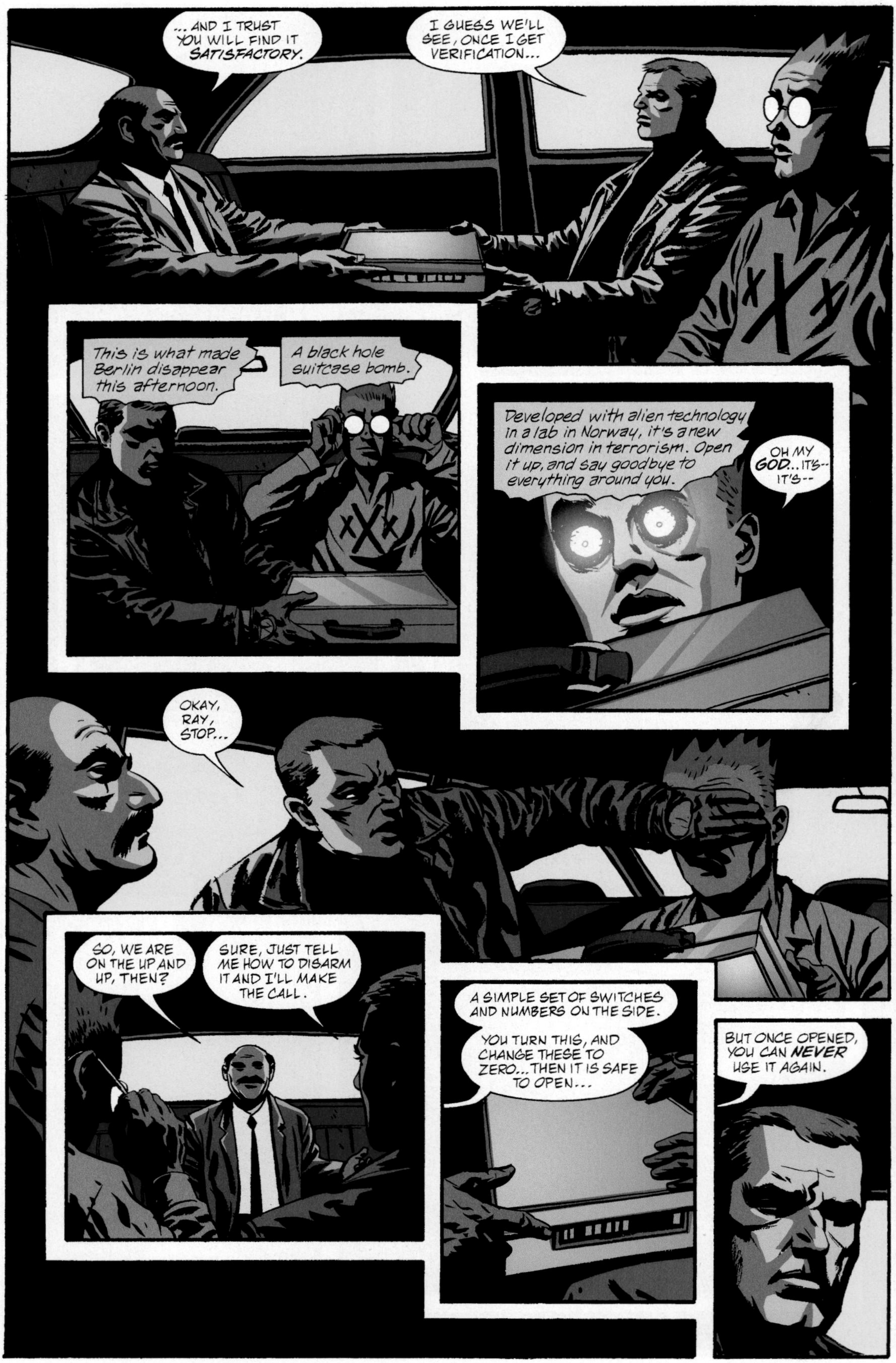
...AND I TRUST YOU WILL FIND IT SATISFACTORY.
I GUESS WE'LL SEE, ONCE I GET VERIFICATION...
This is what made Berlin disappear this afternoon.
A black hole suitcase bomb.
Developed with alien technology in a lab in Norway, it's a new dimension in terrorism. Open it up, and say goodbye to everything around you.
OH MY GOD... IT'S-- IT'S--
OKAY, RAY, STOP...
SO, WE ARE ON THE UP AND UP, THEN?
SURE, JUST TELL ME HOW TO DISARM IT AND I'LL MAKE THE CALL.
A SIMPLE SET OF SWITCHES AND NUMBERS ON THE SIDE.
YOU TURN THIS, AND CHANGE THESE TO ZERO... THEN IT IS SAFE TO OPEN...
BUT ONCE OPENED, YOU CAN NEVER USE IT AGAIN.

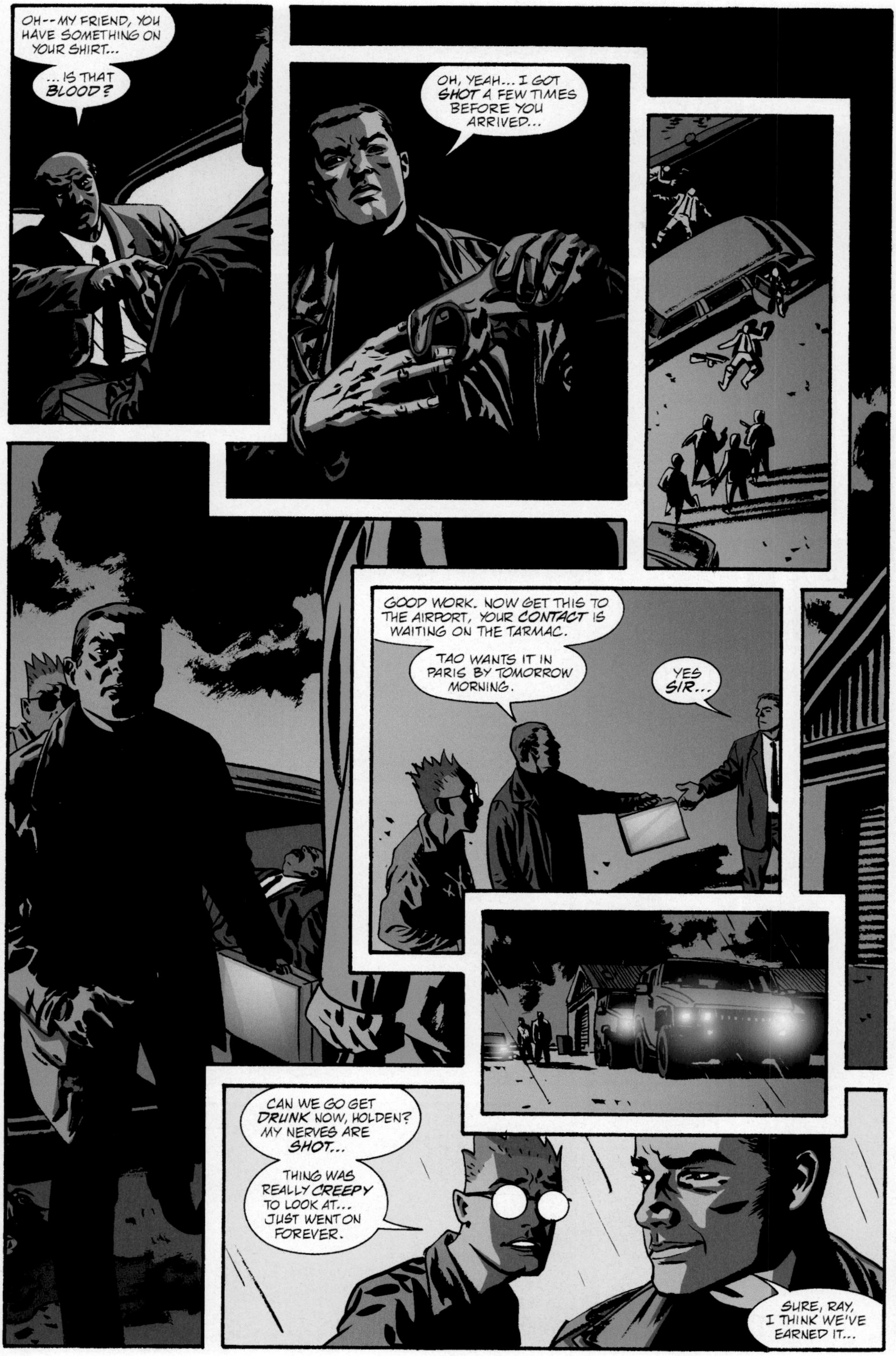
OH--MY FRIEND, YOU HAVE SOMETHING ON YOUR SHIRT...
...IS THAT BLOOD?
OH, YEAH... I GOT SHOT A FEW TIMES BEFORE YOU ARRIVED...
GOOD WORK. NOW GET THIS TO THE AIRPORT, YOUR CONTACT IS WAITING ON THE TARMAC.
TAO WANTS IT IN PARIS BY TOMORROW MORNING.
YES SIR...
CAN WE GO GET DRUNK NOW, HOLDEN? MY NERVES ARE SHOT...
THING WAS REALLY CREEPY TO LOOK AT... JUST WENT ON FOREVER.
SURE, RAY, I THINK WE'VE EARNED IT...

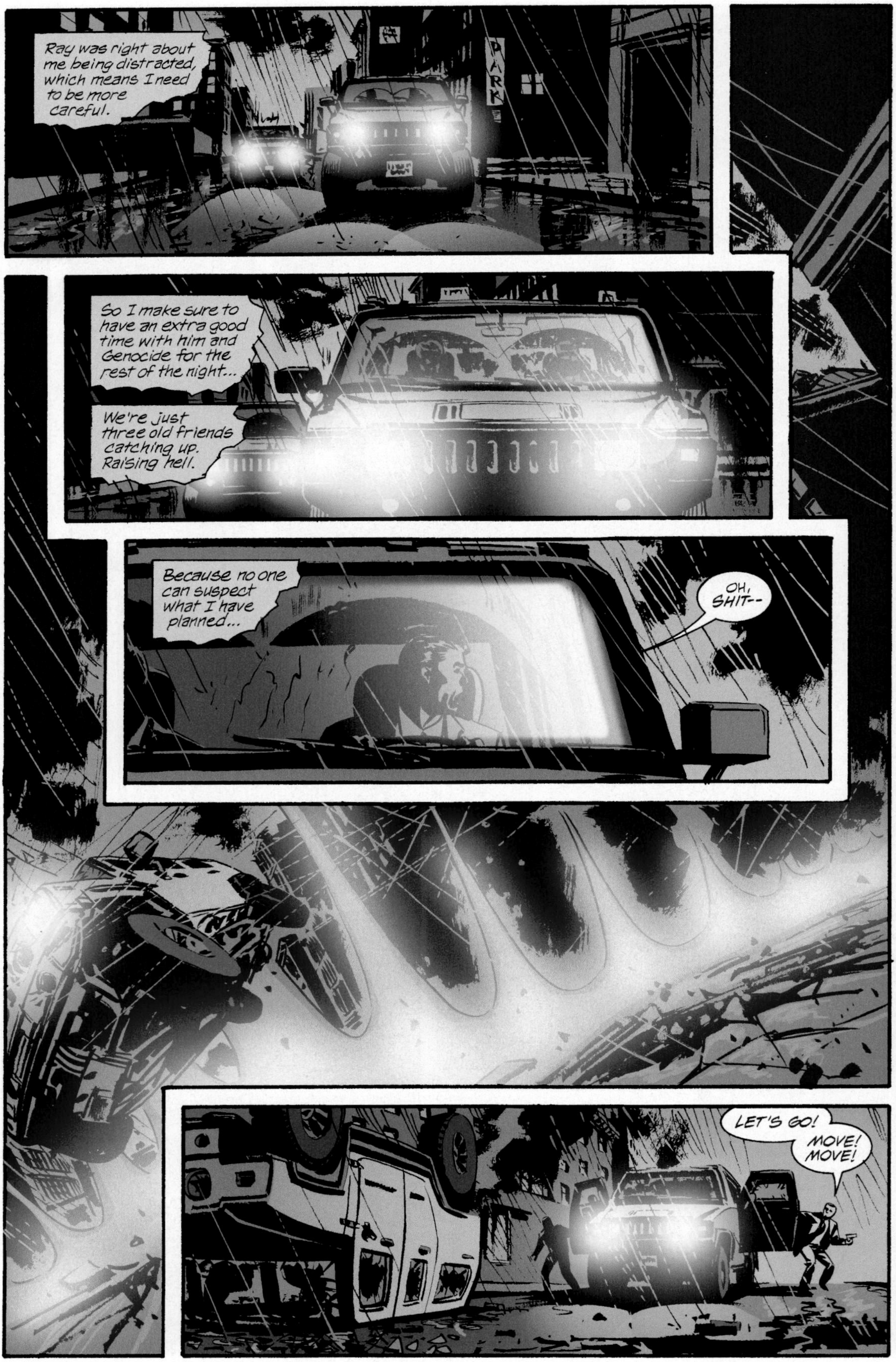
Ray was right about me being distracted, which means I need to be more careful.
So I make sure to have an extra good time with him and Genocide for the rest of the night...
We're just three old friends catching up. Raising hell.
Because no one can suspect what I have planned...
OH, SHIT--
LET'S GO!
MOVE! MOVE!

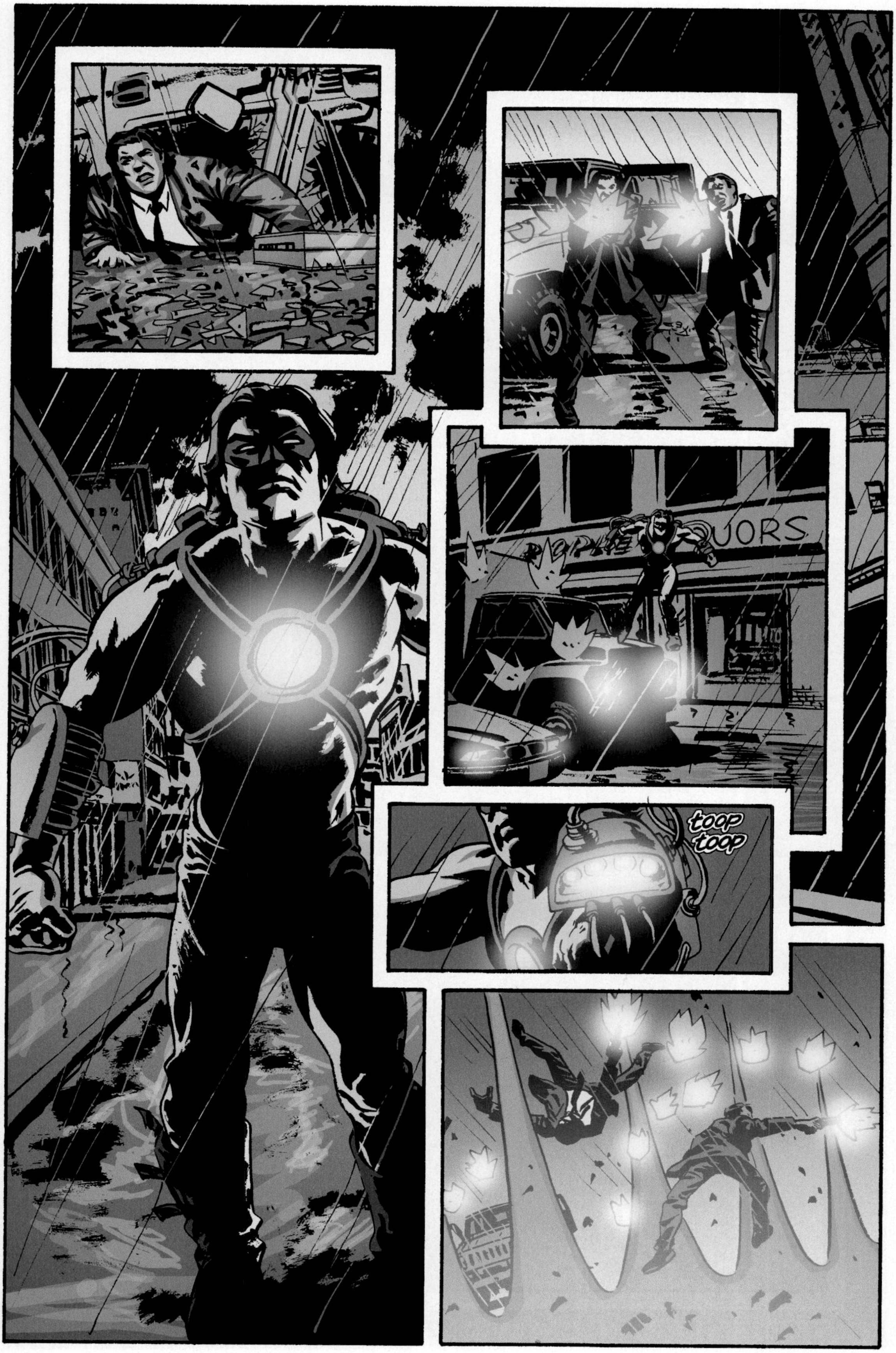
UORS
toop
toop

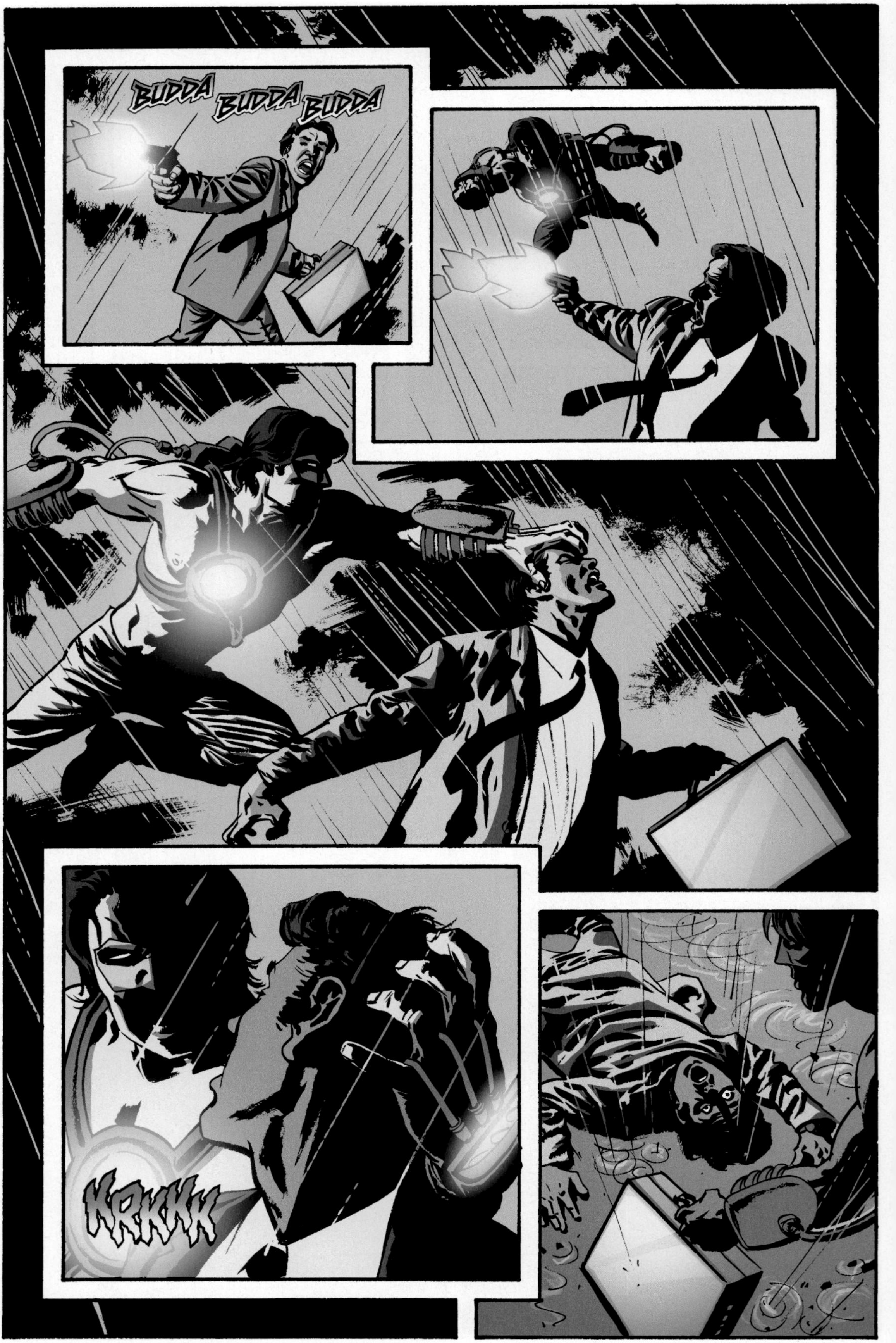
BUDDA BUDDA BUDDA
KRKKK

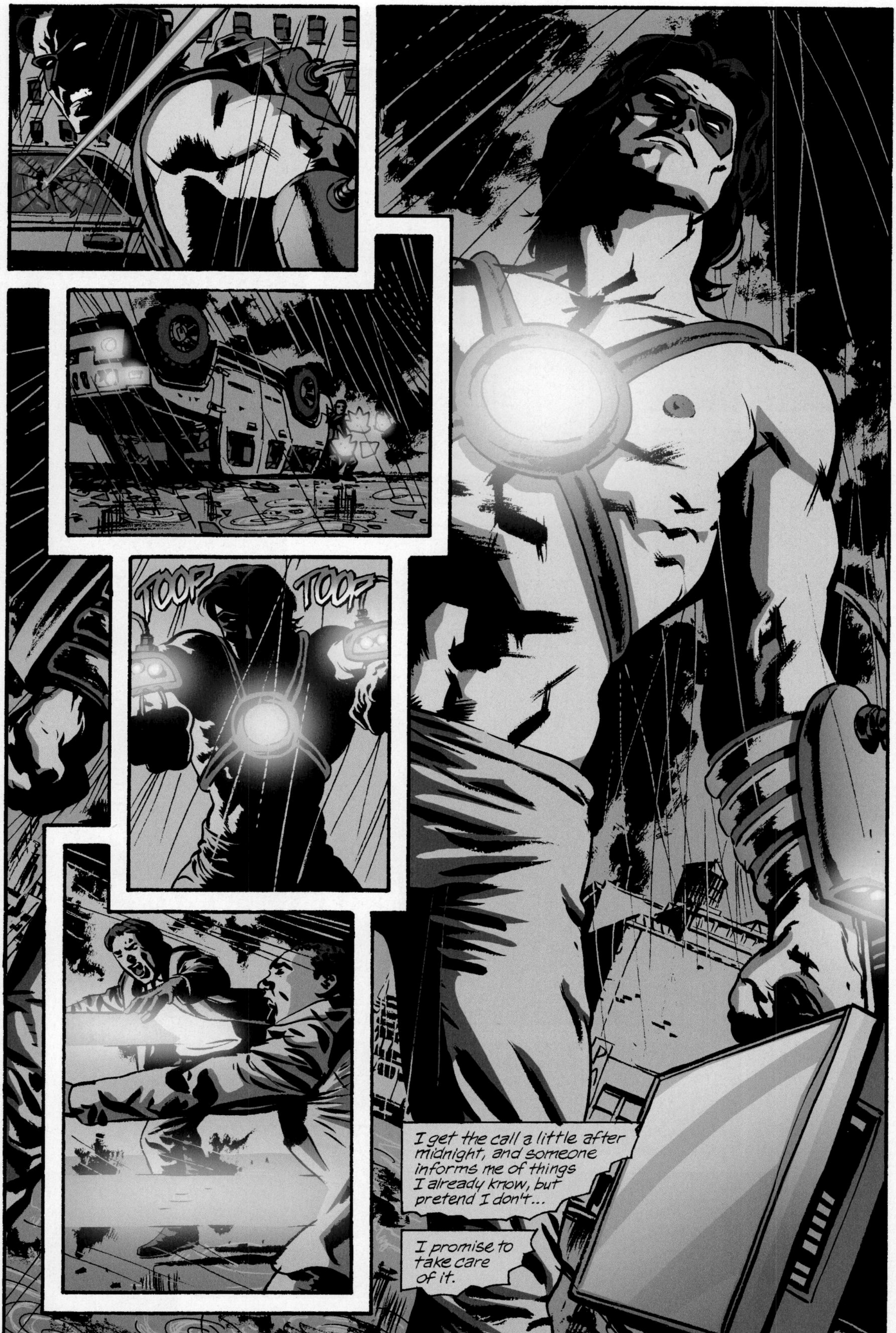
TOOP
TOOP
I get the call a little after midnight, and someone informs me of things I already know, but pretend I don't...
I promise to take care of it.

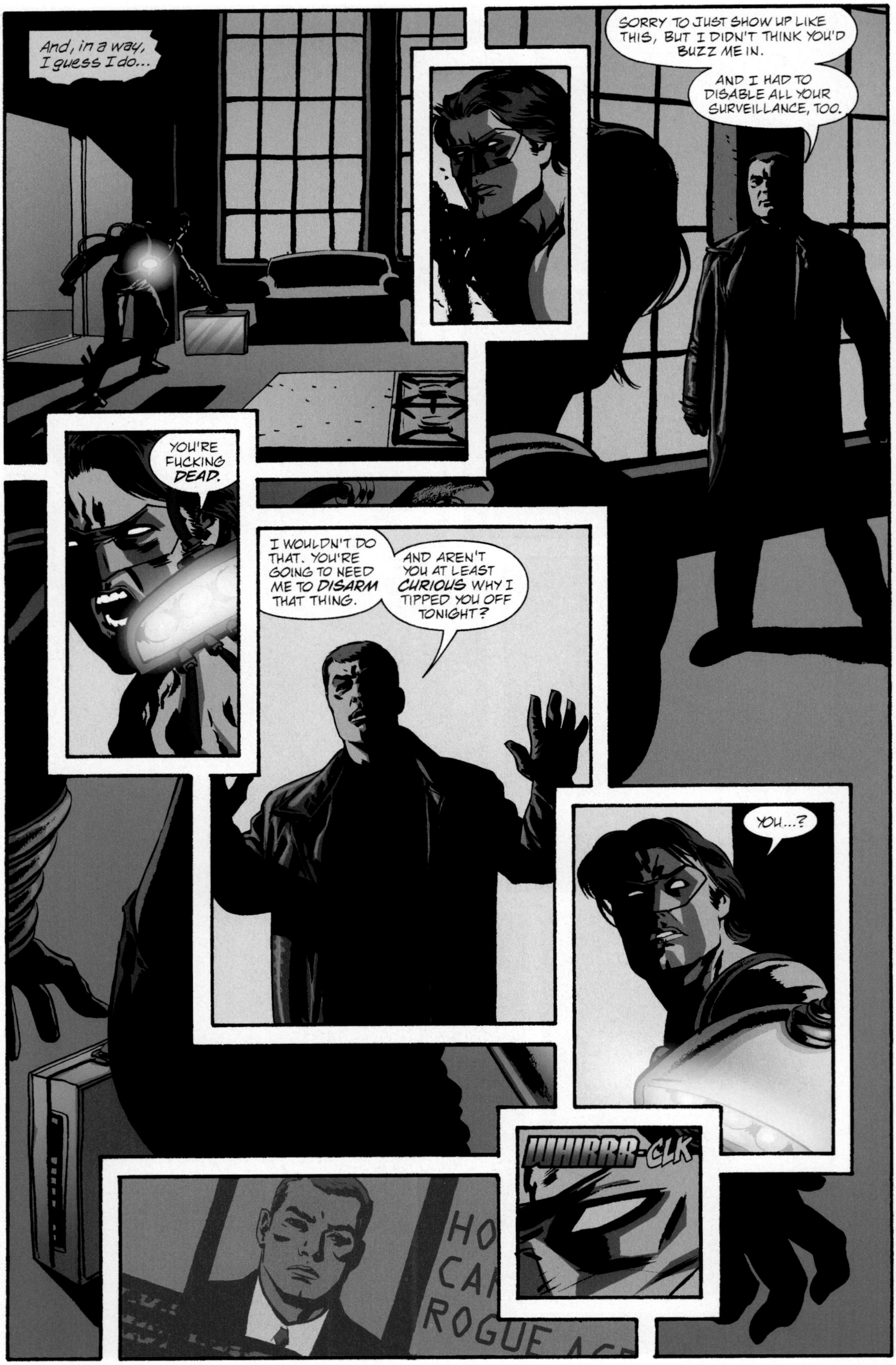
And, in a way, I guess I do...
SORRY TO JUST SHOW UP LIKE THIS, BUT I DIDN'T THINK YOU'D BUZZ ME IN.
AND I HAD TO DISABLE ALL YOUR SURVEILLANCE, TOO.
YOU'RE FUCKING DEAD.
I WOULDN'T DO THAT. YOU'RE GOING TO NEED ME TO DISARM THAT THING.
AND AREN'T YOU AT LEAST CURIOUS WHY I TIPPED YOU OFF TONIGHT?
YOU...?
WHIRRR-CLK
ROGUE

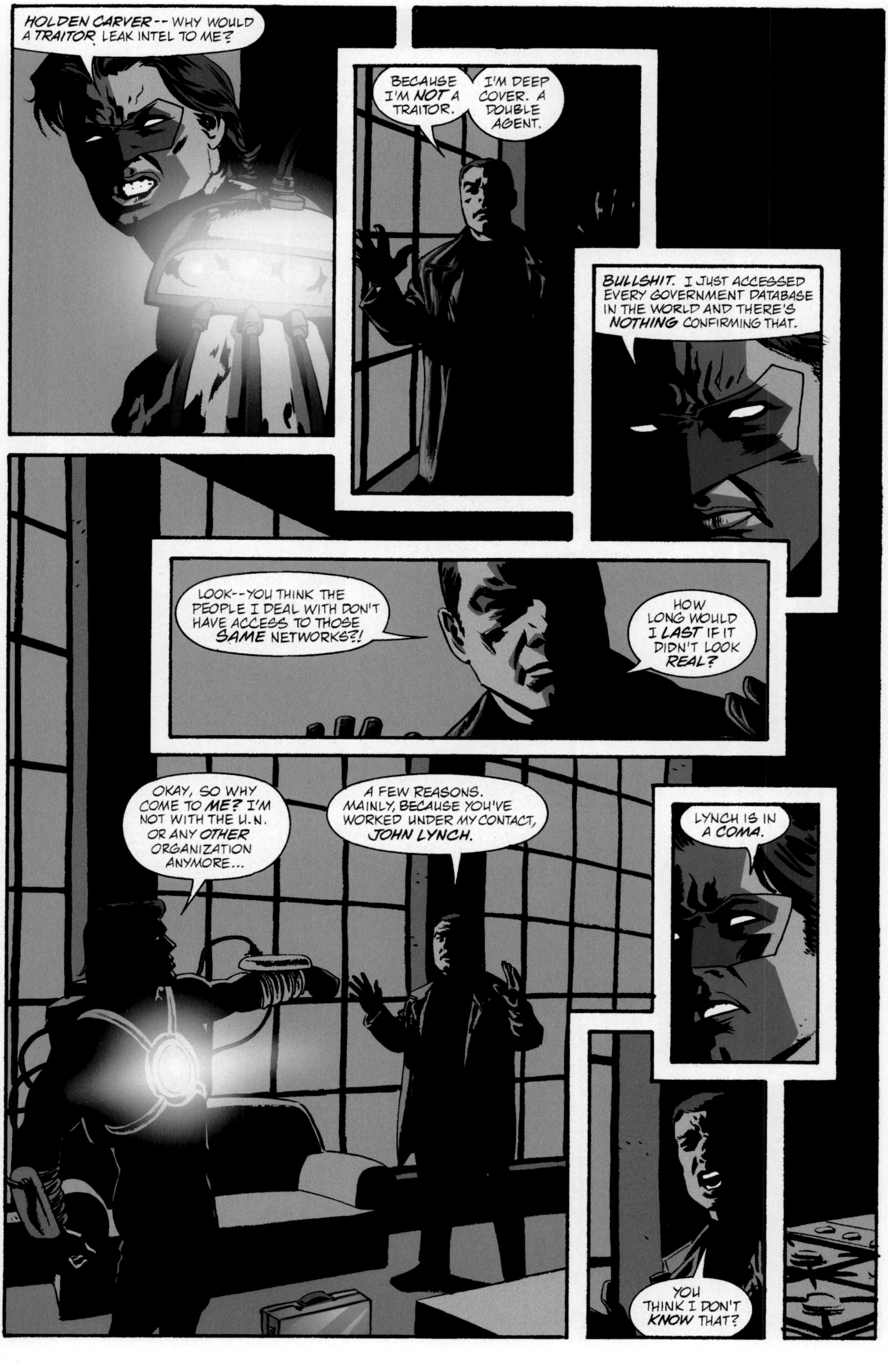
HOLDEN CARVER-- WHY WOULD A TRAITOR LEAK INTEL TO ME?
BECAUSE I'M NOT A TRAITOR.
I'M DEEP COVER. A DOUBLE AGENT.
BULLSHIT. I JUST ACCESSED EVERY GOVERNMENT DATABASE IN THE WORLD AND THERE'S NOTHING CONFIRMING THAT.
LOOK--YOU THINK THE PEOPLE I DEAL WITH DON'T HAVE ACCESS TO THOSE SAME NETWORKS?!
HOW LONG WOULD I LAST IF IT DIDN'T LOOK REAL?
OKAY, SO WHY COME TO ME? I'M NOT WITH THE U.N. OR ANY OTHER ORGANIZATION ANYMORE...
A FEW REASONS. MAINLY, BECAUSE YOU'VE WORKED UNDER MY CONTACT, JOHN LYNCH.
LYNCH IS IN A COMA.
YOU THINK I DON'T KNOW THAT?

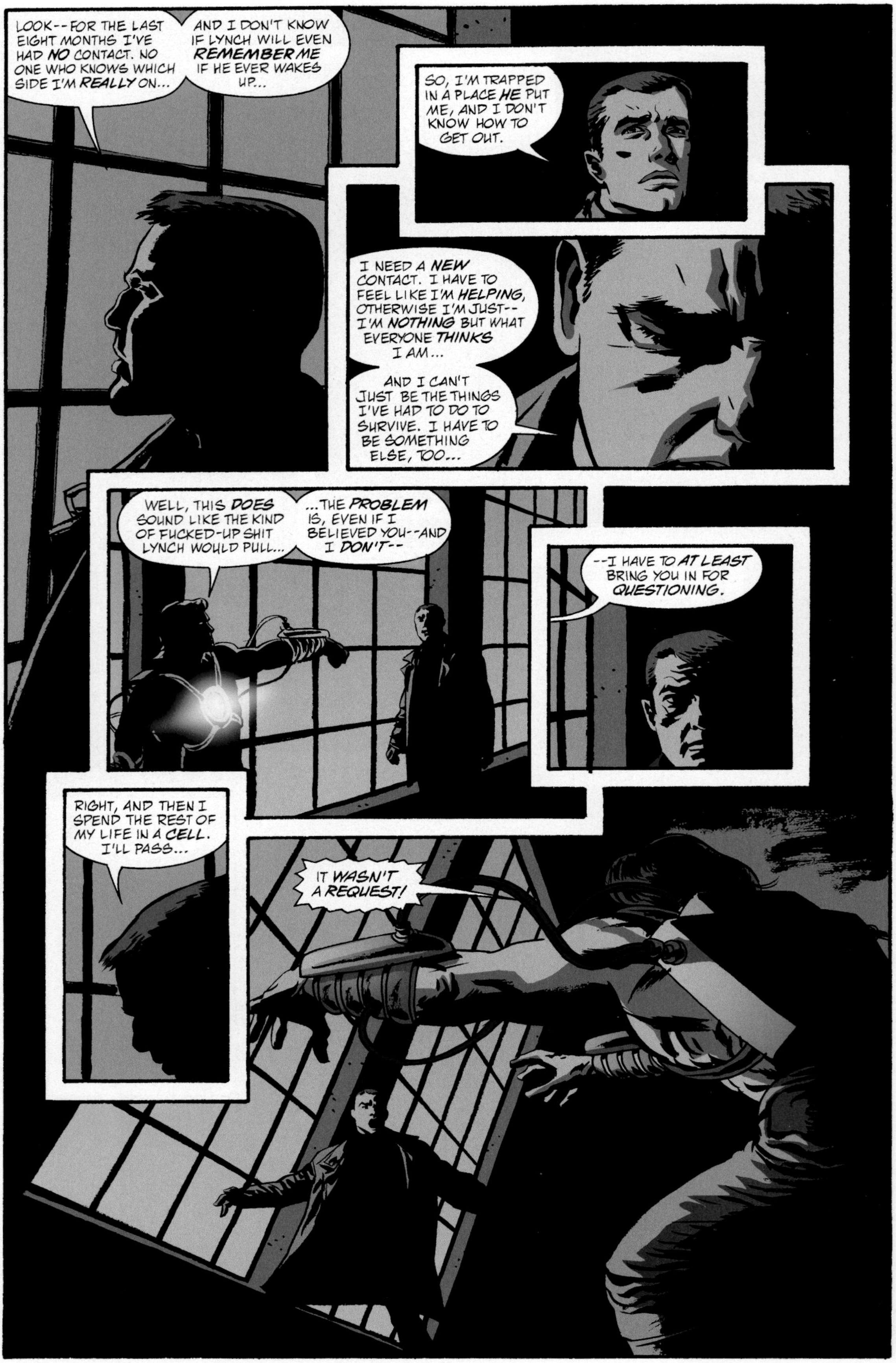
LOOK--FOR THE LAST EIGHT MONTHS I'VE HAD NO CONTACT. NO ONE WHO KNOWS WHICH SIDE I'M REALLY ON...
AND I DON'T KNOW IF LYNCH WILL EVEN REMEMBER ME IF HE EVER WAKES UP...
SO, I'M TRAPPED IN A PLACE HE PUT ME, AND I DON'T KNOW HOW TO GET OUT.
I NEED A NEW CONTACT. I HAVE TO FEEL LIKE I'M HELPING, OTHERWISE I'M JUST-- I'M NOTHING BUT WHAT EVERYONE THINKS I AM...
AND I CAN'T JUST BE THE THINGS I'VE HAD TO DO TO SURVIVE. I HAVE TO BE SOMETHING ELSE, TOO...
WELL, THIS DOES SOUND LIKE THE KIND OF FUCKED-UP SHIT LYNCH WOULD PULL...
...THE PROBLEM IS, EVEN IF I BELIEVED YOU--AND I DON'T--
--I HAVE TO AT LEAST BRING YOU IN FOR QUESTIONING.
RIGHT, AND THEN I SPEND THE REST OF MY LIFE IN A CELL. I'LL PASS...
IT WASN'T A REQUEST!

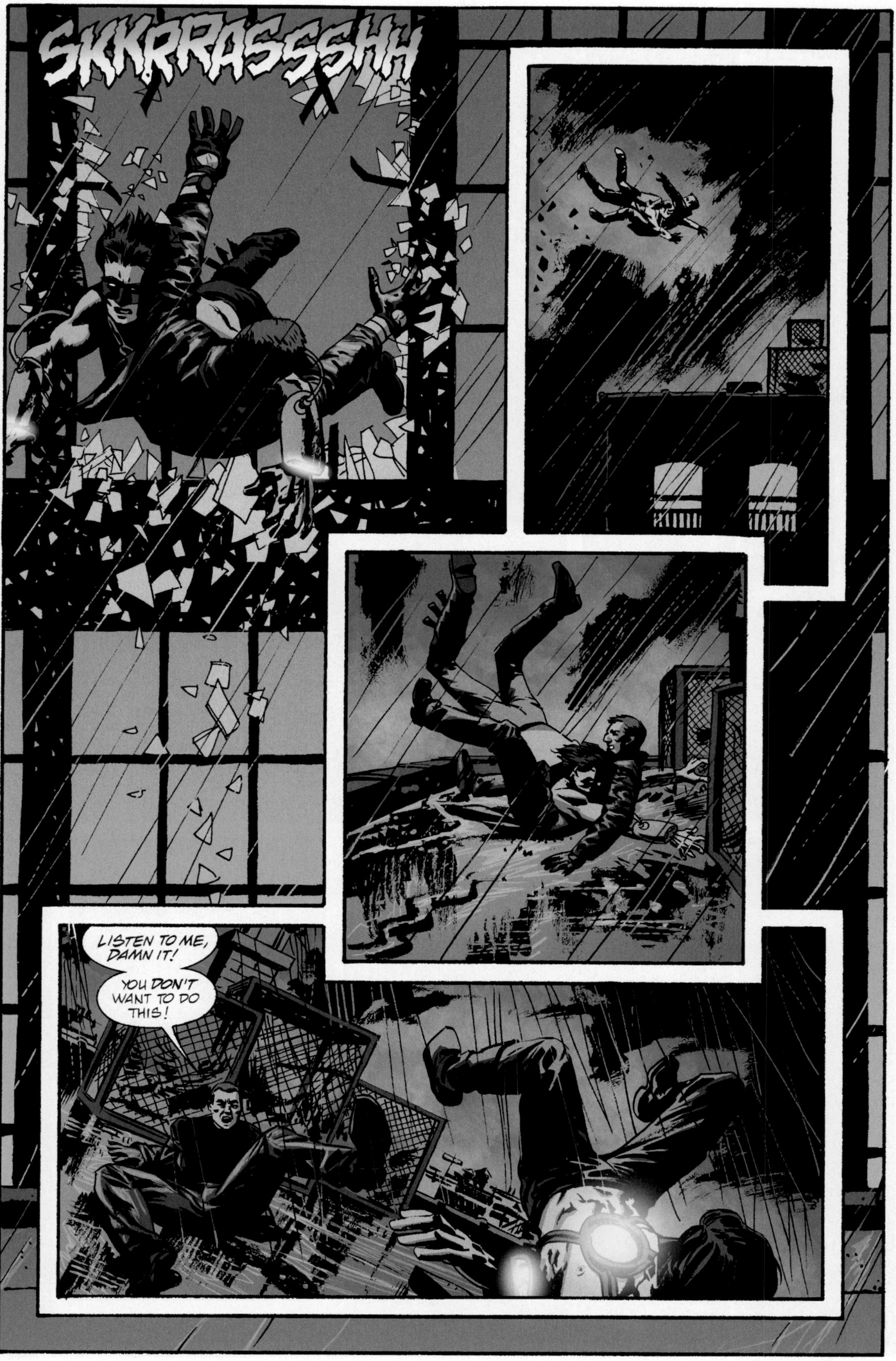
SKKRRASSSHH
LISTEN TO ME, DAMN IT!
YOU DON'T WANT TO DO THIS!

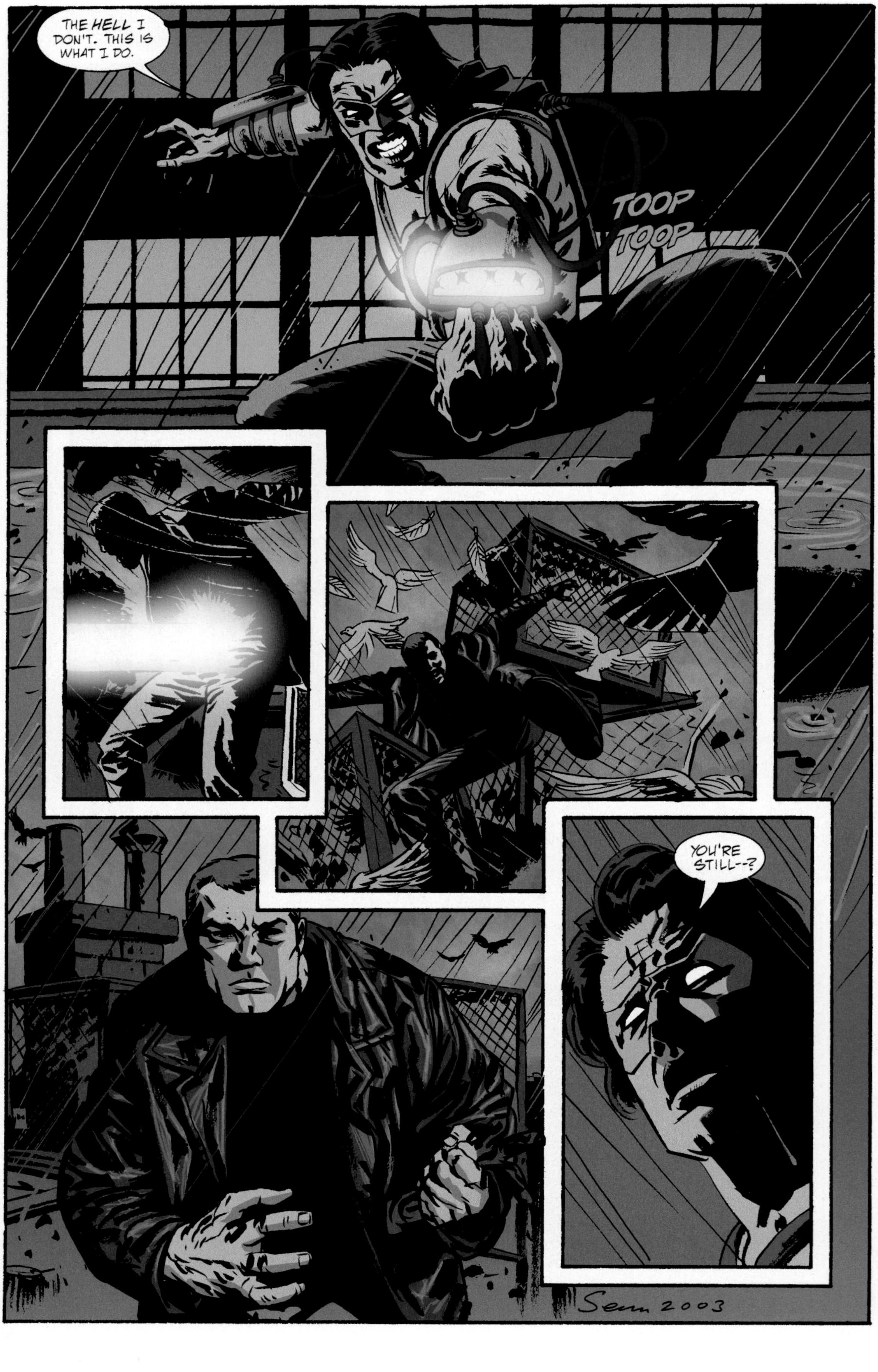
THE HELL I DON'T. THIS IS WHAT I DO.
TOOP TOOP
YOU'RE STILL--?
Sean 2003

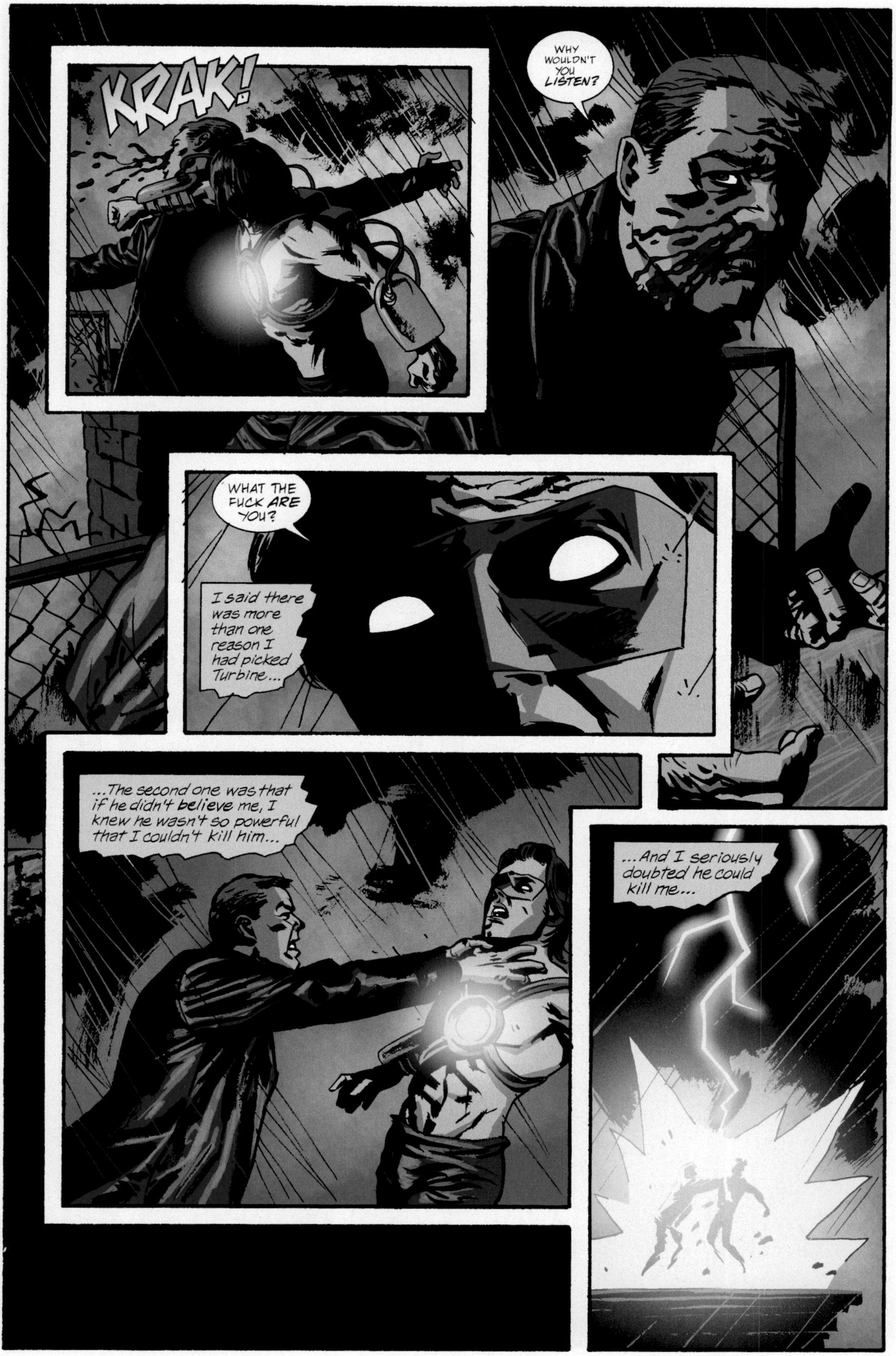
KRAK!
WHY WOULDN'T YOU LISTEN?
WHAT THE FUCK ARE YOU?
I said there was more than one reason I had picked Turbine...
...The second one was that if he didn't believe me, I knew he wasn't so powerful that I couldn't kill him...
...And I seriously doubted he could kill me...

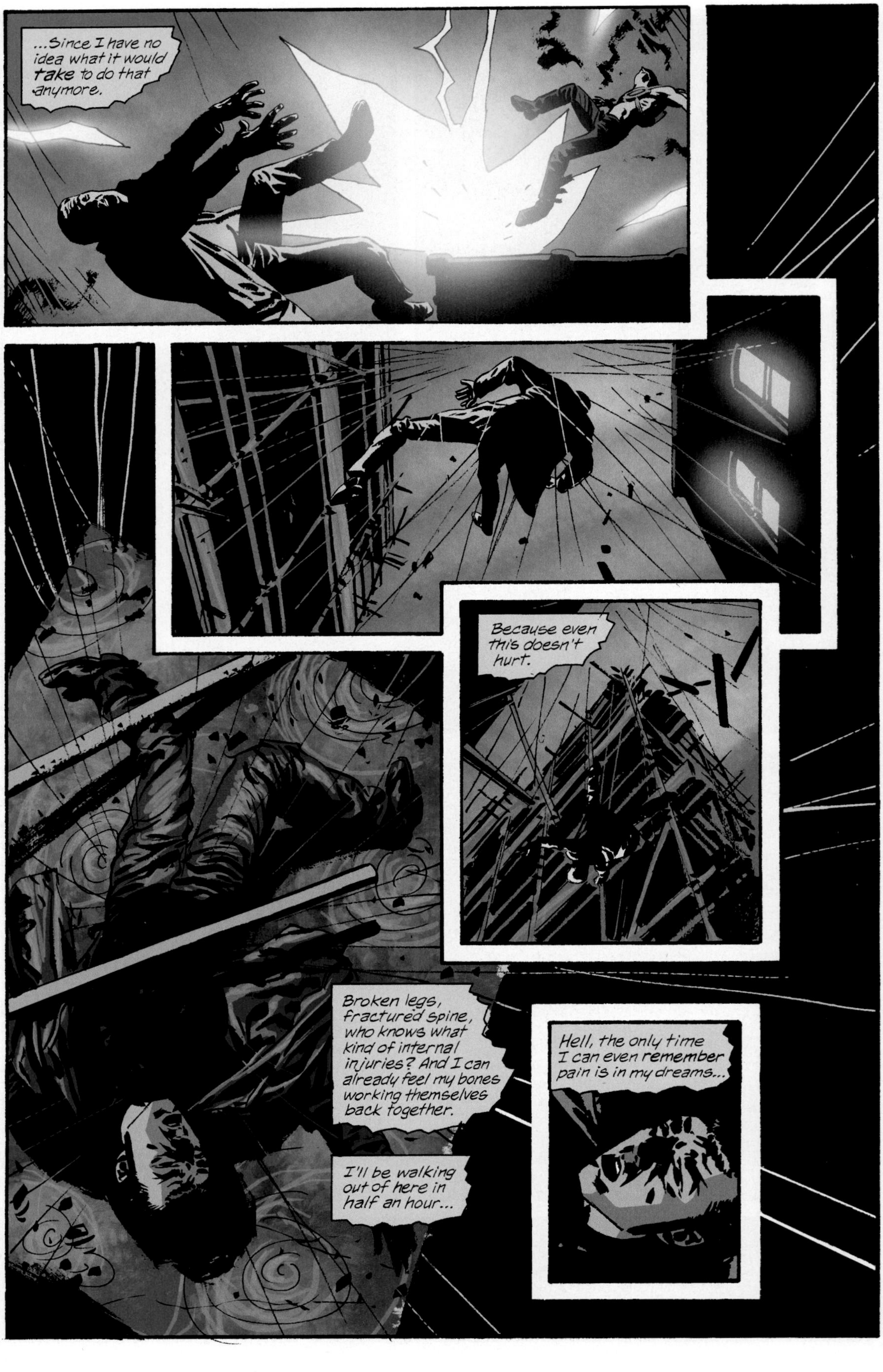
...Since I have no idea what it would take to do that anymore.
Because even this doesn't hurt.
Broken legs, fractured spine, who knows what kind of internal injuries? And I can already feel my bones working themselves back together.
I'll be walking out of here in half an hour...
Hell, the only time I can even remember pain is in my dreams...

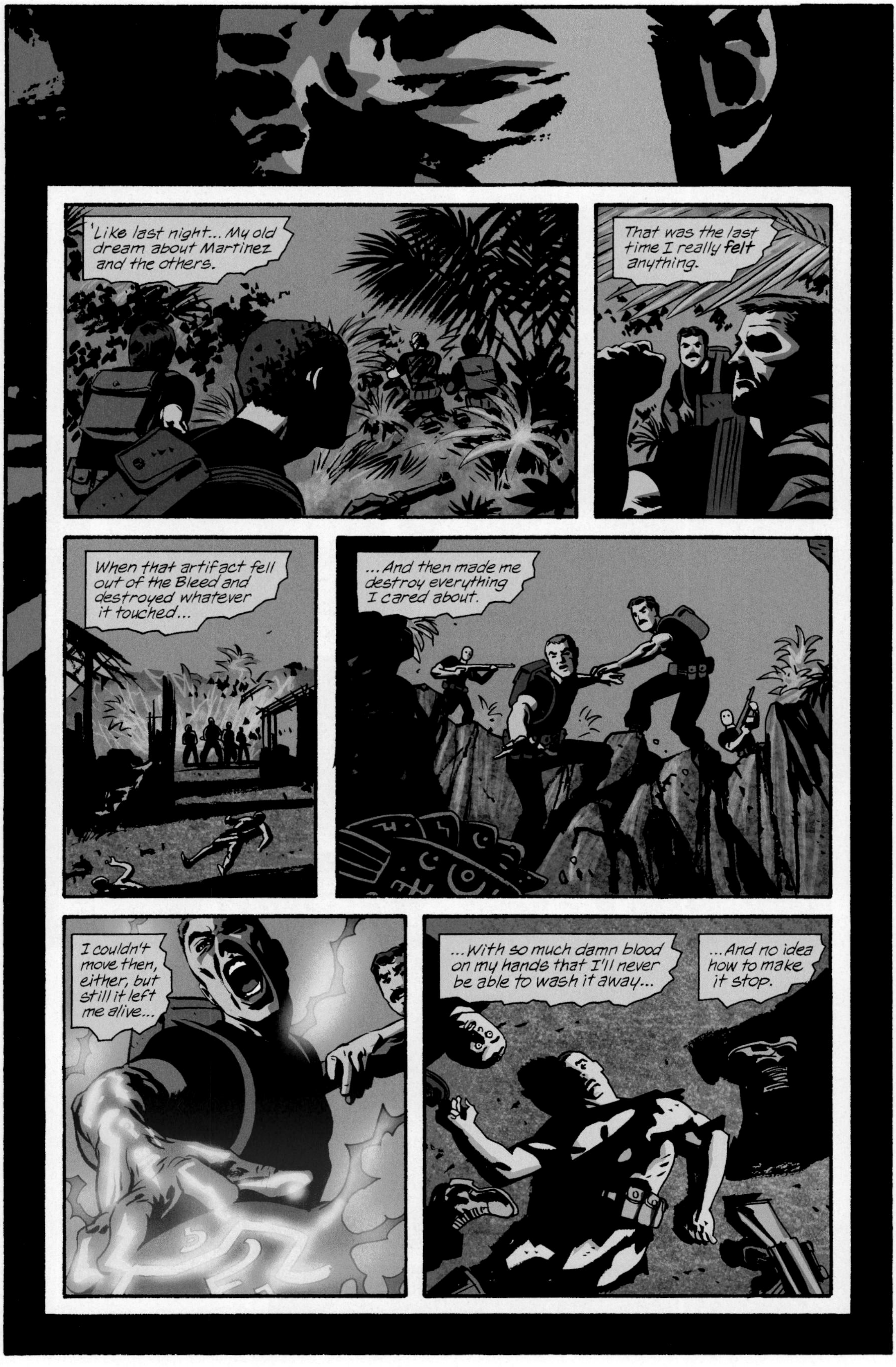
'Like last night... My old dream about Martinez and the others.
That was the last time I really **felt** anything.
When that artifact fell out of the Bleed and destroyed whatever it touched...
...And then made me destroy everything I cared about.
I couldn't move then, either, but still it left me alive...
...With so much damn blood on my hands that I'll never be able to wash it away...
...And no idea how to make it stop.

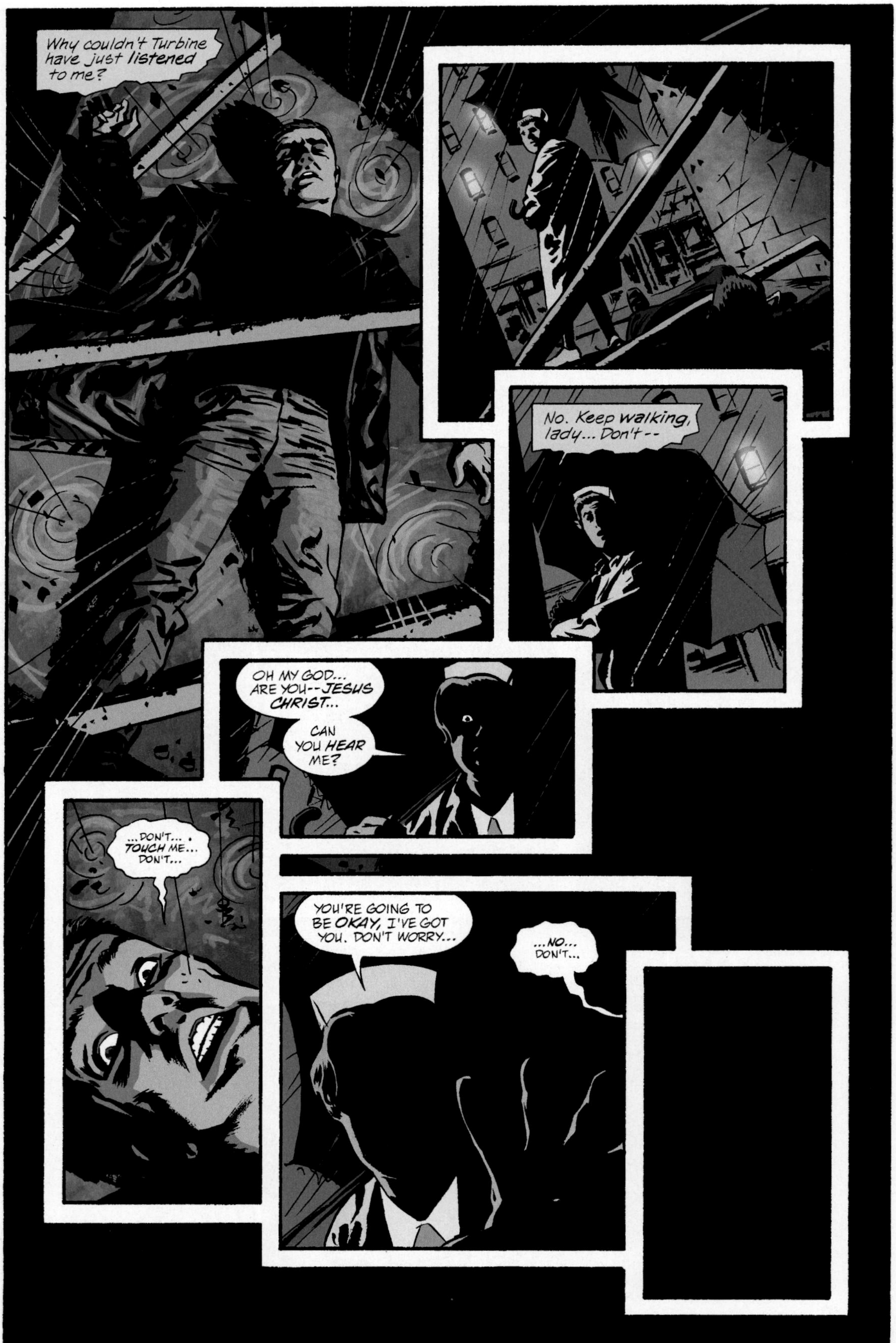

Why couldn't Turbine have just listened to me?
No. Keep walking, lady... Don't--
OH MY GOD... ARE YOU--JESUS CHRIST...
CAN YOU HEAR ME?
...DON'T... TOUCH ME... DON'T...
YOU'RE GOING TO BE OKAY, I'VE GOT YOU. DON'T WORRY...
...NO... DON'T...

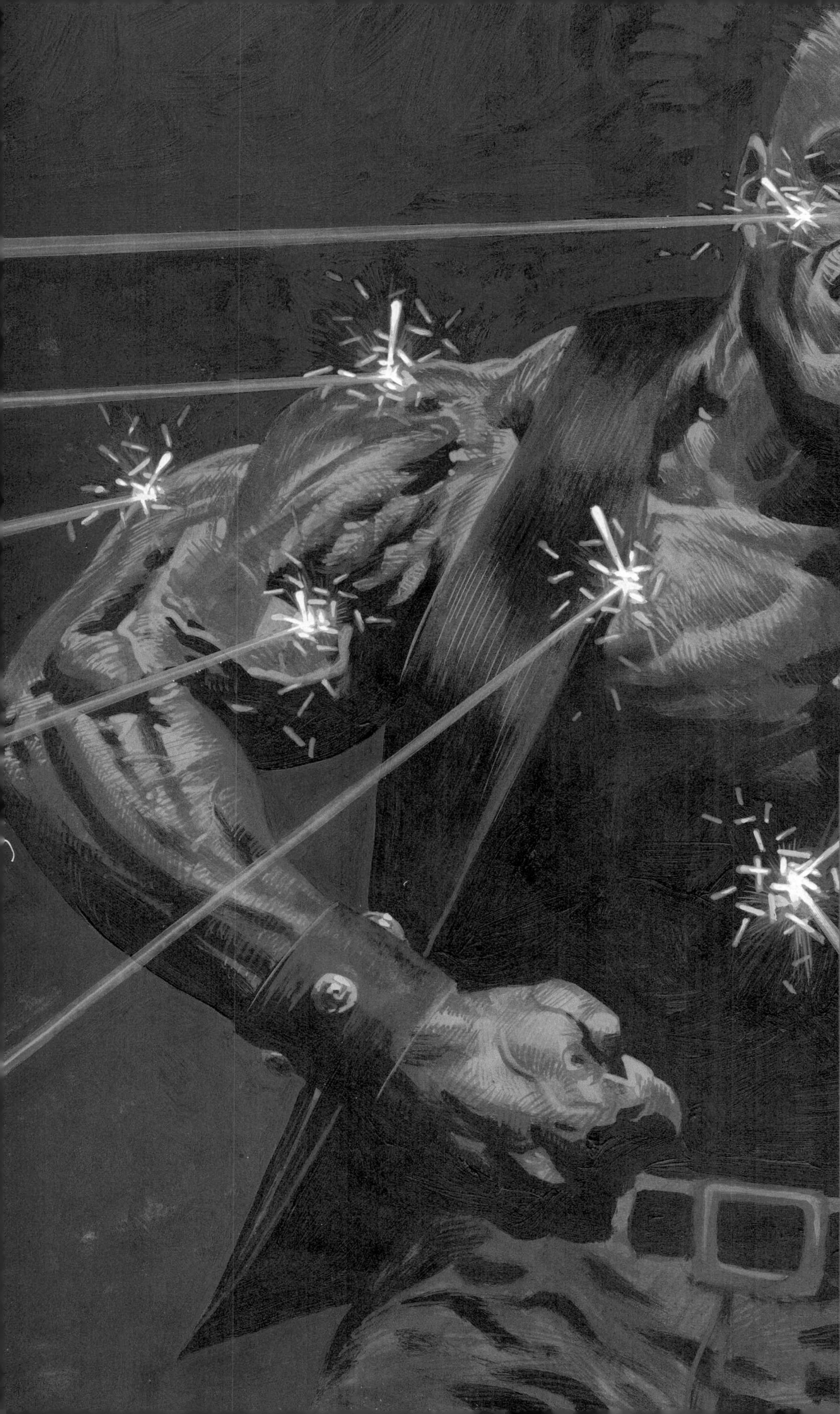

Cover by SEAN PHILLIPS

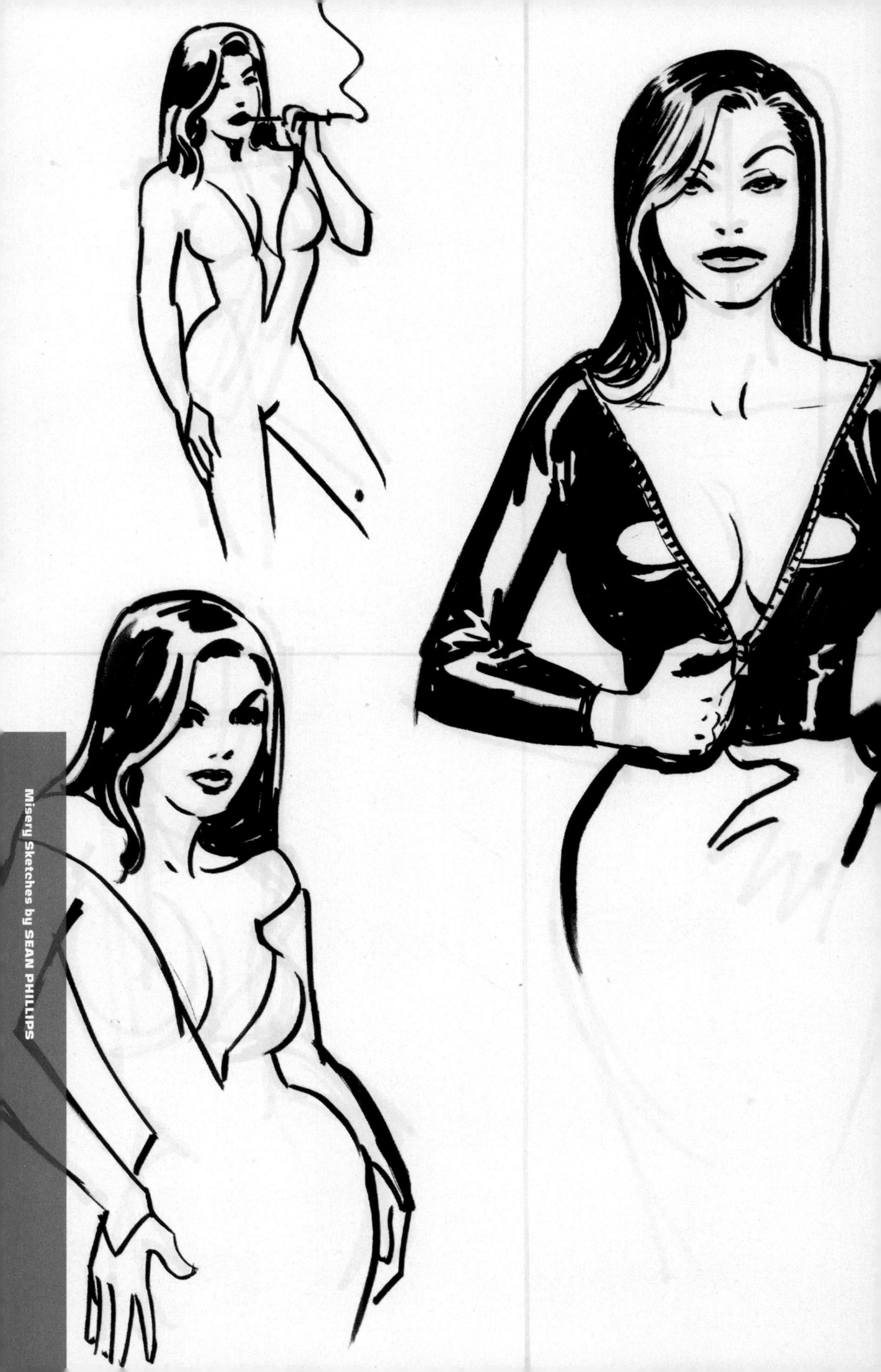

Misery Sketches by SEAN PHILLIPS

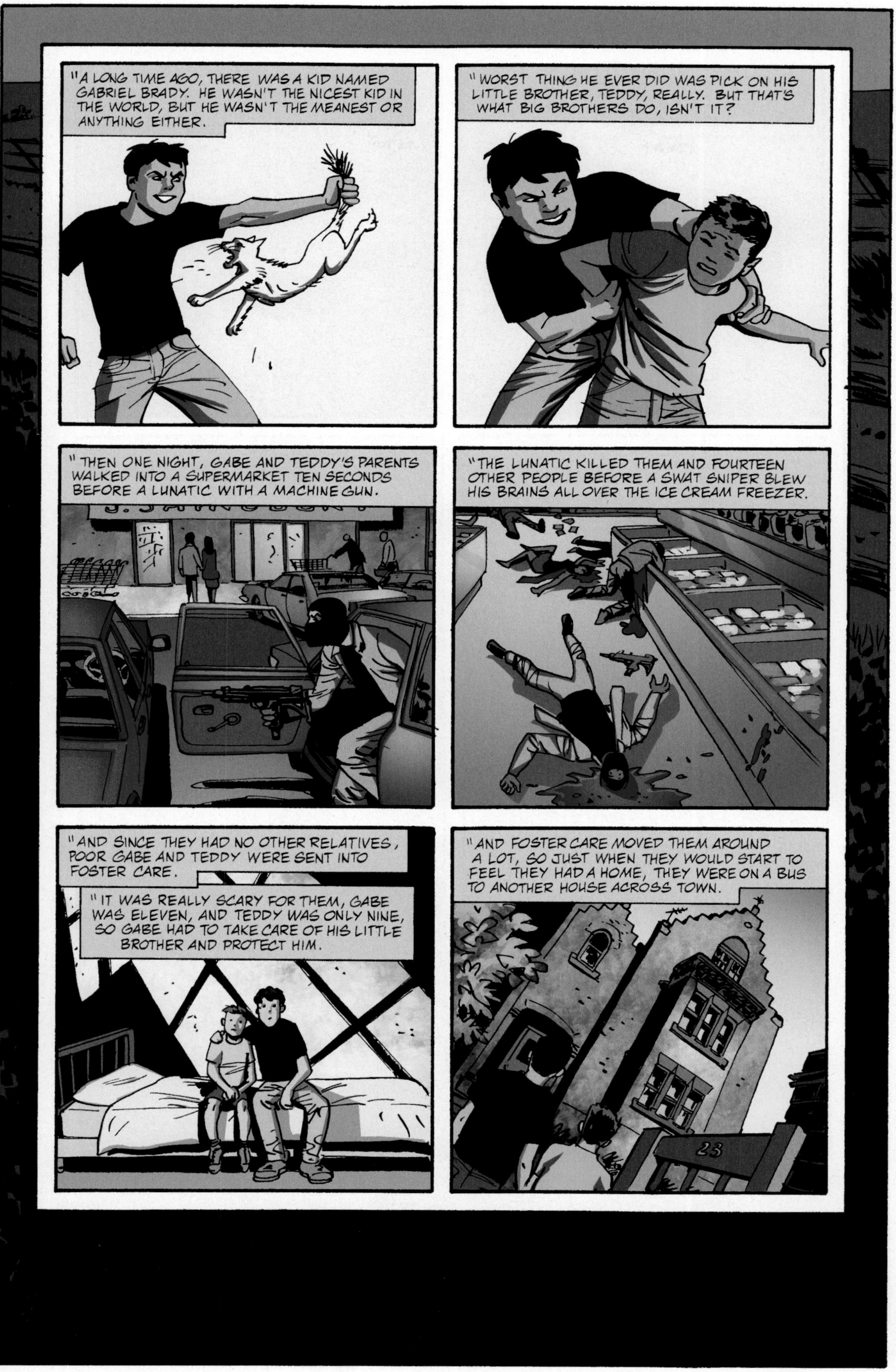
"A LONG TIME AGO, THERE WAS A KID NAMED GABRIEL BRADY. HE WASN'T THE NICEST KID IN THE WORLD, BUT HE WASN'T THE MEANEST OR ANYTHING EITHER.
"WORST THING HE EVER DID WAS PICK ON HIS LITTLE BROTHER, TEDDY, REALLY. BUT THAT'S WHAT BIG BROTHERS DO, ISN'T IT?
"THEN ONE NIGHT, GABE AND TEDDY'S PARENTS WALKED INTO A SUPERMARKET TEN SECONDS BEFORE A LUNATIC WITH A MACHINE GUN.
"THE LUNATIC KILLED THEM AND FOURTEEN OTHER PEOPLE BEFORE A SWAT SNIPER BLEW HIS BRAINS ALL OVER THE ICE CREAM FREEZER.
"AND SINCE THEY HAD NO OTHER RELATIVES, POOR GABE AND TEDDY WERE SENT INTO FOSTER CARE.
"IT WAS REALLY SCARY FOR THEM, GABE WAS ELEVEN, AND TEDDY WAS ONLY NINE, SO GABE HAD TO TAKE CARE OF HIS LITTLE BROTHER AND PROTECT HIM.
"AND FOSTER CARE MOVED THEM AROUND A LOT, SO JUST WHEN THEY WOULD START TO FEEL THEY HAD A HOME, THEY WERE ON A BUS TO ANOTHER HOUSE ACROSS TOWN.
23

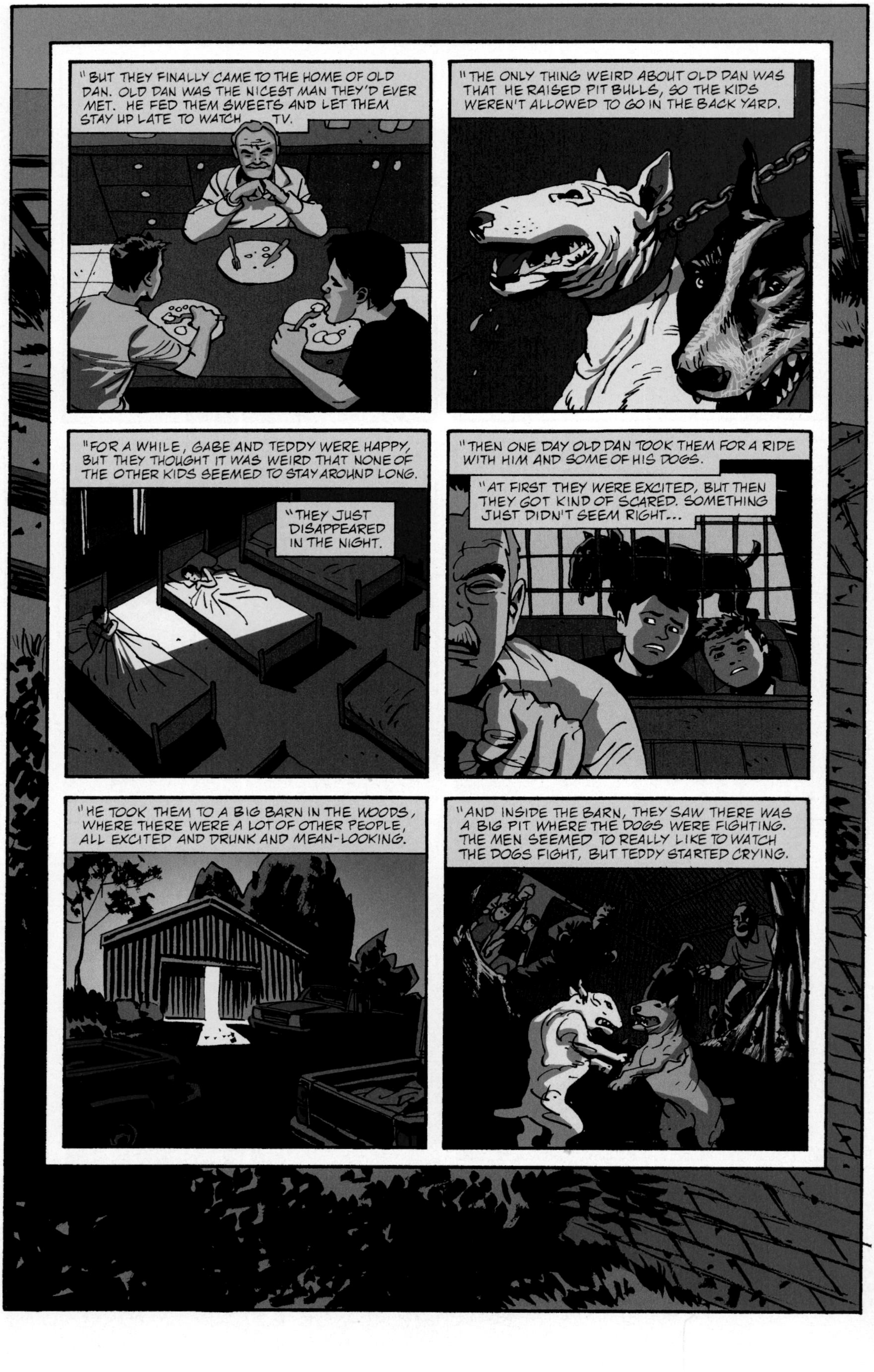
"BUT THEY FINALLY CAME TO THE HOME OF OLD DAN. OLD DAN WAS THE NICEST MAN THEY'D EVER MET. HE FED THEM SWEETS AND LET THEM STAY UP LATE TO WATCH TV.
"THE ONLY THING WEIRD ABOUT OLD DAN WAS THAT HE RAISED PIT BULLS, SO THE KIDS WEREN'T ALLOWED TO GO IN THE BACK YARD.
"FOR A WHILE, GABE AND TEDDY WERE HAPPY, BUT THEY THOUGHT IT WAS WEIRD THAT NONE OF THE OTHER KIDS SEEMED TO STAY AROUND LONG.
"THEY JUST DISAPPEARED IN THE NIGHT.
"THEN ONE DAY OLD DAN TOOK THEM FOR A RIDE WITH HIM AND SOME OF HIS DOGS.
"AT FIRST THEY WERE EXCITED, BUT THEN THEY GOT KIND OF SCARED. SOMETHING JUST DIDN'T SEEM RIGHT...
"HE TOOK THEM TO A BIG BARN IN THE WOODS, WHERE THERE WERE A LOT OF OTHER PEOPLE, ALL EXCITED AND DRUNK AND MEAN-LOOKING.
"AND INSIDE THE BARN, THEY SAW THERE WAS A BIG PIT WHERE THE DOGS WERE FIGHTING. THE MEN SEEMED TO REALLY LIKE TO WATCH THE DOGS FIGHT, BUT TEDDY STARTED CRYING.

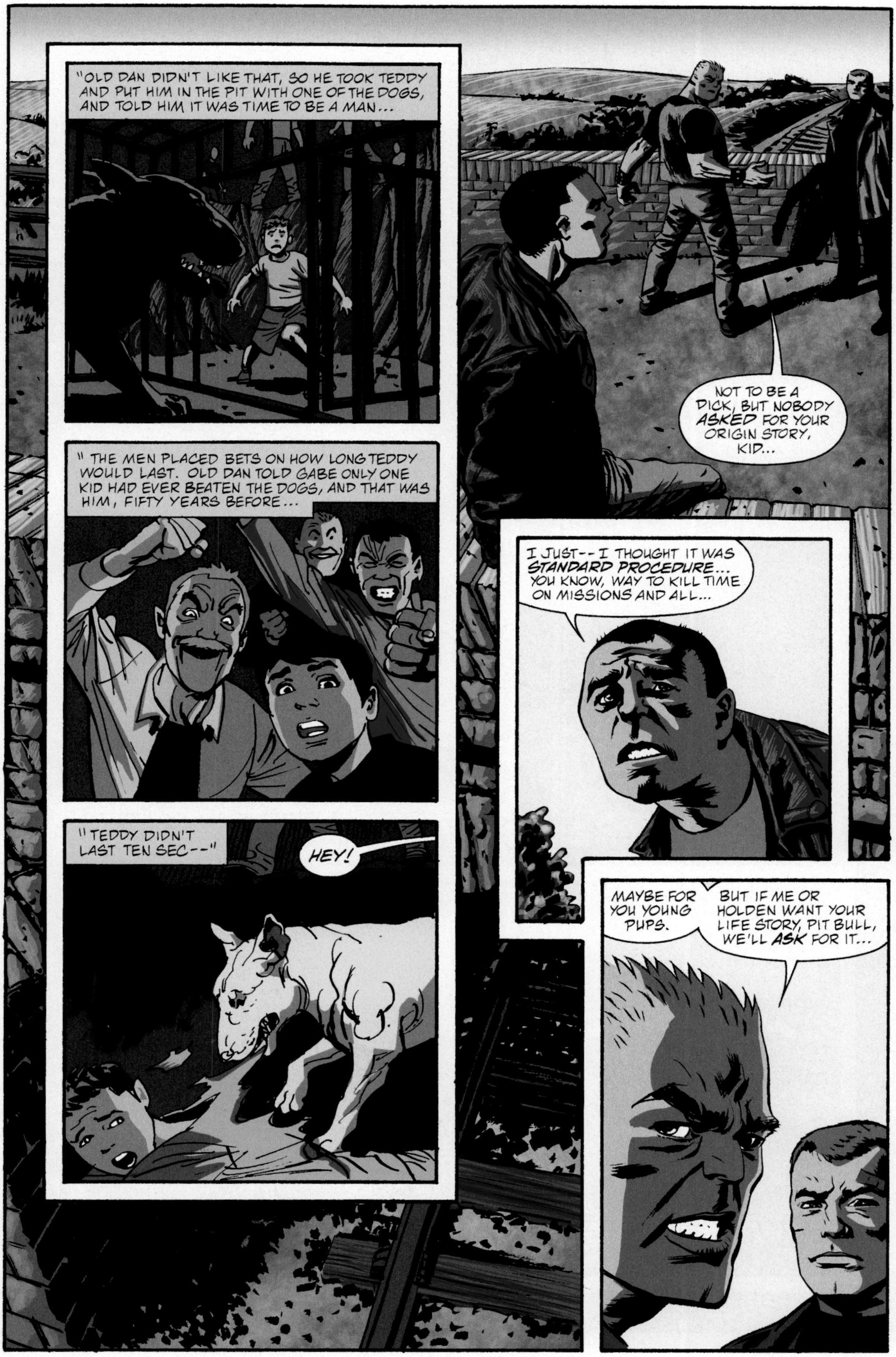
"OLD DAN DIDN'T LIKE THAT, SO HE TOOK TEDDY AND PUT HIM IN THE PIT WITH ONE OF THE DOGS, AND TOLD HIM IT WAS TIME TO BE A MAN...
" THE MEN PLACED BETS ON HOW LONG TEDDY WOULD LAST. OLD DAN TOLD GABE ONLY ONE KID HAD EVER BEATEN THE DOGS, AND THAT WAS HIM, FIFTY YEARS BEFORE...
" TEDDY DIDN'T LAST TEN SEC--"
HEY!
NOT TO BE A DICK, BUT NOBODY ASKED FOR YOUR ORIGIN STORY, KID...
I JUST-- I THOUGHT IT WAS STANDARD PROCEDURE... YOU KNOW, WAY TO KILL TIME ON MISSIONS AND ALL...
MAYBE FOR YOU YOUNG PUPS.
BUT IF ME OR HOLDEN WANT YOUR LIFE STORY, PIT BULL, WE'LL ASK FOR IT...

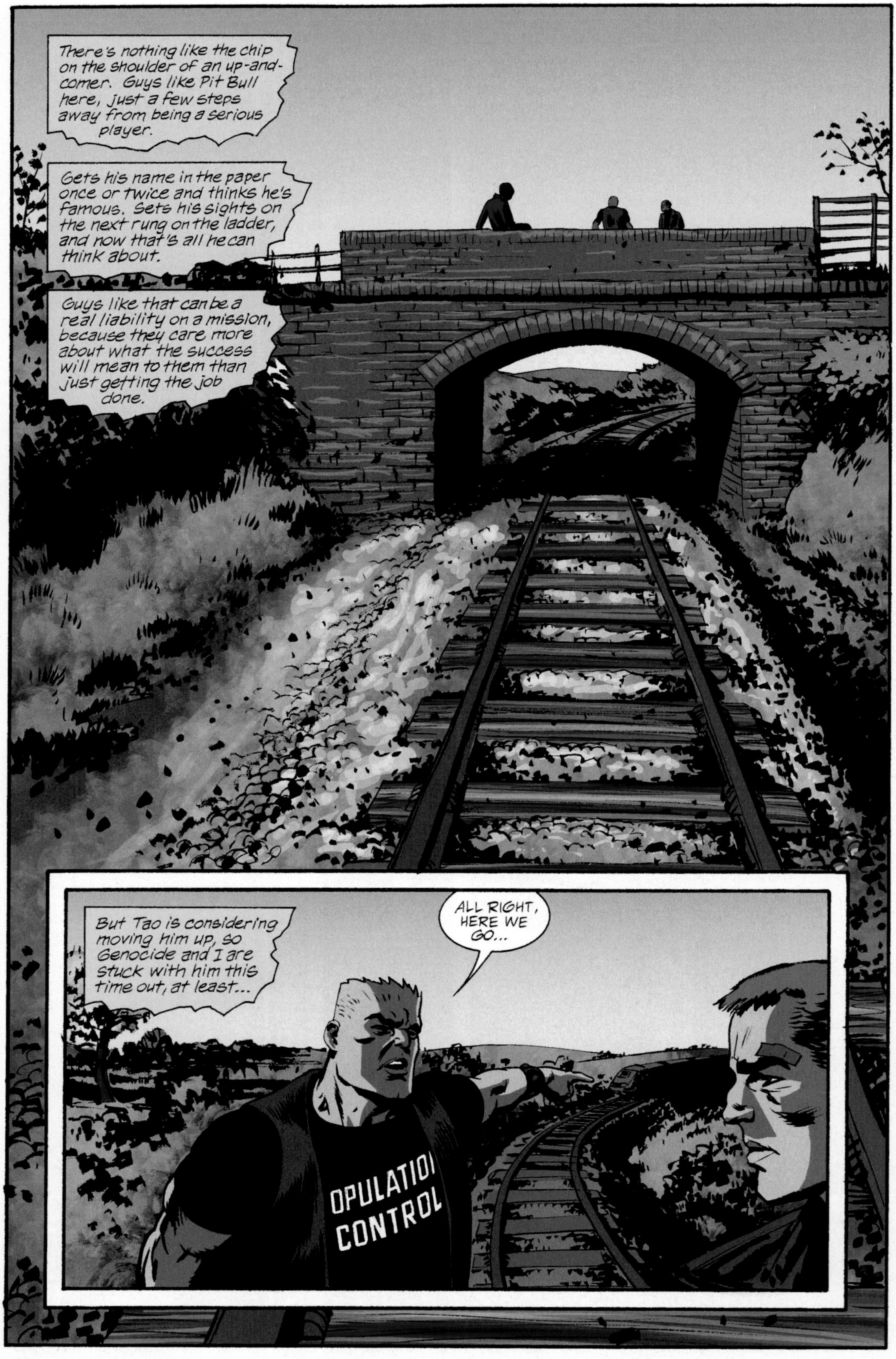
There's nothing like the chip on the shoulder of an up-and-comer. Guys like Pit Bull here, just a few steps away from being a serious player.
Gets his name in the paper once or twice and thinks he's famous. Sets his sights on the next rung on the ladder, and now that's all he can think about.
Guys like that can be a real liability on a mission, because they care more about what the success will mean to them than just getting the job done.
But Tao is considering moving him up, so Genocide and I are stuck with him this time out, at least...
ALL RIGHT, HERE WE GO...
OPULATIO CONTROL

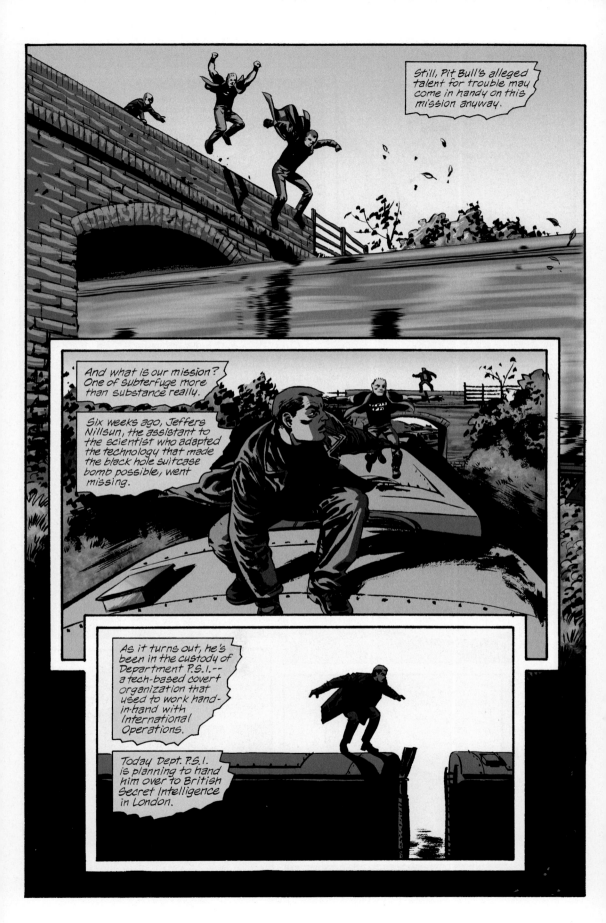

Still, Pit Bull's alleged talent for trouble may come in handy on this mission anyway.

And what is our mission? One of subterfuge more than substance really.

Six weeks ago, Jeffers Nillsun, the assistant to the scientist who adapted the technology that made the black hole suitcase bomb possible, went missing.

As it turns out, he's been in the custody of Department P.S.1.-- a tech-based covert organization that used to work hand-in-hand with International Operations.

Today Dept. P.S.1. is planning to hand him over to British Secret Intelligence in London.

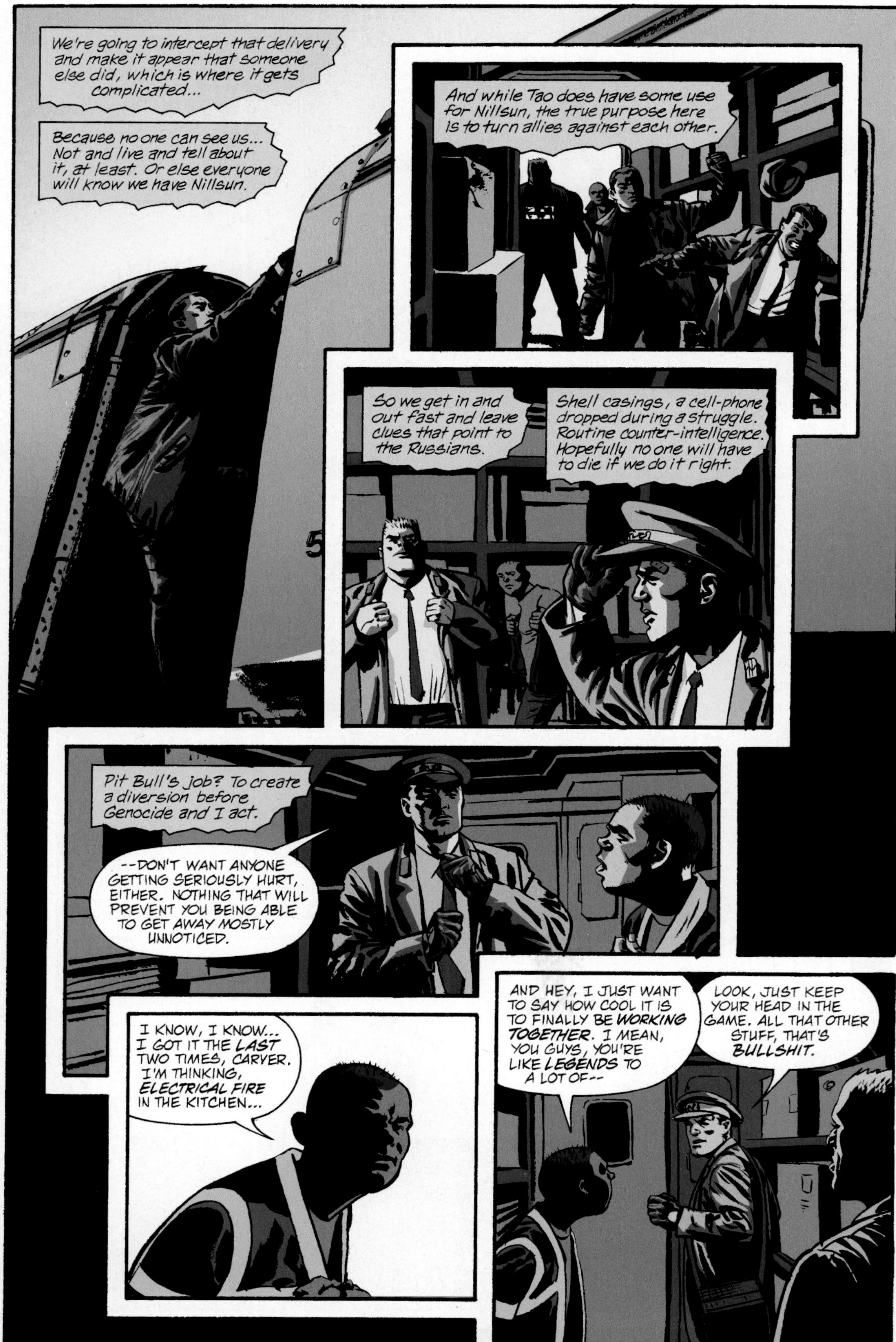
We're going to intercept that delivery and make it appear that someone else did, which is where it gets complicated...
Because no one can see us... Not and live and tell about it, at least. Or else everyone will know we have Nillsun.
And while Tao does have some use for Nillsun, the true purpose here is to turn allies against each other.
So we get in and out fast and leave clues that point to the Russians.
Shell casings, a cell-phone dropped during a struggle. Routine counter-intelligence. Hopefully no one will have to die if we do it right.
Pit Bull's job? To create a diversion before Genocide and I act.
--DON'T WANT ANYONE GETTING SERIOUSLY HURT, EITHER. NOTHING THAT WILL PREVENT YOU BEING ABLE TO GET AWAY MOSTLY UNNOTICED.
I KNOW, I KNOW... I GOT IT THE LAST TWO TIMES, CARVER. I'M THINKING, ELECTRICAL FIRE IN THE KITCHEN...
AND HEY, I JUST WANT TO SAY HOW COOL IT IS TO FINALLY BE WORKING TOGETHER. I MEAN, YOU GUYS, YOU'RE LIKE LEGENDS TO A LOT OF--
LOOK, JUST KEEP YOUR HEAD IN THE GAME. ALL THAT OTHER STUFF, THAT'S BULLSHIT.

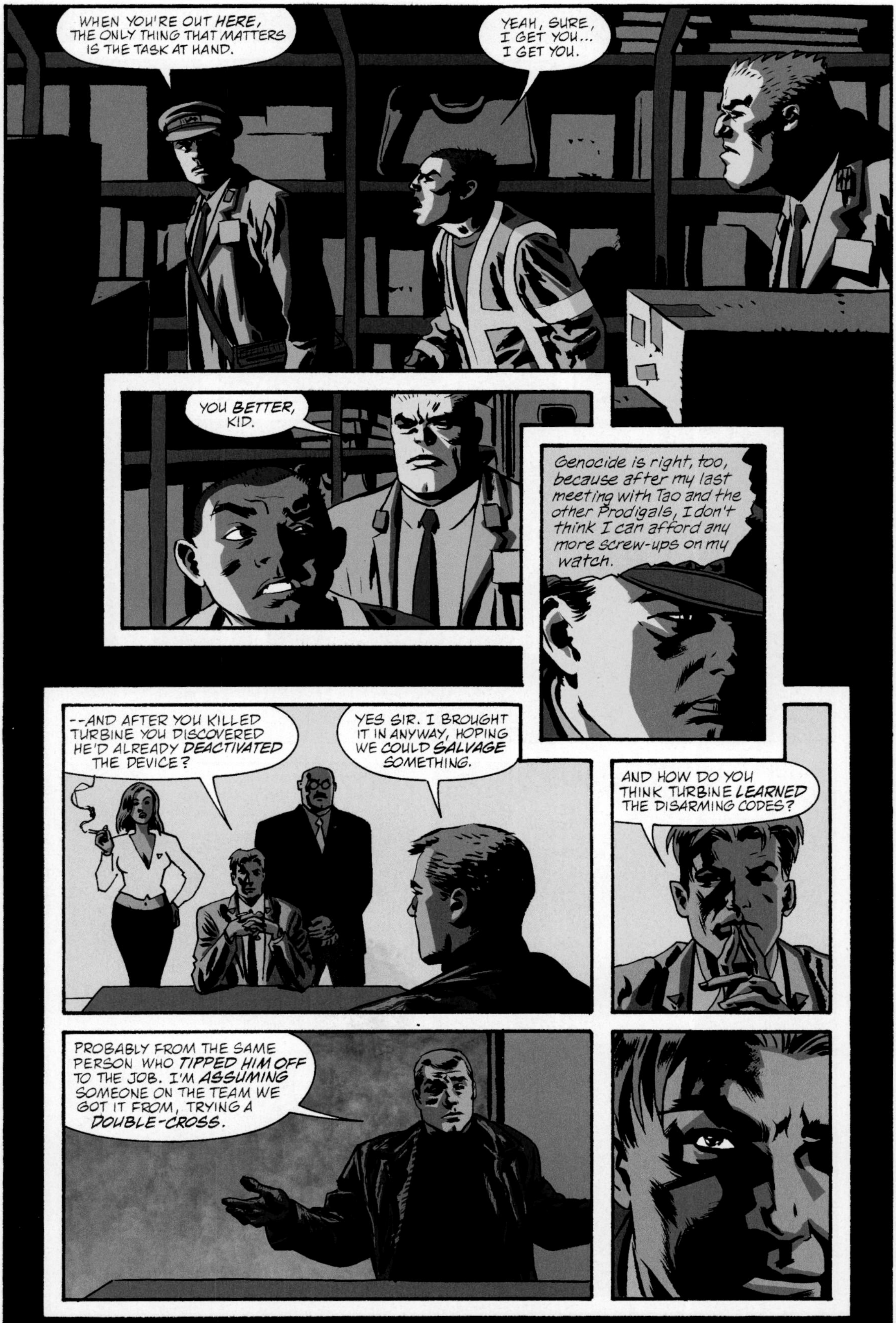
WHEN YOU'RE OUT HERE, THE ONLY THING THAT MATTERS IS THE TASK AT HAND.
YEAH, SURE, I GET YOU... I GET YOU.
YOU BETTER, KID.
Genocide is right, too, because after my last meeting with Tao and the other Prodigals, I don't think I can afford any more screw-ups on my watch.
--AND AFTER YOU KILLED TURBINE YOU DISCOVERED HE'D ALREADY DEACTIVATED THE DEVICE?
YES SIR. I BROUGHT IT IN ANYWAY, HOPING WE COULD SALVAGE SOMETHING.
AND HOW DO YOU THINK TURBINE LEARNED THE DISARMING CODES?
PROBABLY FROM THE SAME PERSON WHO TIPPED HIM OFF TO THE JOB. I'M ASSUMING SOMEONE ON THE TEAM WE GOT IT FROM, TRYING A DOUBLE-CROSS.

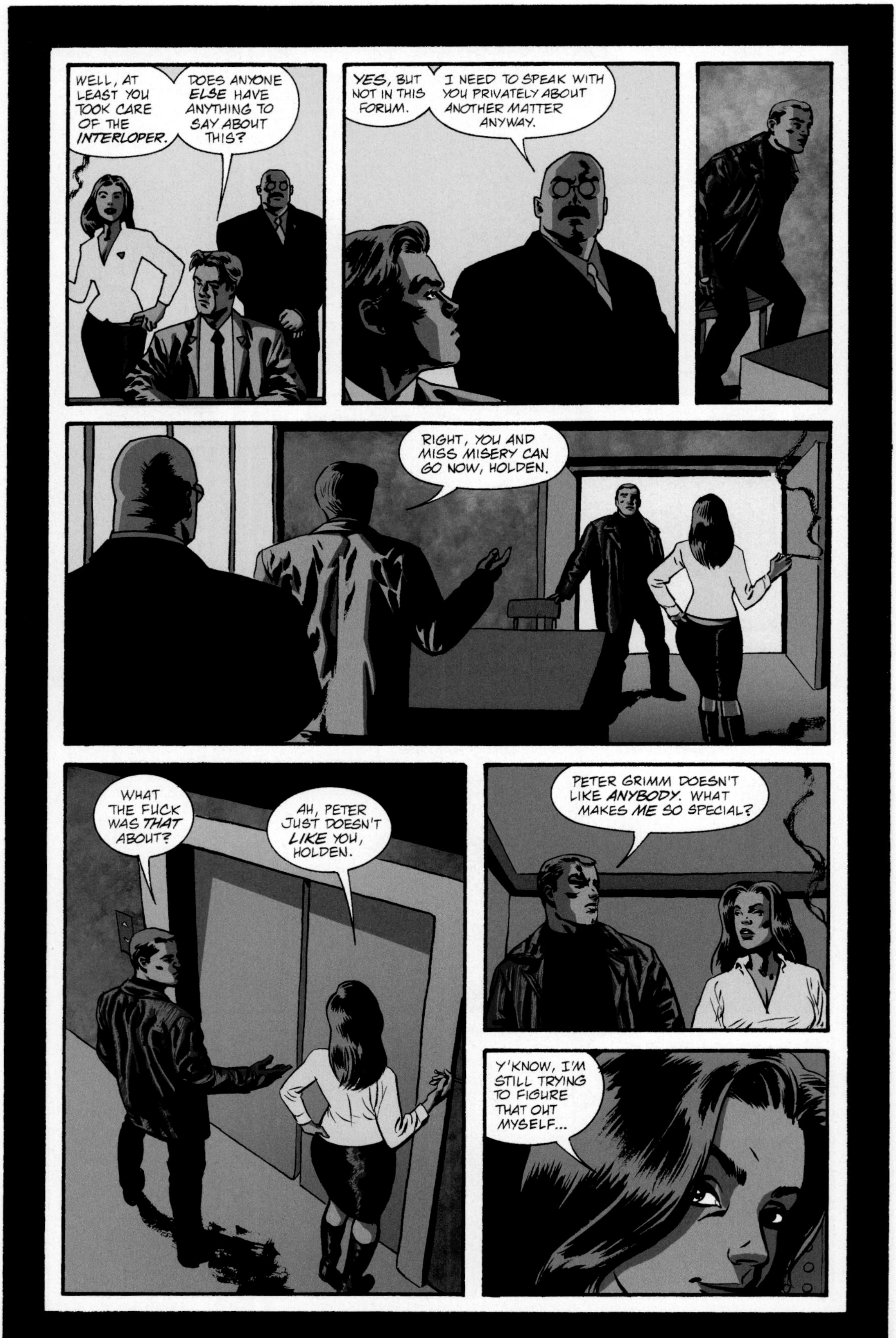
WELL, AT LEAST YOU TOOK CARE OF THE INTERLOPER.
DOES ANYONE ELSE HAVE ANYTHING TO SAY ABOUT THIS?
YES, BUT NOT IN THIS FORUM.
I NEED TO SPEAK WITH YOU PRIVATELY ABOUT ANOTHER MATTER ANYWAY.
RIGHT, YOU AND MISS MISERY CAN GO NOW, HOLDEN.
WHAT THE FUCK WAS THAT ABOUT?
AH, PETER JUST DOESN'T LIKE YOU, HOLDEN.
PETER GRIMM DOESN'T LIKE ANYBODY. WHAT MAKES ME SO SPECIAL?
Y'KNOW, I'M STILL TRYING TO FIGURE THAT OUT MYSELF...

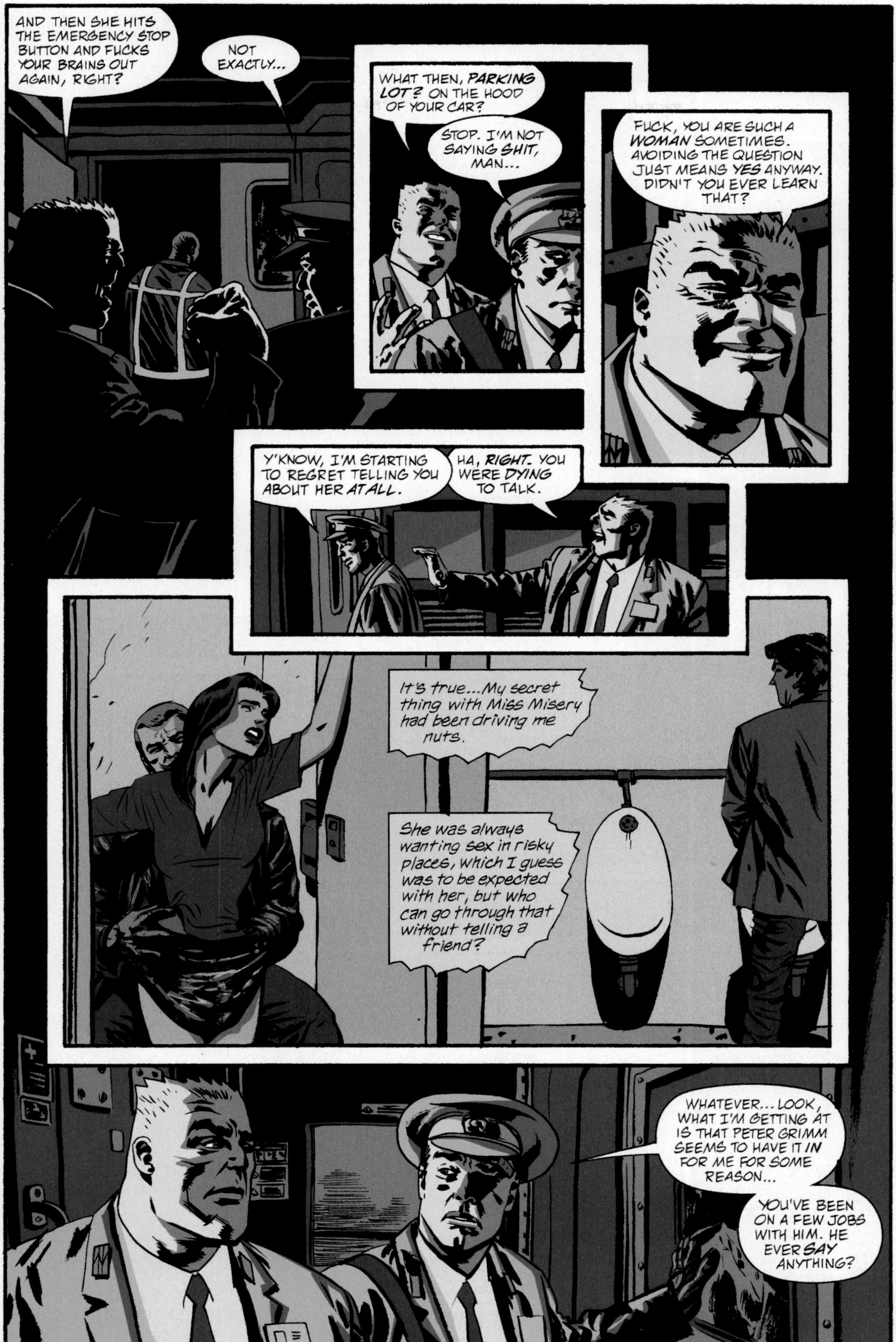
AND THEN SHE HITS THE EMERGENCY STOP BUTTON AND FUCKS YOUR BRAINS OUT AGAIN, RIGHT?
NOT EXACTLY...
WHAT THEN, PARKING LOT? ON THE HOOD OF YOUR CAR?
STOP. I'M NOT SAYING SHIT, MAN...
FUCK, YOU ARE SUCH A WOMAN SOMETIMES. AVOIDING THE QUESTION JUST MEANS YES ANYWAY. DIDN'T YOU EVER LEARN THAT?
Y'KNOW, I'M STARTING TO REGRET TELLING YOU ABOUT HER AT ALL.
HA, RIGHT. YOU WERE DYING TO TALK.
It's true...My secret thing with Miss Misery had been driving me nuts.
She was always wanting sex in risky places, which I guess was to be expected with her, but who can go through that without telling a friend?
WHATEVER... LOOK, WHAT I'M GETTING AT IS THAT PETER GRIMM SEEMS TO HAVE IT IN FOR ME FOR SOME REASON...
YOU'VE BEEN ON A FEW JOBS WITH HIM. HE EVER SAY ANYTHING?

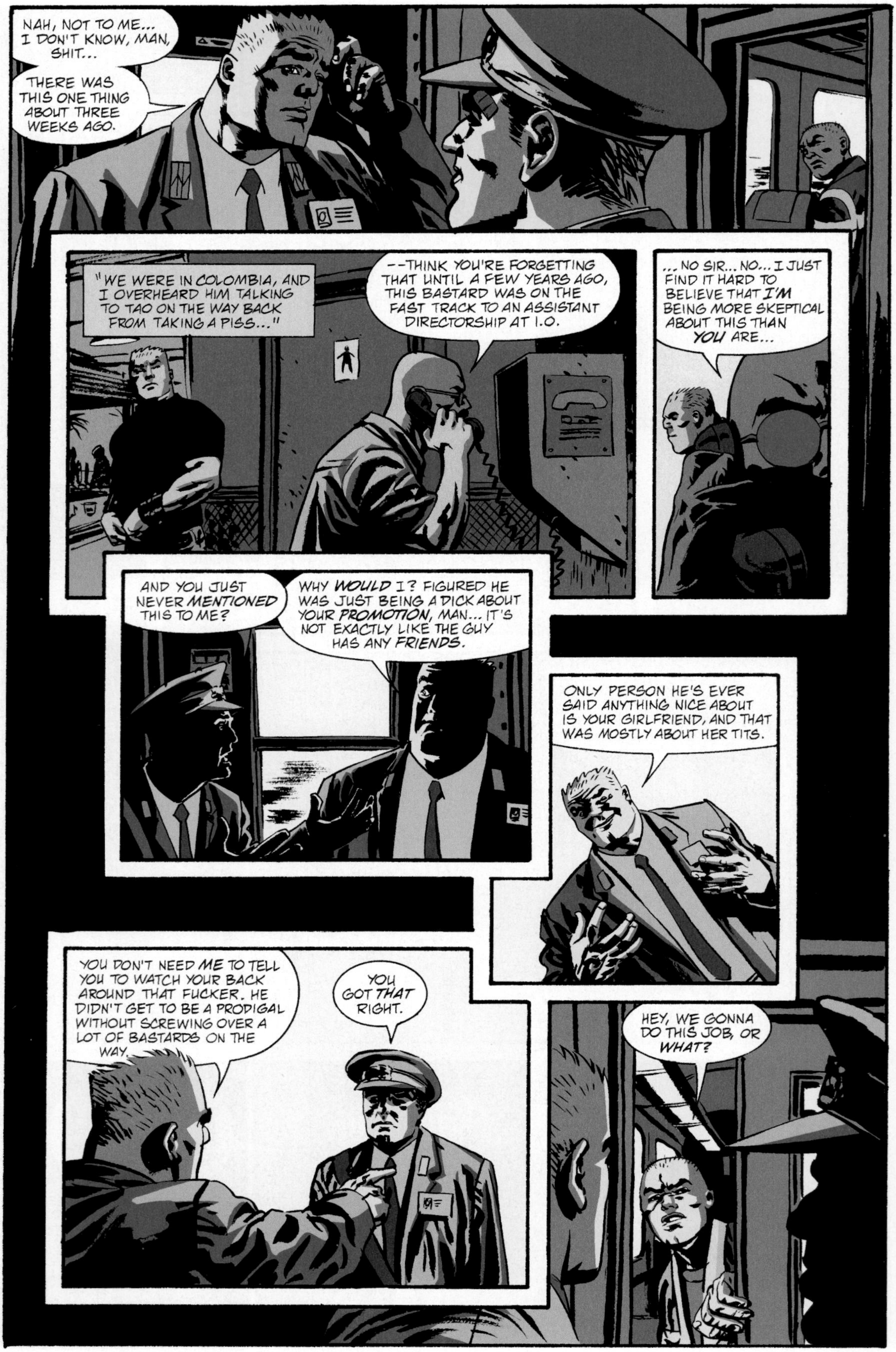
NAH, NOT TO ME... I DON'T KNOW, MAN, SHIT...
THERE WAS THIS ONE THING ABOUT THREE WEEKS AGO.
"WE WERE IN COLOMBIA, AND I OVERHEARD HIM TALKING TO TAO ON THE WAY BACK FROM TAKING A PISS..."
--THINK YOU'RE FORGETTING THAT UNTIL A FEW YEARS AGO, THIS BASTARD WAS ON THE FAST TRACK TO AN ASSISTANT DIRECTORSHIP AT I.O.
...NO SIR... NO... I JUST FIND IT HARD TO BELIEVE THAT I'M BEING MORE SKEPTICAL ABOUT THIS THAN YOU ARE...
AND YOU JUST NEVER MENTIONED THIS TO ME?
WHY WOULD I? FIGURED HE WAS JUST BEING A DICK ABOUT YOUR PROMOTION, MAN... IT'S NOT EXACTLY LIKE THE GUY HAS ANY FRIENDS.
ONLY PERSON HE'S EVER SAID ANYTHING NICE ABOUT IS YOUR GIRLFRIEND, AND THAT WAS MOSTLY ABOUT HER TITS.
YOU DON'T NEED ME TO TELL YOU TO WATCH YOUR BACK AROUND THAT FUCKER. HE DIDN'T GET TO BE A PRODIGAL WITHOUT SCREWING OVER A LOT OF BASTARDS ON THE WAY.
YOU GOT THAT RIGHT.
HEY, WE GONNA DO THIS JOB, OR WHAT?

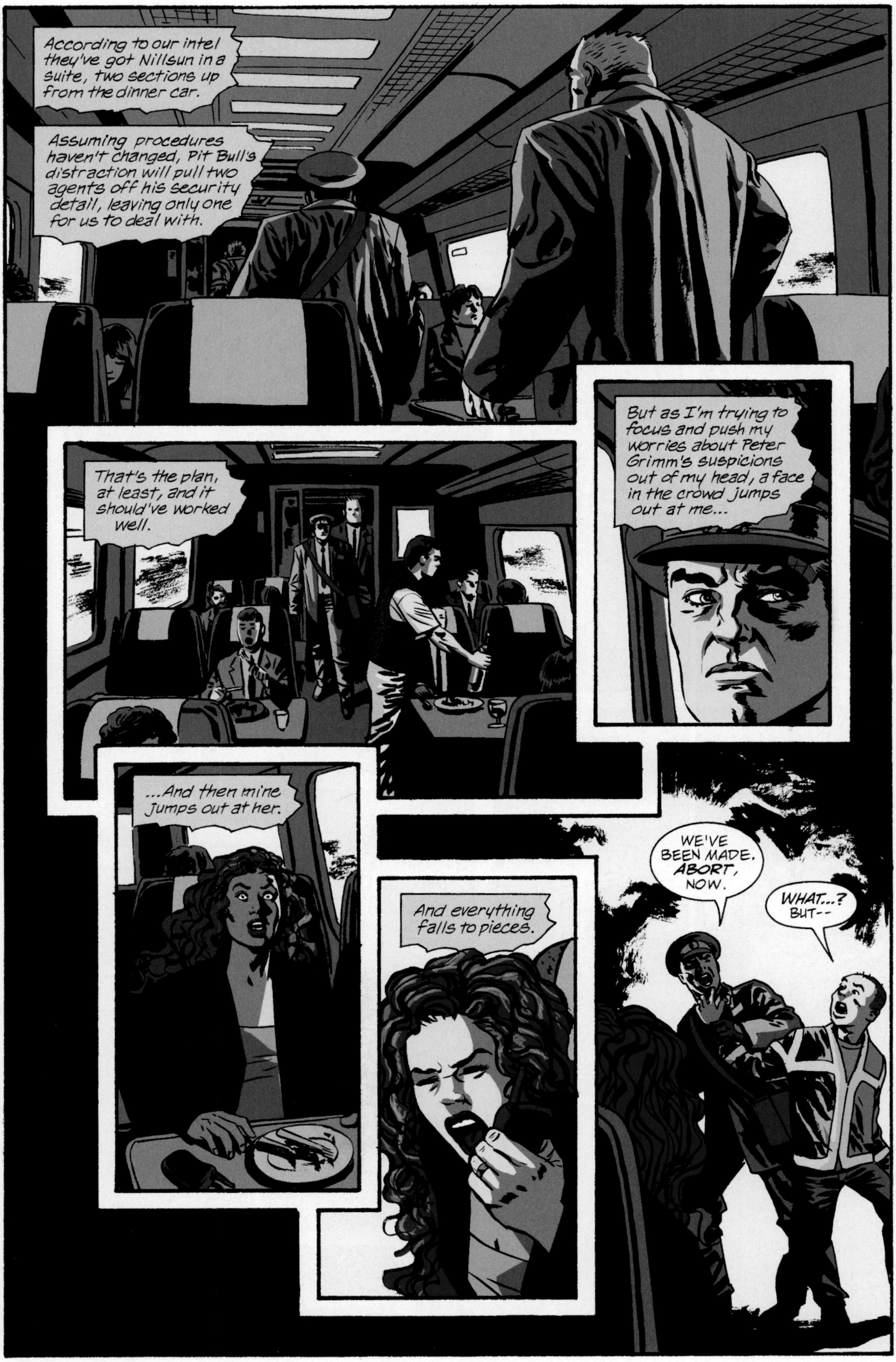
According to our intel they've got Nillsun in a suite, two sections up from the dinner car.
Assuming procedures haven't changed, Pit Bull's distraction will pull two agents off his security detail, leaving only one for us to deal with.
That's the plan, at least, and it should've worked well.
But as I'm trying to focus and push my worries about Peter Grimm's suspicions out of my head, a face in the crowd jumps out at me...
...And then mine jumps out at her.
And everything falls to pieces.
WE'VE BEEN MADE. ABORT, NOW.
WHAT...? BUT--

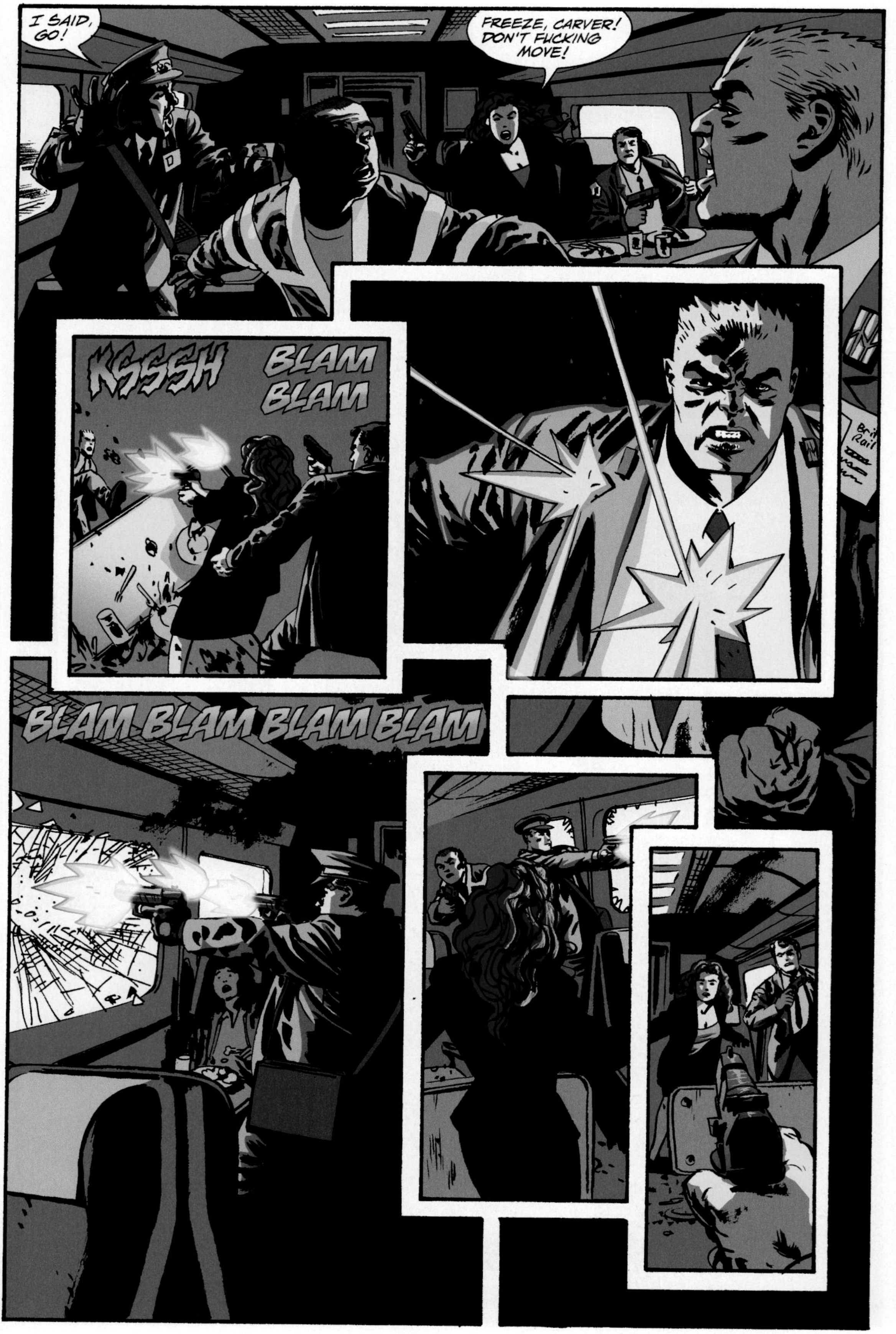
I SAID, GO!
FREEZE, CARVER! DON'T FUCKING MOVE!
KSSSH
BLAM BLAM
BLAM BLAM BLAM BLAM

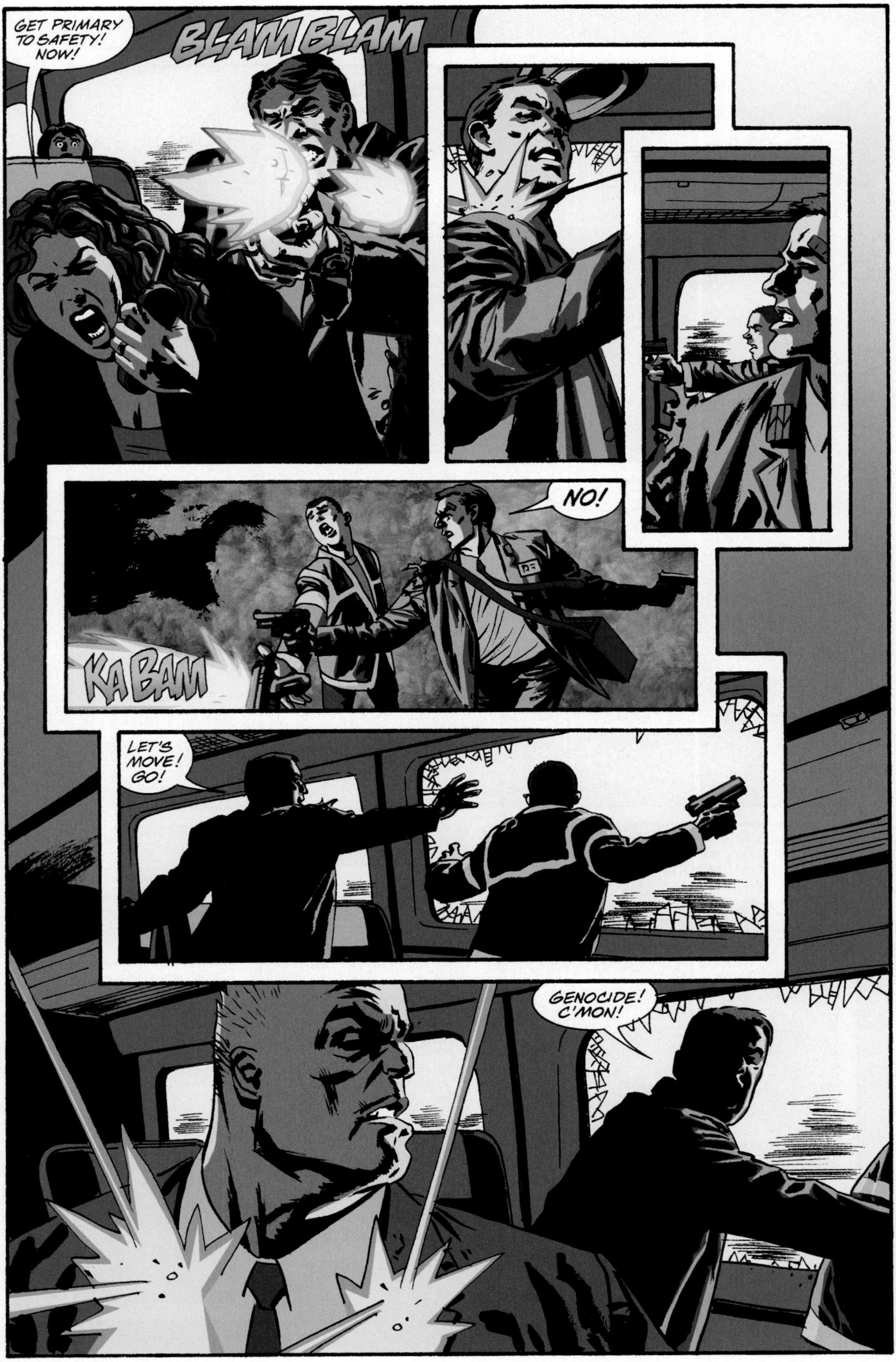
GET PRIMARY TO SAFETY! NOW!
BLAM BLAM
NO!
KA BAM
LET'S MOVE! GO!
GENOCIDE! C'MON!

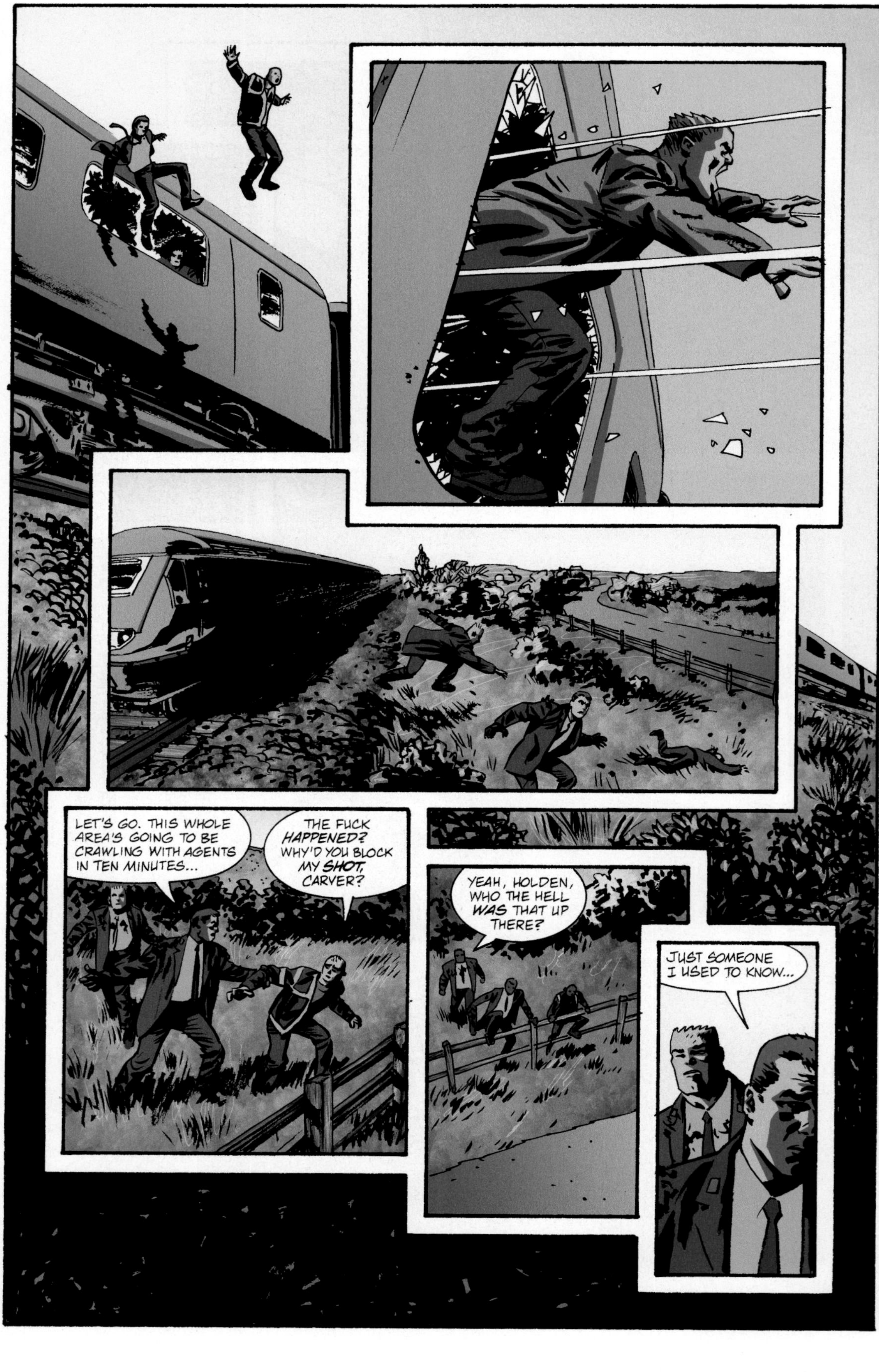
LET'S GO. THIS WHOLE AREA'S GOING TO BE CRAWLING WITH AGENTS IN TEN MINUTES...
THE FUCK HAPPENED? WHY'D YOU BLOCK MY SHOT, CARVER?
YEAH, HOLDEN, WHO THE HELL WAS THAT UP THERE?
JUST SOMEONE I USED TO KNOW...

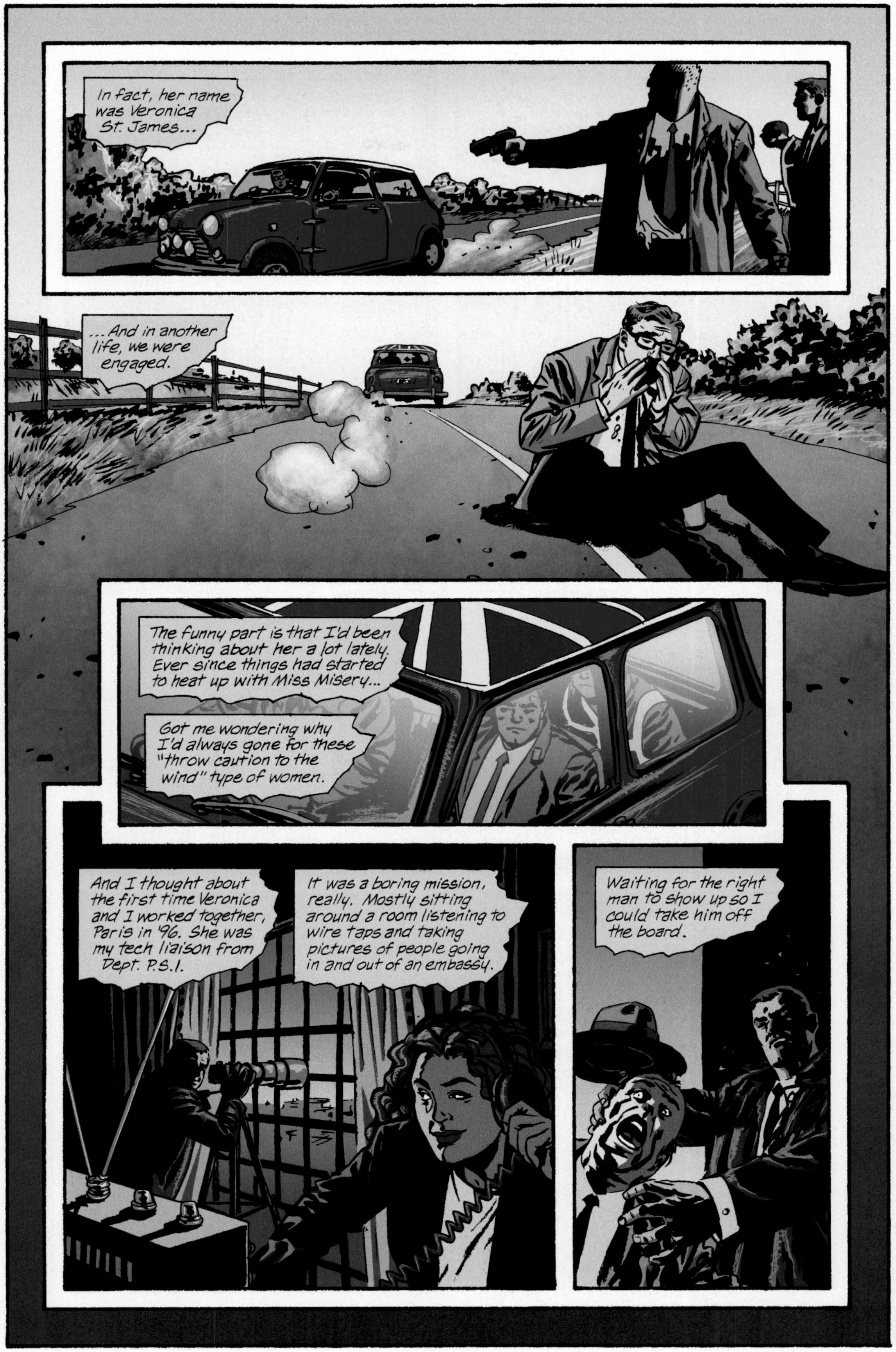
In fact, her name was Veronica St. James...
...And in another life, we were engaged.
The funny part is that I'd been thinking about her a lot lately. Ever since things had started to heat up with Miss Misery...
Got me wondering why I'd always gone for these "throw caution to the wind" type of women.
And I thought about the first time Veronica and I worked together, Paris in '96. She was my tech liaison from Dept. P.S.I.
It was a boring mission, really. Mostly sitting around a room listening to wire taps and taking pictures of people going in and out of an embassy.
Waiting for the right man to show up so I could take him off the board.

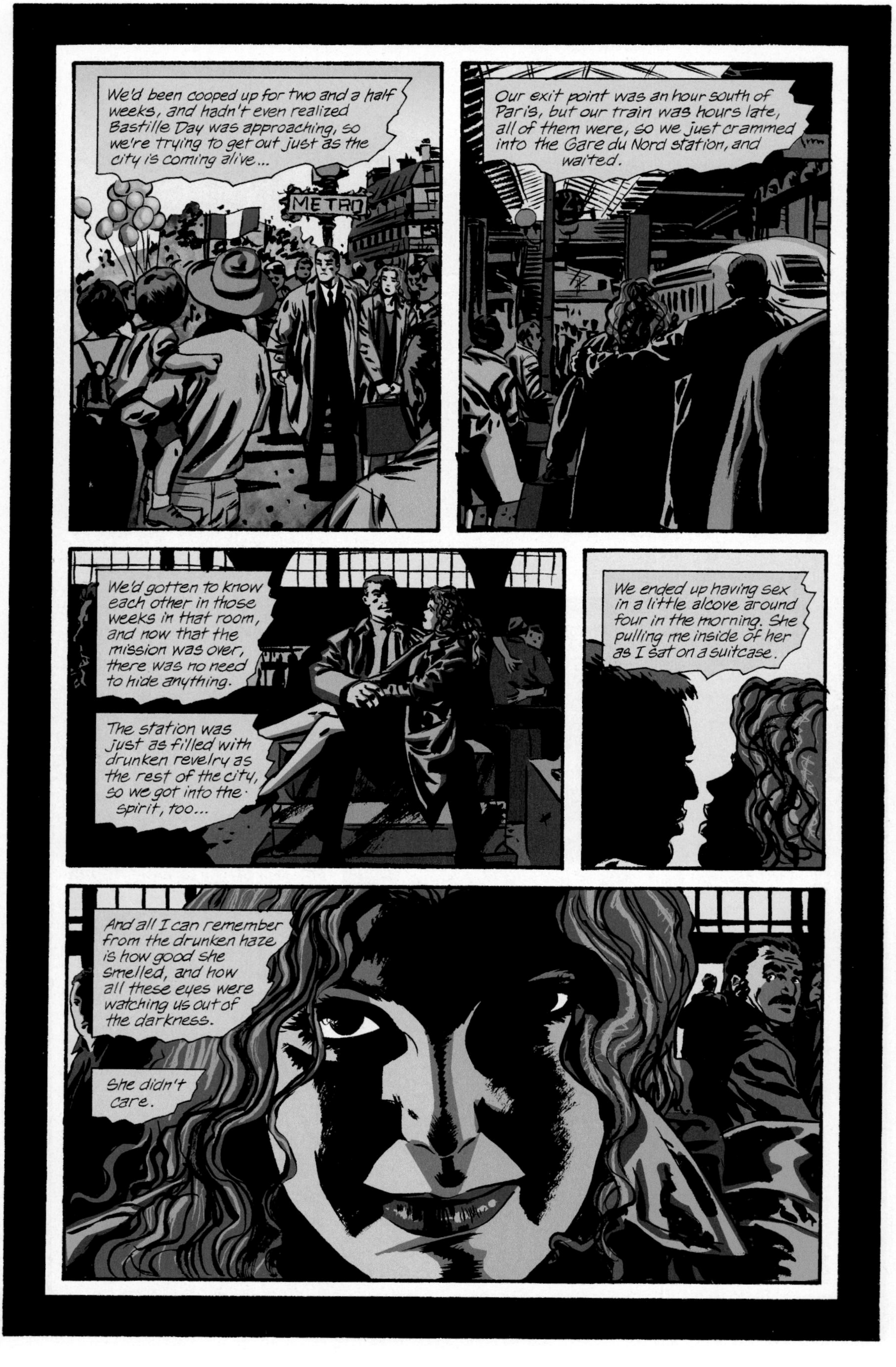
We'd been cooped up for two and a half weeks, and hadn't even realized Bastille Day was approaching, so we're trying to get out just as the city is coming alive...
METRO
Our exit point was an hour south of Paris, but our train was hours late, all of them were, so we just crammed into the Gare du Nord station, and waited.
We'd gotten to know each other in those weeks in that room, and now that the mission was over, there was no need to hide anything.
The station was just as filled with drunken revelry as the rest of the city, so we got into the spirit, too...
We ended up having sex in a little alcove around four in the morning. She pulling me inside of her as I sat on a suitcase.
And all I can remember from the drunken haze is how good she smelled, and how all these eyes were watching us out of the darkness.
She didn't care.

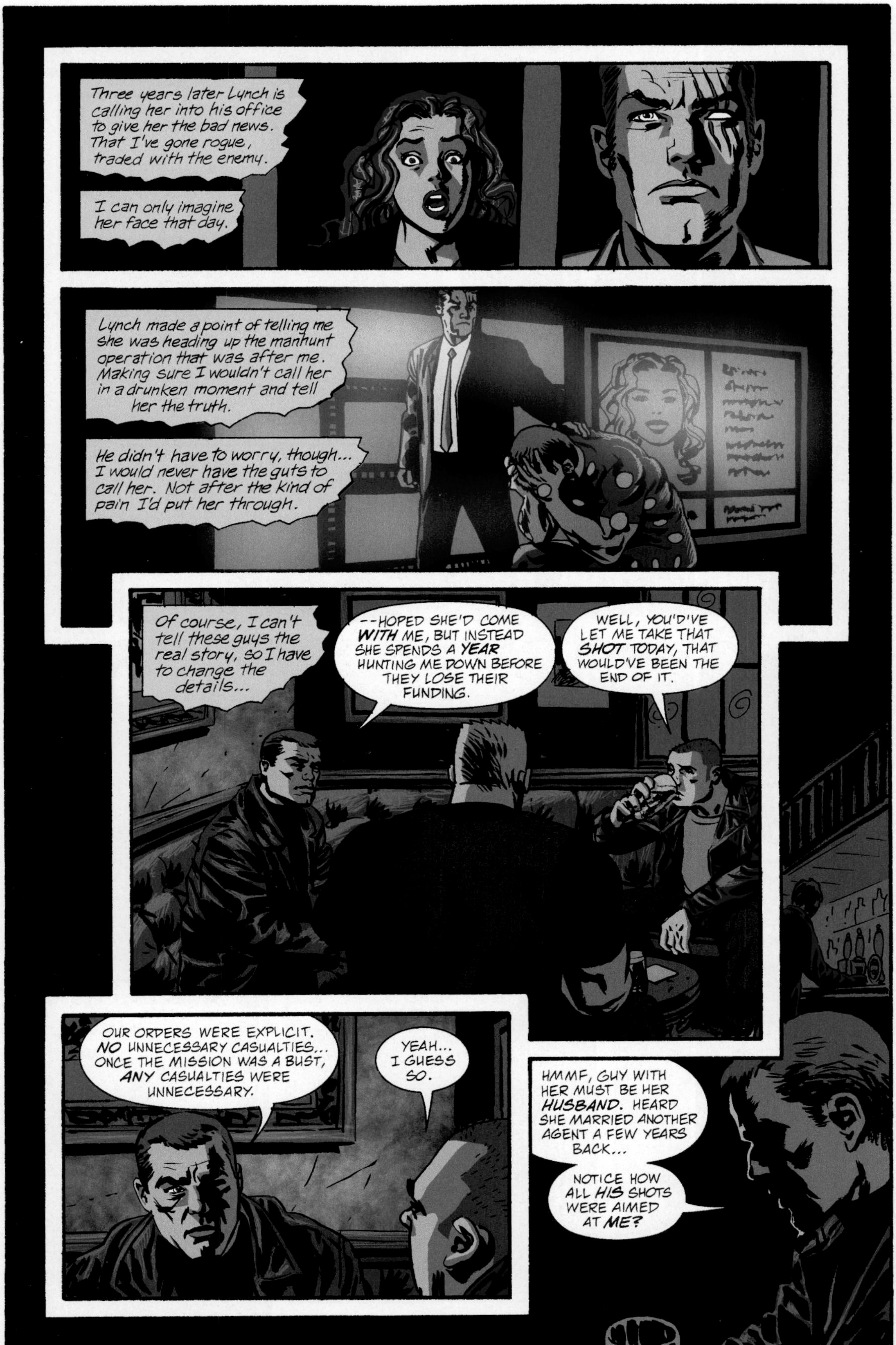

Three years later Lynch is calling her into his office to give her the bad news. That I've gone rogue, traded with the enemy.
I can only imagine her face that day.
Lynch made a point of telling me she was heading up the manhunt operation that was after me. Making sure I wouldn't call her in a drunken moment and tell her the truth.
He didn't have to worry, though... I would never have the guts to call her. Not after the kind of pain I'd put her through.
Of course, I can't tell these guys the real story, so I have to change the details...
--HOPED SHE'D COME WITH ME, BUT INSTEAD SHE SPENDS A YEAR HUNTING ME DOWN BEFORE THEY LOSE THEIR FUNDING.
WELL, YOU'D'VE LET ME TAKE THAT SHOT TODAY, THAT WOULD'VE BEEN THE END OF IT.
OUR ORDERS WERE EXPLICIT. NO UNNECESSARY CASUALTIES... ONCE THE MISSION WAS A BUST, ANY CASUALTIES WERE UNNECESSARY.
YEAH... I GUESS SO.
HMMF, GUY WITH HER MUST BE HER HUSBAND. HEARD SHE MARRIED ANOTHER AGENT A FEW YEARS BACK...
NOTICE HOW ALL HIS SHOTS WERE AIMED AT ME?

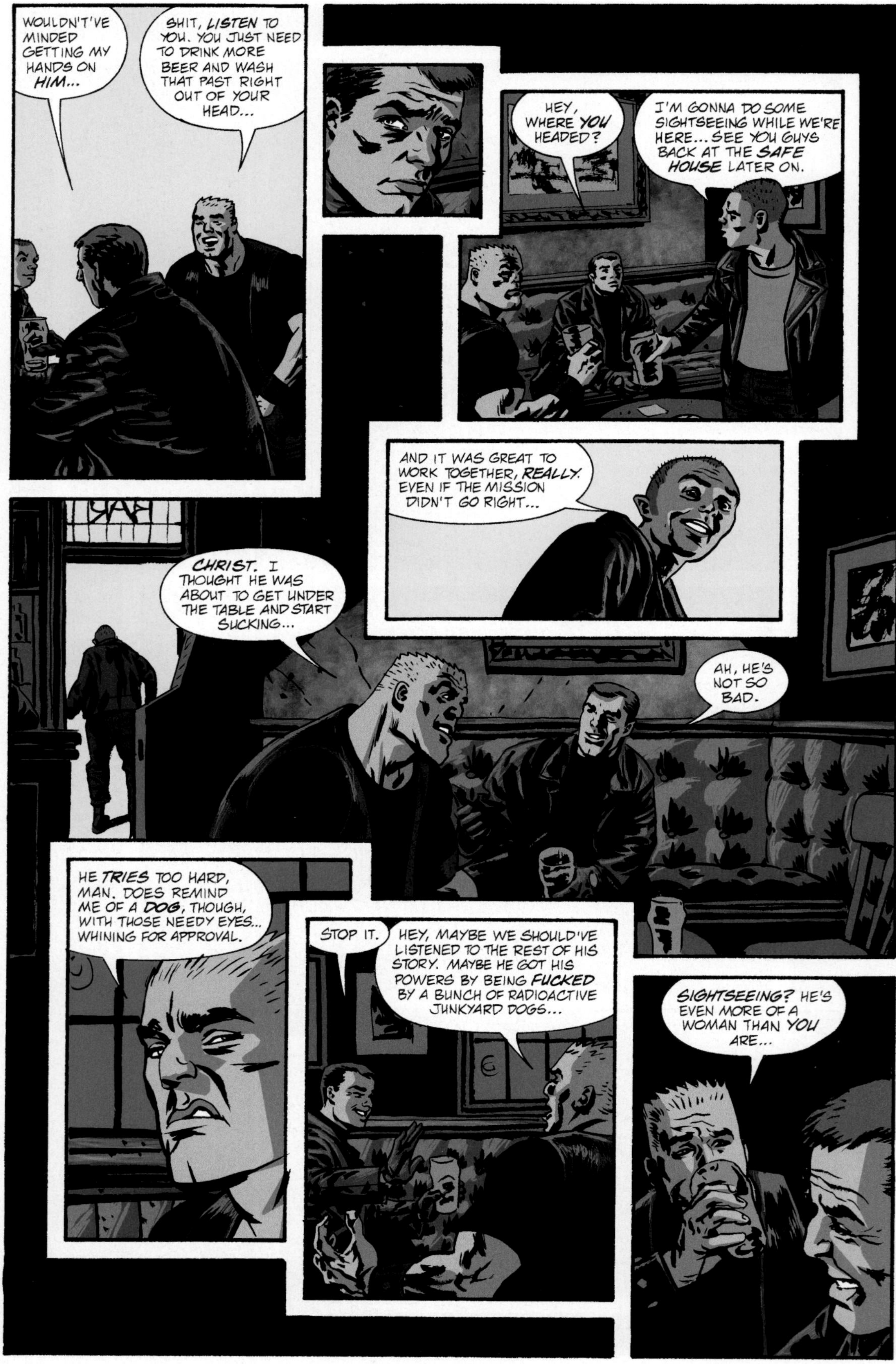
WOULDN'T'VE MINDED GETTING MY HANDS ON HIM...
SHIT, LISTEN TO YOU. YOU JUST NEED TO DRINK MORE BEER AND WASH THAT PAST RIGHT OUT OF YOUR HEAD...
HEY, WHERE YOU HEADED?
I'M GONNA DO SOME SIGHTSEEING WHILE WE'RE HERE... SEE YOU GUYS BACK AT THE SAFE HOUSE LATER ON.
AND IT WAS GREAT TO WORK TOGETHER, REALLY. EVEN IF THE MISSION DIDN'T GO RIGHT...
CHRIST. I THOUGHT HE WAS ABOUT TO GET UNDER THE TABLE AND START SUCKING...
AH, HE'S NOT SO BAD.
HE TRIES TOO HARD, MAN. DOES REMIND ME OF A DOG, THOUGH, WITH THOSE NEEDY EYES... WHINING FOR APPROVAL.
STOP IT.
HEY, MAYBE WE SHOULD'VE LISTENED TO THE REST OF HIS STORY. MAYBE HE GOT HIS POWERS BY BEING FUCKED BY A BUNCH OF RADIOACTIVE JUNKYARD DOGS...
SIGHTSEEING? HE'S EVEN MORE OF A WOMAN THAN YOU ARE...

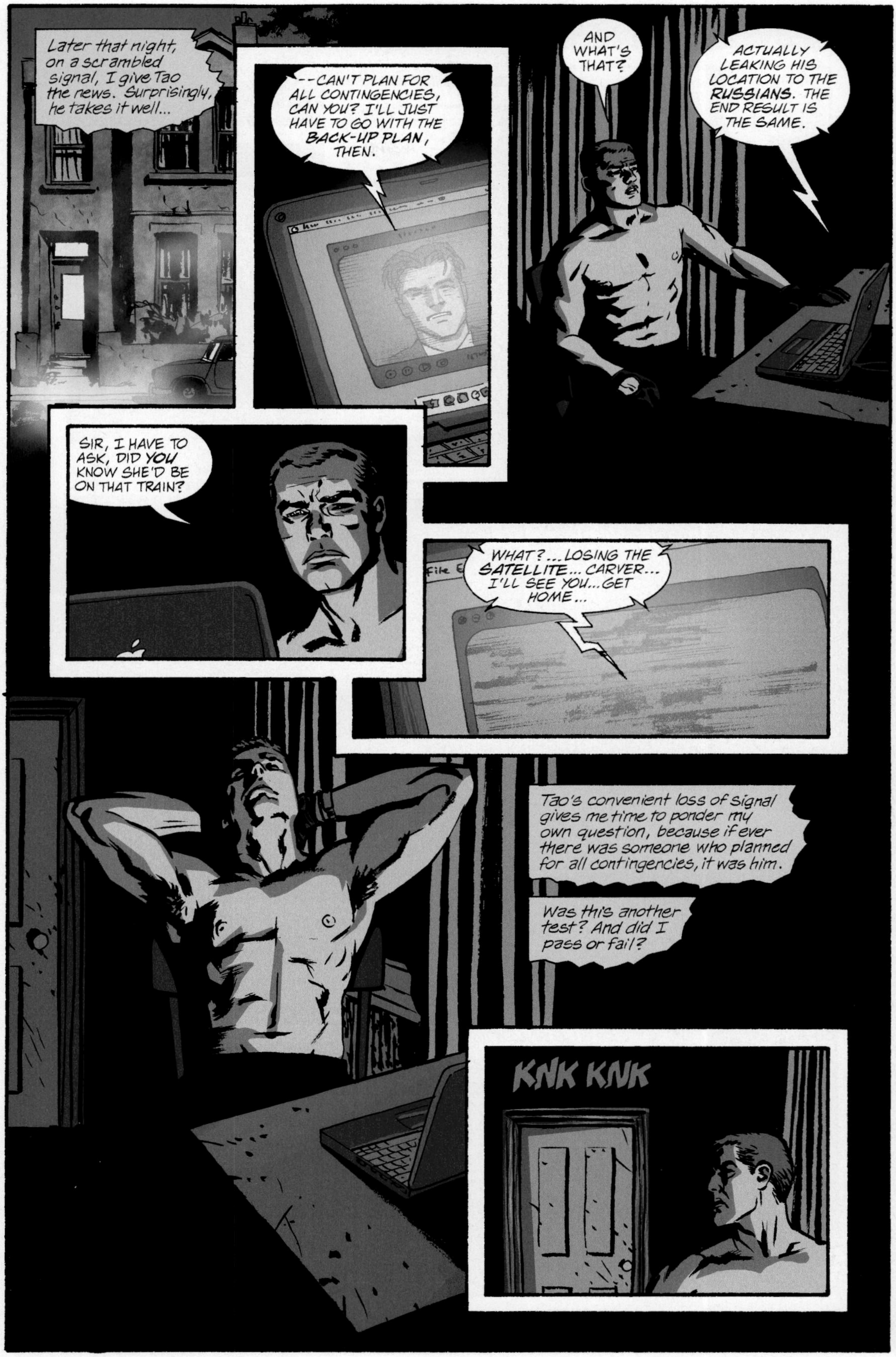
Later that night, on a scrambled signal, I give Tao the news. Surprisingly, he takes it well...
--CAN'T PLAN FOR ALL CONTINGENCIES, CAN YOU? I'LL JUST HAVE TO GO WITH THE BACK-UP PLAN, THEN.
AND WHAT'S THAT?
ACTUALLY LEAKING HIS LOCATION TO THE RUSSIANS. THE END RESULT IS THE SAME.
SIR, I HAVE TO ASK, DID YOU KNOW SHE'D BE ON THAT TRAIN?
WHAT?...LOSING THE SATELLITE... CARVER... I'LL SEE YOU...GET HOME...
Tao's convenient loss of signal gives me time to ponder my own question, because if ever there was someone who planned for all contingencies, it was him.
Was this another test? And did I pass or fail?
KNK KNK

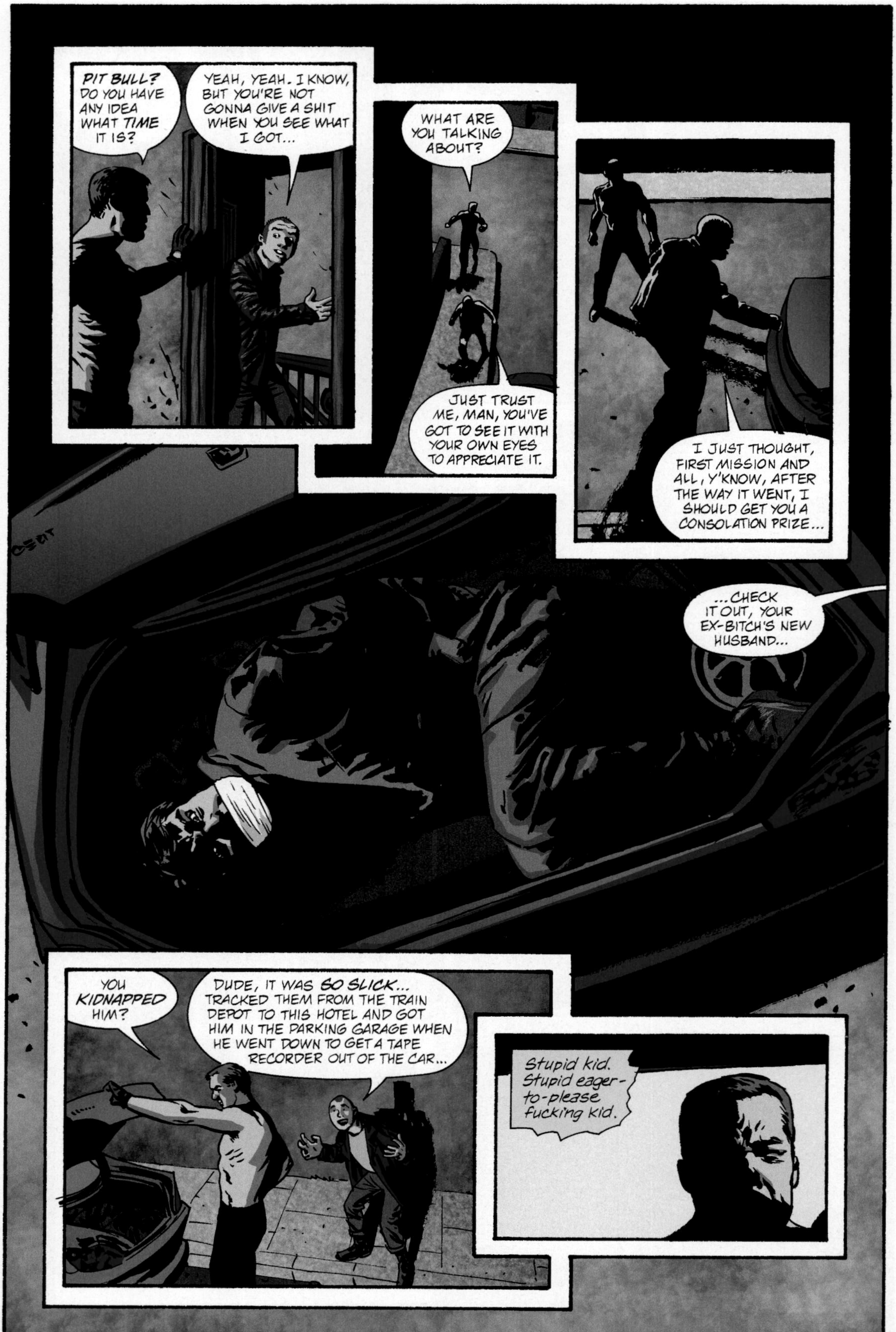
PIT BULL? DO YOU HAVE ANY IDEA WHAT TIME IT IS?
YEAH, YEAH. I KNOW, BUT YOU'RE NOT GONNA GIVE A SHIT WHEN YOU SEE WHAT I GOT...
WHAT ARE YOU TALKING ABOUT?
JUST TRUST ME, MAN, YOU'VE GOT TO SEE IT WITH YOUR OWN EYES TO APPRECIATE IT.
I JUST THOUGHT, FIRST MISSION AND ALL, Y'KNOW, AFTER THE WAY IT WENT, I SHOULD GET YOU A CONSOLATION PRIZE...
...CHECK IT OUT, YOUR EX-BITCH'S NEW HUSBAND...
YOU KIDNAPPED HIM?
DUDE, IT WAS SO SLICK... TRACKED THEM FROM THE TRAIN DEPOT TO THIS HOTEL AND GOT HIM IN THE PARKING GARAGE WHEN HE WENT DOWN TO GET A TAPE RECORDER OUT OF THE CAR...
Stupid kid. Stupid eager-to-please fucking kid.

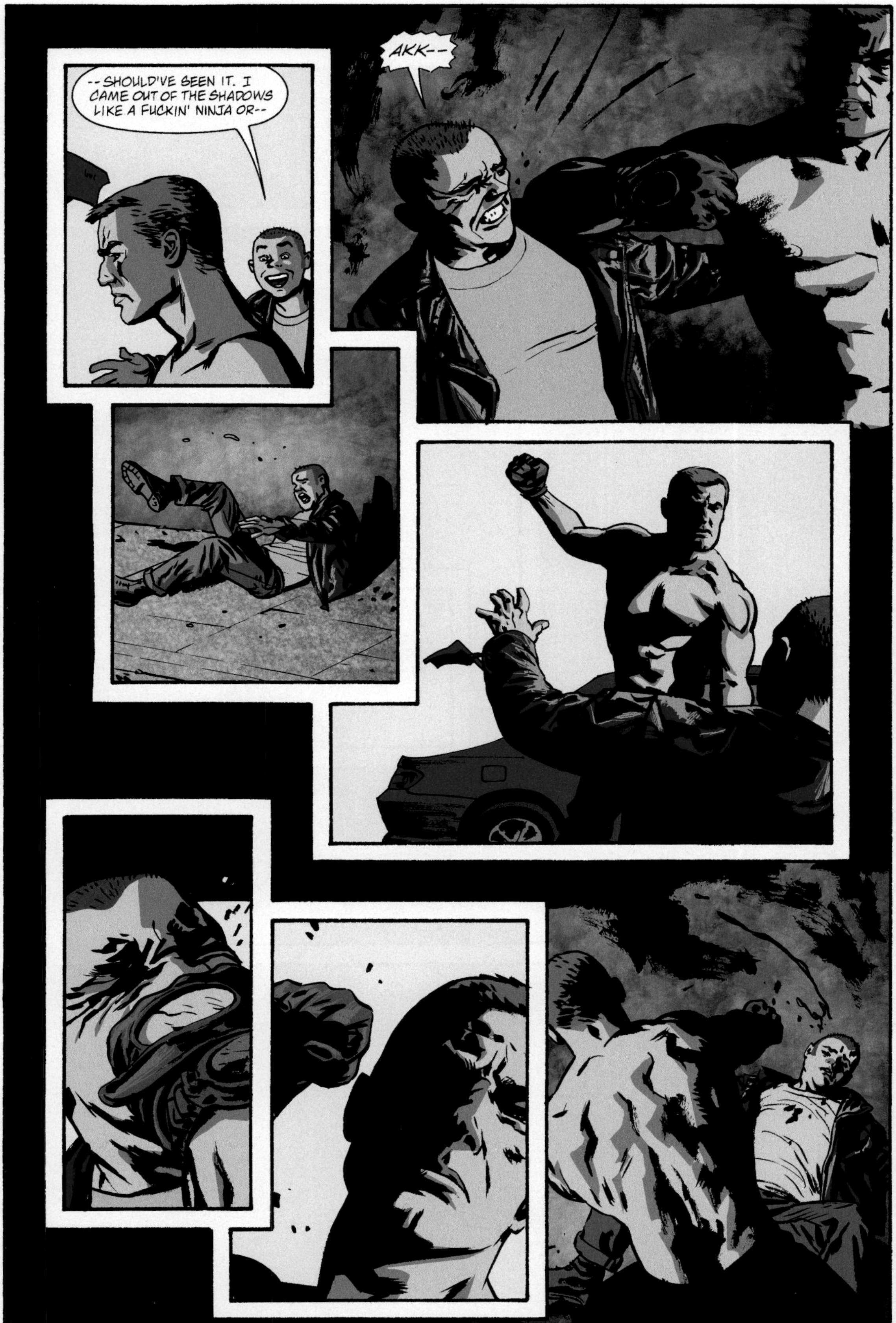
--SHOULD'VE SEEN IT. I CAME OUT OF THE SHADOWS LIKE A FUCKIN' NINJA OR--
AKK--

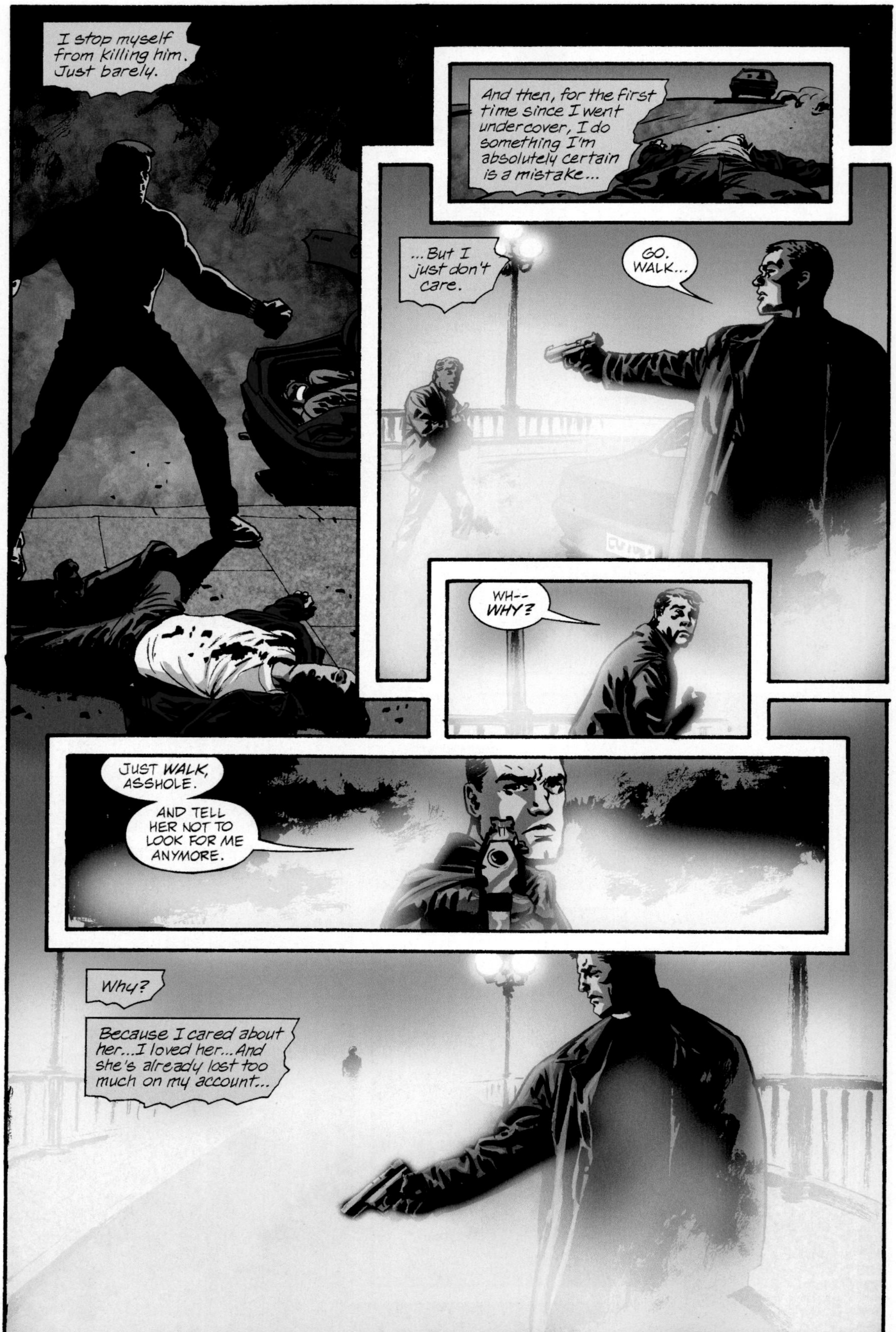
I stop myself from killing him. Just barely.
And then, for the first time since I went undercover, I do something I'm absolutely certain is a mistake...
...But I just don't care.
GO. WALK...
WH-- WHY?
JUST WALK, ASSHOLE.
AND TELL HER NOT TO LOOK FOR ME ANYMORE.
Why?
Because I cared about her...I loved her...And she's already lost too much on my account...

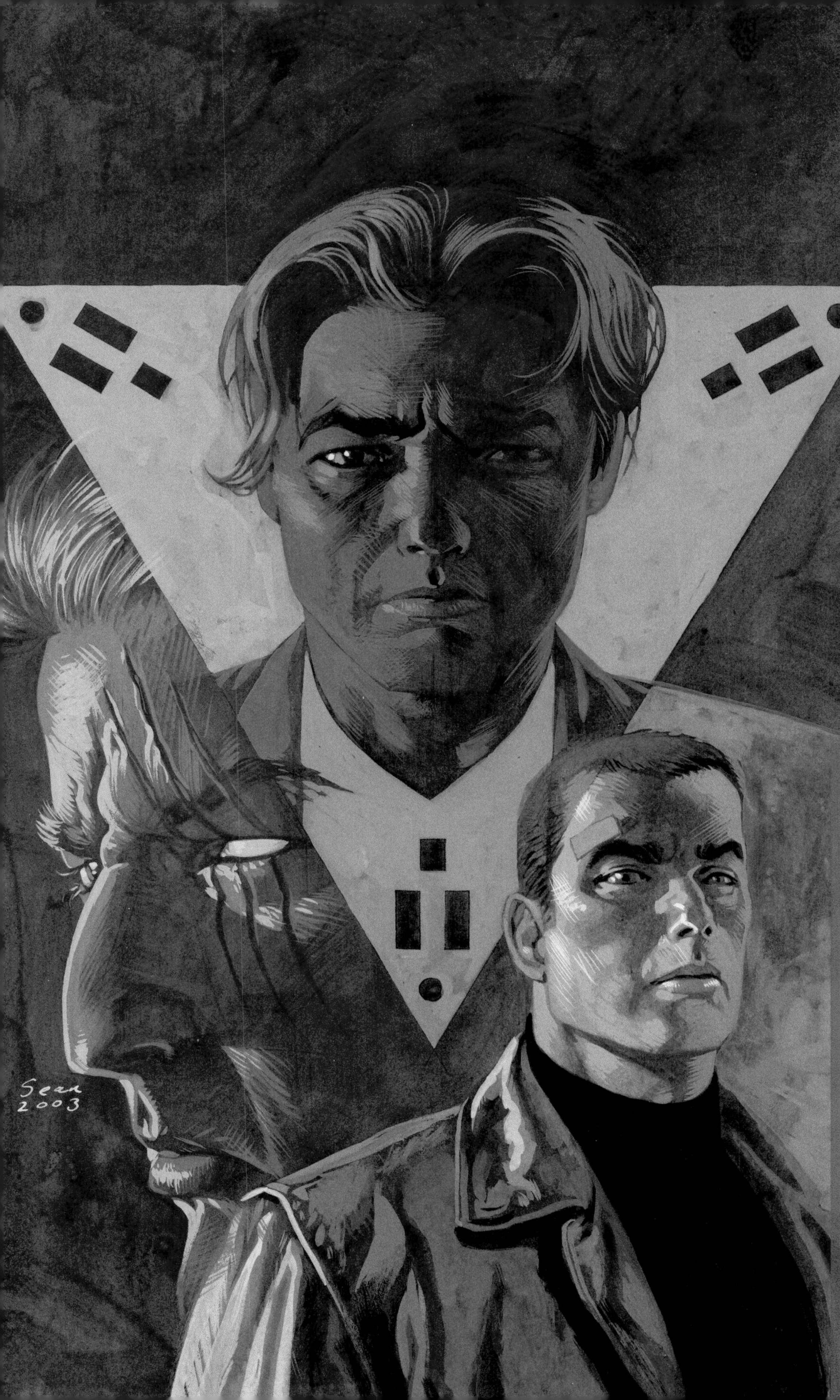
Sean
2003

Cover by SEAN PHILLIPS

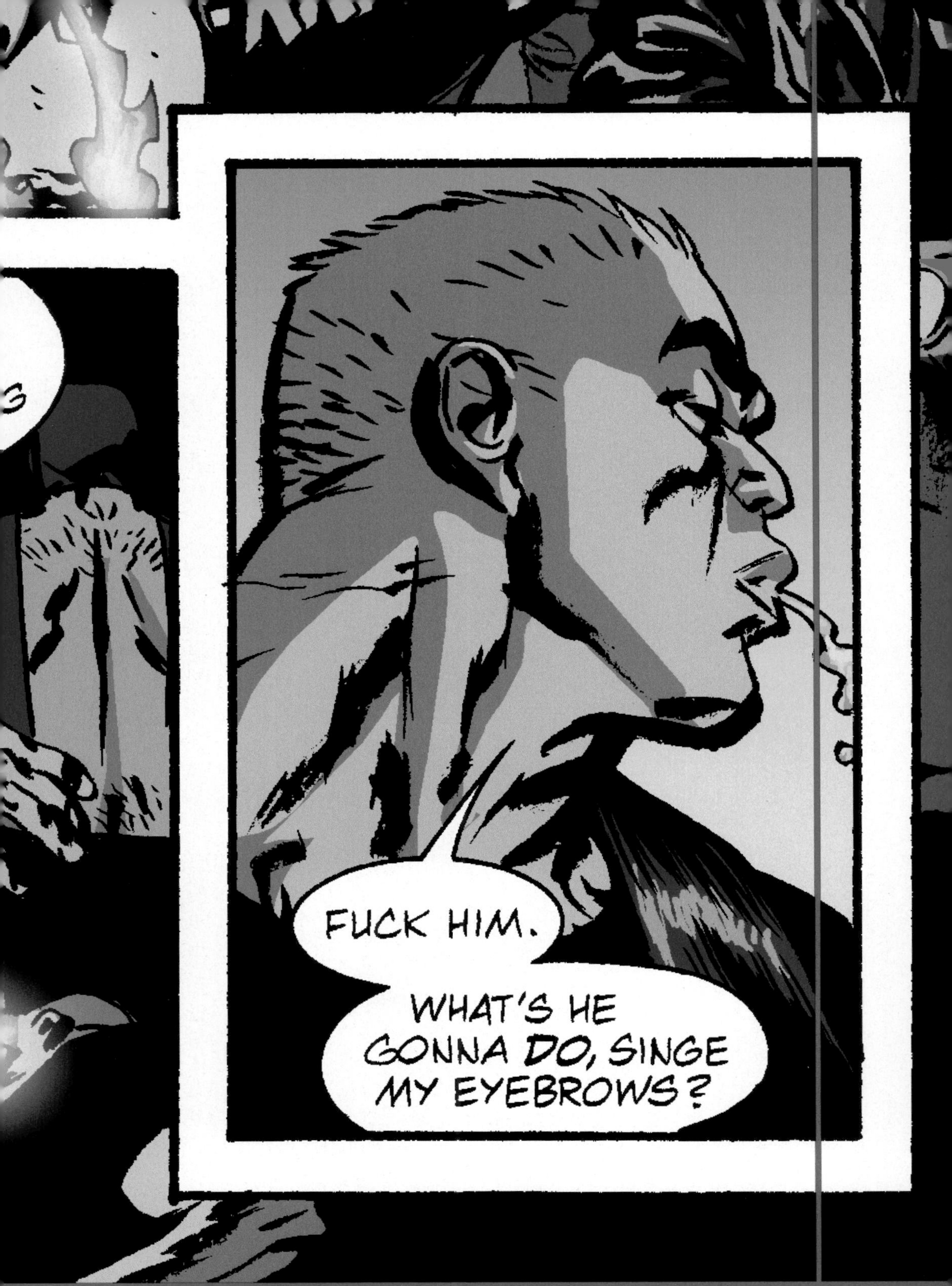
FUCK HIM.
WHAT'S HE GONNA DO, SINGE MY EYEBROWS?

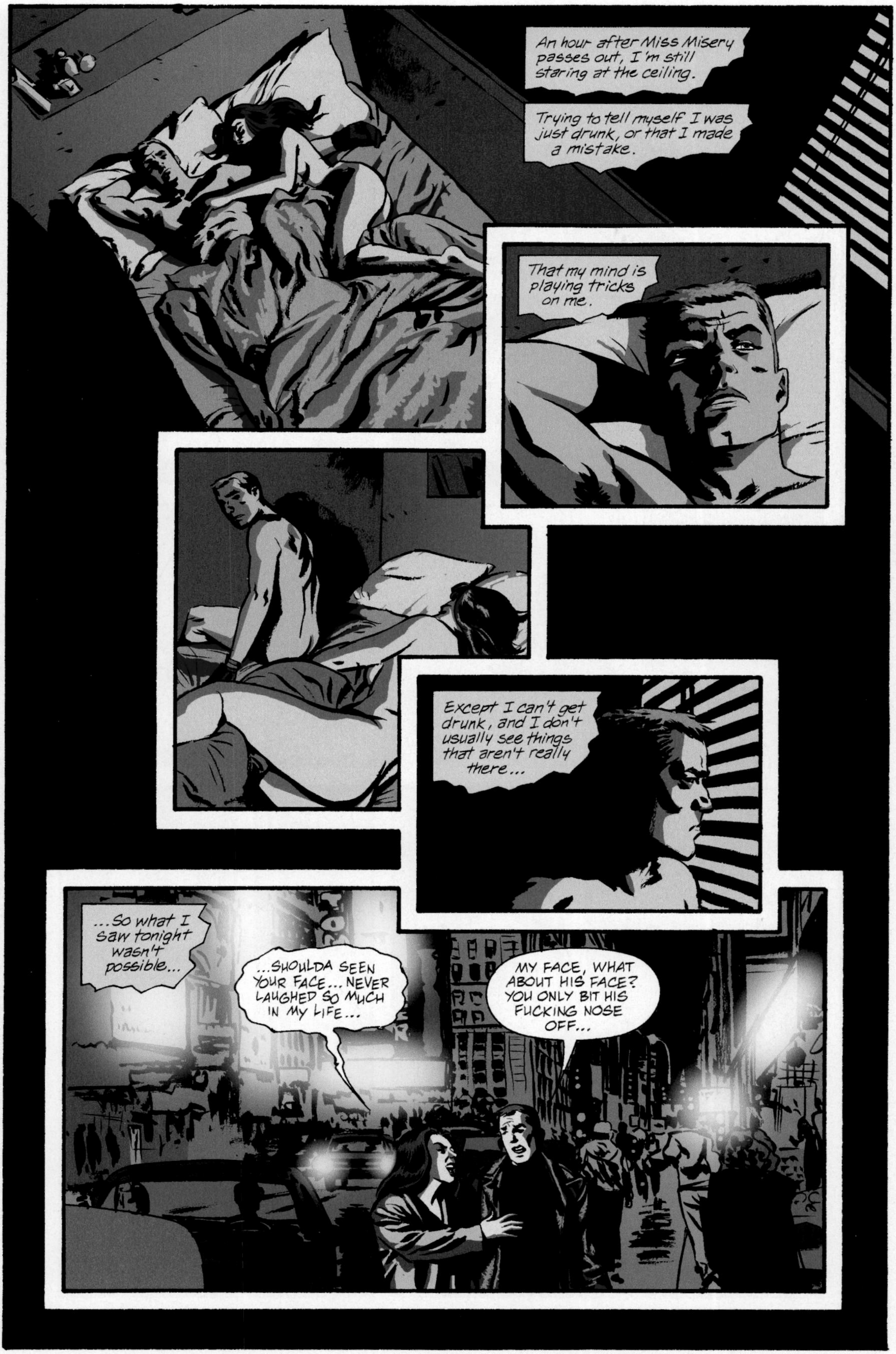
An hour after Miss Misery passes out, I'm still staring at the ceiling.
Trying to tell myself I was just drunk, or that I made a mistake.
That my mind is playing tricks on me.
Except I can't get drunk, and I don't usually see things that aren't really there...
...So what I saw tonight wasn't possible...
...SHOULDA SEEN YOUR FACE... NEVER LAUGHED SO MUCH IN MY LIFE...
MY FACE, WHAT ABOUT HIS FACE? YOU ONLY BIT HIS FUCKING NOSE OFF...

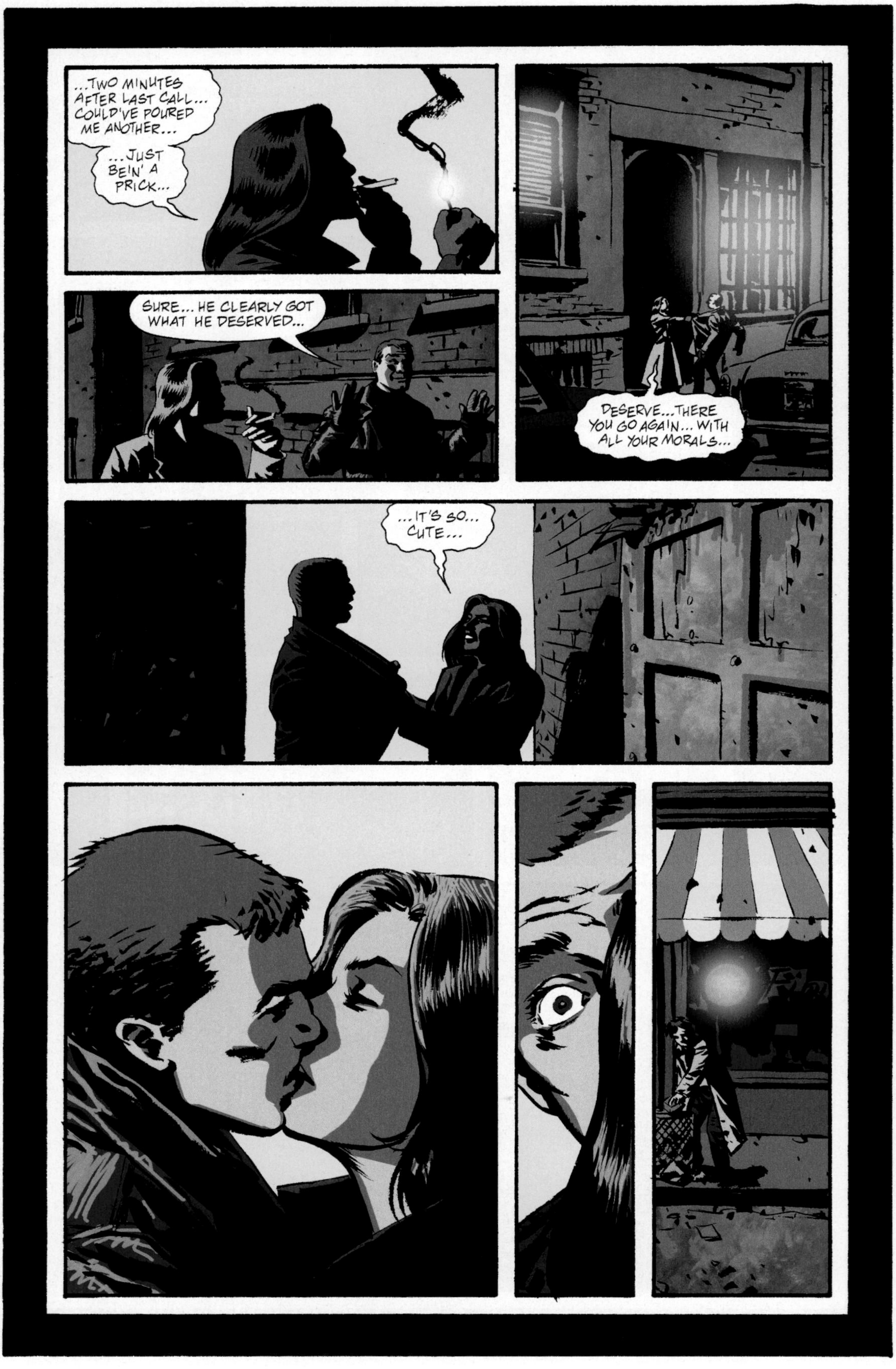
...TWO MINUTES AFTER LAST CALL... COULD'VE POURED ME ANOTHER...
...JUST BEIN' A PRICK...
SURE... HE CLEARLY GOT WHAT HE DESERVED...
DESERVE... THERE YOU GO AGAIN... WITH ALL YOUR MORALS...
...IT'S SO... CUTE...

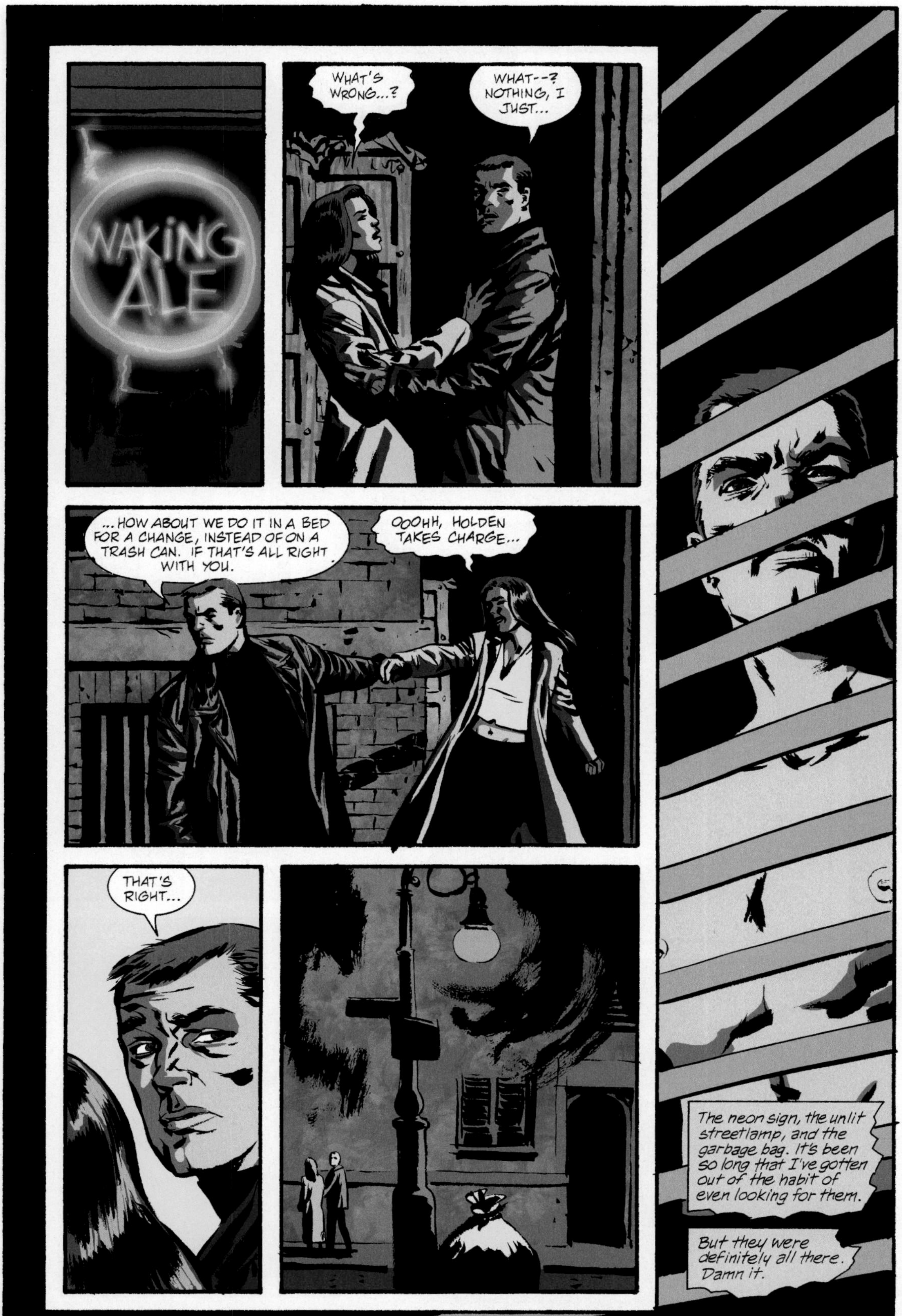
WHAT'S WRONG...?
WHAT--? NOTHING, I JUST...
WAKiNG ALE
...HOW ABOUT WE DO IT IN A BED FOR A CHANGE, INSTEAD OF ON A TRASH CAN. IF THAT'S ALL RIGHT WITH YOU.
OOOHH, HOLDEN TAKES CHARGE...
THAT'S RIGHT...
The neon sign, the unlit streetlamp, and the garbage bag. It's been so long that I've gotten out of the habit of even looking for them.
But they were definitely all there. Damn it.

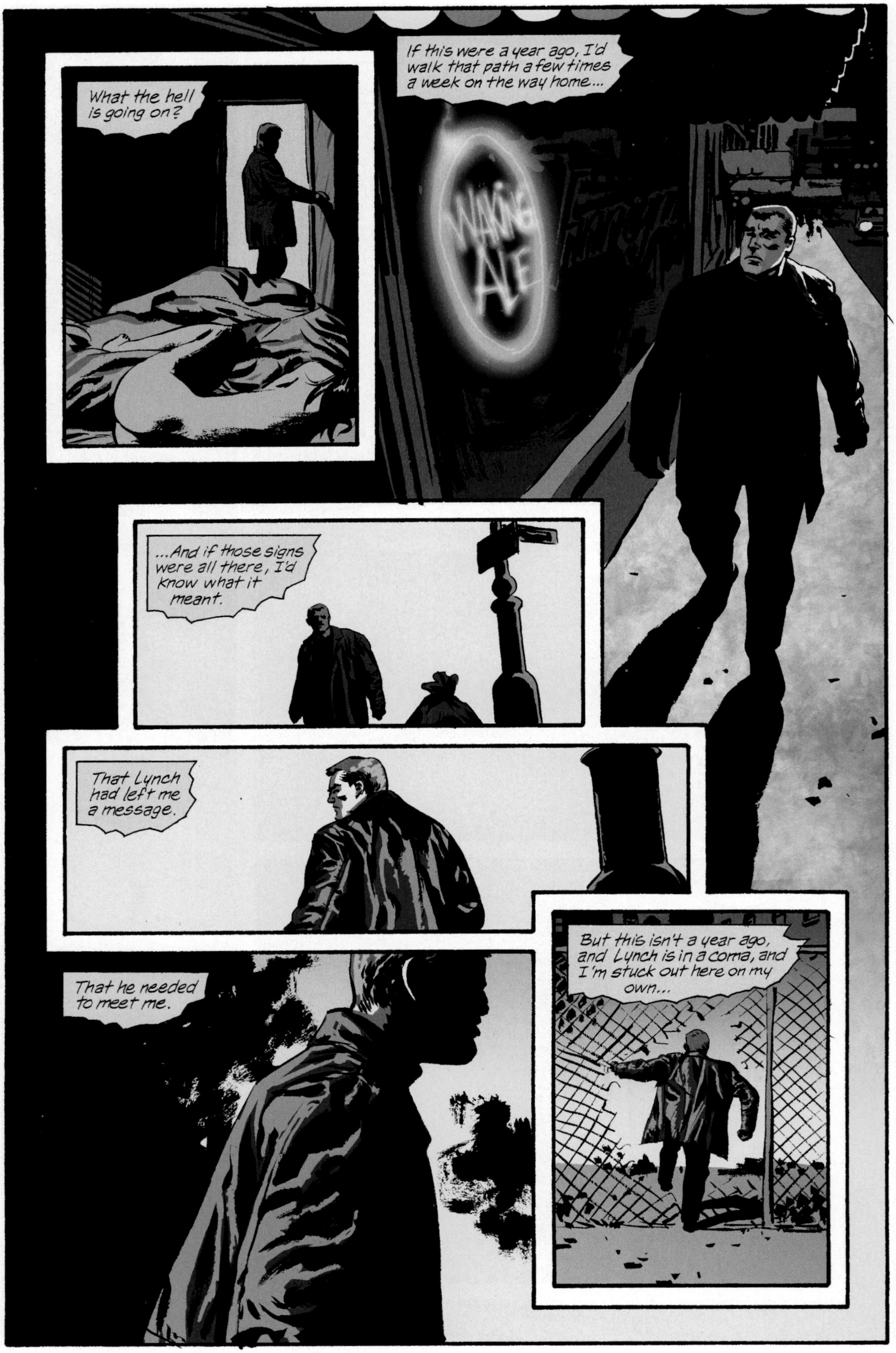
What the hell is going on?
If this were a year ago, I'd walk that path a few times a week on the way home...
...And if those signs were all there, I'd know what it meant.
That Lynch had left me a message.
That he needed to meet me.
But this isn't a year ago, and Lynch is in a coma, and I'm stuck out here on my own...

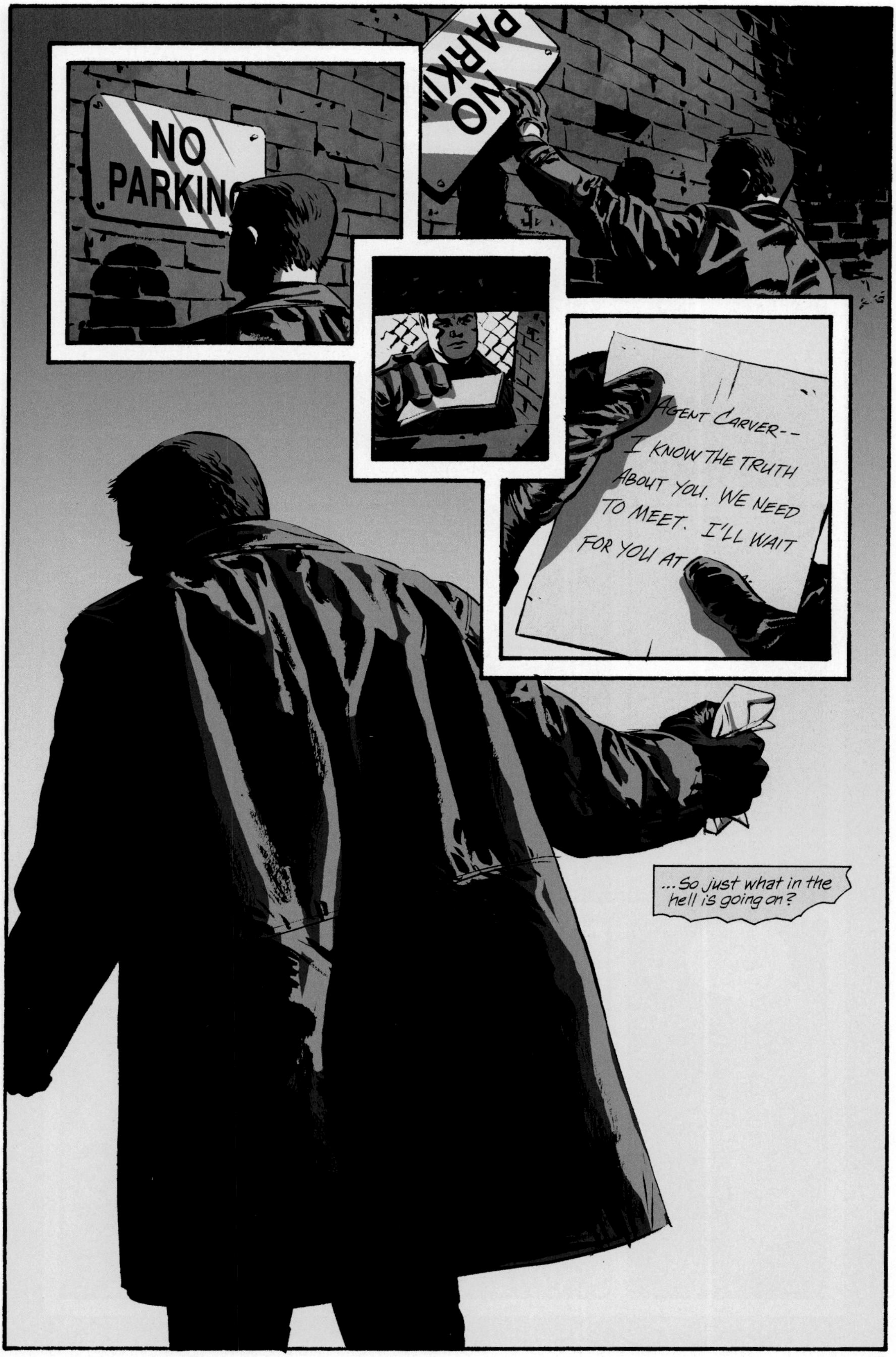
NO PARKING
NO PARKI
AGENT CARVER-- I KNOW THE TRUTH ABOUT YOU. WE NEED TO MEET. I'LL WAIT FOR YOU AT
...So just what in the hell is going on?

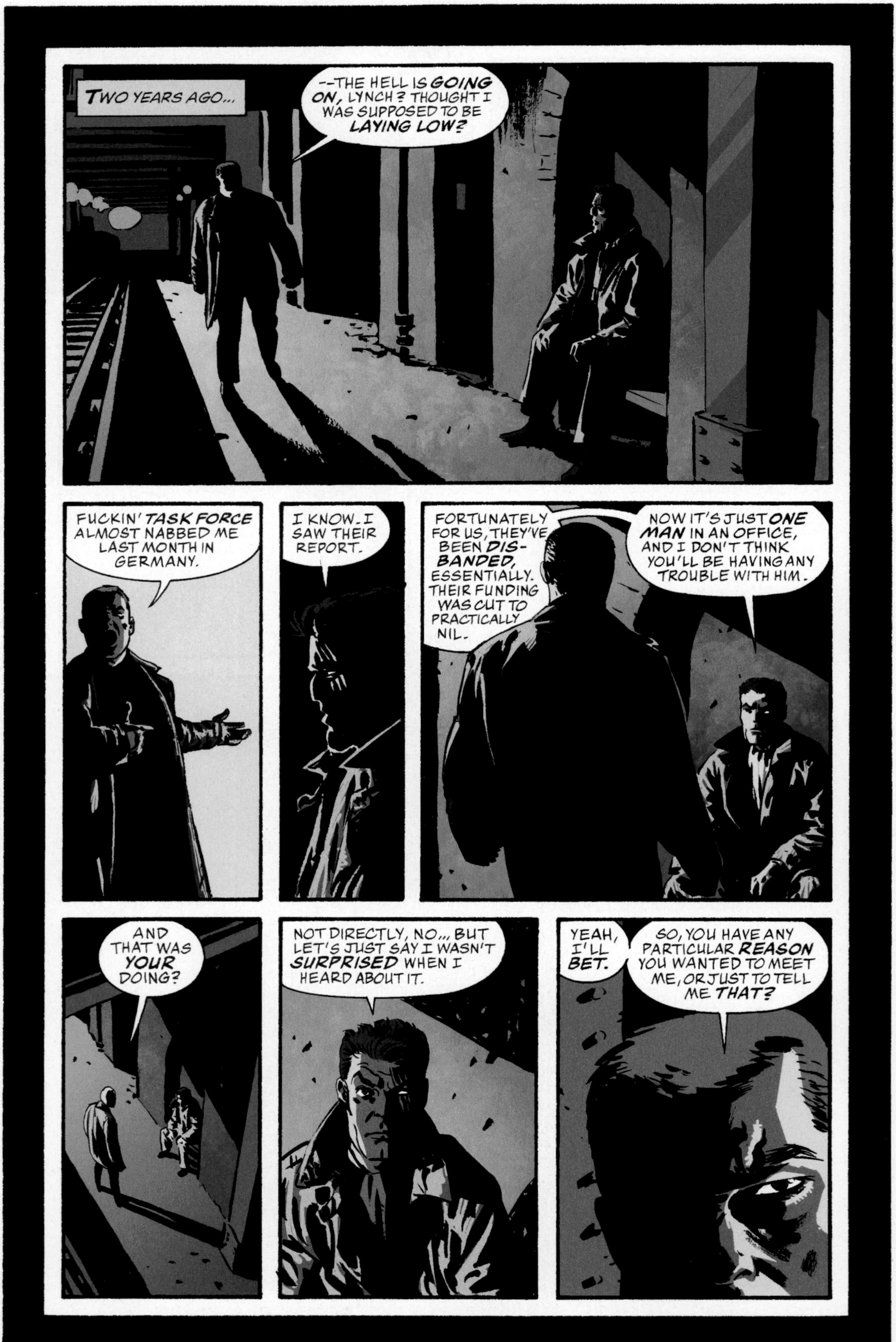

TWO YEARS AGO...
--THE HELL IS GOING ON, LYNCH? THOUGHT I WAS SUPPOSED TO BE LAYING LOW?
FUCKIN' TASK FORCE ALMOST NABBED ME LAST MONTH IN GERMANY.
I KNOW. I SAW THEIR REPORT.
FORTUNATELY FOR US, THEY'VE BEEN DIS-BANDED, ESSENTIALLY. THEIR FUNDING WAS CUT TO PRACTICALLY NIL.
NOW IT'S JUST ONE MAN IN AN OFFICE, AND I DON'T THINK YOU'LL BE HAVING ANY TROUBLE WITH HIM.
AND THAT WAS YOUR DOING?
NOT DIRECTLY, NO... BUT LET'S JUST SAY I WASN'T SURPRISED WHEN I HEARD ABOUT IT.
YEAH, I'LL BET.
SO, YOU HAVE ANY PARTICULAR REASON YOU WANTED TO MEET ME, OR JUST TO TELL ME THAT?

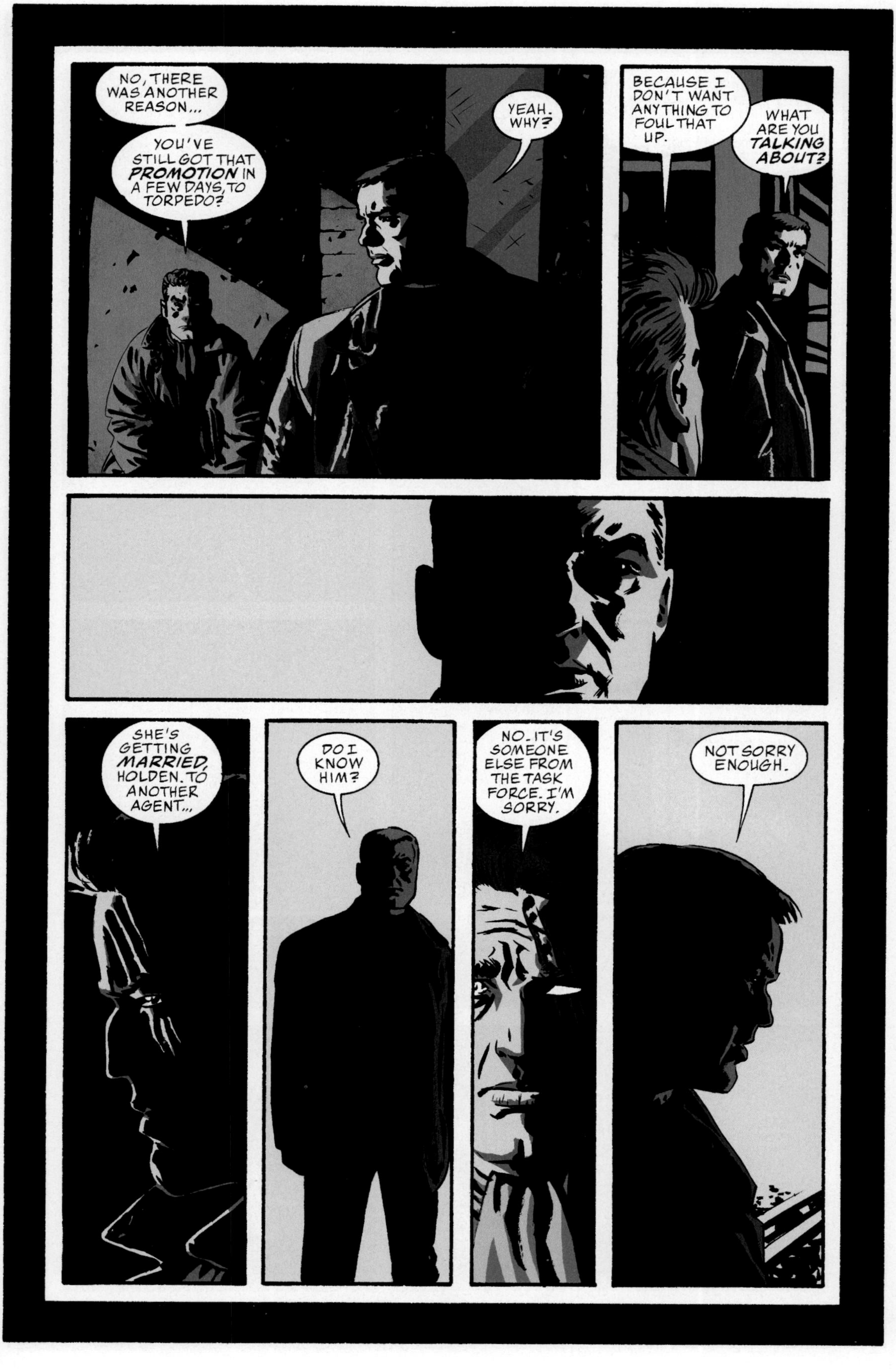

NO, THERE WAS ANOTHER REASON...
YOU'VE STILL GOT THAT PROMOTION IN A FEW DAYS, TO TORPEDO?
YEAH. WHY?
BECAUSE I DON'T WANT ANYTHING TO FOUL THAT UP.
WHAT ARE YOU TALKING ABOUT?
SHE'S GETTING MARRIED, HOLDEN. TO ANOTHER AGENT...
DO I KNOW HIM?
NO. IT'S SOMEONE ELSE FROM THE TASK FORCE. I'M SORRY.
NOT SORRY ENOUGH.

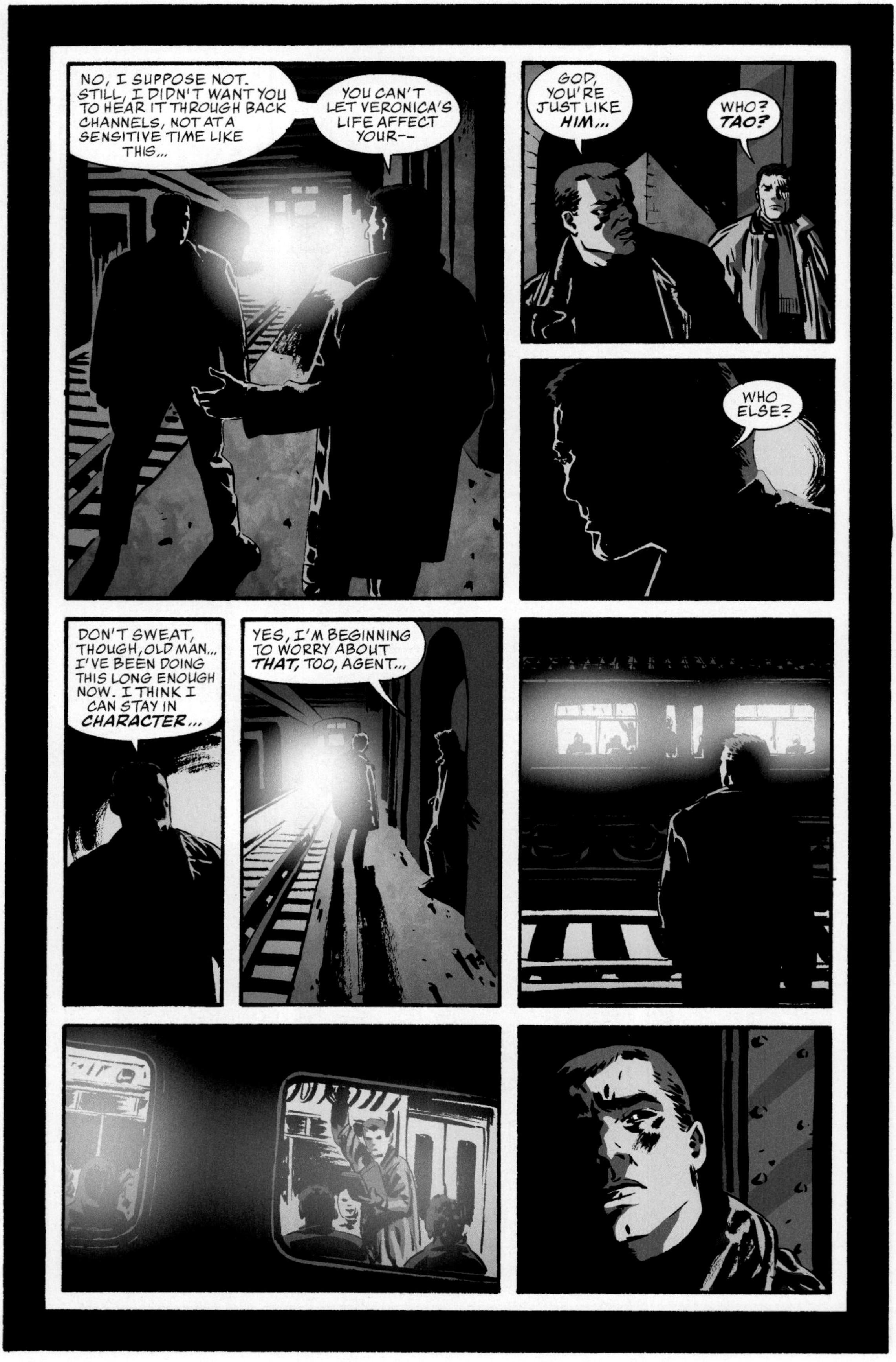
NO, I SUPPOSE NOT. STILL, I DIDN'T WANT YOU TO HEAR IT THROUGH BACK CHANNELS, NOT AT A SENSITIVE TIME LIKE THIS...
YOU CAN'T LET VERONICA'S LIFE AFFECT YOUR--
GOD, YOU'RE JUST LIKE HIM...
WHO? TAO?
WHO ELSE?
DON'T SWEAT, THOUGH, OLD MAN... I'VE BEEN DOING THIS LONG ENOUGH NOW. I THINK I CAN STAY IN CHARACTER...
YES, I'M BEGINNING TO WORRY ABOUT THAT, TOO, AGENT...

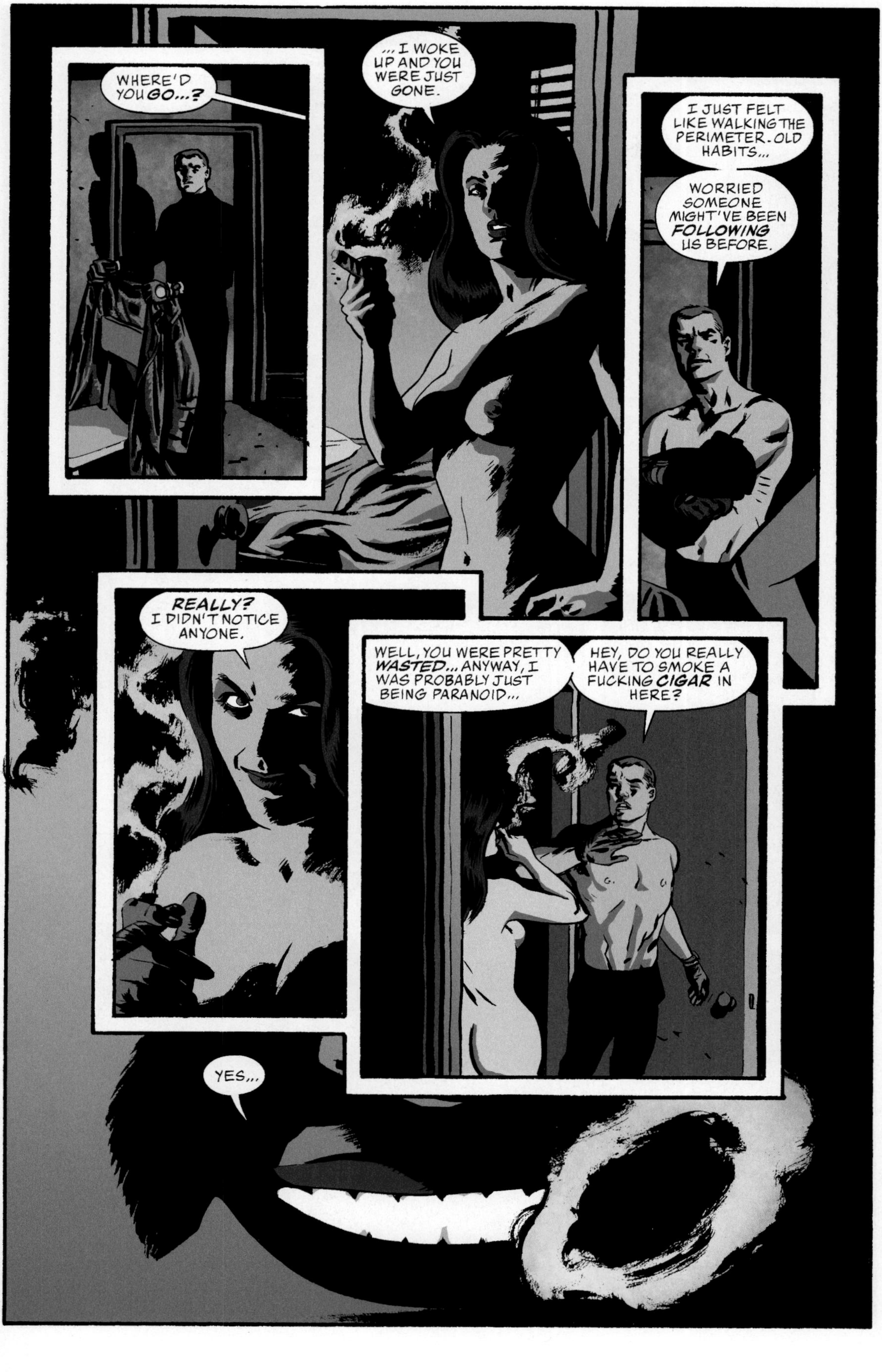
WHERE'D YOU GO...?
...I WOKE UP AND YOU WERE JUST GONE.
I JUST FELT LIKE WALKING THE PERIMETER. OLD HABITS...
WORRIED SOMEONE MIGHT'VE BEEN FOLLOWING US BEFORE.
REALLY? I DIDN'T NOTICE ANYONE.
WELL, YOU WERE PRETTY WASTED... ANYWAY, I WAS PROBABLY JUST BEING PARANOID...
HEY, DO YOU REALLY HAVE TO SMOKE A FUCKING CIGAR IN HERE?
YES...

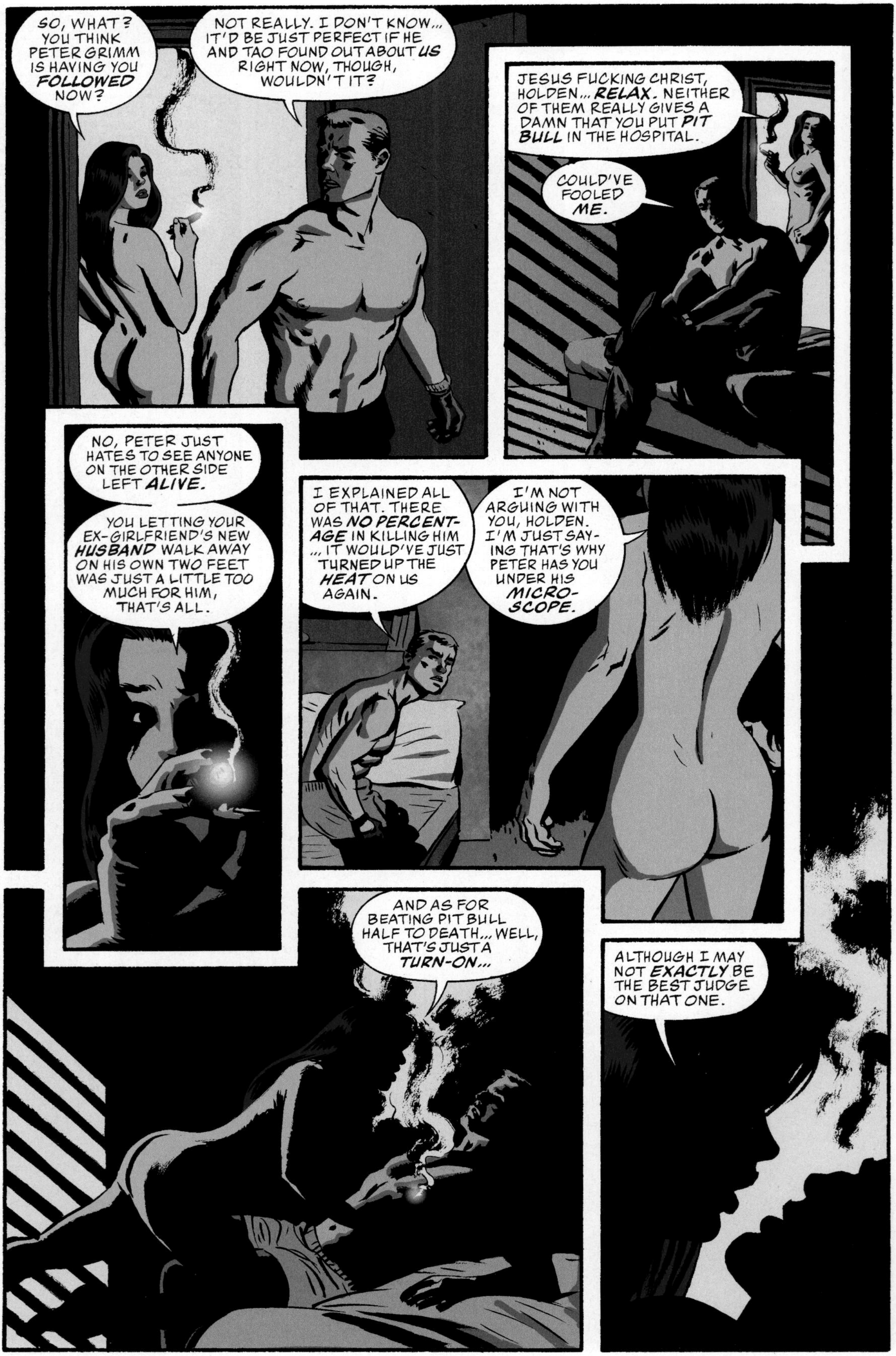
SO, WHAT? YOU THINK PETER GRIMM IS HAVING YOU FOLLOWED NOW?
NOT REALLY. I DON'T KNOW... IT'D BE JUST PERFECT IF HE AND TAO FOUND OUT ABOUT US RIGHT NOW, THOUGH, WOULDN'T IT?
JESUS FUCKING CHRIST, HOLDEN... RELAX. NEITHER OF THEM REALLY GIVES A DAMN THAT YOU PUT PIT BULL IN THE HOSPITAL.
COULD'VE FOOLED ME.
NO, PETER JUST HATES TO SEE ANYONE ON THE OTHER SIDE LEFT ALIVE.
YOU LETTING YOUR EX-GIRLFRIEND'S NEW HUSBAND WALK AWAY ON HIS OWN TWO FEET WAS JUST A LITTLE TOO MUCH FOR HIM, THAT'S ALL.
I EXPLAINED ALL OF THAT. THERE WAS NO PERCENTAGE IN KILLING HIM... IT WOULD'VE JUST TURNED UP THE HEAT ON US AGAIN.
I'M NOT ARGUING WITH YOU, HOLDEN. I'M JUST SAYING THAT'S WHY PETER HAS YOU UNDER HIS MICROSCOPE.
AND AS FOR BEATING PIT BULL HALF TO DEATH... WELL, THAT'S JUST A TURN-ON...
ALTHOUGH I MAY NOT EXACTLY BE THE BEST JUDGE ON THAT ONE.

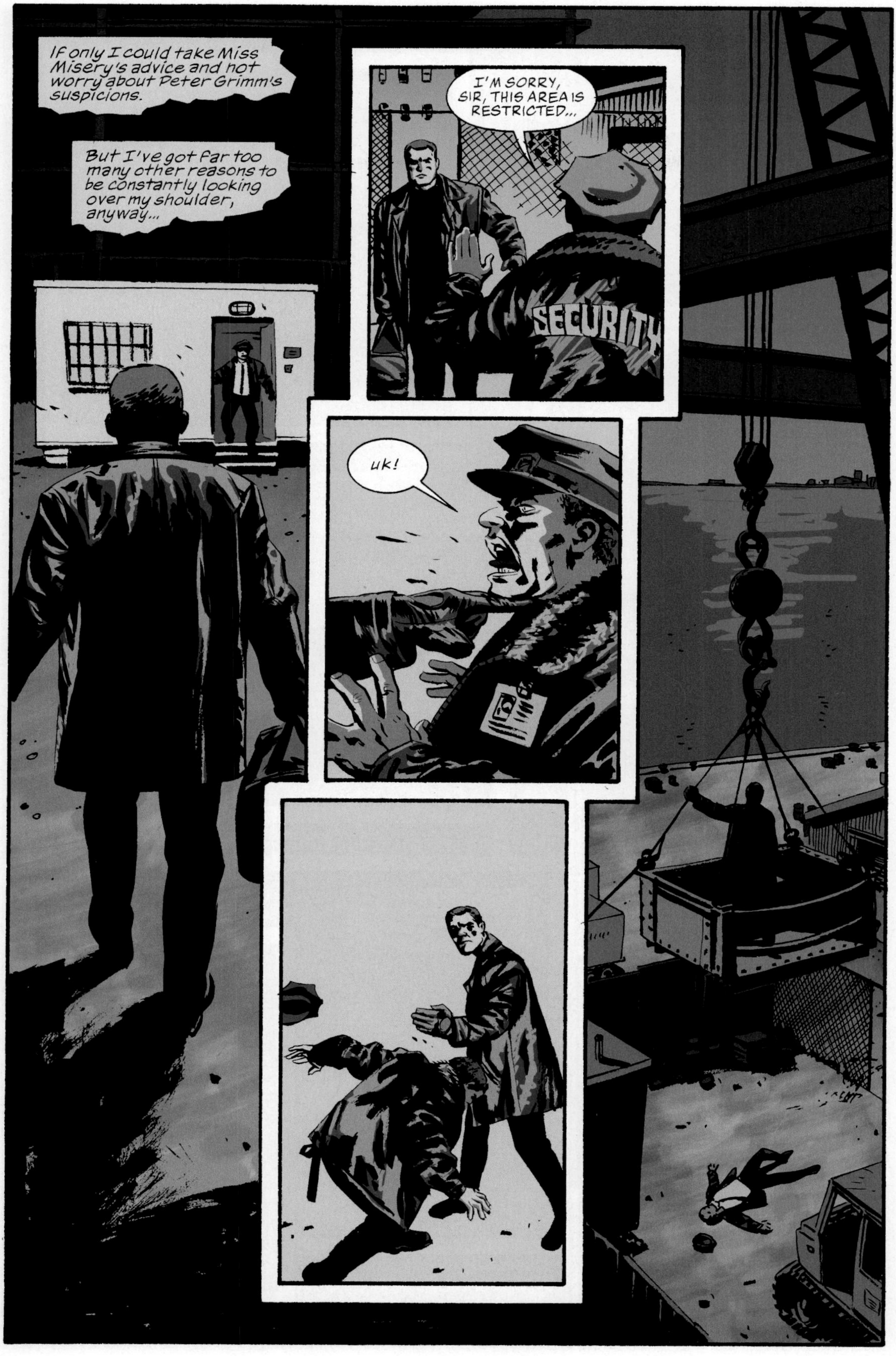
If only I could take Miss Misery's advice and not worry about Peter Grimm's suspicions.
But I've got far too many other reasons to be constantly looking over my shoulder, anyway...
I'M SORRY, SIR, THIS AREA IS RESTRICTED...
SECURITY
uk!

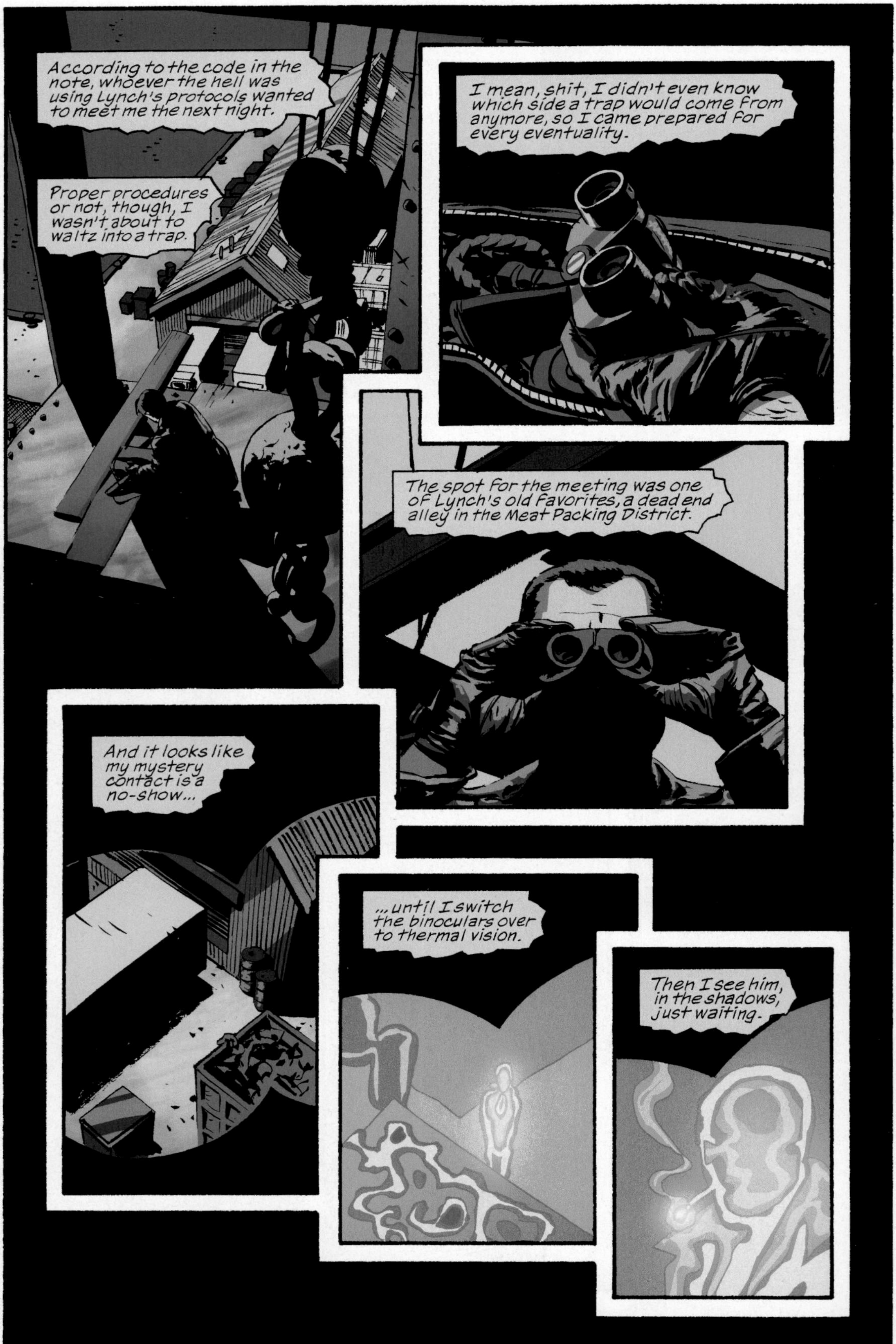
According to the code in the note, whoever the hell was using Lynch's protocols wanted to meet me the next night.
Proper procedures or not, though, I wasn't about to waltz into a trap.
I mean, shit, I didn't even know which side a trap would come from anymore, so I came prepared for every eventuality.
The spot for the meeting was one of Lynch's old favorites, a dead end alley in the Meat Packing District.
And it looks like my mystery contact is a no-show...
...until I switch the binoculars over to thermal vision.
Then I see him, in the shadows, just waiting.

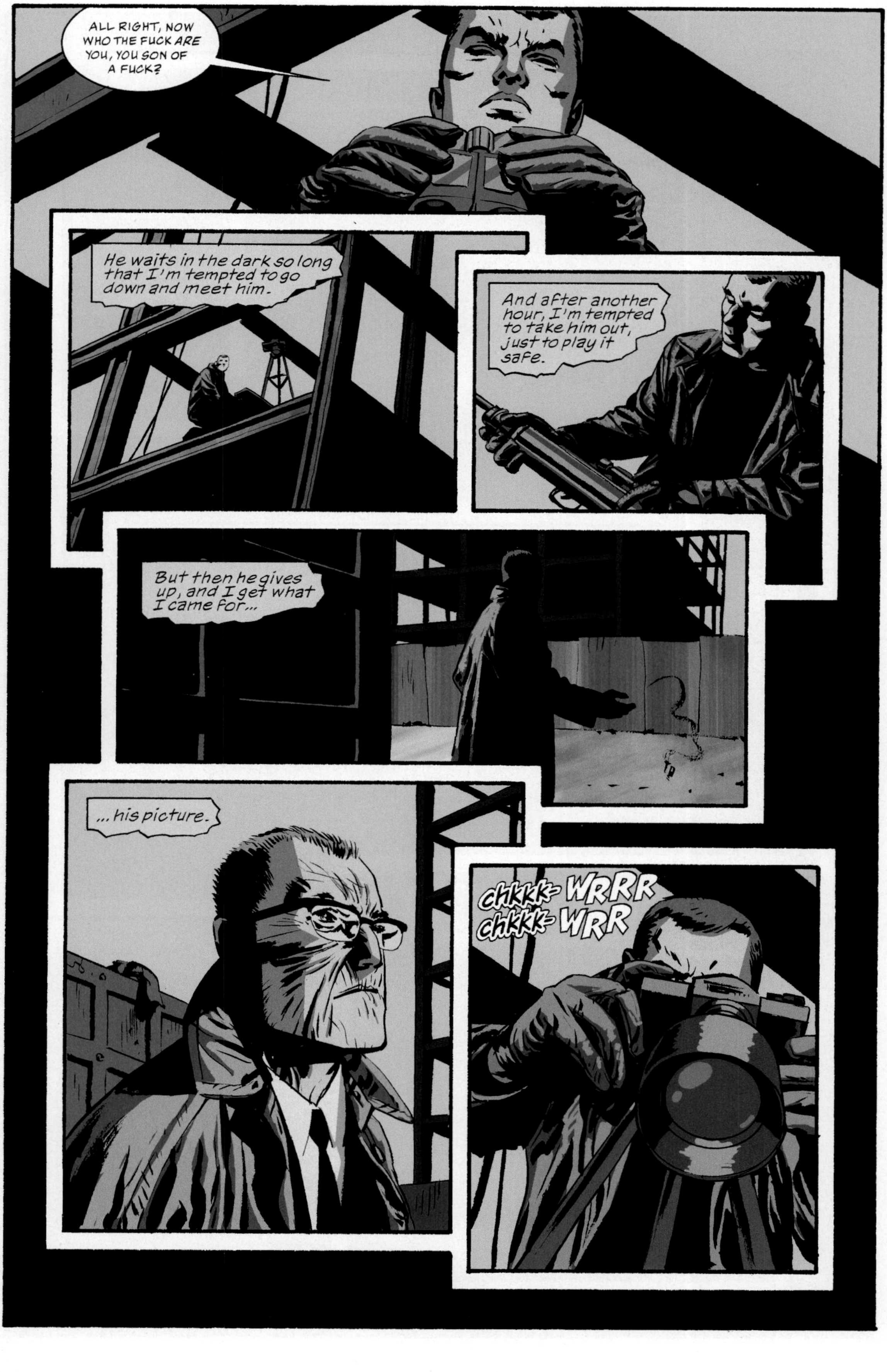
ALL RIGHT, NOW WHO THE FUCK ARE YOU, YOU SON OF A FUCK?
He waits in the dark so long that I'm tempted to go down and meet him.
And after another hour, I'm tempted to take him out, just to play it safe.
But then he gives up, and I get what I came for...
...his picture.
CHKKK- WRRR
CHKKK- WRR

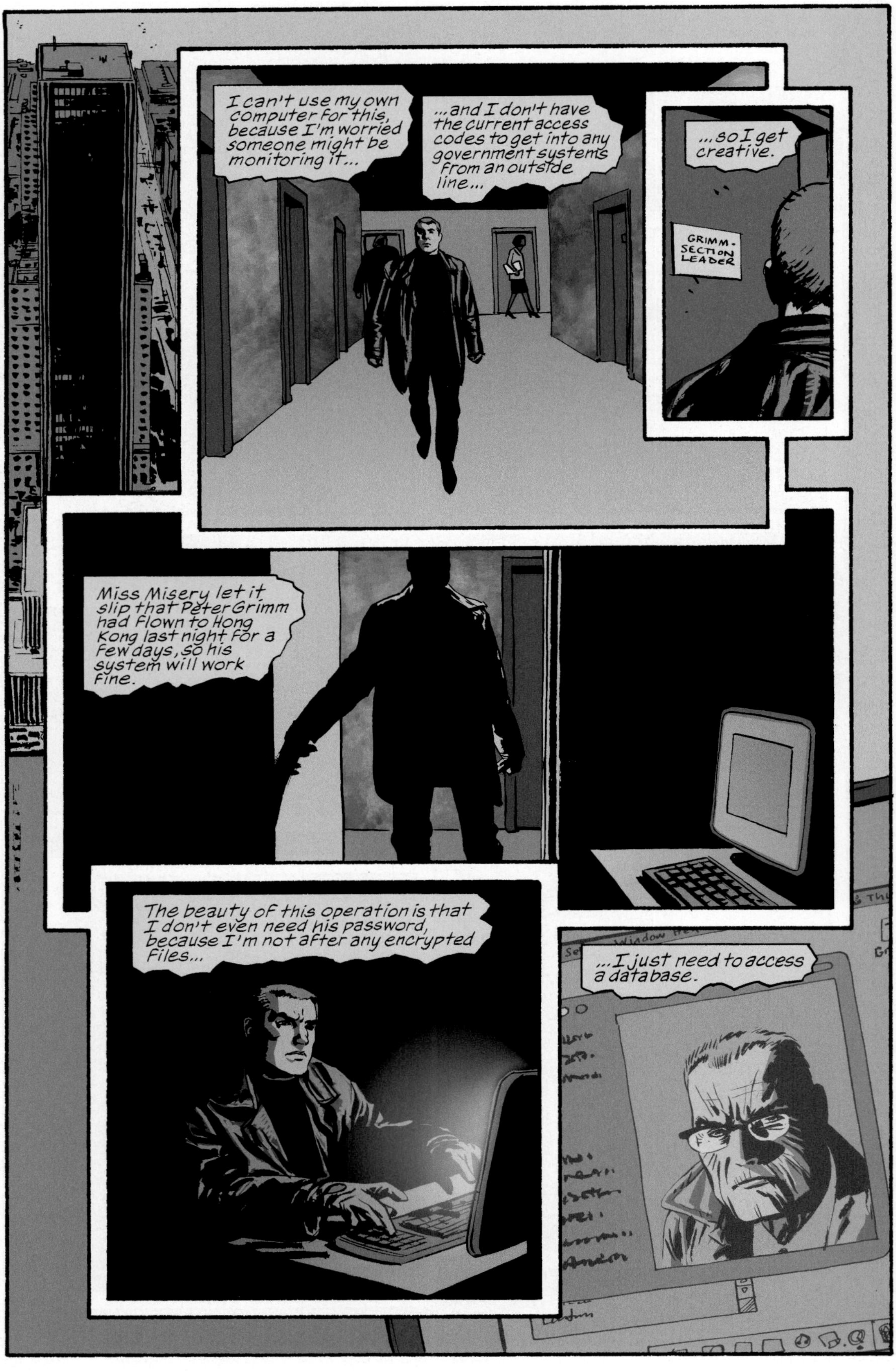

I can't use my own computer for this, because I'm worried someone might be monitoring it...
...and I don't have the current access codes to get into any government systems from an outside line...
...so I get creative.
GRIMM. SECTION LEADER
Miss Misery let it slip that Peter Grimm had flown to Hong Kong last night for a few days, so his system will work fine.
The beauty of this operation is that I don't even need his password, because I'm not after any encrypted files...
...I just need to access a database.

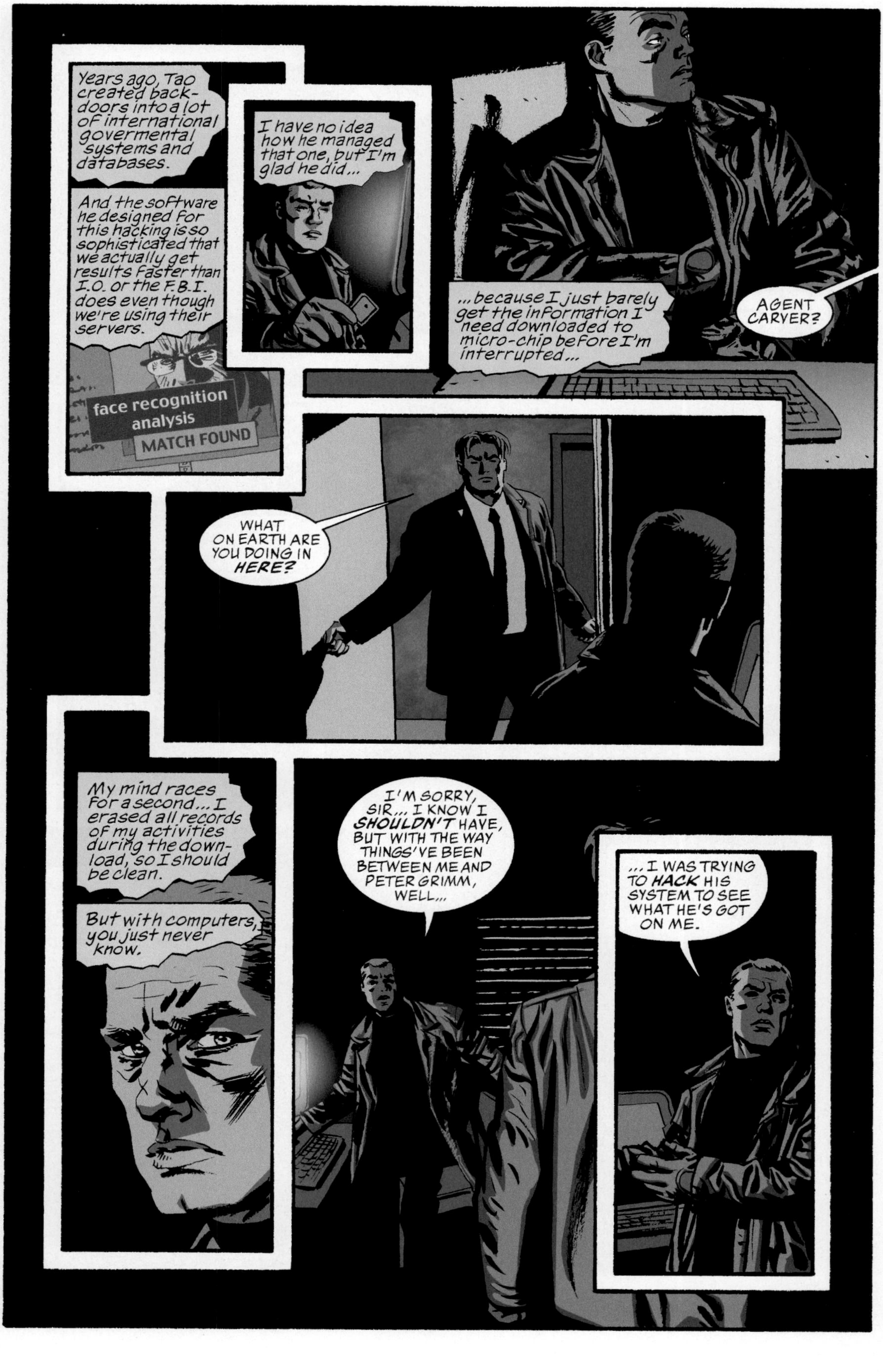
Years ago, Tao created back-doors into a lot of international govermental systems and databases.
And the software he designed for this hacking is so sophisticated that we actually get results faster than I.O. or the F.B.I. does even though we're using their servers.
face recognition analysis
MATCH FOUND
I have no idea how he managed that one, but I'm glad he did...
...because I just barely get the information I need downloaded to micro-chip before I'm interrupted...
AGENT CARVER?
WHAT ON EARTH ARE YOU DOING IN HERE?
My mind races for a second... I erased all records of my activities during the download, so I should be clean.
But with computers, you just never know.
I'M SORRY, SIR... I KNOW I SHOULDN'T HAVE, BUT WITH THE WAY THINGS'VE BEEN BETWEEN ME AND PETER GRIMM, WELL...
...I WAS TRYING TO HACK HIS SYSTEM TO SEE WHAT HE'S GOT ON ME.

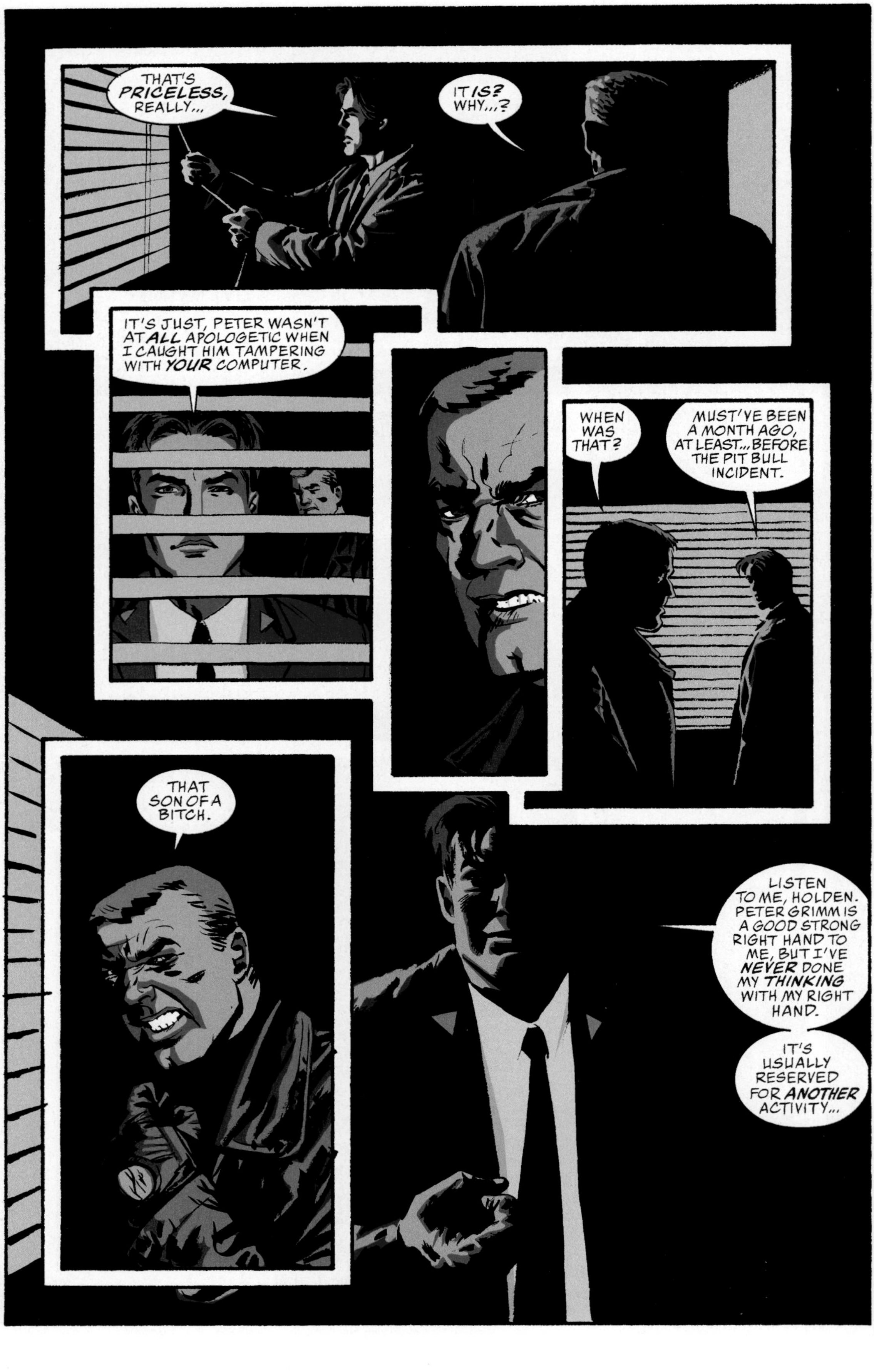
THAT'S PRICELESS, REALLY...
IT IS? WHY...?
IT'S JUST, PETER WASN'T AT ALL APOLOGETIC WHEN I CAUGHT HIM TAMPERING WITH YOUR COMPUTER.
WHEN WAS THAT?
MUST'VE BEEN A MONTH AGO, AT LEAST... BEFORE THE PIT BULL INCIDENT.
THAT SON OF A BITCH.
LISTEN TO ME, HOLDEN. PETER GRIMM IS A GOOD STRONG RIGHT HAND TO ME, BUT I'VE NEVER DONE MY THINKING WITH MY RIGHT HAND.
IT'S USUALLY RESERVED FOR ANOTHER ACTIVITY...

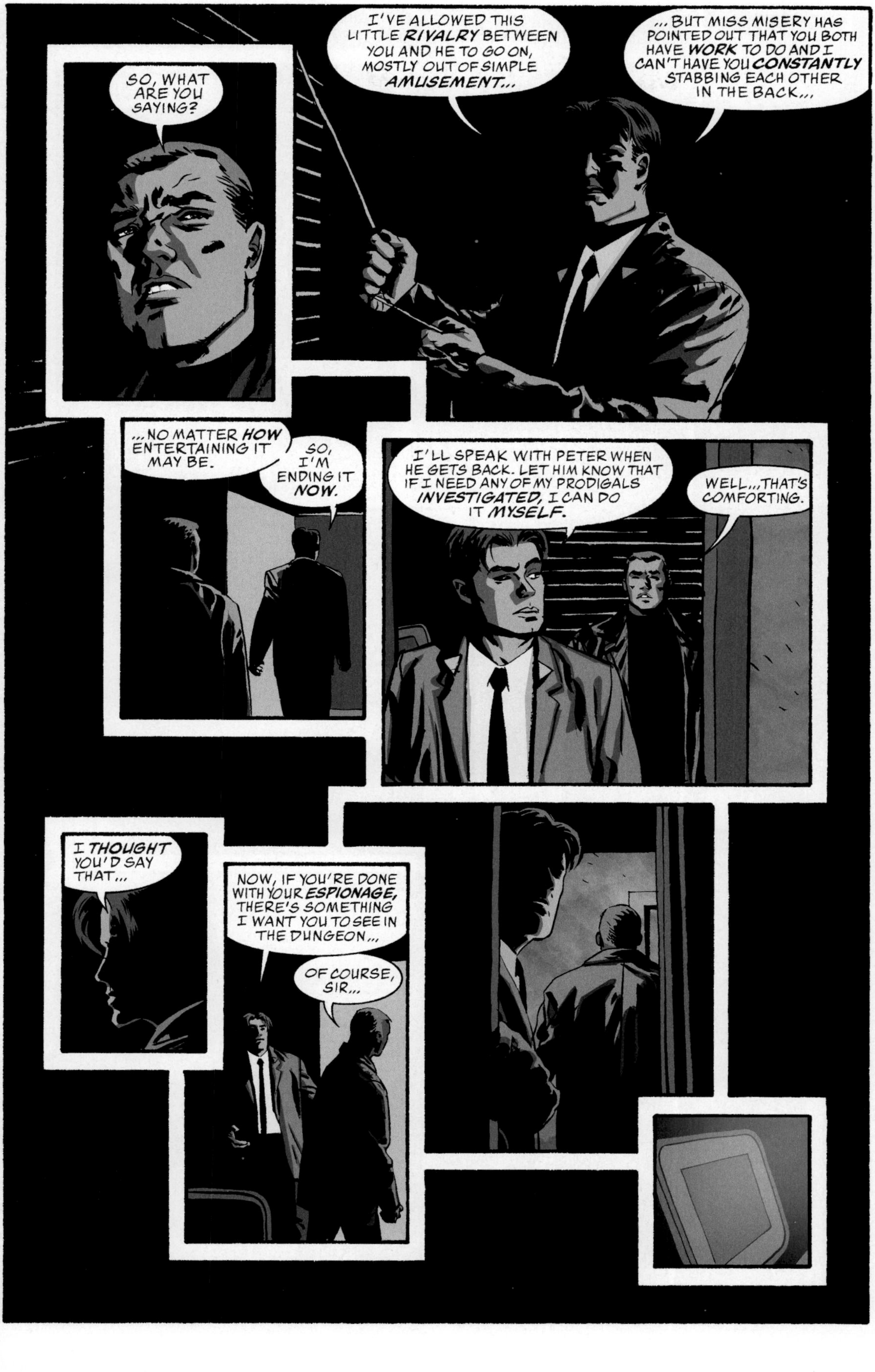
SO, WHAT ARE YOU SAYING?
I'VE ALLOWED THIS LITTLE RIVALRY BETWEEN YOU AND HE TO GO ON, MOSTLY OUT OF SIMPLE AMUSEMENT...
... BUT MISS MISERY HAS POINTED OUT THAT YOU BOTH HAVE WORK TO DO AND I CAN'T HAVE YOU CONSTANTLY STABBING EACH OTHER IN THE BACK...
...NO MATTER HOW ENTERTAINING IT MAY BE.
SO, I'M ENDING IT NOW.
I'LL SPEAK WITH PETER WHEN HE GETS BACK. LET HIM KNOW THAT IF I NEED ANY OF MY PRODIGALS INVESTIGATED, I CAN DO IT MYSELF.
WELL...THAT'S COMFORTING.
I THOUGHT YOU'D SAY THAT...
NOW, IF YOU'RE DONE WITH YOUR ESPIONAGE, THERE'S SOMETHING I WANT YOU TO SEE IN THE DUNGEON...
OF COURSE, SIR...

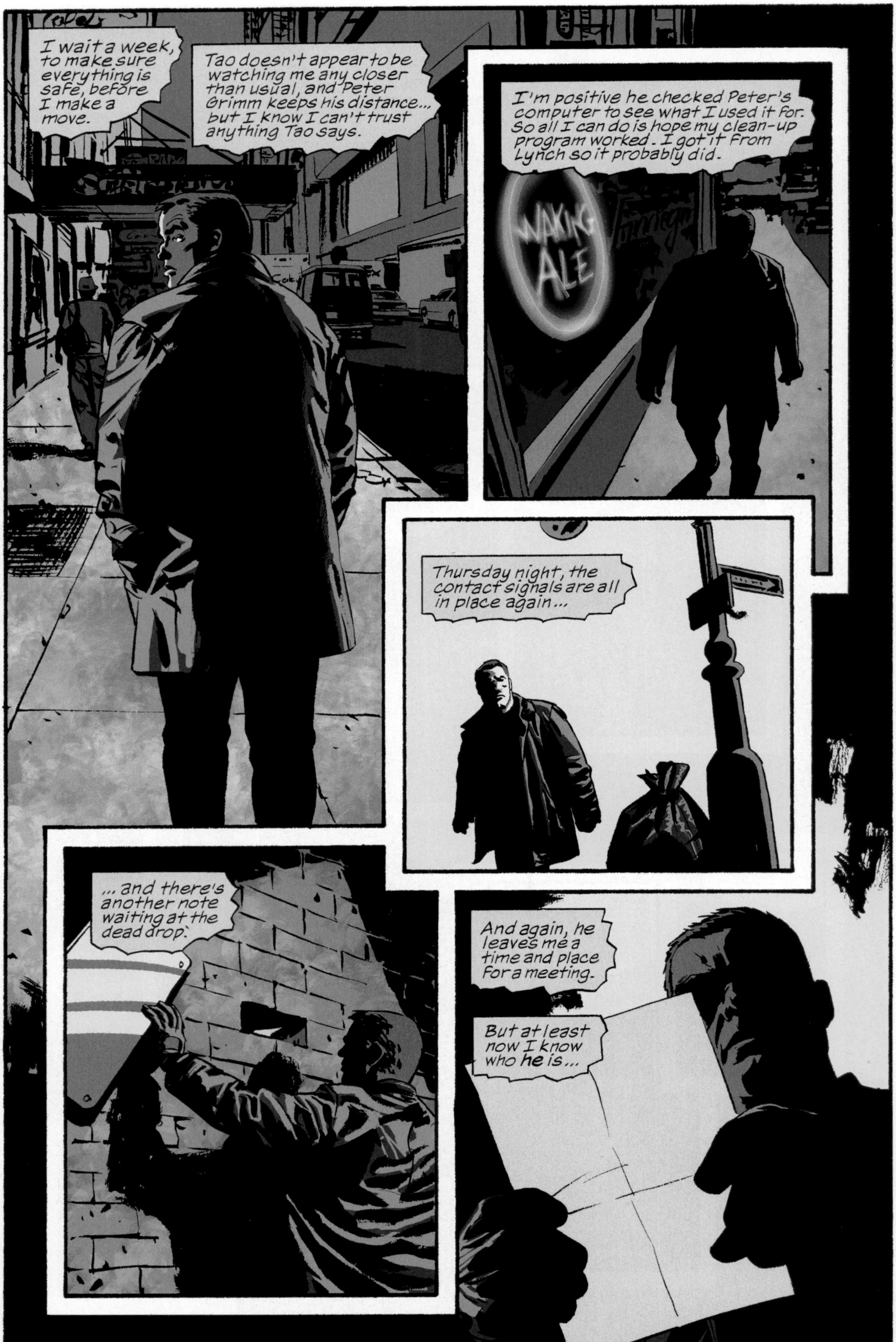
I wait a week, to make sure everything is safe, before I make a move.
Tao doesn't appear to be watching me any closer than usual, and Peter Grimm keeps his distance... but I know I can't trust anything Tao says.
I'm positive he checked Peter's computer to see what I used it for. So all I can do is hope my clean-up program worked. I got it from Lynch so it probably did.
WAKING ALE
Thursday night, the contact signals are all in place again...
...and there's another note waiting at the dead drop.
And again, he leaves me a time and place for a meeting.
But at least now I know who **he** is...

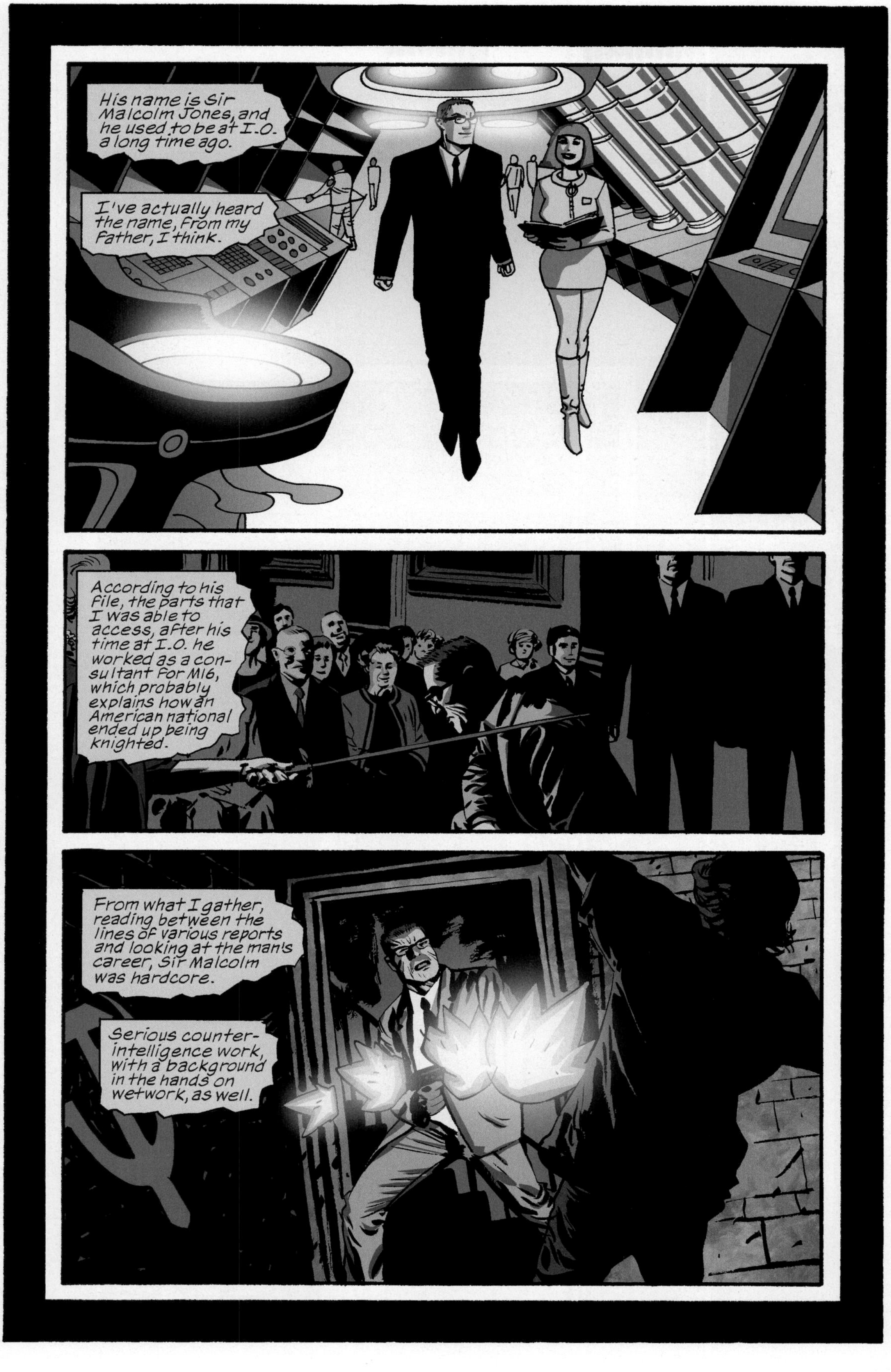
His name is Sir Malcolm Jones, and he used to be at I.O. a long time ago.
I've actually heard the name, from my father, I think.
According to his file, the parts that I was able to access, after his time at I.O. he worked as a consultant for MI6, which probably explains how an American national ended up being knighted.
From what I gather, reading between the lines of various reports and looking at the man's career, Sir Malcolm was hardcore.
Serious counter-intelligence work, with a background in the hands on wetwork, as well.

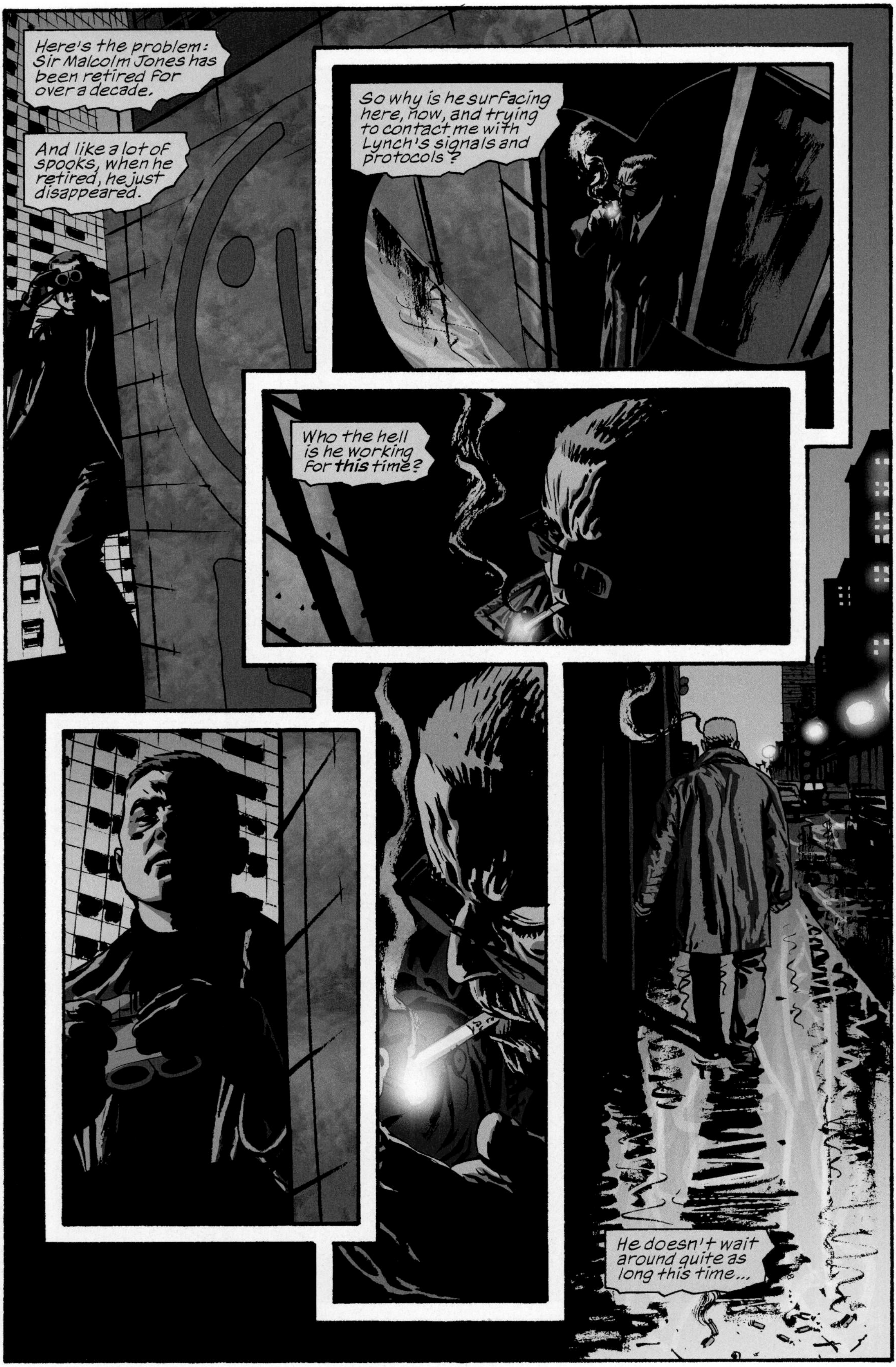
Here's the problem: Sir Malcolm Jones has been retired for over a decade.
And like a lot of spooks, when he retired, he just disappeared.
So why is he surfacing here, now, and trying to contact me with Lynch's signals and protocols?
Who the hell is he working for **this** time?
He doesn't wait around quite as long this time...

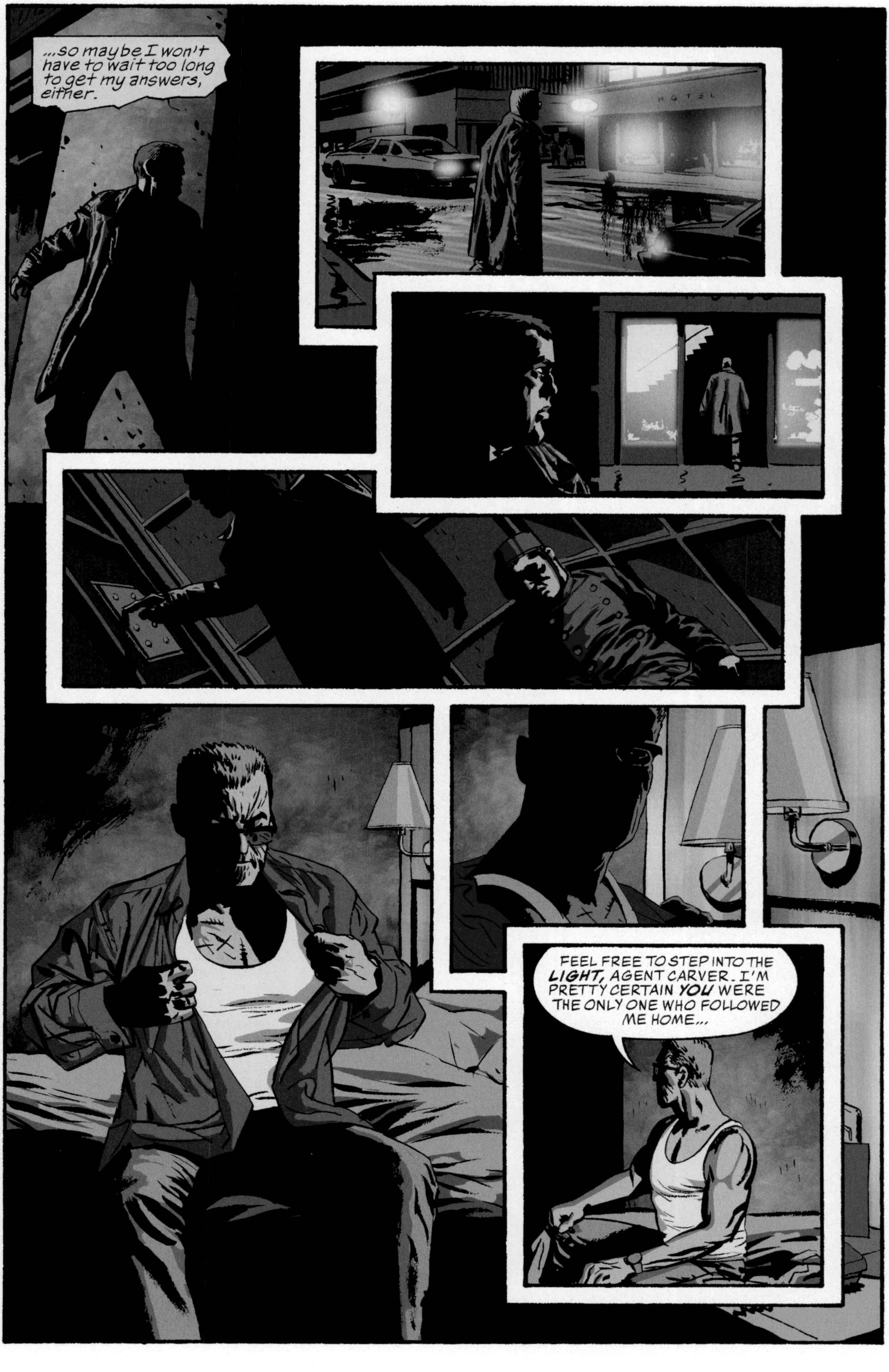
...so maybe I won't have to wait too long to get my answers, either.
FEEL FREE TO STEP INTO THE LIGHT, AGENT CARVER. I'M PRETTY CERTAIN YOU WERE THE ONLY ONE WHO FOLLOWED ME HOME...

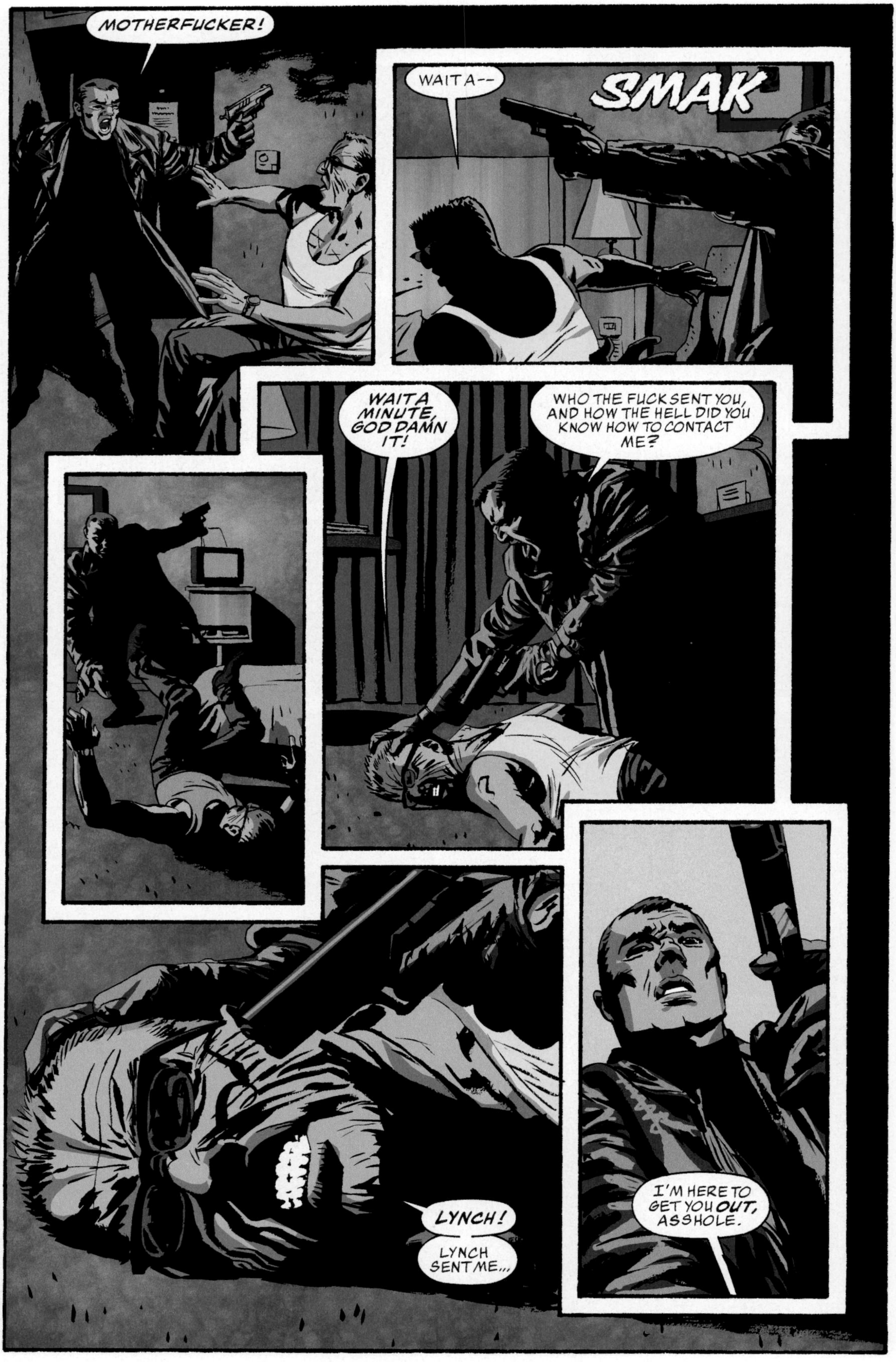
MOTHERFUCKER!
WAIT A--
SMAK
WAIT A MINUTE, GOD DAMN IT!
WHO THE FUCK SENT YOU, AND HOW THE HELL DID YOU KNOW HOW TO CONTACT ME?
LYNCH!
LYNCH SENT ME...
I'M HERE TO GET YOU OUT, ASSHOLE.

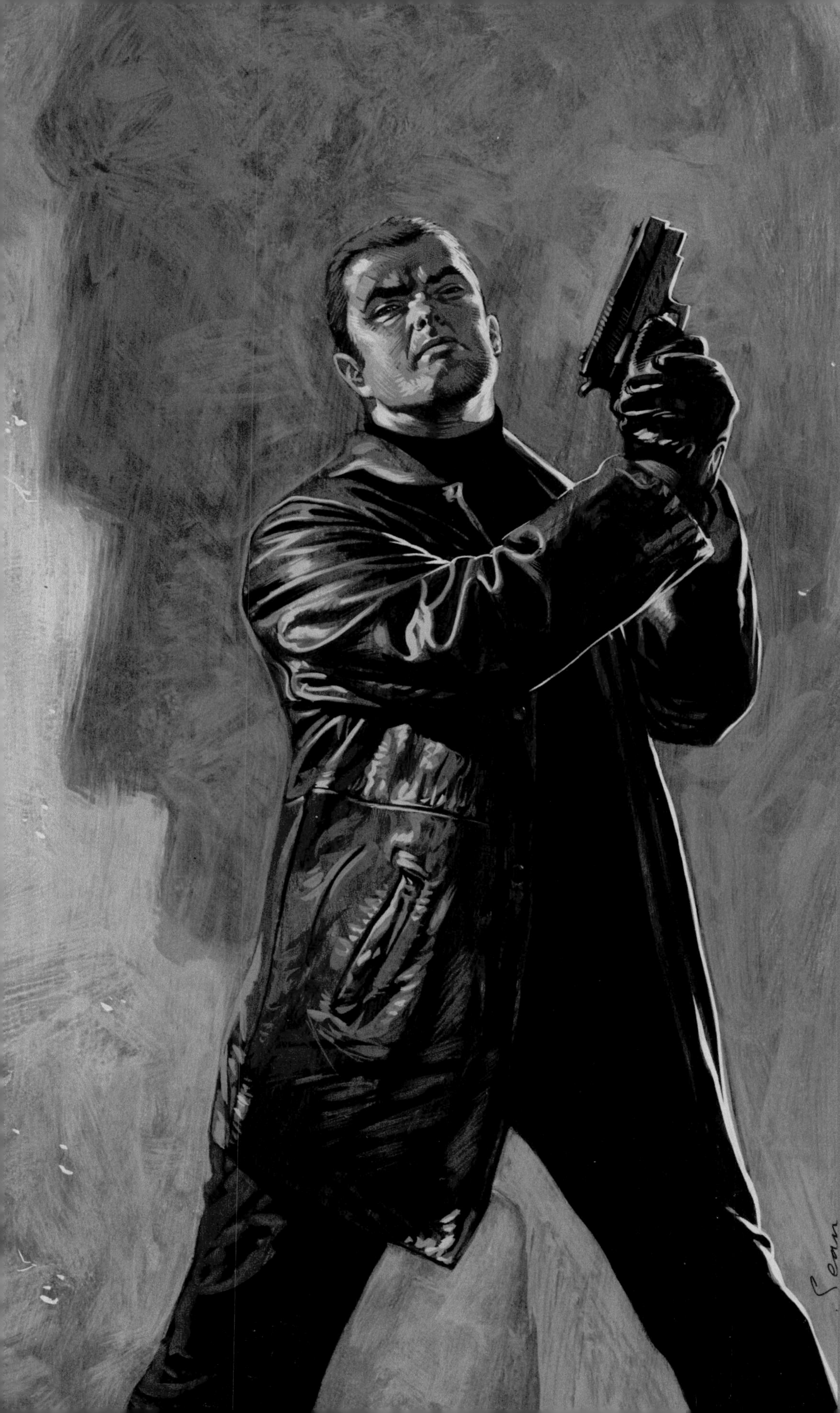
Sean
2003

Cover by SEAN PHILLIPS

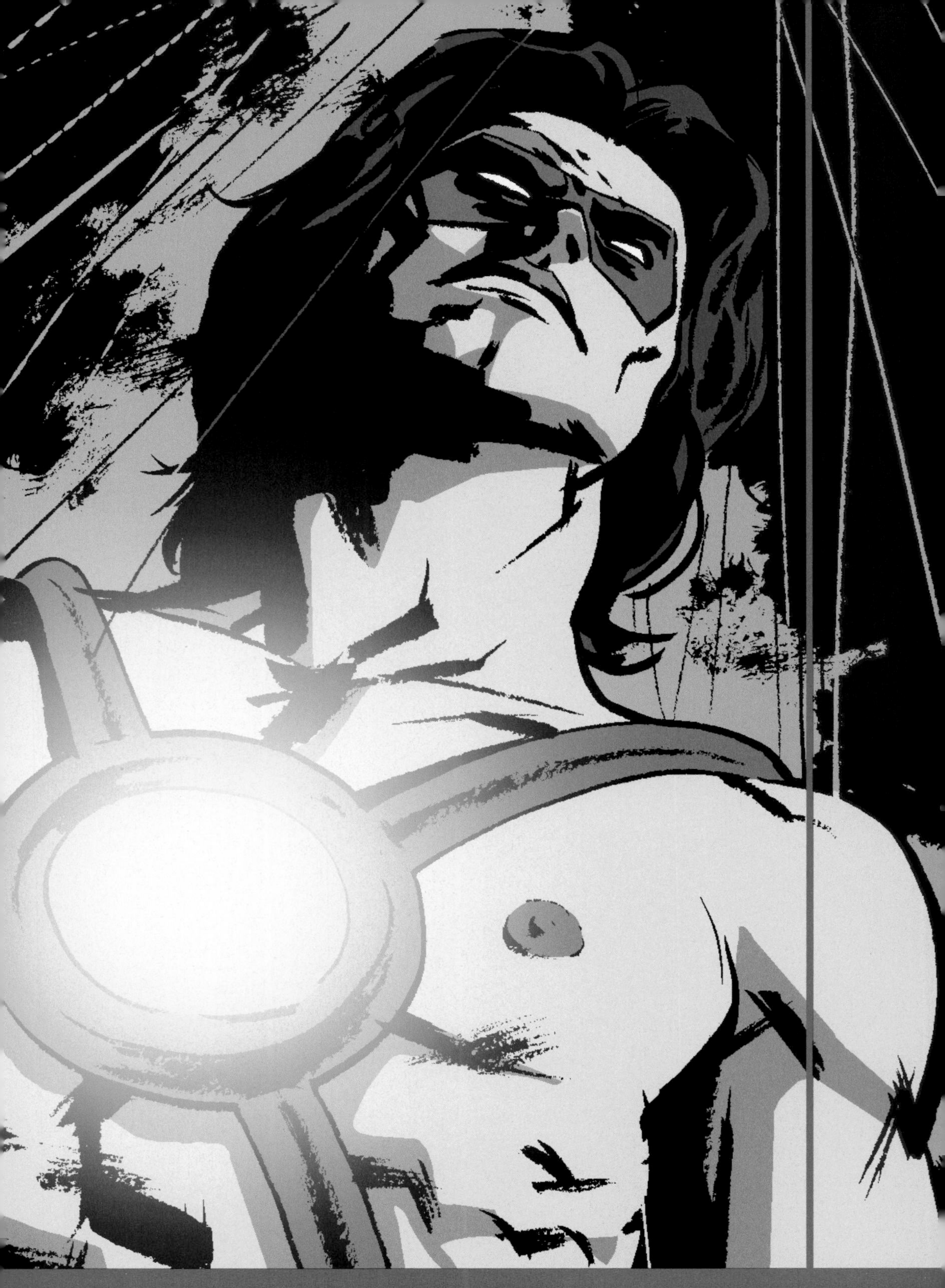

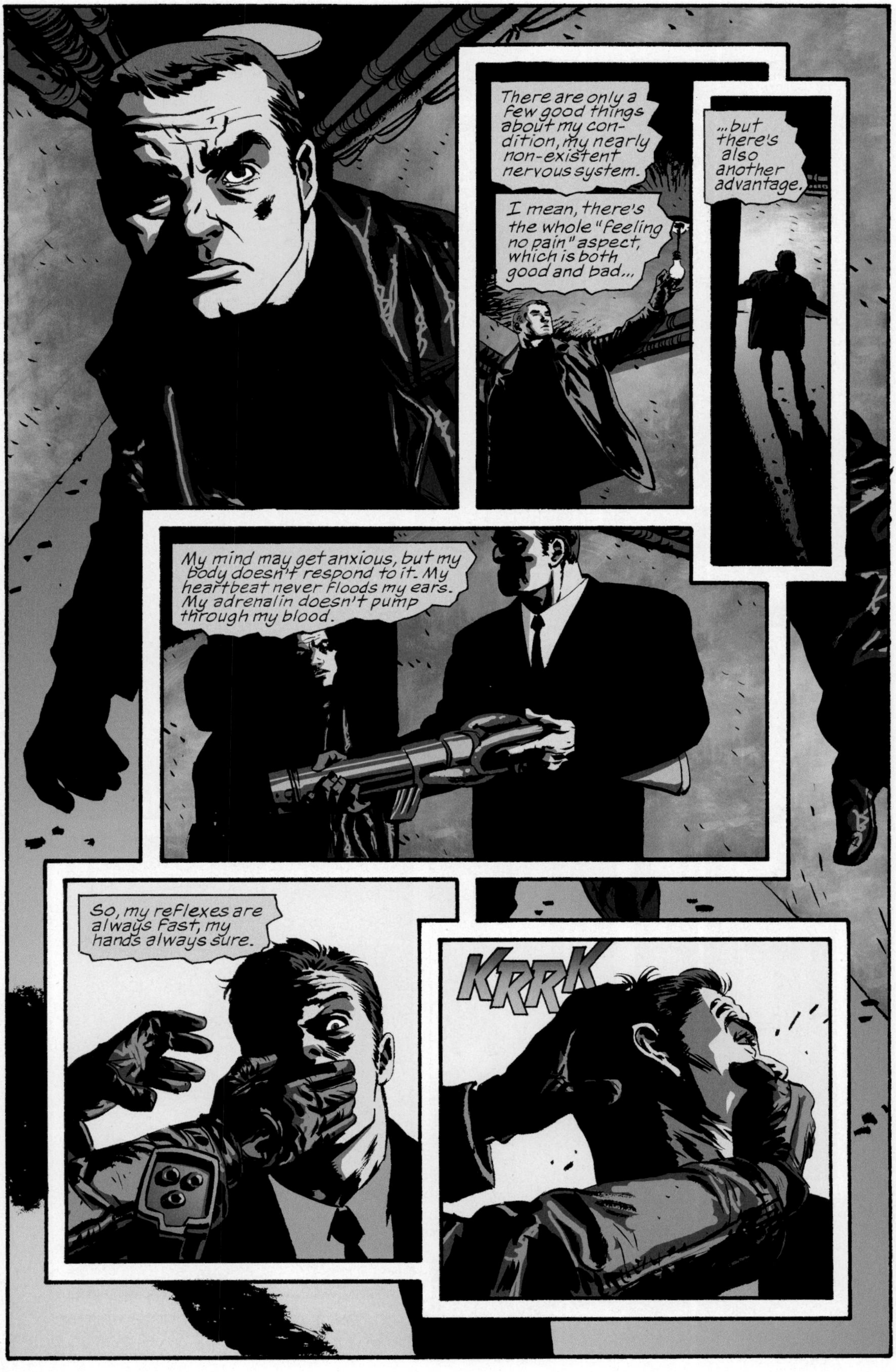
There are only a few good things about my condition, my nearly non-existent nervous system.
I mean, there's the whole "feeling no pain" aspect, which is both good and bad...
...but there's also another advantage.
My mind may get anxious, but my body doesn't respond to it. My heartbeat never floods my ears. My adrenalin doesn't pump through my blood.
So, my reflexes are always fast, my hands always sure.
KRRK

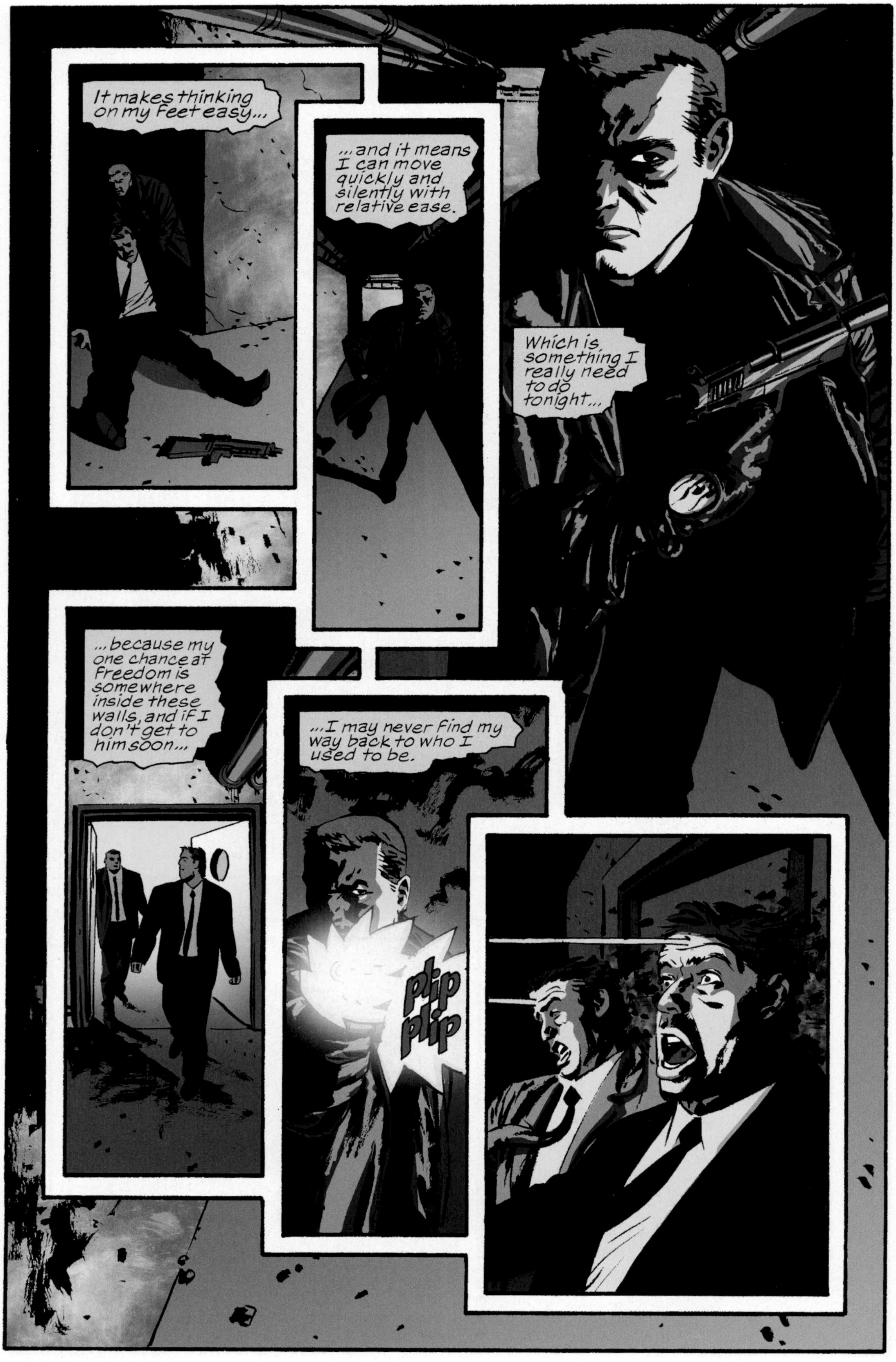
It makes thinking on my feet easy...
...and it means I can move quickly and silently with relative ease.
Which is something I really need to do tonight...
...because my one chance at freedom is somewhere inside these walls, and if I don't get to him soon...
...I may never find my way back to who I used to be.
plip plip

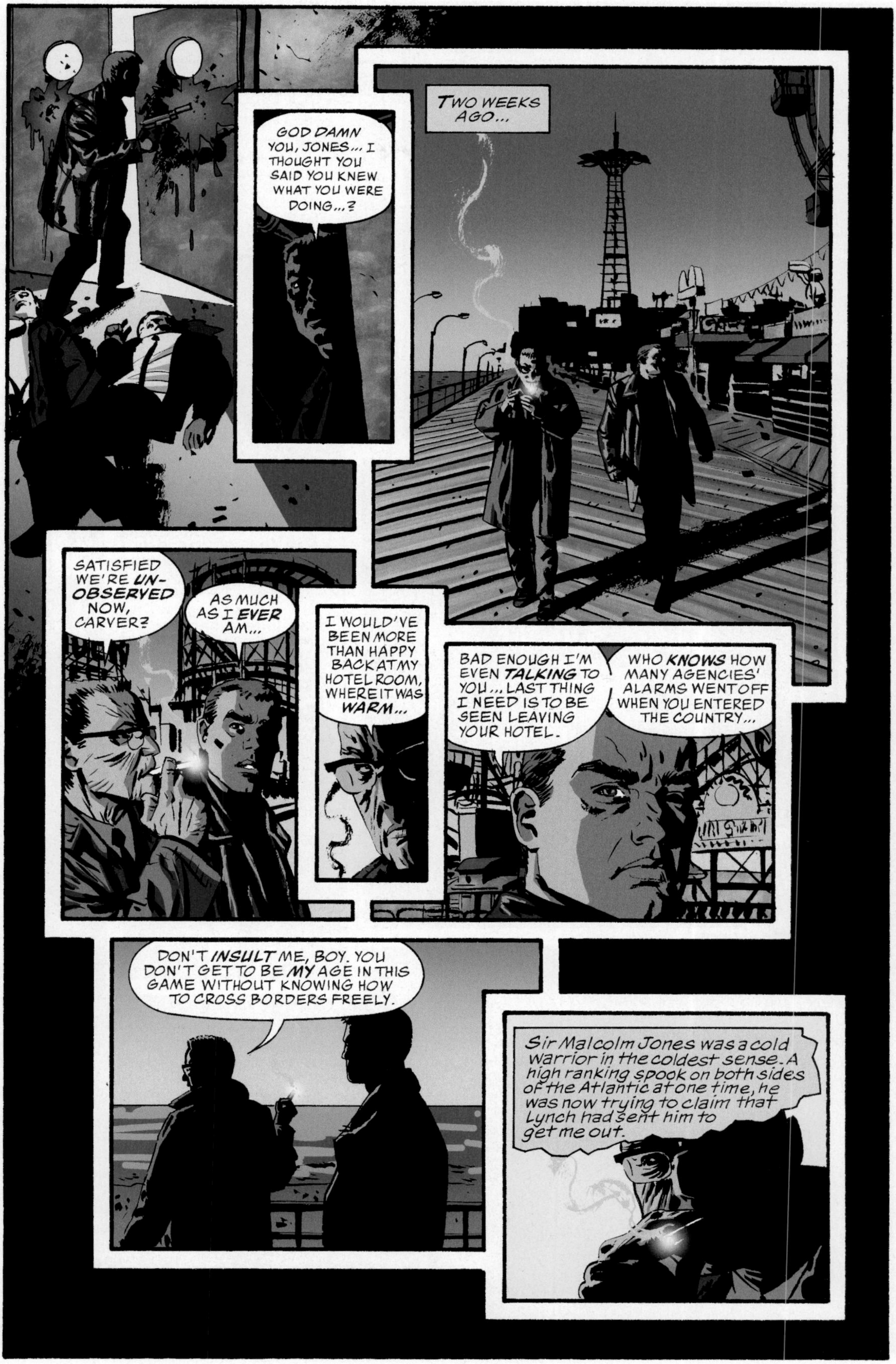
GOD DAMN YOU, JONES... I THOUGHT YOU SAID YOU KNEW WHAT YOU WERE DOING...?
TWO WEEKS AGO...
SATISFIED WE'RE UN-OBSERVED NOW, CARVER?
AS MUCH AS I EVER AM...
I WOULD'VE BEEN MORE THAN HAPPY BACK AT MY HOTEL ROOM, WHERE IT WAS WARM...
BAD ENOUGH I'M EVEN TALKING TO YOU... LAST THING I NEED IS TO BE SEEN LEAVING YOUR HOTEL.
WHO KNOWS HOW MANY AGENCIES' ALARMS WENT OFF WHEN YOU ENTERED THE COUNTRY...
DON'T INSULT ME, BOY. YOU DON'T GET TO BE MY AGE IN THIS GAME WITHOUT KNOWING HOW TO CROSS BORDERS FREELY.
Sir Malcolm Jones was a cold warrior in the coldest sense. A high ranking spook on both sides of the Atlantic at one time, he was now trying to claim that Lynch had sent him to get me out.

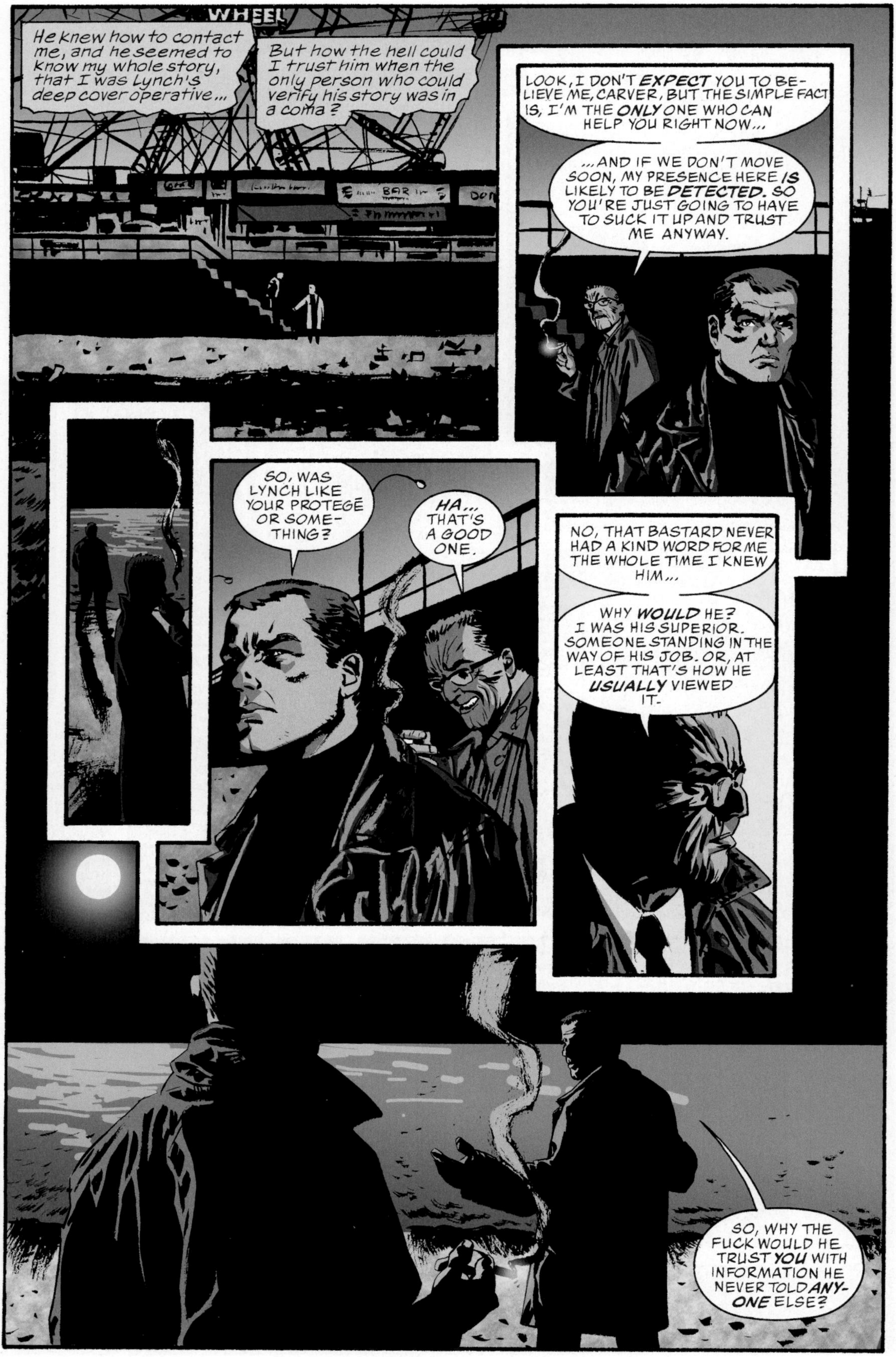
He knew how to contact me, and he seemed to know my whole story, that I was Lynch's deep cover operative...
But how the hell could I trust him when the only person who could verify his story was in a coma?
LOOK, I DON'T EXPECT YOU TO BELIEVE ME, CARVER, BUT THE SIMPLE FACT IS, I'M THE ONLY ONE WHO CAN HELP YOU RIGHT NOW...
...AND IF WE DON'T MOVE SOON, MY PRESENCE HERE IS LIKELY TO BE DETECTED. SO YOU'RE JUST GOING TO HAVE TO SUCK IT UP AND TRUST ME ANYWAY.
SO, WAS LYNCH LIKE YOUR PROTEGE OR SOMETHING?
HA... THAT'S A GOOD ONE.
NO, THAT BASTARD NEVER HAD A KIND WORD FOR ME THE WHOLE TIME I KNEW HIM...
WHY WOULD HE? I WAS HIS SUPERIOR. SOMEONE STANDING IN THE WAY OF HIS JOB. OR, AT LEAST THAT'S HOW HE USUALLY VIEWED IT.
SO, WHY THE FUCK WOULD HE TRUST YOU WITH INFORMATION HE NEVER TOLD ANYONE ELSE?

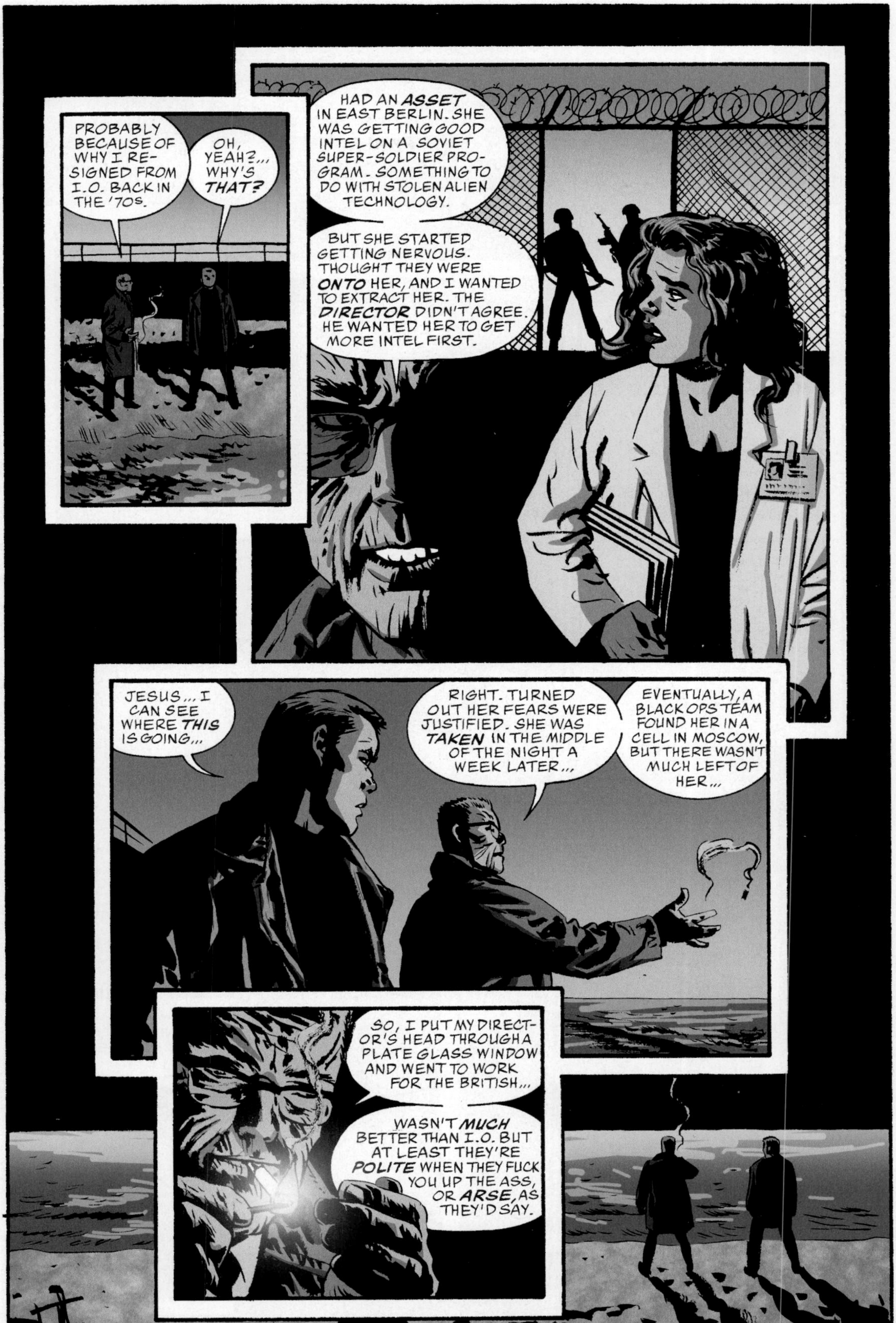
PROBABLY BECAUSE OF WHY I RESIGNED FROM I.O. BACK IN THE '70s.
OH, YEAH?... WHY'S THAT?
HAD AN ASSET IN EAST BERLIN. SHE WAS GETTING GOOD INTEL ON A SOVIET SUPER-SOLDIER PROGRAM. SOMETHING TO DO WITH STOLEN ALIEN TECHNOLOGY.
BUT SHE STARTED GETTING NERVOUS. THOUGHT THEY WERE ONTO HER, AND I WANTED TO EXTRACT HER. THE DIRECTOR DIDN'T AGREE. HE WANTED HER TO GET MORE INTEL FIRST.
JESUS... I CAN SEE WHERE THIS IS GOING...
RIGHT. TURNED OUT HER FEARS WERE JUSTIFIED. SHE WAS TAKEN IN THE MIDDLE OF THE NIGHT A WEEK LATER...
EVENTUALLY, A BLACK OPS TEAM FOUND HER IN A CELL IN MOSCOW, BUT THERE WASN'T MUCH LEFT OF HER...
SO, I PUT MY DIRECTOR'S HEAD THROUGH A PLATE GLASS WINDOW AND WENT TO WORK FOR THE BRITISH...
WASN'T MUCH BETTER THAN I.O. BUT AT LEAST THEY'RE POLITE WHEN THEY FUCK YOU UP THE ASS, OR ARSE, AS THEY'D SAY.

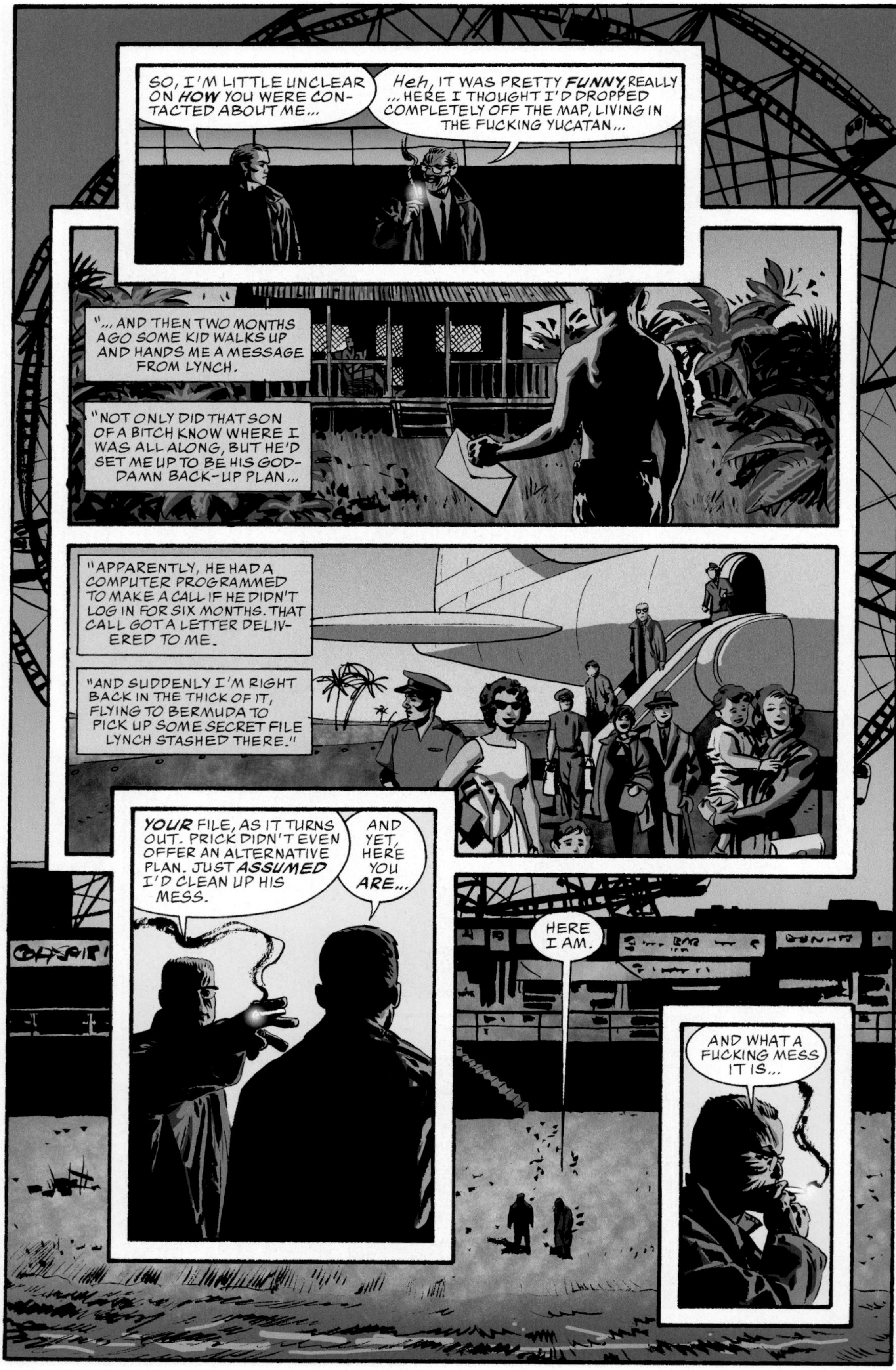
SO, I'M LITTLE UNCLEAR ON HOW YOU WERE CONTACTED ABOUT ME...
Heh, IT WAS PRETTY FUNNY, REALLY ...HERE I THOUGHT I'D DROPPED COMPLETELY OFF THE MAP, LIVING IN THE FUCKING YUCATAN...
"...AND THEN TWO MONTHS AGO SOME KID WALKS UP AND HANDS ME A MESSAGE FROM LYNCH.
"NOT ONLY DID THAT SON OF A BITCH KNOW WHERE I WAS ALL ALONG, BUT HE'D SET ME UP TO BE HIS GOD-DAMN BACK-UP PLAN...
"APPARENTLY, HE HAD A COMPUTER PROGRAMMED TO MAKE A CALL IF HE DIDN'T LOG IN FOR SIX MONTHS. THAT CALL GOT A LETTER DELIVERED TO ME.
"AND SUDDENLY I'M RIGHT BACK IN THE THICK OF IT, FLYING TO BERMUDA TO PICK UP SOME SECRET FILE LYNCH STASHED THERE."
YOUR FILE, AS IT TURNS OUT. PRICK DIDN'T EVEN OFFER AN ALTERNATIVE PLAN. JUST ASSUMED I'D CLEAN UP HIS MESS.
AND YET, HERE YOU ARE...
HERE I AM.
AND WHAT A FUCKING MESS IT IS...

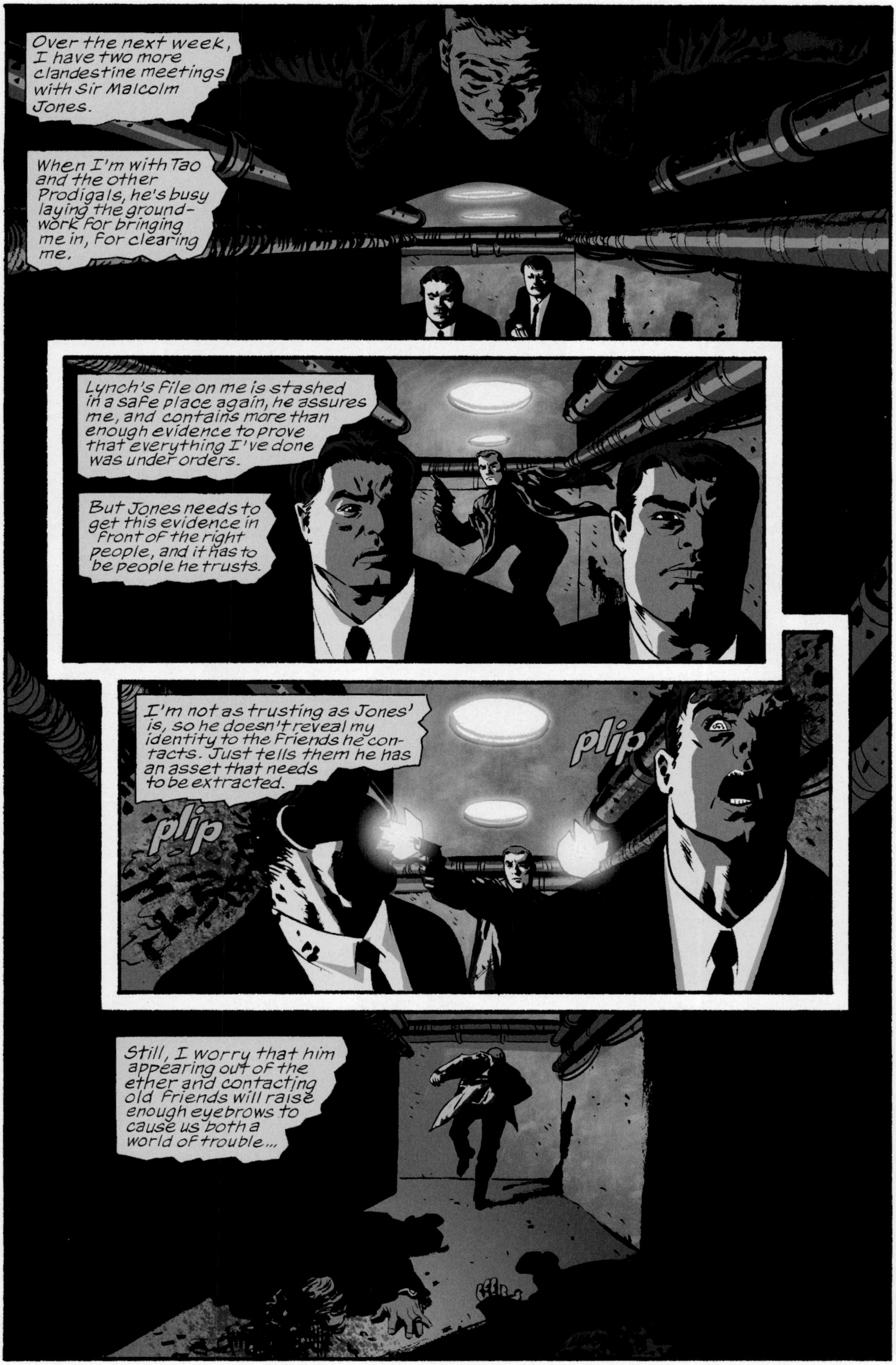
Over the next week, I have two more clandestine meetings with Sir Malcolm Jones.
When I'm with Tao and the other Prodigals, he's busy laying the ground-work for bringing me in, for clearing me.
Lynch's file on me is stashed in a safe place again, he assures me, and contains more than enough evidence to prove that everything I've done was under orders.
But Jones needs to get this evidence in front of the right people, and it has to be people he trusts.
I'm not as trusting as Jones' is, so he doesn't reveal my identity to the Friends he contacts. Just tells them he has an asset that needs to be extracted.
plip
plip
Still, I worry that him appearing out of the ether and contacting old friends will raise enough eyebrows to cause us both a world of trouble...

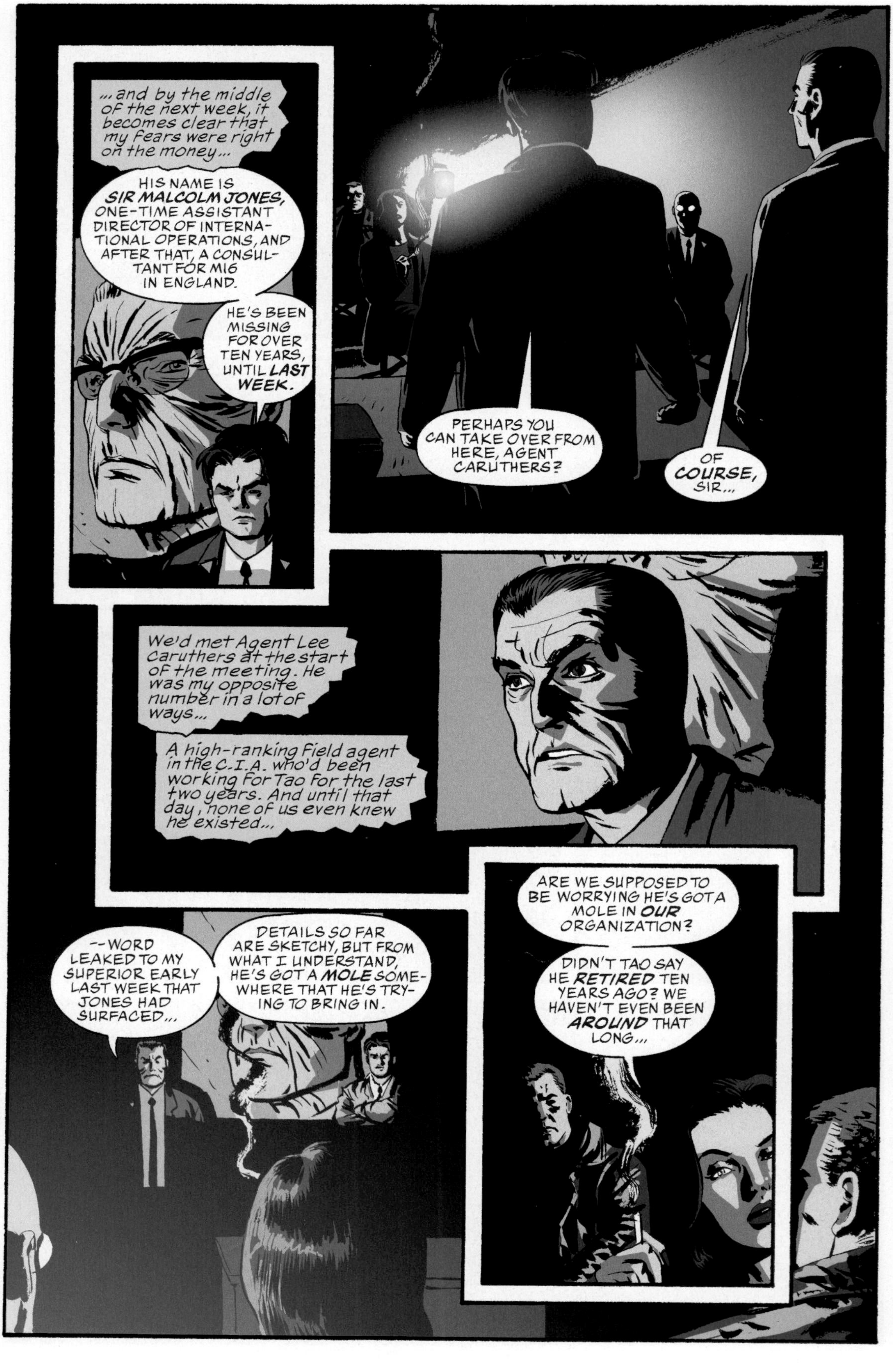
...and by the middle of the next week, it becomes clear that my fears were right on the money...
HIS NAME IS SIR MALCOLM JONES, ONE-TIME ASSISTANT DIRECTOR OF INTERNATIONAL OPERATIONS, AND AFTER THAT, A CONSULTANT FOR MI6 IN ENGLAND.
HE'S BEEN MISSING FOR OVER TEN YEARS, UNTIL LAST WEEK.
PERHAPS YOU CAN TAKE OVER FROM HERE, AGENT CARUTHERS?
OF COURSE, SIR...
We'd met Agent Lee Caruthers at the start of the meeting. He was my opposite number in a lot of ways...
A high-ranking field agent in the C.I.A. who'd been working for Tao for the last two years. And until that day, none of us even knew he existed...
--WORD LEAKED TO MY SUPERIOR EARLY LAST WEEK THAT JONES HAD SURFACED...
DETAILS SO FAR ARE SKETCHY, BUT FROM WHAT I UNDERSTAND, HE'S GOT A MOLE SOMEWHERE THAT HE'S TRYING TO BRING IN.
ARE WE SUPPOSED TO BE WORRYING HE'S GOT A MOLE IN OUR ORGANIZATION?
DIDN'T TAO SAY HE RETIRED TEN YEARS AGO? WE HAVEN'T EVEN BEEN AROUND THAT LONG...

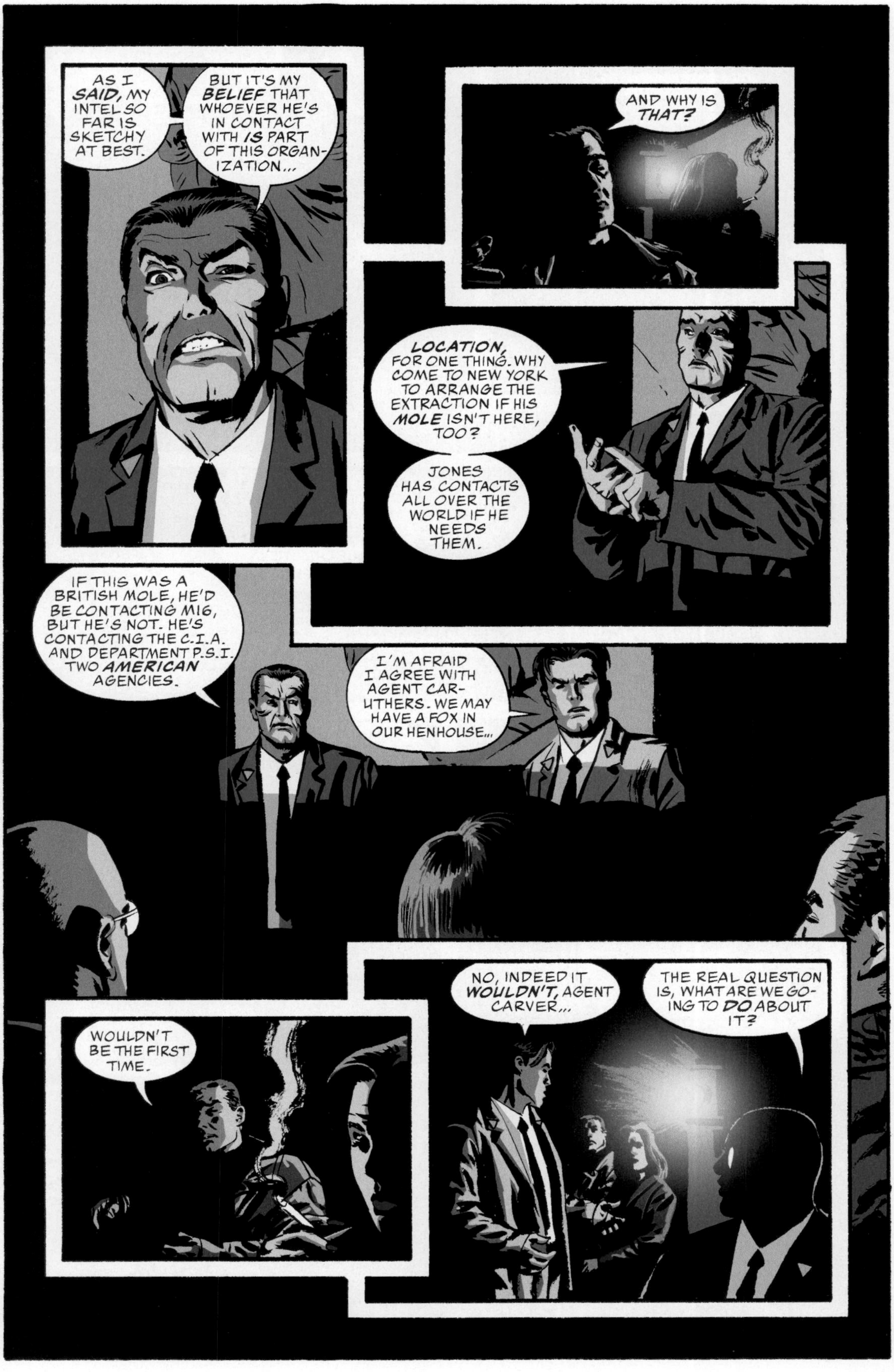
AS I SAID, MY INTEL SO FAR IS SKETCHY AT BEST.
BUT IT'S MY BELIEF THAT WHOEVER HE'S IN CONTACT WITH IS PART OF THIS ORGANIZATION...
AND WHY IS THAT?
LOCATION, FOR ONE THING. WHY COME TO NEW YORK TO ARRANGE THE EXTRACTION IF HIS MOLE ISN'T HERE, TOO?
JONES HAS CONTACTS ALL OVER THE WORLD IF HE NEEDS THEM.
IF THIS WAS A BRITISH MOLE, HE'D BE CONTACTING MI6, BUT HE'S NOT. HE'S CONTACTING THE C.I.A. AND DEPARTMENT P.S.I. TWO AMERICAN AGENCIES.
I'M AFRAID I AGREE WITH AGENT CARUTHERS. WE MAY HAVE A FOX IN OUR HENHOUSE...
WOULDN'T BE THE FIRST TIME.
NO, INDEED IT WOULDN'T, AGENT CARVER...
THE REAL QUESTION IS, WHAT ARE WE GOING TO DO ABOUT IT?

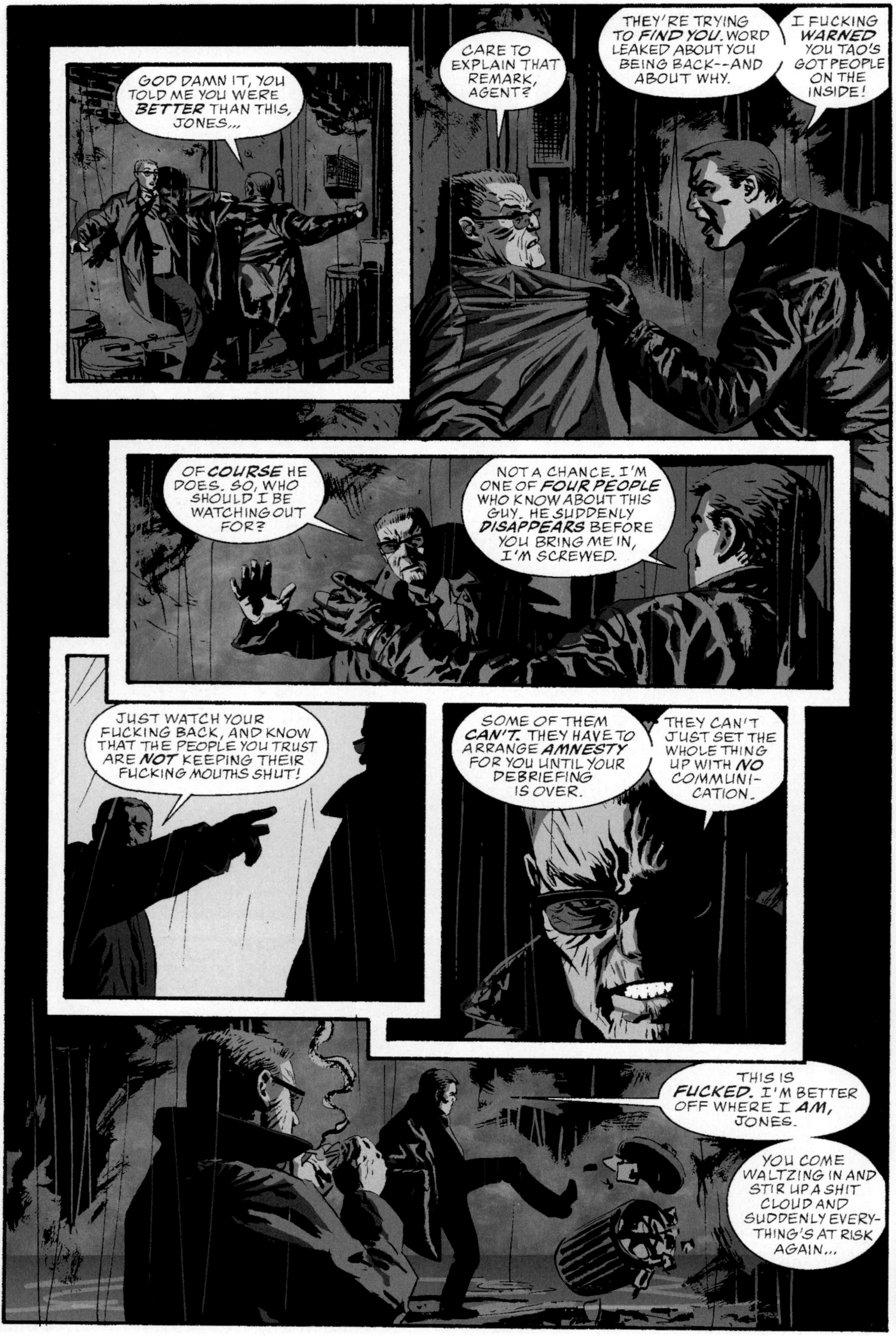
GOD DAMN IT, YOU TOLD ME YOU WERE BETTER THAN THIS, JONES...
CARE TO EXPLAIN THAT REMARK, AGENT?
THEY'RE TRYING TO FIND YOU. WORD LEAKED ABOUT YOU BEING BACK--AND ABOUT WHY.
I FUCKING WARNED YOU TAO'S GOT PEOPLE ON THE INSIDE!
OF COURSE HE DOES. SO, WHO SHOULD I BE WATCHING OUT FOR?
NOT A CHANCE. I'M ONE OF FOUR PEOPLE WHO KNOW ABOUT THIS GUY. HE SUDDENLY DISAPPEARS BEFORE YOU BRING ME IN, I'M SCREWED.
JUST WATCH YOUR FUCKING BACK, AND KNOW THAT THE PEOPLE YOU TRUST ARE NOT KEEPING THEIR FUCKING MOUTHS SHUT!
SOME OF THEM CAN'T. THEY HAVE TO ARRANGE AMNESTY FOR YOU UNTIL YOUR DEBRIEFING IS OVER.
THEY CAN'T JUST SET THE WHOLE THING UP WITH NO COMMUNI-CATION.
THIS IS FUCKED. I'M BETTER OFF WHERE I AM, JONES.
YOU COME WALTZING IN AND STIR UP A SHIT CLOUD AND SUDDENLY EVERY-THING'S AT RISK AGAIN...

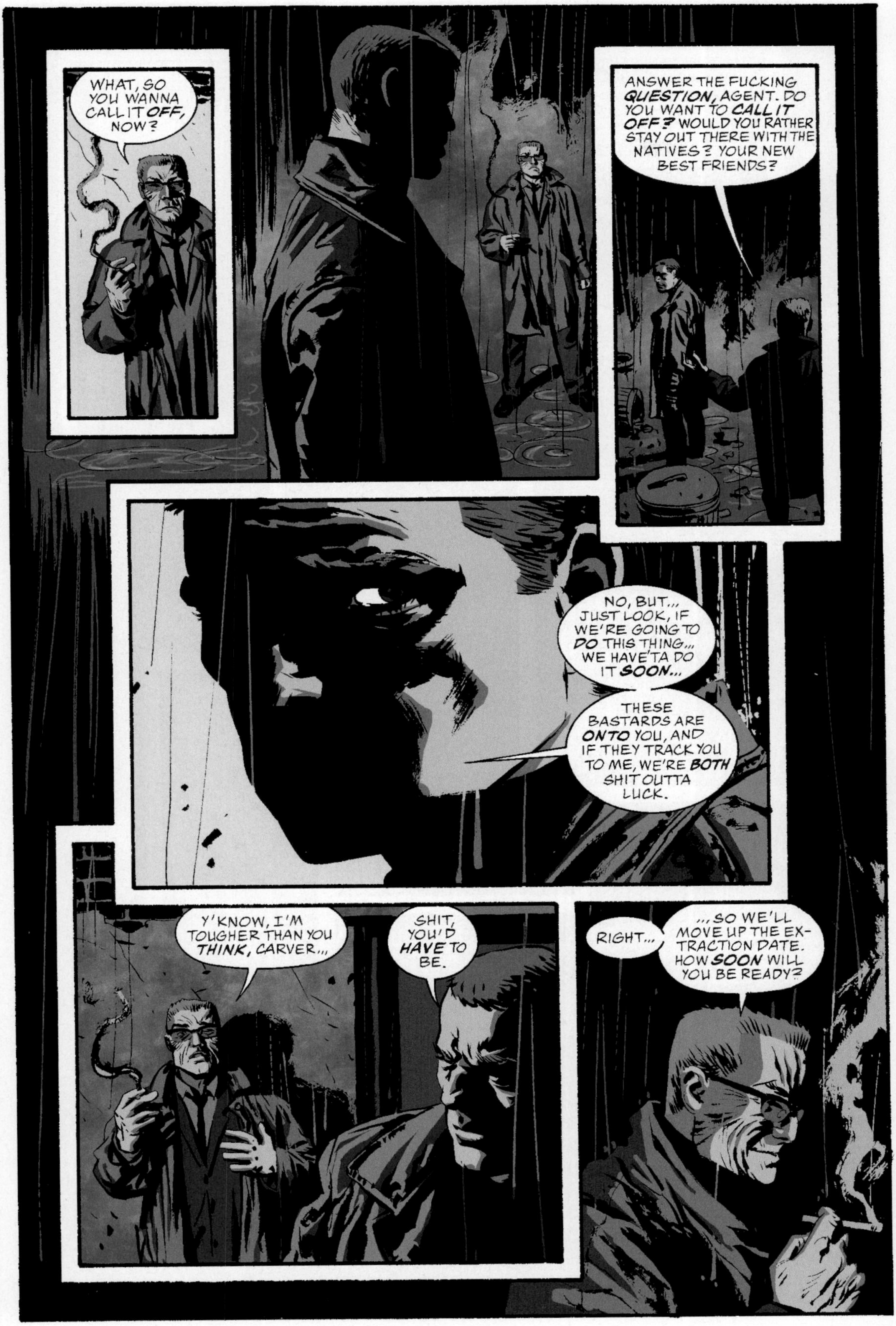
WHAT, SO YOU WANNA CALL IT OFF, NOW?
ANSWER THE FUCKING QUESTION, AGENT. DO YOU WANT TO CALL IT OFF? WOULD YOU RATHER STAY OUT THERE WITH THE NATIVES? YOUR NEW BEST FRIENDS?
NO, BUT... JUST LOOK, IF WE'RE GOING TO DO THIS THING... WE HAVE'TA DO IT SOON...
THESE BASTARDS ARE ONTO YOU, AND IF THEY TRACK YOU TO ME, WE'RE BOTH SHIT OUTTA LUCK.
Y'KNOW, I'M TOUGHER THAN YOU THINK, CARVER...
SHIT, YOU'D HAVE TO BE.
RIGHT...
...SO WE'LL MOVE UP THE EXTRACTION DATE. HOW SOON WILL YOU BE READY?

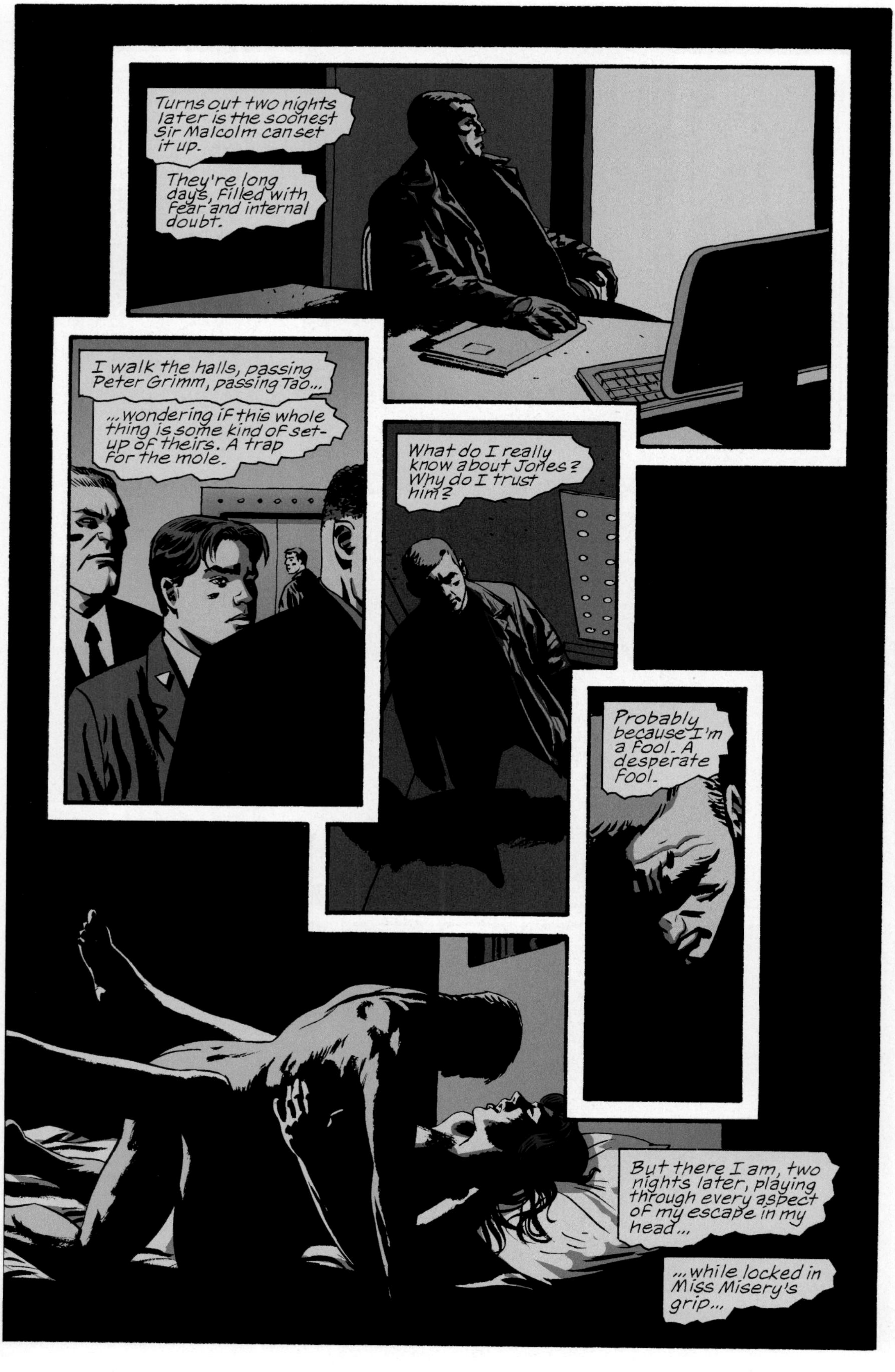
Turns out two nights later is the soonest Sir Malcolm can set it up.
They're long days, filled with fear and internal doubt.
I walk the halls, passing Peter Grimm, passing Tao...
...wondering if this whole thing is some kind of set-up of theirs. A trap for the mole.
What do I really know about Jones? Why do I trust him?
Probably because I'm a fool. A desperate fool.
But there I am, two nights later, playing through every aspect of my escape in my head...
...while locked in Miss Misery's grip...

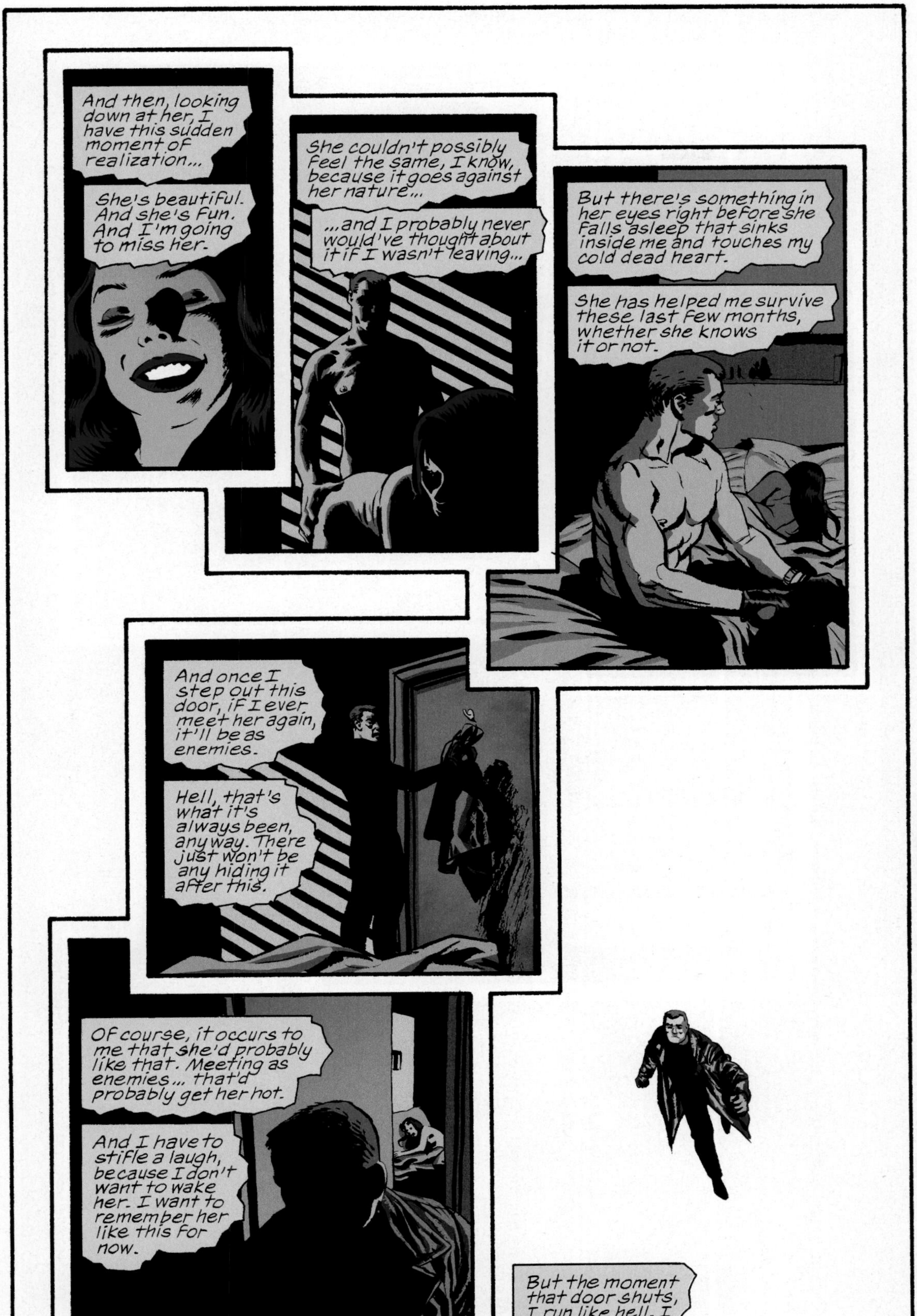

And then, looking down at her, I have this sudden moment of realization...

She's beautiful. And she's fun. And I'm going to miss her.

She couldn't possibly feel the same, I know, because it goes against her nature...

...and I probably never would've thought about it if I wasn't leaving...

But there's something in her eyes right before she falls asleep that sinks inside me and touches my cold dead heart.

She has helped me survive these last few months, whether she knows it or not.

And once I step out this door, if I ever meet her again, it'll be as enemies.

Hell, that's what it's always been, anyway. There just won't be any hiding it after this.

Of course, it occurs to me that she'd probably like that. Meeting as enemies... that'd probably get her hot.

And I have to stifle a laugh, because I don't want to wake her. I want to remember her like this for now.

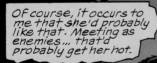

But the moment that door shuts, I run like hell. I run away...

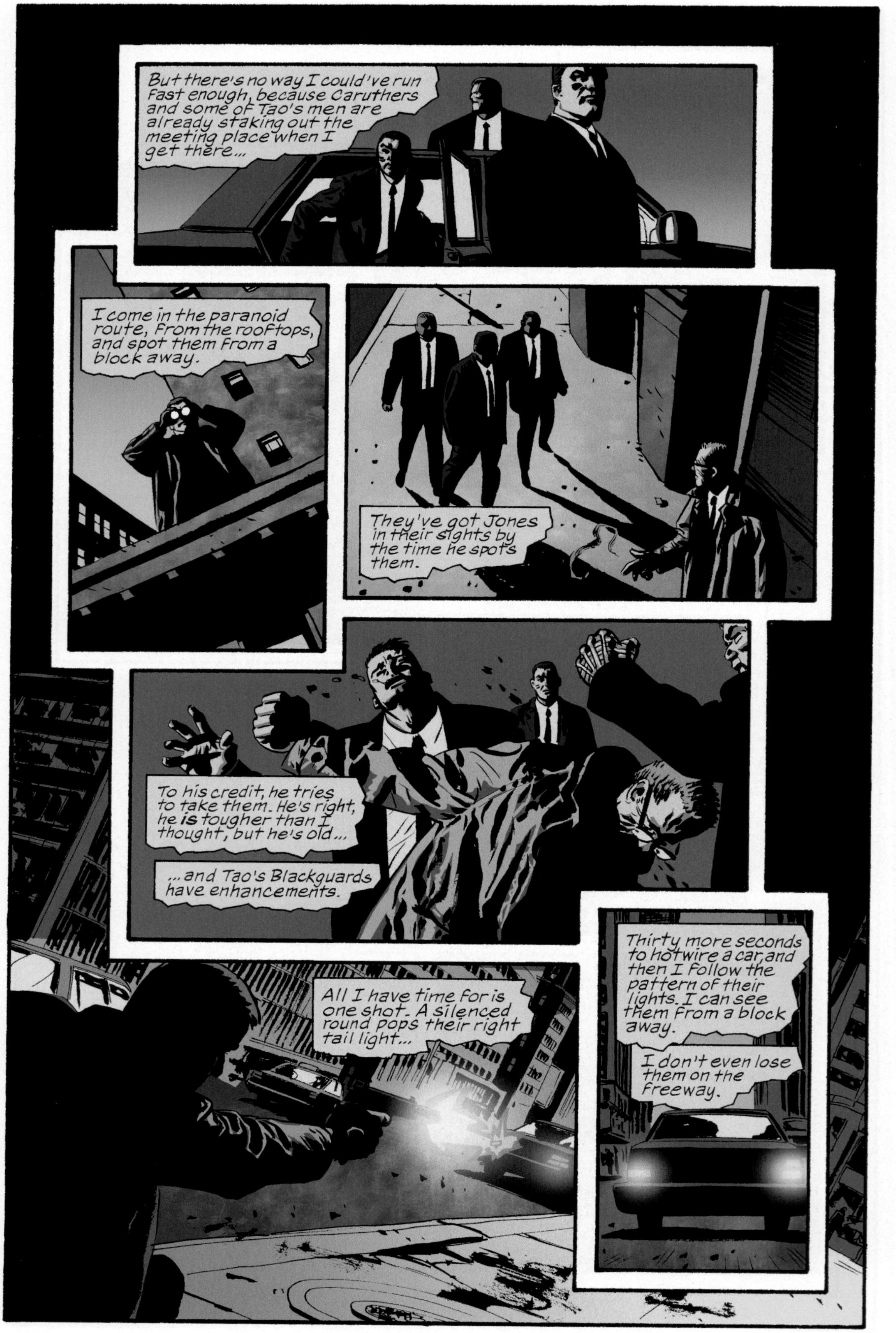
But there's no way I could've run fast enough, because Caruthers and some of Tao's men are already staking out the meeting place when I get there...
I come in the paranoid route, from the rooftops, and spot them from a block away.
They've got Jones in their sights by the time he spots them.
To his credit, he tries to take them. He's right, he **is** tougher than I thought, but he's old...
...and Tao's Blackguards have enhancements.
All I have time for is one shot. A silenced round pops their right tail light...
Thirty more seconds to hotwire a car, and then I follow the pattern of their lights. I can see them from a block away.
I don't even lose them on the freeway.

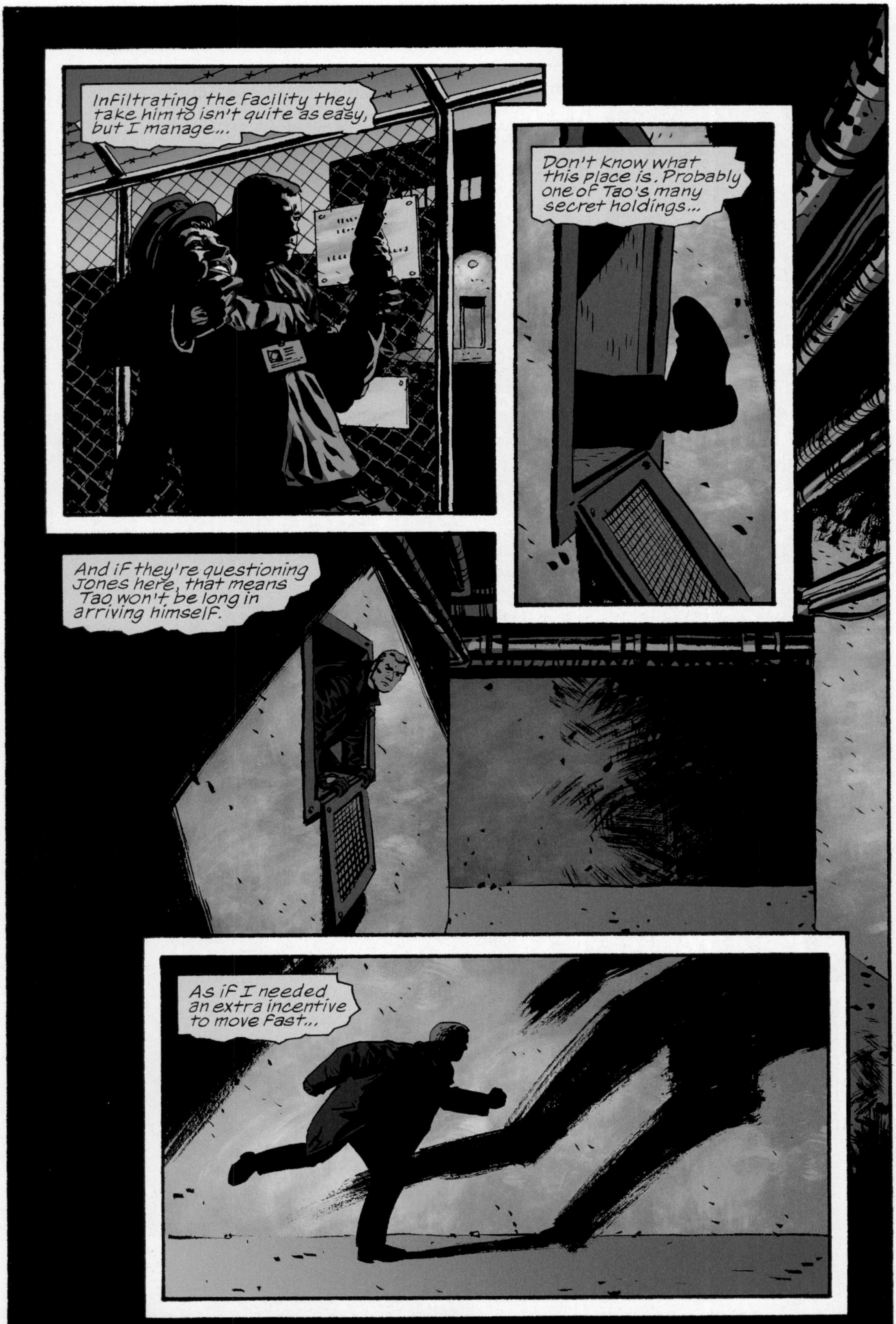
Infiltrating the facility they take him to isn't quite as easy, but I manage...
Don't know what this place is. Probably one of Tao's many secret holdings...
And if they're questioning Jones here, that means Tao won't be long in arriving himself.
As if I needed an extra incentive to move fast...

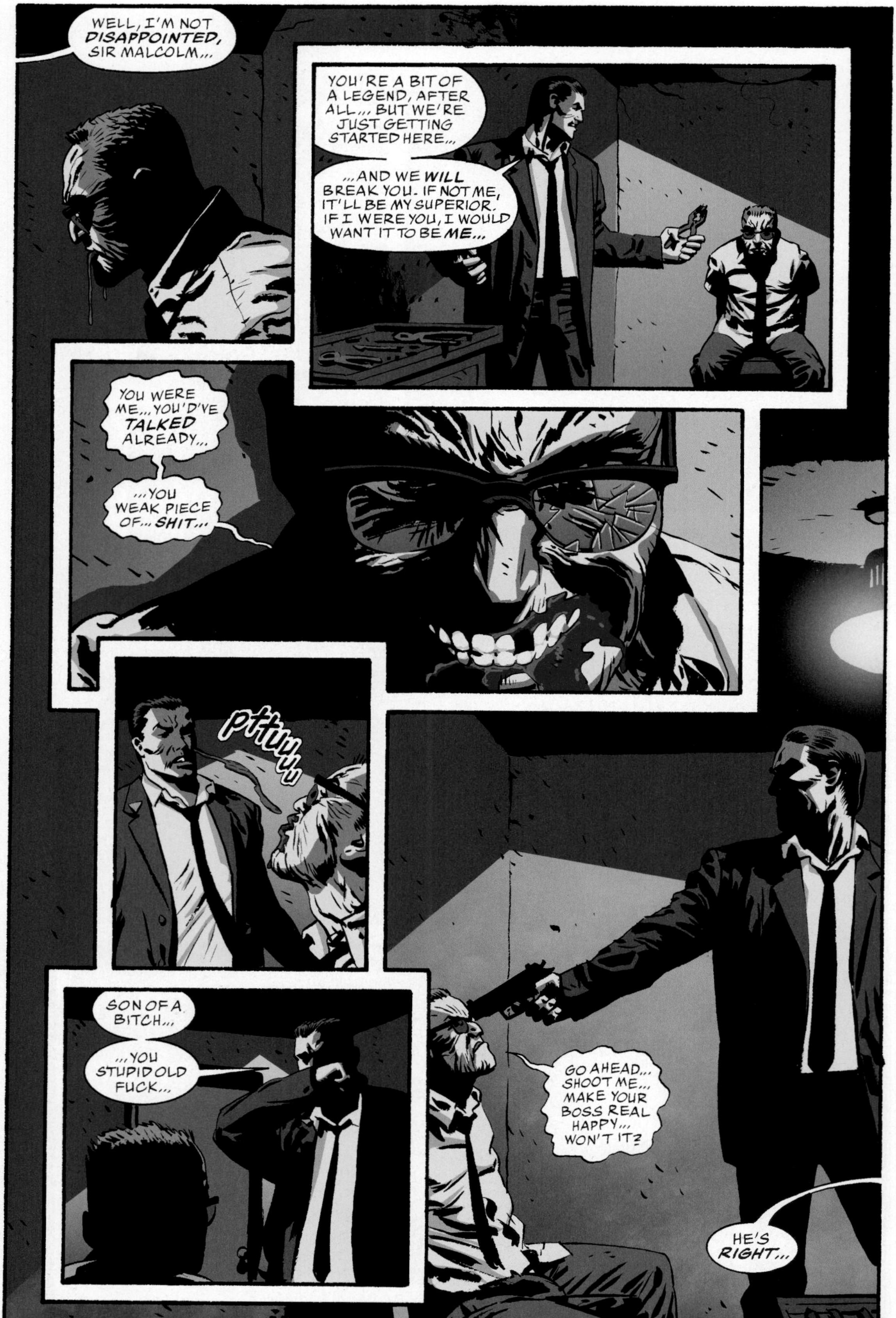
WELL, I'M NOT DISAPPOINTED, SIR MALCOLM...
YOU'RE A BIT OF A LEGEND, AFTER ALL... BUT WE'RE JUST GETTING STARTED HERE...
...AND WE WILL BREAK YOU- IF NOT ME, IT'LL BE MY SUPERIOR. IF I WERE YOU, I WOULD WANT IT TO BE ME...
YOU WERE ME... YOU'D'VE TALKED ALREADY...
...YOU WEAK PIECE OF... SHIT...
pttuyyy
SON OF A BITCH...
...YOU STUPID OLD FUCK...
GO AHEAD... SHOOT ME... MAKE YOUR BOSS REAL HAPPY... WON'T IT?
HE'S RIGHT...

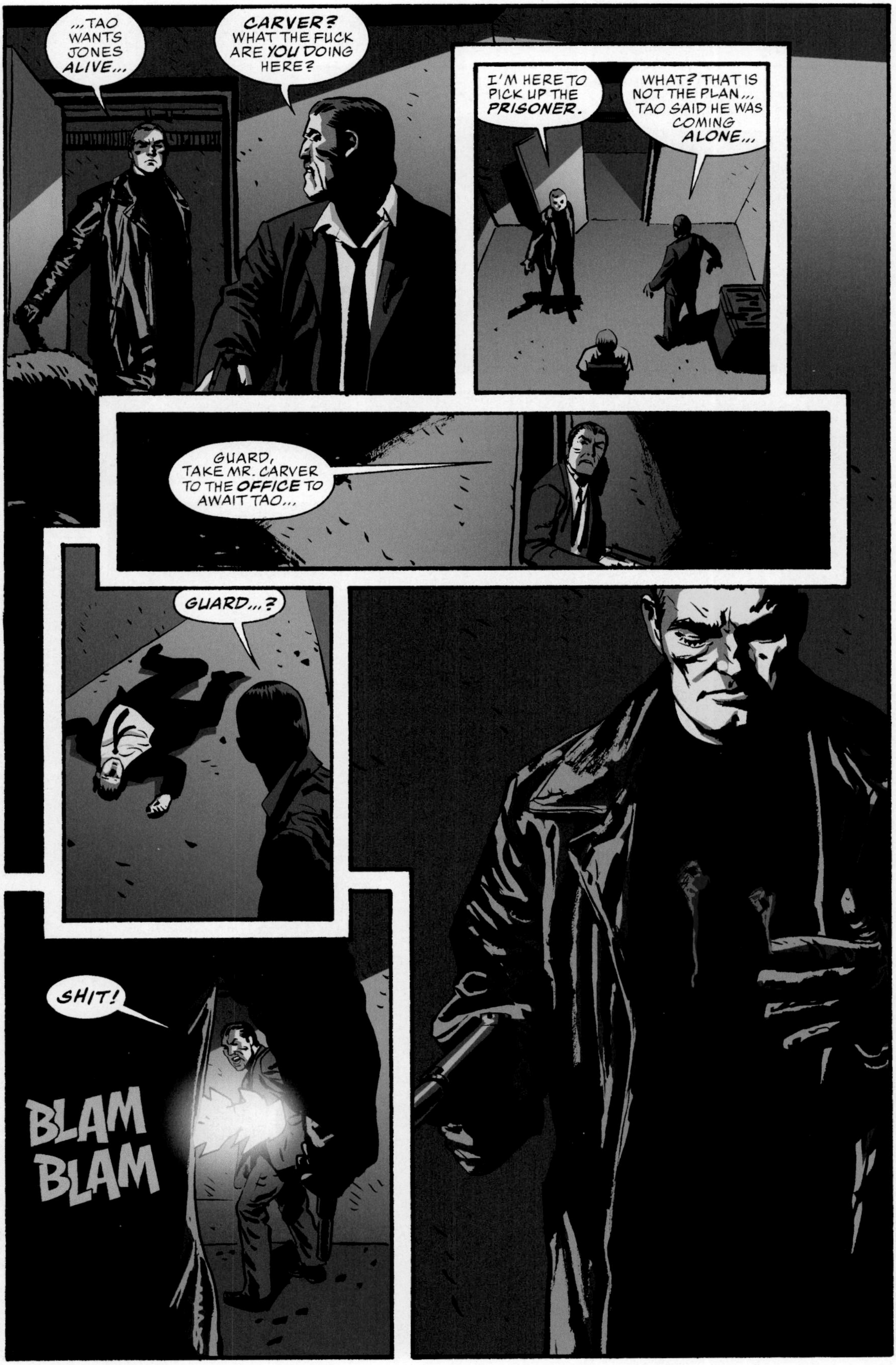
...TAO WANTS JONES ALIVE...
CARVER? WHAT THE FUCK ARE YOU DOING HERE?
I'M HERE TO PICK UP THE PRISONER.
WHAT? THAT IS NOT THE PLAN... TAO SAID HE WAS COMING ALONE...
GUARD, TAKE MR. CARVER TO THE OFFICE TO AWAIT TAO...
GUARD...?
SHIT!
BLAM
BLAM

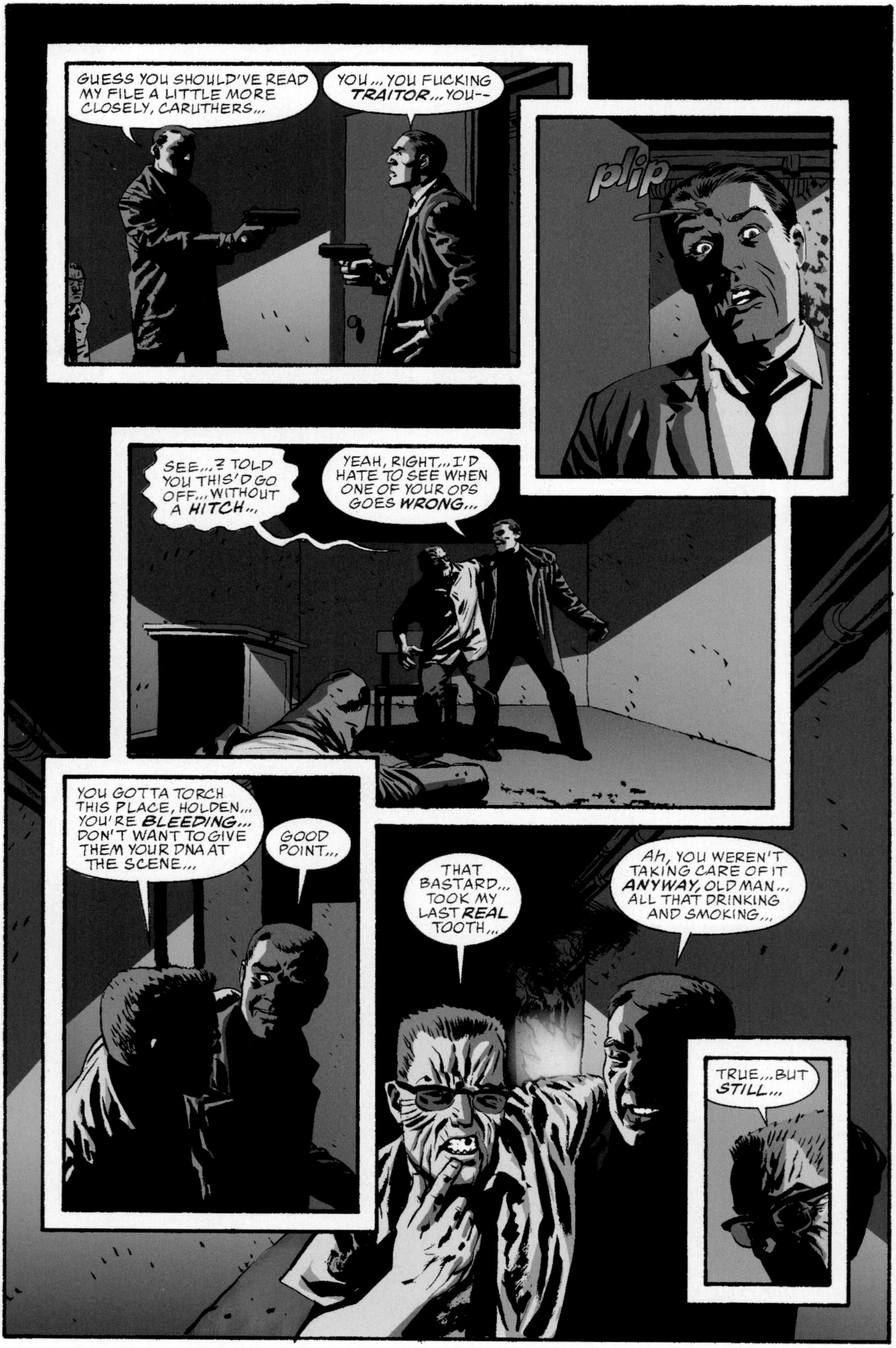
GUESS YOU SHOULD'VE READ MY FILE A LITTLE MORE CLOSELY, CARUTHERS...
YOU... YOU FUCKING TRAITOR... YOU--
plip
SEE... I TOLD YOU THIS'D GO OFF... WITHOUT A HITCH...
YEAH, RIGHT... I'D HATE TO SEE WHEN ONE OF YOUR OPS GOES WRONG...
YOU GOTTA TORCH THIS PLACE, HOLDEN... YOU'RE BLEEDING... DON'T WANT TO GIVE THEM YOUR DNA AT THE SCENE...
GOOD POINT...
THAT BASTARD... TOOK MY LAST REAL TOOTH...
Ah, YOU WEREN'T TAKING CARE OF IT ANYWAY, OLD MAN... ALL THAT DRINKING AND SMOKING...
TRUE... BUT STILL...

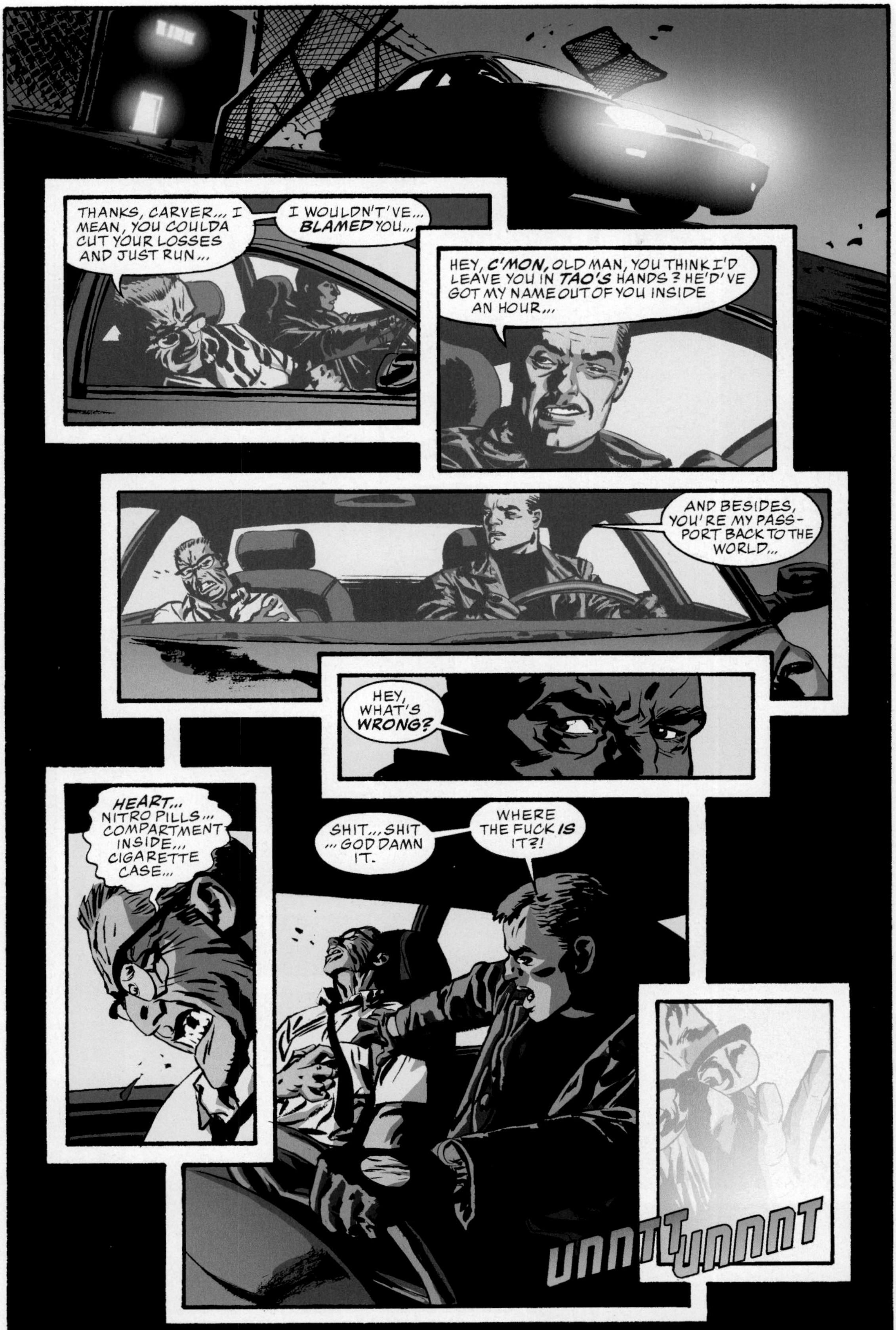
THANKS, CARVER... I MEAN, YOU COULDA CUT YOUR LOSSES AND JUST RUN...
I WOULDN'T'VE... BLAMED YOU...
HEY, C'MON, OLD MAN, YOU THINK I'D LEAVE YOU IN TAO'S HANDS? HE'D'VE GOT MY NAME OUT OF YOU INSIDE AN HOUR...
AND BESIDES, YOU'RE MY PASS-PORT BACK TO THE WORLD...
HEY, WHAT'S WRONG?
HEART... NITRO PILLS... COMPARTMENT INSIDE... CIGARETTE CASE...
SHIT... SHIT ...GOD DAMN IT.
WHERE THE FUCK IS IT?!
UNNNT
UNNNT

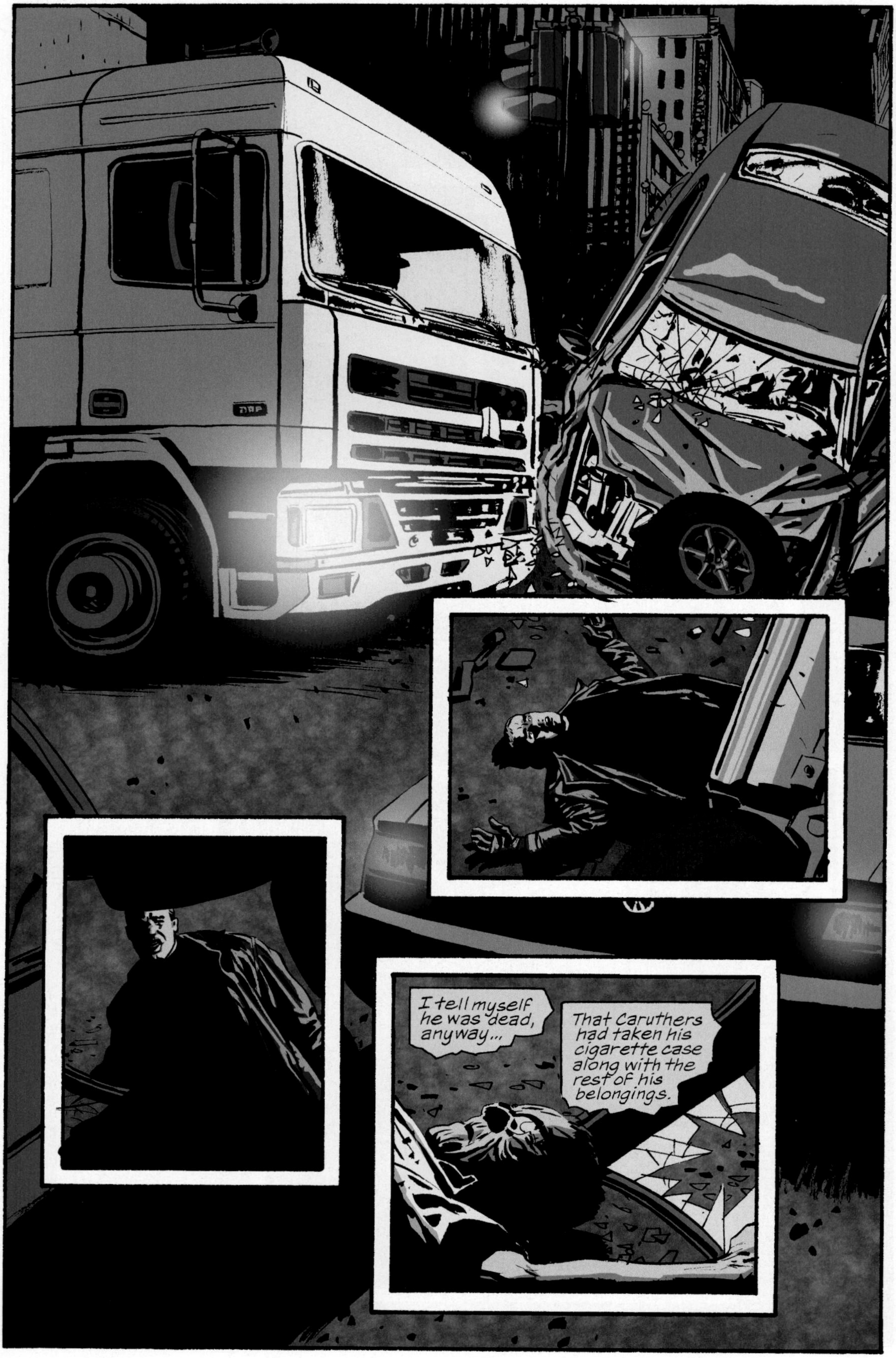
I tell myself he was dead, anyway...
That Caruthers had taken his cigarette case along with the rest of his belongings.

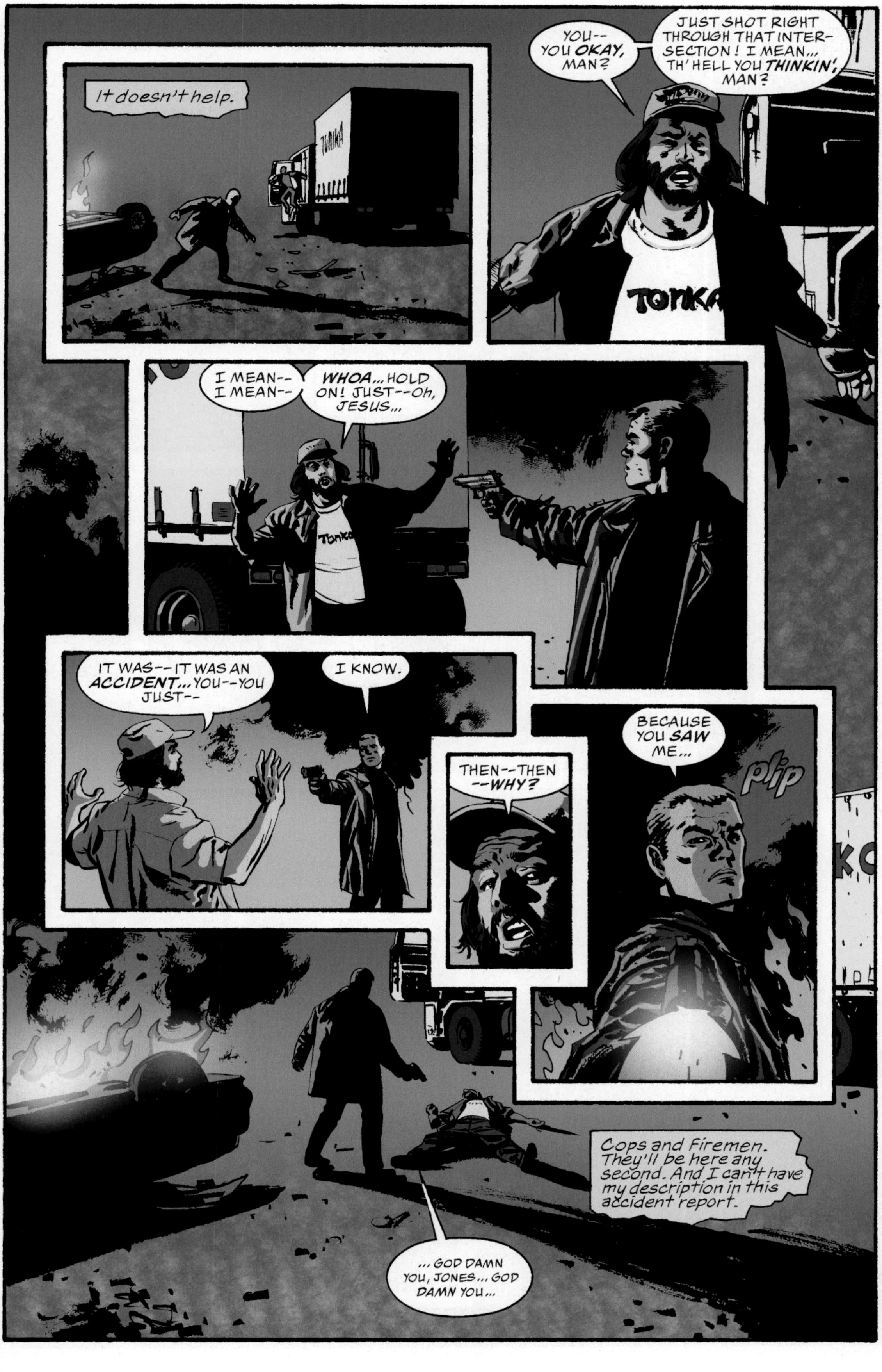
It doesn't help.
YOU-- YOU OKAY, MAN?
JUST SHOT RIGHT THROUGH THAT INTER-SECTION! I MEAN... TH' HELL YOU THINKIN', MAN?
I MEAN-- I MEAN--
WHOA... HOLD ON! JUST--Oh, JESUS...
IT WAS--IT WAS AN ACCIDENT... YOU--YOU JUST--
I KNOW.
THEN--THEN --WHY?
BECAUSE YOU SAW ME...
plip
Cops and Firemen. They'll be here any second. And I can't have my description in this accident report.
...GOD DAMN YOU, JONES... GOD DAMN YOU...

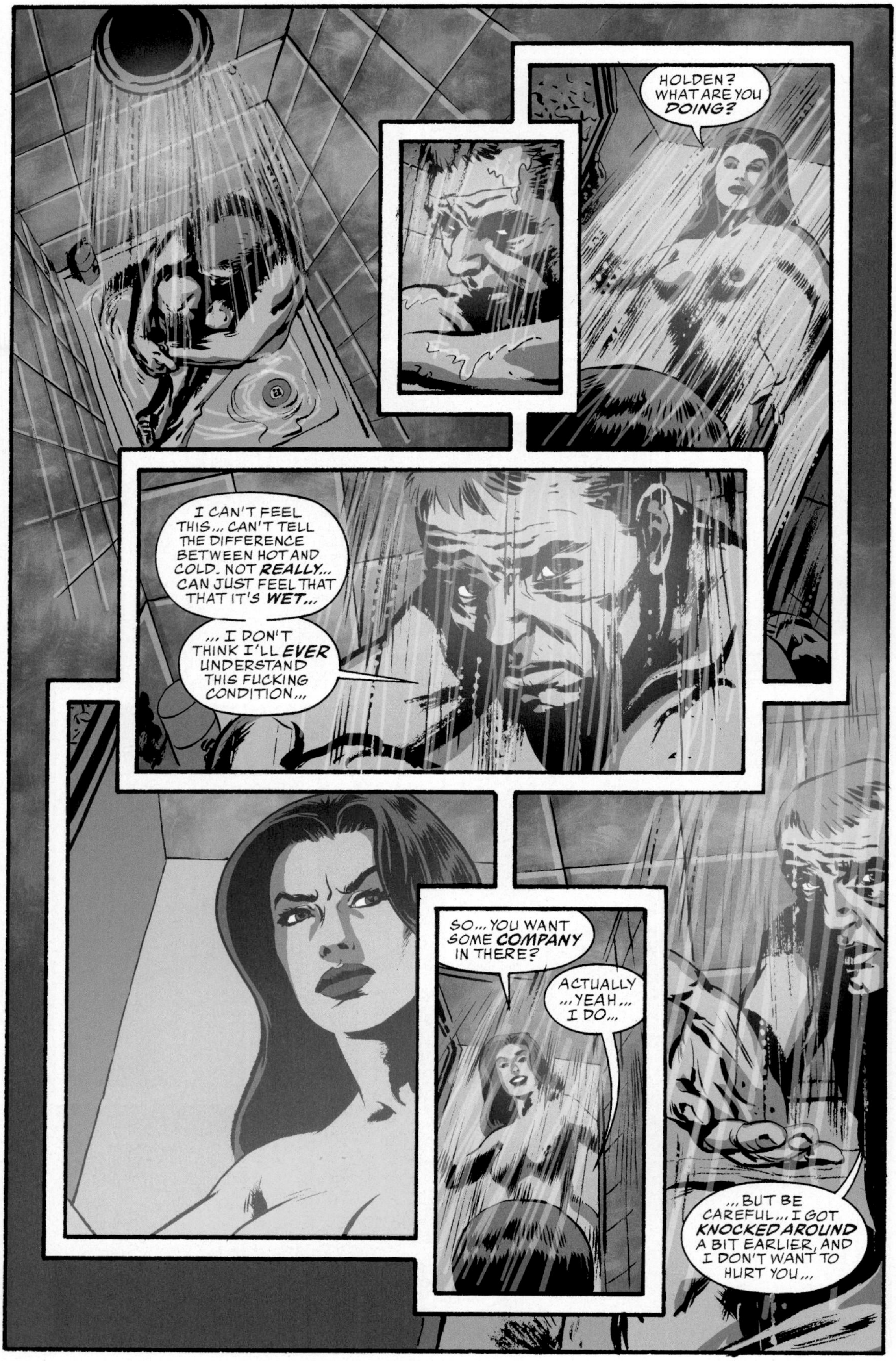

HOLDEN? WHAT ARE YOU DOING?
I CAN'T FEEL THIS... CAN'T TELL THE DIFFERENCE BETWEEN HOT AND COLD. NOT REALLY... CAN JUST FEEL THAT THAT IT'S WET...
... I DON'T THINK I'LL EVER UNDERSTAND THIS FUCKING CONDITION...
SO... YOU WANT SOME COMPANY IN THERE?
ACTUALLY ...YEAH... I DO...
...BUT BE CAREFUL... I GOT KNOCKED AROUND A BIT EARLIER, AND I DON'T WANT TO HURT YOU...

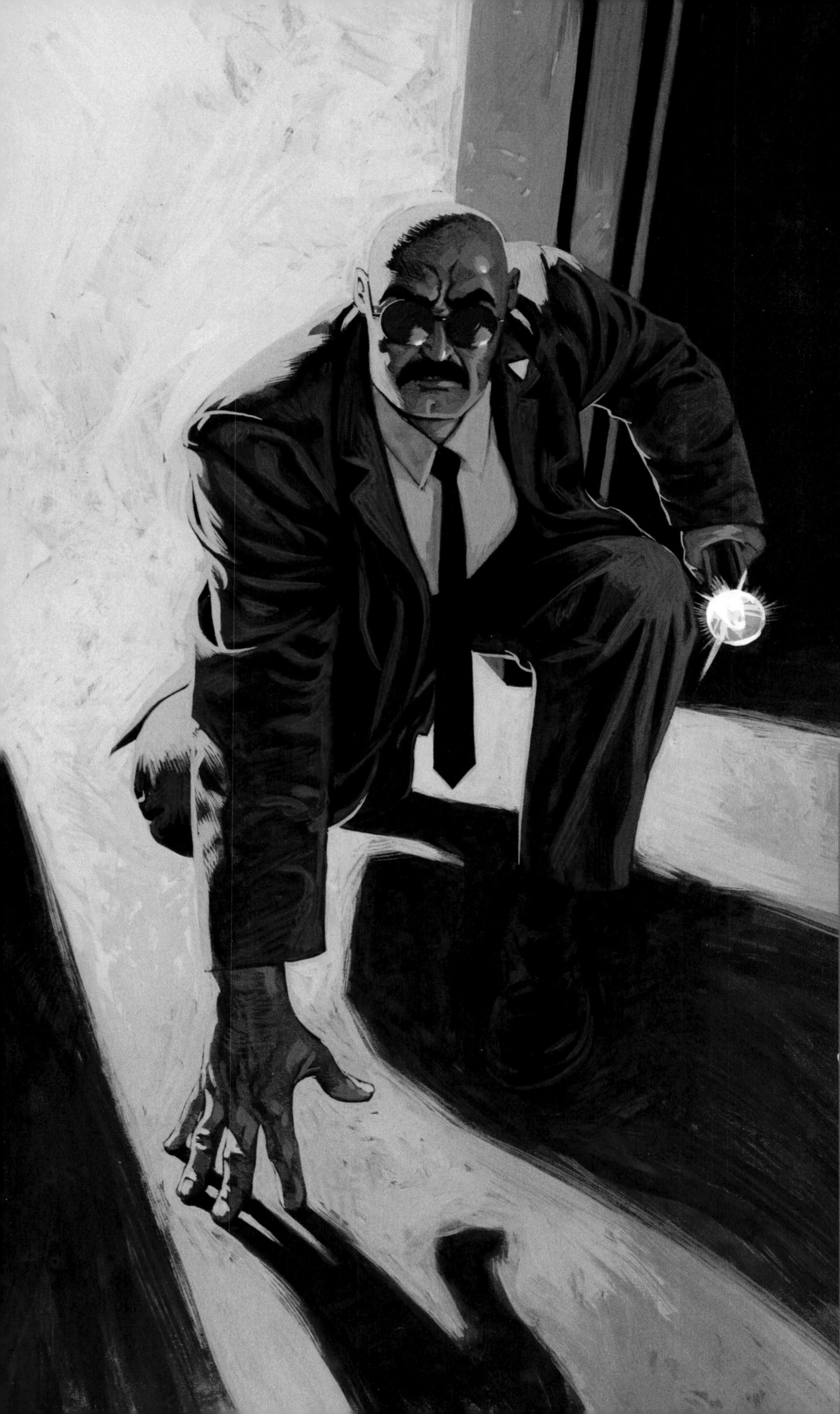

Cover by SEAN PHILLIPS

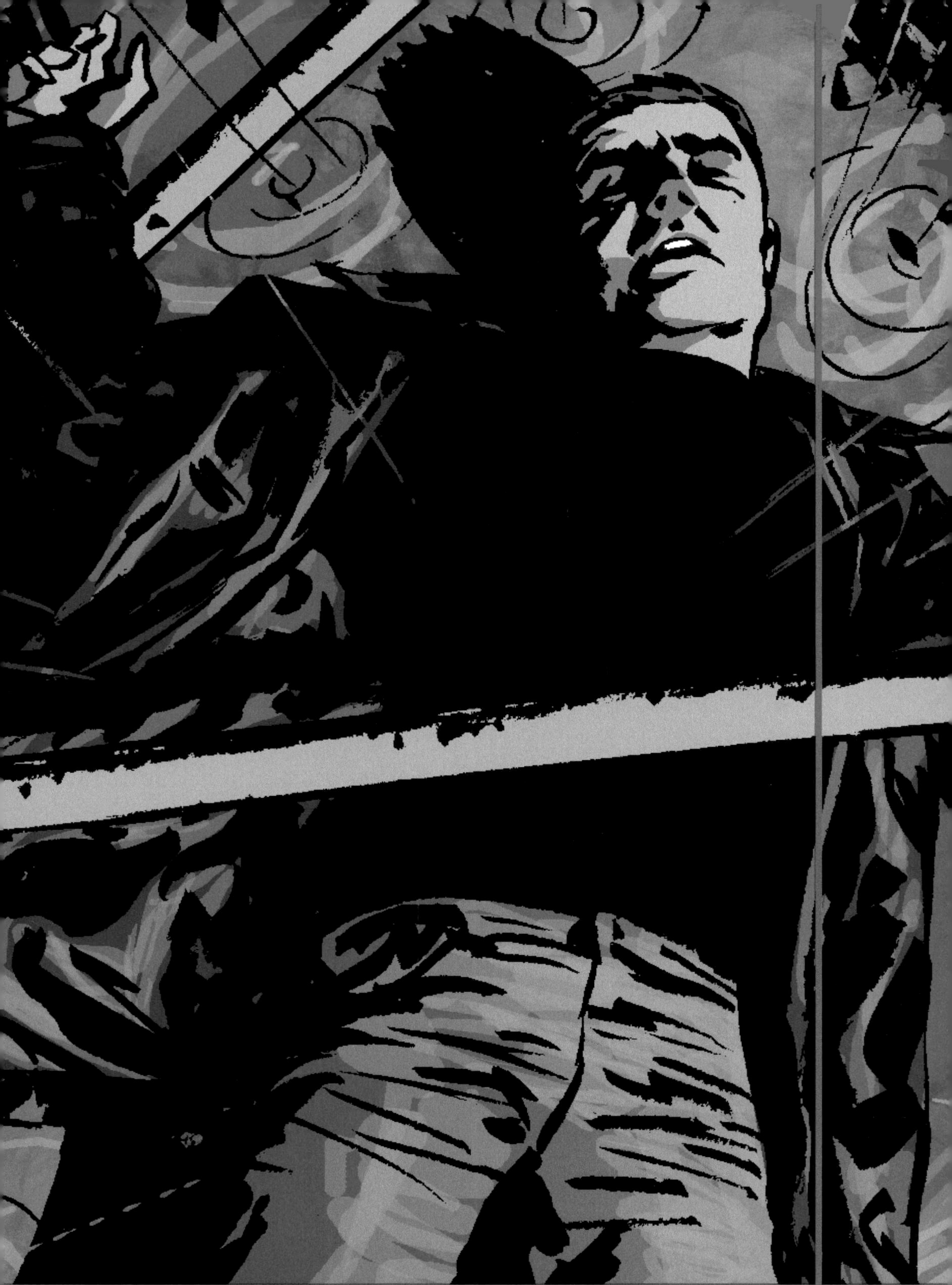

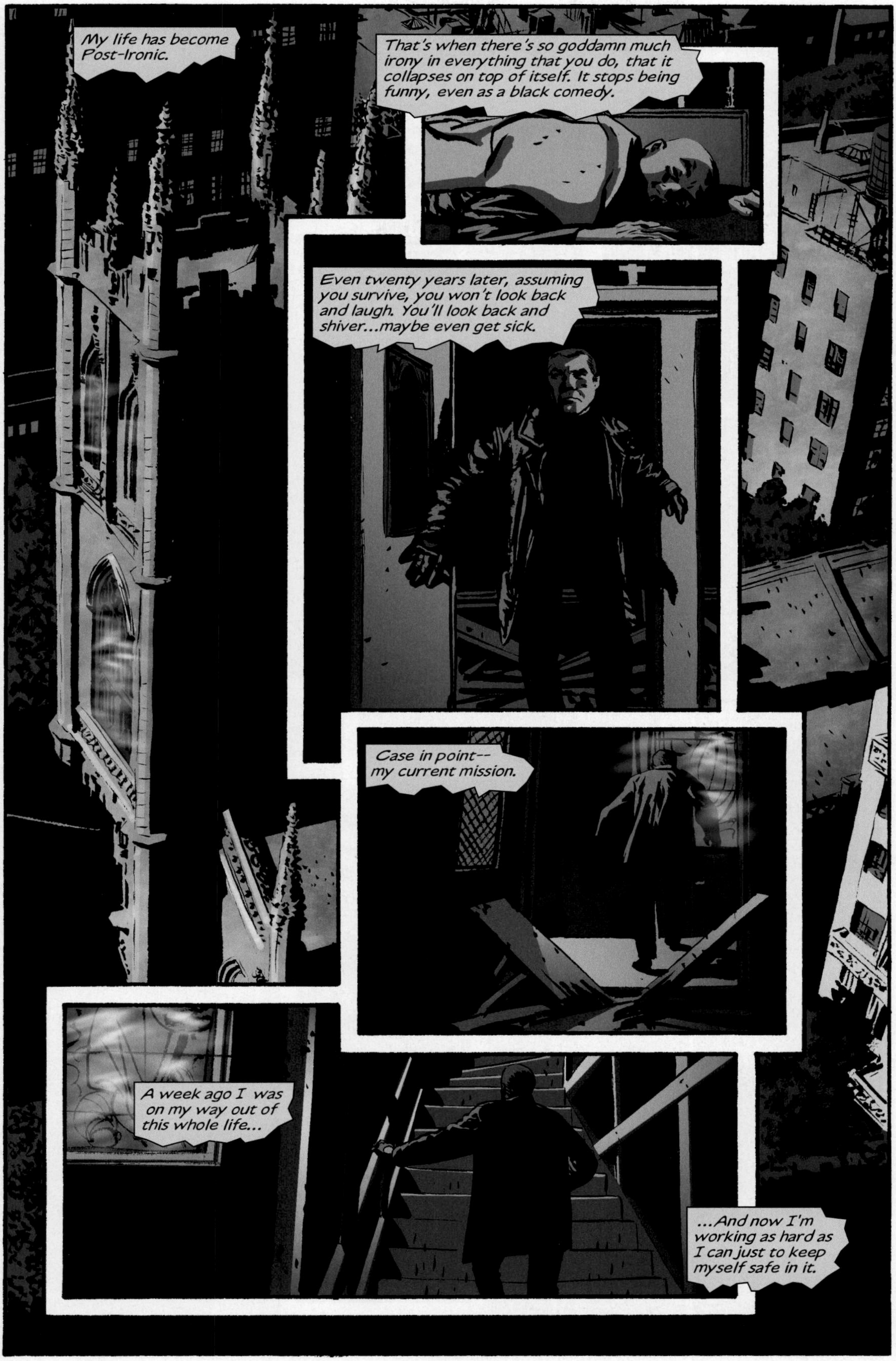
My life has become Post-Ironic.
That's when there's so goddamn much irony in everything that you do, that it collapses on top of itself. It stops being funny, even as a black comedy.
Even twenty years later, assuming you survive, you won't look back and laugh. You'll look back and shiver...maybe even get sick.
Case in point-- my current mission.
A week ago I was on my way out of this whole life...
...And now I'm working as hard as I can just to keep myself safe in it.

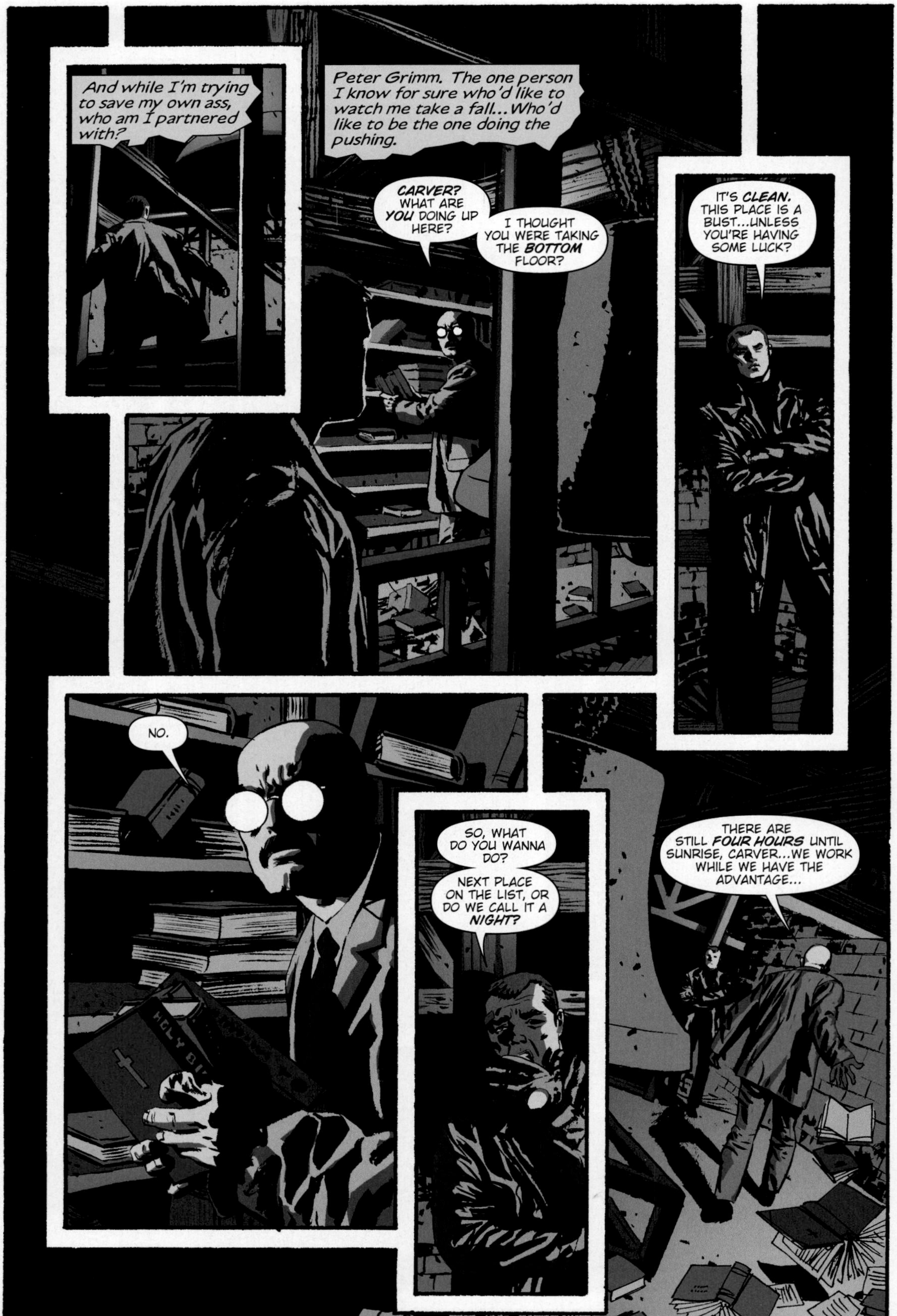
And while I'm trying to save my own ass, who am I partnered with?
Peter Grimm. The one person I know for sure who'd like to watch me take a fall...Who'd like to be the one doing the pushing.
CARVER? WHAT ARE YOU DOING UP HERE?
I THOUGHT YOU WERE TAKING THE BOTTOM FLOOR?
IT'S CLEAN. THIS PLACE IS A BUST...UNLESS YOU'RE HAVING SOME LUCK?
NO.
SO, WHAT DO YOU WANNA DO?
NEXT PLACE ON THE LIST, OR DO WE CALL IT A NIGHT?
THERE ARE STILL FOUR HOURS UNTIL SUNRISE, CARVER...WE WORK WHILE WE HAVE THE ADVANTAGE...

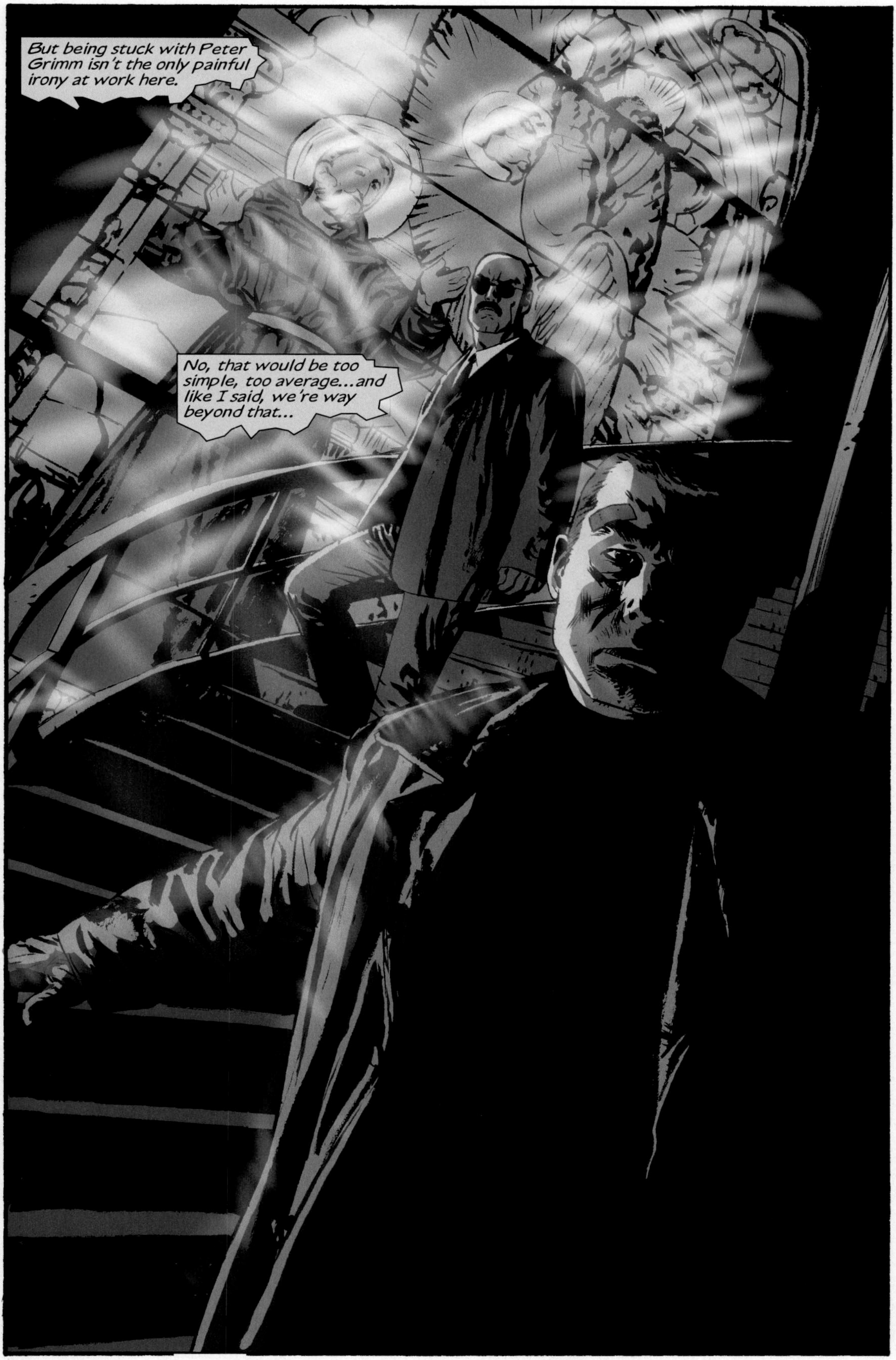
But being stuck with Peter Grimm isn't the only painful irony at work here.
No, that would be too simple, too average...and like I said, we're way beyond that...

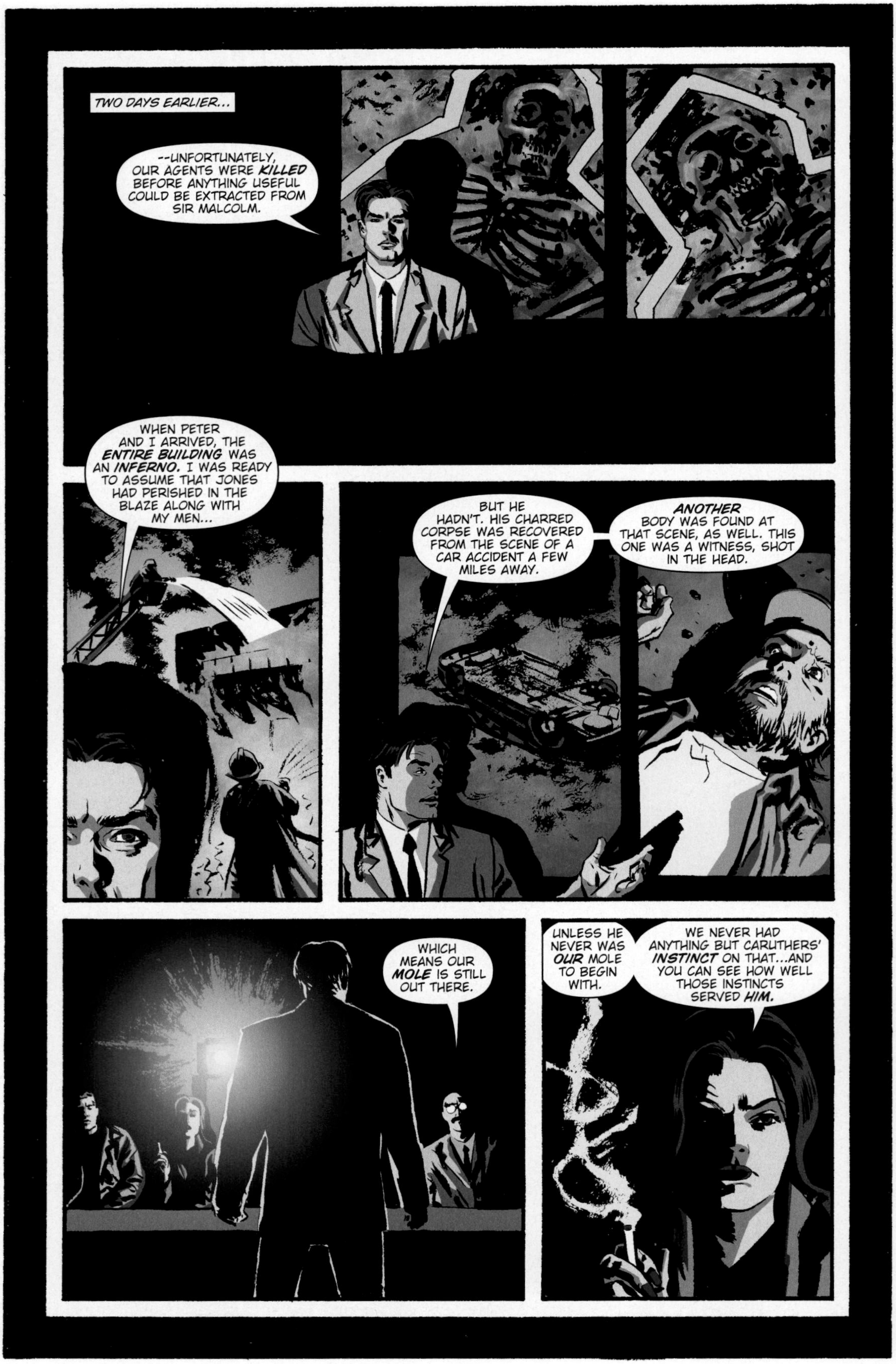
TWO DAYS EARLIER...
--UNFORTUNATELY, OUR AGENTS WERE KILLED BEFORE ANYTHING USEFUL COULD BE EXTRACTED FROM SIR MALCOLM.
WHEN PETER AND I ARRIVED, THE ENTIRE BUILDING WAS AN INFERNO. I WAS READY TO ASSUME THAT JONES HAD PERISHED IN THE BLAZE ALONG WITH MY MEN...
BUT HE HADN'T. HIS CHARRED CORPSE WAS RECOVERED FROM THE SCENE OF A CAR ACCIDENT A FEW MILES AWAY.
ANOTHER BODY WAS FOUND AT THAT SCENE, AS WELL. THIS ONE WAS A WITNESS, SHOT IN THE HEAD.
WHICH MEANS OUR MOLE IS STILL OUT THERE.
UNLESS HE NEVER WAS OUR MOLE TO BEGIN WITH.
WE NEVER HAD ANYTHING BUT CARUTHERS' INSTINCT ON THAT...AND YOU CAN SEE HOW WELL THOSE INSTINCTS SERVED HIM.

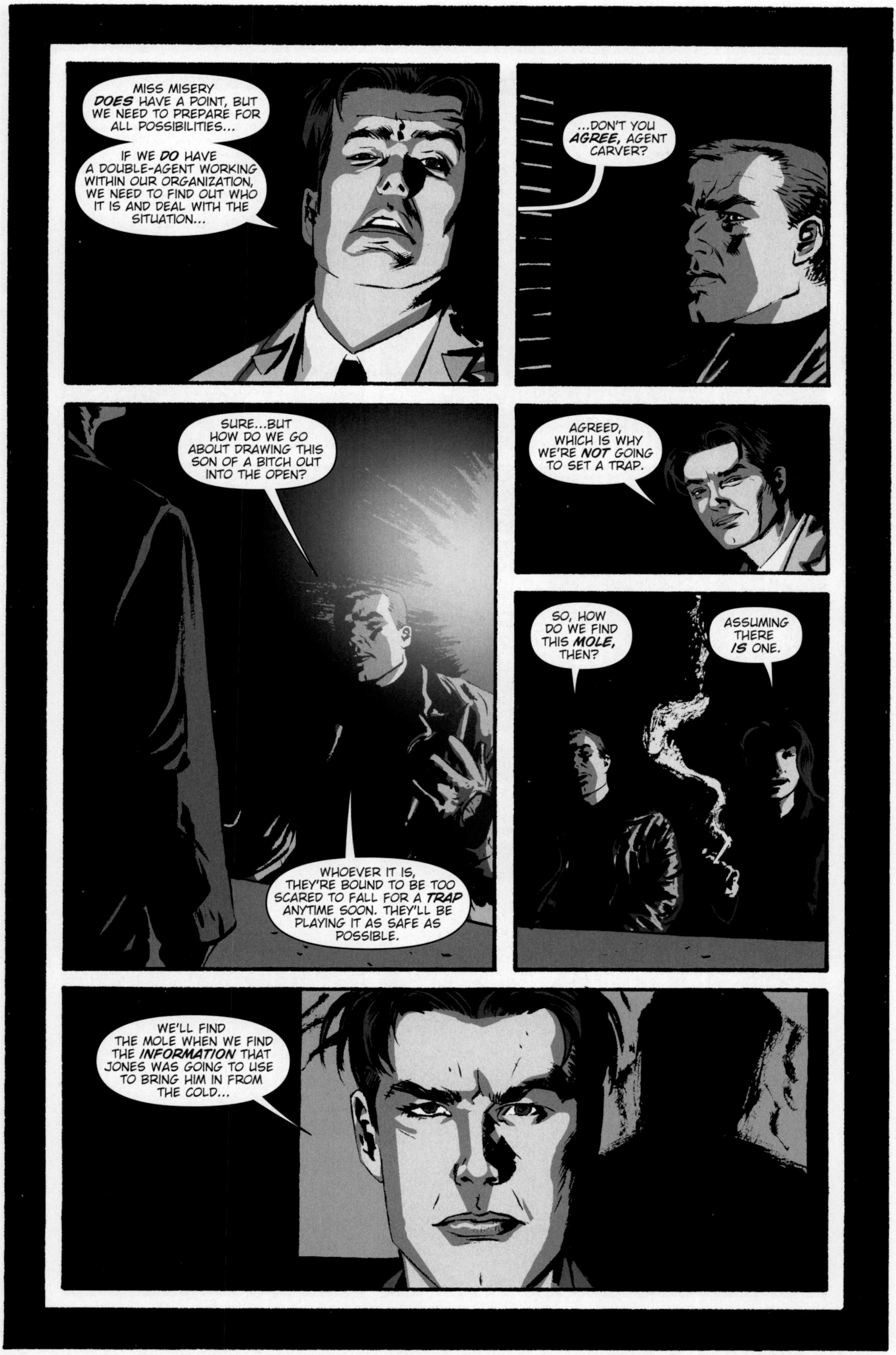
MISS MISERY DOES HAVE A POINT, BUT WE NEED TO PREPARE FOR ALL POSSIBILITIES...
IF WE DO HAVE A DOUBLE-AGENT WORKING WITHIN OUR ORGANIZATION, WE NEED TO FIND OUT WHO IT IS AND DEAL WITH THE SITUATION...
...DON'T YOU AGREE, AGENT CARVER?
SURE...BUT HOW DO WE GO ABOUT DRAWING THIS SON OF A BITCH OUT INTO THE OPEN?
WHOEVER IT IS, THEY'RE BOUND TO BE TOO SCARED TO FALL FOR A TRAP ANYTIME SOON. THEY'LL BE PLAYING IT AS SAFE AS POSSIBLE.
AGREED, WHICH IS WHY WE'RE NOT GOING TO SET A TRAP.
SO, HOW DO WE FIND THIS MOLE, THEN?
ASSUMING THERE IS ONE.
WE'LL FIND THE MOLE WHEN WE FIND THE INFORMATION THAT JONES WAS GOING TO USE TO BRING HIM IN FROM THE COLD...

AND WHAT INFORMATION IS *THIS?*

SOURCES INSIDE THE C.I.A. TELL ME THAT JONES CLAIMED TO HAVE *HARD COPY* EVIDENCE--A *DOSSIER*--ON THE ENTIRE HISTORY OF HIS AGENT.

NO ONE ACTUALLY *SAW* THIS FILE, BUT THEY *DO* BELIEVE IT EXISTS, AND AS WE SPEAK, AGENTS FROM MANY COVERT GOVERNMENT ORGANIZATIONS ARE COMBING NEW YORK CITY LOOKING FOR IT.

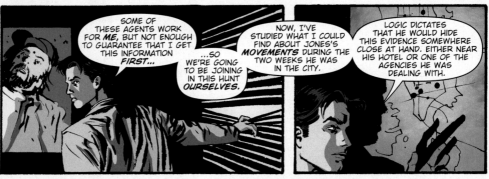

SOME OF THESE AGENTS WORK FOR *ME,* BUT NOT ENOUGH TO GUARANTEE THAT I GET THIS INFORMATION *FIRST...*

...SO WE'RE GOING TO BE JOINING IN THIS HUNT *OURSELVES.*

NOW, I'VE STUDIED WHAT I COULD FIND ABOUT JONES'S *MOVEMENTS* DURING THE TWO WEEKS HE WAS IN THE CITY.

LOGIC DICTATES THAT HE WOULD HIDE THIS EVIDENCE SOMEWHERE CLOSE AT HAND. EITHER NEAR HIS HOTEL OR ONE OF THE AGENCIES HE WAS DEALING WITH.

SO, I'VE COME UP WITH A LIST OF A FEW DOZEN LOCATIONS TO *START* WITH...

AGENTS GRIMM AND CARVER WILL TAKE THE MOST LIKELY ONES, WHILE MISS MISERY OVERSEES THE TORPEDOES AND BLACKGUARDS IN SEARCHING THE REST.

UNLESS ANYONE HAS ANY OBJECTIONS?

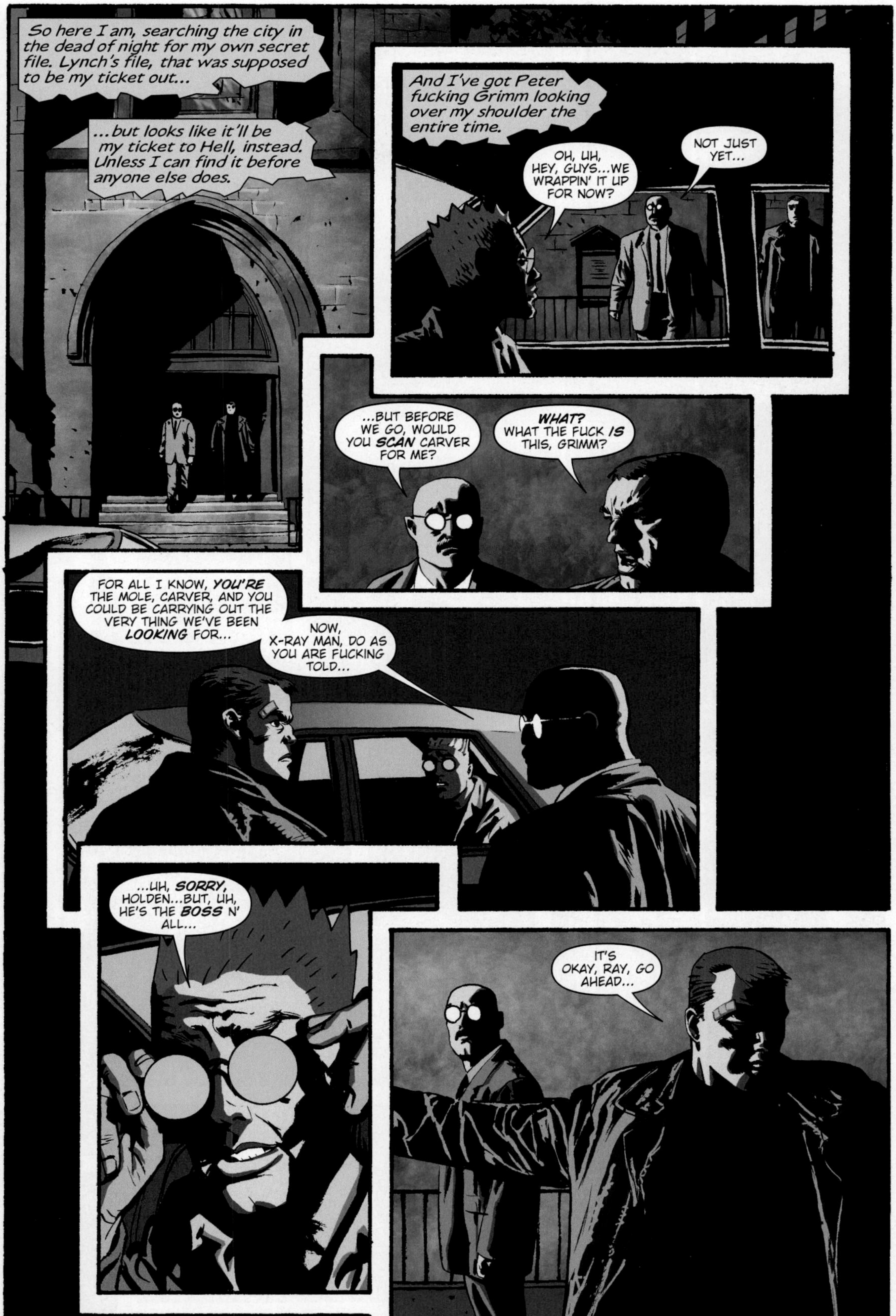
So here I am, searching the city in the dead of night for my own secret file. Lynch's file, that was supposed to be my ticket out...
...but looks like it'll be my ticket to Hell, instead. Unless I can find it before anyone else does.
And I've got Peter fucking Grimm looking over my shoulder the entire time.
OH, UH, HEY, GUYS...WE WRAPPIN' IT UP FOR NOW?
NOT JUST YET...
...BUT BEFORE WE GO, WOULD YOU SCAN CARVER FOR ME?
WHAT? WHAT THE FUCK IS THIS, GRIMM?
FOR ALL I KNOW, YOU'RE THE MOLE, CARVER, AND YOU COULD BE CARRYING OUT THE VERY THING WE'VE BEEN LOOKING FOR...
NOW, X-RAY MAN, DO AS YOU ARE FUCKING TOLD...
...UH, SORRY, HOLDEN...BUT, UH, HE'S THE BOSS N' ALL...
IT'S OKAY, RAY, GO AHEAD...

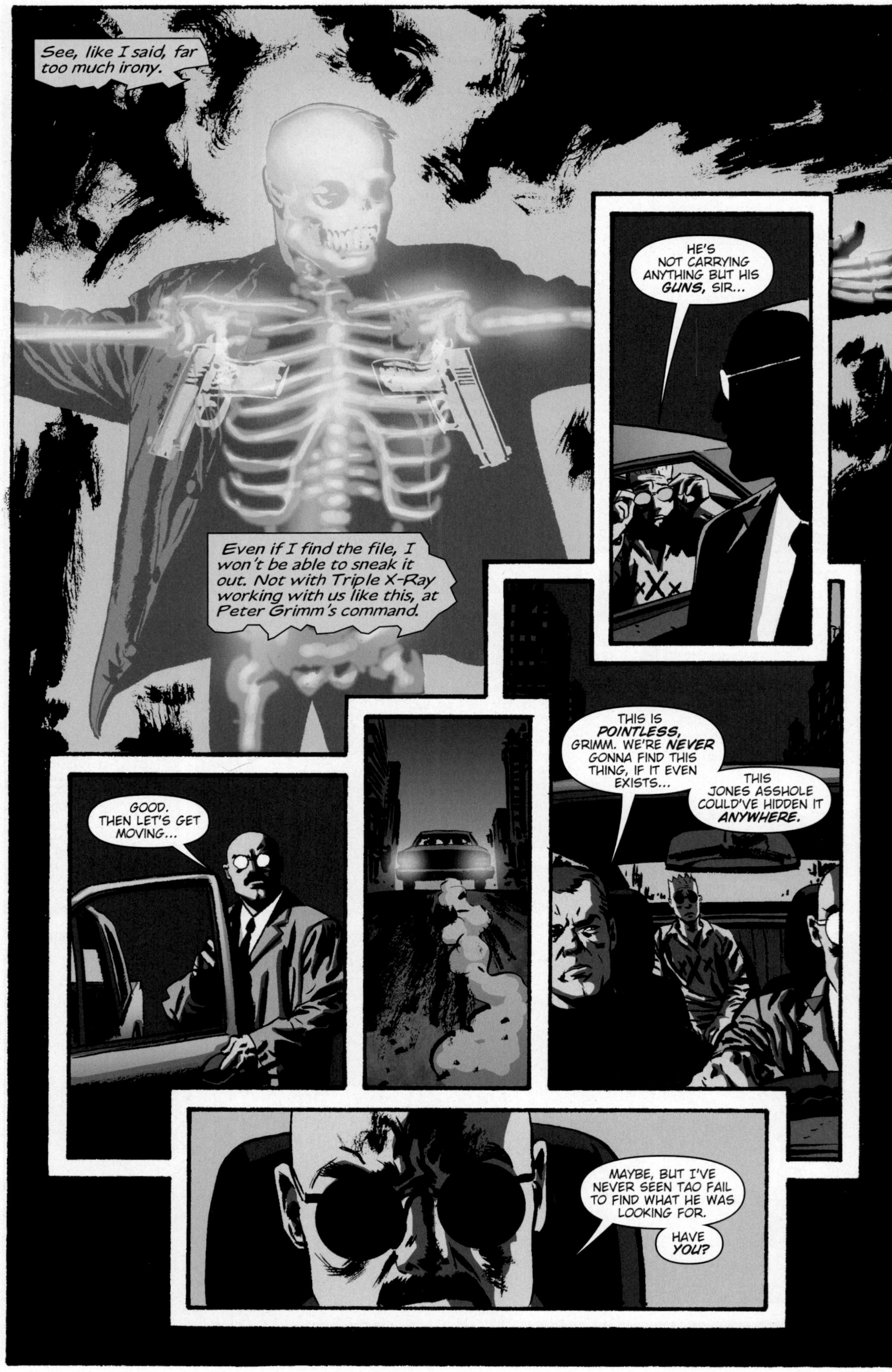
See, like I said, far too much irony.
HE'S NOT CARRYING ANYTHING BUT HIS GUNS, SIR...
Even if I find the file, I won't be able to sneak it out. Not with Triple X-Ray working with us like this, at Peter Grimm's command.
GOOD. THEN LET'S GET MOVING...
THIS IS POINTLESS, GRIMM. WE'RE NEVER GONNA FIND THIS THING, IF IT EVEN EXISTS...
THIS JONES ASSHOLE COULD'VE HIDDEN IT ANYWHERE.
MAYBE, BUT I'VE NEVER SEEN TAO FAIL TO FIND WHAT HE WAS LOOKING FOR.
HAVE YOU?

And the fact was, I hadn't. Tao always got what he was after.

Which was, in a way, my ace in the hole.

Because if the CIA and Dept. PSI and the remnants of I.O. are all in a race to find something, and Tao is on its trail, too...

...I'll put my money on him every time.

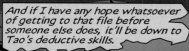

And if I have any hope whatsoever of getting to that file before someone else does, it'll be down to Tao's deductive skills.

That and a lot of luck.

SHNK

NICE *SHOOTIN'*, TEX...

BLOW ME.

SO, *ANYWAY,* I'M ON THE COUCH WAITIN' FOR HER TO GET READY, AND MEANWHILE HER *CAT* KEEPS RUBBING AGAINST ME, WHICH IS BAD ENOUGH...

...BUT IT ALSO KEEPS STICKING ITS FUCKING *BUTT* IN MY FACE.

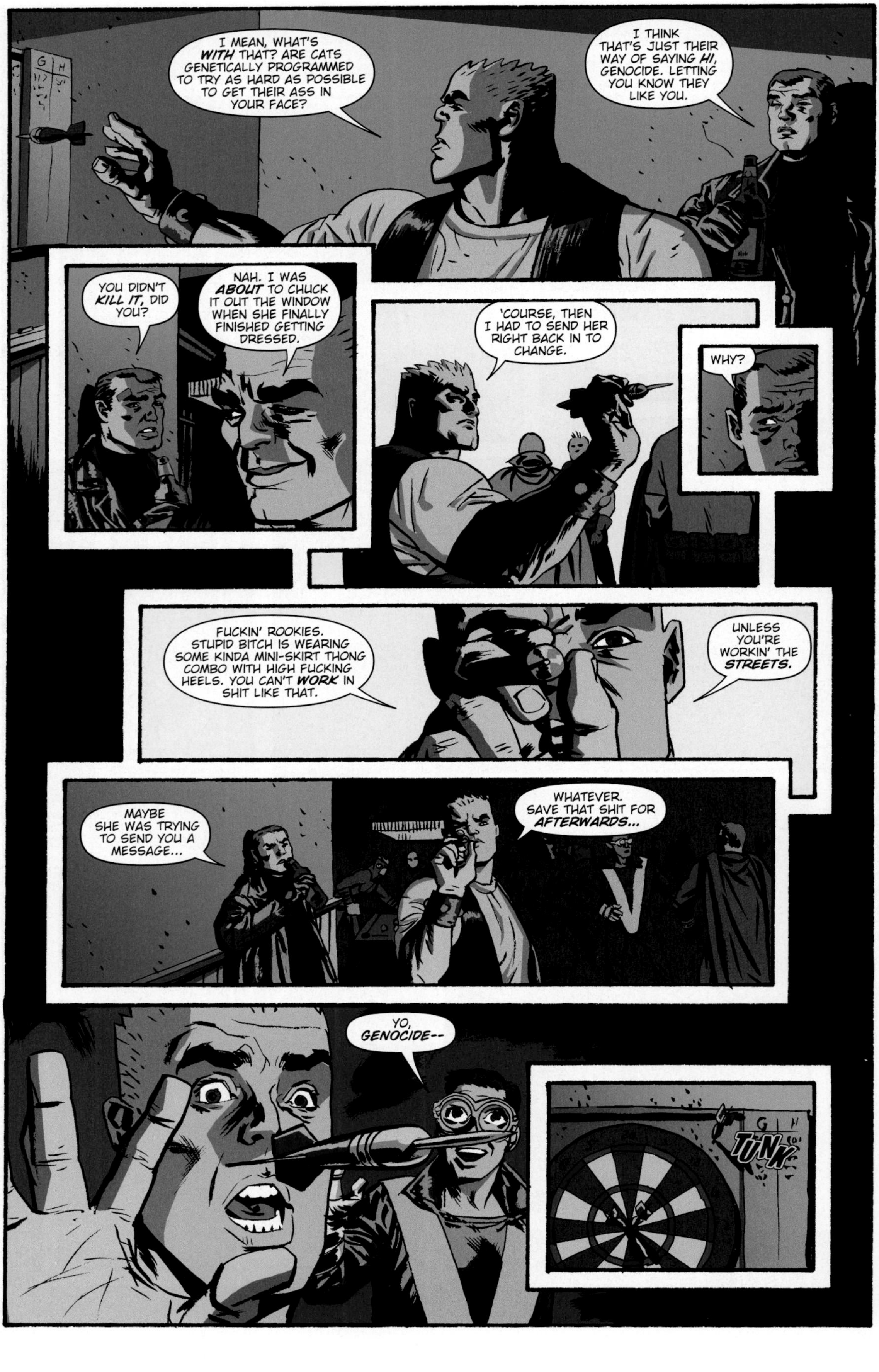
I MEAN, WHAT'S WITH THAT? ARE CATS GENETICALLY PROGRAMMED TO TRY AS HARD AS POSSIBLE TO GET THEIR ASS IN YOUR FACE?
I THINK THAT'S JUST THEIR WAY OF SAYING HI, GENOCIDE. LETTING YOU KNOW THEY LIKE YOU.
YOU DIDN'T KILL IT, DID YOU?
NAH. I WAS ABOUT TO CHUCK IT OUT THE WINDOW WHEN SHE FINALLY FINISHED GETTING DRESSED.
'COURSE, THEN I HAD TO SEND HER RIGHT BACK IN TO CHANGE.
WHY?
FUCKIN' ROOKIES. STUPID BITCH IS WEARING SOME KINDA MINI-SKIRT THONG COMBO WITH HIGH FUCKING HEELS. YOU CAN'T WORK IN SHIT LIKE THAT.
UNLESS YOU'RE WORKIN' THE STREETS.
MAYBE SHE WAS TRYING TO SEND YOU A MESSAGE...
WHATEVER. SAVE THAT SHIT FOR AFTERWARDS...
YO, GENOCIDE--
TUNK

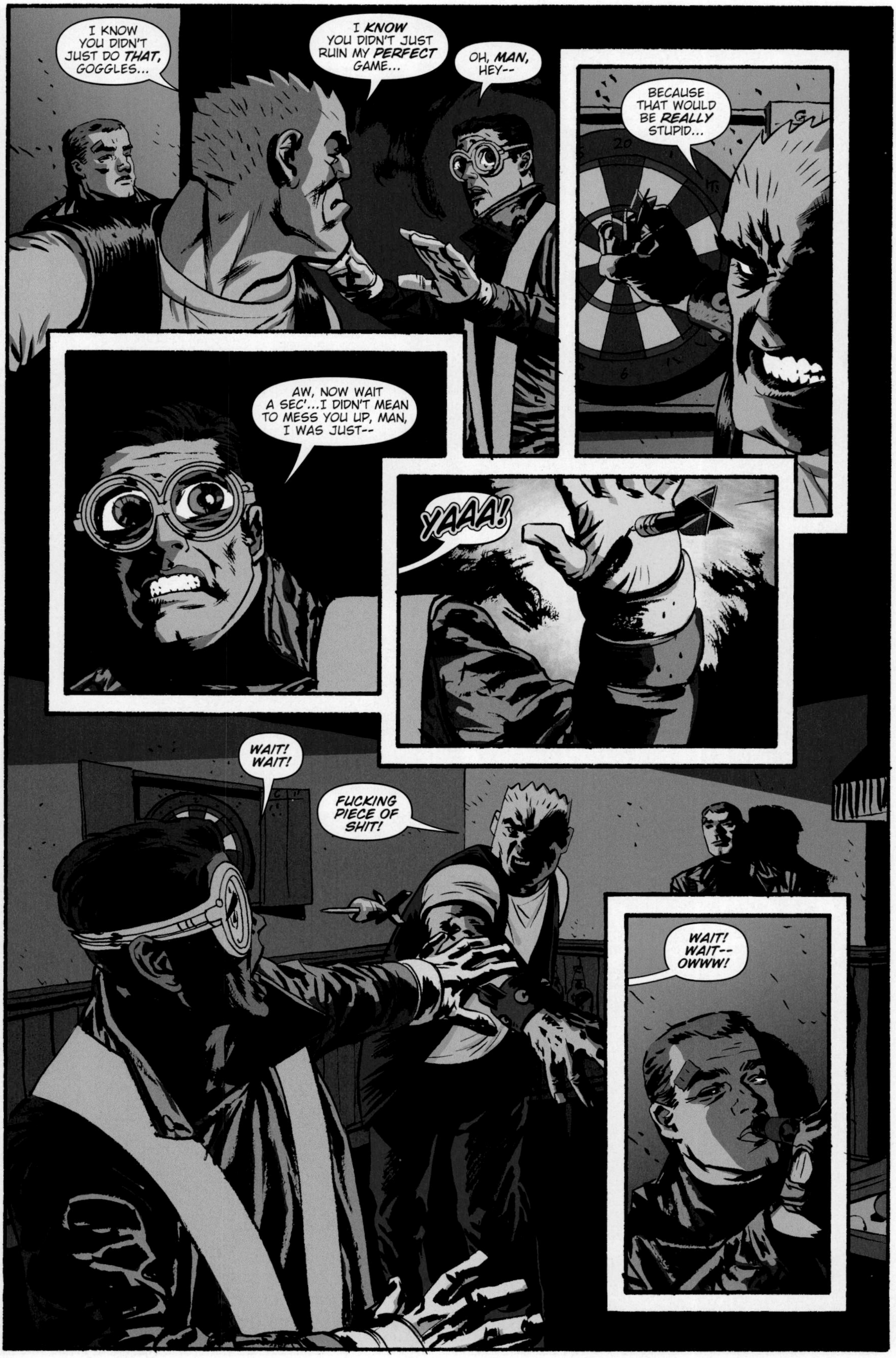
I KNOW YOU DIDN'T JUST DO *THAT*, GOGGLES...
I *KNOW* YOU DIDN'T JUST RUIN MY *PERFECT* GAME...
OH, *MAN*, HEY--
BECAUSE THAT WOULD BE *REALLY* STUPID...
AW, NOW WAIT A SEC'...I DIDN'T MEAN TO MESS YOU UP, MAN, I WAS JUST--
YAAA!
WAIT! WAIT!
FUCKING PIECE OF SHIT!
WAIT! WAIT-- OWWW!

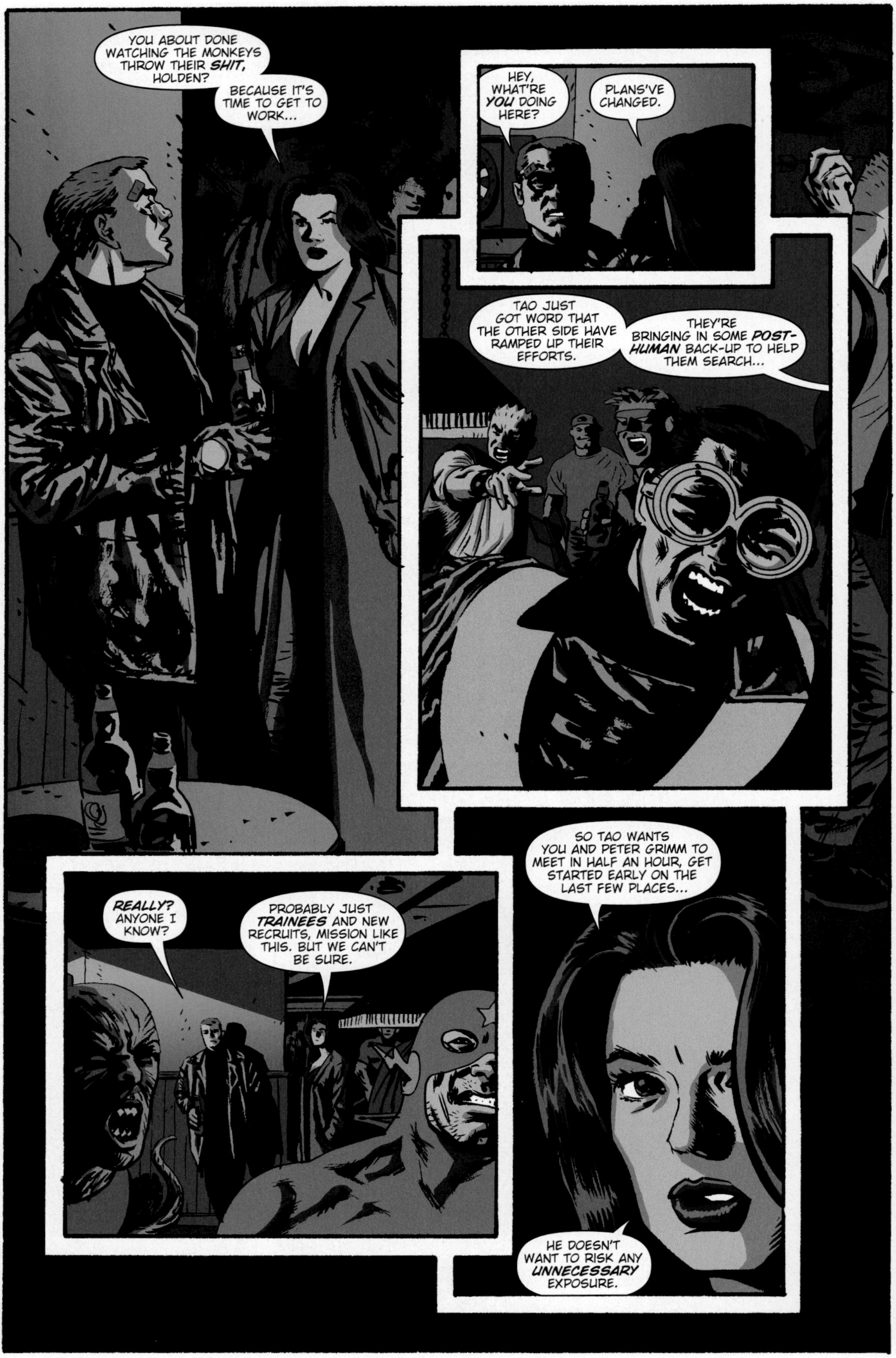
YOU ABOUT DONE WATCHING THE MONKEYS THROW THEIR SHIT, HOLDEN?
BECAUSE IT'S TIME TO GET TO WORK...
HEY, WHAT'RE YOU DOING HERE?
PLANS'VE CHANGED.
TAO JUST GOT WORD THAT THE OTHER SIDE HAVE RAMPED UP THEIR EFFORTS.
THEY'RE BRINGING IN SOME POST-HUMAN BACK-UP TO HELP THEM SEARCH...
REALLY? ANYONE I KNOW?
PROBABLY JUST TRAINEES AND NEW RECRUITS, MISSION LIKE THIS. BUT WE CAN'T BE SURE.
SO TAO WANTS YOU AND PETER GRIMM TO MEET IN HALF AN HOUR, GET STARTED EARLY ON THE LAST FEW PLACES...
HE DOESN'T WANT TO RISK ANY UNNECESSARY EXPOSURE.

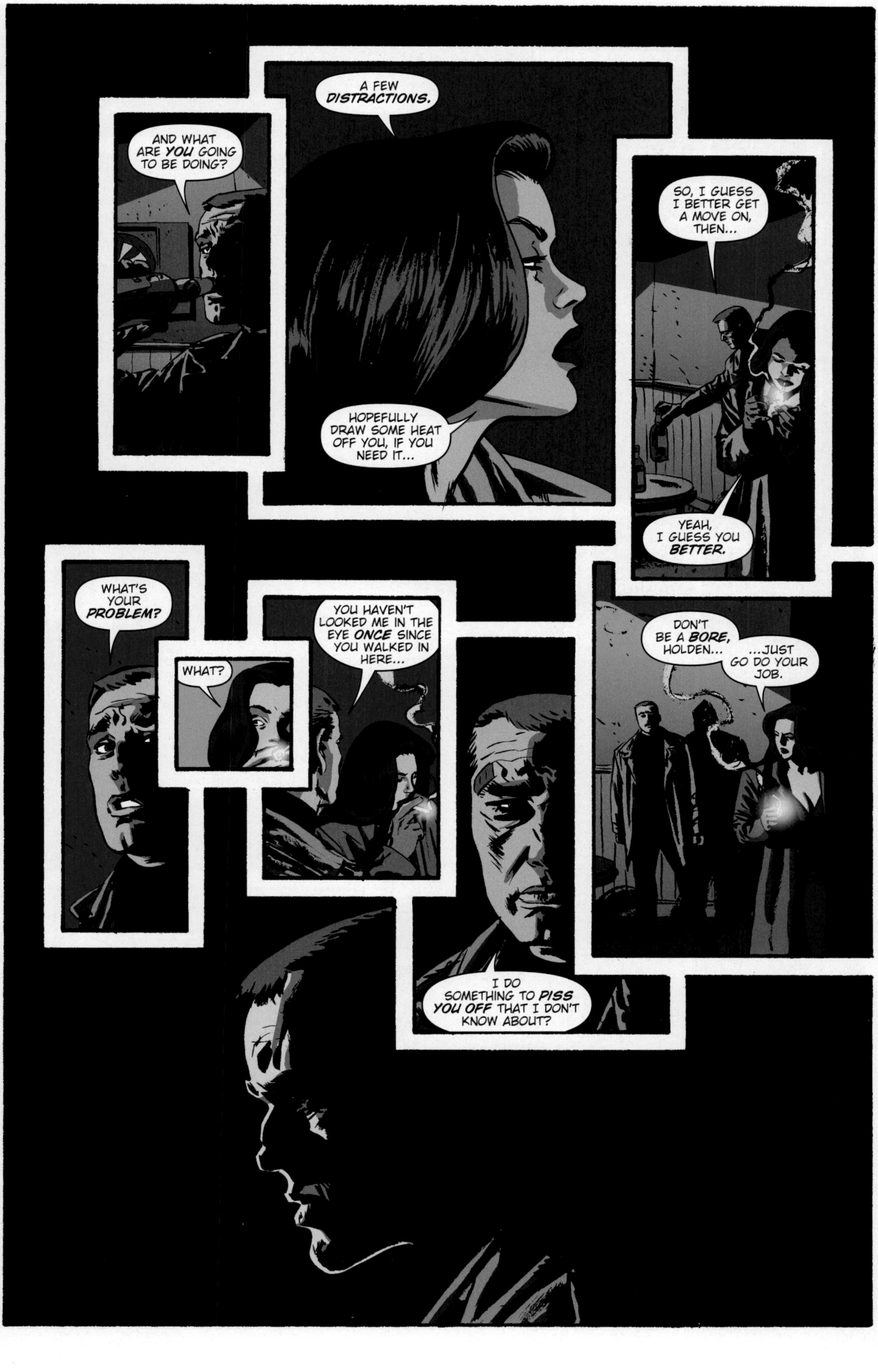
AND WHAT ARE YOU GOING TO BE DOING?
A FEW DISTRACTIONS.
HOPEFULLY DRAW SOME HEAT OFF YOU, IF YOU NEED IT...
SO, I GUESS I BETTER GET A MOVE ON, THEN...
YEAH, I GUESS YOU BETTER.
WHAT'S YOUR PROBLEM?
WHAT?
YOU HAVEN'T LOOKED ME IN THE EYE ONCE SINCE YOU WALKED IN HERE...
I DO SOMETHING TO PISS YOU OFF THAT I DON'T KNOW ABOUT?
DON'T BE A BORE, HOLDEN...
...JUST GO DO YOUR JOB.

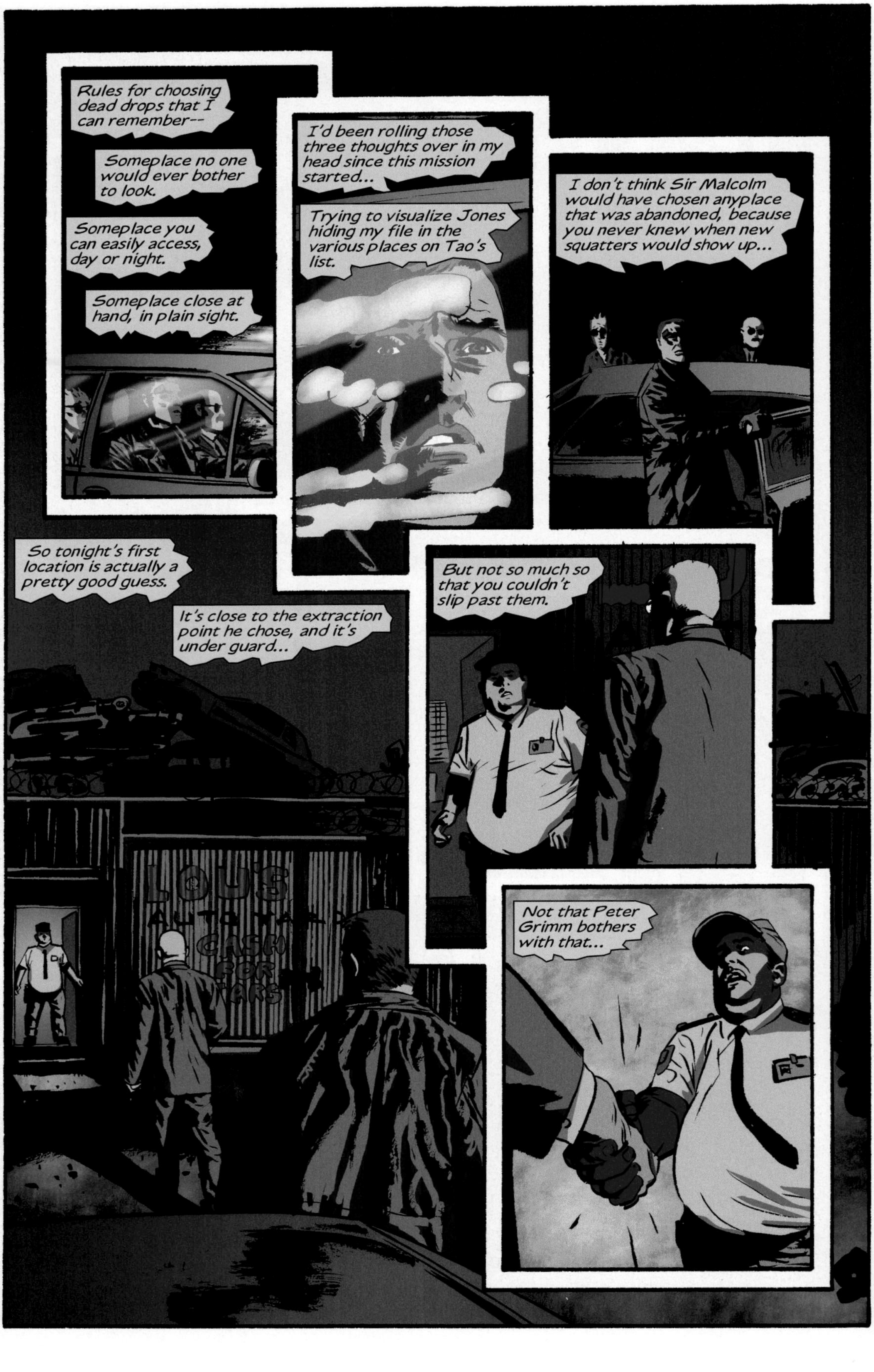
Rules for choosing dead drops that I can remember--
Someplace no one would ever bother to look.
Someplace you can easily access, day or night.
Someplace close at hand, in plain sight.
I'd been rolling those three thoughts over in my head since this mission started...
Trying to visualize Jones hiding my file in the various places on Tao's list.
I don't think Sir Malcolm would have chosen anyplace that was abandoned, because you never knew when new squatters would show up...
So tonight's first location is actually a pretty good guess.
It's close to the extraction point he chose, and it's under guard...
LOU'S
CASH FOR CARS
But not so much so that you couldn't slip past them.
Not that Peter Grimm bothers with that...

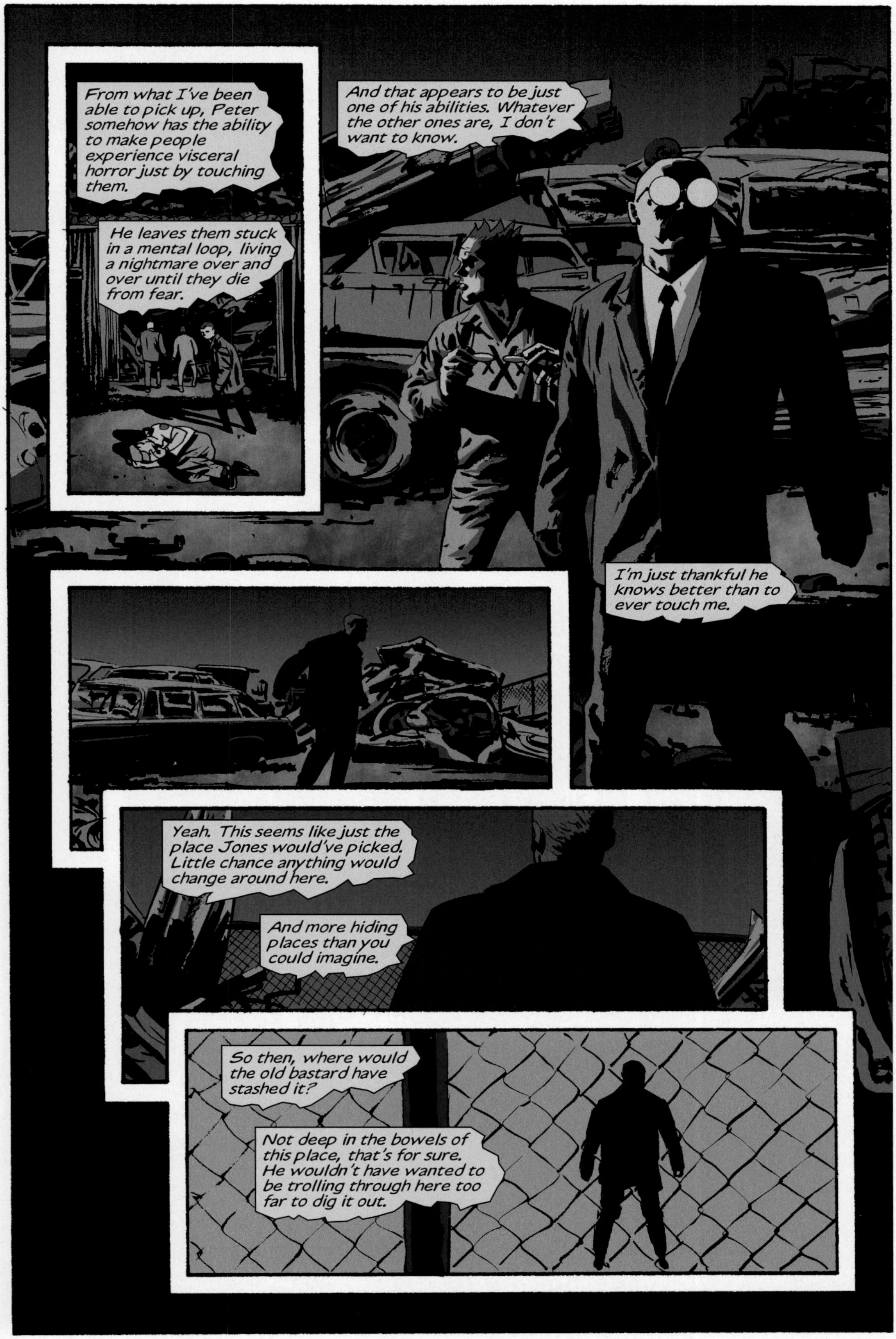
From what I've been able to pick up, Peter somehow has the ability to make people experience visceral horror just by touching them.
He leaves them stuck in a mental loop, living a nightmare over and over until they die from fear.
And that appears to be just one of his abilities. Whatever the other ones are, I don't want to know.
I'm just thankful he knows better than to ever touch me.
Yeah. This seems like just the place Jones would've picked. Little chance anything would change around here.
And more hiding places than you could imagine.
So then, where would the old bastard have stashed it?
Not deep in the bowels of this place, that's for sure. He wouldn't have wanted to be trolling through here too far to dig it out.

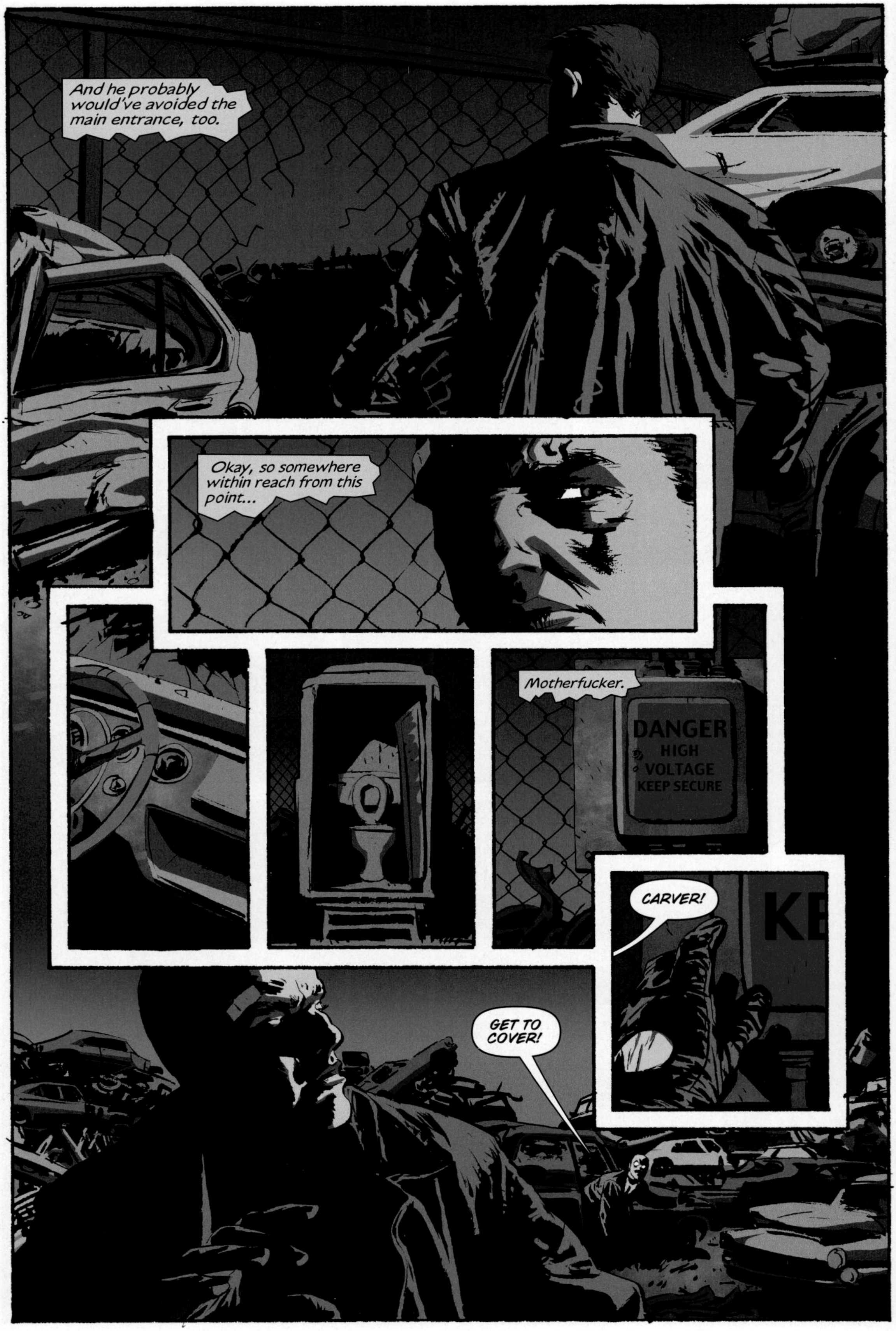
And he probably would've avoided the main entrance, too.
Okay, so somewhere within reach from this point...
Motherfucker.
DANGER
HIGH
VOLTAGE
KEEP SECURE
CARVER!
GET TO COVER!

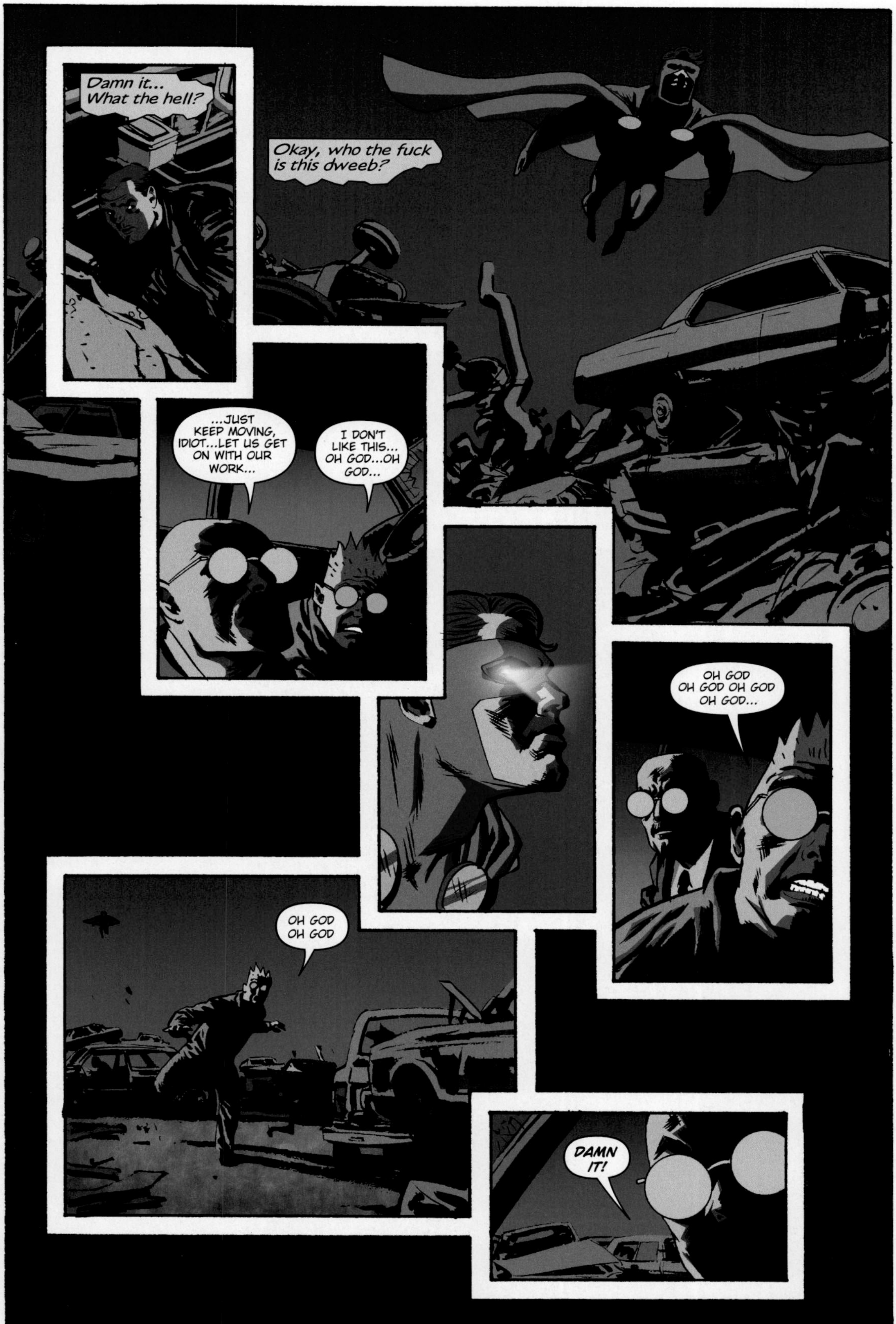
Damn it... What the hell?
Okay, who the fuck is this dweeb?
...JUST KEEP MOVING, IDIOT...LET US GET ON WITH OUR WORK...
I DON'T LIKE THIS... OH GOD...OH GOD...
OH GOD OH GOD OH GOD OH GOD...
OH GOD OH GOD
DAMN IT!

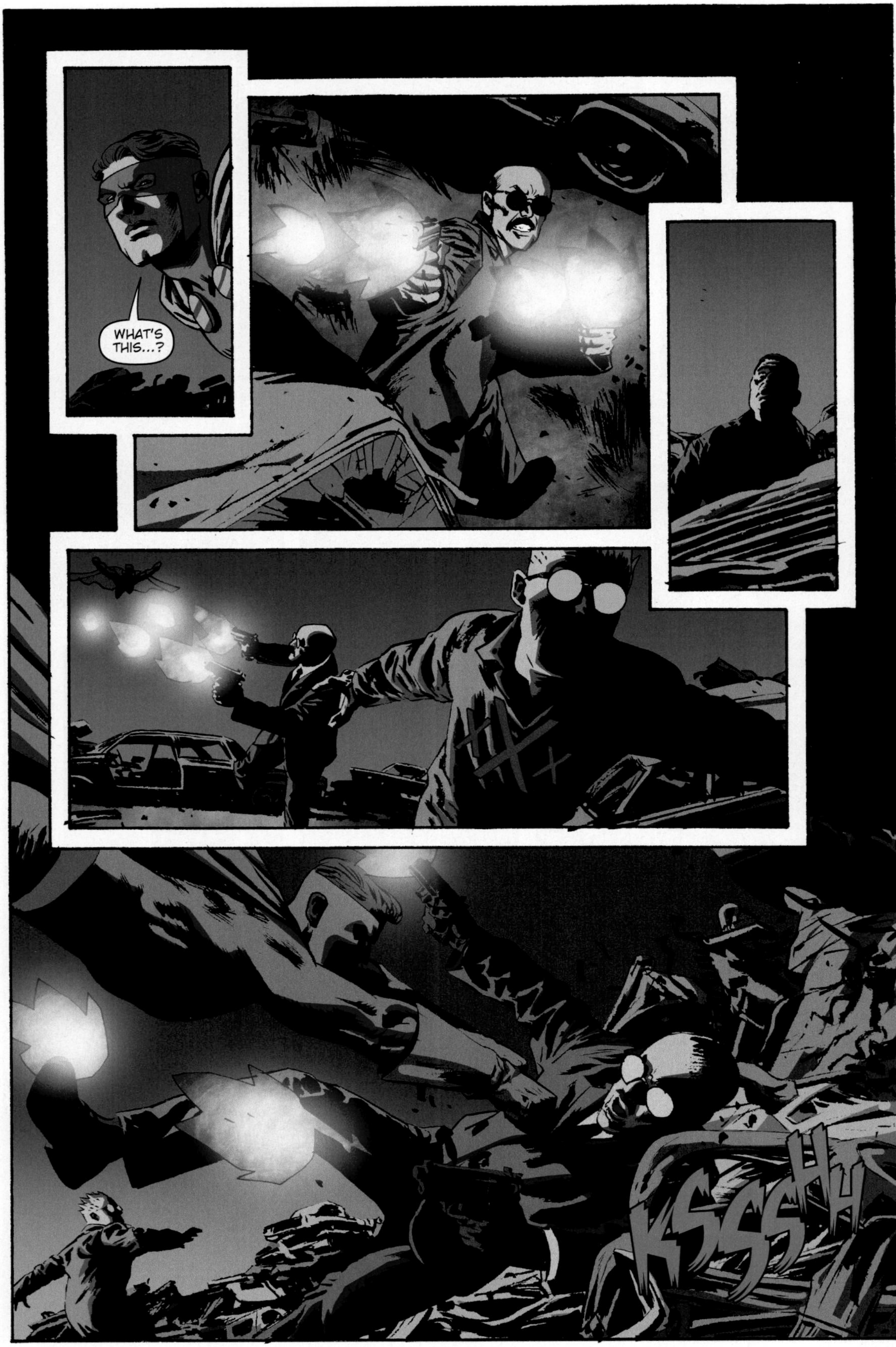
WHAT'S THIS...?
KSSSHH

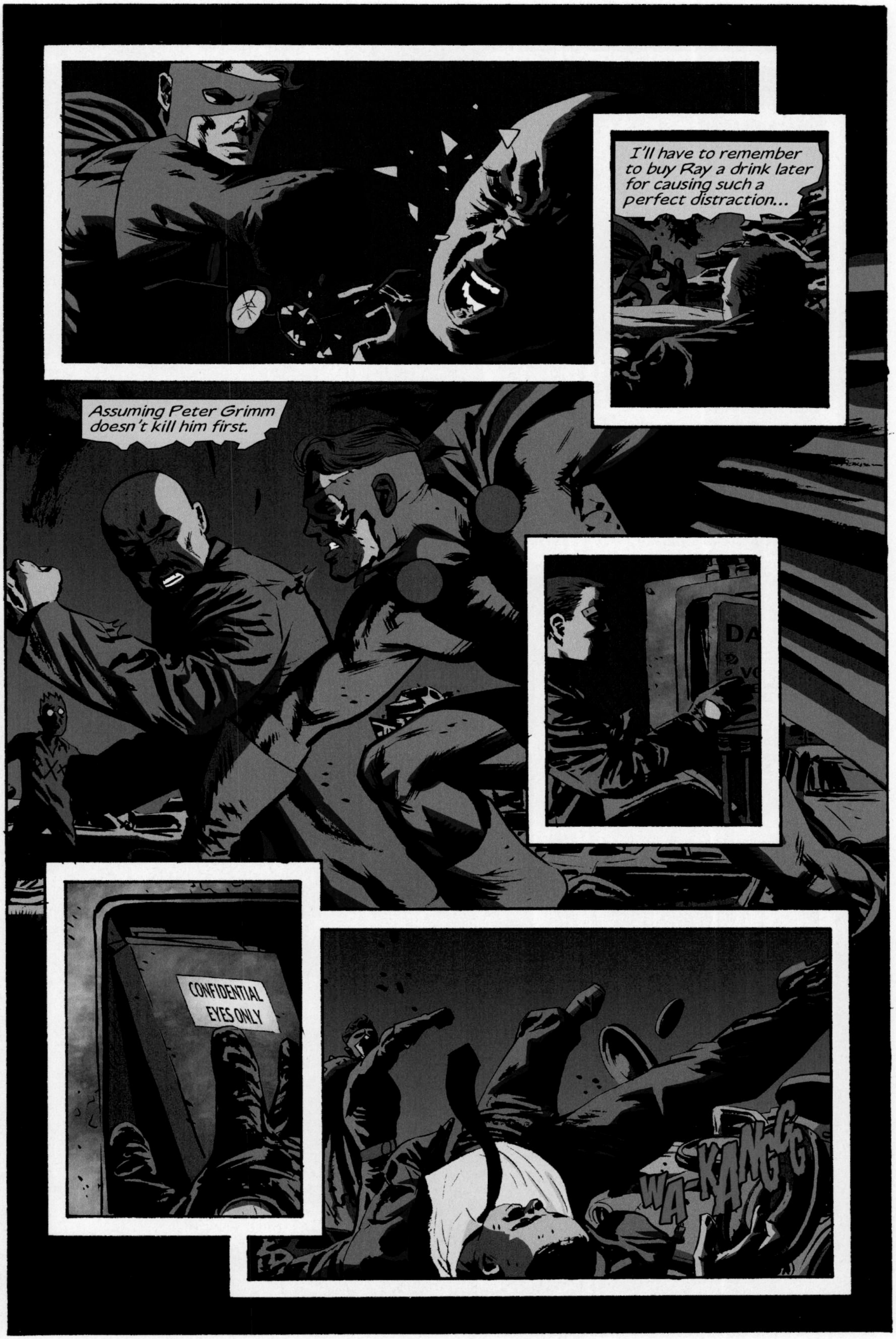
I'll have to remember to buy Ray a drink later for causing such a perfect distraction...
Assuming Peter Grimm doesn't kill him first.
CONFIDENTIAL EYES ONLY
WA-KANGGG

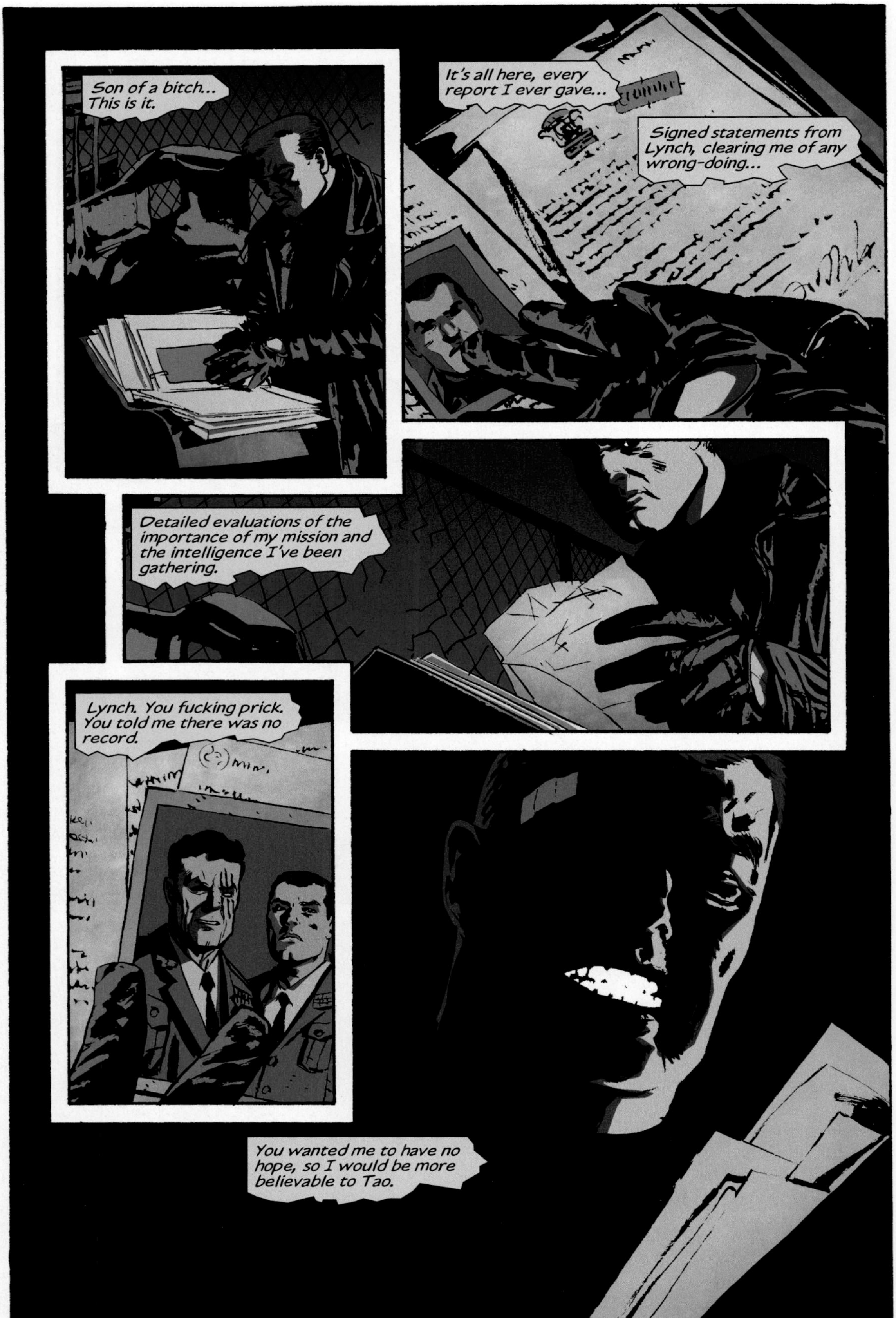
Son of a bitch... This is it.
It's all here, every report I ever gave...
Signed statements from Lynch, clearing me of any wrong-doing...
Detailed evaluations of the importance of my mission and the intelligence I've been gathering.
Lynch. You fucking prick. You told me there was no record.
You wanted me to have no hope, so I would be more believable to Tao.

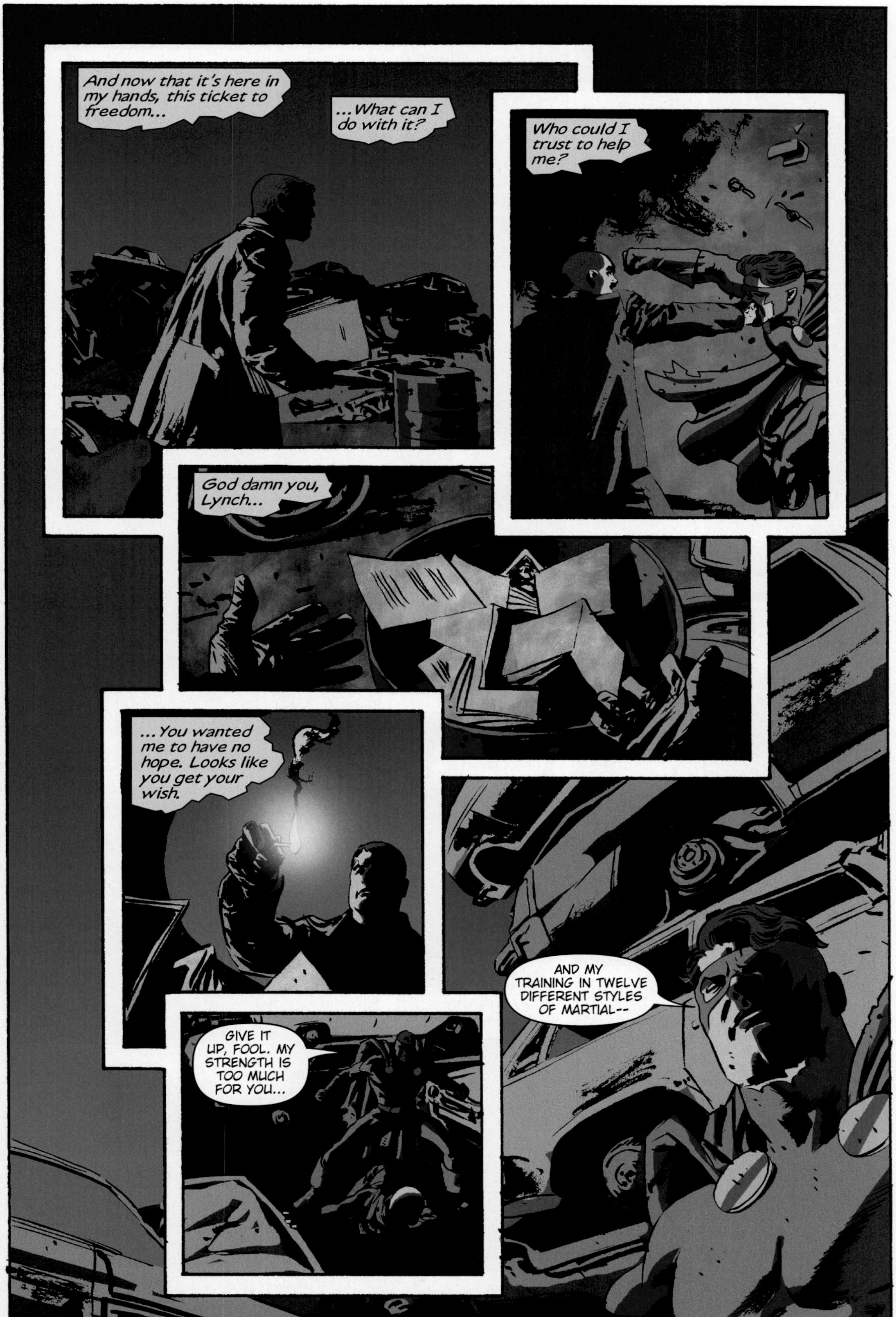
And now that it's here in my hands, this ticket to freedom...
...What can I do with it?
Who could I trust to help me?
God damn you, Lynch...
...You wanted me to have no hope. Looks like you get your wish.
AND MY TRAINING IN TWELVE DIFFERENT STYLES OF MARTIAL--
GIVE IT UP, FOOL. MY STRENGTH IS TOO MUCH FOR YOU...

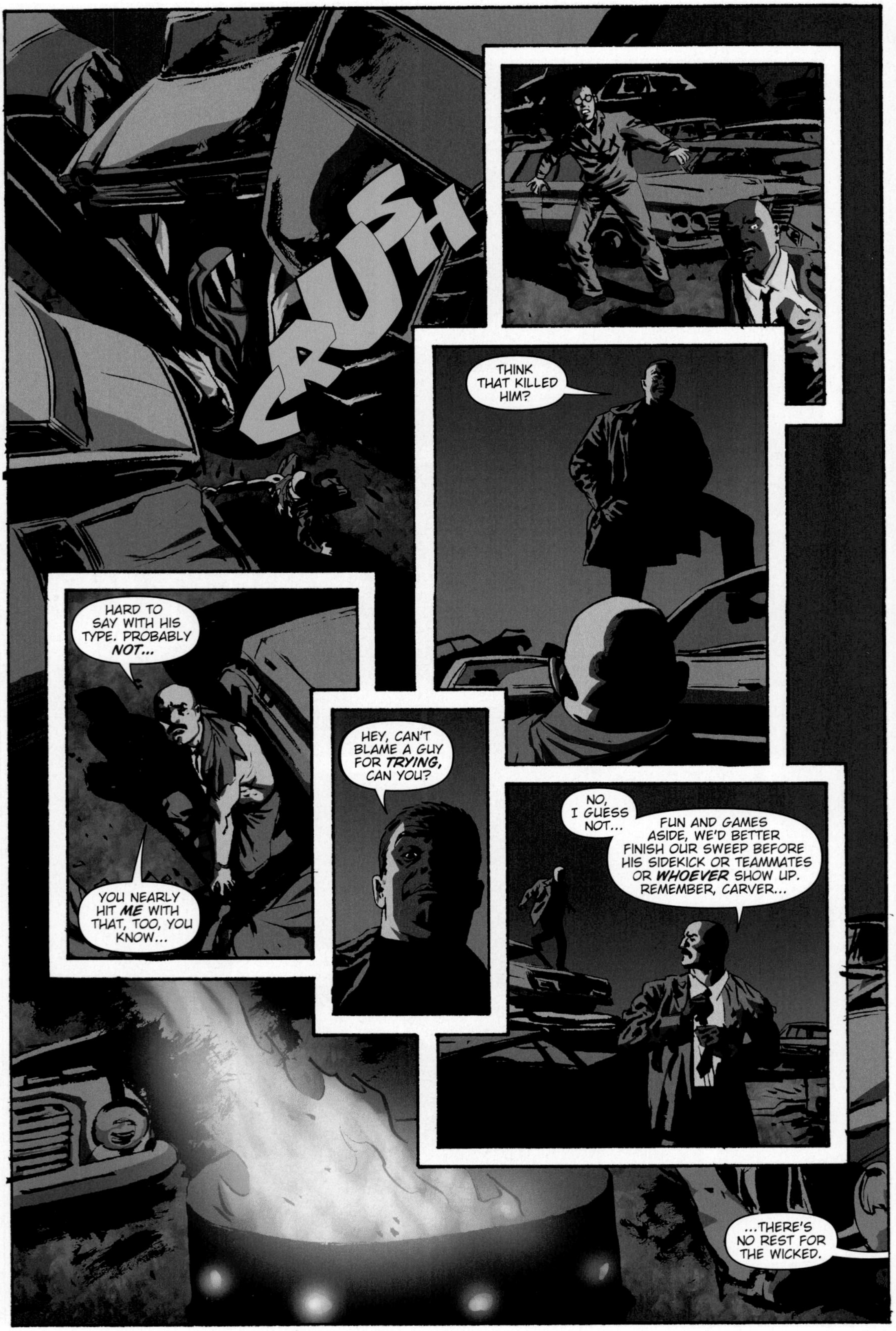
CRUSH
THINK THAT KILLED HIM?
HARD TO SAY WITH HIS TYPE. PROBABLY NOT...
YOU NEARLY HIT ME WITH THAT, TOO, YOU KNOW...
HEY, CAN'T BLAME A GUY FOR TRYING, CAN YOU?
NO, I GUESS NOT...
FUN AND GAMES ASIDE, WE'D BETTER FINISH OUR SWEEP BEFORE HIS SIDEKICK OR TEAMMATES OR WHOEVER SHOW UP. REMEMBER, CARVER...
...THERE'S NO REST FOR THE WICKED.

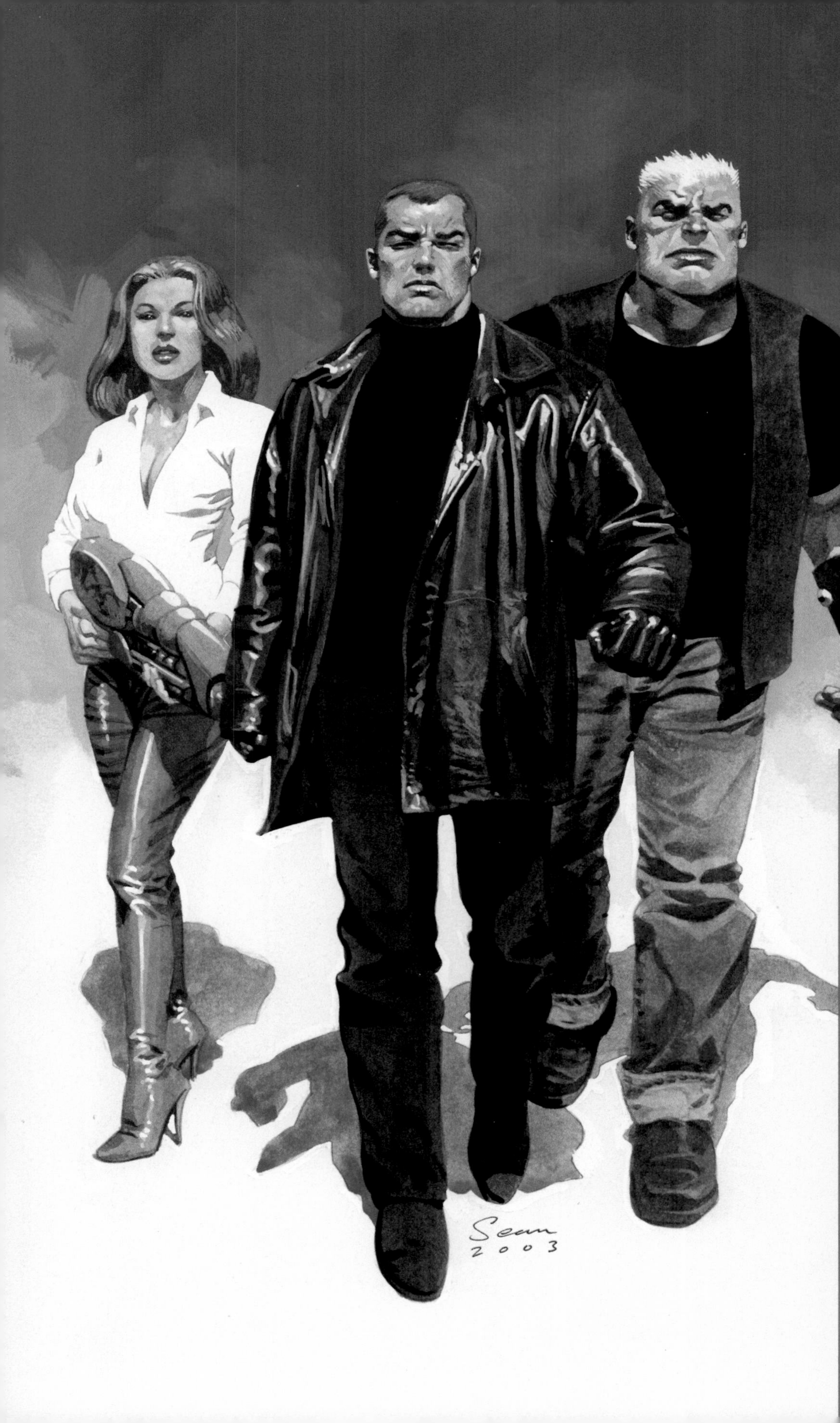
Sean
2003

Cover by SEAN PHILLIPS

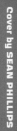

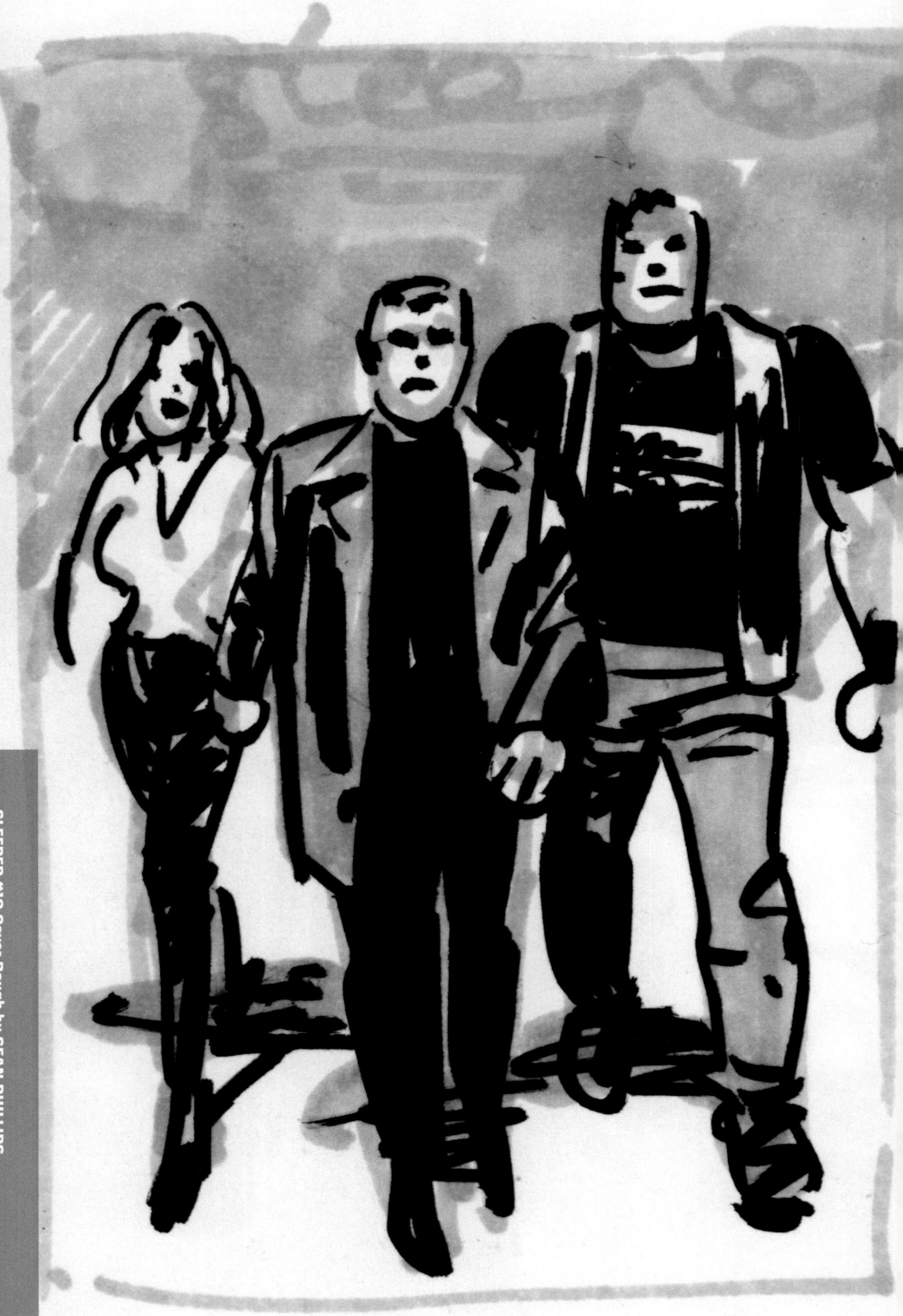

SLEEPER #10 Cover Rough by SEAN PHILLIPS

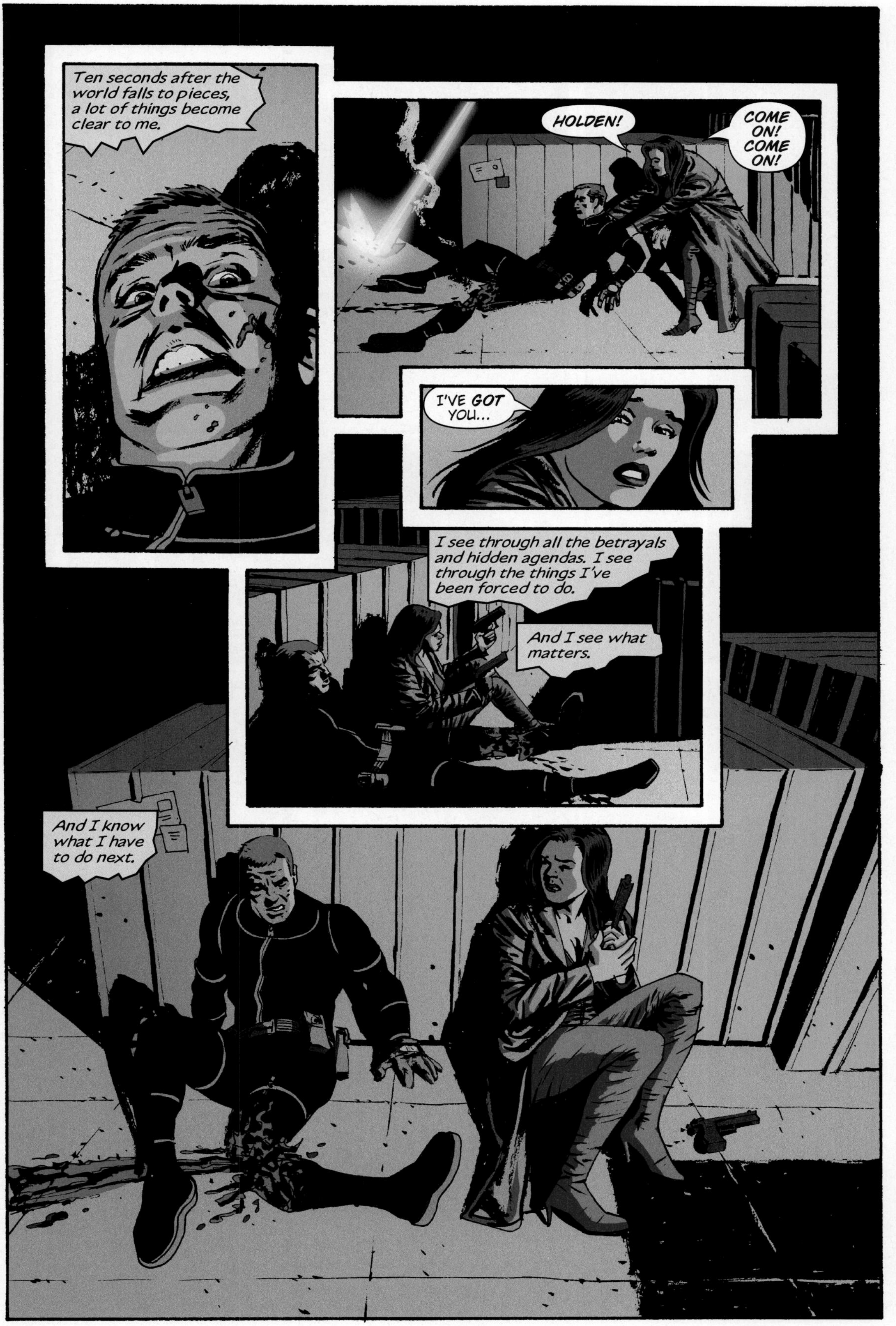
Ten seconds after the world falls to pieces, a lot of things become clear to me.
HOLDEN!
COME ON! COME ON!
I'VE GOT YOU...
I see through all the betrayals and hidden agendas. I see through the things I've been forced to do.
And I see what matters.
And I know what I have to do next.

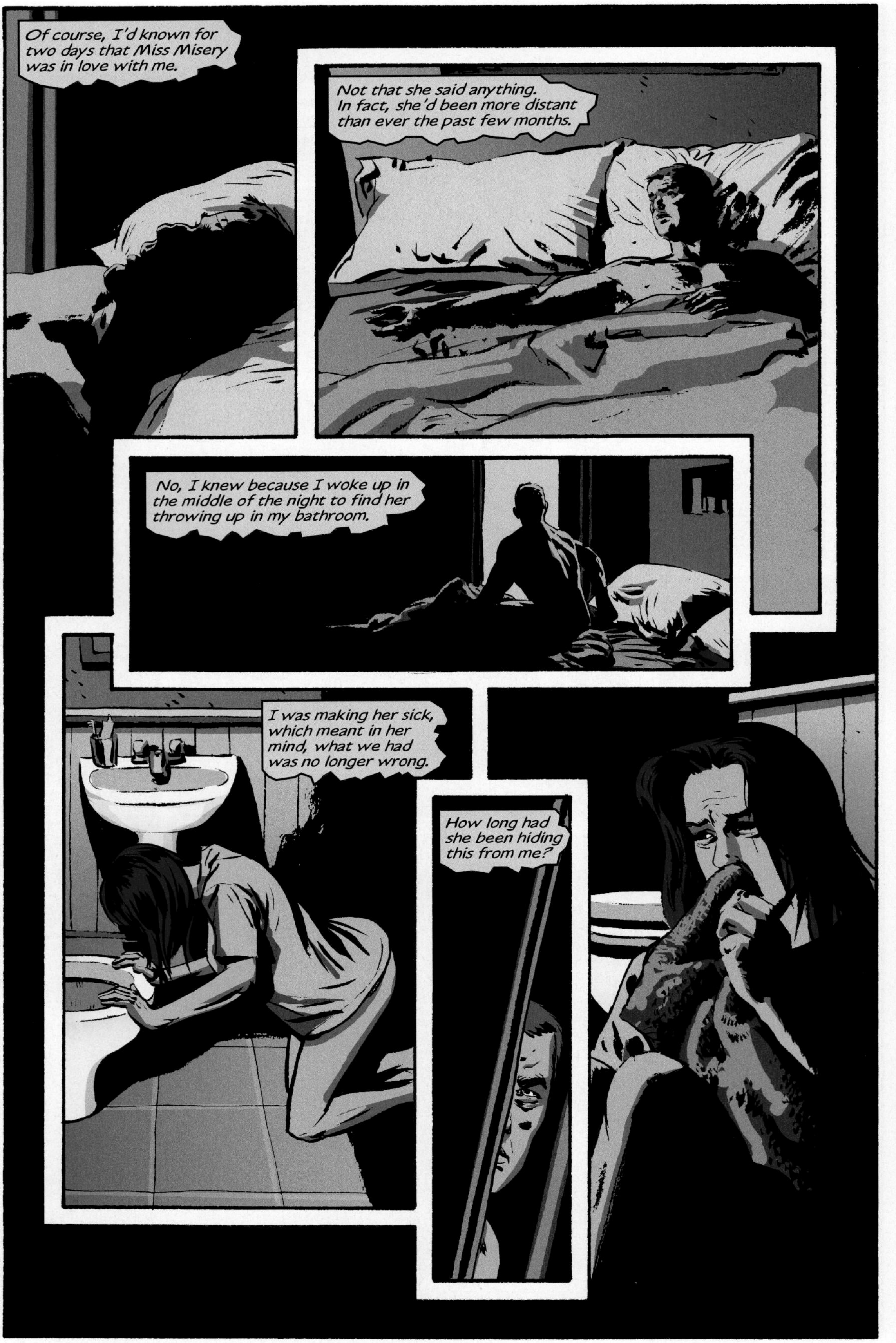
Of course, I'd known for two days that Miss Misery was in love with me.
Not that she said anything. In fact, she'd been more distant than ever the past few months.
No, I knew because I woke up in the middle of the night to find her throwing up in my bathroom.
I was making her sick, which meant in her mind, what we had was no longer wrong.
How long had she been hiding this from me?

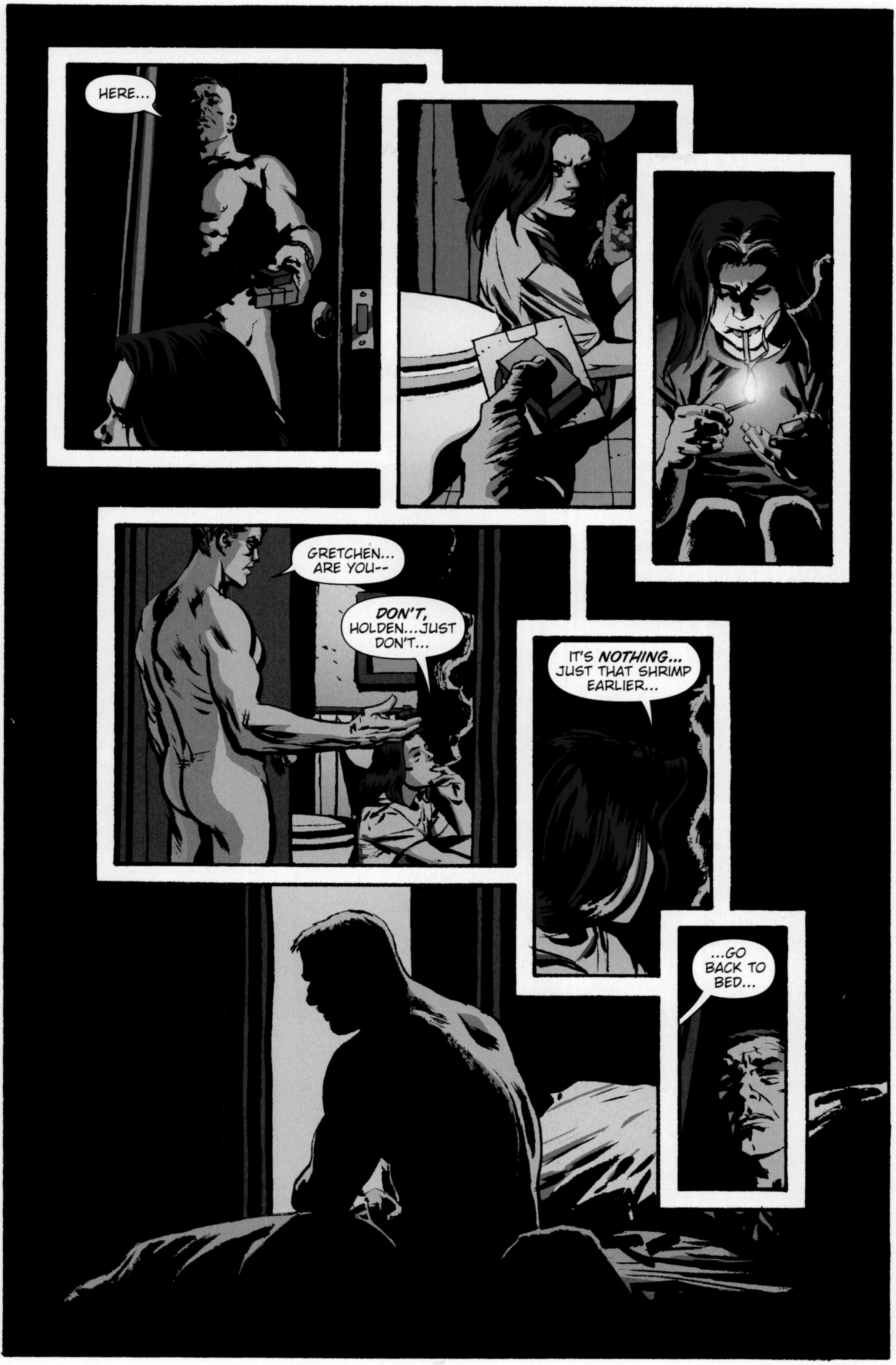
HERE...
GRETCHEN... ARE YOU--
DON'T, HOLDEN...JUST DON'T...
IT'S NOTHING... JUST THAT SHRIMP EARLIER...
...GO BACK TO BED...

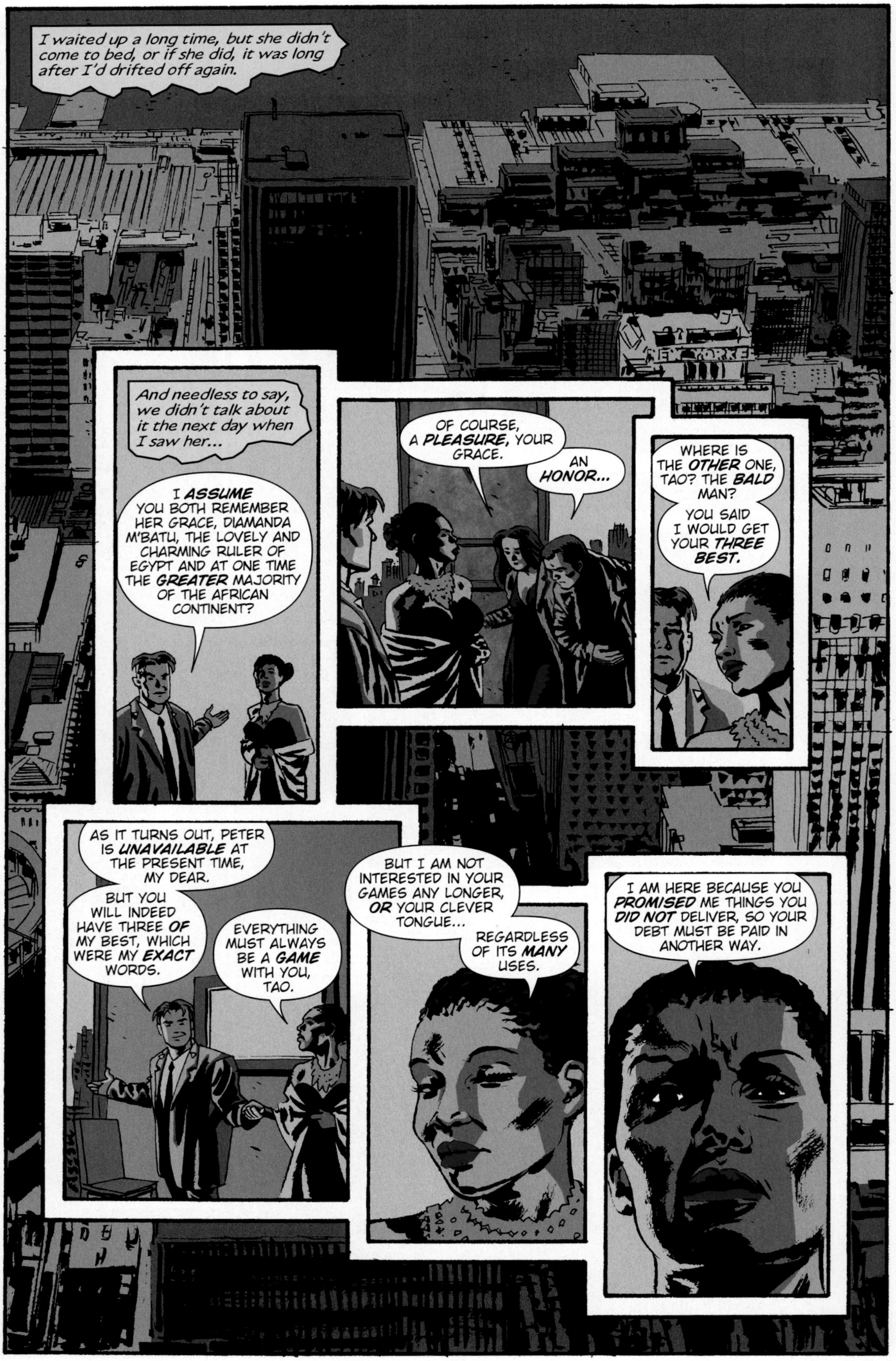
I waited up a long time, but she didn't come to bed, or if she did, it was long after I'd drifted off again.
And needless to say, we didn't talk about it the next day when I saw her...
I ASSUME YOU BOTH REMEMBER HER GRACE, DIAMANDA M'BATU, THE LOVELY AND CHARMING RULER OF EGYPT AND AT ONE TIME THE GREATER MAJORITY OF THE AFRICAN CONTINENT?
OF COURSE, A PLEASURE, YOUR GRACE.
AN HONOR...
WHERE IS THE OTHER ONE, TAO? THE BALD MAN?
YOU SAID I WOULD GET YOUR THREE BEST.
AS IT TURNS OUT, PETER IS UNAVAILABLE AT THE PRESENT TIME, MY DEAR.
BUT YOU WILL INDEED HAVE THREE OF MY BEST, WHICH WERE MY EXACT WORDS.
EVERYTHING MUST ALWAYS BE A GAME WITH YOU, TAO.
BUT I AM NOT INTERESTED IN YOUR GAMES ANY LONGER, OR YOUR CLEVER TONGUE...
REGARDLESS OF ITS MANY USES.
I AM HERE BECAUSE YOU PROMISED ME THINGS YOU DID NOT DELIVER, SO YOUR DEBT MUST BE PAID IN ANOTHER WAY.

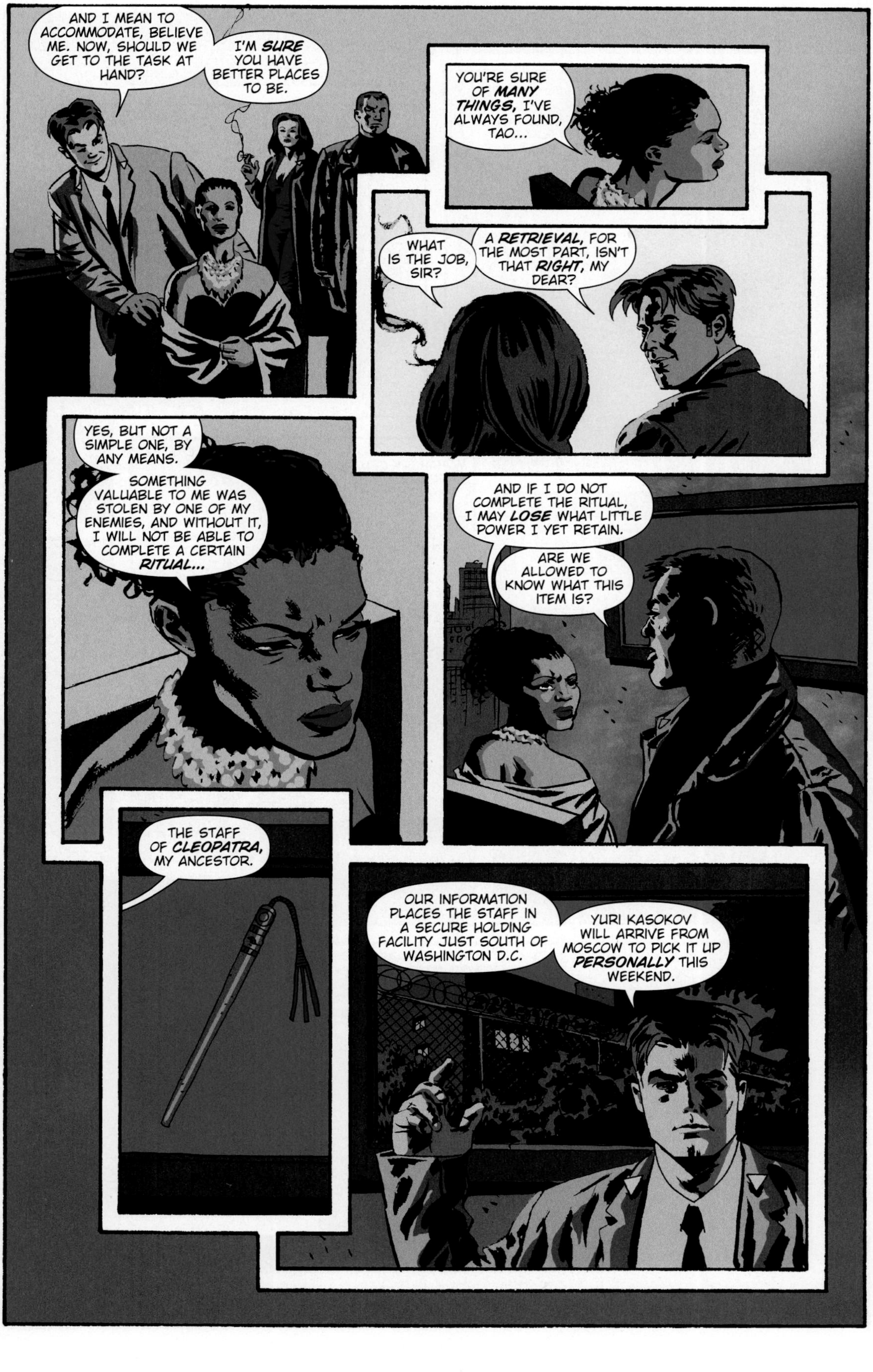
AND I MEAN TO ACCOMMODATE, BELIEVE ME. NOW, SHOULD WE GET TO THE TASK AT HAND?
I'M SURE YOU HAVE BETTER PLACES TO BE.
YOU'RE SURE OF MANY THINGS, I'VE ALWAYS FOUND, TAO...
WHAT IS THE JOB, SIR?
A RETRIEVAL, FOR THE MOST PART, ISN'T THAT RIGHT, MY DEAR?
YES, BUT NOT A SIMPLE ONE, BY ANY MEANS.
SOMETHING VALUABLE TO ME WAS STOLEN BY ONE OF MY ENEMIES, AND WITHOUT IT, I WILL NOT BE ABLE TO COMPLETE A CERTAIN RITUAL...
AND IF I DO NOT COMPLETE THE RITUAL, I MAY LOSE WHAT LITTLE POWER I YET RETAIN.
ARE WE ALLOWED TO KNOW WHAT THIS ITEM IS?
THE STAFF OF CLEOPATRA, MY ANCESTOR.
OUR INFORMATION PLACES THE STAFF IN A SECURE HOLDING FACILITY JUST SOUTH OF WASHINGTON D.C.
YURI KASOKOV WILL ARRIVE FROM MOSCOW TO PICK IT UP PERSONALLY THIS WEEKEND.

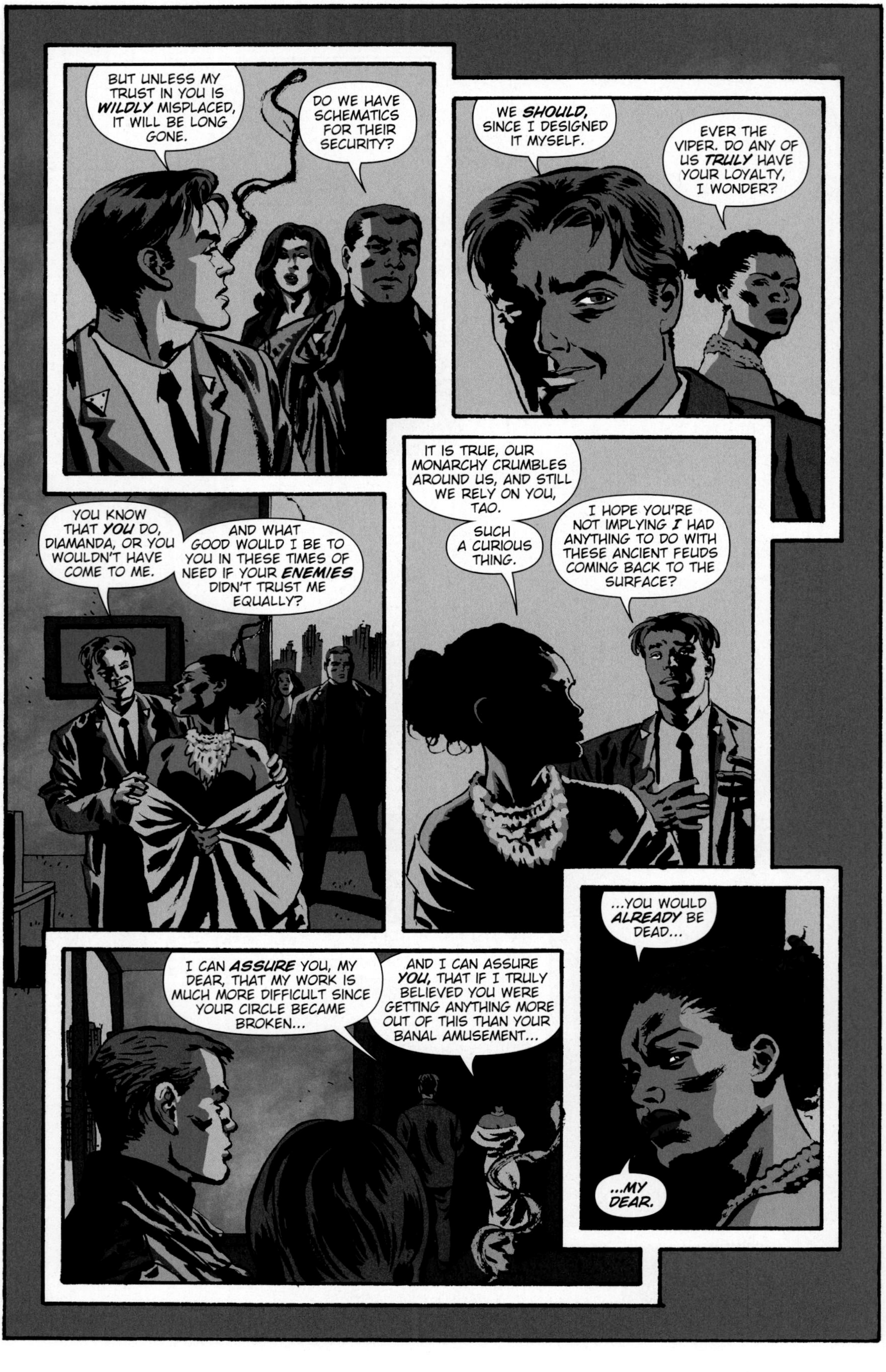
BUT UNLESS MY TRUST IN YOU IS WILDLY MISPLACED, IT WILL BE LONG GONE.
DO WE HAVE SCHEMATICS FOR THEIR SECURITY?
WE SHOULD, SINCE I DESIGNED IT MYSELF.
EVER THE VIPER. DO ANY OF US TRULY HAVE YOUR LOYALTY, I WONDER?
YOU KNOW THAT YOU DO, DIAMANDA, OR YOU WOULDN'T HAVE COME TO ME.
AND WHAT GOOD WOULD I BE TO YOU IN THESE TIMES OF NEED IF YOUR ENEMIES DIDN'T TRUST ME EQUALLY?
IT IS TRUE, OUR MONARCHY CRUMBLES AROUND US, AND STILL WE RELY ON YOU, TAO.
SUCH A CURIOUS THING.
I HOPE YOU'RE NOT IMPLYING I HAD ANYTHING TO DO WITH THESE ANCIENT FEUDS COMING BACK TO THE SURFACE?
I CAN ASSURE YOU, MY DEAR, THAT MY WORK IS MUCH MORE DIFFICULT SINCE YOUR CIRCLE BECAME BROKEN...
AND I CAN ASSURE YOU, THAT IF I TRULY BELIEVED YOU WERE GETTING ANYTHING MORE OUT OF THIS THAN YOUR BANAL AMUSEMENT...
...YOU WOULD ALREADY BE DEAD...
...MY DEAR.

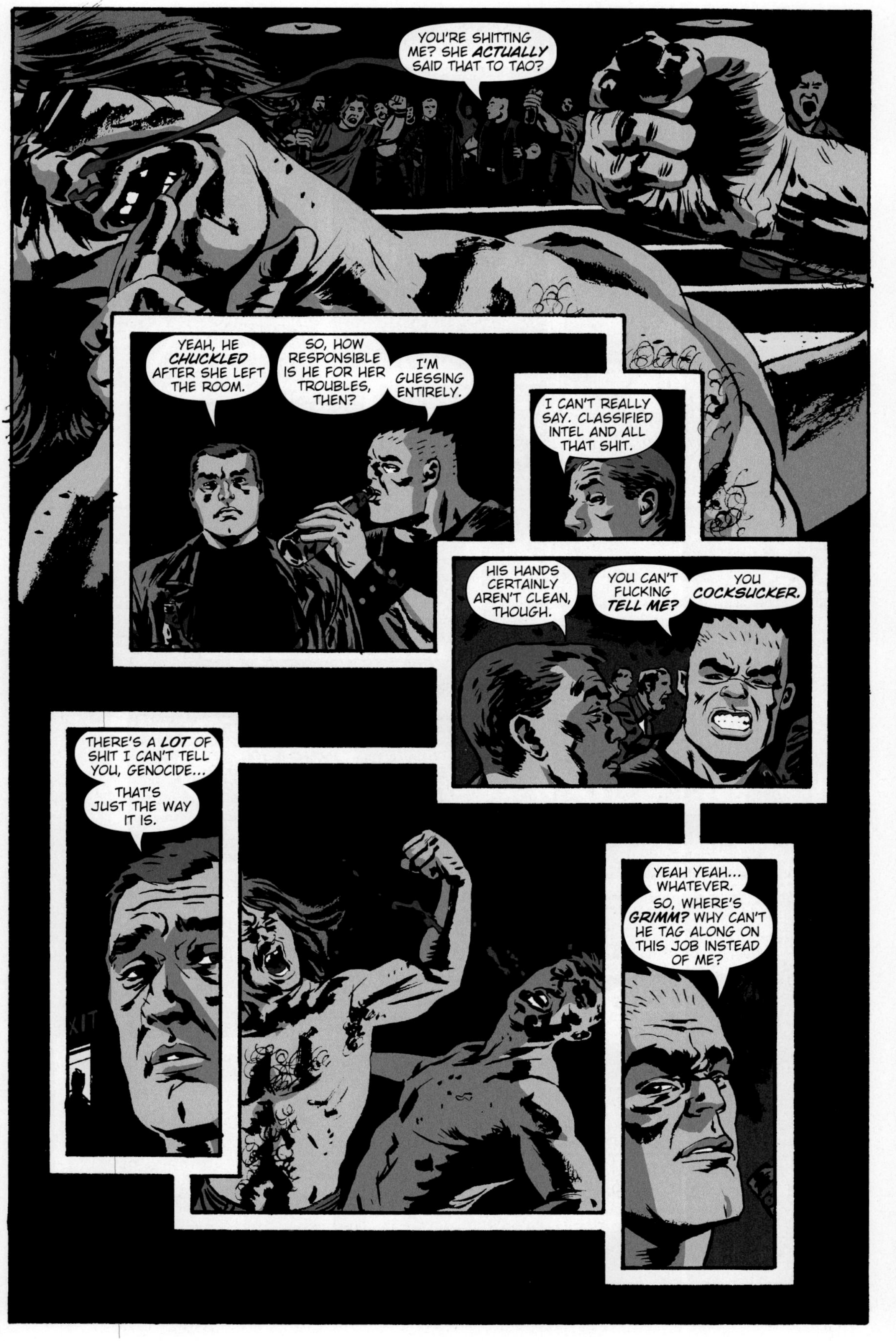
YOU'RE SHITTING ME? SHE ACTUALLY SAID THAT TO TAO?
YEAH, HE CHUCKLED AFTER SHE LEFT THE ROOM.
SO, HOW RESPONSIBLE IS HE FOR HER TROUBLES, THEN?
I'M GUESSING ENTIRELY.
I CAN'T REALLY SAY. CLASSIFIED INTEL AND ALL THAT SHIT.
HIS HANDS CERTAINLY AREN'T CLEAN, THOUGH.
YOU CAN'T FUCKING TELL ME?
YOU COCKSUCKER.
THERE'S A LOT OF SHIT I CAN'T TELL YOU, GENOCIDE...
THAT'S JUST THE WAY IT IS.
YEAH YEAH... WHATEVER.
SO, WHERE'S GRIMM? WHY CAN'T HE TAG ALONG ON THIS JOB INSTEAD OF ME?
EXIT

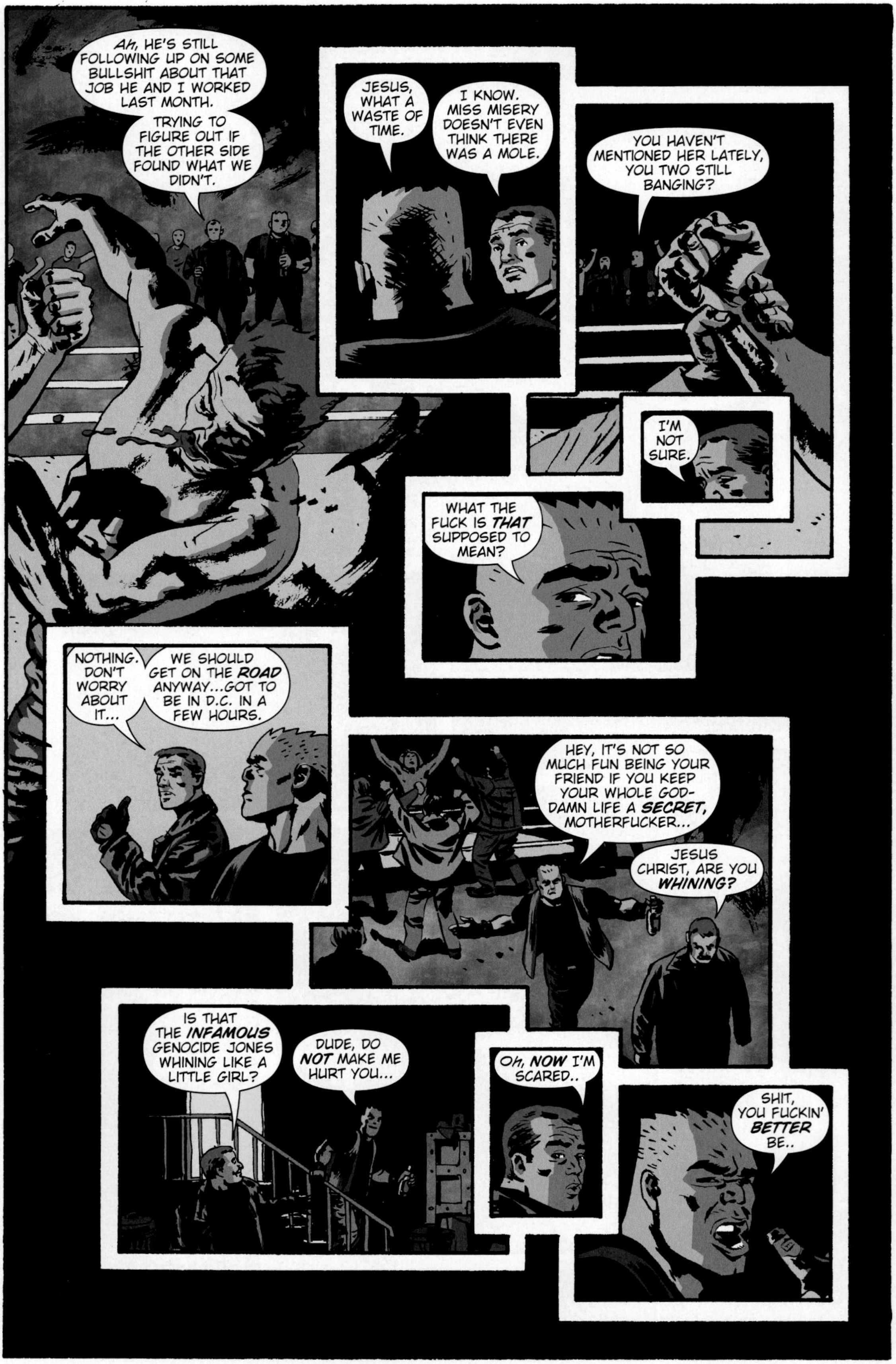

Ah, HE'S STILL FOLLOWING UP ON SOME BULLSHIT ABOUT THAT JOB HE AND I WORKED LAST MONTH.
TRYING TO FIGURE OUT IF THE OTHER SIDE FOUND WHAT WE DIDN'T.
JESUS, WHAT A WASTE OF TIME.
I KNOW. MISS MISERY DOESN'T EVEN THINK THERE WAS A MOLE.
YOU HAVEN'T MENTIONED HER LATELY, YOU TWO STILL BANGING?
I'M NOT SURE.
WHAT THE FUCK IS ***THAT*** SUPPOSED TO MEAN?
NOTHING. DON'T WORRY ABOUT IT...
WE SHOULD GET ON THE ***ROAD*** ANYWAY...GOT TO BE IN D.C. IN A FEW HOURS.
HEY, IT'S NOT SO MUCH FUN BEING YOUR FRIEND IF YOU KEEP YOUR WHOLE GOD-DAMN LIFE A ***SECRET,*** MOTHERFUCKER...
JESUS CHRIST, ARE YOU ***WHINING?***
IS THAT THE ***INFAMOUS*** GENOCIDE JONES WHINING LIKE A LITTLE GIRL?
DUDE, DO ***NOT*** MAKE ME HURT YOU...
Oh, ***NOW*** I'M SCARED..
SHIT, YOU FUCKIN' ***BETTER*** BE..

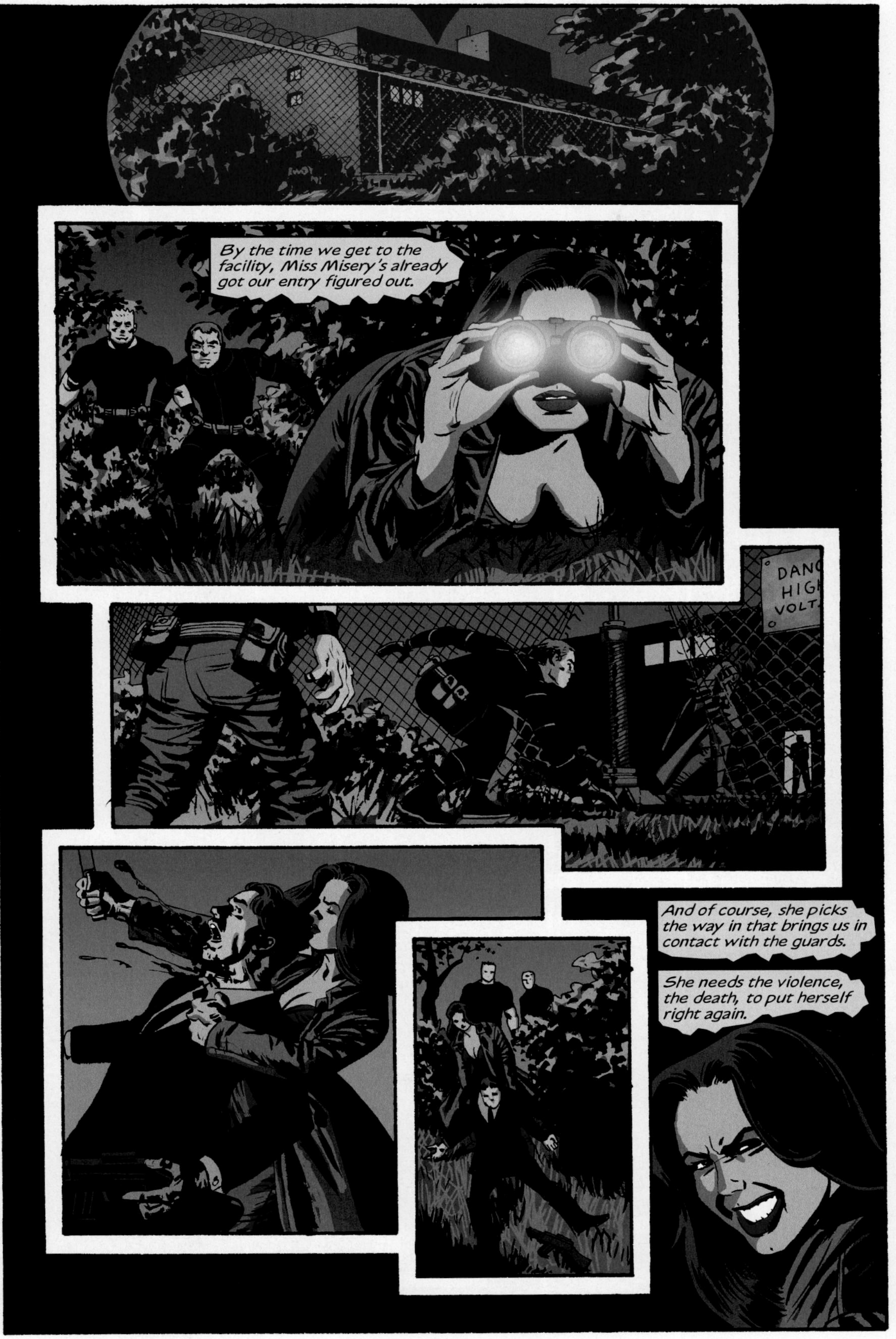
By the time we get to the facility, Miss Misery's already got our entry figured out.
DANG
HIGH
VOLT
And of course, she picks the way in that brings us in contact with the guards.
She needs the violence, the death, to put herself right again.

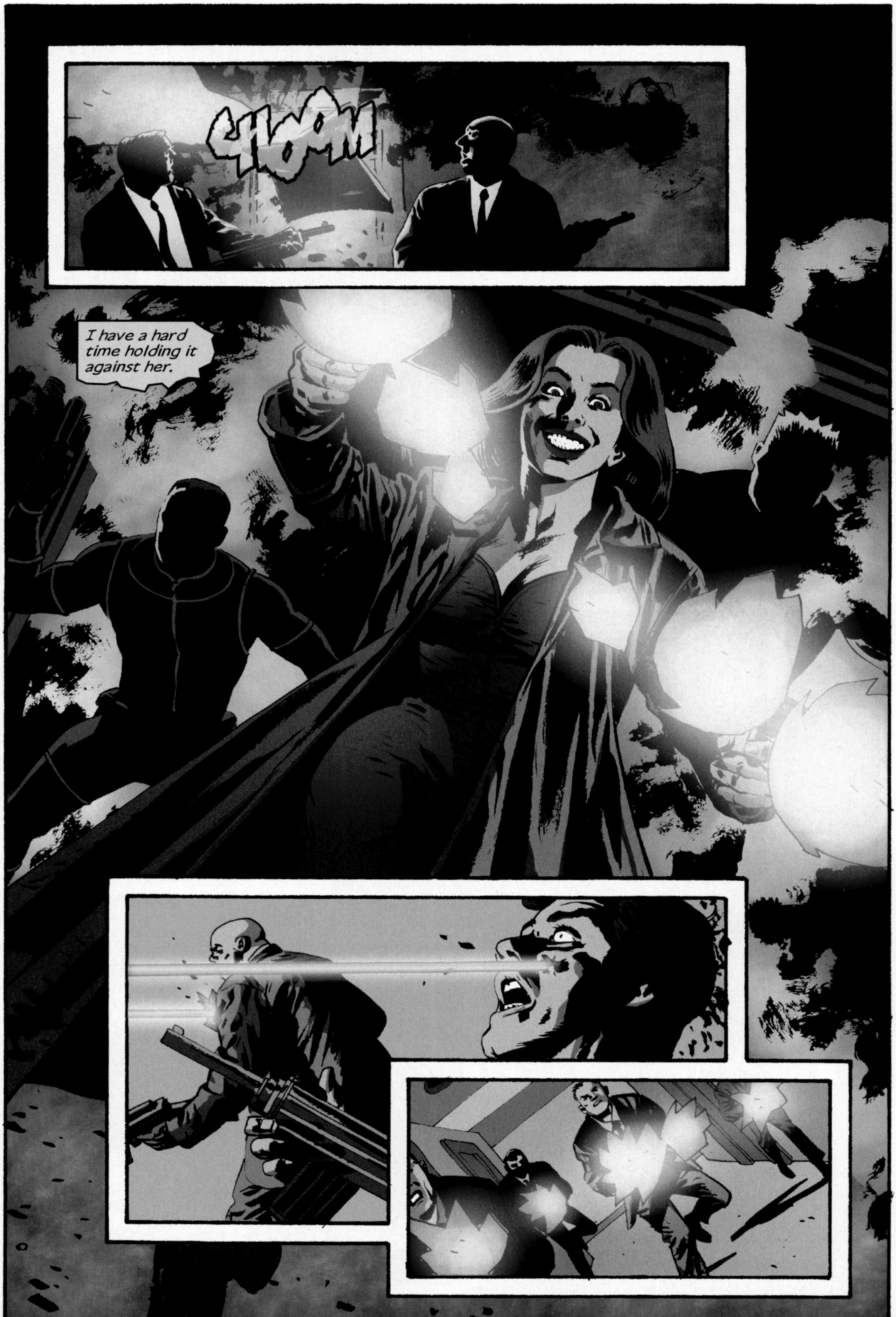
CHOOM
I have a hard time holding it against her.

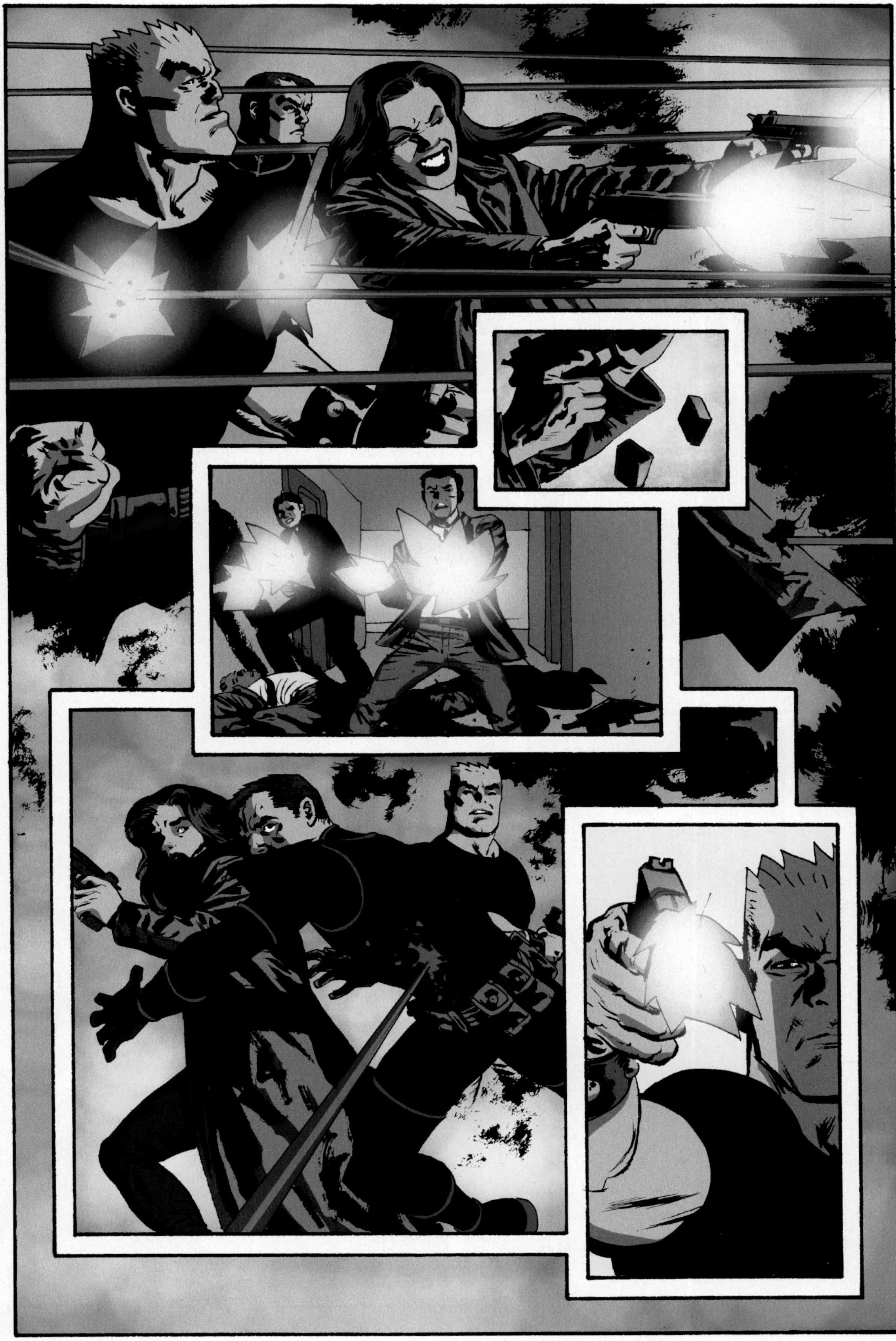

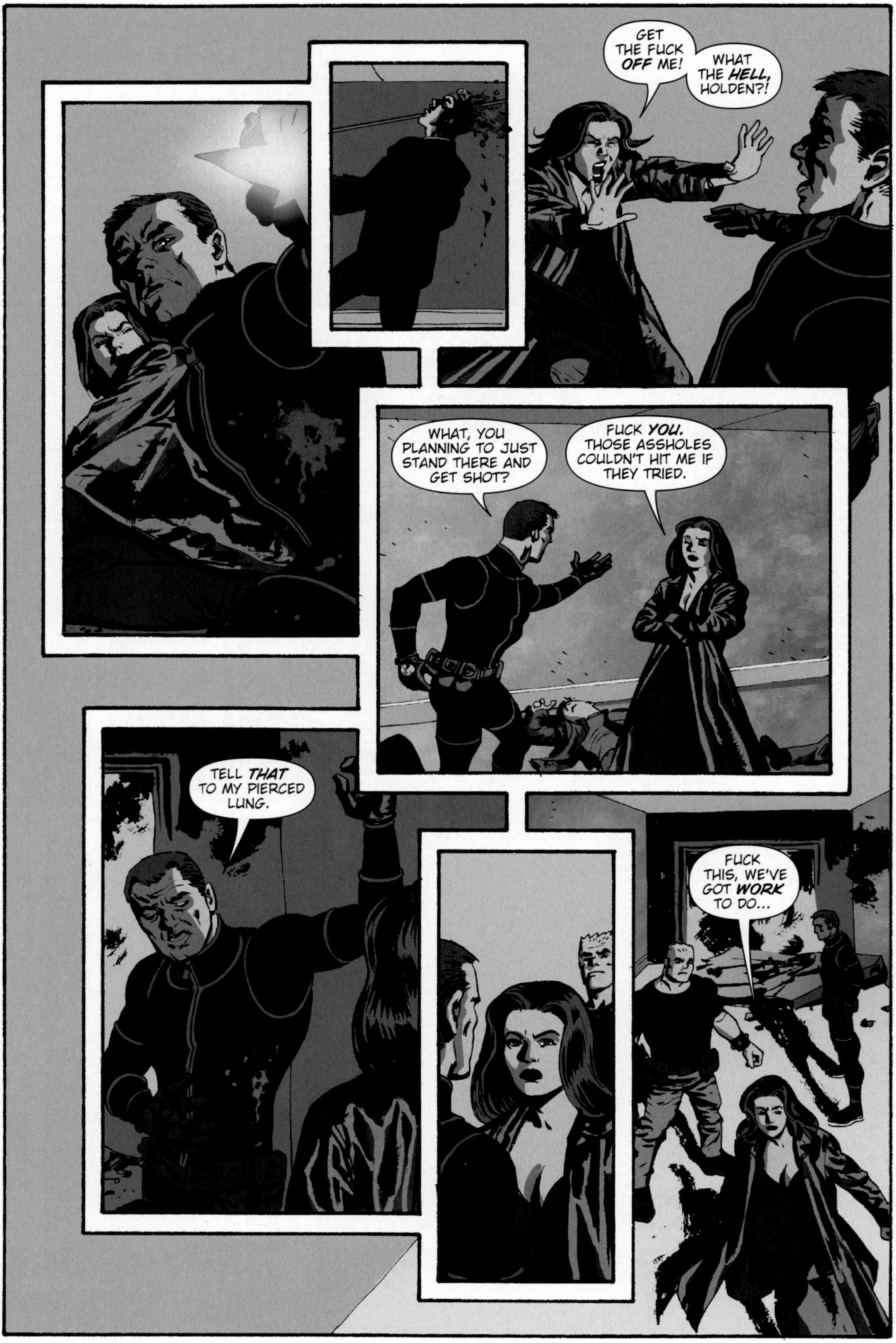
GET THE FUCK OFF ME!
WHAT THE HELL, HOLDEN?!
WHAT, YOU PLANNING TO JUST STAND THERE AND GET SHOT?
FUCK YOU. THOSE ASSHOLES COULDN'T HIT ME IF THEY TRIED.
TELL THAT TO MY PIERCED LUNG.
FUCK THIS, WE'VE GOT WORK TO DO...

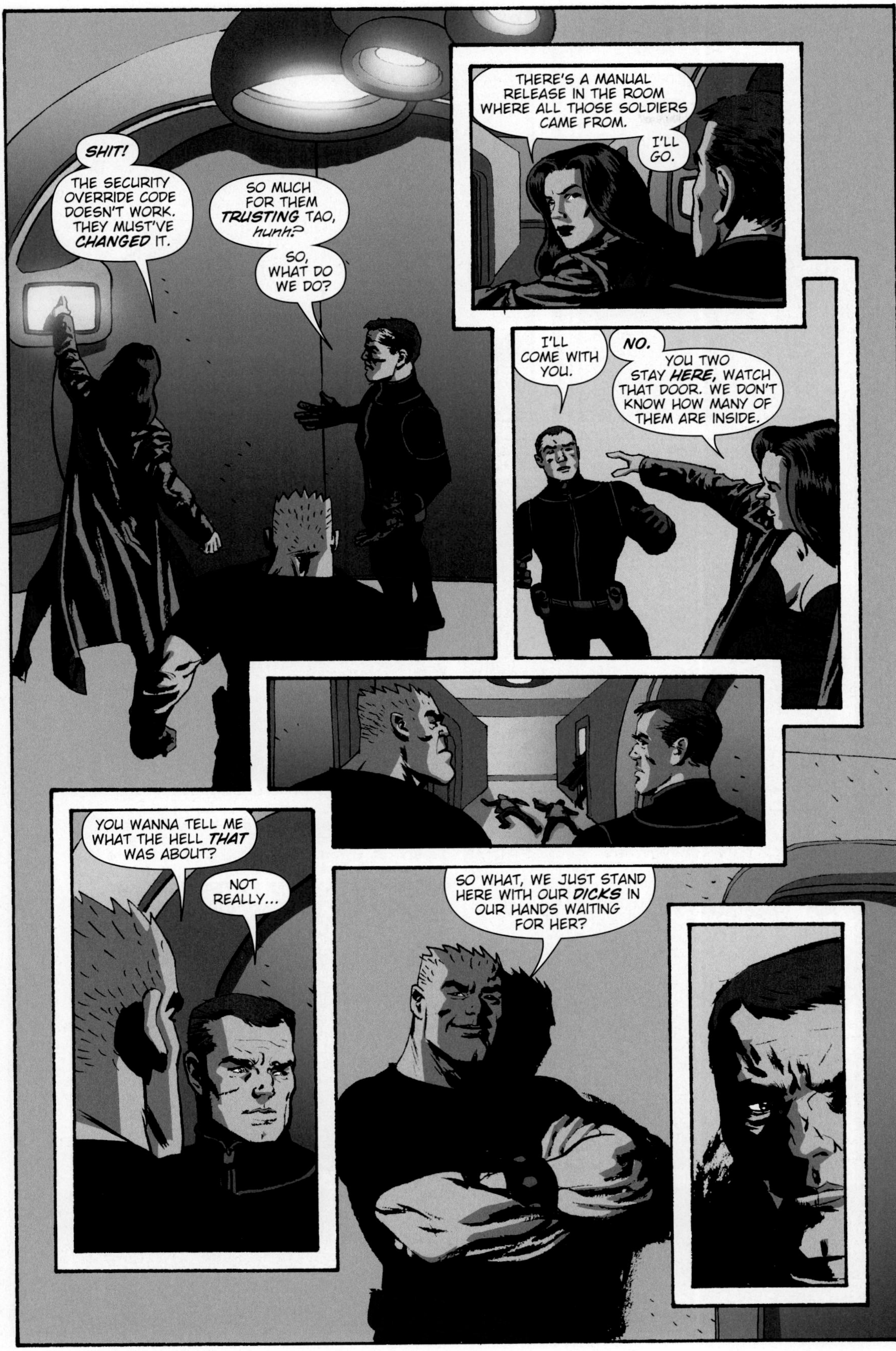
SHIT!
THE SECURITY OVERRIDE CODE DOESN'T WORK. THEY MUST'VE CHANGED IT.
SO MUCH FOR THEM TRUSTING TAO, hunh?
SO, WHAT DO WE DO?
THERE'S A MANUAL RELEASE IN THE ROOM WHERE ALL THOSE SOLDIERS CAME FROM.
I'LL GO.
I'LL COME WITH YOU.
NO.
YOU TWO STAY HERE, WATCH THAT DOOR. WE DON'T KNOW HOW MANY OF THEM ARE INSIDE.
YOU WANNA TELL ME WHAT THE HELL THAT WAS ABOUT?
NOT REALLY...
SO WHAT, WE JUST STAND HERE WITH OUR DICKS IN OUR HANDS WAITING FOR HER?

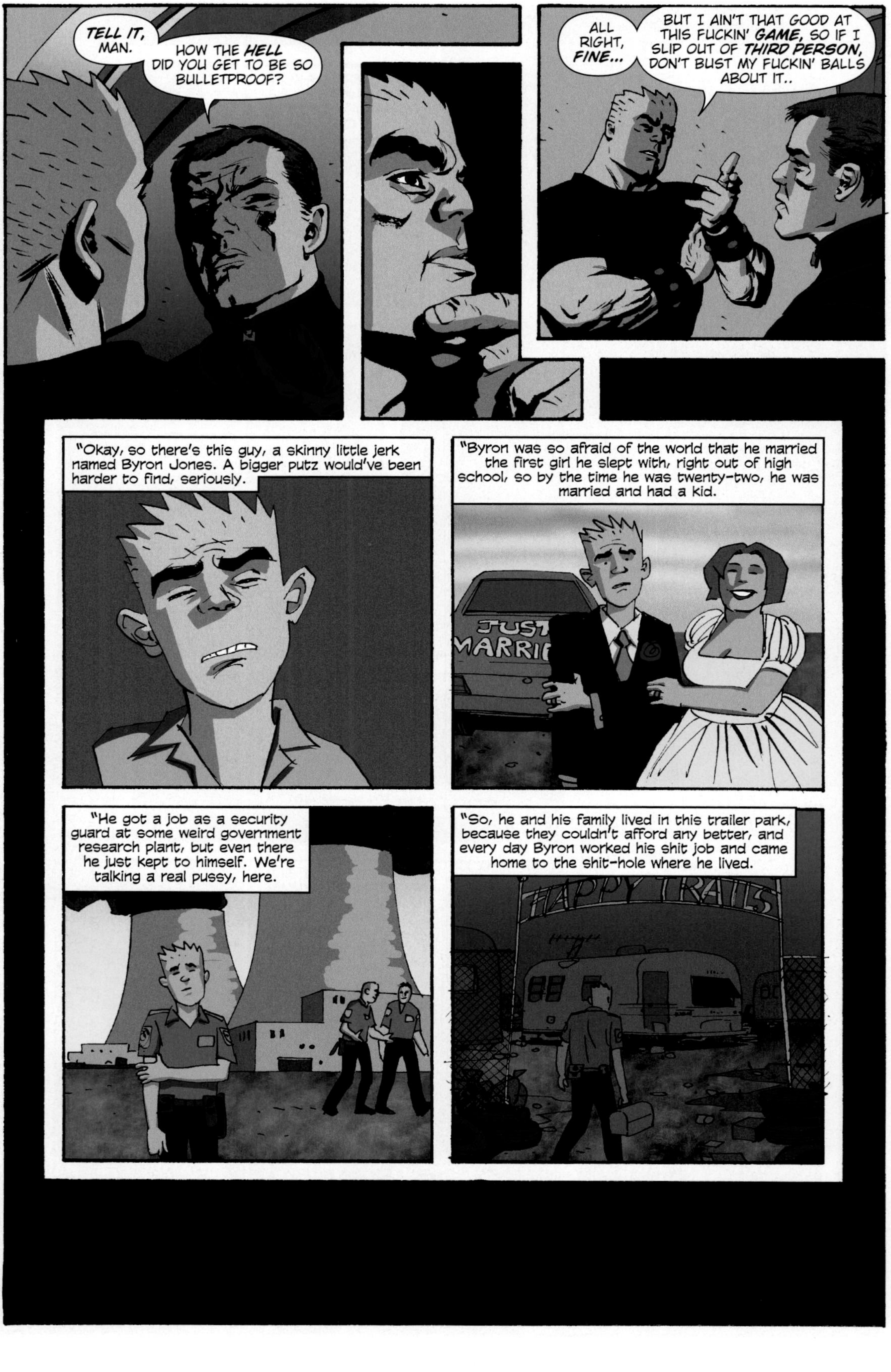
TELL IT, MAN.
HOW THE HELL DID YOU GET TO BE SO BULLETPROOF?
ALL RIGHT, FINE...
BUT I AIN'T THAT GOOD AT THIS FUCKIN' GAME, SO IF I SLIP OUT OF THIRD PERSON, DON'T BUST MY FUCKIN' BALLS ABOUT IT..
"Okay, so there's this guy, a skinny little jerk named Byron Jones. A bigger putz would've been harder to find, seriously.
"Byron was so afraid of the world that he married the first girl he slept with, right out of high school, so by the time he was twenty-two, he was married and had a kid.
JUST MARRI
"He got a job as a security guard at some weird government research plant, but even there he just kept to himself. We're talking a real pussy, here.
"So, he and his family lived in this trailer park, because they couldn't afford any better, and every day Byron worked his shit job and came home to the shit-hole where he lived.
HAPPY TRAILS

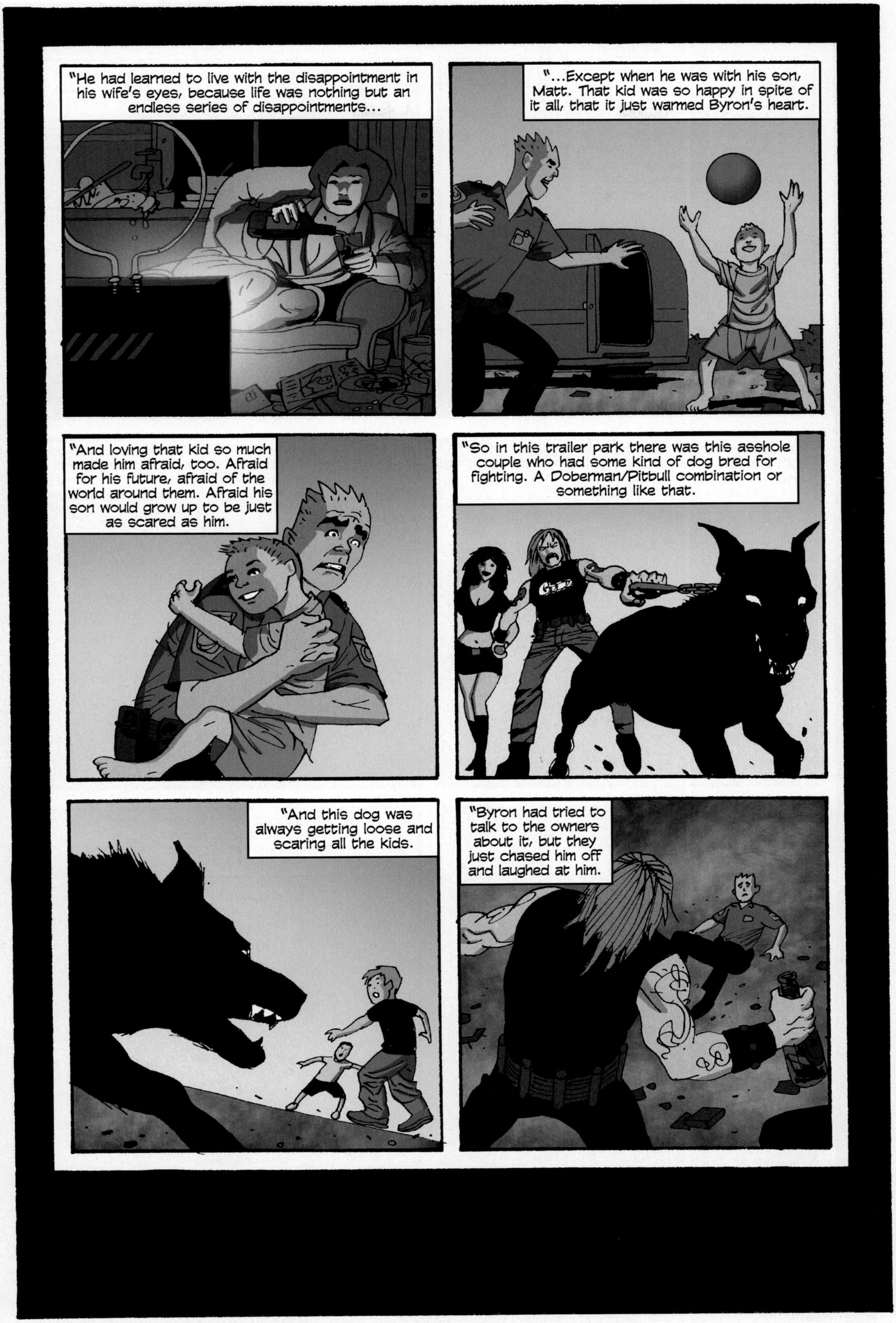
"He had learned to live with the disappointment in his wife's eyes, because life was nothing but an endless series of disappointments...
"...Except when he was with his son, Matt. That kid was so happy in spite of it all, that it just warmed Byron's heart.
"And loving that kid so much made him afraid, too. Afraid for his future, afraid of the world around them. Afraid his son would grow up to be just as scared as him.
"So in this trailer park there was this asshole couple who had some kind of dog bred for fighting. A Doberman/Pitbull combination or something like that.
"And this dog was always getting loose and scaring all the kids.
"Byron had tried to talk to the owners about it, but they just chased him off and laughed at him.

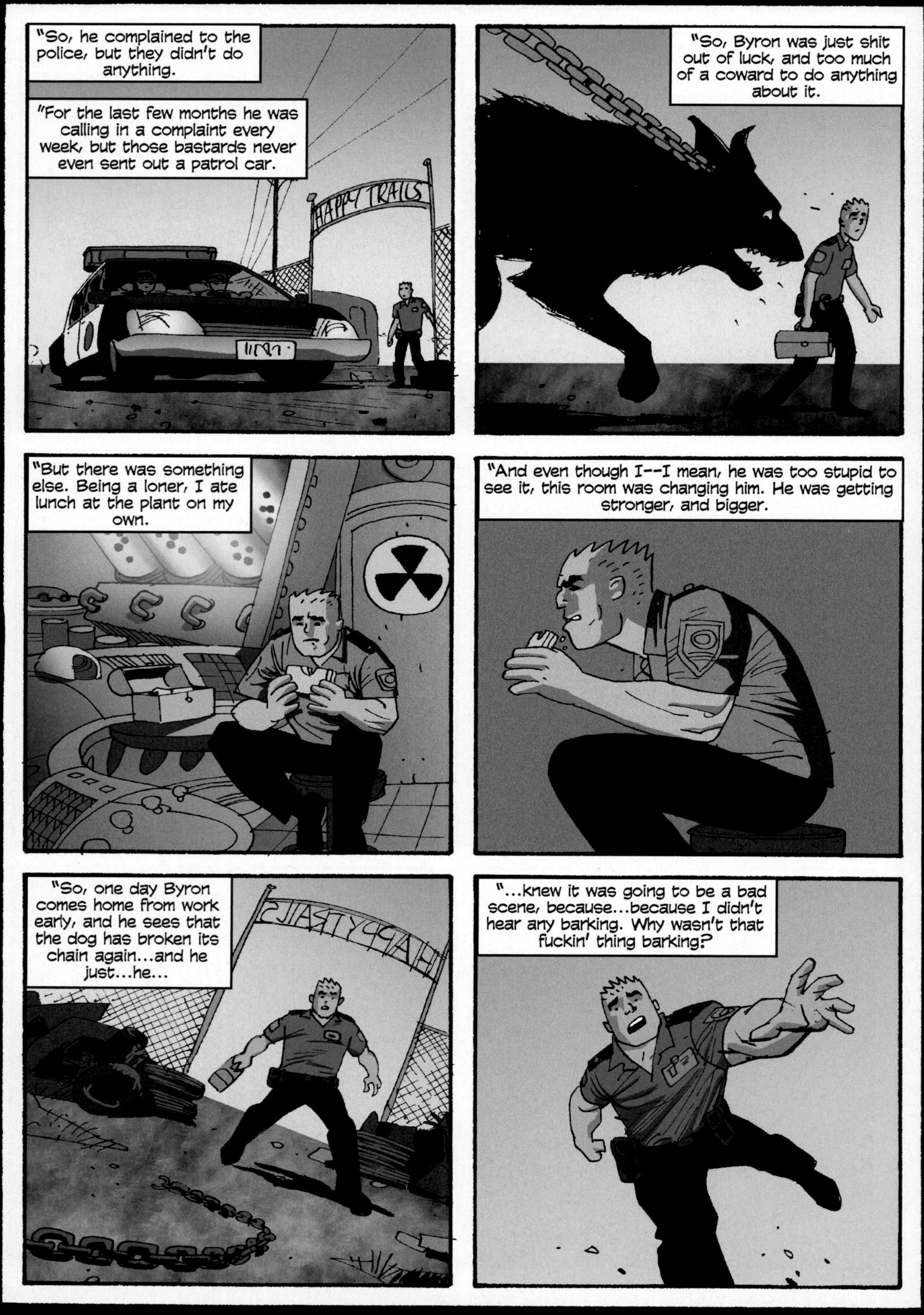
"So, he complained to the police, but they didn't do anything.
"For the last few months he was calling in a complaint every week, but those bastards never even sent out a patrol car.
HAPPY TRAILS
"So, Byron was just shit out of luck, and too much of a coward to do anything about it.
"But there was something else. Being a loner, I ate lunch at the plant on my own.
"And even though I--I mean, he was too stupid to see it, this room was changing him. He was getting stronger, and bigger.
"So, one day Byron comes home from work early, and he sees that the dog has broken its chain again...and he just...he...
"...knew it was going to be a bad scene, because...because I didn't hear any barking. Why wasn't that fuckin' thing barking?

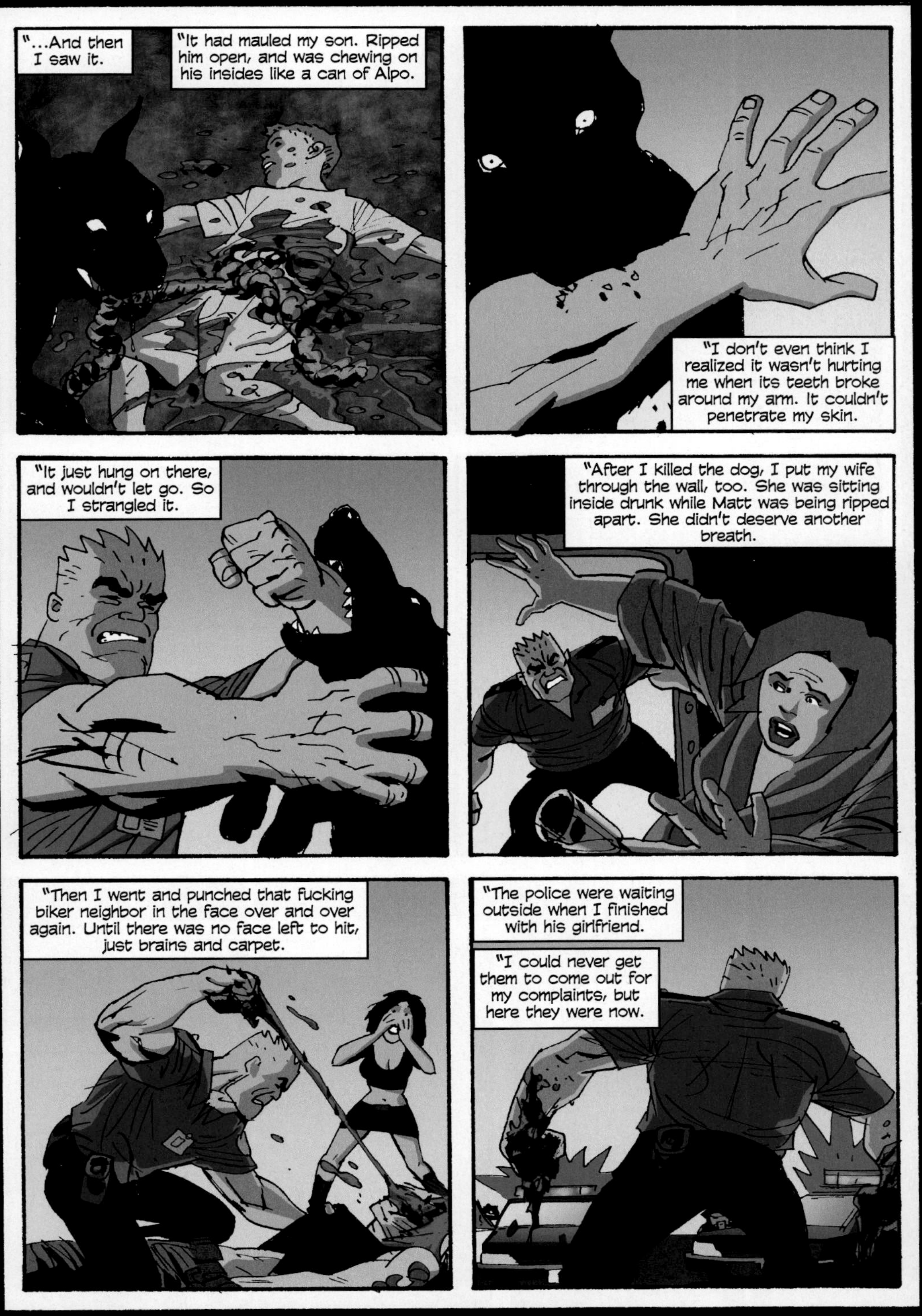
"...And then I saw it.
"It had mauled my son. Ripped him open, and was chewing on his insides like a can of Alpo.
"I don't even think I realized it wasn't hurting me when its teeth broke around my arm. It couldn't penetrate my skin.
"It just hung on there, and wouldn't let go. So I strangled it.
"After I killed the dog, I put my wife through the wall, too. She was sitting inside drunk while Matt was being ripped apart. She didn't deserve another breath.
"Then I went and punched that fucking biker neighbor in the face over and over again. Until there was no face left to hit, just brains and carpet.
"The police were waiting outside when I finished with his girlfriend.
"I could never get them to come out for my complaints, but here they were now.

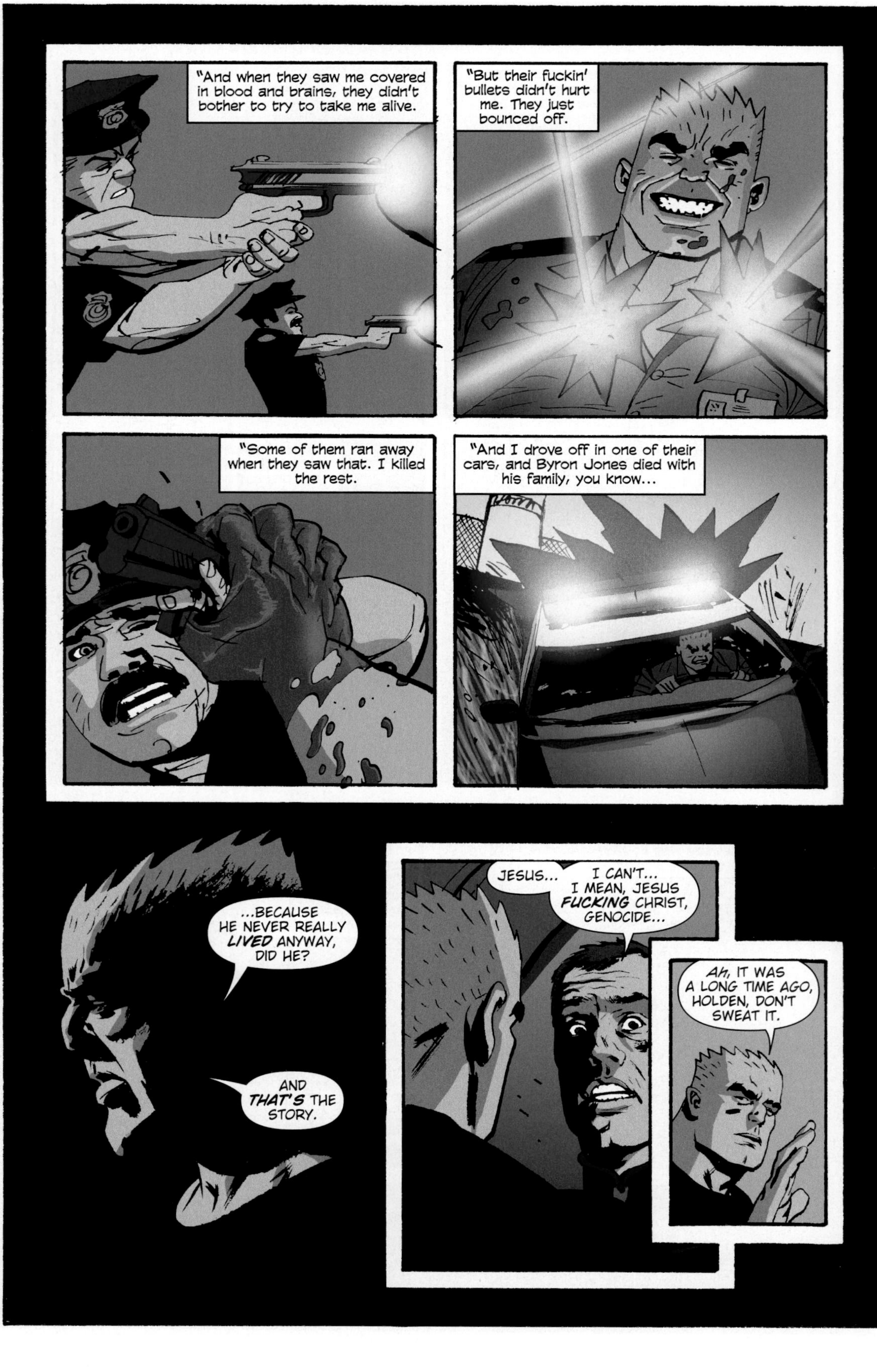
"And when they saw me covered in blood and brains, they didn't bother to try to take me alive.
"But their fuckin' bullets didn't hurt me. They just bounced off.
"Some of them ran away when they saw that. I killed the rest.
"And I drove off in one of their cars, and Byron Jones died with his family, you know...
...BECAUSE HE NEVER REALLY LIVED ANYWAY, DID HE?
AND THAT'S THE STORY.
JESUS...
I CAN'T... I MEAN, JESUS FUCKING CHRIST, GENOCIDE...
AH, IT WAS A LONG TIME AGO, HOLDEN, DON'T SWEAT IT.

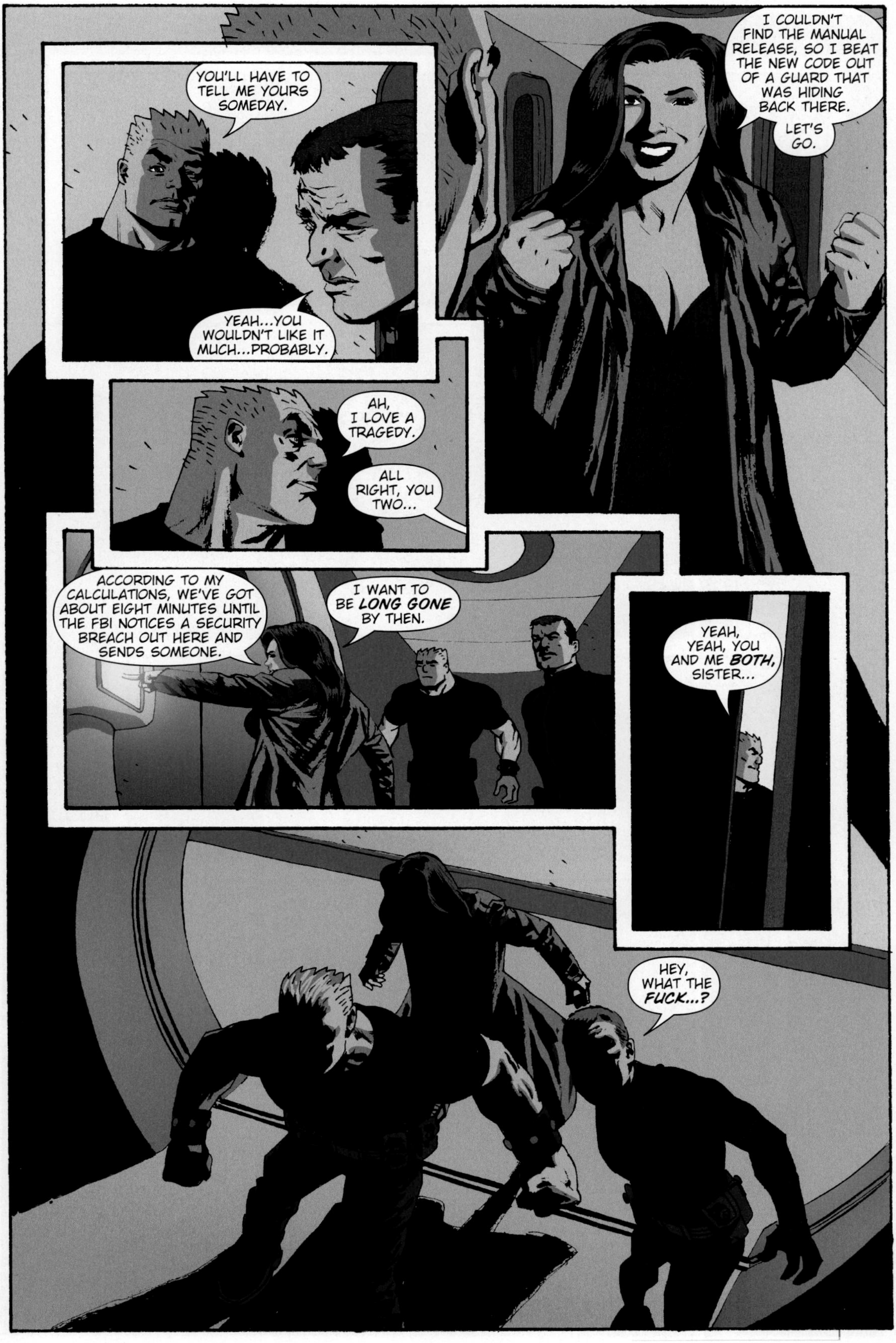
YOU'LL HAVE TO TELL ME YOURS SOMEDAY.
YEAH...YOU WOULDN'T LIKE IT MUCH...PROBABLY.
I COULDN'T FIND THE MANUAL RELEASE, SO I BEAT THE NEW CODE OUT OF A GUARD THAT WAS HIDING BACK THERE.
LET'S GO.
AH, I LOVE A TRAGEDY.
ALL RIGHT, YOU TWO...
ACCORDING TO MY CALCULATIONS, WE'VE GOT ABOUT EIGHT MINUTES UNTIL THE FBI NOTICES A SECURITY BREACH OUT HERE AND SENDS SOMEONE.
I WANT TO BE *LONG GONE* BY THEN.
YEAH, YEAH, YOU AND ME *BOTH,* SISTER...
HEY, WHAT THE *FUCK...?*

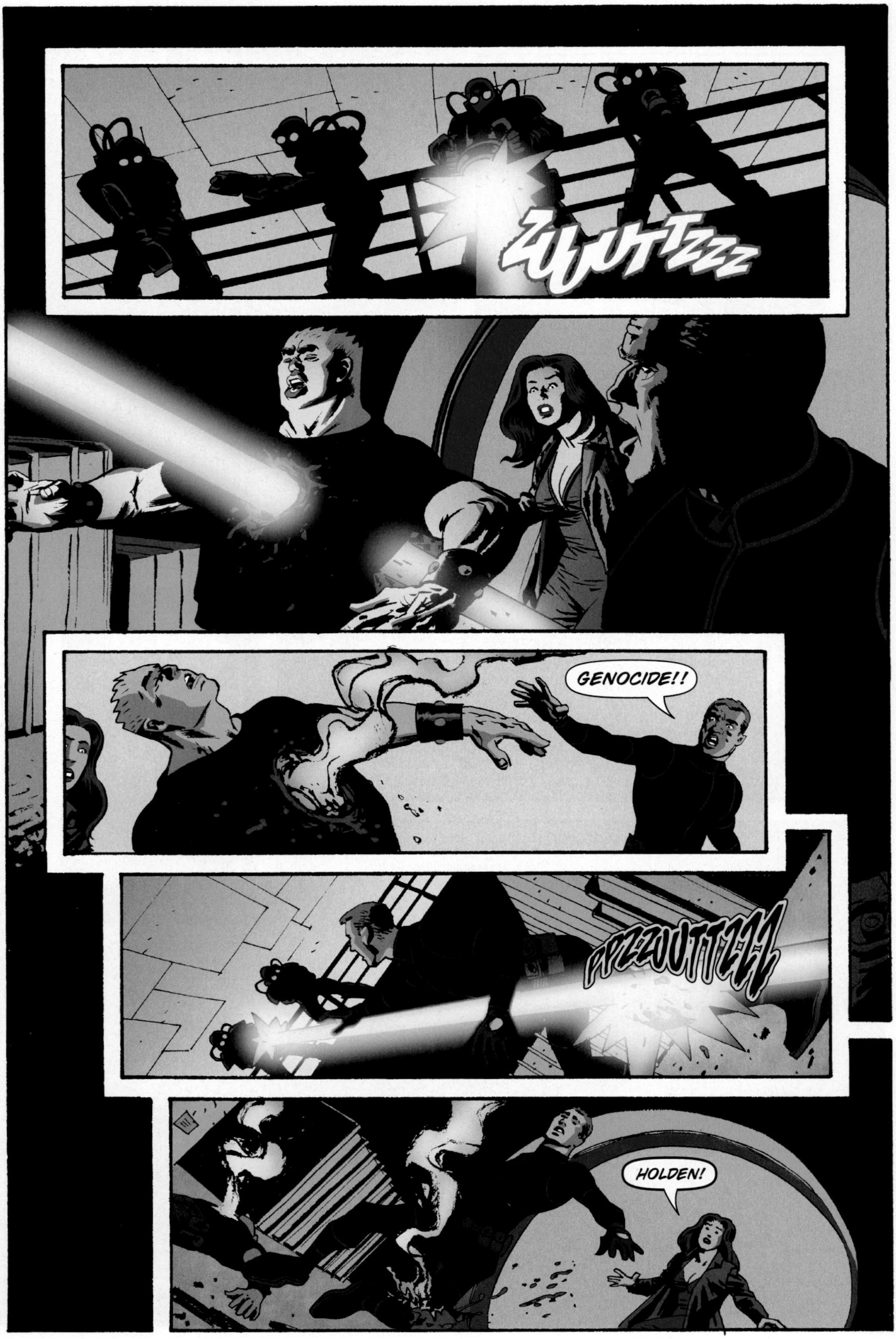
ZUUUTTZZZ
GENOCIDE!!
PPZZZOUTTZZZ
HOLDEN!

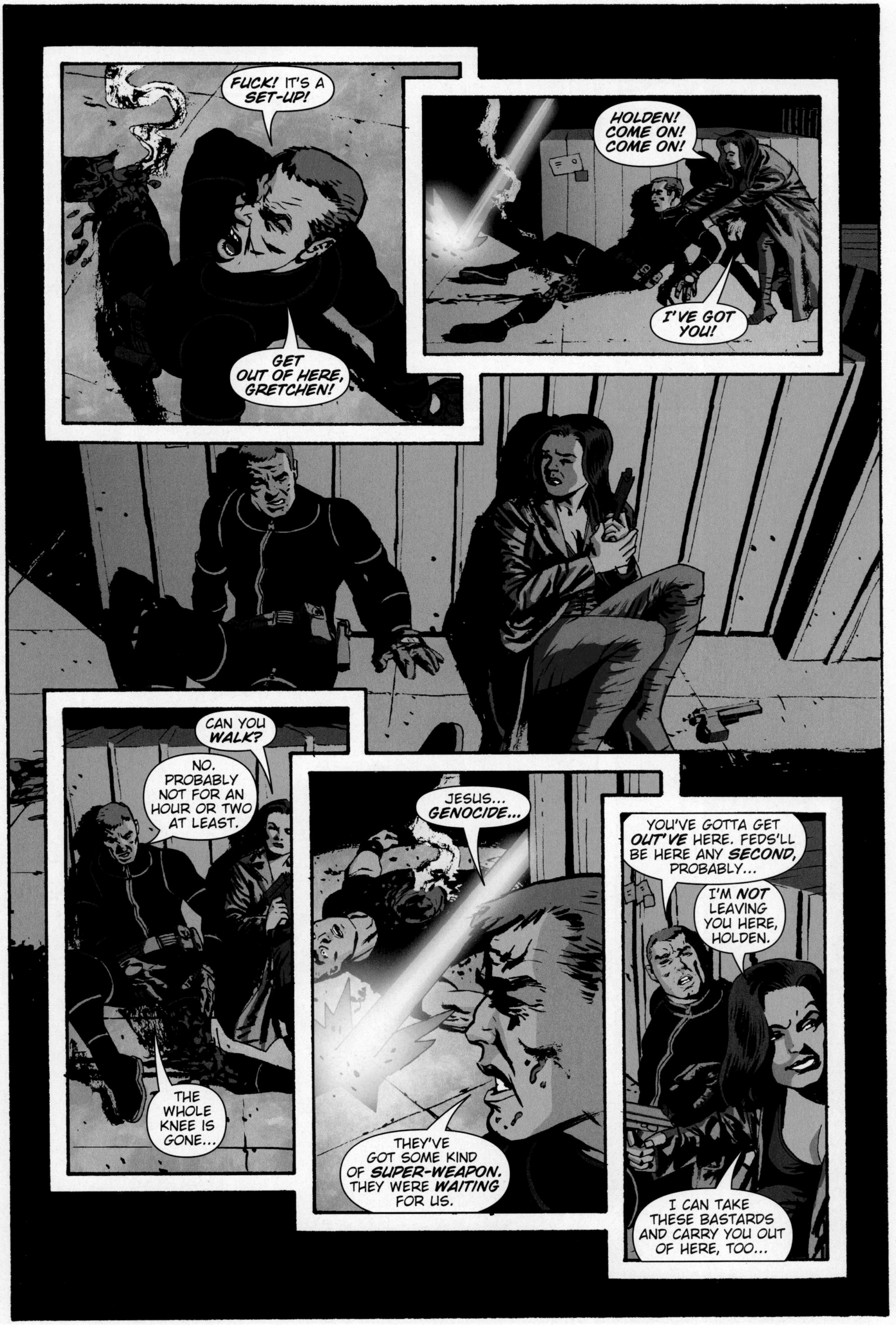

FUCK! IT'S A SET-UP!
GET OUT OF HERE, GRETCHEN!
HOLDEN! COME ON! COME ON!
I'VE GOT YOU!
CAN YOU WALK?
NO. PROBABLY NOT FOR AN HOUR OR TWO AT LEAST.
THE WHOLE KNEE IS GONE...
JESUS... GENOCIDE...
THEY'VE GOT SOME KIND OF SUPER-WEAPON. THEY WERE WAITING FOR US.
YOU'VE GOTTA GET OUT'VE HERE. FEDS'LL BE HERE ANY SECOND, PROBABLY...
I'M NOT LEAVING YOU HERE, HOLDEN.
I CAN TAKE THESE BASTARDS AND CARRY YOU OUT OF HERE, TOO...

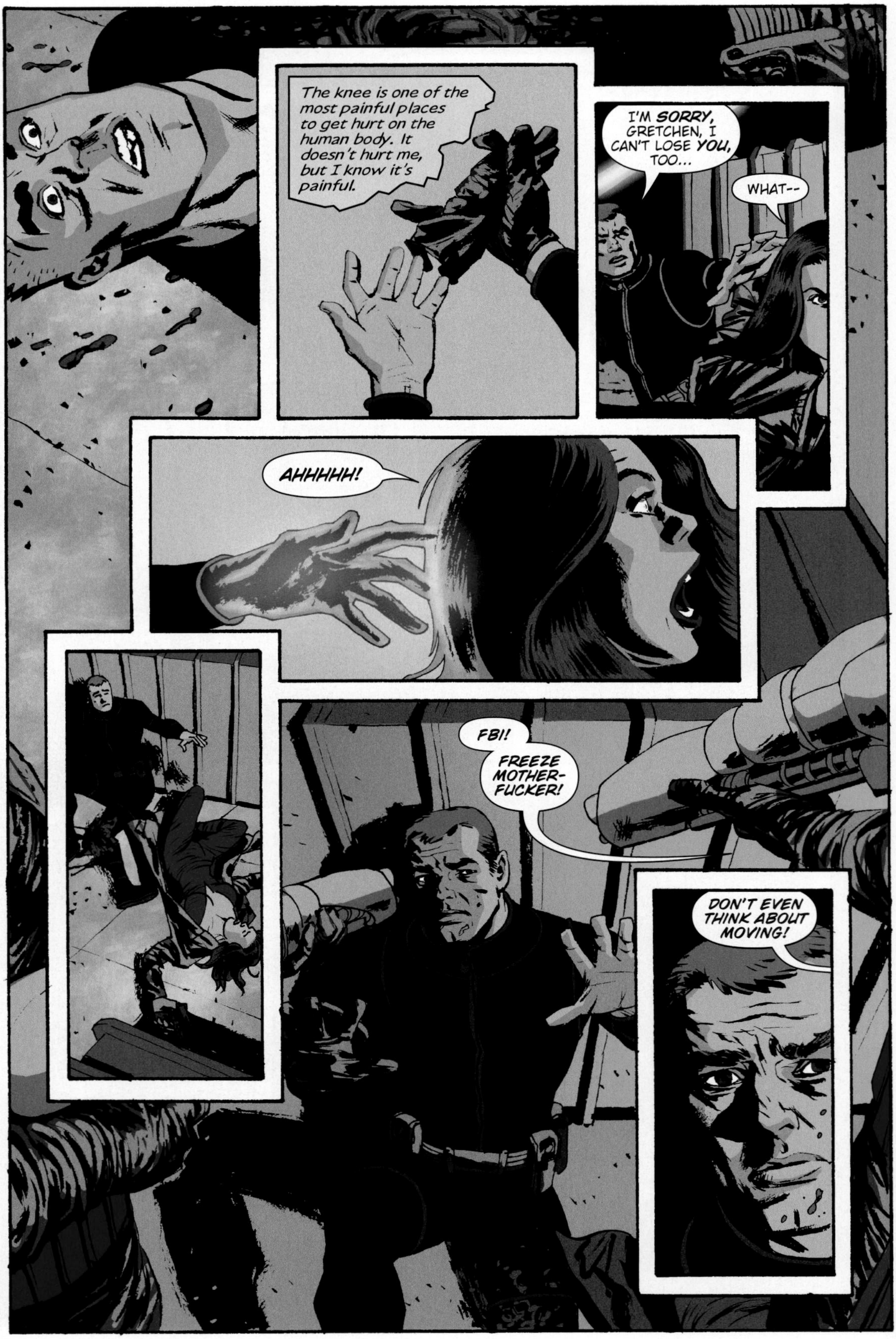
The knee is one of the most painful places to get hurt on the human body. It doesn't hurt me, but I know it's painful.
I'M SORRY, GRETCHEN, I CAN'T LOSE YOU, TOO...
WHAT--
AHHHHH!
FBI! FREEZE MOTHER-FUCKER!
DON'T EVEN THINK ABOUT MOVING!

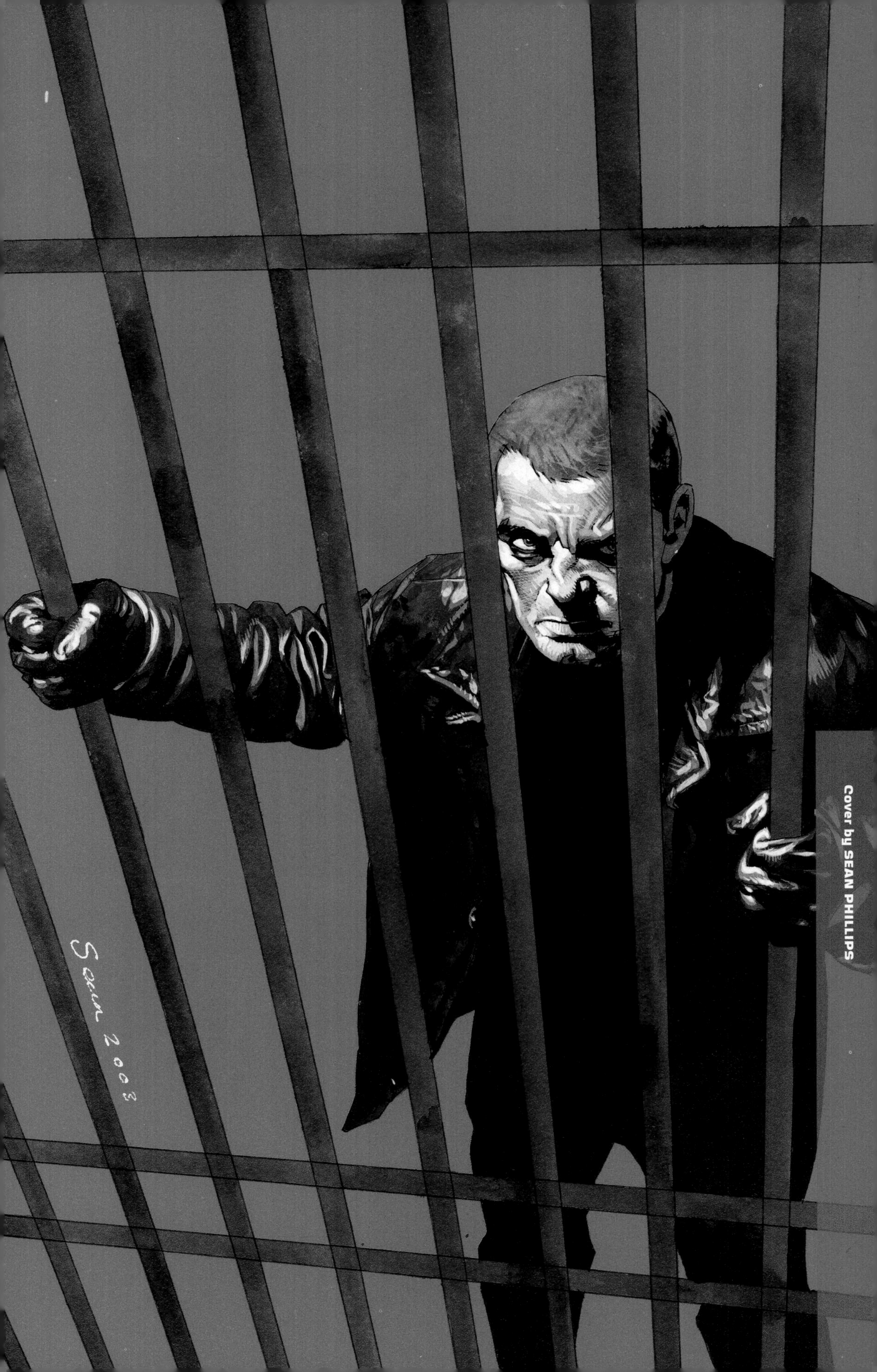
Sean 2003
Cover by SEAN PHILLIPS

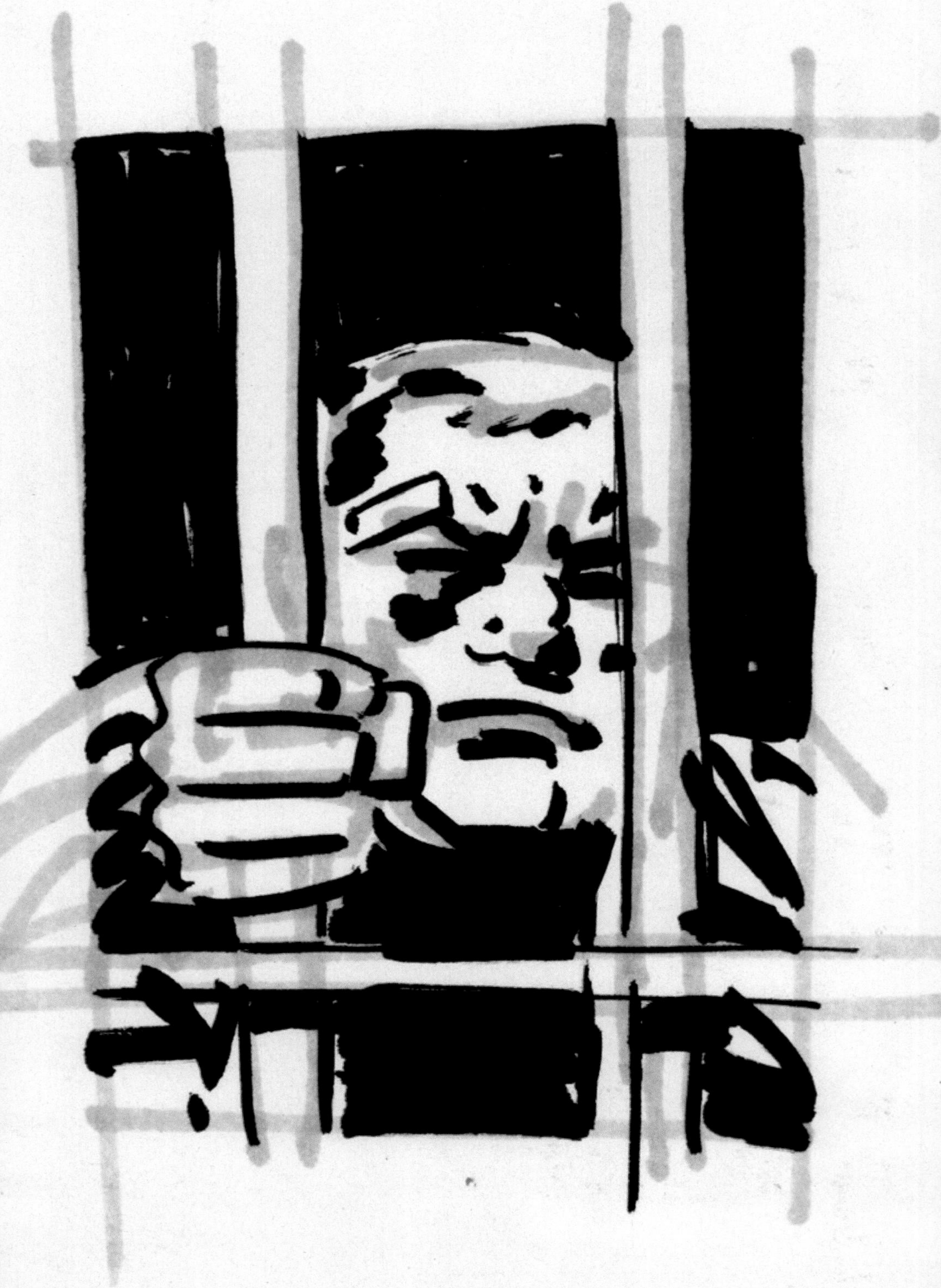

SLEEPER #11 Cover Rough by SEAN PHILLIPS

This is Lynch flying me to my drop-off in a black helicopter. Flying under radar, on an unregistered flight path.

Flying me away from one life and dropping me into another.

And this is his final pep-talk...

FORGET EVERYTHING YOU LEARNED. YOUR ONE GOAL NOW IS TO **BLEND IN.** THAT'S THE ONLY WAY YOU'LL **SURVIVE.**

AND I **NEED YOU** TO SURVIVE, AGENT... OR YOU MIGHT AS WELL HAVE DIED WITH YOUR MEN.

BUT WHEN YOU STEP OUT OF THIS CHOPPER, YOU STEP AWAY FROM **EVERYTHING** YOU'VE KNOWN, AND THERE'S **NO** TURNING BACK...

...NOT UNTIL YOUR MISSION IS COMPLETE.

HOW DO I CONTACT YOU?

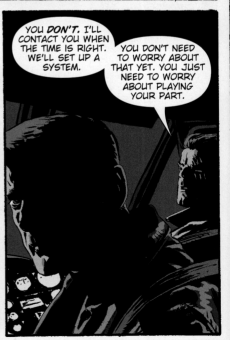

YOU **DON'T.** I'LL CONTACT YOU WHEN THE TIME IS RIGHT. WE'LL SET UP A SYSTEM.

YOU DON'T NEED TO WORRY ABOUT THAT YET. YOU JUST NEED TO WORRY ABOUT PLAYING YOUR PART.

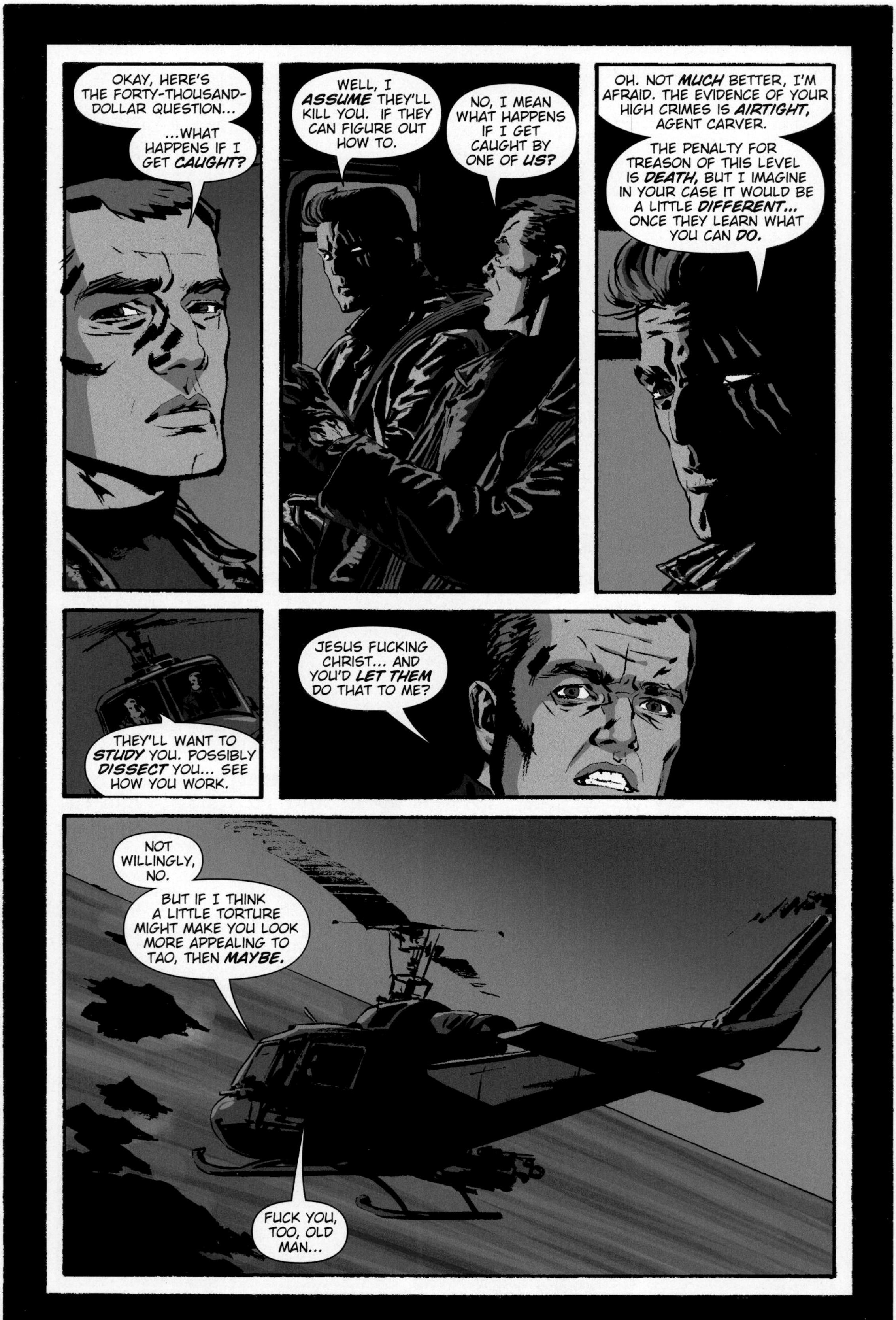
OKAY, HERE'S THE FORTY-THOUSAND-DOLLAR QUESTION...
...WHAT HAPPENS IF I GET CAUGHT?
WELL, I ASSUME THEY'LL KILL YOU. IF THEY CAN FIGURE OUT HOW TO.
NO, I MEAN WHAT HAPPENS IF I GET CAUGHT BY ONE OF US?
OH. NOT MUCH BETTER, I'M AFRAID. THE EVIDENCE OF YOUR HIGH CRIMES IS AIRTIGHT, AGENT CARVER.
THE PENALTY FOR TREASON OF THIS LEVEL IS DEATH, BUT I IMAGINE IN YOUR CASE IT WOULD BE A LITTLE DIFFERENT... ONCE THEY LEARN WHAT YOU CAN DO.
THEY'LL WANT TO STUDY YOU. POSSIBLY DISSECT YOU... SEE HOW YOU WORK.
JESUS FUCKING CHRIST... AND YOU'D LET THEM DO THAT TO ME?
NOT WILLINGLY, NO.
BUT IF I THINK A LITTLE TORTURE MIGHT MAKE YOU LOOK MORE APPEALING TO TAO, THEN MAYBE.
FUCK YOU, TOO, OLD MAN...

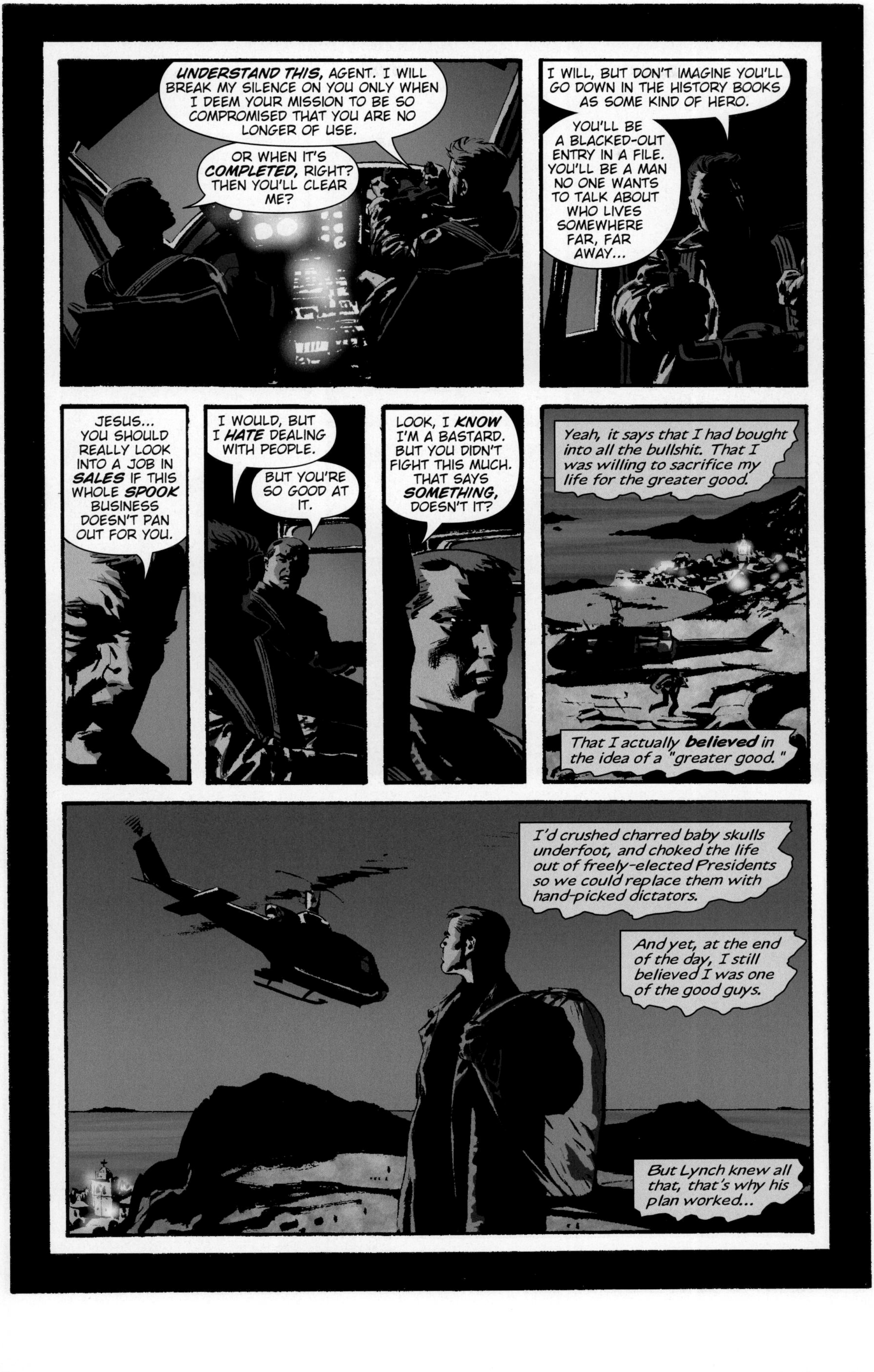
UNDERSTAND THIS, AGENT. I WILL BREAK MY SILENCE ON YOU ONLY WHEN I DEEM YOUR MISSION TO BE SO COMPROMISED THAT YOU ARE NO LONGER OF USE.
OR WHEN IT'S COMPLETED, RIGHT? THEN YOU'LL CLEAR ME?
I WILL, BUT DON'T IMAGINE YOU'LL GO DOWN IN THE HISTORY BOOKS AS SOME KIND OF HERO.
YOU'LL BE A BLACKED-OUT ENTRY IN A FILE. YOU'LL BE A MAN NO ONE WANTS TO TALK ABOUT WHO LIVES SOMEWHERE FAR, FAR AWAY...
JESUS... YOU SHOULD REALLY LOOK INTO A JOB IN SALES IF THIS WHOLE SPOOK BUSINESS DOESN'T PAN OUT FOR YOU.
I WOULD, BUT I HATE DEALING WITH PEOPLE.
BUT YOU'RE SO GOOD AT IT.
LOOK, I KNOW I'M A BASTARD. BUT YOU DIDN'T FIGHT THIS MUCH. THAT SAYS SOMETHING, DOESN'T IT?
Yeah, it says that I had bought into all the bullshit. That I was willing to sacrifice my life for the greater good.
That I actually believed in the idea of a "greater good."
I'd crushed charred baby skulls underfoot, and choked the life out of freely-elected Presidents so we could replace them with hand-picked dictators.
And yet, at the end of the day, I still believed I was one of the good guys.
But Lynch knew all that, that's why his plan worked...

...For the most part, at least.

They gassed me to sleep on my first day and I woke up with bandages on my knee.

Then the next day I woke up to find all the bandages gone and the knee perfectly healed. That must have thrown them for a loop.

I know from I.O. Black Ops training that this is all part of the process of **breaking** me.

They'll keep me isolated and unfed until I start to lose it. Then they'll go to work.

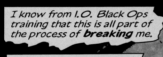

They must be questioning their tactics, though, after observing my condition. Obviously torture won't work. Maybe I don't get hungry, either?

Except I do. I don't get hunger **pain**, but my body doesn't respond as well, my mind races in circles.

I forget how long a man can survive without food or water. Not that long.

I think I could die this way, and maybe through suffocation. I don't think my condition helps with non-physical damage.

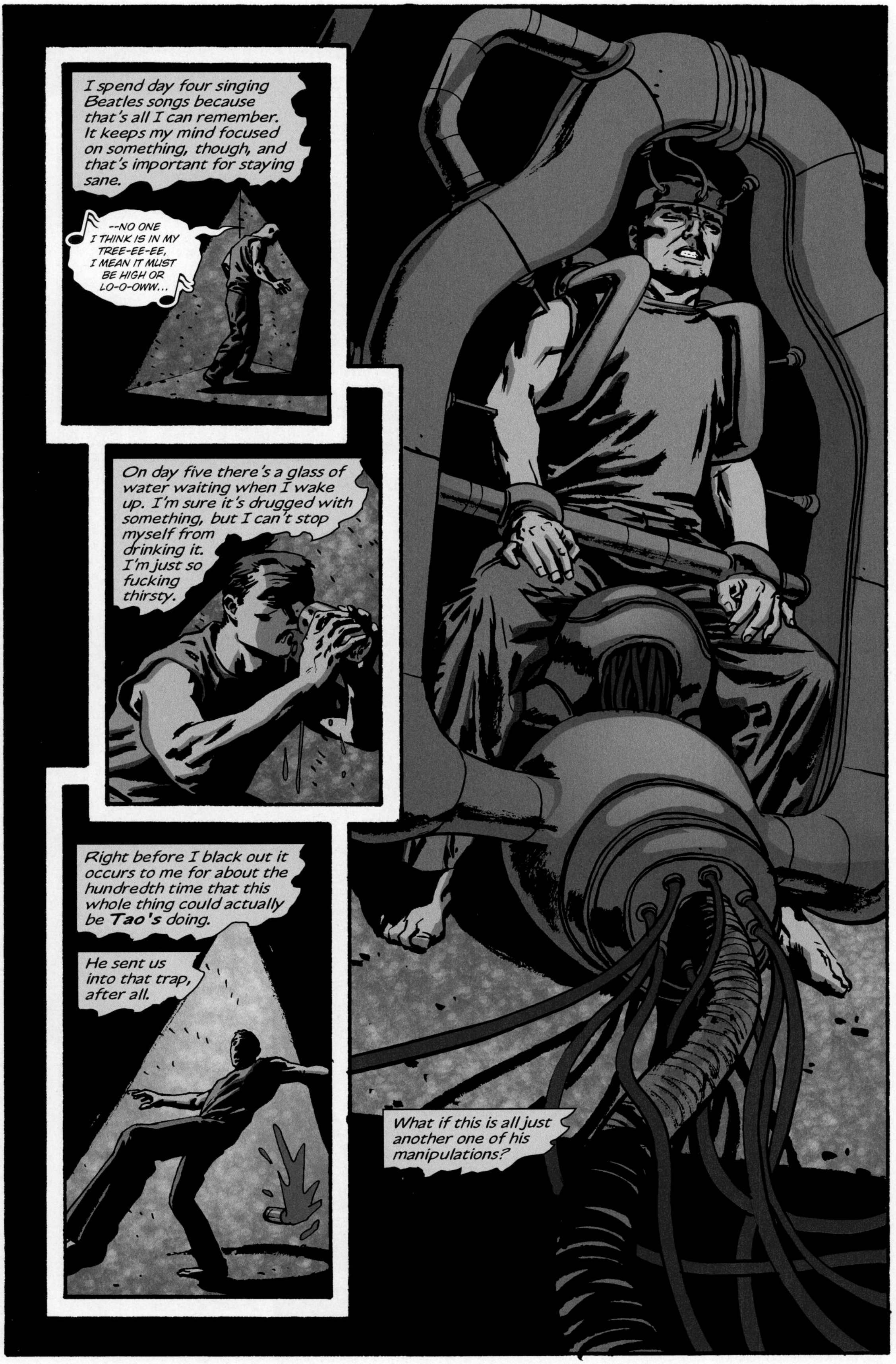

I spend day four singing Beatles songs because that's all I can remember. It keeps my mind focused on something, though, and that's important for staying sane.
--NO ONE I THINK IS IN MY TREE-EE-EE, I MEAN IT MUST BE HIGH OR LO-O-OWW...
On day five there's a glass of water waiting when I wake up. I'm sure it's drugged with something, but I can't stop myself from drinking it. I'm just so fucking thirsty.
Right before I black out it occurs to me for about the hundredth time that this whole thing could actually be Tao's doing.
He sent us into that trap, after all.
What if this is all just another one of his manipulations?

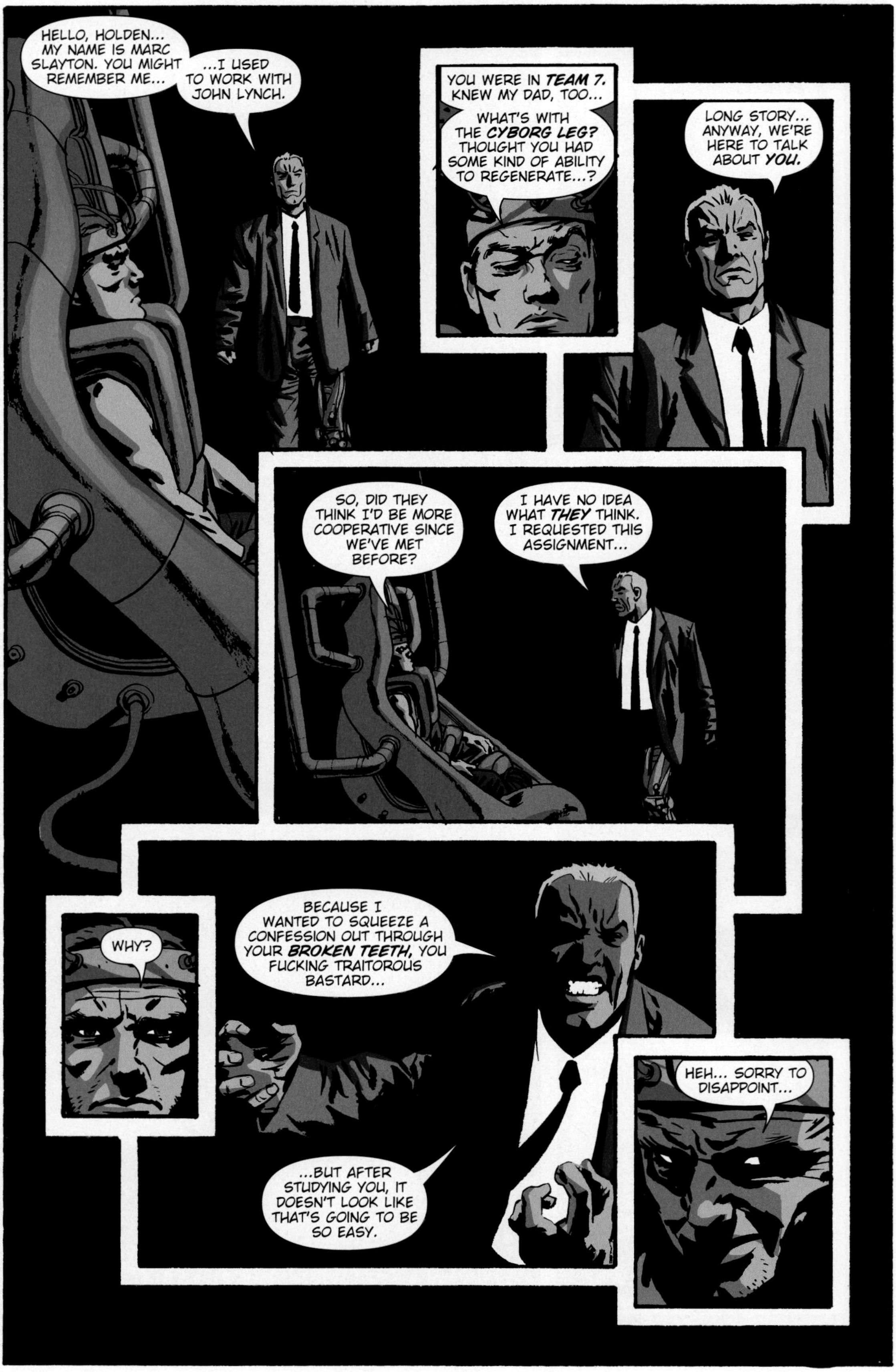

HELLO, HOLDEN... MY NAME IS MARC SLAYTON. YOU MIGHT REMEMBER ME...
...I USED TO WORK WITH JOHN LYNCH.
YOU WERE IN TEAM 7. KNEW MY DAD, TOO...
WHAT'S WITH THE CYBORG LEG? THOUGHT YOU HAD SOME KIND OF ABILITY TO REGENERATE...?
LONG STORY... ANYWAY, WE'RE HERE TO TALK ABOUT YOU.
SO, DID THEY THINK I'D BE MORE COOPERATIVE SINCE WE'VE MET BEFORE?
I HAVE NO IDEA WHAT THEY THINK. I REQUESTED THIS ASSIGNMENT...
WHY?
BECAUSE I WANTED TO SQUEEZE A CONFESSION OUT THROUGH YOUR BROKEN TEETH, YOU FUCKING TRAITOROUS BASTARD...
...BUT AFTER STUDYING YOU, IT DOESN'T LOOK LIKE THAT'S GOING TO BE SO EASY.
HEH... SORRY TO DISAPPOINT...

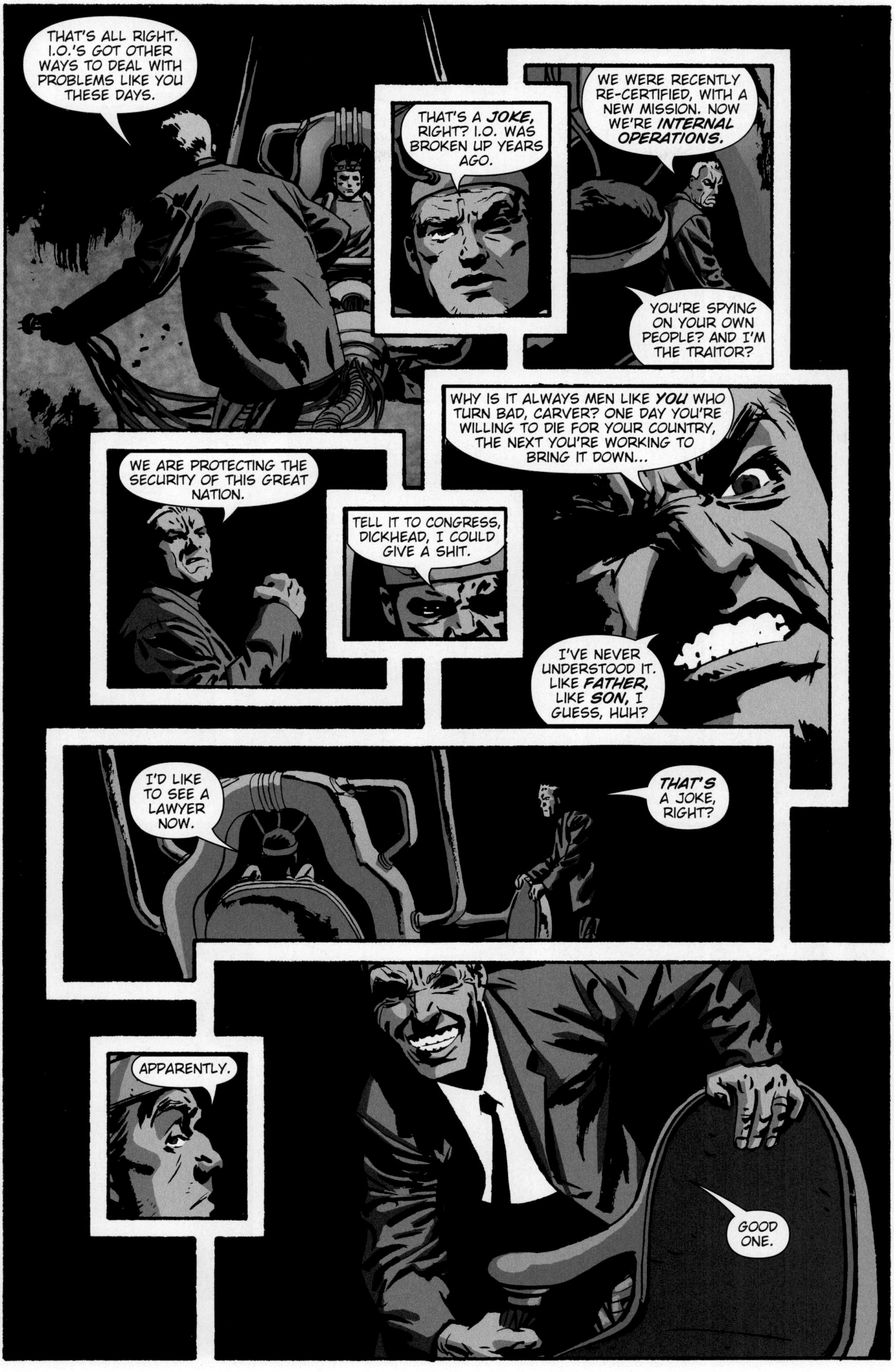
THAT'S ALL RIGHT. I.O.'S GOT OTHER WAYS TO DEAL WITH PROBLEMS LIKE YOU THESE DAYS.
THAT'S A *JOKE,* RIGHT? I.O. WAS BROKEN UP YEARS AGO.
WE WERE RECENTLY RE-CERTIFIED, WITH A NEW MISSION. NOW WE'RE *INTERNAL OPERATIONS.*
YOU'RE SPYING ON YOUR OWN PEOPLE? AND I'M THE TRAITOR?
WHY IS IT ALWAYS MEN LIKE *YOU* WHO TURN BAD, CARVER? ONE DAY YOU'RE WILLING TO DIE FOR YOUR COUNTRY, THE NEXT YOU'RE WORKING TO BRING IT DOWN...
WE ARE PROTECTING THE SECURITY OF THIS GREAT NATION.
TELL IT TO CONGRESS, DICKHEAD, I COULD GIVE A SHIT.
I'VE NEVER UNDERSTOOD IT. LIKE *FATHER,* LIKE *SON,* I GUESS, HUH?
I'D LIKE TO SEE A LAWYER NOW.
THAT'S A JOKE, RIGHT?
APPARENTLY.
GOOD ONE.

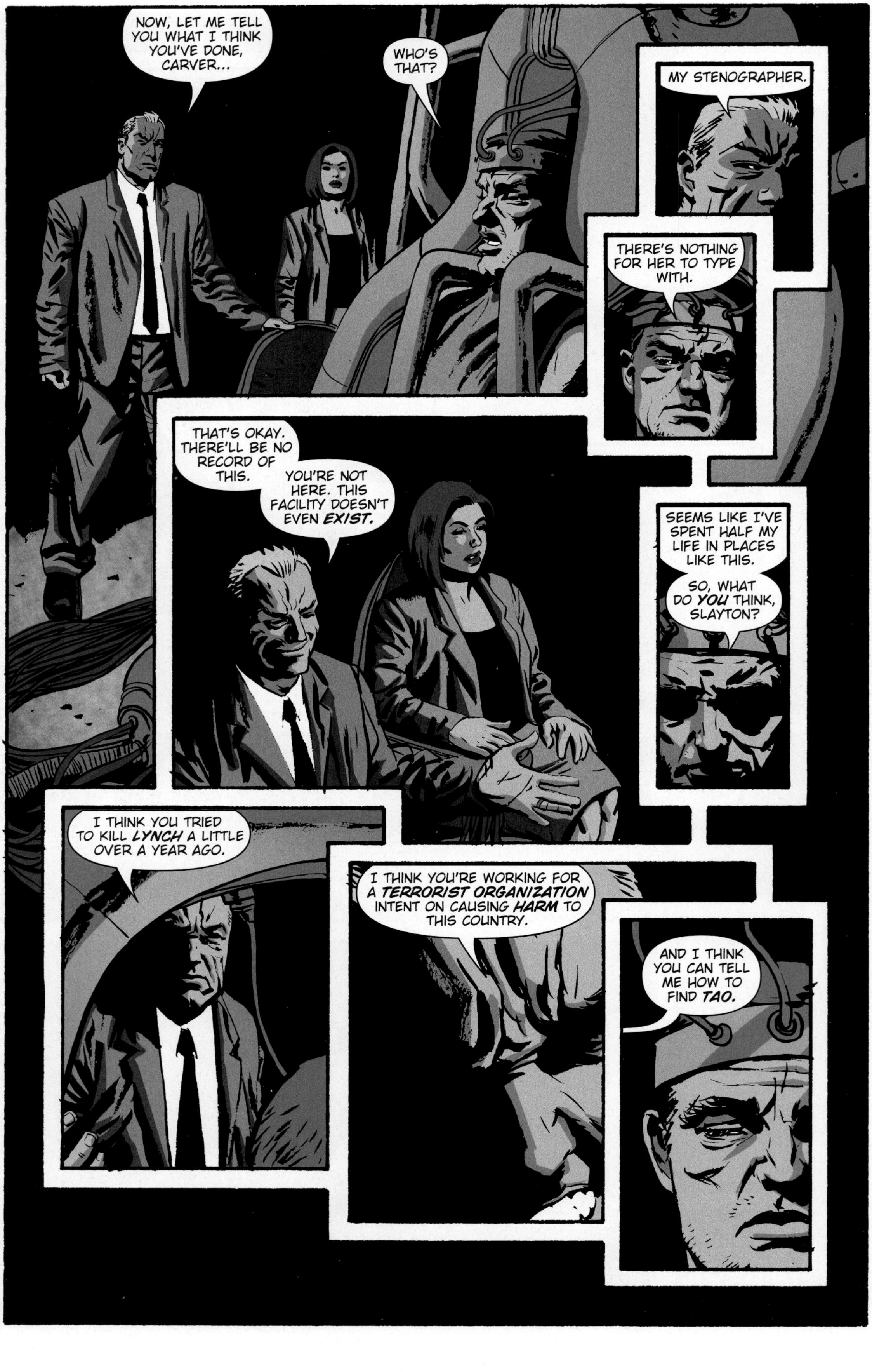
NOW, LET ME TELL YOU WHAT I THINK YOU'VE DONE, CARVER...
WHO'S THAT?
MY STENOGRAPHER.
THERE'S NOTHING FOR HER TO TYPE WITH.
THAT'S OKAY. THERE'LL BE NO RECORD OF THIS.
YOU'RE NOT HERE. THIS FACILITY DOESN'T EVEN EXIST.
SEEMS LIKE I'VE SPENT HALF MY LIFE IN PLACES LIKE THIS.
SO, WHAT DO YOU THINK, SLAYTON?
I THINK YOU TRIED TO KILL LYNCH A LITTLE OVER A YEAR AGO.
I THINK YOU'RE WORKING FOR A TERRORIST ORGANIZATION INTENT ON CAUSING HARM TO THIS COUNTRY.
AND I THINK YOU CAN TELL ME HOW TO FIND TAO.

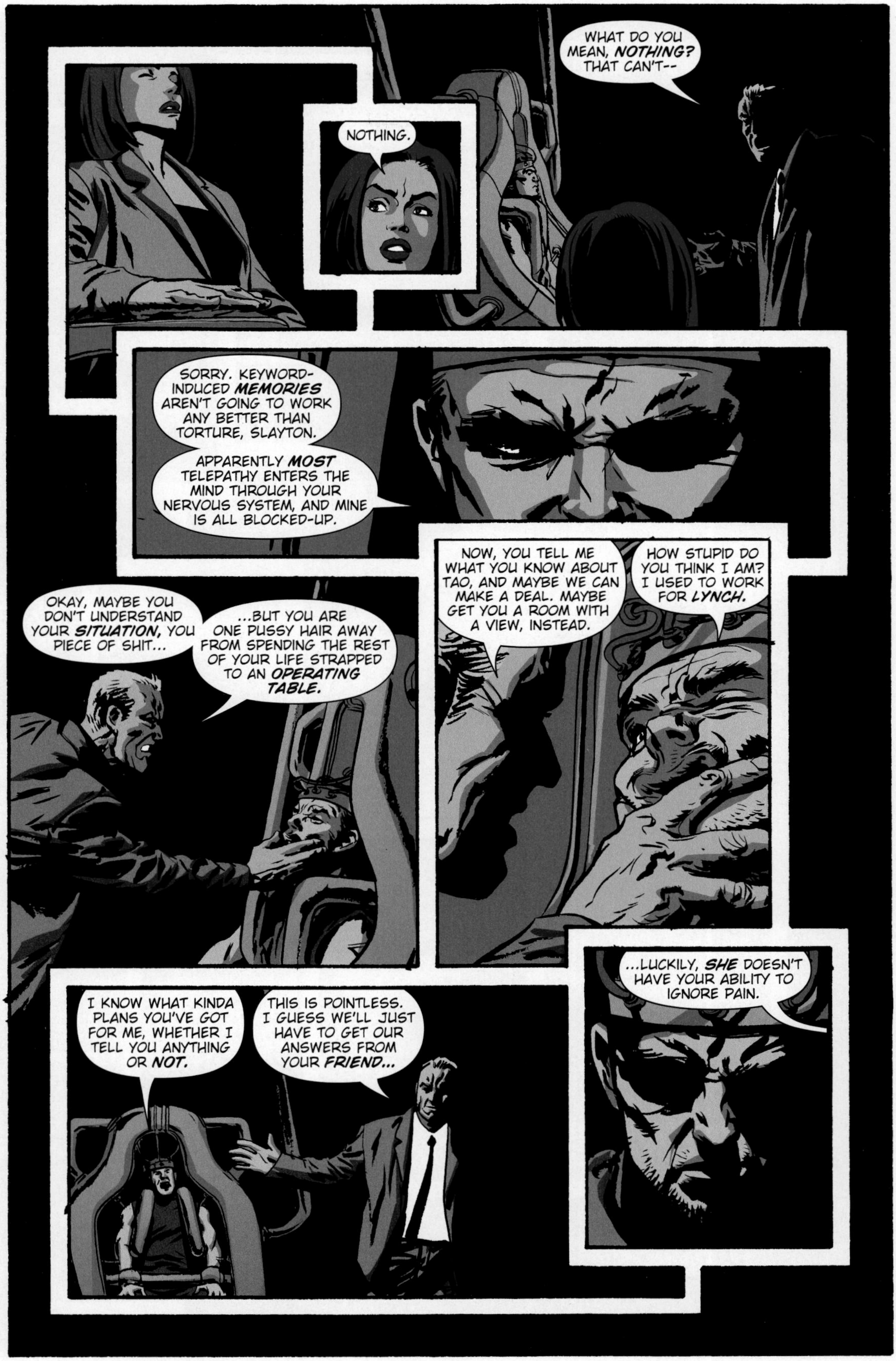
WHAT DO YOU MEAN, NOTHING? THAT CAN'T--
NOTHING.
SORRY. KEYWORD-INDUCED MEMORIES AREN'T GOING TO WORK ANY BETTER THAN TORTURE, SLAYTON.
APPARENTLY MOST TELEPATHY ENTERS THE MIND THROUGH YOUR NERVOUS SYSTEM, AND MINE IS ALL BLOCKED-UP.
OKAY, MAYBE YOU DON'T UNDERSTAND YOUR SITUATION, YOU PIECE OF SHIT...
...BUT YOU ARE ONE PUSSY HAIR AWAY FROM SPENDING THE REST OF YOUR LIFE STRAPPED TO AN OPERATING TABLE.
NOW, YOU TELL ME WHAT YOU KNOW ABOUT TAO, AND MAYBE WE CAN MAKE A DEAL. MAYBE GET YOU A ROOM WITH A VIEW, INSTEAD.
HOW STUPID DO YOU THINK I AM? I USED TO WORK FOR LYNCH.
I KNOW WHAT KINDA PLANS YOU'VE GOT FOR ME, WHETHER I TELL YOU ANYTHING OR NOT.
THIS IS POINTLESS. I GUESS WE'LL JUST HAVE TO GET OUR ANSWERS FROM YOUR FRIEND...
...LUCKILY, SHE DOESN'T HAVE YOUR ABILITY TO IGNORE PAIN.

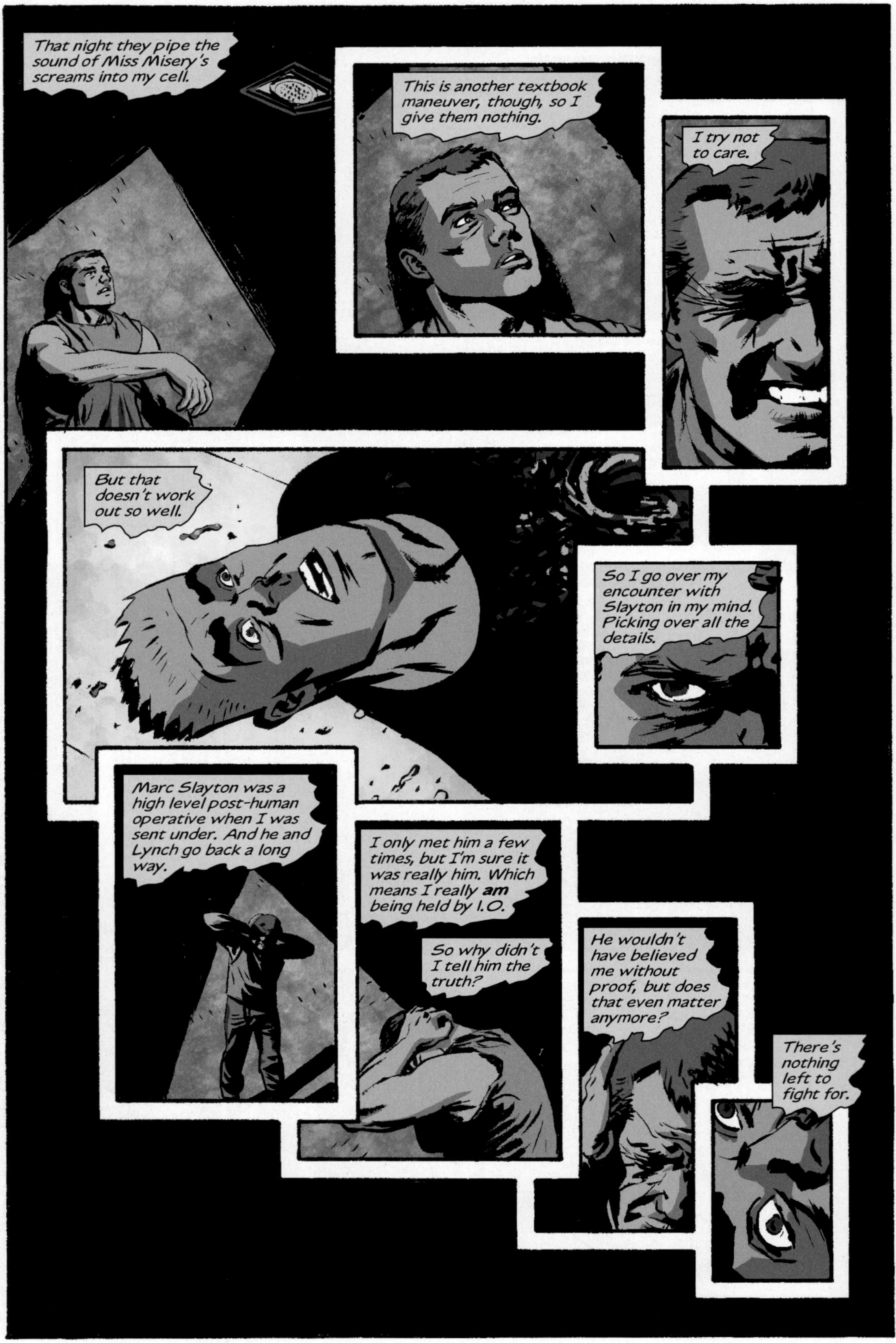
That night they pipe the sound of Miss Misery's screams into my cell.
This is another textbook maneuver, though, so I give them nothing.
I try not to care.
But that doesn't work out so well.
So I go over my encounter with Slayton in my mind. Picking over all the details.
Marc Slayton was a high level post-human operative when I was sent under. And he and Lynch go back a long way.
I only met him a few times, but I'm sure it was really him. Which means I really **am** being held by I.O.
So why didn't I tell him the truth?
He wouldn't have believed me without proof, but does that even matter anymore?
There's nothing left to fight for.

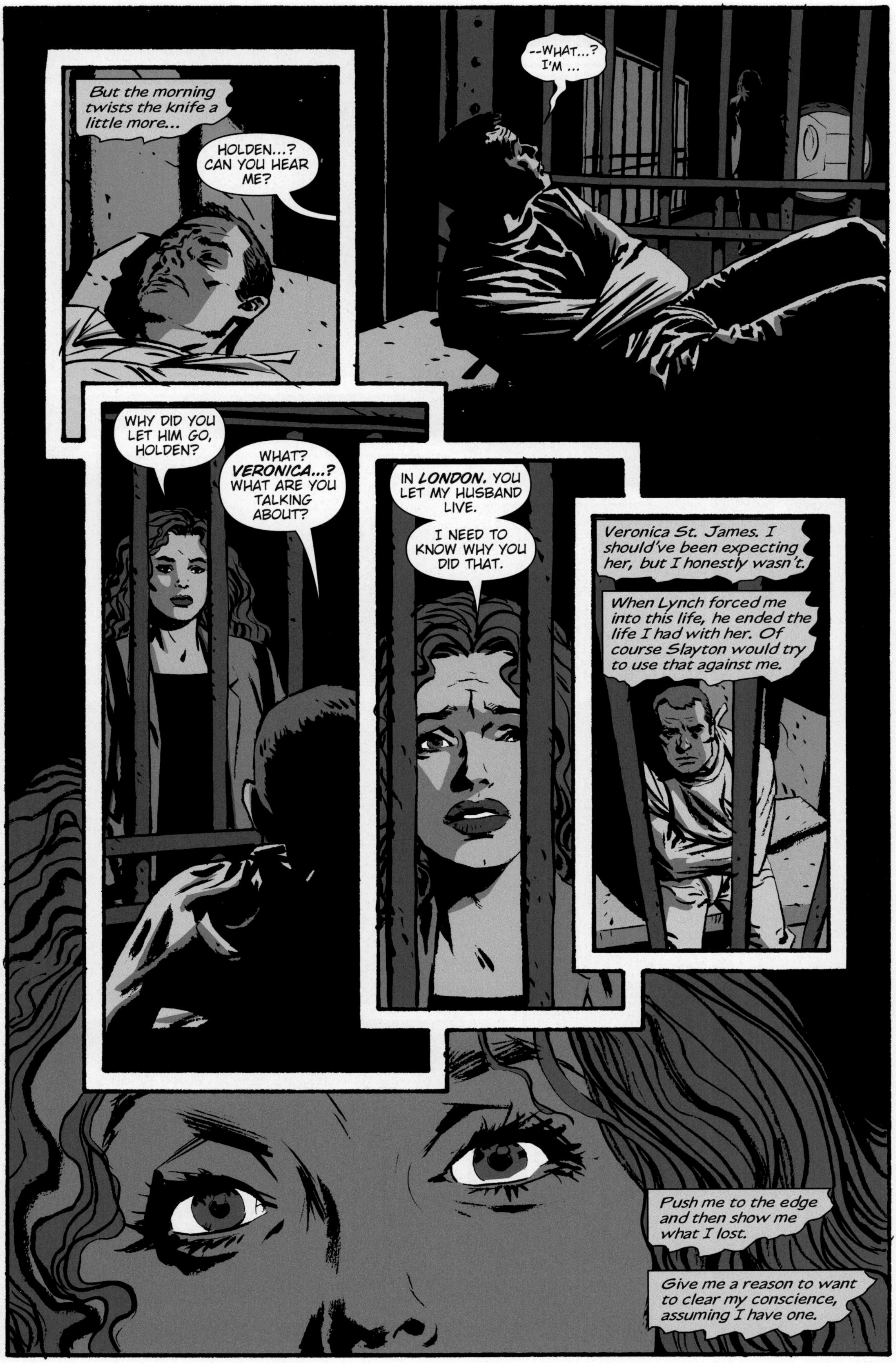
But the morning twists the knife a little more...
HOLDEN...? CAN YOU HEAR ME?
--WHAT...? I'M ...
WHY DID YOU LET HIM GO, HOLDEN?
WHAT? VERONICA...? WHAT ARE YOU TALKING ABOUT?
IN LONDON. YOU LET MY HUSBAND LIVE.
I NEED TO KNOW WHY YOU DID THAT.
Veronica St. James. I should've been expecting her, but I honestly wasn't.
When Lynch forced me into this life, he ended the life I had with her. Of course Slayton would try to use that against me.
Push me to the edge and then show me what I lost.
Give me a reason to want to clear my conscience, assuming I have one.

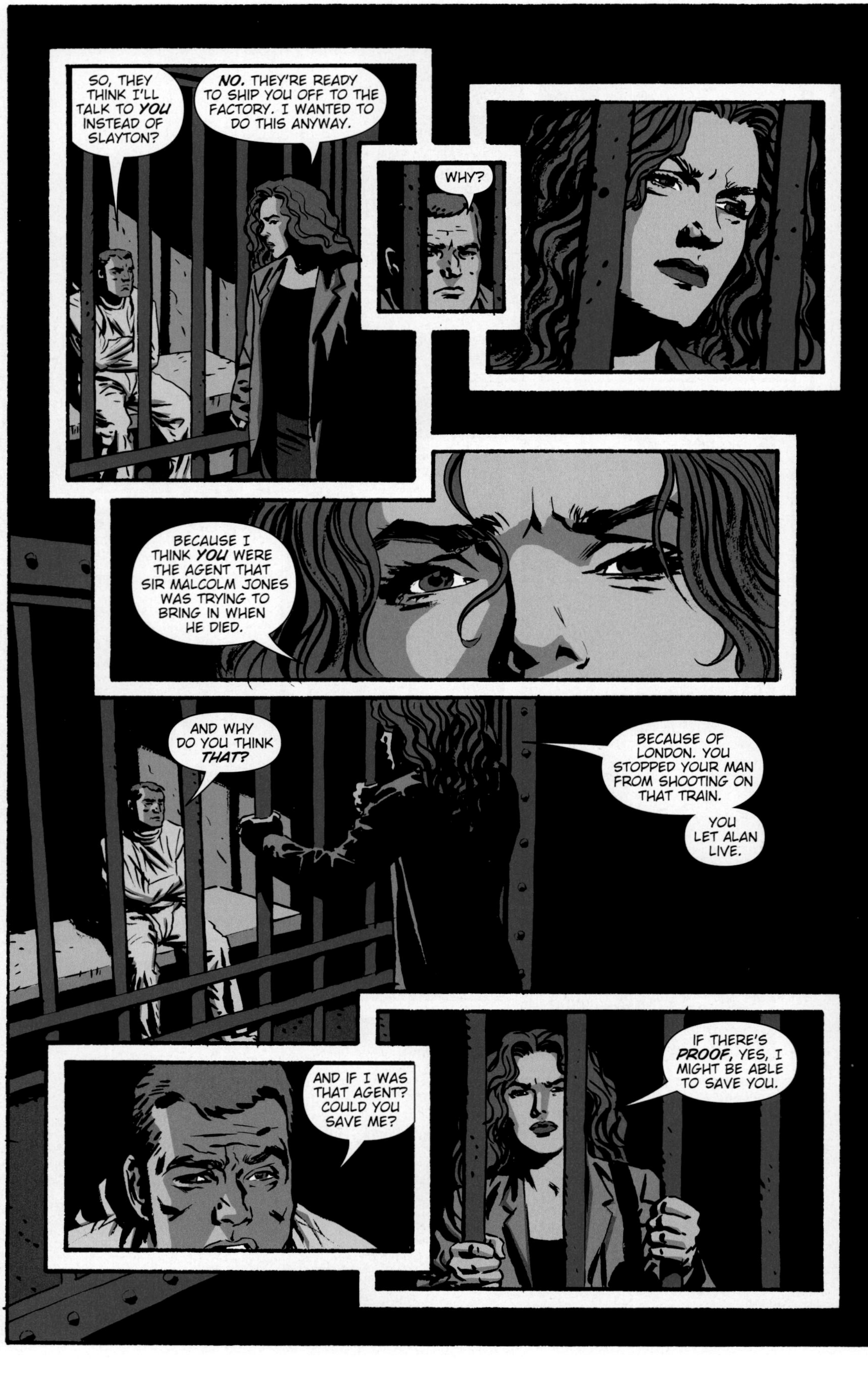
SO, THEY THINK I'LL TALK TO *YOU* INSTEAD OF SLAYTON?
NO. THEY'RE READY TO SHIP YOU OFF TO THE FACTORY. I WANTED TO DO THIS ANYWAY.
WHY?
BECAUSE I THINK *YOU* WERE THE AGENT THAT SIR MALCOLM JONES WAS TRYING TO BRING IN WHEN HE DIED.
AND WHY DO YOU THINK *THAT?*
BECAUSE OF LONDON. YOU STOPPED YOUR MAN FROM SHOOTING ON THAT TRAIN.
YOU LET ALAN LIVE.
AND IF I WAS THAT AGENT? COULD YOU SAVE ME?
IF THERE'S *PROOF,* YES, I MIGHT BE ABLE TO SAVE YOU.

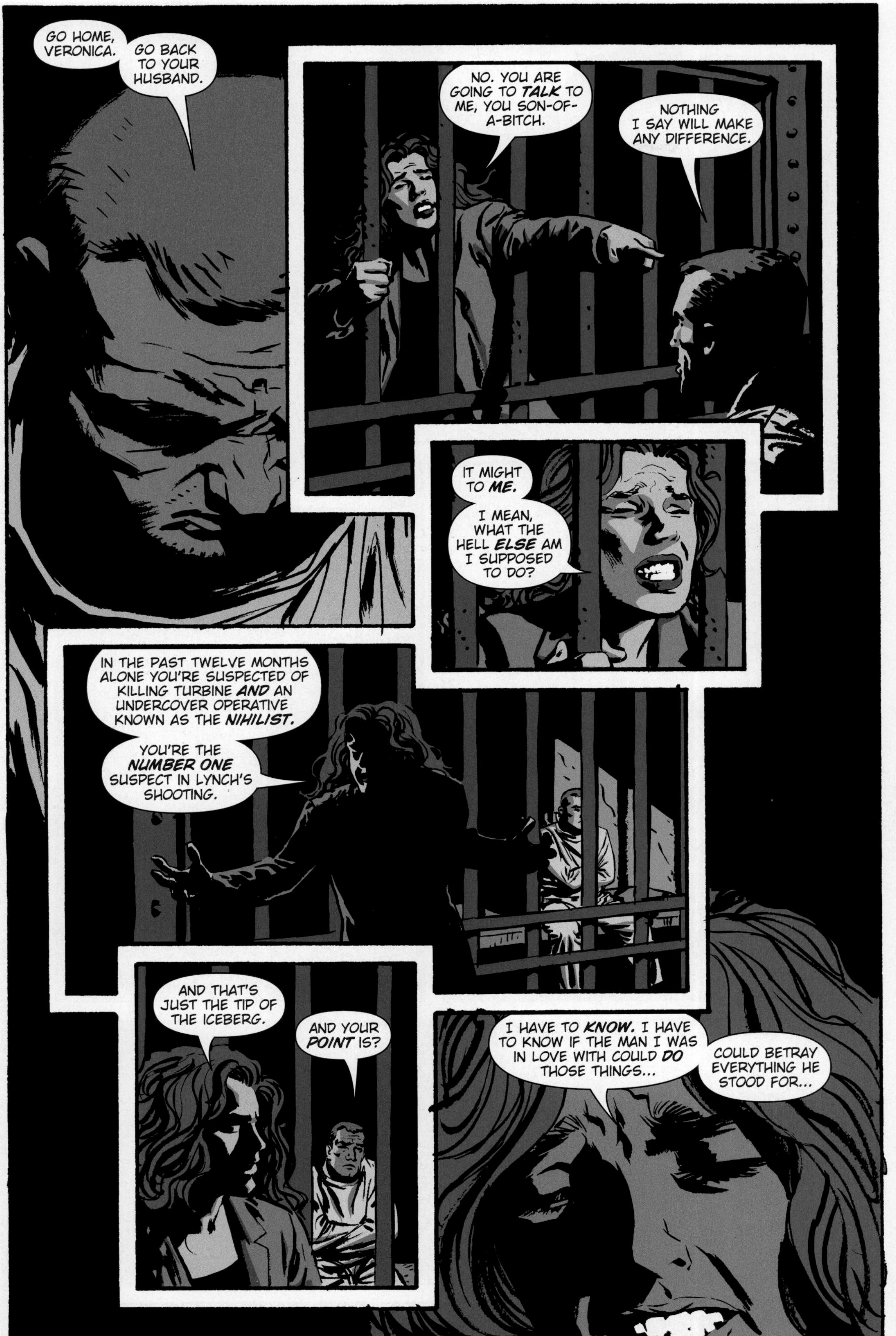
GO HOME, VERONICA.
GO BACK TO YOUR HUSBAND.
NO. YOU ARE GOING TO TALK TO ME, YOU SON-OF-A-BITCH.
NOTHING I SAY WILL MAKE ANY DIFFERENCE.
IT MIGHT TO ME.
I MEAN, WHAT THE HELL ELSE AM I SUPPOSED TO DO?
IN THE PAST TWELVE MONTHS ALONE YOU'RE SUSPECTED OF KILLING TURBINE AND AN UNDERCOVER OPERATIVE KNOWN AS THE NIHILIST.
YOU'RE THE NUMBER ONE SUSPECT IN LYNCH'S SHOOTING.
AND THAT'S JUST THE TIP OF THE ICEBERG.
AND YOUR POINT IS?
I HAVE TO KNOW. I HAVE TO KNOW IF THE MAN I WAS IN LOVE WITH COULD DO THOSE THINGS...
COULD BETRAY EVERYTHING HE STOOD FOR...

YOU'D RATHER BELIEVE I DID ALL THAT ON *ORDERS?*

YES! RATHER THAN THINK I DIDN'T KNOW YOU *AT ALL.*

For a second I almost believe her... And suddenly I want to tell her everything so badly...

I want to tell her about my squad dying in the jungle...

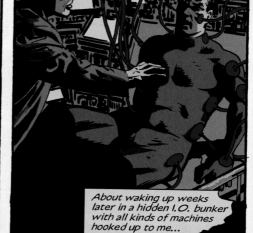

About waking up weeks later in a hidden I.O. bunker with all kinds of machines hooked up to me...

...About Lynch setting me up to be his mole in Tao's operation...

ROGUE AGENT
WANTED DEAD OR ALIVE

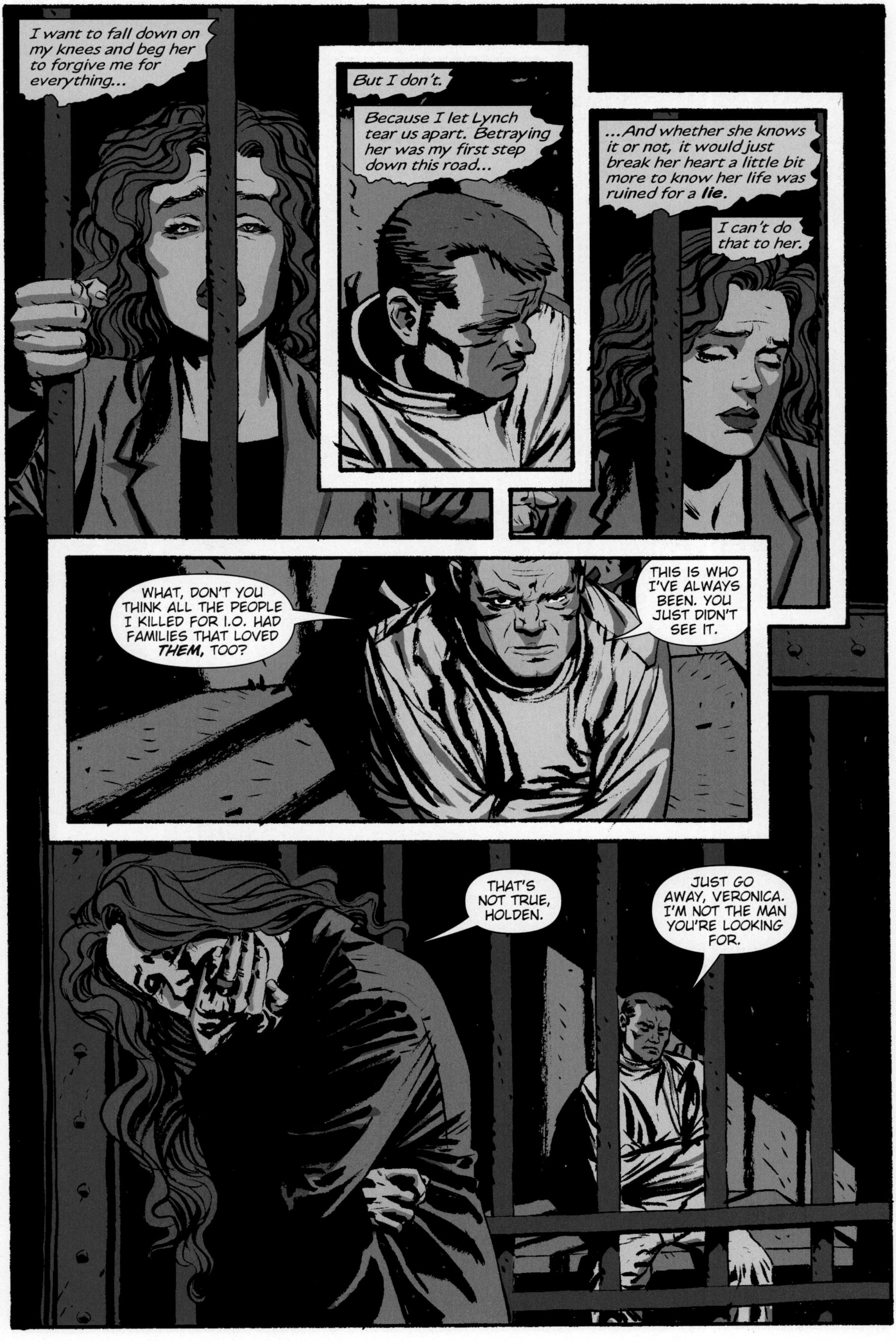
I want to fall down on my knees and beg her to forgive me for everything...
But I don't.
Because I let Lynch tear us apart. Betraying her was my first step down this road...
...And whether she knows it or not, it would just break her heart a little bit more to know her life was ruined for a **lie**.
I can't do that to her.
WHAT, DON'T YOU THINK ALL THE PEOPLE I KILLED FOR I.O. HAD FAMILIES THAT LOVED **THEM**, TOO?
THIS IS WHO I'VE ALWAYS BEEN. YOU JUST DIDN'T SEE IT.
THAT'S NOT TRUE, HOLDEN.
JUST GO AWAY, VERONICA. I'M NOT THE MAN YOU'RE LOOKING FOR.

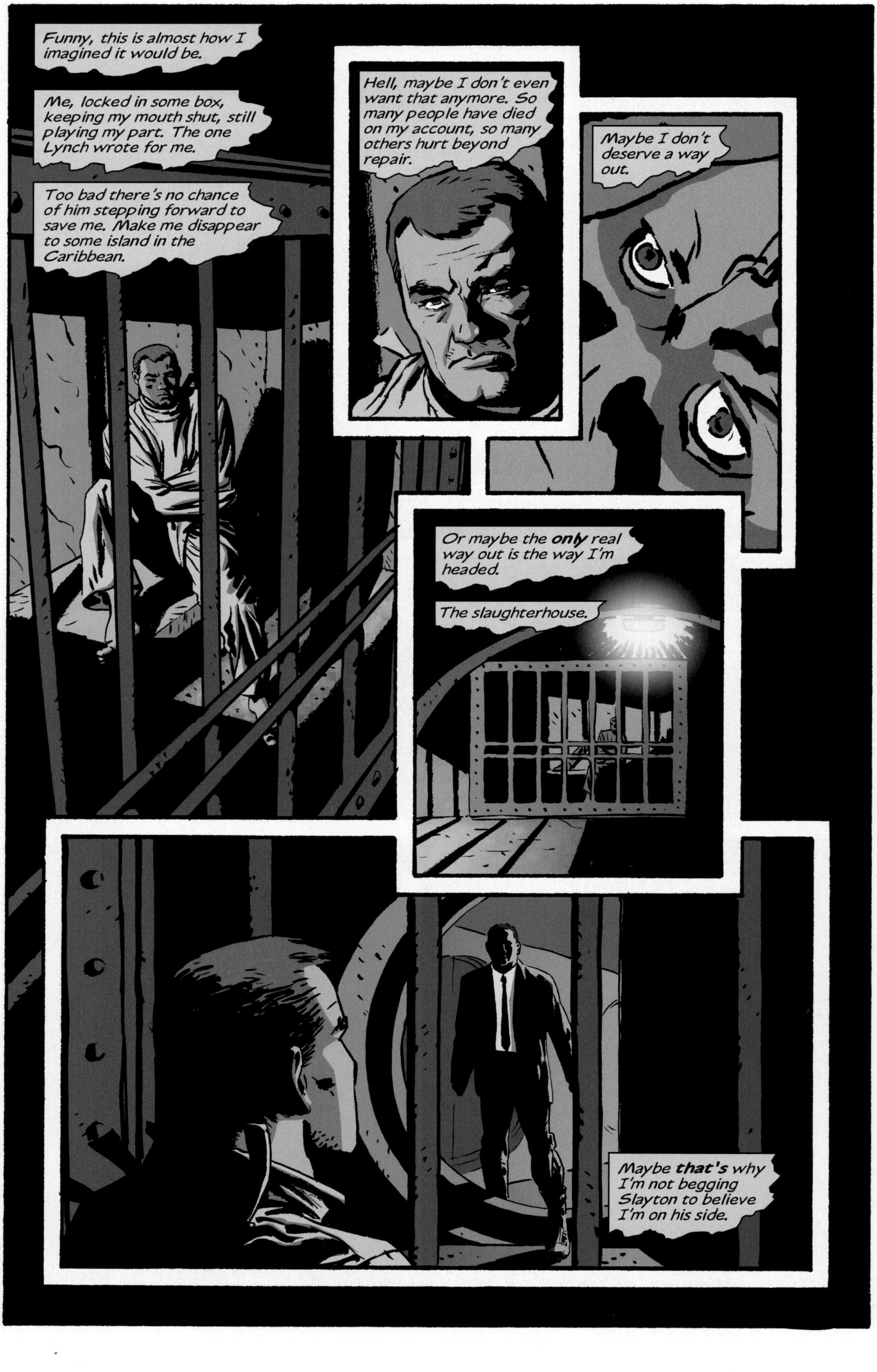
Funny, this is almost how I imagined it would be.
Me, locked in some box, keeping my mouth shut, still playing my part. The one Lynch wrote for me.
Too bad there's no chance of him stepping forward to save me. Make me disappear to some island in the Caribbean.
Hell, maybe I don't even want that anymore. So many people have died on my account, so many others hurt beyond repair.
Maybe I don't deserve a way out.
Or maybe the only real way out is the way I'm headed.
The slaughterhouse.
Maybe that's why I'm not begging Slayton to believe I'm on his side.

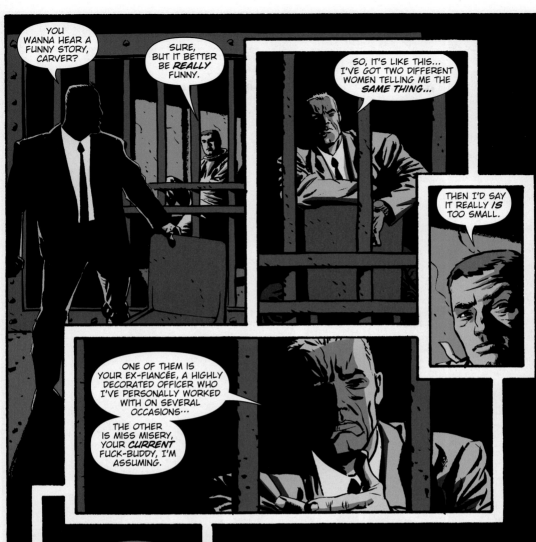

YOU WANNA HEAR A FUNNY STORY, CARVER?

SURE, BUT IT BETTER BE *REALLY* FUNNY.

SO, IT'S LIKE THIS... I'VE GOT TWO DIFFERENT WOMEN TELLING ME THE *SAME THING*...

THEN I'D SAY IT REALLY *IS* TOO SMALL.

ONE OF THEM IS YOUR EX-FIANCÉE, A HIGHLY DECORATED OFFICER WHO I'VE PERSONALLY WORKED WITH ON SEVERAL OCCASIONS...

THE OTHER IS MISS MISERY, YOUR *CURRENT* FUCK-BUDDY, I'M ASSUMING.

AND SEE, THE FUNNY PART IS BOTH OF THEM ARE TRYING TO TELL ME THAT *YOU* ARE AN *UNDERCOVER OPERATIVE*... THAT YOU WORK FOR *US.*

ANY IDEA WHERE THEY'D GET *THAT* IDEA?

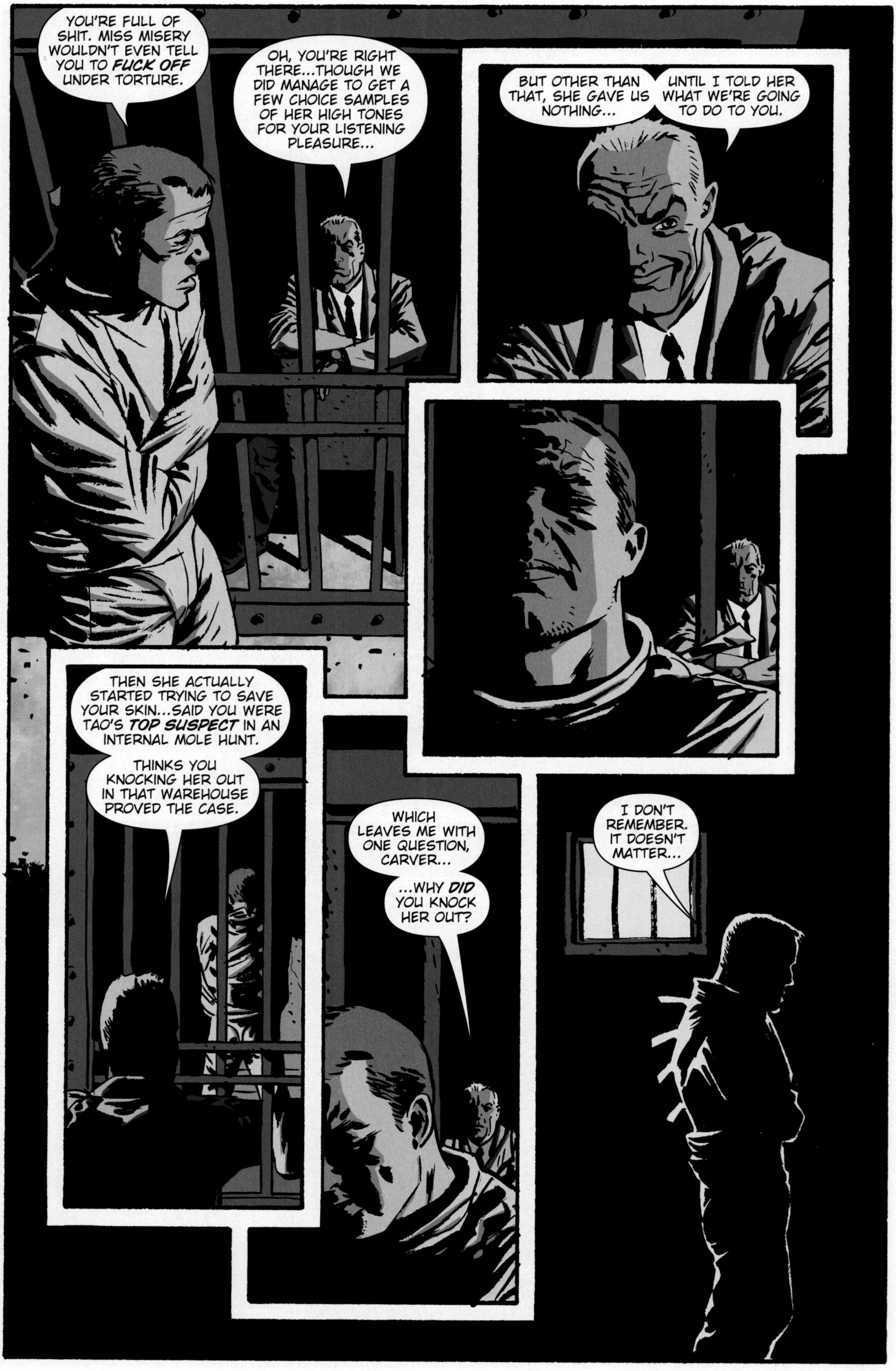
YOU'RE FULL OF SHIT. MISS MISERY WOULDN'T EVEN TELL YOU TO *FUCK OFF* UNDER TORTURE.
OH, YOU'RE RIGHT THERE...THOUGH WE DID MANAGE TO GET A FEW CHOICE SAMPLES OF HER HIGH TONES FOR YOUR LISTENING PLEASURE...
BUT OTHER THAN THAT, SHE GAVE US NOTHING...
UNTIL I TOLD HER WHAT WE'RE GOING TO DO TO YOU.
THEN SHE ACTUALLY STARTED TRYING TO SAVE YOUR SKIN...SAID YOU WERE TAO'S *TOP SUSPECT* IN AN INTERNAL MOLE HUNT.
THINKS YOU KNOCKING HER OUT IN THAT WAREHOUSE PROVED THE CASE.
WHICH LEAVES ME WITH ONE QUESTION, CARVER...
...WHY *DID* YOU KNOCK HER OUT?
I DON'T REMEMBER. IT DOESN'T MATTER...

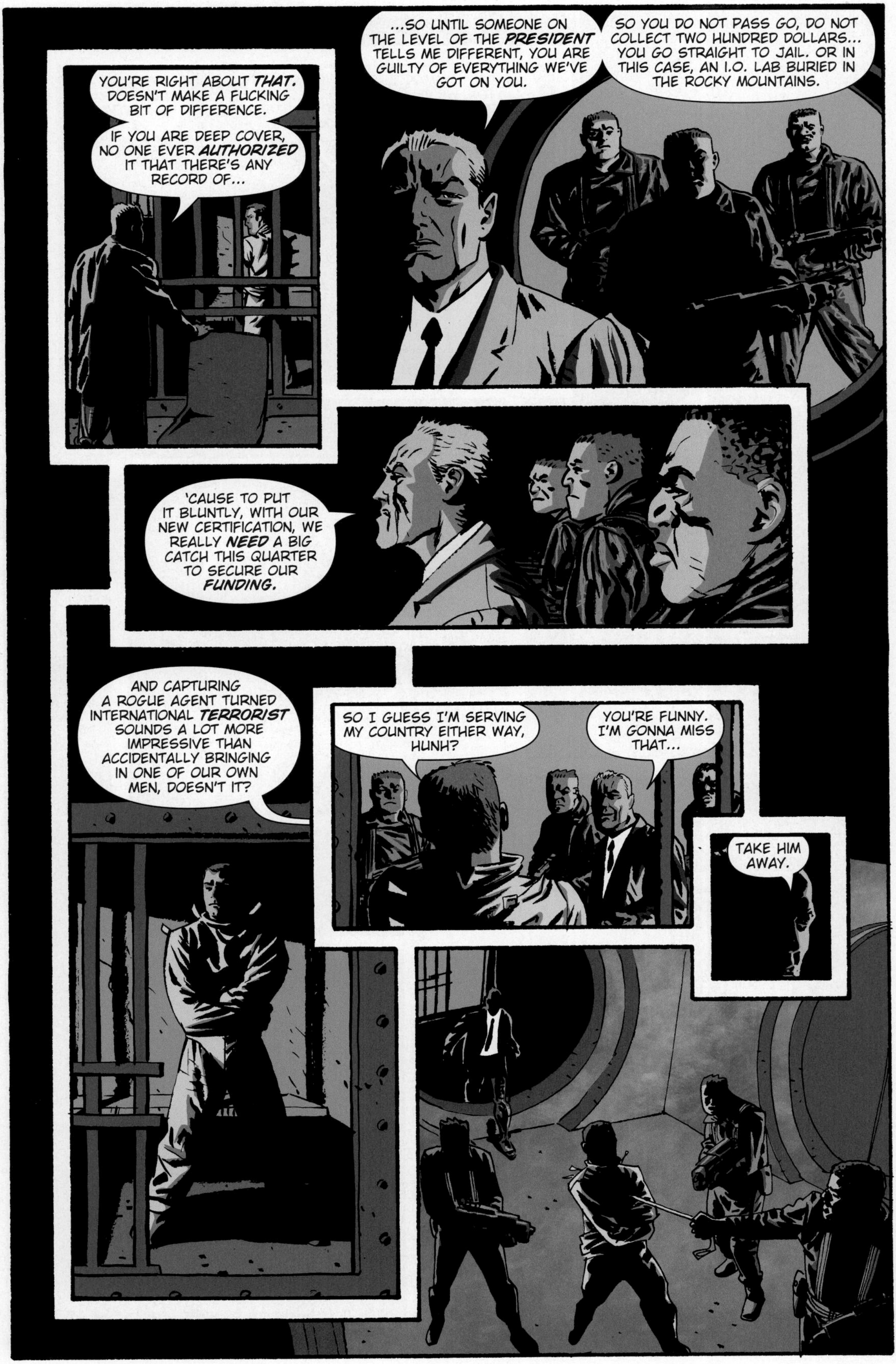
YOU'RE RIGHT ABOUT THAT. DOESN'T MAKE A FUCKING BIT OF DIFFERENCE.
IF YOU ARE DEEP COVER, NO ONE EVER AUTHORIZED IT THAT THERE'S ANY RECORD OF...
...SO UNTIL SOMEONE ON THE LEVEL OF THE PRESIDENT TELLS ME DIFFERENT, YOU ARE GUILTY OF EVERYTHING WE'VE GOT ON YOU.
SO YOU DO NOT PASS GO, DO NOT COLLECT TWO HUNDRED DOLLARS... YOU GO STRAIGHT TO JAIL. OR IN THIS CASE, AN I.O. LAB BURIED IN THE ROCKY MOUNTAINS.
'CAUSE TO PUT IT BLUNTLY, WITH OUR NEW CERTIFICATION, WE REALLY NEED A BIG CATCH THIS QUARTER TO SECURE OUR FUNDING.
AND CAPTURING A ROGUE AGENT TURNED INTERNATIONAL TERRORIST SOUNDS A LOT MORE IMPRESSIVE THAN ACCIDENTALLY BRINGING IN ONE OF OUR OWN MEN, DOESN'T IT?
SO I GUESS I'M SERVING MY COUNTRY EITHER WAY, HUNH?
YOU'RE FUNNY. I'M GONNA MISS THAT...
TAKE HIM AWAY.

UMMM, COMMANDER SLAYTON, WE'VE GOT A PROBLEM WITH THE OTHER PRISONER...

WE CAN'T SEEM TO GET HER TO STOP *VOMITING.*

WHAT? WHO THE FUCK IS *FEEDING* HER?

NO ONE. SHE'S THROWING UP BLOOD AND MUCUS...

I KNOW WHAT'S WRONG WITH HER.

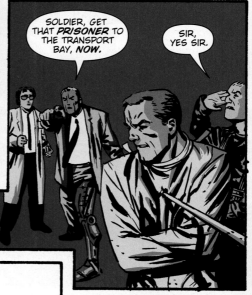

SOLDIER, GET THAT *PRISONER* TO THE TRANSPORT BAY, *NOW.*

SIR, YES SIR.

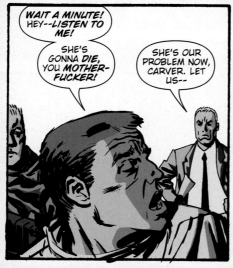

WAIT A MINUTE! HEY--*LISTEN TO ME!*

SHE'S GONNA *DIE,* YOU *MOTHER-FUCKER!*

SHE'S OUR PROBLEM NOW, CARVER. LET US--

KA-WHOOM

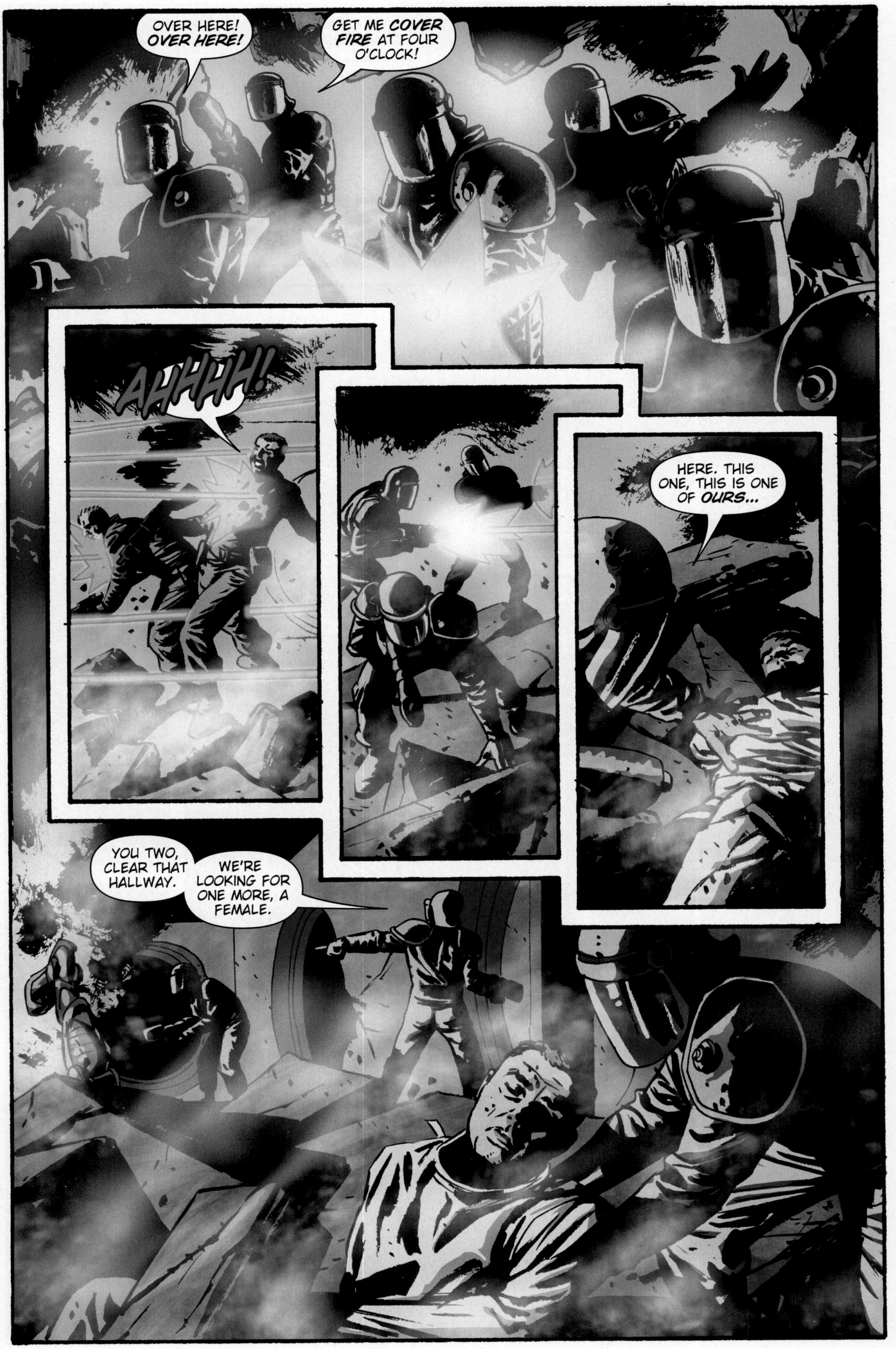
OVER HERE! OVER HERE!
GET ME COVER FIRE AT FOUR O'CLOCK!
AHHHH!
HERE. THIS ONE, THIS IS ONE OF OURS...
YOU TWO, CLEAR THAT HALLWAY.
WE'RE LOOKING FOR ONE MORE, A FEMALE.

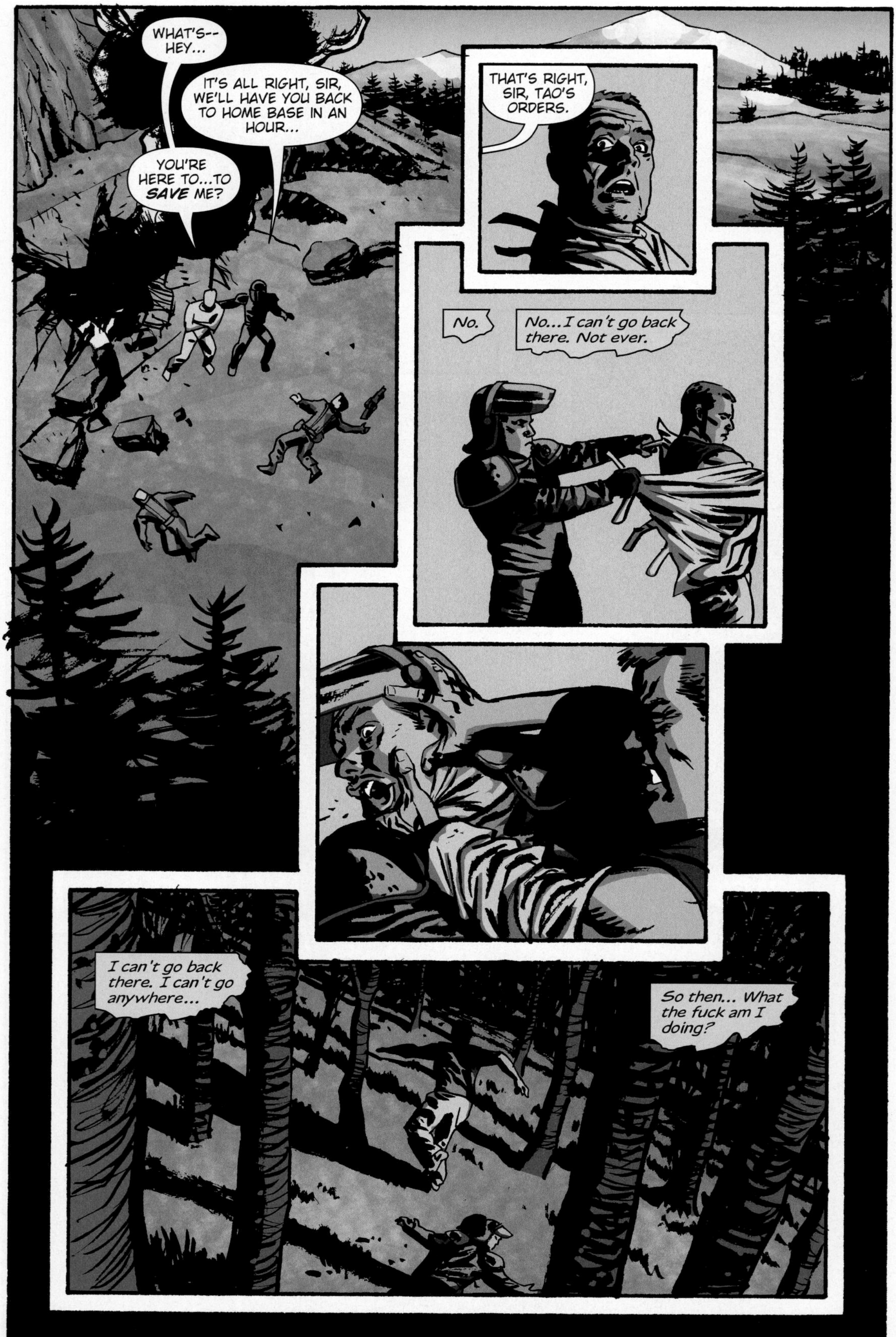
WHAT'S-- HEY...
IT'S ALL RIGHT, SIR, WE'LL HAVE YOU BACK TO HOME BASE IN AN HOUR...
YOU'RE HERE TO...TO SAVE ME?
THAT'S RIGHT, SIR, TAO'S ORDERS.
No.
No...I can't go back there. Not ever.
I can't go back there. I can't go anywhere...
So then... What the fuck am I doing?

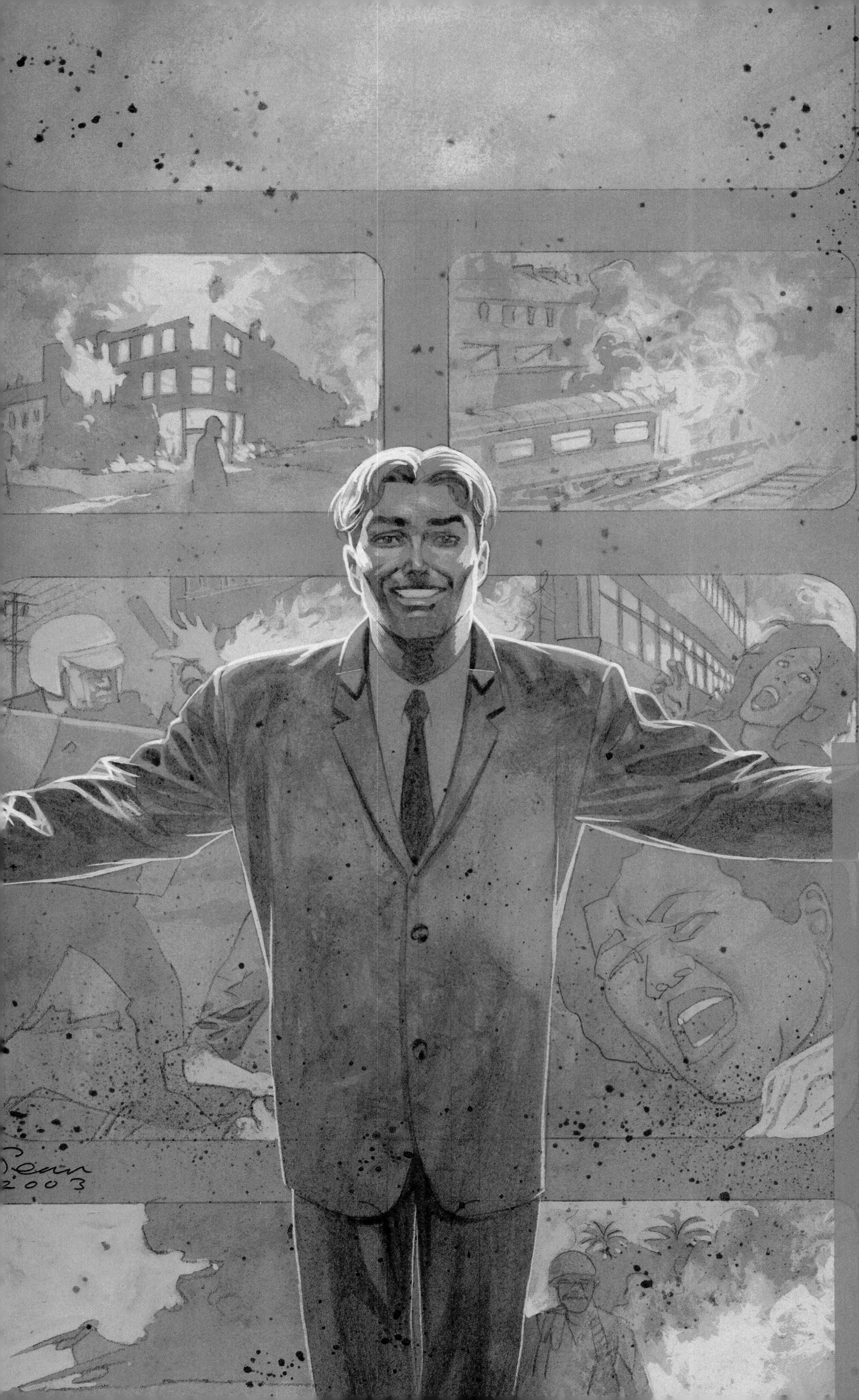
Sean
2003

Cover by SEAN PHILLIPS

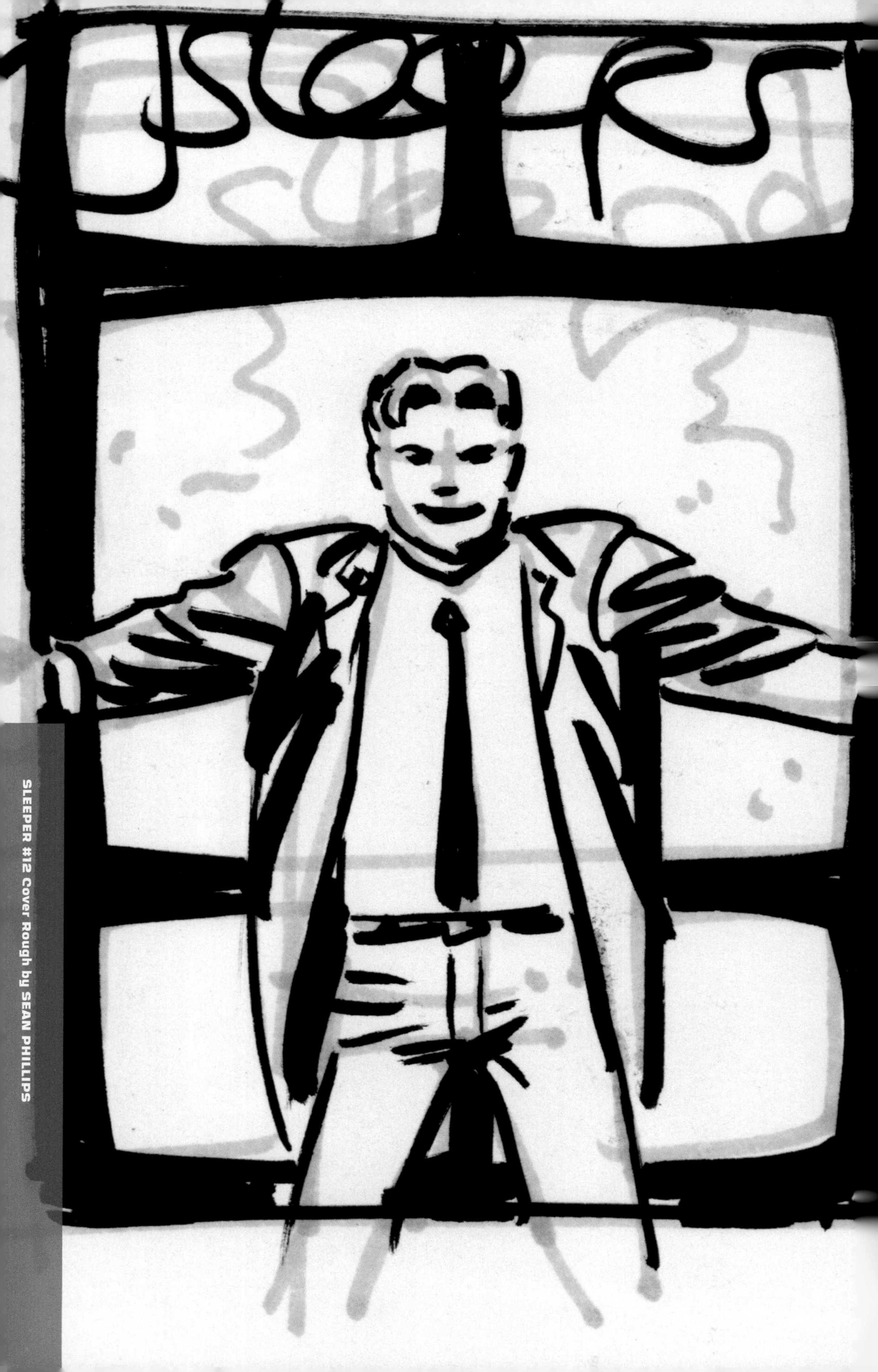

SLEEPER #12 Cover Rough by SEAN PHILLIPS

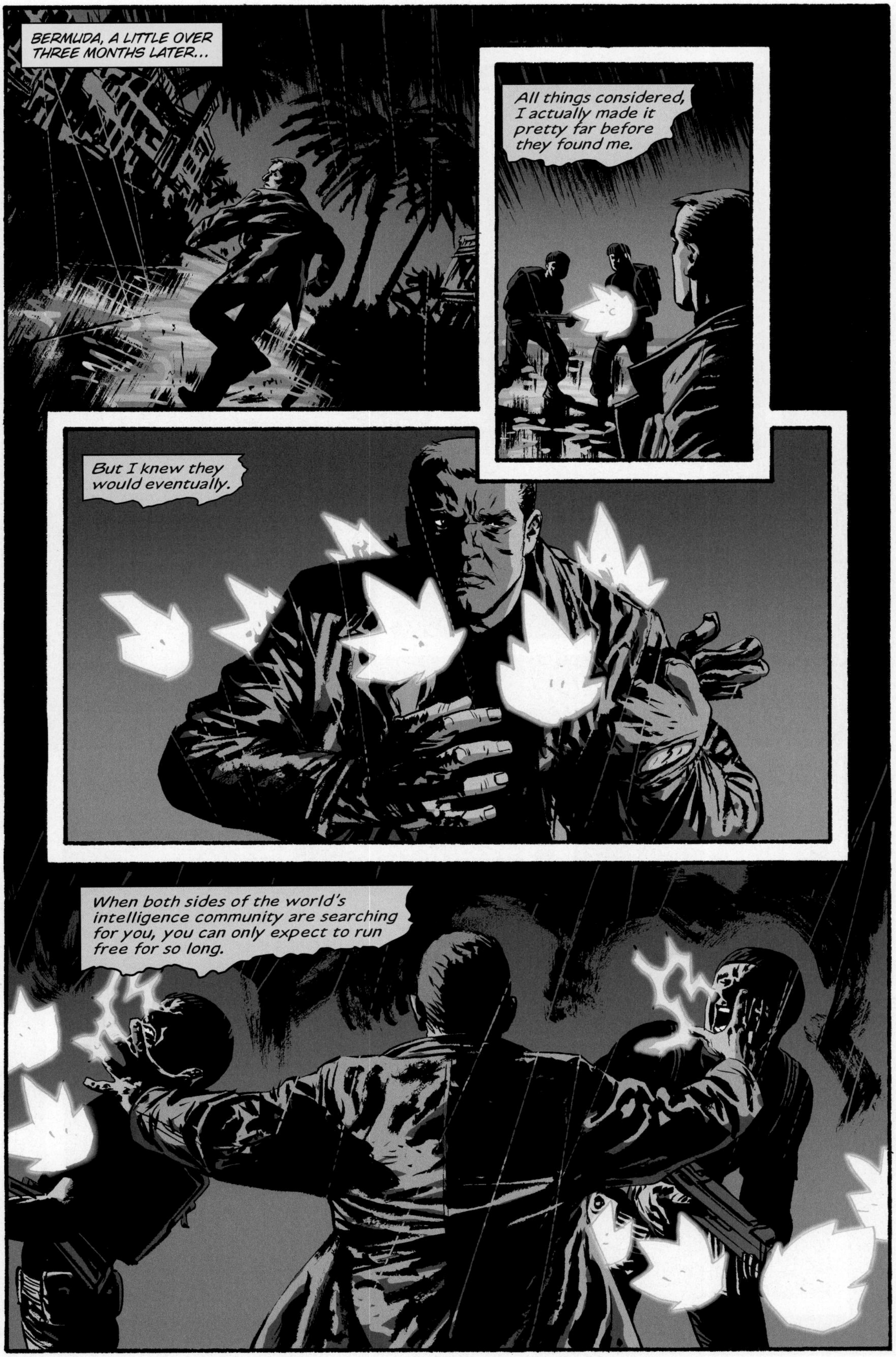
BERMUDA, A LITTLE OVER THREE MONTHS LATER...
All things considered, I actually made it pretty far before they found me.
But I knew they would eventually.
When both sides of the world's intelligence community are searching for you, you can only expect to run free for so long.

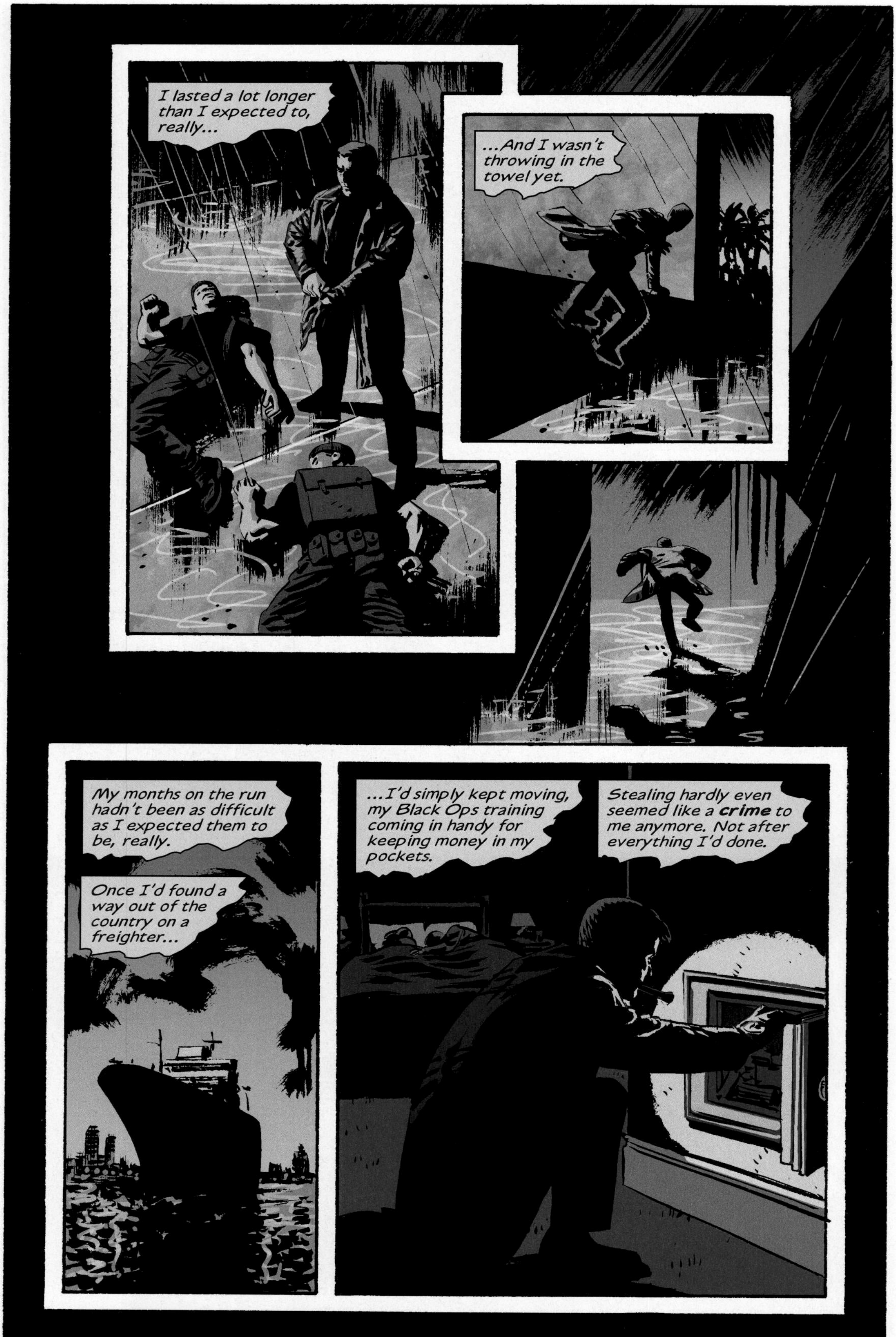

I lasted a lot longer than I expected to, really...
...And I wasn't throwing in the towel yet.
My months on the run hadn't been as difficult as I expected them to be, really.
Once I'd found a way out of the country on a freighter...
...I'd simply kept moving, my Black Ops training coming in handy for keeping money in my pockets.
Stealing hardly even seemed like a **crime** to me anymore. Not after everything I'd done.

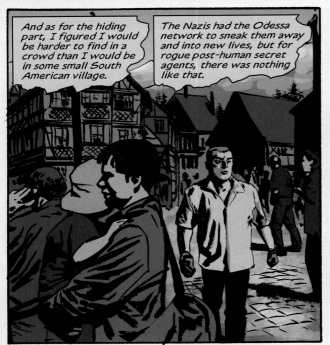

And as for the hiding part, I figured I would be harder to find in a crowd than I would be in some small South American village.

The Nazis had the Odessa network to sneak them away and into new lives, but for rogue post-human secret agents, there was nothing like that.

So, instead my life became like a permanent vacation. I followed the crowds, the tourists...

I went everyplace that I'd never have been caught dead before.

And I tried as hard as I could to seem just as clueless and easy-to-please as the rest of the monkey-mass that surrounded me.

It wasn't living, but it wasn't death, either.

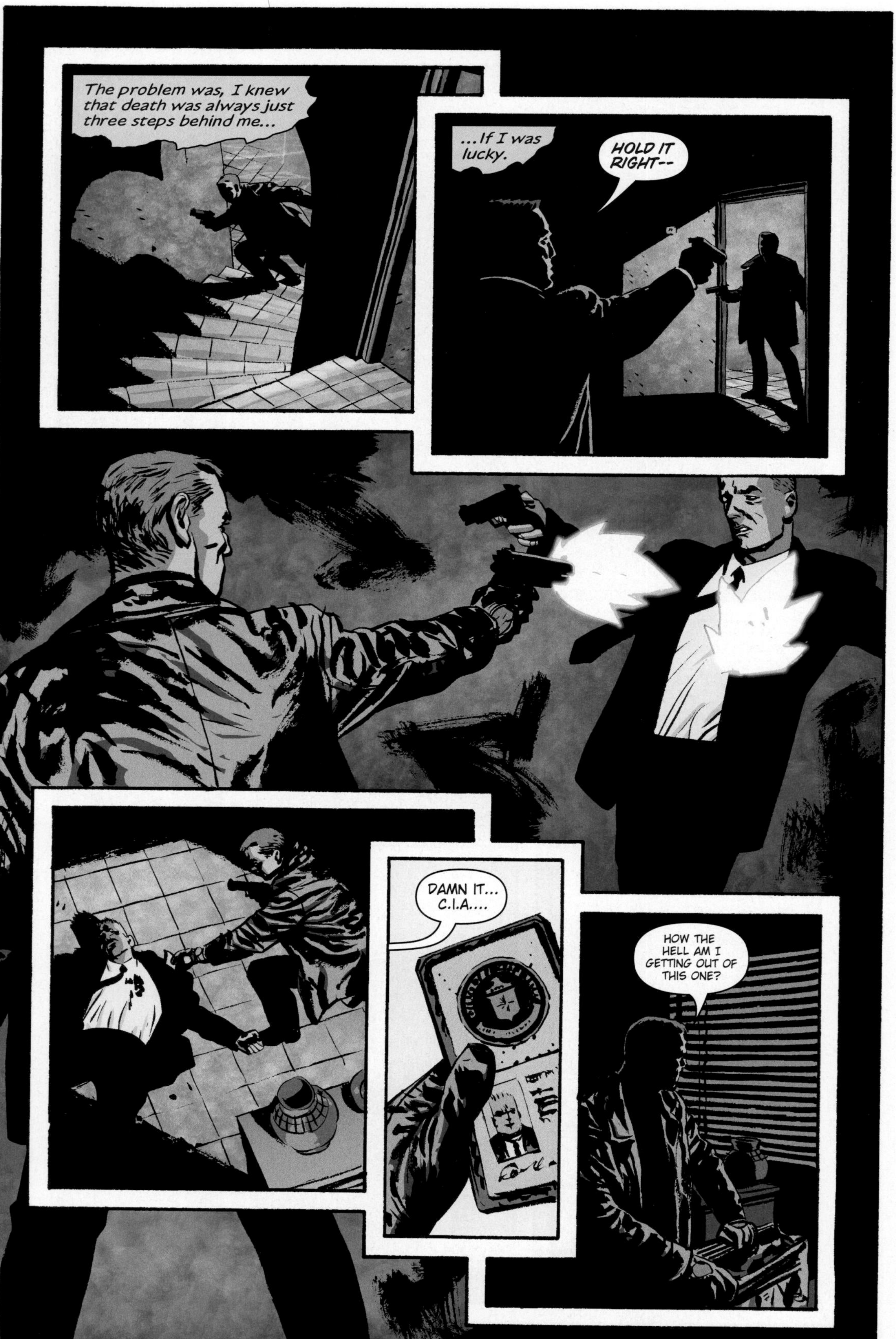
The problem was, I knew that death was always just three steps behind me...
...If I was lucky.
HOLD IT RIGHT--
DAMN IT... C.I.A....
HOW THE HELL AM I GETTING OUT OF THIS ONE?

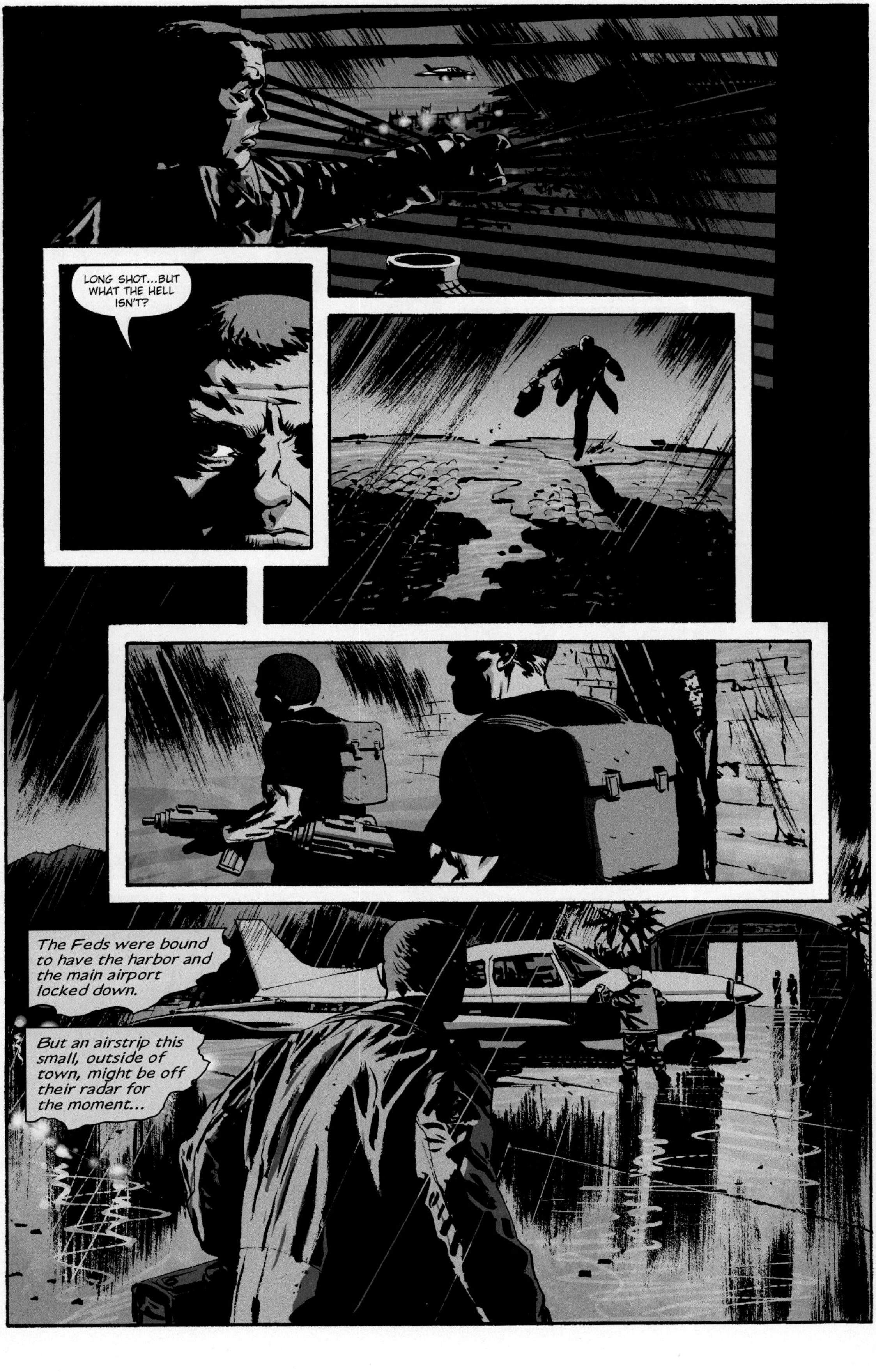
LONG SHOT...BUT WHAT THE HELL ISN'T?
The Feds were bound to have the harbor and the main airport locked down.
But an airstrip this small, outside of town, might be off their radar for the moment...

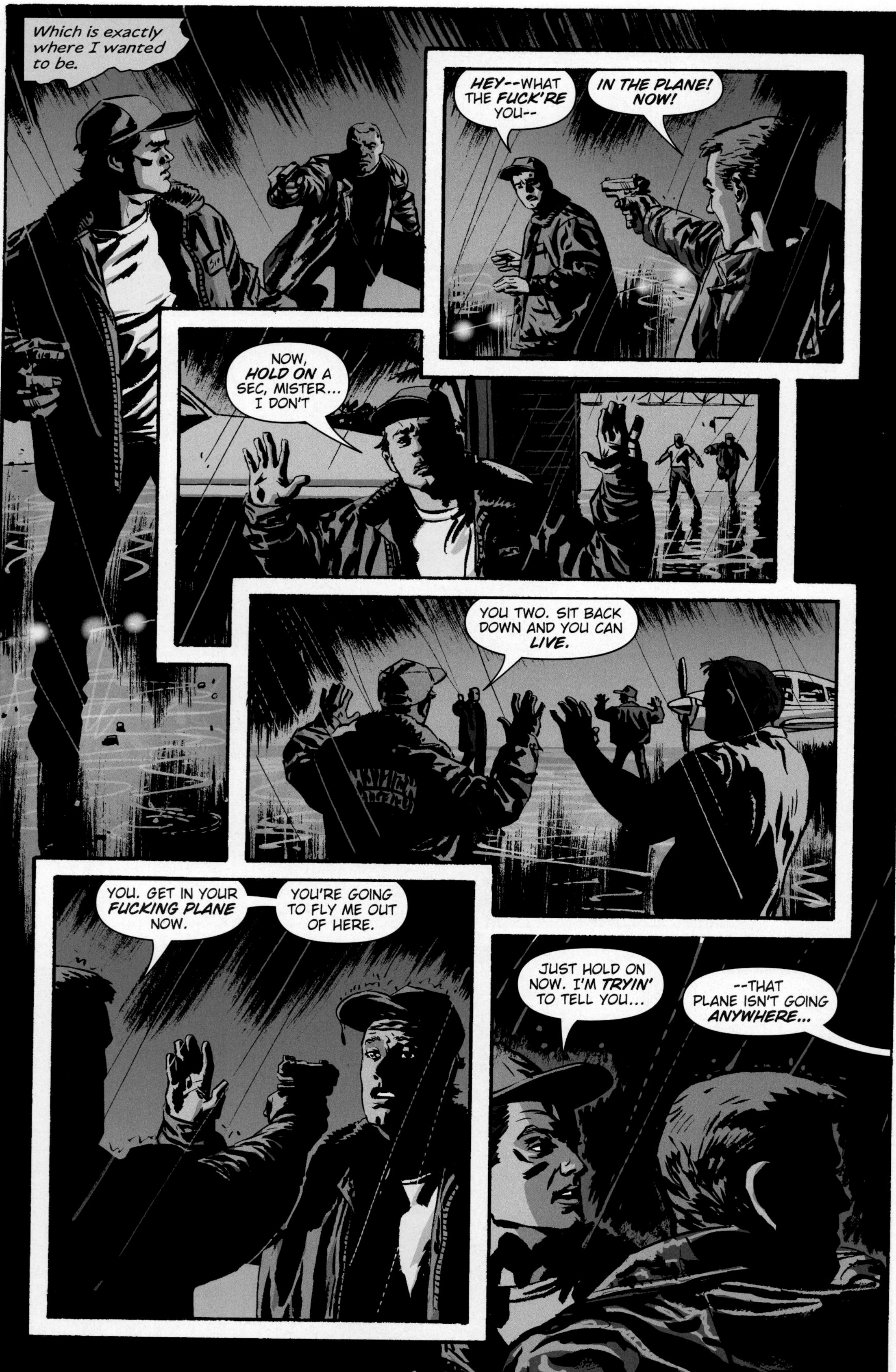
Which is exactly where I wanted to be.
HEY--WHAT THE FUCK'RE YOU--
IN THE PLANE! NOW!
NOW, HOLD ON A SEC, MISTER... I DON'T
YOU TWO. SIT BACK DOWN AND YOU CAN LIVE.
YOU. GET IN YOUR FUCKING PLANE NOW.
YOU'RE GOING TO FLY ME OUT OF HERE.
JUST HOLD ON NOW. I'M TRYIN' TO TELL YOU...
--THAT PLANE ISN'T GOING ANYWHERE...

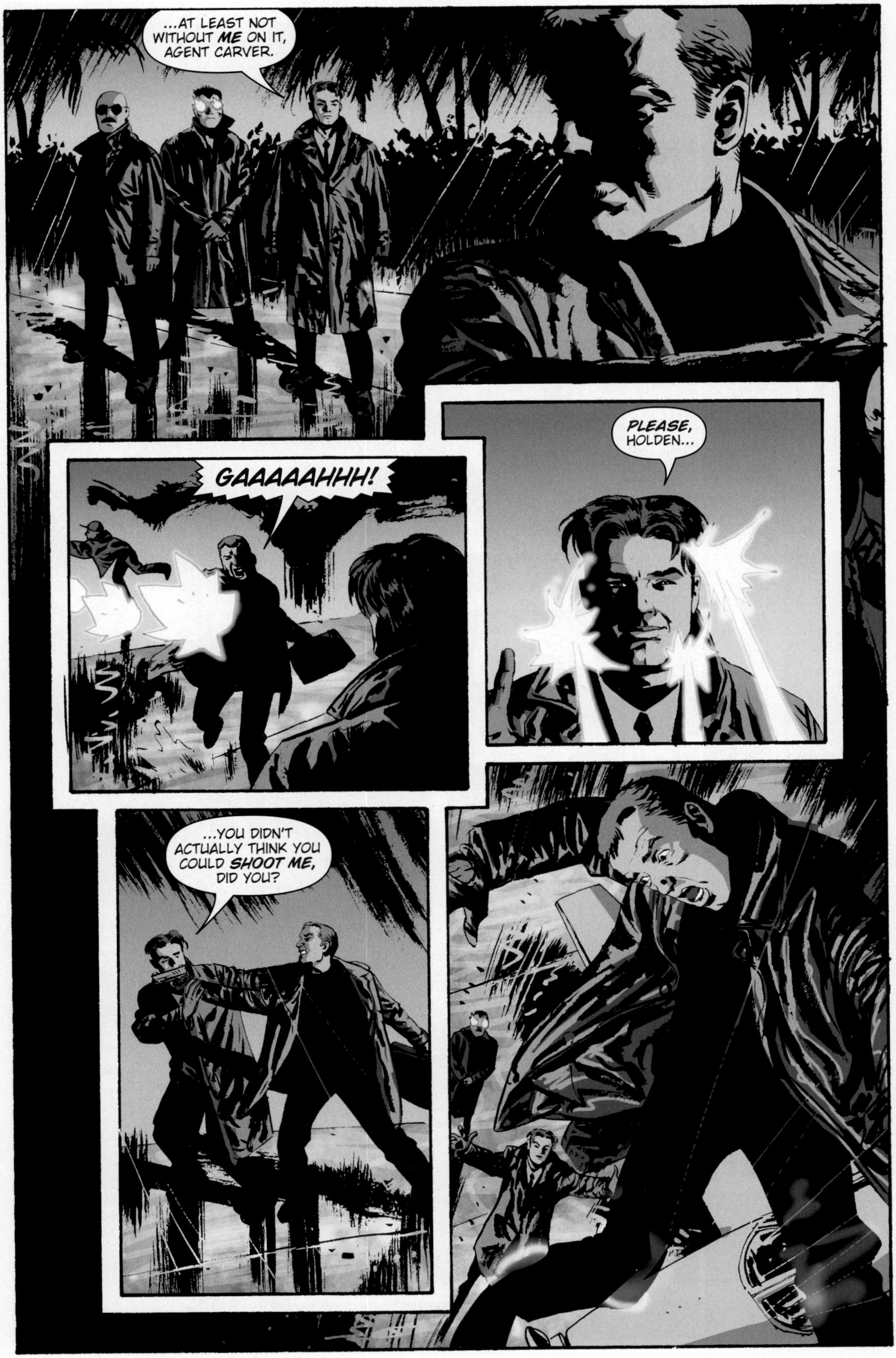
...AT LEAST NOT WITHOUT ME ON IT, AGENT CARVER.
GAAAAAHHH!
PLEASE, HOLDEN...
...YOU DIDN'T ACTUALLY THINK YOU COULD SHOOT ME, DID YOU?

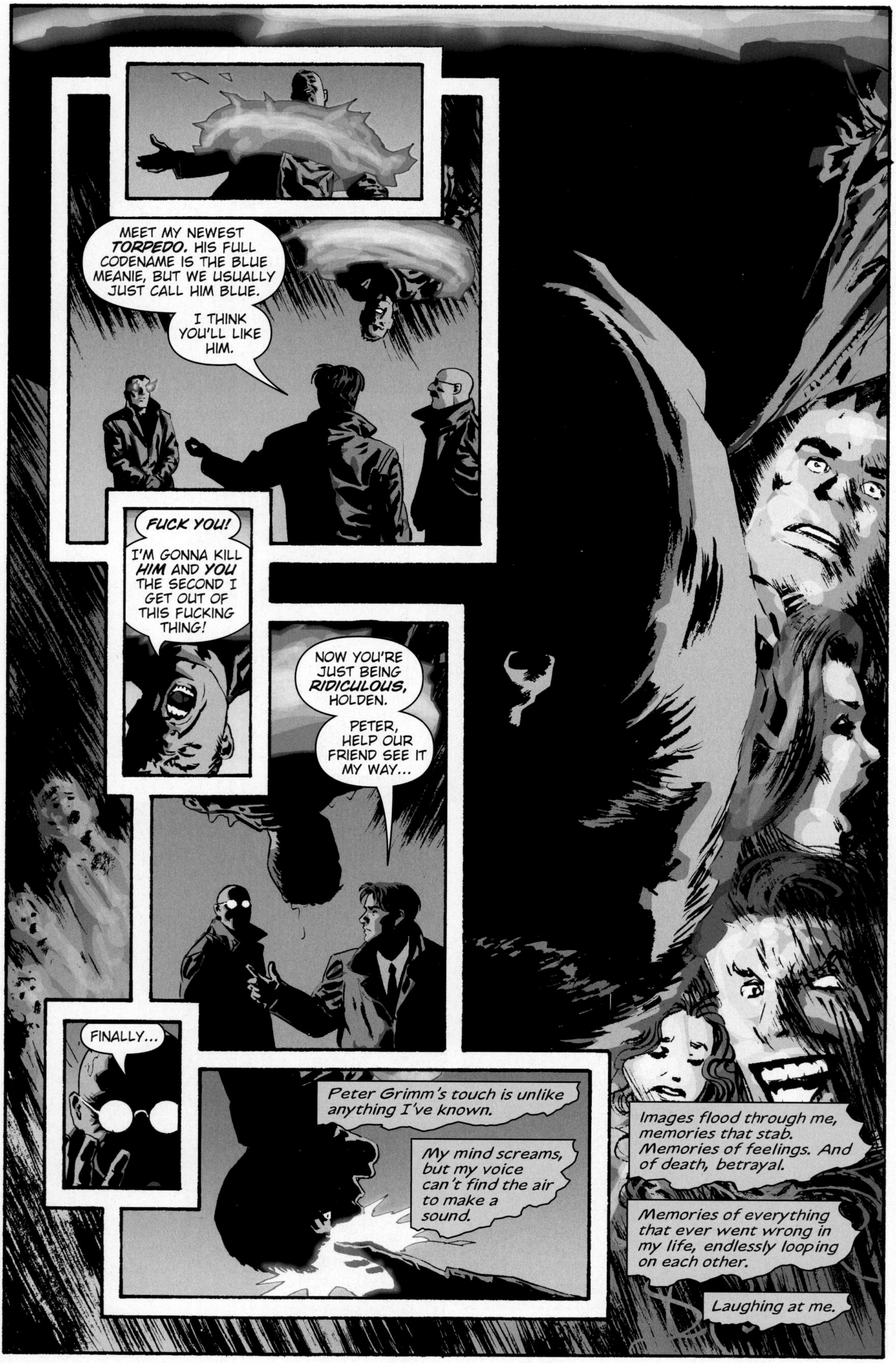
MEET MY NEWEST TORPEDO. HIS FULL CODENAME IS THE BLUE MEANIE, BUT WE USUALLY JUST CALL HIM BLUE.
I THINK YOU'LL LIKE HIM.
FUCK YOU!
I'M GONNA KILL HIM AND YOU THE SECOND I GET OUT OF THIS FUCKING THING!
NOW YOU'RE JUST BEING RIDICULOUS, HOLDEN.
PETER, HELP OUR FRIEND SEE IT MY WAY...
FINALLY...
Peter Grimm's touch is unlike anything I've known.
My mind screams, but my voice can't find the air to make a sound.
Images flood through me, memories that stab. Memories of feelings. And of death, betrayal.
Memories of everything that ever went wrong in my life, endlessly looping on each other.
Laughing at me.

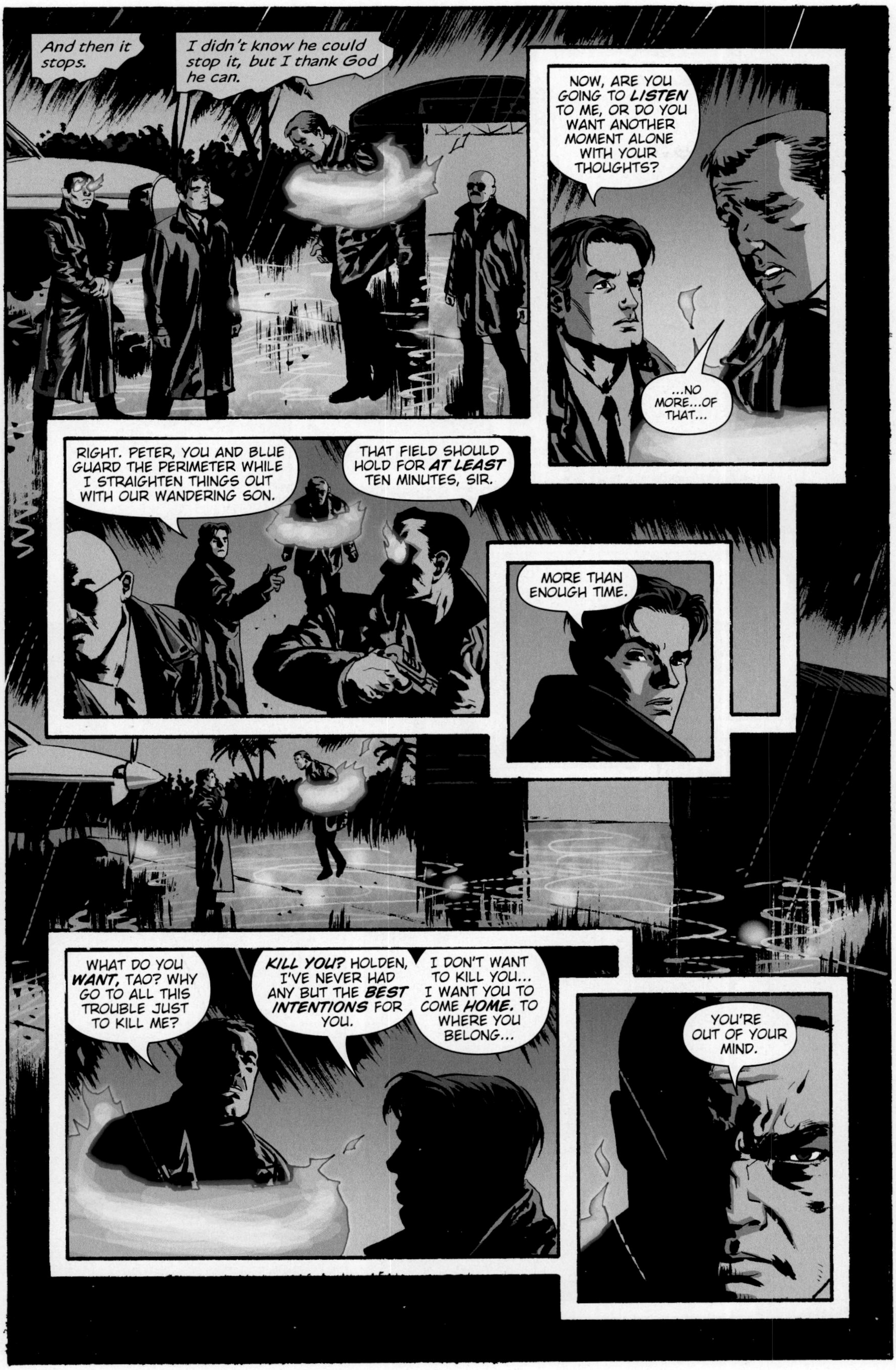
And then it stops.
I didn't know he could stop it, but I thank God he can.
NOW, ARE YOU GOING TO LISTEN TO ME, OR DO YOU WANT ANOTHER MOMENT ALONE WITH YOUR THOUGHTS?
...NO MORE...OF THAT...
RIGHT. PETER, YOU AND BLUE GUARD THE PERIMETER WHILE I STRAIGHTEN THINGS OUT WITH OUR WANDERING SON.
THAT FIELD SHOULD HOLD FOR AT LEAST TEN MINUTES, SIR.
MORE THAN ENOUGH TIME.
WHAT DO YOU WANT, TAO? WHY GO TO ALL THIS TROUBLE JUST TO KILL ME?
KILL YOU? HOLDEN, I'VE NEVER HAD ANY BUT THE BEST INTENTIONS FOR YOU.
I DON'T WANT TO KILL YOU... I WANT YOU TO COME HOME. TO WHERE YOU BELONG...
YOU'RE OUT OF YOUR MIND.

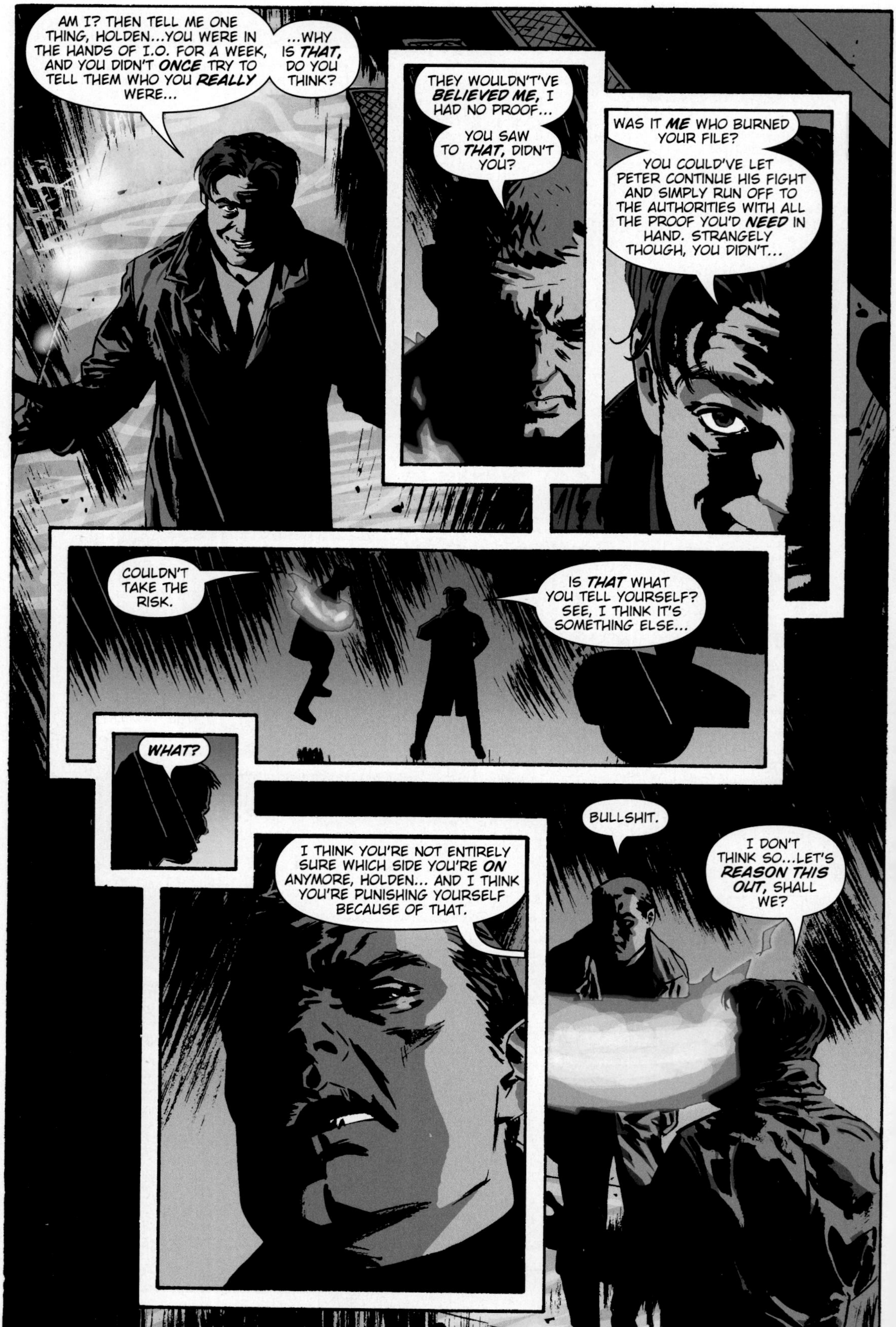
AM I? THEN TELL ME ONE THING, HOLDEN...YOU WERE IN THE HANDS OF I.O. FOR A WEEK, AND YOU DIDN'T ONCE TRY TO TELL THEM WHO YOU REALLY WERE...
...WHY IS THAT, DO YOU THINK?
THEY WOULDN'T'VE BELIEVED ME, I HAD NO PROOF...
YOU SAW TO THAT, DIDN'T YOU?
WAS IT ME WHO BURNED YOUR FILE?
YOU COULD'VE LET PETER CONTINUE HIS FIGHT AND SIMPLY RUN OFF TO THE AUTHORITIES WITH ALL THE PROOF YOU'D NEED IN HAND. STRANGELY THOUGH, YOU DIDN'T...
COULDN'T TAKE THE RISK.
IS THAT WHAT YOU TELL YOURSELF? SEE, I THINK IT'S SOMETHING ELSE...
WHAT?
I THINK YOU'RE NOT ENTIRELY SURE WHICH SIDE YOU'RE ON ANYMORE, HOLDEN... AND I THINK YOU'RE PUNISHING YOURSELF BECAUSE OF THAT.
BULLSHIT.
I DON'T THINK SO...LET'S REASON THIS OUT, SHALL WE?

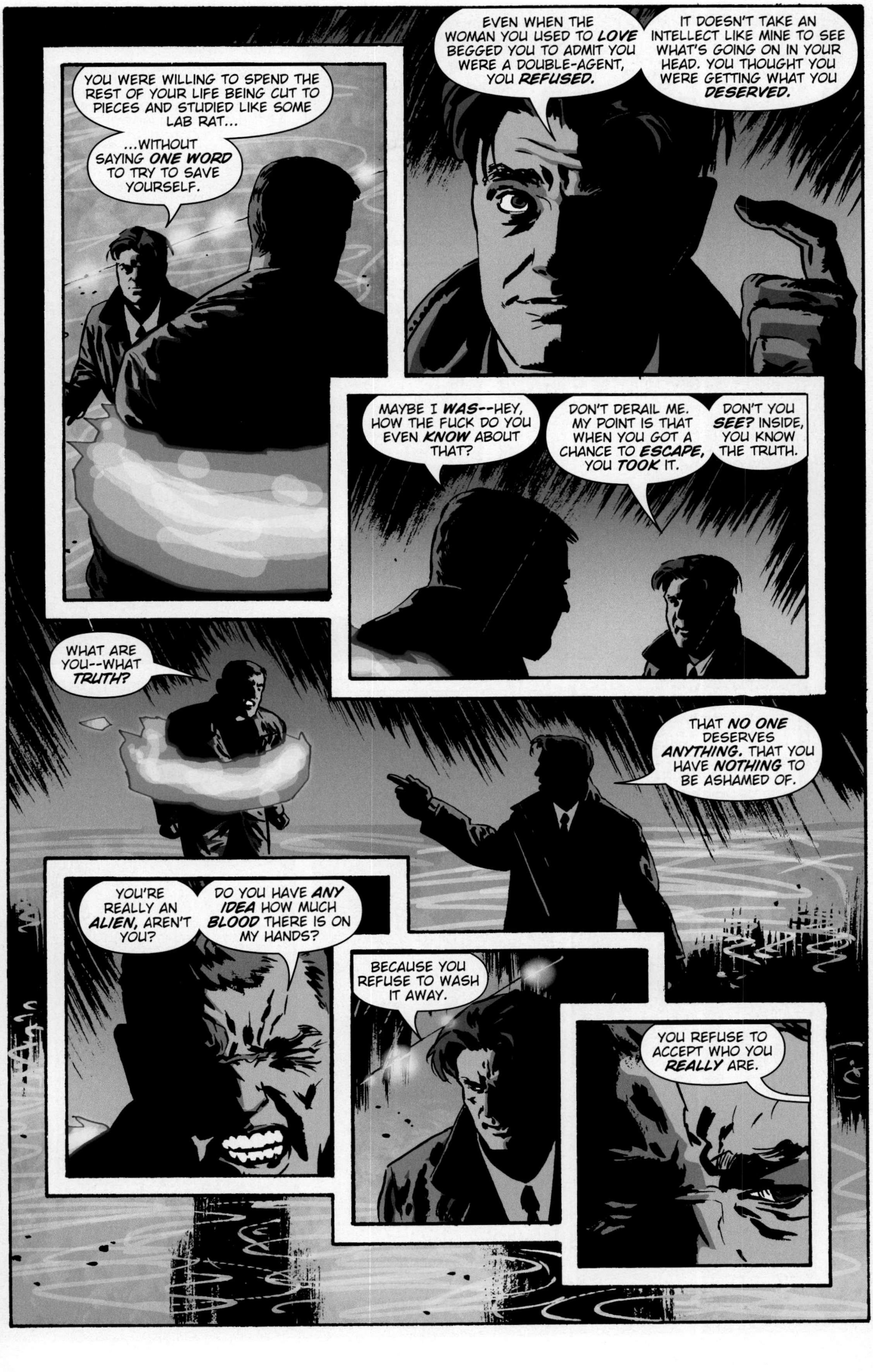
YOU WERE WILLING TO SPEND THE REST OF YOUR LIFE BEING CUT TO PIECES AND STUDIED LIKE SOME LAB RAT...
...WITHOUT SAYING ONE WORD TO TRY TO SAVE YOURSELF.
EVEN WHEN THE WOMAN YOU USED TO LOVE BEGGED YOU TO ADMIT YOU WERE A DOUBLE-AGENT, YOU REFUSED.
IT DOESN'T TAKE AN INTELLECT LIKE MINE TO SEE WHAT'S GOING ON IN YOUR HEAD. YOU THOUGHT YOU WERE GETTING WHAT YOU DESERVED.
MAYBE I WAS--HEY, HOW THE FUCK DO YOU EVEN KNOW ABOUT THAT?
DON'T DERAIL ME. MY POINT IS THAT WHEN YOU GOT A CHANCE TO ESCAPE, YOU TOOK IT.
DON'T YOU SEE? INSIDE, YOU KNOW THE TRUTH.
WHAT ARE YOU--WHAT TRUTH?
THAT NO ONE DESERVES ANYTHING. THAT YOU HAVE NOTHING TO BE ASHAMED OF.
YOU'RE REALLY AN ALIEN, AREN'T YOU?
DO YOU HAVE ANY IDEA HOW MUCH BLOOD THERE IS ON MY HANDS?
BECAUSE YOU REFUSE TO WASH IT AWAY.
YOU REFUSE TO ACCEPT WHO YOU REALLY ARE.

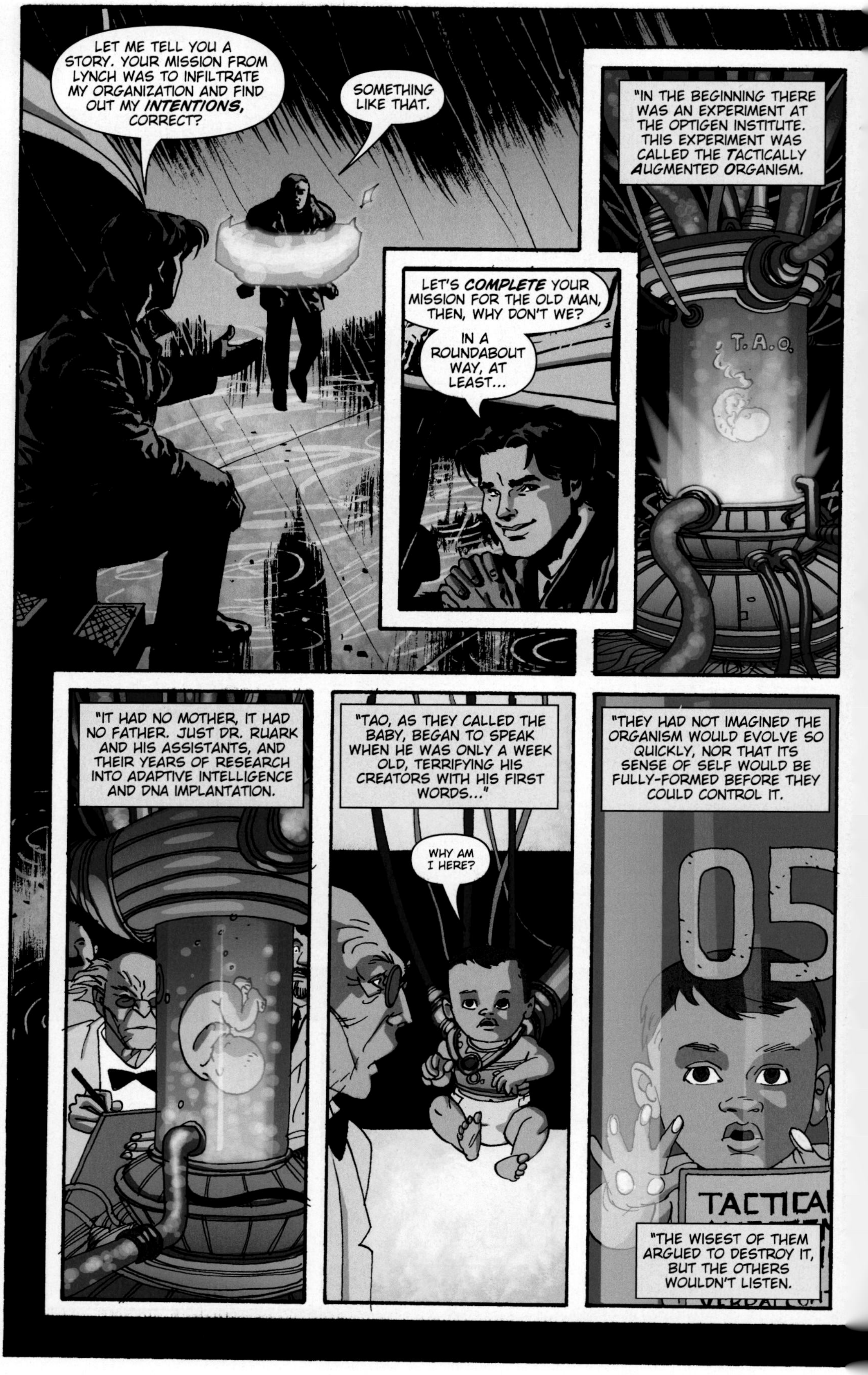
LET ME TELL YOU A STORY. YOUR MISSION FROM LYNCH WAS TO INFILTRATE MY ORGANIZATION AND FIND OUT MY *INTENTIONS,* CORRECT?
SOMETHING LIKE THAT.
LET'S *COMPLETE* YOUR MISSION FOR THE OLD MAN, THEN, WHY DON'T WE?
IN A ROUNDABOUT WAY, AT LEAST...
"IN THE BEGINNING THERE WAS AN EXPERIMENT AT THE OPTIGEN INSTITUTE. THIS EXPERIMENT WAS CALLED THE TACTICALLY AUGMENTED ORGANISM.
T.A.O.
"IT HAD NO MOTHER, IT HAD NO FATHER. JUST DR. RUARK AND HIS ASSISTANTS, AND THEIR YEARS OF RESEARCH INTO ADAPTIVE INTELLIGENCE AND DNA IMPLANTATION.
"TAO, AS THEY CALLED THE BABY, BEGAN TO SPEAK WHEN HE WAS ONLY A WEEK OLD, TERRIFYING HIS CREATORS WITH HIS FIRST WORDS..."
WHY AM I HERE?
"THEY HAD NOT IMAGINED THE ORGANISM WOULD EVOLVE SO QUICKLY, NOR THAT ITS SENSE OF SELF WOULD BE FULLY-FORMED BEFORE THEY COULD CONTROL IT.
05
TACTICA
"THE WISEST OF THEM ARGUED TO DESTROY IT, BUT THE OTHERS WOULDN'T LISTEN.

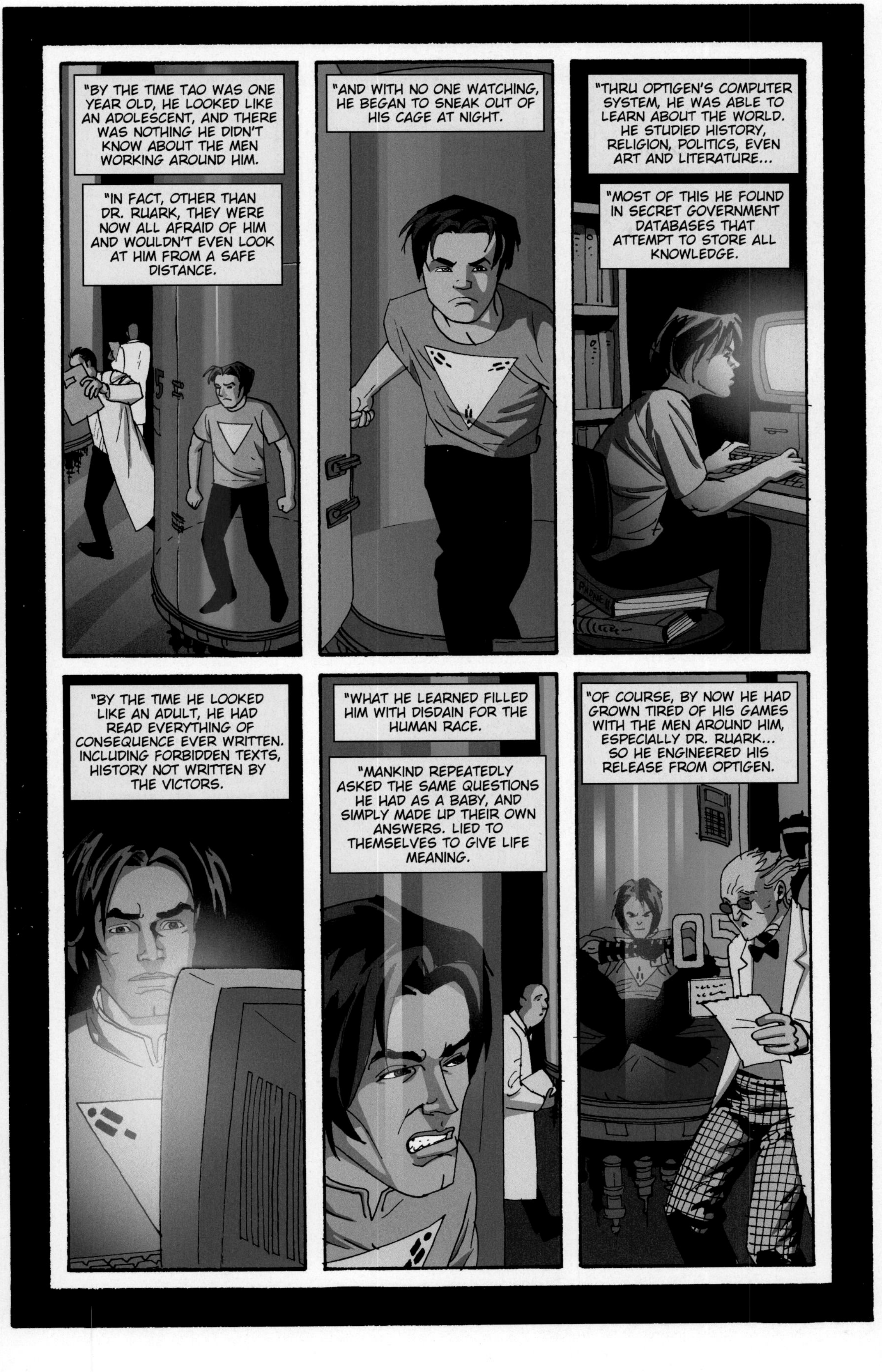
"BY THE TIME TAO WAS ONE YEAR OLD, HE LOOKED LIKE AN ADOLESCENT, AND THERE WAS NOTHING HE DIDN'T KNOW ABOUT THE MEN WORKING AROUND HIM.
"IN FACT, OTHER THAN DR. RUARK, THEY WERE NOW ALL AFRAID OF HIM AND WOULDN'T EVEN LOOK AT HIM FROM A SAFE DISTANCE.
"AND WITH NO ONE WATCHING, HE BEGAN TO SNEAK OUT OF HIS CAGE AT NIGHT.
"THRU OPTIGEN'S COMPUTER SYSTEM, HE WAS ABLE TO LEARN ABOUT THE WORLD. HE STUDIED HISTORY, RELIGION, POLITICS, EVEN ART AND LITERATURE...
"MOST OF THIS HE FOUND IN SECRET GOVERNMENT DATABASES THAT ATTEMPT TO STORE ALL KNOWLEDGE.
"BY THE TIME HE LOOKED LIKE AN ADULT, HE HAD READ EVERYTHING OF CONSEQUENCE EVER WRITTEN. INCLUDING FORBIDDEN TEXTS, HISTORY NOT WRITTEN BY THE VICTORS.
"WHAT HE LEARNED FILLED HIM WITH DISDAIN FOR THE HUMAN RACE.
"MANKIND REPEATEDLY ASKED THE SAME QUESTIONS HE HAD AS A BABY, AND SIMPLY MADE UP THEIR OWN ANSWERS. LIED TO THEMSELVES TO GIVE LIFE MEANING.
"OF COURSE, BY NOW HE HAD GROWN TIRED OF HIS GAMES WITH THE MEN AROUND HIM, ESPECIALLY DR. RUARK... SO HE ENGINEERED HIS RELEASE FROM OPTIGEN.

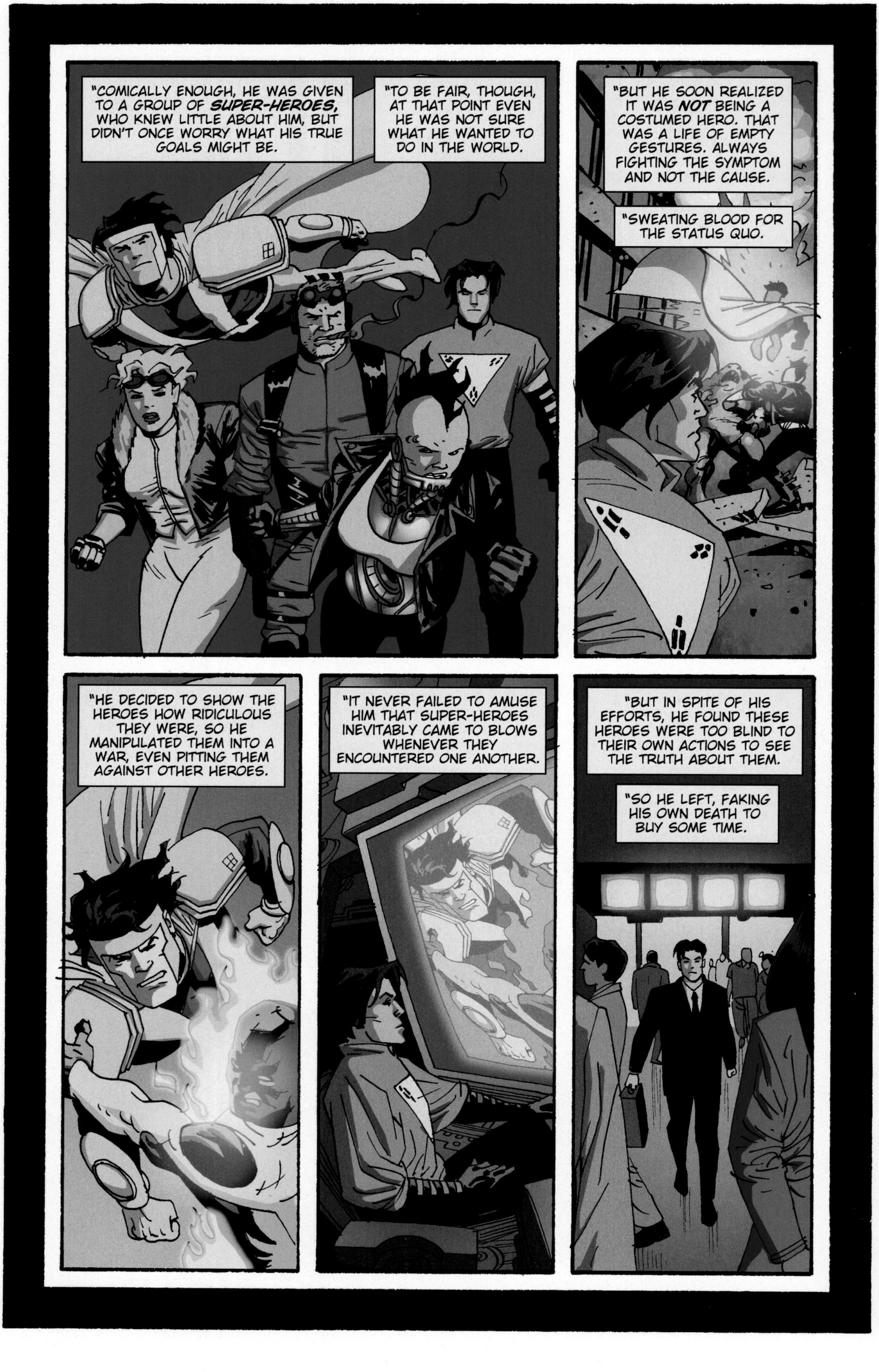
"COMICALLY ENOUGH, HE WAS GIVEN TO A GROUP OF SUPER-HEROES, WHO KNEW LITTLE ABOUT HIM, BUT DIDN'T ONCE WORRY WHAT HIS TRUE GOALS MIGHT BE.
"TO BE FAIR, THOUGH, AT THAT POINT EVEN HE WAS NOT SURE WHAT HE WANTED TO DO IN THE WORLD.
"BUT HE SOON REALIZED IT WAS NOT BEING A COSTUMED HERO. THAT WAS A LIFE OF EMPTY GESTURES. ALWAYS FIGHTING THE SYMPTOM AND NOT THE CAUSE.
"SWEATING BLOOD FOR THE STATUS QUO.
"HE DECIDED TO SHOW THE HEROES HOW RIDICULOUS THEY WERE, SO HE MANIPULATED THEM INTO A WAR, EVEN PITTING THEM AGAINST OTHER HEROES.
"IT NEVER FAILED TO AMUSE HIM THAT SUPER-HEROES INEVITABLY CAME TO BLOWS WHENEVER THEY ENCOUNTERED ONE ANOTHER.
"BUT IN SPITE OF HIS EFFORTS, HE FOUND THESE HEROES WERE TOO BLIND TO THEIR OWN ACTIONS TO SEE THE TRUTH ABOUT THEM.
"SO HE LEFT, FAKING HIS OWN DEATH TO BUY SOME TIME.

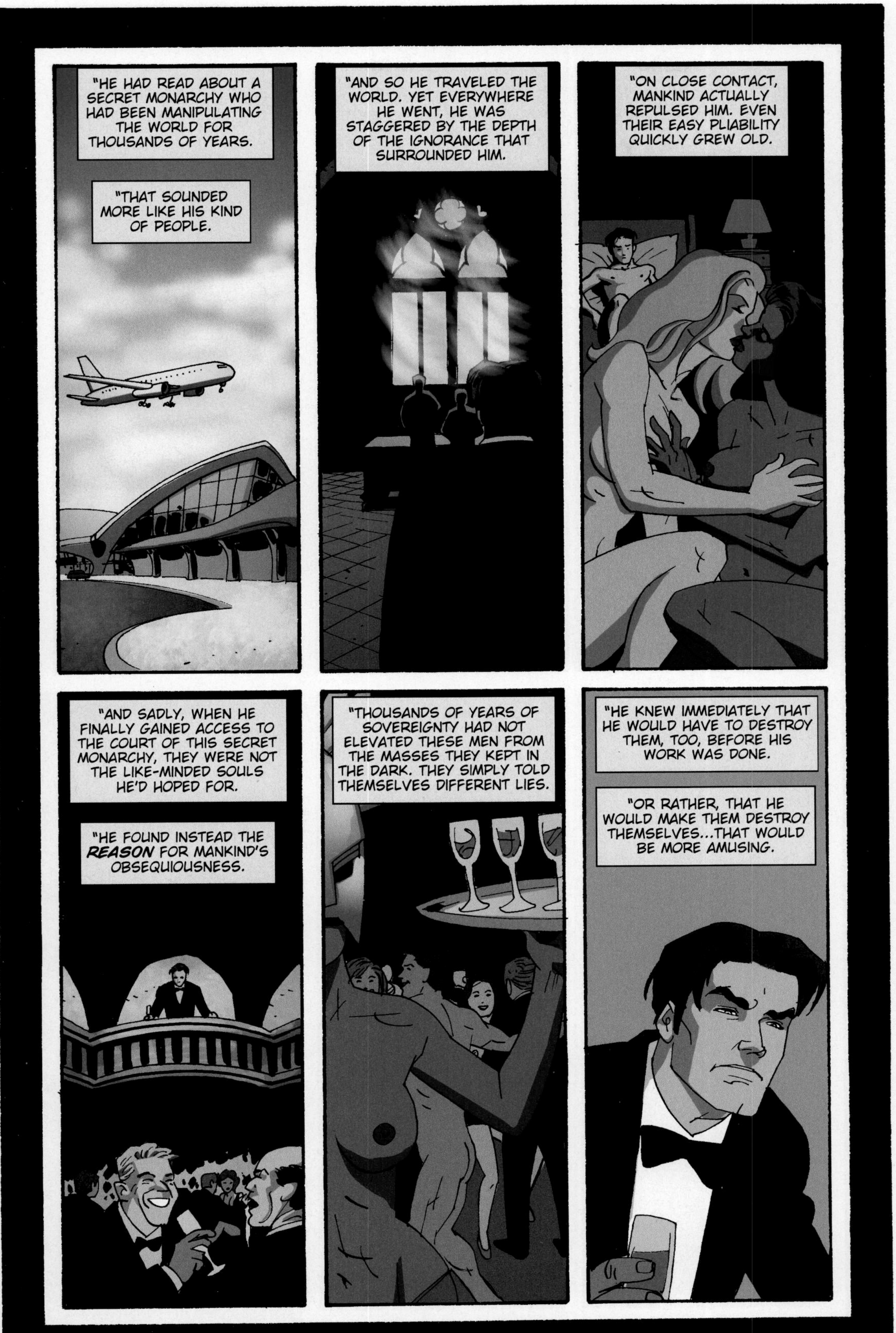
"HE HAD READ ABOUT A SECRET MONARCHY WHO HAD BEEN MANIPULATING THE WORLD FOR THOUSANDS OF YEARS.
"THAT SOUNDED MORE LIKE HIS KIND OF PEOPLE.
"AND SO HE TRAVELED THE WORLD. YET EVERYWHERE HE WENT, HE WAS STAGGERED BY THE DEPTH OF THE IGNORANCE THAT SURROUNDED HIM.
"ON CLOSE CONTACT, MANKIND ACTUALLY REPULSED HIM. EVEN THEIR EASY PLIABILITY QUICKLY GREW OLD.
"AND SADLY, WHEN HE FINALLY GAINED ACCESS TO THE COURT OF THIS SECRET MONARCHY, THEY WERE NOT THE LIKE-MINDED SOULS HE'D HOPED FOR.
"HE FOUND INSTEAD THE ***REASON*** FOR MANKIND'S OBSEQUIOUSNESS.
"THOUSANDS OF YEARS OF SOVEREIGNTY HAD NOT ELEVATED THESE MEN FROM THE MASSES THEY KEPT IN THE DARK. THEY SIMPLY TOLD THEMSELVES DIFFERENT LIES.
"HE KNEW IMMEDIATELY THAT HE WOULD HAVE TO DESTROY THEM, TOO, BEFORE HIS WORK WAS DONE.
"OR RATHER, THAT HE WOULD MAKE THEM DESTROY THEMSELVES...THAT WOULD BE MORE AMUSING.

"SO HE BEGAN GATHERING FOLLOWERS, WHICH WAS SIMPLE. THE ILLUSION OF POWER AND WEALTH BOUGHT THE LOYALTY OF MOST MEN.

"AND HIS TEAMS BEGAN STRIKING AROUND THE GLOBE, LEAVING NO CLUE TO THEIR AGENDA.

"HIS MEN INSIDE VARIOUS AGENCIES TOLD HIM HOW FRUSTRATED THEIR BOSSES WERE. WHAT WAS HE PLANNING? WHAT WAS HE AFTER?

"SOME FEARED HE WANTED TO RULE THE WORLD, BUT NOTHING COULD'VE BEEN FURTHER FROM THE TRUTH.

"WHAT HE REALLY WANTED WAS TO SHATTER THE LIES, TO FRACTURE THE HIDDEN SYSTEMS THAT KEPT THE WORLD TURNING IN SUCH A TEDIOUS WAY.

"BECAUSE WHEN THE TACTICALLY AUGMENTED ORGANISM LOOKED AT LIFE HE SAW ONLY CHAOS AND ORDER. AND HUMANITY'S DENIAL OF CHAOS APPALLED HIM.

"SO HE WOULD TEAR IT ALL DOWN AND FILL THE WHOLE WORLD WITH CHAOS, IF ONLY TO WATCH MANKIND CLING TO THEIR ILLUSIONS AS THEY BURNED AROUND THEM...

...WOULD HE *DESTROY* THE WORLD AT THE SAME TIME? IT'S CERTAINLY A POSSIBILITY.

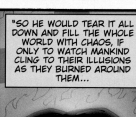

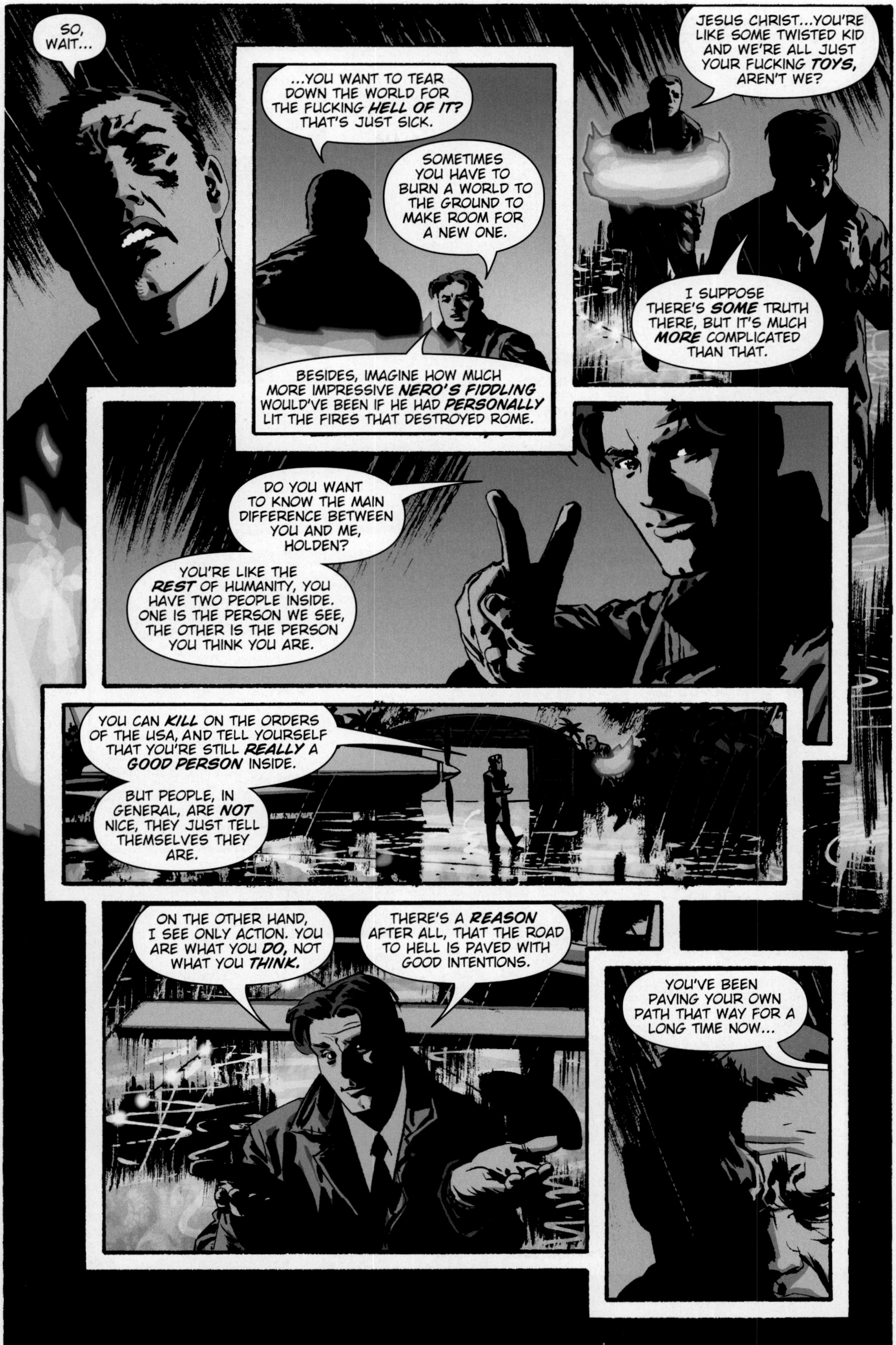
SO, WAIT...
...YOU WANT TO TEAR DOWN THE WORLD FOR THE FUCKING HELL OF IT? THAT'S JUST SICK.
SOMETIMES YOU HAVE TO BURN A WORLD TO THE GROUND TO MAKE ROOM FOR A NEW ONE.
BESIDES, IMAGINE HOW MUCH MORE IMPRESSIVE NERO'S FIDDLING WOULD'VE BEEN IF HE HAD PERSONALLY LIT THE FIRES THAT DESTROYED ROME.
JESUS CHRIST...YOU'RE LIKE SOME TWISTED KID AND WE'RE ALL JUST YOUR FUCKING TOYS, AREN'T WE?
I SUPPOSE THERE'S SOME TRUTH THERE, BUT IT'S MUCH MORE COMPLICATED THAN THAT.
DO YOU WANT TO KNOW THE MAIN DIFFERENCE BETWEEN YOU AND ME, HOLDEN?
YOU'RE LIKE THE REST OF HUMANITY, YOU HAVE TWO PEOPLE INSIDE. ONE IS THE PERSON WE SEE, THE OTHER IS THE PERSON YOU THINK YOU ARE.
YOU CAN KILL ON THE ORDERS OF THE USA, AND TELL YOURSELF THAT YOU'RE STILL REALLY A GOOD PERSON INSIDE.
BUT PEOPLE, IN GENERAL, ARE NOT NICE, THEY JUST TELL THEMSELVES THEY ARE.
ON THE OTHER HAND, I SEE ONLY ACTION. YOU ARE WHAT YOU DO, NOT WHAT YOU THINK.
THERE'S A REASON AFTER ALL, THAT THE ROAD TO HELL IS PAVED WITH GOOD INTENTIONS.
YOU'VE BEEN PAVING YOUR OWN PATH THAT WAY FOR A LONG TIME NOW...

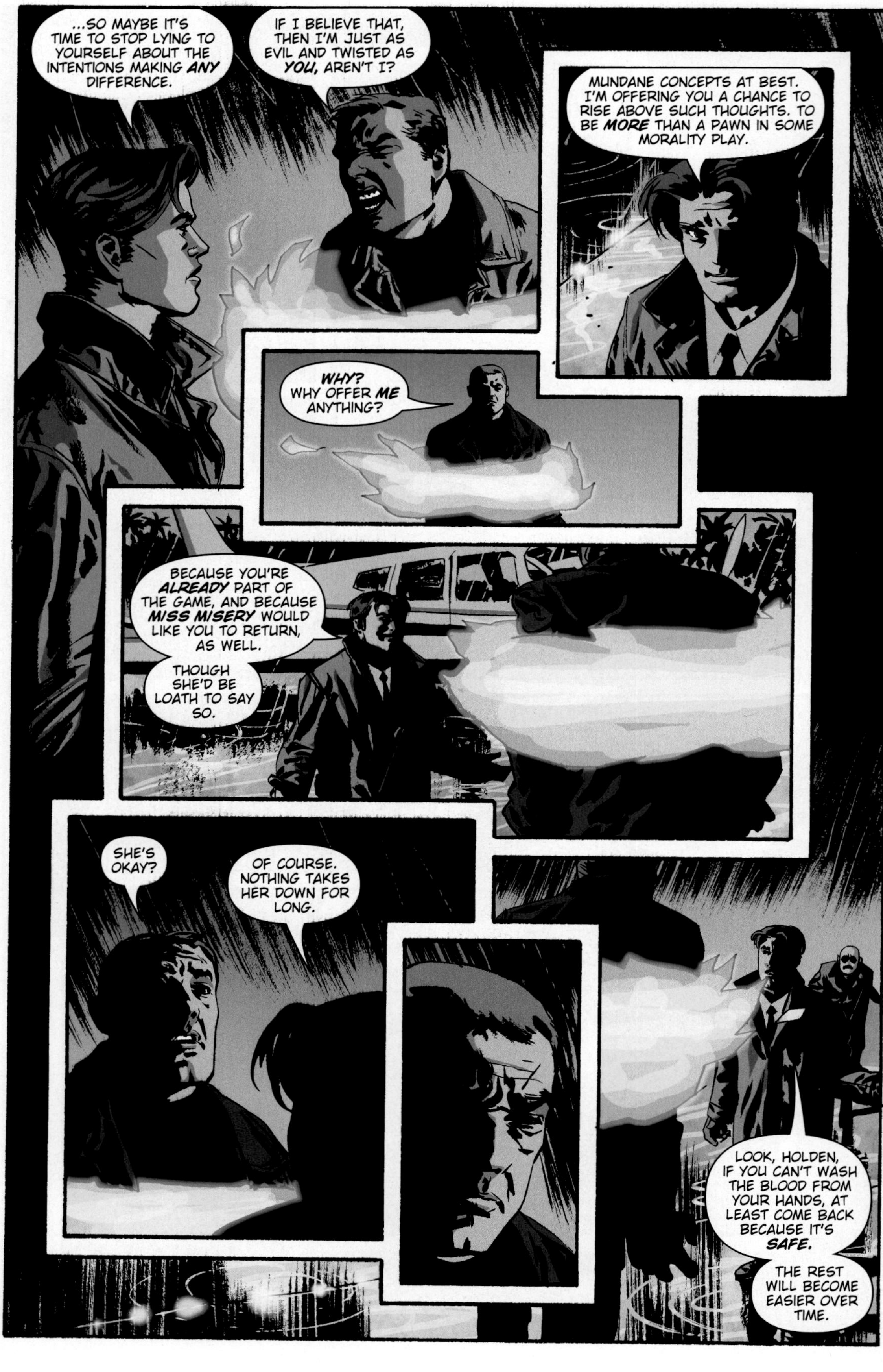
...SO MAYBE IT'S TIME TO STOP LYING TO YOURSELF ABOUT THE INTENTIONS MAKING ANY DIFFERENCE.
IF I BELIEVE THAT, THEN I'M JUST AS EVIL AND TWISTED AS YOU, AREN'T I?
MUNDANE CONCEPTS AT BEST. I'M OFFERING YOU A CHANCE TO RISE ABOVE SUCH THOUGHTS. TO BE MORE THAN A PAWN IN SOME MORALITY PLAY.
WHY? WHY OFFER ME ANYTHING?
BECAUSE YOU'RE ALREADY PART OF THE GAME, AND BECAUSE MISS MISERY WOULD LIKE YOU TO RETURN, AS WELL.
THOUGH SHE'D BE LOATH TO SAY SO.
SHE'S OKAY?
OF COURSE. NOTHING TAKES HER DOWN FOR LONG.
LOOK, HOLDEN, IF YOU CAN'T WASH THE BLOOD FROM YOUR HANDS, AT LEAST COME BACK BECAUSE IT'S SAFE.
THE REST WILL BECOME EASIER OVER TIME.

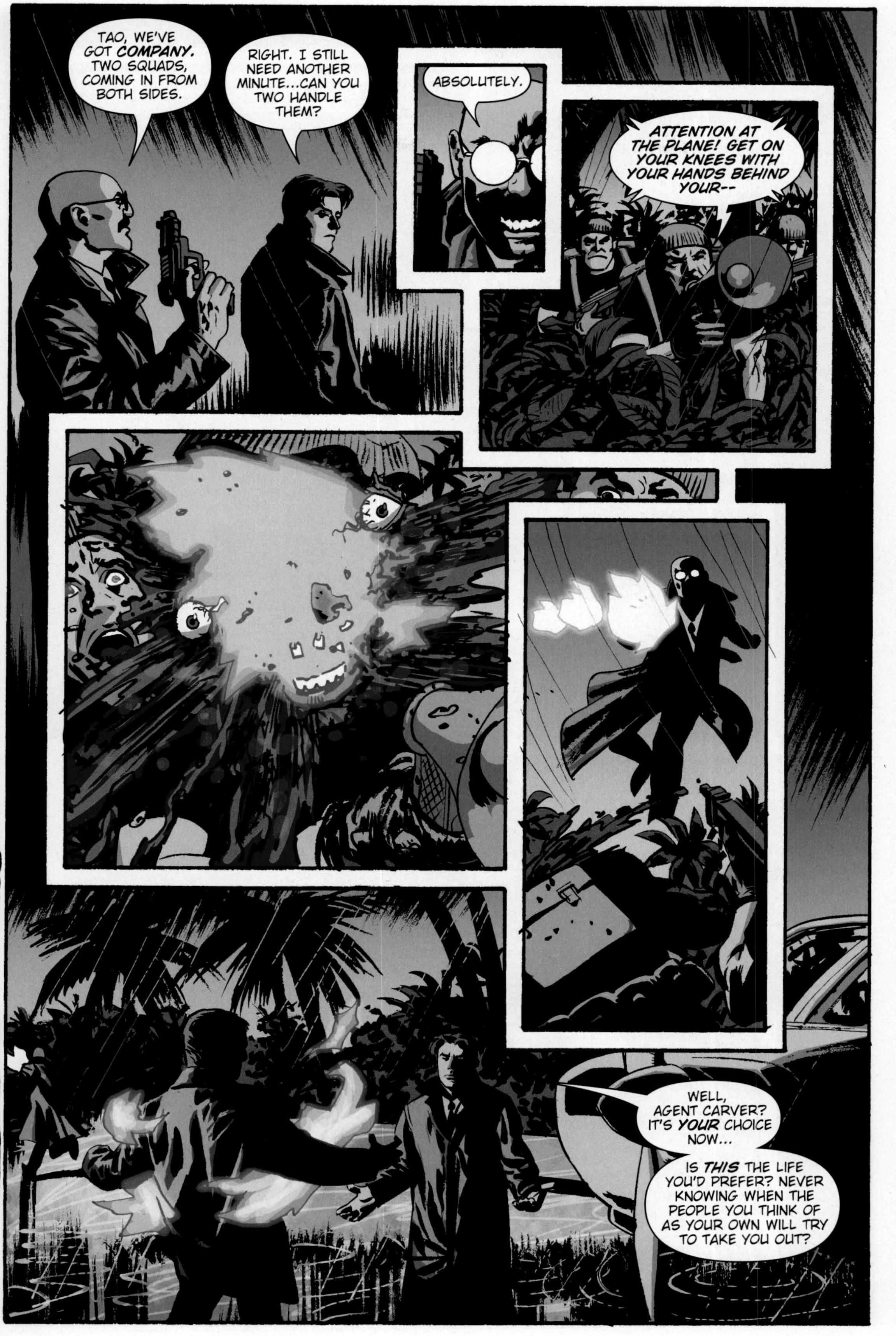
TAO, WE'VE GOT COMPANY. TWO SQUADS, COMING IN FROM BOTH SIDES.
RIGHT. I STILL NEED ANOTHER MINUTE...CAN YOU TWO HANDLE THEM?
ABSOLUTELY.
ATTENTION AT THE PLANE! GET ON YOUR KNEES WITH YOUR HANDS BEHIND YOUR--
WELL, AGENT CARVER? IT'S YOUR CHOICE NOW...
IS THIS THE LIFE YOU'D PREFER? NEVER KNOWING WHEN THE PEOPLE YOU THINK OF AS YOUR OWN WILL TRY TO TAKE YOU OUT?

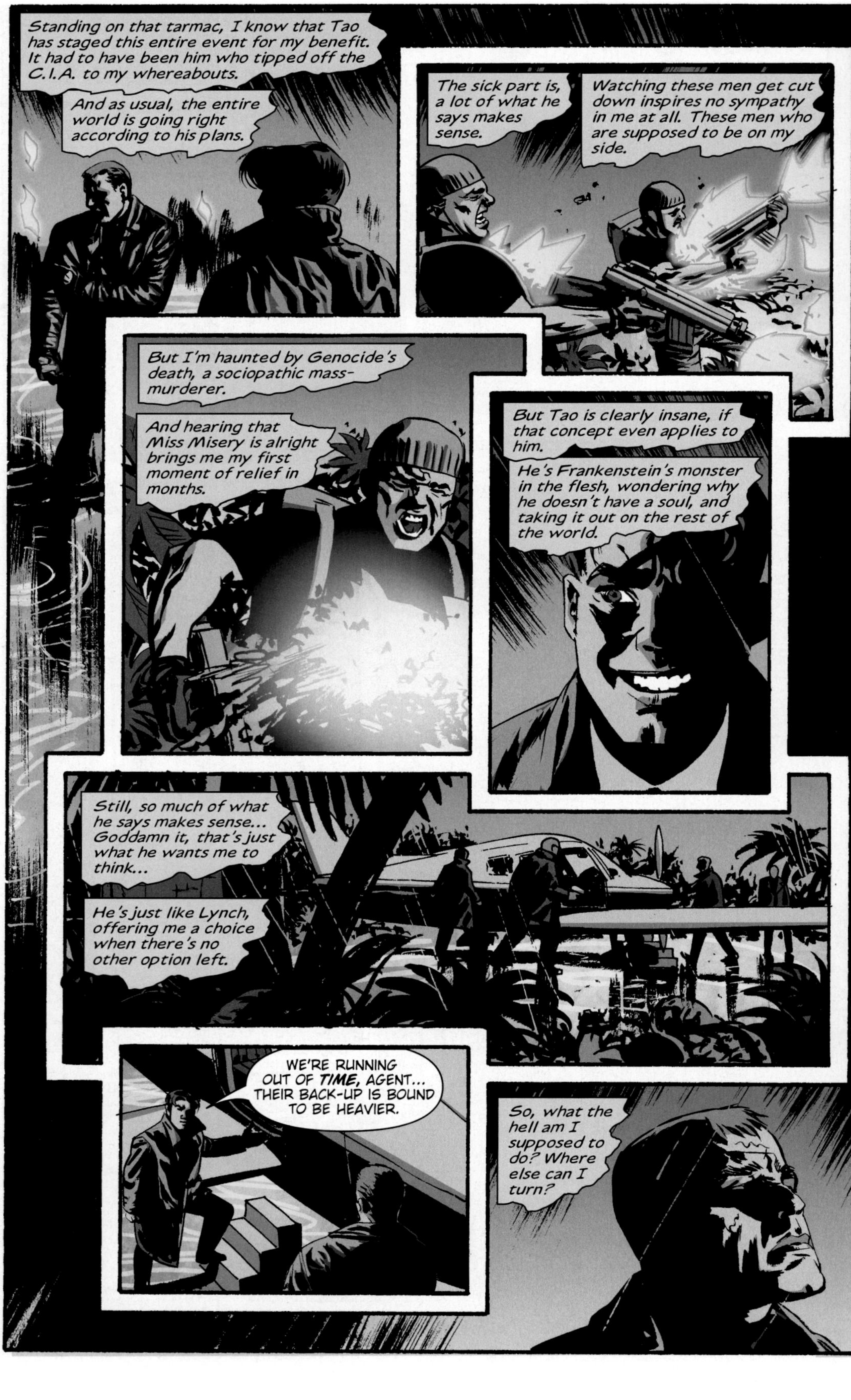
Standing on that tarmac, I know that Tao has staged this entire event for my benefit. It had to have been him who tipped off the C.I.A. to my whereabouts.
And as usual, the entire world is going right according to his plans.
The sick part is, a lot of what he says makes sense.
Watching these men get cut down inspires no sympathy in me at all. These men who are supposed to be on my side.
But I'm haunted by Genocide's death, a sociopathic mass-murderer.
And hearing that Miss Misery is alright brings me my first moment of relief in months.
But Tao is clearly insane, if that concept even applies to him.
He's Frankenstein's monster in the flesh, wondering why he doesn't have a soul, and taking it out on the rest of the world.
Still, so much of what he says makes sense... Goddamn it, that's just what he wants me to think...
He's just like Lynch, offering me a choice when there's no other option left.
WE'RE RUNNING OUT OF *TIME*, AGENT... THEIR BACK-UP IS BOUND TO BE HEAVIER.
So, what the hell am I supposed to do? Where else can I turn?

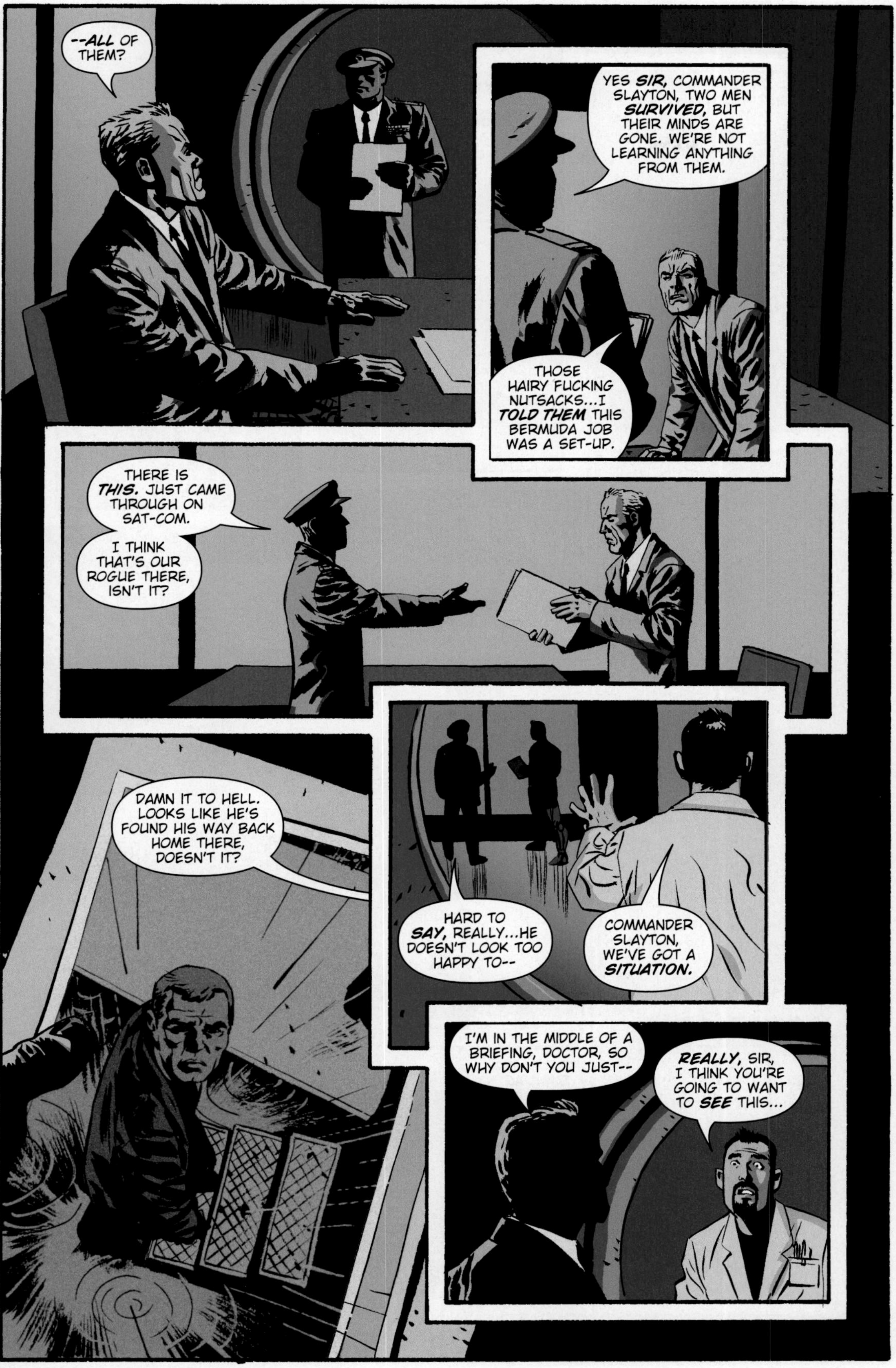
--ALL OF THEM?
YES SIR, COMMANDER SLAYTON, TWO MEN SURVIVED, BUT THEIR MINDS ARE GONE. WE'RE NOT LEARNING ANYTHING FROM THEM.
THOSE HAIRY FUCKING NUTSACKS...I TOLD THEM THIS BERMUDA JOB WAS A SET-UP.
THERE IS THIS. JUST CAME THROUGH ON SAT-COM.
I THINK THAT'S OUR ROGUE THERE, ISN'T IT?
DAMN IT TO HELL. LOOKS LIKE HE'S FOUND HIS WAY BACK HOME THERE, DOESN'T IT?
HARD TO SAY, REALLY...HE DOESN'T LOOK TOO HAPPY TO--
COMMANDER SLAYTON, WE'VE GOT A SITUATION.
I'M IN THE MIDDLE OF A BRIEFING, DOCTOR, SO WHY DON'T YOU JUST--
REALLY, SIR, I THINK YOU'RE GOING TO WANT TO SEE THIS...

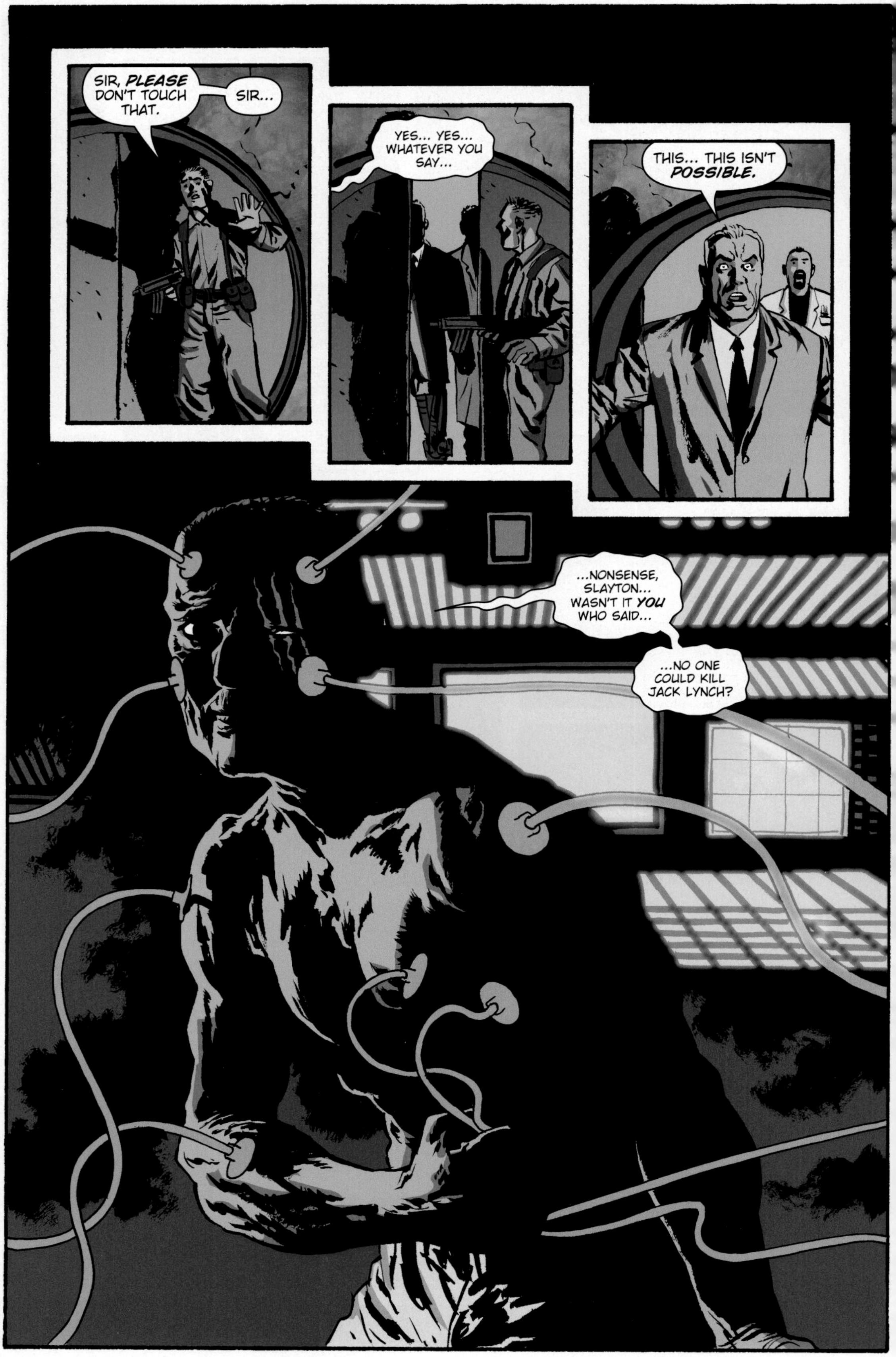
SIR, PLEASE DON'T TOUCH THAT.
SIR...
YES... YES... WHATEVER YOU SAY...
THIS... THIS ISN'T POSSIBLE.
...NONSENSE, SLAYTON... WASN'T IT YOU WHO SAID...
...NO ONE COULD KILL JACK LYNCH?

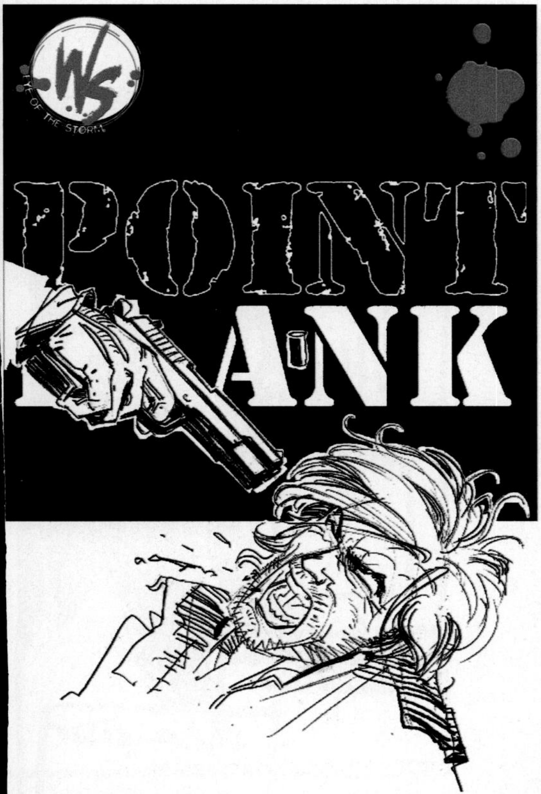
POINT

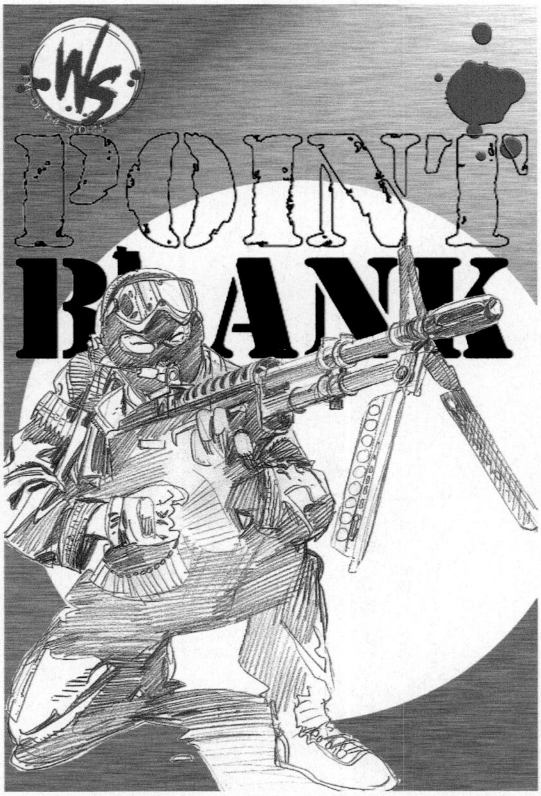
POINT

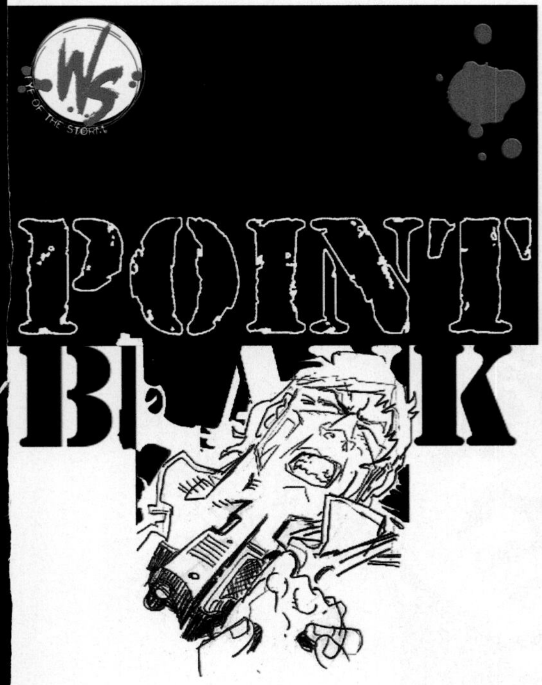
POINT

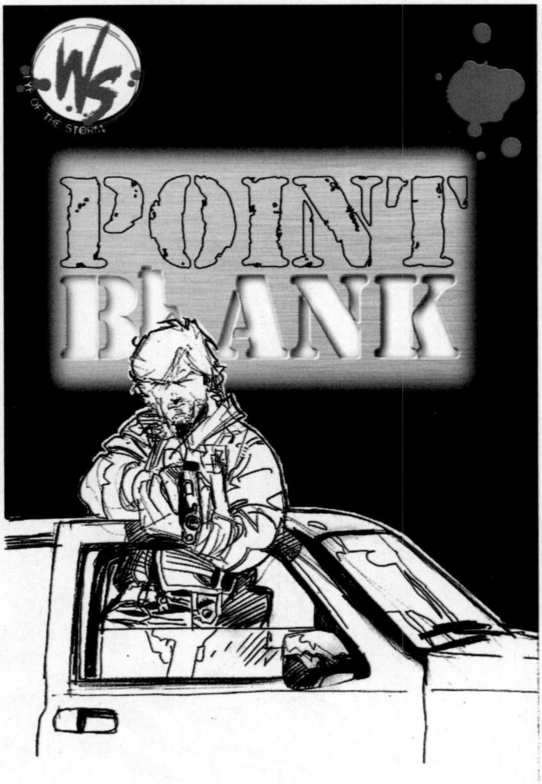
POINT

POINT BLANK #1 Variant Cover Sketches by COLIN WILSON

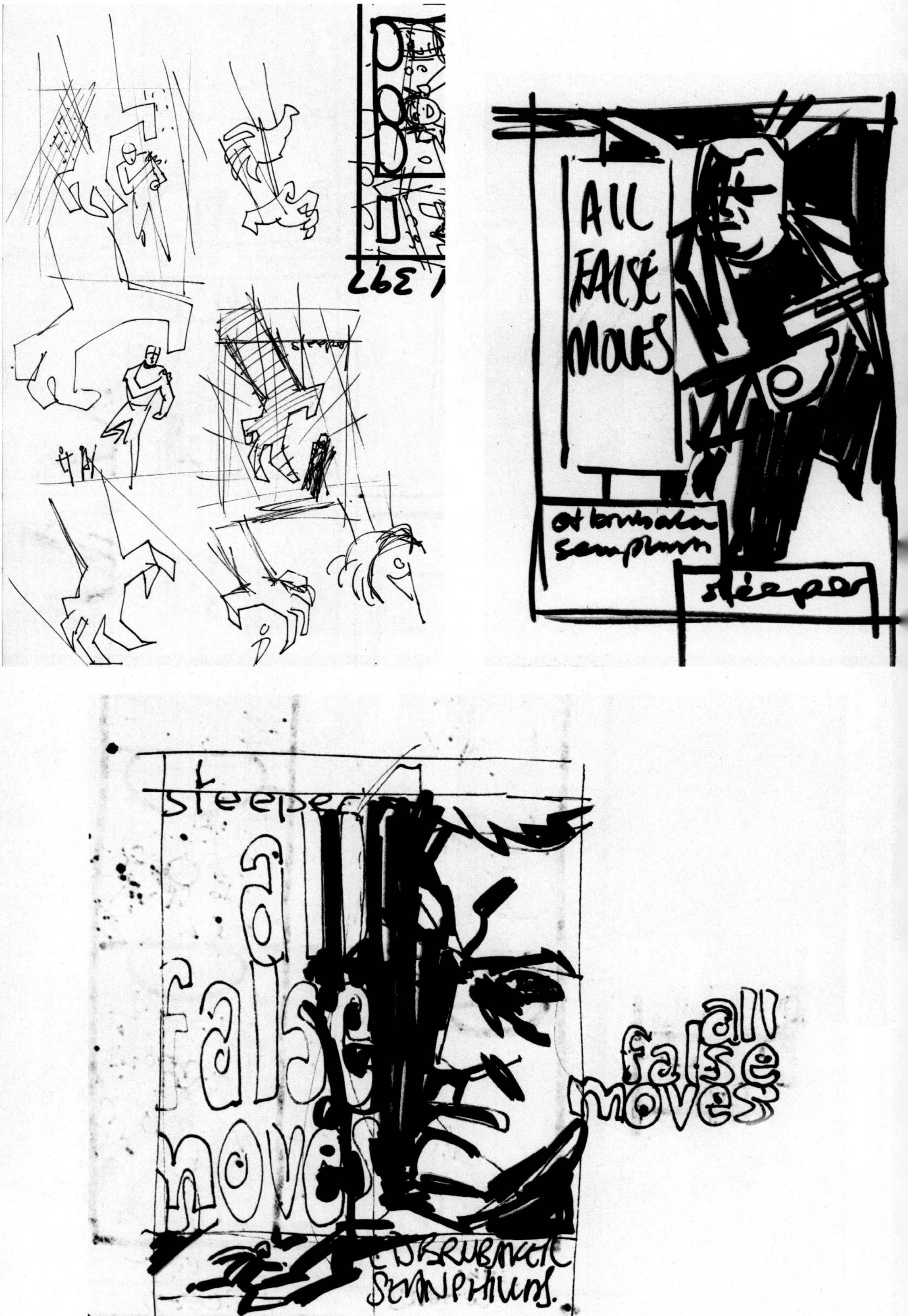
ALL FALSE MOVES
sleeper
sleeper
all false moves
all false moves

Cover Sketches for SLEEPER: OUT IN THE COLD TPB and SLEEPER: ALL THE FALSE MOVES TPB by SEAN PHILLIPS

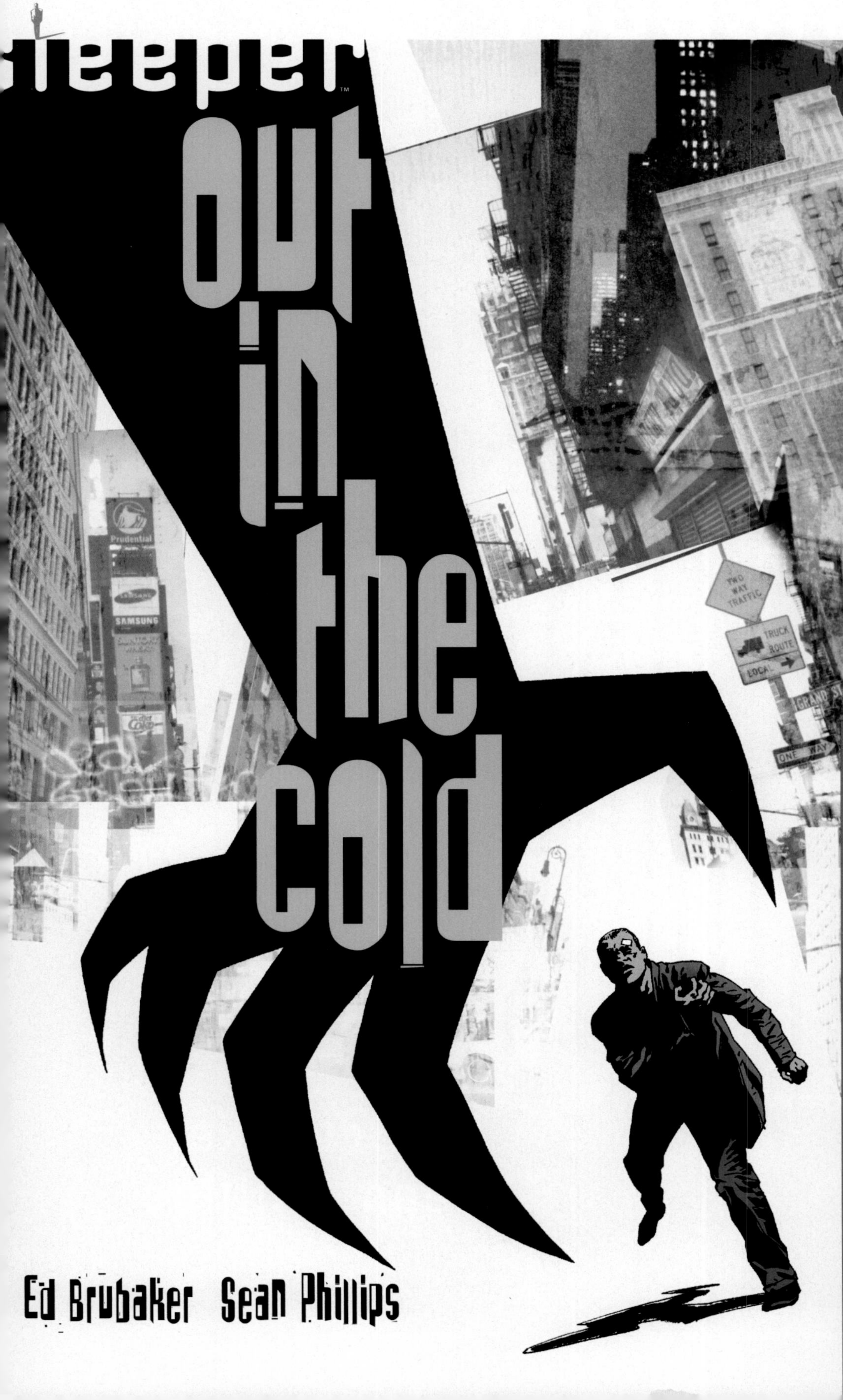
Sleeper™
Out in the Cold
Ed Brubaker Sean Phillips
TWO WAY TRAFFIC
TRUCK ROUTE
LOCAL
ONE WAY
GRAND ST
Prudential
SAMSUNG

SLEEPER: OUT IN THE COLD TPB Cover by SEAN PHILLIPS

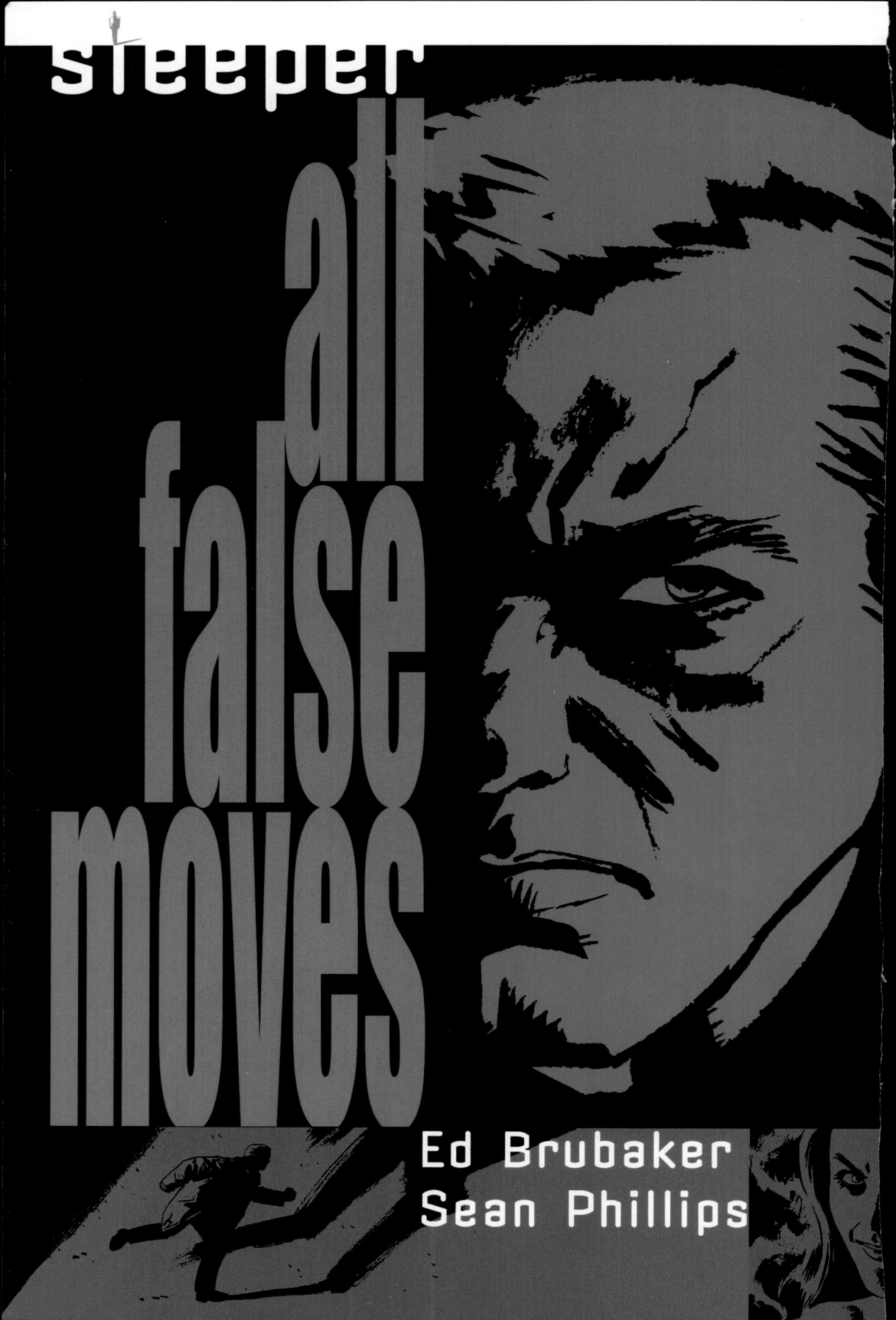
sleeper
all
false
moves
Ed Brubaker
Sean Phillips

SLEEPER: ALL THE FALSE MOVES TPB Cover by SEAN PHILLIPS

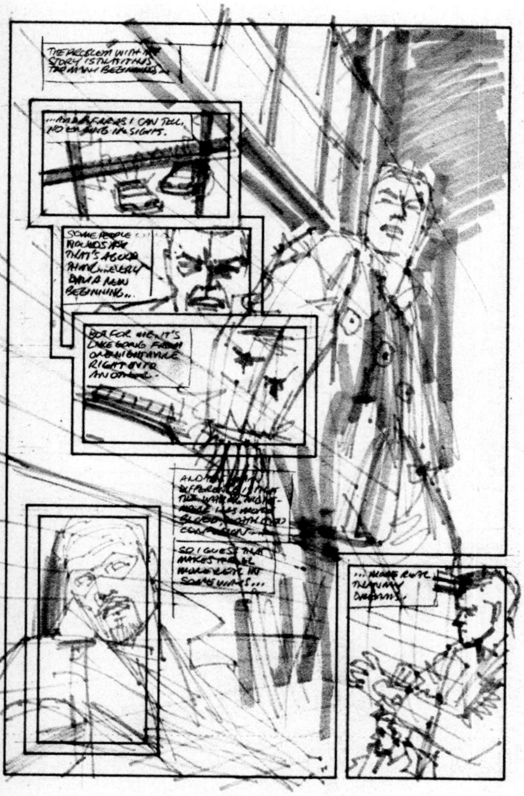

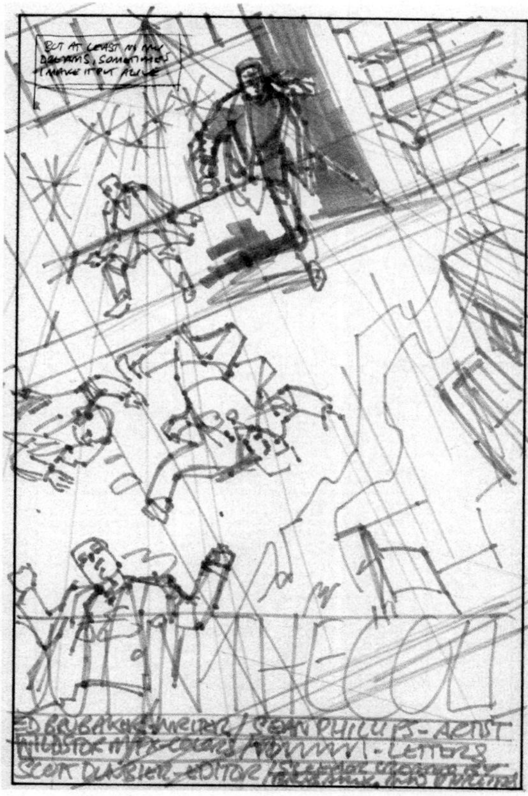
BUT AT LEAST IN MY DREAMS, SOMETIMES I MAKE IT OUT ALIVE
ED BRUBAKER-WRITER / SEAN PHILLIPS - ARTIST

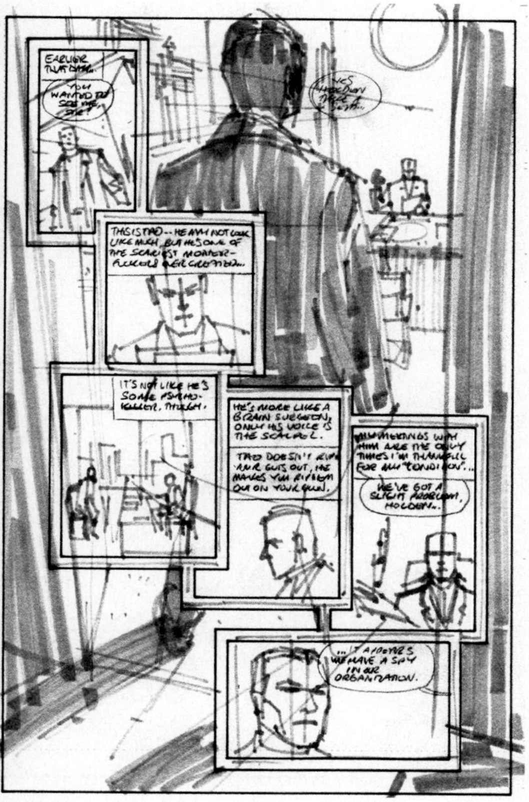
EARLIER THAT DAY...
YOU WANTED TO SEE ME, SIR?
THIS IS TAO-- HE MAY NOT LOOK LIKE MUCH, BUT HE'S ONE OF THE SCARIEST MOTHER-FUCKERS EVER CREATED...
IT'S NOT LIKE HE'S SOME PSYCHO-KILLER, THOUGH.
HE'S MORE LIKE A BRAIN SURGEON, ONLY HIS VOICE IS THE SCALPEL.
TAO DOESN'T RIP YOUR GUTS OUT, HE MAKES YOU RIP THEM OUT ON YOUR OWN.
MY MEETINGS WITH HIM ARE THE ONLY TIMES I'M THANKFUL FOR MY "CONDITION"...
WE'VE GOT A SLIGHT PROBLEM, HOLDEN..
...IT APPEARS WE HAVE A SPY IN OUR ORGANIZATION.

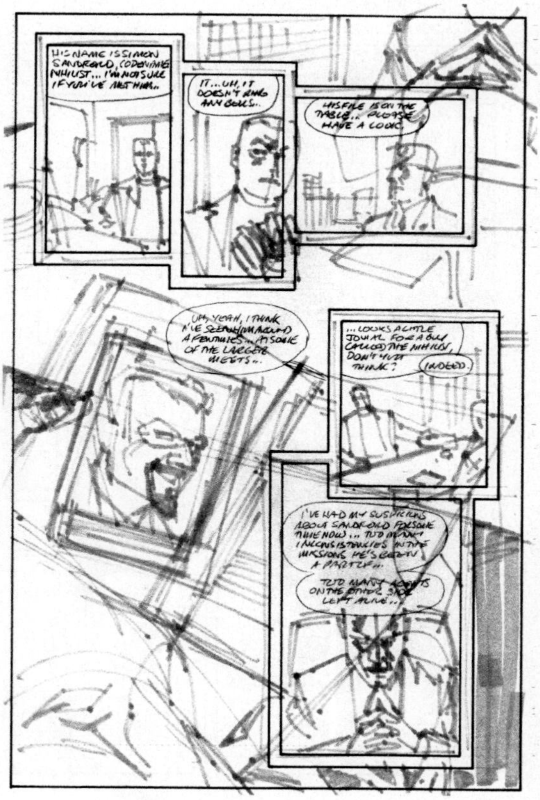
HIS NAME IS SIMON SANDFORD, CODENAME NIHILIST... I'M NOT SURE IF YOU'VE MET HIM..
IT... UH, IT DOESN'T RING ANY BELLS..
HIS FILE IS ON THE TABLE.. PLEASE HAVE A LOOK.
UH, YEAH, I THINK I'VE SEEN HIM AROUND A FEW TIMES... AT SOME OF THE LARGER MEETS..
...LOOKS A LITTLE JOVIAL FOR A GUY CALLED THE NIHILIST, DON'T YOU THINK?
INDEED.
I'VE HAD MY SUSPICIONS ABOUT SANDFORD FOR SOME TIME NOW... TOO MANY INCONSISTENCIES IN THE MISSIONS HE'S BEEN A PART OF..
TOO MANY AGENTS ON THE OTHER SIDE LEFT ALIVE...

SLEEPER #1 Layouts/Pencil Sketches by SEAN PHILLIPS

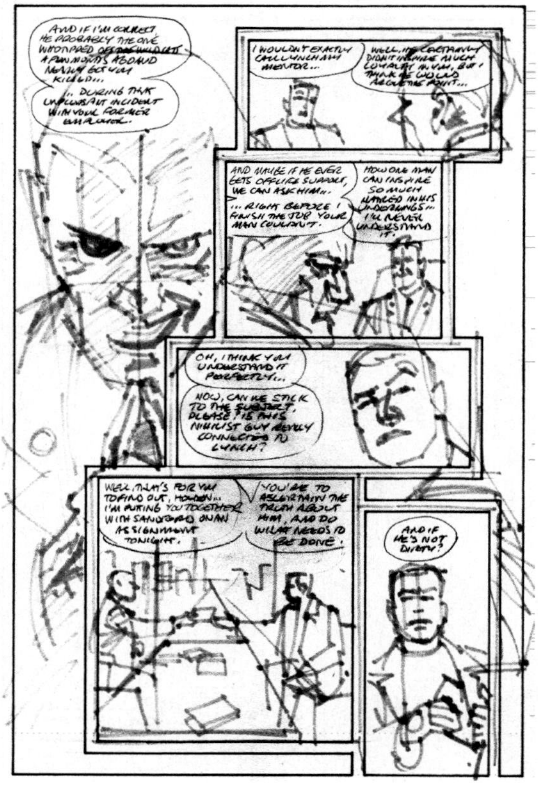
... DURING THAT UNPLEASANT INCIDENT WITH YOUR FORMER EMPLOYER.
I WOULDN'T EXACTLY CALL LYNCH A MENTOR...
AND MAYBE IF HE EVER GETS OFFICE SUPPORT, WE CAN ASK HIM...
... RIGHT BEFORE I FINISH THE JOB YOUR MAN COULDN'T.
HOW ONE MAN CAN INSPIRE SO MUCH HATRED IN HIS UNDERLINGS... I'LL NEVER UNDERSTAND IT.
OH, I THINK YOU UNDERSTAND IT PERFECTLY...
NOW, CAN WE STICK TO THE SUBJECT, PLEASE? IS THIS NIHILIST GUY REALLY CONNECTED TO LYNCH?
WELL, THAT'S FOR YOU TO FIND OUT, HOLDEN... I'M PUTTING YOU TOGETHER WITH SANDFORD ON AN ASSIGNMENT TONIGHT.
YOU'RE TO ASCERTAIN THE TRUTH ABOUT HIM, AND DO WHAT NEEDS TO BE DONE.
AND IF HE'S NOT DIRTY?

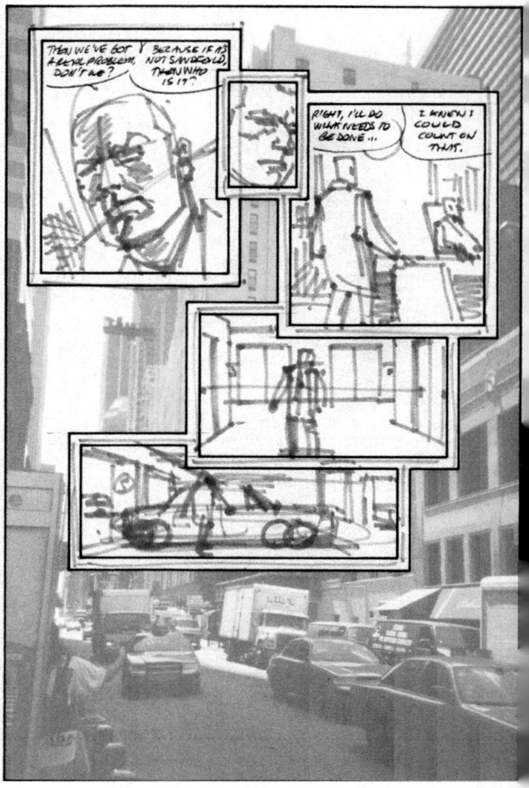
THEN WE'VE GOT A REAL PROBLEM, DON'T WE?
BECAUSE IF IT'S NOT SANDFORD, THEN WHO IS IT?
RIGHT, I'LL DO WHAT NEEDS TO BE DONE...
I KNEW I COULD COUNT ON THAT.

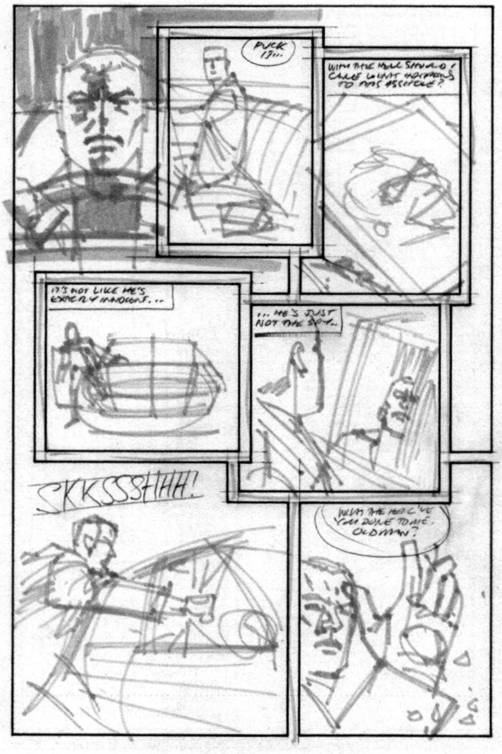
FUCK IT...
IT'S NOT LIKE HE'S EXACTLY INNOCENT...
... HE'S JUST NOT THE SPY...
SKKSSSHHH!

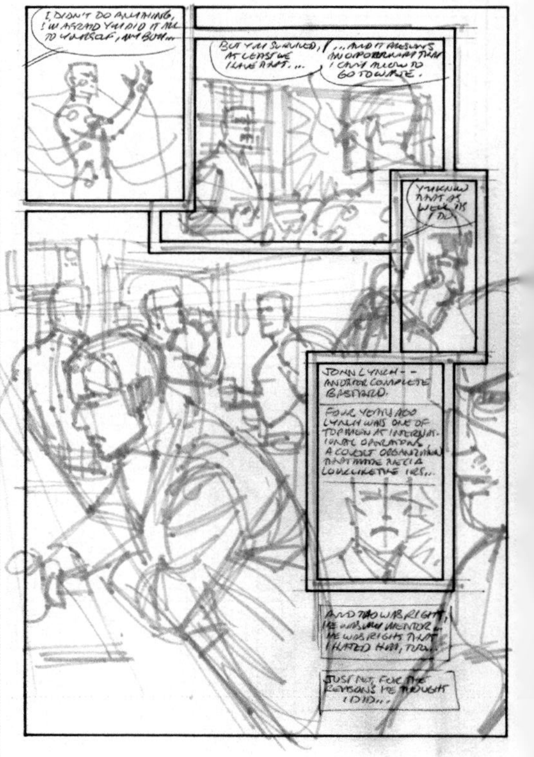
I DIDN'T DO ANYTHING, I'M AFRAID YOU DID IT ALL TO YOURSELF, MY BOY...
BUT YOU SURVIVED, AT LEAST WE HAVE THAT...
... AND IT ALWAYS AN OPPORTUNITY THAT I CAN'T ALLOW TO GO TO WASTE.
Y'KNOW THAT AS WELL AS I DO.
JOHN LYNCH -- ANOTHER COMPLETE BASTARD.
AND TAO WAS RIGHT, HE WAS MY MENTOR... HE WAS RIGHT THAT I HATED HIM, TOO...
JUST NOT FOR THE REASONS HE THOUGHT I DID...

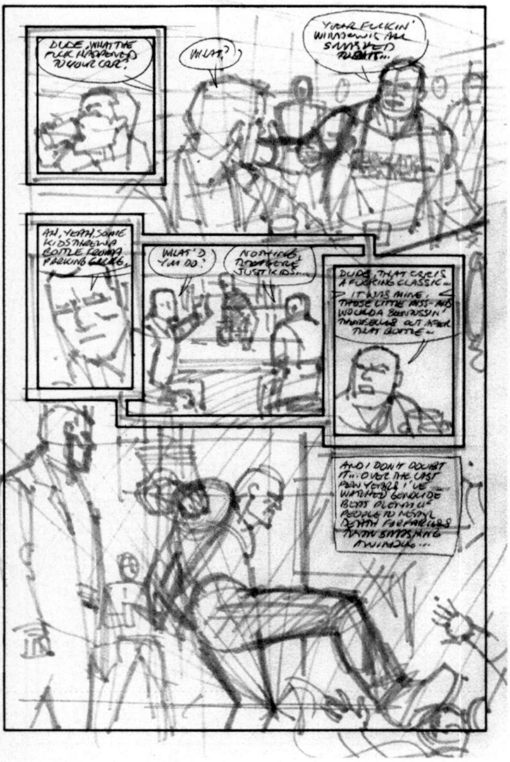
DUDE, WHAT THE FUCK HAPPENED TO YOUR CAR?
WHAT?
YOUR FUCKIN' WINDOWS ALL SMASHED...
AH, YEAH, SOME KIDS THREW A BOTTLE FROM A PARKING GARAGE.
WHAT'D YOU DO?
NOTHING, THEY WERE JUST KIDS...
DUDE, THAT CAR IS A FUCKING CLASSIC... IT WAS MINE, THOSE LITTLE ASS-HATS WOULDA BEEN PISSIN' THEMSELVES OUT AFTER THAT BOTTLE...

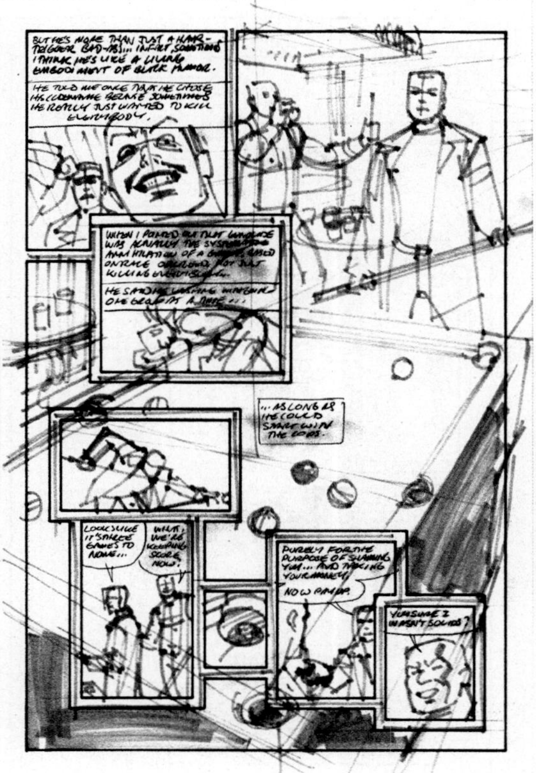
BUT HE'S MORE THAN JUST A HAIR-TRIGGER BAD-ASS... IN FACT, SOMETIMES I THINK HE'S LIKE A LIVING EMBODIMENT OF BLACK HUMOR.
HE TOLD ME ONCE THAT HE CHOSE HIS CODENAME BECAUSE SOMETIMES HE REALLY JUST WANTED TO KILL EVERYBODY.
...AS LONG AS HE COULD START WITH THE COPS.
LOOKS LIKE IT'S THREE GAMES TO NONE...
WHAT, WE'RE KEEPING SCORE NOW?
PURELY FOR THE PURPOSE OF SHAMING YOU... AND TAKING YOUR MONEY.
NOW PAY UP.
YOU SURE I WASN'T SOLIDS?

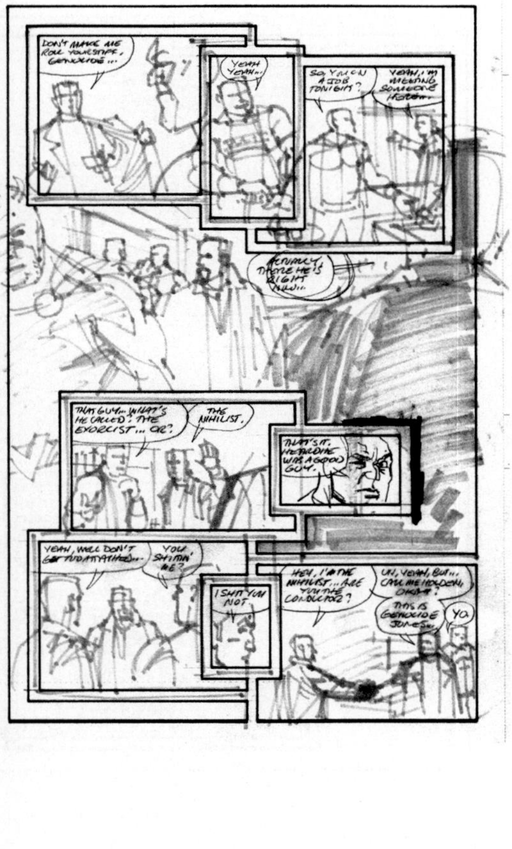
DON'T MAKE ME ROLL YOUR STIFF, GENOCIDE...
YEAH YEAH...
SO, YOU ON A JOB TONIGHT?
ACTUALLY, THERE HE'S RIGHT NOW...
THAT GUY... WHAT'S HE CALLED? THE EXORCIST... OR?
THE NIHILIST.
THAT'S IT.
YOU SHITTIN' ME?
I SHIT YOU NOT.
HEY, I'M THE NIHILIST... ARE YOU THE CONDUCTOR?
THIS IS GENOCIDE JONES...
YO.

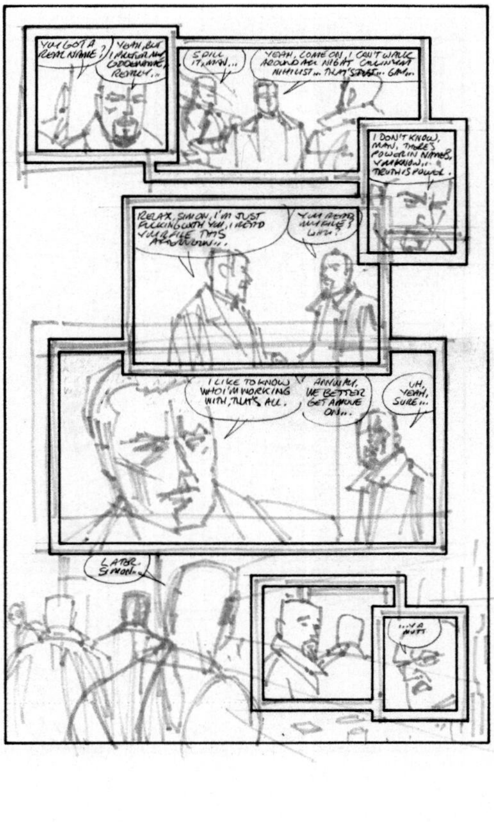
YOU GOT A REAL NAME?
SPILL IT, MAN...
YEAH, COME ON, I CAN'T WALK AROUND ALL NIGHT CALLIN' YOU NIHILIST... THAT'S JUST... GAY...
I DON'T KNOW, MAN, THERE'S POWER IN NAMES, Y'KNOW... TRUTH IS POWER.
RELAX, SIMON, I'M JUST FUCKING WITH YOU, I READ YOUR FILE THIS AFTERNOON...
I LIKE TO KNOW WHO I'M WORKING WITH, THAT'S ALL.
ANYWAY, WE BETTER GET A MOVE ON...
UH, YEAH, SURE...
LATER, SIMON...

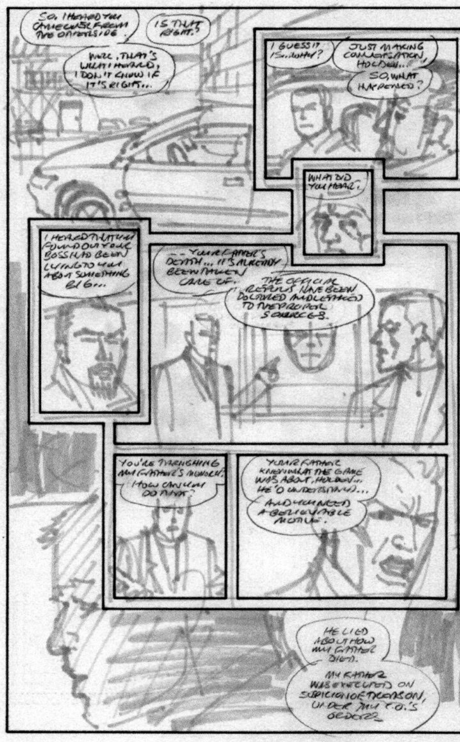
SO, I HEARD YOU CAME BACK FROM THE OTHER SIDE.
IS THAT RIGHT?
WELL, THAT'S WHAT I HEARD, I DON'T KNOW IF IT'S RIGHT...
I GUESS IT IS... WHY?
JUST MAKING CONVERSATION, HOLDEN...
SO, WHAT HAPPENED?
WHAT DID YOU HEAR?
I HEARD THAT YOU FOUND OUT YOUR BOSS HAD BEEN LYING TO YOU ABOUT SOMETHING BIG...
...YOUR FATHER'S DEATH... IT'S ALREADY BEEN TAKEN CARE OF.
THE OFFICIAL REPORTS HAVE BEEN DOCTORED AND LEAKED TO THE PROPER SOURCES.
YOU'RE TARNISHING MY FATHER'S HONOR! HOW CAN YOU DO THAT?
YOUR FATHER KNEW WHAT THE GAME WAS ABOUT, HOLDEN... HE'D UNDERSTAND...
AND YOU NEED A BELIEVABLE MOTIVE.
HE LIED ABOUT HOW MY FATHER DIED.
MY FATHER WAS EXECUTED ON SUSPICION OF TREASON, UNDER MY C.O.'S ORDERS

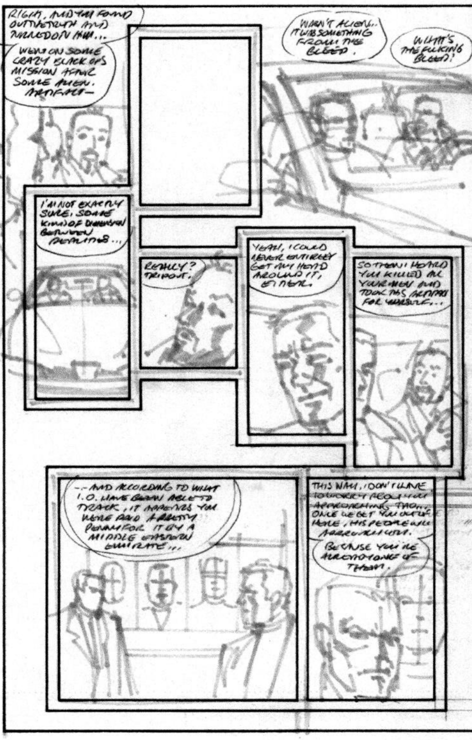
RIGHT, AND YOU FOUND OUT THE TRUTH AND TURNED ON HIM...
WENT ON SOME CRAZY BLACK OPS MISSION AFTER SOME ALIEN ARTIFACT—
WASN'T ALIEN... IT WAS SOMETHING FROM THE BLEED.
WHAT'S THE FUCKING BLEED?
I'M NOT EXACTLY SURE. SOME KIND OF DIMENSION BETWEEN REALITIES...
REALLY? TRIPPY.
YEAH, I COULD NEVER ENTIRELY GET MY HEAD AROUND IT, EITHER.
SO THEN I HEARD YOU KILLED ALL YOUR MEN AND TOOK THIS ARTIFACT FOR YOURSELF...
...AND ACCORDING TO WHAT I.O. HAVE BEEN ABLE TO TRACK, IT APPEARS YOU WERE PAID A PRETTY PENNY FOR IT BY A MIDDLE EASTERN EMIRATE...
BECAUSE YOU'RE ALREADY ONE OF THEM.

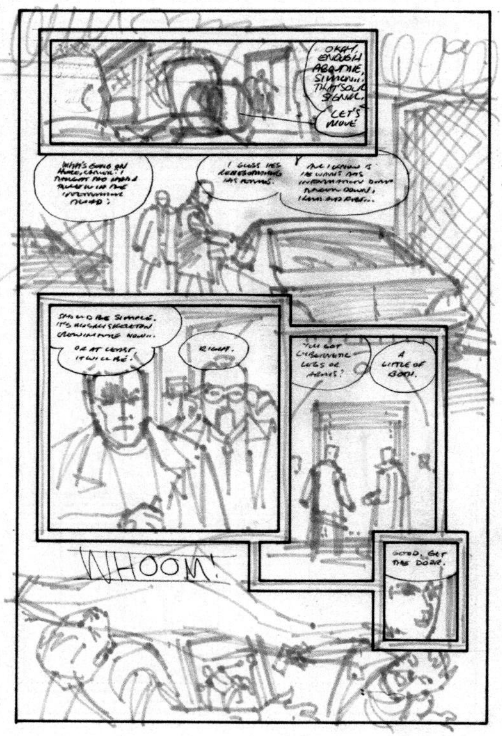
OKAY, ENOUGH ABOUT ME, SIMON... THAT'S OUR SIGNAL.
LET'S MOVE
OR AT LEAST, IT WILL BE!
RIGHT.
YOU GOT CYBERNETIC LEGS OR ARMS?
A LITTLE OF BOTH.
WHOOM!
GOOD, GET THE DOOR.

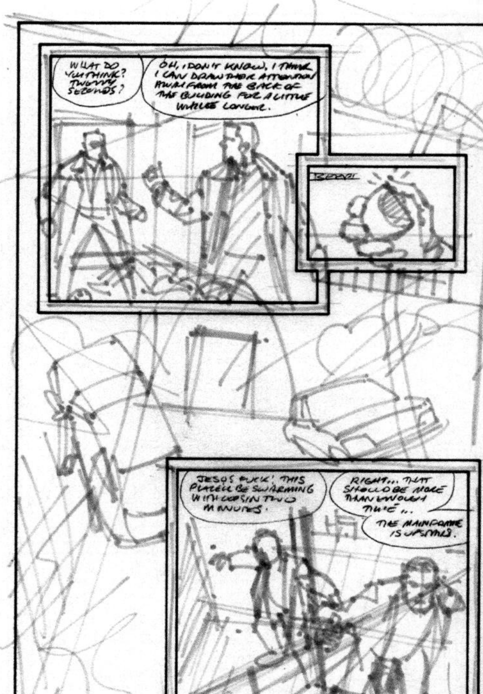
WHAT DO YOU THINK? TWENTY SECONDS?
OH, I DON'T KNOW. I THINK I CAN DRAW THEIR ATTENTION AWAY FROM THE BACK OF THE BUILDING FOR A LITTLE WHILE LONGER.
JESUS FUCK! THIS PLACE'LL BE SWARMING WITH COPS IN TWO MINUTES.
RIGHT... THAT SHOULD BE MORE THAN ENOUGH TIME...
THE MAINFRAME IS UPSTAIRS.

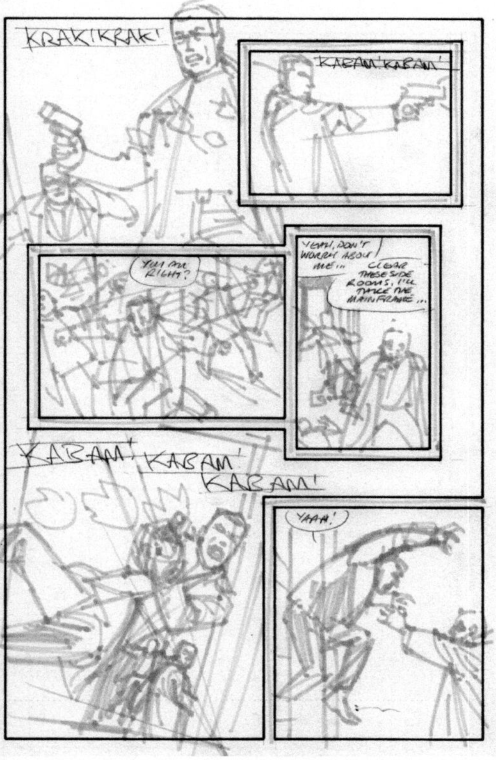
KRAK! KRAK!
KABAM! KABAM!
YOU ALL RIGHT?
YEAH, DON'T WORRY ABOUT ME...
CLEAR THESE SIDE ROOMS, I'LL TAKE THE MAINFRAME...
KABAM! KABAM! KABAM!
YAAH!

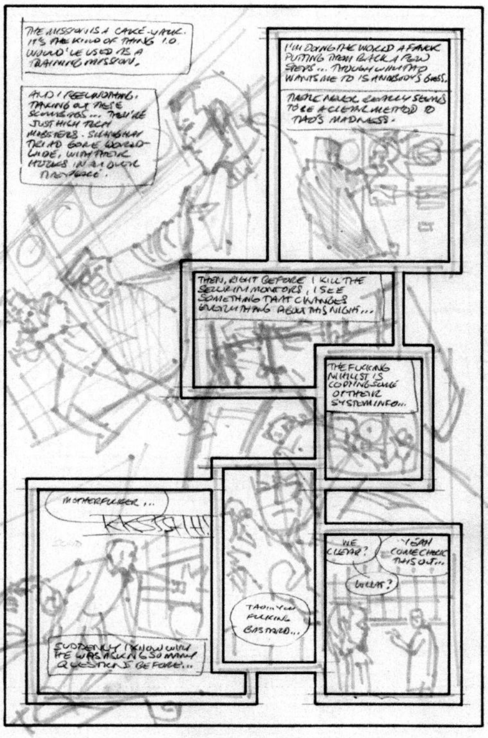
THE MISSION IS A CAKE-WALK. IT'S THE KIND OF THING I.O. WOULD'VE USED AS A TRAINING MISSION.
THEN, RIGHT BEFORE I KILL THE SECURITY MONITORS, I SEE SOMETHING THAT CHANGES EVERYTHING ABOUT THIS NIGHT...
THE FUCKING NIHILIST IS COPYING SOME OF THEIR SYSTEM INFO...
MOTHERFUCKER...
SUDDENLY I KNOW WHY HE WAS ASKING SO MANY QUESTIONS BEFORE...
YOU FUCKING BASTARD...
WE CLEAR?
YEAH. COME CHECK THIS OUT...
WHAT?

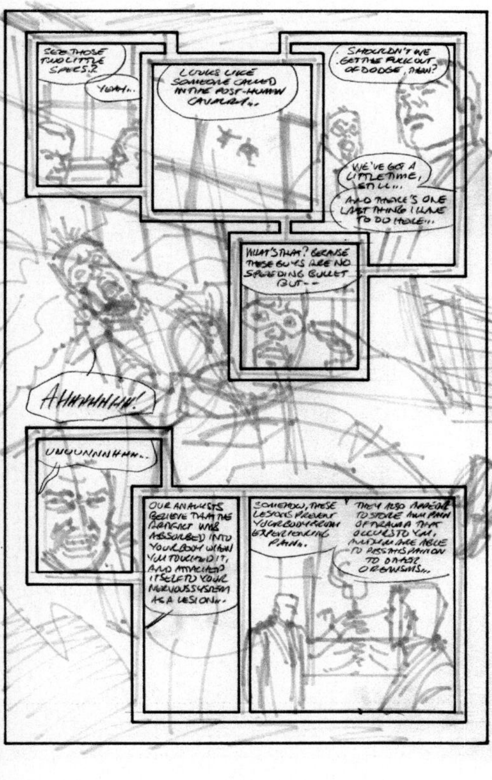
SEE THOSE TWO LITTLE SPECS?
YEAH...
LOOKS LIKE SOMEONE CALLED IN THE POST-HUMAN CAVALRY...
SHOULDN'T WE GET THE FUCK OUT OF DODGE, THEN?
WE'VE GOT A LITTLE TIME, STILL...
AND THERE'S ONE LAST THING I HAVE TO DO HERE...
WHAT'S THAT? BECAUSE THESE GUYS ARE NO SPEEDING BULLET BUT--
AHHHHHHH!
UNUUNNNHHH...
OUR ANALYSTS BELIEVE THAT THE ARTIFACT WAS ABSORBED INTO YOUR BODY WHEN YOU TOUCHED IT, AND ATTACHED ITSELF TO YOUR NERVOUS SYSTEM AS A LESION...
SOMEHOW, THESE LESIONS PREVENT YOUR BODY FROM EXPERIENCING PAIN...
TO OTHER ORGANISMS...

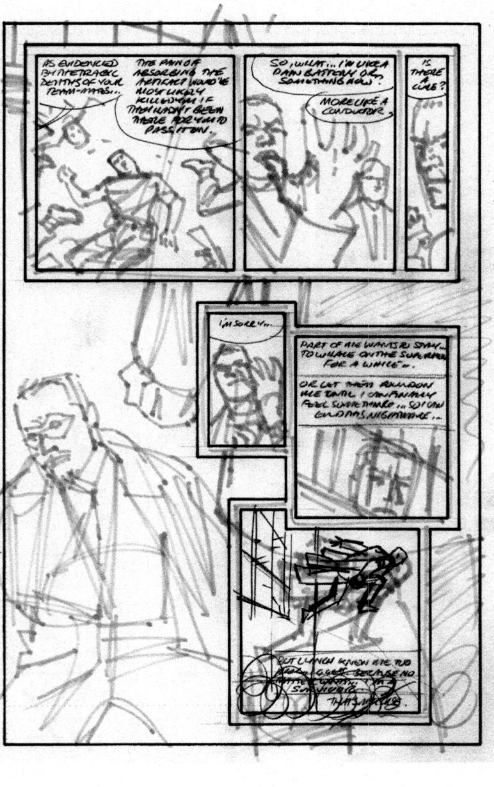
AS EVIDENCED BY THE TRAGIC DEATHS OF YOUR TEAM-MATES...
SO, WHAT... I'M LIKE A PAIN BATTERY OR SOMETHING NOW?
MORE LIKE A CONDUCTOR.
IS THERE A CURE?
I'M SORRY...
FOR A WHILE...

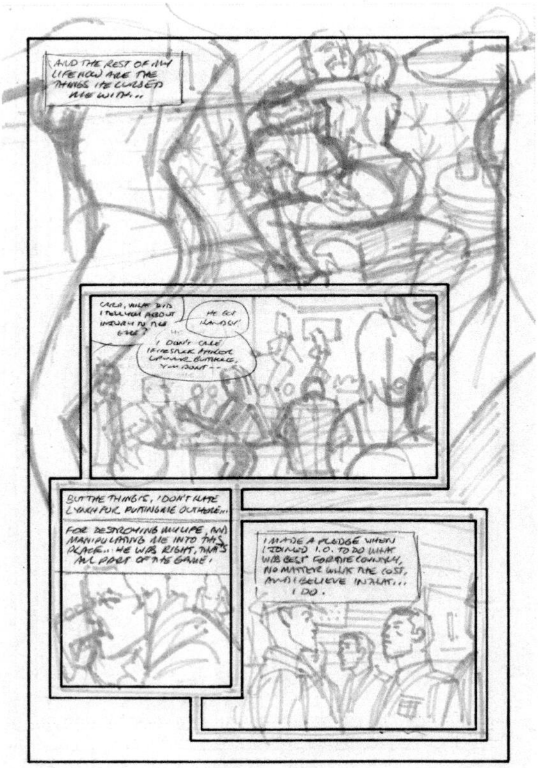
AND THE REST OF MY LIFE NOW ARE THE THINGS HE CURSED ME WITH...
HE GOT HANDSY!
BUT THE THING IS, I DON'T HATE LYNCH FOR PUTTING ME OUT HERE...
FOR DESTROYING MY LIFE, AND MANIPULATING ME INTO THIS PLACE... HE WAS RIGHT, THAT'S ALL PART OF THE GAME.
I MADE A PLEDGE WHEN I JOINED I.O. TO DO WHAT WAS BEST FOR THE COUNTRY, NO MATTER WHAT THE COST, AND I BELIEVE IN THAT... I DO.

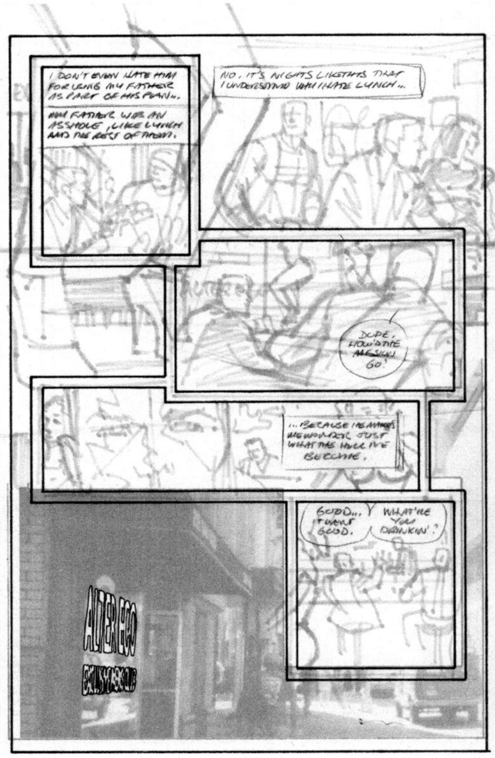
I DON'T EVEN HATE HIM FOR USING MY FATHER AS PART OF HIS PLAN...
MY FATHER WAS AN ASSHOLE, LIKE LYNCH AND THE REST OF THEM.
NO, IT'S NIGHTS LIKE THIS THAT I UNDERSTAND WHY I HATE LYNCH...
DUDE, HOW'D THE MISSION GO?
...BECAUSE HE MAKES ME WONDER JUST WHAT THE HELL I'VE BECOME.
GOOD... IT WENT GOOD.
WHAT'RE YOU DRINKIN'?
ALTER EGO

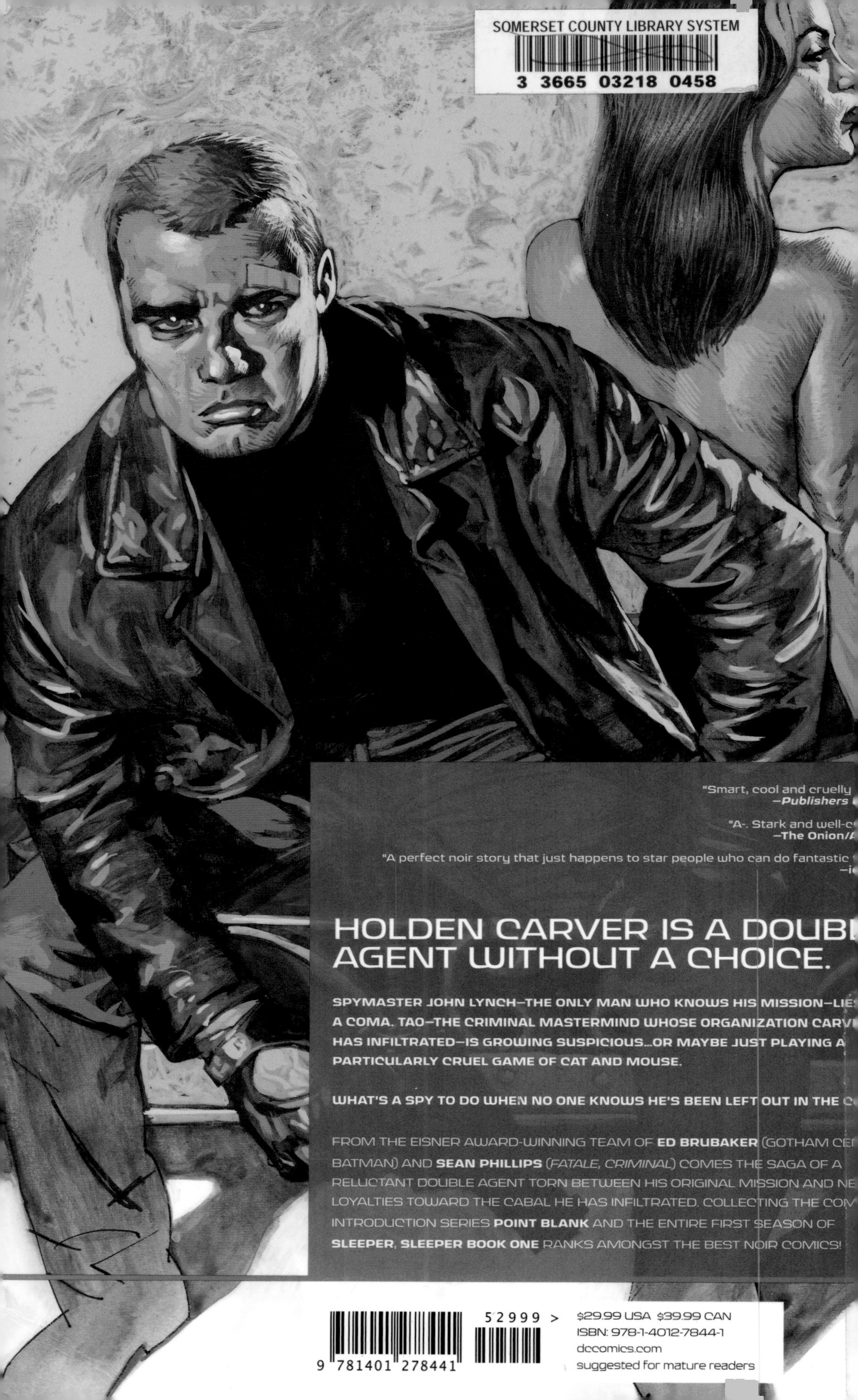

"Smart, cool and cruelly
—*Publishers*

"A-. Stark and well-c
—**The Onion/A**

"A perfect noir story that just happens to star people who can do fantastic
—i

HOLDEN CARVER IS A DOUBL AGENT WITHOUT A CHOICE.

SPYMASTER JOHN LYNCH—THE ONLY MAN WHO KNOWS HIS MISSION—LIES A COMA. TAO—THE CRIMINAL MASTERMIND WHOSE ORGANIZATION CARV HAS INFILTRATED—IS GROWING SUSPICIOUS…OR MAYBE JUST PLAYING A PARTICULARLY CRUEL GAME OF CAT AND MOUSE.

WHAT'S A SPY TO DO WHEN NO ONE KNOWS HE'S BEEN LEFT OUT IN THE C

FROM THE EISNER AWARD-WINNING TEAM OF **ED BRUBAKER** (GOTHAM CE BATMAN) AND **SEAN PHILLIPS** (*FATALE, CRIMINAL*) COMES THE SAGA OF A RELUCTANT DOUBLE AGENT TORN BETWEEN HIS ORIGINAL MISSION AND NE LOYALTIES TOWARD THE CABAL HE HAS INFILTRATED. COLLECTING THE COM INTRODUCTION SERIES **POINT BLANK** AND THE ENTIRE FIRST SEASON OF **SLEEPER, SLEEPER BOOK ONE** RANKS AMONGST THE BEST NOIR COMICS!

52999 >
9 781401 278441
$29.99 USA $39.99 CAN
ISBN: 978-1-4012-7844-1
dccomics.com
suggested for mature readers